Embracing Modern C++ Safely

Embracing Modern C++ *Safely*

John Lakos

Vittorio Romeo

Rostislav Khlebnikov

Alisdair Meredith

✦ Addison-Wesley

Boston • Columbus • New York • San Francisco • Amsterdam • Cape Town
Dubai • London • Madrid • Milan • Munich • Paris • Montreal • Toronto • Delhi • Mexico City
São Paulo • Sydney • Hong Kong • Seoul • Singapore • Taipei • Tokyo

Cover image: Unconventional/Shutterstock
Pages 109, 130: cocktail glass, Laura Humpfer/OpenMojis

For information about buying this title in bulk quantities, or for special sales opportunities (which may include electronic versions; custom cover designs; and content particular to your business, training goals, marketing focus, or branding interests), please contact our corporate sales department at corpsales@pearsoned.com or (800) 382-3419.

For government sales inquiries, please contact governmentsales@pearsoned.com.

For questions about sales outside the U.S., please contact intlcs@pearson.com.

Visit us on the Web: informit.com/aw

Library of Congress Control Number: 2021947542

ISBN-13: 978-0-13-738035-0
ISBN-10: 0-13-738035-6

ScoutAutomatedPrintCode

Pearson's Commitment to Diversity, Equity, and Inclusion

Pearson is dedicated to creating bias-free content that reflects the diversity of all learners. We embrace the many dimensions of diversity, including but not limited to race, ethnicity, gender, socioeconomic status, ability, age, sexual orientation, and religious or political beliefs.

Education is a powerful force for equity and change in our world. It has the potential to deliver opportunities that improve lives and enable economic mobility. As we work with authors to create content for every product and service, we acknowledge our responsibility to demonstrate inclusivity and incorporate diverse scholarship so that everyone can achieve their potential through learning. As the world's leading learning company, we have a duty to help drive change and live up to our purpose to help more people create a better life for themselves and to create a better world.

Our ambition is to purposefully contribute to a world where:

- Everyone has an equitable and lifelong opportunity to succeed through learning.

- Our educational products and services are inclusive and represent the rich diversity of learners.

- Our educational content accurately reflects the histories and experiences of the learners we serve.

- Our educational content prompts deeper discussions with learners and motivates them to expand their own learning (and worldview).

While we work hard to present unbiased content, we want to hear from you about any concerns or needs with this Pearson product so that we can investigate and address them.

- Please contact us with concerns about any potential bias at https://www.pearson.com/report-bias.html.

To my darling wife, Elyse, who I love dearly, always have, and forever will:

"'When I use a word,' Humpty Dumpty said in rather a scornful tone,
'it means just what I choose it to mean—neither more nor less.'"
— Lewis Carroll, *Through the Looking-Glass*

JSL

To my aunts and my dad,
who have always supported me
in every aspect of my life.

VR

To Elena and my parents.

RK

To the late David and Mary Meredith,
loving parents who encouraged me in everything that I did
and would have been so proud to see their son finally in print.

AM

Contents

Foreword by Shawn Edwards   **xiii**

Foreword by Andrei Alexandrescu   **xv**

Acknowledgments   **xix**

About the Authors   **xxv**

Chapter 0 Introduction   **1**

What Makes This Book Different   1

Scope for the First Edition   2

The *EMC++S* Guiding Principles   3

What Do We Mean by *Safely*?   4

A *Safe* Feature   5

A *Conditionally Safe* Feature   5

An *Unsafe* Feature   6

Modern C++ Feature Catalog   6

How to Use This Book   8

Chapter 1 Safe Features   **11**

1.1   C++11   11

Attribute Syntax	Generalized Attribute Support	12
Consecutive >s	Consecutive Right-Angle Brackets	21
`decltype`	Operator for Extracting Expression Types	25
Defaulted Functions	Using `=default` for Special Member Functions	33
Delegating Ctors	Constructors Calling Other Constructors	46
Deleted Functions	Using `=delete` for Arbitrary Functions	53
`explicit` Operators	Explicit Conversion Operators	61
Function `static` '11	Thread-Safe Function-Scope `static` Variables	68
Local Types '11	Local/Unnamed Types as Template Arguments	83
`long long`	The `long long` ($\geq$64 bits) Integral Type	89
`noreturn`	The `[[noreturn]]` Attribute	95

Contents

nullptr	The Null-Pointer-Literal Keyword	99
override	The **override** Member-Function Specifier	104
Raw String Literals	Syntax for Unprocessed String Contents	108
static_assert	Compile-Time Assertions	115
Trailing Return	Trailing Function Return Types	124
Unicode Literals	Unicode String Literals	129
using Aliases	Type/Template Aliases (Extended **typedef**)	133
1.2 C++14		138
Aggregate Init '14	Aggregates Having Default Member Initializers	138
Binary Literals	Binary Literals: The 0b Prefix	142
deprecated	The [[deprecated]] Attribute	147
Digit Separators	The Digit Separator (')	152
Variable Templates	Templated Variable Declarations/Definitions	157

Chapter 2 Conditionally Safe Features		**167**
2.1 C++11		167
alignas	The **alignas** Specifier	168
alignof	The **alignof** Operator	184
auto Variables	Variables of Automatically Deduced Type	195
Braced Init	Braced-Initialization Syntax: {}	215
constexpr Functions	Compile-Time Invocable Functions	257
constexpr Variables	Compile-Time Accessible Variables	302
Default Member Init	Default **class**/**union** Member Initializers	318
enum class	Strongly Typed, Scoped Enumerations	332
extern template	Explicit-Instantiation Declarations	353
Forwarding References	Forwarding References (T&&)	377
Generalized PODs '11	Trivial and Standard-Layout Types	401
Inheriting Ctors	Inheriting Base-Class Constructors	535
initializer_list	List Initialization: std::initializer_list<T>	553
Lambdas	Anonymous Function Objects (Closures)	573
noexcept Operator	Asking if an Expression Cannot **throw**	615
Opaque **enums**	Opaque Enumeration Declarations	660
Range **for**	Range-Based **for** Loops	679
Rvalue References	Move Semantics and *Rvalue* References (&&)	710
Underlying Type '11	Explicit Enumeration Underlying Type	829
User-Defined Literals	User-Defined Literal Operators	835
Variadic Templates	Variable-Argument-Count Templates	873
2.2 C++14		958
constexpr Functions '14	Relaxed Restrictions on **constexpr** Functions	959
Generic Lambdas	Lambdas Having a Templated Call Operator	968
Lambda Captures	Lambda-Capture Expressions	986

Contents

Chapter 3 Unsafe Features   **997**

  3.1 C++11   997

     `carries_dependency`   The `[[carries_dependency]]` Attribute   998

     `final`   Prohibiting Overriding and Derivation   1007

     `friend` '11   Extended `friend` Declarations   1031

     `inline namespace`   Transparently Nested Namespaces   1055

     `noexcept` Specifier   The **noexcept** Function Specification   1085

     Ref-Qualifiers   Reference-Qualified Member Functions   1153

     `union` '11   Unions Having Non-Trivial Members   1174

  3.2 C++14   1182

     `auto` Return   Function (**auto**) Return-Type Deduction   1182

     `decltype(auto)`   Deducing Types Using **decltype** Semantics   1205

Afterword: Looking Back and Looking Forward   **1215**

Glossary   **1217**

Bibliography   **1281**

Index   **1305**

Foreword by Shawn Edwards

I have been writing programs in C++ professionally for more than 25 years, even before it was standardized. The C++ language, in its mission to deliver zero overhead and maximum performance, necessarily provides few guardrails; syntax and type safety go only so far. Using C++ features in unsound ways and creating spectacular failures was always easy. But because the language was relatively stable, good developers — over time — learned how to write reliable C++ software.

The first standardized version, C++98, formalized what many already knew about the language. The second version of the Standard, C++03, included some small corrections and enhancements but did not fundamentally alter the way programs were written. What it meant to know how to program in C++, however, changed drastically with the publication of the C++11 Standard. For the first time in many years, the ISO C++ Standards Committee (WG21) added significant new functionality and removed functionality as well. For example, `noexcept` and `std::unique_ptr` were in, and the days of using dynamic exception specifications and `std::auto_ptr` were numbered.

At the same time, the Standards Committee announced its unprecedented commitment to deliver a new version of the C++ Standard every three years! For a large software organization, like Bloomberg, whose software asset lifetimes are measured in decades, relying on a language standard that is updated with such frequency is especially problematic. Bloomberg has been reliably and accurately providing indispensable information to the professional financial community for nearly 40 years, with services that span such diverse needs as financial analytics, trading solutions, and real-time market data.

To support our global business, Bloomberg has developed high-performance software systems that operate at scale and, for more than two decades now, has written them primarily in C++. As you can imagine, incorporating and validating new tool chains that underpin our company's entire code base is no simple task. Each update risks the stability of the very products upon which our customers depend.

Modern C++ has much to offer — both good and bad. Many of its newer features offer the prospect of improving performance, expressiveness, maintainability, and so on. On the other hand, many of these same features come with potential pitfalls, some of which are obvious, and others less so. With each new release of C++, now every three years, the language gets bigger, and the opportunities for misusing a feature, through lack of knowledge and experience, grow ever larger as well.

Foreword by Shawn Edwards

Using new features of an already sophisticated programming language such as C++, with which many developers might not be fully familiar, introduces its own category of risk. Less-seasoned engineers might unwittingly introduce new features into a mature code base where they could add manifestly negative value in that context. As ever, only time and experience can provide proof as to whether and under what conditions using a new C++ language feature would be prudent. We, as senior developers, team leads, and technical managers of a leading financial technology company, bear responsibility for protecting our Software Capital asset from undue risk.

We cannot justify the instability of rewriting all of our software every time a new version of the language appears, nor can we leave it in perpetual stasis and forgo the important benefits modern C++ has to offer. So we move forward but with expertise and caution, adopting features only after we fully understand them. Bloomberg is committed to extracting all of the benefit that it can from modern C++, but as a company, we must do so *safely*.

Bloomberg sponsored this book, *Embracing Modern C++ Safely*, because we felt that, despite all of the books, conferences, blogs, etc., that covered C++11/14 features, we needed to look at each feature from the point of view of how to apply it *safely* as well as effectively in the context of a large, mature corpus of production code. Therefore, this book provides detailed explanations of each C++11/14 language feature, examples of its effective use, and pitfalls to avoid. Moreover, this book could only have been written *now*, after years of gathering real-world experience. What's more, we knew that we had the right people — some of the best engineers and authors in the world — to write it.

As promised, the C++ Standards Committee has been sticking to its schedule, sometimes in the face of major world events, and two additional versions of the Standard, C++17 and C++20, have been published. As the community gains experience using the new features provided in those standards, I expect that future editions of this book will offer similar guidance and critique.

If you've been writing programs in C++ for more than a decade, you've undoubtedly noticed that being an accomplished C++ programmer is a different challenge than it used to be. This book will help you navigate the modern C++ landscape so that you too can feel confident in applying C++11/14 in ways that truly add value without undue risk to your organization's precious Software Capital investment.

— Shawn Edwards
Chief Technology Officer, Bloomberg LP
August 2021

Foreword by Andrei Alexandrescu

Do you like version control systems — Git, Perforce, Mercurial, and such? I love them! I have no idea how any of today's complex software systems could have ever been built without using version control.

One beneficial artifact of version control software is the *diff view*, that quintessential side-by-side view of a change of a large system as a differential from the previous, known version of the system. The diff view is often the best way to review code, to assess complexity of a feature, to find a bug, and, most importantly, to get familiar with a new system. I pore over diff views almost every working day, perusing them for one or more of their advantages. The diff view is proof that we *can* actually have the proverbial nice things.

The novel concept of this book is a diff view between classic C++ — i.e. C++03, the baseline — and modern C++ — i.e., post-2011 C++, with its added features. A diff view of programming language features! Now that's a cool idea with interesting implications.

Embracing Modern C++ Safely addresses a large category of programmers: those who work daily on complex, long-lived C++ systems and who are familiar with C++03 because said systems were written with that technology. Classes. Inheritance. Polymorphism. Templates. The STL. Yep, they know these notions well and work with them every day in complex problem domains. Rehashing those classic features is unnecessary. But some programmers are perhaps less comfortable with the cornucopia of new features standardized every three years, starting with C++11. They have no time to spend on tracking what the C++ Standards Committee is doing. Every hour spent learning new C++ features is an hour not spent on core systems functionality, so that snazzy new feature better be worth it. *Embracing Modern C++ Safely* is cleverly optimized to maximize the ratio of usefulness in production to time spent learning.

Pedagogically, this book achieves an almost impossible challenge: a *partial* diff (to allow this nerd a mathematically motivated metaphor) for each individual new feature added to C++ after 2003. What do I mean by that? When a book teaches language features, cross talk is inevitable: While discussing any one given feature, most other features interfere by necessity. As Scott Meyers once told me, "When you learn a language, all features come at you in parallel." The authors *modularized* the teaching of each new feature, so if you want to read about, say, generic lambdas, you get to read about generic lambdas with minimal interference from any other new language feature. When necessary, the interaction between the feature being discussed and others is narrowly specified, documented, and cross-referenced. The result is a fractally self-consistent book that can be read cover to cover or chunked by themes, interconnected features, or individual topics.

Foreword by Andrei Alexandrescu

Chapters 1, 2, and 3 mimic a sort of reverse *Divine Comedy*, whereby, as you may recall, the poet Dante is led by trusted guides through Hell (*Inferno*), Purgatory (*Purgatorio*), and Heaven (*Paradiso*). The respective chapters help you navigate from *Safe* to *Conditionally Safe* to *Unsafe* features of Modern C++.

Safe features (Chapter 1) will clearly, definitely, pound-the-table improve your code wherever you use them. Acquiring and applying the teachings of Chapter 1 is the fastest way for a team to start leveraging Modern C++ in production. `override`? Enjoy. Digit separators? Have at 'em. Explicit conversion operators? Knock yourself out. Such features are recommended fully and without reservation. Chapter 2 discusses *conditionally safe* features, those that are good for you but come with caveats. Initializer lists? Let's talk. Range `for`? Couple of things to be mindful of. Rvalue references? Long discussion; grab a coffee. And last but not least, *unsafe* features are those that can be challenging and require skill and utmost attention in usage. Their use should be confined as much as possible and wrapped under interfaces. Standard-layout types? Way trickier than it may seem. The `noexcept` specifier? Careful, you're on your own. Inline namespaces? At best, don't. Extensive details, examples, and discussions are available for every single feature added after C++03.

The authors use "unsafe" in a tongue-in-cheek manner here. Nothing taught in this book is unsafe in the traditional computer science sense; instead, think of the casual meaning of "safety" when used, say, in a hardware store. What's the safety of various tools for someone just starting to use them? A screwdriver is safe; a power drill is conditionally safe; and a welding machine is unsafe.

You may be concerned, thinking, "That sounds authoritative. What is the basis of such a ranking?" In fact, *Embracing Modern C++ Safely* is emphatically not authoritative but *objective* and based on the vast community of experience that the authors collected and curated. They intentionally, sometimes painfully, withhold their opinions. The "Use Cases" and "Potential Pitfalls" sections, taken from production code, are empirical evidence as much as instructive examples to learn from.

Only the passage of time can distill the programming community's practical experience with each feature and how well it fared, which is why this book discusses features added up to C++14, even though C++20 is already out. Using features for years can replace passionate debate on language design ideas with cold, hard experience, which guides this book's remarkably clinical approach. In the words of John Lakos, "We explain the degrees of burns you could get if you put your hand on a hot stove, but we won't tell you not to do it." The result is a refreshingly nonideological read, no more partisan than a book on experimental physics. Consistently avoiding injecting one's own ego and opinion in an analysis takes paradoxically a lot of work. *Ars est celare artem*, the Latin proverb goes in typical brief, cryptic, and slightly confusing manner. (Is Latin the APL of natural languages?) That literally translates to "the art is to conceal the art," but the profound meaning is closer to "good art is not emphatically artsy." Good artists don't leave fingerprints all over their work. In a very concrete way, that has been a design goal of *Embracing Modern C++ Safely*, for you won't find in it any opinion, pontification, or even gratuitously flowery language. (Fierce debates occurred about the perfect, most spartan choice of words in one paragraph or another.) This polished clarity will, I'm sure, shine through to any reader.

That Extra Oomph

"The only kind of writing is rewriting," goes the famous quote. That is doubly true for technical books. The strength of a textbook stands in the willingness of its authors to redo their work and in the depth and breadth of its review team feeding the revision process. And rewriting is not easy! Have you ever written some code and then resisted reviews because you fell in love with it? Multiply that by 1024 and you'll know how book authors feel about rewriting passages they've already poured their souls into. You really need to be committed to quality to keep heart during such a trial.

The authors' insistence on quality brings to mind what I like most about this book, which is also the most difficult to explain. I call it *the extra oomph*.

I noticed something about great work — be it in engineering, art, sports, or any other challenging human endeavor. Almost always, great work is the result of talented people making an extra effort that goes beyond what one might consider reasonable. In appreciating such work, we implicitly acknowledge great capability combined with commensurately great effort in realizing it. Good work can be done glibly; great work cannot.

Through an odd turn of events I ended up getting quite involved with this book — first, for one review. And then another, and another, for a total of four thorough passes through the entire book. The quest for perfection is as contagious as the resignation to sloppiness and incomparably more fun. ("Destroy!" John Lakos pithily emailed me along with each new revision. My often caustic reviews motivated him like nothing else.) Other reviewers — C++ Standards Committee denizens, industry C++ experts, C++03 experts with no prior exposure to C++1x, software-architecture experts, multithreading experts, process experts, even LaTeX experts — have done the same, with the net result that each sentence you'll read has been critically considered dozens of times and probably rewritten a few. For my part, I got so enthused with the project and with the authors' uncompromising take on quality, that I ended up writing a full feature for the book. (Any mistake in Section 2.1. "Variadic Templates" is my fault.) This book project has been a lot of work, more than I might have reasonably expected, which is everything I'd hoped for. I thought I've gotten too old to still pull all-nighters; apparently I was wrong.

Having been thusly involved, I can tell: This book does have that extra oomph baked into it. The talk is being walked, there's no fluff, and the code examples are precise and eloquent. I think *Embracing Modern C++ Safely* is Great Work. Aside from learning from this book, I hope you derive from it inspiration to add more oomph into your own work. I know I did.

— Andrei Alexandrescu
May 2021

Acknowledgments

Embracing Modern C++ Safely is the work of the C++ community as a whole, not just the authors. This book comprises knowledge drawn from the depths of language design to the boundaries of sound software development. Those who are expert at one end of that language-design to application-development spectrum might be relatively unfamiliar with the other. Although we, the four authors named on the front of this book, are each professional senior software engineers, our combined knowledge did not initially span everything presented here, and we relied on many of our colleagues — from our fellow developers at Bloomberg to the Core Working Group of the C++ Standards Committee to Bjarne Stroustrup himself — to fill in holes in our understanding and to correct misconceptions we held.

Everyone on Bloomberg's BDE team, founded in December 2001, contributed directly, in one way or another, to the publication of this book: Parsa Amini, Joshua Berne, Harry Bott, Steven Breitstein, Nathan Burgers, Bill Chapman, Attila Feher, Mungo Gill, Rostislav Khlebnikov, Jeffrey Mendelsohn, Alisdair Meredith, Hyman Rosen, and the BDE team's second manager (since April 2019), Mike Verschell.

Nina Ranns, ISO C++ Standards Committee secretary and ISO C++ Foundation director, was our principal researcher and provided a window into the depths of the C++ core language standard. We relied on her to get to *the truth*: With a release coming every three years and defect reports retroactive to previous standards, *the truth* is a contextual, ephemeral, and elusive beast. Nonetheless, Nina provided us with clarity about what was in effect when and thoroughly reviewed each and every core-language-intensive feature in this book; see Section 2.1. "**constexpr** Functions" on page 257, Section 2.1. "Generalized PODs '11" on page 401, Section 2.1. "*Rvalue* References" on page 710, and Section 3.1. "**noexcept** Specifier" on page 1085, as just a few examples.

Joshua Berne, senior software engineer on Bloomberg's BDE team and an active member of the C++ Standards Committee's Core Working Group (CWG) and Contracts Study Group (SG21), served multiple roles: Josh was our bridge between the core language and software development, performing structural rewrites of major features, including the features mentioned and many others. All benchmarking research conducted for this book was designed, performed, and/or reviewed by Josh. He provided the technical expertise needed to make LaTeX function to its fullest capabilities, designing and implementing the glossary, including automating the references back into the individual sections that use the terms. Importantly, Josh was the voice of reason throughout this entire project.

Lori Hughes, our project manager, frontline technical editor, and LaTeX designer and compositor, would probably tell you that herding cats is child's play compared to what she

Acknowledgments

endured during this project. The tenacity, assertiveness, and roll-up-your-sleeves hard work she demonstrated relentlessly is arguably the only reason this book was published in 2021 (if not this decade). In short, Lori's our rock; she is a veteran of **lakos20**, and we look forward to working with her on *all* of our planned future projects — e.g., allocators (**lakos22**), contracts (**lakos23**), Volumes II and III following **lakos20** (**lakos2a** and **lakos2b**), and anticipated future editions of this book incorporating C++17, C++20, etc.

Pablo Halpern, a former member of Bloomberg's BDE team, an active member of the C++ Standards Committee, the creator of the `std::pmr` allocator model, and now a full-time collaborator with BDE working on language-level support for local memory allocators, served as a ghost writer for several features in this book (e.g., see Section 2.1."User-Defined Literals" on page 835) and provided massive restructuring to many others (e.g., see Section 2.1. "Generalized PODs '11" on page 401. Notably, out of all the nonauthors who contributed drafts in final form, only Pablo was able to write in a style approximating the authors' voice. He also performed the research for a paper, commissioned by the authors of this book, demonstrating that **move operations**, though faster to execute initially, can have negative overall runtime implications due to **memory diffusion**; see **halpern21c**.

Dr. Andrei Alexandrescu — author of the seminal book *Modern C++ Design* (Addison-Wesley, 2001), coauthor of *C++ Coding Standards* (Addison-Wesley, 2005), and major contributor to the D language — was called upon for multiple assists in this endeavor: (1) as an expert author to provide an approachable guide to using variadic templates for those accustomed to their C++03 counterparts (see Section 2.1."Variadic Templates" on page 873); (2) as a technical reviewer whose primary job was to reduce the tedium of John Lakos' writing style and its numerous parenthetical phrases and footnotes; and (3) as a mascot and champion of our effort to imbue, on C++03 folk, the C++11/14 overlay of features. Andrei also generously agreed to write a foreword to this book, advocating its utility for senior developers familiar with classic C++.

Harold Bott, John's TA in his Advanced C++ course during the 1990s at Columbia University, reconnected with John in 2019. Harry has since been a force in driving this book forward to completion. After a month of research with Nina, John entrusted Harry, a former programmer at Goldman Sachs and Executive Director at JP Morgan, with getting the flagship feature of modern C++ (see Section 2.1."*Rvalue* References" on page 710) ready for review — a daunting task indeed. Once reviews were in and revisions were needed, Harry worked with John, nearly around the clock for almost three straight weeks, to incorporate reviewer feedback and to bring this important feature to the state in which it is presented here.

Mungo Gill is one of the newest full-time contributors on the BDE team and brings with him more than 30 years of professional software experience at such notable organizations as Salomon Brothers, Citigroup, Lehman Brothers, Google, and Citadel Securities. Mungo has reviewed every line of this book and has provided valuable feedback from a senior practitioner's perspective. He also coordinated the process of assembling glossary definitions and gaining consensus among a host of eclectic domain experts.

Clay Wilson, a member of the BDE team since 2003, is another veteran of **lakos20**. Clay has, for the past 18 years, been our "closer" when it comes to reviewing software components.

His attention to detail and accuracy is, in our experience, second to none. Clay has reviewed much of this book, and we look forward to the possibility of working with him on future projects.

Steven Breitstein, a member of BDE since 2004 and an alumnus of **lakos20**, has reviewed every line and code snippet in this book and has made innumerable suggestions for manifestly improving the rendering of the material. He also stepped up and singlehandedly applied all the copy edits to our glossary.

Hyman Rosen retired from Bloomberg's BDE team in April 2021 and was the master of pragmatic real-world use cases for some of the otherwise ostensibly *unsafe* features of modern C++, such as using extended friendship (see Section 3.1.`"friend` '11" on page 1031) with the **curiously recurring template pattern (CRTP)**. You'll find many others scattered throughout this book.

Stephen Dewhurst, an internationally recognized expert in C++ programming and popular repeat C++ author, conference speaker, and professional C++ trainer (including, for more than a decade, at Bloomberg), has reviewed *every* feature in this book and provided copious, practically valuable feedback, including a use case; see *Use Cases — Stateless lambdas* on page 605 within Section 2.1."Lambdas."

Jeffrey Olkin, who joined Bloomberg in 2011, is one of its most senior software architects, was the structural editor of **lakos20**, and has been a welcome advocate of this book from the start, reviewing many features, helping to organize the preliminary material, and providing his insightful and always valuable feedback along the way.

Steve Downey, a senior developer at Bloomberg since 2003, C++ Standards Committee member, and multidomain expert, contributed much of the advanced material found in a somewhat niche, *conditionally safe* feature of C++11; see Section 1.1."Unicode Literals" on page 129. Mike Giroux and Oleg Subbotin fleshed out and provided benchmark material for another *conditionally safe* C++11 feature; see Section 2.1.`"extern template"` on page 353.

Sean Parent contributed a subsection assessing the strictness of current requirements on moved-from objects for standard containers; see *Annoyances — Standard Library requirements on a moved-from object are overly strict* on page 807 within Section 2.1."*Rvalue* References." Niall Douglas contributed a subsection detailing his experiences at scale with one of the *unsafe* C++ features; see *Appendix — Case study of using inline namespaces for versioning* on page 1083 within Section 3.1.`"inline namespace."` Niels Dekker reviewed another *unsafe* C++11 feature (see Section 3.1.`"noexcept` Specifier" on page 1085) and provided valuable additional information as well as pointers to his own benchmark research. Kevin Klein helped organize and draft the material of yet another *unsafe* C++11 feature; see Section 3.1.`"final"` on page 1007.

Many senior C++ software engineers, instructors, and professional developers reviewed this work and provided copious feedback: Adil Al-Yasiri, Andrei Alexandrescu, Parsa Amini, Brian Bi, Frank Birbacher, Harry Bott, Steve Breitstein, Tomaz Canabrava, Bill Chapman, Marshall Clow, Stephen Dewhurst, Akshaye Dhawan, Niall Douglas, Steve Downey, Tom Eccles, Attila Feher, Kevin Fleming, J. Daniel Garcia, Mungo Gill, Mike Giroux, Kevin

Acknowledgments

Klein, Jeff Mendelsohn, Jeffrey Olkin, Nina Ranns, Hyman Rosen, Daniel Ruoso, Ben Saks, Richard Smith, Oleg Subbotin, Julian Templeman, Mike Verschell, Clay Wilson, and JC van Winkel.

In addition to reviewing the features of this book as they were being written, the BDE team fleshed out the first draft of the glossary, after which we relied again on Josh Berne, Brian Bi, Harry Bott, Mungo Gill, Pablo Halpern, and Nina Ranns to refine and consolidate it into a final draft before finally reviewing it ourselves in its totality. Jeff Mendelsohn and Nathan Burgers helped to distill the essence of this book onto its back cover. We want to thank all the Standards Committee members who provided valuable information when researching the details, history, etc., surrounding the various language features presented in this book. In particular, we would like to thank Bjarne Stroustrup for affably answering our pointed questions regarding anything related to C++. Howard Hinnant confirmed, among other things, the details of why and how *xvalues* were originally invented and how they have since morphed (a.k.a. "the delta") from their original concept to their definition today. Michael Wong, Paul McKenney, and Maged Michael reviewed and signed off on our presentation of the `[[carries_dependency]]` attribute; see Section 3.1."`carries_dependency`" on page 998. And we cannot thank Richard Smith enough for his thorough review and myriad suggestions on how to correct and improve our treatment of the flagship feature of modern C++ (see Section 2.1."*Rvalue* References" on page 710). We hope that Richard will review *every* feature in subsequent editions of this book.

The team at Pearson — Greg Doench, our editor and fearless leader; Julie Nahil, our production manager; and Kim Wimpsett, our copy editor — have been very supportive of our efforts to get this book done quickly and accurately, despite its unorthodox workflow. We had originally projected that this book would contain 300–400 pages and would be complete by the end of 2020. That didn't happen. Somehow, Greg and Julie found a way to accommodate our process and get this book printed in time for the 2021 winter holidays; thank you!

Online compilers, such as Godbolt (Compiler Explorer) and Wandbox, proved invaluable in the development of this work, allowing the team to rapidly evaluate and share code samples tested with various versions of multiple compilers accepting different dialects of the language.

We want to give a shout-out to the folks at Bloomberg involved in making sure that Bloomberg's intellectual property and customer data were in no way compromised by anything contained herein and that appropriate attributions were made: Tom Arcidiacono, Kevin P. Fleming, and Chaim Haas.

Moreover, we want to recognize and thank our Bloomberg management for providing not just the support but the *imperative* to do this essential work for ourselves and then share it! In 2012, Vladimir Kliatchko, then and still Global Head of Engineering at Bloomberg, directed John Lakos, who collaborated with Rostislav Khlebnikov, to write a paper, **khlebnikov18**, to describe concisely the value proposition of C++11 and how best to exploit it. That short C++11 paper, 11 pages of 11-point type, was indeed well received, widely accepted, and ratified by fully 85 percent of the Standards Committee members who reviewed it. After that, Andrei Basov, Engineering Manager, Middleware and Core Services; Akshaye Dhawan, Engineering Manager, Training, Documentation, and Work Management; and Adam Wolf, Head of Engineering, Software Infrastructure, encouraged and supported us in pursuing a more all-encompassing, practical-engineering-oriented treatment of modern C++, including C++14, in book form.

Finally, this book would not have been possible without the generous patronage of our Chief Technology Officer, Shawn Edwards. Without his support, and especially his sponsorship, the vast technical resources needed for this book to come to fruition could never have been brought to bear. Shawn, with his illustrious career as a developer, team lead, and technical manager, and now, as a senior executive, has graciously provided a foreword to this book.

About the Authors

John Lakos, author of *Large-Scale C++ Software Design* (Addison-Wesley, 1996) and *Large-Scale C++ Volume I: Process and Architecture* (Addison-Wesley, 2020), serves at Bloomberg in New York City as a senior architect and mentor for C++ software development worldwide. He is also an active voting member of the C++ Standards Committee's Evolution Working Group. From 1997 to 2001, Dr. Lakos directed the design and development of infrastructure libraries for proprietary analytic financial applications at Bear Stearns. From 1983 to 1997, Dr. Lakos was employed at Mentor Graphics, where he developed large frameworks and advanced ICCAD applications for which he holds multiple software patents. His academic credentials include a Ph.D. in Computer Science (1997) and an Sc.D. in Electrical Engineering (1989) from Columbia University. Dr. Lakos received his undergraduate degrees from MIT in Mathematics (1982) and Computer Science (1981).

Vittorio Romeo (B.Sc., Computer Science, 2016) is a senior software engineer at Bloomberg in London, where he builds mission-critical C++ middleware and delivers modern C++ training to hundreds of fellow employees. He began programming at the age of 8 and quickly fell in love with C++. Vittorio has created several open-source C++ libraries and games, has published many video courses and tutorials, and actively participates in the ISO C++ standardization process. He is an active member of the C++ community with an ardent desire to share his knowledge and learn from others: He presented more than 20 times at international C++ conferences (including CppCon, C++Now, ++it, ACCU, C++ On Sea, C++ Russia, and Meeting C++), covering topics from game development to template metaprogramming. Vittorio maintains a website (https://vittorioromeo.info/) with advanced C++ articles and a YouTube channel (https://www.youtube.com/channel/UC1XihgHdkNOQd5IBHnIZWbA) featuring well received modern C++11/14 tutorials. He is active on StackOverflow, taking great care in answering interesting C++ questions (75k+ reputation). When he is not writing code, Vittorio enjoys weightlifting and fitness-related activities as well as computer gaming and sci-fi movies.

Rostislav Khlebnikov is the lead of the BDE Solutions team that works on a variety of BDE libraries, such as the library for HTTP/2 communication, and contributes to other projects, including improving interoperability of BDE libraries with the Standard Library vocabulary types. He is an active member of the C++ Standards Committee and presented at CppCon 2019. Prior to his work at Bloomberg, Dr. Khlebnikov received his undergraduate degrees in Applied Mathematics and Computer Science from St. Petersburg State

About the Authors

Polytechnic University, Russia, and his Ph.D. in Computer Science from Graz University of Technology, Austria. He has worked professionally as a C++ software engineer for over 15 years.

Alisdair Meredith has been a member of the C++ Standards Committee since the inception of C++11 at the Oxford 2003 meeting, focusing on feature integration and actively finding and fixing language inconsistencies. Alisdair was the LWG chair when both C++11 and C++14 were published, for which he credits the hard work of the preceding chair, Howard Hinnant. Alisdair has been a perennial conference speaker for nearly 15 years, elucidating new work from the C++ Standards Committee. Alisdair joined Bloomberg's BDE team in 2009. For a decade prior, Alisdair worked as a professional C++ application programmer in F1 motor racing with the Benetton and Renault teams, winning two world championships! Between the two, Alisdair spent a year or so as a product manager at Borland, marketing their C++ products. Alisdair enjoys traveling, dining, and snorkeling.

Chapter 0

Introduction

Welcome! *Embracing Modern C++ Safely* is a reference book designed for professionals who develop and maintain large-scale, complex C++ software systems and want to leverage modern C++ features.

This book focuses on the productive value of each new language feature, starting with C++11, particularly when the systems and organizations involved are considered at scale. We deliberately left aside ideas and idioms — however clever and intellectually intriguing — that could hurt the bottom line when applied to large-scale systems. Instead, we focus on making wise economic and design decisions, with an understanding of the inevitable trade-offs that arise in any engineering discipline. In doing so, we do our best to steer clear of subjective opinions and recommendations.

Richard Feynman famously said, "If it disagrees with experiment, it's wrong. In that simple statement is the key to science."[1] There is no better way to experiment with a language feature than letting time do its work. We took that to heart and decided to cover only the features of modern C++ that have been part of the Standard for at least five years, which we believe provides enough perspective to properly evaluate the practical impact of new features. Thus, we are able to draw from practical experience to provide a thorough and comprehensive treatment that is worthy of your limited professional development time. If you're looking for ways to improve your productivity by using tried and true modern C++ features, we hope this book will be the one you'll reach for.

What's missing from a book is as important as what's present. *Embracing Modern C++ Safely*, known also as *EMC++S*, is not a tutorial on C++ programming or even on new features of C++. We assume you are an experienced developer, team lead, or manager; that you already have a good command of classic C++98/03; and that you are looking for clear, goal-driven ways to integrate modern C++ features into your toolbox.

What Makes This Book Different

The goal of the book you're now reading is to be objective, empirical, and practical. We simply present features, their applicability, and their potential pitfalls as reflected by the analysis of millions of person-hours of using C++11 and C++14 in the development of

---

[1]Richard Feynman, lecture at Cornell University, 1964. Video and commentary available at https://fs.blog/2009/12/mental-model-scientific-method.

varied large-scale software systems; personal preference matters have been neutralized to our best ability. We wrote down the distilled truth that remains, which should shape your understanding of what modern C++ has to offer without being skewed by our subjective opinions or domain-specific inclinations.

The final analysis and interpretation of what is appropriate for your context is left to you, the reader. This book is, by design, not a C++ style or coding-standards guide; it does, however, provide valuable input to any development organization seeking to author or enhance one.

Practicality is important to us in a real-world, economic sense. We examine modern C++ features through the lens of a large company developing and using software in a competitive environment. In addition to showing you how to best utilize a given C++ language feature in practice, our analysis takes into account the costs associated with routinely employing that feature in the ecosystem of a software development organization. Most texts omit the costs of using language features. In other words, we weigh the benefits of successfully using a feature against the hidden cost of its widespread ineffective use (or misuse) and/or the costs associated with training and code review required to reasonably ensure that such ill-conceived use does not occur. We are acutely aware that what applies to one person or a small crew of like-minded individuals is quite different from what works with a large, distributed team. The outcome of this analysis is our signature categorization of features based on how safe they are to adopt — namely, *safe*, *conditionally safe*, or *unsafe* features.

We are not aware of any similar text amid the rich offering of C++ textbooks; we wrote this book because we needed it.

Scope for the First Edition

Given the vastness of C++'s already voluminous and rapidly growing standardized libraries, we have chosen to limit this book's scope to just the language features themselves. A companion book, *Embracing Modern C++ Standard Libraries Safely*, is a separate project that we hope to tackle in the future. To be effective, this book, however, must remain focused on what expert C++ developers need to know well to be successful right now.

We chose to limit the scope of this first edition to only those features that have been included in the language standard since C++11 and widely available in practice for at least five years. This limited focus enables us to better evaluate the real-world impact of these features and to highlight any caveats that might not have been anticipated prior to standardization and sustained, active, and widespread use in industry.

We assume you are quite familiar with essentially all of the basic and important special-purpose features of classic C++98/03, so in this book we confine our attention to just the subset of C++ language features introduced in C++11 and C++14. This book is best for you if you need to know how to safely incorporate C++11/14 language features into a predominately C++98/03 codebase, today.

We are actively planning to cover pre-C++11 material in future editions. For the time being, however, we highly recommend *Effective C++* by Scott Meyers[2] as a concise, practical treatment of many important and useful C++98/03 features.

The *EMC++S* Guiding Principles

Throughout the writing of *Embracing Modern C++ Safely*, we have followed a set of guiding principles, which collectively drive the style and content of this book.

Facts, Not Opinions

This book describes only beneficial uses and potential pitfalls of modern C++ features. The content presented is based on objectively verifiable facts, derived either from standards documents or from extensive practical experience; we explicitly avoid subjective opinions on the relative merits of design trade-offs (restraint that is a good exercise in humility). Although such opinions are often valuable, they are inherently biased toward the author's area of expertise.

Note that *safety* — the rating we use to segregate features by chapter — is the one exception to this objectivity guideline. Although the analysis of each feature aims at being entirely objective, each feature's chapter classification — indicating the relative safety of its quotidian use in a large software-development environment — reflects our combined decades of real-world, hands-on experience developing a variety of large-scale C++ software systems.

Elucidation, Not Prescription

We deliberately avoid prescribing any solutions to address specific feature pitfalls. Instead, we merely describe and characterize such concerns in sufficient detail to equip you to devise a solution suitable for your own development environment. In some cases, we might reference techniques or publicly available libraries that others have used to work around such speed bumps, but we do not pass judgment about which workaround should be considered a best practice.

Thorough, Not Superficial

Embracing Modern C++ Safely is neither designed nor intended to be an introduction to modern C++. This book is a handy reference for experienced C++ programmers who have

---

[2]**meyers92**

familiarity with earlier versions of the language (C++98/03). Our goal is to provide you with facts, detailed objective analysis, and cogent, real-world examples. By doing so, we spare you the task of wading through material that we presume you already know. If you are entirely unfamiliar with the C++ language, we suggest you start with a more elementary and language-centric text such as *The C++ Programming Language* by Bjarne Stroustrup.[3]

Real-World, Not Contrived, Examples

We hope you will find the examples in this book useful in multiple ways. The primary purpose of the examples is to illustrate productive use of each feature as it might occur in practice. We stay away from contrived examples that give equal importance to seldom-used aspects and to the intended, idiomatic uses of the feature. Hence, many of our examples are based on simplified code fragments extracted from real-world codebases. Though we typically change identifier names to be more appropriate to the shortened example (rather than the context and the process that led to the example), we keep the code structure of each example as close as possible to its original, real-world counterpart.

At Scale, Not Overly Simplistic, Programs

As with many aspects of software development, what works for small programs and teams often doesn't scale to larger development efforts. We attempt to simultaneously capture two distinct aspects of size: (1) the sheer product size (e.g., in bytes, source lines, separate units of release) of the programs, systems, and libraries developed and maintained by a software organization; and (2) the size of an organization itself as measured by the number of software developers, quality-assurance engineers, site-reliability engineers, operators, and so on that the organization employs.

What's more, powerful new language features in the hands of a few expert programmers working together on a prototype for their new start-up don't always fare as well when they are wantonly exercised by dozens or hundreds of developers in a large software-development organization. Hence, when we consider the relative safety of a feature, as defined in the next section, we do so with mindfulness that any given feature might be used — and occasionally misused — in large programs and by a large number of programmers having a wide range of knowledge, skill, and ability.

What Do We Mean by *Safely?*

The ISO C++ Standards Committee, of which we are members, would be remiss — and downright negligent — if it allowed any feature of the C++ language to be standardized if that feature were not reliably safe when used as intended. Still, we have chosen the word

[3]stroustrup13

"safely" as the moniker for the signature aspect of our book and the method by which we rank the risk-to-reward ratio for using a given feature in a large-scale development environment. By contextualizing the meaning of the term "safe," we apply it to a real-world economy in which everything has a cost in multiple dimensions: risk of misuse, added maintenance burden borne by using a new feature in an older codebase, and training needs for developers who might not be familiar with that feature.

Several factors impact the value added by the adoption and widespread use of any new language feature, thereby reducing its intrinsic safety. By categorizing features in terms of safety, we strive to capture an appropriately weighted combination of the following factors:

- Number and severity of known deficiencies
- Difficulty in teaching consistent proper use
- Experience level required for consistent proper use
- Risks associated with widespread misuse

In this book, the degree of safety of a given feature is the relative likelihood that widespread use of that feature will have positive impact and no adverse effect on a large software company's codebase.

A *Safe* Feature

Some of the new features of modern C++ add considerable value, are easy to use, and are decidedly hard to misuse unintentionally; hence, ubiquitous adoption of such features is productive, relatively unlikely to become a problem in the context of a large-scale development organization, and generally encouraged — even without training. We identify such staunchly helpful, unflappable C++ features as *safe*.

For example, we categorize the **override** contextual keyword as a safe feature because it prevents bugs, serves as documentation, cannot be easily misused, and has no serious deficiencies. If someone has heard of this feature and tried to use it and the software compiles, the codebase is likely better for it. Using **override** wherever applicable is always a sound engineering decision.

A *Conditionally Safe* Feature

The vast majority of new features available in modern C++ have important, frequently occurring, and valuable uses, yet how these features are used appropriately, let alone optimally, might not be obvious. What's more, some of these features are fraught with inherent dangers and deficiencies, requiring explicit training and extra care to circumnavigate their pitfalls.

For example, we deem default member initializers a *conditionally safe* feature because, although they are easy to use per se, the perhaps less-than-obvious unintended consequences of doing so (e.g., tight compile-time coupling) might be prohibitively costly in certain circumstances (e.g., might prevent relink-only patching in production).

An *Unsafe* Feature

When an expert programmer uses any C++ feature appropriately, the feature typically does no direct harm. Yet other developers — seeing the feature's use in the codebase but failing to appreciate the highly specialized or nuanced reasoning justifying it — might attempt to use it in what they perceive to be a similar way, yet with profoundly less desirable results. Similarly, maintainers might change the use of a fragile feature, altering its semantics in subtle but damaging ways.

Features that are classified as unsafe are those that might have valid — and even important — use cases, yet our experience indicates that routine or widespread use would be counterproductive in a typical, large-scale, software-development enterprise.

For example, we deem the `final` contextual keyword an unsafe feature because the situations in which it would be misused overwhelmingly outnumber those vanishingly few isolated cases in which it is appropriate, let alone valuable. Furthermore, its widespread use would inhibit fine-grained (e.g., hierarchical) reuse, which is critically important to the success of a large organization.

Modern C++ Feature Catalog

This first edition of *Embracing Modern C++ Safely* was designed to serve as a comprehensive catalog of C++11 and C++14 language features, presenting vital information for each in a clear, consistent, and predictable format to which experienced engineers can readily refer during development or technical discourse.

Organization

This book is divided into four chapters, the last three of which form the catalog of modern C++ language features grouped by their respective safety classifications:

- Chapter 0: Introduction
- Chapter 1: *Safe* Features

- Chapter 2: *Conditionally Safe* Features

- Chapter 3: *Unsafe* Features

For this first edition, the language-feature chapters (1, 2, and 3) are divided into two sections containing, respectively, C++11 and C++14 features having the safety level (*safe, conditionally safe,* or *unsafe*) corresponding to that chapter. Recall, however, that Standard Library features are outside the scope of this book.

Each feature is presented in a separate section, rendered in a canonical format:

- **Description** — A brisk but comprehensive introduction of the feature's syntax and semantics, supplemented with abundant code snippets. We do our best to avoid using other new features concurrently with the one being described, so each feature can be read independently and out of order. This might lead, on occasion, to code that is less fluent than it could otherwise be. Make sure you consult the "See Also" section (described below) to learn about crosstalk between features.

- **Use Cases** — A collection of tried-and-true use cases distilled from libraries and applications.

- **Potential Pitfalls** — Misuses of the feature that might lead to serious bugs and other problems.

- **Annoyances** — Shortcomings of the feature and unpleasant quirks that might make the feature less pleasant to use.

- **See Also** — Cross-references to other related features within this book along with a brief description of the connection.

- **Further Reading** — References to external sources discussing the feature.

Constraining our treatment of each individual feature to this canonized format facilitates rapid discovery of whatever particular aspects of a given language feature you are searching for.

Note that cross-references to subsections within a feature are in italics, and cross-references to other features are in normal text font. We refer to each feature within its relevant chapter and section: For example, Section 1.1. "Attribute Syntax" tells you that the "Attributes" feature is located in Chapter 1 (Safe) and within Section 1 (C++11). Terms that are defined within the glossary are set in a **different font**, with the first use in each feature being set in **bold**.

The commenting style is worth noting because it conveys good information in a terse format. Note that "description" or "details" provides additional descriptive information. Placeholders for irrelevant and/or unspecified code are shown with stylized comments in one of the following ways:

```
/*...*/
// ...
// ...                                        (<description>)
```

Code that does not compile will be marked with one of the following two comments:

```
// Error
// Error, <details>
```

Code that does not link will be marked with one of the following two comments:

```
// Link-Time Error
// Link-Time Error, <details>
```

Code that does not behave as expected at run time will be marked with one of the following two comments:

```
// Bug
// Bug, <details>
```

Code that behaves as expected will be marked with one of the following two comments:

```
// OK
// OK, <details>
```

Code that might warn but behaves as expected would be marked "OK, might warn" or similarly. For example, if a feature is deprecated until C++17 and removed in C++20, we might comment it like this:

```
// OK, deprecated⁴ (might warn)
```

How to Use This Book

Depending on your needs, *Embracing Modern C++ Safely* can be handy in a variety of ways.

- **Read the entire book from front to back.** If you are conversant with classic C++, consuming this book in its entirety will provide a complete and nuanced practical understanding of each of the language features introduced by C++11 and C++14.

- **Read the chapters in order but slowly over time.** An incremental, priority-driven approach is also possible and recommended, especially if you're feeling less sure-footed. Understanding and applying first the *safe* features of Chapter 1 gets you the low-hanging fruit. In time, the *conditionally safe* features of Chapter 2 will allow you to ease into the breadth of useful modern C++ language features, prioritizing those that are least likely to prove problematic.

---

⁴Removed in C++20

- **Read the C++11 sections of each of the three catalog chapters first.** If you are a developer whose organization uses C++11 but not yet C++14, you can focus on learning everything that can be applied now and then circle back and learn the rest later when it becomes relevant to your evolving organization.

- **Use the book as a quick-reference guide if and as needed.** Random access is great, too, especially now that you've made it through Chapter 0. If you prefer not to read the book in its entirety (or simply want to refer to it periodically as a refresher), reading any arbitrary individual feature section in any order will provide timely access to all relevant details of whichever feature is of immediate interest.

We believe that you will derive value in several ways from the knowledge we imbued into *Embracing Modern C++ Safely*, irrespective of how you read it. In addition to helping you become a more knowledgeable and therefore safer developer, this book aims to clarify (whether you are a developer, a lead, or a manager) which features demand more training, attention to detail, experience, peer review, and such. The factual, objective presentation style also makes for excellent input into the preparation of coding standards and style guides that suit the particular needs of a company, project, team, or even just a single discriminating developer (which, of course, we all aim at being). Finally, any C++ software-development organization that adopts this book will be taking the first steps toward leveraging modern C++ in a way that maximizes reward while minimizing risks, i.e., by embracing modern C++ *safely*.

Last but definitely not least, this is *your* book in more than one sense of the word. It has been a collaborative effort with input from many engineers just like you, and it was "designed for maintenance" because we plan future revised editions with new features and improved treatment of the existing ones. Those future editions could greatly benefit from your contributions. Found something broken or missing? A clever use case? A hidden pitfall? An annoyance you can't stand? We'd be happy to add it to the book. Point your browser to http://emcpps.com, and follow the instructions to send us feedback. Your input will be well received. You'll find more information about the book on the website. Thank you, and happy coding!

Chapter 1

Safe Features

Modern C++ has a lot to offer. Many of the modern language features provide affirmative value. They enable increased productivity and reliability, are easy to understand and use, and are hard to accidentally misuse in consequential ways. This chapter introduces those C++11 and C++14 features that have few, minor, and readily recognizable pitfalls, making misuse easy to avoid. Moreover, these features bring little systemic risk when introduced widely into a predominantly C++03 codebase, allowing organized training to be optional rather than mandatory. An organization's leadership can feel reasonably comfortable guiding all its engineers toward using features presented in this chapter.

Safe features are characterized primarily by being of low risk. Recall from "A *Safe* Feature" in Chapter 0 that the **override** feature (p. 104) was singled out as epitomizing a *safe* feature. Though applicable only in the context of inheritance and virtual functions, this feature is almost impossible to misuse such that it fails to add value. Another example of a feature having low risk but with exceptionally high reward is static_asssert (p. 115). This particular feature is so universally useful and immune to inadvertent misuse that we use it liberally throughout the book to illustrate important compile-time properties almost as if it were a C++03 feature. Although not all features presented in this chapter are as eminently useful or widely applicable as these two, all of them are usable with minimal risk and thus are considered *safe*.

In short, widespread adoption of *safe* features is a low-risk proposition. All of these features are easy to understand and use profitably and hard to misuse; hence, formal training is generally not required. An organization need not be concerned about incorporating *safe* features into a predominantly C++03 codebase maintained primarily by those largely unfamiliar with modern features. If you're new to the features of modern C++, by all means start here.

Generalized Attribute Support

A new syntax for annotating code with attributes affords the portable provision of supplementary information for compiler implementations and external tools.

Description

Developers are often aware of information that cannot be easily deduced directly from the source code within a given translation unit. Some of this information might be useful to certain compilers, say, to inform diagnostics or optimizations; typical attributes, however, are designed to avoid affecting the semantics of a well-written program. By *semantics*, here we typically mean any observable behavior apart from runtime performance. Generally, ignoring an attribute is a valid and safe choice for a compiler to make. Sometimes, however, an attribute will not affect the behavior of a *correct* program but might affect the behavior of a well-formed yet incorrect one (see *Use Cases — Stating explicit assumptions in code to achieve better optimizations* on page 16). Customized annotations targeted at external tools might be beneficial as well.

C++ attribute syntax

C++ supports a standard syntax for attributes, introduced via a matching pair of [[and]], the simplest of which is a single attribute represented using a simple identifier, e.g., attribute_name:

```
[[attribute_name]]
```

A single annotation can consist of zero or more attributes:

```
[[]]           // permitted in every position where any attribute is allowed
[[foo, bar]]   // equivalent to [[foo]] [[bar]]
```

An attribute might have an argument list consisting of an arbitrary sequence of tokens:

```
[[attribute_name()]]            // zero-argument attribute
[[deprecated("bad API")]]       // single-argument attribute
[[theoretical(1, "two", 3.0)]]  // multiple-argument attribute
[[complicated({1, 2, 3} + 5)]]  // arbitrary tokens[1]
```

Note that having an incorrect number of arguments or an incompatible argument type is a compile-time error for all attributes defined by the Standard; the behavior for all other attributes, however, is **implementation-defined** (see *Potential Pitfalls — Unrecognized attributes have implementation-defined behavior* on page 18).

---

[1] GCC offered no support for certain tokens in the attributes until GCC 9.3 (c. 2020).

Any attribute may be qualified with an attribute namespace,[2] i.e., a single arbitrary identifier:

```
[[gnu::const]]  // (GCC-specific) namespace-gnu-qualified const attribute
[[my::own]]     // (user-specified) namespace-my-qualified own attribute
```

C++ attribute placement

Attributes can be placed in a variety of locations within the C++ grammar. For each such location, the Standard defines the entity or statement to which the attribute is said to *pertain*. For example, an attribute in front of a simple declaration statement pertains to each of the entities declared by the statement, whereas an attribute placed immediately after the declared name pertains only to that entity:

```
[[foo]] void f(), g();    // foo pertains to both f() and g().
void u(), v [[foo]] ();   // foo pertains only to v().
```

Attributes can apply to an entity without a name (e.g., anonymous **union** or **enum**):

```
struct S { union [[attribute_name]] { int a; float b; }; };
enum [[attribute_name]] { SUCCESS, FAIL } result;
```

The valid positions for any particular attribute are constrained to only those locations where the attribute pertains to the entity to which it applies. That is, an attribute such as `noreturn`, which applies only to functions, would be valid syntactically but not semantically if it were used to annotate any other kind of entity or syntactic element. Misplacement of a standard attribute results in an ill-formed program[3]:

```
void [[noreturn]] x() {}   // Error, cannot be applied to a type
     [[noreturn]] int i;   // Error, cannot be applied to a variable
     [[noreturn]] { throw; } // Error, cannot be applied to a statement
```

The empty attribute specifier sequence `[[]]` is allowed to appear anywhere the C++ grammar allows attributes.

Common compiler-dependent attributes

Prior to C++11, no standardized syntax for attributes was available and nonportable compiler intrinsics — such as `__attribute__((fallthrough))`, which is GCC-specific syntax — had to be used instead. Given the new standard syntax, vendors are now able to express

---

[2]Attributes having a namespace-qualified name — e.g., `[[gnu::const]]` — were only **conditionally supported** in C++11 and C++14 but were historically supported by all major compilers, including both Clang and GCC; all C++17-conforming compilers *must* support attribute namespaces.

[3]As of this writing, GCC is lax and merely warns when it sees the standard `noreturn` attribute in an unauthorized syntactic position, whereas Clang correctly fails to compile. Hence, using even a standard attribute might lead to different behavior on different compilers.

these extensions in a syntactically consistent manner. If an unknown attribute is encountered during compilation, it is ignored, emitting a likely[4] nonfatal diagnostic.

Table 1 provides several examples of popular compiler-specific attributes that have been standardized or have migrated to the standard syntax. For additional compiler-specific attributes, see *Further Reading* on page 20.

Table 1: Some standardized compiler-specific attributes

Compiler	Compiler-Specific	Standard-Conforming
GCC	`__attribute__((pure))`	`[[gnu::pure]]`
Clang	`__attribute__((no_sanitize))`	`[[clang::no_sanitize]]`
MSVC	`declspec(deprecated)`	`[[deprecated]]`

Portability is the biggest advantage of preferring standard syntax when it is available for compiler- and external-tool-specific attributes. Because most compilers will simply ignore unknown attributes that use standard attribute syntax (and, as of C++17, they are required to do so), conditional compilation is no longer required.

Use Cases

Prompting useful compiler diagnostics

Decorating entities with certain attributes can give compilers enough additional context to provide more detailed diagnostics; e.g., the GCC-specific `[[gnu::warn_unused_result]]` attribute[5] can be used to inform the compiler and developers that a function's return value should not be ignored[6]:

```
struct UDPListener
{
    [[gnu::warn_unused_result]] int start();
        // Start the UDP listener's background thread, which can fail for a
        // variety of reasons. Return 0 on success and a nonzero value
        // otherwise.

    void bind(int port);
        // The behavior is undefined unless start was called successfully.
};
```

---

[4]Prior to C++17, a conforming implementation was permitted to treat an unknown attribute as ill formed and terminate translation; to the authors' knowledge, however, none of them did.

[5]For compatibility with GCC, Clang supports `[[gnu::warn_unused_result]]` as well.

[6]The C++17 Standard `[[nodiscard]]` attribute serves the same purpose and is portable.

Such annotation of the client-facing declaration can prevent defects caused by a client forgetting to inspect the result of a function[7]:

```cpp
void init()
{
    UDPListener listener;
    listener.start();       // Might fail; return value must be checked!
    listener.bind(27015);   // possible undefined behavior (BAD IDEA)
}
```

For the code above, GCC produces a useful warning:

```
warning: ignoring return value of 'int UDPListener::start()' declared
         with attribute 'warn_unused_result' [-Wunused-result]
```

Hinting at additional optimization opportunities

Some annotations can affect compiler optimizations leading to more efficient or smaller binaries. For example, decorating the function `reportError` below with the GCC-specific `[[gnu::cold]]` attribute (also available on Clang) tells the compiler that the developer believes the function is unlikely to be called often:

```cpp
[[gnu::cold]] void reportError(const char* message) { /*...*/ }
```

Not only might the definition of `reportError` itself be optimized differently (e.g., for space over speed), any use of this function will likely be given lower priority during branch prediction:

```cpp
void checkBalance(int balance)
{
    if (balance >= 0)  // likely branch
    {
        // ...
    }
    else  // unlikely branch
    {
        reportError("Negative balance.");
    }
}
```

Because the annotated `reportError(const char*)` appears on the **else** branch of the **if** statement in the example above, the compiler knows to expect that **balance** is likely *not*

---

[7]Because the [[gnu::warn_unused_result]] attribute does not affect code generation, it is explicitly *not* ill formed for a client to make use of an unannotated declaration and yet compile its corresponding definition in the context of an annotated one or vice versa; such is not always the case for other attributes, however, and best practice might argue in favor of consistency regardless.

to be negative and therefore optimizes its predictive branching accordingly. Note that even if our hint to the compiler turns out to be misleading at run time, the semantics of every well-formed program remain the same.

Stating explicit assumptions in code to achieve better optimizations

Although the presence of an attribute usually has no effect on the behavior of any well-formed program besides its runtime performance, an attribute sometimes imparts knowledge to the compiler, which, if incorrect, could alter the intended behavior of the program. As an example of this more forceful form of attribute, consider the GCC-specific `[[gnu::const]]` attribute, also available in Clang. When applied to a function, this attribute instructs the compiler to *assume* that the function is a **pure function**, which has no **side effects**. In other words, the function always returns the same value for a given set of arguments, and the globally reachable state of the program is not altered by the function. For example, a function performing a linear interpolation between two values may be annotated with `[[gnu::const]]`:

```
[[gnu::const]]
double linearInterpolation(double start, double end, double factor)
{
    return (start * (1.0 - factor)) + (end * factor);
}
```

More generally, the return value of a function annotated with `[[gnu::const]]` is not permitted to depend on any state that might change between its successive invocations. For example, it is not allowed to examine contents of memory supplied to it by address. In contrast, functions annotated with a similar but more lenient `[[gnu::pure]]` attribute are allowed to return values that depend on any nonvolatile state. Therefore, functions such as `strlen` or `memcmp`, which read but do not modify the observable state, may be annotated with `[[gnu::pure]]` but not `[[gnu::const]]`.

The `vectorLerp` function below performs linear interpolation (referred to as LERP) between two bidimensional vectors. The body of this function comprises two invocations to the `linearInterpolation` function in the example above — one per vector component:

```
Vector2D vectorLerp(const Vector2D& start, const Vector2D& end, double factor)
{
    return Vector2D(linearInterpolation(start.x, end.x, factor),
                    linearInterpolation(start.y, end.y, factor));
}
```

If the values of the two components are the same, the compiler is allowed to invoke `linearInterpolation` only once, even if its body is not visible in `vectorLerp`'s translation unit:

```
// pseudocode (hypothetical compiler transformation)
Vector2D vectorLerp(const Vector2D& start, const Vector2D& end, double factor)
{
    if (start.x == start.y && end.x == end.y)
    {
        const double cache = linearInterpolation(start.x, end.x, factor);
        return Vector2D(cache, cache);
    }

    return Vector2D(linearInterpolation(start.x, end.x, factor),
                    linearInterpolation(start.y, end.y, factor));
}
```

If the implementation of a function tagged with the `[[gnu::const]]` attribute does not satisfy limitations imposed by the attribute, however, the compiler will not be able to detect this mistake, and a runtime defect will be the likely result; see *Potential Pitfalls — Some attributes, if misused, can affect program correctness* on page 19.

Using attributes to control external static analysis

Since unknown attributes are ignored by the compiler, external static-analysis tools can define their own custom attributes that can be used to embed detailed information to influence or control those tools without affecting program semantics. For example, the Microsoft-specific `[[gsl::suppress(/* rules */)]]` attribute can be used to suppress unwanted warnings from static-analysis tools that verify *Guidelines Support Library*[8] rules. In particular, consider GSL C26481 (Bounds rule 1),[9] which forbids any pointer arithmetic, instead suggesting that users rely on the `gsl::span` type[10]:

```
void hereticalFunction()
{
    int array[] = {0, 1, 2, 3, 4, 5};

    printElements(array, array + 6);  // elicits warning C26481
}
```

Any block of code for which validating rule C26481 is considered undesirable can be decorated with the `[[gsl::suppress(bounds.1)]]` attribute:

---

[8] *Guidelines Support Library* (see **microsofta**) is an open-source library, developed by Microsoft, that implements functions and types suggested for use by the "C++ Core Guidelines" (see **stroustrup21**).

[9] **microsoftd**

[10] `gsl::span` is a lightweight reference type that observes a contiguous sequence or subsequence of objects of homogeneous type. `gsl::span` can be used in interfaces as an alternative to both pointer/size or iterator-pair arguments and in implementations as an alternative to raw pointer arithmetic. Since C++20, the standard `std::span` template can be used instead.

```
void hereticalFunction()
{
    int array[] = {0, 1, 2, 3, 4, 5};

    [[gsl::suppress(bounds.1)]]              // Suppress GSL C26481.
    {
        printElements(array, array + 6);  // Silence!
    }
}
```

Creating new attributes to express semantic properties

Other uses of attributes for static analysis include statements of properties that cannot otherwise be deduced. Consider a function, f, that takes two pointers, p1 and p2, and has a **precondition** that both pointers must refer to the same contiguous block of memory. Using the standard attribute to inform the analyzer of such a precondition has a distinct advantage of requiring nothing other than the agreement between the developer and the static analyzer regarding the namespace and the name of the attribute. For example, we could choose to designate home_grown::in_same_block(p1, p2) for this purpose:

```
// lib.h:

[[home_grown::in_same_block(p1, p2)]]
int f(double* p1, double* p2);
```

The compiler will simply ignore this unknown attribute. However, because our static-analysis tool knows the meaning of the home_grown::in_same_block attribute, it will report, at analysis time, defects that might otherwise have resulted in **undefined behavior** at run time:

```
// client.cpp:
#include <lib.h>

void client()
{
    double a[10], b[10];
    f(a, b);  // Pointers are unrelated.  Our static analyzer reports an error.
}
```

Potential Pitfalls

Unrecognized attributes have implementation-defined behavior

Although standard attributes work well and are portable across all platforms, the behavior of compiler-specific and user-specified attributes is entirely implementation defined, with unrecognized attributes typically resulting in compiler warnings. Such warnings can typically be disabled (e.g., on GCC using -Wno-attributes), but, if they are, misspellings in even standard attributes will go unreported.[11]

Some attributes, if misused, can affect program correctness

Many attributes are benign in that they might improve diagnostics or performance but cannot themselves cause a program to behave incorrectly. However, misuse of some attributes can lead to incorrect results and/or **undefined** behavior.

For example, consider the myRandom function that is intended to return a new random number in range $[0.0, 0.1)$ on each successive call:

```
double myRandom()
{
    static std::random_device randomDevice;
    static std::mt19937 generator(randomDevice());
    static std::uniform_real_distribution<double> distribution(0, 1);

    return distribution(generator);
}
```

Suppose that we somehow observed that decorating myRandom with the [[gnu::const]] attribute occasionally improved runtime performance and innocently but naively decided to use it in production. Doing so is clearly a misuse of the [[gnu::const]] attribute because the function doesn't inherently satisfy the requirement of producing the same result when invoked with the same arguments — in this case, none. Adding this attribute tells the compiler that it need not call this function repeatedly and is free to treat the first value returned as a constant for all time.

See Also

- "noreturn" (§1.1, p. 95) presents a standard attribute used to indicate that a particular function never returns control flow to its caller.

- "deprecated" (§1.2, p. 147) presents a standard attribute that discourages the use of an entity via compiler diagnostics.

- "carries_dependency" (§3.1, p. 998) presents a standard attribute used to communicate release-consume dependency-chain information to the compiler to avoid unnecessary memory-fence instructions.

---

[11]Ideally, every relevant platform would offer a way to silently ignore a specific attribute on a case-by-case basis.

Further Reading

- For more information on commonly supported function attributes, see section 6.33.1, "Common Function Attributes," **freesoftwarefdn20**.

Consecutive Right-Angle Brackets

In the context of template argument lists, >> is parsed as two separate closing angle brackets.

Description

Prior to C++11, a pair of consecutive right-pointing angle brackets anywhere in the source code was always interpreted as a bitwise right-shift operator, so making an intervening space was required if the brackets were to be treated as separate closing-angle-bracket tokens:

```
// C++03
std::vector<std::vector<int>> v0;    // annoying compile-time error in C++03
std::vector<std::vector<int> > v1;  // OK
```

To facilitate the common use case above, a special rule was added whereby, when parsing a template-argument expression, *non-nested* — i.e., not placed within parentheses — appearances of >, >>, >>>, and so on are to be treated as separate closing angle brackets:

```
// C++11
std::vector<std::vector<int>> v0;                    // OK
std::vector<std::vector<std::vector<int>>> v1;  // OK
```

Using the greater-than or right-shift operators within template-argument expressions

For templates that take only type parameters, there's no issue. When the template parameter is a non-type, however, the greater-than or right-shift operators might be useful. In the unlikely event that we need either the greater-than operator, >, or the right-shift operator, >>, within a non-type template-argument expression, we can achieve our goal by nesting that expression within parentheses:

```
const int i = 1, j = 2;  // arbitrary integer values (used below)

template <int I> class C { /*...*/ };
    // class C taking non-type template parameter I of type int

C<i > j>    a1;  // Error, always has been
C<i >> j>   b1;  // Error in C++11, OK in C++03
C<(i > j)>  a2;  // OK
C<(i >> j)> b2;  // OK
```

In the definition of a1 above, the first > is interpreted as a closing angle bracket, and the subsequent j is and always has been a syntax error. In the case of b1, the >> is, as of C++11, parsed as a pair of separate tokens in this context, so the second > is now considered an error.

For both a2 and b2, however, the would-be operators appear nested within parentheses and thus are blocked from matching any active open angle bracket to the left of the parenthesized expression.

Use Cases

Avoiding annoying whitespace when composing template types

When using nested templated types — e.g., nested containers — in C++03, having to remember to insert an intervening space between trailing angle brackets added no value. What made it even more galling was that every popular compiler was able to tell us confidently that we had forgotten to leave the space. With this new feature (rather, this repaired defect), we can now render closing angle brackets contiguously, just like parentheses and square brackets:

```
// OK in both C++03 and C++11
std::list<std::map<int, std::vector<std::string> > > idToNameMappingList1;

// OK in C++11, compile-time error in C++03
std::list<std::map<int, std::vector<std::string>>>   idToNameMappingList2;
```

Potential Pitfalls

Some C++03 programs might stop compiling in C++11

If a right-shift operator is used in a template expression, the newer parsing rules might result in a compile-time error where before there was none:

```
T<1 >> 5> t;  // worked in C++03, compile-time error in C++11
```

The easy fix is simply to parenthesize the expression:

```
T<(1 >> 5)> t;  // OK
```

This rare syntax error is invariably caught at compile time, avoiding undetected surprises at run time.

The meaning of a C++03 program can, in theory, silently change in C++11

Though pathologically rare, the same valid expression can, in theory, have a different interpretation in C++11 than it had when compiled for C++03. Consider the case[1] where the >> token is embedded as part of an expression involving templates:

```
S<G< 0 >>::c>::b>::a
//  ^~~~~~~
```

---

[1] Example adapted from **gustedt13**

In the expression in the previous example, `0 >>::c` will be interpreted as a *bitwise right-shift operator* in C++03 but not in C++11. Writing a program that compiles under both C++03 and C++11 and exposes the difference in parsing rules is possible:

```
enum Outer { a = 1, b = 2, c = 3 };

template <typename> struct S
{
    enum Inner { a = 100, c = 102 };
};

template <int> struct G
{
    typedef int b;
};

int main()
{
    std::cout << (S<G< 0 >>::c>::b>::a) << '\n';
}
```

The program above will print `100` when compiled for C++03 and `0` for C++11:

```
// C++03

//      (2) instantiation of G<0>
//      ‖~~~~~~~~~~~~~
//      ‖ ‖ ‖   (4) instantiation of S<int>
//   ~~‖ ↓ ‖~~~~~~~~~~~~~~~~~↓
    S< G< 0 >>::c > ::b >::a
//     ~~‖ ↑ ‖~~~~~~~~~~↑
//       ‖ ‖ ‖ (3) type alias for int
//       ‖~~~~~~~
// (1) bitwise right-shift (0 >> 3)


// C++11

//
//
//  (2) compare (>) Inner::c and Outer::b
//  ↓ ~~~~~~~~~~~~~~~~~~~
    S< G< 0 >>::c > ::b >::a
//  ↑ ~~~~~~~~~
//  (1) instantiation of S<G<0>>
//
//
```

Though theoretically possible, programs that are syntactically valid in both C++03 and C++11 and have distinct semantics have not emerged in practice anywhere that we are aware of.

Further Reading

- For alternative design decisions that were considered to allow consecutive right angle brackets, see the original proposal: *Right Angle Brackets,* **vandevoorde05**.

Operator for Extracting Expression Types

The keyword **decltype** enables the compile-time inspection of the **declared type** of an **entity** *or* the type and **value category** of an expression.

Description

What results from the use of **decltype** depends on the nature of its operand.

Use with entities

If the operand is an unparenthesized **id expression** or unparenthesized member access, **decltype** yields the *declared type*, meaning the type of the *entity* indicated by the operand:

```
int i;                  // decltype(i)   -> int
std::string s;          // decltype(s)   -> std::string
int* p;                 // decltype(p)   -> int*
const int& r = *p;      // decltype(r)   -> const int&
struct { char c; } x;   // decltype(x.c) -> char
double f();             // decltype(f)   -> double()
double g(int);          // decltype(g)   -> double(int)
```

Use with expressions

When **decltype** is used with any other expression E of type T, including parenthesized id-expression or parenthesized member access, the result incorporates both the expression's type and its **value category** (see Section 2.1."*Rvalue* References" on page 710):

Value category of E	Result of decltype(E)
prvalue	T
lvalue	T&
xvalue	T&&

In general, *prvalues* can be passed to **decltype** in a number of ways, including numeric literals, function calls that return by value, and explicitly created temporaries:

```
decltype(0)   i; // -> int
int f();
decltype(f()) j; // -> int
struct S{};
decltype(S()) k; // -> S
```

An entity name passed to **decltype**, as mentioned above, produces the type of the entity. If an entity name is enclosed in an additional set of parentheses, however, **decltype** interprets its argument as an expression, and its result incorporates the value category:

```
int i;
decltype(i)   l = i; // -> int
decltype((i)) m = i; // -> int&
```

Similarly, for all other *lvalue* expressions, the result of **decltype** will be an *lvalue* reference:

```
int* pi = &i;
decltype(*pi) j = *pi; // -> int&
decltype(++i) k = ++i; // -> int&
```

Finally, the value category of the expression will be an *xvalue* if it is a cast to or a function returning an *rvalue* reference:

```
int i;
decltype(static_cast<int&&>(i)) j = static_cast<int&&>(i); // -> int&&
int&& g();
decltype(g()) k = g();                                     // -> int&&
```

Much like the **sizeof** operator (which is also resolved at compile time), the expression operand of **decltype** is not evaluated:

```
void test1()
{
    int i = 0;
    decltype(i++) j;  // equivalent to int j;
    assert(i == 0);   // The expression i++ was not evaluated.
}
```

Note that the choice of using the postfix increment is significant; the prefix increment yields a different type:

```
void test2()
{
    int i = 0;
    int m = 1;
    decltype(++i) k = m; // equivalent to int& k = m;
    assert(i == 0);      // The expression ++i was not evaluated.
}
```

Use Cases

Avoiding unnecessary use of explicit typenames

Consider two logically equivalent ways of declaring a vector of iterators into a list of Widgets:

```
std::list<Widget> widgets;
std::vector<std::list<Widget>::iterator> widgetIterators;
    // (1) The full type of widgets needs to be restated, and iterator
    // needs to be explicitly named.

std::list<Widget> widgets;
std::vector<decltype(widgets.begin())> widgetIterators;
    // (2) Neither std::list nor Widget nor iterator need be named
    // explicitly.
```

Notice that, when using **decltype**, if the C++ type representing the widget changes (e.g., from Widget to, say, ManagedWidget) or the container used changes (e.g., from std::list to std::vector), the declaration of widgetIterators does not necessarily need to change.

Expressing type-consistency explicitly

In some situations, repetition of explicit type names might inadvertently result in latent defects caused by mismatched types during maintenance. For example, consider a Packet class exposing a **const** member function that returns a value of type std::uint8_t representing the length of the packet's checksum:

```
class Packet
{
    // ...

public:
    std::uint8_t checksumLength() const;
};
```

This unsigned 8-bit type was selected to minimize bandwidth usage as the checksum length is sent over the network. Next, picture a loop that computes the checksum of a Packet, using the same type for its iteration variable to match the type returned by Packet::checksumLength:

```
void f()
{
    Checksum sum;
    Packet data;

    for (std::uint8_t i = 0; i < data.checksumLength(); ++i)  // brittle
    {
        sum.appendByte(data.nthByte(i));
    }
}
```

Now suppose that, over time, the data transmitted by the Packet type grows to the point where the range of an std::uint8_t value might not be enough to ensure a sufficiently reliable checksum. If the type returned by checksumLength() is changed to, say, std::uint16_t without updating the type of the iteration variable i in lockstep, the loop might silently[1] become infinite.[2]

Had **decltype**(packet.checksumLength()) been used to express the type of i, the types would have remained consistent, and the ensuing defect would naturally have been avoided:

```
// ...
for (decltype(data.checksumLength()) i = 0; i < data.checksumLength(); ++i)
// ...
```

Creating an auxiliary variable of generic type

Consider the task of implementing a generic loggedSum function template that returns the sum of two arbitrary objects, a and b, after logging both the operands and the result value, e.g., for debugging or monitoring purposes. To avoid computing the possibly expensive sum twice, we decide to create an auxiliary function-scope variable, result. Since the type of the sum depends on both a and b, we can use **decltype**(a + b) to infer the type for both the trailing return type of the function (see Section 1.1. "Trailing Return" on page 124) and the auxiliary variable:

```
template <typename A, typename B>
auto loggedSum(const A& a, const B& b)
    -> decltype(a + b)                    // (1) exploiting trailing return types
{
    decltype(a + b) result = a + b;    // (2) auxiliary generic variable
    LOG_TRACE << a << " + " << b << " = " << result;
    return result;
}
```

Using **decltype**(a + b) as a return type is significantly different from relying on automatic **return-type deduction**; see Section 2.1. "**auto** Variables" on page 195. Note that this particular use involves significant repetition of the expression a+b. See *Annoyances — Mechanical repetition of expressions might be required* on page 31 for a discussion of ways in which such repetition might be avoided.

Determining the validity of a generic expression

In the context of generic-library development, **decltype** can be used in conjunction with **SFINAE** ("Substitution Failure Is Not An Error") to validate an expression involving a template parameter.

---

[1]As of this writing, neither GCC 11.2 (c. 2021) nor Clang 12.0.0 (c. 2021) provide a warning (using -Wall, -Wextra, and -Wpedantic) for the comparison between std::uint8_t and std::uint16_t — even if (1) the value returned by checksumLength does not fit in a 8-bit integer, and (2) the body of the function is visible to the compiler. Decorating checksumLength with **constexpr** causes clang++ to issue a warning, which is clearly not a general solution.

[2]The loop variable is promoted to an **unsigned int** for comparison purposes but wraps to 0 whenever its value prior to being incremented is 255.

For example, consider the task of writing a generic sortRange function template that, given a **range**, either invokes the sort member function of the argument (the one specifically optimized for that type) if available or falls back to the more general std::sort:

```
template <typename Range>
void sortRange(Range& range)
{
    sortRangeImpl(range, 0);
}
```

The client-facing sortRange function in the example above delegates its behavior to an overloaded sortRangeImpl function in the example below, invoking the latter with the range and a **disambiguator** of type **int**. The type of this additional parameter, whose value is arbitrary, is used to give priority to the sort member function at compile time by exploiting overload resolution rules in the presence of an implicit, *standard* conversion from **int** to **long**:

```
template <typename Range>
void sortRangeImpl(Range& range, long)  // low priority: standard conversion
{
    // fallback implementation
    std::sort(std::begin(range), std::end(range));
}
```

The fallback overload of sortRangeImpl in the code snippet above will accept a **long** disambiguator, requiring a standard conversion from **int**, and will simply invoke std::sort. The more specialized overload of sortRangeImpl in the code snippet below will accept an **int** disambiguator requiring no conversions and thus will be a better match, provided a range-specific sort is available:

```
template <typename Range>
void sortRangeImpl(Range& range,
                   int,                          // high priority: exact match
                   decltype(range.sort())* = 0)  // check expression validity
{
    // optimized implementation
    range.sort();
}
```

Note that, by exposing **decltype**(range.sort()) as part of sortRangeImpl's declaration, the more specialized overload will be discarded during template substitution if range.sort() is not a valid expression for the deduced Range type.[3]

---

[3]The technique of exposing a possibly unused unevaluated expression — e.g., using **decltype** — in a function's declaration for the purpose of expression-validity detection prior to template instantiation is commonly known as **expression SFINAE**, which is a restricted form of the more general, classical SFINAE, and acts exclusively on expressions visible in a function's signature rather than on frequently obscure template-based type computations.

The relative position of **decltype**(range.sort()) in the signature of sortRangeImpl is not significant as long as it is visible to the compiler during template substitution. The previous example uses a function parameter that is defaulted to 0. Alternatives involving a trailing return type or a default template argument are also viable:

```cpp
#include <utility>  // declval
template <typename Range>
auto sortRangeImpl(Range& range, int) -> decltype(range.sort(), void());
    // The comma operator is used to force the return type to void,
    // regardless of the return type of range.sort().

template <typename Range, typename = decltype(std::declval<Range&>().sort())>
auto sortRangeImpl(Range& range, int) -> void;
    // std::declval is used to generate a reference to Range that can
    // be used in an unevaluated expression.
```

Putting it all together, we see that exactly two possible outcomes exist for the original client-facing sortRange function invoked with a range argument of type R:

- If R does have a sort member function, the more specialized overload of sortRangeImpl will be viable since range.sort() is a well-formed expression and preferred because the disambiguator 0 of type **int** requires no conversion.

- Otherwise, the more specialized overload will be discarded during template substitution because range.sort() is not a well-formed expression, and the only remaining more general sortRangeImpl overload will be chosen instead.

Potential Pitfalls

Perhaps surprisingly, **decltype**(x) and **decltype**((x)) will sometimes yield different results for the same expression, x:

```cpp
int i = 0; // decltype(i) yields int.
           // decltype((i)) yields int&.
```

In the case where the unparenthesized operand is an entity having a declared type, T, and the parenthesized operand is an expression whose value category is represented by **decltype** as the same type T, the results will coincidentally be the same:

```cpp
int& ref = i;  // decltype(ref) yields int&.
               // decltype((ref)) yields int&.
```

Wrapping its operand with parentheses ensures **decltype** yields the value category of a given expression. This technique can be useful in the context of **metaprogramming**, particularly in the case of value category propagation.

Annoyances

Mechanical repetition of expressions might be required

As mentioned in *Use Cases — Creating an auxiliary variable of generic type* on page 28, using **decltype** to capture a value of an expression that is about to be used or for the return value of an expression can often lead to repeating the same expression in multiple places, three distinct ones in the earlier example.

An alternate solution to this problem is to capture the result of the **decltype** expression in a **typedef**, **using** type alias, or as a defaulted template parameter, but such an approach runs into the problem that it can be used only after the expression is valid. A defaulted **template** parameter cannot reference parameter names because it is written before them, and a type alias cannot be introduced prior to the return type being needed. A solution to this problem lies in using Standard Library function std::declval to create expressions of the appropriate type without needing to reference the actual function parameters by name:

```
template <typename A, typename B,
          typename Result = decltype(std::declval<const A&>() +
                                     std::declval<const B&>())>
Result loggedSum(const A& a, const B& b)
{
    Result result = a + b;   // no duplication of the decltype expression
    LOG_TRACE << a << " + " << b << "=" << result;
    return result;
}
```

Here, std::declval, a function that cannot be executed at run time and is only appropriate for use in **unevaluated contexts**, produces an expression of the specified type. When mixed with **decltype**, std::declval lets us determine the result types for expressions without needing to or even being able to construct objects of the needed types.

See Also

- "**using** Aliases" (§1.1, p. 133) explains that often it is useful to give a name to the type yielded by **decltype**, which is done with a **using** alias.

- "**auto** Variables" (§2.1, p. 195) illustrates how **auto** variables have a similar but distinct type deduction to that computed by **decltype**.

- "*Rvalue* References" (§2.1, p. 710) describes **value categories** that can be obtained for arbitrary expressions using **decltype**.

- "**decltype(auto)**" (§3.2, p. 1205) presents **decltype** type computation rules that can be useful in conjunction with an auto variable.

Using = `default` for Special Member Functions

The keyword **default** annotating a declaration of a **special member function** instructs the compiler to attempt to generate the function automatically.

Description

An important aspect of C++ class design is the understanding that the compiler will attempt to generate certain member functions to *create, copy, destroy*, and now *move* (see Section 2.1. "*Rvalue* References" on page 710) an object unless developers implement some or all of these functions themselves. Determining which of the **special member functions** will continue to be generated and which will be suppressed in the presence of **user-provided special member functions** requires remembering the numerous rules the compiler uses.

Declaring a special member function explicitly

The rules specifying what happens in the presence of one or more user-provided special member functions are inherently complex and not necessarily intuitive; in fact, some have been deprecated. Specifically, even in the presence of a user-provided destructor, both the copy constructor and the copy-assignment operator have historically been generated implicitly. Relying on such generated behavior is problematic because it is unlikely that a class requiring a user-provided destructor will function correctly without corresponding user-provided copy operations. As of C++11, reliance on such dubious implicitly generated behavior is deprecated.

Let's briefly illustrate a few common cases and then take a look at Howard Hinnant's now famous table (see page 44 of *Appendix — Implicit Generation of Special Member Functions*) to demystify what's going on under the hood.

Example 1: Providing just the default constructor   Consider a **struct** with a user-provided default constructor:

```
struct S1
{
    S1();  // user-provided default constructor
};
```

A user-provided default constructor has no effect on other special member functions. Providing any other constructor, however, will suppress automatic generation of the default constructor. We can, however, use = **default** to restore the constructor as a **trivial operation**; see *Use Cases — Restoring the generation of a special member function suppressed by another* on page 36. Note that a nondeclared function is nonexistent, which means that it will *not* participate in overload resolution at all. In contrast, a **deleted function** participates in overload resolution and, if selected, results in a compilation failure; see Section 1.1. "Deleted Functions" on page 53.

Example 2: Providing just a copy constructor   Now, consider a **struct** with a user-provided copy constructor:

```
struct S2
{
    S2(const S2&);  // user-provided copy constructor
};
```

A user-provided copy constructor (1) suppresses the generation of the default constructor and both move operations and (2) allows implicit generation of both the copy-assignment operator and the destructor. Similarly, providing just the copy-assignment operator would allow the compiler to implicitly generate both the copy constructor and the destructor, but, in this case, it would also generate the default constructor. Note that — in either of these cases — relying on the compiler's implicitly generated copy operation is deprecated.

Example 3: Providing just the destructor   Finally, consider a **struct** with a user-provided destructor:

```
struct S3
{
    ~S3();  // user-provided destructor
};
```

A user-provided destructor suppresses the generation of move operations but still allows copy operations to be generated. Again, relying on either of these implicitly compiler-generated copy operations is deprecated.

Example 4: Providing more than one special member function   When more than one special member function is declared explicitly, the *union* of their respective declaration suppressions and the *intersection* of their respective implicit generations pertain. For example, if just the default constructor and destructor are provided (S1 + S3 in Examples 1 and 3), then the declarations of both move operations are suppressed, and both copy operations are generated implicitly.

Defaulting the first declaration of a special member function explicitly

Using the =**default** syntax with the first declaration of a special member function instructs the compiler to synthesize such a function automatically without treating it as being user provided. The compiler-generated version for a special member function is required to call the corresponding special member functions on every base class in base-class-declaration order and then every data member of the encapsulating type in declaration order, regardless of any access specifiers. Note that the destructor calls will be in exactly the opposite order of the other special-member-function calls.

For example, consider struct S4 in the code snippet below in which we have chosen to make explicit that the copy operations are to be autogenerated by the compiler; note, in particular, that implicit declaration and generation of each of the other special member functions are left unaffected.

```cpp
struct S4
{
    S4(const S4&) = default;            // copy constructor
    S4& operator=(const S4&) = default; // copy-assignment operator

    // has no effect on other four special member functions, i.e.,
    // implicitly generates the default constructor, the destructor,
    // the move constructor, and the move-assignment operator
};
```

A defaulted declaration may appear with any **access specifier** (i.e., **private**, **protected**, or **public**), and access to that generated function will be regulated accordingly:

```cpp
struct S5
{
private:
    S5(const S5&) = default;            // private copy constructor
    S5& operator=(const S5&) = default; // private copy-assignment operator

protected:
    ~S5() = default;                    // protected destructor

public:
    S5() = default;                     // public default constructor
};
```

In the example above, copy operations exist for use by *member* and *friend* functions only. Declaring the destructor **protected** or **private** limits which functions can create automatic variables of the specified type to those functions with the appropriately privileged access to the class. Declaring the default constructor **public** is necessary to avoid its declaration being suppressed by another constructor — e.g., the private copy constructor in the code snippet above — or *any* move operation.

In short, using =**default** on the first declaration denotes that a special member function is intended to be generated by the compiler, irrespective of any user-provided declarations; in conjunction with =**delete** (see Section 1.1."Deleted Functions" on page 53), using =**default** affords the fine-grained control over which special member functions are to be generated and/or made publicly available.

Defaulting the implementation of a user-provided special member function

The =**default** syntax can also be used after the first declaration but with a distinctly different meaning: The compiler will treat the first declaration as a **user-provided** special member function and thus will suppress the generation of other special member functions accordingly:

```
// example.h:

struct S6
{
    S6& operator=(const S6&);  // user-provided copy-assignment operator

    // suppresses the declaration of both move operations
    // implicitly generates the default and copy constructors and the destructor
};

inline S6& S6::operator=(const S6&) = default;
    // Explicitly request the compiler to generate the default implementation
    // for this copy-assignment operator. This request might fail, e.g., if S6
    // were to contain a non-copy-assignable data member.
```

Alternatively, an explicitly defaulted noninline implementation of this copy-assignment operator may appear in a separate (.cpp) file; see *Use Cases — Physically decoupling the interface from the implementation* on page 40.

Use Cases

Restoring the generation of a special member function suppressed by another

Incorporating =**default** in the declaration of a special member function instructs the compiler to generate its definition regardless of any other user-provided special member functions. As an example, consider a **value-semantic** SecureToken class that wraps a standard string, std::string, and an arbitrary-precision-integer, BigInt, token code that together satisfy certain invariants:

```
class SecureToken
{
    std::string d_value;  // The default-constructed value is the empty string.
    BigInt      d_code;   // The default-constructed value is the integer zero.

public:
    // All six special member functions are implicitly defaulted.

    void setValue(const char* value);
    const char* value() const;
    BigInt code() const;
};
```

By default, a secure token's **value** will be the empty-string value, and the token's **code** will be the numerical value of zero because those are, respectively, the **default-initialized** values of the two data members, d_value and d_code:

```
void f()
{
    SecureToken token;                              // default constructed          (1)
    assert(token.value() == std::string());  // default value: empty string (2)
    assert(token.code() == BigInt());         // default value: zero            (3)
}
```

Now suppose that we get a request to add a **value constructor** that creates and initializes a SecureToken from a specified token string:

```
class SecureToken
{
    std::string d_value;   // The default-constructed value is the empty string.
    BigInt      d_code;    // The default-constructed value is the integer zero.

public:
    SecureToken(const char* value);   // newly added value constructor

    // suppresses the declaration of just the default constructor --- i.e.,
    // implicitly generates all of the other five special member functions

    void setValue(const char* value);
    const char* value() const;
    const BigInt& code() const;
};
```

Attempting to compile function f would now fail on the first line, where it attempts to default-construct the token. Using the =**default** feature, however, we can reinstate the default constructor to work trivially, just as it did before:

```
class SecureToken
{
    std::string d_value;   // The default-constructed value is the empty string.
    BigInt d_code;         // The default-constructed value is the integer zero.

public:
    SecureToken() = default;          // newly defaulted default constructor
    SecureToken(const char* value);   // newly added value constructor

    // implicitly generates all of the other five special member functions

    void setValue(const char* value);
    const char* value() const;
    const BigInt& code() const;
};
```

Making class APIs explicit at no runtime cost

In the early days of C++, coding standards sometimes required that each special member function be declared explicitly so that it could be documented or even just to know that it hadn't been forgotten:

```cpp
class C1
{
    // ...

public:
    C1();
        // Create an empty object.

    C1(const C1& rhs);
        // Create an object having the same value as the specified rhs object.

    ~C1();
        // Destroy this object.

    C1& operator=(const C1& rhs);
        // Assign to this object the value of the specified rhs object.
};
```

Over time, explicitly writing out what the compiler itself could do more reliably became clearly an inefficient use of developer time and a maintenance burden. What's more, even if the function definition was empty, implementing it explicitly often degraded performance compared to a **trivial** default. Hence, such standards tended to evolve toward conventionally commenting out — e.g., using //! — the declarations of functions having an empty body rather than providing it explicitly:

```cpp
class C2
{
    // ...

public:
    //! C2();
        // Create an empty object.

    //! C2(const C2& rhs);
        // Create an object having the same value as the specified rhs object.

    //! ~C2();
        // Destroy this object.

    //! C2& operator=(const C2& rhs);
        // Assign to this object the value of the specified rhs object.
};
```

Note, however, that the compiler does not check the commented code, which is easily susceptible to copy-paste and other errors. By uncommenting the code and defaulting it explicitly in class scope, we regain the compiler's syntactic checking of the function signatures without incurring the cost of turning what would have been **trivial** functions into equivalent non-trivial ones:

```cpp
class C3
{
    // ...

public:
    C3() = default;
        // Create an empty object.

    C3(const C3& rhs) = default;
        // Create an object having the same value as the specified rhs object.

    ~C3() = default;
        // Destroy this object.

    C3& operator=(const C3& rhs) = default;
        // Assign to this object the value of the specified rhs object.
};
```

Preserving type triviality

A particular type being **trivial** can be beneficial. The type is considered **trivial** if its default constructor is **trivial** and it is **trivially copyable** — i.e., it has no non-trivial copy or move constructors, no non-trivial copy or move assignment operators, at least one of those nondeleted, and a trivial destructor. As an example, consider a simple **trivial** Metrics type in the code snippet below containing certain collected metrics for our application:

```cpp
struct Metrics
{
    int d_numRequests;  // number of requests to the service
    int d_numErrors;    // number of error responses

    // All special member functions are generated implicitly.
};
```

Now imagine that we would like to add a constructor to this struct to make its use more convenient:

```
struct Metrics
{
    int d_numRequests;   // number of requests to the service
    int d_numErrors;     // number of error responses

    Metrics(int, int);   // user-provided value constructor

    // Generation of default constructor is suppressed.
};
```

As illustrated in *Appendix — Implicit Generation of Special Member Functions* on page 44, the presence of a user-provided constructor suppressed the implicit generation of the default constructor. Replacing the default constructor with a seemingly equivalent user-provided one might appear to work as intended:

```
struct Metrics
{
    int d_numRequests;   // number of requests to the service
    int d_numErrors;     // number of error responses

    Metrics(int, int);   // user-provided value constructor
    Metrics() {}         // user-provided default constructor

    // Default constructor is user-provided: Metrics is not trivial.
};
```

The user-provided nature of the default constructor, however, renders the `Metrics` type non-trivial, even if the definitions are identical! In contrast, explicitly requesting the default constructor be generated using `= default` restores the triviality of the type:

```
struct Metrics
{
    int d_numRequests;   // number of requests to the service
    int d_numErrors;     // number of error responses

    Metrics(int, int);     // user-provided value constructor
    Metrics() = default;   // defaulted, trivial default constructor

    // Default constructor is defaulted: Metrics is trivial.
};
```

Physically decoupling the interface from the implementation

Sometimes, especially during large-scale development, avoiding compile-time coupling clients to the implementations of individual methods offers distinct maintenance advantages.

Specifying that a special member function is defaulted on its first declaration, i.e., in class scope, implies that making any change to this implementation will force all clients to recompile:

```
// smallscale.h:

struct SmallScale
{
    SmallScale() = default;  // explicitly defaulted default constructor
};
```

The important issue regarding recompilation here is not merely compile time per se but compile-time coupling.[1]

Alternatively, we can choose to declare the function but deliberately *not* default it in class scope or anywhere in the .h file:

```
// largescale.h:

struct LargeScale
{
    LargeScale();  // user-provided default constructor
};
```

We can then default just the noninline implementation in a corresponding[2] .cpp file:

```
// largescale.cpp:
#include <largescale.h>

LargeScale::LargeScale() = default;
    // Generate the default implementation for this default destructor.
```

Using this *insulation* technique, we are free to change our minds and implement the default constructor ourselves in any way we see fit without necessarily forcing our clients to recompile.

Potential Pitfalls

Defaulted special member functions cannot restore trivial copyability

Library classes often rely on whether the type on which they are operating is eligible for being copied with memcpy for optimization purposes. Such could be the case for implementing, say,

---

[1]See **lakos20**, section 3.10.5, "Real-World Example of Benefits of Avoiding Compile-Time Coupling," pp. 783–789.

[2]In practice, every .cpp file, other than the one containing main, typically has a unique associated header, .h, file and often vice versa, with the .cpp and .h pair of files constituting a component; see **lakos20**, section 1.6, "From .h/.cpp Pairs to Components," and section 1.11, "Extracting Actual Dependencies," pp. 209–216 and 256–259, respectively.

vector, which would make a single call to memcpy when growing its buffer. For the memcpy or memmove to be well defined, however, the type of the object that is stored in the buffer must be trivially copyable. One might assume that this trait means that, as long as the copy constructor of the type is trivial, this optimization will apply. Defaulting the copy operations would then allow us to achieve this goal, while allowing the type to have a non-trivial destructor or move operation. Such, however, is not the case.

The requirements for a type to be considered trivially copyable — and thus eligible for use with memcpy — include triviality of all of its nondeleted copy and move operations as well as of its destructor. Furthermore, library authors cannot perform fine-grained dispatch based on which operations on the type are in fact trivial. Even if we detect that the type is trivially copy-constructible with the std::is_trivially_copy_constructible trait and know that our code would use only copy constructors (and not copy assignment nor any move operations), we still would be unable to use memcpy unless the more restrictive std::is_trivially_copyable trait is also **true**.

Annoyances

Generation of defaulted functions is not guaranteed

Using =**default** does not guarantee that the special member function of a type, T, will be generated. For example, a noncopyable member variable or base class of T will inhibit generation of T's copy constructor even when =**default** is used. Such behavior can be observed in the presence of an std::unique_ptr[3] data member:

```cpp
#include <memory>  // std::unique_ptr
class Connection
{
private:
    class Impl;                          // nested implementation class
    std::unique_ptr<Impl> d_impl;  // noncopyable data member

public:
    Connection() = default;
    Connection(const Connection&) = default;
};
```

---

[3] std::unique_ptr<T> is a move-only — movable but noncopyable — class template introduced in C++11. It models unique ownership over a dynamically allocated T instance, leveraging *rvalue* references (see Section 2.1."*Rvalue* References" on page 710) to represent ownership transfer between instances:

```cpp
int* p = new int(42);
std::unique_ptr<int> up(p);              // OK, take ownership of p.
std::unique_ptr<int> upCopy = up;        // Error, copy is deleted.
std::unique_ptr<int> upMove = std::move(up); // OK, transfer ownership.
```

Despite the defaulted copy constructor, `Connection` will not be copy-constructible as `std::unique_ptr` is a noncopyable type. Some compilers *might* produce a warning on the declaration of `Connection(const Connection&)`, but they are not required to do so since the example code on the previous page is well formed and would produce a compilation failure only if an attempt were made to default-construct or copy a `Connection`.[4]

If desired, a possible way to ensure that a defaulted special member function has indeed been generated is to use **static_assert** (see Section 1.1."**static_assert**" on page 115) in conjunction with an appropriate trait from the `<type_traits>` header:

```
class IdCollection
{
    std::vector<int> d_ids;

public:
    IdCollection() = default;
    IdCollection(const IdCollection&) = default;
    // ...
};

static_assert(std::is_default_constructible<IdCollection>::value,
              "IdCollection must be default constructible.");

static_assert(std::is_copy_constructible<IdCollection>::value,
              "IdCollection must be copy constructible.");


// ...
```

Routinely using such compile-time testing techniques can help to ensure that a type will continue to behave as expected at no additional runtime cost, even when member and base types evolve as a result of ongoing software maintenance.

See Also

- "Deleted Functions" (§1.1, p. 53) describes a companion feature, =**delete**, that can be used to suppress access to implicitly generated special member functions.

- "**static_assert**" (§1.1, p. 115) describes a facility that can be used to verify at compile time that undesirable copy and move operations are declared to be accessible.

- "*Rvalue* References" (§2.1, p. 710) provides the basis for **move operations**, namely, the move-constructor and move-assignment special member functions, which too can be defaulted.

---

[4]Clang 8.0.0 (c. 2019) and later produces a diagnostic with no warning flags specified. MSVC 12.0 (c. 2013) produces a diagnostic if /Wall is specified. As of this writing, GCC 12.1 (c. 2021) produces no warning, even with both -Wall and -Wextra enabled.

Further Reading

- For more information on defaulted functions in the context of move operations, see the "Everything You Ever Wanted to Know About Move Semantics" talks by Howard Hinnant, **hinnant14** and **hinnant16**.

Appendix

Implicit Generation of Special Member Functions

The rules a compiler uses to decide if a special member function should be generated implicitly are not entirely intuitive. Howard Hinnant, lead designer and author of the C++11 proposal for move semantics[5] (among other proposals), produced a tabular representation[6] of such rules in the situation where the user provides a single special member function and leaves the rest to the compiler. To understand Table 1, after picking a special member function in the first column, the corresponding row will show what is implicitly generated by the compiler.

Table 1: Implicit generation of special member functions

	Default Ctor	Destructor	Copy Ctor	Copy Assignment	Move Ctor	Move Assignment
Nothing	Defaulted	Defaulted	Defaulted	Defaulted	Defaulted	Defaulted
Any Ctor	Not Declared	Defaulted	Defaulted	Defaulted	Defaulted	Defaulted
Default Ctor	User Declared	Defaulted	Defaulted	Defaulted	Defaulted	Defaulted
Destructor	Defaulted	User Declared	Defaulted[a]	Defaulted[a]	Not Declared	Not Declared
Copy Ctor	Not Declared	Defaulted	User Declared	Defaulted[a]	Not Declared	Not Declared
Copy Assignment	Defaulted	Defaulted	Defaulted[a]	User Declared	Not Declared	Not Declared
Move Ctor	Not Declared	Defaulted	Deleted	Deleted	User Declared	Not Declared
Move Assignment	Defaulted	Defaulted	Deleted	Deleted	Not Declared	User Declared

[a] Deprecated behavior: compilers might warn upon reliance of this implicitly generated member function.

As an example, explicitly declaring a copy-assignment operator would result in the default constructor, destructor, and copy constructor being defaulted and in the move operations not being declared. If more than one special member function is user declared, regardless of whether or how it is implemented, the remaining generated member functions are

---

[5] hinnant02
[6] hinnant16

those in the intersection of the corresponding rows. For example, explicitly declaring both the destructor and the default constructor would still result in the copy constructor and the copy-assignment operator being defaulted and both move operations not being declared. Relying on the compiler-generated copy operations when the destructor is anything but defaulted is dubious; if correct, defaulting them explicitly makes both their existence and intended definition clear.

Constructors Calling Other Constructors

The use of the name of the class in the initializer list of that class's constructor enables delegating initialization to another constructor of the same class.

Description

A **delegating constructor** is a constructor of a **user-defined type (UDT)** — i.e., **class**, **struct**, or **union** — that invokes another constructor defined for the same UDT as part of its initialization of an object of that type. The syntax for invoking another constructor is to specify the name of the type as the only element in the **member initializer list**:

```
#include <string>  // std::string

struct S0
{
  int       d_i;
  std::string d_s;

  S0(int i)        : d_i(i)       {} // nondelegating constructor
  S0()             : S0(0)        {} // OK, delegates to S0(int)
  S0(const char* s) : S0(0), d_s(s) {} // Error, delegation must be on its own
};
```

Multiple delegating constructors can be chained together, one calling exactly one other, so long as cycles are avoided; see *Potential Pitfalls — Delegation cycles* on page 50. Once a *target* — i.e., invoked via delegation — constructor returns, the body of the delegator is invoked:

```
#include <iostream>  // std::cout

struct S1
{
    S1(int, int)            { std::cout << 'a'; }
    S1(int)    : S1(0, 0) { std::cout << 'b'; }
    S1()       : S1(0)    { std::cout << 'c'; }
};

void f()
{
    S1 s;  // OK, prints "abc" to stdout
}
```

If an exception is thrown while executing a nondelegating constructor, the object being initialized is considered only **partially constructed** (i.e., the object is not yet known to be in a valid state), and hence its destructor will *not* be invoked:

```
#include <iostream>  // std::cout

struct S2
{
    S2()  { std::cout << "S2() ";  throw 0; }
    ~S2() { std::cout << "~S2() ";          }
};

void f() try { S2 s; } catch(int) { }
    // prints only "S2() " to stdout (the destructor of S2 is never invoked)
```

Although the destructor of a **partially constructed** object will not be invoked, the destructors of each successfully constructed base and of data members will still be invoked:

```
#include <iostream>  // std::string

using std::cout;
struct A { A() { cout << "A() "; } ~A() { cout << "~A() "; } };
struct B { B() { cout << "B() "; } ~B() { cout << "~B() "; } };

struct C : B
{
    A d_a;

    C()  { cout << "C() "; throw 0; }  // nondelegating constructor that throws
    ~C() { cout << "~C() ";         }  // destructor that never gets called
};

void f() try { C c; } catch(int) { }
    // prints "B() A() C() ~A() ~B()" to stdout
```

Notice that base class B and member d_a of type A were fully constructed, and so their respective destructors are called, even though the destructor for class C itself is never executed.

However, if an exception is thrown in the body of a delegating constructor, the object being initialized is considered **fully constructed**, as the target constructor must have returned control to the delegator; hence, the object's destructor *is* invoked:

```
#include <iostream>  // std::cout

struct S3
{
    S3()          { std::cout << "S3() ";              }
    S3(int) : S3() { std::cout << "S3(int) "; throw 0; }
    ~S3()         { std::cout << "~S3() ";             }
};

void f() try { S3 s(0); } catch(int) { }
    // prints "S3() S3(int) ~S3() " to stdout
```

Use Cases

Avoiding code duplication among constructors

Many consider avoiding gratuitous code duplication a best practice. Having one ordinary member function call another has always been an option, but having one constructor directly invoke another constructor has not. Classic workarounds included repeating the code or else factoring the code into a private member function that would be called from multiple constructors. The drawback with this workaround is that the private member function, not being a constructor, would be unable to make use efficiently of **member initializer lists** to initialize base classes and data members. As of C++11, *delegating constructors* can be used to minimize code duplication when some of the same operations are performed across multiple constructors without having to forgo efficient initialization. Consider an `IPV4Host` class representing a network endpoint that can be constructed either (1) by a 32-bit address and a 16-bit port or (2) by an IPV4 string with `XXX.XXX.XXX.XXX:XXXXX` format[1]:

```
#include <cstdint>  // std::uint16_t, std::uint32_t
#include <string>   // std::string

class IPV4Host
{
    // ...
private:
    int connect(std::uint32_t address, std::uint16_t port);

public:
    IPV4Host(std::uint32_t address, std::uint16_t port)
    {
        if (!connect(address, port))  // code duplication: BAD IDEA
        {
            throw ConnectionException{address, port};
```

---

[1] Note that this initial design might itself be suboptimal in that the representation of the IPV4 address and port value might profitably be factored out into a separate **value-semantic** class, say, `IPV4Address`, that itself might be constructed in multiple ways; see *Potential Pitfalls — Suboptimal factoring* on page 51.

```
            }
        }

    IPV4Host(const std::string& ip)
    {
        std::uint32_t address = extractAddress(ip);
        std::uint16_t port = extractPort(ip);

        if (!connect(address, port))  // code duplication: BAD IDEA
        {
            throw ConnectionException{address, port};
        }
    }
};
```

Prior to C++11, working around such code duplication would require the introduction of a separate, private helper function that would be called by each of the constructors:

```
// C++03 (obsolete)
#include <cstdint>  // std::uint16_t, std::uint32_t

class IPV4Host
{
    // ...

private:
    int connect(std::uint32_t address, std::uint16_t port);
    void init(std::uint32_t address, std::uint16_t port)  // helper function
    {
        if (!connect(address, port))  // factored implementation of needed logic
        {
            throw ConnectionException{address, port};
        }
    }

public:
    IPV4Host(std::uint32_t address, std::uint16_t port)
    {
        init(address, port);  // Invoke factored private helper function.
    }

    IPV4Host(const std::string& ip)
    {
        std::uint32_t address = extractAddress(ip);
        std::uint16_t port = extractPort(ip);

        init(address, port);  // Invoke factored private helper function.
    }
};
```

With C++11 delegating constructors, the constructor accepting a string can be rewritten to delegate to the one accepting `address` and `port`, avoiding repetition without having to use a private function:

```cpp
#include <cstdint>  // std::uint16_t, std::uint32_t
#include <string>   // std::string

class IPV4Host
{
    // ...
private:
    int connect(std::uint32_t address, std::uint16_t port);

public:
    IPV4Host(std::uint32_t address, std::uint16_t port)
    {
        if(!connect(address, port))
        {
            throw ConnectionException{address, port};
        }
    }

    IPV4Host(const std::string& ip)
        : IPV4Host{extractAddress(ip), extractPort(ip)}
    {
    }
};
```

Using delegating constructors results in less boilerplate and fewer runtime operations, as data members and base classes can be initialized directly through the **member initializer list**.

Potential Pitfalls

Delegation cycles

If a constructor delegates to itself either directly or indirectly, the program is **ill formed, no diagnostic required (IFNDR)**. While some compilers can, under certain conditions, detect delegation cycles at compile time, they are neither required nor necessarily able to do so. For example, even the simplest delegation cycles might not result in a diagnostic from a compiler[2]:

---

[2] As of this writing, GCC 11.2 (c. 2021) does not detect this delegation cycle at compile time and produces a binary that, if run, will necessarily exhibit **undefined behavior**. Clang 3.0 (c. 2011) and later, on the other hand, halts compilation with a helpful error message:

```
error: constructor for S creates a delegation cycle
```

```
struct S  // Object
{
    S(int)  : S(true) { }  // delegating constructor
    S(bool) : S(0)    { }  // delegating constructor
};
```

Suboptimal factoring

The need for delegating constructors might result from initially suboptimal factoring —
e.g., in the case where the same **value** is being presented in different forms to a variety of
different **mechanisms**. For example, consider the IPV4Host class in *Use Cases — Avoiding
code duplication among constructors* on page 48. While having two constructors to initialize
the host might be appropriate, if either (1) the number of ways of expressing the same value
increases or (2) the number of consumers of that value increases, we might be well advised
to create a separate **value-semantic** type, e.g., IPV4Endpoint, to represent that value[3]:

```
#include <cstdint>  // std::uint16_t, std::uint32_t
#include <string>   // std::string


class IPV4Endpoint
{
    std::uint32_t d_address;
    std::uint16_t d_port;

public:
    IPV4Endpoint(std::uint32_t address, std::uint16_t port)
        : d_address{address}, d_port{port}
    {
    }

    IPV4Endpoint(const std::string& ep)
        : IPV4Endpoint{extractAddress(ep), extractPort(ep)}
    {
    }
};
```

Note that IPV4Endpoint itself makes use of delegating constructors but as a purely private,
encapsulated implementation detail. With the introduction of IPV4Endpoint into the codebase, IPV4Host (and similar components requiring an IPV4Endpoint value) can be redefined
to have a single constructor (or other previously overloaded member function) taking an
IPV4Endpoint object as an argument.

---

[3]The notion that each component in a subsystem ideally performs one focused function well is sometimes
referred to as separation of logical concerns or fine-grained, physical factoring; see **dijkstra82** and see
lakos20, section 0.4, "Hierarchically Reusable Software," section 3.2.7, "Not Just Minimal, Primitive: The
Utility struct," and section 3.5.9, "Factoring," pp. 20–28, 529–530, and 674–676, respectively.

See Also

- "Forwarding References" (§2.1, p. 377) provides perfect forwarding of arguments from one ctor to another.

- "Variadic Templates" (§2.1, p. 873) describes how to implement constructors that forward an arbitrary list of arguments to other constructors.

Using = delete for Arbitrary Functions

The keyword **delete** annotating a function's first declaration makes any attempt to use or even access it ill formed.

Description

Declaring a particular function or function overload to result in a fatal diagnostic upon invocation can be useful, e.g., to suppress the generation of a **special member function** or to limit the types of arguments a particular overload set is able to accept. In such cases, =**delete** followed by a semicolon (;) can be used in place of the body of any function on first declaration only to force a compile-time error if any attempt is made to invoke it or take its address.

```
void g(double) { }
void g(int) = delete;

void f()
{
    g(3.14);   // OK, f(double) is invoked.
    g(0);      // Error, f(int) is deleted.
}
```

Notice that deleted functions participate in **overload resolution** and produce a compile-time error when selected as the best candidate.

Use Cases

Suppressing special member function generation

When instantiating an object of user-defined type, **special member functions** that have not been declared explicitly are often generated automatically by the compiler. The generation of individual special member functions can be affected by the existence of other user-defined special member functions or by limitations imposed by the specific types of any data members or base types; see Section 1.1."Defaulted Functions" on page 33. For certain kinds of types, the notion of *copying* is not meaningful, and hence permitting the compiler to generate *copy* operations would be inappropriate. The two special member functions controlling **move operations**, introduced in C++11, are typically implemented as effective optimizations of **copy operations** and thus would be similarly contraindicated. Much less frequently, a useful notion of moving exists where copying does not, and so we might choose to have move operations generated, while **copy operations** are explicitly deleted; see Section 2.1. "*Rvalue* References" on page 710.

Consider a class, `FileHandle`, that uses the RAII idiom to safely acquire and release an I/O stream. As **copy semantics** are typically not meaningful for such resources, we will want to suppress generation of both the **copy constructor** and **copy assignment operator**. Prior to C++11, there was no direct way to express suppression of special member functions in C++. The commonly recommended workaround was to **declare** the two methods **private** and leave them unimplemented, typically resulting in a compile-time or link-time error when accessed:

```cpp
#include <cstdio>  // FILE
class FileHandle
{
private:
    // ...

    FileHandle(const FileHandle&);                // not implemented
    FileHandle& operator=(const FileHandle&);  // not implemented

public:
    explicit FileHandle(FILE* filePtr);
    ~FileHandle();

    // ...
};
```

Not implementing a special member function that is declared to be private ensures that there will be at least a link-time error in case that function is inadvertently accessed from within the implementation of the class itself. With the `=`**delete** syntax, we are able to (1) explicitly express our intention to make these special member functions unavailable, (2) do so directly in the **public** region of the class, and (3) enable clearer compiler diagnostics:

```cpp
class FileHandle
{
private:
    // ...
    // Declarations of copy constructor and copy assignment are now public.

public:
    explicit FileHandle(FILE* filePtr);
    ~FileHandle();

    FileHandle(const FileHandle&) = delete;                // make unavailable
    FileHandle& operator=(const FileHandle&) = delete;  // make unavailable

    // ...
};
```

Using the = **delete** syntax on declarations that are private results in error messages concerning privacy, not the use of deleted functions. Care must be exercised to make *both* changes when converting code from the old style to the new syntax.

Preventing a particular implicit conversion

Certain functions — especially those that take a **char** as an argument — are prone to inadvertent misuse. As a truly classic example, consider the C library function memset, which might be used to write the character * five times in a row, starting at a specified memory address, buf:

```
#include <cstdio>   // puts
#include <cstring>  // memset

void f()
{
    char buf[] = "Hello World!";
    memset(buf, 5, '*');  // undefined behavior: buffer overflow
    puts(buf);            // expected output: "***** World!"
}
```

Sadly, inadvertently reversing the order of the last two arguments is a commonly recurring error, and the C language provides no help. As shown above, memset writes the nonprinting character '\x5' 42 (i.e., the integer value of ASCII '*') times, way past the end of buf. In C++, we can target such observed misuse using an extra deleted overload:

```
namespace my {
void* memset(void* str, int ch, std::size_t n);  // Standard Library equivalent
void* memset(void* str, int n, char) = delete;   // defense against misuse
}
```

Pernicious user errors can now be reported during compilation:

```
void f2()
{
    char buf[] = "Hello World!";
    my::memset(buf, 5, '*');            // Error, call to deleted function
    my::memset(buf, '*', (std::size_t)5);  // OK
}
```

Preventing all implicit conversions

The ByteStream::send member function on the next page is designed to work with 8-bit unsigned integers only. Providing a deleted overload accepting an **int** forces a caller to ensure that the argument is always of the appropriate type:

```
class ByteStream
{
public:
    void send(unsigned char byte) { /*...*/ }
    void send(int) = delete;

    // ...
};

void f()
{
    ByteStream stream;
    stream.send(0);    // Error, send(int) is deleted.    (1)
    stream.send('a');  // Error, send(int) is deleted.    (2)
    stream.send(0L);   // Error, ambiguous                (3)
    stream.send(0U);   // Error, ambiguous                (4)
    stream.send(0.0);  // Error, ambiguous                (5)
    stream.send(
        static_cast<unsigned char>(100));  // OK          (6)
}
```

Invoking send with an **int** — noted with (1) in the code above — or any integral type, other
than **unsigned char**, that promotes to **int** (2) will map exclusively to the deleted send(**int**)
overload; all other integral, (3) and (4), and floating-point types (5) are convertible to both
via a **standard conversion** and hence will be ambiguous. Note that implicitly converting
from **unsigned char** to either a **long** or **unsigned** integer involves a **standard conversion**
(not just an **integral promotion**), the same as converting to a **double**. An explicit cast to
unsigned char (6) can always be pressed into service if needed.

Hiding a structural, nonpolymorphic base class's member function

Avoiding deriving publicly from concrete classes is commonly advised because by doing
so, we do not hide the underlying capabilities, which can easily be accessed (potentially
breaking any invariants the derived class might want to keep) via assignment to a pointer or
reference to a base class, with no casting required. Worse, inadvertently passing such a class
to a function taking the base class by value will result in slicing, which can be especially
problematic when the derived class holds data. A more robust approach would be to use
layering or at least private inheritance.[1] Best practices notwithstanding,[2] it can be cost-
effective in the short term to provide an elided "view" on a concrete class for trusted clients.
Imagine a class AudioStream designed to play sounds and music that — in addition to
providing basic "play" and "rewind" operations — sports a large, robust interface:

---

[1]For more on improving compositional designs at scale, see **lakos20**, section 3.5.10.5, "Realizing Multicomponent Wrappers," and section 3.7.3, "Improving Purely Compositional Designs," pp. 687–703 and
726–727, respectively.

[2]See **meyers92**, "Item 38: Never define an inherited default parameter value," pp. 132–135.

```
struct AudioStream
{
    void play();
    void rewind();
    // ...
    // ... (large, robust interface)
    // ...
};
```

Suppose that, on short notice, we must whip up a similar class, `ForwardAudioStream`, to use with audio samples that cannot be rewound, e.g., coming directly from a live feed. Realizing that we can readily reuse most of `AudioStream`'s interface, we pragmatically decide to prototype the new class simply by exploiting public **structural inheritance** and then deleting just the lone unwanted `rewind` member function:

```
struct ForwardAudioStream : AudioStream
{
    void rewind() = delete; // Make just this one function unavailable.
};

void f()
{
    ForwardAudioStream stream = FMRadio::getStream();
    stream.play();   // fine
    stream.rewind(); // Error, rewind() is deleted.
}
```

If the need for a `ForwardAudioStream` type persists, we can always consider reimplementing it more carefully later.[3] As discussed at the beginning of this section, the protection provided by this example is easily circumvented:

```
void g(const ForwardAudioStream &stream)
{
    AudioStream fullStream = stream;
    fullStream.play();   // OK
    fullStream.rewind(); // This code compiles OK, but what happens at run time?
}
```

Hiding non**virtual** functions is something one undertakes only after attaining a complete understanding of what makes such an unorthodox endeavor *safe*; see, in particular, Section 3.1.“**final**” on page 1007.

---

[3]lakos20, section 3.5.10.5, “Realizing Multicomponent Wrappers,” and section 3.7.3, “Improving Purely Compositional Designs,” pp. 687–703 and 726–727, respectively

Annoyances

Deleting a function declares it

It should come as no surprise that when we declare a **free function** followed by =**delete**, we *are* in fact *declaring* it. For example, consider the pair of overloads of functions f declared taking a **char** and **int**, respectively:

```cpp
int f(char);        // (1) accessible declaration of f taking a char
int f(int) = delete; // (2) inaccessible declaration of f taking an int

int x = f('a');     // OK, exact match for (1) f(char), which is accessible
int y = f(123);     // Error, exact match for (2) f(int), which is deleted
```

Both functions above must be *declared* so that both of them can participate in overload resolution; it is only after the inaccessible overload is selected that it will be reported as a compile-time error.

When it comes to deleting certain **special member functions** of a class (or class template), however, what might seem like a tiny bit of extra, self-documenting code can have subtle, unintended consequences as evidenced below. Let's begin by considering an empty **struct**, S0:

```cpp
struct S0 { };  // The default constructor is declared implicitly.

S0 x0;  // OK, invokes the implicitly generated default constructor
```

As S0 defines not constructors, destructors, or assignment operators, the compiler will generate (**declare** and **define**), for S0, all *six* of the **special member functions** available as of C++11; see Section 1.1."Defaulted Functions" on page 33.

Next, suppose we create a second **struct**, S1, that differs from S0 only in that S1 declares a *value* constructor taking an **int**:

```cpp
struct S1  // Implicit declaration of the default constructor is suppressed.
{
    S1(int);  // explicit declaration of value constructor
};

S1 y1(5);  // OK, invokes the explicitly declared value constructor
S1 x1;     // Error, no declaration for default constructor S1::S1()
```

By explicitly declaring a *value* constructor (or any other constructor for that matter), we automatically suppress the implicit declaration of the default constructor for S1. If suppressing the default destructor is *not* our intention, we can always reinstate it via an explicit declaration followed by =**default**; (see Section 1.1."Defaulted Functions" on page 33).

Let's now suppose it *is* our intention to suppress generation of the default constructor, and to make our intention clear, we elect to explicitly **declare** and **delete** it:

```
struct S2  // Implicit declaration of the default constructor is suppressed.
{
    S2() = delete;  // explicit declaration of inaccessible default constructor
    S2(int);        // explicit declaration of value constructor
};

S2 y2(5);  // OK, invokes the explicitly declared value constructor
S2 x2;     // Error, use of deleted function, S2::S2()
```

By declaring and then deleting the default constructor we have, it would appear that we (1) made our intentions clear and (2) improved diagnostics for our clients at the cost of a single extra line of self-documenting code. Ah, if only C++ were that straightforward.

Deleting certain **special member functions** — i.e., *default* constructor, *move* constructor, or *move*-assignment operator — that are not necessarily implicitly declared can have non-obvious consequence that adversely affect subtle compile-time properties of a class. One such subtle property is whether the compiler considers it to be a **literal type**, i.e., a type whose *value* is eligible for use as part of a **constant expression**. This same property of being a **literal type** is what determines whether an arbitrary type may be passed by value in the interface of a **constexpr** function; see Section 2.1."**constexpr** Functions" on page 257.

As a simple illustration of a subtle compile-time difference between S1 and S2, consider this practically useful *pattern* for a developer's "test" function that will compile if and only if its by-value parameter, x, is of a literal type:

```
constexpr int test(S0 x) { return 0; }  // OK,    S0 is   a literal type.
constexpr int test(S1 x) { return 0; }  // Error, S1 is not a literal type.
constexpr int test(S2 x) { return 0; }  // OK,    S2 is   a literal type.
```

For the compiler to treat a given class type as a **literal type**, it must, among other things, have at least one constructor (other than the *copy* or *move* constructor) declared as **constexpr**.

In the case of the empty S0 class, the implicitly generated default constructor is **trivial** and so it is implicitly *declared* **constexpr** too. Class S1's explicitly declared *non***constexpr** value constructor suppresses the declaration of its only **constexpr** constructor, the default constructor; hence, S1 does not qualify as a *literal type*.

Finally, by conspicuously declaring and deleting S2's default constructor, we *declare* it nonetheless. What's more, the declaration brought about by deleting it is the same as if it had been generated implicitly (or declared explicitly and then defaulted); hence, S2, unlike S1, *is* a **literal type**. Go figure!

See Also

- "Defaulted Functions" (§1.1, p. 33) describes a companion feature that enables defaulting, as opposed to deleting, special member functions.

- "*Rvalue* References" (§2.1, p. 710) explains how this feature gives rise to two *move* variants of special member functions, which may also be subject to deletion.

Further Reading

- For comparison of deleting functions to the pre-C++11 approach of using private undefined functions and for techniques for deleting function template specializations, see **meyers15b**, "Item 11: Prefer deleted functions to private undefined ones," pp. 74–79.

Explicit Conversion Operators

Ensure that a user-defined type is convertible to another type only in contexts where the conversion is made obvious in the code.

Description

Though sometimes desirable, implicit conversions achieved via user-defined *conversion functions* — either **converting constructors** accepting a single argument or **conversion operators** — can also be problematic, especially when the conversion involves a commonly used type (e.g., **int** or **double**):

```
class Point  // implicitly convertible from an int or to a double
{
    int d_x, d_y;

public:
    Point(int x = 0, int y = 0);  // default, conversion, and value constructor
    // ...
    operator double() const;  // Return distance from origin as a double.
};
```

Using a conversion operator to calculate distance from the origin in this unrealistically simple `Point` example is for didactic purposes only. In practice, we would typically use a named function for this purpose; see *Potential Pitfalls — Sometimes a named function is better* on page 66.

As ever, calling a function that takes a `Point` but accidentally passing an **int** can lead to surprises:

```
void g0(Point p);        // arbitrary function taking a Point object by value
void g1(const Point& p);  // arbitrary function taking a Point by const reference

void f1(int i)
{
    g0(i);  // oops, called g0 with Point(i, 0) by mistake
    g1(i);  // oops, called g1 with Point(i, 0) by mistake
}
```

This problem could have been solved even in C++03 by declaring the constructor to be **explicit**:

```
explicit Point(int x = 0, int y = 0);  // explicit converting constructor
```

If the conversion is desired, it must now be specified explicitly:

```
void f2(int i)
{
    g0(i);          // Error, could not convert i from int to Point
    g1(i);          // Error, invalid initialization of reference type
    g0(Point(i));   // OK
    g1(Point(i));   // OK
}
```

The companion problem stemming from an *implicit conversion operator*, albeit less severe, remained:

```
void h(double d);

double f3(const Point& p)
{
    h(p);      // OK? Or maybe we mistakenly called h with a hypotenuse.
    return p;  // OK? Or maybe this is a mistake too.
}
```

As of C++11, we can now use the **explicit** specifier when declaring **conversion operators** as well as **converting constructors**, thereby forcing the client to request conversion explicitly, e.g., using **direct initialization** or **static_cast**:

```
struct S0 { explicit operator int(); };

void g()
{
    S0 s0;
    int i = s0;                      // Error, copy initialization
    int k(s0);                       // OK, direct initialization
    double d = s0;                   // Error, copy initialization
    int j = static_cast<int>(s0);    // OK, static cast
    if (s0) { }                      // Error, contextual conversion to bool
    double e(s0);                    // Error, direct initialization
}
```

In contrast, had the conversion operator in the example above not been declared to be **explicit**, all conversions shown above would compile:

```
struct S1 { /* implicit */ operator int(); };

void f()
```

```
{
    S1 s1;
    int i = s1;                         // OK, copy initialization
    double d = s1;                      // OK, copy initialization
    int j = static_cast<int>(s1);       // OK, static cast
    if (s1) { }                         // OK, contextual conversion to bool
    int k(s1);                          // OK, direct initialization
    double e(s1);                       // OK, direct initialization
}
```

Additionally, the notion of **contextual convertibility to bool** applicable to arguments of logical operations — e.g., &&, ||, and ! — and conditions of most control-flow constructs, e.g., **if** and **while**, was extended in C++11 to admit *explicit* user-defined **bool** conversion operators; see *Use Cases — Enabling contextual conversions to* bool *as a test for validity* below:

```
struct S2 { explicit operator bool(); };

void h()
{
    S2 s2;
    int i = s2;                         // Error, copy initialization
    double d = s2;                      // Error, copy initialization
    int j = static_cast<int>(s2);       // Error, static cast
    if (s2) { }                         // OK, contextual conversion to bool
    int k(s2);                          // Error, direct initialization
    double fd(s2);                      // Error, direct initialization
    bool b0 = s2;                       // Error, copy initialization
    bool b1(s2);                        // OK, direct initialization
    !s2;                                // OK, contextual conversion to bool

    s2 && s2;                           // OK, contextual conversion to bool
}
```

Use Cases

Enabling contextual conversions to bool as a test for validity

Having a conventional test for validity that involves testing whether the object itself evaluates to **true** or **false** is an idiom that goes back to the origins of C++. The Standard input/output library, for example, uses this idiom to determine if a given stream is valid:

```
// C++03
#include <ostream>  // std::ostream

std::ostream& printTypeValue(std::ostream& stream, double value)
{
    if (stream)  // relies on an implicit conversion to bool
    {
        stream << "double(" << value << ')';
    }
    else
    {
        // ... (handle stream failure)
    }

    return stream;
}
```

Implementing the implicit conversion to **bool** was, however, problematic as the straight-forward approach of using a **conversion operator** could easily allow accidental misuse to go undetected:

```
class ostream
{
    // ...

    public:

    /* implicit */ operator bool();  // hypothetical (bad) idea
};

int client(ostream& out)
{
    // ...
    return out + 1;  // likely a latent runtime bug: always returns 1 or 2
}
```

The classic workaround, the **safe-bool idiom**,[1] was to return some obscure pointer type (e.g., **pointer to member**) that could not possibly be useful in any context other than one in which **false** and a null pointer-to-member value are treated equivalently. With explicit conversion operators, such workarounds are no longer required. As discussed in *Description* on page 61, a conversion operator to type **bool** that is declared **explicit** continues to act as if it were *implicit* only in those places where we might want it to do so and nowhere else, i.e., exactly those places that enable **contextual conversion to bool**.[2]

---

[1] www.artima.com/cppsource/safebool.html
[2] Note that two consecutive ! operators can be used to synthesize a contextual conversion to **bool** — i.e., if X is an expression that is explicitly convertible to **bool**, then (!!(X)) will be **true** or **false** accordingly.

As a concrete example, consider a `ConnectionHandle` class that can be in either a *valid* or *invalid* state. For the user's convenience and consistency with other proxy types, e.g., raw pointers, that have a similar *invalid* state, representing the invalid or null state via an explicit conversion to **bool** might be desirable:

```
#include <cstddef>  // std::size_t
#include <iostream> // std::cerr
struct ConnectionHandle
{
    std::size_t maxThroughput() const;
        // Return the maximum throughput (in bytes) of the connection.

    explicit operator bool() const;
        // Return true if the handle is valid and false otherwise.
};
```

Instances of `ConnectionHandle` will convert to **bool** only where one might reasonably want them to do so, say, as the predicate of an **if** statement:

```
int ping(const ConnectionHandle& handle)
{
    if (handle)  // OK, contextual conversion to bool
    {
        // ...
        return 0;  // success
    }

    std::cerr << "Invalid connection handle.\n";
    return -1;  // failure
}
```

Having an **explicit** conversion operator prevents unwanted conversions to **bool** that might otherwise happen inadvertently:

```
bool hasEnoughThroughput(const ConnectionHandle& ingress,
                         const ConnectionHandle& egress)
{
    return ingress.throughput() <= egress;  // Error, thankfully
//                                   ^~~~~~
}
```

In the example above, the programmer mistakenly wrote `egress` instead of `egress.maxThroughput()` after `<=`, the relational operator. Fortunately, the conversion operator of `ConnectionHandle` was declared to be **explicit**, and a compile-time error ensued; if the conversion had been *implicit*, the example code above would have compiled, and, if executed, the above faulty implementation of the `hasEnoughThroughput` function would have silently exhibited well-defined but incorrect behavior.

Potential Pitfalls

Sometimes implicit conversion *is* indicated

Implicit conversions to and from common arithmetic types, especially **int**, are generally ill advised given the likelihood of accidental misuse. However, for proxy types that are intended to be drop-in replacements for the types they represent, implicit conversions are precisely what we want. Consider, for example, a `NibbleConstReference` proxy type that represents the 4-bit integer elements of a `PackedNibbleVector`:

```
class NibbleConstReference
{
    // ...
public:
    operator int() const; // implicit

    // ...
};

class PackedNibbleVector
{
    // ...
public:
    bool empty() const;
    NibbleConstReference operator[](int index) const;

    // ...
};
```

The `NibbleConstReference` proxy is intended to interoperate well with other integral types in various expressions, and making its conversion operator **explicit** hinders its intended use as a drop-in replacement by requiring an explicit conversion, a.k.a. cast:

```
int firstOrZero(const PackedNibbleVector& values)
{
    return values.empty()
        ? 0
        : values[0]; // compiles only if conversion operator is implicit
}
```

Sometimes a named function is better

Other kinds of overuse of even *explicit* conversion operators exist. As happens with any user-defined operator, when the operation being implemented is not somehow either canonical or ubiquitously idiomatic for that operator, expressing that operation by a named, i.e., nonoperator, function is often better. Recall from *Description* on page 61 that we used a conversion operator of class `Point` to represent the distance from the origin. This example serves to illustrate how conversion operators might be both ambiguous and insufficient at the same time. Consider that (1) many mathematical operations on a 2-D integral point might return a **double** (e.g., `magnitude`, `angle`) and (2) we might want to represent the same information but in different units (e.g., `angleInDegrees`, `angleInRadians`). Another valid design decision would be to return an object of user-defined type, say, `Angle`, that captures the amplitude and provides named accessory to the different units (e.g., `asDegrees`, `asRadians`).

Rather than employing any conversion *operator* (**explicit** or otherwise), consider instead providing a named function, which (1) is automatically **explicit** and (2) affords both flexibility in writing and clarity in reading for a variety of domain-specific functions — now and in the future — that might well have had overlapping return types:

```
class Point  // only explicitly convertible and from only an int
{
    int d_x, d_y;

public:
    explicit Point(int x = 0, int y = 0);  // explicit converting constructor
    // ...
    double magnitude() const;  // Return distance from origin as a double.
};
```

Note that defining **nonprimitive functionality**, like `magnitude`, in a separate *utility* at a higher level in the physical hierarchy, e.g., `PointUtil::magnitude(const Point& p)`, might be better still.[3]

---

[3]For more on separating out nonprimitive functionality, see **lakos20**, section 3.2.7, "Not Just Minimal, Primitive: The Utility struct," through section 3.2.8, "Concluding Example: An Encapsulating Polygon Interface," pp. 529–552.

Thread-Safe Function-Scope `static` Variables

Initialization of function-scope **static** objects is now guaranteed to be free of data races in the presence of multiple concurrent threads.

Description

A variable declared at function, a.k.a. local, scope has **automatic storage duration**, except when it is marked **static**, in which case it has **static storage duration**. Variables having automatic storage duration are allocated on the stack each time the function is invoked and initialized when that invocation's **flow of control** passes through the **definition** of that object. In contrast, variables with static storage duration, e.g., iLocal, defined at function scope, e.g., f, are instead allocated once per program and are initialized only the first time the flow of control passes through the **definition** of that object:

```
#include <cassert>  // standard C assert macro

int f(int i) // function returning the first argument with which it is called
{
    static int iLocal = i;  // Object is initialized only once, on the first call.
    return iLocal;          // The same iLocal value is returned on every call.
}

int main()
{
    int a = f(10);  assert(a == 10);  // Initialize and return iLocal.
    int b = f(20);  assert(b == 10);  // Return iLocal.
    int c = f(30);  assert(c == 10);  // Return iLocal.

    return 0;
}
```

In the simple example above, the function, f, initializes its **static** object, iLocal, with its argument, i, only the first time it is called and then always returns the same value, e.g., 10. Hence, when that function is called repeatedly with distinct arguments to initialize the a, b, and c variables, all three of them are initialized to the same value, 10, supplied to the first invocation of f. Although the function-scope **static** object, iLocal, was created after main was entered, it will not be destroyed until after main exits.

Concurrent initialization

Historically, initialization of **function-scope** static storage duration objects was not guaranteed to be safe in a **multithreading context** because it was subject to **data races** if the function was called concurrently from multiple threads. These **data races** around initialization can lead to the initializer being invoked multiple times, object construction running concurrently on the same object, and control flow continuing past the variable definition before initialization had completed at all. All of these variations would result in critical software flaws. One common but nonportable pre-C++11 workaround was the *double-checked-lock pattern*; see *Appendix — C++03 double-checked-lock pattern* on page 81.

As of C++11, a conforming compiler is now required to ensure that initialization of function-scope static storage duration objects is performed safely and exactly once before execution continues past the initializer, even when the function is called concurrently from multiple threads.

Destruction

Objects with **automatic storage duration** are destroyed when control leaves the scope in which they are declared. In contrast, **static** local objects that have been initialized are not destroyed until normal program termination, either after the `main` function returns normally or when the `std::exit` function is called. The order of destruction of these objects will be the reverse of the order in which they completed construction. Note that programs can terminate in several other ways, such as a call to `std::quick_exit`, `_Exit`, or `std::abort`, that explicitly do *not* destroy **static storage duration** objects. This behavior is as if each static object is scheduled for destruction by using the C Standard Library function `std::atexit` right after construction.

Logger example

Let's now consider a real-world example in which a single object, e.g., `localLogger` in the example below, is used widely throughout a program; see also *Use Cases — Meyers Singleton* on page 71[1]:

```
Logger& getLogger()  // ubiquitous pattern commonly known as "Meyers Singleton"
{
    static Logger localLogger("log.txt");  // function-local static definition
    return localLogger;
}

int main()
{
    getLogger() << "hello";
        // OK, invokes Logger's constructor for the first and only time

    getLogger() << "world";
        // OK, uses the previously constructed Logger instance
}
```

---

[1]An eminently useful, full-featured logger, known as the `ball` logger, can be found in the `ball` package of the `bal` package group of Bloomberg's open-source BDE libraries (**bde14**, /groups/bal/ball).

Here we have an example of the "Singleton pattern"[2] being used to create the shared `Logger` instance and provide access to it through the `getLogger()` function. The **static** local instance of `Logger`, `localLogger`, will be initialized exactly once and then destroyed after normal program termination. In C++03, it would not be safe to call this function concurrently from multiple threads. Conversely, C++11 *guarantees* that the initialization of `localLogger` will happen exactly once even when multiple threads call `getLogger` concurrently.

Multithreaded contexts

The C++11 Standard Library provides several utilities and abstractions related to multithreading. The `std::thread` class is a portable wrapper for a platform-specific thread handle provided by the operating system. When constructing an `std::thread` object with a **callable object**, a new thread invoking that **callable object** will be spawned. Prior to destroying such `std::thread` objects, invoking the `join` member function on the thread object is necessary and will block until the background thread of execution completes invoking its **callable object**.

This threading facility from the Standard Library can be used with our earlier example in *Logger example* on page 69 to concurrently attempt to access the `getLogger` function:

```
#include <thread>  // std::thread

void useLogger() { getLogger() << "example"; }  // concurrently called function

int main()
{
    std::thread t0(&useLogger);
    std::thread t1(&useLogger);
        // Spawn two new threads, each of which invokes useLogger.

    // ...

    t0.join();  // Wait for t0 to complete execution.
    t1.join();  // Wait for t1 to complete execution.

    return 0;
}
```

Such use prior to the C++11 thread-safety guarantees, with pre-C++11 threading libraries, could have led to a **data race** during the initialization of `localLogger`, which was defined as a local **static** object in `getLogger`. This **undefined behavior** might have resulted in invoking the constructor of `localLogger` multiple times, returning from `localLogger` before

---

[2]**gamma95**, Chapter 3, section "Singleton," pp. 127–134

that constructor had actually been completed, or any other form of misbehavior over which the developer has no control.

If `Logger::operator<<(const char*)` is designed properly for multithreaded use, then, as of C++11, the previous example has no **data races**, even though the `Logger::Logger(const char* logFilePath)` constructor, i.e., the one used to configure the singleton instance of the logger, is not so designed. That is to say, the implicit **critical section** that is guarded by the compiler includes evaluation of the initializer, which is why a recursive call to initialize a function-scope **static** variable is **undefined** behavior and is likely to result in deadlock; see *Potential Pitfalls — Dangerous recursive initialization* on page 77. Such use of function-scope **static**s, however, is not foolproof; see *Potential Pitfalls — Depending on order-of-destruction of local objects after main returns* on page 78.

The destruction of function-scope **static** objects is and always has been guaranteed to be safe *provided* (1) no threads are running after returning from main and (2) function-scope **static** objects do not depend on each other during destruction; see *Potential Pitfalls — Depending on order-of-destruction of local objects after main returns* on page 78.

Use Cases

Meyers Singleton

The guarantees surrounding access across **translation units** to runtime-initialized objects at file or namespace scope are few and weak — especially when that access might occur prior to entering main. Consider a library component, `libcomp`, that defines a file-scope **static** singleton, `globalS`, that is initialized at run time:

```
// libcomp.h:
#ifndef INCLUDED_LIBCOMP
#define INCLUDED_LIBCOMP

struct S { /*...*/ };
S& getGlobalS();  // access to global singleton object of type S

#endif


// libcomp.cpp:
#include <libcomp.h>

static S globalS;
S& getGlobalS() { return globalS; }  // access into this translation unit
```

The interface in the `libcomp.h` file comprises the definition of S along with the declaration of an accessor function, `getGlobalS`. Code outside the `libcomp.cpp` file can access the singleton object `globalS` only by calling the free function `getGlobalS()`. Now consider the `main.cpp` file in the example below, which implements `main` and also makes use of `globalS` prior to entering `main`:

```
// main.cpp:
#include <cassert>    // standard C assert macro
#include <libcomp.h>  // getGlobalS()

bool globalInitFlag = getGlobalS().isInitialized();

int main()
{
    assert(globalInitFlag);   // Bug, or at least potentially so
    return 0;
}
```

Depending on the compiler or the link line, the call initializing `globalInitFlag` might occur and return *prior* to the initialization of `globalS`. C++ does not guarantee that objects at file or namespace scope in separate **translation units** will be initialized just because a function located within that **translation unit** happens to be called.

An effective pattern for helping to ensure that a nonlocal object *is* initialized before it is used from a separate **translation unit** — especially when that use might occur prior to entering `main` — is simply to move the **static** object from file or namespace scope to the scope of the function accessing it, making it a function-scope **static** instead:

```
S& getGlobalS()  // access into this translation unit
{
    static S globalS;  // singleton is now function-scope static
    return globalS;
}
```

Commonly known as the **Meyers Singleton** for author Scott Meyers who popularized it, this pattern ensures that the singleton object will *necessarily* be initialized on the first call to the accessor function that envelopes it, irrespective of when and where that call is made. Moreover, that singleton object will also live past the end of `main`. The Meyers Singleton pattern also gives us a chance to catch and respond to exceptions thrown when constructing the **static** object, rather than immediately terminating the program, as would be the case if declared as a **static** global variable. Much more importantly, however, since C++11, the Meyers Singleton pattern automatically inherits the benefits of effortless race-free initialization of *reusable* program-wide singleton objects. The Meyers Singleton can be safely used both in the programs where the singleton initialization might happen before `main` and those where it might happen after additional threads have already been started.

As discussed in *Description* on page 68, the augmentation of a thread-safety guarantee for the runtime initialization of function-scope **static** objects in C++11 minimizes the effort required to create a thread-safe singleton. Note that, prior to C++11, the simple function-scope **static** implementation would not be safe if concurrent threads were trying to initialize the logger; see *Appendix — C++03 double-checked-lock pattern* on page 81.

The Meyers Singleton is also seen in a slightly different form where the singleton type's constructor is made **private** to prevent more than just the one singleton object from being created:

```
class Logger
{
private:
    Logger(const char* logFilePath);  // configures the singleton
    ~Logger();                         // suppresses copy construction too

public:
    static Logger& getInstance()
    {
        static Logger localLogger("log.txt");
        return localLogger;
    }
};
```

This variant of the function-scope-**static** singleton pattern prevents users from manually creating rogue Logger objects; the only way to get one is to invoke the logger's **static** Logger::getInstance() member function:

```
void client()
{
    Logger::getInstance() << "Hi";  // OK
    Logger myLogger("myLog.txt");    // Error, Logger constructor is private.
}
```

This formulation of the singleton pattern, however, conflates the type of the singleton object with its use and purpose as a singleton. Once we find a use of a singleton object, finding another and perhaps even a third is not uncommon.

Consider, for example, an application on an early model of mobile phone where we want to refer to the phone's camera. Let's presume that a Camera class is a fairly involved and sophisticated mechanism. Initially we use the variant of the Meyers Singleton pattern where at most one Camera object can be present in the entire program. The next generation of the phone, however, turns out to have more than one camera, say, a front Camera and a back Camera. Our brittle design doesn't admit the dual-singleton use of the same fundamental Camera type. A more finely factored solution would be to implement the Camera type separately and then to provide a thin wrapper, e.g., perhaps using the **strong-typedef** idiom (see Section 2.1."Inheriting Ctors" on page 535), corresponding to each singleton use:

```
class PrimaryCamera
{
private:
    Camera& d_camera_r;
    PrimaryCamera(Camera& camera)  // implicit constructor
      : d_camera_r(camera) { }

public:
    static PrimaryCamera getInstance()
    {
        static Camera localCamera{/*...*/};
        return localCamera;
    }
};
```

With this design, adding a second and even a third singleton that is able to reuse the underlying `Camera` mechanism is facilitated.

Although this function-scope-**static** approach provides stronger guarantees than the file-scope-**static** one, it does have its limitations. In particular, when one global facility object, such as a logger, is used in the destructor of another function-scope static object, the logger object might possibly have already been destroyed when it is used.[3] One approach is to construct the logger object by explicitly allocating it and never deleting it:

```
Logger& getLogger()
{
    static Logger& l = *new Logger("log.txt");  // dynamically allocated
    return l;  // Return a reference to the logger (on the heap).
}
```

A distinct advantage of this approach is that once an object is created, it *never* goes away before the process ends. The disadvantage is that, for many classic and current profiling tools (e.g., *Purify*, *Coverity*), this intentionally never-freed dynamic allocation is indistinguishable from a **memory leak**. The ultimate workaround is to create the object itself in **static** memory, in an appropriately sized and aligned region of memory:

```
#include <new>  // placement new

Logger& getLogger()
{
    static std::aligned_storage<sizeof(Logger), alignof(Logger)>::type buf;
    static Logger& logger = *new(&buf) Logger("log.txt");  // allocate in place
    return logger;
}
```

---

[3] An amusing workaround, the so-called *Phoenix Singleton*, is proposed in **alexandrescu01**, section 6.6, "Addressing the Dead Reference Problem (I): The Phoenix Singleton," pp. 137–139.

Note that any memory that the `Logger` itself manages would still come from the global heap and be recognized as memory leaks.[4]

In this final incarnation of a decidedly non-Meyers-Singleton pattern, we first reserve a block of memory of sufficient size and the correct alignment for `Logger` using `std::aligned_storage`. Next we use that storage in conjunction with placement **new** to create the logger directly in that static memory. Notice that this allocation is not from the dynamic store, so typical profiling tools will not track and will not provide a false warning when we fail to destroy this object at program termination time. Now we can return a reference to the logger object embedded safely in static memory knowing that it will be there until application exit.

Potential Pitfalls

static storage duration objects are not guaranteed to be initialized

Despite C++11's guarantee that each individual function-scope **static** initialization will occur at most once and before control can reach a point where the variable can be referenced, no analogous guarantees are made of nonlocal objects of **static storage duration**. Absence of this guarantee makes any interdependency in the initialization of such objects, especially across **translation units** (TUs), an abundant source of insidious errors.

Objects that undergo **constant initialization** have no such issue: Such objects will never be accessible at run time before having their initial values. Objects that are not constant initialized[5] will instead be **zero initialized** until their constructors run, which itself might lead to **undefined behavior** that is not necessarily conspicuous.

As a demonstration of what can happen when we depend on the relative order of initialization of variables at file or namespace scope used before `main`, consider the **cyclically dependent** pair of source files, `a.cpp` and `b.cpp`:

```cpp
// a.cpp:
extern int setB(int);   // declaration only of setter in other TU
int *a = new int;       // runtime initialization of file-scope variable
int setA(int i)         // Initialize a; then b.
{
    *a = i;             // Populate the allocated heap memory.
    setB(i);            // Invoke setter to populate the other one.
    return 0;           // Return successful status.
}
```

---

[4]If the global heap is to be entirely avoided, we could leverage a polymorphic-allocator implementation such as `std::pmr` in C++17. We would first create a fixed-size array of memory having static storage duration. Then we would create a **static** memory-allocation mechanism, e.g., `std::pmr::monotonic_buffer_resource`. Next we would use placement **new** to construct the logger within the static memory pool using our static allocation mechanism and supply that same mechanism to the `Logger` object so that it could get all its internal memory from that static pool as well; a discussion of this topic is planned for **lakos22**.

[5]C++20 added a new keyword, **constinit**, that can be placed on a variable declaration to *require* that the variable in question undergo constant initialization and thus can never be accessed at run time prior to the start of its lifetime.

```
// b.cpp:
int *b = new int;        // runtime initialization of file-scope variable
int setB(int i)          // Initialize b.
{
    *b = i;              // Populate the allocated heap memory.
    return 0;            // Return successful status.
}

extern int setA(int);    // declaration (only) of setter in other TU
int x = setA(5);         // Initialize a and b.
int main()               // main program entry point
{
    return 0;            // Return successful status.
}
```

These two **translation units** will be initialized before **main** is entered in some order, but regardless of that order, the program in the example above will wind up dereferencing a null pointer before entering **main**:

```
$ g++ a.cpp b.cpp main.cpp
$ ./a.out
  Segmentation fault (core dumped)
```

Suppose we were to instead move the file-scope **static** pointers, corresponding to both setA and setB, inside their respective function bodies:

```
// a.cpp:
extern int setB(int);    // declaration only of setter in other TU
int setA(int i)          // Initialize this static variable; then that one.
{
    static int *p = new int;   // runtime init of function-scope static
    *p = i;                    // Populate this static-owned heap memory.
    setB(i);                   // Invoke setter to populate the other one.
    return 0;                  // Return successful status.
}

// b.cpp: (make analogous changes)
```

Now the program reliably executes without incident:

```
$ g++ a.cpp b.cpp main.cpp
$ ./a.out
$
```

In other words, even though no order exists in which the **translation units** as a whole could have been initialized prior to entering **main** such that the *file*-scope variables would be valid before they were used, by instead making them *function*-scope **static**, we are able to guarantee that each variable is itself initialized before it is used, regardless of translation-unit-initialization order.

On the surface it may seem as though local and nonlocal objects of static storage duration are effectively interchangeable, but clearly they are not. Even when clients cannot directly access the nonlocal object due to giving it **internal linkage** by marking it **static** or putting it in an **unnamed namespace**, the initialization behaviors make such objects behave differently.

Dangerous recursive initialization

As with all other initialization, control flow does not continue *past* the definition of a **static** local object until after the initialization is complete, making recursive **static** initialization — or any initializer that might eventually call back to the same function — dangerous:

```cpp
int fz(int i)  // The behavior of the first call is undefined unless i is 0.
{
    static int dz = i ? fz(i - 1) : 0;  // Initialize recursively. (BAD IDEA)
    return dz;
}

int main()  // The program is ill formed.
{
    int x = fz(5);  // Bug, e.g., due to possible deadlock
}
```

In the example above, the second recursive call of `fz` to initialize `dz` has undefined behavior because the control flow reached the same definition again before the initialization of the **static** object was completed; hence, control flow cannot continue to the **return** statement in `fz`. Given a likely implementation with a nonrecursive mutex or similar lock, the program can potentially deadlock, though many implementations provide better diagnostics with an exception or assertion violation when this form of error is encountered.[6]

Subtleties with recursion

Even when not recursing within the initializer itself, the rule for the initialization of **static** objects at function scope becomes more subtle for self-recursive functions. Notably, the initialization happens based on when flow of control first passes the variable definition and *not* based on the first invocation of the containing function. Due to this, when a recursive call happens in relation to the definition of a **static** local variable impacts which values might be used for the initialization:

---

[6]Prior to standardization (see **ellis90**, section 6.7, "Declaration Statement," pp. 91–92), C++ allowed control to flow past a **static** function-scope variable even during a recursive call made as part of the initialization of that variable. This behavior would result in the rest of such a function executing with a zero-initialized and possibly partially constructed local object. Even modern compilers, such as GCC with `-fno-threadsafe-statics`, allow turning off the locking and protection from concurrent initialization and retaining some of the pre-C++98 behavior. This optional behavior is, however, dangerous and unsupported in any standard version of C++.

```
int fx(int i)  // self-recursive after creating function-static variable, dx
{
    static int dx = i;    // Create dx first.
    if (i) { fx(i - 1); }  // Recurse second.
    return dx;            // Return dx third.
}

int fy(int i)  // self-recursive before creating function-static variable, dy
{
    if (i) { fy(i - 1); }  // Recurse first.
    static int dy = i;    // Create dy second.
    return dy;            // Return dy third.
}

int main()
{
    int x = fx(5);  assert(x == 5);  // dx is initialized before recursion.
    int y = fy(5);  assert(y == 0);  // dy is initialized after recursion.
    return 0;
}
```

If the self-recursion takes place *after* the **static** variable is initialized (e.g., fx in the example above), then the **static** object (e.g., dx) is initialized on the *first* recursive call; if the recursion occurs *before* (e.g., fy in the example above), the initialization (e.g., of dy) occurs on the *last* recursive call.

Depending on order-of-destruction of local objects after main returns

Within any given translation unit, the relative order of initialization of objects at file or namespace scope having **static storage duration** is well defined and predictable. As soon as we have a way to reference an object outside of the current translation unit, before main is entered, we are at risk of using the object before it has been initialized. Provided the initialization itself is not cyclic in nature, we can make use of function-scope **static** objects (see *Use Cases — Meyers Singleton* on page 71) to ensure that no such uninitialized use occurs, even across translation units before main is entered. The relative order of destruction of such function-scope **static** variables — even when they reside within the same translation unit — is not clearly known at compile time, as it will be the reverse of the order in which they are initialized, and reliance on such order can easily lead to undefined behavior in practice.

This specific problem occurs when a **static** object at file, namespace, or function scope uses (or might use) in its destructor another **static** object that is either (1) at file or namespace scope and resides in a separate translation unit or (2) any other function-scope **static** object, i.e., including one in the same translation unit. For example, suppose we have implemented a low-level logging facility as a Meyers Singleton:

```
Logger& getLogger()
{
    static Logger local("log.txt");
    return local;
}
```

Now suppose we implement a higher-level file-manager type that depends on the function-scope **static** logger object:

```
struct FileManager
{
    FileManager()
    {
        getLogger() << "Starting up file manager...";
        // ...
    }

    ~FileManager()
    {
        getLogger() << "Shutting down file manager...";
        // ...
    }
};
```

Now, consider a Meyers Singleton implementation for FileManager:

```
FileManager& getFileManager()
{
    static FileManager fileManager;
    return fileManager;
}
```

Whether getLogger or getFileManager is called first doesn't really matter; if getFileManager is called first, the logger will be initialized as part of FileManager's constructor. However, whether the Logger or FileManager object is destroyed first *is* important.

- If the FileManager object is destroyed prior to the Logger object, the program will have well-defined behavior.

- Otherwise, the program will have **undefined behavior** because the destructor of FileManager will invoke getLogger, which will now return a reference to a previously destroyed object.

Logging in the constructor of the FileManager makes it certain that the logger's function-local **static** will be initialized before that of the file manager; hence, since destruction occurs in reverse relative order of creation, the logger's function-local **static** will be destroyed after that of the file manager. But suppose that `FileManager` didn't always log at construction and was created before anything else logged. In that case, we have no reason to think that the logger would be around for the `FileManager` to log during its destruction after `main`.

In the case of low-level, widely used facilities, such as a logger, a conventional Meyers Singleton is contraindicated. The two most common alternatives discussed at the end of *Use Cases — Meyers Singleton* on page 71 involve never ending the lifetime of the mechanism at all. It is worth noting that truly global objects — such as `cout`, `cerr`, and `clog` — from the Standard `iostream` Library are typically not implemented using conventional methods and are in fact treated specially by the runtime system.

Annoyances

Overhead in single-threaded applications

A single-threaded application invoking a function containing a function-scope static storage duration variable might have unnecessary synchronization overhead, such as an **atomic** load operation. For example, consider a program that accesses a simple Meyers Singleton for a user-defined type with a **user-provided** default constructor:

```cpp
struct S  // user-defined type
{
    S() { }  // inline default constructor
};

S& getS()  // free function returning local object
{
    static S local;  // function-scope local object
    return local;
}

int main()
{
    getS();    // Initialize the file-scope static singleton.
    return 0;  // successful status
}
```

Although it is clearly visible to the compiler that `getS()` is invoked by only one thread, the generated assembly instructions might still contain **atomic** operations or other forms of synchronization, and the call to `getS()` might not be inlined.[7]

---

[7]Both GCC 11.2 (c. 2021) and Clang 12.0.1 (c. 2021), using the `-Ofast` optimization level, generate assembly instructions for a **memory barrier** and fail to inline the call to `getS`. Using `-fno-threadsafe-statics` reduces considerably the number of operations performed but still does not lead to the compilers' inlining of the function call. Both popular compilers will, however, reduce the program to just two x86 assembly instructions if the **user-provided** constructor of S is either removed or defaulted (see Section 1.1."Defaulted Functions" on page 33); doing so will turn S into a **trivially-constructible** type, implying that no code needs to be executed during initialization:

Further Reading

- For an in-depth discussion of the difficulties of implementing double-checked locking in C++03, see **meyers04a** and **meyers04b**.

- For a discussion of the Singleton pattern and a variety of implementations in C++03, see Chapter 6 of **alexandrescu01**.

Appendix

C++03 double-checked-lock pattern

Prior to the introduction of the function-scope **static** object initialization guarantees discussed in *Description* on page 68, preventing multiple initializations of **static** objects and use before initialization of those same objects was still needed. Guarding access using a `mutex` was often a significant performance cost, so using the unreliable, double-checked-lock pattern was often attempted to avoid the overhead:

```
Logger& getInstance()
{
    static Logger* volatile loggerPtr = 0;   // hack, used to simulate atomics

    if (!loggerPtr)   // Does the logger need to be initialized?
    {
        static std::mutex m;
        std::lock_guard<std::mutex> guard(m);   // Lock the mutex.

        if (!loggerPtr)   // We are first, as the logger is still uninitialized.
        {
            static Logger logger("log.txt");
            loggerPtr = &logger;
        }
    }                       // Either way, the lock guard unlocks the mutex here.

    return *loggerPtr;
}
```

```
xor eax, eax  ; zero out 'eax' register
ret           ; return from 'main'
```

A sufficiently smart compiler might, however, not generate synchronization code in a single-threaded context or else provide a flag to control this behavior.

In this example, we are using a **volatile** pointer as a partial substitute for an atomic variable, a nonportable solution that is not correct in standard C++ but has historically been moderately effective. The C++11 Standard Library does, however, provide the `<atomic>` header, which is a far superior alternative, and many implementations have historically provided extensions to support atomic types even prior to C++11. Where available, compiler extensions are typically preferable over home-grown solutions.

In addition to being difficult to write, this decidedly complex workaround would often prove unreliable. The problem is that, even though the logic appears sound, architectural changes in widely used CPUs allowed for the CPU itself to optimize and reorder the sequence of instructions. Without additional support, the hardware would not see the dependency that the second test of `loggerPtr` has on the locking behavior of the mutex and would do the read of `loggedPtr` prior to acquiring the lock. This reordering of instructions would then allow multiple threads to acquire the lock while each thinking the **static** variable still needs to be initialized.

To solve this subtle issue, concurrency library authors are expected to issue ordering hints, such as **fences** and **barriers**. A well-implemented threading library would provide atomics equivalent to the modern `std::atomic` that would issue the correct instructions when accessed and modified. The C++11 Standard makes the compiler aware of these concerns and provides portable *atomics* and support for threading that enables users to handle such issues correctly. The above `getInstance` function could be corrected by changing the type of `loggerPtr` to `std::atomic<Logger*>`. Prior to C++11, despite being complicated, the same function would reliably implement the Meyers Singleton (see *Use Cases — Meyers Singleton* on page 71) in C++03 on contemporary hardware.

Local/Unnamed Types as Template Arguments

C++11 allows function-scope and unnamed types to be used as template arguments.

Description

Historically, types without **linkage**, i.e., local and unnamed types, were forbidden as template arguments due to implementability concerns using the compiler technology available at that time.[1] Modern C++ lifts this restriction, making use of local or unnamed types consistent with nonlocal, named ones, thereby obviating the need to gratuitously name or enlarge the scope of a type.

```cpp
template <typename T>
void f(T) { }                // function template

template <typename T>
class C { };                 // class template

struct { } obj;              // object obj of unnamed C++ type

void g()
{
    struct S { };            // local type

    f(S());                  // OK in C++11; was error in C++03
    f(obj);                  // OK in C++11; was error in C++03

    C<S>            cs;      // OK in C++11; was error in C++03
    C<decltype(obj)> co;     // OK in C++11; was error in C++03
}
```

Notice that we have used the ***decltype*** *keyword* (see Section 1.1."**decltype**" on page 25) to extract the unnamed type of the object obj.

These new relaxed rules for template arguments are essential to the ergonomics of **lambda expressions** (see Section 2.1."Lambdas" on page 573), as such types are both unnamed and local in typical usage:

---

[1] narkive

```
#include <algorithm>  // std::sort
#include <string>     // std::string
#include <vector>     // std::vector

struct Person { std::string d_name; };

void sortByName(std::vector<Person>& people)
{
    std::sort(people.begin(), people.end(),
            [](const Person& lhs, const Person& rhs)
            {
                return lhs.d_name < rhs.d_name;
            });
}
```

In the example above, the lambda expression passed to the `std::sort` algorithm is a local unnamed type, and the algorithm itself is a function template.

Use Cases

Encapsulating a type within a function

Limiting the scope and visibility of an **entity** to the body of a function actively prevents its direct use, even when the function body is exposed widely, say, as an **inline** function or function template defined within a header file.

Consider, for instance, an implementation of Dijkstra's algorithm that uses a local type to keep track of metadata for each vertex in the input graph:

```
// dijkstra.h:

#include <vector>  // std::vector

inline int dijkstra(std::vector<Vertex>* path, const Graph& graph)
{
    struct VertexMetadata        // implementation-specific helper class
    {
        int  d_distanceFromSource;
        bool d_inShortestPath;
    };

    std::vector<VertexMetadata> vertexMetadata(graph.numNodes());
        // standard vector of local VertexMetadata objects --- one per vertex

    // ... (body of algorithm)
}
```

Defining `VertexMetadata` outside of the body of `dijkstra`, e.g., to comply with C++03 restrictions, would make that implementation-specific helper class directly accessible to anyone including the `dijkstra.h` header file. As Hyrum's law[2] suggests, if the implementation-specific `VertexMetadata` detail is defined outside the function body, it is to be expected that some user somewhere will depend on it in its current form, making it problematic, if not impossible, to change.[3] Conversely, encapsulating the type within the function body avoids unintended use by clients, while improving human cognition by colocating the definition of the type with its sole purpose.[4]

Instantiating templates with local function objects as type arguments

Suppose that we have a program that makes wide use of an aggregate data type, `City`:

```cpp
#include <algorithm>   // std::copy
#include <iostream>    // std::ostream
#include <iterator>    // std::ostream_iterator
#include <set>         // std::set
#include <string>      // std::string
#include <vector>      // std::vector

struct City
{
    int         d_uniqueId;
    std::string d_name;
};
std::ostream& operator<<(std::ostream& stream,
                         const City&   object);
```

Consider now the task of writing a function to print unique elements of an `std::vector<City>`, ordered by name:

---

[2]"With a sufficient number of users of an API, it does not matter what you promise in the contract: all observable behaviors of your system will be depended on by somebody" (**wight**).

[3]The C++20 *modules* facility enables the encapsulation of helper types, such as `metadata` in the `dijkstra.h` example on the previous page, used in the implementation of other locally defined types or functions, even when the helper types appear at namespace scope within the module.

[4]For a detailed discussion, see **lakos20**, section 0.5, "Malleable vs. Stable Software," pp. 29–43.

```
void printUniqueCitiesOrderedByName(const std::vector<City>& cities)
{
    struct OrderByName
    {
        bool operator()(const City& lhs, const City& rhs) const
        {
            return lhs.d_name < rhs.d_name;
                // increasing order (subject to change)
        }
    };

    const std::set<City, OrderByName> tmp(cities.begin(), cities.end());

    std::copy(tmp.begin(), tmp.end(),
            std::ostream_iterator<City>(std::cout, "\n"));
}
```

Absent reasons to make the `OrderByName` function object more generally available, rendering its definition alongside the one place where it is used, i.e., directly within function scope, again enforces and readily communicates its tightly encapsulated and therefore *malleable* status.

As an aside, note that using a lambda (see Section 2.1."Lambdas" on page 573) in such scenario requires using **decltype** and passing the closure to the set's constructor:

```
void printUniqueCitiesOrderedByName(const std::vector<City>& cities)
{
    auto compare = [](const City& lhs, const City& rhs) {
        return lhs.d_name < rhs.d_name;
    };
    const std::set<City, decltype(compare)>
        tmp(cities.begin(), cities.end(), compare);
}
```

We discuss the topic of lambda expressions further in the next section.

Configuring algorithms via lambda expressions

Suppose we are representing a 3D environment using a *scene graph* and managing the graph's nodes via an `std::vector` of SceneNode objects. A *scene graph* data structure, commonly used in computer games and 3D-modeling software, represents the logical and spatial hierarchy of objects in a scene. Our SceneNode class supports a variety of **const** member functions used to query its status, e.g., isDirty and isNew. Our task is to implement a **predicate function**, mustRecalculateGeometry, that returns **true** if and only if at least one of the nodes is either "dirty" or "new."

These days, we might reasonably elect to implement this functionality using the C++11 standard algorithm `std::any_of`[5]:

```
template <typename InputIterator, typename UnaryPredicate>
bool any_of(InputIterator first, InputIterator last, UnaryPredicate pred);
    // Return true if any of the elements in the range satisfies pred.
```

Prior to C++11, however, using a function template, such as `any_of`, would have required a separate function or function object, defined *outside* of the scope of the function:

```
// C++03 (obsolete)
namespace {

struct IsNodeDirtyOrNew
{
    bool operator()(const SceneNode& node) const
    {
        return node.isDirty() || node.isNew();
    }
};


}  // close unnamed namespace

bool mustRecalculateGeometry(const std::vector<SceneNode>& nodes)
{
    return any_of(nodes.begin(), nodes.end(), IsNodeDirtyOrNew());
}
```

Because unnamed types can serve as arguments to this function template, we can also employ a lambda expression instead of a function object that would be required in C++03:

```
#include <algorithm> // std::any_of
bool mustRecalculateGeometry(const std::vector<SceneNode>& nodes)
{
    return std::any_of(nodes.begin(),              // start of range
                       nodes.end(),                // end of range
                       [](const SceneNode& node)   // lambda expression
                       {
                           return node.isDirty() || node.isNew();
                       }
                       );
}
```

By creating a **closure** of unnamed type via a lambda expression, unnecessary boilerplate, excessive scope, and even local symbol visibility are avoided.

---

[5]cpprefa

See Also

- "**decltype**" (§1.1, p. 25) describes how developers may query the type of any expression or entity, including objects with unnamed types.

- "Lambdas" (§2.1, p. 573) provides strong practical motivation for the relaxations discussed here.

The long long (≥64 bits) Integral Type

A new fundamental integral type, **long long** is guaranteed to have at least 64 bits on all platforms.

Description

The **integral type long long** and its companion type **unsigned long long** are the only two fundamental integral types in C++ that are guaranteed to have at least 64 bits on all conforming platforms[1]:

```
#include <climits>  // CHAR_BIT, a.k.a. ~8

long long          a;  // sizeof(a) * CHAR_BIT >= 64
unsigned long long b;  // sizeof(b) * CHAR_BIT >= 64

static_assert(sizeof(a) == sizeof(b), "");
    // I.e., a and b necessarily have the same size in every program.
```

On all conforming platforms, CHAR_BIT — the number of bits in a byte — is at least 8 and, on virtually all commonly available commercial platforms today, is exactly 8.

The corresponding integer-literal suffixes indicating type **long long** are ll and LL; for **unsigned long long**, any of eight alternatives are accepted: ull, ULL, uLL, Ull, llu, LLU, LLu, llU:

```
auto i = 0LL;   // long long, sizeof(i) * CHAR_BIT >= 64
auto u = 0uLL;  // unsigned long long, sizeof(u) * CHAR_BIT >= 64
```

Note that **long long** and **unsigned long long** are also candidates for the type of an integer literal having a large enough value. As an example, the type of the literal 2147483648 (one more than the upper bound of a 32-bit integer) is likely to be **long long** on a 32-bit platform. To understand how integral types have evolved — and continue to evolve — over time, see *Appendix — Historical perspective on the evolution of use of fundamental integral types* on page 93.

Use Cases

Storing values that won't safely fit in 32 bits

For many quantities that need to be represented as an integral value in a program, plain **int** is a natural choice. For example, such quantities could be the case for years of a person's age,

---

[1] **long long** has been available in C since the C99 standard, and many C++ compilers supported it as an extension prior to C++11.

score in a ten-pin bowling game, or number of stories in a building. For efficient storage in a **class** or **struct**, however, we may well decide to represent such quantities more compactly using a **short** or **char**; see also the aliases found in C++11's <cstdint>.

Sometimes the size of the virtual address space for the underlying architecture itself dictates how large an integer we will need. For example, on a 64-bit platform, specifying the *distance* between two pointers into a contiguous array or the size of the array itself could well exceed the size of an **int** or **unsigned int**, respectively. Using either **long long** or **unsigned long long** here would, however, not be indicated as the respective platform-dependent integer types (**typedef**s) std::ptrdiff_t and std::size_t are provided expressly for such use and avoid wasting space where it cannot be used by the underlying hardware.

Occasionally, however, the decision of whether to use an **int** is neither platform dependent nor clear cut, in which case using an **int** is almost certainly a bad idea. Suppose we were asked to provide a function, as part of a financial library, that, given a date, returns the number of shares of some particular stock, identified by its security id, SecId, traded on the New York Stock Exchange (NYSE).[2] Since the average daily volume of even the most heavily traded stocks — roughly 70 million shares — appears to be well under the maximum value a signed **int** supports (more than 2 billion on our production platforms), we might at first think to write the function to return **int**:

```cpp
int volYMD(SecId equity, int year, int month, int day);  // (1) BAD IDEA
```

One obvious problem with this interface is that the daily fluctuations in turbulent times might exceed the maximum value representable by a 32-bit **int**, which, unless detected internally, would result in **signed integer overflow**, which is both **undefined behavior** and potentially a pervasive defect enabling avenues of deliberate attack from outside sources.[3] What's more, the growth rate of some companies, especially technology startups, has been at times seemingly exponential. To gain an extra insurance factor of two, we might opt to replace the return type **int** with an **unsigned int**:

```cpp
unsigned volYMD(SecId stock, int year, int month, int day);  // (2) BAD IDEA!
```

Use of an **unsigned int**, however, simply delays the inevitable as the number of shares being traded is almost certainly going to grow over time.

Furthermore, the algebra for unsigned quantities is entirely different from what one would normally expect from an **int**. For example, if we were to try to express the day-over-day change in volume by subtracting two calls to this function and if the number of shares traded were to have decreased, then the **unsigned int** difference would wrap, and the result would be a typically large, erroneous value. Because integer literals are themselves of type **int** and not **unsigned**, comparing an unsigned value with a negative signed one does not

---

[2]There are more than 3,200 listed symbols on the NYSE. Composite daily volume of NYSE-listed securities across all exchanges ranges from 3.5 to 6 billion shares, with a high reached in March 2020 of more than 9 billion shares.

[3]For an overview of integer overflow in C++, see **ballman**. For a more focused discussion of secure coding in CPP using CERT standards, see **seacord13**, Chapter 5, "Integer Security," pp. 225–307.

typically go well; hence, many compilers will warn when the two types are mixed, which itself is problematic.

If we happen to be on a 64-bit platform, we might choose to return a **long**:

```
long volYMD(SecId stock, int year, int month, int day);  // (3) NOT A GOOD IDEA
```

The problems using **long** as the return type are that it (1) is not yet generally considered a **vocabulary type** (see *Appendix — Historical perspective on the evolution of use of fundamental integral types* on page 93) and (2) would reduce portability (see *Potential Pitfalls — Relying on the relative sizes of **int**, **long**, and **long long*** below).

Prior to C++11, we might have considered returning a **double**:

```
double volYMD(SecId stock, int year, int month, int day);  // (4) OK
```

At least with **double** we know that we will have sufficient precision (53 bits) to express integers accurately into the quadrillions, which will certainly cover us for any foreseeable future. The main drawback is that **double** doesn't properly describe the nature of the type that we are returning, i.e., a whole integer number of shares, and so its algebra, although not as dubious as **unsigned int**, isn't ideal either.

With the advent of C++11, we might consider using one of the type aliases in <cstdint>:

```
std::int64_t volYMD(SecId stock, int year, int month, int day);  // (4) OK
```

This choice addresses most of the issues discussed above except that, instead of being a specific C++ type, it is a platform-dependent alias that is likely to be a **long** on a 64-bit platform and almost certainly a **long long** on a 32-bit one. Such exact size requirements are often necessary for packing data in structures and arrays but are not as useful when reasoning about them in the interfaces of functions where having a common set of fundamental vocabulary types becomes much more important, e.g., for interoperability.

All of this leads us to our final alternative, **long long**:

```
long long volYMD(SecId stock, int year, int month, int day);  // (5) GOOD IDEA
```

In addition to being a signed fundamental integral type of sufficient capacity on all platforms, **long long** is the same C++ type *relative* to other C++ types on all platforms.

Potential Pitfalls

Relying on the relative sizes of int, long, and long long

As discussed at some length in *Appendix — Historical perspective on the evolution of use of fundamental integral types* on page 93, the fundamental integral types have historically been a moving target. On older, 32-bit platforms, a **long** was often 32 bits, and **long long**, which was nonstandard prior to C++11, or its platform-dependent equivalent was needed to ensure that 64 bits were available. When the correctness of code depends on either `sizeof(int) < sizeof(long)` or `sizeof(long) < sizeof(long long)`, portability is needlessly restricted. Relying instead on only the guaranteed[4] property that `sizeof(int) < sizeof(long long)` avoids such portability issues since the relative sizes of the **long** and **long long** integral types continue to evolve.

When precise control of size *in the implementation* (as opposed to in the interface) matters, consider using one of the standard signed, `intn_t`, or unsigned, `uintn_t`, integer aliases provided, since C++11, in `<cstdint>` and summarized here in Table 1.

Table 1: Useful `typedefs` found in `<cstdint>` (since C++11)

Exact Size (optional)[a]	Fastest integral type having at least N bits	Smallest integer type having at least N bits
int8_t	int_fast8_t	int_least8_t
int16_t	int_fast16_t	int_least16_t
int32_t	int_fast32_t	int_least32_t
int64_t	int_fast64_t	int_least64_t
uint8_t	uint_fast8_t	uint_least8_t
uint16_t[a]	uint_fast16_t	uint_least16_t
uint32_t	uint_fast32_t	uint_least32_t
uint64_t	uint_fast64_t	uint_least64_t

[a] The compiler doesn't need to fabricate the exact-width type if the target platform doesn't support it.

Note: Also see `intmax_t`, the maximum width integer type, which might be different from all of the above.

See Also

- "Binary Literals" (§1.2, p. 142) explains how programmers can specify binary constants directly in the source code; large binary values might fit only in a **long long** or even **unsigned long long**.

- "Digit Separators" (§1.2, p. 152) describes visually separating digits of large **long long** literals.

Further Reading

- For rationale behind adding the 64-bit integral type to the language, see the original proposal, "Adding the **long long** type to C++," **adamczyk05**.

---

[4]Due to the unfathomable amount of software that would stop working if an **int** were ever anything but exactly *four* bytes, we — along with the late Richard Stevens of Unix fame (see **stevens93**, section 2.5.1., "ANSI C Limits," pp. 31–32, specifically row 6, column 4 of Figure 2.2, p. 32) — are prepared to *guarantee* that it will never become as large as a **long long** for any general-purpose computer.

Appendix

Historical perspective on the evolution of use of fundamental integral types

The designers of C got it right back in 1972 when they created a portable **int** type that could act as a bridge from a single-word, 16-bit, integer, **short**, to a double-word, 32-bit, integer, **long**. Just by using **int**, one would get the optimal space versus speed trade-off as the 32-bit computer *word* was on its way to becoming the norm. As an example, the Motorola 68000 series (c. 1979) was a hybrid CISC architecture employing a 32-bit instruction set with 32-bit registers and a 32-bit external data bus; internally, however, it used only 16-bit ALUs and a 16-bit data bus.

During the late 1980s and into the 1990s, the word size of the machine and the size of an **int** were synonymous. Some of the earlier mainframe computers, such as IBM 701 (c. 1954), had a word size of 36 characters (1) to allow accurate representation of a signed 10-digit decimal number or (2) to hold up to six 6-bit characters. Smaller computers, such as Digital Equipment Corporation's PDP-1, PDP-9, and PDP-15 used 18-bit words, so a double word held 36 bits; memory addressing, however, was limited to just 12–18 bits, i.e., a maximum 4K–256K 18-bit words of DRAM. With the standardization of 7-bit ASCII (c. 1967), its adoption throughout the 1970s, and its last update (c. 1986), the common typical notion of character size moved from 6 to 7 bits. Some early conforming implementations of C would choose to set CHAR_BIT to 9 to allow two characters per half word. (On some early vector-processing computers, CHAR_BIT is 32, making every type, including a **char**, at least a 32-bit quantity.) As double-precision floating-point calculations — enabled by type **double** and supported by floating-point coprocessors — became typical in the scientific community, machine architectures naturally evolved from 9-, 18-, and 36-bit words to the familiar 8-, 16-, 32-, and now 64-bit addressable integer words we have today. Apart from embedded systems and digital signal processors, a **char** is now almost universally considered to be exactly 8 bits. Instead of scrupulously and actively using CHAR_BIT for the number of bits in a **char**, consider statically asserting it instead:

```
static_assert(CHAR_BIT == 8, "A char is not 8-bits on this CrAzY platform!");
```

As cost of *main memory* was decreasing exponentially throughout the final two decades of the 20th century,[5] the need for a much larger *virtual address space* quickly followed. Intel began its work on 64-bit architectures in the early 1990s and realized one a decade later. As we progressed into the 2000s, the common notion of word size, i.e., the width (in bits) of typical registers within the CPU itself, began to shift from "the size of an **int**" to "the size of a simple (nonmember) pointer type," e.g., 8 * **sizeof**(**void***), on the host platform. By this time, 16-bit **int** types — like 16-bit architectures for **general-purpose machines**, i.e., excluding **embedded systems** — were long gone, but a **long int** was still expected to be 32 bits on a 32-bit platform. Embedded systems are designed specifically to work with high-performance hardware, such as digital-signal processors. Sadly, **long** was often

---

[5] Moore's law (c. 1965) — the observation that the number of transistors in densely packed integrated circuits (e.g., DRAM) grows exponentially over time, doubling every 1–2 years or so — held for nearly a half century, until finally saturating in the 2010s.

improperly used to hold an address; hence, the size of **long** is associated with a de facto need (due to immeasurable amounts of legacy code) to remain in lockstep with pointer size.

Something new was needed to mean at least 64 bits on all platforms. Enter **long long**. We have now come full circle. On 64-bit platforms, an **int** is still 4 bytes, but a **long** is now — for practical reasons — typically 8 bytes unless requested explicitly[6] to be otherwise. To ensure portability until 32-bit machines go the way of 16-bit ones, we have **long long** to (1) provide a common *vocabulary type*, (2) make our intent clear, and (3) avoid the portability issue for at least the next decade or two; still, see *Potential Pitfalls — Relying on the relative sizes of* **int**, **long**, *and* **long long** on page 91 for some alternative ideas.

---

[6]On 64-bit systems, **sizeof(long)** is typically 8 bytes. Compiling with the -m32 flag on either GCC or Clang emulates compiling on a 32-bit platform: **sizeof(long)** is likely to be 4, while **sizeof(long long)** remains 8.

The [[noreturn]] Attribute

The standard attribute `[[noreturn]]` indicates that the function to which it pertains does not return normally.

Description

The presence of the standard `[[noreturn]]` attribute as part of a function declaration informs both the compiler and human readers that such a function never returns control flow to the caller:

```cpp
[[noreturn]] void f()
{
    throw 1;
}
```

The `[[noreturn]]` attribute is not part of a function's type and is also, therefore, not part of the type of a function pointer. Applying `[[noreturn]]` to a function pointer is not an error, though doing so has no actual effect in standard C++; see *Potential Pitfalls — Misuse of [[noreturn]] on function pointers* on page 98. Using it on a pointer might have benefits for external tooling, code expressiveness, and future language evolution:

```cpp
void (*fp [[noreturn]])() = f;
```

Use Cases

Better compiler diagnostics

Consider the task of creating an assertion handler that, when invoked, always aborts execution of the program after printing some useful information about the source of the assertion. Since this specific handler will never return because it unconditionally invokes a `[[noreturn]]std::abort` function, it is a viable candidate for `[[noreturn]]`:

```cpp
[[noreturn]] void abortingAssertionHandler(const char* filename, int line)
{
    LOG_ERROR << "Assertion fired at " << filename << ':' << line;
    std::abort();
}
```

The additional information provided by the attribute will allow a compiler to warn if it determines that a code path in the function would allow it to return normally:

```
[[noreturn]] void abortingAssertionHandler(const char* filename, int line)
{
    if (filename)
    {
        LOG_ERROR << "Assertion fired at " << filename << ':' << line;
        std::abort();
    }
} // compile-time warning made possible
```

This information can also be used to warn in case unreachable code is present after abortingAssertionHandler is invoked:

```
int main()
{
    // ...
    abortingAssertionHandler("main.cpp", __LINE__);
    std::cout << "We got here.\n"; // compile-time warning made possible
    // ...
}
```

Note that this warning is made possible by decorating just the declaration of the handler function, i.e., even if the definition of the function is not visible in the current translation unit.

Improved runtime performance

If the compiler knows that it is going to invoke a function that is guaranteed not to return, the compiler is within its rights to optimize that function by removing what it can now determine to be dead code. As an example, consider a utility component, util, that defines a function, throwBadAlloc, that is used to **insulate** the throwing of an std::bad_alloc exception in what would otherwise be template code fully exposed to clients:

```
// util.h:
[[noreturn]] void throwBadAlloc();

// util.cpp:
#include <util.h> // [[noreturn]] void throwBadAlloc()

#include <new> // std::bad_alloc

void throwBadAlloc() // This redeclaration is also [[noreturn]].
{
    throw std::bad_alloc();
}
```

The compiler is within its rights to elide code that is rendered unreachable by the call to the `throwBadAlloc` function due to the function being decorated with the `[[noreturn]]` attribute on its declaration:

```
// client.cpp:
#include <util.h>  // [[noreturn]] void throwBadAlloc()

void client()
{
    // ...
    throwBadAlloc();
    // ... (Everything below this line can be optimized away.)
}
```

Notice that even though `[[noreturn]]` appeared only on the first declaration — that in the `util.h` header — the `[[noreturn]]` attribute carries over to the redeclaration used in the `throwBadAlloc` function's definition because the header was included in the corresponding `.cpp` file.

Potential Pitfalls

`[[noreturn]]` can inadvertently break an otherwise working program

Unlike many attributes, using `[[noreturn]]` *can* alter the semantics of a well-formed program, potentially introducing a runtime defect and/or making the program ill formed. If a function that can potentially return is decorated with `[[noreturn]]` and then, in the course of executing a program, it ever does return, that behavior is **undefined**.

Consider a `printAndExit` function whose role is to print a fatal error message before aborting the program:

```
[[noreturn]] void printAndExit()
{
    std::cout << "Fatal error. Exiting the program.\n";
    assert(false);
}
```

The programmer chose to sloppily implement termination by using an assertion, which would not be incorporated into a program compiled with the preprocessor definition NDEBUG active, and thus `printAndExit` would return normally in such a build mode. If the compiler of the client is informed that function will not return, the compiler is free to optimize accordingly. If the function then does return, any number of hard-to-diagnose defects, e.g., due to incorrectly elided code, might materialize as a consequence of the ensuing **undefined behavior**. Furthermore, if a function is declared `[[noreturn]]` in some translation units within a program but not in others, that program is **ill formed, no diagnostic required (IFNDR)**.

Misuse of [[noreturn]] on function pointers

Although the [[noreturn]] attribute is permitted to syntactically pertain to a function pointer for the benefit of external tools, it has no effect in standard C++; fortunately, most compilers will issue a warning:

```
void (*fp [[noreturn]])();  // no effect in standard C++; will likely warn
```

What's more, assigning the address of a function that is not decorated with [[noreturn]] to an otherwise suitable function pointer that is so decorated is perfectly fine:

```
void f() { return; };  // function that always returns

void g()
{
    fp = f;  // [[noreturn]] on fp is silently ignored.
}
```

Any reliance on [[noreturn]] to have any effect in standard C++ when applied to other than a function's declaration is misguided.

See Also

- "Attribute Syntax" (§1.1, p. 12) explains that [[noreturn]] is a built-in attribute that follows the general syntax and placement rules of C++ attributes.

Further Reading

- The original proposal for this feature — elucidating its rationale and history — is presented in **svoboda10**.

- Herb Sutter opines on this attribute being one of comparative few that cannot be ignored in **sutter12**.

The Null-Pointer-Literal Keyword

The **nullptr** literal, unlike 0 or NULL, unambiguously denotes a *null-address* value.

Description

The **nullptr** keyword is a *prvalue* (pure *rvalue*) of type std::nullptr_t representing the implementation-defined bit pattern corresponding to a **null address** on the host platform; **nullptr** and other values of type std::nullptr_t, along with the integer literal 0 and the macro NULL, can be converted implicitly to any pointer or pointer-to-member type:

```cpp
#include <cstddef> // NULL
int data;  // nonmember data

int* pi0 = &data;    // Initialize with non-null address.
int* pi1 = nullptr;  // Initialize with null address.
int* pi2 = NULL;     //      "        "    "      "
int* pi3 = 0;        //      "        "    "      "

double f(int x);  // nonmember function

double (*pf0)(int) = &f;       // Initialize with non-null address.
double (*pf1)(int) = nullptr;  // Initialize with null address.

struct S
{
    short d_data;    // member data
    float g(int y);  // member function
};

short S::*pmd0 = &S::d_data;  // Initialize with non-null address.
short S::*pmd1 = nullptr;     // Initialize with null address.

float (S::*pmf0)(int) = &S::g;   // Initialize with non-null address.
float (S::*pmf1)(int) = nullptr;  // Initialize with null address.
```

Because `std::nullptr_t` is its own distinct type, overloading on it is possible:

```
#include <cstddef>  // std::nullptr_t

void g(void*);        // (1)
void g(int);          // (2)
void g(std::nullptr_t); // (3)

void f()
{
    char buf[] = "hello";
    g(buf);      // OK, (1) void g(void*)
    g(0);        // OK, (2) void g(int)
    g(nullptr);  // OK, (3) void g(std::nullptr_t)
    g(NULL);     // Error, ambiguous --- (1), (2), or (3)
}
```

Use Cases

Improvement of type safety

In pre-C++11 codebases, using the `NULL` macro was a common way of indicating, mostly to the human reader, that the literal value the macro conveys is intended specifically to represent a *null address* rather than the literal **int** value 0. In the C Standard, the macro `NULL` is defined as an **implementation-defined** integral or **void*** constant. Unlike C, C++ forbids conversions from **void*** to arbitrary pointer types and instead, prior to C++11, defined `NULL` as an "integral constant expression rvalue of integer type that evaluates to zero"; any integer literal, e.g., 0, 0L, 0U, or 0LLU, satisfies this criterion. From a type-safety perspective, its implementation-defined definition, however, makes using `NULL` only marginally better suited than a raw literal 0 to represent a null pointer. It is worth noting that as of C++11, the definition of `NULL` has been expanded to, in theory, permit **nullptr** as a conforming definition; as of this writing, however, no major compiler vendors do so.[1]

As just one specific illustration of the added type safety provided by **nullptr**, imagine that the coding standards of a large software company historically required that values returned via output parameters (as opposed to a **return** statement) are always returned via pointer to a modifiable object. Functions that return via argument typically do so to reserve the function's return value to communicate status.[2] A function in this codebase might "zero" the output parameter's local pointer variable to indicate and ensure that nothing more is to be written. The function below illustrates three different ways of doing this:

---

[1]Both GCC and Clang default to 0L (**long int**), while MSVC defaults to 0 (**int**). Such definitions are unlikely to change since existing code could cease to compile or possibly silently present altered runtime behavior.

[2]See **lakos96**, section 9.1.11, "Pass Argument by Value, Reference, or Pointer," pp. 621–628, specifically the *Guideline* at the bottom of p. 623: "Be consistent about returning values through arguments (e.g., avoid declaring non**const** reference parameters)."

```
int illustrativeFunction(int* x)    // pointer to modifiable integer
{
    // ...
    if (/*...*/)
    {
        x = 0;        // OK, set pointer x to null address.
        x = NULL;     // OK, set pointer x to null address.
        x = nullptr;  // Bug, set pointer x to null address.
    }
    // ...
    return 0;     // success
}
```

Now suppose that the function signature is changed (e.g., due to a change in coding standards in the organization) to accept a reference instead of a pointer:

```
int illustrativeFunction(int& x)    // reference to modifiable integer
{
    // ...
    if (/*...*/)
    {
        x = 0;        // OK, always compiles; makes what x refers to 0
        x = NULL;     // OK, implementation-defined; might warn
        x = nullptr;  // Error, always a compile-time error
    }
    // ...
    return 0;     // SUCCESS
}
```

As the example above demonstrates, how we represent the notion of a null address matters.

1. 0 — Portable across all implementations but minimal type safety

2. NULL — Implemented as a macro; added type safety, if any, is platform specific

3. **nullptr** — Portable across all implementations and fully type-safe

Using **nullptr** instead of 0 or NULL to denote a null address maximizes type safety and readability, while avoiding both macros and implementation-defined behavior.

Disambiguation of (int)0 vs. (T*)0 during overload resolution

The platform-dependent nature of NULL presents additional challenges when used to call a function whose overloads differ only in accepting a pointer or an integral type as the same positional argument, which might be the case, e.g., in a poorly designed third-party library:

```
void uglyLibraryFunction(int* p);  // (1)
void uglyLibraryFunction(int  i);  // (2)
```

Calling this function with the literal 0 will always invoke overload (2), but that might not always be what casual clients expect:

```
void f()
{
    uglyLibraryFunction(0);        // unambiguously invokes (2)
    uglyLibraryFunction((int*) 0); // unambiguously invokes (1)
    uglyLibraryFunction(nullptr);  // unambiguously invokes (1)
    uglyLibraryFunction(NULL);     // Might invoke (1), (2), or be ambiguous;
                                   // implementation-defined
    uglyLibraryFunction(0U);       // Error, ambiguous call on all platforms
}
```

nullptr is especially useful when such problematic overloads are unavoidable because it obviates explicit casts. (Note that explicitly casting 0 to an appropriately typed pointer — other than **void*** — was at one time considered by some to be a best practice, especially in C.)

Overloading for a literal null pointer

Being a distinct type, std::nullptr_t can itself participate in an overload set:

```
#include <cstddef> // std::nullptr_t
void f(int* v);         // (1)
void f(std::nullptr_t); // (2)

void g()
{
    int* ptr = nullptr;
    f(ptr);     // unambiguously invokes (1)
    f(nullptr); // unambiguously invokes (2)
}
```

Given the relative ease with which a **nullptr** can be converted to a typed pointer having the same null-address value, such overloads are dubious when used to control essential behavior. Nonetheless, we can envision such use to, say, aid in compile-time diagnostics when passing a null address would otherwise result in a runtime error (see Section 1.1."Deleted Functions" on page 53):

```
std::size_t strlen(const char* s);
    // The behavior is undefined unless s is null-terminated.

std::size_t strlen(std::nullptr_t) = delete;
    // The function is not defined but still participates in overload resolution.
```

Another arguably safe use of such an overload for a **nullptr** is to avoid a null-pointer check. However, for cases where the client knows the address is null at compile time, better ways typically exist for avoiding the often insignificant overhead of testing for a null pointer at run time.

Further Reading

- Scott Meyers advocates always preferring **nullptr** over use of either 0 or NULL in **meyers15b**, "Item 8: Prefer nullptr to 0 and NULL," pp. 58–62.

The override Member-Function Specifier

Decorating a function in a derived class with the contextual keyword **override** ensures that
a **virtual** function having a compatible declaration exists in one or more of its base classes.

Description

The **contextual keyword override** can be provided at the end of a member-function declaration to ensure that the decorated function is indeed *overriding* a corresponding **virtual**
member function in a base class, as opposed to *hiding* it or otherwise inadvertently introducing a distinct function declaration:

```
struct Base
{
    virtual void f(int);
            void g(int);
    virtual void h(int) const;
    virtual void i(int) = 0;
};

struct DerivedWithoutOverride : Base
{
    void f();              // hides Base::f(int) (likely mistake)
    void f(int);           // OK, implicitly overrides Base::f(int)

    void g();              // hides Base::g(int) (likely mistake)
    void g(int);           // hides Base::g(int) (likely mistake)

    void h(int);           // hides Base::h(int) const (likely mistake)
    void h(int) const;     // OK, implicitly overrides Base::h(int) const

    void i(int);           // OK, implicitly overrides Base::i(int)
};

struct DerivedWithOverride : Base
{
    void f()          override;   // Error, Base::f() not found
    void f(int)       override;   // OK, explicitly overrides Base::f(int)

    void g()          override;   // Error, Base::g() not found
    void g(int)       override;   // Error, Base::g() is not virtual.

    void h(int)       override;   // Error, Base::h(int) not found
    void h(int) const override;   // OK, explicitly overrides Base::h(int)
```

```
    void i(int)         override;    // OK, explicitly overrides Base::i(int)
};
```

Using this feature expresses design intent so that (1) human readers are aware of it and (2) compilers can validate it.

As noted, **override** is a contextual keyword. C++11 introduces keywords that have special meaning only in certain contexts. In this case, **override** is a keyword in the context of a declaration, but not otherwise using it as the identifier for a variable name, for example, is perfectly fine:

```
int override = 1;   // OK
```

Use Cases

Ensuring that a member function of a base class is being overridden

Consider the following polymorphic hierarchy of error-category classes, as we might have defined them using C++03:

```
struct ErrorCategory
{
    virtual bool equivalent(const ErrorCode& code, int condition);
    virtual bool equivalent(int code, const ErrorCondition& condition);
};

struct AutomotiveErrorCategory : ErrorCategory
{
    virtual bool equivalent(const ErrorCode& code, int condition);
    virtual bool equivolent(int code, const ErrorCondition& condition);
};
```

Notice that there is a defect in the last line of the example above: equivalent has been misspelled. Moreover, the compiler did not catch that error. Clients calling equivalent on AutomotiveErrorCategory will incorrectly invoke the base-class function. If the function in the base class happens to be defined, the code might compile and behave unexpectedly at run time. Now, suppose that over time the interface is changed by marking the equivalence-checking function **const** to bring the interface closer to that of std::error_category:

```
struct ErrorCategory
{
    virtual bool equivalent(const ErrorCode& code, int condition) const;
    virtual bool equivalent(int code, const ErrorCondition& condition) const;
};
```

Without applying the corresponding modification to all classes deriving from
ErrorCategory, the semantics of the program change due to the derived classes now hiding
the base class's **virtual** member function instead of overriding it. Both errors discussed
above would be detected automatically if the **virtual** functions in all derived classes were
decorated with **override**:

```
struct AutomotiveErrorCategory : ErrorCategory
{
    bool equivalent(const ErrorCode& code, int condition) override;
        // Error, failed when base class changed

    bool equivolent(int code, const ErrorCondition& code) override;
        // Error, failed when first written
};
```

What's more, **override** serves as a clear indication of the derived-class author's intent to
customize the behavior of ErrorCategory. For any given member function, using **override**
necessarily renders any use of **virtual** for that function syntactically and semantically
redundant. The only cosmetic reason for retaining **virtual** in the presence of **override**
would be that **virtual** appears to the left of the function declaration, as it always has,
instead of all the way to the right, as **override** does now.

Potential Pitfalls

Lack of consistency across a codebase

Relying on **override** as a means of ensuring that changes to base-class interfaces are propagated across a codebase can prove unreliable if this feature is used inconsistently, i.e., not
applied in every circumstance where its use would be appropriate. In particular, altering the
signature of a **virtual** member function in a base class and then compiling the entire code
base will always flag as an error any nonmatching derived-class function where **override**
was used but might fail even to warn where it is not.

Further Reading

- Various relationships among **virtual**, **override**, and **final** (see Section 3.1."**final**" on page 1007) are presented in **boccara20**.

- Scott Meyers advocates the use of the **override** specifier in **meyers15b**, "Item 12: Declare overriding functions **override**," pp. 79–85.

Syntax for Unprocessed String Contents

Supplying a leading R adjacent to a double-quoted string having augmented delimiters —
typically "(and)" — disables interpretation of special characters, obviating escaping each
individually.

Description

A *raw* string literal is a new form of syntax for string literals that allows developers to embed
arbitrary character sequences in a program's source code, without having to modify them
by escaping individual special characters. As an example, suppose that we want to write a
small program that outputs the following text into the standard output stream:

```
printf("Hello, %s%c\n", "World", '!');
```

In C++03, capturing the line of C code above in a string literal would require five escape
characters (\) distributed throughout the string:

```
#include <iostream>  // std::cout, std::endl

void printRegularStringLiteral()
{
    std::cout << "printf(\"Hello, %s%c\\n\", \"World\", '!');" << std::endl;
    //                     ^                 ^   ^    ^     ^
    //                              escape characters
}
```

If we use C++11's *raw* string-literal syntax, no escaping is required:

```
void printRawStringLiteral()
{
    std::cout << R"(printf("Hello, %s%c\n", "World", '!');)" << std::endl;
    //            ^ ^                                      ^
    //        additional raw string-literal syntax (C++11)
}
```

To represent the original character data as a raw string literal, we typically need only to add
a capital R immediately and adjacently before the starting quote (") and nest the character
data within parentheses, ( ), with some exceptions; see *Collisions* on page 109. Sequences of
characters that would be escaped in a regular string literal are instead interpreted verbatim:

```
const char s0[] = R"({ "key": "value" })";
    // OK, equivalent to "{ \"key\": \"value\" }"
```

Recall that, to incorporate a newline character into a conventional string literal, one must
represent that newline using the escape sequence, \n. Attempting to do so by entering a

newline into the source, i.e., making the string literal span lines of source code, is an error. In contrast to conventional string literals, *raw* string literals (1) treat unescaped embedded double quotes (") as literal data, (2) do not interpret special-character escape sequences (e.g., \n, \t), and (3) interpret both vertical and horizontal whitespace characters present in the source file as part of the string contents:

```cpp
const char s1[] = R"(line one
line two
    line three)";
    // OK
```

In this example, we assume that all trailing whitespace has been stripped since even trailing whitespace in a raw literal would be captured. Note that any literal tab characters are treated the same as a \t and hence can be problematic, especially when developers have inconsistent tab settings; see *Potential Pitfalls — Unexpected indentation* on page 112. Finally, all string literals are concatenated with adjacent ones in the same way the conventional ones are in C++03:

```cpp
const char s2[] = R"(line one)"        "\n"
                  "line two"           "\n"
                R"(    line three)";
    // OK, equivalent to "line one\nline two\n    line three"
```

These same rules apply to both raw *wide* string literals and raw *Unicode* ones (see Section 1.1. "Unicode Literals" on page 129) that are introduced by placing their corresponding prefix before the R character:

```cpp
const wchar_t  ws [] = LR"(Raw\tWide\tLiteral)";
    // represents "Raw\tWide\tLiteral", not "Raw    Wide    Literal"


const char     u8s[] = u8R"(\U0001F378)"; // Represents "\U0001F378", not " Y "
const char16_t us [] =  uR"(\U0001F378)"; //         "          "       "    "
const char32_t Us [] =  UR"(\U0001F378)"; //         "          "       "    "
```

Collisions

Although unlikely, the data to be expressed within a string literal might itself contain the character sequence)" embedded within it:

```cpp
#include <cstdio>   // printf

void emitHelloWorld()
{
    printf("printf(\"Hello, World!\")");
    //                              ^^
    // The )" character sequence terminates a typical raw string literal.
}
```

If we use the basic syntax for a *raw* string literal, we will get a syntax error:

```
const char s3[] = R"(printf("printf(\"Hello, World!\")"))";  // collision
//                                                     ^^
//                          syntax error after literal ends
```

To circumvent this problem, we could escape every special character in the string separately, as in C++03, but the result is difficult to read and error prone:

```
const char s4[] = "printf(\"printf(\\\"Hello, World!\\\")\")";  // error prone
```

Instead, we can use the extended disambiguation syntax of *raw* string literals to resolve the issue:

```
const char s5[] = R"###(printf("printf(\"Hello, World!\")"))###";  // cleaner
```

This disambiguation syntax allows us to insert an essentially arbitrary sequence of characters between the outermost quote/parenthesis pairs such that the combined sequence — e.g.,)###" — avoids the collision with the literal data:

```
//                          delimiter and parenthesis
//                    v~~~                         ~~~v
const char s6[] = R"xyz(<-- Literal String Data -->)xyz";
//                ^    ^~~~~~~~~~~~~~~~~~~~~~~~~~~^
//                |            string contents
//                |
//                | uppercase R
```

The delimiter of a raw string literal can comprise any member of the **basic source character set** except space, backslash, parentheses, and the control characters representing horizontal tab, vertical tab, form feed, and new line.

The value of s6 above is equivalent to "<-- Literal String Data -->". Every raw string literal comprises these syntactical elements in order:

- An uppercase R

- The opening double quotes, "

- An optional arbitrary sequence of characters called the *delimiter* (e.g., xyz)

- An opening parenthesis, (

- The contents of the string

- A closing parenthesis,)

- The same delimiter specified previously, if any (i.e., xyz, not reversed)

- The closing double quotes, "

The delimiter can be — and, in practice, often is — an empty character sequence:

```
const char s7[] = R"("Hello, World!")";
    // OK, equivalent to \"Hello, World!\"
```

A nonempty delimiter — e.g., ! — can be used to disambiguate any appearance of the)" character sequence within the literal data:

```
const char s8[] = R"!("--- R"(Raw literals are not recursive!)" ---")!";
    // OK, equivalent to \"--- R\"(Raw literals are not recursive!)\" ---\"
```

Had an empty delimiter been used to initialize s8 in the example above, the compiler would have produced a perhaps obscure compile-time error:

```
const char s8a[] = R"("---R"( Raw literals are not recursive!)" ---")";
    //                                                               ^~
    // Error, decrement of read-only location
```

In fact, it could turn out that a program with an unexpectedly terminated *raw* string literal could still be valid and compile quietly:

```
void emitPith()
{
    printf(R"("Live-Free, don't (ever)","Die!");
        // prints "Live-Free, don't (ever

    printf((R"("Live-Free, don't (ever)","Die!"));
        // prints Die!
}
```

Fortunately, examples like the one above are invariably contrived, not accidental.

Use Cases

Embedding code in a C++ program

When a source code snippet needs to be embedded as part of the source code of a C++ program, use of a *raw* string literal can significantly reduce the syntactic noise that would otherwise be caused by repeated escape sequences. As an example, consider a regular expression for an online shopping product ID represented as a conventional string literal:

```
const char* productIdRegex = "[0-9]{5}\\(\".*\"\\)";
    // This regular expression matches strings like 12345("Product").
```

Not only do the backslashes obscure the meaning to human readers, a mechanical translation is often needed when transforming between source and data, such as when copying the contents of the string literal into an online regular-expression validation tool, and introduces significant opportunities for human error. Using a raw string literal solves these problems:

```
const char* productIdRegex = R"([0-9]{5}\(".*"\))";
```

Another format that benefits from raw string literals is JSON, due to its frequent use of double quotes:

```
const char* testProductResponse = R"!(
{
    "productId": "58215(\"Camera\")",
    "availableUnits": 5,
    "relatedProducts": ["59214(\"CameraBag\")", "42931(\"SdStorageCard\")"]
})!";
```

With a conventional string literal, the JSON string above would require every occurrence of " and \ to be escaped and every new line to be represented as \n, resulting in visual noise, less interoperability with other tools accepting or producing JSON, and heightened risk during manual maintenance.

Finally, raw string literals can also be helpful for whitespace-sensitive languages, such as Python, but see *Potential Pitfalls — Encoding of new lines and whitespace* on page 113:

```
const char* testPythonInterpreterPrint = R"(def test():
    print("test printing from Python")
)";
```

Potential Pitfalls

Unexpected indentation

Consistent indentation and formatting of source code facilitates human comprehension of program structure. Space and tabulation (\t) characters used for the purpose of source code formatting are, however, always interpreted as part of a raw string literal's contents:

```
void emitPythonEvaluator0(const char* expression)
{
    std::cout << R"(
        def evaluate():
            print("Evaluating...")
            return )" << expression << '\n';
}
```

Despite the intention of the programmer to aid readability by indenting the above raw string literal consistently with the rest of the code, the streamed data will contain a large number of spaces or tabulation characters, resulting in an invalid Python program:

```
        def evaluate():
            print("Evaluating...")
            return someExpression
# ^~~~~~
# Error, excessive indentation
```

Correct Python code would start unindented and then be indented the same number of spaces, e.g., exactly four:

```python
def evaluate():
    print("Evaluating...")
    return someExpression
```

Correct, albeit visually jarring, Python code can be expressed with a single *raw* string literal, but visualizing the final output requires some effort:

```cpp
void emitPythonEvaluator1(const char* expression)
{
    std::cout << R"(def evaluate():
print("Evaluating...")
return )" << expression << '\n';
}
```

Always representing indentation as the precise number of spaces (instead of tab characters) — especially when committed to source-code control systems — goes a long way toward avoiding unexpected indentation issues.

When more explicit control is desired, we can use a mixture of **raw string literals** and explicit new lines represented as **conventional string literals**:

```cpp
void emitPythonEvaluator2(const char* expression)
{
    std::cout <<
        R"(def evaluate():)"                "\n"
        R"(    print("Evaluating...")))"     "\n"
        R"(    return )" << expression << '\n';
}
```

Encoding of new lines and whitespace

The intent of the feature is that new lines should map to a single \n character regardless of how new lines are encoded in the platform-specific encoding of the source file, e.g., \r\n. The wording of the C++ Standard, however, is not entirely clear.[1] While all major compiler implementations act in accordance with the original intent of the feature, relying on a specific newline encoding might lead to nonportable code until clarity is achieved.

In a similar fashion, the type of whitespace characters, e.g., tabs versus spaces, used as part of a raw string literal can be significant. As an example, consider a unit test verifying that a string representing the status of the system is as expected:

---

[1]See CWG issue 1655 (**miller13**).

```
void verifyDefaultOutput()
{
    const std::string output = System::outputStatus();
    const std::string expected = R"(Current status:
    - No violations detected.)";

    assert(output == expected);
}
```

The unit test might pass for years, until, for instance, the company's indentation style changes from tabulation characters to spaces, leading the `expected` string to contain spaces instead of tabs and thus resulting in test failures.

A well-designed unit test will typically be imbued with *expected values,* rather than values that were produced by the previous run. The latter is sometimes referred to as a **benchmark test,** and such tests are often implemented as *diffs* against a file containing output from a previous run. This file has presumably been reviewed and is considered to be correct; the file is sometimes called the **golden file.** Though ill advised, when trying to get a new version of the software to pass the benchmark test and when the precise format of the output of a system changes subtly, the golden file might be summarily jettisoned — and the new output installed in its stead — with little if any detailed review. Hence, well-designed unit tests will often hard code exactly what is to be expected, nothing more or less, directly in the **test-driver** source code.

Compile-Time Assertions

This compile-time analog to the classic runtime **assert** causes compilation to terminate with a user-supplied error message whenever its **constant-expression** argument evaluates to **false**.

Description

Assumptions are inherent in every program, whether we explicitly document them or not. A common way of validating certain assumptions at run time is to use the classic **assert** macro found in <cassert>. Such runtime assertions are not always ideal because (1) the program must already be built and running for them to even have a chance of being triggered and (2) executing a **redundant check** at run time typically[1] results in a slower program. Being able to validate an assertion at compile time avoids several drawbacks.

1. Validation occurs at compile time within a single translation unit and therefore doesn't need to wait until a complete program is linked and executed.

2. Compile-time assertions can exist in many more places than runtime assertions and are unrelated to program control flow.

3. No runtime code will be generated due to a **static_assert**, so program performance will not be impacted.

Syntax and semantics

We can use **static assertion declarations** to conditionally trigger controlled compilation failures depending on the truthfulness of a **constant expression**. Such declarations are introduced by the **static_assert** keyword, followed by a parenthesized list consisting of (1) a constant Boolean expression and (2) a mandatory **string literal** (see *Annoyances — Mandatory string literal* on page 123), which will be part of the compiler diagnostics if the compiler determines that the assertion fails to hold:

```
static_assert(true, "Never fires.");
static_assert(false, "Always fires.");
```

---

[1]It is not unheard of for a program having runtime assertions to run faster with them enabled than disabled. For example, asserting that a pointer is not null enables the optimizer to elide all code branches that can be reached only if that pointer were null.

Static assertions can be placed anywhere in the scope of a namespace, block, or class:

```
static_assert(1 + 1 == 2, "Never fires.");  // global namespace scope

template <typename T>
struct S
{
    void f0()
    {
        static_assert(1 + 1 == 3, "Always fires.");  // block scope
    }

    static_assert(!Predicate<T>::value, "Might fire.");  // class scope
};
```

Providing a nonconstant expression to a **static_assert** is itself a compile-time error:

```
extern bool x;
static_assert(x, "Nice try.");  // Error, x is not a compile-time constant.
```

Evaluation of static assertions in templates

The C++ Standard does not explicitly specify at precisely what point during the compilation process the expressions tested by static assertion declarations are evaluated. In particular, when used within the body of a template, the expression tested by a **static_assert** declaration might not be evaluated until **template instantiation time**. In practice, however, a **static_assert** that does not depend on any template parameters is essentially always[2] evaluated immediately, i.e., as soon as it is parsed and irrespective of whether any subsequent template instantiations occur:

```
void f1()
{
    static_assert(false, "Impossible!");  // always evaluated immediately
}                                         // even if f1() is never invoked

template <typename T>
void f2()
{
    static_assert(false, "Impossible!");  // always evaluated immediately
}                                         // even if f2() is never instantiated
```

The evaluation of a static assertion that is located within the body of a class or function template and depends on at least one template parameter is almost always bypassed during its initial parse since the assertion predicate might evaluate to true or false depending on the template argument:

---

[2]E.g., GCC 11.2 (c. 2021), Clang 12.0.1 (c. 2021), and MSVC 19.29 (c. 2021)

```
template <typename T>
void f3()
{
    static_assert(sizeof(T) >= 8, "Size < 8.");  // depends on T
}
```

However, see *Potential Pitfalls — Static assertions in templates can trigger unintended compilation failures* on page 120. In the example above, the compiler has no choice but to wait until each time f3 is instantiated because the truth of the predicate will vary depending on the type provided:

```
void g()
{
    f3<double>();               // OK
    f3<long double>();          // OK
    f3<std::complex<float>>();  // OK
    f3<char>();                 // Error, static assertion failed: Size < 8.
}
```

The Standard does, however, specify that a program containing any template definition for which no valid specialization exists is **ill formed, no diagnostic required (IFNDR)**, which was the case for f2 but not f3 in the example above. Contrast each of the h*n* definitions below with its correspondingly numbered f*n* definition above[3]:

```
void h1()
{
    int a[!sizeof(int) - 1];  // Error, same as int a[-1];
}
```

```
template <typename T>
void h2()
{
    int a[!sizeof(int) - 1];  // Error, always reported
}
```

```
template <typename T>
void h3()
{
    int a[!sizeof(T) - 1];    // typically reported only if instantiated
}
```

Both f1 and h1 are ill-formed nontemplate functions, and both will always be reported at compile time, albeit typically with decidedly different error messages as demonstrated by GCC 10.x's output:

```
f1: error: static assertion failed: Impossible!
h1: error: size -1 of array a is negative
```

---

[3]The formula used — int a[-1]; — leads to −1, not 0, to avoid a nonconforming extension to GCC that allows a[0].

Both f2 and h2 are ill-formed template functions; the cause of their being ill formed has nothing to do with the template type and hence will always be reported as a compile-time error in practice. Finally, f3 can be only contextually ill formed, whereas h3 is always necessarily ill formed, and yet neither is reported by typical compilers as such unless and until it has been instantiated. Reliance on a compiler not to notice that a program is ill formed is dubious; see *Potential Pitfalls — Static assertions in templates can trigger unintended compilation failures* on page 120.

Use Cases

Verifying assumptions about the target platform

Some programs rely on specific properties of the native types provided by their target platform. Static assertions can help ensure portability and prevent such programs from being compiled into a malfunctioning binary on an unsupported platform. As an example, consider a program that relies on the size of an **int** to be exactly 32 bits, e.g., due to the use of inline **asm** blocks. Placing a **static_assert** in namespace scope in any of the program's translation units will ensure that the assumption regarding the size of **int** is valid, and also serve as documentation for readers:

```
#include <climits>  // CHAR_BIT

static_assert(sizeof(int) * CHAR_BIT == 32,
    "An int must have exactly 32 bits for this program to work correctly.");
```

More typically, statically asserting the *size* of an **int** avoids having to write code to handle an **int** type's having greater or fewer bytes when no such platforms are likely ever to materialize:

```
static_assert(sizeof(int) == 4, "An int must have exactly 4 bytes.");
```

Preventing misuse of class and function templates

Static assertions are often used in practice to constrain class or function templates to prevent their being instantiated with unsupported types. If a type is not syntactically compatible with the template, static assertions provide clear customized error messages that replace compiler-issued diagnostics, which are often absurdly long and notoriously hard to read. More critically, static assertions actively avoid erroneous runtime behavior.

As an example, consider the SmallObjectBuffer<N> class templates,[4] which provide storage, aligned properly using **alignas** (see Section 2.1.“**alignas**” on page 168), for arbitrary objects whose size does not exceed N:

---

[4] A SmallObjectBuffer is similar to C++17's std::any (**cpprefc**) in that it can store any object of any type. Instead of performing dynamic allocation to support arbitrarily sized objects, however, SmallObjectBuffer uses an internal fixed-size buffer, which can lead to better performance and cache locality provided the maximum size of all of the types involved is known.

```
#include <cstddef> // std::size_t, std::max_align_t
#include <new>        // placement new

template <std::size_t N>
class SmallObjectBuffer
{
private:
    alignas(std::max_align_t) char d_buffer[N];

public:
    template <typename T>
    void set(const T& object);

    // ...
};
```

To prevent buffer overruns, it is important that **set** accepts only those objects that will fit in **d_buffer**. The use of a static assertion in the **set** member function template catches at compile time any such misuse:

```
template <std::size_t N>
template <typename T>
void SmallObjectBuffer<N>::set(const T& object)
{
    static_assert(sizeof(T) <= N, "object does not fit in the small buffer.");
    // Destroy existing object, if any; store how to destroy this new object of
    // type T later; then...
    new (&d_buffer) T(object);
}
```

The principle of constraining inputs can be applied to most class and function templates. **static_assert** is particularly useful in conjunction with standard **type traits** provided in <type_traits>. In the **rotateLeft** function template in the example below, we have used two static assertions to ensure that only unsigned integral types will be accepted:

```
#include <climits>       // CHAR_BIT
#include <type_traits>  // std::is_integral, std::is_unsigned

template <typename T>
T rotateLeft(T x)
{
    static_assert(std::is_integral<T>::value, "T must be an integral type.");
    static_assert(std::is_unsigned<T>::value, "T must be an unsigned type.");

    return (x << 1) | (x >> (sizeof(T) * CHAR_BIT - 1));
}
```

Potential Pitfalls

Static assertions in templates can trigger unintended compilation failures

As mentioned in *Description* on page 115, any program containing a template for which no valid specialization can be generated is IFNDR. Attempting to prevent the use of, say, a particular function template overload by using a static assertion that never holds produces such a program:

```
template <bool>
struct SerializableTag { };

template <typename T>
void serialize(char* buffer, const T& object, SerializableTag<true>);  // (1)

template <typename T>
void serialize(char* buffer, const T& object, SerializableTag<false>)  // (2a)
{
    static_assert(false, "T must be serializable.");  // independent of T
        // too obviously ill formed: always a compile-time error
}
```

In the example above, the second overload (2a) of `serialize` is provided with the intent of eliciting a meaningful compile-time error message in the event that an attempt is made to serialize a nonserializable type. The program, however, is technically **ill formed** and, in this simple case, will likely result in a compilation failure, irrespective of whether either overload of `serialize` is ever instantiated.

A commonly attempted workaround is to make the predicate of the assertion somehow dependent on a template parameter, ostensibly forcing the compiler to withhold evaluation of the **static_assert** unless and until the template is actually instantiated, a.k.a. **instantiation time**:

```
template <typename>  // N.B., we make no use of the nameless type parameter:
struct AlwaysFalse   // This class exists only to make 'value' a dependent name.
{
    enum { value = false };
};

template <typename T>
void serialize(char* buffer, const T& object, SerializableTag<false>)  // (2b)
{
    static_assert(AlwaysFalse<T>::value, "T must be serializable.");  // OK
        // less obviously ill formed: compile-time error when instantiated
}
```

To implement this version of the second overload, we have provided an intermediary class template `AlwaysFalse` that, when instantiated on any type, contains an enumerator named value, whose value is **false**. Although this second implementation is more likely to produce the desired result (i.e., a controlled compilation failure only when `serialize` is invoked with unsuitable arguments), sufficiently sophisticated compilers looking at just the current translation unit would still be able to know that no valid instantiation of `serialize` exists and would therefore be well within their rights to refuse to compile this still technically ill formed program.

Equivalent workarounds achieving the same result without a helper class are possible.

```
template <typename T>
void serialize(char* buffer, const T& object, SerializableTag<false>)  // (2c)
{
    static_assert(0 == sizeof(T), "T must be serializable.");  // OK
        // not too obviously ill formed: compile-time error when instantiated
}
```

Using this sort of obfuscation is not guaranteed to be either portable or future-proof.

Misuse of static assertions to restrict overload sets

Even if we are careful to *fool* the compiler into thinking that a specialization is wrong *only* if instantiated, we still cannot use this approach to remove a candidate from an overload set because translation will terminate if the static assertion is triggered. Consider this flawed attempt at writing a `process` function that will behave differently depending on the size of the given argument:

```
template <typename T>
void process(const T& x)  // (1) first definition of process function
{
    static_assert(sizeof(T) <= 32, "Overload for small types");  // BAD IDEA
    // ... (process small types)
}

template <typename T>
void process(const T& x)  // (2) compile-time error: redefinition of function
{
    static_assert(sizeof(T) > 32, "Overload for big types");    // BAD IDEA
    // ... (process big types)
}
```

While the intention of the developer might have been to statically dispatch to one of the two mutually exclusive overloads, the ill-fated implementation above will not compile because the signatures of the two overloads are identical, leading to a redefinition error. The semantics of **static_assert** are not suitable for the purposes of **compile-time dispatch**, and SFINAE-based approaches might be used instead.

To achieve the goal of removing up front a specialization from consideration, we will need to employ SFINAE. To do that, we must instead find a way to get the failing compile-time expression to be part of the function's **declaration**:

```
template <bool> struct Check { };
    // helper class template having a non-type Boolean template parameter
    // representing a compile-time predicate

template <> struct Check<true> { typedef int Ok; };
    // specialization of Check that makes the type Ok manifest only if
    // the supplied predicate (Boolean template argument) evaluates to true

template <typename T,
          typename Check<(sizeof(T) <= 32)>::Ok = 0>  // SFINAE
void process(const T& x)  // (1)
{
    // ... (process small types)
}

template <typename T,
          typename Check<(sizeof(T) > 32)>::Ok = 0>  // SFINAE
void process(const T& x)  // (2)
{
    // ... (process big types)
}
```

The empty **Check** helper class template in the example above in conjunction with just one of its two possible specializations conditionally exposes the **Ok** type alias *only* if the provided Boolean template parameter evaluates to **true**. (Otherwise, by default, it does not.) C++11 provides a library function, **std::enable_if**, that more directly addresses this use case.[5]

During the substitution phase of template instantiation, exactly one of the two overloads of the **process** function will attempt to access a nonexisting **Ok** type alias via the **Check<false>** instantiation, which again, by default, is nonexistent. Although such an error would typically result in a compilation failure, in the context of template argument substitution it will instead result in only the offending overload's being discarded, giving other valid overloads a chance to be selected:

```
void client()
{
    process(SmallType());  // discards (2), selects (1)
    process(BigType());    // discards (1), selects (2)
}
```

This general technique of pairing template specializations is used widely in modern C++ programming. For another, often more convenient way of constraining overloads using **expression SFINAE**, see Section 1.1."Trailing Return" on page 124.

---

[5]**Concepts**, a language feature introduced in C++20, provides a far less baroque alternative to SFINAE that allows for overload sets to be governed by the syntactic properties of their compile-time template arguments.

Annoyances

Mandatory string literal

Many compilation failures caused by static assertions are self-explanatory since the offending line, which necessarily contains the predicate code, is displayed as part of the compiler diagnostic. In those situations, the message required[6] as part of **static_assert**'s grammar is redundant:

```
static_assert(std::is_integral<T>::value, "T must be an integral type.");
```

Developers commonly provide an empty string literal in these cases:

```
static_assert(std::is_integral<T>::value, "");
```

There is no universal consensus as to the parity of the user-supplied error message. Should it restate the asserted condition, or should it state what went amiss?

```
static_assert(0 < x, "x is negative");
    // misleading when 0 == x
```

See Also

- "Trailing Return" (§1.1, p. 124) describes how enabling expression SFINAE directly as part of a function's declaration allows simple and fine-grained control over overload resolution.

Further Reading

- The original proposal recommending that a static-assertion facility, complementing the runtime **assert** macro and **#error** preprocessor directive, be added to to the C++ language to support constraints on template type arguments is presented in **klarer04**.

---

[6] As of C++17, the message argument of a static assertion is optional.

Trailing Function Return Types

This syntactically more convenient yet semantically equivalent alternative of using -> to declare a function's return type *after* its parameter list enables that type to refer to the individual parameters by name along with other class or namespace members without explicit qualification.

Description

C++11 offers an alternative function-declaration syntax in which the return type of a function is located to the right of its **signature** (name, parameters, and qualifiers), offset by the arrow token (->); the function itself is introduced by the keyword **auto**, which acts as a type placeholder:

```cpp
auto f() -> void;  // equivalent to void f();
```

When using the alternative, trailing-return-type syntax, any **const**, **volatile**, and reference qualifiers (see Section 3.1."Ref-Qualifiers" on page 1153) are placed to the left of the -> *<return-type>*, and any contextual keywords, such as **override** and **final** (see Section 1.1."**override**" on page 104 and Section 3.1."**final**" on page 1007), are placed to its right:

```cpp
struct Base
{
    virtual int e() const;     // const qualifier
    virtual int f() volatile;  // volatile qualifier
    virtual int g() &;         // lvalue-reference qualifier
    virtual int h() &&;        // rvalue-reference qualifier
};

struct Derived : Base
{
    auto e() const    -> int override;  // override contextual keyword
    auto f() volatile -> int final;     // final            "        "
    auto g() &        -> int override;  // override         "        "
    auto h() &&       -> int final;     // final            "        "
};
```

Using a trailing return type allows the parameters of a function to be named as part of the specification of the return type, which can be useful in conjunction with **decltype**:

```cpp
auto g(int x) -> decltype(x);  // equivalent to int g(int x);
```

When using the trailing-return-type syntax in a member function definition outside the class definition, names appearing in the return type, unlike with the classic notation, will be looked up in class scope by default:

```
struct S
{
    typedef int T;
    auto h1() -> T;  // trailing syntax for member function
    T h2();          // classical syntax for member function
};

auto S::h1() -> T { /*...*/ }  // equivalent to S::T S::h1() { /.../ }
T    S::h2()       { /*...*/ }  // Error, T is unknown in this context.
```

The same advantage would apply to a nonmember function[1] defined outside of the name-space in which it is declared:

```
namespace N
{
    typedef int T;
    auto h3() -> T;  // trailing syntax for free function
    T h4();          // classical syntax for free function
}

auto N::h3() -> T { /*...*/ }  // equivalent to N::T N::h3() { /.../ }
T    N::h4()       { /*...*/ }  // Error, T is unknown in this context.
```

Finally, since the syntactic element to be provided after the arrow token is a separate type unto itself, return types involving pointers to functions are somewhat simplified. Suppose, for example, we want to describe a **higher-order function**, f, that takes as its argument a **long long** and returns a pointer to a function that takes an **int** and returns a **double**[2]:

```
// [function(long long) returning]
//     [pointer to] [function(int x) returning] double   f;
//     [pointer to] [function(int x) returning] double   f(long long);
//                  [function(int x) returning] double*  f(long long);
//                                              double (*f(long long))(int x);
```

Using the alternate trailing syntax, we can conveniently break the declaration of f into two parts: (1) the declaration of the function's signature, **auto f(long long)**, and (2) that of the return type, say, R for now:

```
// [pointer to] [function (int) returning] double   R;
//              [function (int) returning] double*  R;
//                                         double (*R)(int);
```

---

[1] A **static** member function of a **struct** can be a viable alternative implementation to a free function declared within a namespace; see **lakos20**, section 1.4, "Header Files," pp. 190–201, especially Figure 1-37c on p. 199, and section 2.4.9, "Only Classes, **struct**s, and Free Operators at Package-Namespace Scope," pp. 312–321, especially Figure 2-23 on p. 316.

[2] Coauthor John Lakos first used the shown verbose declaration notation while teaching Advanced Design and Programming Using C++ at Columbia University (1991–1997).

The two equivalent forms of the same declaration are shown below:

```
double (*f(long long))(int x);        // classic return-type syntax
auto f(long long) -> double (*)(int); // trailing return-type syntax
```

Note that both syntactic forms of the same declaration may appear together within the same scope. Note also that not all functions that can be represented in terms of the trailing syntax have a convenient equivalent representation in the classic one:

```
#include <utility>  // declval

template <typename A, typename B>
auto foo(A a, B b) -> decltype(a.foo(b));
    // trailing return-type syntax

template <typename A, typename B>
decltype(std::declval<A&>().foo(std::declval<B&>())) foo(A a, B b);
    // classic return-type syntax using C++11's std::declval
```

In the example above, we were essentially forced to use the C++11 Standard Library template `std::declval`[3] to express our intent with the classic return-type syntax.

Use Cases

Function template whose return type depends on a parameter type

Declaring a function template whose return type depends on the types of one or more of its parameters is not uncommon in generic programming. For example, consider a mathematical function that linearly interpolates between two values of possibly different types:

```
template <typename A, typename B, typename F>
auto linearInterpolation(const A& a, const B& b, const F& factor)
    -> decltype(a + factor * (b - a))
{
    return a + factor * (b - a);
}
```

The return type of `linearInterpolation` is the type of expression inside the ***decltype*** *specifier*, which is identical to the expression returned in the body of the function. Hence, this interface necessarily supports any set of input types for which `a + factor * (b - a)` is valid, including types such as mathematical vectors, matrices, or expression templates. As an added benefit, the presence of the expression in the function's declaration enables **expression SFINAE**, which is typically desirable for generic template functions (see Section 1.1."**decltype**" on page 25).

---

[3]cpprefd

Avoiding having to qualify names redundantly in return types

When defining a function outside the **class**, **struct**, or **namespace** in which it is first declared, any unqualified names present in the return type might be looked up differently depending on the particular choice of function-declaration syntax used. When the return type precedes the qualified name of the function definition as is the case with classic syntax, all references to types declared in the same scope where the function itself is declared must also be qualified. By contrast, when the return type follows the qualified name of the function, the return type is looked up in the same scope in which the function was first declared, just like its parameter types would. Avoiding redundant qualification of the return type can be beneficial, especially when the qualifying name is long.

As an illustration, consider a class representing an abstract syntax tree node that exposes a type alias:

```
struct NumericalASTNode
{
    using ElementType = double;
    auto getElement() -> ElementType;
};
```

Defining the `getElement` member function using traditional function-declaration syntax would require repetition of the `NumericalASTNode` name:

```
NumericalASTNode::ElementType NumericalASTNode::getElement() { /*...*/ }
```

Using the trailing-return-type syntax handily avoids the repetition:

```
auto NumericalASTNode::getElement() -> ElementType { /*...*/ }
```

By ensuring that name lookup within the return type is the same as for the parameter types, we avoid needlessly having to qualify names that should be found correctly by default.

Improving readability of declarations involving function pointers

Declarations of functions returning a pointer to either a function, a member function, or a data member are notoriously hard to parse, even for seasoned programmers. As an example, consider a function called `getOperation` that takes a `kind` of enumerated `Operation` as its argument and returns a pointer to a member function of `Calculator` that takes a **double** and returns a **double**:

```
double (Calculator::*getOperation(Operation kind))(double);
```

As we saw in the description, such declarations can be constructed systematically but do not exactly roll off the fingers. On the other hand, by partitioning the problem into (1) the declaration of the function itself and (2) the type it returns, each individual problem becomes far simpler than the original:

```
auto getOperation(Operation kind)   // (1) function taking a kind of Operation
  -> double (Calculator::*)(double);
      // (2) returning a pointer to a Calculator member function taking a
      //     double and returning a double
```

Using this divide-and-conquer approach, writing such functions becomes fairly straightforward. Declaring a **higher-order function** that takes a function pointer as an argument might be even easier to read if a type alias is used via **typedef** or, as of C++11, **using**.

See Also

- "**decltype**" (§1.1, p. 25) describes how function declarations might use **decltype** either in conjunction with, or as an alternative to, trailing return types.

- "**auto** Return" (§3.2, p. 1182) explains that leaving the return type to deduction shares syntactical similarities with trailing return types but brings with it significant pitfalls when migrating from C++11 to C++14.

Further Reading

- Those interested in consistency of style — a la east **const** versus **const** west — can find such a discussion involving *trailing* versus *classic* return types in **mertz18**.

Unicode String Literals

C++11 introduces a portable mechanism for ensuring that a literal is encoded as UTF-8, UTF-16, or UTF-32.

Description

According to the C++ Standard, the character encoding of string literals is unspecified and can vary with the target platform or the configuration of the compiler. In essence, the C++ Standard does not guarantee that the string literal `"Hello"` will be encoded as the ASCII sequence 0x48, 0x65, 0x6C, 0x6C, 0x6F or that the character literal `'X'` has the value 0x58. In fact, C++ still fully supports platforms using EBCDIC, a rarely used alternative encoding to ASCII, as their primary text encoding.

Table 1 illustrates three new *Unicode*-compliant *string literals*, each delineating the precise encoding of each character.

Table 1: Three new Unicode-compliant literal strings

Encoding	Syntax	Underlying Type
UTF-8	u8"Hello"	char[a]
UTF-16	u"Hello"	char16_t
UTF-32	U"Hello"	char32_t

[a] char8_t in C++20

A Unicode literal value is guaranteed to be encoded in UTF-8, UTF-16, or UTF-32, for u8, u, and U literals, respectively:

```
char s0[] = "Hello";
    // unspecified encoding, albeit likely ASCII

char s1[] = u8"Hello";
    // guaranteed to be encoded as {0x48, 0x65, 0x6C, 0x6C, 0x6F, 0x0}
```

C++11 also introduces *universal character names* that provide a reliably portable way of embedding Unicode **code points** in a C++ program. They can be introduced by the \u character sequence followed by four hexadecimal digits or by the \U character sequence followed by eight hexadecimal digits:

```
#include <cstdio>  // std::puts
void f()
{
    std::puts(u8"\U0001F378"); // Unicode code point in a UTF8-encoded literal
}
```

This output statement is guaranteed to emit the cocktail emoji (🍸) to **stdout**, assuming that the receiving end is configured to interpret output bytes as UTF-8.

Use Cases

Guaranteed-portable encodings of literals

The encoding guarantees provided by the Unicode literals can be useful, such as in communication with other programs or network and/or IPC protocols that expect character strings having a particular encoding.

As an example, consider an instant-messaging program in which both the client and the server expect messages to be encoded in UTF-8. As part of broadcasting a message to all clients, the server code uses UTF-8 Unicode literals to guarantee that all clients will receive a sequence of bytes they are able to interpret and display as human-readable text:

```
void Server::broadcastServerMessage(const std::string& utf8Message)
{
    Packet data;
    data << u8"Message from the server: '" << utf8Message << u8"'\n";

    broadcastPacket(data);
}
```

Not using u8 literals in the code snippet above could potentially result in nonportable behavior and might require compiler-specific flags to ensure that the source is UTF-8 encoded.

Potential Pitfalls

Embedding Unicode graphemes

The addition of Unicode string literals to the language did not bring along an extension of the **basic source character set**: Even in C++11, the default **basic source character set** is a subset of ASCII.[1]

Developers might incorrectly assume that u8" 🍸 " is a portable way of embedding a string literal representing the cocktail emoji in a C++ program. The representation of the string literal, however, depends on what encoding the compiler assumes for the source file, which can

---

[1]Implementations are free to map characters outside the basic source character set to sequences of its members, resulting in the possibility of embedding other characters, such as emojis, in a C++ source file.

generally be controlled through compiler flags. The only portable way of embedding the cocktail emoji is to use its corresponding Unicode code point escape sequence (u8"\U0001F378").

Lack of library support for Unicode

Essential **vocabulary types**, such as std::string, are completely unaware of encoding. They treat any stored string as a sequence of bytes. Even when correctly using Unicode string literals, programmers unfamiliar with Unicode might be surprised by seemingly innocent operations, such as asking for the size of a string representing the cocktail emoji:

```
#include <cassert>  // standard C assert macro
#include <string>   // std::string

void f()
{
    std::string cocktail(u8"\U0001F378"); // big character
    assert(cocktail.size() == 1);         // assertion failure
}
```

Even though the cocktail emoji is a *single* code point, std::string::size returns the number of code units (bytes) required to encode it. The lack of Unicode-aware vocabulary types and utilities in the Standard Library can be a source of defects and misunderstandings, especially in the context of international program localization.

Problematic treatment of UTF-8 in the type system

UTF-8 string literals use **char** as their **underlying type**. Such a choice is inconsistent with UTF-16 and UTF-32 literals, which provide their own distinct character types, **char16_t** and **char32_t**, respectively. Lack of a UTF-8-specific character type precludes providing distinct behavior for UTF-8 encoded strings using function overloading or template specialization because they are indistinguishable from strings having the encoding of the execution character set. Furthermore, whether the underlying type of **char** is a **signed** or **unsigned** type is itself implementation defined. Note that **char** is distinct from both **signed char** and **unsigned char**, but its behavior is guaranteed to be the same as one of those.

C++20 fundamentally changes how UTF-8 string literals work, by introducing a new non-aliasing **char8_t** character type whose representation is guaranteed to match **unsigned char**. The new character type provides several benefits.

- Ensures an **unsigned** and distinct type for UTF-8 character data

- Enables overloading for regular string literals versus UTF-8 string literals

- Potentially achieves better performance due to the lack of special aliasing rules

Unfortunately, the changes brought by C++20 are not backward-compatible and might cause code targeting previous versions of the language using u8 literals either to fail to compile or to silently change its behavior when targeting C++20:

```
template <typename T> void print(const T*);    // (0)
void print(const char*);                       // (1)

void f()
{
    print(u8"text");   // invokes (1) prior to C++20, (0) afterwards
}
```

Type/Template Aliases (Extended `typedef`)

The **using** keyword may now be used to introduce type aliases and alias templates, providing a more general alternative to **typedef** that might also improve readability, especially for function aliases.

Description

The keyword **using** has historically supported the introduction of an alias for a named entity, e.g., type, function, or data, from some named scope into the current one. As of C++11, we can employ the **using** keyword to achieve everything that could previously be accomplished with a **typedef** declaration but in a syntactic form that many people find more natural and intuitive but that offers nothing profoundly new:

```cpp
using Type1 = int;      // equivalent to typedef int Type1;
using Type2 = double;   // equivalent to typedef double Type2;
```

In contrast to **typedef**, the name of the synonym created via the **using** syntax always appears on the left side of the = token and separate from the type declaration itself, the advantage of which becomes apparent with more involved types, such as *pointer-to-function*, *pointer-to-member-function*, or *pointer-to-data-member*:

```cpp
struct S { int i; void f(); };  // user-defined type S defined at file scope

using Type3 = void(*)();        // equivalent to typedef void(*Type3)();
using Type4 = void(S::*)();     // equivalent to typedef void(S::*Type4)();
using Type5 = int S::*;         // equivalent to typedef int S::*Type5;
```

Just as with a **typedef**, the name representing the type can be qualified, but the symbol representing the synonym cannot:

```cpp
namespace N { struct S { }; }   // original type S defined with namespace N

using Type6 = N::S;             // equivalent to typedef N::S Type6;
using ::Type7 = int;            // Error, the alias's name must be unqualified.
```

Unlike a **typedef**, however, a type alias introduced via **using** can itself be a template, known as an *alias template*:

```cpp
template <typename T>
using Type8 = T;  // "identity" alias template

Type8<int>    i;  // equivalent to int i;
Type8<double> d;  // equivalent to double d;
```

Note, however, that neither partial nor full specialization of alias templates is supported:

```
template <typename, typename>   // general alias template
using Type9 = char;             // OK

template <typename T>           // attempted partial specialization of above
using Type9<T, int> = char;     // Error, expected = before < token

template <>                     // attempted full specialization of above
using Type10<int, int> = char;  // Error, expected unqualified id before using
```

Used in conjunction with existing class templates, alias templates allow programmers to *bind* one or more template parameters to a fixed type, while leaving others open:

```
#include <utility>  // std::pair

template <typename T>
using PairOfCharAnd = std::pair<char, T>;
    // alias template that binds char to the first type parameter of std::pair

PairOfCharAnd<int>    pci;  // equivalent to std::pair<char, int> pci;
PairOfCharAnd<double> pcd;  // equivalent to std::pair<char, double> pcd;
```

Finally, note that similar functionality can be achieved in C++03; it suppresses type deduction and requires additional boilerplate code at both the point of definition and the call site:

```
// C++03 (obsolete)
template <typename T>
struct PairOfCharAnd
    // template class holding an alias, Type, to std::pair<char, T>
{
    typedef std::pair<char, T> Type;
        // type alias binding char to the first type parameter of std::pair
};

PairOfCharAnd<int>::Type    pci;  // equivalent to std::pair<char, int> pci;
PairOfCharAnd<double>::Type pcd;  // equivalent to std::pair<char, double> pcd;
```

Use Cases

Simplifying convoluted `typedef` declarations

Complex **typedef** declarations involving pointers to functions, member functions, or data members require looking in the middle of the declaration to find the alias name. As an example, consider a *callback* type alias intended to be used with asynchronous functions:

```
typedef void(*CompletionCallback)(void* userData);
```

Developers coming from a background other than C or C++03 might find the above declaration hard to parse since the name of the alias, `CompletionCallback`, is embedded in the function pointer type. Replacing **typedef** with **using** results in a simpler, more consistent formulation of the same alias:

```
using CompletionCallback = void(*)(void* userData);
```

The `CompletionCallback` alias declaration above reads almost completely left-to-right, and the name of the alias is clearly specified after the **using** keyword. To make the `CompletionCallback` alias read left-to-right, a trailing return (see Section 1.1."Trailing Return" on page 124) can be used:

```
using CompletionCallback = auto(*)(void* userData) -> void;
```

The alias declaration above can be read as, "`CompletionCallback` is an alias for a pointer to a function taking a **void*** parameter named `userData` and returning **void**."

Binding arguments to template parameters

An alias template can be used to *bind* one or more template parameters of, say, a commonly used class template, while leaving the other parameters open to variation. Suppose, for example, we have a class, `UserData`, that contains several distinct instances of `std::map`, each having the same key type, `UserId`, but with different payloads:

```
class UserData  // class having excessive code repetition (BAD IDEA)
{
private:
    std::map<UserId, Message>        d_messages;
    std::map<UserId, Photos>         d_photos;
    std::map<UserId, Article>        d_articles;
    std::map<UserId, std::set<UserId>> d_friends;
};
```

The example above, though clear and regular, involves significant repetition, making it more difficult to maintain should we later opt to change data structures. If we were to instead use an **alias template** to bind the `UserId` type to the first type parameter of `std::map`, we could both reduce code repetition and enable the programmer to consistently replace `std::map` to another container, e.g., `std::unordered_map`,[1] by performing the change in only one place:

---

[1] An `std::unordered_map` is an STL container type that became available on all conforming platforms along with C++11. The functionality is similar except that since it is not required to support ordered traversal or, worst case, O[log(n)] lookups and O[n*log(n)] insertions, `std::unordered_map` can be implemented as a hash table instead of a balanced tree, yielding significantly faster average access times. See **cppreflb**.

```
class UserData  // class with well-factored implementation (GOOD IDEA)
{
private:
    template <typename V>
    using Mapping = std::map<UserId, V>;    // using a template alias to bind
                                            // UserId as the key type

    Mapping<Message>        d_messages;
    Mapping<Photos>         d_photos;
    Mapping<Article>        d_articles;
    Mapping<std::set<UserId>> d_friends;
};
```

Providing a shorthand notation for type traits

Alias templates can provide a shorthand notation for **type traits**, avoiding **boilerplate code** in the usage site. As an example, consider a simple type trait that adds a pointer to a given type (similar to std::add_pointer):

```
template <typename T>
struct AddPointer
{
    typedef T* Type;
};
```

To use the trait above, the AddPointer class template must be instantiated, and its nested Type alias must be accessed. Furthermore, in the generic context, it has to be prepended with the **typename** keyword::

```
template <typename T>void f()
{
    T t;
    typename AddPointer<T>::Type p = t;
}
```

The syntactical overhead of AddPointer can be removed by creating an alias template for its nested type alias, such as AddPointer_t:

```
template <typename T>
using AddPointer_t = typename AddPointer<T>::Type;
```

Using AddPointer_t instead of AddPointer results in shorter code devoid of boilerplate:

```
void g()
{
    int i;
    AddPointer_t<int> p = &i;
}
```

Note that, since C++14, all the standard type traits defined in the `<type_traits>` header provide a corresponding alias template with the goal of reducing boilerplate code. For instance, C++14 introduces the `std::remove_reference_t` alias template for the C++11 `std::remove_reference` type trait:

```
typename std::remove_reference<int&>::type i0 = 5; // OK in both C++11 and C++14
std::remove_reference_t<int&> i1 = 5;               // OK in C++14
```

See Also

- "Trailing Return" (§1.1, p. 124) offers an alternative syntax for function declaration, which can help improve readability in type aliases and alias templates involving function types.

- "Inheriting Ctors" (§2.1, p. 535) provides another meaning for the **using** keyword to allow base-class constructors to be invoked as part of the derived class.

Aggregates Having Default Member Initializers

C++14 enables the use of **aggregate initialization** with classes employing default member initializers.

Description

Prior to C++14, classes that used default member initializers, i.e., initializers that appear directly within the scope of the class (see Section 2.1."Default Member Init" on page 318), were not considered **aggregate** types:

```
struct S                 // aggregate type in C++14 but not C++11
{
    int i;
    bool b = false;      // uses default member initializer
};

struct A                 // aggregate type in C++11 and C++14
{
    int  i;
    bool b;              // does not use default member initializer
};
```

Because A but not S is considered an **aggregate** in C++11, instances of A can be created via aggregate initialization, whereas instances of S cannot:

```
A a={100, true};  // OK, in both C++11 and C++14
S s={100, true};  // Error, in C++11; OK, in C++14
```

Note that since C++11, direct list initialization can be used to perform aggregate initialization; see Section 2.1."Braced Init" on page 215:

```
A a{100, true};  // OK in both C++11 and C++14 but not in C++03
```

As of C++14, the requirements for a type to be categorized as an **aggregate** are relaxed, allowing classes employing default member initializers to be considered as such; hence, both A and S are considered **aggregates** in C++14 and eligible for **aggregate initialization**:

```
void f()
{
    S s0{100, true};        // OK in C++14 but not in C++11
    assert(s0.i == 100);    // set via explicit aggregate initialization
    assert(s0.b == true);   // set via explicit aggregate initialization

    S s1{456};              // OK in C++14 but not in C++11
    assert(s1.i == 456);    // set via explicit aggregate initialization
    assert(s1.b == false);  // set via default member initializer
}
```

In the code snippet above, the C++14 aggregate S is initialized in two ways: s0 is created using aggregate initialization for both data members, and s1 is created using aggregate initialization for only the first data member, the second being set via its default member initializer.

Use Cases

Configuration structs

Aggregates in conjunction with default member initializers (see Section 2.1."Default Member Init" on page 318) can be used to provide concise customizable configuration structs, packaged with typical default values. As an example, consider a configuration struct for an HTTP request handler:

```cpp
struct HTTPRequestHandlerConfig
{
    int maxQueuedRequests = 1024;
    int timeout           = 60;
    int minThreads        = 4;
    int maxThreads        = 8;
};
```

When creating objects of type HTTPRequestHandlerConfig (shown in the example above), aggregate initialization can be used to override one or more of the defaults in definition order[1]:

```cpp
HTTPRequestHandlerConfig getRequestHandlerConfig(bool inLowMemoryEnvironment)
{
    if (inLowMemoryEnvironment)
    {
        return HTTPRequestHandlerConfig{128};
            // timeout, minThreads, and maxThreads have their default value.
    }
    else
    {
        return HTTPRequestHandlerConfig{2048, 120};
            // minThreads and maxThreads have their default value.
    }
}

// ...
```

---

[1]In C++20, the designated initializers feature adds flexibility (e.g., for configuration structs, such as HTTPRequestHandlerConfig) by enabling explicit specification of the names of the data members:

```cpp
HTTPRequestHandlerConfig lowTimeout{.timeout = 15};
    // maxQueuedRequests, minThreads, and maxThreads have their default value.

HTTPRequestHandlerConfig highPerformance{.timeout = 120, .maxThreads = 16};
    // maxQueuedRequests and minThreads have their default value.
```

Potential Pitfalls

Empty list-initializing members do not use the default initializer

When we add default member initializers to members of an aggregate, those initializers are in effect *only* if that member has no corresponding initializer in the braced-initializer list. We cannot explicitly *request* the default value by placing empty braces into the list because that will value-initialize the member with an empty initializer, not use its default member initializer. Any case where we want to explicitly initialize a later member variable's value during aggregate initialization means we must manually determine the proper default for all prior members:

```
struct A
{
    int i{1};
    int j{2};
    int k{3};
};

A a1{};         // OK,  result is i=1, j=2,       k=3
A a2{ 4 };      // OK,  result is i=4, j=2,       k=3
A a3{ 4, {}, 8 }; // Bug, result is i=4, j=0 (not 2), k=3
```

Annoyances

Syntactical ambiguity in the presence of brace elision

During the initialization of multilevel **aggregates**, braces around the initialization of a nested aggregate can be omitted, which is called **brace elision**:

```
struct S
{
    int data[3];
};

S s0{{0, 1, 2}};  // OK, nested data initialized explicitly
S s1{0, 1, 2};    // OK, brace elision for nested data
```

The possibility of brace elision creates an interesting syntactical ambiguity when used alongside **aggregates** with default member initializers (see Section 2.1."Default Member Init" on page 318). Consider a **struct** X containing three data members, one of which has a default value:

```
struct X
{
    int a;
    int b;
    int c = 0;
};
```

Now, consider various ways in which an array of elements of type X can be initialized:

```
X xs0[] = {{0, 1}, {2, 3}, {4, 5}};
    // OK, clearly 3 elements having the respective values:
    // {0, 1, 0}, {2, 3, 0}, {4, 5, 0}

X xs1[] = {{0, 1, 2}, {3, 4, 5}};
    // OK, clearly 2 elements with values:
    // {0, 1, 2}, {3, 4, 5}

X xs2[] = {0, 1, 2, 3, 4, 5};
    // ...?
```

Upon seeing the definition of xs2, a programmer not versed in the details of the C++ Language Standard might be unsure as to whether the initializer of xs2 is three elements, like xs0, or two elements, like xs1. The Standard is, however, clear that the compiler will interpret xs2 the same as xs1, and, thus, the default values of X::c for the two array elements will be replaced with 2 and 5, respectively.

See Also

- "Braced Init" (§2.1, p. 215) introduces a syntactically similar feature for initializing objects in a uniform manner.

- "Default Member Init" (§2.1, p. 318) explains how developers can provide a default initializer for a data member directly in the definition of a class.

Binary Literals: The 0b Prefix

The 0b (or 0B) prefix, modeled after 0x, enables integer literals to be expressed in base 2.

Description

A binary literal is an integral value represented in code in a binary numeral system. A binary literal consists of a 0b or 0B prefix followed by a nonempty sequence of binary digits, namely, 0 and 1[1]:

```
int i = 0b11110000;  // equivalent to 240, 0360, or 0xF0
int j = 0B11110000;  // same value as above
```

The first digit after the 0b prefix is the most significant one:

```
static_assert(0b0     == 0, "");  // 0*2^0
static_assert(0b1     == 1, "");  // 1*2^0
static_assert(0b10    == 2, "");  // 1*2^1 + 0*2^0
static_assert(0b11    == 3, "");  // 1*2^1 + 1*2^0
static_assert(0b100   == 4, "");  // 1*2^2 + 0*2^1 + 0*2^0
static_assert(0b101   == 5, "");  // 1*2^2 + 0*2^1 + 1*2^0
// ...
static_assert(0b11010 == 26, "");  // 1*2^4 + 1*2^3 + 0*2^2 + 1*2^1 + 0*2^0
```

Leading zeros — as with octal and hexadecimal (but not decimal) literals — are ignored but can be added for readability:

```
static_assert(0b00000000 ==   0, "");
static_assert(0b00000001 ==   1, "");
static_assert(0b00000010 ==   2, "");
static_assert(0b00000100 ==   4, "");
static_assert(0b00001000 ==   8, "");
static_assert(0b10000000 == 128, "");
```

The type of a binary literal is by default an **int** unless that value cannot fit in an **int**. In that case, its type is the first type in the sequence {**unsigned int**, **long**, **unsigned long**, **long long**, **unsigned long long**} in which it will fit. This same type list applies for both octal and hex literals but not for decimal literals, which, if initially **signed**, skip over any **unsigned** types, and vice versa. If neither of those is applicable, the compiler may use implementation-defined extended integer types such as __int128 to represent the literal if it fits; otherwise, the program is ill formed:

---

[1]Prior to being introduced in C++14, GCC supported binary literals — with the same syntax as the standard feature — as a nonconforming extension since version 4.3.0, released in March 2008; for more details, see https://gcc.gnu.org/gcc-4.3/.

```
// example platform 1:
// (sizeof(int): 4; sizeof(long): 4; sizeof(long long): 8)
auto i32   = 0b0111...[ 24 1-bits]...1111;  // i32 is int.
auto u32   = 0b1000...[ 24 0-bits]...0000;  // u32 is unsigned int.
auto i64   = 0b0111...[ 56 1-bits]...1111;  // i64 is long long.
auto u64   = 0b1000...[ 56 0-bits]...0000;  // u64 is unsigned long long.
auto i128  = 0b0111...[120 1-bits]...1111;  // Error, integer literal too large
auto u128  = 0b1000...[120 0-bits]...0000;  // Error, integer literal too large

// example platform 2:
// (sizeof(int): 4; sizeof(long): 8; sizeof(long long): 16)
auto i32   = 0b0111...[ 24 1-bits]...1111;  // i32  is int.
auto u32   = 0b1000...[ 24 0-bits]...0000;  // u32  is unsigned int.
auto i64   = 0b0111...[ 56 1-bits]...1111;  // i64  is long.
auto u64   = 0b1000...[ 56 0-bits]...0000;  // u64  is unsigned long.
auto i128  = 0b0111...[120 1-bits]...1111;  // i128 is long long.
auto u128  = 0b1000...[120 0-bits]...0000;  // u128 is unsigned long long.
```

Purely for convenience of exposition, we have employed the C++11 **auto** feature to conveniently capture the type implied by the literal itself; see Section 2.1."**auto** Variables" on page 195. Separately, the precise initial type of a binary literal, like any other literal, can be controlled explicitly using the common integer-literal suffixes {u, l, ul, ll, ull} in either lower- or uppercase:

```
auto i    = 0b101;          // type: int;                 value: 5
auto u    = 0b1010U;        // type: unsigned int;        value: 10
auto l    = 0b1111L;        // type: long;                value: 15
auto ul   = 0b10100UL;      // type: unsigned long;       value: 20
auto ll   = 0b11000LL;      // type: long long;           value: 24
auto ull  = 0b110101ULL;    // type: unsigned long long;  value: 53
```

Finally, note that affixing a minus sign to a binary literal (e.g., -b1010) — just like any other integer literal (e.g., -10, -012, or -0xa) — is parsed as a non-negative value first, after which a unary minus is applied:

```
static_assert(sizeof(int) == 4, "");   // true on virtually all machines today
static_assert(-0b1010 == -10, "");     // as if: 0 - 0b1010 == 0 - 10
static_assert( 0b0111...[ 24 1-bits]...1111      //   signed
            != -0b0111...[ 24 1-bits]...1111, ""); //   signed

static_assert( 0b1000...[ 24 0-bits]...0000      //   unsigned
            != -0b1000...[ 24 0-bits]...0000, ""); //   unsigned
```

Use Cases

Bit masking and bitwise operations

Prior to the introduction of binary literals, hexadecimal and octal literals were commonly used to represent bit masks or specific bit constants in source code. As an example, consider a function that returns the least significant four bits of a given **unsigned int** value:

```
unsigned int lastFourBits(unsigned int value)
{
    return value & 0xFu;
}
```

The correctness of the *bitwise and* operation above might not be immediately obvious to a developer inexperienced with hexadecimal literals. In contrast, using a binary literal more directly states our intent to mask all but the four least-significant bits of the input:

```
unsigned int lastFourBits(unsigned int value)
{
    return value & 0b1111u;
}
```

Similarly, other bitwise operations, such as setting or getting individual bits, might benefit from the use of binary literals. For instance, consider a set of flags used to represent the state of an avatar in a game:

```
struct AvatarStateFlags
{
    enum Enum
    {
        e_ON_GROUND   = 0b0001,
        e_INVULNERABLE = 0b0010,
        e_INVISIBLE   = 0b0100,
        e_SWIMMING    = 0b1000,
    };
};

class Avatar
{
    unsigned char d_state;

public:
    bool isOnGround() const
    {
        return d_state & AvatarStateFlags::e_ON_GROUND;
    }
```

```
    // ...
};
```

Note that the choice of using a nested classic **enum** was deliberate; see Section 2.1."**enum class**" on page 332.

Replicating constant binary data

Especially in the context of **embedded development** or emulation, a programmer will commonly write code that needs to deal with specific constants, e.g., provided as part of the specification of a CPU or virtual machine, that must be incorporated in the program's source code. Depending on the original format of such constants, a binary representation can be the most convenient or most easily understandable one.

As an example, consider a function decoding instructions of a virtual machine whose opcodes are specified in binary format:

```
#include <cstdint>  // std::uint8_t

void VirtualMachine::decodeInstruction(std::uint8_t instruction)
{
    switch (instruction)
    {
        case 0b00000000u:  // no-op
            break;

        case 0b00000001u:  // add(register0, register1)
            d_register0 += d_register1;
            break;

        case 0b00000010u:  // jmp(register0)
            jumpTo(d_register0);
            break;

        // ...
    }
}
```

Replicating the same binary constant specified as part of the CPU's or virtual machine's manual or documentation directly in the source avoids the need to mentally convert such constant data to and from, say, a hexadecimal number.

Binary literals are also suitable for capturing bitmaps. For instance, consider a bitmap representing the uppercase letter C:

```
const unsigned char letterBitmap_C[] =
{
    0b00011111,
    0b01100000,
    0b10000000,
    0b10000000,
    0b10000000,
    0b01100000,
    0b00011111
};
```

Using *binary* literals makes the shape of the image that the bitmap represents apparent directly in the source code.

See Also

- "Digit Separators" (§1.2, p. 152) explains grouping digits visually to make long binary literals much more readable.

Further Reading

- Example use of binary literals in conjunction with digit separators (see Section 1.2. "Digit Separators" on page 152) along with another loosely related C++14 feature, variable templates (see Section 1.2. "Variable Templates" on page 157), can be found in **kalev14**.

The [[deprecated]] Attribute

The standard attribute [[deprecated]] indicates that the use of the entity to which the attribute pertains is discouraged, typically in the form of a compiler warning.

Description

The standard [[deprecated]] attribute is used to portably indicate that a particular **entity** is no longer recommended and to actively discourage its use. Such deprecation typically follows the introduction of alternative constructs that are superior to the original one, providing time for clients to migrate to them *asynchronously* before the deprecated one is removed in some subsequent release.

An asynchronous process for ongoing improvement of legacy codebases, sometimes referred to as **continuous refactoring**, often allows time for clients to migrate — on their own respective schedules and time frames — from existing *deprecated* constructs to newer ones, rather than having every client change in lock step. Allowing clients time to move *asynchronously* to newer alternatives is often the only viable approach unless (1) the codebase is a closed system, (2) all of the relevant code is governed by a single authority, and (3) the change can be made mechanically.

Although not strictly required, the Standard explicitly encourages[1] conforming compilers to produce a diagnostic message in case a program refers to any **entity** to which the [[deprecated]] attribute pertains. For instance, most popular compilers emit a warning whenever a [[deprecated]] function or object is used:

```
                 void f();
[[deprecated]] void g();

                 int a;
[[deprecated]] int b;

void h()
{
    f();
    g();   // Warning: g is deprecated.
    a;
    b;     // Warning: b is deprecated.
}
```

---

[1] The C++ Standard characterizes what constitutes a well-formed program, but compiler vendors require a great deal of leeway to facilitate the needs of their users. In case any feature induces warnings, command-line options are typically available to disable those warnings (-Wno-deprecated in GCC), or methods are in place to suppress those warnings locally, e.g., **#pragma** GCC diagnostic ignored "-Wdeprecated".

The [[deprecated]] attribute can be used portably to decorate other entities: **class**, **struct**, **union**, type alias, variable, data member, function, enumeration, template specialization.[2]

A programmer can supply a **string literal** as an argument to the [[deprecated]] attribute — e.g., [[deprecated("message")]] — to inform human users regarding the reason for the deprecation:

```
[[deprecated("too slow, use algo1 instead")]] void algo0();
                                               void algo1();

void f()
{
    algo0();   // Warning: algo0 is deprecated; too slow, use algo1 instead.
    algo1();
}
```

An entity that is initially *declared* without [[deprecated]] can later be redeclared with the attribute and vice versa:

```
void f();
void g0() { f(); }   // OK, likely no warnings

[[deprecated]] void f();
void g1() { f(); }   // Warning: f is deprecated.

void f();
void g2() { f(); }   // Warning: f is deprecated still.
```

As shown in g2 in the example above, redeclaring an entity that was previously decorated with [[deprecated]] without the attribute leaves the entity still deprecated.

Use Cases

Discouraging use of an obsolete or unsafe entity

Decorating any entity with the [[deprecated]] attribute serves both to indicate a particular feature should not be used in the future and to actively encourage migration of existing uses to a better alternative. Obsolescence, lack of safety, and poor performance are common motivators for deprecation.

As an example of productive deprecation, consider the RandomGenerator class having a static nextRandom member function to generate random numbers:

---

[2]Applying [[deprecated]] to a specific enumerator or namespace, however, is guaranteed to be supported only since C++17; see **smith15a**.

```
struct RandomGenerator
{
    static int nextRandom();
        // Generate a random value between 0 and 32767 (inclusive).
};
```

Although such a simple random number generator can be useful, it might become unsuitable for heavy use because good pseudorandom number generation requires more state (and the overhead of synchronizing such state for a single **static** function can be a significant performance bottleneck), while good random number generation requires potentially high overhead access to external sources of entropy. The rand function, inherited from C and available in C++ through the <cstdlib> header, has many of the same issues as our RandomGenerator::nextRandom function, and similarly developers are guided to use the facilities provided in the <random> header since C++11.

One solution is to provide an alternative random number generator that maintains more state, allows users to decide where to store that state (the random number generator objects), and overall offers more flexibility for clients. The downside of such a change is that it comes with a functionally distinct API, requiring that users update their code to move away from the inferior solution:

```
class StatefulRandomGenerator
{
    // ... (internal state of a quality pseudorandom number generator)

public:
    int nextRandom();
        // Generate a quality random value between 0 and 32767, inclusive.
};
```

Any user of the original random number generator can migrate to the new facility with little effort, but that is not a completely trivial operation, and migration will take some time before the original feature is no longer in use. The empathic maintainers of RandomGenerator can decide to use the [[deprecated]] attribute to discourage continued use of RandomGenerator::nextRandom() instead of removing it completely:

```
struct RandomGenerator
{
    [[deprecated("Use StatefulRandomGenerator class instead.")]]
    static int nextRandom();
        // ...
};
```

By using [[deprecated]] as shown in the previous example, existing clients of RandomGenerator are informed that a superior alternative, BetterRandomGenerator, is available, yet they are granted time to migrate their code to the new solution rather than having their code broken by the removal of the old solution. When clients are notified of the deprecation (thanks to a compiler diagnostic), they can schedule time to rewrite their applications to consume the new interface.

Continuous refactoring is an essential responsibility of a development organization, and deciding when to go back and fix what's suboptimal instead of writing new code that will please users and contribute more immediately to the bottom line will forever be a source of tension. Allowing disparate development teams to address such improvements in their own respective time frames, perhaps subject to some reasonable overall deadline date, is a proven real-world practical way of ameliorating this tension.

Potential Pitfalls

Interaction with treating warnings as errors

In some code bases, compiler warnings are promoted to errors using compiler flags, such as -Werror for GCC and Clang or /WX for MSVC, to ensure that their builds are warning-clean. For such code bases, use of the [[deprecated]] attribute by their dependencies as part of the API might introduce unexpected compilation failures.

Having the compilation process completely stopped due to use of a deprecated entity defeats the purpose of the attribute because users of such an entity are given no time to adapt their code to use a newer alternative. On GCC and Clang, users can selectively demote deprecation errors back to warnings by using the -Wno-error=deprecated-declarations compiler flag. On MSVC, however, such demotion of warnings is not possible, and the available workarounds, such as entirely disabling the effects of the /WX flag or the deprecation diagnostics using the -wd4996 flag, are often unsuitable.

Furthermore, this interaction between [[deprecated]] and treating warnings as errors makes it impossible for owners of a low-level library to deprecate a function when releasing their code requires that they do not break the ability for *any* of their higher-level clients to compile; a single client using the to-be-deprecated function in a code base that treats warnings as errors prevents the release of the code that uses the [[deprecated]] attribute. With the frequent advice given in practice to aggressively treat warnings as errors, the use of [[deprecated]] might be completely unfeasible.

This page is intentionally blank.

The Digit Separator (')

A digit separator is a single-character token (') that can appear as part of a numeric literal without altering its value.

Description

A digit separator — i.e., an instance of the single-quote character (') — may be placed anywhere within a numeric literal to visually separate its digits without affecting its value:

```
int          i = -12'345;                      // same as -12345
unsigned int u = 1'000'000u;                   // same as 1000000u
long         j = 500'000L;                      // same as 500000L
long long    k = 9'223'372'036'854'775'807;    // same as 9223372036854775807
float        f = 3.14159'26535f;                // same as 3.1415926535f
double       d = 3.14159'26535'89793;           // same as 3.141592653589793
long double  e = 20'812.80745'23204;            // same as 20812.8074523204
int          hex = 0x8C'25'00'F9;               // same as 0x8C2500F9
int          oct = 044'73'26;                   // same as 0447326
int          bin = 0b1001'0110'1010'0111;       // same as 0b1001011010100111
```

Multiple digit separators within a single literal are allowed, but they cannot be contiguous, nor can they appear either before or after the *numeric* part, i.e., digit sequence, of the literal:

```
int e0 = 10''00;    // Error, consecutive digit separators
int e1 = -'1000;    // Error, before numeric part
int e2 = 1000'u;    // Error, after numeric part
int e3 = 0x'abc;    // Error, before numeric part
int e4 = 0'xdef;    // Error, way before numeric part
int e5 = 0'89;      // Error, nonoctal digits
int e6 = 0'67;      // OK, valid octal literal
```

Although the leading 0x and 0b prefixes for hexadecimal and binary literals, respectively, are not considered part of the *numeric* part of the literal, a leading 0 in an octal literal is. As a side note, remember that on some platforms an integer literal that is too large to fit in a **long long int** but that does fit in an **unsigned long long int** might generate a warning or error[1]:

```
unsigned long long big1 = 9'223'372'036'854'775'808;  // 2^63
    // warning: integer constant is so large that it is an
    // unsigned long long big1 = 9'223'372'036'854'775'808;
    //                          ^~~~~~~~~~~~~~~~~~~~~~~~~~~~
```

---

[1] Tested on GCC 7.4.0 (c. 2018).

Such warnings can typically be suppressed by adding a `ull` suffix to the literal:

```
unsigned long long big2 = 9'223'372'036'854'775'808ull;  // OK
```

Warnings like the one above, however, are not typical when the implied precision of a floating-point literal exceeds what can be represented:

```
float reallyPrecise = 3.141'592'653'589'793'238'462'643'383'279'502'884;  // OK
    // Everything after 3.141'592'6 is typically ignored silently.
```

See *Appendix — Silent loss of precision in floating-point literals* on page 154.

Use Cases

Grouping digits together in large constants

When embedding large constants in source code, consistently placing digit separators, e.g., every thousand, might improve readability, as illustrated in Table 1.

Table 1: Use of digit separators to improve readability

Without Digit Separator	With Digit Separators
10000	10'000
100000	100'000
1000000	1'000'000
1000000000	1'000'000'000
18446744073709551615ULL	18'446'744'073'709'551'615ULL
1000000.123456	1'000'000.123'456
3.141592653589793238462L	3.141'592'653'589'793'238'462L

Use of digit separators is especially useful with binary literals to group bits in octets (**bytes**) or quartets (**nibbles**), as shown in Table 2. In addition, using a binary literal with digits grouped in triplets instead of an octal literal to represent UNIX file permissions might improve code readability, e.g., `0b111'101'101` instead of `0755`.

Table 2: Use of digit separators in binary data

Without Digit Separator	With Digit Separators
0b1100110011001100	0b1100'1100'1100'1100
0b0110011101011011	0b0110'0111'0101'1011
0b1100110010101010	0b11001100'10101010

See Also

- "Binary Literals" (§1.2, p. 142) describes how binary literals represent a binary constant for which digit separators are commonly used to group bits in octets (**bytes**) or quartets (**nibbles**).

Further Reading

- A thorough discussion of the IEEE754 standard for binary floating-point arithmetic can be found in **kahan97**.

- The IEEE Standard for floating-point arithmetic itself is delineated in **ieee19**.

Appendix

Silent loss of precision in floating-point literals

Just because we can keep track of precision in floating-point literals doesn't mean that the compiler can. As an aside, it is worth pointing out that the binary representation of floating-point types is not mandated by the Standard nor are the precise minimums on the ranges and precisions they must support. Although the C++ Standard says little that is normative, the macros in `<cfloat>` are defined by reference to the C Standard.[2,3]

There are, however, normal and customary minimums that one can typically rely upon in practice. On conforming compilers that employ the IEEE 754 floating-point standard representation[4] as most do, a **float** can typically represent up to 7 significant decimal digits accurately, while a **double** typically has nearly 15 decimal digits of precision. For any given program, **long double** is required to hold whatever a **double** can hold but is typically larger, e.g., 10, 12, or 16 bytes, and typically adds at least 5 decimal digits of precision, i.e., supports a total of at least 20 decimal digits. A notable exception is Microsoft Visual C++ where **long double** is a distinct type whose representation is identical to **double**.[5] A table summarizing typical precisions for various IEEE-conforming floating-point types is presented for convenient reference in Table 3. The actual bounds on a given platform can be found using the standard `std::numeric_limits` class template found in `<limits>`.

---

[2]**iso20b**, section 6.8.2, "Fundamental types [basic.fundamental]," pp. 73–75; section 17.3.5.2, "numeric_limits members [numeric.limits.members]," pp. 513–516; and section 17.3.7, "Header <cfloat> synopsis [cfloat.syn]," p. 519

[3]**iso18b**, section 7.7, "Characteristics of floating types <float.h>," p. 157

[4]**ieee19**

[5]**microsoftc**

Table 3: Available precisions for various IEEE-754 floating-point types

Name	Common Name	Significant Bits[a]	Decimal Digits	Exponent Bits	Dynamic Range
binary16	Half precision	11	3.31	5	$\sim 6.5 \times 10^5$
binary32	Single precision	24	7.22	8	$\sim 3.4 \times 10^{38}$
binary64	Double precision	53	15.95	11	$\sim 10^{308}$
binary80	Extended precision	69	20.77	11	$\sim 10^{308}$
binary128	Quadruple precision	113	34.02	15	$\sim 10^{4932}$

[a] Note that the most significant bit of the **mantissa** is always a 1 for normalized numbers and 0 for denormalized ones and, hence, is not stored explicitly. Thus one additional bit remains to represent the sign of the overall floating-point value; the sign of the exponent is encoded using **excess-n** notation.

Determining the minimum number of decimal digits needed to accurately approximate a transcendental value, such as π, for a given type on a given platform can be tricky and require some binary-search-like detective work, which is likely why overshooting the precision without warning is the default on most platforms. One way to establish that *all* of the decimal digits in a given floating-point literal are relevant for a given floating-point type is to compare that literal and a similar one with its least significant decimal digit removed[6]:

```cpp
static_assert(3.1415926535f != 3.141592653f, "too precise for float");
    // This assert will fire on a typical platform.

static_assert(3.141592653f != 3.14159265f, "too precise for float");
    // This assert too will fire on a typical platform.

static_assert(3.14159265f != 3.1415926f, "too precise for float");
    // This assert will not fire on a typical platform.

static_assert(3.1415926f != 3.141592f, "too precise for float");
    // This assert too will not fire on a typical platform.
```

If the values are *not* the same, then that floating-point type can make use of the precision suggested by the original literal; if they *are* the same, however, then it is likely that the available precision has been exceeded. Iterative use of this technique by developers can help them to empirically narrow down the maximal number of decimal digits a particular platform

---

[6]Note that affixing the f (*literal suffix*) to a floating-point literal is equivalent to applying a `static_cast<float>` to the (unsuffixed) literal:

```cpp
static_assert(3.14'159'265'358f == static_cast<float>(3.14'159'265'358),"");
```

will support for a particular floating-point type and value. Note, however, that because the compiler is not required to use the floating-point arithmetic of the target platform *during compilation*, this approach might not be applicable for a cross-compilation scenario.

One final useful tidbit pertains to the safe, i.e., lossless, conversion between binary and decimal floating-point representations; note that "Single" in the extract below corresponds to a single-precision IEEE-754-conforming (32-bit) **float**[7]:

> If a decimal string with at most 6 sig. dec. is converted to Single and then converted back to the same number of sig. dec., then the final string should match the original. Also, ...
>
> If a Single Precision floating-point number is converted to a decimal string with at least 9 sig. dec. and then converted back to Single, then the final number must match the original.

The ranges corresponding to 6–9 for a single-precision, i.e., 32-bit, **float** described in the extract above, when applied to a double-precision, i.e., 64-bit, **double** and a quad-precision, i.e., 128-bit, **long double**, are 15–17 and 33–36, respectively.

---

[7]**kahan97**, section "Representable Numbers," p. 4

Templated Variable Declarations/Definitions

Traditional **template** syntax is extended to define, in namespace or class (but not function) scope, a family of like-named variables that can be instantiated explicitly.

Description

By beginning a variable declaration with the familiar **template-head** syntax (e.g., **template** <**typename** T>), we can create a *variable template*, which defines a family of variables having the same name (e.g., exampleOf):

```
template <typename T> T exampleOf;  // variable template defined at file scope
```

Like any other kind of template, a variable template can be instantiated explicitly by providing an appropriate number of type or non-type arguments:

```
#include <iostream>  // std::cout

void initializeExampleValues()
{
    exampleOf<int>   = -1;
    exampleOf<char>  = 'a';
    exampleOf<float> = 12.3f;
}

void printExampleValues()
{
    initializeExampleValues();
    std::cout << "int = "   << exampleOf<int>   << "; "
              << "char = "  << exampleOf<char>  << "; "
              << "float = " << exampleOf<float> << ';';

    // outputs "int = -1; char = a; float = 12.3;"
}
```

In the example above, the type of each instantiated variable is the same as its template parameter, but this matching is not required. For example, the type might be the same for all instantiated variables or derived from its parameters, such as by adding **const** qualification:

```
#include <type_traits>  // std::is_floating_point
#include <cassert>      // standard C assert macro

template <typename T>
const bool sane_for_pi = std::is_floating_point<T>::value;  // same type

template <typename T> const T pi(3.1415926535897932385);    // distinct types

void testPi()
{
    assert(!sane_for_pi<bool>);
    assert(!sane_for_pi<int>);

    assert( sane_for_pi<float>);
    assert( sane_for_pi<double>);
    assert( sane_for_pi<long double>);

    const float       pi_as_float       = 3.1415927;
    const double      pi_as_double       = 3.141592653589793;
    const long double pi_as_long_double = 3.1415926535897932385;

    assert(pi<float>       == pi_as_float);
    assert(pi<double>      == pi_as_double);
    assert(pi<long double> == pi_as_long_double);
}
```

Variable templates may be declared at namespace-scope or as **static** members of a **class**, **struct**, or **union** but are not permitted as non**static** members nor at all in function scope:

```
template <typename T> T vt1;              // OK, external linkage
template <typename T> static T vt2;       // OK, internal linkage

namespace N
{
    template <typename T> T vt3;          // OK, external linkage
    template <typename T> static T vt4;   // OK, internal linkage
}

struct S
{
    template <typename T> T vt5;          // Error, not static
    template <typename T> static T vt6;   // OK, external linkage
};
```

```
void f3()  // Variable templates cannot be defined in functions.
{
    template <typename T> T vt7;          // Error
    template <typename T> static T vt8;   // Error

    vt1<bool> = true;                     // OK
    N::vt3<bool> = true;
    N::vt4<bool> = true;
    S::vt6<bool> = true;
}
```

Like other templates, variable templates may be defined with multiple parameters consisting of arbitrary combinations of type and non-type parameters, including a **parameter pack** in the last position:

```
namespace N
{
    template <typename V, int I, int J> V factor;  // namespace scope
}
```

Variable templates can even be defined recursively, but see *Potential Pitfalls — Recursive variable template initializations require **const** or **constexpr*** on page 163:

```
namespace {
template <int N>
const int sum = N + sum<N - 1>;    // recursive general template

template <> const int sum<0> = 0;  // base case specialization
}  // close unnamed namespace

void f()
{
    std::cout << sum<4> << '\n';  // prints 10
    std::cout << sum<5> << '\n';  // prints 15
    std::cout << sum<6> << '\n';  // prints 21
}
```

Note that while variable templates do not add new functionality, they significantly reduce the boilerplate associated with achieving the same goals without them. For example, compare the definition of **pi** on the previous page with the pre-C++14 code:

```
// C++03 (obsolete)
#include <cassert>  // standard C assert macro

template <typename T>
struct Pi {
    static const T value;
};

template <typename T>
const T Pi<T>::value(3.1415926535897932385);  // separate definition

void testCpp03Pi()
{
    const float       piAsFloat      = 3.1415927;
    const double      piAsDouble     = 3.141592653589793;
    const long double piAsLongDouble = 3.1415926535897932385;

    // additional boilerplate on use (::value)
    assert(Pi<float>::value       == piAsFloat);
    assert(Pi<double>::value      == piAsDouble);
    assert(Pi<long double>::value == piAsLongDouble);
}
```

Use Cases

Parameterized constants

A common effective use of variable templates is in the definition of type-parameterized constants. As discussed in *Description* on page 157, the mathematical constant π serves as our example. Here we want to initialize the constant as part of the variable template; the literal chosen is the shortest decimal string to do so accurately for an 80-bit **long double**:

```
template <typename T>
constexpr T pi(3.1415926535897932385);
    // smallest digit sequence to accurately represent pi as a long double
```

For portability, a floating-point literal value of π that provides sufficient precision for the longest **long double** on any relevant platform — e.g., 34 decimal digits for 128 bits of precision: 3.141'592'653'589'793'238'462'643'383'279'503 — might be used; see Section 1.2. "Digit Separators" on page 152.

Notice that we have elected to use **constexpr** variables in place of **const** to guarantee that the floating-point **pi** is a compile-time constant that will be usable as part of a constant expression.

With the definition in the previous example, we can provide a `toRadians` function template that performs at maximum runtime efficiency by avoiding needless type conversions during the computation:

```
template <typename T>
constexpr T toRadians(T degrees)
{
    return degrees * (pi<T> / T(180));
}
```

Reducing verbosity of type traits

A **type trait** is an empty type carrying compile-time information about one or more aspects of another type. The way in which type traits have been specified historically has been to define a class template having the trait name and a public **static** data member conventionally called **value**, which is initialized in the primary template to **false**. Then, for each type that wants to advertise that it has this trait, the header defining the trait is included, and the trait is specialized for that type, initializing **value** to **true**. We can achieve precisely this same usage pattern replacing a trait **struct** with a variable template whose name represents the type trait and whose type of variable itself is always **bool**. Preferring variable templates in this use case decreases the amount of **boilerplate code**, both at the point of definition and at the call site.[1]

Consider, for example, a Boolean trait designating whether a particular type T can be serialized to JSON:

```
// isSerializableToJson.h:

template <typename T>
constexpr bool isSerializableToJson = false;
```

The header above contains the general variable template trait that, by default, concludes that a given type is not serializable to JSON. Next we consider the streaming utility itself:

---

[1]As of C++17, the Standard Library provides a more convenient way of inspecting the result of a type trait, by introducing variable templates named the same way as the corresponding traits but with an additional _v suffix:

```
// C++11/14
bool dc1 = std::is_default_constructible<T>::value;
```

```
// C++17
bool dc2 = std::is_default_constructible_v<T>;
```

This delay is a consequence of the train release model of the Standard: Thoughtful application of the new feature throughout the vast Standard Library required significant effort that could not be completed before the next release date for the Standard and thus was delayed until C++17.

```
// serializeToJson.h:
#include <isSerializableToJson.h>  // general trait variable template

template <typename T>
JsonObject serializeToJson(const T& object)  // serialization function template
{
    static_assert(isSerializableToJson<T>,
                  "T must support serialization to JSON.");

    // ...

    return { /*...*/ };
}
```

Notice that we have used the C++11 **static_assert** feature to ensure that any type used to instantiate this function will have specialized the general variable template associated with the specific type to be **true**; see the next code snippet.

Now imagine that we have a type, CompanyData, that we would like to advertise at compile time as being serializable to JSON. Like other templates, variable templates can be specialized explicitly:

```
// companyData.h:
#include <isSerializableToJson.h>  // general trait variable template

struct CompanyData { /*...*/ };    // type to be JSON serialized

template <>
constexpr bool isSerializableToJson<CompanyData> = true;
    // Let anyone who needs to know that this type is JSON serializable.
```

Finally, our **client** function incorporates all of the above and attempts to serialize both a CompanyData object and an std::map<int, char>:

```
// client.h:
#include <isSerializableToJson.h>  // general trait template
#include <companyData.h>           // JSON serializable type
#include <serializeToJson.h>       // serialization function
#include <map>                     // std::map (not JSON serializable)
```

```
void client()
{
    JsonObject jsonObj0 = serializeToJson(CompanyData());         // OK
    JsonObject jsonObj1 = serializeToJson(std::map<int, char>()); // Error
}
```

In the `client()` function above, `CompanyData` works fine, but because the variable template `isSerializableToJson` was never specialized to be **true** for type `std::map<int, char>`, the client header will, as desired, fail to compile.

Potential Pitfalls

Recursive variable template initializations require `const` or `constexpr`

Instantiating variable templates that are defined recursively might have a subtle issue that could produce different results[2] despite having no undefined behavior:

```
#include <iostream>  // std::cout

template <int N>
int fib = fib<N - 1> + fib<N - 2>;

template <> int fib<2> = 1;
template <> int fib<1> = 1;

int main()
{
    std::cout << fib<4> << '\n';  // 3 expected
    std::cout << fib<5> << '\n';  // 5 expected
    std::cout << fib<6> << '\n';  // 8 expected

    return 0;
}
```

The root cause of this instability is that the relative order of the initialization of the recursively generated variable template instantiations is not guaranteed. Therefore, a similar issue might have occurred in C++03 using **static** members of a **struct**:

---

[2]For example, GCC 4.7.0 (c. 2017) produces the expected results, whereas Clang 12.0.1 (c. 2021) produces 1, 3, and 4, respectively.

```cpp
#include <iostream>  // std::cout

template <int N> struct Fib
{
    static int value;                             // BAD IDEA: not const
};

template <> struct Fib<2> { static int value; };  // BAD IDEA: not const
template <> struct Fib<1> { static int value; };  // BAD IDEA: not const

template <int N> int Fib<N>::value = Fib<N - 1>::value + Fib<N - 2>::value;
int Fib<2>::value = 1;
int Fib<1>::value = 1;

int main()
{
    std::cout << Fib<4>::value << '\n';  // 3 expected
    std::cout << Fib<5>::value << '\n';  // 5 expected
    std::cout << Fib<6>::value << '\n';  // 8 expected

    return 0;
}
```

However, using **enum**s avoids this issue since enumerators are always compile-time constants:

```cpp
#include <iostream>  // std::cout

template <int N> struct Fib
{
    enum { value = Fib<N - 1>::value + Fib<N - 2>::value };  // OK, const
};

template <> struct Fib<2> { enum { value = 1 }; };           // OK, const
template <> struct Fib<1> { enum { value = 1 }; };           // OK, const

int main()
{
    std::cout << Fib<4>::value << '\n';  // 3 guaranteed
    std::cout << Fib<5>::value << '\n';  // 5 guaranteed
    std::cout << Fib<6>::value << '\n';  // 8 guaranteed

    return 0;
}
```

For integral variable templates, this issue can be resolved simply by adding a **const** qualifier because the C++ Standard requires that any integral variable declared as **const** and initialized with a compile-time constant is itself to be treated as a compile-time constant within the translation unit:

```
#include <iostream>  // std::cout

template <int N>
const int fib = fib<N - 1> + fib<N - 2>;  // OK, compile-time const

template <> const int fib<2> = 1;       // OK, compile-time const
template <> const int fib<1> = 1;       // OK, compile-time const

int main()
{
    std::cout << fib<4> << '\n';  // guaranteed to print out 3
    std::cout << fib<5> << '\n';  // guaranteed to print out 5
    std::cout << fib<6> << '\n';  // guaranteed to print out 8

    return 0;
}
```

Note that replacing each of the three **const** keywords with **constexpr** in the example above also achieves the desired goal, does not consume memory in the **static data space**, and would also be applicable to nonintegral constants.

Annoyances

Variable templates do not support template template parameters

Although a class or function template can accept a **template template parameter**, no equivalent construct is available for variable templates[3]:

```
template <typename T> T vt(5);

template <template <typename> class>
struct S { };

S<vt> s1;  // Error
```

Providing a wrapper **struct** around a variable template might therefore be necessary in case the variable template needs to be passed to an interface accepting a template template parameter:

```
template <typename T>
struct Vt { static constexpr T value = vt<T>; };

S<Vt> s2;  // OK
```

---

[3]A method to increase consistency between variable templates and class templates when used as template template parameters has been proposed for C++23; see **pusz20a**.

See Also

- "**constexpr** Variables" (§2.1, p. 302) discusses an alternative to **const** template variables that can reduce unnecessary consumption of the **static** data space.

Chapter 2

Conditionally Safe Features

With great power comes great responsibility. Several modern C++ language features afford immense opportunities for expressiveness, performance, and maintainability; however, they come at a cost. For these features to add value without introducing unacceptable risk, they require a comprehensive understanding of their behavior, effective uses, and consequential pitfalls. This chapter introduces those C++11 and C++14 features that can yield significant, sometimes prodigious, benefits, yet are dangerous when used naively by the uninitiated; the sometimes-latent defects that result might not be discovered until much later in the software development life cycle. As these features offer a moderately high degree of systemic risk when introduced widely into a predominantly C++03 codebase, some form of organized training is an essential prerequisite. An organization's leadership — to feel reasonably comfortable supporting its experienced engineers' use of these features — is well advised to ensure each engineer has been suitably trained in their respective behaviors, effective use cases, and known pitfalls.

Conditionally safe features are characterized by being of moderate to high risk but with rewards that could justify the education and training costs needed to effectively mitigate those risks. Recall from "A *Conditionally Safe* Feature" in Chapter 0 that the default member initializers feature (p. 318) was chosen as representative of *conditionally safe* features. This feature is of moderately low complexity and, though not immune to misuse, addresses a need that often occurs in practice. At the high end of the complexity spectrum, we find the variadic templates feature (p. 873). Though this feature is not especially error prone, the effort needed to master its effective use is substantial for implementors and maintainers alike, yet it offers a degree of power and flexibility that is simply unavailable in C++03. Of moderately high complexity is the flagship feature of modern C++, *rvalue* references (p. 710). This feature fairly demands a substantial training investment, yet its ubiquitous applicability and widespread use typically justify the up-front costs. Although the features presented in this chapter differ widely in their complexities, risks, and general applicability, all provide a plausible value proposition and thus are considered *conditionally safe.*

In short, widespread adoption of *conditionally safe* features offers a sensible risk–reward ratio. All of these features, to be used safely, require some amount of training, hence this book. An organization considering incorporating *conditionally safe* features into a predominantly C++03 codebase would be well advised to ensure its engineers are fully apprised of the behaviors, effective uses, and known pitfalls of these features. Even if you're familiar with the features of modern C++, you will be rewarded by a thorough reading of any section corresponding to a *conditionally safe* feature you might want to employ.

The alignas Specifier

The keyword **alignas** can be used in the declaration of a **class type**, a **data member**, an enumeration, or a variable to strengthen its **alignment**.

Description

Each object type in C++ has an **alignment requirement** that restricts the addresses at which an object of that type is permitted to reside within the virtual-memory-address space. The alignment requirement is imposed by the object type on all objects of that type. The **alignas** specifier provides a means of specifying a stricter alignment requirement than dictated by the type itself for a particular variable of the type or an individual data member of a **user-defined type (UDT)**. The **alignas** specifier can also be applied to a UDT itself, but see *Potential Pitfalls — Applying **alignas** to a* type *might be misleading* on page 177.

Supported alignments

An alignment value is an integral of type std::size_t that represents the number of bytes between the addresses at which a given object may be allocated. In practice, the alignment value will always evenly divide the numerical value of the address of any object of that type. All alignment values in C++ are non-negative powers of two and are divided into two categories depending on whether they are larger than the alignment requirement of the std::max_align_t type. The std::max_align_t type's alignment requirement is at least as strict as that of every **scalar type**. An alignment value of less than or equal to the alignment requirement of std::max_align_t is a **fundamental alignment**; otherwise, it is an **extended alignment**. The std::max_align_t type is typically an alias to the largest scalar type, which is **long double** on most platforms, and its alignment requirement is usually 8 or 16.

Fundamental alignments are required to be supported in *all* contexts, i.e., for variables with automatic, static, and dynamic storage durations as well as for nonstatic data members of a class and for function arguments. While all fundamental and pointer types have fundamental alignments, their specific values are **implementation defined** and might differ between platforms. For example, the alignment requirement of type **long** might be 4 on MSVC and 8 on GCC.

In contrast, whether *any* extended alignment is supported at all and, if so, in which contexts, is implementation defined.[1] For example, the strictest supported extended alignment for a variable with static storage duration might be as large as 2^{28} or 2^{29} or as small as 2^{13}.

Since many aspects pertaining to the alignment requirements are implementation defined, we will use a specific platform to illustrate the behavior of **alignas** throughout this feature's section. Accordingly, the examples below show the behavior observed for the Clang compiler targeting desktop x86-64 Linux.

Strengthening the alignment of a particular object

In its most basic form, the **alignas** specifier strengthens the alignment requirement of a particular object. The desired alignment requirement is an **integral constant expression** provided as an argument to **alignas**:

```cpp
alignas(8) int i;        // OK, i is aligned on an 8-byte address boundary.
int j alignas(8), k;     // OK, j is 8 byte aligned; alignment of k is unchanged.
```

If more than one alignment pertains to a given object, the strictest alignment value is applied:

```cpp
alignas(4) alignas(8) alignas(2) char m;    // OK, m is 8-byte aligned.
alignas(8) int n alignas(16);               // OK, n is 16-byte aligned.
```

For a program to be **well formed**, a specified alignment value must satisfy three requirements.

1. Be either zero or a non-negative integral power of two of type std::size_t (0, 1, 2, 4, 8, 16...)

2. Be larger or equal to what the alignment requirement would be without the **alignas** specifier

3. Be supported on the platform in the context in which the entity appears

---

[1]Implementations might warn when the alignment of a global object exceeds some maximal hardware threshold, such as the size of a physical memory page, e.g., 4096 or 8192. For automatic variables defined on the program stack, making alignment more restrictive than what would naturally be employed is seldom desired because at most one thread is able to access proximately located variables there unless explicitly passed in via address to separate threads; see *Use Cases — Avoiding false sharing among distinct objects in a multithreaded program* on page 174. Note that, in the case of i0 in the **alignas**(32) line in the first code snippet on page 170, a conforming platform that did not support an extended alignment of 32 would be required to report an error at compile time.

Additionally, if the specified alignment value is zero, the **alignas** specifier is ignored:

```
// static variables declared at namespace scope
alignas(32) int i0; // OK, 32-byte aligned (extended alignment)
alignas(16) int i1; // OK, 16-byte aligned (strictest fundamental alignment)
alignas(8)  int i2; // OK,  8-byte aligned (fundamental alignment)
alignas(7)  int i3; // Error, not a power of two
alignas(4)  int i4; // OK, no change to alignment requirement
alignas(2)  int i5; // Error, less than alignment would be without alignas
alignas(0)  int i6; // OK, alignas specifier ignored

alignas(1024 * 16) int i7;
    // OK, might warn on other platforms, e.g., exceeds physical page size

alignas(1 << 30) int i8;
    // Error, exceeds maximum supported extended alignment

alignas(8) char buf[128]; // OK, 8-byte-aligned, 128-byte character buffer

void f()
{
  // automatic variables declared at function scope
  alignas(4)  double e0; // Error, less than alignment would be without alignas
  alignas(8)  double e1; // OK, no change to 8-byte alignment requirement
  alignas(16) double e2; // OK, 16-byte aligned (fundamental alignment)
  alignas(32) double e3; // OK, 32-byte aligned (extended alignment)
}
```

Strengthening the alignment of individual data members

Within a user-defined type (**class**, **struct**, or **union**), using the **alignas** keyword to specify the alignments of individual data members is possible:

```
struct T2
{
    alignas(8)  char   x; // size 1; alignment 8
    alignas(16) int    y; // size 4; alignment 16
    alignas(64) double z; // size 8; alignment 64
}; // size 128; alignment 64
```

The effect here is the same as if we had added the padding explicitly and then set the alignment of the structure overall:

```
struct alignas(64) T3
{
    char   x;      // size 1; alignment 8
    char   a[15];  // padding
```

```
    int    y;       // size 4; alignment 16
    char   b[44];   // padding
    double z;       // size 8; alignment 64
    char   c[56];   // padding (optional)
}; // size 128; alignment 64
```

Again, if more than one alignment specifier pertains to a given data member, the strictest applicable alignment value is applied:

```
struct T4
{
    alignas(2) char
        c1 alignas(1),  // size 1; alignment 2
        c2 alignas(2),  // size 1; alignment 2
        c4 alignas(4);  // size 1; alignment 4
};                      // size 8; alignment 4
```

Strengthening the alignment of a user-defined type

The **alignas** specifier can also be used to specify alignment for UDTs, such as a **class**, **struct**, **union**, or **enum**. When specifying the alignment of a UDT, the **alignas** keyword is placed *after* the type specifier (e.g., **class**) and just before the name of the type (e.g., C):

```
class  alignas( 2) C { };  // OK, aligned on a  2-byte boundary; size = 2
struct alignas( 4) S { };  // OK, aligned on a  4-byte boundary; size = 4
union  alignas( 8) U { };  // OK, aligned on an 8-byte boundary; size = 8
enum   alignas(16) E { };  // OK, aligned on a 16-byte boundary; size = 4
```

Notice that, for each of **class**, **struct**, and **union** in the example above, the **sizeof** objects of that type increased to match the alignment; in the case of the **enum**, however, the size remains that of the default **underlying type**, e.g., 4 bytes, on the current platform. When **alignas** is applied to an enumeration E, the Standard does not indicate whether padding bytes are added to E's object representation, affecting the result of **sizeof**(E).[2]

Again, specifying an alignment that is less than what would be without the **alignas** specifier is ill formed:

```
struct alignas(2) T0 { int i; };
    // Error, alignment of T0 (2) is less than that of int (4).
struct alignas(1) T1 { C c; };
    // Error, alignment of T1 (1) is less than that of C (2).
```

---

[2]The implementation variance resulting from this lack of clarity in the Standard was captured in CWG issue 2354 (**miller17**). The outcome of the core issue was to completely remove permission for **alignas** to be applied to enumerations; see **iso18a**. Therefore, conforming implementations will eventually stop accepting the **alignas** specifier on enumerations in the future.

Matching the alignment of another type

The **alignas** specifier also accepts a type identifier as an argument. In its alternate form, **alignas**(T) is strictly equivalent to **alignas**(**alignof**(T)) (see Section 2.1.“**alignof**” on page 184):

```
alignas(int) char c;   // equivalent to alignas(alignof(int)) char c;
```

Use Cases

Creating a sufficiently aligned object buffer

One of the motivating use cases for introducing the **alignas** feature was creating static capacity, dynamic size containers that do not use dynamic allocations. To avoid the overhead of initializing the unused elements, such a generic container needs to have a character buffer data member and use placement **new** to construct the elements as needed. This buffer needs to be of sufficient size to store the elements, which one can easily compute using CAPACITY * **sizeof**(TYPE). In addition, however, ensuring that the buffer is sufficiently aligned to store elements of the supplied TYPE is important. With **alignas**, ensuring this requirement is straightforward:

```
#include <cassert>   // standard C assert macro
#include <new>       // placement new


template <typename TYPE, std::size_t CAPACITY>
class FixedVector {

    alignas(TYPE) char d_buffer[CAPACITY * sizeof(TYPE)];
        // raw memory buffer of proper size and alignment for TYPE elements

    std::size_t        d_size;
        // current size of the vector

    TYPE *rawElementPtr(std::size_t index)
        // Return the pointer to the element with the specified index.
    {
        return reinterpret_cast<TYPE*>(d_buffer) + index;
    }

public:
    // ...

    void resize(std::size_t size)
    {
        assert(size <= CAPACITY);
```

```
        while (d_size < size) new (rawElementPtr(d_size++)) TYPE;
        while (d_size > size) rawElementPtr(--d_size)->~TYPE();
    }

    // ...

};
```

Without the use of **alignas**, d_buffer (in the code snippet above), which is an array of characters, would itself have an alignment requirement of 1. The compiler would therefore be free to place it on any address boundary, which is problematic for any TYPE argument with an alignment requirement stricter than 1.

Ensuring proper alignment for architecture-specific instructions

Architecture-specific instructions or compiler intrinsics might require the data they act on to have a specific alignment. One example of such intrinsics is the Streaming SIMD Extensions (SSE)[3] instruction set available on the x86 architecture. SSE instructions operate on groups of four 32-bit single-precision floating-point numbers at a time, which are required to be 16-byte aligned.[4] The **alignas** specifier can be used to create a type satisfying this requirement:

```
struct SSEVector
{
    alignas(16) float d_data[4];
};
```

Each object of the SSEVector type above is guaranteed always to be aligned to a 16-byte boundary and can therefore be safely and conveniently used with SSE intrinsics:

```
#include <cassert>    // standard C assert macro
#include <xmmintrin.h> // __m128 and _mm_XXX functions

void f()
{
    const SSEVector v0 = {0.0f, 1.0f, 2.0f, 3.0f};
    const SSEVector v1 = {10.0f, 10.0f, 10.0f, 10.0f};

    __m128 sseV0 = _mm_load_ps(v0.d_data);
    __m128 sseV1 = _mm_load_ps(v1.d_data);
        // _mm_load_ps requires the given float array to be 16-byte aligned.
        // The data is loaded into a dedicated 128-bit CPU register.

    __m128 sseResult = _mm_add_ps(sseV0, sseV1);
        // sum two 128-bit registers; typically generates an addps instruction
```

---

[3]**inteliig**, "Technologies: SSE"

[4]"Data must be 16-byte aligned when loading to and storing from the 128-bit XMM registers used by SSE/SSE2/SSE3/SSSE3": see **intel16**, section 4.4.4, "Data Alignment for 128-Bit Data," pp. 4-19–4-20.

```
SSEVector vResult;
_mm_store_ps(vResult.d_data, sseResult);
    // Store the result of the sum back into a float array.

assert(vResult.d_data[0] == 10.0f);
assert(vResult.d_data[1] == 11.0f);
assert(vResult.d_data[2] == 12.0f);
assert(vResult.d_data[3] == 13.0f);
}
```

Avoiding false sharing among distinct objects in a multithreaded program

In the context of an application where multithreading has been employed to improve performance, seeing a previously single-threaded workflow become even less performant after a parallelization attempt can be surprising and disheartening. One possible insidious cause of such disappointing results comes from **false sharing**, a situation in which multiple threads unwittingly harm each other's performance while writing to logically independent variables that happen to reside on the same **cache line**; see *Appendix — Cache lines; L1, L2, and L3 cache; pages; and virtual memory* on page 181.

As a simple illustration of the potential performance degradation resulting from **false sharing**, consider a function that spawns separate threads to repeatedly increment (concurrently) logically distinct variables that happen to reside in close proximity on the program stack:

```
#include <thread>  // std::thread

void incrementJob(int* p);
    // Repeatedly increment *p a large, fixed number of times.

void f()
{
    int i0 = 0;  // Here, i0 and i1 likely share the same cache line,
    int i1 = 0;  // i.e., byte-aligned memory block on the program stack.

    std::thread t0(&incrementJob, &i0);
    std::thread t1(&incrementJob, &i1);
        // Spawn two parallel jobs incrementing the respective variables.

    t0.join();
    t1.join();
        // Wait for both jobs to be completed.
}
```

In the simplistic example above, the proximity in memory between i0 and i1 can result in their belonging to the same **cache line**, thus leading to **false sharing**. By using **alignas** to strengthen the alignment requirement of both integers to the cache line size, we ensure that the two variables reside on distinct cache lines:

```
// ...

enum { k_CACHE_LINE_SIZE = 64 };  // A cache line on this platform is 64 bytes.

void f()
{
    alignas(k_CACHE_LINE_SIZE) int i0 = 0; // i1 and i2 are on separate
    alignas(k_CACHE_LINE_SIZE) int i1 = 0; // cache lines.

    // ...
}
```

As an empirical demonstration of the effects of false sharing, a benchmark program repeatedly calling f completed its execution seven times faster on average when compared to the same program without use of **alignas**.[5] Note that because supported extended alignments are implementation defined, using **alignas** is not a strictly portable solution. Opting for less elegant and more wasteful padding approach instead of **alignas** might be preferrable for portability.

Avoiding false sharing within a single-thread-aware object

A real-world scenario where the need for preventing false sharing is fundamental occurs in the implementation of high-performance concurrent data structures. As an example, a thread-safe ring buffer might make use of **alignas** to ensure that the indices of the head and tail of the buffer are aligned at the start of a cache line (typically 64, 128, or 256 bytes),[6] thereby preventing them from occupying the same one.

```
#include <atomic>   // std::atomic
class ThreadSafeRingBuffer
{
    alignas(k_CACHE_LINE_SIZE) std::atomic<std::size_t> d_head;
    alignas(k_CACHE_LINE_SIZE) std::atomic<std::size_t> d_tail;

    // ...
};
```

Not aligning d_head and d_tail in the code snippet above to the CPU cache size might result in poor performance of the ThreadSafeRingBuffer because CPU cores that need to access only one of the variables will inadvertently load the other one as well, triggering expensive hardware-level coherency mechanisms between the cores' caches. On the other hand,

---

[5]The benchmark program was compiled using Clang 11.0.0 (c. 2020) using -Ofast, -march=native, and -std=c++11. The program was then executed on a machine running Windows 10 x64, equipped with an Intel Core i7-9700k CPU (8 cores, 64-byte cache line size). Over the course of multiple runs, the version of the benchmark without **alignas** took an average of 18.5967ms to complete, while the version with **alignas** took an average of 2.45333ms to complete.

[6]In C++17, one can portably retrieve the minimum offset between two objects to avoid false sharing through the std::hardware_destructive_interference_size constant defined in the <new> header.

specifying such substantially stricter alignment on consecutive data members necessarily increases the size of the object; see *Potential Pitfalls — Overlooking alternative approaches to avoid false sharing* on page 178.

Potential Pitfalls

Underspecifying alignment is not universally reported

The Standard is clear when it comes to underspecifying alignment[7]:

> The combined effect of all *alignment-specifiers* in a declaration shall not specify an alignment that is less strict than the alignment that would be required for the entity being declared if all *alignment-specifiers* were omitted (including those in other declarations).

The compiler is required to honor the specified value if it is a **fundamental alignment**,[8] so imagining how underspecifying alignment would lead to anything other than an ill-formed program is difficult:

```cpp
alignas(4) void* p;               // Error, alignas(4) is below minimum, 8.

struct alignas(2) S { int x; };   // Error, alignas(2) is below minimum, 4.

struct alignas(2) T { };
struct alignas(1) U { T e; };     // Error, alignas(1) is below minimum, 2.
```

Each of the three errors above are reported by Clang. MSVC and ICC issue a warning, whereas GCC provides no diagnostic at all, even in the most pedantic warning mode. Thus, one could write a program, involving statements like those above, that happens to work on one platform, e.g., GCC, but fails to compile on another, e.g., Clang.[9]

Incompatibly specifying alignment is IFNDR

It is permissible to forward declare a UDT without an **alignas** specifier so long as all defining declarations of the type either have no **alignas** specifier or have the same one. Similarly, if any forward declaration of a UDT has an **alignas** specifier, then all defining declarations of the type must have the same specifier, and that specifier must be *equivalent to*, not necessarily *the same as*, that in the forward declaration:

---

[7]**iso11a**, section 7.6.2, "Alignment Specifier," paragraph 5, pp. 179

[8]"If the constant expression evaluates to a fundamental alignment, the alignment requirement of the declared entity shall be the specified fundamental alignment": **iso11a**, section 7.6.2, "Alignment Specifier," paragraph 2, item 2, p. 178.

[9]Underspecifying alignment is not reported at all by GCC 10.2 (c. 2020), using the -std=c++11 -Wall -Wextra -Wpedantic flags. This behavior is reported as a compiler defect; see **wakely15**. With the same set of options, Clang 10.1 (c. 2020) produces a compilation failure. ICC 2021.1.2 (c. 2020) and MSVC 19.29 (c. 2021) will produce a warning and ignore any alignment less than the minimum one.

```
struct Foo;                    // OK, does not specify an alignment
struct alignas(double) Foo;    // OK, must be equivalent to every definition
struct alignas(8) Foo;         // OK, all definitions must be identical.

struct alignas(8) Foo { };     // OK, def. equiv. to each decl. specifying alignment

struct Foo;                    // OK, has no effect
struct alignas(8) Foo;         // OK, has no effect; might warn after definition
```

Specifying an alignment in a forward declaration without specifying an equivalent one in the defining declaration is **ill formed, no diagnostic required (IFNDR)** if the two declarations appear in distinct translation units:

```
struct alignas(4) Bar;    // OK, forward declaration
struct Bar { };           // Error, missing alignas specifier

struct alignas(4) Baz;    // OK, forward declaration
struct alignas(8) Baz { }; // Error, nonequivalent alignas specifier
```

Both of the errors above are flagged by Clang. MSVC and ICC warn on the first one and produce an error on the second one, whereas neither of them is reported by GCC. Note that when the inconsistency *occurs across translation units*, no mainstream compiler is likely to diagnose the problem:

```
// file1.cpp:
struct Bam { char ch; } bam, *p = &bam;

// file2.cpp:
struct alignas(int) Bam;  // Error, definition of Bam lacks alignment specifier.
extern Bam* p;            //          (no diagnostic required)
```

Any program incorporating both translation units above is IFNDR.

Applying alignas to a *type* might be misleading

When applying the **alignas** specifier to a user-defined type having no base classes, one might be convinced that it is equivalent to applying **alignas** to its first declared data member:

```
struct S0 {
    alignas(16) char d_buffer[128]; // guaranteed to be 16-byte aligned
                int  d_index;
};

struct alignas(16) S1 {
    char d_buffer[128];             // guaranteed to be 16-byte aligned
    int  d_index;
};
```

Indeed, for all objects of the S0 and S1 types in the example above, their respective d_buffer data members will be aligned on a 16-byte boundary. Such equivalency, however, holds only for **standard-layout types**. Adding a virtual function or even simply changing the access control for some of the data members[10] might break this equivalency:

```
struct S2 {
    alignas(16) char d_buffer[128];  // guaranteed to be 16-byte aligned
                int d_index;

    virtual ~S2();
};

struct alignas(16) S3 {
    char d_buffer[128];              // not guaranteed to be 16-byte aligned
    int  d_index;

    virtual ~S3();
};

struct S4 {
    alignas(16) char d_buffer[128];  // guaranteed to be 16-byte aligned
private:
                int  d_index;
};

struct alignas(16) S5 {
    char d_buffer[128];              // not guaranteed to be 16-byte aligned
private:
    int  d_index;
};
```

Any code that relies on the d_buffer member of instances of the S3 and S5 types, in the code example above, being 16-byte aligned is defective.

Overlooking alternative approaches to avoid false sharing

User-defined types having artificially stricter alignments than would naturally occur on the host platform means that fewer of them can fit within any given level of physical cache within the hardware. Types having data members whose alignment is artificially strengthened tend to be larger and thus suffer the same lost cache utilization. As an alternative to enforcing stricter alignment to avoid false sharing, consider organizing a multithreaded program such

---

[10]According to the C++20 Standard, compilers are allowed to reorder data members having different access control. However, no compilers take advantage of this ability in practice, and C++23 might mandate that the data members are always laid out in declaration order; see **balog20**.

that tight clusters of repeatedly accessed objects are always acted upon by only a single thread at a time, e.g., using local (arena) memory allocators; see *Appendix — Cache lines; L1, L2, and L3 cache; pages; and virtual memory* on page 181.

See Also

- "**alignof**" (§2.1, p. 184) inspects the alignment of a given type.

Appendix

Natural alignment

Many micro-architectures are optimized for working with data that has **natural alignment**; i.e., objects reside on an address boundary that divides their size rounded up to the nearest power of two. With the additional restriction that no padding is allowed between C++ array elements, the alignment requirements of fundamental types are often equal to their respective size on most platforms:

```
char        c;  // size 1;  alignment 1;  boundaries: 0x00, 0x01, 0x02, ...
short       s;  // size 2;  alignment 2:  boundaries: 0x00, 0x02, 0x04, ...
int         i;  // size 4;  alignment 4;  boundaries: 0x00, 0x04, 0x08, ...
float       f;  // size 4;  alignment 4;  boundaries: 0x00, 0x04, 0x08, ...
double      d;  // size 8;  alignment 8;  boundaries: 0x00, 0x08, 0x10, ...
long double l;  // size 16; alignment 16; boundaries: 0x00, 0x10, 0x20, ...
```

The alignment requirement of an array of objects is the same as that of its elements:

```
char  arrC[4];  // size 4; alignment 1
short arrS[4];  // size 8; alignment 2
```

For user-defined types, compilers compute the alignment and add appropriate padding between the data members and after the last one, such that all alignment requirements of the data members are satisfied and no padding would be required should an array of the type be created. Typically, the resulting alignment requirement of a UDT is the same as that of the most strictly aligned nonstatic data member:

```
struct S0
{
    char a;     // size 1; alignment 1
    char b;     // size 1; alignment 1
    int  c;     // size 4; alignment 4
};              // size 8; alignment 4
```

```
struct S1
{
    char a;    // size  1; alignment 1
    int  b;    // size  4; alignment 4
    char c;    // size  1; alignment 1
};             // size 12; alignment 4

struct S2
{
    int  a;    // size 4; alignment 4
    char b;    // size 1; alignment 1
    char c;    // size 1; alignment 1
};             // size 8; alignment 4

struct S3
{
    char a;    // size 1; alignment 1
    char b;    // size 1; alignment 1
};             // size 2; alignment 1

struct S4
{
    char a[2]; // size 2; alignment 1
};             // size 2; alignment 1
```

Size and alignment behave similarly with respect to **structural inheritance**:

```
struct D0 : S0
{
    double d;  // size  8; alignment 8
};             // size 16; alignment 8

struct D1 : S1
{
    double d;  // size  8; alignment 8
};             // size 24; alignment 8

struct D2 : S2
{
    int d;     // size  4; alignment 4
};             // size 12; alignment 4

struct D3 : S3
{
    int d;     // size 4; alignment 4
};             // size 8; alignment 4
```

```
struct D4 : S4
{
    char d;     // size 1; alignment 1
};              // size 3; alignment 1
```

Finally, virtual functions and virtual base classes invariably introduce an implicit virtual-table-pointer member having a size and alignment corresponding to that of a memory address (e.g., 4 or 8) on the target platform:

```
struct S5
{
    virtual ~S5();
};              // size 8; alignment 8

struct D5 : S5
{
    char d;     // size  1; alignment 1
};              // size 16; alignment 8
```

Cache lines; L1, L2, and L3 cache; pages; and virtual memory

Modern computers are highly complex systems, and a detailed understanding of their intricacies is unnecessary to achieve most of the performance benefits. Still, certain general themes and rough thresholds aid in understanding how to squeeze just a bit more out of the underlying hardware. In this section, we sketch fundamental concepts that are common to all modern computer hardware; although the precise details will vary, the general ideas remain essentially the same.

In its most basic form, a computer consists of central processing unit (CPU) having internal registers that access main memory (MM). Registers in the CPU (on the order of hundreds of bytes) are among the fastest forms of memory, while MM, typically many gigabytes, is orders of magnitude slower. An almost universally observed phenomenon is that of **locality of reference**, which suggests that data that resides in close proximity in the virtual address space is more likely to be accessed together in rapid succession than more distant data.

To exploit the phenomenon of locality of reference, computers introduce the notion of a cache that, while much faster than MM, is also much smaller. Programs that attempt to amplify locality of reference will, in turn, often be rewarded with faster run times. The organization of a cache and, in fact, the number of levels of cache, e.g., L1, L2, L3,..., will vary, but the basic design parameters are, again, more or less the same. A given level of cache will have a certain total size in bytes, invariably an integral power of two. The cache will be segmented into what are called **cache lines** whose size — a smaller power of two — divides that of the cache itself. When the CPU accesses MM, it first looks to see if that memory is in the cache; if it is, the value is returned quickly, known as a **cache hit**. Otherwise, the cache lines containing that data are fetched from the next higher level of cache or from MM and placed into the cache (known as a **cache miss**), possibly ejecting other less recently used ones.[11]

Data residing in distinct cache lines is physically independent and can be written concurrently by multiple threads, possibly running on separate cores or even processors. Logically unrelated data residing in the same cache line, however, is nonetheless physically coupled; two threads that write to such logically unrelated data will find themselves synchronized by the hardware. Such unexpected and typically undesirable sharing of a cache line by unrelated data acted upon by two concurrent threads is known as **false sharing**. One way of avoiding **false sharing** is to align such data on a cache-line boundary, thus rendering impossible the accidental colocation of such data on the same cache line. Another, more broad-based design approach that avoids lowering cache utilization is to ensure that data acted upon by a given thread is kept physically separate, e.g., through the use of local, arena memory allocators.[12]

Finally, even data that is not currently in cache but resides nearby in MM can benefit from locality. The virtual address space, synonymous with the size of a **void*** (typically 64 bits on modern general-purpose hardware), has historically well exceeded the physical memory available to the CPU. The operating system must therefore maintain a mapping in MM from what is resident in physical memory and what resides in secondary storage, e.g., on disc. In addition, essentially all modern hardware provides a translation-lookaside buffer (TLB)[13] that caches the addresses of the most recently accessed physical pages, providing yet another advantage to having the **working set**, i.e., the current set of frequently accessed

---

[11]Conceptually, the cache is often thought of as being able to hold any arbitrary subset of the most recently accessed cache lines. This kind of cache is known as **fully associative**. Although it provides the best hit rate, a fully associative cache requires the most power along with significant additional chip area to perform the fully parallel lookup. **Direct-mapped** cache associativity is at the other extreme. In direct mapped, each memory location has exactly one location available to it in the cache. If another memory location mapping to that location is needed, the current cache line must be flushed from the cache. This approach has the lowest hit rate, but lookup times, chip area, and power consumption are all optimally minimized. Between these two extremes is a continuum that is referred to as **set associative**. A set associate cache has more than one — typically 2, 4, or 8; see **solihin15**, section 5.2.1, "Placement Policy," pp. 136–141, and **hruska20** — location in which each memory location in main memory can reside. Note that, even with a relatively small N, as N increases, an N-way **set associative** cache quickly approaches the hit rate of a fully associative cache at greatly reduced collateral cost; for most software-design purposes, any loss in hit rate due to set associativity of a cache can be safely ignored.

[12]**lakos17b**, **lakos19**, **lakos22**

[13]A TLB is a kind of address-translation cache that is typically part of a chip's memory management unit. A TLB holds a recently accessed subset of the complete mapping, itself maintained in MM, from virtual memory address to physical ones. A TLB is used to reduce access time when the requisite pages are already resident in memory; its size, e.g., 4K, is capped at the number of bytes of physical memory, e.g., 32Gb, divided by the number of bytes in each physical page, e.g., 8Kb, but could be smaller. Because it resides on chip, is typically an order of magnitude faster (SRAM versus DRAM), and requires only a single lookup (as opposed to two or more when going out to MM), there is an enormous premium on minimizing TLB misses.

pages, remain small and densely packed with relevant data.[14] What's more, dense working sets, in addition to facilitating hits for repeat access, increase the likelihood that data that is coresident on a page or cache line will be needed soon, i.e., in effect acting as a prefetch. Table 1 provides a summary of typical physical parameters found in modern computers today.

Table 1: Various sizes and access speeds of typical memory for modern computers

Memory Type	Typical Memory Size (Bytes)	Typical Access Times
CPU Registers	512 ... 2048	~250ps
Cache Line	64 ... 256	NA
L1 Cache	16Kb ... 64Kb	~1ns
L2 Cache	1Mb ... 2Mb	~10ns
L3 Cache	8Mb ... 32Mb	~80ns ... 120ns
L4 Cache	32Mb ... 128Mb	~100ns ... 200ns
Set Associativity	2 ... 64	NA
TL	4 words ... 65536 words	~10ns ... 50ns
Physical Memory Page	512 ... 8192	~100ns ... 500ns
Virtual Memory	2^{32} bytes ... 2^{64} bytes	~10μs ... 50μs
Solid-State Disc (SSD)	256Gb ... 16Tb	~25μs ... 100μs
Mechanical Disc	Huge	~5ms ... 10ms
Clock Speed	NA	~4GHz

---

[14]Note that memory for handle-body types (e.g., `std::vector` or `std::deque`) and especially node-based containers (e.g., `std::map` and `std::unordered_map`), originally allocated within a single page, can — through deallocation and reallocation or even move operations — become scattered across multiple, perhaps many, pages, thus causing what was originally a relatively small working set to no longer fit within physical memory. This phenomenon, known as **diffusion** (which is a distinct concept from **fragmentation**), is what typically leads to a substantial runtime performance degradation due to cache line **thrashing** in large, long-running programs. Such **diffusion** can be mitigated by judicious use of local arena memory allocators and deliberate avoidance of **move operations** across disparate localities of frequent memory usage.

The alignof Operator

The keyword **alignof** serves as a compile-time operator used to query the **alignment requirements** of a type on the current platform.

Description

The **alignof** operator, when applied to a type, evaluates to an **integral constant expression** that represents the alignment requirement of its argument type. Similar to **sizeof**, the compile-time value of **alignof** is of type std::size_t; unlike **sizeof** that can accept an arbitrary expression, **alignof** is defined for only type identifiers but often works on expressions anyway (see *Annoyances — alignof is defined only on types* on page 193). The argument type, T, supplied to **alignof** must be a **complete type**, a **reference type**, or an array type. If T is a **complete type**, the result is the alignment requirement for T. If T is a **reference type**, the result is the alignment requirement for the referenced type. If T is an array type, the result is the alignment requirement for every element in the array. For example, on a platform where **sizeof(short)** == 2 and **alignof(short)** == 2, the following assertions pass:

```
static_assert(alignof(short)    == 2, "");  // complete type   (sizeof is 2)
static_assert(alignof(short&)   == 2, "");  // reference type  (sizeof is 2)
static_assert(alignof(short[5]) == 2, "");  // array type      (sizeof is 10)
static_assert(alignof(short[])  == 2, "");  // array type      (sizeof fails)
```

According to the C++11 Standard, "An object of array type contains a contiguously allocated nonempty set of N subobjects of type T."[1] Note that, for every type T, **sizeof**(T) is always a multiple of **alignof**(T); otherwise, storing multiple T instances in an array would be impossible without padding, and the Standard explicitly prohibits padding between array elements.

alignof Fundamental Types

Like their size, the alignment requirements of a **char**, **signed char**, and **unsigned char** are guaranteed to be 1 on every conforming platform. For any other fundamental or pointer type FPT, **alignof**(FPT) is platform-dependent but is typically approximated well by the type's **natural alignment** — i.e., **sizeof**(FPT) == **alignof**(FPT):

```
static_assert(alignof(char)   == 1, "");  // guaranteed to be 1
static_assert(alignof(short)  == 2, "");  // platform-dependent
static_assert(alignof(int)    == 4, "");  //      "          "
static_assert(alignof(double) == 8, "");  //      "          "
static_assert(alignof(void*)  >= 4, "");  //      "          "
```

---

[1] iso11a, section 8.3.4, "Arrays," paragraph 1, p. 188

alignof **User-Defined Types**

When applied to user-defined types, alignment is always at least that of the strictest alignment of any of its arguments' base or member objects. Compilers will by default avoid nonessential padding because any extra padding would be wasteful of memory, e.g., cache:

```cpp
struct S0 { };                          // sizeof(S0) is  1; alignof(S0) is  1
struct S1 { char c; };                  // sizeof(S1) is  1; alignof(S1) is  1
struct S2 { short s; };                 // sizeof(S2) is  2; alignof(S2) is  2
struct S3 { char c; short s; };         // sizeof(S3) is  4; alignof(S3) is  2
struct S4 { short s1; short s2; };      // sizeof(S4) is  4; alignof(S4) is  2
struct S5 { int i; char c; };           // sizeof(S5) is  8; alignof(S5) is  4
struct S6 { char c1; int i; char c2; }; // sizeof(S6) is 12; alignof(S6) is  4
struct S7 { char c; short s; int i; };  // sizeof(S7) is  8; alignof(S7) is  4
struct S8 { double d; };                // sizeof(S8) is  8; alignof(S8) is  8
struct S9 { double d; char c; };        // sizeof(S9) is 16; alignof(S9) is  8
struct SA { long double ld; };          // sizeof(SA) is 16; alignof(SA) is 16
struct SB { long double ld; char c; };  // sizeof(SB) is 32; alignof(SB) is 16
```

The sizes of empty types, such as S0 in the example above, are defined to have the size and alignment of 1 to ensure that each object and member subobject of type S0 has a unique address. However, if an empty type is used as a base, the size of the derived type will not be affected (with some exceptions) due to the **empty-base optimization**:

```cpp
struct D0 : S0 { int i; };  // sizeof(D0) is 4; alignof(D0) is 4
```

The alignment of the base type always affects the derived type's alignment. However, this effect is observable for an empty base only if it is **over-aligned**; see Section 2.1."**alignas**" on page 168:

```cpp
struct alignas(8) E { };   // sizeof(E)  is 8; alignof(E)  is 8
struct D1 : E { int i; };  // sizeof(D1) is 8; alignof(D1) is 8
```

Compilers are permitted to increase alignment — e.g., in the presence of virtual functions, which typically implies a virtual function table pointer — but have certain restrictions on padding. For example, they must ensure that each comprised type is itself sufficiently aligned. Furthermore, sufficient padding must be added so that the alignment of the parent type divides its size, ensuring that storing multiple instances in an array does not require any padding between array elements, which is explicitly prohibited by the Standard. In other words, the following identities hold for all types, T, and positive integers, N:

```cpp
#include <cstddef>  // std::size_t

template <typename T, std::size_t N>
void f()
{
    static_assert(0 == sizeof(T) % alignof(T), "guaranteed");

    T a[N];
    static_assert(N == sizeof(a) / sizeof(*a), "guaranteed");
}
```

The alignment of user-defined types can be made artificially stricter but not weaker using the **alignas** specifier; see Section 2.1."**alignas**" on page 168. Also note that, for **standard-layout types**, the address of the first member object is guaranteed to be the same as that of the parent object; see Section 2.1."Generalized PODs '11" on page 401:

```cpp
struct S { int i; };
class T { public: S s; };
T t;
static_assert(static_cast<void*>(&t.s) == &t, "guaranteed");
static_assert(static_cast<void*>(&t.s) == &t.s.i, "guaranteed");
```

This property also holds for unions:

```cpp
struct { union { char c; float f; double d; }; } u;
static_assert(static_cast<void*>(&u) == &u.c, "guaranteed");
static_assert(static_cast<void*>(&u) == &u.f, "guaranteed");
static_assert(static_cast<void*>(&u) == &u.d, "guaranteed");
```

Use Cases

Probing the alignment of a type during development

Both **sizeof** and **alignof** are often used informally during development and debugging to confirm the values of those attributes for a given type on the current platform:

```cpp
#include <iostream>  // std::cout

void f()
{
    std::cout << " sizeof(double): " <<  sizeof(double) << '\n';  // always 8
    std::cout << "alignof(double): " << alignof(double) << '\n';  // usually 8
}
```

Printing the size and alignment of a **struct** along with those of each of its individual data members can lead to the discovery of suboptimal ordering of data members, resulting in wasteful extra padding. As an example, consider two **struct**s, Wasteful and Optimal, having the same three data members but in different order:

```cpp
struct Wasteful
{
    char   d_c; // size = 1;  alignment = 1
    double d_d; // size = 8;  alignment = 8
    int    d_i; // size = 4;  alignment = 4
};             // size = 24;  alignment = 8

struct Optimal
{
```

```
    double d_d;  // size =  8;  alignment = 8
    int    d_i;  // size =  4;  alignment = 4
    char   d_c;  // size =  1;  alignment = 1
};               // size = 16;  alignment = 8
```

Both **alignof**(Wasteful) and **alignof**(Optimal) are 8 on our platform, but **sizeof**(Wasteful) is 24, whereas **sizeof**(Optimal) is only 16. Even though these two **struct**s contain the very same data members, the individual alignment requirements of these members forces the compiler to insert more total padding between the data members in Wasteful than is necessary in Optimal:

```
struct Wasteful
{
    char   d_c;           // size =  1;  alignment = 1
    char   padding_0[7];  // size =  7
    double d_d;           // size =  8;  alignment = 8
    int    d_i;           // size =  4;  alignment = 4
    char   padding_1[4];  // size =  4
};                        // size = 24;  alignment = 8

struct Optimal
{
    double d_d;           // size =  8;  alignment = 8
    int    d_i;           // size =  4;  alignment = 4
    char   d_c;           // size =  1;  alignment = 1
    char   padding_0[3];  // size =  3
};                        // size = 16;  alignment = 8
```

Determining if a given buffer is sufficiently aligned

The **alignof** operator can be used to determine if a given, e.g., **char**, buffer is suitably aligned for storing an object of arbitrary type. As an example, consider the task of creating a **value-semantic** class, MyAny, that represents an object of arbitrary type[2]:

---

[2]The C++17 Standard Library provides the nontemplate class std::any, which is a type-safe container for single values of *any* **regular type**. The implementation strategies surrounding alignment for std::any in both libstdc++ and libc++ closely mirror those used to implement the simplified MyAny class presented here. Note that std::any also records the current **typeid** on construction or assignment, which can be queried with the type member function to determine, at run time, whether a specified type is currently the active one:

```
#include <any>  // std::any
void f(const std::any& object)
{
    if (object.type() == typeid(int)) { /*...*/ }
}
```

```
#include <cassert>   // standard C assert macro
#include <string>    // std::string
#include <my_any.h>  // MyAny
void f()
{
    MyAny obj = 10;                     // can be initialized with values of any type
    assert(obj.as<int>() == 10);  // Inner data can be retrieved at run time.

    obj = std::string{"hello"};   // can be reassigned from a value of any type
    assert(obj.as<std::string>() == "hello");
}
```

A straightforward implementation of MyAny would be to allocate an appropriately sized block
of dynamic memory each time a value of a new type is assigned. Such a naive implementation
would force memory allocations even though the vast majority of values assigned in practice
are small (e.g., fundamental types), most of which would fit within the space that would
otherwise be occupied by just the pointer needed to refer to dynamic memory. As a practical
optimization, we might instead consider reserving a small buffer within the footprint of the
MyAny object to hold the value provided (1) it will fit and (2) the buffer is sufficiently aligned.
The natural implementation of this type, typically having a **union** of a **char** array and a
char pointer as a data member, will naturally result in the alignment requirement of at least
that of the **char***, e.g., 4 on a 32-bit platform and 8 on a 64-bit one:

```
// my_any.h:

class MyAny  // nontemplate class
{
    union {
        char* d_buf_p;      // pointer to dynamic memory if needed
        char  d_buffer[39]; // small buffer

    }; // Size of union is 39; alignment of union is alignof(char*).

    char d_onHeapFlag;              // Boolean (discriminator) for union (above)

public:
    template <typename T>
    MyAny(const T& x);                        // member template constructor

    template <typename T>
    MyAny& operator=(const T& rhs);  // member template assignment operator
```

```
    template <typename T>
    const T& as() const;                   // member template accessor

    // ...

}; // Size of MyAny is 40; alignment of MyAny is alignof(char*), e.g., 8.
```

We could, in addition, use the **alignas** attribute to ensure that the minimal alignment of d_buffer is at least 8 (or even 16):

```
    // ...
    alignas(8) char d_buffer[39];  // small buffer aligned to, at least, 8
    // ...
```

We chose the size of d_buffer in the example above to be 39 for two reasons. First, we decided that we want 32-byte types to fit into the buffer, meaning that the size of d_buffer should be at least 32. Combined with the use of **char** for the d_onHeapFlag, which is guaranteed to have the size of 1, we require that **sizeof**(MyAny) >= 33. Second, we want to ensure that no space is wasted on padding. On platforms where **alignof**(MyAny) is 8, which will be the case for many 64-bit platforms, **sizeof**(MyAny) would be 40, which we choose to achieve by increasing the useful capacity to 39 instead of having the compiler add unused padding.

The templated constructor of MyAny can then decide, potentially at compile time, whether to store the given object x in the internal small buffer storage or on the heap, depending on x's size and alignment:

```
template <typename T>
MyAny::MyAny(const T& x)
{
    if (sizeof(x) <= 39 && alignof(T) <= alignof(char*))
    {
        // Store x in place in the small buffer.
        new(d_buffer) T(x);
        d_onHeapFlag = false;
    }
    else
    {
        // Store x on the heap and its address in the buffer.
        d_buf_p = reinterpret_cast<char*>(new T(x));
        d_onHeapFlag = true;
    }
}
```

In a real-world implementation, among other improvements, a *forwarding reference* would be used as the parameter type of MyAny's constructor to *perfectly forward* the argument object into the appropriate storage; see Section 2.1."Forwarding References" on page 377.

Using the **alignof** operator in the constructor above to check whether the alignment of T is compatible with the alignment of the small buffer is necessary to avoid attempting to store overly aligned objects in place, even if they would fit in the 39-byte buffer. As an example, consider **long double**, which on typical platforms has both a size and alignment of 16. Even though **sizeof(long double)** at 16 bytes is not greater than 39, **alignof(long double)** at 16 bytes is greater than that of d_buffer at 8 bytes; hence, attempting to store an instance of **long double** in the small buffer, d_buffer, might, depending on where the MyAny object resides in memory, result in **undefined behavior**. User-defined types that either contain a **long double** or have had their alignments artificially extended beyond 8 bytes are also unsuitable candidates for the internal buffer even if they might otherwise fit:

```
struct Unsuitable1 { long double d_value; };
    // Size is 16 (<= 39), but alignment is 16 (> 8).

struct alignas(32) Unsuitable2 { };
    // Size is  1 (<= 39), but alignment is 32 (> 8).
```

Monotonic memory allocation

A common pattern in software, e.g., request/response in client/server architectures, is to quickly build up a complex data structure, use it, and then quickly destroy it. A **monotonic allocator** is a special-purpose memory allocator that returns a monotonically increasing sequence of addresses into an arbitrary buffer, subject to specific size and alignment requirements.[3] Especially when the memory is allocated by a single thread, there are prodigious[4] performance benefits to having unsynchronized raw memory be taken directly off the program stack. In what follows, we will provide the building blocks of a monotonic memory allocator wherein the **alignof** operator plays an essential role.

As a practically useful example, suppose that we want to create a lightweight MonotonicBuffer class template that will allow us to allocate raw memory directly from the footprint of the object. Just by creating an object of an appropriately sized instance of this type on the program stack, memory will naturally come from the stack. For didactic reasons, we will start with a first pass at this class, ignoring alignment, and then go back and fix it using **alignof** so that it returns properly aligned memory:

---

[3]C++17 introduces an alternate interface to supply memory allocators via an abstract base class. The C++17 Standard Library provides a complete version of standard containers using this more interoperable design in a subnamespace, std::pmr, where pmr stands for **polymorphic memory resource**. Also adopted as part of C++17 are two concrete memory resources, std::pmr::monotonic_buffer_resource and std::pmr::unsynchronized_pool_resource.

[4]See **lakos16**.

```
#include <cstddef>  // std::size_t

template <std::size_t N>
struct MonotonicBuffer  // first pass at a monotonic memory buffer
{
    char  d_buffer[N];  // fixed-size buffer
    char* d_top_p;       // next available address

    MonotonicBuffer() : d_top_p(d_buffer) { }
        // Initialize the next available address to be the start of the buffer.

    template <typename T>
    void* allocate()              // BAD IDEA, doesn't address alignment
                                  // doesn't check buffer limit
    {
        void* result = d_top_p;   // Remember the current next-available address.
        d_top_p += sizeof(T);     // Reserve just enough space for this type.
        return result;            // Return the address of the reserved space.
    }
};
```

MonotonicBuffer is a class template with one integral template parameter that controls the size of the d_buffer member from which it will dispense memory. Note that, while d_buffer has an alignment of 1, the d_top_p member, used to keep track of the next available address, has an alignment that is typically 4 or 8, corresponding to 32-bit and 64-bit architectures, respectively. The constructor merely initializes the next-address pointer, d_top_p, to the start of the local memory pool, d_buffer. The interesting part is how the allocate function manages to return a monotonically increasing sequence of addresses corresponding to objects allocated sequentially from the local pool:

```
void test1()
{
    MonotonicBuffer<20> mb;  // On a 64-bit platform, the alignment will be 8.
    char*   cp = static_cast<char*  >(mb.allocate<char  >());  // &d_buffer[ 0]
    double* dp = static_cast<double*>(mb.allocate<double>());  // &d_buffer[ 1]
    short*  sp = static_cast<short* >(mb.allocate<short >());  // &d_buffer[ 9]
    int*    ip = static_cast<int*   >(mb.allocate<int   >());  // &d_buffer[11]
    float*  fp = static_cast<float* >(mb.allocate<float >());  // &d_buffer[15]
}
```

The predominant problem with this first attempt at an implementation of allocate is that the addresses returned do not necessarily satisfy the alignment requirements of the supplied type. A secondary concern is that there is no internal check to see if sufficient room remains. To patch this faulty implementation, we will need a function that, given an initial address and an alignment requirement, returns the amount by which the address must be rounded up, i.e., necessary padding, for an object having that alignment requirement to be properly aligned:

```
#include <cstdint>  // std::uintptr_t
std::size_t calculatePadding(const char* address, std::size_t alignment)
    // Requires: alignment is a non-negative, integral power of 2.
{
    return (alignment - reinterpret_cast<std::uintptr_t>(address)) &
           (alignment - 1);
}
```

Armed with the `calculatePadding` helper function in the example above, we are all set to write the final version of the `allocate` method of the `MonotonicBuffer` class template:

```
template <std::size_t N>
template <typename T>
void* MonotonicBuffer<N>::allocate()
{
    // Calculate just the padding space needed for alignment.
    const std::size_t padding = calculatePadding(d_top_p, alignof(T));

    // Calculate the total amount of space needed.
    const std::size_t delta = padding + sizeof(T);

    // Check to make sure the properly aligned object will fit.
    if (delta > d_buffer + N - d_top_p)  // if (Needed > Total - Used)
    {
        return 0;  // not enough properly aligned unused space remaining
    }

    // Reserve needed space; return the address for a properly aligned object.
    void* alignedAddress = d_top_p + padding;  // Align properly for T object.
    d_top_p += delta;                          // Reserve memory for T object.
    return alignedAddress;                     // Return memory for T object.
}
```

Using this corrected implementation that uses **alignof** to pass the alignment of the supplied type `T` to the `calculatePadding` function, the addresses returned from the benchmark example above would be different[5]:

```
void test2()
{
    MonotonicBuffer<20> mb;  // Assume 64-bit platform, 8-byte aligned.
    char*   cp = static_cast<char* >(mb.allocate<char  >());  // &d_buffer[ 0]
    double* dp = static_cast<double*>(mb.allocate<double>());  // &d_buffer[ 8]
```

---

[5]Note that on a 32-bit architecture, the `d_top_p` character pointer would be only four-byte aligned, which means that the entire buffer might be only four-byte aligned. In that case, the respective offsets for `cp`, `dp`, `sp`, `ip`, and `bp` in the example for the aligned use case might sometimes instead be 0, 4, 12, 16, and **nullptr**, respectively. If desired, we can use the **alignas** keyword to artificially constrain the `d_buffer` data member always to reside on a maximally aligned address boundary, thereby improving consistency of behavior, especially on 32-bit platforms.

```
    short*  sp = static_cast<short* >(mb.allocate<short >());;  // &d_buffer[16]
    int*    ip = static_cast<int*   >(mb.allocate<int   >());;  // 0 (no space)
    bool*   bp = static_cast<bool*  >(mb.allocate<bool  >());;  // &d_buffer[18]
}
```

In practice, an object that allocates memory, such as a vector or a list, will be constructed to use an allocator that provides memory that is guaranteed to have either **maximal fundamental alignment**, natural alignment, or alignment that satisfies an optionally specified alignment requirement.

Finally, instead of returning a null pointer when the buffer was exhausted, we would typically have the allocator fall back to a geometrically growing sequence of dynamically allocated blocks; the allocate method would then fail, i.e., an std::bad_alloc exception would somehow be thrown, only if all available memory were exhausted and the **new handler** were unable to acquire more memory yet still opted to return control to its caller.

Annoyances

alignof is defined only on types

Unlike the **sizeof** operator, the **alignof** operator can accept only a *type*, not an *expression*, as its argument[6]:

```
static_assert(sizeof(int)  == 4, "");   // OK, int is a type.
static_assert(alignof(int) == 4, "");   // OK, int is a type.
static_assert(sizeof(3 + 2) == 4, "");  // OK, 3 + 2 is an expression.
static_assert(alignof(3 + 2) == 4, ""); // Error, 3 + 2 is not a type.
```

This asymmetry can result in a need to leverage **decltype** (see Section 1.1."**decltype**" on page 25) when inspecting an expression instead of a type:

```
void f()
{
    enum { e_SUCCESS, e_FAILURE } result;
    std::cout << "size: " << sizeof(result) << '\n';
    std::cout << "alignment:" << alignof(decltype(result)) << '\n';
}
```

The same sort of issue occurs in conjunction with modern **type inference** features such as **auto** (see Section 2.1."**auto** Variables" on page 195) and generic lambdas (see Section 2.2. "*Generic* Lambdas" on page 968). As a real-world example, consider C++14's generic lambda being used to introduce a small *local function* that prints out information regarding the size and alignment of a given **object**, likely for debugging purposes:

---

[6]Although the Standard does not require **alignof** to work on arbitrary expressions, **alignof** is a common GNU extension, and most compilers support it. Both Clang and GCC will warn only if -Wpedantic is set.

```
auto printTypeInformation = [](auto object)
{
    std::cout << "     size: " << sizeof(object) << '\n'
             << "alignment: " << alignof(decltype(object)) << '\n';
};
```

Because there is no explicit type available within the body of the `printTypeInformation` lambda,[7] a programmer aiming to remain entirely within the C++ Standard[8] is forced to use the **decltype** construct explicitly to first obtain the type of `object` before passing it on to **alignof**.

See Also

- "**decltype**" (§1.1, p. 25) explains how **decltype** helps work around **alignof**'s limitation of accepting only a type, not an expression (see *Annoyances — **alignof** is defined only on types* on page 193).

- "**alignas**" (§2.1, p. 168) discusses how **alignas** can be used to provide an artificially stricter alignment, e.g., more than natural alignment.

---

[7]In C++20, referring to the type of a generic lambda parameter explicitly is possible, due to the addition to lambdas of some familiar template syntax:

```
auto printTypeInformation = []<typename T>(T object)
{
    std::cout << "     size: " << sizeof(T) << '\n'
             << "alignment: " << alignof(T) << '\n';
};
```

[8]Note that **alignof**(object) will work on every major compiler — GCC 11.2 (c. 2021), Clang 12.0.1 (c. 2021), and MSVC 19.29 (c. 2021) — as a nonstandard extension.

Variables of Automatically Deduced Type

The keyword **auto** was repurposed in C++11 to act as a **placeholder type** such that, when used in place of a type as part of a variable declaration, the compiler will deduce the variable's type from its initializer.

Description

Prior to C++11, the rarely used **auto** keyword could be used as a **storage class specifier** for objects declared at block scope and in function parameter lists to indicate automatic storage duration, which is the default for these kinds of declarations. The **auto** keyword was repurposed in C++11 alongside the deprecation of the **register** keyword as a storage class specifier.[1]

Starting with C++11, the **auto** keyword may be used instead of an explicit type's name when declaring variables. In such cases, the variable's type is deduced from its initializer by the compiler applying the **placeholder type** deduction rules, which, apart from a single exception for list initializers (see *Potential Pitfalls — Surprising deduction for list initialization* on page 210), are the same as the rules for **function template argument type deduction**:

```
auto two = 2;     // Type of two is deduced to be int.
auto pi = 3.14f;  // Type of pi is deduced to be float.
```

The types of the two and pi variables above are deduced in the same manner as they would be if the same initializers were passed to a function template taking a single argument of the template type by value:

```
template <typename T> void deducer(T);

void testDeduction()
{
    deducer(2);      // T is deduced to be int.
    deducer(3.14f);  // T is deduced to be float.
}
```

The program is ill formed if the variable declared with **auto** does not have an initializer, if its name appears in the expression used to initialize it, or if the initializers of multiple variables in the same declaration don't deduce the same type:

```
auto x;                // Error, declaration of auto x has no initializer.
auto n = sizeof(n);    // Error, use of n before deduction of auto
auto i = 3, f = 0.3f;  // Error, inconsistent deduction for auto
```

---

[1]The deprecated keyword **register** was removed as of C++17, but the name remains reserved for future use.

Just as how function template argument deduction never deduces a reference type for its by-value argument, a variable declared with an unqualified **auto** is never deduced to have a reference type:

```
int  val = 3;
int& ref = val;
auto tmp = ref;  // Type of tmp is deduced to be int, not int&.
```

Augmenting **auto** with reference qualifiers and cv-qualifiers, however, enables us to control whether the deduced type is a reference and whether it is **const** and/or **volatile**:

```
auto val = 3;
    // Type of val is deduced to be int,
    // the same as the argument for template <typename T> void deducer(T).

const auto cval = val;
    // Type of cval is deduced to be const int,
    // the same as the argument for template <typename T> void deducer(const T).

auto& ref = val;
    // Type of ref is deduced to be int&,
    // the same as the argument for template <typename T> void deducer(T&).

auto& cref1 = cval;
    // Type of cref1 is deduced to be const int&,
    // the same as the argument for template <typename T> void deducer(T&).

const auto& cref2 = val;
    // Type of cref2 is deduced to be const int&,
    // the same as the argument for template <typename T> void deducer(const T&).
```

Note that qualifying **auto** with **&&** does *not* result in deduction of an *rvalue* reference (see Section 2.1."*Rvalue* References" on page 710), but, in line with function template argument deduction rules, would be treated as a *forwarding reference* (see Section 2.1."Forwarding References" on page 377). A variable declared with **auto&&** will, therefore, result in an *lvalue* reference or an *rvalue* reference depending on the value category of its initializer:

```
double doStuff();

      int val  = 3;
const int cval = 7;

// Deduction rules are the same as for template <typename T> void deducer(T&&):

auto&& lref1 = val;
    // Type of lref1 is deduced to be int&.

auto&& lref2 = cval;
    // Type of lref2 is deduced to be const int&.
```

```
auto&& rref = doStuff();
    // Type of rref is deduced to be double&&.
```

Similarly to references, explicitly specifying that a pointer type is to be deduced is possible. If the supplied initializer is not a pointer type, the compiler will issue an error:

```
const auto* cptr = &val;
    // Type of cptr is deduced to be const int*,
    // the same as the argument for template <typename T> void deducer(const T*).

auto* cptr2 = cval;  // Error, cannot deduce auto* from cval
```

The compiler can also be instructed to deduce pointers to functions, data members, and member functions, but see *Annoyances — Not all template argument deduction constructs are allowed for **auto*** on page 212:

```
float freeF(float);

struct S
{
    double d_data;
    int memberF(long);
};

auto (*fptr)(float) = &freeF;
    // Type of fptr is deduced to be float (*)(float),
    // the same as the argument for template <typename T> void deducer(T (*)(float)).

const auto S::* mptr = &S::d_data;
    // Type of mptr is deduced to be const double S::*,
    // the same as the argument for template <typename T> void deducer(const T S::*).

auto (S::* mfptr)(long) = &S::memberF;
    // Type of mfptr is deduced to be int (S::*)(long),
    // the same as the argument for template <typename T> void deducer(T (S::*)(long)).

auto (*gptr)(float) = 2; // Error, must be a function address

float freeH(double) { return 0.0; }

auto (*hptr)(float) = &freeH; // Error, the function must have the
                              // specified parameters.

double freeG(float ) { return 0.0; }

auto (*itpr)(float) = &freeG;  // OK, the return value is not constrained.
```

Unlike references, pointer types can be deduced by **auto** alone. Therefore, different forms of **auto** can be used to declare a variable of a pointer type:

```
auto  cptr1 = &cval;  // const int*
auto* cptr2 = &cval;  //   "       "

auto   fptr1          = &freeF;  // float (*)(float)
auto  *fptr2          = &freeF;  //    "            "
auto (*fptr3)(float) = &freeF;  //    "            "

auto      mptr1 = &S::d_data;  // double S::*
auto S::* mptr2 = &S::d_data;  //    "       "

auto          mfptr1         = &S::memberF;  // int (S::*)(long)
auto (S::* mfptr2)(long) = &S::memberF;  //   "      "     "
```

Note, however, that because regular and member pointers are fundamentally different in the C++ type system, **auto*** cannot be used to deduce pointers to data members and member functions:

```
auto* mptr3  = &S::d_data;   // Error, cannot deduce auto* from &S::d_data
auto* mfptr3 = &S::memberF;  // Error, cannot deduce auto* from &S::memberF
```

Pointers might also be deduced from array and function initializers without explicit use of the address-of operator due to function-to-pointer and array-to-pointer conversions applied prior to deduction of nonreference types:

```
auto   fptr4          = freeF;  // float (*)(float)
auto  *fptr5          = freeF;  //    "            "
auto (*fptr6)(float) = freeF;  //    "            "

int array[4];

auto  aptr1 = array;  // int*
auto* aptr2 = array;  //   "

auto  sptr1 = "hello";  // const char*
auto* sptr2 = "world";  // const char*
```

These conversions are not applied when deducing a reference type, and function and array references are deduced instead:

```
auto& fref = freeF;  // float (&)(float)

auto& aref = array;  // int (&)[4]

auto& sref = "meow";  // const char (&)[5]
```

Storage class specifiers as well as the **constexpr** (see Section 2.1."**constexpr** Variables" on page 302) specifier can also be applied to variables that use **auto** in their declaration:

```
thread_local     auto localCounter = 0L;                    // long
static constexpr auto pi          = 3.1415926535f;  // float
```

Finally, **auto** variables may be declared in any location that allows declaring a variable supplied with an initializer with a single exception of nonstatic data members; see *Annoyances — **auto** is disallowed for nonstatic data members* on page 212:

```
// namespace scope
auto globalNamespaceVar = 3.;  // double

namespace ns
{
    static auto nsNamespaceVar = "...";  // const char*
}

enum Status { /*...*/ };

int    sendRequest();
Status responseStatus();
bool   haveMoreWork();
void f()
{
    // block scope
    constexpr auto blockVar = 'a';  // char

    // condition of if, switch, and while statements
    if     (auto rc       = sendRequest())    { /*...*/ }  // int
    switch (auto status   = responseStatus()) { /*...*/ }  // Status
    while  (auto keepGoing = haveMoreWork())   { /*...*/ }  // bool

    // init-statement of for loops
    std::vector<int> v;
    for (auto it = v.begin(); it != v.end(); ++it)  // std::vector<int>::iterator
    { /*...*/ }

    // range declaration of range-based for loops
    for (const auto& constVal : v) { /*...*/ }  // const int&
}

struct S
{
    // static data members
    static const auto k_CONSTANT = 11u;  // unsigned int&
};
```

Use Cases

Ensuring variable initialization

Consider a defect introduced due to mistakenly leaving a variable uninitialized:

```cpp
#include <functional>  // std::function
#include <vector>      // std::vector

int accumulateWith0(const std::vector<int>&                 data,
                    const std::function<void(int&, int)>& apply)
{
    int accumulator;  // Bug, accumulator not initialized
    for (int datum : data)
    {
        apply(accumulator, datum);
    }
    return accumulator;
}
```

Variables declared with **auto** must be initialized. Using **auto** might, therefore, prevent such defects:

```cpp
int accumulateWith1(const std::vector<int>&                 data,
                    const std::function<void(int&, int)>& apply)
{
    auto accumulator;  // Error, declaration of accumulator has no initializer
    for (int datum : data)
    {
        apply(accumulator, datum);
    }
    return accumulator;
}
```

In addition, the initialization requirement encourages the good practice of reducing the scope of local variables.

Avoiding redundant type name repetition

Certain function templates require that the caller explicitly specify the type that the function uses as its return type. For example, the `std::make_shared<TYPE>` function returns an `std::shared_ptr<TYPE>`. If a variable's type is specified explicitly, such declarations redundantly repeat the type. The use of **auto** obviates this repetition:

```cpp
#include <memory>  // std::make_shared, std::make_unique, std::unique_ptr

// Without auto:
std::shared_ptr<RequestContext> context1 = std::make_shared<RequestContext>();
std::unique_ptr<Socket>         socket1  = std::make_unique<Socket>();
```

```
// With auto:
auto context2 = std::make_shared<RequestContext>();
auto socket2  = std::make_unique<Socket>();
```

Preventing unexpected implicit conversions

Using **auto** might prevent defects arising from explicitly specifying a variable's type that is distinct, yet implicitly convertible, from its initializer. As an example, the code below has a subtle defect that can lead to performance degradation or incorrect semantics:

```
#include <map>  // std::map

void testManualForLoop()
{
    std::map<int, User> users{/*...*/};
    for (const std::pair<int, User>& idUserPair : users)
    {
        // ...
    }
}
```

On every iteration, the idUserPair will be bound to a *copy* of the corresponding pair in the users map. A copy is made because the type returned by dereferencing the map's iterator is std::pair<**const int**, User>, which is implicitly convertible to std::pair<**int**, User>. Using **auto** would allow the compiler to deduce the correct type and avoid this unnecessary and potentially expensive copy[2]:

```
void testAutoForLoop()
{
    std::map<int, User> users{/*...*/};
    for (const auto& idUserPair : users)
    {
        // auto is deduced as std::pair<const int, User>.
    }
}
```

---

[2]The C++17 structured bindings allow us to not only avoid the type mismatch when using the range-based **for** loop to iterate over map structures, but also to give the pair elements names that are more meaningful in the context of the loop:

```
void testStructuredBindingForLoop(const std::map<int,User> &users)
{
    for (const auto& [id, user] : users) { /*...*/ }
}
```

Declaring variables of implementation-defined or compiler-synthesized types

Using **auto** is the only way to declare variables of implementation-defined or compiler-synthesized types, such as lambda expressions (see Section 2.1."Lambdas" on page 573). While in some cases using type erasure to avoid the need to spell out the type is possible, doing so typically comes with additional overhead. For example, storing a lambda closure in an `std::function` might entail an allocation on construction and virtual dispatch upon every call:

```cpp
#include <functional>  // std::function

void saveCurrentWork();
void testCallbacks()
{
    std::function<void()> errorCallback0 = [&]{ saveCurrentWork(); };
        // OK, implicit conversion from anonymous closure type to
        // std::function<void()>, which incurs additional overhead

    auto errorCallback1 = [&]{ saveCurrentWork(); };
        // Better, deduces the compiler-synthesized type
}
```

Declaring variables of complex and deeply nested types

auto can be used to declare variables of types that are impractical to spell and/or do not convey useful information to the reader. A typical example is avoiding the need for spelling out the iterator type of a container:

```cpp
#include <vector>  // std::vector

void doWork(const std::vector<int>& data)
{
    // without auto:
    for (std::vector<int>::const_iterator it = data.begin();
         it != data.end(); ++it)
    {
        // ...
    }

    // with auto:
    for (auto it = data.begin(); it != data.end(); ++it) { /*...*/ }
}
```

Furthermore, the need for such types can arise, for example, when storing intermediate results of **expression templates** whose types can be deeply nested and unreadable and might even differ between versions of the same library:

```
// without auto:
MyRanges::TransformRange<
    MyRanges::FilterRange<decltype(employees), JoinedInYear>,
    &Employee::name
> newEmployeeNames1 =
    employees | MyRanges::filter(JoinedInYear(2019))
              | MyRanges::transform(&Employee::name);

// with auto:
auto newEmployeeNames2 =
    employees | MyRanges::filter(JoinedInYear(2019))
              | MyRanges::transform(&Employee::name);
```

Improving resilience to library code changes

auto might be used to indicate that code using the variable doesn't rely on a specific type but rather on certain requirements that the type must satisfy. Such an approach might give library implementers more freedom to change return types without affecting the semantics of their clients' code in projects where automated large-scale refactoring tools are not available, but see *Potential Pitfalls — Lack of interface restrictions* on page 208. As an example, consider the following library function:

```
std::vector<Node> getNetworkNodes();
    // Return a sequence of nodes in the current network.
```

As long as the return value of the getNetworkNodes function is only used for iteration, it is not pertinent that an std::vector is returned. If clients use **auto** to initialize variables storing the return value of this function, the implementers of getNetworkNodes can migrate from std::vector to, for example, std::deque, requiring their clients to recompile only and make no changes to their code.

```
// without auto:
void testConcreteContainer()
{
    const std::vector<Node>& nodes = getNetworkNodes();
    for (const Node& node : nodes) { /*...*/ }
        // prevents migration
}

// with auto:
void testDeducedContainer()
{
    const auto& nodes = getNetworkNodes();
    for (const Node& node : nodes) { /*...*/ }
        // The return type of getNetworkNodes can be silently
        // changed while retaining correctness of the user code.
}
```

Potential Pitfalls

Compromised readability

Using **auto** might sometimes hide important semantic information contained in a variable's type, which could increase the cognitive load for readers. In conjunction with unclear variable naming, use of **auto** can make code difficult to read and maintain.

```cpp
int main(int argc, char** argv)
{
    const auto args0 = parseArgs(argc, argv);
        // The behavior of parseArgs and operations available on args0 is unclear.

    const std::vector<std::string> args1 = parseArgs(argc, argv);
        // It is clear what parseArgs does and what can be done with args1.
}
```

Although reading the contract of the `parseArgs` function at least once might be necessary to fully understand its behavior, using an explicit type's name at the call site helps readers understand its purpose. Modern IDEs might help with understanding the code by providing contextual information about the deduced type, e.g., by displaying a tooltip. However, such information is not readily available in nonIDE contexts, such as, for example, in simple text editors and code review tools, when browsing code on GitHub, or when the code is printed in a book.

Unintentional copies

Since the rules for function template type deduction apply to **auto**, appropriate cv-qualifiers and declarator modifiers — &, &&, *, etc. — must be applied to avoid unnecessary copies that might negatively affect both code performance and correctness. For example, consider a function that capitalizes a user's name:

```cpp
#include <cctype>  // std::toupper
#include <string>  // std::string

class User
{
    std::string d_name;
public:
    // ...
    std::string& name() { return d_name; }
};
void capitalizeName0(User& user)
{
    if (user.name().empty())
```

```
    {
        return;
    }

    user.name()[0] = std::toupper(user.name()[0]);
}
```

This function was then incorrectly refactored to avoid repetition of the user.name() invocation. However, a missing reference qualification leads not only to an unnecessary copy of the string, but also to the function failing to perform its job:

```
void capitalizeName1(User& user)
{
    auto name = user.name();   // Bug, unintended copy

    if (name.empty())
    {
        return;
    }

    name[0] = std::toupper(name[0]);   // Bug, changes the copy
}
```

Furthermore, even a fully cv-ref-qualified **auto** might still prove inadequate in cases as simple as introducing a variable for a returned-temporary value. As an example, consider refactoring the contents of this simple function:

```
void testExpression()
{
    useValue(getValue());
}
```

For debugging or readablity, it can help to use an intermediate variable to store the results of getValue():

```
void testRefactoredExpression()
{
    auto&& tempValue = getValue();
    useValue(tempValue);
}
```

The above invocation of useValue is not equivalent to the original expression; the semantics of the program might have changed because tempValue is an *lvalue* expression. To get close to the original semantics, std::forward and **decltype** must be used to propagate the original value category of getValue() to the invocation of useValue; see Section 2.1. "Forwarding References" on page 377:

```
#include <utility>  // std::forward

void testBetterRefactoredExpression()
{
    auto&& tempValue = getValue();
    useValue(std::forward<decltype(tempValue)>(tempValue));
}
```

Note that, even with the latest changes, the code above achieves the same result but in a somewhat different way because std::forward<**decltype**(tempValue)>(tempValue) is an *xvalue* expression whereas getValue() is a *prvalue* expression; see Section 2.1.*"Rvalue References"* on page 710.

Unexpected conversions and the lack of expected ones

Compulsively declaring variables using **auto**, even in cases where the desired type has to be spelled out in the initializer, allows potentially lossy or expensive explicit conversions to be used where they would not otherwise be applicable. To appreciate the consequences of allowing such conversions, consider a function template, combineDurations0, that is intended to combine two chrono duration values. The original code deliberately uses copy initialization for the sum variable to inhibit **explicit** conversions:

```
#include <chrono>  // std::chrono::seconds

template <typename Duration1, typename Duration2>
std::chrono::seconds combineDurations0(Duration1 d1, Duration2 d2)
{
    std::chrono::seconds sum = d1 + d2;  // only implicit conversions allowed

    // ...                     (more processing)
}
```

The author of combineDurations0 intended that callers would have to pass in types from std::chrono, e.g., to specify clearly the desired units. Using **auto** and forcing the deduction of std::chrono::seconds by specifying it in the initializer results in seemingly equivalent code, e.g., combineDurations1. However, the updated code now allows explicit conversions in initialization of the sum variable despite it still using copy initialization:

```
template <typename Duration1, typename Duration2>
std::chrono::seconds combineDurations1(Duration1 d1, Duration2 d2)
{
    auto sum = std::chrono::seconds(d1 + d2);  // explicit conversions allowed

    // ...                     (more processing)
}
```

With this not-just-stylistic difference, combineDurations1 incorrectly compiles even when its arguments are two integers, potentially masking a defect resulting from a client forgetting to specify units. In fairness, a better solution for this particular problem would be to declare the function template, e.g., combineDurations2, in a more restrictive manner:

```
template <typename Rep1, typename Period1, typename Rep2, typename Period2>
std::chrono::seconds combineDurations2(std::chrono::duration<Rep1, Period1> d1,
                                       std::chrono::duration<Rep2, Period2> d2)
{
    auto sum = std::chrono::seconds(d1 + d2);

    // ...                       (more processing)
}
```

By factoring out and making explicit the respective duration units, we obviate possible risks related to the use of **auto** because calls having such undesirable argument types will simply fail to compile.

Conversely, some conversions that would be expected to happen might be missed when using **auto** instead of an explicitly specified type. For example, **auto** might deduce a proxy type that might lead to difficult-to-diagnose defects:

```
void testProxyDeduction()
{
    std::vector<bool> flags = loadFlags();

    auto firstFlag = flags[0];  // deduces a proxy type, not bool
    flags.clear();

    if (firstFlag) // Bug, use-after-free: flags vector released its memory.
    {
        // ...
    }
}
```

The type of the firstFlag variable above is deduced from its initializer to be std::vector<**bool**>::reference. For types other than **bool**, the reference type alias defined by the vector is an *lvalue* reference to the type, and similar use of **auto** would simply make a copy of the value. The std::vector class template is, however, partially specialized for **bool** to use a packed representation where each Boolean element is represented as a single bit. Since C++ does not allow references to individual bits, std::vector<**bool**>::reference is a special proxy type that behaves mostly as a reference to **bool**. Making a copy of this proxy type, which happens when we initialize the firstFlag variable, creates another reference to the bit despite the use of plain **auto** which normally strips references. Thus, once the underlying flags vector is cleared, accessing the bit through the firstFlag proxy leads to undefined behavior. Explicitly specifying the type of firstFlag to be **bool** resolves the issue:

```
void proxyAvoided()
{
    std::vector<bool> flags = loadFlags();

    bool firstFlag = flags[0];  // OK, makes a copy of the first Boolean
    flags.clear();

    if (firstFlag) // OK, simply accessing a local variable
    {
        // ...
    }
}
```

Lack of interface restrictions

Lack of any restrictions placed by **auto** on the type that is deduced might result in defects that could otherwise be detected at compile time. Consider refactoring the getNetworkNodes function illustrated in *Use Cases — Improving resilience to library code changes* on page 203 to return std::deque<Node> instead of std::vector<Node>:

```
std::deque<Node> getNetworkNodes();  // Return type changed from std::vector<Node>.
    // Return a sequence of nodes in the current network.
```

While code that uses **auto** to store the result returned by getNetworkNodes only to subsequently iterate over it with a range-based **for** wouldn't be affected, the behavior of code that relies on the contiguous layout of elements in std::vector objects *silently* becomes undefined:

```
void testUseContiguousMemory()
{
    auto nodes = getNetworkNodes();
    CLibraryProcessNodes(&nodes[0], nodes.size());
        // Bug, exhibits UB when getNetworkNodes returns an std::deque
}
```

While specifying constraints on types deduced by **auto** with **static_assert** is possible, doing so is often cumbersome[3]:

---

[3]C++20 introduced **concepts**, i.e., named type requirements, as well as means to constrain **auto** with a specific concept, which can be used instead of **static_assert** in such circumstances. For example, one can constrain **auto** to accept only random access iterators:

```
#include <iterator>  // std::random_access_iterator
std::random_access_iterator auto it = std::begin(d_packets);
```

```
const Packet* PacketCache::findFirstCorruptPacket() const
{
    auto it = std::begin(d_packets);

    static_assert(
        std::is_base_of<
            std::random_access_iterator_tag,
            std::iterator_traits<decltype(it)>::iterator_category>::value,
        "'it' must satisfy the requirements of a random access iterator.");

    // ...

    return it == std::end(d_packets) ? nullptr : &*it;
}
```

Important properties of fundamental types might be hidden

Using **auto** for variables of fundamental types might hide important, context-sensitive considerations, such as overflow behavior or a mix of signed and unsigned arithmetic. For example, consider a library that provides functions for encoding a string and, separately, for computing the length of an encoded result for a certain input:

```
// encoder.h:
#include <string>  // std::string

// ...

struct Encoder
{
    template <typename ITERATOR>
    static void encode(ITERATOR result, const std::string& input);

    static int encodedLengthFor(const std::string& input);
};

// ...
```

We then write a function that uses the Encoder to encode its input and follows that up with converting the result to lowercase:

```
#include <cctype>  // std::tolower

#include <encoder.h>

void lowercaseEncode(std::string* result, const std::string& input)
{
    auto encodedLength = Encoder::encodedLengthFor(input);

    result->resize(encodedLength);
    Encoder::encode(result->begin(), input);

    while (--encodedLength >= 0)  // (1)
    {
        (*result)[encodedLength] = std::tolower((*result)[encodedLength]);
    }
}
```

The encodedLength variable in the example above uses **auto** to deduce its type from the return value of Encoder::encodedLengthFor. If the maintainers of the Encoder library changed the return type of encodedLengthFor function to an unsigned type, e.g., std::size_t, instead of **int**, the lowercaseEncode function would become defective due to different behavior of decrementing 0 for unsigned types.

Surprising deduction for list initialization

auto type-deduction rules differ from those of function templates if brace-enclosed initializer lists are used. Function template argument deduction will always fail, whereas, according to C++11 rules, std::initializer_list will be deduced for **auto**.

```
auto example0 = 0; // copy initialization, deduced as int
auto example1(0);  // direct initialization, deduced as int
auto example2{0};  // list initialization, deduced as std::initializer_list<int>

template <typename T> void func(T);

void testFunctionDeduction()
{
    func(0);    // T deduced as int
    func({0});  // Error
}
```

This surprising behavior was, however, widely regarded as a mistake.[4]

---

[4]This erroneous behavior was formally rectified in C++17 with, e.g., **auto** i0 deducing **int**. Furthermore, mainstream compilers had applied this deduction-rule change retroactively as early as GCC 5.1 (c. 2015), Clang 3.8 (c. 2016), and MSVC 19.00 (c. 2015), with the revised rule being applied even if std=c++11 flag is explicitly supplied.

Nonetheless, even with this retroactive fix, the effects of the deduction rules when applied to braced-initializer lists might be puzzling. In particular, std::initializer_list is deduced when **copy initialization** is used instead of **direct initialization**, which requires including <initializer_list>:

```
auto x1 = 1;                    // int
auto x2(1);                     //  "
auto x3{1};                     //  "

#include <initializer_list>    // std::initializer_list
auto x4 = {1};                 // OK, deduced as std::initializer_list<int>

auto x5{1, 2};                 // Error, direct-list-init requires exactly 1 element.
auto x6 = {1, 2};              // OK, deduced as std::initializer_list<int>
```

Deducing built-in arrays is problematic

Deducing built-in array types using **auto** presents multiple challenges. First, declaring an array of **auto** is ill formed:

```
auto arr1[]  = {1, 2};  // Error, array of auto is not allowed.
auto arr2[2] = {1, 2};  // Error, array of auto is not allowed.
```

Second, if the array bound is not specified, either the program does not compile or std::initializer_list is deduced instead of a built-in array:

```
#include <initializer_list>  // std::initializer_list
auto arr3 = {1, 2};  // OK, deduced as std::initializer_list<int>
auto arr4{1, 2};     // Error, direct-list init requires exactly 1 element.
```

Finally, attempting to circumvent this deficiency by using an alias template (see Section 1.1. "**using** Aliases" on page 133) will result in code that compiles but has undefined behavior:

```
template <typename TYPE, std::size_t SIZE>
using BuiltInArray = TYPE[SIZE];

auto arr5 = BuiltInArray<int, 2>{1, 2};
    // Bug, taking the address of a temporary array
```

The type deduced for arr5 is **int*** because array-to-pointer conversion is performed prior to deduction for nonreference types. Binding a pointer to a temporary array does not extend its lifetime, and the array is destroyed at the end of the full expression. Thus, any attempt to access elements of arr5 will lead to undefined behavior. Furthermore, even if this trick were to work, such code would also almost entirely defeat the purpose of **auto** since neither the array element's type nor the array's bound would be deduced.

With that said, using **auto** to deduce references to built-in arrays is straightforward:

```
int data[] = {1, 2};

        auto& arr6 = data;                        //          int (&) [2]
const auto& arr7 = BuiltInArray<int, 2>{1, 2};    // const int (&) [2]
        auto&& arr8 = BuiltInArray<int, 2>{1, 2}; //          int (&&)[2]
```

Note that the `arr7` and `arr8` references in the code snippet immediately above extend the lifetime of the temporary arrays that they bind to, so subscripting them does not have the undefined behavior that subscripting `arr5` in the previous code snippet has.

Annoyances

auto is disallowed for nonstatic data members

Despite C++11 allowing nonstatic data members to be initialized within class definitions, **auto** cannot be used to declare them:

```
class C
{
    auto d_i = 1;  // Error, nonstatic data member is declared with auto.
};
```

Not all template argument deduction constructs are allowed for **auto**

Despite **auto** type deduction largely following the template argument deduction rules, certain constructs that are allowed for templates are not allowed for **auto**. For example, when deducing a pointer-to-data-member type, templates allow for deducing both the data member type and the class type, whereas **auto** can deduce only the former:

```
struct Node
{
    int   d_data;
    Node* d_next;
};

template <typename TYPE>
void deduceMemberTypeFn(TYPE Node::*);

void testDeduceMemberType()
{
                deduceMemberTypeFn  (&Node::d_data); // OK, int Node::*
    auto Node::* deduceMemberTypeVar = &Node::d_data; // OK, "         "
}

template <typename TYPE>
void deduceClassTypeFn(int TYPE::*);
```

```
void testDeduceClassType()
{
                deduceClassTypeFn   (&Node::d_data);  // OK, int Node::*
    int auto::* deduceClassTypeVar = &Node::d_data;   // Error, not allowed
}

template <typename TYPE>
void deduceBothTypesFn(TYPE* TYPE::*);

void testDeduceBothTypes()
{
                 deduceBothTypesFn   (&Node::d_next);  // OK, Node* Node::*
    auto* auto::* deduceBothTypesVar = &Node::d_next;  // Error, not allowed
}

template <typename ARG>
void deduceFunctionArgFn(void (*)(ARG));

void test(int);

void testDeduceFunctionArg()
{
            deduceFunctionArgFn            (&test);  // OK, ARG is int.
    void (*deduceFunctionArgVar)(auto) = &test;    // Error, not allowed
}
```

Furthermore, deducing the parameter of a class template is also not allowed:

```
std::vector<int> vectorOfInt;

template <typename TYPE>
void deduceVectorArgFn(const std::vector<TYPE>&);

void testDeduceVectorArg()
{
                     deduceVectorArgFn   (vectorOfInt); // OK, TYPE is int.
    std::vector<auto> deduceVectorArgVar = vectorOfInt;  // Error, not allowed
}
```

Instead, if **auto** type deduction is desired in such cases, **auto** alone is suitable to deduce the type from the initializer:

```
auto deduceClassTypeVar   = &Node::d_data;  // OK, int Node::*
auto deduceBothTypesVar   = &Node::d_next;  // OK, Node* Node::*

auto deduceFunctionArgVar = &test;          // OK, void (*)(int)

auto deduceVectorArgVar   = vectorOfInt;    // OK, std::vector<int>
```

See Also

- "Trailing Return" (§1.1, p. 124) explains how the **auto** placeholder can be used to specify a function's return type at the end of its signature.

- "*Generic* Lambdas" (§2.2, p. 968) illustrates how the **auto** placeholder can be used in the parameter list of a lambda to make its function call operator a template.

- "**auto** Return" (§3.2, p. 1182) describes how the **auto** placeholder can be used to deduce a function's return type.

Further Reading

- For additional analysis of **auto** type deduction and its use, see **meyers15b**, "Item 1: Understand template type deduction," pp. 9–18; "Item 2: Understand **auto** type deduction," pp. 18–23; "Item 5: Prefer **auto** to explicit type declarations," pp. 37–43; and "Item 6: Use the explicitly typed initializer idiom when **auto** deduces undesired types," pp. 43–48.

Braced-Initialization Syntax: {}

Braced initialization, a generalization of C++03 initialization syntax, was designed with the intention of being used safely and uniformly in any initialization context.

Description

List initialization, originally dubbed **uniform initialization**, is the use of curly braces for initialization, is colloquially referred to as braced initialization, and is sometimes used in close collaboration with the C++ Standard Library's `std::initializer_list` template (see Section 2.1."initializer_list" on page 553). Braced initialization aims to provide a uniform syntax to initialize objects irrespective of (1) the context in which the syntax is used or (2) the type of the object being initialized. As we will see, this design goal was largely achieved albeit with some idiosyncrasies and rough edges.

C++03 initialization syntax review

Classic C++ affords several forms of initialization, each having its own syntax, some of which is syntactically interchangeable yet belying subtle differences. At the highest level, there are two dual categories of initialization: (1) copy/direct, when at least one initializer is present, and (2) default/value, when no initializer is available.

The first dual category of initialization comprises **copy initialization** and **direct initialization**. Direct initialization is produced when initializing an object with one or more arguments within parentheses, such as initializing a data member or base class in a constructor's initializer list, or in a **new** expression. Copy initialization is in effect when initializing from a value without using parentheses, such as passing an argument to a function or returning a value from a function. Both forms can be used to initialize a variable:

```
void test0()
{
    int i = 23;   // copy initialization
    int j(23);    // direct initialization
}
```

In both cases in the example above, we are initializing the variable, i or j, with the literal value 23.

For scalar types, there is no observable difference between these two dual forms of initialization in C++03, but for user-defined types, there is. First, **direct initialization** considers all valid user-defined conversion sequences as part of the overload set, whereas **copy initialization** excludes explicit conversions:

```
struct S
{
    explicit S(int);        //    explicit value constructor (from int)
             S(double);     // nonexplicit value constructor (from double)
             S(const S&);   // nonexplicit copy  constructor
};

S s1(1);     // direct init of s1: calls S(int);     copy constructor is not called
S s2(1.0);   // direct init of s2: calls S(double);  "       "      "  "    "
S s3 = 1;    // copy init of s3: calls S(double); copy constructor might be called
S s4 = 1.0;  // copy init of s4: calls S(double);   "       "      "  "    "
```

Exclusion of explicit conversions for copy initialization manifests in initialization of s1 calling a different constructor than s3 in the example above. What's more, copy initialization is defined as if a temporary object is constructed; the compiler is permitted to elide this temporary and, in practice, typically does. Note, however, that copy initialization is not permitted unless there is an accessible *copy* or *move* constructor, even if the temporary would have been elided.[1] If the *move* constructor for a user-defined type is declared and not accessible, copy initialization is ill formed; see Section 2.1."*Rvalue* References" on page 710 and Section 1.1."Deleted Functions" on page 53. Note that function arguments and return values are initialized using copy initialization.

Reference types are also initialized by copy and direct initialization, binding the declared reference to an object or function. For an *lvalue* reference to a non-**const**-qualified type, the referenced type must match exactly or be derived from that type. However, if binding an *rvalue* reference or an *lvalue* reference to a **const**-qualified type, the compiler copy-initializes a temporary object of the target type of the reference and binds the reference to that temporary; in such cases, the lifetime of the temporary object is extended to the end of the lifetime of the reference:

```
void test1()
{
    int i = 0;          // OK, copy initialization of int
    int& x(i);          // OK, direct initialization of reference
    const long& y = x;  // OK, y binds to a temporary whose lifetime it extends.
    long& z = x;        // Error, incompatible types
}
```

The second dual category of initialization comprises **default initialization** and **value initialization**. Both default and value initialization pertain to situations in which *no* initializer is supplied, and these distinct types of initialization are distinguished by the presence or absence of parentheses, where the absence of parentheses indicates default initialization and the presence indicates value initialization. Note that in simple contexts such as declaring a variable, empty parentheses might also indicate a function declaration instead (see *Use Cases — Avoiding the most vexing parse* on page 237):

---

[1] In C++17, **guaranteed copy elision** omits the temporary object construction and obviates the need for an accessible copy or move constructor.

```
int i;           // default initialization
int j();         // Oops, function declaration
int k = int();   // copy initialization of k with a value-initialized temporary

int* pd = new int;      // default initialization of dynamic int object
int* pv = new int();  // value            "          "       "        "        "
```

For **scalar types**, *default* initialization does not actually initialize an object, and *value* initialization will initialize the object as if by the literal 0. Note that the representation of this value is not necessarily all zero bits, as some platforms use distinct trap values for the null pointer value for pointers and for pointer-to-member objects.

For class having an accessible **user-provided** default constructor, default initialization and value initialization behave identically, calling the default constructor. If there is no accessible default constructor, both forms are ill formed. For objects of class types having an implicitly defined default constructor, each base and member subobject will be default initialized or value initialized according to the form of initialization indicated for the complete object; if any of those initializations produces an error, then the program is ill formed. Note that when a union with an implicitly defined default constructor is value initialized, the first member of the union will be value initialized as the active member of that union:

```
struct B
{
    int i;
    B() : i() { }  // User-provided default constructor: i is value initialized.
};

struct C
{
    int i;
    C() { }  // User-provided default constructor: i is default initialized.
};

struct D : B { int j; };  // derived class with no user-provided constructors

int* pdi = new int;     // default init of dynamic int, *pdi is uninitialized
int* pvi = new int();   // value   init of dynamic int, *pvi is 0
B* pdb = new B;         // default init of dynamic B, pdb->i is 0
B* pvb = new B();       // value   init of dynamic B, pvb->i is 0
C* pdc = new C;         // default init of dynamic C, pdc->i is uninitialized
C* pvc = new C();       // value   init of dynamic C, pvc->i is uninitialized
D* pdd = new D;         // default init of dynamic D, pdd->i is uninitialized
D* pvd = new D();       // value   init of dynamic D, pvd->i is 0
```

In the case of an object of type B, both default and value initialization will invoke the user-provided default constructor, which initializes the subobject i to 0. In the case of an object of type C, both default and value initialization will invoke the user-provided default constructor, which does not initialize the subobject i. In the case of an object of type D, which has an implicitly defined default constructor, the initialization of the subobject j depends on whether the D object is initialized by default initialization or by value initialization.

Any attempt to read the value of an *uninitialized* object has **undefined behavior**. The compiler will issue an error if a constant having such an uninitialized value is created implicitly, even if it is a member of a user-defined type. The types for which a constant can be default initialized are **const**-default-constructible. A type is **const**-default-constructible if it has a user-provided default constructor or if all its bases and members are **const**-default-constructible themselves. For example, the **int** member j, being a scalar type and thus not having a user-provided default constructor, makes D not **const**-default-constructible, whereas both base and member of D2 below have user-provided default constructors:

```
struct D2 : B { B j; };  // derived class with no user-provided constructors

const D  w;         // Error, w.j is not initialized.
const D  x = D();   // OK, x is value initialized.
const D2 y;         // OK, y is default initialized; subobjects invoke default ctor.
const D2 z = D2();  // OK, z is value initialized.
```

Note that, prior to a **defect report**[2] for C++17, relying on default initialization for a **const** object of an empty type was also ill formed. As this **defect report** was resolved at the end of 2016 and applies retroactively to earlier dialects, most current compilers no longer enforce this restriction, and some compilers, notably, GCC, had already stopped enforcing this rule several years prior to the **defect report**:

```
struct E { };

const E ce1;        // Error on some compilers
const E ce2 = E(); // OK, copy init of ce2 with a value-initialized temporary
```

Objects of static storage duration at file, namespace, or function scope (see Section 1.1. "Function **static** '11" on page 68) are **zero initialized** before any other initialization takes place. Note that zero-initialized pointer objects have a *null* address value (see Section 1.1. "**nullptr**" on page 99), even if that representation on the host platform is not numerically zero:

```
struct E
{
    int i;
};

struct F
{
    int i;
    F() : i(42) { }
};
```

---

[2]CWG issue 253; **miller00**

```
E globalE;
    // Zero initialization also zero-initializes globalE.i.
    // Default initialization provides no further initializations.

F globalF;
    // Zero initialization initializes globalF.i.
    // After that, default constructor is invoked.

int globalI;
    // Zero initialization initializes globalI.
    // Default initialization provides no further initializations.
```

Note the implication that default initialization for a static storage duration object will always initialize an object ready for use, either calling the default constructor of a type with a user-provided default constructor or zero-initializing scalars; see Table 1.

Table 1: Summary of C++03 initialization types

Initialization Type	No Arguments	≥ 1 Arguments
With Parentheses	*value* `int i = int();`	*direct* `int i(23);`
Without Parentheses	*default* `int i;`	*copy* `int i = 23;`

C++03 aggregate initialization

Aggregates are a special kind of object in C++03 that generally do not use constructors but follow a different set of rules for initialization, typically denoted by braces. There are two varieties of aggregates: (1) arrays and (2) user-defined class types that have no **private** or **protected** non**static** data members, no base classes, no user-provided constructors, and no virtual functions. Aggregates are similar to a classic C **struct**, potentially with additional, non**virtual** member functions. Note that members of an aggregate are not themselves required to be an aggregate:

```
#include <string>  // std::string

int a[5];           // Arrays are aggregates.

struct A
{
    int        i;   // public data member
    std::string s;  // A is an aggregate even though std::string is not.

private:
    static int j;   // Private data member is static.
    void f();       // Member functions are OK, even if private.
};
```

A quick note on terminology: Strictly speaking, arrays comprise *elements*, and classes comprise *members*, but for ease of exposition in this text, we refer to both as *members*.

When an aggregate is copied by either direct or copy initialization, rather than calling copy constructors, the corresponding members of each aggregate are copied using direct initialization, which corresponds to the behavior of an implicitly defined copy constructor for a class. Note that this process might be applied recursively, if members are aggregates themselves. Further note that the result of copy-initializing one array with another depends on the context. If this initialization happens as a part of copy initialization of an encompassing aggregate, the array elements are copy initialized. Otherwise, the source array undergoes array-to-pointer decay and becomes unsuitable to initialize the target array, resulting in an ill-formed program. This array-copy behavior is one of the motivations for the addition of the std::array template in C++11.

When an aggregate is *default* initialized, each of its members is *default* initialized. When an aggregate is *value* initialized, each of its members is *value* initialized. This behavior follows the usual rules for an implicitly defined constructor for a class type and defines the corresponding behavior for array initialization:

```
int n = 17;
int* pid = new int[n];       // default initialization of dynamic array object and
                             // its elements

int* piv = new int[n]();     // value initialization of dynamic array object and
                             // its elements

A* pd = new A;               // default initialization of dynamic A object and
                             // its members

A* pv = new A();             // value initialization of dynamic A object
                             // and its members
```

Otherwise, an aggregate must be *aggregate* initialized by a braced list — in the form = { list-of-values }; — where members of the aggregate will be initialized by *copy* initialization from the corresponding value in the list of values. If the aggregate has more members than are provided by the list, the remaining members are *value* initialized. It is an error to provide more values in the list than there are members in the aggregate. A union has only one active member, and thus its first member will be initialized by no more than a single value from the list; this behavior becomes relevant for unions as data members of an aggregate initialized by *brace elision*:

```
union U
{
    int i;
    const char* s;
};
```

```
U x = {    };  // OK, value-initializes x.i = 0
U y = { 1  };  // OK, copy-initializes x.i = 1
U z = { "" };  // Error, cannot initialize z.i with ""
```

Let's review the various ways in which we might attempt to initialize an object of aggregate type A2 in the body of a function, **test**, i.e., defined at function scope:

```
struct A2 { int i; };  // aggregate with a single data member

void test()
{
            A2  a1;              // default init: i is not initialized!
    const   A2& a2 = A2();       // value init: i is 0.
            A2  a3 = A2();       // value init followed by copy init: i is 0.
            A2  a4();            // Oops, function declaration!
            A2  a5 = { 5 };      // aggregate initialization employing copy init
            A2  a6 = { };        //     "              "            "    value  "
            A2  a7 = { 5, 6 };   // Error, too many initializers for aggregate A2
    static  A2  a8;              // zero-initialized, then (no-op) default init
}
```

Note the following in the sample code above.

- a1 — Since a1 is **default initialized**, each data member within the aggregate is itself independently **default initialized**. For scalar types, such as an **int**, the effect of default initialization at function scope is a no-op, i.e., a1.i is not initialized. Any attempt to access the contents of a1.i has **undefined** behavior.

- a2 and a3 — In the cases of both a2 and a3, a temporary of type A2 is first **value initialized**. Then, the temporary is bound to a reference for a2, extending its lifetime, whereas for a3, the temporary is used to **copy-initialize** the named variable. Both a2.i and a3.i are initialized to the value 0.

- a4 — Notice that we are unable to create a **value-initialized** local variable, a4, by applying parentheses since that would be interpreted as declaring a function taking no arguments and returning an object of type A2 by value; see *Use Cases — Avoiding the most vexing parse* on page 237.

- a5, a6, and a7 — C++03 supports **aggregate initialization** using braced syntax, as illustrated by a5, a6, and a7 in the code snippet above. The local variable a5 is copy initialized such that a5.i has the *user-supplied* value 5, whereas a6 is value initialized since there are no supplied initializers; hence, a6.i is initialized to 0. Attempting to pass a7 two values to initialize a single data member results in a compile-time error. Note that had class A2 held a second data member, the statement initializing a5 would have resulted in **copy initialization** of the first and **value initialization** of the second.

- **a8** — Because **a8** has static storage duration, it is first *zero* initialized, i.e., **a8.i** is set to 0, and then it is *default* initialized, which is a no-op for the same reasons that it is a no-op for **a1**.

Finally, note that a scalar can be thought of as if it were an array of one element, though note that scalars are never subject to **array-to-pointer decay**; in fact, if we were to take the address of any scalar and add **1** to it, the new pointer value would represent the one-past-the-end iterator for that scalar's implied array of length 1. Similarly, scalars can be initialized using aggregate initialization, just as if they were single-element arrays, where the braced list for a scalar can contain zero or one elements. In C++03, however, scalars cannot be initialized from an empty brace:

```
int    i = { };        // Error in C++03; OK in C++11 (i is 0).
int    j = { 1 };      // OK, i is 1.
double k = { 3.14 };   // OK, k is 3.14.
```

Braced initialization in C++11

Everything we've discussed so far, including braced initialization of aggregates, is well defined in C++03. This same braced-initialization syntax — modified slightly so as to preclude narrowing conversions (see the next section) — is extended in C++11 to work consistently and uniformly in many new situations. This enhanced braced-initialization syntax is designed to better support the two dual initialization categories discussed in *C++03 initialization syntax review* on page 215 as well as entirely new capabilities including language-level support for lists of initial values implemented using the C++ Standard Library's `std::initializer_list` class template.

C++11 restrictions on narrowing conversions

Narrowing conversions, a.k.a. **lossy conversions**, are a notorious source of runtime errors. One of the important properties of list initializations implemented using the C++11 braced-initialization syntax is that error-prone narrowing conversions are no longer permitted. Consider, for example, an **int** array, **ai**, initialized with various built-in *literal* values:

```
int ai[] =
{          //    C++03    C++11
    5,     // (0) OK      OK
    5.0,   // (1) OK      Error, narrowing double to int conversion is not allowed.
    5.5,   // (2) OK      Error, narrowing double to int conversion is not allowed.
    "5",   // (3) Error   Error, no const char* to int conversion exists.
};
```

In C++03, floating-point literals would be coerced to fit within an integer even if the conversion was known to be lossy, e.g., line (2) in the code snippet above would initialize **ai[2]** to **5**. By contrast, C++11 disallows *any* such implicit conversions in braced initializations even when the conversion is known *not* to be lossy, e.g., element **ai[1]** above.

Narrowing conversions within the integral and floating-point type families, respectively, are generally disallowed except where it can be verified at compile time that overflow does not occur and, in the case of integers and classic **enum**s, the initializer value can be represented exactly[3]:

```
const unsigned long ulc = 1;   // compile-time integral constant: 1UL

short as[] = //          C++03      C++11                     Stored Value
{
    32767,   // (0)  OK         OK                        as[0] == 32767
    32768,   // (1)  Warning?   Error, overflow
    -32768,  // (2)  OK         OK                        as[2] == -32768
    -32769,  // (3)  Warning?   Error, underflow
    1UL,     // (4)  OK         OK                        as[4] == 1
    ulc,     // (5)  OK         OK                        as[5] == 1
    1.0      // (6)  OK         Error, narrowing
};
```

Notice that both *overflow*, line (1), and *underflow*, line (3), are rejected for integral values in C++11, whereas neither is ill formed in C++03. An integral literal, line (4), or an **integral constant**, line (5), of a wider type, e.g., **unsigned long**, can be used to initialize a narrower type, e.g., **signed short**, provided that the value can be represented exactly; however, even a floating-point literal that can be *represented exactly*, line (6), is nonetheless rejected in C++11 when used to initialize any integral scalar.

On the other hand, initializing floating-point scalars with integral initializers is allowed but only if the initializer's value can be represented *exactly* by the target type; initializing floating-point scalars with floating-point initializers does not require that the initializer is represented exactly as long as no overflow occurs:

```
float af[] =
{              //          C++03  C++11              Stored value
    3L,        // (0)  OK     OK                 af[0] == 3L
    16777216,  // (1)  OK     OK                 af[1] == 16777216
    16777217,  // (2)  OK     Error, lossy
    0.75,      // (3)  OK     OK                 af[3] == 0.75
    2.4,       // (4)  OK     OK, but lossy      af[4] != 2.4
    1e-46,     // (5)  OK     OK, but underflow  af[5] == 0
    1e+39      // (6)  OK     Error, overflow
};
```

In the example above, lines (0) to (2) represent initialization from an integral type, which requires that the initialized value be represented exactly. Lines (3) to (6) are instead initialized from a floating-point type, e.g., **double**, and therefore are restricted only from overflow.

---

[3]As of C++20, implicit conversion from either a pointer or pointer-to-member type to **bool** is considered narrowing. This change has been accepted as a **defect report** (see **yuan20**) and was applied to earlier versions of the Standard.

When an initializer is *not* a **constant expression**, braced initialization could potentially result in a narrowing conversion at run time and is therefore ill formed. For example, initializing a **float** with a **double** or a **long double**, a **double** with a **long double**, or *any* floating-point type with an integral one is always ill formed for an initializer that is not a constant expression. By the same token, an integral type, e.g., **int**, is not permitted to be initialized by a nonconstant-expression integer value of any other potentially larger integral type (e.g., **long**), even if the number of bits in the representation for the two types on the current platform is the same. Finally, a nonconstant expression of integral type, e.g., **short**, cannot be used to initialize an unsigned version of the same type, e.g., **unsigned short**, and vice versa.

To illustrate the constraints imposed on nonconstant expressions described above, consider a simple aggregate class, S, comprising an **int**, i, and a **double**, d:

```
struct S // aggregated class
{
    int    i; // integral scalar type
    double d; // floating-point scalar type
};
```

A function, test, declaring a variety of arithmetic parameter types illustrates restrictions imposed by C++11 braced initialization on narrowing initializations that were well formed in C++03:

```
void test(short s, int i, long j, unsigned u, float f, double d, long double ld)
{                        //        C++03 C++11
    S s0 = { i, d };     // (0)    OK    OK
    S s1 = { s, f };     // (1)    OK    OK
    S s2 = { u, d };     // (2)    OK    Error, u  causes narrowing.
    S s3 = { i, ld };    // (3)    OK    Error, ld causes narrowing.
    S s4 = { f, d };     // (4)    OK    Error, f  causes narrowing.
    S s5 = { i, s };     // (5)    OK    Error, s  causes narrowing.
}
```

In the test function above, lines (0) and (1) are OK because there is no possibility of narrowing on any conforming platform unlike lines (2) to (5), despite that, in practice, it is more than likely that a **double** will be able to exactly represent every value representable by a **short int**.

C++11 aggregate initialization

Aggregate initialization in C++11, including initialization of arrays, is subject to the rules prohibiting narrowing conversions:

```
int  i  = { 1 };     // OK
long j  = { 2 };     // OK

int  a[] = { 0, 1, 2 }; // OK
```

```
int b[] = { 0, i, j };  // Error, cannot narrow j from long to int

struct S { int a; };
S s1 = { 0  };  // OK
S s2 = { i  };  // OK
S s3 = { 0L };  // OK, 0L is an integer constant expression.
S s4 = { j  };  // Error, narrowing
```

In addition, the rules for **value initialization** now state that members without a specific initializer value in the braced list are "as-if" copy initialized from {}. These rules will result in an error when initializing a member that has an **explicit** default constructor. Furthermore, from C++14 onward, if such a member has a default member initializer, then that member is initialized from the default member initializer; see Section 1.2. "Aggregate Init '14" on page 138. Note that if the member is of reference type and no initializer is provided, the initialization is ill formed.

Regardless of whether the aggregate itself is initialized using a copy initialization or direct initialization, the members of the aggregate will be copy initialized from the corresponding initializer:

```
struct E { };                      // empty type
struct AE { int x; E y; E z; };    // aggregate comprising several empty objects
struct S { explicit S(int = 0) {} }; // class with explicit default constructor
struct AS{ int x; S y; S z; };     // aggregate comprising several S objects

AE aed;                   // OK
AE ae0 = {};              // OK
AE ae1 = { 0 };           // OK
AE ae2 = { 0, {} };       // OK
AE ae3 = { 0, {}, {} };   // OK

AS asd;                   // OK
AS as0 = {};              // OK in 03; Error in 11 calling explicit ctor for S
AS as1 = { 0 };           // OK in 03; Error in 11 calling explicit ctor for S
AS as2 = { 0, S() };      // OK in 03; Error in 11 calling explicit ctor for S
AS as3 = { 0, S(), S() }; // OK, all the aggregate's members have an initializer.
```

To better support generalizing the syntax of brace initialization in a style similar to aggregate initialization, an aggregate can be initialized from an object of the same type through *aggregate* initialization in C++11 as well as through *direct* initialization per C++03:

```
S x{};     // OK, value initialization
S y = {x}; // OK in C++11; copy initialization via aggregate-initialization syntax
```

Otherwise, initialization of aggregates in C++11 is the same where it would have a meaning in C++03 and is correspondingly extended into new places where braced initialization is permitted, as documented in the following subsections.

Copy list initialization

For C++03, only aggregates and scalars could be initialized via braced-initialization syntax:

```
Type var = { /*...*/ };   // C++03-style aggregate-only initialization
```

The first part of generalizing braced-initialization syntax for C++11 is to allow the same syntactic form used to initialize aggregates to be used for *all* user-defined types. This extended form of braced initialization, known as **copy list initialization**, follows the rules of copy initialization:

```
Class var1 = val;       // C++03 copy initialization
Class var2 = { val };   // C++11 copy list initialization
```

For a nonaggregate class type, C++11 allows the use of a braced list provided that its sequence of values serves as a suitable argument to a non**explicit** constructor of the class being initialized. Importantly, this use of copy list initialization provides meaning to **explicit** constructors when taking other than a single argument. For example, consider a **struct** S having constructors with zero to three parameters, only the last of which is **explicit**:

```
struct S
{
         S();                                // default ctor
         S(int);                             // 1-argument ctor
         S(int, const char*);                // 2-argument ctor
    explicit S(int, const char*, double);    // 3-argument ctor
};
```

We can use copy list initialization only if the selected constructor is *not* declared to be **explicit**, e.g., s0, s1, and s2 but not s3:

```
S s0 = { };                // OK, copy list initialization
S s1 = { 1 };              // OK, copy list initialization
S s2 = { 1, "two" };       // OK, copy list initialization
S s3 = { 1, "two", 3.14 }; // Error, constructor is explicit
```

Had we instead declared our default constructor or any of the others to be **explicit**, the corresponding *copy* (or *copy list*) initialization above would have failed too.

Another important difference between C++11 copy list initialization and C++03 copy initialization is that the braced-list syntax considers all constructors, including those that are declared to be **explicit**. Consider a **struct** Q having two overloaded single-argument constructors, i.e., one taking an **int** and the other a member template taking a single deduced type, T, by value:

```
struct Q  // class containing both explicit and implicit constructor overloads
{
    explicit Q(int);               // value constructor taking an int
    template <typename T> Q(T);    // value constructor taking a  T
};
```

Employing direct initialization, e.g., x0 in the code snippet below, selects the most appropriate constructor, regardless of whether it is declared to be **explicit**, and successfully uses that one; employing copy initialization, e.g., x1, drops explicit constructors from the overload set before determining a best match; and employing copy list initialization, e.g., x2, again includes all constructors in the overload set but is ill formed if the selected constructor is **explicit**:

```
Q x0(0);      // OK, direct initialization calls Q(int).
Q x1 = 1;     // OK, copy initialization calls Q(T).
Q x2 = {2};   // Error, copy list initialization selects but cannot call Q(int).
Q x3{3};      // Same idea as x0; direct list initialization calls Q(int).
```

In other words, the presence of the = coupled with the braced notation, e.g., x2 in the code example above, forces the compiler to choose the constructor *as if* it were direct initialization, e.g., x0, but then forces a compilation failure if the selected constructor turns out to be **explicit**. This "consider-but-fail-if-selected" behavior of copy list initialization is analogous to that of functions declared using = **delete**; see Section 1.1."Deleted Functions" on page 53. Using braces but omitting the = (e.g., x3) puts us back in the realm of *direct* rather than *copy* initialization; see *Direct list initialization* on page 228.

When initializing references, copy list initialization, i.e., braced syntax, behaves similarly to copy initialization, i.e., no braces, with respect to the generation of temporaries. For example, when using a braced list to initialize an *lvalue* reference, e.g., **int**& ri or **const int**& cri in the code example below, to a scalar of a type that exactly matches it (e.g., **int** i), no temporary is created, just as it would not have been without the braces; otherwise, a temporary will be created, provided that a viable conversion exists and is not narrowing:

```
#include <cassert>  // standard C assert macro

void test()
{
    int  i = 2;           assert(i   == 2);
    int& ri = { i };      assert(ri  == 2);  // OK, no temporary created
    ri = 3;               assert(i   == 3);  // Original i is affected.

    const int& cri = { i };  assert(cri == 3);  // OK, no temporary created
    ri = 4;                  assert(cri == 4);  // Other reference is affected.

    short s = 5;          assert(s   == 5);
    const int& crs = { s };  assert(crs == 5);  // OK, temporary is created.
    s = 6;                   assert(crs == 5);  // Temporary is unchanged.

    long j = 7;           assert(j   == 7);
    const int& crj = { j };  // Error, narrowing conversion from long to int
}
```

As evidenced by the C-style asserts in the example above, no temporary is created when initializing either ri or cri since modifying the reference affects the variable supplied as the initializer, and vice versa. The C++ type of `crs`, on the other hand, does *not* match exactly the type of its initializer; a temporary *is* created, and hence the value accessed through the reference is not affected by changes to the object supplied as the initializer. Lastly, unlike the case involving `s` (of type **short**), attempting to initialize a **const** *lvalue* reference of type **int**, `crj`, with `j` (of type **long**) is a narrowing conversion and thus ill formed.

Finally, *rvalue* and **const** *lvalue* references to scalars and aggregates initialized via braced lists of literal values follow the rules of aggregates (see *C++11 aggregate initialization* on page 224); a temporary is materialized having the indicated value and bound to the reference with the temporary's lifetime extended:

```
const int& i0 = { };     // OK, materialized temporary is value initialized.
const int& i1 = { 5 };   // OK,         "           "        " copy        "
```

In the example above, a temporary is *value* initialized to 0 and bound to `i0`; another temporary is then *copy* initialized to 5 and bound to `i1`.

Nonmodifiable references to *aggregate UDTs* exploit the generalization of *copy* and *direct* list initialization. Consider an aggregate `A` that comprises three **int** data members:

```
struct A            // struct A is an aggregate data type.
{
    int i, j, k;  // This struct contains three data members of type int.
};
```

We can now use braced initialization to materialize a temporary object of aggregate type `A` using aggregate initialization:

```
const A& s0 = { };          // i, j, and k are value initialized.
const A& s1 = { 1 };        // i is copy and j and k are value initialized.
const A& s2 = { 1, 2 };     // i and j are copy and k is value initialized.
const A& s3 = { 1, 2, 3 };  // i, j, and k are copy initialized.
```

In the example above, each of the references, `s0` through `s3`, is initialized to a temporary **struct** of type A holding the respective aggregate value `{0,0,0}`, `{1,0,0}`, `{1,2,0}`, and `{1,2,3}`.

Direct list initialization

Of the two dual forms of initialization, *direct* versus *copy*, *direct* initialization is the stronger since it enables use of all accessible constructors, i.e., including those declared to be **explicit**. The next step in generalizing the use of braced initialization is to allow use of a braced list without the intervening = character between the variable and the opening brace to denote direct initialization too:

```
Class var1(/*...*/);  // C++03-style direct initialization
Class var2{/*...*/};  // C++11-style direct list initialization
```

Note that C++11 does *not* similarly relax the rules to allow for initialization of aggregates with parentheses.[4]

The syntax suggested in the previous example is known as **direct list initialization** and follows the rules of direct initialization rather than copy initialization in that all constructors of the named type are considered:

```
struct Q  // class containing explicit constructor
{
    explicit Q(int);  // value constructor taking an int
    // ...
};

Q x(5);     // OK  direct initialization can call explicit constructors.
Q y{5};     // OK, direct list initialization can call explicit constructors.
Q z = {5};  // Error, copy list initialization can't call explicit constructors.
```

Either form of direct initialization, shown for x and y in the code example above, can invoke an **explicit** constructor of class Q, whereas *copy list* initialization will necessarily result in a compile-time error.

However, following the rules of C++11 braced initialization, narrowing conversions are rejected by direct *list* initialization:

```
long a = 3L;

Q b(a);  // OK, direct initialization
Q c{a};  // Error, direct list initialization cannot use a narrowing conversion.
```

Similarly, **explicit** conversion operators (see Section 1.1."**explicit** Operators" on page 61) can be considered when direct list initialization (or direct initialization) is employed on a scalar, but not so with copy list initialization (or copy initialization). Consider, for example, class W that can convert to either an **int** or a **long** where conversion to **int** is explicit:

```
struct W
{
    explicit operator int()  const;  // used via direct initialization only
             operator long() const;  // used via direct or copy initialization
};
```

Initializing a **long** variable with an expression of type W can be accomplished via either *direct* or *copy* initialization (e.g., jDirect and jCopy, respectively, in the code snippet below), but initializing an **int** variable with such an expression can be accomplished only via *direct* initialization (e.g., iDirect):

```
long jDirect {W()};  // OK, considers both operators, calls operator long
long jCopy = {W()};  // OK, considers implicit op only, calls operator long
int  iDirect {W()};  // OK, considers both operators, calls operator int
int  iCopy = {W()};  // Error, considers implicit op only, narrowing conversion
```

---

[4]C++20 finally allows for aggregates to be initialized with parentheses.

In the previous example, attempting to use copy list initialization, e.g., iCopy, forces the conversion to **long** as the only option, which results in a narrowing conversion and an ill-formed program.

Note that, for **aggregate** types, even direct list initialization will not allow the explicit constructors of the individual member types to be considered since such *member-wise* initialization is invariably copy initialization; see *C++11 aggregate initialization* on page 224.

We can use direct list initialization as part of **member initialization lists** for base classes and data members of a class; note that there is no equivalent to allow copy list initialization in such a context:

```
struct B { int i; };        // aggregate type
struct C { C(); C(int); };  // nonaggregate type

struct D : B  // class publicly derived from aggregate B
{
    C m;  // data member of nonaggregate type C

    D()      : B{},  m{} { } // direct-initialized base/member objects
    D(int x) : B{x}, m{x} { } //    "         "         "       "
};
```

In the definition of class D above, both constructors employ direct list initialization; the first is also an example of *value* initialization for both aggregate class B and nonaggregate class C. Note that in C++03, aggregate initialization could not be used for bases and members.

Direct list initialization, i.e., with braces, or direct initialization, i.e., with parentheses, can also occur in **new** expressions for both **aggregate** and **nonaggregate** types. If no initializer is provided, the allocated object is **default initialized**; if empty braces or parentheses are supplied, the object is **value initialized**; otherwise, the object is initialized from the contents of the braced or, where permitted, parenthesized list.

As an illustrative example, let's consider the scalar type **int**, which itself can be **default initialized**, i.e., not initialized, **value initialized** to 0 via empty braces or parentheses, or **direct initialized** via a single element within either parentheses or braces:

```
int* s0  = new int;         // default initialized (no initializer)

int* t0 = new int();        // direct-(value)-initialized from ()
int* t1 = new int{};        // direct-(value)-list-initialized from {}

int* u0 = new int(7);       // direct initialized from 7
int* u1 = new int{7};       // direct-list-initialized from {7}

int* v0 = new int[5];       // All 5 elements are default initialized.

int* w0 = new int[5]();     // All 5 elements are value initialized.
int* w1 = new int[5]{};     // Array is direct-list-initialized from {}.
```

```cpp
int* x0 = new int[5](9);      // Error, invalid initializer for an array
int* x1 = new int[5]{9};      // Array is direct-list-initialized from {9}.

int* y1 = new int[5]{1,2,3};  // array direct-list-initialized from {1,2,3}

int* z1 = new int[5]{1,2,3,4,5};  // direct-list-initialized from {1,2,3,4,5}
```

All the comments in the example above apply to the object being created in the **new** expression; the pointer is copy initialized with the address of the dynamically allocated object in all cases. Note that, in C++03, we could default-initialize (e.g., v0) or value-initialize (e.g., w0) the elements of an array in a **new** expression, but there was no way to initialize the elements of such an array to anything other than a default value (e.g., x0); as of C++11, direct list initialization with braces (e.g., x1, y1, z1) makes a more flexible, heterogeneous initialization of array elements in **new** expressions possible.

Contrasting copy and direct list initialization

Applicability of copy list initialization and direct list initialization strongly depends on whether constructors are declared **explicit**:

```cpp
struct C
{
    explicit C() { }
    explicit C(int) { }
};

struct A  // aggregate of C
{
    C x;
    C y;
};

int main()
{
    C c1;          // OK, default initialization
    C c2{};        // OK, value initialization
    C c3{1};       // OK, direct list initialization
    C c4 = {};     // Error, copy list initialization cannot use explicit
                   // default ctor.
    C c5 = {1};    // Error, copy list initialization cannot use explicit ctor.

    C c6[5];       // OK, default initialization
    C c7[5]{};     // Error, aggregate initialization requires a nonexplicit
                   // default ctor.
    C c8[5]{1};    // Error, aggregate initialization requires nonexplicit ctors.
    C c9[5] = {};  // Error, aggregate initialization requires a nonexplicit
                   // default ctor.
```

```
C ca[5] = {1};   // Error, aggregate initialization requires nonexplicit ctors.

A a1;            // OK, default initialization
A a2{};          // Error, aggregate initialization requires a nonexplicit
                 // default ctor.
A a3{1};         // Error, aggregate initialization requires nonexplicit ctors.
A a4 = {};       // Error, aggregate initialization requires a nonexplicit
                 // default ctor.
A a5 = {1};      // Error, aggregate initialization requires nonexplicit ctors.
}
```

Note that if the constructors for C were not marked explicit, then all of the variables in the example above would be safely initialized. If only the **int** constructor of C were explicit, then the initializations that did not depend on the **int** constructor would be valid:

```
struct C
{
    C() { }
    explicit C(int) { }
};

struct A  // aggregate of C
{
    C x;
    C y;
};

int main()
{
    C c1;          // OK, default initialization
    C c2{};        // OK, value initialization
    C c3{1};       // OK, direct list initialization
    C c4 = {};     // OK, copy list initialization
    C c5 = {1};    // Error, copy list initialization cannot use explicit ctor.

    C c6[5];       // OK, default initialization
    C c7[5]{};     // OK, value initialization
    C c8[5]{1};    // Error, aggregate initialization requires nonexplicit ctors.
    C c9[5] = {};  // OK, copy list initialization
    C ca[5] = {1}; // Error, aggregate initialization requires nonexplicit ctors.

    A a1;          // OK, default initialization
    A a2{};        // OK, value initialization
    A a3{1};       // Error, aggregate initialization requires nonexplicit ctors.
    A a4 = {};     // OK, copy list initialization
    A a5 = {1};    // Error, aggregate initialization requires nonexplicit ctors.
}
```

Integrating default member initialization with braced initialization

Another new feature for C++11 is *default member initializers* for data members in a class; see Section 2.1."Default Member Init" on page 318. This new syntax supports both copy list initialization and direct list initialization. However, initialization with parentheses is not permitted in this context:

```cpp
struct S
{
    int i = { 13 };

    S() { }                    // OK, i == 13.
    explicit S(int x) : i(x) { } // OK, i == x.
};


struct W
{
    S a{};          // OK, by default j.i == 13.
    S b{42};        // OK, by default j.i == 42.
    S c = {42};     // Error, constructor for S is explicit.
    S d = S{42};    // OK, direct initialization of temporary for initializer
    S e(42);        // Error, fails to parse as a function declaration
    S f();          // OK, declares member function f
};
```

List initialization where the list itself is a single argument to a constructor

Another new form of initialization for C++11 is list initialization with a braced list of arguments to populate a container; see Section 2.1."initializer_list" on page 553. If a braced list contains arguments that are all of the same type, then the compiler will look for a constructor taking an argument of type std::initializer_list<T>, where T is that common type. Similarly, if a braced list of values can be implicitly converted to a common type, then a constructor for an std::initializer_list of that type will be preferred. When initializing from a nonempty braced-initializer list, a matching initializer list constructor always wins overload resolution. However, *value* initializing from a pair of empty braces will prefer a default constructor:

```cpp
#include <initializer_list>  // std::initializer_list

struct S
{
  S() {}
  S(std::initializer_list<int>) {}
  S(int, int);
};
```

```
S a;                // default initialization with default constructor
S b();              // function declaration!
S c{};              // value initialization with default constructor
S d = {};           // copy list initialization with std::initializer_list
S e{1,2,3,4,5};     // direct list initialization with std::initializer_list
S f{1,2};           // direct list initialization with std::initializer_list
S g = {1,2};        // copy list initialization with std::initializer_list
S h(1,2);           // direct initialization with two ints
```

Omitting the type name when braced initializing a temporary

In addition to supporting new forms of initialization, C++11 allows for braced lists to implicitly construct an object where the type is known from the context, such as for function arguments and return values. This use of a braced list without explicitly specifying a type is equivalent to constructing a temporary object of the destination type from a braced-initializer list. As these contexts use copy initialization, such a temporary will be initialized using copy list initialization, and it will reject explicit constructors:

```
struct S
{
    S(int, int) {}
    explicit S(const char*, const char*) {}
};

S foo(bool b)
{
    if (b)
    {
        // return { "hello", "world" };   // Error, copy list init calls expl ctor.
        return S{ "hello", "world" };      // OK, direct list init of a temporary
    }
    else
    {
        return {0, 0};  // OK, int constructor is not explicit.
    }
}

void bar(S s) { }

int main()
{
    bar( S{0,0} );  // OK, direct list initialization, then copy initialization
    bar( {0,0} );  // OK, copy list initialization
    bar( S{"Hello", "world"} );  // OK, direct list initialization
    bar( {"Hello", "world"} );  // Error, copy list initialization cannot use
                                 // explicit ctor.
}
```

Initializing variables in conditional expressions

As a final tweak to make initialization consistent across the language, initializing a variable in the condition of a **while** or **if** statement in C++03 supported only copy initialization and required using the = token. For C++11, those rules are relaxed to allow any valid form of braced initialization. Conversely, the declaration of a control variable in a **for** loop has supported all forms of initialization permitted for a variable declaration since the original C++ standard[5]:

```
void f()
{
    for (int i = 0; ; ) {}      // OK in all versions of C++
    for (int i = {0}; ; ) {}    // OK for aggregates in C++03 and all types from C++11
    for (int i{0}; ; ) {}       // OK from C++11, direct list initialization
    for (int i{}; ; ) {}        // OK from C++11, value initialization
    for (int i(0); ; ) {}       // OK in all versions of C++
    for (int i(); ; ) {}        // OK in all versions of C++
    for (int i; ; ) {}          // OK in all versions of C++

    if (int i = 0) {}      // OK in all versions of C++
    if (int i = {0}) {}    // OK from C++11, copy list initialization
    if (int i{0}) {}       // OK from C++11, direct list initialization
    if (int i{}) {}        // OK from C++11, value initialization
    if (int i(0)) {}       // Error in all versions of C++
    if (int i()) {}        // Error in all versions of C++
    if (int i) {}          // Error in all versions of C++

    while (int i = 0) {}      // OK in all versions of C++
    while (int i = {0}) {}    // OK from C++11, copy list initialization
    while (int i{0}) {}       // OK from C++11, direct list initialization
    while (int i{}) {}        // OK from C++11, value initialization
    while (int i(0)) {}       // Error in all versions of C++
    while (int i()) {}        // Error in all versions of C++
    while (int i) {}          // Error in all versions of C++
}
```

Copy initialization and scalars

With the addition of explicit conversion operators to C++11 (see Section 1.1."**explicit** Operators" on page 61), it becomes possible for *copy* initialization and *copy list* initialization to fail for scalars and similarly for *direct list* initialization:

```
struct S
{
    explicit operator int() const { return 1; }
};
```

---

[5]Note that GCC would traditionally accept the C++11-only syntaxes, even when using C++03.

```
S one{};

int a(one);     // OK, a = 1.
int b{one};     // OK, b = 1.
int c = {one};  // Error, copy list initialization used with
                // explicit conversion operator.
int d = one;    // Error, copy initialization used with
                // explicit conversion operator.

class C {
    int x;
    int y;

public:
    C(const S& value) : x(value)  // OK, x = 1
                      , y{value}   // OK, y = 1
    {
    }
};
```

Use Cases

Defining a value-initialized variable

The C++ grammar has a pitfall where an attempt to value-initialize a variable turns out
to be a function declaration:

```
struct S{};

S s1();        // Oops! function declaration
S s2 = S();    // variable declaration using value initialization and then
               // copy initialization
```

The declaration of s1 looks like an attempt to value-initialize a local variable of type S, but,
in fact, it is a forward declaration of a function s1 that takes no arguments and returns an S
object by value. This behavior is particularly surprising for folks who do not realize we can
declare (but not define) a function within the body of another function, a feature retained
from the original C Standard. Clearly, there would be an ambiguity in the grammar at this
point unless the language provided a rule to resolve the ambiguity, and the rule opts in favor
of the function declaration in all circumstances, including at function local scope. While this
rule would be essential at namespace and class scope because otherwise functions taking no
arguments could not be so easily declared, the same rule also applies at function local scope,
first for consistency and second for compatibility with pre-existing C code that we might
want to compile with a C++ compiler.

By switching from parentheses to braces, the risk of confusion between a vexing parse and a variable declaration is avoided:

```
S s{};  // object of type S
```

Avoiding the most vexing parse

Value initializing constructor arguments can lead to another pitfall, often called *the most vexing parse*. C++ will parse the intended value initialization of a constructor argument as the declaration of an unnamed parameter of a function type instead, which would otherwise not be legal but for the language rule that such a parameter implicitly decays to a pointer to a function of that type:

```
struct S{};
struct V { V(const S&) { } };

void foo()
{
    V v1(S());     // most vexing parse, function v1 taking a function pointer
    V v2((S()));   // workaround, object of type V due to parentheses on argument

    S x = S();     // declare a variable of type S
    V v3(x);       // workaround, object of type V, but S has longer lifetime
}
```

In the example above, v1 is the forward declaration of a function in the surrounding namespace that returns an object of type V and has a parameter of type pointer-to-function-returning-S-and-taking-no-arguments, S(*)(). That is, we can use an equivalent declaration — V v1(S(*)()); — to express this type.

This most vexing of parses can be disambiguated by having the arguments clearly form an expression, not a type. One simple way to force the argument to be parsed as an expression is to add an otherwise redundant pair of parentheses. Note that declaring the constructor of V as **explicit** in the hopes of forcing a compile error is no help here since the declaration of v1 is not interpreted as a declaration of an object of type V, so the **explicit** constructor is never considered.

With the addition of generalized braced initialization in C++11, using a coding convention to prefer empty braces, rather than parentheses, for all value initializations avoids the question of the most vexing parse arising:

```
V v4(S{});  // direct-initialize object of type V with value initialized temporary
```

Note that the most vexing parse can also apply to constructors taking multiple arguments, but the issue arises less often since any one supplied argument clearly being an expression, rather than a function type, resolves the whole parse:

```cpp
struct W { W(const S&, const S&) { } };

W w1( S(),  S());  // most vexing parse, declares function w1 taking two
                   // function pointers

W w2((S()), S());  // workaround, object of type W due to nonredundant
                   // parentheses on argument

W w3( S{},  S());  // workaround, even a single use of S{} disambiguates
                   // further use of S()
```

Uniform initialization in generic code

One of the design concerns facing an author of generic code is which form of syntax to choose to initialize objects of a type dependent on template parameters. Different C++ types behave differently and accept different syntaxes, so providing a single consistent syntax for all cases is not possible. Consider the following example of a simple test harness for a unit testing framework:

```cpp
#include <initializer_list>  // std::initializer_list

template <typename T, typename U>
bool run_Test(bool (*test)(const T&), std::initializer_list<U> values)
{
    for (const auto& val : values)
    {
        T obj = val;      // initialize the test value
        if (!test(obj))
        {
            return false;
        }
    }

    return true;
}
```

In this example, a test function is provided for an object of parameter type T along with an `initializer_list` of test values. The **for** loop will construct a test object with each test value, in turn, and call the test function, returning early if any value fails. The question is which syntax to use to create the test object `obj`.

- As written, the example uses *copy* initialization — `T obj = val;` — and will thus fail to compile if `T` is not implicitly convertible from `U`.

- Switching to *direct* initialization — `T obj(val);` — would allow explicit constructors to also be considered.

- Using *direct list* initialization — `T obj{val};` — would allow aggregates to be supported as well as explicit constructors but not narrowing conversions; `initializer_list` constructors are also considered and preferred.

- Switching to *copy list* initialization — `T obj = {val};` — would allow aggregates to be supported but would result in an error if an explicit constructor is the best match, rather than considering the non**explicit** constructors for the best viable match. An error would arise if a narrowing conversion is required; `initializer_list` constructors are also considered and preferred.

Table 2 summarizes the different initialization types and highlights the options and trade-offs. In general, there is no one true, universal syntax for initialization in generic template code. The library author should make a deliberate choice among the trade-offs described in this section and document that as part of their contract.

Table 2: Summary of the different initialization types

Initialization Type	Syntax	Aggregate Support	Explicit Constructor Used	Narrowing	`initializer_list` Constructor Used
Copy	`T obj = val;`	only if T==U	no	allow	no
Direct	`T obj(val);`	only if T==U	yes	allow	no
Direct List	`T obj{val};`	yes	yes	error	yes
Copy List	`T obj = {val}`	yes	error if best match	error	yes

Uniform initialization in factory functions

One of the design concerns facing an author of generic code is which form of syntax to choose to initialize objects of a type dependent on template parameters. Different C++ types behave differently and accept different syntaxes, so providing a single consistent syntax for all cases is not possible. Here we present the different trade-offs to consider when writing a factory function that takes an arbitrary set of type arguments to create an object of a user-specified type:

```
#include <utility>  // std::forward

template <typename T, typename... ARGS>
T factory1(ARGS&&... args)
{
    return T(std::forward<ARGS>(args)...);  // direct initialization
}

template <typename T, typename... ARGS>
T factory2(ARGS&&... args)
{
    return T{std::forward<ARGS>(args)...};  // direct list initialization
}

template <typename T, typename... ARGS>
T factory3(ARGS&&... args)
{
    return {std::forward<ARGS>(args)...};  // copy list initialization
}
```

All three factory functions are defined using **perfect forwarding** (see Section 2.1. "Forwarding References" on page 377) but support different subsets of C++ types and might interpret their arguments differently.

function1 returns a value created by direct initialization but, because it uses parentheses, cannot return an aggregate unless, as a special case, the args list is empty or contains exactly one argument of the same type T or one convertible to T; otherwise, the attempt to construct the return value will result in a compilation error.[6]

function2 returns an object created by direct list initialization. Hence, function2 supports the same types as function1, plus aggregates. However, due to the use of braced initialization, function2 will reject any types in ARGS that require narrowing conversion when passed to the constructor (or to initialize the aggregate member) of the return value. Also, if the supplied arguments can be converted into a homogeneous std::initializer_list that matches a constructor for T, then that constructor will be selected, rather than the constructor best matching that list of arguments.

function3 behaves the same as function2 except that it uses *copy list initialization* and will thus also produce a compile error if the selected constructor or conversion operator for the return value is declared as **explicit**.

There is no one true form of initialization that works best in all circumstances for such a factory function, and library developers must choose and document in their contract the form that best suits their needs. Note that the Standard Library runs into this same problem when implementing factory functions like std::make_shared or the emplace function of any container. The Standard Library consistently chooses parentheses initialization like

---

[6]Note that C++20 will allow aggregates to be initialized with parentheses as well as with braces, which will result in this form being accepted for aggregates as well.

function1 in the previous code example, so these functions do not work for aggregates prior to C++20.

Uniform member initialization in generic code

With the addition of general braced initialization to C++11, class authors should consider whether constructors should use *direct* initialization or *direct list* initialization to initialize their bases and members. Note that since copy initialization and copy list initialization are not options, whether or not the constructor for a given base or member is **explicit** will never be a concern.

Prior to C++11, writing code that initialized aggregate subobjects, including arrays, with a set of data in the constructor's member initializer list was not really possible. We could only *default*-initialize, *value*-initialize, or *direct*-initialize from another aggregate of the same type.

Starting with C++11, we are able to initialize aggregate members with a list of values, using aggregate initialization in place of direct list initialization for members that are aggregates:

```
struct S
{
    int         i;
    std::string str;
};

class C
{
    int j;
    int a[3];
    S   s;

public:
    C(int x, int y, int z, int n, const std::string t)
    : j(0)
    , a{ x, y, z }  // ill formed in C++03, OK in C++11
    , s{ n, t }     // ill formed in C++03, OK in C++11
    {
    }
};
```

Note that as the initializer for `C.j` shows in the code example above, there is no requirement to consistently use either braces or parentheses for all member initializers.

As with the case of factory functions, the class author must make a choice for constructors between adding support for initializing aggregates versus narrowing conversion being ill formed. As mentioned earlier, since member initialization supports only *direct* list initialization, there is never a concern regarding **explicit** conversions in this context:

```
template <typename T>
class Wrap
{
    T data;
public:

    template <typename... ARGS>
    Wrap(ARGS&&... args)
    : data(std::forward<ARGS>(args)...)
        // must be empty list or copy for aggregate T
    {
    }
};

template <typename T>
class WrapAggregate
{
    T data;
public:

    template <typename... ARGS>
    WrapAggregate(ARGS&&... args)
    : data{std::forward<ARGS>(args)...}  // no narrowing conversions
    {
    }
};
```

Again, there is no universal best answer, and an explicit choice should be made and documented so that consumers of the class know what to expect.

Potential Pitfalls

Inadvertently calling initializer-list constructors

Classes with `std::initializer_list` constructors (see Section 2.1.“initializer_list” on page 553) follow some special rules to disambiguate overload resolution, which contain subtle pitfalls for the unwary. This pitfall describes how overload resolution might or might not select those constructors in ways that might be surprising.

When an object is initialized by braced initialization, the compiler will first look to find an `std::initializer_list` constructor that could be called, with the exception that if the braced list is empty, a default constructor, if available, would have priority:

```
#include <initializer_list>  // std::initializer_list

struct S
{
    explicit S() { }
```

```
    explicit S(int) { }
    S(std::initializer_list<int> iL) { if (0 == iL.size()) { throw 13; } }
};

S a{};          // OK, value initialization
S b = {};       // Error, default constructor is explicit.
S c{1};         // OK, std::initializer_list
S d = {1};      // OK, std::initializer_list
S e{1, 2, 3};   // OK, std::initializer_list
S f = {1, 2, 3}; // OK, std::initializer_list
```

In the presence of initializer-list constructors, the overload resolution to select which constructor to call will be a two-step process. First, all initializer-list constructors are considered, and only if no matching `std::initializer_list` constructor has been found will non-initializer-list constructors be considered. This process has some possibly surprising consequences since implicit conversions are allowed when performing the overload matching. It is possible that an `std::initializer_list` constructor requiring an implicit conversion will be selected over a non-initializer-list constructor that does not require a conversion:

```
#include <initializer_list>  // std::initializer_list

struct S
{
    S(std::initializer_list<int>); // (1)
    S(int i, char c);              // (2)
};

S s1{1, 'a'};  // calls (1), even though (2) requires no conversions
```

In the example above, due to braced initialization preferring initializer-list constructors and because S has an `initializer_list` constructor that can match the initializer of s1, the constructor that would have been a better match otherwise is not considered.

The other possibly surprising consequence is related to checking for narrowing conversion only *after* the constructor has been selected. Hence, an `initializer_list` constructor that matches but requires a narrowing conversion will cause an error even in the presence of a `noninitializer_list` constructor that would be a match without requiring a narrowing conversion:

```
#include <initializer_list>  // std::initializer_list

struct S
{
    S(std::initializer_list<int>); // (1)
    S(int i, double d);            // (2)
};

S s2{1, 3.2};  // Error, call to (1) with narrowing conversion, even though
               // invoking (2) would be well formed
```

In the previous example, due to braced initialization first selecting a constructor and then checking for narrowing conversion, the non-initializer-list constructor, which would not require a narrowing conversion, is not considered.

Both of these situations can be resolved by using parentheses or other forms of initialization than brace lists, which cannot be interpreted as `initializer_lists`:

```cpp
#include <initializer_list>  // std::initializer_list

struct S
{
    S(std::initializer_list<int>); // (1)
    S(int i, char c);              // (2)
    S(int i, double d);            // (3)
};

S s3(1, 'c'); // calls (2)
S s4(1, 3.2); // calls (3)
```

This consideration often comes up with `std::vector`:

```cpp
std::vector<char> v{std::size_t(3), 'a'};  // contains 2 elements: '\x03' 'a'
std::vector<char> w(std::size_t(3), 'a');  // contains 3 elements: 'a' 'a' 'a'
```

For variable v in the code snippet above, the `std::initializer_list<char>` constructor overload is selected, even though one creating a `vector` with a specified number of elements, e.g., `std::size_t(3)`, having a particular value, e.g., `'a'`, matches the arguments perfectly. In contrast, direct initialization of the variable w in the code snippet above does not consider the `std::initializer_list<char>` constructor, resulting in w containing three elements with value `'a'`.

Implicit move and named return value optimization might be disabled in return statements

Using extra braces in a return statement around a value might disable the named return value optimization or an implicit move into the returned object. Named return value optimization (NRVO) is an optimization that compilers are allowed to perform when the operand of a return statement is just the name (i.e., id-expression) of a nonvolatile local variable (i.e., an object of automatic storage duration that is not a parameter of the function or a **catch** clause) and the type of that variable, ignoring cv-qualification, is the same as the function return type. In such cases, the compiler is allowed to elide the copy implied by the return expression. Naturally this optimization applies only to functions returning objects, not pointers or references.

Note that this optimization is allowed to change the meaning of programs that might rely on observable side effects on the elided copy constructor. Most modern compilers are capable of performing this optimization in at least simple circumstances, such as where there is only one return expression for the whole function.

In the example below, we see that the `notBraced()` function returns using the name of a local variable from within that function. As we call `notBraced()`, we can observe, with a compiler that performs the optimization, that only one object of the `S` class is created, using its default constructor. There is no copy, no move, and no other object created. Essentially the local variable, `a`, inside the `notBraced()` function is created directly in the memory region of the variable `m1` of the `main()` function.

In the `braced()` function, we use the same local variable, but in the return statement we put braces around its name; therefore, the operand of the return is no longer a name (i.e., id-expression), so the rules that allow NRVO do not apply. By calling `braced()`, we see that now two copies, and so two objects, are created, the first being `a`, the local variable, using the default constructor, and the second being `m2`, which is created as a copy of `a`, demonstrating that NRVO is not in effect:

```
#include <iostream>  // std::cout

struct S
{
    S()         { std::cout << "S()\n"; }
    S(const S &) { std::cout << "S(copy)\n"; }
    S(S &&)     { std::cout << "S(move)\n"; }
};

S notBraced()
{
    S a;
    return a;
}

S braced()
{
    S a;
    return { a };  // disables NRVO
}

int main()
{
    S m1 = notBraced();  // S()
    S m2 = braced();     // S(), S(copy)
}
```

Implicit move (see Section 2.1. "*Rvalue* References" on page 710) in a return statement is a subtler operation, so much so that it required a **defect report**[7] to actually make it work as originally intended. We demonstrate implicit moves in a return statement from a local variable by using two types. The class type `L` will be used for the local variable, whereas the class type `R`, which can be move- or copy-constructed from `L`, is used as the return type.

---

[7]CWG issue 1579; **yasskin12**

Essentially, we are forcing a type conversion in the return statement, one that might be a copy or a move:

```cpp
#include <iostream>  // std::cout

struct L
{
    L()         { std::cout << "L()\n"; }
};

struct R
{
    R(const L &) { std::cout << "R(L-copy)\n"; }
    R(L &&)      { std::cout << "R(L-move)\n"; }
};

R notBraced()
{
    L a;
    return a;
}

R braced()
{
    L a;
    return { a };  // disables implicit move from l
}

int main()
{
    R r1 = notBraced();  // L(), R(L-move)
    R r2 = braced();     // L(), R(L-copy)
}
```

The notBraced() function just creates a local variable and returns it. By calling the function, we observe that an L object is created, which is then moved into an R object. Note that the wording of the C++ Standard allows this implicit move only if the return statement's operand is a name, i.e., an id-expression.

The braced() function is identical to the notBraced function, except for adding curly braces around the operand of the return statement. Calling the function shows that the *move-from-L* return expression turned into a *copy-from-L* return expression because a braced initializer is not a name of an object.

Surprising behavior of aggregates having deleted constructors

Value initialization of aggregates is allowed with a braced-initializer list, even if the default constructor is deleted[8]:

```
struct S
{
    int data;
    S() = delete; // don't want "empty"
};

S s{}; // surprisingly works (until C++20), and 0 == s.data
```

This surprising pitfall occurs for two reasons.

1. A deleted constructor is *user declared* but not *user provided*, so it does not break the requirements for a class to be an aggregate.

2. The rules state that aggregate initialization is not defined in terms of constructors but directly in terms of the initialization of its members.

Annoyances

Narrowing aggregate initialization might break C++03 code

When compiling existing C++03 code with a C++11 compiler, previously valid code might report errors for narrowing conversions in aggregate (and, therefore, also array) initialization:

```
unsigned u = 128;          // u is set to an int-friendly value.
int ia[] = { 1, 2, u, 9 }; // OK in C++03, narrowing is allowed.
                           // Error in C++11, narrowing conversion
```

Suppose that the computation in the example above ensures that the value that u holds at the point of initialization is in the range of values an **int** is able to represent. Yet, the code will not compile in C++11 or later modes. Unfortunately each and every case has to be fixed by applying the appropriate type cast or changing the types involved to be "compatible."

No easy way to allow narrowing conversions

In generic code, curly braces have to be used if support for aggregates is required, but if our interface definition requires supporting narrowing conversions (for example, std::tuple), there is no direct way to enable them:

---

[8]Note that C++20 finally addresses the issue so the presence of deleted constructors causes a class to no longer qualify as an aggregate.

```
struct S
{
    short data;
};

class X
{
    S m;

public:
    template <typename U>
    X(const U& a) : m{a}  // no narrowing allowed
    {
    }
};

int i;
X x(i);  // Error, would narrow in initializing S.m
```

The workaround is to **static_cast** to the target type if it is known or to use parentheses and give up aggregate support in the generic code.[9]

Breaks macro-invocation syntax

The macro-invocation syntax of the C++ preprocessor (inherited from C) "understands" parentheses and thus ignores commas within parentheses but does not understand any other list markers, such as braces for braced initialization, square brackets, or the angle bracket notation of templates. If we attempt to use commas in other contexts, macro parsing will interpret such commas as separators for multiple macro arguments and will likely complain that the macro does not support that many arguments:

```
#define MACRO(oneArg) /*...*/

struct C
{
    C(int, int, int);
};

struct S
{
    int i1, i2, i3;
};

MACRO(C x(a, b, c))           // OK, commas inside parentheses ignored
MACRO(S y{a, b, c})           // Error, 3 arguments but MACRO needs 1
MACRO(std::map<int, int> z)   // Error, 2 arguments but MACRO needs 1
```

---

[9]C++20 enables the use of parentheses to initialize aggregates.

As the previous example demonstrates, on the first macro invocation, the commas within the parentheses are ignored, and the macro is invoked with one argument: C x(a, b, c).

In the second macro invocation, we attempt to use braced initialization, but because the syntax of the preprocessor does not recognize curly braces as special delimiters, the commas are interpreted as separating macro arguments, so we end up with three unusual arguments: first C y{a, second b, and third c}. This problematic interaction between braced initialization and macros has existed forever, even back in C code when initializing arrays or **structs**. However, with braced initialization becoming used more widely in C++, it is much more likely that a programmer will encounter this annoyance.

The third invocation of MACRO in the example is just a reminder that the same issue exists in C++ with the angle brackets of templates.

The workaround, as is so often the case with the C preprocessor, is more use of the C preprocessor. We need to define macros to help us hide the commas. Such macros will use the **variadic macros** C99 preprocessor feature that was adopted for C++11 to turn a comma-separated list into a braced-initializer list (and similarly for a template instantiation):

```
#define BRACED(...) { __VA_ARGS__ }
#define TEMPLATE(name, ...) name<__VA_ARGS__>

MACRO(X y BRACED(a, b, c))              // OK, X y { a, b, c }
MACRO(TEMPLATE(std::map, int, int) z)  // OK, std::map<int, int> z
```

A common way this annoyance might show up is using the Standard Library **assert** macro:

```
#include <cassert>  // standard C assert macro

bool operator==(const C&, const C&);

void f(const C& x, int i, int j, int k)
{
    assert(C(i, j, k) == x);  // OK
    assert(C{i, j, k} == x);  // Error, too many arguments to assert macro
}
```

No copy list initialization in member initializer lists

The syntax for base and member initializers allows for both direct initialization with parentheses since C++03 and direct list initialization with braces since C++11. However, there is no syntax corresponding to copy list initialization, which would allow member initializers to report errors for using an unintended **explicit** constructor or conversion operator. It would seem relatively intuitive to extend the syntax to support = { ... } for member initializers to support such use, but so far there have been no proposals to add this feature to the language. That lack of change to the language might be a sign that there is simply no demand and that we, the authors of this book, are the only ones annoyed since member initializer lists are the only part of the language that supports *direct* initializations without a corresponding syntax for *copy* initializations:

```cpp
class C
{
public:
    explicit C(int);
    C(int, int);
};

class X
{
    C a;
    C b;
    C c;

public:
    X(int i)
    : a(i)          // OK, direct initialization
    , b{i}          // OK, direct list initialization
    , c = {i, i}    // Error, copy list initialization is not allowed.
    {
    }
};
```

Accidental meaning for explicit constructors passed multiple arguments

In C++03, marking a default or multi-argument constructor **explicit**, typically as a result of supplying default arguments, had no useful meaning, and compilers did not warn about them because they were harmless. However, C++11 takes notice of the **explicit** keyword for such constructors when invoked by copy list initialization. This design point is generally not considered when migrating code from C++03 to C++11 and might require programmers to invest more thought and potentially split constructors with multiple default arguments into multiple constructors, applying **explicit** to only the intended overloads:

```cpp
class C
{
public:
    explicit C(int = 0, int = 0, int = 0);
};

C c0 = {};           // Error, constructor is explicit.
C c1 = {1};          // Error, constructor is explicit.
C c2 = {1, 2};       // Error, constructor is explicit.
C c3 = {1, 2, 3};    // Error, constructor is explicit.
```

```
class D
{
public:
    D();
    explicit D(int i) : D(i, 0) { }  // delegating constructor
    D(int, int, int = 0);
};

D d0 = {};          // OK
D d1 = {1};         // Error, constructor is explicit.
D d2 = {1, 2};      // OK
D d3 = {1, 2, 3};   // OK

C f(int i, C arg)
{
    switch (i)
    {
        case 0: return {};          // Error, constructor is explicit.
        case 1: return {1};         // Error, constructor is explicit.
        case 2: return {1, 2};      // Error, constructor is explicit.
        case 3: return {1, 2, 3};   // Error, constructor is explicit.
    }
}

D g(int i, D arg)
{
    switch (i)
    {
      case 0: return {};          // OK
      case 1: return {1};         // Error, constructor is explicit.
      case 2: return {1, 2};      // OK
      case 3: return {1, 2, 3};   // OK
    }
}

void test()
{
    f(0, {});           // Error, constructor is explicit.
    f(0, {1});          // Error, constructor is explicit.
    f(0, {1, 2});       // Error, constructor is explicit.
    f(0, {1, 2, 3});    // Error, constructor is explicit.

    g(0, {});           // OK
    g(0, {1});          // Error, constructor is explicit.
    g(0, {1, 2});       // OK
    g(0, {1, 2, 3});    // OK
}
```

Note that this topic is deemed an annoyance, rather than a pitfall, because it affects only code newly written for C++11 or later using the new forms of initialization syntax, so it does not break existing C++03 code recompiled with a more modern language dialect. However, also note that many containers and other types in the C++ Standard Library inherited such a design and have not been refactored into multiple constructors, although some such refactoring occurs in later versions of the Standard.

Obfuscation due to opaque use of braced list intializers

Use of braced initializers for function arguments, omitting any hint of the expected object type at the call site, requires deep familiarity with functions being called to understand the actual types of arguments being initialized, especially when overload resolution must disambiguate several viable candidates. Such usage might produce more fragile code as further overloads are added, silently changing the type initialized by the brace list as a different function wins overload resolution. Such code is also much harder for a subsequent maintainer, or casual code reader, to understand:

```cpp
struct C
{
    C(int, int) { }
};

int test(C, long) { return 0; }

int main()
{
    int a = test({1, 2}, 3);
    return a;
}
```

This program compiles and runs, returning the intended result. However, consider how the behavior changes if we add a second overload during subsequent maintenance:

```cpp
struct C
{
    C(int, int) { }
};

int test(C, long) { return 0; }

struct A  // additional aggregate class
{
    int x;
    int y;
};
```

```
int test(A, int) { return -1; }   // overload for the aggregate class

int callTest1()
{
    int a = test({1, 2}, 3);      // overload resolution prefers the aggregate
    return a;
}
```

Because the overload for A must now be considered, overload resolution might pick a different result. If we are lucky, then the choice of the A and C overloads becomes ambiguous, and an error is diagnosed. However, in this case, there was an integer promotion on the second argument, and the new A overload is now a better match, producing a different program result. If this overload is added through maintenance of an included header file, this code will have silently changed meaning without touching the file. If the above flexibility is not the desired intent, the simple way to avoid this risk is to always name the type of any temporary variables:

```
int callTest2()
{
    int a = test(C{1, 2}, 3);  // Overload resolution prefers struct C.
    return a;
}
```

auto **deduction and braced initialization**

C++11 introduces type inference, where an object's type is deduced from its initialization, using the **auto** keyword; see Section 2.1."**auto** Variables" on page 195. When presented with a homogeneous, nonempty list using *copy* list initialization, **auto** will deduce the type of the supplied argument list as an std::initializer_list of the same type as the list values. When presented with a braced list of a single value using *direct* list initialization, **auto** will deduce the variable type as the same type as the list value:

```
#include <initializer_list>  // std::initializer_list

auto g{1};          // OK, deduces g is int
auto h{1, 2, 3};    // Error, auto requires exactly one element in braced list.
auto i = {1};       // OK, deduces i is initializer_list<int>
auto j = {1, 2, 3}; // OK, deduces j is initializer_list<int>
```

Note that the declarations of i and j in the code example above would also be errors if the <initializer_list> header had not been included to supply the std::initializer_list class template.

Finally, observe that for **auto** deduction from *direct* list initialization, an initializer_list constructor might still be called in preference to copy constructors, even though the syntax seems restricted to making copies:

```cpp
#include <iostream>         // std::cout
#include <initializer_list> // std::initializer_list

struct S
{
    S() { }
    S(std::initializer_list<S>) { std::cout << "init list\n"; }
    S(const S&) { std::cout << "copy\n"; }
};

int main()
{
    S s;
    auto s2{s}; // std::initializer_list<S> constructor is called after
                // deduction. (Note: s2 is deduced to be of type S.)
}
```

The program above prints `copy` followed by `init list` because (1) the type of `s2` is deduced to be `S` per **auto** type deduction rules, (2) overload resolution selects the `initializer_list` constructor as the best match due to use of a braced initializer, and (3) the single element of the `initializer_list` is copy-initialized from `s`. If direct or copy initialization were used for initializing `s2`, the copy constructor would be selected instead.

Compound assignment but not arithmetic operators accept braced lists

Braced initializers can be used to provide arguments to the assignment operator and additionally to compound assignment operators such as +=, where they are treated as calls to the overloaded operator function for class types, or as += T{value} for a scalar type T.[10] Note that assigning to scalars supports brace lists of no more than a single element and does not support compound assignment for pointer types, since the brace lists are converted to a pointer type, which cannot appear on the right-hand side of a compound assignment operator.

While the intent of compounded assignment is to be semantically equivalent to the expression a = a + b (or * b, or - b, and so on), brace lists cannot be used in regular arithmetic expressions since the grammar does not support brace lists as arbitrary expressions:

---

[10] Although valid, the two x += {3} and x *= {3} lines in the example compile successfully on Clang but not on any version of GCC or MSVC at the time of writing. The C++11 Standard currently states:

A braced-init-list may appear on the right-hand side of

— an assignment to a scalar, in which case the initializer list shall have at most a single element. The meaning of x={v}, where T is the scalar type of the expression x, is that of x=T{v} except that no narrowing conversion (8.5.4) is allowed. The meaning of x={} is x=T{}.

(**iso11a**, paragraph 9, section 5.17, "Assignment and Compound Assignment Operators," p. 126). There is currently a defect report to clarify the Standard and explicitly state that this rule also applies to compound assignments; see CWG issue 1542 (**miller12b**) and **miller21**.

```
#include <initializer_list>  // std::initializer_list

struct S
{
    S(std::initializer_list<int>) { }
    S& operator+=(const S&) { return *this; }
};

S operator+(const S&, const S&) { return S{}; }

void demo()
{
    S s1{};             // OK, calls initializer_list constructor
    s1 += {1, 2, 3};    // OK, equivalent to s1.operator+=({1, 2, 3})
    s1 = s1 + {1, 2, 3}; // Error, expecting an expression, not an
                         // std::initializer_list
    s1 = operator+(s1, {1, 2, 3}); // OK, braces allowed as function argument

    int x = 0;
    x += {3};  // OK, equivalent to x += int{3};
    x *= {5};  // OK, equivalent to x *= int{5};

    char y[4] = {1, 2, 3, 4};
    char*p = y;
    p += {3};  // Error, equivalent to p += (char*){3};
}
```

See Also

- "Deleted Functions" (§1.1, p. 53) explains how deleted functions might restrict the available initialization syntaxes.

- "**explicit** Operators" (§1.1, p. 61) describes how **explicit** operators participate in direct initialization but not in copy initialization.

- "Function **static** '11" (§1.1, p. 68) addresses how braced initialization can be used for function static variables.

- "**nullptr**" (§1.1, p. 99) explains how **nullptr** is used as default initializer for pointer values with static duration.

- "**auto** Variables" (§2.1, p. 195) describes how **auto** variables use the same deduction rules as initializers in an initializer list.

- "Default Member Init" (§2.1, p. 318) addresses how default member initialization interacts with braced initialization and illustrates how braced initialization can be used to initialize a data member directly in the class definition.

- "initializer_list" (§2.1, p. 553) illustrates how `initializer_list` works in conjunction with braced initialization and covers the `std::initializer_list` library type, used in conjunction with braced initialization to initialize objects with a set of values.

- "*Rvalue* References" (§2.1, p. 710) explains how *rvalue* references affect copying versus moving during certain initialization operations and describe implicit moves and various ways in which they might be disabled other than by braced initialization in return statements.

Further Reading

- Scott Meyers discusses important subtle differences between two visually similar initialization styles in **meyers15b**, "Item 7: Distinguish between ( ) and { } when creating objects," pp. 49–58.

Compile-Time Invocable Functions

Functions decorated with **constexpr** are eligible to be invoked as part of a **constant expression**.

Description

A constant expression is an expression whose value is determined at compile time — i.e., one that could be used, say, to define the size of a C-style array or as the argument to a **static_assert**:

```
enum { e_SIZE = 5 };          // e_SIZE is a constant expression of value 5.
int a[e_SIZE];                // e_SIZE must be a constant expression.
static_assert(e_SIZE == 5, "");  //     "       "    "  "      "
```

Prior to C++11, evaluating a conventional function at compile time as part of a **constant expression** was not possible:

```
inline const int z() { return 5; }  // OK, returns a nonconstant expression
int a[z()];                         // Error, z() is not a constant expression.
static_assert(z() == 5, "");        // Error,  "    "   "   "        "
int a[0 ? z() : 9];                 // Error,  "    "   "   "       "
```

Developers, in need of such functionality, would use other means, such as template metaprogramming, external code generators, preprocessor macros, or hard-coded constants (as shown in the example above), to work around this deficiency.

As an example, consider a **metaprogram** to calculate the nth factorial number:

```
template <int N>
struct Factorial { enum { value = N * Factorial<N-1>::value }; };  // recursive

template <>
struct Factorial<0> { enum { value = 1 }; };  // base case
```

Evaluating the Factorial metafunction in the example above on a **constant expression** results in a **constant expression**:

```
static_assert(Factorial<5>::value == 120, "");  // OK
int a[Factorial<5>::value];                     // OK, array of 120 ints
```

Note, however, that the metafunction can be used only with template arguments that themselves must be **constant expressions**:

```
int factorial(const int n)
{
    static_assert(n >= 0, "");   // Error, n is not a constant expression.
    return Factorial<n>::value;  // Error, "   "   "   "       "
}
```

Employing this cumbersome work-around leads to code that is difficult both to write and to read and is also non-trivial to compile, often resulting in long compile times. What's more, a separate implementation will be needed for inputs whose values are not compile-time constants.

C++11 introduces a new keyword, **constexpr**, that gives users enhanced control over compile-time evaluation. Prepending a function declaration with the **constexpr** keyword informs both the compiler and prospective users that the function is eligible for compile-time evaluation and, under the right circumstances, can and will be evaluated *at compile time* to determine the value of a constant expression:

```
constexpr int factorial(int n)  // can be evaluated in a constant expression
{
    return n == 0 ? 1 : n * factorial(n - 1);  // single return statement
}
```

In C++11, the body of a **constexpr** function is effectively restricted to a single **return** statement, and any other language construct, such as **if** statements, loops, variable declarations, and so on, are forbidden; see *Restrictions on **constexpr** function bodies (C++11 only)* on page 268. These seemingly overly strict limitations, although much preferred to the Factorial metafunction (e.g., in the code example above), might make optimizing a function's runtime performance infeasible; see *Potential Pitfalls — Prematurely committing to **constexpr*** on page 297. As of C++14, however, many of these restrictions were lifted, though some runtime tools remain unavailable during compile-time evaluation. At the time **constexpr** was added to the language, it was a feature under development, and it still is; see Section 2.2."**constexpr** Functions '14" on page 959.

Note that semantic validation of **constexpr** functions occurs only at the point of *definition*. It is therefore possible to *declare* a member or free function to be **constexpr** for which there can be no valid *definition* — e.g., **constexpr void** f(); — as the return type of a **constexpr** function's *definition* must satisfy certain requirements, including (in C++11 only) that its return type must not be **void**; see *Restrictions on **constexpr** function bodies (C++11 only)* on page 268.

Simply declaring a function to be **constexpr** does not automatically mean that the function will necessarily be evaluated at compile time. A **constexpr** function is *guaranteed* to be evaluated at compile time *only* when invoked in a context where a constant expression is required.[1] Examples of such contexts include the value of a non-type template parameter, array bounds, the first argument to a **static_assert**, **case** labels in **switch** statements, or the initializer for a **constexpr** variable; see Section 2.1."**constexpr** Variables" on page 302. If one attempts to invoke a **constexpr** function in a context where a constant expression is required with an argument that is not a constant expression, the compiler will report an error:

---

[1]C++20 formalized this notion with the term **manifestly constant evaluated** to capture all places where the value of an expression must be determined at compile time. This new term coalesces descriptions in several places in the Standard where this concept had previously been used without being given a common name.

```
#include <cassert>    // standard C assert macro
#include <iostream>   // std::cout

void f(int n)
{
    assert(factorial(5) == 120);
        // OK, factorial(5) might be evaluated at compile time since 5 is a
        // constant expression but the argument of assert does not have to be
        // a constant expression.

    static_assert(factorial(5) == 120, "");
        // OK, factorial(5) is evaluated at compile time since arguments of
        // static_assert must be constant expressions.

    std::cout << factorial(n);
        // OK, likely evaluated at run time since n is not a constant
        // expression

    static_assert(factorial(n) > 0, "");
        // Error, n is not a constant expression.
}
```

As illustrated above, simply invoking a **constexpr** function with arguments that are constant expressions does *not* guarantee that the function will be evaluated at compile time. The only way to *guarantee* compile-time evaluation of a **constexpr** function is to invoke it in places where a constant expression is mandatory.

If the value of a constant expression is needed at compile time (e.g., for the bounds of an array) and computing that value involves the execution of an operation that is not available at compile time (e.g., **throw**), the compiler will have no choice but to report an error:

```
constexpr int h(int x) { return x < 5 ? x : throw x; }  // OK, constexpr func

int a4[h(4)];  // OK, creates an array of four integers
int a6[h(6)];  // Error, unable to evaluate h on 6 at compile time
```

In the code snippet above, although we are able to size the file-scope[2] a4 array because the path of execution within the valid **constexpr** function h does not involve a **throw**, such is

---

[2]A common extension of popular compilers to allow, by default, variable-length arrays within function bodies but, as illustrated above, *never* at file or namespace scope:

```
void g()
{
    int a4[h(4)];  // OK, creates an array of four integers
    int a6[h(6)];  // Warning: ISO C++ forbids variable-length array a6.
                   // But with some compilers, h(6) might be invoked at
                   // run time and throw.
}
```

It is only by compiling with -Wpedantic that GCC issues a warning.

not the case with a6. That a valid **constexpr** function can be invoked with compile-time constant arguments and still not be evaluable at compile time is noteworthy.

So far we have discussed **constexpr** functions in terms of free functions. As we shall see, **constexpr** can also be applied to free-function templates, member functions (importantly, constructors), and member-function templates; see *constexpr member functions* on page 266. Just as with free functions, only **constexpr** member functions are eligible to be evaluated at compile time.

What's more, we'll see that there is a category of user-defined types, called **literal types**, whose *operational definition* — i.e., for now, a rule of thumb that would typically hold in practice but see *Literal types defined* on page 278 — is that at least one of its values can participate in constant expressions:

```
struct Int  // example of a literal type
{
    int d_val;                             // plain old int data member
    constexpr Int(int val) : d_val(val) { }    // constexpr value constructor
    constexpr int val() const { return d_val; } // constexpr value accessor
             int dat() const { return d_val; } // nonconstexpr accessor
};

constexpr int f(){ return Int(5).d_val; } // OK, constexpr value constructor
constexpr int g(Int i){ return i.val(); } // OK, constexpr value accessor
constexpr int h(Int i){ return i.dat(); } // Error, nonconstexpr accessor
```

The basic, intuitive idea of what makes the user-defined **Int** type above a **literal type** is that it is possible to initialize objects of this type during **constant expression** evaluation. Such initialization can be made possible with a **constexpr** constructor or via a type that can be **list initialized** without needing to invoke any non**constexpr** constructors; see Section 2.1. "Braced Init" on page 215 and Section 1.2. "Aggregate Init '14" on page 138. The value of the object of this **Int** literal type is usable at compile time because there is at least one way of extracting a value — either directly or via a **constexpr** accessor — at compile time. We might, however, imagine a use for a valid **literal type** that could be constructed at compile time but not otherwise *used* until run time:

```
class StoreForRt   // compile-time constructible literal type
{
    int d_value;   // There is no way of accessing this value at compile time.

public:
    constexpr StoreForRt(int value) : d_value(value) { } //    constexpr
    int value() const { return d_value; }             // not constexpr
};
```

Contrived though it might seem, the example code above is representative of an application of **constexpr** where the construction of an object can benefit from compile-time optimization, whereas access to the constructed data cannot. First proving, however, that such an object can in fact be constructed at compile time without employing other C++11 features is instructive.

```
static_assert((StoreForRt(1), true), "");
    // OK, can create StoreForRt during constexpr eval. so it is a literal type

static_assert(StoreForRt(5).value() == 5, "");  // Error, value not constexpr
    // There is no way we can access d_value at compile time.
```

As the example code above shows, `StoreForRt` is a literal type because it has been demonstrated to be *used* in a context that requires a constant expression. It is not, however, possible to do anything more with that constructed object at compile time, except for obtaining certain generic compile-time properties, such as its size (**sizeof**) or alignment (see Section 2.1. "**alignof**" on page 184).

To demonstrate that the same object can be (1) *constructed* at compile time and (2) *used* only at run time, we will need to resort to using a C++11 companion feature of **constexpr** functions, namely, **constexpr** variables (see Section 2.1."**constexpr** Variables" on page 302):

```
constexpr StoreForRt x(5);  // OK, object x constructed at compile time

int main() { return x.value(); }  // OK, x.value() used only at run time
```

Only literal types are permitted as parameters and return types for **constexpr** functions; see ***constexpr**-function parameter and return types* on page 277:

```
constexpr int  f11(StoreForRt x) { return 0; }  // OK, x is of a literal type.
constexpr void f14(StoreForRt x) { }            // OK, in C++14 void return allowed
```

constexpr is part of the contract

When a **constexpr** function is invoked with an argument that is *not* known at compile time, compile-time evaluation of the function itself is not possible, and that invocation simply cannot be used in a context where a compile-time constant is required; runtime evaluation, however, is still permitted:

```
      int  i = 10;      // not compile-time constant
const int  j = 10;      //     compile-time constant
      bool mb = false;  // not compile-time constant

constexpr int f(bool b) { return b ? i : 5; }  // conditionally works as constexpr
constexpr int g(bool b) { return b ? j : 5; }  // always works as constexpr

static_assert(f(mb),    "");  // Error, mb not usable in a constant expression
static_assert(f(false), "");  // OK
static_assert(f(true),  "");  // Error, i not usable in a constant expression
```

```
static_assert(g(mb),    "");  // Error, mb not usable in a constant expression
static_assert(g(false), "");  // OK
static_assert(g(true),  "");  // OK, j is usable in a constant expression.

int xf = f(mb);  // OK, runtime evaluation of f
int xg = g(mb);  // OK, runtime evaluation of g
```

In the example above, f can sometimes be used as part of a constant expression but only if its argument is itself a constant expression and b evaluates to **false**, thereby avoiding use of the global variable i, which is not a compile-time constant. Function g, on the other hand, requires only that its argument be a constant expression for it to always be usable as part of a constant expression. If there is not at least one set of compile-time constant argument values that would be usable at compile time, then it is **ill formed, no diagnostic required** (IFNDR):

```
constexpr int h1(bool b) { return f(b); }
    // OK, there is a value of b for which h1 can be evaluated at compile time.

constexpr int h2() { return f(true); }
    // There's no way to invoke h2 so that it can be evaluated at compile time.
    // (This function is ill formed, no diagnostic required.)
```

Here h1 is well formed since it can be evaluated at compile time when the value of b is **false**; h2, on the other hand, is ill formed because it can *never* be evaluated at compile time. A sophisticated analysis would, however, be required to establish such a proof, and modern compilers issue a diagnostic only for reasonably simple cases.

Guaranteeing compile-time evaluation for certain arguments is an essential part of a function's contract. Declaring a function to be **constexpr** might lead prospective clients to conclude that such a function can be evaluated at compile time with *any* compile-time-constant arguments. Such assumptions can prove erroneous as evidenced by h1 in the example above. Subsequently guaranteeing compile-time evaluation for a wider set of inputs than was originally promised is typically not a problematic change. By contrast, however, providing compile-time evaluation for a narrower set of inputs than was originally available, even if not explicitly promised, can lead to compilation errors for those clients that chose to rely on compile-time usage of the function. It is therefore incumbent on library authors to consider carefully whether to mark a function **constexpr** and for which arguments to support compile-time evaluation, since improving the implementation of the function while respecting the restrictions imposed by **constexpr** might prove insurmountable, especially with the limitations imposed by C++11; see *Potential Pitfalls — Prematurely committing to constexpr* on page 297.

Inlining and definition visibility

A function that is declared **constexpr** is (1) implicitly declared **inline** and (2) automatically eligible for compile-time evaluation. Note that adding the **inline** specifier to a function that is already declared **constexpr** has no effect:

```
        constexpr int f1() { return 0; } // automatically inline
inline constexpr int f1();                // redeclares the same f1() above
```

As with all **inline** functions, it is a **one-definition rule (ODR)** violation if definitions in different translation units within a program are not token for token the same. If definitions do differ across translation units, the program is IFNDR:

```
// file1.h:
       inline int f2() { return 0; }
    constexpr int f3() { return 0; }
```

```
// file2.h:
       inline int f2() { return 1; }  // Error, no diagnostic required
    constexpr int f3() { return 1; }  // Error, no diagnostic required
```

When a function is declared **constexpr**, *every* declaration of that function, including its definition, must also be explicitly declared **constexpr**, or else the program is ill formed:

```
constexpr int f4();
constexpr int f4() { return 0; }  // OK, constexpr matching exactly

constexpr int f5();
          int f5() { return 0; }  // Error, constexpr missing

          int f6();
constexpr int f6() { return 0; }  // Error, constexpr added
```

An explicit specialization of a function template declaration may, however, differ with respect to its **constexpr** specifier. For example, a general function template, e.g., ft1 in the code snippet below, might be declared **constexpr**, whereas one of its explicit specializations, e.g., ft1**<int>**, might not be:

```
template <typename T>     // general function template declaration/definition
constexpr bool ft1(T)     // general template is declared constexpr
{
    return true;
}

template <>               // explicit specialization declaration/definition
bool ft1<int>(int)        // The explicit specialization is not constexpr.
{
    return true;
}

static_assert(ft1('a'), "");  // OK, general function template is constexpr.
static_assert(ft1(123), "");  // Error, int specialization is not constexpr.
```

Similarly, the roles can be reversed where only an explicit specialization, e.g., ft2**<int>** in the next example, is **constexpr**:

```
template <typename T> bool ft2(T)        { return true; }  // general template
template <> constexpr bool ft2<int>(int) { return true; }  // specialization

static_assert(ft2('a'), "");  // Error, general template is not constexpr.
static_assert(ft2(123), "");  // OK, int specialization is constexpr.
```

Just as with any other function, a **constexpr** function may appear in an expression before its body has been seen, including from within the body of a recursive function. A **constexpr** function's definition, however, must appear and be complete before that function is evaluated to determine the value of a constant expression. Recursive functions and even sets of mutually recursive functions can be declared **constexpr** as well, so long as none are called in a context requiring a **constant expression** until the completed definitions of all invoked definitions have been seen:

```
constexpr int f7();                    // declared but not yet defined
constexpr int f8() { return f7(); }    // defined with a call to f7
constexpr int f9();                    // declared but not defined in this TU
constexpr int f10(int n)
{
    return (n > 0) ? f10(n - 1) : 0;   // recursive call, incomplete definition
}

int main()
{
    return f8() + f9();  // OK, presumes f7 and f9 are defined and linked
                         // with this TU
}

static_assert(f8() == 0, "");  // Error, body of f7 has not yet been seen.
static_assert(f9() == 0, "");  // Error,    "    "  f9  "    "    "    "    "

constexpr int f7()  // definition matching forward declaration
{
    static_assert(0 == f7(), "");  // Error, body of f7 has not yet been seen.
    return 0;
}

static_assert(f8() == 0, "");  // OK, body of f7 is visible from here.
static_assert(f9() == 0, "");  // Error, body of f9 has not yet been seen.

// Oops, failed to define f9 in this translation unit; compiler might warn
```

In the example code above, we have declared three **constexpr** functions: f7, f8, and f9. Of the three, only f8 is defined ahead of its first use. Any attempt to evaluate a **constexpr** function whose definition has not yet been seen — either directly (e.g., f9) or indirectly (e.g., f7 via f8) — in a context requiring a **constant expression** results in a compile-time error. Notice that, when used in expressions whose values do not need to be determined at compile time (e.g., the **return** statement in **main**), there is no requirement to have seen the body. In this case, **f9** was not defined anywhere within the translation unit (TU). Just as with any other **inline** function whose definition is never seen, many popular compilers will warn if they see any expressions that might invoke such a function, but it is not ill formed because the definition could, by design, reside in some other TU (see also Section 2.1. "**extern template**" on page 353).

However, when a **constexpr** function is *evaluated* to determine the value of a **constant expression**, its body and anything upon which its body depends must have already been seen; notice that we didn't say "appears as part of a **constant expression**" but instead said "is evaluated to determine the value of a **constant expression**."

We *can* have something that is not itself a **constant expression** *appear* as a part of a **constant expression** *provided* that it never actually gets evaluated at compile time:

```
static_assert(true  ?  true : throw, "");  // OK
static_assert(true  ?  throw : true,  "");  // Error, throw not constexpr

extern bool x;
static_assert((true, x), "");        // Error, x not constexpr
static_assert((x, true), "");        // Error, "   "        "

static_assert(true || x,    "");  // OK
static_assert(x    || true, "");  // Error, x not constexpr
```

Note that the *comma* (**,**) **sequencing operator** incurs evaluation of both of its arguments, whereas the *logical-or* (**||**) **operator** requires only that its two arguments be convertible to **bool**, where actual evaluation of the second argument might be short circuited.

The type system and function pointers

Similarly to the **inline** keyword, marking a function **constexpr** does *not* affect its type; hence, it is not possible to have, say, two overloads of a function that differ only on whether they are **constexpr** or to define a pointer to exclusively **constexpr** functions:

```
constexpr int f(int) { return 0; }  // OK
int f(int)            { return 0; }  // Error, int f(int) is now multiply defined.

typedef constexpr int(*MyFnPtr)(int);
    // Error, constexpr cannot appear in a typedef declaration.

void g(constexpr int(*MyFnPtr)(int));
    // Error, a parameter cannot be declared constexpr.
```

Just as with objects of other types, the value of a function pointer can be read as part of evaluating a **constant expression** only if that pointer is a compile-time constant. Furthermore, a function can be invoked at compile time via a function pointer only if the pointer is a compile-time constant and the function is declared **constexpr**:

```
constexpr bool cf() { return true; }  //    constexpr function returning true
          bool nf() { return true; }  // nonconstexpr function returning true

typedef bool (*Fp)(); // pointer to function taking no args. and returning bool

constexpr Fp cpcf = cf;  //    constexpr pointer to a    constexpr function
          Fp npcf = cf;  // nonconstexpr pointer to a    constexpr function
constexpr Fp cpnf = nf;  //    constexpr pointer to a nonconstexpr function
          Fp npnf = nf;  // nonconstexpr pointer to a nonconstexpr function
constexpr Fp cpz  = 0;   //    constexpr pointer having null pointer value

static_assert(cpcf == &cf, "");  // OK, reading a constexpr pointer
static_assert(npcf == &cf, "");  // Error, npcf is not a constexpr pointer.
static_assert(cpz  == 0,   "");  // OK, reading a constexpr pointer

static_assert(cpcf(),      "");  // OK, invoking a constexpr function through a
                                 //     constexpr pointer
static_assert(npcf(), "");       // Error, npcf is not a constexpr pointer.
static_assert(cpnf(), "");       // Error, can't invoke nonconstexpr function
static_assert(npnf(), "");       // Error, npnf is not a constexpr pointer.
static_assert(cpz(),  "");       // Error, 0 doesn't designate a function.
```

constexpr member functions

Member functions — including certain **special member functions**, such as *constructors* but not *destructors* — can be declared to be **constexpr**; see *Literal types defined* on page 278:

```
class Point1
{
    int d_x, d_y; // two ordinary int data members
public:
    constexpr Point1(int x, int y) : d_x(x), d_y(y) { }  // OK, is constexpr

    constexpr int x()       { return d_x; }  // OK, is constexpr
              int y() const { return d_y; }  // OK, is not constexpr
};
```

Simple classes, such as Point1 above, having at least one **constexpr** constructor that is neither a *copy* nor a *move* constructor and satisfies all other requirements of being a literal type — see *Literal types defined* on page 278 — can be evaluated as part of **constant expressions**. However, it is only when combined with a means to access a data member at compile time (e.g., via a public data member, a **constexpr** accessor, or a free **constexpr** **friend** function) that an object of even literal type can contribute to a constant expression's *value*:

```
int ax[Point1(5, 6).x()]; // OK, array of 5 ints
int ay[Point1(5, 6).y()]; // Error, accessor y is not declared constexpr.
```

Member functions decorated with **constexpr** are implicitly **const**-qualified in C++11 but
not in C++14; see Section 2.2."**constexpr** Functions '14" on page 959:

```
struct Point2
{
    int d_x, d_y;                                    // same as for Point1
    constexpr Point2(int x, int y) : d_x(x), d_y(y) { }  //   "    "  "       "

    constexpr int& x() { return d_x; }                   // accessor (1)
        // Error, binding int& reference to const int discards qualifiers.

    constexpr const int& y() const { return d_y; }       // accessor (2)
        // OK, the 2nd const qualifier is redundant (but only in C++11).

    constexpr const int& y() { return d_y; }             // accessor (3)
        // Error, redefinition of constexpr const int& Point::y() const
};
```

In the `Point2` **struct** example above, accessor (1) is implicitly declared **const** in C++11
(but not C++14); hence, the attempt to return a modifiable *lvalue* reference to the implicitly
const d_x data member discards the **const** qualifier, resulting in a compilation error. Had
we declared the **constexpr** function to return a **const** reference, as we did for accessor
(2), the code would have compiled just fine. Note that the explicit **const** member-function
qualifier, i.e., the second **const**, in accessor (2) is redundant in C++11 (but not in C++14);
having it there ensures that the meaning will not change when this code is recompiled
under a subsequent version of the language. Lastly, note that omitting the member-function
qualifier in accessor (3) fails to produce a distinct overload in C++11 (but would in C++14).

Because declaring a member function to be **constexpr** implicitly makes it **const**-qualified
(C++11 only), there can be unintended consequences:

```
struct Point3
{
    int d_x, d_y;                                    // same as for Point1
    constexpr Point3(int x, int y) : d_x(x), d_y(y) { }  //   "    "  "       "

    constexpr int x() const { return d_x; }  // OK
    constexpr int y()       { return d_y; }  // OK, const is implied in C++11.

             int setX(int x) { return d_x = x; }  // OK, but not constexpr
    constexpr int setY(int y) { return d_y = y; }  // Error, implied const

    constexpr Point3& operator=(const Point3& p);
        // constexpr copy and move assignment cannot be
        // implemented properly in C++11.

};
```

Notice that declaring a member function, such as setY in the code example above, to be **constexpr** implicitly qualifies the member function as being **const**, thereby making it an error for any **constexpr** member function to attempt to modify its own object's data members. The inevitable corollary is that any appropriate implementation of *copy* or *move* assignment cannot be declared **constexpr** in C++11 but can be as of C++14.

Finally, **constexpr** member functions cannot be **virtual**[3] but can co-exist in the same class with other member functions that *are* virtual.

Restrictions on constexpr function bodies (C++11 only)

The list of C++ programming features permitted in the bodies of **constexpr** functions for C++11 is small and reflective of the nascent state of this feature when it was first standardized. To begin, the body of a **constexpr** function is not permitted to be a **function-try-block**:

```
          int g1()     { return 0; }                  // OK
constexpr int g2()     { return 0; }                  // OK, no try block
          int g3() try { return 0; } catch(...) {}    // OK, not constexpr
constexpr int g4() try { return 0; } catch(...) {}    // Error, not allowed
```

C++11 **constexpr** functions that are not *deleted* or *defaulted* (see Section 1.1."Deleted Functions" on page 53 and Section 1.1."Defaulted Functions" on page 33, respectively) may consist of only **null statements**, static assertions (see Section 1.1."**static_assert**" on page 115), **using declarations**, **using directives**, and **typedef** and alias declarations (see Section 1.1."**using** Aliases" on page 133) that do not define a class or enumeration. Other than constructors, the body of a **constexpr** function must include exactly one **return** statement. A **constexpr** constructor may have a member-initializer list but no other additional statements, but see *Constraints specific to constructors* on page 269. Use of the **ternary operator**, **comma operator**, and recursion is allowed:

```
constexpr int f(int x)
{
    ;                                     // OK, null statement
    static_assert(sizeof(int) == 4, "");  // OK, static assertion
    using MyInt = int;                    // OK, type alias
    return x > 5 ? x : f(x + 2), f(x + 1); // OK, ternary, comma, and recursion
}
```

Many familiar programming constructs such as runtime assertions, local variables, **if** statements, modifications of function parameters, and **using** directives that define a type are, however, *not* permitted in C++11:

```
#include <cassert> // standard C assert macro
constexpr int g(int x)
{
```

---

[3]C++20 allows **constexpr** member functions to be **virtual** (**dimov18**).

```
    assert(x < 100);            // Error, no runtime asserts
    int y = x;                  // Error, no local variables
    if (x > 5) { return x; }    // Error, no if statements
    using S = struct { };       // Error, no aliases that define types
    return x += 3;              // Error, no compound assignment
}
```

The good news is that the aforementioned restrictions on the kinds of constructs that are permitted in **constexpr** function bodies are significantly relaxed as of C++14; see Section 2.2. "**constexpr** Functions '14" on page 959.

Irrespective of the *kinds* of constructs that are allowed to appear in a **constexpr** function body, every invocation of a function, a constructor, or an implicit conversion operator in the **return** statement must itself be usable in at least one **constant expression**, which means the corresponding function *must*, at a minimum, be declared **constexpr**:

```
          int ga() { return 0; }  // nonconstexpr function returning 0
constexpr int gb() { return 0; }  //    constexpr function returning 0

struct S1a {           S1a() { } };  // nonconstexpr default constructor
struct S1b { constexpr S1b() { } };  //    constexpr default constructor

struct S2a { operator int() { return 5; } };           // nonconstexpr conversion
struct S2b { constexpr operator int() { return 5; } }; // constexpr conversion

constexpr int f1a() { return ga(); }  // Error, ga is not constexpr.
constexpr int f1b() { return gb(); }  // OK, gb is constexpr.

constexpr int f2a() { return S1a(), 5; }  // Error, S1a ctor is not constexpr.
constexpr int f2b() { return S1b(), 5; }  // OK, S1b ctor is constexpr.

constexpr int f3a() { return S2a(); } // Error, S2a conversion is not constexpr.
constexpr int f3b() { return S2b(); } // OK, S2b conversion is constexpr.
```

Note that non**constexpr** implicit conversions, as illustrated by **f3a** above, can also result from a non**constexpr**, non**explicit** constructor that accepts a single argument.

Constraints specific to constructors

In addition to the general restrictions on a **constexpr** function's body (see *Restrictions on constexpr function bodies (C++11 only)* on page 268) and its allowed parameter and return types (see ***constexpr**-function parameter and return types* on page 277), several additional requirements are specific to constructors.

1. The body of a **constexpr** constructor is restricted in the same way as any other **constexpr** function, except that the **return** statement is disallowed. Hence, the body of a **constexpr** constructor must be essentially empty with few exceptions:

```
namespace n          // enclosing namespace
{

class C { /*...*/ };  // arbitrary class definition

struct S
{
    constexpr S(bool) try { } catch (...) { }  // Error, function try block
             S(char) try { } catch (...) { }  // OK, not declared constexpr

    constexpr S(int)
    {
        ;                        // OK, null statement
        static_assert(1, "");    // OK, static_assert declaration
        typedef int Int;         // OK, simple typedef alias
        using Int = int;         // OK, simple using alias
        typedef enum {} E;       // Error, typedef used to define enum E
        using n::C;              // OK, using declaration
        using namespace n;       // OK, using directive
    }
};

}  // close namespace
```

2. All non**static** data members and base-class subobjects of a class must be initialized by a **constexpr** constructor,[4] and the initializers themselves must be usable in a *constant expression*. Scalar members must be explicitly initialized in the member-initializer list or via a **default member initializer**, i.e., they cannot be left in an uninitialized state:

```
struct B  // constexpr constructible only from argument convertible to int
{
    B() { }
    constexpr B(int) { }  // constexpr constructor taking an int
};

struct C  // constexpr default constructible
{
    constexpr C() { }  // constexpr default constructor
};

struct D1 : B  // public derivation
{
```

---

[4]The requirement that all members and base classes be initialized by a constructor that is explicitly declared **constexpr** is relaxed in C++20 provided that uninitialized entities are not accessed at compile time.

```
        constexpr D1() { }  // Error, B has nonconstexpr default constructor
};

struct D2 : B  // public derivation
{
    int d_i;  // nonstatic, scalar data member
    constexpr D2(int i) : B(i) { }  // Error, doesn't initialize d_i
};

        int f1() { return 5; }  // nonconstexpr function
constexpr int f2() { return 5; }  //    constexpr function

struct D3 : C  // public derivation
{
    int d_i = f1();  // initialization using nonconstexpr function
    int d_j = f2();  // initialization using   constexpr function

    constexpr D3() { }  // Error, d_i not constant initialized

    constexpr D3(int i) : d_i(i) { }  // OK, d_i set from init list
};
```

The example code above illustrates various ways in which a base class or non**static**
data member might fail to be initialized by a constructor that is explicitly declared
constexpr. In the final derived class, D3, we note that there are two data members,
d_i and d_j, having member initializers that use a non**constexpr** function, f1, and
a **constexpr** function, f2, respectively. The implementation of the **constexpr** *default*
constructor, D3(), is erroneous because data member d_i would be initialized by the
non**constexpr** function f1 at run time. On the other hand, the implementation of
the *value* constructor, D3(**int**), is fine because the data member d_i is set in the
member-initializer list, thereby enabling compile-time evaluation.

3. Defining a constructor to be **constexpr** requires that the class have no **virtual** base
   classes[5]:

```
struct B { constexpr B(); /*...*/ };  // some arbitrary base class

struct D : virtual B
{
    constexpr D(int) { }   // Error, class D has virtual base class B.
};
```

4. A constructor that is explicitly declared to be **constexpr** can always be suppressed
   using =**delete** (see Section 1.1."Deleted Functions" on page 53). Deleting a function

---

[5]C++20 removes the restriction that a constructor cannot be **constexpr** if the class has any virtual base
classes.

explicitly declares it, makes that declaration inaccessible, and suppresses generation of an implementation; see *Identifying literal types* on page 282. If a constructor is implemented using =**default**, however, a compilation error will result unless the defaulted definition would have been implicitly **constexpr**; see Section 1.1."Defaulted Functions" on page 33:

```
struct S1
{
    S1() { };            // nonconstexpr default constructor
    S1(const S1&) { }; //      "      copy       "
    S1(char) { };        //      "      value      "
};

struct S2
{
    S1 d_s1;
    constexpr S2() = default;        // default constructor
        // Error, S1's default constructor isn't constexpr.

    constexpr S2(const S2&) = delete;  // copy constructor
        // OK, make declaration inaccessible and suppress implementation

    S2(char c) : d_s1(c) { }           // value constructor
        // OK, this constructor is not declared to be constexpr.
};
```

In the example above, explicitly declaring the default constructor of S2 to be **constexpr** is an error because an implicitly defined default constructor would not have been **constexpr**. Using =**delete** *declares* but does not *define* a **constexpr** function; hence, no semantic validation with respect to **constexpr** is applied to S2's suppressed copy constructor. Because S2's value constructor (from **char**) is not explicitly declared **constexpr**, there is no issue with delegating to its non**constexpr** member value-constructor counterpart.

5. An implicitly defined default constructor (generated by the compiler) performs the set of initializations of the class that would be performed by a user-written default constructor for that class having no member-initializer list and an empty function body. If such a user-defined default constructor would satisfy the requirements of a **constexpr** constructor, the implicitly defined default constructor is a **constexpr** constructor (and similarly for the implicitly defined copy and move constructors) irrespective of whether it is explicitly declared **constexpr**. Explicitly declaring a defaulted constructor **constexpr** that is *not* inherently **constexpr** is, however, a compile-time error; see Section 1.1."Defaulted Functions" on page 33:

```
struct I0  { int i; /* implicit default ctor */ };  // OK, literal type

struct I1a { int i;            I1a()        { } };  // OK, i is not init
```

```
    struct I1b { int i;   constexpr I1b()        { } };   // Error, i is not init

    struct I2a { int i;             I2a() = default; };   // OK, but not constexpr
    struct I2b { int i;   constexpr I2b() = default; };   // Error, i is not init

    struct I3a { int i;             I3a() : i(0) { } };   // OK, i is init
    struct I3b { int i;   constexpr I3b() : i(0) { } };   // OK, literal type

    struct S0  { I3b v; /* implicit default ctor */ };    // OK, literal type

    struct S1a { I3b v;             S1a()        { } };   // OK, v is init
    struct S1b { I3b v;   constexpr S1b()        { } };   // OK, literal type

    struct S2a { I3b v;             S2a() = default; };   // OK, literal type
    struct S2b { I3b v;   constexpr S2b() = default; };   // OK, literal type
```

The example code above illustrates the subtle differences between a data member of
scalar literal type, e.g., **int** and one of *user-defined* literal type, e.g., I3b. Unlike I1a,
which leaves its own data member, i, uninitialized, S1a invariably zero-initializes its
i. Therefore, attempting to apply **constexpr** to the constructor of I1a is ill formed,
which is not the case for S1a, as illustrated by I1b and S1b above.

Note that, although every literal type needs to have a way to be constructed in a
context requiring a constant expression, not *every* constructor of a literal type needs
to be **constexpr**; see *Literal types defined* on page 278.

6. **Value initialization** and **aggregate initialization**, although not always resulting
   in constructor invocation, can still occur at compile time. These kinds of initialization
   must involve only those operations that can occur during constant evaluation.

   For types having a user-provided default constructor, **value initialization** implies invoking that constructor, thus requiring it to be declared **constexpr** for it to be evaluated
   as part of a constant expression. For types having an implicitly defined (or defaulted;
   see Section 1.1."Defaulted Functions" on page 33) default constructor, value initialization will first zero-initialize all base-class objects and members and will then **default-
   initialize** the object itself, which places similar restriction on the constructor being
   constexpr. If, however, an implicitly defined or defaulted constructor is also **trivial**,
   its invocation will be skipped.[6] A default constructor is trivial if (a) it is implicitly

---

[6]The original intent was to enable any initialization that involved only those operations that could be
evaluated at compile time to be a valid initialization for a literal type. That a trivial default constructor
was insufficient to make a class a literal type, as it was not going to be a **constexpr** constructor, was a
flaw originally noted by Alisdair Meredith; see CWG issue 644 (**meredith07**). The resolution for this issue
was inadvertently undone before C++11 shipped by mistakenly allowing aggregate initialization in lieu of
trivial initialization with other resolutions; see CWG issues 981 (**dosreis09**) and 1071 (**krugler10a**). This
flaw was identified again (CWG issue 1452; **smith11b**), and all relevant compilers adopted the proposed
resolution as a fix, but the Standard itself did not. C++20 removes the requirement that all members and
base classes be initialized in a **constexpr** constructor (**johnson19**), removing the flaw by making trivial
default constructors **constexpr**.

defined, defaulted, or deleted, (b) all non**static** data members have trivial default constructors and no default member initializers, and (c) all base classes are non**virtual** and have trivial default constructors. Hence, it is possible to value-initialize a type that has an explicitly defaulted but not explicitly **constexpr** default constructor:

```cpp
struct S1  // example of a nonconstexpr trivial default constructor
{
    int d_i;          // not initialized by S1()
    S1() = default;  // trivial, nonconstexpr
};
static_assert(S1().d_i == 0, "");  // OK, value initialization
static_assert(S1{}.d_i == 0, "");  // OK, value initialization
```

Aggregate initialization might produce the even more surprising effect of successful initialization even when matching constructors are deleted (see Section 1.1."Deleted Functions" on page 53), including a deleted default constructor[7]:

```cpp
struct S2  // a type having a non-trivial default constructor
{
    constexpr S2() { }  // non-trivial, constexpr
};

struct S3  // example of an aggregate having deleted constructors
{
    int d_i;   // not initialized
    S2  d_s2;  // has non-trivial constructor

    S3()       = delete;  // non-trivial, nonconstexpr
    S3(int a) = delete;   //                nonconstexpr
};
static_assert(S3().d_i  == 0, "");  // Error, invokes deleted constructor
static_assert(S3{}.d_i  == 0, "");  // OK, aggregate initialization
static_assert(S3{7}.d_i == 7, "");  // OK, aggregate initialization
```

Notice that failing to use braced initialization results in **value initialization**, rather than **aggregate initialization**, and therefore attempts to invoke the deleted default constructor of S3.

7. For a **union**, exactly one of its data members must be initialized with a constant expression via (1) a default member initializer (see Section 2.1."Default Member Init" on page 318), (2) a **constexpr** constructor, or (3) aggregate initialization:

```cpp
// unions having no explicit constructors
union U0 { bool b;      char c;      };  // OK, neither member initialized
```

---

[7]Since C++20, a type having any **user-declared** constructors, which includes defaulted and deleted constructors, is no longer considered an aggregate and thus **aggregate initialization** does not apply to such types.

```
union U1 { bool b = 0;  char c;        };  // OK, first member initialized
union U2 { bool b;      char c = 'A'; };  // OK, second    "         "
union U3 { bool b = 0;  char c = 'A'; };  // Error, multiple initialized

// unions having constexpr constructors
union U4 { bool b; char c;        constexpr U4() { } };  // Error, uninit
union U5 { bool b; char c = 'A';  constexpr U5() { } };            // OK
union U6 { bool b; char c;        constexpr U6() : c('A') { } };   // OK
union U7 { bool b; char c;        constexpr U7(bool v) : b(v) { } };  // OK

struct S                          // S is a literal type.
{
    U0 u0{};                      // value-initialized
    U1 u1; U2 u2; U5 u5; U6 u6;   // default-initialized
    U7 u7;                        // initialized in constructor
    constexpr S() : u7(true) { }  // OK, all members are initialized.
};

constexpr int test(S t) { return 0; }  // OK, confirms S is a literal type
```

The example code above illustrates various ways in which unions, e.g., U0–U2 and U5–U7, can be used that allow them to be initialized by a **constexpr** constructor, e.g., S(). The existence of at least one non*copy*, non*move* **constexpr** constructor implies that the class, e.g., S, comprising these unions is a literal type, which we have confirmed using the C++11 interface test idiom; see *Identifying literal types* on page 282.

8. If the constructor *delegates* to another constructor in the same class (see Section 1.1. "Delegating Ctors" on page 46), that target constructor must be **constexpr**:

```
struct C0  // Only the default constructor is constexpr.
{
            C0(int)    { }  // OK, but not declared constexpr
    constexpr C0() : C0(0) { }  // Error, delegating to nonconstexpr ctor
};

struct C1  // Both default and value constructor are constexpr.
{
    constexpr C1(int)    { }  // OK, declared constexpr
    constexpr C1() : C1(0) { }  // OK, delegating to constexpr constructor
};
```

9. When initializing data members of a class (e.g., S below), any nonconstructor functions needed for implicitly converting the type of the initializing expression (e.g., V in the code snippet below) to that of a data member (e.g., **int** or **double**) must also be **constexpr**:

```
struct V
{
    int v;
                operator    int() const { return v; }  // implicit conversion
    constexpr operator double() const { return v; }  // implicit conversion
};

struct S
{
    int i; double d;  // A constexpr constructor must initialize both members.

    constexpr S(const V& x, double y) : i(x), d(y) { }  // Error, the needed
        // int implicit conversion is not declared constexpr.

    constexpr S(int x, const V& y) : i(x), d(y) { }    // OK, the needed
        // double implicit conversion is declared constexpr.
};
```

constexpr **function templates**

Function templates, member function templates, and constructor templates can all be declared **constexpr** and more liberally than nontemplated entities. That is, if a particular instantiation of such a template doesn't meet the requirements of a **constexpr** function, member function, or constructor, it will not be invocable at compile time.[8] For example, consider a function template, sizeOf, that can be evaluated at compile time only if its argument type, T, is a literal type:

```
template <typename T> constexpr int sizeOf(T t) { return sizeof(t); }
    // This function is constexpr only if T is a literal type.

struct S0 { int i;           S0() : i(0) { } };  // not a literal type
struct S1 { int i; constexpr S1() : i(0) { } };  // a literal type

int a[sizeOf(int())];  // OK,    int is    a literal type.
int b[sizeOf( S0())];  // Error, S0 is not a literal type.
int c[sizeOf( S1())];  // OK,    S1 is     a literal type.
```

If no specialization of such a function template would yield a **constexpr** function, then the program is IFNDR. For example, if this same function template were implemented in C++11 with a function body consisting of more than just a single **return** statement, it would be ill formed:

---

[8]A specialization that cannot be evaluated at compile time is, however, still considered **constexpr**. This idiosyncracy is not readily observable but does enable some generic code to remain well formed as long as the particular specializations are not actually required to be evaluated at compile time. This rule was adopted with the resolution of CWG issue 1358 (**smith11a**).

```
template <typename T>
constexpr int badSizeOf(T t) { const int s = sizeof(t); return s; }
    // This constexpr function template is IFNDR.
```

Most compilers, when compiling such a specialization for runtime use, will not attempt to determine if the **constexpr** would ever be valid. When invoked with arguments that are themselves constant expressions, they do, however, often detect this ill formed nature and report the error:

```
int d[badSizeOf(S1())];  // Error, badSizeOf<S1>(S1) body not return statement
int e[badSizeOf(S0())];  // Error, badSizeOf<S0>(S0) body not return statement
int f = badSizeOf(S1()); // Oops, same issue but might work on some compilers
int g = badSizeOf(S0()); // Oops, same issue but often works without warnings
```

Importantly, note that each of the four statements in the code snippet above is ill formed because the badSizeOf function template is itself ill formed. Although the compiler is not required to diagnose the general case, it is ill formed to attempt to use an instantiation of badSizeOf in a context requiring a constant expression, e.g., d or e. When used in a context not requiring a constant expression (e.g., f or g), whether the compiler fails, warns, or proceeds is a matter of **quality of implementation** (QoI).

constexpr-function parameter and return types

At this point, we arrive at what is perhaps the most confounding part of the seemingly *cyclical* definition of **constexpr** functions: A function cannot be declared **constexpr** unless the return type and every parameter of that function satisfies the criteria for being a literal type, i.e., the category of types whose objects are permitted to be created and destroyed when evaluating a constant expression:

```
struct  Lt { int v; constexpr  Lt() : v(0) { } };  // literal type
struct Nlt { int v;           Nlt() : v(0) { } };  // nonliteral type

          Lt  f1() { return Lt();  }  // OK, no issues
constexpr Lt  f2() { return Lt();  }  // OK, returning literal type
          Nlt f3() { return Nlt(); }  // Ok, function is nonconstexpr.
constexpr Nlt f4() { return Nlt(); }  // Error, constexpr returning nonliteral

          int g1(Lt  x) { return x.v; }  // OK, no issues
constexpr int g2(Lt  x) { return x.v; }  // OK, parameter is a literal type.
          int g3(Nlt x) { return x.v; }  // OK, function is nonconstexpr.
constexpr int g4(Nlt x) { return x.v; }  // Error, constexpr taking nonliteral
```

Consider that all *pointer* and *reference* types — being *built-in types* — are literal types and therefore can appear in the interface of a **constexpr** function irrespective of whether they point to a literal type:

```
constexpr int h1(Lt*  p) { return p->v; }  // OK, parameter is a literal type.
constexpr int h2(Nlt* p) { return p->v; }  // OK,    "      "  "    "    "
constexpr int h3(Lt&  r) { return r.v; }   // OK,    "      "  "    "    "
constexpr int h4(Nlt& r) { return r.v; }   // OK,    "      "  "    "    "
```

However, note that, because constructing an object of nonliteral type at compile time is not
possible, there is no way to invoke h2 or h4 as part of a **constant expression** since the access
of the member v in all of the above functions requires an already created object to exist.
Pointers and references to nonliteral types can be **constexpr** provided they are not used to
access their values at compile time:

```
Nlt arr[17];
constexpr Nlt& arr_0 = arr[0];                // OK, initializing a reference
constexpr Nlt* arr_0_ptr = &arr[0];           // OK, taking an address
constexpr Nlt& arr_0_ptr_deref = *arr_0_ptr;  // OK, dereferencing but not using
static_assert(&arr[17] - &arr[4] == 13,"");   // OK, pointer arithmetic

constexpr int arr_0_v = arr_0.v;              // Error, arr[0] is not usable.
constexpr int arr_0_ptr_v = arr_0_ptr->v;     // Error,   "    "   "   "
```

Literal types defined

As discussed understanding which types are literal types is important for knowing what can
and cannot be done during compile-time evaluation. We now elucidate how the language
defines a literal type and, as such, how they are usable in two primary use cases:

- Literal types are eligible to be created and destroyed during the evaluation of a *constant
  expression.*

- Literal types are suitable to be used in the *interface* of a **constexpr** function, either
  as the return type or as a parameter type.

The criteria for determining whether a given type is a literal type can be divided into six
parts:

1. Every scalar type is a literal type. Scalar types include all fundamental arithmetic
   (integral and floating point) types, all enumerated types, and all pointer types.

int	int is a *literal type.*
double	double is a *literal type.*
short*	short* is a *literal type.*
enum E { e_A };	E is a *literal type.*
T*	T* *is a literal type* (for any T).

Note that a pointer T* is *always* a literal type, even when it points to a type T that
itself is *not* a literal type.

2. Just as with pointers, every reference type is a literal type irrespective of whether the type to which it refers is itself a literal type.

`int&`	`int&` is a *literal type*
`T&`	`T&` is a *literal type* (for any `T`).
`T&&`	`T&&` is a *literal type* (for any `T`).

3. A **class**, **struct**, or **union** is a literal type if it meets each of these four requirements.

    (a) It has a trivial destructor.[9]

    (b) Each non**static** data member is a non**volatile** literal type.[10]

    (c) Each base class is a literal type.

    (d) There is some way to initialize an object of the type during constant evaluation; either it is an **aggregate type**, thereby affording aggregate initialization, or it has at least one **constexpr** constructor (possibly a template) that is not a *copy* or *move* constructor:

```cpp
#include <string>  // std::string
struct LiteralUDT
{
    static std::string s_cache;
        // OK, static data member can have a nonliteral type.

    int d_datum;
        // OK, nonstatic data member of nonvolatile literal type

    constexpr LiteralUDT(int datum) : d_datum(datum) { }
        // OK, has at least one constexpr constructor

    LiteralUDT() : d_datum(-1) { }
        // OK, can have nonconstexpr constructors

    // constexpr ~LiteralUDT() { }   // not permitted until C++20
        // No need to define: implicitly generated destructor is trivial.
};

struct LiteralAggregate
{
    int d_value1;
    int d_value2;
};
```

---

[9]As of C++20, a destructor can be declared **constexpr** and even both **virtual** and **constexpr**.

[10]In C++17, this restriction is relaxed: For a **union** to be a literal type, only one, rather than all, of its non**static** data members needs to be of a non**volatile** literal type.

```
union LiteralUnion
{
    int   d_x;  // OK, int is a literal type.
    float d_y;  // OK, float is a literal type.
};
```

4. A cv-qualified literal type is also a literal type.[11]

const int	is a *literal type*
volatile int	is a *literal type*
const volatile int	is a *literal type*
const LiteralUDT	is a *literal type* (since LiteralUDT is)

5. Arrays of objects of literal type are also literal types:

```
char a[5];  // An array of scalar type, e.g., char, is a literal type.

struct { int i; bool b; } b[7];
    // An array of aggregate type is a literal type.
```

6. In C++14 and thereafter, **void** and thus cv-qualified **void** are also literal types, thereby enabling functions that return **void**:

```
constexpr const volatile void f() { }  // OK, in C++14
```

The overarching goal of the above six-part definition of what constitutes a literal type is to capture those types that might be *eligible* to be created and destroyed during evaluation of a *constant expression*. This definition does not, however, guarantee that every literal type satisfying the above criteria will necessarily be constructible in a constant expression, let alone in a meaningful way.

- A user-defined literal type is not required to have any **constexpr** member functions or publicly accessible members. It is quite possible that the only thing one might be able to do with a user-defined literal type as part of a constant expression is to create it:

```
class C { };  // C is a literal type.

int a[(C(), 5)];  // OK, create an array of five int objects.
```

Such "barely literal" types, though severely limited in their usefulness in constant expressions, do allow for useful compile-time initialization of **constexpr** variables in C++14; see Section 2.1."**constexpr** Variables" on page 302.

---

[11]Note that cv-qualified scalar types are still scalar types, and cv-qualified **class** types were noted as being literal types in a **defect report** that resolved CWG issue 1951 (**smith14**).

- The requirement to have at least one **constexpr** constructor that is not a *copy* or *move* constructor is just that: to have at least one. There is no requirement that such a constructor be invocable at compile time, e.g., it could be declared **private**, or even that it be defined; in fact, a deleted constructor (see Section 1.1."Deleted Functions" on page 53) satisfies the requirement:

```
struct UselessLiteralType
{
    constexpr UselessLiteralType() = delete;
};
```

- Many uses of literal types in **constexpr** functions will require additional **constexpr** functions to be defined (not merely declared), such as a *move* or *copy* constructor:

```
struct Lt  // literal type having nonconstexpr copy constructor
{
    constexpr Lt(int c) { }  // valid constexpr value constructor
    Lt(const Lt& ) { }       // nonconstexpr copy constructor
};

constexpr int processByValue(Lt t) { return 0; }  // valid constexpr function

static_assert(processByValue(Lt(7)) == 0, "");
    // Error, but might work on some platforms due to elided copy

constexpr Lt s{7};  // braced-initialized object of type Lt

static_assert(processByValue(s) == 0, "");  // Error, nonconstexpr copy ctor
```

In the code example above, we have a literal type, Lt, for which we have explicitly declared a non**constexpr** copy constructor. We then defined a valid **constexpr** function, processByValue, taking an Lt (by value) as its only argument. Invoking the function by constructing an object of Lt from a literal **int** value enables the compiler to elide the copy. Platforms where the copy is elided might allow this evaluation at compile time, while on other platforms there will be an error. When we consider using an independently constructed **constexpr** variable (i.e., s), the copy can no longer be elided, and since the copy constructor is declared explicitly to be non**constexpr**, the compile-time assertion fails to compile on all platforms; see Section 2.1."**constexpr** Variables" on page 302.

- Although a pointer or reference is always (by definition) a *literal type*, if the type being pointed to is not itself a literal type, then the referenced object cannot be used during constant expression evaluation.

Identifying literal types

Knowing what is and what is not a literal type is not always obvious given all the various rules we have covered and how the rules have changed from one version of the Standard to another. Having a concrete way of identifying literal types other than becoming a language lawyer and interpreting the full Standard definition can be immensely valuable during development, especially when trying to prototype a facility that we intend to be usable at compile time. We identify two means for ensuring that a type is a literal type and, often more importantly for a user, identifying if a type is a **usable literal type**.

1. Only literal types can be used in the interface of a **constexpr** function (i.e., either as the return type or as a parameter type), and any literal type can be used in the interface of such a function. The first approach one might take to determine if a given type is a literal type would be to define a function that returns the given type *by value*. This approach has the downside of requiring that the type in question also be *copyable* or at least *movable*; see Section 2.1.*"Rvalue* References" on page 710[12]:

   ```
   struct LiteralType    { constexpr LiteralType(int i)    {} };
   struct NonLiteralType {           NonLiteralType(int i) {} };
   struct NonMovableType { constexpr NonMovableType(int i) {}
                           NonMovableType(NonMovableType&&) = delete; };


   constexpr LiteralType    f(int i) { return LiteralType(i);    } // OK
   constexpr NonLiteralType g(int i) { return NonLiteralType(i); } // Error
   constexpr NonMovableType h(int i) { return NonMovableType(i); } // Error
   ```

   In the above example, `NonMovableType` is a literal type but is not movable or copyable, so it cannot be the return type of a function. Passing the type as a *by-value* parameter works more reliably and even consistently identifies non*copyable*, non*movable* literal types:

   ```
   constexpr int test(LiteralType t)    { return 0; } // OK
   constexpr int test(NonLiteralType t) { return 0; } // Error
   constexpr int test(NonMovableType t) { return 0; } // OK
   ```

   This approach is appealing in that it provides a general way for a programmer to query the compiler whether it considers a given type, `S`, *as a whole* to be a literal type and can be succinctly written[13]:

   ```
   constexpr int test(S) { return 0; } // compiles only if S is a literal type
   ```

   Note that all of these tests require providing a function body, since compilers will validate that the declaration of the function is valid for a **constexpr** function only

---

[12]As of C++17, the requirement that the type in question be *copyable* or *movable* to return it as a *prvalue* is removed; see Section 2.1.*"Rvalue* References" on page 710.

[13]As of C++14, we can **return void** — **constexpr void** test(S) { } — and omit the **return** statement entirely; see Section 2.2.*"***constexpr** Functions '14" on page 959.

when they are processing the *definition* of the function. A declaration without a body will not produce the expected error for *non-literal-type* parameters and return types:

```
constexpr NonLiteralType quietly(NonLiteralType t);  // OK, declaration only
constexpr NonLiteralType quietly(NonLiteralType t) { return t; }  // Error
```

Finally, the C++11 Standard Library provides a type trait — std::is_literal_type — that attempts to serve a similar purpose[14]:

```
#include <type_traits>  // std::is_literal_type
static_assert( std::is_literal_type<LiteralType>::value, "");     // OK
static_assert(!std::is_literal_type<NonLiteralType>::value, "");  // OK
```

The important takeaway is that we can use a trivial test in C++11 (made even more trivial in C++14) to find out if the compiler deems that a given type is a literal type.

2. To ensure that a type under development is meaningful in a compile-time facility, confirming that objects of a given literal type can actually be constructed at compile time becomes imperative. This confirmation requires identifying a particular form of initialization and corresponding **witness arguments** that should allow a user-defined type to assume a valid compile-time value. For this example, we can use the interface test to help prove that our class, e.g., Lt, is a literal type:

```
class Lt  // An object of this type can be used in a constant expression.
{
    int d_value;

public:
    constexpr Lt(int i) : d_value(i != 75033 ? throw 0 : i) { }  // OK
};

constexpr int checkLiteral(Lt) { return 0; }  // OK, literal type
```

Proving that Lt in the code example above is a usable literal type next involves choosing a **constexpr** constructor (e.g., Lt(**int**)), selecting appropriate witness arguments (e.g., 75033), and then using the result in a constant expression. The compiler will indicate if our type cannot be constructed at compile time by producing an error:

```
char x[(Lt(75033), 1)];          // OK, usable in constant expr
static_assert((Lt(75033), true), "");  // OK,  "     "      "      "
```

---

[14]Note that the std::is_literal_type trait is deprecated in C++17 and removed in C++20. The rationale is stated in **meredith16**:

> The is_literal_type trait offers negligible value to generic code, as what is really needed is the ability to know that a specific construction would produce constant initialization. The core term of a literal type having at least one **constexpr** constructor is too weak to be used meaningfully.

For types that are not usable literal types, there will be no such proof. When a particular constructor that is *explicitly* declared to be **constexpr** has no set of witness arguments that can be used to prove that the type is usable, the constructor (and any program in which it resides) is IFNDR. Forcing the compiler to perform such a proof in general — even if such were possible — would not be a wise use of compile-time compute resources. Hence, compilers will generally not diagnose the ill-formed constructor and instead simply produce an error on each attempt to provide a set of witnesses for a literal type that fails to be usable at compile time:

```
int a = 1, b = 2;  // a and b are not constexpr.

class PathologicalType  // ill formed, no diagnostic required
{
    int d_value;

public:
    constexpr PathologicalType(int i)
        : d_value( (i <  2) ? a
                 : (i >= 2) ? b
                 : (i * 2) ) { }
};
```

The compiler is unlikely to have logic to discover that there is no way to invoke the above **constexpr** constructor as part of the evaluation of a **constant expression**; the constructor is considered ill formed, but no diagnostic is likely to be produced. Supplying any witness arguments, however, will force the compiler to evaluate the constructor and discover no *particular* invocations are valid:

```
static_assert((PathologicalType(1),true), "");  // Error, a is not constexpr.
static_assert((PathologicalType(2),true), "");  // Error, b is not constexpr.
static_assert((PathologicalType(3),true), "");  // Error, b is not constexpr.
```

Compile-time evaluation

All of the restrictions on the constructs that are valid in a **constexpr** function exist to enable the portable evaluation of such functions at compile time. Appreciating this motivation requires an understanding of compile-time calculations in general and **constant expressions** in particular.

First, a **constant expression** is *required* in specific contexts.

- Any arguments to **static_assert**, **noexcept** operator, and the **alignas** specifier

- The size of a built-in array

- The expression for a **case** label in a **switch** statement

- The initializer for an enumerator

- The length of a bit field

- Nontype template parameters

- The initializer of a **constexpr** variable (see Section 2.1."**constexpr** Variables" on page 302)

Computing the value of expressions in these contexts requires that all of their subexpressions be known and evaluable at compile time, except those that are short-circuited by the logical *or* operator (||), the logical *and* operator (&&), and the *ternary* operator (?:):

```
constexpr int f(int x) { return x || (throw x, 1); }
constexpr int g(int x) { return x && (throw x, 1); }
constexpr int h(int x) { return x ? 1 : throw x; }

static_assert(f(true), "");    // OK, throw x is never evaluated.
static_assert(!g(false), ""); // OK,   "    "   "   "        "
static_assert(h(true), "");    // OK,   "    "   "   "        "
```

Note that the **controlling constant expression** for the preprocessor directives **#if** and **#elif**, while similar to general constant expressions, are computed before any functions — **constexpr** or not — are even parsed. Consequently, **constexpr** functions cannot be invoked as part of the **controlling constant expression** for preprocessor directives.

Second, the C++11 Standard identifies a clear set of operations that are not available for use in **constant expressions** and, therefore, cannot be relied upon for compile-time evaluation. Any operation that does the following is unavailable.

- Throws an exception

- Invokes the **new** and **delete** operators

- Invokes a lambda function

- Depends on runtime polymorphism, such as **dynamic_cast**, **typeid** on a polymorphic type, or invokes a virtual function, which cannot be **constexpr**

- Uses **reinterpret_cast**

- Modifies an object (increment, decrement, and assignment), including function parameters, member variables, and global variables

- Has *undefined behavior* such as integer overflow, dereferencing **nullptr**, or indexing outside the bounds of an array

- Invokes a non**constexpr** function or constructor, or a **constexpr** function whose definition has not yet been seen

Note that being marked **constexpr** enables a function to be evaluated *at compile time* only if (1) the argument values are **constant expressions** known before the function is evaluated and (2) no operations performed when invoking the function with those arguments involve any of the excluded ones listed above.

Global variables can be used in a **constexpr** function only if they are (1) *non***volatile const** objects of *integral* or *enumerated* type that are initialized by a **constant expression** (generally treated as **constexpr** even if only marked as **const**), or (2) **constexpr** objects of literal type; see *Literal types defined* on page 278 and Section 2.1."**constexpr** Variables" on page 302. In either case, any **constexpr** global object used within a **constexpr** function must be initialized with a **constant expression** prior to the definition of the function. C++14[15] relaxes some of these restrictions; see Section 2.2."**constexpr** Functions '14" on page 959.

Use Cases

A better alternative to function-like macros

Computations that are useful both at run time and at compile time and/or that must be inlined for performance reasons were typically implemented using preprocessor macros. For instance, consider the task of converting mebibytes to bytes:

```
#define MEBIBYTES_TO_BYTES(mebibytes) ((mebibytes) * 1024 * 1024)
```

The macro above can be used in contexts where both a **constant expression** is required and the input is known only during program execution:

```
#include <cstddef>  // std::size_t
#include <vector>   // std::vector
void example0(std::size_t input)
{
    unsigned char fixedBuffer[MEBIBYTES_TO_BYTES(2)];  // compile-time constant

    std::vector<unsigned char> dynamicBuffer;
    dynamicBuffer.resize(MEBIBYTES_TO_BYTES(input));  // usable at run time
}
```

While a single-line macro with a reasonably unique (and long) name like MEBIBYTES_TO_BYTES is unlikely to cause any problems in practice, it harbors all the disadvantages macros have compared to regular functions. Macro names are not scoped; hence, they are subject to global name collisions. There is no well-defined input and output type and thus no type safety. Perhaps most tellingly, the lack of expression safety makes writing even simple macros tricky; a common error, for example, is to forget the () around mebibytes in the implementation of MEBIBYTES_TO_BYTES, resulting in an unintended result if applied to a non-trivial expression such as MEBIBYTES_TO_BYTES(2+2) — yielding a value of (2+2 * 1024 * 1024) = 2097154 without the () and the intended value of ((2+2) * 1024 * 1024) = 4194304 with them.

---

[15]C++17 and C++20 each further relax these restrictions.

A single **constexpr** function is sufficient to replace the MEBIBYTES_TO_BYTES macro, avoiding the aforementioned disadvantages without any additional runtime overhead:

```
constexpr std::size_t mebibytesToBytes(std::size_t mebibytes)
{
    return mebibytes * 1024 * 1024;
}

void example1(std::size_t input)
{
    unsigned char fixedBuffer[mebibytesToBytes(2)];
        // OK, guaranteed to be invocable at compile time

    std::vector<unsigned char> dynamicBuffer;
    dynamicBuffer.resize(mebibytesToBytes(input));
        // OK, can also be invoked at run time
}
```

The generally unstructured and unhygienic nature of macros has led to significant language evolution aimed at supplanting their use with proper language features where practicable. We are not suggesting that macros have no place in the ecosystem; in fact, many of the C++ language features — not the least of which were templates and, more recently, contract checks — were initially prototyped using preprocessor macros.

Compile-time string traversal

Beyond simple numeric calculations, many compile-time libraries might need to accept strings as input and manipulate them in various ways. Applications can range from simply pre-calculating string-related values to powerful compile-time regular-expression libraries.[16] To begin, we will consider the simplest of string operations: calculating the length of a string. An initial implementation might attempt to leverage the type of a string constant (array of **char**) with a template:

```
#include <cstddef>  // std::size_t

template <std::size_t N>
constexpr std::size_t constStrlenLit(const char (&lit)[N])
{
    return N - 1;
}
static_assert(constStrlenLit("hello") == 5, "");  // OK
```

This approach, however, fails when attempting to apply it to any number of other ways in which a variable might contain a compile-time or runtime string constant:

---

[16]See **dusikova19** for one example of how far such techniques can evolve and might be incorporated into a future Standard Library release.

```
constexpr const char* hw1      = "hello";
              char    hw2[20] = "hello";
        const char*   hw3      = hw2;

static_assert(constStrlenLit(hw1) == 5, "");  // Error, hw1 not a char[N]

std::size_t len2 = constStrlenLit(hw2);  // Bug, returns 19
std::size_t len3 = constStrlenLit(hw3);  // Error, hw3 not a char[N]
```

The type-based approach is clearly deficient. A better approach is simply to loop over the characters in the string, counting them until we find the terminating \0 character. Here, we'll take the liberty of illustrating the simpler solution (using local variables and loops) that is available with the relaxed rules for **constexpr** functions in C++14 alongside the recursive solution that works in C++11; see Section 2.2."**constexpr** Functions '14" on page 959:

```
constexpr std::size_t constStrlen(const char* str)
{
#if __cplusplus > 201103L
    const char* strEnd = str;
    while (*strEnd) ++strEnd;
    return strEnd - str;
#else
    return (str[0] == '\0') ? 0 : 1 + constStrlen(str + 1);
#endif
}

static_assert(constStrlen("hello") == 5, "");  // OK
static_assert(constStrlen(hw1)     == 5, "");  // OK

std::size_t len2b = constStrlen(hw2);  // OK, returns 5
std::size_t len3b = constStrlen(hw3);  // OK, returns 5
```

With this most basic function implemented, let's move on to the more interesting problem of counting the number of lowercase letters in a string in such a way that it can be evaluated at compile time if the string is a constant expression. We'll need a simple helper function that determines if a given **char** is a lowercase letter:

```
constexpr bool isLowercase(char c)
    // Return true if c is a lowercase ASCII letter, and false otherwise.
{
    return 'a' <= c && c <= 'z';  // true if c is in ASCII range 'a' to z
}
```

Note that we are using a simplistic definition here that is designed to handle only the *ASCII* letters a through z; significantly more work would be required to handle other character sets or locales at compile time. Unfortunately, the std::islower function inherited from C is not **constexpr**.

Now we can apply a similar construct to what we used for constStrlen to count the number of lowercase letters in a string:

```
constexpr std::size_t countLowercase(const char* str)
{
    return (str[0] == '\0') ? 0 : isLowercase(str[0]) + countLowercase(str + 1);
}
```

Now we have a function that will count the lowercase letters in a string at either compile time or run time for *any* null-terminated string:

```
static_assert(countLowercase("") == 0, "");
static_assert(countLowercase("HELLO, WORLD") == 0, "");
static_assert(countLowercase("Hello, World") == 8, "");

#include <cassert>   // standard C assert macro
void test1()
{
    const char* p1 = "";              assert(countLowercase(p1) == 0);
    const char* p2 = "HELLO, WORLD";  assert(countLowercase(p2) == 0);
    const char* p3 = "Hello, World";  assert(countLowercase(p3) == 8);
}
```

The first three invocations of countLowercase, in the code snippet above, illustrate that when given a **constexpr** argument, the function can compute the correct result at compile time. The other three invocations show that countLowercase can be invoked on non-**constexpr** strings and compute the correct results at run time.

Despite severe limitations on C++11 **constexpr** function bodies, much of the power of the language is still available at compile time. For example, counting values in an array that match a function predicate can be converted to a **constexpr** function template in the same way we might do so with a runtime-only template:

```
template <typename T, typename F>
constexpr std::size_t countIf(T* arr, std::size_t len, const F& func)
{
    return (len==0) ? 0 : (func(arr[0]) ? 1 : 0) + countIf(arr+1,len-1,func);
}
```

In just one dense line, countIf recursively determines if the current length, len, is 0 and, if not, whether the first element satisfies the predicate, func. If so, 1 is added to the result of recursively invoking countIf for the rest of the elements in arr.

This countIf function template can now be used at compile time with a **constexpr** function pointer to produce a more modern-looking version of our countLowercase function:

```
constexpr std::size_t countLowercase(const char* str)
{
    return countIf(str, constStrlen(str), isLowercase);
}
```

Rather than a null-terminated array of **char**, we might want a more flexible string representation consisting of a **class** containing a **const char*** pointing to the start of a sequence of **char**s and an std::size_t holding the length of the sequence.[17] We can define such a class as a literal type even in C++11:

```
#include <stdexcept>  // std::out_of_range

class ConstStringView
{
    const char* d_string_p;  // address of the string supplied at construction
    std::size_t d_length;    // length    "    "       "        "     "        "
public:
    constexpr ConstStringView(const char* str)
    : d_string_p(str)
    , d_length(constStrlen(str)) {}

    constexpr ConstStringView(const char* str, std::size_t length)
    : d_string_p(str)
    , d_length(length) {}

    constexpr char operator[](std::size_t n) const
    {
        return n < d_length ? d_string_p[n] : throw std::out_of_range("");
    }

    constexpr const char* data() const { return d_string_p; }
    constexpr std::size_t length() const { return d_length; }

    constexpr const char* begin() const { return d_string_p; }
    constexpr const char* end()  const { return d_string_p + d_length; }
};
```

The ConstStringView class shown above provides some basic functionality to inspect and pass around the contents of a string constant at compile time. The implicitly declared **constexpr** copy constructor of this literal type allows us to overload our countIf function template and countLowercase function to take a ConstStringView by value:

```
template <typename F>
constexpr std::size_t countIf(ConstStringView sv, const F& func)
{
    return countIf(sv.data(), sv.length(), func);
}

constexpr std::size_t countLowercase(ConstStringView sv)
{
    return countIf(sv, isLowercase);
}
```

---

[17]C++17's std::string_view is an example of such string-related utility functionality.

Thanks to the implicit **converting constructors**, all of the earlier **static_assert** statements that were used with previous countLowercase implementations work with this one as well, and we gain the ability to further use ConstStringView as a **vocabulary type** for our **constexpr** functions.

Precomputing tables of data at compile time

Often, compile-time evaluation through the use of **constexpr** functions can be used to replace otherwise complex template metaprogramming or preprocessor tricks. While yielding more readable and more maintainable source code, **constexpr** functions also enable useful computations that previously were simply not practicable at compile time.

Calculating single values and using them at compile time is straightforward. Storing such values to use at run time can be done with a **constexpr** variable; see Section 2.1."**constexpr** Variables" on page 302.

Consider a part of a date and time library that provides utilities to deal with timestamps of type std::time_t — an integer type expressing a number of seconds since some point in time, e.g., the **POSIX epoch**, 00:00:00 UTC on 1 January 1970. An important tool in this library would be a function to determine the year of a given timestamp:

```
#include <ctime>  // std::time_t

int yearOfTimestamp(std::time_t timestamp);
    // Return the year of the specified timestamp. The behavior is undefined
    // if timestamp < 0.
```

Among other features, this library would provide a number of constants, both for its internal use as well as for direct client use. These could be implemented as enumerations, as integral constants at namespace scope, or as static members of a **struct** or **class**. Since we will be leveraging them within **constexpr** functions, we will also illustrate making use of **constexpr** variables here:

```
// constants defining the date and time of the epoch
constexpr int k_EPOCH_YEAR  = 1970;
constexpr int k_EPOCH_MONTH = 1;
constexpr int k_EPOCH_DAY   = 1;

// constants defining conversion ratios between various time units
constexpr std::time_t k_SECONDS_PER_MINUTE = 60;
constexpr std::time_t k_SECONDS_PER_HOUR   = 60  * k_SECONDS_PER_MINUTE;
constexpr std::time_t k_SECONDS_PER_DAY    = 24  * k_SECONDS_PER_HOUR;
constexpr std::time_t k_SECONDS_PER_YEAR   = 365 * k_SECONDS_PER_DAY;
static_assert(31536000L == k_SECONDS_PER_YEAR, "");  // seconds per common year
```

For practical reasons related to the limits that compilers put on template expansion and constant expression evaluation, this library will support only a moderate number of future years:

```
// constant defining the largest year supported by our library
constexpr int k_MAX_YEAR = 2200;
```

To begin implementing `yearOfTimestamp`, it helps to start with an implementation of a solution to the reverse problem, i.e., calculating the timestamp of the start of each year, which requires an adjustment to account for leap days:

```
constexpr int numLeapYearsSinceEpoch(int year)
{
    return (year        / 4) - (year        / 100) + (year        / 400)
        - ((k_EPOCH_YEAR / 4) - (k_EPOCH_YEAR / 100) + (k_EPOCH_YEAR / 400));
}

constexpr std::time_t startOfYear(int year)
    // Return the number of seconds between the epoch and the start of the
    // specified year.  The behavior is undefined if year < k_EPOCH_YEAR or
    // year > k_MAX_YEAR.
{
    return (year - k_EPOCH_YEAR) * k_SECONDS_PER_YEAR
        + numLeapYearsSinceEpoch(year - 1) * k_SECONDS_PER_DAY;
}
```

Given these tools, we could implement `yearOfTimestamp` naively with a simple loop:

```
int yearOfTimestamp(std::time_t timestamp)
{
    int year = k_EPOCH_YEAR;
    for (; timestamp > startOfYear(year + 1); ++year) {}
    return year;
}
```

This implementation, however, has algorithmically poor performance. While a closed-form solution to this problem is certainly possible, for expository purposes we will consider how we might, at compile time, build a lookup table of the results of `startOfYear` so that `yearOfTimestamp` can be implemented as a **binary search** on that table.

Populating a built-in array at compile time is feasible by manually writing each initializer, but a decidedly better option is to generate the sequence of numbers we want as an `std:array` where all we need is to provide the **constexpr** function that will take an index and produce the value we want stored at that location within the array. We will start by implementing the pieces needed to make a generic **constexpr** function for initializing `std::array` instances with the results of a **function object** applied to each index:

```
#include <array>   // std::array
#include <cstddef> // std::size_t

template <typename T, std::size_t N, typename F>
constexpr std::array<T, N> generateArray(const F& func);
    // Return an array arr of size N such that arr[i] == func(i) for
    // each i in the half-open range [0, N).
```

The common idiom to do this initialization is to exploit a type that encodes indices as a variadic parameter pack (see Section 2.1."Variadic Templates" on page 873), along with the help of some **using** aliases (see Section 1.1."**using** Aliases" on page 133):

```
template <std::size_t...>
struct IndexSequence
{
    // This type serves as a compile-time container for the sequence of size_t
    // values that form its template parameter pack.
};

template <std::size_t N, std::size_t... Seq>
struct MakeSequenceHelper : public MakeSequenceHelper<N-1u, N-1u, Seq...>
{
    // This type is a metafunction to prepend a sequence of integers 0 to N-1
    // to the Seq... parameter pack by prepending N-1 to Seq... and
    // recursively instantiating itself.  The resulting integer sequence is
    // available in the type member inherited from the recursive instantiation.
    // The type member has type IndexSequence<FullSequence...>, where
    // FullSequence is the sequence of integers 0 .. N-1, Seq....
};

template <std::size_t ... Seq>
struct MakeSequenceHelper<0U, Seq...>
{
    // This partial specialization is the base case for the recursive
    // inheritance of MakeSequenceHelper.  The type member is an alias for
    // IndexSequence<Seq...>, where the Seq... parameter pack is typically
    // built up through recursive invocations of the MakeSequenceHelper
    // primary template.

    using type = IndexSequence<Seq...>;
};

template <std::size_t N>
using MakeIndexSequence = typename MakeSequenceHelper<N>::type;
    // alias for an IndexSequence<0 .. N-1> (or IndexSequence<> if N is 0)
```

The idiom shown above is, in fact, so common that it is available in the Standard Library as std::index_sequence in C++14.[18] Note that this solution is not lightweight, so the Standard Library types are generally implemented using compiler intrinsics that make them usable for significantly larger values.

To implement our array initializer, we will need another helper function that has, as a template argument, a variadic parameter pack of indices. To enable the deduction of template parameter pack std::size_t... I, our function has an unnamed parameter of type

---

[18]wakely13

IndexSequence<I...>. With this parameter pack in hand, we can then use a simple pack expansion expression and braced initialization to populate our std::array return value:

```
template <typename T, std::size_t... I, typename F>
constexpr std::array<T, sizeof...(I)> generateArrayImpl(const F& func,
                                                        IndexSequence<I...>)
    // Return the results of calling F(i) for each i in the pack deduced as
    // the template parameter pack I.
{
    return { func(I)... };
}
```

The return statement in generateArrayImpl calls func(I) for each I in the range from 0 to the length of the returned std::array. The resulting pack of values is used to list-initialize the return value of the function; see Section 2.1."Braced Init" on page 215.

Finally, our implementation of generateArray forwards func to generateArrayImpl, using MakeIndexSequence to generate an object of type IndexSequence<0,...,N-1>:

```
template <typename T, std::size_t N, typename F>
constexpr std::array<T, N> generateArray(const F& func)
{
    return generateArrayImpl<T>(func, MakeIndexSequence<N>());
}
```

With these tools in hand and a support function to offset the array index with the year, it is now simple to define an array that is initialized at compile time with an appropriate range of results from calls to startOfYear:

```
constexpr std::time_t startOfEpochYear(int epochYear)
{
    return startOfYear(k_EPOCH_YEAR + epochYear);
}

constexpr std::array<std::time_t, k_MAX_YEAR - k_EPOCH_YEAR> k_YEAR_STARTS =
    generateArray<std::time_t, k_MAX_YEAR - k_EPOCH_YEAR>(startOfEpochYear);

static_assert(k_YEAR_STARTS[0]  == startOfYear(1970), "");
static_assert(k_YEAR_STARTS[50] == startOfYear(2020), "");
```

With this table available for our use, the implementation of yearOfTimestamp becomes a simple application of std::upper_bound to perform a binary search on the sorted array of start-of-year timestamps[19]:

---

[19] Among other improvements to language and library support for **constexpr** programming, C++20 added **constexpr** to many of the standard algorithms in <algorithm>, including std::upper_bound, which would make switching this implementation to be **constexpr** also trivial. Implementing a **constexpr** version of most algorithms in C++14 is, however, relatively simple (and in C++11 is still possible), so, given a need, providing **constexpr** versions of functions like this with less support from the Standard Library is straightforward.

```
#include <algorithm>  // std::upper_bound
int yearOfTimestamp(std::time_t timestamp)
{
    std::size_t ndx = std::upper_bound(k_YEAR_STARTS.begin(),
                                       k_YEAR_STARTS.end(),
                                       timestamp)
                    - k_YEAR_STARTS.begin();
    return k_EPOCH_YEAR + ndx - 1;
}
```

When implementing a library of this sort, carefully making key decisions, such as whether to place the **constexpr** calculations in a header or to insulate them in an implementation file, is important; see *Potential Pitfalls — Overzealous use* on page 298. When building tables such as this, it's also worth considering more classical alternatives, such as simply generating code using an external script. Such external approaches can yield significant reductions in compile time and improved insulation; see *Potential Pitfalls — One time is cheaper than compile time or run time* on page 298.

Potential Pitfalls

Low compiler limits on compile-time evaluation

A major restriction on compile-time evaluation, beyond the linguistic restrictions already discussed, is the set of **implementation-defined** limitations specific to the compiler. In particular, the Standard allows implementations to limit the following:

- **Maximum number of recursively nested constexpr function invocations** — The expected value for this limit is 512, and in practice that is the default for most implementations. While 512 might seem like a large call depth, C++11 **constexpr** functions must use recursion instead of iteration, making it easy to exceed this limit when attempting to do involved computations at compile time.

- **Maximum number of subexpressions evaluated within a single constant expression** — The suggested value for this limit as well as the default value for most implementations is 1,048,576, but it is important to note that this value can depend in surprising ways on the way that the number of subexpressions is calculated by each individual compiler. Expressions that stay within the limit reliably with one compiler might be counted differently in the constant expression evaluator of a different compiler, resulting in nonportable code. Compilers generally refer to this limit as the number of **constexpr** steps and do not always support adjusting it.

Though these limits can usually be increased with compiler flags, a significant overhead is introduced in terms of managing build options that can hinder how easily usable a library intended to be portable will be. Small differences in terms of how each compiler might count these values also hinder the ability to write portable **constexpr** code.

Difficulty implementing **constexpr** functions

Many algorithms are simple to express iteratively and/or implement efficiently using dynamic data structures outside of what is possible within a **constexpr** function. Naive (and even non-naive) implementations often exceed the wide-ranging limits that various compilers put on **constexpr** evaluation. Consider this straightforward implementation of isPrime:

```
template <typename T>
constexpr bool isPrime(T input)
{
    if (input < 2) return false;              // too small
    if (input == 2) return true;              // is two
    if (input % 2 == 0) return false;         // is even
    for (T i = 3; i <= input / i; i += 2)     // odd numbers up to square root
    {
        if (input % i == 0) { return false; } // found divisor?
    }
    return true;                              // no divisors, input is prime
}
```

This implementation is iterative, fails to meet the requirements for being a C++11 **constexpr** function, and while meeting the relaxed requirements for being a C++14 **constexpr** function (see Section 2.2."**constexpr** Functions '14" on page 959), is likely to hit default compiler limits on execution steps when input approaches 2^{40} (approximately 10^{12}).

To make this **constexpr** isPrime function implementation valid for C++11, we might start by switching to a recursive implementation for the same algorithm:

```
template <typename T>
constexpr bool isPrimeHelper(T n, T i)
{
    return n % i                           // i is not a divisor.
        && (   i > n / i                   // i is not larger than sqrt(n).
            || isPrimeHelper(n, i + 2));   // tail recursion on next i
}

template <typename T>
constexpr bool isPrime(T input)
{
    return input < 2                     ? false  // too small
        : (input == 2 || input == 3) ? true   // 2 or 3
        : (input % 2 == 0)           ? false  // even
        : isPrimeHelper(input, 3);            // Call recursive helper.
}
```

The recursive implementation above works correctly, albeit slowly, up to an input value of around 2^{19} (approximately 10^6), hitting recursion limits on **constexpr** evaluation on most compilers. With significant effort, we might conceivably be able to push the upper limit slightly higher, e.g., by prechecking more factors than just 2. More importantly, recursively checking every other number below the square root of the input for divisibility is so slow compared to better algorithms that this approach is fundamentally inferior to a runtime solution.[20]

A final approach to working around the **constexpr** recursion limit is to implement a **divide and conquer** algorithm when searching the space of possible factors. While this approach has the same algorithmic performance as the directly recursive implementation and executes a comparable number of steps, the maximum recursion depth it needs is logarithmic in terms of the input value and will stay within the general compiler limits on recursion depth:

```cpp
template <typename T>
constexpr bool hasFactor(T n, T begin, T end)
    // Return true if the specified n has a factor in the
    // closed range [begin, end], and false otherwise.
{
    return (begin > end)      ? false              // empty range [begin, end]
         : (begin > n/begin) ? false              // begin > sqrt(n)
         : (begin == end)     ? (n % begin == 0)   // [begin, end] has one element.
         :     // Otherwise, split into two ranges and recurse.
               hasFactor(n, begin, begin + (end - begin) / 2) ||
               hasFactor(n, begin + 1 + (end - begin) / 2, end);
}

template <typename T>
constexpr bool isPrime(T input)
    // Return true if the specified input is prime.
{
    return input < 2                    ? false  // too small
         : (input == 2 || input == 3) ? true   // 2 or 3
         : (input % 2 == 0)             ? false  // even
         : !hasFactor(input, static_cast<T>(3), input - 1);
}
```

This C++11 implementation will generally work up to the same limits as the more readable iterative C++14 implementation in the example above.

Prematurely committing to constexpr

Declaring a function to be **constexpr** comes with significant collateral costs that, to some, might not be obvious. Marking an eligible function **constexpr** would seem like a sure way to get compile-time evaluation, when possible (i.e., when constant expressions are passed into a function as parameters), without any additional cost for functions that currently meet the requirements of a **constexpr** function, essentially giving us a "free" runtime performance

---

[20]The C++20 Standard adds std::is_constant_evaluated(), a tool to allow a function to branch to different implementations at compile time and run time, enabling the compile-time algorithm to be different from the runtime algorithm with the same API.

boost. The often-overlooked downside, however, is that this choice, once made, is not easily reversed. After a library is released and a **constexpr** function is evaluated as part of a **constant expression**, no clean way of turning back is available because clients now depend on this compile-time property.

Overzealous use

Overzealous application of **constexpr** can also have a significant impact on compilation time. Compile-time calculations can easily add seconds — or in extreme cases much more — to the compilation time of any translation unit that needs to evaluate them. When placed in a header file, these calculations need to be performed for all translation units that include that header file, vastly increasing total compilation time and hindering developer productivity.

Similarly, making public APIs that are **constexpr** usable without making it clear that they are suboptimal implementations can lead to both (1) excessive runtime overhead compared to a highly optimized non**constexpr** implementation (e.g., for isPrime in *Difficulty implementing* **constexpr** *functions* on page 296) that might already exist in an organization's libraries and (2) increased compile time wherever algorithmically complex **constexpr** functions are invoked.

Compilation limits on compile-time evaluation are typically per *constant expression* and can easily be compounded unreasonably within just a single translation unit through the evaluation of numerous constant expressions. For example, when using the generateArray function in *Use Cases — Precomputing tables of data at compile time* on page 291, compile-time limits apply to each individual array element's computation, allowing total compilation to grow linearly with the number of values requested.

One time is cheaper than compile time or run time

Overall, the ability to use a **constexpr** function to do calculations before run time fills in a spectrum of possibilities for who pays for certain calculations and when they pay for them, both in terms of computing time and maintenance costs.

Consider a possible set of five evolutionary steps for a computationally expensive function that produces output values for a moderate number of unique input values. Examples include returning the timestamp for the start of a calendar year or returning the nth prime number up to some maximum n.

1. An initial version directly computes the output value each time it is needed. While correct and written entirely in maintainable C++, this version has the highest runtime overhead. Heavy use will quickly lead the developer to explore optimizations.

2. Where precomputing values might seem beneficial, a subsequent version initializes an array once at run time to avoid the extra computations. Aggregate runtime performance can be greatly improved but at the cost of slightly more code as well as a

possibly noteworthy amount of runtime startup overhead. This hit at startup or on first use of the library can quickly become the next performance bottleneck that needs tackling. Initialization at startup can become increasingly problematic when linking large applications with a multitude of libraries, each of which might have moderate initialization times.

3. At this point **constexpr** comes into play as a tool to develop an option that avoids as much runtime overhead as possible. An initial such implementation puts the initialization of a **constexpr** array of values into the corresponding **inline** implementation in a library header. While this option minimizes the runtime overhead, the compile-time overhead now becomes significantly larger for every translation unit that depends on this library.

4. When faced with crippling compile times, the likely next step is to **insulate** the compile-time-generated table in an implementation file and to provide runtime access to it through accessor functions. While this refactoring removes the compilation overhead from clients who consume a binary distribution of the library, anyone who needs to build the library is still paying this cost each time they do a clean build. In modern environments, with widely disparate operating systems and build toolchains, source distributions have become much more common, and this overhead is imposed on a wide range of clients for a popular library.

5. Finally, the data table generation is moved into a separate program, often written in Python or some other non-C++ language. The output of this outboard program is then embedded as raw data, e.g., a sequence of numbers initializing an array, in a C++ implementation file. This solution eliminates the compile-time overhead for the C++ program; the cost of computing the table is paid only once by the developer. On the one hand, this solution adds to the maintenance costs for the initial developer, since a separate toolchain is often needed. On the other hand, the code becomes simpler, since the programmer is free to choose the best language for the job and is free from the constraints of **constexpr** in C++.

Thus, as attractive as being able to precompute values directly in compile-time C++ might seem, complex situations often dictate against that choice. Note that a programmer with this knowledge might skip all of the intermediate steps and jump straight to the last one. For example, a list of prime numbers is readily available on the Internet without needing even to write a script; a programmer need only cut and paste it once, knowing that it will *never* change.

Annoyances

Penalizing run time to enable compile time

When adopting **constexpr** functions, programmers commonly forget that these functions are also called at run time, often more frequently than at compile time. Restrictions on the operations that are supported in a **constexpr** function definition, especially prior to the looser restrictions of C++14, will often lead to correct results that are less than optimally computed when executed at run time. A good example would be a **constexpr** implementation of the C function strcmp. Writing a recursive **constexpr** function to walk through two strings and return a result for the first characters that differ is relatively easy. However, most common implementations of this function are highly optimized, often taking advantage of inline assembly using architecture-specific vector instructions to handle multiple characters per CPU clock cycle. All of that fine-tuning is given up if we rewrite the function to be **constexpr** compatible. Worse yet, the recursive nature of such functions prior to C++14 leads to a much greater risk of exceeding the limits of the stack, leading to program corruption and security risks when comparing long strings.

One possible workaround for these restrictions is to create different versions of the same function: a **constexpr** version usable at compile time and a non**constexpr** version optimized for run time. Since the language does not support overloading on **constexpr**, the end result is intrusive, requiring the different implementations to have different names. This complication can be mitigated by having a coding convention, such as placing all **constexpr** overloads in a namespace, say, cexpr, or giving all such functions the _c suffix. If the regular version of the function is also **constexpr**, the marked overload can simply forward all arguments to the regular function to ease maintenance, but overhead and complexity still come from having users manage multiple versions of the same function. It is not clear in all cases that the extra complexity covers its cost.

The relaxed restrictions in C++14 for implementing the bodies of **constexpr** functions is a welcome relief when optimizing for compile time and run time simultaneously; see Section 2.2."**constexpr** Functions '14" on page 959. Even then, though, many runtime performance improvements (e.g., dynamic memory allocation, stateful caching, hardware intrinsics) are still not available to functions that need to execute at both run time and compile time. Note that a language-based solution that avoids the need to create separately named **constexpr** and non**constexpr** functions is introduced in C++20 with the std::is_constant_evaluated intrinsic library function.

constexpr member functions are implicitly const-qualified (C++11 only)

A design flaw in C++11 and corrected in C++14 is that any member function declared **constexpr** is, where applicable, implicitly **const**-qualified, leading to unexpected behavior for member functions intended for use during constant expression evaluation; see Section 2.2. "**constexpr** Functions '14" on page 959. This surprising restriction impacts code portability between language standards and makes the naive approach of just marking all member functions **constexpr** into something that unwittingly breaks what would otherwise be correct code.

See Also

- "**constexpr** Variables" (§2.1, p. 302) covers the companion use of the **constexpr** keyword applied to variables.

- "Variadic Templates" (§2.1, p. 873) describes how variadic templates are often needed for complex metaprogramming used in some compile-time computations.

- "**constexpr** Functions '14" (§2.2, p. 959) enumerates the significantly richer syntax permitted for implementing **constexpr** function bodies in C++14.

Further Reading

- Scott Meyers advocates for aggressive use of **constexpr** in **meyers15b**, "Item 15: Use constexpr whenever possible," pp. 97–103.

Compile-Time Accessible Variables

A variable or **variable template** of **literal type** can be declared to be **constexpr**, ensuring it is initialized and can be used at compile time.

Description

Variables of *all* built-in types and certain user-defined types, collectively known as literal types, can be declared **constexpr**, allowing them to be initialized at compile-time and subsequently used in **constant expressions**:

```cpp
          int i0 = 5;           // i0 is not a compile-time constant.
    const int i1 = 5;           // i1 is a compile-time constant.
constexpr int i2 = 5;           // i2 "  "     "       "      "

          double d0 = 5.0;      // d0 is not a compile-time constant.
    const double d1 = 5.0;      // d1 "  "  "  "      "       "      "
constexpr double d2 = 5.0;      // d2 is a compile-time constant.

          const char* s1 = "help";  // s1 is not a compile-time constant.
constexpr const char* s2 = "help";  // s2 is a compile-time constant.
```

Although **const** variables of integral types having preceding initialization with a **constant** expression can be used within constant expressions (e.g., as the first argument to **static_assert**, as the size of an array, or as a non-type template parameter), such is not the case for any other type:

```cpp
static_assert(i0 == 5, "");     // Error, i0 is not a compile-time constant.
static_assert(i1 == 5, "");     // OK, const is "magical" for integers (only).
static_assert(i2 == 5, "");     // OK

static_assert(d1 == 5, "");     // Error, d1 is not a compile-time constant.
static_assert(d2 == 5, "");     // OK

static_assert(s1[1] == 'e', ""); // Error, s1 is not a compile-time constant.
static_assert(s2[1] == 'e', ""); // OK

int a1[s1[1]];                  // Error, s1 is not a compile-time constant.
int a2[s2[1]];                  // OK, a C-style array of 101 (e) integers.

std::array<int, s1[1]> sa1;     // Error, s1 is not a compile-time constant.
std::array<int, s2[1]> sa2;     // OK, an std::array of 101 (e) integers.
```

Prior to C++11, the types of variables usable in a **constant expression** were quite limited:

```
const int b;              // Error, const scalar variable must be initialized.
extern const int c;       // OK, declaration
const int d = c;          // OK, not constant initialized (c initializer not seen)

int ca1[c];               // Error, initializer of c is not visible.
int da1[d];               // Error, initializer of d is not a compile-time constant.

const int c = 7;
int ca2[c];               // OK, initializer is visible
int da2[d];               // Error, initializer of d is not a compile-time constant.

const int e = 17;         // OK
int ea[e];                // OK
```

For an **integral constant** to be usable at compile time (i.e., as part of constant expression), three requirements must be satisfied.

1. The variable must be marked **const**.

2. The initializer for a variable must have been seen by the time it is used, and it must be a **constant expression**; this information is needed for a compiler to be able to make use of the variable in other **constant expressions**.

3. The variable must be of *integral* type, e.g., **bool**, **char**, **short**, **int**, **long**, **long long**, as well as the **unsigned** variations on these and any additional **char** types; see also Section 1.1."**long long**" on page 89.

This restriction to integral types provides support for those values where compile-time constants are most frequently needed while limiting the complexity of what compilers were required to support at compile time.

Use of **constexpr** when declaring a variable or **variable template** (see Section 1.2."Variable Templates" on page 157) enables a much richer category of types to participate in **constant expressions**. This generalization, however, was not made for mere **const** variables because they are not *required* to be initialized by compile-time constants:

```
int f() { return 0; }  // f() is not a compile-time constant expression.
```

```
                int x0 = f();  // OK
          const int x1 = f();  // OK, but x1 is not a compile-time constant.
constexpr       int x2 = f();  // Error, f() is not a constant expression.
constexpr const int x3 = f();  // Error, f()  "   "   "      "         "
```

As the example code above demonstrates, variables marked **constexpr** *must* satisfy the same requirements needed for integral constants to be usable in **constant expressions**. Unlike other integral constants, their initializers *must* be constant expressions, or else the program is **ill formed**.

For a variable of other than **const** integral type to be usable in a **constant expression**, certain criteria must hold:

1. The variable must be annotated with **constexpr**, which implicitly also declares the variable to be **const**[1]:

```
struct S  // simple (aggregate) literal type
{
    int i;  // built-in integer data member
};

void test1()
{
    constexpr S s{1};  // OK, literal type constant expression initialized
    s = S();           // Error, constexpr implies const.
    static_assert(s.i == 1, "");  // OK, subobjects of constexpr objects are
    constexpr int j = s.i;        //      usable in constant expressions.
    constexpr const int k = 1;    // OK, redundant keyword const
    const constexpr int l = 2;    // OK, keywords in either order
}
```

In the example above, we have, for expedience of exposition, used braced initialization to initialize the aggregate; see Section 2.1."Braced Init" on page 215. Note that non**mutable** subobjects of **constexpr** objects are also effectively **constexpr** and can be used freely in **constant expressions** even though they themselves are not explicitly declared **constexpr**.

2. All **constexpr** variables must be initialized with a **constant expression** when they are defined. Hence, every **constexpr** variable must have an initializer, and that initializer must be a valid **constant expression**; see Section 2.1."**constexpr** Functions" on page 257:

```
            int g() { return 17; }  // a nonconstexpr function
constexpr int h() { return 34; }  // a constexpr function

constexpr int v1;        // Error, v1 is not initialized.
constexpr int v2 = 17;   // OK
constexpr int v3 = g();  // Error, g() is not constexpr.
constexpr int v4 = h();  // OK

void test2(int c)
{
    constexpr int v5 = c;          // Error, c is not a compile-time constant.
    constexpr int v6 = sizeof(c);  // OK, c is not evaluated.
}
```

---

[1]C++20 added the **constinit** keyword to identify a variable that is initialized at compile time (with a constant expression) but may subsequently be modified at run time.

3. Any variable declared **constexpr** must be of literal type; all literal types are, among other things, **trivially destructible**:

```
struct Lt  // literal type
{
    constexpr Lt() { }  // constexpr constructor
    ~Lt() = default;    // default trivial destructor
};

constexpr Lt lt;  // OK, Lt is a literal type.

struct Nlt  // nonliteral type
{
    Nlt() { }  // cannot initialize at compile time
    ~Nlt() { }  // cannot skip non-trivial destruction
};

constexpr Nlt nlt;  // Error, Nlt is not a literal type.
```

Since all literal types are trivially destructible, the compiler does not need to emit any special code to manage the end of the lifetime of a **constexpr** variable, which can essentially live "forever" — i.e., until the program exits.[2]

4. Unlike integral constants, non**static** data members cannot be **constexpr**. Only variables at global or **namespace** scope, automatic variables, or **static** data members of a **class** or **struct** may be declared **constexpr**. Consequently, any given **constexpr** variable is a top-level object, never a subobject of another, possibly non**constexpr**, object:

```
            constexpr int i = 17;    // OK, file scope
namespace ns { constexpr int j = 34; }  // OK, namespace scope

struct C
{
    static constexpr int k = 51;  // OK, static data member
           constexpr int l = 68;  // Error, constexpr nonstatic data member
};

void g()
{
    static constexpr int m = 85;  // OK
           constexpr int n = 92;  // OK
}
```

Recall, however, that **nonstatic data members** of **constexpr** objects are implicitly **constexpr** and therefore can be used directly in any constant expressions:

---

[2]In C++20, literal types can have non-trivial destructors, and the destructors for **constexpr** variables will be invoked under the same conditions that a destructor would be invoked for a non**constexpr** global or **static** variable.

```
constexpr struct D { int i; } x{1};  // brace-initialized aggregate x
constexpr int k = x.i;  // Subobjects of constexpr objects are constexpr.
```

Initializer undefined behavior

It is important to note the significance of one of the differences between a **constexpr** integral variable and a **const** integral variable. Because the initializer of a **constexpr** variable is *required* to be a **constant expression**, it is not subject to the possibility of undefined behavior, e.g., integer overflow or out-of-bounds array access, at run time and will instead result in a compile-time error:

```
        const int iA = 1 << 15;  // 2^15 = 32,768 fits in 2 bytes.
        const int jA = iA * iA;  // OK

        const int iB = 1 << 16;  // 2^16 = 65,536 doesn't fit in 2 bytes.
        const int jB = iB * iB;  // Bug, overflow (might warn)

  constexpr const int iC = 1 << 16;
  constexpr const int jC = iC * iC;  // Error, overflow in constant expression

  constexpr       int iD = 1 << 16;  // Example D is the same as C, above.
  constexpr       int jD = iD * iD;  // Error, overflow in constant expression
```

The code example above shows that an integer constant-expression overflow, absent **constexpr**, is not required by the C++ Standard to be treated as ill formed. When signed integer overflow happens in an initializer of a **constexpr** variable, however, the compiler is required to report it as an error (not just a warning).

A strong association exists between **constexpr** variables and functions; see Section 2.1. "**constexpr** Functions" on page 257. Using a **constexpr** variable rather than just a **const** one forces the compiler to detect overflow — and more generally, any undefined behavior — within the body of a **constexpr** function and report that overflow as an error in a way that the compiler would not otherwise be required to do.

For example, suppose we have two similar functions, squareA and squareB, defined for the built-in type **int** that each return the integral product of multiplying the single argument with itself:

```
        int squareA(int i) { return i * i; }  // nonconstexpr function
  constexpr int squareB(int i) { return i * i; }  // constexpr function
```

Declaring a variable to be just **const** — and not **constexpr** — does nothing to force the compiler to check the evaluation of either function for overflow:

```
        int xA0 = squareA(1 << 15);  // OK
  const int xA1 = squareA(1 << 15);  // OK
  constexpr   int xA2 = squareA(1 << 15);  // Error, squareA, not constexpr
```

```
            int yB0 = squareB(1 << 15);   // OK
      const int yB1 = squareB(1 << 15);   // OK
  constexpr int yB2 = squareB(1 << 15);   // OK

            int zC0 = squareB(1 << 16);   // Bug, zC0 is likely 0.
      const int zC1 = squareB(1 << 16);   // Bug, zC1  "      "   "
  constexpr int zC2 = squareB(1 << 16);   // Error, int overflow detected!
```

The compiler must evaluate the `squareB` function in the example above at compile time when it is used to initialize a **constexpr** variable and, consequently, report any UB that would arise during such evaluation as an error. Such is not the case for initialization of non**constexpr** variables even if they are **const**. In such cases, the initialization must happen **as if** it were evaluated at run time and the compiler might choose to do so. Therefore, when initializing a non**constexpr** variable of an integral type, the presence of UB will determine whether the variable will be a compile-time constant but will not lead to a compilation error.

Internal linkage

When a variable at file or namespace scope is either **const** or **constexpr** and nothing explicitly gives it external linkage (e.g., by being marked **extern**), it will have **internal linkage**, meaning that each translation unit will have its own copy of the variable.[3]

Oftentimes, only the values of such variables are relevant: Their initializers are seen, they are used at compile time, and there is no effect if different translation units use different objects having the same name and a different value. After compile-time evaluation is completed, the variables themselves will no longer be needed, and no actual address will be allocated for them at run time. Only in cases where the address of the variable is used will the effects of internal linkage be observable (and can lead to **ODR** violations).

Notably, **static** member variables have external linkage except when inside an unnamed namespace. Therefore, if they are used in a way that requires they have an address allocated at run time, then a definition needs to be provided for them outside of their class irrespective of whether they are **constexpr**; see *Annoyances — **static** member variables require external definitions* on page 314.

Use Cases

Alternative to enumerated compile-time integral constants

It is not uncommon to want to express specific integral constants at compile time — e.g., for precomputed operands to be used in algorithms, mathematical constants, configuration variables, or any number of other reasons. A naive, brute-force approach might be to hard-code the constants where they are used:

---

[3]In C++17, all **constexpr** variables are instead automatically **inline** as well, guaranteeing that there is only one instance in a program.

```
int hoursToSeconds0(int hours)
    // Return the number of seconds in the specified hours.  The behavior is
    // undefined unless the result can be represented as an int.
{
    return hours * 3600;
}
```

This use of *magic constants* has, however, long been known[4] to make finding uses of the constants and the relationships between related ones needlessly difficult. For integral values only, we could always represent such compile-time constants symbolically by using a classic **enum** type, in deliberate preference to the modern, type-safe enumerator; see Section 2.1. "**enum class**" on page 332:

```
struct TimeRatios1  // explicit scope for single classic anonymous enum type
{
    enum  // anonymous enumeration comprising related symbolic constants
    {
        k_SECONDS_PER_MINUTE = 60,      // Underlying type (UT) might be int.
        k_MINUTES_PER_HOUR   = 60,
        k_SECONDS_PER_HOUR   = 60*60  // These enumerators have the same UT.
    };
};

int hoursToSeconds1(int hours)
    // ...
{
    return hours * TimeRatios1::k_SECONDS_PER_HOUR;
}
```

This traditional solution, while often effective, gives little control over the underlying integral type of the enumerator used to represent the symbolic compile-time constant, leaving it at the mercy of the totality of values used to initialize the members of the enumeration. Such inflexibility might lead to compiler warnings and nonintuitive behavior resulting from **enum**-specific integral promotion rules, especially when the **underlying type (UT)** used to represent the time ratios differs from the integral types with which they are ultimately used; see Section 2.1."Underlying Type '11" on page 829.

In this particular example, extending the **enum** to cover ratios up to a week and conversions down to microseconds would manifestly change its UT (because there are far more than 2^{32} microseconds in a week), altering how all of the enumerators behave when used in expressions with, say, values of type **int**:

```
struct TimeRatios2  // explicit scope for single classic anonymous enum type
{
    enum  // Anonymous enumeration --- UT is governed by all of the enumerators.
    {
```

---

[4]**kernighan99**, section 1.5, pp. 19–22

```
            k_SECONDS_PER_MINUTE = 60,     // UT might be long or long long.
            k_MINUTES_PER_HOUR   = 60,
            k_SECONDS_PER_HOUR   = 60*60,
            // ...
            k_USEC_PER_WEEK = 1000L*1000*60*60*24*7  // same UT as all of the above
        };
    };
```

The original *values* will remain unchanged after the enumeration is extended, but the burden of all of the compiler warnings resulting from the change in UT and rippling throughout a large codebase could be expensive to repair.

We would like the original values to remain unchanged (e.g., remain as **int** if that's what they were), and we want only those values that do *not* fit in an **int** to morph into a larger integral type. We might achieve this effect by placing each enumerator in its own separate anonymous enumeration:

```
struct TimeRatios3  // explicit scope for multiple classic anonymous enum types
{
    enum { k_SECONDS_PER_MINUTE = 60              }; // UT: int (likely)
    enum { k_MINUTES_PER_HOUR   = 60              }; // "   "     "
    enum { k_SECONDS_PER_HOUR   = 60*60           }; // "   "     "
    // ...
    enum { k_USEC_PER_SEC  = 1000*1000            }; // UT: int (likely)
    enum { k_USEC_PER_MIN  = 1000*1000*60         }; // "   "     "
    enum { k_USEC_PER_HOUR = 1000U*1000*60*60     }; // UT: unsigned int
    enum { k_USEC_PER_DAY  = 1000L*1000*60*60*24  }; // UT: long or long long
    enum { k_USEC_PER_WEEK = 1000L*1000*60*60*24*7 }; // UT: long or long long
};
```

In this case, the original values as well as their respective UTs will remain unchanged, and each new enumerated value will independently take on its own independent UT, which is either implementation defined or else dictated by the number of bits required to represent the value.

A modern alternative to having separate anonymous **enum**s for each distinct value (or class of values) is to instead encode each ratio as an explicitly typed **constexpr** variable:

```
struct TimeRatios4
{
    static constexpr int k_SECONDS_PER_MINUTE     = 60;
    static constexpr int k_MINUTES_PER_HOUR       = 60;
    static constexpr int k_SECONDS_PER_HOUR       = k_MINUTES_PER_HOUR *
                                                    k_SECONDS_PER_MINUTE;
    // ...
    static constexpr long long k_NANOS_PER_SECOND = 1000*1000*1000;
    static constexpr long long k_NANOS_PER_HOUR   = k_NANOS_PER_SECOND *
                                                    k_SECONDS_PER_HOUR;
};
```

```
int hoursToSeconds(int hours)
    // ...
{
    return hours * TimeRatios4::k_SECONDS_PER_HOUR;
}


long long hoursToNanos(int hours)
    // Return the number of nanoseconds in the specified hours.  The behavior
    // is undefined unless the result can be represented as a long.
{
    return hours * TimeRatios4::k_NANOS_PER_HOUR;
}
```

In the example above, we've rendered the **constexpr** variables as **static** members of a **struct** rather than placing them at namespace scope primarily to show that, from a user perspective, the two are syntactically indistinguishable, the substantive difference here being that a client would be prevented from unilaterally adding logical content to the "namespace" of a TimeRatio **struct**.[5]

Nonintegral symbolic numeric constants

Not all symbolic numeric constants that are needed at compile time are necessarily integral. Consider, for example, the mathematical constants pi and e, which are typically represented using a floating-point type, such as **double** or **long double**.

The classical solution to avoid encoding this type of constant value as a *magic number* is to instead use a macro, such as is done in the math.h header on most operating systems:

```
#define M_E   2.71828182845904523536 /* e */
#define M_PI  3.14159265358979323846 /* pi */

double circumferenceOfCircle(double radius)
{
    return 2 * M_PI * radius;
}
```

While this approach can be effective, it comes with all the well-known downsides of using the C preprocessor, such as potential name collisions. Furthermore, since these constants are not a part of the C or C++ Standard, some platforms do not provide them at all or require additional preprocessor definitions prior to including math.h to provide them.

A safer and far less error-prone approach is to instead use a **constexpr** variable for this form of nonintegral constant. Note that, while macros for mathematical constants in math.h are defined with sufficiently large precision to be able to initialize variables of possibly

---

[5]lakos20, section 2.4.9, pp. 312–321, specifically Figure 2-23

higher-precision floating-point types, here we need only enough digits to uniquely identify the appropriate **double** constant:

```
struct NumericConstants
{
    static constexpr double k_E  = 2.718'281'828'459'045;  /* e */
    static constexpr double k_PI = 3.141'592'653'589'793;  /* pi */
};

double circumferenceOfCircle(double radius)
{
    return 2 * NumericConstants::k_PI * radius;
}
```

In the example above, we have made valuable use of a safe C++14 feature to help identify the needed precision of the numeric literal; see Section 1.2."Digit Separators" on page 152. Beyond the potential name collisions and global name pollution, preferring a **constexpr** variable over a C preprocessor macro has the added benefit of making explicit the C++ type of constant being defined. Note that supplying digits beyond what are significant will be silently ignored.

Storing **constexpr** data structures

Precomputing values at compile time for subsequent use at run time is one impactful use of **constexpr** *functions*, but see *Potential Pitfalls — constexpr function pitfalls* on page 314. Storing the values in explicitly **constexpr** variables ensures that the values are (1) guaranteed to be computed at compile time and not, for example, at startup as the result of a dangerous runtime initialization of a file- or namespace-scoped variable (see Section 1.1. "Function **static** '11" on page 68) and (2) usable as part of the evaluation of any constant expression; see Section 2.1."**constexpr** Functions" on page 257.

Rather than attempting to circumvent the draconian limitations of the C++11 version of **constexpr** functions, we will make use of the relaxed restrictions of C++14. We will define a class template that initializes an array member with the results of a **constexpr** functor applied to each array index[6]:

```
#include <cstddef> // std::size_t

template <typename T, std::size_t N>
struct ConstexprArray
{
```

---

[6]Note that, in C++17, most of the manipulators of std::array have been changed to be **constexpr** and, when combined with the relaxation of the rules for **constexpr** evaluation in C++14 (see Section 2.2. "**constexpr** Functions '14" on page 959), this compile-time-friendly container provides a simple way to define functions that populate tables of values.

```
private:
    T d_data[N];  // data initialized at construction

public:
    template <typename F>
    constexpr ConstexprArray(const F &func)
    : d_data{}
    {
        for (int i = 0; i < N; ++i)
        {
            d_data[i] = func(i);
        }
    }

    constexpr const T& operator[](std::size_t ndx) const
    {
        return d_data[ndx];
    }
};
```

The numerous alternative approaches to writing such data structures vary in their complexity, trade-offs, and understandability. In this case, we default-initialize our elements before populating them but do not need to rely on any other significant new language infrastructure. Other approaches could be taken; see Section 2.1."**constexpr** Functions" on page 257.

Given this utility class template, we can then precompute at compile time any function that we can express as a **constexpr** function, such as a simple table of the first N squares:

```
constexpr int square(int x) { return x * x; }

constexpr ConstexprArray<int, 500> squares(square);

static_assert(squares[1]   == 1,     "");
static_assert(squares[289] == 83521,"");
```

Note that, as with many applications of **constexpr** functions, attempting to initialize a large array of **constexpr** variables will quickly bump up against a number of possible compiler-imposed limits.

Diagnosing undefined behavior at compile time

Avoiding overflow during intermediate calculations is an important consideration, especially from a security perspective, and yet is a generally difficult-to-solve problem. Forcing computations to occur at compile time brings the full power of the compiler to bear in addressing such undefined behavior.

As an academically interesting example of this practical security problem, suppose we want to write a compile-time function in C++ to compute the **Collatz length** of an arbitrary positive integer and generate a compilation error if any intermediate calculation would result in signed integer overflow.

First let's take a step back to understand what we mean by Collatz length. Suppose we have a function, cf, that takes a positive **int**, n, and for even n returns n/2 and for odd n returns 3n+1:

```cpp
int cf(int n) { return n % 2 ? 3 * n + 1 : n / 2; }  // Collatz function
```

Given a positive integer, n, the **Collatz sequence**, cs(n), is defined as the sequence of integers generated by repeated application of the **Collatz function** — e.g., cs(1) = { 4, 2, 1, 4, 2, 1, 4, ... };, cs(3) = { 10, 5, 16, 8, 4, 2, 1, 4, ... }, and so on. A classic but as yet unproven conjecture in mathematics states that, for every positive integer, n, the Collatz sequence for n will eventually reach 1. The Collatz length of the positive integer n is the number of iterations of the Collatz function needed to reach 1, starting from n. Note that the Collatz length for n = 1 is 0.

This example showcases the need for a **constexpr** variable in that its initializer is required to be a constant expression, ensuring that the evaluation of a **constexpr** function occurs at compile time. Again, to avoid distractions related to implementing more complex functionality within the limitations of C++11 **constexpr** functions, we will make use of the relaxed restrictions of C++14; see Section 2.1."**constexpr** Functions" on page 257:

```cpp
constexpr int collatzLength(long long number)
    // Return the length of the Collatz sequence of the specified number. The
    // behavior is undefined unless each intermediate sequence member can be
    // expressed as a long long and number > 0.
{
    int length = 0;        // collatzLength(1) is 0.

    while (number > 1)     // The current value of number is not 1.
    {
        ++length;          // Keep track of the length of the sequence so far.

        if (number % 2)    // if the current number is odd
        {
            number = 3 * number + 1;    // advance from odd sequence value
        }
        else
        {
            number /= 2;                // advance from even sequence value
        }
    }

    return length;
}
```

```
const    int c1 = collatzLength(942488749153153);  // OK, 1862
constexpr int x1 = collatzLength(942488749153153);  // OK, 1862

const int c2 = collatzLength(104899295810901231);
    // Bug, program has undefined behavior.

constexpr int x2 = collatzLength(104899295810901231);
    // Error, overflow in constant-expression evaluation
```

In the example above, the variables c1 and x1 can be initialized correctly at compile time, but c2 and x2 cannot. The non**constexpr** nature of c2 allows the overflow to occur and exhibit undefined behavior — integer overflow — at run time. On the other hand, the variable x2, due to its being declared **constexpr**, forces the computation to occur at compile time, thereby discovering the overflow, which generates the desired error at compile time.

Potential Pitfalls

constexpr function pitfalls

Many of the uses of **constexpr** variables involve a corresponding use of **constexpr** functions (see Section 2.1."**constexpr** Functions" on page 257). The pitfalls related to **constexpr** functions are similarly applicable to the variables in which their results might be stored. In some circumstances, it might even be advantageous to forgo use of the **constexpr** function feature altogether, do the precomputation externally to the program, and embed the calculated results — along with a comment containing source text of the (e.g., Perl or Python) script that performed the calculation — into the C++ program source itself.

Annoyances

static member variables require external definitions

In most situations, there is little behavioral difference between a variable at file or namespace scope and a **static** member variable; primarily they differ only in name lookup and access-control restrictions. When they are **constexpr**, however, they behave differently when they need to exist at run time. A file or namespace scope variable will have internal linkage, allowing free use of its address with the understanding that that address will be different in different translation units:

```
// common.h:

constexpr int c = 17;
const int *f1();
const int *f2();
```

```
// file1.cpp:
#include <common.h>

const int *f1() { return &c; }

// file2.cpp:
#include <common.h>

const int *f2() { return &c; }

// main.cpp:
#include <common.h>
#include <cassert>  // standard C assert macro

int main()
{
    assert( f1() != f2() );    // different addresses in memory per TU
    assert( *f1() == *f2() );  // same value
    return 0;
}
```

For **static** data members, however, things become more difficult. While the **declaration** in the class **definition** needs to have an initializer, that is not itself a **definition** and will not result in static storage being allocated at run time for the object, ending in a link-time error when we try to build an application that tries to reference the **static** data member[7]:

```
struct S {
    static constexpr int d_i = 17;
};
void useByReference(const int& i) { /*...*/ }

int main()
{
    const int local = S::d_i;  // OK, value is only used at compile time.
    useByReference(S::d_i);    // Link-Time Error, S::d_i not defined
    return 0;
}
```

This link-time error would be averted by adding a **definition** of S::d_i. Note that the initializer needs to be omitted, as it has already been specified in the definition of S:

```
constexpr int S::d_i;  // Define constexpr data member.
```

---

[7]The C++17 change to make **constexpr** variables **inline** also applies to **static** member variables, removing the need to provide external definitions when they are used.

No static constexpr member variables defined in their own class

When implementing a class using the singleton pattern, it might be desirable to have the single object of that type be a **constexpr private static** member of the class itself, with guaranteed compile-time, data-race-free initialization and no direct accessibility outside the class. This approach does not work as easily as planned because **constexpr static** data members must have a complete type, and the class being defined is not complete until its closing brace:

```
class S
{
private:
    static const    S constVal;      // OK, initialized outside class below
    static constexpr S constexprVal; // Error, constexpr must be initialized.
    static constexpr S constInit{};  // Error, S is not complete.
};


const S S::constVal{};  // OK, initialize static const member.
```

The "obvious" workaround of applying a more traditional singleton pattern, where the singleton object is a static local variable at function scope, also fails (see Section 1.1. "Function **static** '11" on page 68) because **constexpr** functions are not allowed to have static variables (see Section 2.1."**constexpr** Functions" on page 257):

```
constexpr const S& singleton()
{
    static constexpr S object{};  // Error, even in C++14, static is not allowed.
    return object;
}
```

The only solution available for **constexpr** objects of static storage duration is to put them outside of their type, either at global scope, at **namespace** scope, or nested within a befriended helper class[8]:

```
class S
{
    friend struct T;
    S() = default;  // private
    // ...
};


struct T
{
    static constexpr S constInit{};
};
```

---

[8]C++20 provides an alternate partial solution with the **constinit** keyword, allowing for compile-time initialization of static data members, but that still does not make such objects usable in a constant expression.

See Also

- "**constexpr** Functions" (§2.1, p. 257) describes how this feature can be used to initialize a **constexpr** variable.

- "User-Defined Literals" (§2.1, p. 835) explains a convenient way of initializing a **constexpr** variable of a UDT with a compile-time value.

Default **class/union** Member Initializers

Non**static** class data members might specify a default initializer, which is used for constructors that don't initialize the member explicitly.

Description

The traditional means for initializing non**static** data members and base class objects within a class is a constructor's **member initializer list**:

```
struct B
{
    int d_i;

    B(int i) : d_i(i) { }      // Initialize d_i with i.
};

struct D : B
{
    char d_c;

    D() : B(2), d_c('3') { }  // Initialize base B with 2 and d_c with '3'.
};
```

Starting with C++11, non**static** data members — except for bit fields — can also be initialized using a **default member initializer**, by using **copy initialization**, **copy list initialization**, or **direct list initialization**; see Section 2.1."Braced Init" on page 215:

```
struct S0
{
    int   d_i = 10;      // OK, uses copy initialization
    char  d_c = {'a'};   // OK, uses copy list initialization
    float d_f{2.f};      // OK, uses direct list initialization
};
```

Note that although braced initialization is supported, **direct initialization** with a parenthesized list is not:

```
struct S1
{
    char d_c('a');  // Error, invalid syntax
};
```

For any member m that has a default member initializer, constructors that don't initialize m in their **member initializer list** will implicitly initialize m by using the default member initializer value:

```
struct S2
{
    int d_i = 1;
    int d_j = 1;

    S2() { }                                  // Initialize d_i with 1, d_j with 1.
    S2(int) : d_i(2) { }                      // Initialize d_i with 2, d_j with 1.
    S2(int, int) : d_i(2), d_j(3) { }         // Initialize d_i with 2, d_j with 3.
};
```

Note that initialization of all member variables including those using the default member initializers happen in the order in which they are declared in the class definition. Accordingly, previously initialized non**static** data members can be used in subsequent initializer expressions:

```
struct S4 {
    const char* d_s{"hello"};
    int         d_i{2};
    char        d_c{d_s[1]};  // OK, d_c initialized to d_s's second character

    S4()                      { }
    S4(const char* s) : d_s(s) { }
};

S4 s4d;              // OK, s4d.d_c initialized to 'e'
S4 s4v("goodbye");   // OK, s4v.d_c initialized to 'o'
```

The default member initializer, just like member function bodies and member initialization lists, executes in a **complete-class context**. Since the initializer sees its enclosing class as a **complete type**, it can therefore reference the size of the enclosing type and invoke member functions that have not yet been seen:

```
struct S5
{
    int d_a[4];
    int d_i = sizeof(S5) + seenBelow();  // OK
    int seenBelow();
};
```

Name lookup in default member initializers will find members of the enclosing class and its bases before looking in namespace scope:

```
char i = 4;

struct S6
{
    int j = sizeof(i);  // refers to S6::i, not ::i
    int i = 5;
};

S6 s6;  // OK, s6.j initialized to 4.
```

The **this** pointer can also be safely used as part of a default member initializer. As with any other uses of **this** inside a constructor, care must be exercised because the object referred to by **this** will be in a partially constructed state:

```
int getSomeRuntimeValue();

struct S7
{
    S7* d_selfPtr = this;                  // OK
    int d_bad = this->d_later;             // Bug, d_later not yet initialized
    int d_later = getInitialDLaterValue(); // OK
    static int getInitialDLaterValue();
};
```

Unlike variables at function or global scope and unlike static data members, a default member initializer for a member that is an array of unknown bound will not determine the array bound:

```
struct S8
{
    static int d_s[];        // OK, d_s has unknown bounds.
    int d_a[]  = {1, 2, 3};  // Error, d_a is an array of unknown bound.
    int d_b[3] = {1, 2, 3};  // OK, bound explicitly specified
};

int a[]       = {1, 2, 3};  // OK, the length of a is deduced to 3.
int S8::d_s[] = {4, 5, 6};  // OK, the length of S8::d_s is deduced to 3.
```

Interactions with unions

Default member initializers can also be used with union members. However, only one variant member of a union can have a default member initializer, since that will determine the default initialization of the entire union:

```
union U0
{
    char d_c = 'a';
```

```
    int  d_d = 1;
        // Error, only one member of U0 can have a default initializer.
};
```

Note that members of an anonymous union are considered to be variant members of the parent union:

```
union U1
{
    union { int d_x = 1; };

    union
    {
        int d_y;
        int d_z = 1;
            // Error, only one member of U1 can have a default initializer.
    };

    char d_c = 'a';
        // Error, only one member of U1 can have a default initializer.
};
```

The default member initializer of a variant member will be used unless the same or a different variant member of the union is initialized explicitly, e.g., via a constructor having a member initializer list or via aggregate initialization (allowed for types with default member initializers only since C++14; see Section 1.2."Aggregate Init '14" on page 138). In all cases, the initialized variant member becomes the active member of the union:

```
union U2
{
    char d_c;
    int  d_i = 10;
};

U2 x;      // initializes d_i with 10
U2 y{};    // initializes d_i with 10

U2 z{'a'}; // initializes d_c with 'a', default initializer ignored

union U3
{
    char d_c;
    int  d_i = 10;

    U3() { }                 // default member initializer used for d_i

    U3(char c) : d_c{c} { }  // default member initializer ignored
};
```

Use Cases

Concise initialization of simple `structs`

Default member initializers provide a concise and effective way of initializing all the members of a simple **struct**. Consider, for instance, a **struct** used to configure a thread pool:

```
struct ThreadPoolConfiguration
{
    int  d_numThreads        = 8;     // number of worker threads
    bool d_enableWorkStealing = true; // enable work stealing
    int  d_taskSize          = 64;    // buffer size for an enqueued task
};
```

Compared to the use of a constructor, the above definition of `ThreadPoolConfiguration` provides sensible default values with minimal **boilerplate code**.[1]

Ensuring initialization of a non**static** data member

Non**static** data members that do not have a default member initializer or appear in any constructor member initializer list are **default initialized**. For **user-defined types**, default initialization is equivalent to the default constructor being invoked. For built-in types, default initialization results in an indeterminate value.

As an example, consider a **struct** tracking the number of times a user accesses a website:

```
#include <string>  // std::string

struct UsageTracker
{
    std::string d_token;
    std::string d_websiteURL;
    int         d_clicks;
};
```

The programmer intended `UsageTracker` to be used as a simple aggregate. Forgetting to explicitly initialize `d_clicks` can result in a defect:

---

[1]In C++20, designated initializers can be used to tweak one or more default settings in a configuration **struct** like `ThreadPoolConfiguration` in a clear and concise manner:

```
void testDesignatedInitializer()
{
    ThreadPoolConfiguration tpc = {.d_taskSize = 128};
    assert(tpc.d_numThreads == 8);
    assert(tpc.d_enableWorkStealing);
    assert(tpc.d_taskSize == 128);
}
```

```
#include <map>      // std::map
#include <vector>   // std::vector

std::map<std::string, std::vector<UsageTracker>> usageTrackers;
// ...

void onVisitWebsite(const std::string& username, const std::string& token)
{
    UsageTracker ut = {token, "https://emcpps.com"};
    usageTrackers[username].push_back(ut);
        // Bug, ut.d_clicks has indeterminate value.
}
```

Consistent use of default member initializers for built-in types can avoid such defects:

```
#include <string>  // std::string

struct UsageTracker
{
    std::string d_token;
    std::string d_websiteURL;
    int         d_clicks = 0;  // OK, will not have an indeterminate value
};
```

Avoiding boilerplate repetition across multiple constructors

Certain member variables of a type might be used to track the state of the object during its lifetime, independently of the initial state of the object. In such cases, we might want all constructors to set such variables to the same value, irrespective of constructor arguments. Consider a state machine that controls execution of a background process:

```
class StateMachine
{
    enum State { e_INIT = 1, e_RUNNING, e_DONE, e_FAIL };
    State           d_state;
    MachineProgram d_program;  // instructions to execute

public:
    StateMachine()  // Create a machine to run the default program.
    : d_state(e_INIT)
    , d_program(getDefaultProgram())
    { }

    StateMachine(const MachineProgram& program)  // Run the specified program.
    : d_state(e_INIT)
    , d_program(program)
    { }
```

```
    StateMachine(MachineProgram&& program)  // Run the specified program.
    : d_state(e_INIT)
    , d_program(std::move(program))
    { }

    StateMachine(const char* filename)  // read program to run from filename
    : d_state(e_INIT)
    , d_program(loadProgram(filename))
    { }
};
```

For member variables such as d_state, which always start at the same value and then are updated as the object is used, using a default initializer reduces boilerplate and reduces the risk of accidentally initializing with an incorrect value:

```
class StateMachine
{
    enum State { e_INIT = 1, e_RUNNING, e_DONE, e_FAIL };
    State           d_state = e_INIT;  // default member initializer
    MachineProgram d_program;          // instructions to execute

public:
    StateMachine() : d_program(getDefaultProgram()) { }
    StateMachine(const MachineProgram& program) : d_program(program) { }
    StateMachine(MachineProgram&& program) : d_program(std::move(program)) { }
    StateMachine(const char* filename) : d_program(loadProgram(filename)) { }
};
```

Other members that are updated during an object's lifetime, such as mutable members for caching expensive calculations, can also benefit from being initialized once as opposed to having individual initializers in each constructor. Suppose we define a class, NetSession, that caches resolved IP addresses (v4 and v6), so it doesn't need to perform a DNS lookup every time the IP address is needed. In all constructors, the IP address is not resolved yet, meaning the cached IP address is invalid. A simple convention is to set both IP addresses to 0 because no valid IP address has that value:

```
#include <string>   // std::string
#include <cstdint>  // std::uint32_t, std::uint64_t

class NetSession
{
    std::string d_address;                  // such as "example.com"
    mutable std::uint32_t d_ip      = 0;    // cache of resolved IPv4 address
    mutable std::uint64_t d_ipv6[2] = {0, 0};  // cache of resolved IPv6 address

public:
    NetSession() { }
    NetSession(const std::string& address) : d_address(address) { }
```

```
   // ...
};
```

Making default values obvious for documentation purposes

Configuration objects that bundle a large number of different properties are a popular artifact in large systems. Though the values might be loaded from, e.g., an appropriate configuration file, they often have meaningful default values. In C++03, the default values for these properties would typically be documented in the header file (.h) but actually effected in the implementation file (.cpp), which opens the opportunity for the documentation to become out of sync with the implementation:

```
// my_config.h:

#include <string>  // std::string

struct Config
{
    std::string d_organization;  // default value "ACME"
    long long   d_maxTries;      // default value 1
    double      d_costRatio;     // default value 13.2

    Config();
};

// my_config.cpp:

#include <my_config.h>

Config::Config()
    : d_organization("Acme")    // Bug, doesn't match documentation
    , d_maxTries(3)             // Bug, went out of sync in maintenance
{ }                             // Bug, d_costRatio not initialized
```

Default initializers can be used in such cases to work as active documentation:

```
#include <string>  // std::string

struct Config
{
    std::string d_organization = "Acme";
    long long   d_maxTries     = 3;
    double      d_costRatio    = 13.2;

    Config() = default;  // no user-provided definition needed any longer
};
```

Potential Pitfalls

Loss of insulation

Although convenient, placing default values in a header file — and thus potentially also using a **default** default constructor — can result in a loss of insulation that can have severe consequences, especially at scale. For instance, consider a hash table with a non**static** data member representing the growth factor:

```
// hashtable.h:

class HashTable
{
private:
    float d_growthFactor;
    // ...

public:
    HashTable();
    // ...
};
```

Without using default member initializers, the default growth factor is provided as part of the member initialization list of the default constructor:

```
// hashtable.cpp:
#include <hashtable.h>  // HashTable

HashTable::HashTable() : d_growthFactor(2.0f) { }
```

In the eventuality that the default growth factor is too large and results in excessive memory consumption in production, relinking the affected applications with a new version of the library-provided `HashTable`, rather than recompiling them, is sufficient. Subject to a company's compilation and deployment infrastructure, relinking alone can be significantly less expensive than having to recompile the entire program prior to relinking it.

Had the default member initializer been used, the otherwise trivial default constructor might be defined in the header with `=` **default**, effectively removing any insulation of these values that might allow speedy relinking in lieu of expensive recompilation, should these values need to change in a crisis.[2]

Inconsistent subobject initialization

An approach occasionally taken to avoid keeping globally shared state is to have objects keep a handle to a `Context` object holding data that would otherwise be application-global:

```
struct Context
{
```

---

[2]For a complete description of this real-world example, see **lakos20**, section 3.10.5, pp. 783–789.

```
    bool d_isProduction;
    long d_userId;
    int  d_dataCenterId;
    // ... other information about the context being run in

    static Context* defaultContext();
};
```

Each type that needs `Context` information would take an optional argument to specify a local context; otherwise, it would use the default context:

```
#include <string>  // std::string

struct ContextualObject
{
// ...
    ContextualObject(const std::string& name,
                     Context* context = Context::defaultContext());
// ...
};
```

When combining many objects, all of which might need to access the same context for configuration, it becomes important to pass the context specified at construction to each subobject:

```
struct CompoundObject
{
// ...
    ContextualObject d_o1;
    ContextualObject d_o2;
// ...
    CompoundObject(Context* context = Context::defaultContext())
    : d_o1("First", context)
    , d_o2("Second", context)
    { }
// ...
};
```

This situation might seem well suited for using default member initializers, but the naive approach would have a serious flaw:

```
struct CompoundObject
{
// ...
    ContextualObject d_o1{"first"};   // Bug, does not use context passed to
    ContextualObject d_o2{"second"};  // CompoundObject constructor
// ...
    CompoundObject(Context* context = Context::defaultContext());
// ...
};
```

This defect, frustratingly, will impact only those applications that use multiple contexts, which might be a small subset of applications and libraries that use contextual objects. The only nonintrusive approach that avoids this defect is to forgo default member initializers for subobjects that can take a `context` parameter. The other — still error-prone — alternative is to store a context pointer as the *first* member, initialize it in all constructors, and use that in the default member initializer of the subobjects:

```cpp
struct CompoundObject
{
// ...
    Context*        d_context;
    ContextualObject d_o1{"first", d_context};   // OK
    ContextualObject d_o2{"second", d_context};  // OK
    // ...
    CompoundObject(Context* context = Context::defaultContext())
    : d_context(context)
    { }
// ...
};
```

This approach has the downside of requiring an extra copy of the `Context*` member to transmit the passed-in value from the constructor to the subobject initializers. Additionally, now the correctness of the code strongly depends on the subobjects of `CompoundObject` being initialized after the `d_context` member variable, so the order of members is subtly constrained. Consequently, innocuous changes in member order during maintenance are liable to introduce bugs.[3]

Annoyances

Parenthesized direct-initialization syntax cannot be used

Direct-initialization syntax is not allowed in default member initialization, which makes it tedious to copy code from automatic variables into class members. For example, suppose we set out to transform a function into an equivalent **function object**, which might be useful for applications needing callbacks. This transformation entails migrating a function's automatic variables to member variables of the corresponding function object:

```cpp
void function() // before
{
    int i1 = 17;
    int i2(18);
    int i3{42};
```

---

[3]C++17 introduces the **polymorphic memory resource** allocator model, which is a **scoped allocator model** with issues similar to `ContextualObject`.

```
    // ... do stuff
}

class Functor  // after
{
    int i1 = 17;   // OK
    int i2(18);    // Error, invalid syntax
    int i3{42};    // OK

    void operator()(int step)
    {
        // ... do stuff
    }
};
```

Cutting and pasting the definitions of the locals i1, i2, and i3 will result in compile-time errors. The code initializing i2 needs to be adjusted to use either copy initialization (like i1) or braced initialization (like i3).

Limitations of applicability

Default member initializers can be used to replace the initialization of almost all members that can be placed in a constructor's **member initializer list**, except for two cases.

1. Bit-field data members[4]

2. Base classes

Both of these situations continue to require initialization in member initializer lists, which translates to boilerplate that might be inconsistent with the rest of the codebase.

Loss of triviality

Having member initializers makes the default constructor nontrivial. The presence of a nontrivial constructor can prevent some optimizations that might otherwise be possible; see Section 2.1."Generalized PODs '11" on page 401:

---

[4]In C++20, bit fields can be initialized through a default member initializer:

```
struct S
{
    int d_i : 4 = 8;   // Error, before C++20; OK, in C++20
    int d_j : 4 {8};   // Error, before C++20; OK, in C++20
};
```

```
#include <type_traits>  // std::is_trivial

struct S0 { int d_i;     };
struct S1 { int d_i = 0; };
struct S2 { int d_i; S2() : d_i(0) { } };

static_assert(std::is_trivial<S0>::value, "");
static_assert(!std::is_trivial<S1>::value, "");
static_assert(!std::is_trivial<S2>::value, "");
```

Loss of aggregate status

In C++11, classes using default member initializers are not considered **aggregates**, and therefore **aggregate initialization** can't be used. Fortunately, this restriction has been lifted in C++14; see Section 1.2."Aggregate Init '14" on page 138:

```
struct ThreadPoolConfiguration
{
    int  d_numThreads        = 8;     // number of worker threads
    bool d_enableWorkStealing = true;  // enable work stealing
    int  d_taskSize          = 64;    // buffer size for an enqueued task
};

void f()
{
    ThreadPoolConfiguration tpc0;                  // OK in C++11
    ThreadPoolConfiguration tpc1{16, true, 64};   // Error, in C++11; OK in C++14
}
```

Default member initializer does not deduce array size

Default member initializers do not allow deduction of the size of an array member:

```
struct S
{
    char s[]{"Idle"};  // Error, must specify array size
};
```

The rationale is that there is no guarantee that the default member initializer will be used to initialize the member; hence, it cannot be a definitive source of information about the size of such a member in the object layout.

See Also

- "Delegating Ctors" (§1.1, p. 46) discusses how to reduce code repetition in initialization of non**static** data members by chaining constructors together.

- "Aggregate Init '14" (§1.2, p. 138) illustrates how default member initializers are used during aggregate initialization in C++14.

- "Braced Init" (§2.1, p. 215) shows how default member initializers support **list ini-tialization**, which is part of the uniform initialization effort.

- "Opaque **enum**s" (§2.1, p. 660) provides another means of insulating clients from unnecessary implementation details.

Strongly Typed, Scoped Enumerations

An **enum class** is an alternative enumeration type that provides simultaneously (1) an enclosing scope for its enumerators and (2) stronger typing compared to a classic **enum**.

Description

C++11 introduces a novel enumeration construct, **enum class** or, equivalently, **enum struct**:

```
enum class  Ec { A, B, C }; // scoped enumeration, Ec, containing three enumerators
```

The enumerators of the **enum class** Ec in the line above — namely, A, B, and C — do not automatically become part of the enclosing scope and must be qualified to be referenced:

```
Ec e0 = A;      // Error, A not found
Ec e1 = Ec::A;  // OK
```

Moreover, attempting to use an expression of type **enum class** E as, say, an **int** or in an arithmetic context will be flagged as an error, thus necessitating an explicit cast:

```
int  i0 = Ec::B;                    // Error, conversion to int not supported
int  i1 = static_cast<int>(Ec::B);  // OK, i1 is 1.
int  i2 = 1 + Ec::B;                // Error, conversion to int not supported
int  i3 = -Ec::B;                   // Error, unsupported arithmetic operations

bool b0 = Ec::B != 2;               // Error, comparison with int unsupported
bool b1 = Ec::B != Ec::C;           // OK, b1 is 'true'.
```

The **enum class** *complements* but does not replace the classical, C-style **enum**:

```
enum E { e_Enumerator0 /*= value0 */, /*...*/ e_EnumeratorN /* = valueN */ };
    // Classic, C-style enum: enumerators are neither type safe nor scoped.
```

For examples where the classic **enum** shines, see *Potential Pitfalls — Strong typing of an* **enum class** *can be counterproductive* on page 344 and *Annoyances — Scoped enumerations do not necessarily add value* on page 351.

Still, innumerable practical situations occur in which enumerators that are both scoped and more type safe would be preferred; see *Introducing the C++11 scoped enumerations* on page 335 and *Use Cases* on page 337.

Drawbacks and workarounds relating to unscoped C++03 enumerations

Since the enumerators of a classic **enum** leak out into the enclosing scope, if two unrelated enumerations that happen to use the same enumerator name appear in the same scope, an ambiguity could ensue:

```
enum Color { e_RED, e_ORANGE, e_YELLOW };    // OK
enum Fruit { e_APPLE, e_ORANGE, e_BANANA };  // Error, e_ORANGE is redefined.
```

Note that we use a lowercase, single-letter prefix — such as **e_** — to ensure that the uppercase enumerator name is less likely to collide with a legacy macro, which is especially useful in header files. The problems associated with the use of unscoped enumerations is exacerbated when those enumerations are placed in their own respective header files in the global or some other large namespace scope, such as **std**, for general reuse. In such cases, latent defects will typically not manifest unless and until the two enumerations are included in the same translation unit.

If the only issue were the leakage of the enumerators into the enclosing scope, then the long-established workaround of enclosing the enumeration within a **struct** would suffice:

```
struct Color { enum Enum { e_RED, e_ORANGE, e_YELLOW }; };    // OK (scoped)
struct Fruit { enum Enum { e_APPLE, e_ORANGE, e_BANANA }; };  // OK (scoped)
```

Employing the C++03 workaround in the above code snippet implies that when passing such an explicitly scoped, classical **enum** into a function, the distinguishing name of the **enum** is subsumed by its enclosing **struct** and the **enum** name itself, such as Enum, becomes **boilerplate code**:

```
int enumeratorValue1 = Color::e_ORANGE;  // OK
int enumeratorValue2 = Fruit::e_ORANGE;  // OK

void colorFunc(Color::Enum color);  // enumerated (scoped) Color parameter
void fruitFunc(Fruit::Enum fruit);  // enumerated (scoped) Fruit parameter
```

Hence, adding *just* scope to a classic, C++03 **enum** is easily doable and might be exactly what is indicated; see *Potential Pitfalls — Strong typing of an **enum class** can be counterproductive* on page 344.

Drawbacks relating to weakly typed, C++03 enumerators

Historically, C++03 enumerations have been employed to represent at least two distinct concepts:

1. A collection of related, but not necessarily unique, named integral values

2. A pure, perhaps ordered, set of named entities in which cardinal value has no relevance

It will turn out that the modern **enum class** feature, which we will discuss in *Introducing the C++11 scoped enumerations* on page 335, is more closely aligned with this second concept.

A classic enumeration, by default, has an implementation-defined **underlying type (UT)** (see Section 2.1.“Underlying Type ’11” on page 829), which it uses to represent variables of that enumerated type as well as the values of its enumerators. Although implicit conversion *to* an enumerated type is never permitted, when implicitly converting *from* a classic **enum** type to some arithmetic type, the **enum** promotes to integral types in a way similar to how its underlying type would promote using the rules of **integral promotion** and **standard conversion**:

```
void f()
{
    enum A { e_A0, e_A1, e_A2 };  // classic, C-style C++03 enum
    enum B { e_B0, e_B1, e_B2 };  //    "     "      "    "     "

    A a;  // Declare object a to be of type A.
    B b;  //    "       "    b  "  "   "   "  B.

    a = e_B2;  // Error, cannot convert e_B2 to enum type A
    b = e_B2;  // OK, assign the value e_B2 (numerically 2) to b.
    a = b;     // Error, cannot convert enum type B to enum type A
    b = b;     // OK, self-assignment
    a = 1;     // Error, invalid conversion from int 1 to enum type A
    a = 0;     // Error, invalid conversion from int 0 to enum type A

    bool     v = a;     // OK
    char     w = e_A0;  // OK
    int      i = e_B0;  // OK
    unsigned y = e_B1;  // OK
    float    x = b;     // OK
    double   z = e_A2;  // OK
    char*    p = e_B0;  // Error, unable to convert e_B0 to char*
    char*    q = +e_B0; // Error, invalid conversion of int to char*
}
```

Notice that, in this example, the final two diagnostics for the attempted initializations of p and q, respectively, differ slightly. In the first, we are trying to initialize a pointer, p, with an enumerated type, B. In the second, we have creatively used the built-in unary-plus operator to explicitly promote the enumerator to an integral type before attempting to assign it to a pointer, q. Even though the numerical value of the enumerator is 0 and such is known at compile time, implicit conversion to a pointer type from anything but the literal integer constant 0 is not permitted. Excluding esoteric user-defined types, only a literal 0 or, as of C++11, a value of type std::nullptr_t is implicitly convertible to an arbitrary pointer type; see Section 1.1."**nullptr**" on page 99.

C++ fully supports comparing values of *classic* **enum** types with values of arbitrary **arithmetic type** as well as those of the same enumerated type; the operands of a comparator will be promoted to a sufficiently large integer type, and the comparison will be done with those values. Comparing values having distinct enumerated types, however, is deprecated and will typically elicit a warning.[1]

Introducing the C++11 scoped enumerations

With the advent of modern C++, we now have a new, alternative enumeration construct, **enum class**, that simultaneously addresses strong type safety and lexical scoping, two distinct and often desirable properties:

```
enum class Name { e_Enumerator0 /* = value0 */, e_EnumeratorN /* = valueN */ };
    // enum class enumerators are both type-safe and scoped
```

Another major distinction is that the default underlying type for a C-style **enum** is implementation defined, whereas, for an **enum class**, it is always an **int**. See *enum class and underlying type* on page 337 and *Potential Pitfalls — External use of opaque enumerators* on page 350.

Unlike unscoped enumerations, **enum class** does not leak its enumerators into the enclosing scope and can therefore help avoid collisions with other enumerations having like-named enumerators defined in the same scope:

```
enum       VehicleUnscoped  { e_CAR, e_TRAIN, e_PLANE };
struct     VehicleScopedExplicitly { enum Enum { e_CAR, e_TRAIN, e_PLANE }; };
enum class VehicleScopedImplicitly { e_CAR, e_BOAT, e_PLANE };
```

Just like an unscoped **enum** type, an object of a scoped enumeration type is passed as a parameter to a function using the enumeration name itself:

```
void f1(VehicleUnscoped value);          // unscoped enumeration passed by value
void f2(VehicleScopedImplicitly value);  // scoped enumeration passed by value
```

If we use the approach for adding scope to enumerators that is described in *Drawbacks relating to weakly typed, C++03 enumerators* on page 333, the name of the enclosing **struct**

---

[1]As of C++20, attempting to compare two values of distinct classically enumerated types is a compile-time error. Note that explicitly converting at least one of them to an integral type — for example, using built-in unary plus — both makes our intentions clear and avoids warnings.

```
void test()
{
  if (e_A0 < 0)      { /*...*/ }  // OK, comparison with integral type
  if (1.0 != e_B1)   { /*...*/ }  // OK, comparison with arithmetic type
  if (A() <= e_A2)   { /*...*/ }  // OK, comparison with same enumerated type
  if (e_A0 == e_B0)  { /*...*/ }  // warning, deprecated (error as of C++20)
  if ( e_A0 == +e_B0) { /*...*/ } // OK, unary + converts to integral type
  if (+e_A0 ==  e_B0) { /*...*/ } // OK,   "        "      "      "       "
  if (+e_A0 == +e_B0) { /*...*/ } // OK,   "        "      "      "       "
}
```

together with a consistent name for the enumeration, such as Enum, has to be used to indicate an enumerated type:

```
void f3(VehicleScopedExplicitly::Enum value);
    // classically scoped enum passed by value
```

Qualifying the enumerators of a scoped enumeration is the same, irrespective of whether the scoping is explicit or implicit:

```
void g()
{
    f3(VehicleScopedExplicitly::e_PLANE);
        // call f3 with an explicitly scoped enumerator

    f2(VehicleScopedImplicitly::e_PLANE);
        // call f2 with an implicitly scoped enumerator
}
```

Apart from implicit scoping, the modern, C++11 scoped enumeration deliberately does *not* support implicit conversion, in any context, to its **underlying type**:

```
void h()
{
    int i1 = VehicleScopedExplicitly::e_PLANE;
        // OK, scoped C++03 enum (implicit conversion)

    int i2 = VehicleScopedImplicitly::e_PLANE;
        // Error, no implicit conversion to underlying type

    if (VehicleScopedExplicitly::e_PLANE > 3) {} // OK
    if (VehicleScopedImplicitly::e_PLANE > 3) {} // Error, implicit conversion
}
```

Enumerators of an **enum class** do, however, admit equality and ordinal comparisons within their own type:

```
enum class E { e_A, e_B, e_C };  // By default, enumerators increase from 0.

static_assert(E::e_A < E::e_C, "");  // OK, comparison between same-type values
static_assert(0 == E::e_A, "");      // Error, no implicit conversion from E
static_assert(0 == static_cast<int>(E::e_A), "");  // OK, explicit conversion

void f(E v)
{
    if (v > E::e_A) { /*...*/ }  // OK, comparing values of same type, E
}
```

Note that incrementing an enumeration variable from one strongly typed enumerator's value to the next requires an explicit cast; see *Potential Pitfalls — Strong typing of an **enum class** can be counterproductive* on page 344.

enum class and underlying type

Since C++11, both scoped and unscoped enumerations permit explicit specification of their integral underlying type (see Section 2.1."Underlying Type '11" on page 829):

```
enum Ec : char { e_X, e_Y, e_Z };
    // Underlying type is char.

static_assert(1 == sizeof(Ec),     "");
static_assert(1 == sizeof Ec::e_X, "");

enum class Es : short { e_X, e_Y, e_Z };
    // Underlying type is short int.

static_assert(sizeof(short) == sizeof(Es),     "");
static_assert(sizeof(short) == sizeof Es::e_X, "");
```

Unlike a classic **enum**, which has an implementation-defined default underlying type, the default underlying type for an **enum class** is always **int**:

```
enum class Ei { e_X, e_Y, e_Z };
    // When not specified, the underlying type of an enum class is int.

static_assert(sizeof(int) == sizeof(Ei),     "");
static_assert(sizeof(int) == sizeof Ei::e_X, "");
```

Note that, because the default underlying type of an **enum class** is specified by the Standard, eliding the enumerators of an **enum class** in a local redeclaration is *always* possible; see *Potential Pitfalls — External use of opaque enumerators* on page 350 and Section 2.1. "Opaque **enum**s" on page 660.

Use Cases

Avoiding unintended implicit conversions to arithmetic types

Suppose that we want to represent the result of selecting one of a fixed number of alternatives from a drop-down menu as a simple unordered set of uniquely valued named integers. For example, this might be the case when configuring a product, such as a vehicle, for purchase:

```
struct Transmission
{
    enum Enum { e_MANUAL, e_AUTOMATIC };  // classic, C++03 scoped enum
};
```

Although automatic promotion of a classic enumerator to **int** works well when typical use of the enumerator involves knowing its cardinal value, such promotions are less than ideal when cardinal values have no role in intended usage:

```
class Car { /*...*/ };

struct Transmission
{                                      // explicitly scoped
    enum Enum { e_MANUAL, e_AUTOMATIC };  // classic enum
};                                     // (BAD IDEA)

int buildCar(Car* result, int numDoors, Transmission::Enum transmission)
{
    int status = Transmission::e_MANUAL;    // Bug, accidental misuse

    for (int i = 0; i < transmission; ++i)  // Bug, accidental misuse
    {
        attachDoor(i);
    }

    return status;
}
```

As shown in the example above, it is never correct for a value of type `Transmission::Enum` to be assigned to, compared with, or otherwise modified like an integer; hence, *any* such use would necessarily be considered a mistake and, ideally, flagged by the compiler as an error. The stronger typing provided by **enum class** achieves this goal:

```
class Car { /*...*/ };

enum class Transmission { e_MANUAL, e_AUTOMATIC };  // modern enum class (GOOD IDEA)

int buildCar(Car* result, int numDoors, Transmission transmission)
{
    int status = Transmission::e_MANUAL;    // Error, incompatible types

    for (int i = 0; i < transmission; ++i)  // Error, incompatible types
    {
        attachDoor(i);
    }

    return status;
}
```

By deliberately choosing the **enum class** in the examle above over the *classic* **enum**, we automate the detection of many common kinds of accidental misuse. Secondarily, we slightly simplify the interface of the function signature by removing the extra `::Enum` boilerplate qualifications required of an explicitly scoped, less-type-safe, classic **enum**, but see *Potential Pitfalls — Strong typing of an **enum class** can be counterproductive* on page 344.

In the event that the numeric value of a strongly typed enumerator is needed (e.g., for serialization), it can be extracted explicitly via a **static_cast**:

```
const int manualIntegralValue    = static_cast<int>(Transmission::e_MANUAL);
const int automaticIntegralValue = static_cast<int>(Transmission::e_AUTOMATIC);
static_assert(0 == manualIntegralValue,    "");
static_assert(1 == automaticIntegralValue, "");
```

Avoiding namespace pollution

Classic, C-style enumerations do not provide scope for their enumerators, leading to unintended latent name collisions:

```
// vehicle.h:
// ...
enum Vehicle  { e_CAR, e_TRAIN, e_PLANE };  // classic, C-style enum
// ...


// geometry.h:
// ...
enum Geometry { e_POINT, e_LINE, e_PLANE };  // classic, C-style enum
// ...


// client.cpp:
#include <vehicle.h>  // OK
#include <geometry.h> // Error, e_PLANE redefined
// ...
```

The common workaround is to wrap the **enum** in a **struct** or **namespace**:

```
// vehicle.h:
// ...
struct Vehicle {                          // explicitly scoped
    enum Enum { e_CAR, e_TRAIN, e_PLANE };  // classic, C-style enum
};
// ...

// geometry.h:
// ...
struct Geometry {                         // explicitly scoped
    enum Enum { e_POINT, e_LINE, e_PLANE };  // classic, C-style enum
};
// ...

// client.cpp:
#include <vehicle.h>    // OK
#include <geometry.h>   // OK, enumerators are scoped explicitly.
// ...
```

If implicit conversions of enumerators to integral types are not required, we can achieve the same scoping effect with much more type safety and slightly less boilerplate, i.e., without the ::Enum when declaring a variable, by employing **enum class** instead:

```
// vehicle.h:
// ...
enum class Vehicle { e_CAR, e_TRAIN, e_PLANE };
// ...


// geometry.h:
// ...
enum class Geometry { e_POINT, e_LINE, e_PLANE };
// ...


// client.cpp:
#include <vehicle.h>  // OK
#include <geometry.h> // OK, enumerators are scoped implicitly.
// ...
```

Improving overloading disambiguation

Stronger type safety of scoped enumerations might prevent mistakes when calling overloaded functions, especially when the overload set accepts multiple arguments. As an illustration of the compounding of such maintenance difficulties, suppose that we have a widely used, named type, `Color`, and the numeric values of its enumerators are small, unique, and irrelevant. Imagine we have chosen to represent `Color` as an unscoped **enum**:

```
struct Color
{                                           // explicitly scoped
    enum Enum { e_RED, e_BLUE /*...*/ };  // classic, C-style enum
};                                          // (BAD IDEA)
```

Suppose further that we have provided two overloaded functions, each having two parameters, with one signature's parameters including the enumeration `Color`:

```
void clearScreen(int pattern, int orientation);          // (0)
void clearScreen(Color::Enum background, double alpha);  // (1)
```

Depending on the types of the arguments supplied, one of the functions will be selected, or else the call will be ambiguous, and the program will fail to compile[2]:

---

[2]GCC 11.2 (c. 2021) incorrectly diagnoses both ambiguity errors as warnings, although it states in the warning that it is an error:

```
warning: ISO C++ says that these are ambiguous, even though the worst conversion for the
         first is better than the worst conversion for the second:

note: candidate 1: void clearScreen(int, int)
void clearScreen(int pattern, int orientation);
     ^~~~~~~~~~~
note: candidate 2: void clearScreen(Color::Enum, double)
void clearScreen(Color::Enum background, double alpha;
     ^~~~~~~~~~~
```

```
void f0()
{
    clearScreen(1              , 1              );  // calls (0) above
    clearScreen(1              , 1.0            );  // calls (0) above
    clearScreen(1              , Color::e_RED);  // calls (0) above

    clearScreen(1.0            , 1              );  // calls (0) above
    clearScreen(1.0            , 1.0            );  // calls (0) above
    clearScreen(1.0            , Color::e_RED);  // calls (0) above

    clearScreen(Color::e_RED, 1              );  // Error, ambiguous call
    clearScreen(Color::e_RED, 1.0            );  // calls (1) above
    clearScreen(Color::e_RED, Color::e_RED);  // Error, ambiguous call
}
```

Now suppose that we had instead defined our `Color` enumeration as a modern **enum class**:

```
enum class Color { e_RED, e_BLUE /*...*/ };

void clearScreen(int pattern, int orientation);     // (2)
void clearScreen(Color background, double alpha);  // (3)
```

The function that will be called from a given set of arguments becomes clear:

```
void f1()
{
    clearScreen(1              , 1              );  // calls (2) above
    clearScreen(1              , 1.0            );  // calls (2) above
    clearScreen(1              , Color::e_RED);  // Error, no matching function

    clearScreen(1.0            , 1              );  // calls (2) above
    clearScreen(1.0            , 1.0            );  // calls (2) above
    clearScreen(1.0            , Color::e_RED);  // Error, no matching function

    clearScreen(Color::e_RED, 1              );  // calls (3) above
    clearScreen(Color::e_RED, 1.0            );  // calls (3) above
    clearScreen(Color::e_RED, Color::e_RED);  // Error, no matching function
}
```

Returning to our original, classic-**enum** design, suppose that we find we need to add a third parameter, **bool** z, to the second overload:

```
void clearScreen(int pattern, int orientation);                         // (0)
void clearScreen(Color::Enum background, double alpha, bool z);  // (4) classic
```

If our plan is that any existing client calls involving `Color::Enum` will now be flagged as errors, we are going to be disappointed:

```
void f2()
{
    clearScreen(Color::e_RED, 1.0);  // calls (0) above
}
```

In fact, every combination of arguments above — all nine of them — will call function (0) above, often with no warnings at all:

```
void f3()
{
    clearScreen(1          , 1          );  // calls (0) above
    clearScreen(1          , 1.0        );  // calls (0) above
    clearScreen(1          , Color::e_RED);  // calls (0) above

    clearScreen(1.0        , 1          );  // calls (0) above
    clearScreen(1.0        , 1.0        );  // calls (0) above
    clearScreen(1.0        , Color::e_RED);  // calls (0) above

    clearScreen(Color::e_RED, 1          );  // calls (0) above
    clearScreen(Color::e_RED, 1.0        );  // calls (0) above
    clearScreen(Color::e_RED, Color::e_RED);  // calls (0) above
}
```

Finally, let's suppose again that we have used **enum class** to implement our Color enumeration:

```
void clearScreen(int pattern, int orientation);          // (2)
void clearScreen(Color background, double alpha, bool z);  // (5) modern

void f4()
{
    clearScreen(Color::e_RED, 1.0);  // Error, no matching function
}
```

And in fact, the *only* calls that succeed unmodified are precisely those that do not involve the enumeration Color, as desired:

```
void f5()
{
    clearScreen(1          , 1          );  // calls (2) above
    clearScreen(1          , 1.0        );  // calls (2) above
    clearScreen(1          , Color::e_RED);  // Error, no matching function

    clearScreen(1.0        , 1          );  // calls (2) above
    clearScreen(1.0        , 1.0        );  // calls (2) above
    clearScreen(1.0        , Color::e_RED);  // Error, no matching function
```

```
    clearScreen(Color::e_RED, 1            );  // Error, no matching function
    clearScreen(Color::e_RED, 1.0          );  // Error, no matching function
    clearScreen(Color::e_RED, Color::e_RED);  // Error, no matching function
}
```

Bottom line: Having a *pure* enumeration be strongly typed — such as `Color`, used widely in function signatures — can help to expose accidental misuse but, again, see *Potential Pitfalls — Strong typing of an **enum class** can be counterproductive* on page 344.

Note that strongly typed enumerations help to avoid accidental misuse by requiring an explicit *cast* should conversion to an arithmetic type be desired:

```
void f6()
{
    clearScreen(Color::e_RED, 1.0);                     // Error, no match
    clearScreen(static_cast<int>(Color::e_RED), 1.0);  // OK, calls (2) above
    clearScreen(Color::e_RED, 1.0, false);             // OK, calls (5) above
}
```

Encapsulating implementation details within the enumerators themselves

In rare cases, providing a pure, ordered enumeration having unique (but not necessarily contiguous) numerical values that exploit lower-order bits to categorize and make readily available important individual properties might offer an advantage, such as in performance. Note that to preserve the ordinality of the enumerators overall, the higher-level bits must encode their relative order. The lower-level bits are then available for arbitrary use in the implementation.

For example, suppose that we have a `MonthOfYear` enumeration that encodes in the least-significant bit the months that have 31 days and an accompanying **inline** function to quickly determine whether a given enumerator represents such a month:

```
#include <type_traits>  // std::underlying_type

enum class MonthOfYear : unsigned char  // optimized to flag long months
{
    e_JAN = ( 1 << 4) + 0x1,
    e_FEB = ( 2 << 4) + 0x0,
    e_MAR = ( 3 << 4) + 0x1,
    e_APR = ( 4 << 4) + 0x0,
    e_MAY = ( 5 << 4) + 0x1,
    e_JUN = ( 6 << 4) + 0x0,
    e_JUL = ( 7 << 4) + 0x1,
    e_AUG = ( 8 << 4) + 0x1,
    e_SEP = ( 9 << 4) + 0x0,
```

```
    e_OCT = (10 << 4) + 0x1,
    e_NOV = (11 << 4) + 0x0,
    e_DEC = (12 << 4) + 0x1
};

bool hasThirtyOneDays(MonthOfYear month)
{
    return static_cast<std::underlying_type<MonthOfYear>::type>(month) & 0x1;
}
```

In the example above, we are using a new cross-cutting feature of all enumerated types that allows the client defining the type to specify its underlying type precisely. In this case, we have chosen an **unsigned char** to maximize the number of flag bits while keeping the overall size to a single byte. Three bits remain available. Had we needed more flag bits, we could have just as easily used a larger underlying type, such as **unsigned short**; see Section 2.1. "Underlying Type '11" on page 829.

In case **enum**s are used for encoding purposes, the public clients are not intended to make use of the cardinal values; hence, clients are well advised to treat them as implementation details, potentially subject to change without notice. Representing this enumeration using the modern **enum class**, instead of an explicitly scoped classic **enum**, deters clients from making any use (apart from same-type comparisons) of the cardinal values assigned to the enumerators. Notice that implementors of the hasThirtyOneDays function will require a verbose but efficient **static_cast** to resolve the cardinal value of the enumerator and thus make the requested determination as efficiently as possible.

Potential Pitfalls

Strong typing of an enum class can be counterproductive

The additive value in using a scoped enumeration is governed *solely* by whether the stronger typing of its enumerators, *not* the implicit scoping, would be beneficial in typical anticipated usage. If the expectation is that the client will never need to know the specific values of the enumerators, then use of the modern **enum class** is often just what's needed. But if the cardinal values themselves are ever needed during typical use, extracting them will require the client to perform an explicit cast. Beyond mere inconvenience, encouraging clients to use casts invites defects.

Suppose, for example, we have a function, setPort, from an external library that takes an integer port number:

```
int setPort(int portNumber);
    // Set the current port; return 0 on success and a nonzero value otherwise.
```

Suppose further that we have used the modern **enum class** feature to implement an enumeration, SysPort, that identifies well-known ports on our system:

```
enum class SysPort { e_INPUT = 27, e_OUTPUT = 29, e_ERROR = 32, e_CTRL = 6 };
    // enumerated port values used to configure our systems
```

Now suppose we want to call the function `setPort` using one of these enumerated values:

```
void setCurrentPortToCtrl()
{
    setPort(SysPort::e_CTRL);  // Error, cannot convert SysPort to int
}
```

Unlike the situation for a *classic* **enum**, no implicit conversion occurs from an **enum class** to its underlying integral type, so anyone using this enumeration will be forced to somehow explicitly **cast** the enumerator to some arithmetic type. There are, however, multiple choices for performing this cast:

```
#include <type_traits>  // std::underlying_type

void test()
{
    setPort(int(SysPort::e_CTRL));                                    // (1)
    setPort((int)SysPort::e_CTRL);                                    // (2)
    setPort(static_cast<int>(SysPort::e_CTRL));                       // (3)
    setPort(static_cast<std::underlying_type<SysPort>::type>(         // (4)
                                          SysPort::e_CTRL));
    setPort(static_cast<int>(                                         // (5)
            static_cast<std::underlying_type<SysPort>::type>(SysPort::e_CTRL)));
}
```

Any of the above casts would work in this case, but consider a future where a platform changed `setPort` to take a **long** and the control port was changed to a value that cannot be represented as an **int**:

```
int setPort(long portNumber);
enum class SysPort : unsigned { e_INPUT = 27, e_OUTPUT = 29, e_ERROR = 32,
                                e_CTRL = 0x80000000 };
    // enumerated port values used to configure our systems
```

Only the casting method, line (4) in the example on this page, will pass the correct value for `e_CTRL` to this new `setPort` implementation. The other variations will all pass a negative number for the port, which would certainly not be the intention of the user writing this code. A classic, C-style **enum** would have avoided any manually written cast entirely, and the proper value would propagate into `setPort` even as the range of values used for ports changes:

```
struct SysPort  // explicit scoping for a classic, C-style enum
{
    enum Enum { e_INPUT = 27, e_OUTPUT = 29, e_ERROR = 32,
                e_CTRL = 0x80000000 };
```

```
    // Note that the underlying type of Enum is implicit and will be
    // large enough to represent all of these values.
    static_assert(
        std::is_same<std::underlying_type<Enum>::type,unsigned>::value, "");
};

void setCurrentPortToCtrl()
{
    setPort(SysPort::e_CTRL);  // OK, SysPort::Enum promotes to long.
}
```

When the intended client will depend on the cardinal values of the enumerators during routine use, we can avoid tedious, error-prone, and repetitive casting by instead employing a classic, C-style **enum**, possibly nested within a **struct** to achieve explicit scoping of its enumerators. The sections that follow highlight specific cases in which classic, C-style, C++03 **enum**s are appropriate.

Misuse of enum class for collections of named constants

When constants are truly independent, we are often encouraged to avoid enumerations altogether, preferring instead individual constants; see Section 2.1."**constexpr** Variables" on page 302. On the other hand, when the constants all participate within a coherent theme, the expressiveness achieved using a *classic* **enum** to aggregate those values is compelling. Another advantage of an enumerator over an individual constant is that the enumerator is guaranteed to be a **compile-time constant** (see Section 2.1."**constexpr** Variables" on page 302) and a *prvalue* (see Section 2.1."*Rvalue* References" on page 710), which never needs static storage and cannot have its address taken.

For example, suppose we want to collect the coefficients for various numerical suffixes representing *thousands*, *millions*, and *billions* using an enumeration:

```
enum class S0 { e_K = 1000, e_M = e_K * e_K, e_G = e_M * e_K };  // (BAD IDEA)
```

A client trying to access one of these enumerated values would need to cast it explicitly:

```
void client0()
{
    int distance = 5 * static_cast<int>(S0::e_K);  // casting is error-prone
    // ...
}
```

By instead making the enumeration an explicitly scoped, *classic* **enum** nested within a **struct**, no casting is needed during typical use:

```
struct S1  // scoped
{
    enum Enum { e_K = 1000, e_M = e_K * e_K, e_G = e_M * e_K };
```

```
                      // classic enum (GOOD IDEA)
};

void client1()
{
    int distance = 5 * S1::e_K;  // no casting required during typical use
    // ...
}
```

If the intent is that these constants will be specified and used in a purely local context, we might choose to drop the enclosing scope, along with the name of the enumeration itself:

```
void client2()
{
    enum { e_K = 1000, e_M = e_K * e_K, e_G = e_M * e_K };  // function scoped

    double salary = 95 * e_K;
    double netWorth = 0.62 * e_M;
    double companyRevenue = 47.2 * e_G;
    // ...
}
```

We sometimes use the lowercase prefix k_ instead of e_ to indicate salient **compile-time constants** that are not considered part of an enumerated set, irrespective of whether they are implemented as enumerators:

```
enum { k_NUM_PORTS = 500, k_PAGE_SIZE = 512 };      // compile-time constants
static const double k_PRICING_THRESHOLD = 0.03125; // compile-time constant
```

Misuse of enum class in association with bit flags

Using **enum class** to implement enumerators that are intended to interact closely with arithmetic types will typically require the definition of arithmetic and bitwise operator overloads between values of the same enumeration and between the enumeration and arithmetic types, leading to yet more code that needs to be written, tested, and maintained. This situation often arises for bit flags. Consider, for example, an enumeration used to control a file system:

```
enum class Ctrl { e_READ = 0x1, e_WRITE = 0x2, e_EXEC = 0x4 };  // (BAD IDEA)
    // low-level bit flags used to control file system

void chmodFile(int fd, int access);
    // low-level function used to change privileges on a file
```

We could conceivably write a series of functions to combine the individual flags in a type-safe manner:

```
#include <type_traits>  // std::underlying_type

int flags() { return 0; }
int flags(Ctrl a) { return static_cast<std::underlying_type<Ctrl>::type>(a); }
int flags(Ctrl a, Ctrl b) { return flags(a) | flags(b); }
int flags(Ctrl a, Ctrl b, Ctrl c) { return flags(a, b) | flags(c); }

void setRW(int fd)
{
    chmodFile(fd, flags(Ctrl::e_READ, Ctrl::e_WRITE));  // (BAD IDEA)
}
```

Alternatively, a *classic*, C-style **enum** nested within a **struct** achieves what's needed:

```
struct Ctrl // scoped
{
    enum Enum { e_READ = 0x1, e_WRITE = 0x2, e_EXEC = 0x4 };  // classic enum
        // low-level bit flags used to control file system (GOOD IDEA)
};

void chmodFile(int fd, int access);
    // low-level function used to change privileges on a file

void setRW(int fd)
{
    chmodFile(fd, Ctrl::e_READ | Ctrl::e_WRITE);  // (GOOD IDEA)
}
```

Misuse of enum class in association with iteration

Sometimes the relative values of enumerators are considered important as well. For example, let's again consider enumerating the months of the year grouped by astronomical seasons in the north temperate zone:

```
enum class MonthOfYear  // modern, strongly typed enumeration
{
    e_JAN, e_FEB, e_MAR,  // winter
    e_APR, e_MAY, e_JUN,  // spring
    e_JUL, e_AUG, e_SEP,  // summer
    e_OCT, e_NOV, e_DEC   // autumn
};
```

If all we need to do is compare the ordinal values of the enumerators, there's no problem:

```
bool isSummer(MonthOfYear month)
{
```

```
        return MonthOfYear::e_JUL <= month && month <= MonthOfYear::e_SEP;
    }
```

Although the **enum class** features allow for relational and equality operations between like-typed enumerators, no arithmetic operations are supported directly, which becomes problematic when we need to iterate over the enumerated values:

```
    void doSomethingWithEachMonth()
    {
        for (MonthOfYear i =  MonthOfYear::e_JAN;
                         i <= MonthOfYear::e_DEC;
                    ++i)  // Error, no match for ++
        {
            // ...
        }
    }
```

To make this code compile, an explicit cast from and to the enumerated type will be required:

```
    void doSomethingWithEachMonth()
    {
        for (MonthOfYear i =  MonthOfYear::e_JAN;
                         i <= MonthOfYear::e_DEC;
                         i = static_cast<MonthOfYear>(static_cast<int>(i) + 1))
        {
            // ...
        }
    }
```

Alternatively, an auxiliary, helper function could be supplied to allow clients to bump the enumerator:

```
    MonthOfYear nextMonth(MonthOfYear value)
    {
        return static_cast<MonthOfYear>((static_cast<int>(value) + 1) % 12);
    }

    void doSomethingWithEachMonth()
    {
        for (MonthOfYear i =  MonthOfYear::e_JAN;
                         i <= MonthOfYear::e_DEC;
                         i = nextMonth(i))
        {
            // ...
        }
    }
```

If, however, the cardinal value of the MonthOfYear enumerators is likely to be relevant to clients, an explicitly scoped *classic* **enum** might be considered as a viable alternative:

```
struct MonthOfYear  // explicit scoping for enum
{
    enum Enum
    {
        e_JAN, e_FEB, e_MAR,   // winter
        e_APR, e_MAY, e_JUN,   // spring
        e_JUL, e_AUG, e_SEP,   // summer
        e_OCT, e_NOV, e_DEC    // autumn
    };
};

bool isSummer(MonthOfYear::Enum month)  // must now pass nested Enum type
{
    return MonthOfYear::e_JUL <= month && month <= MonthOfYear::e_SEP;
}

void doSomethingWithEachMonth()
{
    for (int i =  MonthOfYear::e_JAN;  // iteration variable is now an int
             i <= MonthOfYear::e_DEC;
           ++i)  // OK, convert to underlying type
    {
        // ... (might require cast back to enumerated type)
    }
}
```

Note that such code presumes that the enumerated values will (1) remain in the same order and (2) have contiguous numerical values irrespective of the implementation choice.

External use of opaque enumerators

Since scoped enumerations have a UT of **int** by default, clients are always able to (re)declare it, as a **complete type**, without its enumerators. Unless the opaque form of an **enum class**'s definition is exported in a header file separate from the one implementing the publicly accessible full definition, external clients wishing to exploit the opaque version will experience an *attractive nuisance* in that they can provide it locally, along with its **underlying type**, if any.

If the underlying type of the full definition were to subsequently change, any program incorporating the original elided definition locally and also the new, full one from the header would become silently **ill formed, no diagnostic required (IFNDR)**; see Section 2.1. "Opaque **enum**s" on page 660.

Annoyances

Scoped enumerations do not necessarily add value

When the enumeration is local, say, within the scope of a given function, forcing an additional scope on the enumerators is superfluous. For example, consider a function that returns an integer status 0 on success and a nonzero value otherwise:

```cpp
int f()
{
    enum { e_ERROR = -1, e_OK = 0 } result = e_OK;
    // ...
    if (/* error 1 */) { result = e_ERROR; }
    // ...
    if (/* error 2 */) { result = e_ERROR; }
    // ...
    return result;
}
```

Use of **enum class** in this context would require potentially needless qualification — and perhaps even casting — where it might not be warranted:

```cpp
int f()
{
    enum class RC { e_ERROR = -1, e_OK = 0 } result = RC::e_OK;
    // ...
    if (/* error 1 */) { result = RC::e_ERROR; } // undesirable qualification
    // ...
    if (/* error 2 */) { result = RC::e_ERROR; } // undesirable qualification
    // ...
    return static_cast<int>(result);  // undesirable explicit cast
}
```

See Also

- "Opaque **enum**s" (§2.1, p. 660) illustrates how entirely insulating individual enumerators from clients is sometimes useful.

- "Underlying Type '11" (§2.1, p. 829) shows how, absent implicit conversion to integrals, **enum** class values might use **static_cast** in conjunction with their underlying type.

Further Reading

- The original authors of this feature present its motivation and describe its interaction with the standard library along with its impact on classic enumerations in **miller07**.

- Scott Meyers illustrates effective use of strongly typed enumerations in **meyers15b**, "Item 10: Prefer scoped `enums` to unscoped `enums`," pp. 67–74.

Explicit-Instantiation Declarations

The **extern template** prefix can be used to suppress *implicit* generation of local object code for the definitions of particular specializations of class, function, or variable templates used within a translation unit, with the expectation that any suppressed object-code-level definitions will be provided elsewhere within the program by template definitions that are instantiated *explicitly*.

Description

Inherent in the current ecosystem for supporting template programming in C++ is the need to generate redundant definitions of fully specified function and variable templates within .o files. For common instantiations of popular templates, such as std::vector, the increased object-file size, a.k.a. **code bloat**, and potentially extended link times might become significant:

```
#include <vector>        // std::vector is a popular template.
std::vector<int> v;      // std::vector<int> is a common instantiation.

#include <string>        // std::basic_string is a popular template.
std::string s;           // std::string, an alias for std::basic_string<char>, is
                         // a common instantiation.
```

The intent of the **extern template** feature is to *suppress* the implicit generation of duplicative object code within every translation unit in which a fully specialized class template, such as std::vector<int> in the code snippet above, is used. Instead, **extern template** allows developers to choose a single translation unit in which to explicitly *generate* object code for all the definitions pertaining to that specific template specialization as explained next.

Explicit-instantiation definition

Creating an **explicit-instantiation definition** was possible prior to C++11.[1] The requisite syntax is to place the keyword **template** in front of the name of the fully specialized class template, function template, or, in C++14, variable template (see Section 1.2. "Variable Templates" on page 157):

---

[1]The C++03 Standard term for the syntax used to create an explicit-instantiation definition, though rarely used, was **explicit-instantiation directive**. The term explicit-instantiation directive was clarified in C++11 and can now also refer to syntax that is used to create a *declaration* — i.e., **explicit-instantiation declaration**.

```
#include <vector>  // std::vector (general template)

template class std::vector<int>;
    // Deposit all definitions for this specialization into the .o for this
    // translation unit.
```

This explicit-instantiation directive compels the compiler to instantiate *all* functions defined by the named `std::vector` class template having the specified **int** template argument; any collateral object code resulting from these instantiations will be deposited in the resulting `.o` file for the current translation unit. Importantly, even functions that are never used are still instantiated, so this solution might not be the correct one for many classes; see *Potential Pitfalls — Accidentally making matters worse* on page 373.

Explicit-instantiation declaration

C++11 introduced the explicit-instantiation declaration, a complement to the explicit-instantiation definition. The newly provided syntax allows us to place **extern template** in front of the declaration of an explicit specialization of a class template, a function template, or a variable template:

```
#include <vector>  // std::vector (general template)

extern template class std::vector<int>;
    // Suppress depositing of any object code for std::vector<int> into the
    // .o file for this translation unit.
```

Using the modern **extern template** syntax above instructs the compiler to *refrain* from depositing any object code for the named specialization in the current translation unit and instead to rely on some other translation unit to provide any missing object-level definitions that might be needed at link time; see *Annoyances — No good place to put definitions for unrelated classes* on page 373.

Note, however, that declaring an explicit instantiation to be an **extern template** *in no way* affects the ability of the compiler to instantiate and to inline visible function-definition bodies for that template specialization in the translation unit:

```
// client.cpp:
#include <vector>  // std::vector (general template)

extern template class std::vector<int>;

void client(std::vector<int>& inOut)  // fully specialized instance of a vector
{
    if (inOut.size())             // This invocation of size can inline.
    {
        int value = inOut[0];  // This invocation of operator[] can be inlined.
    }
}
```

In the previous example, the two tiny member functions of vector, namely, size and operator[], will typically be inlined — in precisely the same way they would have been had the **extern template** declaration been omitted. The *only* purpose of an **extern template** declaration is to suppress object-code generation for this particular template instantiation for the current translation unit.

Finally, note that the use of explicit-instantiation directives has absolutely no effect on the logical meaning of a well-formed program; in particular, when applied to specializations of function templates, they have no effect on overload resolution:

```
template <typename T> bool f(T v) {/*...*/}  // general template definition

extern template bool f(char c);  // specialization of f for char
extern template bool f(int v);   // specialization of f for int

bool bc = f((char)    0);  // exact match: Object code is suppressed locally.
bool bs = f((short)   0);  // not exact match: Object code is generated locally.
bool bi = f((int)     0);  // exact match: Object code is suppressed locally.
bool bu = f((unsigned)0);  // not exact match: Object code is generated locally.
```

As the example above illustrates, overload resolution and template argument deduction occur independently of any explicit-instantiation declarations. Only *after* the template to be instantiated is determined does the **extern template** syntax take effect; see also *Potential Pitfalls — Corresponding explicit-instantiation declarations and definitions* on page 371.

A more complete illustrative example

So far, we have seen the use of explicit-instantiation declarations and explicit-instantiation definitions applied to only a standard *class* template, std::vector. The same syntax shown in the previous code snippet applies also to full specializations of individual function templates and variable templates.

As a more comprehensive, albeit largely pedagogical, example, consider the overly simplistic my::Vector class template along with other related templates defined within a header file, my_vector.h:

```
// my_vector.h:
#ifndef INCLUDED_MY_VECTOR  // internal include guard
#define INCLUDED_MY_VECTOR

#include <cstddef>  // std::size_t
#include <utility>  // std::swap

namespace my  // namespace for all entities defined within this component
{

template <typename T>
class Vector
```

```
{
    static std::size_t s_count;        // track number of objects constructed
    T*               d_data_p;         // pointer to dynamically allocated memory
    std::size_t      d_length;         // current number of elements in the vector
    std::size_t      d_capacity;       // number of elements currently allocated

public:
    // ...

    std::size_t length() const { return d_length; }
        // Return the number of elements.

    // ...
};

// ...           Any partial or full specialization definitions
// ...           of the class template Vector go here.

template <typename T>
void swap(Vector<T> &lhs, Vector<T> &rhs) { return std::swap(lhs, rhs); }
        // free function that operates on objects of type my::Vector via ADL

// ...           Any [full] specialization definitions
// ...           of free function swap would go here.

template <typename T>
const std::size_t vectorSize = sizeof(Vector<T>);  // C++14 variable template
        // This nonmodifiable static variable holds the size of a my::Vector<T>.

// ...           Any [full] specialization definitions
// ...           of variable vectorSize would go here.

template <typename T>
std::size_t Vector<T>::s_count = 0;
        // definition of static counter in general template

// ... We might opt to add explicit-instantiation declarations here.
// ...

}  // Close my namespace.

#endif  // Close internal include guard.
```

In the `my_vector` component in the code snippet above, we have defined the following, in the my namespace.

1. A **class** template, Vector, parameterized on element type

2. A free-function template, swap, that operates on objects of corresponding specialized Vector type

3. A **const** C++14 variable template, vectorSize, that represents the number of bytes in the **footprint** of an object of the corresponding specialized Vector type

Any use of these templates by a client might and typically will trigger the depositing of equivalent definitions as object code in the client translation unit's resulting .o file, irrespective of whether the definition being used winds up getting inlined.

To eliminate object code for specializations of entities in the my_vector component, we must first decide where the unique definitions will go; see *Annoyances — No good place to put definitions for unrelated classes* on page 373. In this specific case, we own the component that requires specialization, and the specialization is for a ubiquitous built-in type; hence, the natural place to generate the specialized definitions is in a .cpp file corresponding to the component's header:

```cpp
// my_vector.cpp:
#include <my_vector.h>  // We always include the component's own header first.
    // By including this header file, we have introduced the general template
    // definitions for each of the explicit-instantiation declarations below.

namespace my  // namespace for all entities defined within this component
{

template class Vector<int>;
    // Generate object code for all nontemplate member functions and definitions
    // of static data members of template my::Vector having int elements.

template std::size_t Vector<double>::length() const;  // BAD IDEA
    // In addition, we could generate object code for just a particular member
    // function definition of my::Vector (e.g., length) for some other
    // argument type (e.g., double).

template void swap(Vector<int>& lhs, Vector<int>& rhs);
    // Generate object code for the full specialization of the swap free-
    // function template that operates on objects of type my::Vector<int>.

template const std::size_t vectorSize<int>;  // C++14 variable template
    // Generate the object-code-level definition for the specialization of the
    // C++14 variable template instantiated for built-in type int.

template std::size_t Vector<int>::s_count;
    // Generate the object-code-level definition for the specialization of the
    // static member variable of Vector instantiated for built-in type int.

}  // Close my namespace.
```

Each of the constructs introduced by the keyword **template** within the my namespace in the previous example represents a separate **explicit-instantiation definition**. These constructs instruct the compiler to generate object-level definitions for general templates declared in my_vector.h specialized on the built-in type **int**. Explicit instantiation of individual member functions, such as length() in the example, is, however, only rarely useful; see *Annoyances — All members of an explicitly defined template class must be valid* on page 374.

Having installed the necessary **explicit-instantiation definitions** in the component's my_vector.cpp file, we must now go back to its my_vector.h file and, without altering any of the previously existing lines of code, *add* the corresponding **explicit-instantiation declarations** to suppress redundant local code generation:

```
// my_vector.h:
#ifndef INCLUDED_MY_VECTOR  // internal include guard
#define INCLUDED_MY_VECTOR

namespace my  // namespace for all entities defined within this component
{

// ...
// ...  everything that was in the original my namespace
// ...


                    // ------------------------------------
                    // explicit-instantiation declarations
                    // ------------------------------------

extern template class Vector<int>;
    // Suppress object code for this class template specialized for int.

extern template std::size_t Vector<double>::length() const;  // BAD IDEA
    // Suppress object code for this member, only specialized for double.

extern template void swap(Vector<int>& lhs, Vector<int>& rhs);
    // Suppress object code for this free function specialized for int.

extern template std::size_t vectorSize<int>;  // C++14
    // Suppress object code for this variable template specialized for int.

extern template std::size_t Vector<int>::s_count;
    // Suppress object code for this static member definition w.r.t. int.

}  // Close my namespace.

#endif  // Close internal include guard.
```

Each of the constructs that begins with **extern template** in the example above are **explicit-instantiation declarations**, which serve only to suppress the generation of any object code emitted to the .o file of the current translation unit in which such specializations are used. These added **extern template** declarations must appear in my_header.h *after* the declaration of the corresponding general template and, importantly, before whatever relevant definitions are ever used.

The effect on various .o files

To illustrate the effect of explicit-instantiation declarations and explicit-instantiation definitions on the contents of object and executable files, we'll use a simple lib_interval library **component** consisting of a header file, lib_interval.h, and an implementation file, lib_interval.cpp. The latter, apart from including its corresponding header, is effectively empty:

```
// lib_interval.h:
#ifndef INCLUDED_LIB_INTERVAL  // internal include guard
#define INCLUDED_LIB_INTERVAL

namespace lib  // namespace for all entities defined within this component
{

template <typename T>  // elided definition of a class template
class Interval
{
    T d_low;   // interval's low value
    T d_high;  // interval's high value

public:
    explicit Interval(const T& p) : d_low(p), d_high(p) { }
        // Construct an empty interval.

    Interval(const T& low, const T& high) : d_low(low), d_high(high) { }
        // Construct an interval having the specified boundary values.

    const T& low() const { return d_low; }
        // Return this interval's low value.

    const T& high() const { return d_high; }
        // Return this interval's high value.

    int length() const { return d_high - d_low; }
        // Return this interval's length.

    // ...
};

template <typename T>  // elided definition of a function template
bool intersect(const Interval<T>& i1, const Interval<T>& i2)
    // Determine whether the specified intervals intersect.
```

```
{
    bool result = false;  // nonintersecting until proven otherwise
    // ...
    return result;
}

} // Close lib namespace.

#endif  // INCLUDED_LIB_INTERVAL


// lib_interval.cpp:
#include <lib_interval.h>
```

This library component above defines, in the namespace `lib`, an implementation of (1) a class template, `Interval`, and (2) a function template, `intersect`.

Let's also consider a trivial application that uses this library component:

```
// app.cpp:
#include <lib_interval.h>  // Include the library component's header file.

int main(int argv, const char** argc)
{
    lib::Interval<double> a(0, 5);  // instantiate with double type argument
    lib::Interval<double> b(3, 8);  // instantiate with double type argument
    lib::Interval<int>    c(4, 9);  // instantiate with int    type argument

    if (lib::intersect(a, b))  // instantiate deducing double type argument
    {
        return 0;  // Return "success" as (0.0, 5.0) does intersect (3.0, 8.0).
    }

    return 1;  // Return "failure" status as function apparently doesn't work.
}
```

The purpose of this application is merely to exhibit a couple of instantiations of the library *class* template, `lib::Interval`, for type arguments **int** and **double**, and of the library *function* template, `lib::intersect`, for just **double**.

Next, we compile the application and library translation units, **app.cpp** and **lib_interval.cpp**, and inspect the symbols in their respective corresponding object files, **app.o** and **lib_interval.o**:

```
$ gcc -I. -c app.cpp lib_interval.cpp
$ nm -C app.o lib_interval.o

app.o:
0000000000000000 W lib::Interval<double>::Interval(double const&, double const&)
```

```
0000000000000000 W lib::Interval<int>::Interval(int const&, int const&)
0000000000000000 W bool lib::intersect<double>(lib::Interval<double> const&,
                                                lib::Interval<double> const&)
0000000000000000 T main

lib_interval.o:
```

Looking at `app.o` in the previous example, the class and function templates used in the `main` function, which is defined in the `app.cpp` file, were instantiated *implicitly*, and the relevant code was added to the resulting object file, `app.o`, with each instantiated function definition in its own separate **section**. In the `Interval` *class* template, the generated symbols correspond to the two unique instantiations of the constructor, i.e., for **double** and **int**, respectively. The `intersect` function template, however, was implicitly instantiated for only type **double**. Note that all of the implicitly instantiated functions have the W symbol type, indicating that they are *weak* symbols, which are permitted to be present in multiple object files. By contrast, this file also defines the *strong* symbol `main`, marked here by a T. Linking `app.o` with any other object file containing such a symbol would cause the linker to report a multiply-defined-symbol error. On the other hand, the `lib_interval.o` file corresponds to the `lib_interval` library component, whose `.cpp` file served only to include its own `.h` file, and is again effectively empty.

Let's now link the two object files, `app.o` and `lib_interval.o`, and inspect the symbols in the resulting executable, `app`[2]:

```
$ gcc -o app app.o lib_interval.o
$ nm -C app
000000000040056e W lib::Interval<double>::Interval(double const&, double const&)
00000000004005a2 W lib::Interval<int>::Interval(int const&, int const&)
00000000004005ce W bool lib::intersect<double>(lib::Interval<double> const&,
                                                lib::Interval<double> const&)
00000000004004b7 T main
```

As the textual output above confirms, the final program contains exactly one copy of each weak symbol. In this tiny illustrative example, these weak symbols have been defined in only a single object file, thus not requiring the linker to select one definition out of many.

More generally, if the application comprises multiple object files, each file will potentially contain their own set of weak symbols, often leading to duplicate code **sections** for implicitly instantiated class, function, and variable templates instantiated on the same type arguments. When the linker combines object files, it will arbitrarily choose at most one of each of these respective and ideally identical weak-symbol **sections** to include in the final executable.

Imagine now that our program includes a large number of object files, many of which make use of our `lib_interval` component, particularly to operate on **double** intervals.

---

[2]We have stripped out extraneous unrelated information that the `nm` tool produces; note that the `-C` option invokes the symbol demangler, which turns encoded names like `_ZN3lib8IntervalIdEC1ERKdS3_` into something more readable like `lib::Interval<`**double**`>::Interval(`**double const&**`, `**double const&**`)`.

Suppose, for now, we decide we would like to suppress the generation of object code for templates related to just **double** type with the intent of later putting them all in one place, i.e., the currently empty `lib_interval.o`. Achieving this objective is precisely what the **extern template** syntax is designed to accomplish.

Returning to our `lib_interval.h` file, we need not change one line of code; we need only to *add* two explicit-instantiation declarations — one for the *class* template, `Interval<`**double**`>`, and one for the *function* template, `intersect<`**double**`>(`**const double**`&,` **const double**`&)` — to the header file anywhere *after* their respective corresponding general template declaration and definition:

```
// lib_interval.h:  // No change to existing code.
#ifndef INCLUDED_LIB_INTERVAL  // internal include guard
#define INCLUDED_LIB_INTERVAL

namespace lib  // namespace for all entities defined within this component
{

template <typename T>
class Interval
{
    // ...  (same as before)
};

template <typename T>
bool intersect(const Interval<T>& i1, const Interval<T>& i2)
{
    // ...  (same as before)
}

extern template class Interval<double>;  // explicit-instantiation declaration

extern template                 // explicit-instantiation declaration
bool intersect(const Interval<double>&, const Interval<double>&);

}  // close lib namespace

#endif  // INCLUDED_LIB_INTERVAL
```

Let's again compile the two `.cpp` files and inspect the corresponding `.o` files:

```
$ gcc -I. -c app.cpp lib_interval.cpp
$ nm -C app.o lib_interval.o

app.o:
                U lib::Interval<double>::Interval(double const&, double const&)
```

```
0000000000000000 W lib::Interval<int>::Interval(int const&, int const&)
                 U bool lib::intersect<double>(lib::Interval<double> const&,
                                               lib::Interval<double> const&)
0000000000000000 T main

lib_interval.o:
```

Notice that this time some of the symbols, specifically those relating to the class and function templates instantiated for type **double**, have changed from W, indicating a *weak* symbol, to U, indicating an *undefined* one. This symbol type change means that instead of generating a weak symbol for the explicit specializations for **double**, the compiler left those symbols undefined, as if only the *declarations* of the member and free-function templates had been available when compiling **app.cpp**, yet inlining of the instantiated definitions is in no way affected. **Undefined symbols** are expected to be made available to the linker from other object files. Attempting to link this application expectedly fails because no object files being linked contain the needed definitions for those instantiations:

```
$ gcc -o app app.o lib_interval.o

app.o: In function 'main':
app.cpp:(.text+0x38): undefined reference to
  `lib::Interval<double>::Interval(double const&, double const&)'
app.cpp:(.text+0x69): undefined reference to
  `lib::Interval<double>::Interval(double const&, double const&)'
app.cpp:(.text+0xa1): undefined reference to
  `bool lib::intersect<double>(lib::Interval<double> const&,
                               lib::Interval<double> const&)'

collect2: error: ld returned 1 exit status
```

To provide the missing definitions, we will need to instantiate them explicitly. Since the type for which the class and function are being specialized is the ubiquitous built-in type, **double**, the ideal place to sequester those definitions would be within the object file of the **lib_interval** library component itself, but see *Annoyances — No good place to put definitions for unrelated classes* on page 373. To force the needed template definitions into the **lib_interval.o** file, we will need to use **explicit-instantiation definition** syntax, i.e., the **template** prefix:

```
// lib_interval.cpp:
#include <lib_interval.h>

template class lib::Interval<double>;
    // example of an explicit-instantiation definition for a class

template bool lib::intersect(const Interval<double>&, const Interval<double>&);
    // example of an explicit-instantiation definition for a function
```

We recompile once again and inspect our newly generated object files:

```
$ gcc -I. -c app.cpp lib_interval.cpp
$ nm -C app.o lib_interval.o

app.o:
                 U lib::Interval<double>::Interval(double const&, double const&)
0000000000000000 W lib::Interval<int>::Interval(int const&, int const&)
                 U bool lib::intersect<double>(lib::Interval<double> const&,
                                               lib::Interval<double> const&)
0000000000000000 T main

lib_interval.o:
0000000000000000 W lib::Interval<double>::Interval(double const&)
0000000000000000 W lib::Interval<double>::Interval(double const&, double const&)
0000000000000000 W lib::Interval<double>::low() const
0000000000000000 W lib::Interval<double>::high() const
0000000000000000 W lib::Interval<double>::length() const
0000000000000000 W bool lib::intersect<double>(lib::Interval<double> const&,
                                               lib::Interval<double> const&)
```

The application object file, `app.o`, naturally remained unchanged. What's new here is that the functions that were missing from the `app.o` file are now available in the `lib_interval.o` file, again as *weak* (W), as opposed to strong (T), symbols. Notice, however, that explicit instantiation forces the compiler to generate code for all of the member functions of the class template for a given specialization. These symbols might all be linked into the resulting executable unless we take explicit precautions to exclude those that aren't needed[3]:

```
$ gcc -o app app.o lib_interval.o -Wl,--gc-sections
$ nm -C app
00000000004005ca W lib::Interval<double>::Interval(double const&, double const&)
000000000040056e W lib::Interval<int>::Interval(int const&, int const&)
000000000040063d W bool lib::intersect<double>(lib::Interval<double> const&,
                                               lib::Interval<double> const&)
00000000004004b7 T main
```

The **extern template** feature is provided to enable software architects to reduce code bloat in individual object files for common instantiations of class, function, and, as of C++14, variable templates in large-scale C++ software systems. The practical benefit is in reducing the physical size of libraries, which *might* lead to improved link times. Explicit-instantiation declarations do *not* (1) affect the meaning of a program, (2) suppress inline template implicit instantiation, (3) impede the compiler's ability to **inline**, or (4) meaningfully improve

---

[3]To avoid including the explicitly generated definitions that are being used to resolve undefined symbols, we have instructed the linker to remove all unused code sections from the executable. The -Wl option passes comma-separated options to the linker. The --gc-sections option instructs the compiler to compile and assemble and instructs the linker to omit individual unused sections, where each section contains, for example, its own instantiation of a function template.

compile time. To be clear, the *only* purpose of the **extern template** syntax is to suppress object-code generation for the current translation unit, which is then selectively overridden in the translation unit(s) of choice.

Use Cases

Reducing template code bloat in object files

The motivation for the **extern template** syntax is as a purely compile-time, not runtime, optimization, i.e., to reduce the amount of redundant code within individual object files resulting from common template instantiations in client code. As an example, consider a fixed-size-array class template, FixedArray, that is used widely, i.e., by many clients from separate translation units, in a large-scale **game** project for both integral and floating-point calculations, primarily with type arguments **int** and **double** and array sizes of either 2 or 3:

```cpp
// game_fixedarray.h:
#ifndef INCLUDED_GAME_FIXEDARRAY  // internal include guard
#define INCLUDED_GAME_FIXEDARRAY

#include <cstddef>  // std::size_t

namespace game  // namespace for all entities defined within this component
{

template <typename T, std::size_t N>  // widely used class template
class FixedArray
{
    // ... (elided private implementation details)
public:
    FixedArray()                                     { /*...*/ }
    FixedArray(const FixedArray<T, N>& other)        { /*...*/ }
    T& operator[](std::size_t index)                 { /*...*/ }
    const T& operator[](std::size_t index) const     { /*...*/ }
};

template <typename T, std::size_t N>
T dot(const FixedArray<T, N>& a, const FixedArray<T, N>& b) { /*...*/ }
    // Return the scalar ("dot") product of the specified 'a' and 'b'.

// Explicit-instantiation declarations for full template specializations
// commonly used by the game project are provided below.

extern template class FixedArray<int, 2>;               // class template
extern template int dot(const FixedArray<int, 2>& a,    // function template
                        const FixedArray<int, 2>& b);   // for int and 2
```

```
extern template class FixedArray<int, 3>;              // class template
extern template int dot(const FixedArray<int, 3>& a,   // function template
                  const FixedArray<int, 3>& b);        // for int and 3

extern template class FixedArray<double, 2>;           // for double and 2
extern template double dot(const FixedArray<double, 2>& a,
                  const FixedArray<double, 2>& b);

extern template class FixedArray<double, 3>;           // for double and 3
extern template double dot(const FixedArray<double, 3>& a,
                  const FixedArray<double, 3>& b);

} // Close game namespace.

#endif  // INCLUDED_GAME_FIXEDARRAY
```

Specializations commonly used by the **game** project are provided by the **game** library. In the component header in the example above, we have used the **extern template** syntax to suppress object-code generation for instantiations of both the class template FixedArray and the function template dot for element types **int** and **double**, each for array sizes 2 and 3. To ensure that these specialized definitions are available in every program that might need them, we use the **template** syntax counterpart to *force* object-code generation within just the one .o corresponding to the game_fixedarray library component[4]:

```
// game_fixedarray.cpp:
#include <game_fixedarray.h>  // included as first substantive line of code

// Explicit-instantiation definitions for full template specializations
// commonly used by the game project are provided below.

template class game::FixedArray<int, 2>;               // class template
template int game::dot(const FixedArray<int, 2>& a,    // function template
                  const FixedArray<int, 2>& b);        // for int and 2

template class game::FixedArray<int, 3>;               // class template
template int game::dot(const FixedArray<int, 3>& a,    // function template
                  const FixedArray<int, 3>& b);        // for int and 3

template class game::FixedArray<double, 2>;            // for double and 2
template double game::dot(const FixedArray<double, 2>& a,
                  const FixedArray<double, 2>& b);
```

---

[4]Notice that we have chosen *not* to nest the explicit specializations — or any other definitions — of entities already declared directly within the game namespace, preferring instead to qualify each entity explicitly to be consistent with how we render free-function definitions to avoid self-declaration; see **lakos20**, section 2.5, "Component Source-Code Organization," pp. 333–342, specifically Figure 2-36b, p. 340. See also *Potential Pitfalls — Corresponding explicit-instantiation declarations and definitions* on page 371.

```
template class game::FixedArray<double, 3>;              // for double and 3
template double game::dot(const FixedArray<double, 3>& a,
                         const FixedArray<double, 3>& b);
```

Compiling `game_fixedarray.cpp` and examining the resulting object file shows that the code for all explicitly instantiated classes and free functions was generated and placed into the object file, `game_fixedarray.o`, of which we show a subset of the relevant symbols:

```
$ gcc -I. -c game_fixedarray.cpp
$ nm -C game_fixedarray.o
0000000000000000 W game::FixedArray<double, 2ul>::FixedArray(
  game::FixedArray<double, 2ul> const&)
0000000000000000 W game::FixedArray<double, 2ul>::FixedArray()
0000000000000000 W game::FixedArray<double, 2ul>::operator[](unsigned long)
0000000000000000 W game::FixedArray<double, 3ul>::FixedArray(
  game::FixedArray<double, 3ul> const&)
0000000000000000 W game::FixedArray<int, 3ul>::FixedArray()
                              :
0000000000000000 W double game::dot<double, 2ul>(
  game::FixedArray<double, 2ul> const&, game::FixedArray<double, 2ul> const&)
0000000000000000 W double game::dot<double, 3ul>(
  game::FixedArray<double, 3ul> const&, game::FixedArray<double, 3ul> const&)
0000000000000000 W int game::dot<int, 2ul>(
  game::FixedArray<int, 2ul> const&, game::FixedArray<int, 2ul> const&)
                              :
0000000000000000 W game::FixedArray<int, 2ul>::operator[](unsigned long) const
0000000000000000 W game::FixedArray<int, 3ul>::operator[](unsigned long) const
```

This `FixedArray` class template is used in multiple translation units within the `game` project. The first one contains a set of geometry utilities:

```
// app_geometryutil.cpp:

#include <game_fixedarray.h>  // game::FixedArray
#include <game_unit.h>        // game::Unit

using namespace game;

void translate(Unit* object, const FixedArray<double, 2>& dst)
    // Perform precise movement of the object on 2D plane.
{
    FixedArray<double, 2> objectProjection;
    // ...
}

void translate(Unit* object, const FixedArray<double, 3>& dst)
    // Perform precise movement of the object in 3D space.
```

```
{
    FixedArray<double, 3> delta;
    // ...
}

bool isOrthogonal(const FixedArray<int, 2>& a1, const FixedArray<int, 2>& a2)
    // Return true if 2d arrays are orthogonal.
{
    return dot(a1, a2) == 0;
}

bool isOrthogonal(const FixedArray<int, 3>& a1, const FixedArray<int, 3>& a2)
    // Return true if 3d arrays are orthogonal.
{
    return dot(a1, a2) == 0;
}
```

The second one deals with physics calculations:

```
// app_physics.cpp:

#include <game_fixedarray.h>  // game::FixedArray
#include <game_unit.h>        // game::Unit

using namespace game;

void collide(Unit* objectA, Unit* objectB)
    // Calculate the result of object collision in 3D space.
{
    FixedArray<double, 3> centerOfMassA = objectA->centerOfMass();
    FixedArray<double, 3> centerOfMassB = objectB->centerOfMass();
    // ..
}

void accelerate(Unit* object, const FixedArray<double, 3>& force)
    // Calculate the position after applying a specified force for the
    // duration of a game tick.
{
    // ...
}
```

Note that the object files for the application components throughout the game project do not contain any of the implicitly instantiated definitions that we had chosen to uniquely sequester externally, i.e., within the game_fixedarray.o file:

```
$ nm -C app_geometryutil.o
000000000000003e T isOrthogonal(game::FixedArray<int, 2ul> const&,
  game::FixedArray<int, 2ul> const&)
```

```
0000000000000068 T isOrthogonal(game::FixedArray<int, 3ul> const&,
  game::FixedArray<int, 3ul> const&)
0000000000000000 T translate(game::Unit*, game::FixedArray<double, 2ul> const&)
000000000000001f T translate(game::Unit*, game::FixedArray<double, 3ul> const&)
                 U game::FixedArray<double, 2ul>::FixedArray()
                 U game::FixedArray<double, 3ul>::FixedArray()
                 U int game::dot<int, 2ul>(game::FixedArray<int, 2ul> const&,
  game::FixedArray<int, 2ul> const&)
                 U int game::dot<int, 3ul>(game::FixedArray<int, 3ul> const&,
  game::FixedArray<int, 3ul> const&)

$ nm -C app_physics.o
0000000000000039 T accelerate(game::Unit*,
  game::FixedArray<double, 3ul> const&)
0000000000000000 T collide(game::Unit*, game::Unit*)
                 U game::FixedArray<double, 3ul>::FixedArray()
0000000000000000 W game::Unit::centerOfMass()
```

Whether optimization involving **explicit-instantiation directives** reduces library sizes on disk has no noticeable effect or actually makes matters worse will depend on the particulars of the system at hand. Having this optimization applied to frequently used templates across a large organization has been known to decrease object file sizes, storage needs, link times, and overall build times, but see *Potential Pitfalls — Accidentally making matters worse* on page 373.

Insulating template definitions from clients

Even before the introduction of **explicit-instantiation declarations**, strategic use of **explicit-instantiation definitions** made it possible to **insulate** the *definition* of a template from client code, presenting instead just a limited set of instantiations against which clients may link. Such insulation enables the definition of the template to change without forcing clients to recompile. What's more, new explicit instantiations can be added without affecting existing clients.

As an example, suppose we have a single free-function template, transform, that operates on only floating-point values:

```
// transform.h:
#ifndef INCLUDED_TRANSFORM
#define INCLUDED_TRANSFORM

template <typename T>  // declaration only of free-function template
T transform(const T& value);
    // Return the transform of the specified floating-point value.

#endif
```

Initially, this function template will support just two built-in types, **float** and **double**, but it is anticipated to eventually support the additional built-in type **long double** and perhaps even supplementary user-defined types (e.g., Float128) to be made available via separate headers (e.g., float128.h). By placing only the declaration of the transform function template in its component's header, clients will be able to link against only two supported explicit specializations provided in the transform.cpp file:

```cpp
// transform.cpp:
#include <transform.h>  // Ensure consistency with client-facing declaration.

template <typename T>   // redeclaration/definition of free-function template
T transform(const T& value)
{
    // insulated implementation of transform function template
}

// explicit-instantiation definitions
template float transform(const float&);    // Instantiate for type float.
template double transform(const double&);  // Instantiate for type double.
```

Without the two explicit-instantiation declarations in the transform.cpp file above, its corresponding object file, transform.o, would be empty.

Note that, as of C++11, we *could* place the corresponding explicit-instantiation declarations in the header file for, say, documentation purposes:

```cpp
// transform.h:
#ifndef INCLUDED_TRANSFORM
#define INCLUDED_TRANSFORM

template <typename T>  // declaration only of free-function template
T transform(const T& value);
    // Return the transform of the specified floating-point value.

// explicit-instantiation declarations, available as of C++11
extern template float transform(const float&);    // user documentation only;
extern template double transform(const double&);  // has no effect whatsoever

#endif
```

Because no definition of the transform free-function template is visible in the header, no *implicit* instantiation can result from client use; hence, the two explicit-instantiation declarations above for **float** and **double**, respectively, do nothing.

Potential Pitfalls

Corresponding explicit-instantiation declarations and definitions

To realize a reduction in object-code size for individual translation units and yet still be able to link all valid programs successfully into a well-formed program, four moving parts have to be brought together correctly.

1. Each general template, C<T>, whose object code bloat is to be optimized must be declared within some designated component's header file, c.h.

2. The specific definition of each C<T> relevant to an explicit specialization being optimized — including general, partial-specialization, and full-specialization definitions — must appear in the header file prior to its corresponding **explicit-instantiation declaration**.

3. Each **explicit-instantiation declaration** for each specialization of each separate top-level — i.e., class, function, or variable — template must appear in the component's .h file *after* the corresponding general template declaration and the relevant general, partial-specialization, or full-specialization definition, but, in practice, always after *all* such definitions, not just the relevant one.

4. Each template specialization having an **explicit-instantiation declaration** in the header file must have a corresponding **explicit-instantiation definition** in the component's implementation file, c.cpp.

Absent items (1) and (2), clients would have no way to safely separate out the usability and inlineability of the template definitions yet consolidate the otherwise redundantly generated object-level definitions within just a single translation unit. Moreover, failing to provide the relevant definition would mean that any clients using one of these specializations would either fail to compile or, arguably worse, pick up the general definitions when a more specialized definition was intended, likely resulting in an ill-formed program.

Failing item (3), the object code for that particular specialization of that template will be generated locally in the client's translation unit as usual, negating any benefits with respect to local object-code size, irrespective of what is specified in the c.cpp file.

Finally, unless we provide a matching **explicit-instantiation definition** in the c.cpp file for each and every corresponding **explicit-instantiation declaration** in the c.h file as in item (4), our optimization attempts might well result in a library component that compiles, links, and even passes some unit tests but, when released to our clients, fails to link. Additionally, any **explicit-instantiation definition** in the c.cpp file that is not accompanied by a corresponding explicit-instantiation declaration in the `c.h` file will inflate the size of the `c.o` file with no possibility of reducing code bloat in client code:

```
// c.h:
#ifndef INCLUDED_C                              // internal include guard
#define INCLUDED_C

template <typename T> void f(T v) {/*...*/}  // general template definition

extern template void f<int>(int v);           // OK, matched in c.cpp
extern template void f<char>(char c);         // Error, unmatched in .cpp file

#endif


// c.cpp:
#include <c.h>                                 // incorporate own header first

template void f<int>(int v);                   // OK, matched in c.h
template void f<double>(double v);             // Bug, unmatched in c.h file


// client.cpp:
#include <c.h>

void client()
{
    int    i = 1;
    char   c = 'a';
    double d = 2.0;

    f(i);  // OK, matching explicit-instantiation directives
    f(c);  // Link-Time Error, no matching explicit-instantiation definition
    f(d);  // Bug, size increased due to no matching explicit-instantiation
           // declaration.
}
```

In the example above, `f(i)` works as expected, with the linker finding the definition of `f<int>` in `c.o`; `f(c)` fails to link because no definition of `f<char>` is guaranteed to be found anywhere; and `f(d)` accidentally works by silently generating a *redundant* local copy of `f<double>` in `client.o`, while another, identical definition is generated explicitly in `c.o`. These extra instantiations do not result in multiply-defined symbols because they still reside in their own **sections** and are marked as *weak* symbols. Importantly, note that **extern template** has *absolutely no effect* on overload resolution because the call to `f(c)` did *not* resolve to `f<int>`.

Accidentally making matters worse

When making the decision to explicitly instantiate common specializations of popular templates within some designated object file, it is important to consider that not all programs necessarily need every (or even any) such instantiation. Classes that have many member functions but typically use only a few require special attention.

For such classes, it might be beneficial to explicitly instantiate individual member functions instead of the entire class template. However, selecting *which* member functions to explicitly instantiate and with *which* template arguments they should be instantiated without carefully measuring the effect on the overall object size might result in not only overall pessimization, but also to an unnecessary maintenance burden. Finally, remember that one might need to explicitly tell the linker to strip unused sections resulting, for example, from forced instantiation of common template specializations, to avoid inadvertently bloating executables, which could adversely affect load times.

Annoyances

No good place to put definitions for unrelated classes

When we consider the implications of physical dependency,[5,6] determining in which component to deposit the specialized definitions can be problematic. For example, consider a codebase implementing a core library that provides both a nontemplated `String` class and a `Vector` container class template. These fundamentally unrelated entities would ideally live in separate physical **components** (i.e., .h/.cpp pairs), neither of which depends physically on the other. That is, an application using just one of these components could be compiled, linked, tested, and deployed entirely independently of the other. Now, consider a large codebase that makes heavy use of `Vector<String>`: In what component should the object-code-level definitions for the `Vector<String>` specialization reside?[7] There are two obvious alternatives.

1. vector — In this case, `vector.h` would hold **extern template class** Vector<String>; — the explicit-instantiation declaration. `vector.cpp` would hold **template class** Vector<String>; — the explicit-instantiation definition. With this approach, we would create a physical dependency of the `vector` component on `string`. Any client program wanting to use a `Vector` would also depend on `string` regardless of whether it was needed.

---

[5]See **lakos96**.

[6]See **lakos20**.

[7]Note that the problem of determining in which component to instantiate the object-level implementation of a template for a user-defined type is similar to that of specializing an arbitrary user-defined trait for a user-defined type.

2. `string` — In this case, `string.h` and `string.cpp` would instead be modified so as to depend on `vector`. Clients wanting to use a `string` would also be forced to depend physically on `vector` *at compile time*.

Another possibility might be to create a third component, called `stringvector`, that itself depends on both `vector` and `string`. By **escalating**[8] the mutual dependency to a higher level in the physical hierarchy, we avoid forcing any client to depend on more than what is actually needed. The practical drawback to this approach is that only those clients that proactively include the composite `stringvector.h` header would realize any benefit; fortunately, in this case, there is no **one-definition rule (ODR)** violation if they don't.

Finally, complex machinery could be added to both `string.h` and `vector.h` to conditionally include `stringvector.h` whenever both of the other headers are included; such heroic efforts would, nonetheless, involve a **cyclic physical dependency** among all three of these components. Circular intercomponent collaborations are best avoided.[9]

All members of an explicitly defined template class must be valid

In general, when using a class template, only those members that are actually used get implicitly instantiated. This hallmark allows class templates to provide functionality for parameter types having certain capabilities, e.g., default constructible, while also providing partial support for types lacking those same capabilities. When providing an **explicit-instantiation definition**, however, *all* members of a class template are instantiated.

Consider a simple class template having a data member that can be either default-initialized via the template's default constructor or initialized with an instance of the member's type supplied at construction:

```
template <typename T>
class W
{
    T d_t;  // a data member of type T

public:
    W() : d_t() {}
        // Create an instance of W with a default-constructed T member.

    W(const T& t) : d_t(t) {}
        // Create an instance of W with a copy of the specified t.

    void doStuff() { /* do stuff */ }
};
```

This class template can be used successfully with a type, such as `U` in the following code snippet, that is not default constructible:

---

[8]**lakos20**, section 3.5.2, "Escalation," pp. 604–614
[9]**lakos20**, section 3.4, "Avoiding Cyclic Link-Time Dependencies," pp. 592–601

```
struct U
{
    U(int i) { /* construct from i */ }
    // ...
};

void useWU()
{
    W<U> wu1(U(17));   // OK, using copy constructor for U
    wu1.doStuff();
}
```

As it stands, the code above is well formed even though W<U>::W() would fail to compile if instantiated. Consequently, although providing an explicit-instantiation declaration for W<U> is valid, a corresponding explicit-instantiation definition for W<U> fails to compile, as would an implicit instantiation of W<U>::W():

```
extern template class W<U>;   // Valid: Suppress implicit instantiation of W<U>.

template class W<U>;          // Error, U::U() not available for W<U>::W()

void useWU0()
{
    W<U> wu0;        // Error, U::U() not available for W<U>::W()
}
```

Unfortunately, the only workaround to achieve a comparable reduction in code bloat is to provide explicit-instantiation directives for each valid member function of W<U>, an approach that would likely carry a significantly greater maintenance burden:

```
extern template W<U>::W(const U& u);    // suppress individual member
extern template void W<U>::doStuff();   //      "           "           "
// ... Repeat for all other functions in W except W<U>::W().

template W<U>::W(const U& u);            // instantiate individual member
template void W<U>::doStuff();           //      "           "           "
// ... Repeat for all other functions in W except W<U>::W().
```

The power and flexibility to make it all work — albeit annoyingly — are there nonetheless.

See Also

- "Variable Templates" (§1.2, p. 157) covers an extension of the template syntax for defining a family of like-named variables or static data members that can be instantiated explicitly.

Further Reading

- For a different perspective on this feature, see **lakos20**, section 1.3.16, "extern Templates," pp. 183–185.

- For a more complete discussion of how compilers and linkers work with respect to C++, see **lakos20**, Chapter 1, "Compilers, Linkers, and Components," pp. 123–268.

Forwarding References (T&&)

A forwarding reference (T&&) — distinguishable from an *rvalue* reference (&&) (see Section 2.1."*Rvalue* References" on page 710) based only on context — is a distinct, special kind of reference that (1) binds universally to the result of an expression of *any* **value category** and (2) preserves aspects of that **value category** so that the bound object can be *moved from*, if appropriate.

Description

Sometimes we want the same reference to bind to either an *lvalue* or an *rvalue* and then later be able to discern, from the reference itself, whether the result of the original expression was eligible to be *moved from*. A *forwarding reference*, e.g., forRef in the example below, used in the interface of a function *template*, e.g., myFunc below, affords precisely this capability and will prove invaluable for the purpose of conditionally moving, or else copying, an object from within the function template's body:

```
template <typename T>
void myFunc(T&& forRef)
{
    // It is possible to check if forRef is eligible to be moved from or not
    // from within the body of myFunc.
}
```

In the definition of the myFunc function template in the example above, the parameter forRef appears syntactically to be a non**const** reference to an *rvalue* of type T; in this precise context, however, the same T&& syntax designates a **forwarding reference**, with the effect of retaining the original value category of the object bound to forRef; see *Identifying forwarding references* on page 382. The T&& syntax represents a *forwarding* reference, as opposed to an *rvalue* reference, when an *individual* function template has a type parameter, e.g., T, and an unqualified function parameter of type that is exactly T&&, e.g., **const** T&& would be an *rvalue* reference, not a forwarding reference.

Consider, for example, a function template f that takes a single argument by reference and then attempts to use it to invoke one of two overloads of a function g, depending on whether the original argument was an *lvalue* or *rvalue*:

```
struct S { /* some type that might benefit from being able to be moved */ };

void g(const S&);    // target function; overload for const S lvalues
void g(S&&);         // target function; overload for S rvalues only

template <typename T>
void f(T&& forRef); // forwards to target overload g based on value category
```

Note that a function may be overloaded on the reference type alone (see Section 2.1."*Rvalue References*" on page 710); however, overloading on a **const** *lvalue* reference and an *rvalue* reference occur most often in practice. In this specific case — where f is a function template, T is a template type parameter, and the type of the parameter itself is exactly T&& — the forRef function parameter in the code snippet above denotes a *forwarding reference*. If f is invoked with an *lvalue*, forRef is an *lvalue* reference; otherwise, forRef is an *rvalue* reference.

Given the dual nature of forRef, one rather verbose way of determining the original value category of the passed argument would be to use the std::is_lvalue_reference **type trait** on forRef itself:

```cpp
#include <type_traits>  // std::is_lvalue_reference
#include <utility>  // std::move

template <typename T>
void f(T&& forRef)       // forRef is a forwarding reference.
{
    if (std::is_lvalue_reference<T>::value)  // using a C++11 type trait
    {
        g(forRef);                 // propagates forRef as an lvalue
    }                              // invokes g(const S&)
    else
    {
        g(std::move(forRef));  // propagates forRef as an rvalue
    }                              // invokes g(S&&)
}
```

The std::is_lvalue_reference<T>::value predicate above asks if the object bound to forRef originated from an *lvalue* expression and allows the developer to branch on the answer. A better solution that captures this logic at compile time is generally preferred; see *The* std::forward *utility* on page 385:

```cpp
#include <utility>  // std::forward

template <typename T>
void f(T&& forRef)
{
    g(std::forward<T>(forRef));
        // same as g(std::move(forRef)) if and only if forRef is an rvalue
        // reference; otherwise, equivalent to g(forRef)
}
```

A client function invoking f will enjoy the same behavior with either of the two implementation alternatives offered above:

```
void client()
{
    S s;
    f(s);   // Instantiates f<S&> -- forRef is an lvalue reference (S&).
            // The function f<S&> will end up invoking g(S&).

    f(S()); // Instantiates f<S> -- forRef is an rvalue reference (S&&).
            // The function f<S> will end up invoking g(S&&).
}
```

Use of `std::forward` in combination with forwarding references is typical in the implementation of industrial-strength generic libraries; see *Use Cases* on page 386.

A brief review of function template argument deduction

Invoking a function template without explicitly providing template arguments at the call site will compel the compiler to attempt, if possible, to *deduce* those template *type* arguments from the function arguments:

```
template <typename T> void f();
template <typename T> void g(T x);
template <typename T> void h(T y, T z);

void example0()
{
    f();        // Error, couldn't infer template argument T
    f<short>(); // OK, T is specified explicitly.
    g(0);       // OK, T is deduced as int from literal 0; x is an int.
    h(0, 'a');  // Error, deduced conflicting types for T (int vs. char)
    h('A', 'B'); // OK, both arguments have same type.
}
```

Any **cv-qualifiers** — **const**, **volatile**, or both — on a *deduced* function parameter will be applied *after* type deduction is performed:

```
template <typename T> void cf(const T x);
template <typename T> void vf(volatile T y);
template <typename T> void wf(const volatile T z);

void example1()
{
    cf(0);  // OK, T is deduced as int; x is a const int.
    vf(0);  // OK, T is deduced as int; y is a volatile int.
    wf(0);  // OK, T is deduced as int; z is a const volatile int.
}
```

Similarly, **ref-qualifiers** other than &&, i.e., & or && along with any cv-qualifiers, do not alter the deduction process, and they too are applied after deduction:

```
template <typename T> void rf(T& x);
template <typename T> void crf(const T& x);

void example2(int i)
{
    rf(i);   // OK, T is deduced as int; x is an int&.
    crf(i);  // OK, T is deduced as int; x is a const int&.

    rf(0);   // Error, expects an lvalue for 1st argument
    crf(0);  // OK, T is deduced as int; x is a const int&.
}
```

Type deduction works differently for *forwarding* references where the only qualifier on the template parameter is &&. For the sake of exposition, consider a function template declaration, f, accepting a forwarding reference, forRef:

```
template <typename T> void f(T&& forRef);
```

We saw in the example on page 378 that, when f is invoked with an *lvalue* of type S, then T is deduced as S& and forRef becomes an *lvalue* reference. When f is instead invoked with an *xvalue* of type S (see Section 2.1."*Rvalue* References" on page 710), then T is deduced as S and forRef becomes an *rvalue* reference. The underlying process that results in this duality relies on **reference collapsing** (see the next section) and special **type deduction** rules introduced for this particular case. When the type T of a *forwarding* reference is being deduced from an expression E, T itself will be deduced as an *lvalue* reference if E is an *lvalue*; otherwise, normal type-deduction rules will apply, and T will be deduced as a nonreference type:

```
void g()
{
    int i;
    f(i); // i is an lvalue expression.
          // T is therefore deduced as int& --- special rule!
          // T&& becomes int& &&, which collapses to int&.

    f(0); // 0 is an rvalue expression.
          // T is therefore deduced as int.
          // T&& becomes int&&, which is an rvalue reference.
}
```

For more on general type deduction, see Section 2.1."**auto** Variables" on page 195.

Reference collapsing

As we saw in the previous section, when a function having a *forwarding* reference parameter, forRef, is invoked with a corresponding *lvalue* argument (e.g., a named variable), an interesting phenomenon occurs: After type deduction, we temporarily get what appears syntactically to be an *rvalue* reference to an *lvalue* reference. As references to references are *not* allowed in C++, the compiler uses **reference collapsing** to resolve the *forwarding* reference parameter, forRef, into a single reference, thus providing a way to infer, from T itself, the original **value category** of the argument passed to f.

The process of **reference collapsing** is performed by the compiler in any situation where a reference to a reference would be formed. Table 1 illustrates the simple rules for collapsing unstable references into stable ones. Notice, in particular, that an *lvalue* reference always overpowers an *rvalue* reference. The only situation in which two references collapse into an *rvalue* reference is when they are both *rvalue* references.

Table 1: Collapsing unstable reference pairs into a single, stable one

First Reference Type	Second Reference Type	Result of Reference Collapsing
&	&	&
&	&&	&
&&	&	&
&&	&&	&&

Writing a reference-to-reference type in C++ explicitly is not possible:

```cpp
int   i   = 0;   // OK
int&  ir  = i;   // OK
int& & irr = ir; // Error, irr declared as a reference to a reference
```

Doing so, however, is easy with type aliases and template parameters, and that is where reference collapsing comes into play:

```cpp
#include <type_traits>  // std::is_same
using T1 = int&;  // OK
using T2 = T1&;   // OK, int& & becomes int&.
static_assert(std::is_same<T2, int&>::value, "");
```

Furthermore, references to references can occur during computations involving **metafunctions** or as part of language rules, such as type deduction:

```cpp
template <typename T>
struct AddLvalueRef { typedef T& type; };
    // metafunction that transforms to an lvalue reference to T

template <typename T>
void f(T input)
{
    typename AddLvalueRef<T>::type ir1 = input;    // OK, adds & to make T&
    typename AddLvalueRef<T&>::type ir2 = input;   // OK, collapses to T&
    typename AddLvalueRef<T&&>::type ir3 = input;  // OK, collapses to T&
}
```

Notice that we are using the **typename** keyword in the previous example as a generalized way of indicating, during **template instantiation**, that a dependent name is a type as opposed to a value.[1]

Identifying forwarding references

The syntax for a *forwarding* reference (**&&**) is the same as that for *rvalue* references; the only way to discern one from the other is by observing the surrounding context. When used in a manner where **type deduction** can take place, the **T&&** syntax does not designate an *rvalue* reference; instead, it represents a *forwarding* reference. For type deduction to be in effect, a function template must have a type parameter (e.g., **T**) and a function parameter of a type that exactly matches that parameter followed by **&&** (e.g., **T&&**):

```
struct S0
{
    template <typename T>
    void f(T&& forRef);
        // Fully eligible for template-argument type deduction: forRef
        // is a forwarding reference.
};
```

Note that if the function parameter is qualified, the syntax reverts to the usual meaning of *rvalue* reference:

```
struct S1
{
    template <typename T>
    void f(const T&& crRef);
        // Eligible for type deduction but is not a forwarding reference: due
        // to the const qualifier, crRef is an rvalue reference.
};
```

If a member function of a class template is not itself also a template, then its template type parameter will not be deduced:

```
template <typename T>
struct S2
{
    void f(T&& rRef);
        // Not eligible for type deduction because T is fixed and known as part
        // of the instantiation of S2: rRef is an rvalue reference.
};
```

---

[1]In C++20, the **typename** disambiguator is no longer required in some of the contexts where a dependent qualified name must be a type. For example, a dependent name used as a function return type — **template <typename T> T::R f();** — requires no **typename**.

More generally, note that the **&&** syntax can *never* imply a *forwarding* reference for a function that is not itself a template; see *Annoyances — Forwarding references look just like rvalue references* on page 397.

auto&& — a forwarding reference in a nonparameter context

Outside of template function parameters, *forwarding* references can also appear in the context of variable definitions using the **auto** keyword (see Section 2.1."**auto** Variables" on page 195) because they too are subject to type deduction:

```
void f()
{
    auto&& i = 0;   // i is a forwarding reference because the type of i must
                    // be deduced from the initialization expression 0.
}
```

Just like function parameters, **auto**&& resolves to either an *lvalue* reference or *rvalue* reference depending on the **value category** of the initialization expression:

```
void g()
{
    int i = 0;
    auto&& lv = i;   // lv is an int&.

    auto&& rv = 0;   // rv is an int&&.
}
```

Similarly to **const auto&**, the **auto**&& syntax binds to anything. In the case of **auto**&&, however, the reference will be **const** *only* if it is initialized with a **const** object:

```
void h()
{
    int       i = 0;
    const int ci = 0;

    auto&& lv  = i;   // lv is an int&.
    auto&& clv = ci;  // clv is a const int&.
}
```

Just as with function parameters, the original **value category** of the expression used to initialize a *forwarding* reference variable can be propagated during subsequent function invocation, e.g., using std::forward (see *The std::forward utility* on page 385):

```
#include <utility> // std::forward
template <typename T>
T get();          // Produce an lvalue or rvalue depending on T.
template <typename T>
void use(T&& t); // Here use also takes a forwarding reference parameter
                 // to do with as it pleases.

template <typename T>
void l()
{
    auto&& fr = get<T>();
        // get<T>() might be either an lvalue or rvalue depending on T.

    use(std::forward<decltype(fr)>(fr));  // decltype is a C++11 feature.
        // Propagate the original value category of get<T>() into use.
}
```

Notice that because (1) `std::forward` requires the type of the object that's going to be forwarded as a user-provided template argument and (2) it is not possible to name the type of `fr`, **decltype** (see Section 1.1."**decltype**" on page 25) was used in the example above to retrieve the type of `fr`.

Forwarding references without forwarding

Sometimes deliberately *not* forwarding (see *The `std::forward` utility* on page 385) an **auto&&** variable or a forwarding reference function parameter at all can be useful. In such cases, *forwarding* references are employed solely for their **const**-preserving and universal binding semantics. As an example, consider the task of obtaining iterators over a range of an unknown value category:

```
#include <iterator>  // std::begin, std::end

template <typename T>
void m()
{
    auto&& r = getRange<T>();
        // getRange<T>() might be either an lvalue or rvalue depending on T.

    auto b = std::begin(r);
    auto e = std::end(r);

    traverseRange(b, e);
}
```

Using `std::forward` in the initialization of both b and e in the example above might result in moving from r twice, which is potentially unsafe; see Section 2.1."*Rvalue* References" on page 710:

```
auto b = std::begin(std::forward<decltype(r)>(r));
auto e = std::end  (std::forward<decltype(r)>(r));   // BAD IDEA:
                                                     // r might be moved from.
```

Forwarding r only in the initialization of e might avoid issues caused by moving an object twice but might result in inconsistent behavior with b:

```
auto b = std::begin(r);
auto e = std::end(std::forward<decltype(r)>(r));   // BAD IDEA: e might have
                                                   // a different type than b.
```

The std::forward utility

The final piece of the forwarding reference infrastructure is the std::forward utility function. Since the expression naming a forwarding reference x is always an *lvalue* due to its reachability by either name or address and since our intention is to move x in case it was originally an *rvalue*, we need a conditional *move* operation that will move x only in that case and otherwise let x pass through as an *lvalue*.

The Standard Library provides two overloads of the std::forward function in the <utility> header:

```
namespace std {
template <class T> T&& forward(typename remove_reference<T>::type&  t) noexcept;
template <class T> T&& forward(typename remove_reference<T>::type&& t) noexcept;
}
```

Note that, to avoid ambiguity, the second overload will be deliberately removed from the overload set if T is an *lvalue* reference type.

Recall that the type T associated with a forwarding reference is deduced as a reference type if given an *lvalue* reference and as a nonreference type otherwise. So for a forwarding reference forRef of type T&&, we have two cases.

1. An *lvalue* of type U was used for initializing forRef, so T is U&; thus, the first overload of forward will be selected and will be of the form U& forward(U& u) noexcept, thus just returning the original *lvalue* reference. Notice the effect of reference collapsing in the return type: (U&)&& becomes simply U&.

2. An *rvalue* of type U was used for initializing forRef, so T is U, and the second overload of forward will be selected and will be of the form U&& forward(U&& u) noexcept, essentially equivalent to std::move.

Note that, in the body of a function template accepting a forwarding reference T&& named x, std::forward<T>(x) could be replaced with **static_cast**<T&&>(x) to achieve the same effect. Due to reference collapsing rules, T&& will resolve to T& whenever the original value category of x was an *lvalue* and to T&& otherwise, thus achieving the *conditional move* behavior elucidated in *Description* on page 377. Using std::forward over **static_cast**, however, expresses the programmer's intent explicitly.

Use Cases

Perfectly forwarding an expression to a downstream consumer

A frequent use of forwarding references and `std::forward` is to propagate an object, whose value category is invocation-dependent, down to one or more service providers that will behave differently depending on the value category of the original argument.

As an example, consider an overload set for a function, `sink`, that accepts an `std::string` either by **const** *lvalue* reference, e.g., with the intention of *copying* from it, or by *rvalue* reference, e.g., with the intention of *moving* from it:

```
void sink(const std::string& s) { target = s; }
void sink(std::string&& s)       { target = std::move(s); }
```

Now, let's assume that we want to create an intermediary function template, `pipe`, that will accept an `std::string` of any value category and will dispatch its argument to the corresponding overload of `sink`. By accepting a *forwarding* reference as a function parameter and invoking `std::forward` as part of `pipe`'s body, we can achieve our original goal without any code duplication:

```
template <typename T>
void pipe(T&& x)
{
    sink(std::forward<T>(x));
}
```

Invoking `pipe` with an *lvalue* will result in `x` being an *lvalue* reference and thus `sink(`**const** `std::string&)` being called. Otherwise, `x` will be an *rvalue* reference and `sink(std::string&&)` will be called. This idea of enabling *move* operations without code duplication, as `pipe` does, is commonly referred to as perfect forwarding; see *Perfect forwarding for generic factory functions* on page 388.

Handling multiple parameters concisely

Suppose we have a **value-semantic type (VST)** that holds a collection of attributes where some (not necessarily proper) subset of them need to be changed together to preserve some class invariant[2]:

```
#include <type_traits>  // std::decay, std::enable_if, std::is_same
#include <utility>      // std::forward

struct Person { /* UDT that benefits from move semantics */ };

class StudyGroup
```

---

[2]This type of value-semantic type can be classified more specifically as a *complex-constrained* attribute class; a discussion of this topic is planned for **lakos2a**, section 4.2.

```
{
    Person d_a;
    Person d_b;
    Person d_c;
    Person d_d;
    // ...

public:
    static bool isValid(const Person& a, const Person& b,
                        const Person& c, const Person& d);
        // Return true if these specific people form a valid study group under
        // the guidelines of the study-group commission, and false otherwise.
    // ...

    template <typename PA, typename PB, typename PC, typename PD,
        typename = typename std::enable_if<
            std::is_same<typename std::decay<PA>::type, Person>::value &&
            std::is_same<typename std::decay<PB>::type, Person>::value &&
            std::is_same<typename std::decay<PC>::type, Person>::value &&
            std::is_same<typename std::decay<PD>::type, Person>::value>::type>
    int setPersonsIfValid(PA&& a, PB&& b, PC&& c, PD&& d)
    {
        enum { e_SUCCESS = 0, e_FAIL };

        if (!isValid(a, b, c, d))
        {
            return e_FAIL;  // no change
        }

        // Move or copy each person into this object's Person data members.

        d_a = std::forward<PA>(a);
        d_b = std::forward<PB>(b);
        d_c = std::forward<PC>(c);
        d_d = std::forward<PD>(d);

        return e_SUCCESS;  // Study group was updated successfully.
    }
};
```

Because the template arguments used in each successive function parameter are deduced interdependently from the types of their corresponding function arguments, the setPersonsIfValid function template can be instantiated for a full Cartesian product of variations of qualifiers that can be on a Person object. Any combination of *lvalue* and *rvalue* Persons can be passed, and a template will be instantiated that will copy the *lvalues* and move from the *rvalues*. To make sure the Person objects are created externally, the function is restricted, using std::enable_if, to instantiate only for types that decay to Person, i.e., types that are cv-qualified or ref-qualified `Person`. Because each parameter is a forwarding reference, they can all implicitly convert to **const** `Person&` to pass to `isValid`, creating no additional temporaries. Finally, `std::forward` is then used to do the actual moving or copying as appropriate to data members.

Perfect forwarding for generic factory functions

Consider the prototypical standard-library generic factory function, `std::make_shared<T>`. On the surface, the requirements for this function are fairly simple: Allocate a place for a `T` and then construct it with the same arguments that were passed to `make_shared`. Correctly passing arguments to the constructor, however, gets reasonably complex to implement efficiently when `T` can have a wide variety of ways in which it might be initialized.

For simplicity, we will show how a two-argument `my::make_shared` might be defined, knowing that a full implementation would employ variadic template arguments for this purpose; see Section 2.1."Variadic Templates" on page 873. Furthermore, our simplified `make_shared` creates the object on the heap with **new** and constructs an `std::shared_ptr` to manage the lifetime of that object.

Let's now consider how we would structure the declaration of this form of `make_shared`:

```
namespace my {
template <typename OBJECT_TYPE, typename ARG1, typename ARG2>
std::shared_ptr<OBJECT_TYPE> make_shared(ARG1&& arg1, ARG2&& arg2);
}
```

Notice that we have two forwarding reference arguments, `arg1` and `arg2`, with deduced types `ARG1` and `ARG2`. Now, the body of our function needs to carefully construct our `OBJECT_TYPE` object on the heap and then create our output `shared_ptr`:

```
template <typename OBJECT_TYPE, typename ARG1, typename ARG2>
std::shared_ptr<OBJECT_TYPE> my::make_shared(ARG1&& arg1, ARG2&& arg2)
{
    OBJECT_TYPE* object_p = new OBJECT_TYPE(std::forward<ARG1>(arg1),
                                            std::forward<ARG2>(arg2));
    try
    {
        return std::shared_ptr<OBJECT_TYPE>(object_p);
    }
    catch (...)
    {
        delete object_p;
        throw;
    }
}
```

Notice that this simplified implementation needs to clean up the allocated object if the constructor for the return value throws; normally a **RAII** proctor to manage this ownership would be a more robust solution to this problem.

Importantly, using `std::forward` to construct the object means that the arguments passed to `make_shared` will be used to find the appropriate matching two-parameter constructor of `OBJECT_TYPE`. When those arguments are *rvalues*, the constructor found will again search for one that takes an *rvalue*, and the arguments will be moved from. What's more, because this function wants to forward exactly the **const**ness and reference type of the input arguments, we would have to write 12 distinct overloads, one for each argument, if we were not using perfect forwarding — the full Cartesian product of **const** (or not), **volatile** (or not), and **&** or **&&** (or neither). A full implementation of just this two-parameter variation would require 144 distinct overloads, all almost identical and most never used. Using forwarding references reduces that to just one overload for each number of arguments.

Wrapping initialization in a generic factory function

Occasionally we might want to initialize an object with an intervening function call wrapping the actual construction of that object. Suppose we have a tracking system that we want to use to monitor how many times certain initializers have been invoked:

```
struct TrackingSystem
{
    template <typename T>
    static void trackInitialization(int numArgs);
        // Track the creation of a T with a constructor taking numArgs
        // arguments.
};
```

Now we want to write a general utility function that can be used to construct an arbitrary object and notify the tracking system of the construction for us. Here we will use a variadic pack (see Section 2.1."Variadic Templates" on page 873) of forwarding references to handle calling the constructor for us:

```
template <typename OBJECT_TYPE, typename... ARGS>
OBJECT_TYPE trackConstruction(ARGS&&... args)
{
    TrackingSystem::trackInitialization<OBJECT_TYPE>(sizeof...(args));
    return OBJECT_TYPE(std::forward<ARGS>(args)...);
}
```

This use of a variadic pack of forwarding references lets us add tracking easily to convert any initialization to a tracked one by inserting a call to this function around the constructor arguments:

```
void myFunction()
{
    BigObject untracked("Hello", "World");
    BigObject tracked = trackConstruction<BigObject>("Hello","World");
}
```

On the surface there does seem to be a difference between how objects untracked and tracked are constructed. The first variable is having its constructor directly invoked, while the second is being constructed from an object being returned by-value from trackConstruction. This construction, however, has long been something that has been optimized away to avoid any additional objects and construct the object in question just once. In this case, because the object being returned is initialized by the **return** statement of trackConstruction, the optimization is called **return value optimization (RVO)**. C++ has always allowed this optimization by enabling **copy elision**. Ensuring that this elision actually happens (on all current compilers of which the authors are aware) is possible by publicly **declaring** but not **defining** the copy constructor for BigObject.[3] We find that this code will still compile and link with such an object, providing observable proof that the copy constructor is never actually invoked with this pattern.

Emplacement

Prior to C++11, inserting an object into a Standard Library container always required the programmer to first create such an object and then copy it inside the container's storage. As an example, consider inserting a temporary std::string object in an std::vector<std::string>:

```
void f(std::vector<std::string>& v)
{
    v.push_back(std::string("hello world"));
        // invokes std::string::string(const char*) and the copy constructor
}
```

In the function above, a temporary std::string object is created on the stack frame of f and is then copied to the dynamically allocated buffer managed by v. Additionally, the buffer might have insufficient capacity and hence might require reallocation, which would in turn require every element of v to be copied from the old buffer to the new, larger one.

In C++11, the situation is significantly better thanks to *rvalue* references. The temporary will be moved into v, and any subsequent buffer reallocation will *move* the elements between buffers rather than copy them, assuming that the element's move constructor has a **noexcept** specifier (see Section 3.1."**noexcept** Specifier" on page 1085). The amount of work can, however, be further reduced: What if, instead of first creating an object externally, we constructed the new std::string object directly in v's buffer?

This is where **emplacement** comes into play. All standard library containers, including std::vector, now provide an emplacement API powered by variadic templates (see Section 2.1."Variadic Templates" on page 873) and perfect forwarding (see *Perfect forwarding for generic factory functions* on page 388). Rather than accepting a fully-constructed element, **emplacement** operations accept an arbitrary number of arguments, which will in turn

---

[3]In C++17, this copy elision can be guaranteed and is allowed to be done for objects that have no copy or move constructors.

be used to construct a new element directly in the container's storage, thereby avoiding unnecessary copies or even moves:

```
void g(std::vector<std::string>& v)
{
    v.emplace_back("hello world");
        // invokes only the std::string::string(const char*) constructor
}
```

Calling `std::vector<std::string>::emplace_back` with a **const char*** argument results in a new `std::string` object being created in-place in the next empty spot of the vector's storage. Internally, `std::allocator_traits::construct` is invoked, which typically employs **placement new** to construct the object in raw dynamically allocated memory. As previously mentioned, `emplace_back` makes use of both variadic templates and forwarding references; it accepts any number of forwarding references and internally *perfectly forwards* them to the constructor of T via `std::forward`:

```
template <typename T>
template <typename... Args>
void std::vector<T>::emplace_back(Args&&... args)
{
    // ...
    (void) new (d_data_p[d_size]) T(std::forward<Args>(args)...);  // pseudocode
    // ...
}
```

Emplacement operations remove the need for copy or move operations when inserting elements into containers, potentially increasing the performance of a program and sometimes, depending on the container, even allowing even noncopyable or nonmovable objects to be stored in a container.

As previously mentioned, declaring without defining the *copy* or *move* constructor of a noncopyable or nonmovable type to be private is often a way to guarantee that a C++11/14 compiler constructs an object in place. Containers that might need to move elements around for other operations, such as `std::vector` or `std::deque`, will still need movable elements, while node-based containers that never move the elements themselves after initial construction, such as `std::list` or `std::map`, can use emplace along with noncopyable or nonmovable objects.

Decomposing complex expressions

Many modern C++ libraries have adopted a more functional style of programming, chaining the output of one function as the arguments of another function to produce complex expressions that accomplish a great deal in relatively concise fashion. Consider a function that reads a file, does some spell-checking for every unique word in the file, and gives us a list of incorrect words and corresponding suggested proper spellings, implemented using a range-like[4] library having common utilities similar to standard UNIX processing utilities:

```
SpellingSuggestion checkSpelling(const std::string& word);

std::map<std::string, SpellingSuggestion> checkFileSpelling(
                                            const std::string& filename)
{
    return makeMap(
        filter(transform(
            uniq(sort(filterRegex(splitRegex(openFile(filename),"\\s+"),"\\w+")))),
        [](const std::string& x)
        {
            return std::tuple<std::string, SpellingSuggestion>(x,
                                            checkSpelling(x));
        }
    ), [](auto&& x) { return !std::get<1>(x).isCorrect(); }));
}
```

Each of the functions in this range library — makeMap, transform, uniq, sort, filterRegex, splitRegex, and openFile — is a set of complex templated overloads and deeply subtle metaprogramming that becomes hard to unravel for a nonexpert C++ programmer.

To better understand, document, and debug what is happening here, we decide to decompose this expression into many, capturing the implicit temporaries returned by all of these functions and ideally not changing the actual semantics of what is being done. To do that properly, we need to capture the type and value category of each subexpression appropri-

---

[4]The C++20 ranges library that provides a variety of range utilities and adaptors allows for composition using the pipe (|) operators instead of nested function calls, resulting in code that might be easier to read:

```
#include <algorithm>  // std::ranges::equal
#include <cassert>    // standard C assert macro
#include <ranges>       // std::ranges::views::transform, std::ranges::views::filter

void f()
{
    int data[] = {1, 2, 3, 4, 5};
    int expected[] = {1, 9, 25};

    auto isOdd  = [](int i) { return i % 2 == 1; };
    auto square = [](int i) { return i * i; };

    using namespace std::ranges;

    // function-call composition
    assert(equal(views::transform(views::filter(data, isOdd), square), expected));

    // pipe operator composition
    assert(equal(data | views::filter(isOdd) | views::transform(square), expected));
}
```

ately, without necessarily being able to easily decode it manually from the expression. Here is where **auto&&** forwarding references can be used effectively to decompose and document this expression while achieving the same result:

```
std::map<std::string, SpellingSuggestion> checkFileSpelling(
                                            const std::string& filename)
{
    // Create a range over the contents of filename.
    auto&& openedFile = openFile(filename);

    // Split the file by whitespace.
    auto&& potentialWords = splitRegex(
        std::forward<decltype(openedFile)>(openedFile), "\\s+");

    // Filter out only words made from word-characters.
    auto&& words = filterRegex(
        std::forward<decltype(potentialWords)>(potentialWords), "\\w+");

    // Sort all words.
    auto&& sortedWords = sort(std::forward<decltype(words)>(words));

    // Skip adjacent duplicate words so as to create a sequence of unique words.
    auto&& uniqueWords = uniq(std::forward<decltype(sortedWords)>(sortedWords));

    // Get a SpellingSuggestion for every word.
    auto&& suggestions = transform(
        std::forward<decltype(uniqueWords)>(uniqueWords),
        [](const std::string&x) {
            return std::tuple<std::string,SpellingSuggestion>(
                x,checkSpelling(x));
        });

    // Filter out correctly spelled words, keeping only elements where the
    // second element of the tuple, which is a SpellingSuggestion, is not
    // correct.
    auto&& corrections = filter(
        std::forward<decltype(suggestions)>(suggestions),
        [](auto&& suggestion){ return !std::get<1>(suggestion).isCorrect(); });

    // Return a map made from these two-element tuples:
    return makeMap(std::forward<decltype(corrections)>(corrections));
}
```

Now each step of this complex expression is documented, each temporary has a name, but the net result of the lifetimes of each object is functionally the same. No new conversions have been introduced, and every object that was used as an *rvalue* in the original expression will still be used as an *rvalue* in this much longer and more descriptive implementation of the same functionality.

Potential Pitfalls

Surprising number of template instantiations with string literals

When forwarding references are used as a means to avoid code repetition between exactly two overloads of the same function (one accepting a **const** T& and the other a T&&), it can be surprising to see more than two template instantiations for that particular template function, in particular when the function is invoked using string literals.

Consider, as an example, a `Dictionary` class containing two overloads of an **addWord** member function:

```
class Dictionary
{
    // ...

public:
    void addWord(const std::string& word);  // (0) copy word in the dictionary
    void addWord(std::string&& word);        // (1) move word in the dictionary
};

void f()
{
    Dictionary d;

    std::string s = "car";
    d.addWord(s);                     // invokes (0)

    const std::string cs = "toy";
    d.addWord(cs);                    // invokes (0)

    d.addWord("house");               // invokes (1)
    d.addWord("garage");              // invokes (1)
    d.addWord(std::string{"ball"});   // invokes (1)
}
```

Now, imagine replacing the two overloads of **addWord** with a single *perfectly forwarding* template member function, with the intention of avoiding code repetition between the two overloads:

```
class Dictionary
{
    // ...

public:
    template <typename T>
    void addWord(T&& word);
};
```

Perhaps surprisingly, the number of template instantiations skyrockets:

```
void f()
{
    Dictionary d;

    std::string s = "car";
    d.addWord(s);   // instantiates addWord<std::string&>

    const std::string cs = "toy";
    d.addWord(cs);  // instantiates addWord<const std::string&>

    d.addWord("house");                   // instantiates addWord<char const(&)[6]>
    d.addWord("garage");                  // instantiates addWord<char const(&)[7]>
    d.addWord(std::string{"ball"});  // instantiates addWord<std::string&&>
}
```

Depending on the variety of argument types supplied to `addWord`, having many call sites could result in an undesirably large number of distinct template instantiations, perhaps significantly increasing object code size, compilation time, or both.

`std::forward<T>` can enable move operations

Invoking `std::forward<T>(x)` is equivalent to conditionally invoking `std::move` if `T` is an *lvalue* reference. Hence, any subsequent use of `x` is subject to the same caveats that would apply to an *lvalue* cast to an unnamed *rvalue* reference; see Section 2.1."*Rvalue* References" on page 710:

```
template <typename T>
void f(T&& x)
{
    g(std::forward<T>(x));   // OK
    g(x);                    // Oops! x could have already been moved from.
}
```

Once an object has been passed as an argument using `std::forward`, it should typically not be accessed again because it could now be in a moved-from state.

A perfect-forwarding constructor can hijack the copy constructor

A single-parameter constructor of a class `S` accepting a forwarding reference can unexpectedly be a better match during overload resolution compared to `S`'s copy constructor:

```
struct S
{
    S();                               // default constructor
    template <typename T> S(T&&);  // forwarding constructor
    S(const S&);                       // copy constructor
};
```

```
void f()
{
    S a;
    const S b;

    S x(a);   // invokes forwarding constructor
    S y(b);   // invokes copy constructor
}
```

Despite the programmer's intention to copy from a into x, the forwarding constructor of S was invoked instead, because a is a non**const** *lvalue* expression, and instantiating the forwarding constructor with T = S& results in a better match than even the copy constructor.

This potential pitfall can arise in practice, for example, when writing a value-semantic wrapper template, e.g., Wrapper, that can be initialized by *perfectly forwarding* the object to be wrapped into it:

```
#include <string>   // std::string
#include <utility>  // std::forward
template <typename T>
class Wrapper   // wrapper for an object of arbitrary type 'T'
{
private:
    T d_datum;

public:
    template <typename U>
    Wrapper(U&& datum) : d_datum(std::forward<U>(datum)) { }
        // perfect-forwarding constructor to optimize runtime performance

    // ...
};

void f()
{
    std::string s("hello world");
    Wrapper<std::string> w0(s);   // OK, s is copied into d_datum.

    Wrapper<std::string> w1(std::string("hello world"));
        // OK, the temporary string is moved into d_datum.
}
```

Similarly to the example involving class S in the example above, attempting to copy-construct a non**const** instance of Wrapper, e.g., wr in the example above, results in an error:

```
void g(Wrapper<int>& wr)   // The same would happen if wr were passed by value.
{
```

```
    Wrapper<int> w2(10);    // OK, invokes perfect-forwarding constructor
    Wrapper<int> w3(wr);    // Error, no conversion from Wrapper<int> to int
}
```

The compilation failure above occurs because the perfect-forwarding constructor template, instantiated with `Wrapper<int>&`, is a better match than the implicitly generated copy constructor, which accepts a **const** `Wrapper<int>&`. Constraining the perfect forwarding constructor via **SFINAE**, e.g., with `std::enable_if`, to explicitly *not* accept objects whose type is `Wrapper` fixes this problem:

```cpp
#include <type_traits> // std::enable_if,  std::is_same
#include <utility>      // std::forward
template <typename T>
class Wrapper
{
private:
    T d_datum;

public:
    template <typename U,
        typename = typename std::enable_if<
            !std::is_same<typename std::decay<U>::type, Wrapper>::value
        >::type
    >
    Wrapper(U&& datum) : d_datum(std::forward<U>(datum)) { }
        // This constructor participates in overload resolution only if U,
        // after being decayed, is not the same as Wrapper<T>.
};

void h(Wrapper<int>& wr)    // The same would happen if wr were passed by value.
{
    Wrapper<int> w4(10);    // OK, invokes the perfect-forwarding constructor
    Wrapper<int> w5(wr);    // OK, invokes the copy constructor
}
```

Notice that function h replicates what had been a problematic scenario in the earlier function g. Also notice that the `std::decay` metafunction was used as part of the constraint; for more information on the using `std::decay`, see *Annoyances — Metafunctions are required in constraints* on page 398.

Annoyances

Forwarding references look just like *rvalue* references

Despite *forwarding* references and *rvalue* references having significantly different semantics, as discussed in *Description — Identifying forwarding references* on page 382, they share the same syntax. For any given type T, whether the T&& syntax designates an *rvalue* reference or a *forwarding* reference depends entirely on the surrounding context.[5]

```
template <typename T> struct S0 { void f(T&&); };   // rvalue reference
struct S1 { template <typename T> void f(T&&); };   // forwarding reference
```

Furthermore, even if T is subject to template argument deduction, the presence of *any* qualifier will suppress the special *forwarding*-reference deduction rules:

```
template <typename T> void f(T&&);            // forwarding reference
template <typename T> void g(const T&&);      // const rvalue reference
template <typename T> void h(volatile T&&);   // volatile rvalue reference
```

It is remarkable that we still do not have some unique syntax — hypothetically, &&& — that we could use, at least optionally, to imply unequivocally a *forwarding* reference that is independent of its context.

Metafunctions are required in constraints

As we showed in *Use Cases* on page 386, being able to perfectly forward arguments of the same general type and effectively leave only the value category of the argument up to type deduction is a frequent need.

The challenge of correctly forwarding only the value category, however, is significant. The template must be constrained using SFINAE and the appropriate type traits to disallow types that aren't some form of a cv-qualified or ref-qualified version of the type that we want to accept. As an example, let's consider a function intended to *copy* or *move* a Person object into a data structure:

---

[5]In C++20, developers might be subject to additional confusion due to the new terse concept notation syntax, which allows function templates to be defined without any explicit appearance of the **template** keyword. As an example, a constrained function parameter, like Addable **auto**&& a in the example below, is a forwarding reference; looking for the presence of the mandatory **auto** keyword is helpful in identifying whether a type is a forwarding reference or *rvalue* reference:

```
template <typename T>
concept Addable = requires(T a, T b) { a + b; };

void f(Addable auto&& a);  // C++20 terse concept notation

void example()
{
    int i;

    f(i);  // OK, decltype(a) is int& in f.
    f(0);  // OK, decltype(a) is int&& in f.
}
```

```
#include <type_traits> // std::decay, std::enable_if, std::is_same

class Person;
class PersonManager {
    // ...
public:
    template <typename T, typename = typename std::enable_if<
            std::is_same<typename std::decay<T>::type, Person>::value>::type>
    void addPerson(T&& person) { /*...*/ }
        // This function participates in overload resolution only if T is
        // (possibly cv- or ref-qualified) Person.
    // ...
};
```

This pattern that constrains T has five layers to it, so let's unpack them one at a time.

1. T is the template argument we are trying to deduce. We'd like to limit it to being a Person that is **const**, **volatile**, &, &&, or some possibly empty combination of those.

2. std::decay<T>::type is then the application of the standard metafunction (defined in <type_traits>) std::decay to T. This metafunction removes all cv-qualifiers and ref-qualifiers from T, and so, for the types to which we want to limit T, the result of applying decay will *always* be Person. Note that decay will also allow some other implicitly convertible transformations, such as converting an array type to the corresponding pointer type. For types we are concerned with (i.e., those that decay to a Person), this metafunction is equivalent to std::remove_cv<std::remove_reference<T>::type>::type.[6] Due to historical availability and readability, we will continue with our use of decay for this purpose.

3. std::is_same<std::decay<T>::type, Person>::value is then the application of another metafunction, std::is_same, to two arguments (i.e., our decay expression and Person, which results in a value that is either std::true_type or std::false_type), special types that can at compile time convert expressions to **true** or **false**. For the types T that we care about, this expression will be **true**, and for all other types, this expression will be **false**.

4. std::enable_if<X>::type is yet another metafunction that evaluates to a valid type if and only if X is true. Unlike the **value** in std::is_same, this expression is simply not valid if X is false.

5. Finally, by using this enable_if expression as a default argument for the final template parameter (unused, so left unnamed), the expression is going to be instantiated for any deduced T considered during overload resolution for addPerson. For any T that

---

[6]C++20 provides the std::remove_cvref<T> metafunction that can be used to remove cv and reference qualifiers in a terse manner.

is not a (possibly) cv-ref-qualified `Person`, `enable_if` will not define the `type` member `typedef`, leading to a failure during the substitution process. Rather than being a compile-time error, such substitution failure will just remove `addPerson` from the overload set being considered, hence the term "substitution failure is not an error," or SFINAE. If a client attempts to pass a non`Person` as an argument to the `addPerson` function, the compiler will issue an error that there is no matching function for call to `addPerson`, which is exactly the result we want.

Putting this all together means we get to call `addPerson` with *lvalues* and *rvalues* of type `Person`, and the value category will be appropriately usable within `addPerson`, generally with use of `std::forward` within that function's definition.

See Also

- "**auto** Variables" (§2.1, p. 195) covers a feature that can introduce a forwarding reference with the **auto&&** syntax.

- "*Rvalue* References" (§2.1, p. 710) details how *rvalue* references can be confused with forwarding references due to similar syntax.

- "Variadic Templates" (§2.1, p. 873) explores how variadic templates are commonly used in conjunction with forwarding references to provide highly generic interfaces.

Further Reading

- Scott Meyers provides valuable insight on how to spot a forwarding reference as opposed to the **rvalue reference** (see Section 2.1."*Rvalue* References" on page 710) in **meyers15b**, "Item 24: Distinguish universal references from rvalue references," pp. 164–168.

- The original authors of this feature explain (1) that they "intentionally overloaded the **&&** syntax with this special case" (p. 2) but didn't give it a distinct name, (2) why a distinct name would be useful in the standard itself, and (3) why they prefer the term forwarding reference over **universal reference** in **sutter14b**.

- Eric Niebler drills down on a pernicious pitfall involving the overloading of functions having a forwarding reference parameter — particularly when the function is a single argument constructor that can be used as a copy constructor — in **niebler13**.

Trivial and Standard-Layout Types

The classical notion of **POD** has been expanded and refined to comprise two important new categories, **trivial types** (i.e., both **trivially default constructible** and **trivially copyable**) and **standard-layout types**, each of which characterizes objects that can be accessed and manipulated in ways not supported for more general user-defined types.

Description

Data does not reside solely within computer programs. Data is often transmitted over networks to other programs and stored in files and databases. Even within programs, data tends to migrate while being copied or moved from place to place.

Programmers eventually ask themselves, since they know the address and size of a given object, why not simply copy the bytes of the object to the destination to send that object or to save it somewhere? Similarly, to reconstruct an object, why not just copy those saved bytes into the object? Perhaps these same programmers observe that they can use a C++ **union** in the manner of FORTRAN *equivalence* to overlay one object on another to reinterpret the contents as a different type, a.k.a. **type punning**; see *Potential Pitfalls — Misuse of unions* on page 505.

C++, like C before it, strives to be second to none as a language that is close to the hardware, making such machinations tempting, especially when they are perceived to have always worked as intended. At the same time, C++ intends to have a robust object model, in which data is accessed in well-defined ways specified by the language. Furthermore, compiler writers, well represented on the C++ Standards Committee, are eager to restrict accessing and modifying data as nothing more than a bag of bits, because doing so limits the optimizations that they can perform on behalf of their users. The C++ Standards Committee has tried to bridge the gap by inventing the concept of POD (plain old data), a restricted subset of C++ objects that can, in some ways, be treated *naively* as a bag of bits.

Before we go on to discuss PODs, however, a word of warning is necessary. Even POD types do not give license to programmers to violate other C++ rules, such as the rules that fit under the **strict aliasing** umbrella. The boundary between legal programs and those that have **undefined behavior** is fraught and fractal. Compilers are allowed to assume that no program ever executes code having **undefined behavior**, so if a program violates that assumption, the code may be silently compiled in a way contrary to the intentions of the programmer.

Moreover, unrelenting improvements in compilers will, over time, exploit every advantage permitted them; hence, newer versions of compilers may subvert the intent of older programs written in the days of more permissive compilers. What's more, under these conditions, even thoroughly testing code is entirely inadequate because testing cannot demonstrate the absence of **undefined behavior**: One possible outcome of **undefined behavior** is that the program behaves, at least for now, exactly as the programmer intended. It is therefore necessary for programmers to understand and stay within the boundaries of the appropriate leniency conferred by the C++ Standard.

Finally, the notion of what constitutes a POD has been refined over several versions of the C++ Standard. In C++03, the set of POD types encompasses possibly cv-qualified scalar types, such as **int**, **void***, and **enum**, and a limited subset of possibly cv-qualified **aggregates** of POD types — e.g., a **struct**, a **union**, or an array; see Section 2.1. "Braced Init" on page 215. C++11 widens the definition of POD to accommodate many more user-defined types. Separately, a C++11 POD is defined in terms of the intersection of two much larger and more targeted type categories, **standard-layout types** and **trivial types**, with the intention that they might each be used much more widely for the respective benefits that they confer. The trivial-type category is further subdivided into **trivially copyable** — which implies **trivially destructible** — and trivially default constructible, each of which affords its own more focused and, therefore, even more widely applicable capabilities.

Privileges enjoyed by POD types

The term POD types has been used historically to encompass the category of C++ data types that are required to be **ABI** and **API** compatible with their corresponding C-language types when translation units of both languages appear in a single program compiled using the same backend toolchain on a given platform. Such C-language-compatible types form a proper subset of C++03 POD types; see *C++03 POD types* on page 412.

For example, consider a cross-language project in which a C++ application program, main (defined in main.cpp and compiled in C++), invokes a C-language library function, printPODtype (defined in podtype.c and compiled in C), using a common datatype, PODtype (defined in podtype.h and compilable in both C and C++):

```
// podtype.h:
#ifndef INCLUDED_PODTYPE  // internal include guard
#define INCLUDED_PODTYPE

#ifdef __cplusplus  // Ensure that this header can be consumed by both C and C++.
extern "C"
{
#endif

typedef struct { int x; double y; } PODtype;
    // UDT compatible with both C++ and C

void printPODtype(PODtype* data);  // C function prototype (has C linkage)

#ifdef __cplusplus  // needed to close the extern "C" block when opened above
}
#endif

#endif  // end of internal include guard
```

In the example above, `podtype.h` follows the common convention to detect when it is being parsed by a C++ compiler, rather than a C compiler, by checking whether the `__cplusplus` macro is defined, as required by the C++ Standard. If the macro is defined, we wrap the declarations within the file in an **extern** `"C"` block to ensure C-language linkage for all of the declared entities. If this header is consumed by a C compiler, the `__cplusplus` macro will not be defined, and the syntax specific to C++ for **C linkage** is elided. Thus, this header can be consumed simultaneously, with compatible meanings, by both C and C++ compilers.

Next, we consider the C-language implementation file, `podtype.c`, which includes the bilingual `podtype.h` header:

```
// podtype.c:
#include <podtype.h>   // PODtype, printPODtype (component header)
#include <stdio.h>     // printf()

#ifdef __cplusplus     // guards against accidentally compiling this file in C++
#error This is not a C++ file; use a C compiler instead.
#endif

void printPODtype(PODtype* data)
{
    printf("data = { %d, %f }\n", data->x, data->y);
}
```

Since the `podtype.c` implementation file above is intended to be compiled by only a C compiler, it need not concern itself with **extern** `"C"` syntax; we have, however, used conditional compilation along with the C preprocessor's **#error** guard against accidental compilation in C++.

Let's now turn to our C++ application, which resides in `main.cpp`:

```
// main.cpp:
#include <podtype.h>   // PODtype, printPODtype

int main()             // our C++ application main program
{
    PODtype d;         // Create a POD type.

    d.x = 17;          // Populate it in C++.
    d.y = 3.14;
    printPODtype(&d);  // Call a C-language function to print its contents.
}
```

The example above demonstrates creating, populating, and destroying an object of type `PODtype` within C++ code and accessing and printing it by calling code compiled in C. In this example, the `printPODtype` function is available in a precompiled C library (e.g., `lib.a`) and a corresponding suite of headers including `podtype.h`. The `main` program, written in

C++, is able to call the C-linkage `printPODtype` function by dint of the classic **extern "C"** syntax conditionally compiled within `podtype.h`.

Sometimes, however, we might be supplied with a legacy C library that was written without regard for C++ support. In such cases, we would be forced to adopt a slightly different idiom to resolve the linkage:

```
// legacypodtype.h:                  // ancient C-only legacy header file (no C++)
#ifndef INCLUDED_LEGACYPODTYPE       // internal include guard for legacy header
#define INCLUDED_LEGACYPODTYPE

typedef struct { int x; double y; } PODtype;
    // UDT compatible with both C++ and C

void printPODtype(PODtype* data);  // C function prototype (has C linkage)

#endif                             // end internal include guard
```

```
// main2.cpp:
extern "C"  // forces printPODtype to be declared as having C linkage
{
#include <legacypodtype.h>  // PODtype, printPODtype
}

int main()  // C++ application using ancient C library having no support for C++
{
    PODtype d{ 17, 3.14 };  // Create a POD type in C++.
    printPODtype(&d);       // Call C-language function to print its contents.
}
```

In the alternative dual-language example above, the entire `legacypodtype.h` header is **#include**d inside an **extern "C"** block. The `printPODtype` function is now declared to have C linkage; the **extern "C"** specification has no effect on the definition of types such as `PODtype` that contain no function declarators. This alternative approach works in pressing situations but can become problematic should any ostensibly C-only header some day have an **#include** statement in a header that contains C++ code.

Interestingly, not every C++ POD **type** is representable in C, so saying that every POD **type** has the property exhibited above would be an overstatement. For example, a **struct** having a user-declared member function cannot be represented in C yet might well be a POD in C++. Every[1] type that can be represented in C is a POD **type** in C++, and virtually[2]

---

[1]C99 introduces the possibility of having an open array at the end of a dynamically allocated **struct** to store data of arbitrary length, called a *flexible array member* (see **iso99**, section 6.7.2.1, "Structure and union specifiers," subsection "Semantics," paragraph 16, p. 103). Such types are an exception to C++ compatibility in that they cannot directly be compiled in C++14.

[2]Note that C++ provides additional scalar types — such as pointer to member, std::nullptr_t (see Section 1.1."**nullptr**" on page 99), and scoped enumerations (see Section 2.1."**enum class**" on page 332) — that are not representable in C.

every POD type in C++ has a corresponding type in C that — at least in practice — is structurally compatible with it, even if its C rendering lacks certain member functions, access controls, empty base classes, and so on that might otherwise pertain in C++; see *Use Cases — Translating a C++-only type to C (standard layout)* on page 452.

Being a C++ POD-**struct**, though almost always an overly strict constraint, is sufficient to guarantee many other useful properties not generally afforded to other **class types**. The details of the minimal requirements needed for any given property to hold are discussed in subsequent sections; e.g., see *Standard-layout types* on page 417 and *Trivial types* on page 425. Let's now consider some of the special properties and advantages that *all* PODs enjoy.

1. **Contiguous storage** — All objects of POD type, a.k.a. POD objects, occupy contiguous bytes of storage. The **value representation** of a POD object is a subset of the bits in that storage, and the valid values of a POD object are an implementation-defined set of values that those bits can take on. Consider a POD-**struct**, S1, containing a **char** and a **short**:

   ```
   struct S1      // POD-struct whose size is typically 4 bytes
   {
       char  a;      // always exactly 1 byte
                     // typically 1 byte of padding for alignment purposes
       short b;      // at least (and typically exactly) 2 bytes
   };
   ```

   Objects of this POD type are typically stored in exactly 4 contiguous bytes and have a **value representation** of 24 noncontiguous bits. The 8 extra padding bits are not part of the **value representation**.

   Objects with virtual base classes might potentially have not just a noncontiguous **value representation** but also a noncontiguous **object representation**, since the virtual base subobject might not be adjacent to the rest of the object. This reason is one of a few that explains why types with virtual base classes are not POD **types**.

2. **Predictable layout** — The layout of every POD object is stable and in some important ways predictable. For example, the first non**static** data member (e.g., x) of a POD-**struct** (e.g., X) is guaranteed to reside at the same address as does the POD-**struct** object (e.g., pso) itself:

   ```
   struct X { int x; } pso;  // POD-struct object
   static_assert(static_cast<void*>(&pso) == static_cast<void*>(&pso.x), "");
   ```

   This property of a POD-**struct** predates C++03 and is true even in C. Although base classes are not permitted for C++03 POD types, in C++11 the address of a POD-**struct** having one or more base classes is the same as that of its first base class:

```
struct B11 { /*...*/ };     // arbitrary POD-struct
struct C11 : B11 { } c11;   // empty derived POD-struct
static_assert(static_cast<void*>(&c11) == static_cast<B11*>(&c11), "");

struct E11 { };                     // empty POD-struct
struct D11 : E11 { /*...*/ } d11;   // arbitrary derived POD-struct
static_assert(static_cast<void*>(&d11) == static_cast<E11*>(&d11), "");
```

As another generally applicable example of the advantages of the predictable layout of a POD type, consider a POD-**union** comprising multiple POD-**struct** members having a **common initial member sequence (CIMS)**, which enables access to the common members through any of those union members provided one of them is the **active member**; i.e., the last union member written was one that started with the common initial sequence. For example, consider three **struct**s, AA, BB, and CC, each consisting of three scalar values:

```
struct AA { float f;  int g;  int    h; };  // POD-struct type
struct BB { int   x;  int y;  char   z; };  //  "      "      "
struct CC { int   t;  int u;  double v; };  //  "      "      "
```

All three of these POD-**struct**s have an **int** as their second data member, but only BB and CC share a common initial member sequence. Now suppose we create a **union**, MM, comprising each of these POD-**struct** types:

```
union MM { AA aa; BB bb; CC cc; };  // union of all three POD-struct types
```

We can now write a function, test1, to illustrate what is and isn't permitted with respect to cross-accessing common members within a **union**:

```
#include <cassert>  // standard C assert macro
void test1()
{
    BB b = { 1, 2, '3'};  // Initialize an object, b, of type BB.
    MM m;                 // union m of type MM; aa is the active member
    m.bb = b;            // assign to bb to make it the active member of m
    assert(m.bb.y == 2); // OK, value as assigned
    assert(m.cc.u == 2); // OK, access through matching initial sequence
    assert(m.aa.g == 2); // Bug, might work but has undefined behavior
    m.aa.h = 3;          // OK, changes active member to aa
    assert(m.cc.u == 2); // Bug, might work but cc member is no longer active
}
```

Because BB and CC have the first two data members in common, it is valid to write to one and subsequently read one of the common members from the other; see also *Use Cases — Vertical encoding for non-trivial types (standard layout)* on page 448. Note that, even though a **float** and an **int** will typically both occupy the same amount of space (four bytes) on common platforms, and thus m.aa.g and m.bb.y will occupy the same location in memory, an attempt to access the second data member when the initial member sequence is other than an exact match nonetheless has **undefined** behavior. Moreover, writing to any part of any other, noncompatible union member, irrespective of its relative physical position in its POD-**struct** (e.g., writing to aa.h), renders the previously active member of the union (e.g., bb) inactive, thereby precluding access to *any* members of the original pair of partially compatible POD-**structs** (e.g., bb and cc). On most platforms, however, the buggy code in the previous example is likely to compile and perform as though there was no **undefined** behavior; see *Potential Pitfalls — Misuse of unions* on page 505.

3. **Lifetime of an object begins at allocation** — Scalar types are trivial types, which means no code need run to either construct or destroy scalar objects. POD-**struct** types, like the scalars they comprise, also are trivial. The lifetime of a POD object starts when memory is first acquired for it, such as by a variable declaration or a call to the **new** operator. However, starting the lifetime of a POD does not guarantee that it has been initialized. Consider the case of declaring an **int** as a local variable:

```
void test2()
{
    int  x;         // x is not initialized, but lifetime begins.
    int* p = &x;    // We cannot read x but can take its address.
    int  y = x;     // Bug, read of uninitialized x
    *p = 5;         // We can write to x, thereby initializing it.
    int  z = x;     // Now we can read x.
}
```

Similarly, the lifetime of a POD object ends when its memory is reclaimed, such as by going out of scope, or when it is repurposed by constructing a new object in that memory; the destructor of a POD is always trivial, and nothing will execute when a POD object is destroyed. Note that explicit invocation of a trivial destructor will not end the lifetime of an object, including a POD object.[3]

Although a POD can be declared **const** or contain a non**static const** data member, such a POD cannot exist in an uninitialized state; attempting to create an object that requires **const** data member initialization will fail to compile if the initializer is omitted:

```
struct S2          // POD type containing two scalar data members
{
    const int* p;  // Pointers, but not references, can be POD data members.
    const int  i;  // Note that const data members must be initialized.
};

S2 s2a;            // Error, uninitialized const data member, s2a.i
S2 s2b = { 0, 5 }; // OK, const data member s2b.i is initialized to 5.
```

---

[3]As of C++20, running the destructor of any object — even a POD — ends its lifetime, and assigning a value to it after the fact would have **undefined** behavior; see CWG issue 2256 (**smith16b**).

The POD-**struct** S2 above contains two data members, the second of which, S2::i, is **const** and must be initialized explicitly when created. Nonetheless, S2 satisfies the requirements of a POD type; hence, its lifetime starts the moment storage for its footprint is allocated:

```
S2 s2c =        // Initialize POD object by accessing its member address first.
{
    &s2c.i,     // Initialize first data member with address of second one.
    0           // must provide initializer for const member i, or ill formed
};              // In general, C++ object lifetimes would typically begin here.
```

As the code snippet above illustrates, we are permitted to access the internal data members of the object for the purpose of extracting their address even before the object is initialized.

Another property of the subset of POD types whose objects do *not* require initialization is that the flow of control is permitted to jump over them (e.g., using a **goto** statement) when not initialized explicitly:

```
void func3()  // OK, valid C++ function; jumping over uninitialized POD
{
    goto Label;  // OK, jump over definition of uninitialized POD object.
    S1 s1;       // POD type with no need for code to run at construction
Label:           // Jump to here, no problem.
    ;
}
```

In the function func3 in the example above, no code is required to run to initialize s1; hence, it is permissible to jump over the object's definition.[4] When the POD object is initialized explicitly, however, jumping over that initialization is not an option:

```
void func3b()  // Error, ill formed; attempt to jump over initialized POD
{
    goto Label;           // Error, cannot jump over initialized POD object
    S2 s = { &s.i, 0 };   // This POD-type requires const initialization.
Label:                    // cannot jump over code required to initialize
    ;
}
```

In the function func3b in the example above, even though S2 is of POD type, it contains a **const** data member and therefore must be initialized; hence, not every POD type is suitable for this Byzantine use of **goto**. There are, however, other, more practical applications of the same property that we used **goto** to illustrate here; see *Use Cases — Secure buffer (trivially constructible)* on page 460.

---

[4]Although no longer required by the C++ Standard, many common implementations still require that the type of object whose definition the **goto** bypasses has a **trivial destructor** as well as a **trivial constructor**; see *Annoyances — The C++ Standard has not yet stabilized in this area* on page 521.

Any object that requires a **vtable pointer** or **virtual base pointer** cannot have a trivial constructor, as the values of those pointers would be left uninitialized by a trivial constructor. Due to this need to initialize the hidden pointers within an object, such types cannot be POD types.

4. **Bitwise copyablity** — All of the bits within the value representation of the footprint of a POD object, i.e., excluding any padding, contribute to its usable value. For non-POD types, some of those usable bits might refer to aspects of the implementation such as the address of an object-owned resource. Because such a resource is typically released upon the object's destruction, cavalierly overwriting such administrative information with, say, a bitwise copy of another object could result in resources being leaked or in multiple objects claiming ownership of the same resource, resulting in program misbehavior. However, because POD types have trivial destructors, we can reasonably assume that they do not hold such resource information, and thus we do not need to concern ourselves about overwriting one object with another. Nor do we need to concern ourselves about having multiple objects sharing a bitwise-identical value representation active within a program at any given time:

```
#include <cassert>  // standard C assert macro
#include <cstring>  // std::memcpy

void func4()
{
    int x = 123;               // Create initialized POD object x.
    unsigned char b[sizeof x]; // Create uninitialized byte buffer b.
    std::memcpy(b, &x, sizeof b); // Copy POD object x to byte buffer b.

    int y = 456;               // Create initialized POD object y.
    std::memcpy(&y, b, sizeof b); // Copy byte buffer b to POD object y.
    assert(y == x);            // value 123 successfully copied to y

    int z;                     // Create uninitialized POD object z.
    std::memcpy(&z, &y, sizeof(int)); // Copy bytes directly from y to z.
    assert(z == x);            // value 123 successfully copied to z
}
```

In the example code above, we first create an object of POD type, x, and initialize it to the value 123. Then, we create an **unsigned char** buffer,[5] b, having the same number of bytes as the footprint of x and use std::memcpy to copy all the bits from x to b. Next, we create another object, y, of the *same* POD type and initialize it to a different value, 456. Then we std::memcpy the bytes from b into y and observe that the original value of x, 123, has been successfully transferred. What's more, we are also able to create an object, z, in an *uninitialized* state and then initialize it from an initialized object, y, of the same POD type by copying the bytes directly from y

---

[5]It is safe to copy **trivial** objects into arrays of **char**, **unsigned char**, and std::byte (C++17) but not **signed char** or **char8_t** (C++20).

to z using std::memcpy. Recall, however, that not all objects of POD type can be created in an uninitialized state (see item 3). Objects of any type that might need to execute code (e.g., acquire or release a resource) during construction, destruction, or assignment — such as std::string or std::vector — explicitly have **undefined behavior** when used with std::memcpy, whether or not the object can be created in an uninitialized state; see *Use Cases — Fixed-capacity string (trivially copyable)* on page 470.

5. **Use with offsetof macro** — The standard C offsetof macro may be applied reliably to **accessible** non**static** data members of any POD-**struct**. For example, consider an **aggregate type**, A, comprising five scalar types and a **char** array:

```
struct A { char c; double d; short s; char a[2]; int i; bool b; };
    // simple aggregate POD-struct
```

Because A is of POD type, we are guaranteed to be able to use offsetof to get the offset of each member from the start of the **struct**, shown in the example code below, and the size and alignment values are typical of a 64-bit platform:

```
#include <cassert>  // standard C assert macro
#include <cstddef>  // standard C offsetof macro

                                      // type    size    alignment
static_assert( 0 ==  offsetof(A, c),     "");  // char    1        1
static_assert( 8 ==  offsetof(A, d),     "");  // double  8        8
static_assert(16 ==  offsetof(A, s),     "");  // short   2        2
static_assert(18 ==  offsetof(A, a),     "");  // char[2] 2        1
static_assert(18 ==  offsetof(A, a[0]),  "");  // char    1        1
static_assert(19 ==  offsetof(A, a[1]),  "");  // char    1        1
static_assert(20 ==  offsetof(A, a[2]),  "");  // Bug, beyond array range
static_assert(51 ==  offsetof(A, a[33]), "");  // Bug, beyond array range
static_assert(20 ==  offsetof(A, i),     "");  // int     4        4
static_assert(24 ==  offsetof(A, b),     "");  // bool    1        1

// Verify that our platform assumptions are correct:
static_assert(32 == sizeof(A),           "");  // A       32       8
static_assert( 8 == alignof(A),          "");  // "       "        "

void test3()
{
    A a;
    assert(  reinterpret_cast<char*>(&a.i)
          == reinterpret_cast<char*>(&a) + offsetof(A, i));
}
```

Here we are using `offsetof` at compile time to determine the relative position of the various subfields within the aggregate. Within `test3`, we verify that if we add the offset of field `i` to the starting address of object `a`, we get the address of `a.i`.

As a shortcut, in this specific case, we are able to avoid the second **reinterpret_cast** by cheating and using the address of the first data member, `c`, which we know, given that A is a POD, to have the same address as the enclosing A object and patently has type **char***:

```
void test4()
{
    A a;

    // clever trick to avoid second reinterpret_cast
    assert(reinterpret_cast<char*>(&a.i) == &a.c + offsetof(A, i));
}
```

Had the first data member been anything but a **char** or other byte-sized object, we could not have omitted the second cast:

```
struct A2 { int i; char c; };
    // aggregate where first data member has size greater than 1

void test5()
{
    A2 a2;
    assert(reinterpret_cast<void*>(&a2.c) == &a2.i + offsetof(A2, c));
    //                                              ^^
    // Bug, adding offset to address of int, whose size is greater than one
}
```

In the code snippet above, we need to make sure that we traffic exclusively in byte-sized entities of like kind, which requires us to explicitly cast the address of the object or its first member to a pointer to a byte-sized type:

```
void test6()
{
    A2 a2;
    assert(   reinterpret_cast<unsigned char*>(&a2.c)
           == reinterpret_cast<unsigned char*>(&a2) + offsetof(A2, c));
    //         ^^^^^^^^^^^^^^^^^^^^^^^^^^^^^^^^^^^^^^^^
}
```

This more verbose, two-cast approach is explicitly supported by the C++ Standard and generalizes to POD-type aggregates of arbitrary nesting levels:

```
struct A3 { int i; A2 a2; };
    // POD-type aggregate containing nonscalar data members

void test7()
{
    A3 a3;
    assert(   reinterpret_cast<unsigned char*>(&a3.a2.i)
           == reinterpret_cast<unsigned char*>(&a3) + offsetof(A3, a2.i));
}
```

Notice that we were able to obtain the offset of the integer i nested within the aggregate a2 of type A2. More general class types, especially those involving virtual base classes, do not lend themselves to use with offsetof; see *Use Cases — Navigating a compound object using offsetof (standard layout)* on page 456 and *Potential Pitfalls — Aggressive use of offsetof* on page 520.

6. **Other advantages** — POD types, with their trivial nature and predictable layouts, are suitable for many applications. As an example, the "character" type of std::basic_string<CharT> (i.e., CharT) may be of any nonarray POD type; see *Use Cases — Elements of fixed-capacity string (trivial)* on page 476 and *Use Cases — Secure buffer (trivially constructible)* on page 460.

C++03 POD types

In C++03, the requirements for a user-defined type to be of POD type were as restrictive as they were simple: Every **struct** or **union** that was to be considered of POD type needed to be of **aggregate type** with only POD type members:

```
+----------------------------------------------------+
| All C++03 (Non-Enumeration) User-Defined Types |
|                a.k.a. "class types"                |
|       .----------------------------------.         |
|       |          C++03 Aggregates        |         |
|       |       .--------------------.      |         |
|       |       ( C++03 POD classes   )     |         |
|       |       `--------------------'      |         |
|       `----------------------------------'         |
+----------------------------------------------------+
```

That is, every POD-**struct** in C++03 must, first and foremost, be of **aggregate type**, i.e., precisely those types that classically could be **value initialized** using an empty braced initializer; see Section 2.1."Braced Init" on page 215:

```
struct X { int i, j; double d[2]; };      X x = {};   // OK, X is an aggregate.
class  Y { int i; public: Y(); ~Y(); };   Y y = {};   // Error, Y isn't.
```

A *C++03 aggregate* is an array, **class**, **struct**, or **union** having no user-declared[6] constructors, no **private** or **protected** non**static** data members, no base classes, and no **virtual**
functions:

```
// Class declaration                  Is a C++03 aggregate?
class  A0  { };                       // Yes, empty class is an aggregate.
class  A1  { int x; };                // no, private data member
class  A2  { protected: int x; };     // no, protected data member
class  A3  { public: int x; };        // yes, public data
class  A4  { int f(); };              // yes, private nonvirtual function
class  A5  { static A1 x; };          // Yes, static members don't matter.
struct A6  { A6() { } };              // no, user-declared default ctor
struct A7  { A7(const A7&) { } };     // no, user-declared copy ctor
struct A8  { A8(int) { } };           // no, user-declared value ctor
struct A9  { ~A9(); };               // Yes, destructor can be declared.
struct A10 { A10& operator=(const A10&); };
                                      // yes, user-declared copy assignment allowed
struct A11 { int* x; };               // Yes, pointers are allowed in aggregates.
struct A12 : A0 { };                  // no, base class
struct A13 { virtual void f(); };     // no, virtual function
struct A14 { A1  x; };                // Yes, data members need not be aggregates.
struct A15 { A13 x; };                // Yes,   "       "       "   "   "      "

struct A16 { const int x; };          // yes, but must initialize const values
struct A17 { int& x; };               // yes,  "      "         "    references
union  A18 { int x; double y; };      // Yes, unions can be aggregates.
```

As the example types above illustrate, an aggregate may contain arbitrary public data members, private nonvirtual functions, and static members of any kind. Although an aggregate
may not declare any constructors, it is permitted to declare a copy-assignment operator and
a destructor. Importantly, an aggregate is permitted to contain elements that are themselves not of aggregate type. Hence, an array of any C++ type would itself be considered
an aggregate:

```
#include <string>  // std::string
std::string a[10] = {};  // a is an aggregate.
```

---

[6]The C++03 term **user-declared** is replaced in C++11 by **user-provided** because a **special member
function** that is explicitly declared and immediately defaulted (see Section 1.1."Defaulted Functions" on
page 33) or deleted (see Section 1.1."Deleted Functions" on page 53) is considered user-declared and yet
is not user-provided; hence, a class with, e.g., explicitly defaulted constructors can still be an aggregate in
C++11.

Now that we have classified what kinds of user-defined types are considered **aggregate types** in C++03, let's step back and appreciate the complete set of **C++03 POD types**. We begin by observing that all of the scalar types are POD types in every version of C++:

```
+----------------------------------------------------------+
|                    All C++03 Types                       |
|                                                          |
|       .------------------------------------.             |
|       |       C++03 Aggregate Types        |             |
|       |                                    |             |
|       |   .----------------------------.   |             |
|       |   |    C++03 POD classes       |   |             |
|       |   |                            |   |             |
|       `--+ - - C++03 POD Types - - +--'             |
|       |   |                        |   |             |
|       |   |      C++03 Scalars     |   |             |
|       |   `------------------------'   |             |
|       `------------------------------------'             |
+----------------------------------------------------------+
```

A *C++03 scalar* is a possibly **const** or **volatile** arithmetic type, enumeration type, pointer type, or pointer-to-member type:

```
         int        i   = { 0   };   // integer
const short          cs  = { 0   };   // const short
         double     d   = { 0.0 };   // floating point
         enum E { }  e   = { E()  };   // enumeration
         char*      p   = { 0   };   // pointer to char
const char*         pc  = { 0   };   // pointer to const char
         char* const cp  = { 0   };   // const pointer to char
class C; int       C::*pm  = { 0   };   // pointer to int member data
         void (C::*pmf)() = { 0   };   // pointer to void member function
```

As it turns out, scalars can also be initialized using the braced notation in C++03, just not with empty braces. A C++03 POD-**struct** is an aggregate class, declared with either the **struct** or **class class key**, that has no non-POD-**struct** members, no non-POD-**union** members, no array members having non-POD elements, no non**static** *reference* members, and no user-declared copy-assignment operator or destructor:

```
// Class declaration              Is a C++03 POD?
class  B0 { };                    // Yes, an empty (aggregate) class is a POD.
class  B1 { public: int x; };     // Yes, public data
class  B2 { int f(); };           // Yes, private non-virtual function
class  B3 { static B1 x; };       // Yes, static members don't matter
struct B4 { ~B4(); };             // No, a destructor cannot be declared.
struct B5 { B5& operator=(const B5&); };
                                  // No, copy assignment cannot be declared.
struct B6 { int* x; };            // Yes, pointers are allowed in PODs too.
struct B7 { B1   x; };            // No, any data members must also be PODs.
```

```
struct B8 { const int x; };          // Yes, but must initialize const values
struct B9 { int& x; };               // No, references are not permitted in PODs.
```

The examples shown here are a subset of the same examples used above to illustrate what is and is not a C++03 aggregate. The additional restrictions are (1) no copy-assignment operator or destructor may be declared, (2) all nested objects must also be PODs, and (3) non**static** reference members are not permitted.

A C++03 POD-**union** is an **aggregate class** declared with the **union** class key and having the same restrictions as a POD-**struct**, above:

```
// Union declaration               Is a C++03 POD?
union U0 { };                       // Yes, an empty (aggregate) union is a POD.
union U1 { public: int x; };        // yes, public data
union U2 { private: int f(); };     // yes, private nonvirtual function
union U3 { static int x; };         // Error, static members not allowed in C++03
union U4 { int* x; };               // Yes, pointers are allowed in PODs too.
union U5 { const int x; };          // yes, but must initialize const values
union U6 { int x; ~U6(); };         // No, POD cannot have user-defined destructor.
```

The C++03 Standard defines a POD **class** as a class that is either a POD-**struct** or a POD-**union**.

Finally, we have our complete set of C++03 POD types: a possibly cv-qualified (1) scalar type, (2) POD-**struct**, (3) POD-**union**, or (4) array of the preceding:

```
const double              cd    = { 5.0 };        // scalar
class C { }               c     = { };            // POD-struct
union U { int i; char* p; } u    = { 5 };          // POD-union
volatile int              via[] = { 0, 1, 2 };    // array of scalar
struct S { int x, y; }    sa[3] = { {1}, {2, 3} }; // array of POD-struct
```

C++11 generalized POD types

Prior to C++11, the benefits of POD types listed above were available only by eschewing many of the features that distinguish C++ from C. Over time it became clear that many of the restrictions on PODs were unnecessary and could be relaxed while still preserving essentially all of its desirable properties. C++11 widens the set of types that can be treated as POD types. In particular, C++11 no longer requires that a POD **class** be an aggregate:

```
class A { int x; };   // C++11 POD but not an aggregate; contains private data
class B : A { };      // C++11 POD but not an aggregate; has a base class
```

Neither A nor B above are aggregates, so they are not C++03 POD types, but each is a C++11 POD type.

What's more, it was also observed that not every property of PODs is necessary for every use case. In making its definition more general and formal, C++11 defines the POD type category as the intersection of two more focused type categories: **standard-layout types**, for which members have a predictable memory-layout order, and **trivial types**, which can be constructed and destroyed without executing any code and which can be bitwise copied:

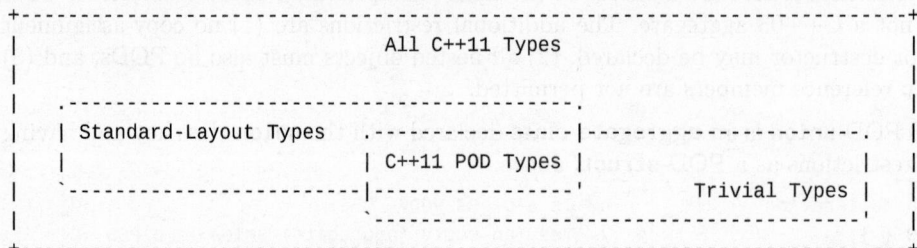

By partitioning the requirements necessary for a type to be considered a POD into two orthogonal sets of requirements, we widen the applicability of the subset of POD properties associated with each respective type category.

1. **Standard layout** — In general, the C++ Standard avoids discussing the layout of a class object. To provide compatibility with other languages, however, certain guarantees do need to be made for a subset of types. These guarantees can extend to types that are not entirely representable in other languages. For example, empty nonvirtual base classes typically take up no space in the physical layout of an object. Similarly, nonvirtual member functions do not affect the physical layout of an object in any way.

   Given an object of **standard-layout type**, we can reliably predict the order in which each of the subobjects appears in that object. It is these kinds of types that allow access via identical leading sequences in **union**s; see *Use Cases — Vertical encoding for non-trivial types (standard layout)* on page 448. It is also precisely these kinds of objects that are guaranteed to be, in some sense, physically translatable to a C-style **struct**; see *Use Cases — Translating a C++-only type to C (standard layout)* on page 452. Finally, in addition to predicting the order, we can use the C **offsetof** macro to reliably and portably extract the offset of each subobject from the base address of its enclosing object, though there is no guarantee that such an offset will be the same across nonidentical builds of the same program; see *Use Cases — Navigating a compound object using* **offsetof** *(standard layout)* on page 456.

2. **Trivial types** — While there is no standard-defined term, we use the word *triviality* to describe **special member functions** where no bespoke work needs to be done by compiler-provided implementations. Operations being **trivial** entails not needing to invoke any **user-provided** functions and having no need to manage the **dynamic type** of an object through the updating of a **vtable** pointer or virtual base pointer; see *Use Cases — Fixed-capacity string (trivially copyable)* on page 470. A trivial type is essentially one where all of its **special member functions** are trivial.

As it happens, trivial types themselves are too coarse a category to be sufficiently practicable, and subdividing that category further into two subcategories — namely, trivially copyable, which implies trivially destructible, and trivially default constructible
— adds substantial utility and flexibility. Default construction or destruction is considered trivial if it can be performed without having to execute any code, e.g., to
initialize an object's members, its **vtable pointer**, or its **virtual base pointer**, or otherwise manage resources. Similarly, copy construction and copy-assignment operations
are trivial if they may be performed using bitwise-copy algorithms, such as but not
limited to `std::memcpy`; see *Trivial subcategories* on page 429.

Standard-layout types

All **scalar types** are standard-layout types:

```
// Type         Is standard layout?
int   x; // yes, scalar type
double y; // yes,    "    "
char* z; // Yes, pointers are scalar types.
```

Moreover, arrays and cv-qualified versions of **standard-layout types** are also **standard-layout**
types:

```
class X;
```

```
// Type              Is standard layout?
volatile int a[5];  // yes, array of volatile scalar type
X*          p;      // yes, const pointer to arbitrary type
```

For a **class**, **struct**, or **union** type to be deemed a **standard-layout type**, each of several
independent properties must hold.

1. The type has no non**static** data members that are of reference type:

```
// Type                          Is standard layout?
struct S0a { };                  // yes
struct S0b { int   x; };         // yes
struct S0c { int*  x; };         // yes
struct S0d { int&  x; };         // no, has lvalue reference member
struct S0e { const int  x; };    // yes, but must be initialized
struct S0f { const int* x; };    // yes
struct S0g { const int& x; };    // no, has lvalue reference member
struct S0h { int&& x; };         // no, has rvalue reference member
struct S0i { static int&& x; };  // Yes, reference member is static.
```

2. The type has no virtual base classes:

```
// Type                          Is standard layout?
struct B1                { };  // yes
struct S1a :         B1 { };  // Yes, base class is not virtual.
struct S1b : virtual B1 { };  // No, base class is virtual.
```

3. The type has no virtual functions:

```
// Type                          Is standard layout?
struct S2a {         void f(); };  // yes, has function that is not virtual
struct S2b { virtual void f(); };  // no, has virtual function
```

4. All non**static** data members, including bit fields, within the type have the same access control, i.e., any of **public**, **protected**, or **private**:

```
// Type                                          Is standard layout?
struct S3a { private: int x; private: int y; };  // yes, all members private
struct S3b { private: int x; public:  int y; };  // no, not same access
struct S3c { int x; private: public:  int y; };  // yes, all members public
```

5. All non**static** data members, including bit fields, of the type, e.g., class S, are direct members of a single class within the class hierarchy of S; i.e., if any non**static** data members reside in any direct or indirect base class of S, then no non**static** data members reside in S or any other base class of S. Otherwise, any base classes of S must be empty:

```
// Type                   Is standard layout?
struct A4 { };            // yes, empty class
struct B4 { char c; };    // yes, no base classes
struct S4a : A4 { };      // Yes, base and derived classes are empty.
struct S4b : B4 { };      // Yes, only base class is nonempty.
struct S4c : A4 { int i; };  // Yes, only derived class is nonempty.
struct S4d : B4 { int i; };  // no, nonempty base and derived classes
struct S4e : A4, B4 { };  // Yes, only one base class is nonempty.
struct S4f : B4, S4c { }; // No, two base classes are nonempty.
```

6. The type has no direct or indirect base classes with the same type as a subobject that would have a 0 offset within the type, e.g., the first non**static** data member of a **class** type, any member of a **union** type, and any base classes of those members. This requirement of **standard-layout types** is a consequence of the **unique-object-address** requirement, which states that no two *distinct* objects of the same type B within a class C are ever permitted to share the same address, even if B is an empty class type; hence, if this criterion would otherwise be violated, the compiler is required to adjust the object layout in a way that necessarily prevents C from satisfying the required property of **standard-layout types** that the address of an object is the same as the address of its first non**static** data member (see *Standard-layout class special properties* on page 420):

```
// Type                                Is standard layout?
struct X5 { };                         // yes
struct Y5 { };                         // yes
struct S5a            { X5 x; Y5 y; }; // yes, no base class
struct S5b : X5       { X5 x; Y5 y; }; // No, base is same type as first member.
struct S5c : Y5       { X5 x; Y5 y; }; // Yes, base is not same as first member.
struct S5d : X5, Y5 { X5 x; Y5 y; };   // No, base is same type as first member.
struct S5e : Y5, X5 { X5 x; Y5 y; };   // No,  "   "   "    "   "   "   "   "
```

Note that extra padding needs to be added to S5b precisely because the base class X5 subobject and the member X5 subobject x cannot exist at the same location. The member y of s5c does not cause such padding because it is not the first member, so it would not have the same offset as the base class Y5 subobject:

```
static_assert(1 == sizeof(X5), "");  // OK
static_assert(1 == sizeof(Y5), "");  // OK
static_assert(2 == sizeof(S5a), ""); // OK
static_assert(3 == sizeof(S5b), ""); // OK, S5b has an extra byte.
static_assert(2 == sizeof(S5c), ""); // OK, base class takes up no space.
static_assert(3 == sizeof(S5d), ""); // OK, S5d has an extra byte.
static_assert(3 == sizeof(S5e), ""); // OK, S5e "   "   "    "
```

Additional padding to prevent the overlap of a base class subobject and a member, which prevents a type from being a **standard-layout type**, can also occur for members of a different base class or for **union** data members:

```
// Type                  Is standard layout?
struct A5 { };           // yes
struct B5 { A5 a; };     // yes
struct S5f : A5, B5 { }; // No, A5::a would be at offset 0 without padding.

union U5 { char c; A5 a; }; // yes
struct S5g : A5 { U5 u; };  // No, u.a would be at offset 0 without padding.
```

7. The type has no two direct or indirect base classes of the same type. This restriction is again a consequence of the **unique-object-address** requirement combined with additional padding preventing the first non**static** data member from having an offset of 0:

```
// Type                     Is standard layout?
struct E6 { };              // Yes, size = 1.
struct F6 { };              // Yes, size = 1.
struct B6E : E6 { };        // Yes, size = 1.
struct B6F : F6 { };        // Yes, size = 1.
struct B6G : E6 { };        // Yes, size = 1.
struct S6a : B6E, B6F { }; // Yes, size = 1, derived from E6 and F6.
struct S6b : B6E, B6G { }; // No,  size = 2, derived twice from E6.
```

8. The type has no non**static** data members or direct base classes that are not themselves of standard-layout type:

```
// Type                                      Is standard layout?
struct Y7 { int i; public:  int j; };  // yes, same access control
struct N7 { int i; private: int j; };  // no, not same access control
struct S7a { Y7 d; };                  // yes, standard-layout member
struct S7b { N7 d; };                  // no, non-standard-layout member
struct S7c : Y7 { };                   // yes, standard-layout base class
struct S7d : N7 { };                   // no, non-standard-layout base class
```

Standard-layout class special properties

Although standard-layout types can be classes or scalars, the C++ type category known as **standard-layout class types** identifies an important category that is a subset of other important categories — each affording its own specific set of supported properties:

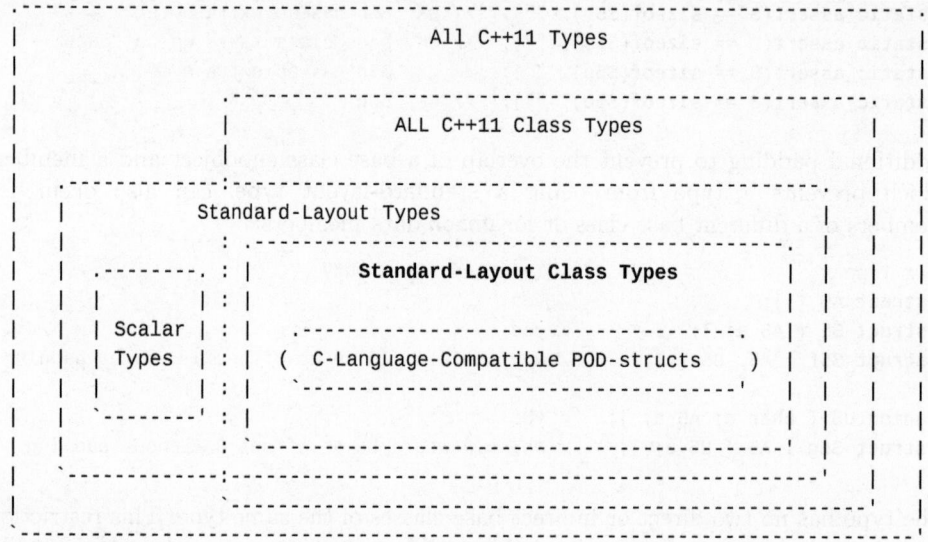

Importantly, for a class type to be considered **standard layout**, it does not need to be trivial or look like a C type in any way:

```
#include <cstddef>   // std::size_t

class String  // non-trivial standard-layout class type
{
    char*       d_array_p;   // scalar (standard layout)
    std::size_t d_length;    //    "        "       "
    std::size_t d_capacity;  //    "        "       "
```

```
public:
    String();                               // non-trivial
    String(const String& other);           //    "      "
    String& operator=(const String& other);  //   "      "
    ~String();                              //    "      "
};
```

In the definition of the `String` class shown above, there are no base classes or virtual functions, and all of the data members are scalars of the same access level, **private**; hence, this `String` class is of **standard-layout type** despite its having user-provided (and therefore non-trivial) default constructor, destructor, copy constructor, and copy-assignment special member functions; see *Trivial subcategories* on page 429. Similarly, `std::vector<T>` where `T` is any viable element type is almost certainly of **standard-layout type**, e.g., all private scalar member data with no virtual table; it's just not *trivial* as it potentially owns and manages a resource.

Standard-layout class types are guaranteed by the C++ Standard to have certain important properties.

1. **The first data member shares the address of the enclosing object.** That is, if a given class type, C, is of standard-layout type and if there are any data members in C or any base class, B, from which C derives, then the first data member in the sequence of data members defined in that scope will have the same address as the enclosing object:

   ```
   struct A { };
   struct C : A { int i, j; };  // All data members are in the derived class.

   struct B { double x, y; };
   struct D : B { };                // All data members are in the base class.

   #include <cassert>  // standard C assert macro
   void test1()
   {
       C c;
       D d;

       assert(&c == static_cast<void*>(&c.i));  // i is first member of c.
       assert(&d == static_cast<void*>(&d.x));  // x is first member of d.
   }
   ```

2. **Within a union, members can share a common initial member sequence.** When a **union** has two or more members of standard-layout class type and one is *active*, any other standard-layout class type that shares a CIMS with the type of the active member can be used to access any data member in that CIMS provided it

has been initialized. For example, consider a simple **standard-layout class**, SS, containing three public data members, of types **int**, **double**, and **void***, along with some other similar standard-layout class types, S0, S1, S2, and S3, that are in turn comprised into a union, U:

```
struct SS { int  i; double d; void* p; };

struct S0 { long i; double d; void* p; };          // 0 member CIMS
struct S1 { int  j; float  d; void* p; };          // 1   "       " w/ all but S0
struct S2 { int  j; double e; char* p; };          // 2   "       " with SS, S3
struct S3 { int  j; double e; void* q; S0 s; };    // 3   "       " with SS

union U { SS ss; S0 s0; S1 s1; S2 s2; S3 s3; };  // all standard-layout types
```

In the example above, the type of the first data member of S0 differs from that of SS and therefore shares no CIMS with SS or any of the other members of U. The first data member of S1 matches exactly that of SS (and all of the other members of U except S0) but differs in the type of its second member; hence, SS and S1 share a CIMS of length 1: **int**. The first two data members of S2 exactly match those of SS (but differ after that), so they share a CIMS of length 2: **int**, **double**. Finally, the first three data members of S3 exactly match those of SS, so they share a CIMS of length 3: **int**, **double**, **void***.

If we create an instance of our **union** U (e.g., u) with ss as the active member and initialize the three data members of SS, we are able to safely access none, some, or all of those values via the other members of U depending on the length of their mutual CIMS:

```
U u = { 3, 5.5, 0 };  // braced initialization of SS standard-layout member

int    i0 = u.s0.i;  // Bug, no CIMS with SS

int    i1 = u.s1.j;  // OK, j member of S1 is part of CIMS with SS.
double d1 = u.s1.d;  // Bug, d member of S1 is not part of CIMS with SS.
void*  p1 = u.s1.p;  // Bug, p    "    "  " " " "    "      "    " "   "

int    i2 = u.s2.j;  // OK, j member of S2 is part of CIMS with SS.
double d2 = u.s2.e;  // OK, e    "    "  " " " "    "    "      "    " "
void*  p2 = u.s2.p;  // Bug, p member of S2 is not part of CIMS with SS.

int    i3 = u.s3.j;  // OK, j member of S3 is part of CIMS with SS.
double d3 = u.s3.e;  // OK, e    "    "  " " " "    "    "      "    " "
void*  p3 = u.s3.q;  // OK, q    "    "  " " " "    "    "      "    " "
```

According to the definition of **standard-layout class types** (see *Standard-layout types* on page 417, above), at most one class in any class hierarchy is permitted to contain non**static** member data; hence, the CIMS is independent of where in an inheritance hierarchy the CIMS is defined:

```
struct E0 { };              // empty base class
struct E1 { };              //    "     "    "
struct AA { int x; };       // First non-static data member has type int.
struct BB : E0 { int x; };  //   "    "       "      "    "     "    "   "
struct CC : AA { };         //   "    "       "      "    "     "    "   "
struct DD : E1, CC { };     //   "    "       "      "    "     "    "   "
```

All of the standard-layout types AA, BB, CC, and DD (above) share a CIMS of length 1:
int. Hence, it is permissible, with a **union** of these types, to initialize or write to the
first data member of any one of them and then read the member from the same **union**
member or from any of the others:

```
const union UU { AA a; BB b; CC c; DD d; } uu = { 17 };   // Initialize uu.a.
const int xa = uu.a.x, xb = uu.b.x, xc = uu.c.x, xd = uu.d.x; // Read from any.
```

For a CIMS to pertain, the types of the members must match exactly:

```
struct FF { AA          x; };  // First non-static data member is AA.
struct GG { unsigned int x; }; //   "      "       "      "     " unsigned
struct HH { const int    x; }; //   "      "       "      "     " const
```

None of the standard-layout classes FF, GG, or HH shares a CIMS with any of AA, BB,
CC, or DD. Moreover, each standard-layout member of a union must be of *class* type to
qualify; hence, a raw **int** member of a **union** would not qualify:

```
union NoCIMS { int x; AA a; FF f; GG g; HH h; }; // no CIMS, different members
```

Note in particular that x is not of class type and hence has no members to participate in
a CIMS; writing to x does not give license to read from any of the other data members
and vice versa. What's more, adding a trailing data member of non-standard-layout
type to a class type that would otherwise have a CIMS renders the class type to be
non-standard-layout and, therefore, invalidates this special use of CIMS in unions:

```
struct NonSlct { int i; private: int j; };   // not standard-layout class type

struct Sx  { int x; };                        // is standard-layout class type
struct Sxy { int x; NonSlct y; };             // not   "        "       "    "

union NoCIMS2 { Sx a; Sxy b; };  // No CIMS because Sxy is not standard-layout
NoCIMS2 nc2 = { 3 };
int i4 = nc2.b.x;                // Bug, b.x is not part of a CIMS
```

Such misuse is not uncommon and is usually inadvertent; see *Potential Pitfalls —
Misuse of unions* on page 505.

3. **Standard-layout class types are guaranteed to support the standard C
offsetof macro.** The offsetof macro, defined in <cstddef>, takes a type argument (e.g., a type name, template parameter, or **decltype** expression) and a member
designator, returning the offset, in bytes, of that member within the named type. A

conforming implementation of the C++ Standard must support this macro for any type that is a **standard-layout class**. For example, consider a **standard-layout** Point class that happens to have a non-*trivial* destructor:

```
#include <cstddef>  // standard C offsetof macro

struct Point  // standard-layout type having all public data members
{
    int d_x, d_y;
    ~Point() { }  // user-provided (non-trivial) destructor
};

const std::size_t xoff = offsetof(Point, d_x);  // OK, return 0.
const std::size_t yoff = offsetof(Point, d_y);  // OK, return 4.
```

As we've seen, the address of the first member of a **standard-layout class**, d_x in this case, always has the same address as the class object itself, so the offset of d_x within Point is 0. Assuming **int** has a size of 4 bytes on our platform, we would expect d_y to be at offset 4 within any object of type Point.

If the data member is not accessible at the site that offsetof is called, the program is ill formed. As all of the data members of Point are **public**, we are able to use offsetof to access them (e.g., to initialize xoff and yoff) at file scope. Now consider a class Box that consists entirely of **private** data members and happens to have a non-trivial copy constructor. As before, **int** is assumed to have a size of 4 bytes:

```
class Box  // standard-layout type having all private data members
{
    int   d_length;
    int   d_width;
    Point d_origin;  // nested standard-layout class type

public:
    Box() // user-provided (non-trivial) constructor
    {
        static_assert(8 == offsetof(Box, d_origin.d_x), "");
                        // OK, d_origin is accessible within the constructor.
    }

    friend void boxUtil();  // grant function boxUtil private access
};

void boxUtil() { static_assert(12 == offsetof(Box, d_origin.d_y), ""); } // OK

std::size_t woff = offsetof(Box, d_width);  // Error, d_width is private.
```

Even with private data, the offsetof macro is viable when used from within (1) a member function (e.g., the Box constructor) or (2) a friend function (e.g., boxUtil) but not when used in any scope that doesn't have access to a private member of Box (e.g., the initializer for woff). Note that offsetof also works with a member of a member — e.g., it is able to return the offset within Point of the d_x member of the d_origin member.

In C++11 and C++14, use of offsetof on a non-standard-layout type is classified as having **undefined behavior**; in practice, however, most popular compilers will produce a usable result when using offsetof on some subset of non-standard-layout types, often accompanied by a warning.[7] Getting the offset of a member of a **virtual** base class is typically not supported, however, even on the most lenient compilers.

Trivial types

All scalar types are trivial types:

```
// Type        Is trivial?
int     x;  // yes, scalar type
double  y;  // yes,      "      "
char*   z;  // Yes, pointers are scalar types too.
```

Moreover, arrays and cv-qualified versions of trivial types are also trivial types:

```
// Type                 Is trivial?
double       a1[20];  // yes, array of trivial type
const int    i1 = 2;  // yes, const-qualified trivial type
volatile int a2[5];   // yes, array of volatile-qualified trivial type
```

For a **class**, **struct**, or **union** type to be deemed a trivial type, each of several independent properties must hold; see Section 1.1."Defaulted Functions" on page 33 and Section 1.1. "Deleted Functions" on page 53[8]:

1. The type has no **virtual** functions:

    ```
    // Type                         Is trivial?
    struct S0a { void f(); };        // yes, has no virtual functions
    struct S0b { virtual void f(); }; // no, has a virtual function
    ```

2. The type has no **virtual** base classes:

    ```
    // Type                         Is trivial?
    struct S1a { };                  // yes, empty class
    struct S1b : S1a { };            // yes, nonvirtual base class
    struct S1c : virtual S1a { };    // no, virtual base class
    ```

---

[7] In C++17, using offsetof for certain non-standard-layout types is classified as **conditionally supported**; i.e., it must either work as specified or be ill formed.

[8] C++17 updates the rules governing what constitutes a trivial type and makes them retroactive to previous standards; for simplicity, we are presenting them as they are in C++17, with the understanding that older compilers might treat edge cases somewhat differently; see *Annoyances — The C++ Standard has not yet stabilized in this area* on page 521.

3. The type has no non**static** data members employing a **default member initializer** (see Section 2.1."Default Member Init" on page 318):

```
// Type                                   Is trivial?
struct S2a { int i; };                    // yes
struct S2b { int i = 0; };                // no, default member initializer
struct S2c { int i = {}; };               // no, default member initializer
struct S2d { static const int i = 0; };   // yes, static const data member
struct S2e { static const int i{}; };     // yes,    "      "      "      "
```

4. The type has no user-provided default constructors:

```
struct S3a { int i; };          // yes
struct S3b { int i; S3b(); };   // no, user-provided default constructor
```

5. The type has at least one nondeleted trivial default constructor. A trivial constructor is one that is not user-provided and invokes a trivial default constructor for each base class and non**static** data member. Additionally, the presence of **virtual** functions, **virtual** base classes, or default member initializers (items 1–3 above) prevents the default constructor from being trivial, with the **virtual** entities necessitating the constructor to properly initialize the vtable pointer or the virtual base pointer:

```
// Type                          Is trivial?
struct S4a { };                  // yes
struct S4b { S4b(); };           // no, user-provided default constructor
struct S4c { S4c() = default; }; // yes, defaulted default constructor
struct S4d { S4d() = delete; };  // no, deleted default constructor
struct S4e { S4e() = default; S4e(int = 0) = delete; };  // yes, but ambiguous
struct S4f { S4f() = delete; S4f(int = 0) = default; };  // Error, bad syntax
```

```
// Type                    Is trivial?
struct S4g : S4a { };   // Yes, S4a base class has trivial default constructor.
struct S4h : S4b { };   // No, S4b base class has non-trivial default ctor.
struct S4i { S4c c; };  // Yes, S4c member has trivial default constructor.
struct S4j { S4d d; };  // No, S4d missing nondeleted default ctor.
struct S4k : S4e { };   // No, S4e default constructor is ambiguous, so S4k
                        //     default constructor is implicitly deleted.
```

Note that S4e above is trivial, but the default constructor is ambiguous and therefore cannot be used. This unusable default constructor prevents S4k from being trivial because the compiler cannot synthesize a default constructor for S4k. Also note that S4f(**int** = 0) cannot be defaulted and is thus ill formed; see Section 1.1."Defaulted Functions" on page 33.

6. The class has a trivial destructor — i.e., a destructor that is not user-provided, is not **virtual**, and for which each base class and non**static** member destructor is trivial.

The defaulted destructor must be nondeleted, which requires that each base class and non**static** member destructor also be nondeleted and accessible:

```
// Type                                                  Is trivial?
struct S5a { S5a() = default; };                         // yes
struct S5b { S5b() = default; ~S5b(); };                 // no, user-provided dtor
struct S5c { S5c() = default; ~S5c() = default; }; // yes
struct S5d { S5d() = default; ~S5d() = delete; };  // no, deleted dtor
struct S5e { private: ~S5e() = default; };               // Yes, but dtor is private.


// Type                        Is trivial?
struct S5f : S5a { };          // Yes, S5a base class has trivial destructor.
struct S5g : S5b { };          // No, S5b base class has non-trivial destructor.
struct S5h { S5c c; };         // Yes, S5c member has trivial destructor.
struct S5i { S5d d[5]; };      // No, S5d has a deleted destructor.
struct S5j : S5e { };          // No, S5e base class destructor is not accessible.
```

Note that S5e above is trivial, but the destructor is private and cannot be used except by **friend**s. The destructor for S5j is deleted because it cannot access the destructor for base class S5e, making S5j non-trivial.

7. The class has no user-provided copy constructors, move constructors, copy-assignment operators, or move-assignment operators:

```
// Type                                      Is trivial?
struct S6a { };                              // yes
struct S6b { S6b() = default;
             S6b(const S6b&) = default; }; // yes
struct S6c { S6c() = default;
             S6c(const S6c&); };             // no, has user-provided copy ctor
struct S6d { S6d() = default;
             S6d(const S6d&) = delete; };  // yes, no user-provided copy ctor
struct S6e { S6e& operator=(S6e&&); };       // no, user-provided move assignment
```

8. There is at least one nondeleted trivial copy constructor, move constructor, copy-assignment operator, or move-assignment operator. Each of these operations is trivial if it is not user-provided and if it invokes only trivial constructors or assignment operators for each base class and non**static** data member. Additionally, the presence of either **virtual** functions or **virtual** base classes (items 0 and 1, above) prevent the copy/move constructors and copy/move-assignment operators from being trivial:

```
// Type                               Is trivial?
struct S7a
{
    S7a()                  = default;  // trivial default constructor
    S7a(const S7a&)        = delete;   // deleted copy constructor
```

```
    S7a& operator=(const S7a&) = default;   // trivial copy assignment
};                                          // yes, one trivial copy operation

struct S7b
{
    S7b()                      = default;   // trivial default constructor
    S7b(const S7b&)            = delete;    // deleted copy constructor
    S7b& operator=(const S7b&) = delete;    // deleted copy assignment
};                                          // no, no nondeleted copy ops

struct S7c
{
    S7c()                      = default;   // trivial default constructor
    S7c(const S7c&)            = delete;    // deleted copy constructor
    S7c(S7c&&)                 = default;   // trivial move constructor
    S7c& operator=(const S7c&) = delete;    // deleted copy assignment
};                                          // yes, one trivial copy operation

struct S7d
{
    S7d()                      = default;   // trivial default constructor
    S7d(const S7d&);                        // user-provided copy ctor
    S7d(S7d&&)                 = default;   // trivial move constructor
};                                          // no, user-provided copy operation

struct S7e
{
    S7e()                      = default;   // trivial default constructor
    S7e(const S7e&)            = default;   // trivial copy constructor
    S7e& operator=(S7e&&);                  // user-provided move assignment
};                                          // no, user-provided move operation

struct S7f { const int i; };                // Yes, but assignment is deleted.

struct S7g : S7a { S7g()   = default; };    // yes, trivial base copy

struct S7h : S7b { S7h()   = default; };    // No, S7b copy ops are deleted.

struct S7i { S7d x; S7i()  = default; };    // No, copy ctor is not trivial.
```

In the example code above, S7b is not trivial because there are no nondeleted trivial copy operations; S7d and S7e are not trivial because each has at least one non-trivial copy/move operation (i.e., the copy constructor in the case of S7d and the move-assignment operator in the case of S7e).

Though uncommon, it is possible to create a trivial type having base classes or members with non-trivial copy/move operations by deleting those operations in the new type:

```
// Type                                              Is trivial?
struct S7j { S7d x; S7j()         = default;        // Yes, non-trivial copy ctor
             S7j(const S7j&)      = delete;  };     // deleted in outer class.

struct S7k : S7d { S7k()          = default;        // yes, deletes non-trivial
                   S7k(const S7k&) = delete;  };     // copy ctor

struct S7l { S7e y; S7l()         = default;        // yes, deletes non-trivial
             S7l& operator=(S7l&&) = delete;  };     // move assignment
```

Normally, a class having S7d as a member or base class would have a copy constructor that is non-trivial because it invokes the non-trivial copy constructor of S7d. However, both S7j and S7k are trivial because they delete the copy constructor, leaving the trivial copy-assignment operator as the only nondeleted copy/move operation. Similarly, S7l is trivial because it deletes what would otherwise be a non-trivial move-assignment operator.

Trivial subcategories

By partitioning the requirements for POD types into two orthogonal categories, standard-layout and trivial types, we dramatically increase the applicability of functionality associated with either one separately. Requiring a type to be entirely trivial is rarely necessary, and segregating the aspects of triviality into finer-grained requirements increases the applicability of the individual properties enabled by the various trivial subcategories:

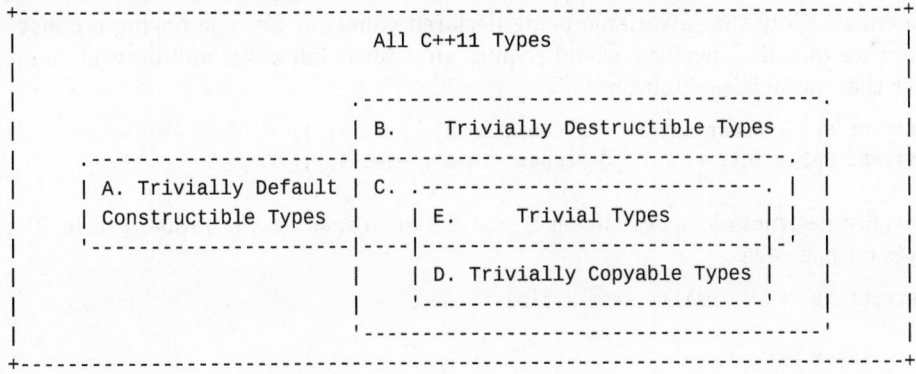

As the Venn diagram above suggests, types that support any sort of triviality can be partitioned as shown:

A. Trivially default constructible

B. Trivially destructible

C. Trivially default constructible and trivially destructible

D. Trivially copyable, which implies trivially destructible

E. Trivial, which implies trivially default constructible and trivially copyable

Each of these subtypes is required to satisfy a different subset of the requirements needed for entirely **trivial types**, making them separately more functionally complete and therefore more generally applicable.

A. **Trivially default constructible** types have a trivial default constructor, satisfying properties 1–5 in *Trivial types* on page 425:

```
struct SA  // trivially default constructible
{
    int x, y;
    SA() = default;               // trivial default constructor
    SA(const SA&);                // user-provided copy constructor
    SA& operator=(const SA&);     // user-provided assignment operator
    ~SA();                        // user-provided destructor
};
```

The lifetime of an object of **trivially default constructible** type begins when storage for it is allocated for the object and persists until its storage is reclaimed or repurposed. Unless the **trivially default constructible** type is also **trivially destructible**, we can end its lifetime by calling the destructor.[9] Objects of this category have an indeterminate value unless and until they are written to. It is also permissible to jump over the definition of variables of such types that do not have initializers, e.g., via a **goto** statement. Note that a variable being declared **const**, or its type having a **const**- or reference-qualified member, would require an explicit initializer and prevent jumping over that variable's definition:

```
struct SA2 { const int i; SA2(const SA2&); ~SA2(); }; // must initialize
struct SA3 { int& r;      SA3(const SA3&); ~SA3(); }; //    "        "
```

B. **Trivially destructible** types have a trivial destructor, satisfying property 6 in *Trivial types* on page 425:

```
struct SB  // trivially destructible
{
    int x, y;
    SB();                         // user-provided default constructor
    SB(const SB&);                // user-provided copy constructor
    SB& operator=(const SB&);     // user-provided assignment operator
    ~SB() = default;              // trivial destructor
};
```

---

[9]As of C++20, explicitly calling a destructor on any object, including one of **trivially destructible type**, ends its lifetime such that accessing it in a way that depends on its value is considered to have undefined behavior; taking the address of the destroyed object is allowed, however, provided that the storage had not yet been released or reused.

Trivially destructible types are potentially candidates to be **literal types**, objects of which are usable at compile time in **constant expressions**. More generally, invoking the destructor of such objects can be safely omitted; see Section 2.1."**constexpr** Functions" on page 257 and Section 2.1."**constexpr** Variables" on page 302.

Finally, trivially destructible types simplify the use of **union**s. Although C++11 no longer requires **union** members to be trivial types (see Section 3.1."**union** '11" on page 1174), the presence of any member in a **union** that is of a type such as SA that is not trivially destructible causes the **union**'s implicitly defined destructor to be deleted:

```cpp
union U1a { SA s; int i; };              // OK, but U1a's destructor is deleted.
union U1b { SA s; int i; ~U1b() { } };   // OK, user-defined no-op destructor
union U1c { SB s; int i; };              // OK, SB is trivially destructible.

void f1()
{
    U1a u1a{SA{}};   // Error, destructor for U1a is deleted.
    U1b u1b{SA{}};   // OK, U1b has a user-defined destructor.
    U1c u1c{SB{}};   // OK, U1c is trivially destructible.
    u1b.s.~SA();     // explicit destructor call to avoid leaking resources
}
```

A local variable of type U1a cannot be defined because the compiler cannot generate code to destroy it at the end of the current scope. The definition of u1b is valid, but because the destructor for U1b cannot know the current active member, we explicitly invoke the non-trivial destructor for the active member to avoid potentially leaking resources. The definition of u1c, conversely, has neither of these problems because all of the members of U1c (and, consequently, U1c itself) have trivial destructors; regardless of the active member at the end of the scope, u1c can be destroyed without invoking any code.

C. Trivially default constructible and trivially destructible types satisfy properties 1–6 in *Trivial types* on page 425:

```cpp
struct SC // trivially default constructible and destructible
{
    int x, y;
    SC() = default;              // trivial default constructor
    SC(const SC&);               // user-provided copy constructor
    SC& operator=(const SC&);    // user-provided assignment operator
    ~SC() = default;             // trivial destructor
};
```

There are comparatively few use cases where types that are both trivially default constructible and trivially destructible but not trivially copyable are needed. Although a variable must be **trivially constructible** without requiring explicit initialization for its definition to be jumped over (e.g., by a **goto** statement), C++ no longer requires that the type also be **trivially destructible**[10]; many implementations, however, still impose this requirement (see *Annoyances — The C++ Standard has not yet stabilized in this area* on page 521):

```
int func()  // works even when dtor is still required to be trivial
{
    goto L;         // Jump over definition of obj.
    SC obj;         // definition having trivial default ctor (and destructor)
 L: obj.x = 5;      // Initialize public x data member with value 5.
    return obj.x;   // Return value of initialized x data member.
}
```

In a conforming compiler, the only requirement for type `SC` is that it be **trivially constructible** without explicit initialization.

Another situation that might elicit a need for types that are both **trivially default constructible** and **trivially destructible** occurs when changing the active member of a **union** via assignment. In such cases, the type of the original active member must be **trivially destructible** to avoid resource leaks, and the type of the newly active member must be **trivially default constructible** to avoid **undefined** behavior:

```
struct TD  // trivially destructible (only)
{
    TD();                       // user-provided default constructor
    ~TD() = default;            // trivial destructor
    TD& operator=(const TD&);   // user-provided assignment operator
};

struct TC  // trivially default constructible (only)
{
    TC() = default;             // trivial default constructor
    ~TC();                      // user-provided destructor
    TC& operator=(const TC&);   // user-provided assignment operator
};

union U2
{
    TD orig;  // trivially destructible; holds no resources
    TC next;  // trivially constructible; enables assignment to raw memory
    ~U2();    // user-provided destructor required for U2
};

void f2()  // Initialize union U2 and change the active member once.
{
    U2 u{TD()};     // OK, u.orig is copy initialized and active.
```

---

[10]This requirement was initially added in 2012 (for C++14), removed in 2016 (for C++17), and reinstated in 2019 (with the resolution as a **defect report** of CWG issue 2256; **smith16b**).

```
    u.next = TC();   // OK, make u.next the active member of union u.
    u.next.~TC();    // Destroy the active member before u goes out of scope.
}
```

A user-provided destructor is required for U2 because one of its members is not trivially destructible. Note that the two member types in U2, TD and TC, are not symmetric because TD is only initialized and never assigned to, whereas TC is only assigned to and never initialized within the **union**. Safely assigning to u.next requires that u.orig be trivially destructible and that u.next be trivially default constructible. At the end of the function, we destroy u.next to avoid leaking resources.

Each time an assignment changes the **active member** of a **union**, the lifetime of one member ends and the lifetime of another member begins, but no member destructors or constructors will be invoked. Thus, changing the active member of u from next back to orig using assignment is problematic because (a) the non-trivial destructor for next is not run, possibly resulting in a resource leak, and (b) orig is not initialized prior to being used as the target of an assignment, resulting in **undefined behavior**:

```
void f3()   // Attempt to change the active member of union U2 twice.
{
    U2 u{TD()};      // OK, u.orig is copy initialized and active.
    u.next = TC();   // OK, make u.next the active member of union u.
    u.orig = TD();   // Bug (UB), u.next is not destroyed, and u.orig is not
                     //    constructed prior to assignment.
}
```

The safe way to change the active member in this circumstance is to explicitly destroy the original active member (i.e., u.next) and explicitly construct the new active member (i.e., u.orig) in place:

```
#include <new>         // placement new
void f4()   // Initialize union U2 and change the active member twice.
{
    U2 u{TD()};           // OK, u.orig is copy initialized and active.
    u.next = TC();        // OK, make u.next the active member of union u.
    u.next.~TC();         // OK, destroy active member having non-trivial dtor.
    new(&u.orig) TD();    // OK, construct new active member in place.
} // u goes out of scope with orig as its active member.
```

At the end of the function above, u.orig is the active member and so, because TD is trivially destructible, it is not necessary to call u.orig.~TD() before u goes out of scope.

To safely use *assignment* (as opposed to the destructor/constructor idiom shown in f4) for switching back and forth among *all* of the members of a **union**, every member must be both trivially destructible and trivially default constructible. Such a **union** would itself be trivially destructible and would not require a user-provided destructor:

```cpp
struct TDC1 { TDC1& operator=(const TDC1&); };  // trivial ctor and destructor
struct TDC2 { TDC2& operator=(const TDC2&); };  // trivial ctor and destructor

union U3 { TDC1 orig; TDC2 next; };

void f5()  // Initialize union U3 and change the active member multiple times.
{
    U3 u{TDC1()};      // Initialize with orig as the active member.
    u.next = TDC2();   // OK, make u.next the active member of union u.
    u.orig = TDC1();   // OK, make u.orig the active member of union u.
    // ...     (repeat as needed)
    // OK, u is trivially destructible, regardless of its active member.
}
```

D. Trivially copyable types have at least one copy or move special member function
(i.e., copy/move constructor or assignment operator), and any of those operations
that they do have are trivial. In addition, all **trivially copyable** types are also **trivially
destructible**. These types satisfy properties 1, 2, and 6–8 in *Trivial types* on page 425[11]:

```cpp
class SD  // trivially copyable
{
    int x, y;  // private data members
public:
    SD(int u, int v) : x(u), y(v) { }  // not default constructible
    int xValue() const { return x; }   // OK, nonvirtual member function
    int yValue() const { return y; }   //   "        "        "        "

    // trivial: destructor, copy constructor, and copy-assignment operator
};
```

Trivially copyable types are eligible to have their underlying **object representations**,
i.e., the byte values making up the entire footprint of an object, "bitwise" copied (e.g.,
via `std::memcpy`) either (1) directly to another object of the same type or (2) to an
intermediate array of **char** or **unsigned char** and then back to an object of the same
type:

```cpp
#include <cstring>  // std::memcpy

void exerciseTriviallyCopyable()
{
    SD a(3, 5), c(0, 0);                                    // value init
    SD b(a);                                                // copy init
```

---

[11]When it was first ratified, the C++14 Standard additionally required that a **trivially copyable** type have
no **volatile** data members. This new restriction was reversed as a **defect report** via the resolution of CWG
issue 2094 (**vandevoorde15**). A 2018 proposal (**odwyer18**) would effectively reverse CWG issue 2094 by
deleting the implicit copy and move operations for a class having **volatile** members; see *Annoyances —
The C++ Standard has not yet stabilized in this area* on page 521.

```
    SD& d = *static_cast<SD*>(::operator new(sizeof(SD)));  // uninitialized
    c = b;                                    // copy assignment
    std::memcpy(&d, &b, sizeof(SD));  // Copy-initialize via memcpy.

    // Each of a, b, c, and d now have the value (x = 3, y = 5).

    unsigned char buf[sizeof(SD)];  // must be char or unsigned char array
    std::memcpy(buf, &b, sizeof(SD));  // eligible use of memcpy
    SD e(0, 0);                        // value construction
    std::memcpy(&e, buf, sizeof(SD));  // eligible use of memcpy

    // Now e too has the value (x = 3, y = 5).
    ::operator delete(&d);
}
```

Types that are **trivially copyable** might afford certain advantages, such as better performance; see *Use Cases — Fixed-capacity string (trivially copyable)* on page 470. Using `std::memcpy` when not supported by the Standard, however, has **undefined behavior**; see *Potential Pitfalls — Ineligible use of* `std::memcpy` on page 497. Finally, `std::memcpy` is not the only way to transfer bytes of *arbitrary* or even **indeterminate value**; see *Potential Pitfalls — Naive copying via other than* `std::memcpy` on page 501.

E. **Trivial types** are trivially copyable and **trivially default constructible** and satisfy all of the properties (i.e., 1–8) in *Trivial types* on page 425:

```
class SE // trivial
{
    int x, y;  // private data members

    // All special member functions are implicitly trivial.
public:
    void setX(int u)    { x = u;  } // OK, nonvirtual member function
    void setY(int v)    { y = v;  } // OK, nonvirtual member function
    int xValue() const { return x; }  // "     "      "       "
    int yValue() const { return y; }  // "     "      "       "
};
```

A fully **trivial type** can be copied (e.g., using `std::memcpy`) to other objects of like type directly or to an array of specifically **unsigned char** or **char** and then back to an object of the same type; note that, because the default constructor is **trivial**, the original object may have an **indeterminate value**, in which case the resulting object will also hold an **indeterminate value**. Elements of the byte array may be indeterminate as well, even if the object copied into them has been initialized, making any attempt to "inspect" such bytes have **undefined behavior**. Said bytes can, however, be safely copied back to the same object, or one of the same type, and that object will hold the original, possibly **indeterminate**, value:

```
void exerciseTrivial()
{
    SE a, b;  // a and b are uninitialized; each has indeterminate value.

    a.setX(3); a.setY(5);  // a now holds the value (x = 3, y = 5).

    unsigned char buf[sizeof(SE)];  // must be char or unsigned char array

    std::memcpy(buf, &a, sizeof(SE));  // buf now holds "inspectable" bytes.
    std::memcpy(buf, &b, sizeof(SE));  // buf now has indeterminate value.

    std::memcpy(&a, buf, sizeof(SE));  // a again has indeterminate value.
}
```

Type traits

C++11 provides **type traits** — templates that define classes that contain a **value** member, which is **true** if instantiated with a complete type of the queried category and **false** otherwise — to identify the various categories described above, but, sadly, in practice they all have a number of issues. Each of these traits is defined in <type_traits> and typically inherits from std::true_type or std::false_type to provide the appropriate **value** member:

```
#include <type_traits>  // std::is_pod, std::is_standard_layout, std::is_trivial

class  Pod1 { double x; char* y; };       // POD type
struct SL1 { SL1(); };                    // standard-layout, not trivial
class  Tr1 { int x; public: int y; };     // trivial, not standard-layout
class  Antipod { virtual ~Antipod(); };   // not standard-layout, not trivial

static_assert( std::is_pod<Pod1>::value, "");              // OK
static_assert( std::is_standard_layout<Pod1>::value, "");  // OK
static_assert( std::is_trivial<Pod1>::value, "");          // OK

static_assert(!std::is_pod<SL1>::value, "");               // OK
static_assert( std::is_standard_layout<SL1>::value, "");   // OK
static_assert(!std::is_trivial<SL1>::value, "");           // OK

static_assert(!std::is_pod<Tr1>::value, "");               // OK
static_assert(!std::is_standard_layout<Tr1>::value, "");   // OK
static_assert( std::is_trivial<Tr1>::value, "");           // OK

static_assert(!std::is_pod<Antipod>::value, "");              // OK
static_assert(!std::is_standard_layout<Antipod>::value, "");  // OK
static_assert(!std::is_trivial<Antipod>::value, "");          // OK
```

According to the C++ Standard, the value `std::is_standard_layout<T>::value` is intended to be **true** for any `T` that is a **standard-layout type**. There are, however, certain seldom encountered cases where the incorrect value is produced by this trait. In particular, some popular compilers[12] produce the wrong value for the trait (**true**) when the compiler is forced to pad an object with empty space to prevent overlapping footprints for an otherwise empty base class and the first non**static** data member.

The value `std::is_trivial<T>::value` is supposed to be **true** for any `T` that is a **trivial type**. This trait too is often flawed for some edge cases. In particular, on the same contemporary versions of popular compilers,[13] `std::is_trivial` too yields a false positive (evaluates to **true**) for a class having a deleted default constructor, deleted copy and move operations, or deleted destructor (e.g., S4d, S4j, S4k, S5d, S5i, S5j, S7b, S7h, S7j, S7k, and S7l in the examples above). Using these same compilers, `std::is_trivial` yields a false negative (evaluates to **false**) when a class deletes a copy or move operation that would invoke a non-trivial operation for a base class or a data member (e.g., S7j, S7k, and S7l in the examples above).

For querying if an arbitrary constructor is trivial, the Standard Library provides another type trait, `is_trivially_constructible`, which identifies if construction with a given sequence of arguments and subsequent destruction is well defined and trivial for a given type `T`:

```
namespace std {

template <typename T, typename... Args>
struct is_trivially_constructible
{
    // The value is true if T t(std::declval<Args>()...) invokes no non-trivial
    // operations.
};

}
```

Because it is defined in terms of a variable declaration, this trait tests the triviality of both construction and destruction. The construction combines a **template parameter pack** with the Standard Library utility `std::declval` to specify a variable declaration initialized by a sequence of arguments of the specified types; see Section 2.1."Variadic Templates" on page 873. Three more specific type traits are provided to identify the various types of constructors that could potentially be trivial; note that nothing other than a **default constructor**, **copy constructor**, or **move constructor** can be trivial:

```
namespace std {

template <typename T>
struct is_trivially_default_constructible
    : std::is_trivially_constructible<T> { };                // possible definition
```

---

[12]E.g., GCC 11.1 (c. 2021) and Clang 12.0 (c. 2021).
[13]E.g., GCC 11.1 (c. 2021) and Clang 12.0 (c. 2021).

```
template <typename T>
struct is_trivially_copy_constructible
    : std::is_trivially_constructible<T, const T&> { };   // possible definition

template <typename T>
struct is_trivially_move_constructible
    : std::is_trivially_constructible<T, T&&> { };        // possible definition

}
```

The value of `std::is_pod<T>::value`, being a combination of `std::is_trivial` and `std::is_standard_layout`, exhibits incorrect results for the same general situations that those two traits misidentify.[14]

Summary and future directions

The original notion of a POD type was essentially a scalar, **struct**, or **union** that could be compiled using either a C or C++ compiler and where the interpretation of the members would result in few surprises. A C++03 POD type is a superset of C-compatible types, and C++11 extends what may be considered a POD type to include, e.g., private or protected data members and a limited form of (structural) inheritance. Importantly, a C++11 POD type no longer needs to be of aggregate type.

Although C++11 widens the definition of POD substantially, it is nonetheless a highly restricted subset of useful C++ types. C++11 redefined the meaning of POD as the intersection of two more precise and targeted subcategories of C++ types: (1) standard-layout types and (2) trivial types.

We observed that standard-layout types enjoy certain structural properties that are independent of triviality. What's more, many compilers provide support for using `offsetof` with an implementation-specific superset of types beyond standard-layout classes; see *Standard-layout class special properties* on page 420.

We also observed that trivial types could be further subdivided into separate useful subcategories — trivially default constructible, trivially destructible, and trivially copyable — each of which is more widely applicable than requiring a type to be fully trivial. For example, consider a seemingly nondescript class type, Foo:

```
class Foo  // nothing particularly special here
{
    int d_a;                      // private data
public:
    int d_b;                      // public data
    Foo(int x) : d_a{x}, d_b{x} { } // user-provided value constructor
};
```

---

[14]C++20 removed all core-language usage of the term POD, replacing all such uses with more specific requirements. Because of this removal, the type trait `std::is_pod` is deprecated in C++20 and is likely to be removed in a future standard.

Type `Foo` above is not of **standard-layout type** because it has both **public** and **private** data members. `Foo` is not of **trivial type** because, by declaring a constructor, the implicit declaration of a default constructor (which would have been trivial) is suppressed. Hence, it is not **trivially constructible**; it is, however, **trivially copyable** (which implies **trivially destructible**):

```
#include <type_traits>  // std::is_standard_layout, std::is_trivial, etc.

static_assert(!std::is_pod<Foo>::value,                     "");
static_assert(!std::is_standard_layout<Foo>::value,         "");
static_assert(!std::is_trivial<Foo>::value,                 "");
static_assert(!std::is_trivially_constructible<Foo>::value, "");

static_assert(std::is_trivially_destructible<Foo>::value,   "");
static_assert(std::is_trivially_copyable<Foo>::value,       "");
```

Every trivial type is trivially copyable, but not every trivially copyable type is *trivial*. Note that `Foo` could be made trivial simply by adding a defaulted constructor declaration: `Foo() = default;` — see Section 1.1."Defaulted Functions" on page 33. Making `Foo` a POD is less straightforward and would require uniting both data members under one access specifier — i.e., either **public** or **private**.

Although types such as `Foo` are not even close to satisfying the requirements of a C++11 POD type, being able to identify that `Foo` satisfies one or more of the subrequirements of a POD, and in this case specifically the **trivially copyable** property, means that `Foo` is eligible to be properly byte-copied via, e.g., `std::memcpy`; see both *Use Cases — Fixed-capacity string (trivially copyable)* on page 470 and *Potential Pitfalls — Ineligible use of* `std::memcpy` on page 497.

The notion of what constitutes a POD continues to evolve. Rather than attempting to further reduce the requirements that, if satisfied, anoint a given C++ type with POD status, the trend has been away from ever referring to a POD directly, preferring instead to more precisely identify the specific subcategories – e.g., **standard layout**, **trivially constructible**, **trivially destructible**, and/or **trivially copyable** — required by each particular corner of the language.[15]

Use Cases

Vertical encoding within a union (POD)

Support for inheritance and dynamic binding through virtual functions in C++ affords a qualitatively more powerful form of abstraction than is supported or easily achievable in purely procedural languages, such as C. There are times, however, when employing such abstractions is excessive and contraindicated. A more conventionally procedural approach

---

[15]As of C++20, `std::is_pod` is officially deprecated, and no other mention of POD appears normatively in that version of the standard.

to achieving runtime polymorphism is through the disciplined use of **union**s of standard-layout class types in a manner that we'll refer to here as **vertical encoding** — i.e., an initial sequence of data whose respective types are (1) common to all encodings and (2) may affect the interpretation of subsequent data in those encodings.

To readily compare the benefits of **vertical encoding** with those of an **object-oriented** design, we begin with the classic introductory **object-oriented** "shapes" example, which provides a pure abstract (a.k.a. **protocol**) base class, VShape:

```
#include <iostream>  // std::ostream

struct VShape  // pure abstract base class (a.k.a. protocol)
{
    virtual ~VShape() { }
    virtual std::ostream& draw(std::ostream& stream) const = 0;
        // Format this shape to the specified output stream.

    // ... (any additional methods common across all shapes)
};
```

Even though VShape is an abstract class, the destructor, ~VShape, must be defined, not just declared, because derived classes' destructors will invoke the base class's destructor. Note that the destructor for an abstract base class is never called via virtual-function dispatch; it is called only from derived-class destructors. In our example, the empty destructor is **inline** so as to minimize the cost of destroying derived-class objects.

Next, we derive, from our abstract VShape base class, the various concrete shapes in our application:

```
struct VCircle    : VShape    // size 16, alignment 8
{
    double d_radius;
    VCircle(double radius);
    virtual std::ostream& draw(std::ostream& stream) const;
    // ...
};

struct VRectangle : VShape    // size 16, alignment 8
{
    short d_len, d_width;
    VRectangle(short length, short width);
    virtual std::ostream& draw(std::ostream& stream) const;
    // ...
};

struct VTriangle  : VShape    // size 24, alignment 8
{
    int d_side1, d_side2, d_side3;
```

```
    VTriangle(int side1, int side2, int side3);
    virtual std::ostream& draw(std::ostream& stream) const;
    // ...
};
```

Calls to virtual functions are typically dispatched via a **virtual-function table** (a.k.a. *vtable*) that is generated by the compiler for each derived class. All popular compilers store the address of the vtable as a hidden pointer member in the base-class subobject; this pointer is initialized, by the derived-class's constructor, to the address of the corresponding derived-class's virtual-function table. The derived classes in our example have just a few small data members — typically 2 bytes for a **short** member, 4 bytes for an **int**, and 8 bytes for a **double** — so both the size and alignment of our VTriangle, VRectangle, and VCircle types are significantly affected by those of the hidden vtable pointer, presumed here to be 8 bytes.

An application using this framework would first construct concrete shapes and then pass them into functions or subroutines (e.g., doSomethingV, below) via a pointer or reference to the abstract VShape base class:

```
void doSomethingV(const VShape& shape);  // arbitrary subroutine on a VShape

void testV()
{
    VCircle t(3);      // Create a concrete object derived from VShape.
    doSomethingV(t);   // Invoke function on circle via VShape base.
    // ...
}
```

Support for object-oriented programming in C++ affords distinct advantages. For example, new shapes can be added easily without affecting clients of the protocol, and changes to derived concrete shapes need not force clients of the protocol to recompile. However, not all use cases can benefit from this form of factoring, and these potential benefits come at the cost of increased object size and the potential added runtime overhead resulting from virtual-function dispatch. In cases when the suite of shapes is fixed and only the set of procedures on shapes is expected to grow over time, the primary advantage of this design is diminished. Moreover, the use of vtable pointers in each object footprint might, for small objects, overwhelm object size (and alignment). Additionally, we might want a design that is robust across languages, including those, such as C, that do not readily support the **object-oriented** paradigm and generally do not support the C++ object model natively. When the set of derived objects (but *not* necessarily the functionality they provide) is stable, minimizing data size is a priority, language portability is important, or compile-time coupling is a nonissue, we might want to consider an alternative to the familiar **object-oriented** syntax supported by C++.

Let's now consider **vertical encoding** — an implementation technique that can produce an alternative, yet largely equivalent, *procedural* shape framework based on a **union** (e.g., UShape):

```
struct UShapeTag
{ char d_type; };                              // size 1, alignment 1

struct UCircle
{ char d_type; double d_radius; };             //   "  16    "    8

struct URectangle
{ char d_type; short d_length, d_width; };     //   "   6,   "    2

struct UTriangle
{ char d_type; int d_side1, d_side2, d_side3; }; //  " 16,    "    4

enum { k_CI = 1, k_RE, k_TR };                 // discriminating values

union UShape                                   // union of all shapes
{
    UShapeTag  tg;  // char
    UCircle    ci;  // char, double
    URectangle re;  // char, short, short
    UTriangle  tr;  // char, int, int, int
};                                             // size 16, alignment 8
```

Notice that both the size and alignment of our UShape objects are substantially smaller than those derived from VShape. The tg member holds only the common portion of all the members of the **union**. Strictly speaking, tg is not needed since any of the other members contain the same first field, but having such a member is common practice for this vertical-encoding idiom because accessing tg clearly indicates that only the common fields are being used. The size benefit can be illusory, however, because a UShape is always as large as its *largest* member, whereas an object of a class derived from VShape is only as large as needed to hold its data members plus the vtable pointer.

Operations on the composite UShape **union** are now implemented as independent **free functions** employing a **switch** statement on the common first data member, **char** d_type, of all UShape members, ci, re, and tr:

```
std::ostream& draw(std::ostream& stream, const UShape& shape)
    // Format the specified shape to the specified output stream.
{
    switch (shape.tg.d_type)  // Use tg to access vertical encoding.
    {
      case k_CI: {
        stream << "Circle(" << shape.ci.d_radius << ')';
      } break;
      case k_RE: {
        stream << "Rectangle(" << shape.re.d_length <<
                  ", "         << shape.re.d_width  << ')';
      } break;
      case k_TR: {
```

```
        stream << "Triangle(" << shape.tr.d_side1 <<
                ", "          << shape.tr.d_side2 <<
                ", "          << shape.tr.d_side3 << ')';
    } break;
    default: {
        stream << "Error, unknown discriminator value: " << shape.tg.d_type;
    } break;
    }
    return stream;
}
```

An application using this framework would look quite similar to the program we saw previously for the **VShape** framework except that, instead of constructing a derived-class object, we construct one of the specific shapes and assign it to a **UShape** member before passing the **UShape** to a polymorphic subroutine:

```
void doSomethingU(const UShape& shape);   // arbitrary subroutine on a UShape

void testU()
{
    UShape u;                     // Default-initialize union; tg is active.
    u.ci = UCircle{ k_CI, 3.0 };  // Assign a concrete shape to a union member.
    doSomethingU(u);              // Invoke function on a circle via UShape.
    // ...
}
```

Importantly, all of the **struct**s participating in our vertically encoded **union** are of standard-layout type. Moreover, it so happens that all of the **struct**s are also of trivial type. Being both standard-layout and trivial, these **struct**s meet the definition of POD. What's more, because they comprise only public, non**static**, data members, they are syntactically and structurally compatible with **struct**s in the C language; with the addition of a few **typedef**s (e.g., **typedef struct** UCircle UCircle), the same declarations can be compiled by both C and C++ compilers to produce data structures whose source code is interoperable between the two languages. That said, the technique shown here can be modified slightly to work with standard-layout types that are *not* trivial, and, therefore, not POD types; see *Vertical encoding for non-trivial types (standard layout)* on page 448.

Note that the **union**-based **UShape** design has a somewhat different usage model than its protocol-based **VShape** counterpart. While the **VShape** base class does not depend on the set of concrete derived-class shapes, just the opposite is true for **UShape** and the set of concrete shape **struct**s. Hence, unlike with **VShape**, the **UShape** model doesn't offer reduced **physical dependencies** for clients that merely operate on shapes compared to those that create them.

Also note the different maintenance trade-offs: In the object-oriented design, adding a new function for all shapes affects every concrete shape derived from **VShape**, whereas in the **union**-based vertical-encoding design, adding a new shape affects every common operation on shapes and requires adding a new enumerator to the type tag. The primary advantages of the **union**-based vertical-encoding approach over the **object-oriented** one are language portability, function-oriented extensibility,[16] and sometimes memory efficiency.

Extending this illustration, let's now suppose that every concrete shape (e.g., VShape2) maintains its location in a 2-D coordinate system represented by a Point:

```cpp
struct Point { short d_x, d_y; };  // location in x-y coordinate system


class VShape2
{
public:
    virtual ~VShape2() { }
    // ...
    virtual Point getOrigin() const = 0;
    // ...
};
```

For simplicity, we'll represent the origin as a Point **struct** directly in each derived class (e.g., VCircle2):

```cpp
struct VCircle2 : VShape2
{
    Point  d_origin;  // common location of shape in x-y coordinate system
    double d_radius;  // circle-specific data member

    VCircle2(const Point& xy, double r) : d_origin(xy), d_radius(r) { }
    // ...
    Point getOrigin() const override;
    //
};

Point VCircle2::getOrigin() const { return d_origin; }
```

The analogous **union**-based vertical encoding achieves essentially this same functionality simply by extending the common initial member sequence:

```cpp
struct UShapeTag2
{
    char d_type; Point d_orig;  // common initial member sequence
};                              // size: 6

struct UCircle2
{
```

---

[16]The qualities of vertical encoding are similar to those of the visitor pattern, as described in **alexandrescu01**, in that it is easy to add operations but more difficult to add new types.

```
    char d_type; Point d_orig;    // common initial member sequence
    double d_radius;
};                                // size: 16


struct URectangle2
{
    char d_type; Point d_orig;    // common initial member sequence
    short d_length, d_width;
};                                // size: 10


struct UTriangle2
{
    char d_type; Point d_orig;    // common initial member sequence
    int d_side1, d_side2, d_side3;
};                                // size: 20



union UShape2 { UShapeTag2 tg; UCircle2 ci; URectangle2 re; UTriangle2 tr; };

Point origin(const UShape2& shape) { return shape.tg.d_orig; }
    // Return the origin of the specified shape.
```

If it is efficiency we're after, the code doesn't get any smaller or faster; moreover, the **union**-based vertical-encoding design above is entirely compatible with C.[17]

Vertical encoding in the wild --- the Xlib library   The use of vertical encoding can be found in the X Window system, ubiquitous on Unix-like platforms. This graphics framework sports a C API (application programming interface) trafficking in a variety of event structures, each of which represents an input action such as a keypress, mouse-button press, mouse movement, or window movement. The Xlib API takes liberal advantage of the common initial member sequence permission granted to **union**s. Every event **struct** begins with the same five fields: `type`, `serial` number, `send_event`, `display`, and `window`:

---

[17]Having certain parts of the data affect the interpretation of other parts is applicable in the field of microprocessor instructions, where there are two common approaches: *horizontal* and *vertical* microprogramming. With horizontal microcode, each bit of an instruction represents a control signal that is independent of any other. Vertical microcode trades concurrency for compactness by decoding a small opcode and then interpreting the remaining bits accordingly:

```
[ opcode ] [ <- read instruction -> ]
[ opcode ] [ <----- write instruction -----> ]
[ opcode ] [ <------- execute instruction ----------->]
[ opcode ] [ <------ i/o instruction ------> ]
```

```
// X11/Xlib.h:

// ...

typedef struct
{
    int          type;
    unsigned long serial;
    Bool         send_event;   // Bool is a C typedef defined in Xlib.h.
    Display*     display;
    Window       window;
} XAnyEvent;

typedef struct
{
    int          type;
    unsigned long serial;
    Bool         send_event;
    Display*     display;
    Window       window;

    Window       root;
    Window       subwindow;
    Time         time;
    int          x, y;
    int          x_root, y_root;
    unsigned int state;
    unsigned int button;
    Bool         same_screen;
} XButtonEvent;

// ...            (many other kinds of events)
```

Because X11/Xlib.h is a C header, it uses the C syntax for defining named **struct** types —
typedef struct {...} *name*; rather than **struct** *name* {...};. In C++, these two syntaxes
have essentially the same meaning, so the X11/Xlib.h header can be **#include**d into either
a C or C++ program.

Functions that handle general events take the address of an XEvent, a discriminating **union**
comprising every possible X-Window event, as well as an initial **int** type field, which is
common with the first element of every specific X Window standard-layout event **struct**.

```
// X11/Xlib.h:
typedef union
{
    int          type;      // int (not a struct)
    XAnyEvent    xany;      // has 5 fields
```

```
    XButtonEvent xbutton;   // has 5-field common initial sequence
    // ...                   // other events having same 5-field initial sequence
} XEvent;
```

If we are passed the address of an XEvent that was populated via any of its **standard-layout** event **struct** types, we can reliably determine its event type as well as manipulate any of the data in the initial common member sequence:

```
#include <X11/Xlib.h>

int process(XEvent* event)   // reliable access guaranteed by C/C++ Standards
{
    int           t = event->xany.type;
    unsigned long s = event->xany.serial;
    Bool          e = event->xany.send_event;
    Display*      d = event->xany.display;
    Window        w = event->xany.window;

    switch (t)
    {
        case ButtonPress:
        case ButtonRelease:
        {
            XButtonEvent* buttonEvent = &event->xbutton;
            // ...      (access fields in buttonEvent)
        } break;
        // ...        (access fields specific to other event types)
    }

    return t;   // Reliably return the type of this event struct.
}
```

Data that is specific to the event type is handled in a vertical fashion via the runtime **switch** statement.

Note that examining the same event via the (*non***struct**) **int** member **type** technically has undefined behavior in C++:

```
int getType(XEvent* event)   // common practice not supported by the Standard
{
    return event->type;   // undefined unless type member is active in union
                          // Better: return event->xany.type;
}
```

The getType function above is dubious because the rules guaranteeing access to common initial member sequences apply only to identical members of an object of **standard-layout** class type sharing a CIMS with the active member of the **union**; see *Potential Pitfalls —*

Misuse of unions on page 505. Although `getType` does not follow the rules in either C or C++, it nevertheless illustrates a common idiom found in X Window programming.

Because the `XEvent` **union** comprises standard-layout POD-**struct** types that all share a common (horizontal) initial member sequence, many useful *standalone* (a.k.a. *free*) functions can be written without the runtime overhead of a **switch** statement:

```
bool is_sent(XEvent& event)  // Determine if an event has been sent.
{
    return event.xany.send_event != 0;  // OK, regardless of the event type
}

void fake_button()
{
    XEvent e;
    e.xbutton = XButtonEvent{ButtonPress, 0, true};
    assert(is_sent(e));
    // ...
}
```

The analogous `object-oriented` implementation would be to derive publicly from a base **struct** that encapsulates the common event data.

Finally, Xlib — being a C-language library — has no supported `object-oriented` alternative, leaving this **procedural union**–based approach as an eminently suitable design choice.[18]

Vertical encoding for non-trivial types (standard layout)

In the previous use case, we saw how standard-layout **struct**s having a common initial member sequence can be united in a **union** to achieve vertical encoding. The examples were simple but had a few limitations, which we'll explore here, along with an approach to lift such limitations.

The API for `UShape` and for the individual shapes is manifestly C-like: All data members are public, there are no constructors to ensure that `UShape` is in a usable state, and the shapes cannot manage external resources because they are required to be trivial types and, thus, do not have destructors for releasing such resources. Though usable, the framework lacks C++'s renowned automatic resource-management capabilities. Consider the implementations of a generic `draw` function for objects of type `UShape` along with a function, `f1`, that haplessly endeavors to use it:

```
#include <iostream>  // std::ostream, std::cout

std::ostream& draw(std::ostream& stream, const UShape& shape)
{
    switch (shape.tg.d_type)
```

---

[18]The X Toolkit Intrinsics (Xt) took a different approach: implementing an `object-oriented` interface in C, complete with virtual-table-like data structures; see **mccormack94**.

```
        {
            // ...   (process ci, re, or tr)
        }
        return stream;
    }

    void f1()
    {
        UShape s1;
        draw(std::cout, s1);            // Bug, s1.tg.d_type is not initialized.

        UShape s2;
        s2.ci = UCircle{ k_TR, 1.2 }; // Bug, UCircle pretending to be UTriangle
        draw(std::cout, s2);            // Bug, misinterprets stored shape
    }
```

Both calls to `draw` in the `f1` function above have undefined behavior — the first by reading an uninitialized `d_type` field, the second by treating a `UCircle` as though it were a `UTriangle` because of an errant tag supplied by the user. We can address this initialization problem by giving our individual shape classes constructors that always set the `d_type` field appropriately instead of leaving it uninitialized. Taking matters a step further, we will provide appropriate constructors for `UShape` and make its data members private, thereby ensuring that every instance holds a well-formed instance of exactly one of the three shape objects:

```
#include <cassert>  // standard C assert macro

enum : char { k_CI = 1, k_RE, k_TR };                    // discriminating values

struct UShapeTag { char d_type; };

struct UCircle
{
    char    d_type;
    double d_radius;
    UCircle(double r) : d_type(k_CI), d_radius(r) { }  // Set d_type correctly.
};

struct URectangle { char d_type; /*...*/ }; // details elided
struct UTriangle  { char d_type; /*...*/ }; //      "        "

union UShape  // safer, more user-friendly reimplementation
{
private:
    UShapeTag  tg;  // never one of these
    UCircle    ci;
    URectangle re;
    UTriangle  tr;
```

```
public:
    UShape(const UCircle& c)    : ci(c) { assert(c.d_type == k_CI); }
    UShape(const URectangle& r) : re(r) { assert(r.d_type == k_RE); }
    UShape(const UTriangle& t)  : tr(t) { assert(t.d_type == k_TR); }

    char getType()              const { return tg.d_type; }
    UCircle&       getCircle()        { assert(tg.d_type == k_CI); return ci; }
    const UCircle& getCircle() const { assert(tg.d_type == k_CI); return ci; }

    // ... (additional member functions, e.g., for triangles and rectangles)
};
```

Although C++ has always allowed defining constructors and private members in **union**s, such definitions have become more prevalent now that, as of C++11, **union**s can have non-trivial members; see Section 3.1."**union** '11" on page 1174. Our modified UShape is guaranteed to represent a valid UCircle, URectangle, or UTriangle; the assert precondition checks to ensure that the d_type member holds the correct tag for the object supplied to each function.

Let's now suppose we need to keep track of how many UCircle objects exist. Defining constructors that increment a **static** variable belonging to the UCircle **struct** (e.g., s_count) and a destructor that decrements that variable is straightforward.

```
struct UCircle
{
    char   d_type;
    double d_radius;

    static int s_count;  // count of live UCircle objects

    UCircle(double r)         : d_type(k_CI),d_radius(r)          { ++s_count; }
    UCircle(const UCircle& c) : d_type(k_CI),d_radius(c.d_radius) { ++s_count; }
    ~UCircle()                                                    { --s_count; }
};

int UCircle::s_count = 0;
```

The existence of a **value constructor**, a copy constructor, and a **destructor** — all needed to manage the s_count resource — means that UCircle is no longer a trivial type and hence no longer a POD; UCircle is, however, still a **standard-layout** type and therefore can still participate in our **vertical-encoding** scheme. Unfortunately, UShape, as we have just reimplemented it above, will not compile with this new augmented definition of UCircle because UCircle is no longer trivially destructible, which in turn suppresses the implicit generation of a destructor for the **union**. We correct this problem by supplying a user-provided destructor for UShape itself:

```
union UShape
{
    // ...                              (same as above)
    ~UShape()
    {
        switch (tg.d_type)
        {
            case k_CI: ci.~UCircle();    break;
            case k_RE: re.~URectangle(); break;
            case k_TR: tr.~UTriangle();  break;
        }
    }
    // ...
};
```

Our **union** destructor delegates to the destructor of the active member of the **union**, which is determined via the d_type field in the common initial member sequence. Similarly, the compiler can no longer generate a copy constructor or **copy-assignment operator**, so we must supply those for UShape too:

```
union UShape
{
    // ...                              (same as above)
    UShape(const UShape& original) : tg()  // new user-provided copy constructor
    {
        switch (original.tg.d_type)
        {
            case k_CI: new (&ci) UCircle(original.ci);    break;
            case k_RE: new (&re) URectangle(original.re); break;
            case k_TR: new (&tr) UTriangle(original.tr); break;
        }
    }

    UShape& operator=(const UShape& rhs)    // new user-provided assignment op
    {
        if (this == &rhs) return *this;
        this->~UShape();                    // Invoke destructor.
        return *(new (this) UShape(rhs));   // Invoke copy constructor.
    }
    // ...
};
```

The copy constructor of UShape above dispatches on the active member of the *original* object. Because the members are non-trivial, we cannot simply change the active member of the **union** by assigning to the appropriate member. Instead, we must *construct* the new active member by means of **placement operator new**. The copy-assignment operator must destroy the current active member and construct the new one — tasks that it delegates to the USshape's destructor and copy constructor, respectively. If the **union** will have the same active member after the assignment, we could avoid this destroy/construct dance, at the cost of significantly more logic, including another **switch** statement.

Our revised USshape **union** has the same compact representation as the original USshape described in the previous use case but is now a fully abstract data type having private data members, enforced invariants, and the ability to manage resources, but at the cost of significantly more code and complexity. Moreover, this type is no longer source-code compatible with C; however, there are techniques for making such types available in C; see *Translating a C++-only type to C (standard layout)*[19] below.

Translating a C++-only type to C (standard layout)

Well-designed C++ classes typically encapsulate private data behind an easy-to-understand, easy-to-use public interface. Many C++ classes naturally happen to be of **standard-layout type**. To be otherwise, the class would need to have non**static** data members with different **access levels**, partake in implementation inheritance that involves non**static** data in a base class, or have one or more virtual functions or virtual base classes.

Suppose that we have a C++ date and time library that includes a **value-semantic type**, Date, representing a calendar date in which a date value is encoded directly within the **value representation** of the **footprint** of an object. This particular type (for didactic purpose only) happens to inherit publicly from a **struct** DateEncoder that provides a **static** function for encoding a date as an integer:

```
// datetime.h:

struct DateEncoder  // empty base class
{
    static int encode(int year, int month, int day);
        // Return an encoding of a year, month, and day as a single integer
        // such that, if two encoded dates compare equal, they represent the
        // same date and, if one encoded date compares less than another encoded
        // date, then the first date comes before the second date in the
        // calendar.
};
```

The Date class encodes its date value within a single **int** data member. Having a single chronologically ordered integer to represent the encoding provides good performance for certain operations such as equality comparison and is particularly well suited for deter-

---

[19]The C++17 library template std::variant provides similar functionality without using an intrusive tag type, but doesn't allow straightforward access to additional fields that are common across variant members — e.g., the d_orig field in USshape2 from *Vertical encoding for non-trivial types (standard layout)* on page 448.

mining date difference when the encoding represents a **serial date**[20] — i.e., consecutive calendar dates are represented by consecutive integer values:

```cpp
// datetime.h:
class Date : DateEncoder
{
    int d_encodedDate;  // Encoding is not part of the public interface.

public:
    Date(int year, int month, int day)
        : d_encodedDate(encode(year, month, day)) { }

    int year() const;
    int month() const;
    int day() const;

    friend bool operator<(const Date&, const Date&);
    // ...
};
```

The `Date` class above, which (again, for didactic purposes only) is defined in the same header (`datetime.h`) as `DateEncoder`, satisfies the criteria for being a **standard-layout** type; see *Description — Standard-layout types* on page 417.

Ignoring maintainability considerations, suppose we decide that we need to use, in non-C++ code, the encapsulated (private) integer encoding from `Date` as, say, a key to order files by date, but are not authorized to modify `datetime.h` (e.g., because we don't own the library). How might we extract the encoded value in a well-defined manner? We can exploit the property of **standard-layout types** that the address of the first — and in this case only — data member is that of the derived type itself:

```cpp
int extractDateEncoding(const Date& date)  // Legally extract private data.
{
    return *reinterpret_cast<const int*>(&date);  // legal larceny
}

Date d(1969, 7, 20);  // Construct a date value in C++.

int privateEncoding = extractDateEncoding(d);  // Extract its private member.

// ...          (Use privateEncoding in, say, C code.)
```

Being that `d_encodedDate` is the first member of our **standard-layout** `Date` class, it is well-defined behavior to take the address of the overall `Date` object, d, and then **reinterpret_cast** that address to get the address of a **const int**; we can then deference that constant-integer address to return the *value* of the original **int** data member. Note that we don't even need

---

[20] pacifico12

to copy Date objects, which means that the **standard-layout class**, the value of whose first data element we are stealing, need not even be *copyable*. This approach would also pertain if there were subsequent data members of no interest, provided that the overall type and, hence, each subsequent data member, is of **standard-layout type**; see *Potential Pitfalls — Abuse of **reinterpret_cast*** on page 506.

Let's now turn to cases where we need to access other than just the first of several private data members of a **standard-layout class**. For these, we will need to fall back on another property of **standard-layout class types**.

The date and time library that we are using defines a **Datetime** class that has two private **int** members — an encoded date value and a time offset from midnight in milliseconds.

```cpp
// datetime.h:
class Datetime
{
    int d_encodedDate;  // ordered encoding not part of the public interface
    int d_timeOffset;   // offset from midnight in milliseconds

public:
    Datetime(int year, int month, int day, int ms);

    int year() const;
    int month() const;
    int day() const;
    int milliseconds() const;

    friend bool operator<(const Datetime&, const Datetime&);
    // ...
};
```

First, we create a C-language-style **standard-layout struct** (e.g., **Doppelganger**) having a footprint that is member-wise type-compatible with **Datetime**, but where the members are publicly accessible:

```cpp
struct Doppelganger  // C-style POD-struct layout-compatible with Datetime
{
    int d_extractedDate;  // public data corresponding to Datetime::d_encodedDate
    int d_extractedTime;  // public data corresponding to Datetime::d_timeOffset
};
```

Then, we create a simple **union** (e.g., **Equivalence**) comprising *first* the original **Datetime** type (e.g., **d_priv**) and *second* the **Doppelganger** imposter (e.g., **d_publ**):

```
union Equivalence  // enables public access to private encoding of a datetime
{
    Datetime    d_priv;  // original standard-layout type having private data
    Doppelganger d_publ; // compatible POD-struct having public data members
};
```

Note that the definition of `Equivalence` above relies on `Datetime`'s being trivially destructible; otherwise, `Equivalence` would need a user-defined destructor to explicitly delete the active member on destruction. This example also requires that `Datetime` be copy constructible, though it need not be trivially copyable or trivially constructible.

Writing functions in C++ to extract the private data is now straightforward:

```
int extractPrivateDateEncoding(const Datetime& datetime)
{
    return Equivalence{datetime}.d_publ.d_extractedDate;
}

int extractPrivateTimeOffset(const Datetime& datetime)
{
    return Equivalence{datetime}.d_publ.d_extractedTime;
}
```

In each of the functions above, a temporary `Equivalence` **union** is **direct braced initialized** (see Section 2.1."Braced Init" on page 215) to hold a copy of the supplied `Datetime`, which, by design, is the type of the *first* alternative `Equivalence` **union** member. Once copied into the **union**, both **int** data members, which are part of the common initial member sequence, are then legally accessed publicly via the equivalenced (`Doppelganger`) type, using the `d_publ` member, and returned from their respective functions:

```
void test1()
{
    const Datetime dt(1969, 7, 20, 73'060'000);  // July 20, 1969, 20:17:40 UTC
    int privateDate = extractPrivateDateEncoding(dt);
    int privateTime = extractPrivateTimeOffset(dt);
}
```

Note the *optional* use of the C++14 digit-separator feature (`'`) to partition the milliseconds digits during construction; see Section 1.2."Digit Separators" on page 152.

More generally, once the private information of the **standard-layout struct** has been equivalenced to a C-style POD-**struct**, that same POD-**struct** can be passed directly into a function compiled in C; see *Description — Privileges enjoyed by POD types* on page 402:

```
Doppelganger extractPrivateDatetimeEncoding(const Datetime& datetime)
{
    return Equivalence{datetime}.d_publ;
}


extern "C" void createMapping(const char* filename, const Doppelganger* ts);
    // Insert a file-to-timestamp mapping of filename into a data structure
    // maintained by a C-language component.


void test2()
{
    const Datetime dt(1969, 7, 20, 73'060'000);  // July 20, 1969, 20:17:40 UTC
    Doppelganger cdt = extractPrivateDatetimeEncoding(dt);
                                        // Extract C representation of dt.
    createMapping("test.txt", &cdt);       // Pass to C code.
}
```

Navigating a compound object using `offsetof` (standard layout)

C++ provides the notion of **pointers to members** as a structured way to identify the relative offset of a data member within an object. C has no such construct and instead provides the simpler notion of an integral offset from the address of an object of the enclosing type. The standard C macro `offsetof`, defined in `<cstddef>`, can be used on any **standard-layout** C++ class type (i.e., **class**, **struct**, or **union**) to obtain a **constant** expression of type `std::size_t` denoting the offset in bytes of a named member from the beginning of an object of the named class type. Taking advantage of the guarantees provided by **standard-layout class types**, we can in practice use the `offsetof` macro to navigate around compound objects, going both from the address of an object to one of its data members and vice versa.

As an illustration of using `offsetof`, imagine that we have a system that consumes ASCII characters, and we want to create a function, `countCategories`, that reads a string and counts the respective category of each character we encounter. For example, we might classify each character as alphabetic, numeric, punctuation, etc. To represent our respective counts, we will use a **standard-layout struct**, `CharacterCategoryCounts`:

```
struct CharacterCategoryCounts
{
    int d_numAlphabetic;   // number of alphabetic characters encountered
    int d_numNumeric;      //     "    "  numeric       "          "
    int d_numPunctuation;  //     "    "  punctuation   "          "
    int d_numWhitespace;   //     "    "  whitespace    "          "
    int d_numOther;        //     "    "  other         "          "
};
```

Because we know there are 128 characters in the ASCII character set, we can create an array, `counterOffsetArray`, indexed by ASCII character code, and set the value of each array element to be the offset within the CharacterCategoryCounts **struct** of the field we want to increment for that specific character:

```cpp
#include <cstddef>  // offsetof macro

std::size_t counterOffsetArray[128] =
{
    /* 0x00 */  offsetof(CharacterCategoryCounts, d_numOther),
    /* 0x01 */  offsetof(CharacterCategoryCounts, d_numOther),
    // ...
    /* '\t' */  offsetof(CharacterCategoryCounts, d_numWhitespace),
    // ...
    /* '!' */   offsetof(CharacterCategoryCounts, d_numPunctuation),
    // ...
    /* '0' */   offsetof(CharacterCategoryCounts, d_numNumeric),
    // ...
    /* 'A' */   offsetof(CharacterCategoryCounts, d_numAlphabetic),
    // ...
    /* 0x7F */  offsetof(CharacterCategoryCounts, d_numOther)
};
```

The counterOffsetArray, above, begins (at ASCII 0 = NUL) by storing the offsetof for CharacterCategoryCounts::d_numOther. When we reach the horizontal tab (i.e., '\t'), which is *whitespace*, we store the offsetof to CharacterCategoryCounts::d_numWhitespace, and so on.

In our countCategories function, below, we take a string as input and return a CharacterCategoryCounts object by value:

```cpp
CharacterCategoryCounts countCategories(const char* s)
{
    CharacterCategoryCounts ccc = { };  // Initialize each member counter to 0.

    do
    {
        if (*s & 0x80)
        {
            ++ccc.d_numOther;  // out of ASCII range
            continue;
        }

        std::size_t cOffset = counterOffsetArray[std::size_t(*s)];
        ++*reinterpret_cast<int*>(reinterpret_cast<char*>(&ccc) + cOffset);
    }
    while (*s++);

    return ccc;
}
```

The body of `countCategories` begins by creating a `CharacterCategoryCounts` object initialized to all 0s. For each successive character in the string (including the null terminator), its ASCII code is used to look up, in the `counterOffsetArray`, the offset of the appropriate counter data member in the `CharacterCategoryCounts` object. The offset is added to the byte address of the `ccc` **struct** to get the address of the desired data member. The address arithmetic must be performed on byte (i.e., **char**) locations, so the address of `ccc` must be cast to **char*** before adding the offset, then to **int*** afterward, in order to return an **int** member of `CharacterCategoryCounts`.

Unfortunately, address arithmetic in C++ is well defined only for elements in an array. A `CharacterCategoryCounts` is not an array, so treating it as an array of **char** using a **reinterpret_cast** technically has **undefined** behavior, although it will work on all architectures with which we are familiar; see *Potential Pitfalls — Aggressive use of offsetof* on page 520. Instead of an array of offsets whose values are computed using `offsetof`, as typical in C, in C++ we can define an array of pointer-to-member objects (e.g., `counterMemPtrArray`):

```
// array of 128 pointer-to-int members of CharacterCategoryCounts

int CharacterCategoryCounts::*counterMemPtrArray[128] =
{
    /* 0x00 */   &CharacterCategoryCounts::d_numOther,
    /* 0x01 */   &CharacterCategoryCounts::d_numOther,
    // ...
    /* '\t' */   &CharacterCategoryCounts::d_numWhitespace,
    // ...
    /* '!' */    &CharacterCategoryCounts::d_numPunctuation,
    // ...
    /* '0' */    &CharacterCategoryCounts::d_numNumeric,
    // ...
    /* 'A' */    &CharacterCategoryCounts::d_numAlphabetic,
    // ...
    /* 0x7F */   &CharacterCategoryCounts::d_numOther
};
```

Using the pointer-to-member array above, we can now reimplement our counting function to avoid even theoretically **undefined** behavior:

```
CharacterCategoryCounts countCategories2(const char* s)
{
    CharacterCategoryCounts ccc = { };  // Initialize each member counter to 0.

    do
    {
        if (*s & 0x80)
        {
            ++ccc.d_numOther;  // out of ASCII range
```

```
            continue;
        }

        ++(ccc.*counterMemPtrArray[std::size_t(*s)]);
    }
    while (*s++);

    return ccc;
}
```

A pointer to member is a welcome abstraction that adds type safety and helps avoid rampant casting, so why would one ever choose to use `offsetof` over pointers to members? On a 64-bit architecture, the size of a pointer to member will typically be 8 bytes, while the offset within a **struct** will seldom be larger than a few thousand — easily fitting within two bytes. In our example, we could have declared the original `counterOffsetArray` to have elements of type **unsigned char** instead of `std::size_t`, typically reducing the size by a factor of 8 and making it fit within far fewer **cache lines**.

We now turn to the complementary case where we have a pointer to a member of a **struct**, and we need to get a pointer to its enclosing object. We can in practice use `offsetof` to go back to the beginning of the **struct** to reach other fields within the object. Suppose, for example, we are using the `XClientMessageEvent` from the X Window interface (Xlib). The `XClientMessageEvent` represents a message as a **union**, `data`, of three short arrays of different types:

```
typedef struct
{
    int           type;          // ClientMessage
    unsigned long serial;        // # of last request processed by server
    Bool          send_event;    // true if this event came from a SendEvent request
    Display*      display;       // display with which the event is associated
    Window        window;
    Atom          message_type;
    int           format;
    union
    {
        char  b[20];  // message as a string
        short s[10];
        long  l[5];   // (A long is typically the size of a pointer.)
    } data;
} XClientMessageEvent;
```

The user is responsible for supplying a callback to handle `XClientMessageEvent` events. The callback is represented as a `ClientMessageDataProcessor` — a pointer to function that takes an array of 20 bytes:

```
typedef void (*ClientMessageDataProcessor)(char cdm[20]);
```

Each time the X Window event loop pops an `XClientMessageEvent` from the queue, it calls the registered callback handler and passes it the `data.b` member of the `XClientMessageEvent` object. However, we wish to access the `display` member and other fields of the enclosing `XClientMessageEvent` **struct**, not just the `data.b` member. Recognizing that our callback function will be called only within a context where `cdm` is part of an `XClientMessageEvent`, we write our function to use `offsetof` to compute the address of the enclosing object from the `b.data` member address:

```
void ourClientMessageDataProcessor(char cdm[20])
{
    std::size_t dataOffset = offsetof(XClientMessageEvent, data);
    XClientMessageEvent* event =
        reinterpret_cast<XClientMessageEvent*>(cdm - dataOffset);

    // Check that it's probably an event struct and that the data is intended
    // to be interpreted as bytes.
    assert(event->type == ClientMessage);
    assert(event->format == 8);

    // ...    (access event->display and other fields)
}
```

Note that our function takes advantage of `b`'s member within the `data` **union** having the same address as the **union** itself. In this example, we *subtract* the offset from a data member's address to get the enclosing object's address. We could not have accomplished this feat using pointers to members because there is no syntax to obtain an enclosing object from a pointer to member.

As in the case of the previous example, we violate the rules by performing pointer arithmetic among different fields within an object. It is fairly common practice, however, to use **reinterpret_cast** and pointer arithmetic in this fashion, and it is unlikely a compiler will produce unexpected results. Regardless of whether they adhere to the letter of the C++ Standard, the examples we have shown reflect code that is deployed in real-world legacy codebases. They work and must continue to work, lest vast quantities of existing code break; hence, there is activity within the community to make this kind of pointer arithmetic well defined within the Standard.[21]

Secure buffer (trivially constructible)

Some of the most common security vulnerabilities in software occur when malformed input causes a program to read or write past the end of a buffer. For example, the famous Heartbleed vulnerability, discovered in 2014 in the OpenSSL cryptographic software library,[22] allowed an attacker to see the contents of up to 64 KB of memory to which a foe should not have had access by using a malformed request that would cause the software to read past the

---

[21]See **stasiowski19**.
[22]https://heartbleed.com/

end of a much smaller buffer. If the stolen memory contents contained sensitive data, such as passwords or encryption keys, system security would have been effectively compromised.

To avoid such security holes, programming languages, libraries, virtual machine monitors, and operating systems implement a variety of measures, having varying safety/performance trade-offs. One simple defensive measure is to minimize the time that sensitive information remains in memory. As soon as a chunk of memory — potentially holding a password or other sensitive data — is no longer needed, its contents is explicitly overwritten, e.g., zeroed.

A simple and robust library solution in C++ is to define a low-level buffer type (e.g., `SecureBuffer`) whose destructor scrubs the buffer by filling it with zeros; this simple type can become the basis of a variety of higher-level classes for which memory is to be scrubbed after each use:

```cpp
#include <cstddef>   // std::size_t
#include <string.h>  // memset_s

template <std::size_t N>
struct SecureBuffer
{
    char d_buffer[N];  // data buffer of size N

    ~SecureBuffer()
    {
        memset_s(d_buffer, N, '\0', N);  // scrub memory
    }
};
```

The `memset_s` function, defined in the C11 (not C++11) Standard,[23] is a variant of `memset` that guarantees memory will be overwritten. The `memset_s` function has the same API as `memset` and guarantees that it will always perform the writes requested of it. `memset_s` is defined in an optional annex (Annex K) of the C11 Standard that has seen little implementation uptake. Similar secure functions, though not portable, are available on most platforms, e.g., `explicit_bzero` on OpenBSD and FreeBSD, and `SecureZeroMemory` on Windows. P1315 proposes `secure_clear` for a future C++ Standard. If plain `memset` were used, an aggressive optimizer — whether a human or a compiler — might detect that the values written by `memset` are not later read in the normal flow of control and will elide the call. Such an optimization is generally desirable, as write-only operations represent useless work ("dead code"), but defeats our purpose here, which is to limit the damage from access *outside* the normal flow of control.

Importantly, the `SecureBuffer` class has a **trivial default constructor** because all of the class's members are **trivially constructible** and it has no user-provided constructors.[24]

---

[23]**iso11b**, section K.3.7.4.1, "The memset_s function," pp. 621–622

[24]Despite `SecureBuffer` being trivially default constructible, this case is noteworthy because the Standard Library traits are unable to recognize this property due to how the traits are specified. The `std::is_trivially_constructible` trait also requires a trivial destructor. This schism with the traits is under ongoing discussion; see LWG issue 2827 (**smith16d**) and *Potential Pitfalls — Using the wrong type trait* on page 482.

The usage model for a `SecureBuffer` is the same as for a local array of **char**: no code is executed upon creation, and the comprised **char** elements start out in an uninitialized state. It is only upon destruction that the difference becomes important:

```
#include <iostream>  // std::cin

void authenticatedAccess()  // security-sensitive function
{
    SecureBuffer<31> pwBuffer;  // Create a buffer that erases itself.

    std::cin.getline(pwBuffer.d_buffer, 31, '\n');  // Read up to 31 bytes.
    if (!std::cin) { return; }                       // Return on input error.

    // ...   (use password from pwBuffer.d_buffer)

}  // pwBuffer is erased automatically when it goes out of scope.
```

Initializing `pwBuffer` would be wasteful — its contents being immediately overwritten by the `getline` function — so the definition creating `pwBuffer` does nothing other than allocate space on the program stack; the values of the bytes within the buffer are deliberately *not* initialized and therefore **indeterminate**. Nevertheless, the object's lifetime has begun, and the call to `getline` can fill the buffer. Upon return from `authenticatedAccess`, the destructor for `SecureBuffer` will clear any residual password data left in `pwBuffer` — even in the case of an input error, which might otherwise leave a partial password in the buffer.

Compile-time constructible, literal types (trivially destructible)

It is often convenient to be able to use a scalar type in a **constant expression** such as that required to size a static array, or as an argument to **static_assert**; see Section 1.1. "**static_assert**" on page 115:

```
char a[3 + 2];                    // 3 + 2 is a constant expression.
static_assert(5 == sizeof a, "");  // 5 == sizeof a is a constant expression.
```

There might also be times when we want to have a **user-defined literal (UDL)** that can be used at compile time. As an example of such a compile-time **UDT**, let's define a class, `Fraction`, comprising two integral data members, `d_numerator` and `d_denominator`:

```
struct Fraction  // trivial aggregate type (has a trivial destructor)
{
    int d_numerator;    // scalar member (has a trivial destructor)
    int d_denominator;  //    "     "      "   "     "      "
};
```

Because the `Fraction` class is a simple aggregate of two scalar types, it too can be constructed at compile time and used in a **constant expression** such as an array size or **static_assert**:

```
int array[Fraction{ 2, 3 }.d_denominator];          // array of 3 ints
static_assert(2 == Fraction{ 2, 3 }.d_numerator, "");  // OK, compile-time eval
```

Compile-time-usable types, such as Fraction, can also be used to define a **constexpr** variable — i.e., a compile-time constant that itself is required to be initialized at compile time via a constant expression; see Section 2.1."**constexpr** Variables" on page 302:

```
constexpr Fraction oneHalf      = { 1, 2 };
constexpr Fraction oneQuarter   = { 1, 4 };
constexpr Fraction threeQuarters = { 3, 4 };
```

Any such compile-time manipulation will require, among other things, that the UDT is trivially destructible and, in some way, compile-time constructible. Fraction is a POD type and is, therefore, **trivially destructible**. Our Fraction class is also an **aggregate** of scalar members, which allows for **aggregate initialization** at compile time.

Note, however, that participating in compile-time evaluation does not specifically require either a POD or an aggregate, but rather a literal type, which is essentially either a scalar, an aggregate, or a class type that has at least one compile-time-usable (**constexpr**) constructor, a trivial destructor, and contains only other literal types (or arrays of literal types); see Section 2.1."**constexpr** Functions" on page 257. For example, adding a *non*-trivial **constexpr** value constructor would result in a variation of the type that, while neither a POD type nor an aggregate, would nonetheless still be of literal type:

```
struct FractionB  // non-POD class that can participate in constant expressions
{
    int d_numerator;   // scalar data member (of literal type)
    int d_denominator; //    "       "       "       "       "       "

    constexpr FractionB(int n, int d) : d_numerator(n), d_denominator(d) { }
        // value constructor that can initialize the object at compile time
};

constexpr FractionB oneHalfB{ 1, 2 };  // OK, FractionB is a literal type.
```

Providing a *non*-trivial **destructor** would, however, prevent such compile-time usage — even if the type were trivial in all other respects[25]:

```
struct FractionC  // nonliteral type because destructor is non-trivial
{
    int d_numerator;   // scalar data member (of literal type)
    int d_denominator; //    "       "       "       "       "       "

    ~FractionC() { }   // user-provided (non-trivial) destructor
};

constexpr FractionC oneHalfC{1, 2};  // Error, FractionC is not a literal type.
```

---

[25]Starting with C++20, destructors can be declared **constexpr**. A C++20 literal type is defined in terms of a **constexpr** destructor, which need not be trivial. Note that a trivial destructor is implicitly **constexpr**, so a literal type in C++11 is also a literal type in C++20.

Trivially destructible is also a precondition for being trivially copyable; see *Fixed-capacity string (trivially copyable)* on page 470.

Skippable destructors (notionally trivially destructible)

Sometimes it's possible to skip invoking an object's destructor (e.g., to improve runtime performance) without impacting the correctness of a program. Consider a 2-D line-drawing system that consumes closed shapes, each a sequence of point values representing the vertices of the shape. In our application, it is convenient to store shapes as an array in which each successive shape is represented by an **int** value, indicating the number of its vertices, followed by a sequence of point values, represented by a trivial **Point** class, corresponding to the vertices themselves. Because each array element might hold either an **int** value or a **Point** value, we chose to implement the array element, **ShapeElem**, as a **union**:

```
struct Point { int d_x, d_y; };  // trivial user-defined type (UDT)

union ShapeElem  // dual representation of either the vertex count or a vertex
{
    int   d_numVertices;  // number of vertices to follow in streamed shape
    Point d_vertex;       // coordinate of current vertex in streamed shape
};
```

Shapes are read from an input stream using a simple dual-function API: **nextShapeSize** reads the size (i.e., number of vertices) of the next shape, and **nextVertex** reads the next individual vertex:

```
#include <istream>  // std::istream

int nextShapeSize(std::istream& stream);
    // Return the number of vertices in the next shape to be read from the
    // specified input stream, or a negative value if stream.eof() is true.
    // Set stream.fail() to true if the input is malformed.

Point nextVertex(std::istream& stream);
    // Unconditionally read the next shape vertex from the specified input
    // stream.  Set stream.fail() to true if the input is malformed.
```

We can now create a function (e.g., **readAndProcess**) to read and process multiple shapes at once by repeatedly calling the appropriate API functions and accumulating raw results into an array (e.g., **shapeEncodings**) of **ShapeElem** objects. Each shape will begin with a **ShapeElem** with the vertex count stored in the **d_numVertices** member, followed by that many **ShapeElem** elements in the array with the vertex locations in the **d_vertex** member. For didactic purposes only (i.e., to avoid complexities associated with dynamic memory allocation), we have chosen to employ a fixed-sized array having an arbitrary implementation-defined size, **maxElems**, thus providing an upper bound on the sum of the number of shapes and the number of vertices:

```
#include <cassert>  // standard C assert macro

void batchProcessShapes(ShapeElem* array, int numCompleteShapes);
    // Process, as a single transaction, the specified array encoding the
    // specified numCompleteShapes.

void readAndProcess(std::istream& stream)
    // Read all of the shapes available from the specified input stream into
    // memory, then process them all at once (e.g., as a transaction).
{
    const std::size_t maxElems = 100;      // arbitrary implementation limit
    ShapeElem  shapeEncodings[maxElems];   // accumulation of 0 or more shapes

    std::size_t elemIdx  = 0;  // index of next unread elem in shapeEncodings
    int         numShapes = 0; // number of complete shapes read so far

    // Outer loop reads shapes (note: n must be signed or won't terminate).
    for (int n = nextShapeSize(stream); n >= 0; n = nextShapeSize(stream))
    {
        assert(elemIdx + n + 1 <= maxElems);  // Assert that next shape fits.

        // Make d_numVertices the active member of shapeEncodings[elemIdx].
        shapeEncodings[elemIdx++].d_numVertices = n;  // encode # of vertices

        // Inner loop reads vertices within current shape.
        for ( ; n > 0; --n)
        {
            // Make d_vertex the active member of shapeEncodings[elemIdx].
            shapeEncodings[elemIdx++].d_vertex = nextVertex(stream);
        }

        ++numShapes;                                  // complete shape read
    }

    // Process all numShapes accumulated complete shapes as one transaction.
    batchProcessShapes(shapeEncodings, numShapes);

}  // The local shapeEncodings array goes out of scope (no elements destroyed).
```

Each iteration of the outer loop assigns an **int** value to the d_numVertices member of the next array element, thereby making it the **active member** of the **union**. Each iteration of the inner loop makes **d_vertex** the **active member** of the next array element via assignment from the next value read from the input stream. The implementation of batchProcessShapes can then carefully access the proper **active member** of each ShapeElem, knowing that the array has been populated in a structured fashion.

The implicit destructor for ShapeElem does not invoke the destructor for either of its members because a **union** does not know which of them is active; see Section 3.1. "**union** '11" on page 1174. Thus, when the `shapeEncodings` array goes out of scope upon return from the `readAndProcess` function, no destructors are invoked, including those of any `Point` objects stored within its **union** elements. Because `Point` is trivially destructible, invoking its destructor executes no code; hence, skipping the explicit invocation of an object of trivially destructible type is always valid. To illustrate the impact of this eminently useful, trivially destructible property of class `Point`, let's look at what happens when we use a variation of `Point` (e.g., `Point2`) that is *not* trivially destructible:

```cpp
struct Point2  // like Point except no longer trivially destructible
{
    int d_x, d_y;           // same data as Point
    ~Point2() { /*...*/ }  // non-trivial destructor
};
```

In this variation, we must also revise `ShapeElem` to have a **user-provided** destructor, lest our **union**, which now contains a member that is *not* trivially destructible, have an implicitly deleted destructor and thus fail to compile (see Section 3.1."**union** '11" on page 1174):

```cpp
union ShapeElem2  // like ShapeElem except no longer trivially destructible
{
    int    d_numVertices;
    Point2 d_vertex;   // revised point having a non-trivial destructor

    ~ShapeElem2() { }  // needed since Point2 is non-trivially destructible
};
```

Just as for the implicit destructor for `ShapeElem`, the **user-provided** destructor for `ShapeElem2` doesn't invoke the destructor for either of its members. Skipping the destruction of an arbitrary type that is not **trivially destructible** — though not in and of itself having **undefined behavior** — might lead to unintended consequences, such as a resource leak that would otherwise be addressed by invoking the destructor. To make sure that any `Point2` objects we created are eventually destroyed, therefore, we add a second set of nested loops iterating over the `shapeEncodings` array for the purpose of explicitly destroying all `Point2` objects within those **union** elements for which `d_vertex` is the **active member**. This change is reflected in a second (heavily elided) implementation of our read-and-process function, `readAndProcess2`:

```cpp
void readAndProcess2(std::istream& stream)
{
    // ...          (same as in readAndProcess)

    // Cleanup: Explicitly destroy any Point2 objects in shapeEncodings.
    for (elemIdx = 0; numShapes > 0; --numShapes)
    {
        int n = shapeEncodings[elemIdx++].d_numVertices;
        for ( ; n > 0; --n)
        {
            // Explicitly destroy Point2 active member of current element.
```

```
              shapeEncodings[elemIdx++].d_vertex.~Point2();
        }
    }
} // The local shapeEncodings array goes out of scope.
```

But what if we know that our point class doesn't manage any resources that might leak? A common practice during software testing, and sometimes even in production, is to check the invariants of a class within its destructor to verify that no class operation or spurious program defect has left the object in an invalid state. Imagine applying this technique to a variation on the original **Point** class for which d_x and d_y are always within the range -5000 to +5000. We might choose to instrument our revised class (e.g., **Point3**) to enforce these invariants during development:

```
#include <cassert>  // standard C assert macro

struct Point3  // trivially constructible but not trivially destructible
{
    int d_x, d_y;  // same data as before

    ~Point3()       // Destructor is user-provided; hence, non-trivial.
    {
        assert(-5000 <= d_x);  assert(d_x <= 5000);
        assert(-5000 <= d_y);  assert(d_y <= 5000);
    }
};
```

Class **Point3** checks that both d_x and d_y satisfy their object invariants during destruction, but only in a *debug* build — i.e., one in which the NDEBUG macro is *not* defined.[26] The addition of this **user-provided** destructor again makes our point class *non*-**trivially destructible** in *any* build mode. Just as for **ShapeElem2**, we must provide a destructor for a **union** element (e.g., **ShapeElem3**) employing **Point3** as the type of its d_vertex member:

```
union ShapeElem3  // like ShapeElem except no longer trivially destructible
{
    int     d_numVertices;
    Point3 d_vertex;   // revised point having a non-trivial destructor

    ~ShapeElem3() { }  // required since Point3's non-trivially destructible
};
```

Again, **ShapeElem3**'s empty destructor does not invoke the destructor for either of its members, but, unlike **ShapeElem2**, failing to destroy a possibly active **Point3** member is acceptable because **Point3** has a destructor that neither releases a resource nor produces a side effect that would — in *any* way — affect the correctness of an already-correct program. Thus,

---

[26] A proposal for a more general C++ assertion facility — known widely as "contracts" — narrowly missed being included in C++20 and is the focus of an ongoing study group (SG21) for future inclusion in C++; see **dosreis18**.

we can return to our original implementation of readAndProcess eschewing the cleanup code while retaining program correctness.

We might refer to a class like Point3, which validates its invariants on destruction, as **notionally trivially destructible** because it can be used *as if* it were trivially destructible. In generic software that does not know that a type is notionally trivially destructible, the Point3 class might suffer some performance loss relative to Point, especially in a debug build, but the semantics of a *correct* program do not change. Note, however, that when we skip Point3's destructor invocation, we give up — even in debug mode — the **defensive checks** in Point3's destructor that might catch a bug in our program.

Though useful for human discourse, notionally trivially destructible types are not considered trivially destructible by the compiler or by any general-purpose library and thus are neither literal types (see Section 2.1."**constexpr** Functions" on page 257) nor **trivially copyable types**, as both of these properties require **trivial destructibility**. An notionally trivially destructible type cannot, therefore, be used where either of these properties is an arbiter of correctness:

```
#include <cstring>  // std::memcpy


char array1[Point {1, 2}.d_x];  // OK,    Point is  a literal type.
char array2[Point3{1, 2}.d_x];  // Error, Point3 isn't a literal type.


void f(Point* d, const Point* s) { std::memcpy(d, s, sizeof *s); }  // OK
void f(Point3* d, const Point3* s) { std::memcpy(d, s, sizeof *s); }  // Bug, UB
    // Point3 is not trivially copyable; hence, f's behavior is undefined (UB).
```

In the code snippet above, using Point3 in an array-size computation will fail to compile, whereas the original Point class will work just fine; see *Compile-time constructible, literal types (trivially destructible)* on page 462. Although using std::memcpy to copy objects of trivially copyable type such as Point is valid (see *Fixed-capacity string (trivially copyable)* on page 470), using std::memcpy to propagate values of a *non*-trivially copyable type such as Point3 has **undefined behavior**; see *Potential Pitfalls — Ineligible use of std::memcpy* on page 497.

In a more aggressive version of this runtime optimization technique, even types that allocate memory can be considered **notionally trivially destructible** when the memory that would be deallocated by the destructor can somehow be reclaimed in other ways.[27]

Finally, since the code in the destructor for Point3 is active *only* in a **debug build**, we might be tempted to define a point class (e.g., Point4) for which the entire **user-provided** destructor

---

[27]The introduction of std::pmr::monotoni_resource and std::pmr::unsynchronized_pool_resource in C++17 enables omitting destructor invocation for some *non*-trivially destructible types through the use of local allocators supplied at construction that reclaim all associated memory when they are destroyed, independently of whether the objects that requested the memory ever freed the memory themselves; see **lakos17a**, time 00:38:19. Note that this optimization technique can also be applied at the design level — e.g., to implement efficient garbage collection of cyclically connected networks of objects allocated from a single local memory arena; see **lakos19**, time 01:12:45.

disappears if NDEBUG is defined during compilation, thus recovering the trivial destructibility for our point class in production builds:

```
#ifndef NDEBUG
#include <cassert>  // standard C assert macro
#endif

struct Point4  // trivially constructible, maybe trivially destructible
{
    int d_x, d_y;  // same data as before

#ifndef NDEBUG
    ~Point4()  // Destructor is defaulted, hence trivial, in production builds.
    {
        assert(-5000 <= d_x);  assert(d_x <= 5000);
        assert(-5000 <= d_y);  assert(d_y <= 5000);
    }
#endif  // end of conditionally compiled destructor
};
```

Note that Point4 (1) is of **trivially destructible type** if and only if NDEBUG is defined and (2) enforces object invariants if and only if NDEBUG isn't defined. Correspondingly, if we want our shapes application (e.g., readAndProcess3) to benefit from a performance boost in a **production build** and still perform runtime checking in a debug build, we will need to somehow propagate the **conditional compilation** so as to selectively keep the cleanup code from the readAndProcess2 function only during a debug build:

```
void readAndProcess3(std::istream& stream)
{
    // ...           (same as in readAndProcess2)

#ifndef NDEBUG  // conditional cleanup
    // Cleanup: Explicitly destroy any Point2 objects in shapeEncodings.
    for (elemIdx = 0; numShapes > 0; --numShapes)
    {
        // ...           (same as in readAndProcess2)
    }
#endif  // conditional

}  // The local shapeEncodings array goes out of scope.
```

An important caveat to defining a type that is **trivially destructible** in only certain build modes (e.g., with and without the -DNDEBUG switch on the command line) is that a generic library will likely instantiate different code, employ a different algorithm, or even take an entirely different path based on querying a (compile-time) **metafunction** such as std::is_trivially_destructible. A class such as Point4, having a **conditionally compiled** destructor, could cause substantially different code to be generated and run in a debugging build compared to a production one, perhaps inconspicuously subverting adequate testing of the version of the program to be deployed and/or making defects difficult to reproduce in a debugger:

```
#include <type_traits>  // std::is_trivially_destructible
template <typename T>
void libraryFunc(const T& x)  // generic function that tests for triviality
{
    if (std::is_trivially_destructible<T>::value) { /* code-path A ... */ }
    else                                          { /* code-path B ... */ }
}

void f()
{
    Point4 pt{1, 2};
    libraryFunc(pt);  // executes code-path A in production but B in debug mode
}
```

To minimize failures in the field, it is essential that the build configuration(s) used to test a program (e.g., unit, integration, and stress testing) include at least the *identical* build configuration(s) in which it will be deployed.

The point classes shown so far have each had a **trivial destructor**, **trivial copy constructor**, and **trivial copy-assignment operator**, but none of these is required for us to take advantage of skippable destructors. All of the examples would work equally well if constructing and copying point objects were non-trivial, except that setting the **active member** to **d_vertex** in our shape-element **union** would require using placement **::operator new** instead of simple assignment:

```
//  shapeEncodings[elemIdx++].d_vertex = nextVertex(stream);        // old
    new(&shapeEncodings[elemIdx++].d_vertex) Point(nextVertex(stream));  // new
```

The code snippet above shows, commented out, the assignment statement within the inner loop from our original **readAndProcess** implementation, and the new statement, using placement **::operator new**, that would be required for a non-trivially constructible point class but that also works for a **trivially constructible** one. For example, we might decide that if our point class is never **trivially default constructible**, always supply user-provided *default* and *value* constructors, and conditionally compile any desired precondition checks into the bodies of those constructors (e.g., using the standard C **assert** macro). Note that our shape-element **union** would also need at least an empty **user-provided default constructor** for a *non*-trivially constructible point class.

Regardless of other properties, the destructor of a type can safely be skipped if it is **trivially destructible**, notionally trivially destructible, or conditionally compiled to be either of the two.

Fixed-capacity string (trivially copyable)

Trivially copyable types have the advantage of being duplicated more rapidly than the more general memberwise copy would allow. Consider an application that must quickly copy a large number of application-specific data records. Suppose further that, after some interaction between the developer and the client, it is determined that there exists some bounded (i.e., fixed or maximum) record size that can be known at compile time. Our application will employ arrays of objects — including those representing such data records — where generic functions on arrays will determine (e.g., using `std::is_trivially_copyable`) whether the objects they hold are of **trivially copyable type** and, if so, employ a highly efficient bitwise copy using, e.g., `std::memcpy`. For our application data records to benefit from any bitwise copy optimization in generic libraries, we must therefore design a class of **trivially copyable type** to represent them.

A trivially copyable data record might be a scalar or a POD **struct**. In our application, however, we will need a record that functions as a string albeit having a fixed maximum size, N, of at most 255 characters (not including the null terminator):

```cpp
#include <cassert>     // standard C assert macro
#include <cstring>     // std::strlen, std::memcpy, std::memcmp
#include <cstddef>     // std::size_t
#include <iostream>    // std::ostream, std::cout
#include <type_traits> // std::is_trivially_copyable

template <std::size_t N>   // N is the fixed capacity of this string.
class FixedCapacityString  // implementation type for trivially copyable records
{
    static_assert(N <= 255, "Capacity N is too large.");  // requirement check

    unsigned char d_size;        // compact length value; 1-byte aligned
    char          d_buffer[N + 1]; // same alignment as d_size; no padding

public:
    FixedCapacityString() : d_size(0) { d_buffer[0] = '\0'; } // default ctor
    FixedCapacityString(const char* str) : d_size(std::strlen(str)) // val ctor
    {
        assert(d_size <= N);                      // precondition
        std::memcpy(d_buffer, str, d_size + 1);   // includes null terminator
    }

    std::size_t size() const { return d_size; }    // current length of string
    const char* c_str() const { return d_buffer; } // address of first char

    // free functions (employing the hidden-friend idiom)
    friend bool operator==(const FixedCapacityString& lhs,
                           const FixedCapacityString& rhs)
    {
        return (lhs.d_size == rhs.d_size &&
                0 == std::memcmp(lhs.d_buffer, rhs.d_buffer, lhs.d_size));
    }

    friend bool operator!=(const FixedCapacityString& lhs,
                           const FixedCapacityString& rhs)
```

```
    {
        return !(lhs == rhs);
    }

    friend std::ostream& operator<<(std::ostream&              os,
                                    const FixedCapacityString& s)
    {
        return os << s.c_str();
    }
};

static_assert(std::is_trivially_copyable<FixedCapacityString<255>>::value, "");
    // trait verification

static_assert(sizeof(FixedCapacityString<255>) == 255 + 2, "");
    // verify no padding
```

Assuming the string passed as `str` to the `value constructor` satisfies the **precondition** that it is null-terminated and of length no larger than `N`, both **user-provided** constructors above ensure that (1) the `d_size` data member (which represents the current length of the string) is initialized to a valid value (e.g., 0) and (2) `d_buffer` is always null-terminated — both of these properties being **object invariants** of `FixedCapacityString`. Note that such **preconditions** and **object invariants** can often benefit from runtime enforcement (e.g., during testing) in a `debug build` (e.g., using the standard C `assert` macro).

Although a `FixedCapacityString<N>` is *not* trivially default constructible and, thus, not of trivial type, it does, however, satisfy the requirements for being **trivially copyable** because it has a nondeleted **trivial destructor**, a nondeleted **trivial copy constructor**, and no *non-trivial copy operations* (see *Description — Trivial subcategories* on page 429); we confirm this property at compile time for a single instantiation of `FixedCapacityString` with a **static_assert**.

A `FixedCapacityString` object can thus be constructed, queried, copied, compared, and even printed to an `std::ostream` — the key components of a usable string class (see *Description — C++11 generalized POD types* on page 415). Notice that we have chosen to employ the **hidden-friend idiom** for the operators of `FixedCapacityString`, making them accessible only through **ADL** when a `FixedCapacityString` is an operand of the corresponding operator.[28] By thus limiting the overload set, we defend against extended compile times during overload resolution, especially at scale. Moreover, **hidden friends** guard against ambiguities resulting from implicit conversions to the class that defines them; see Section 1.1. "**explicit** Operators" on page 61.

Let's now consider a function, `f1`, that illustrates how our newly minted `FixedCapacityString` class template might be used:

---

[28]See **brown19** and **williams19**.

```
#include <cassert>   // standard C assert macro

void f1()
{
    FixedCapacityString<30> s1;          // non-trivial default initialization
    FixedCapacityString<30> s2("hello"); // non-trivial value initialization
    FixedCapacityString<30> s3(s2);      // trivial copy construction

    assert(0 == s1.size());              // size accessor
    assert(5 == s2.size());              //   "      "

    assert('\0' == *s1.c_str());         // null-terminated-string accessor
    assert('h'  == *s2.c_str());         //   "        "        "        "

    assert(s2 != s1);                    // inequality comparison operator
    s2 = s1;                             // trivial copy assignment
    assert(s2 == s1);                    // equality comparison operator

    std::cout << s2 << '\n';             // prints '\n'      to standard output
    std::cout << s3 << '\n';             //   "    "hello\n" "   "        "
}
```

So far, none of the functionality we have implemented exploits any of the privileges afforded a trivially copyable type; let's now create a function, copyArrayOfRecords, that does:

```
template <std::size_t N>
void copyArrayOfRecords(FixedCapacityString<N>*       dst,    // destination
                        const FixedCapacityString<N>* src,    // source
                        std::size_t                   numStr) // # of records
    // Copy an array of numStr FixedCapacityString records.
{
    std::memcpy(dst, src, numStr * sizeof(FixedCapacityString<N>));  // fast
}
```

Notice above that, because our record type, FixedCapacityString<N>, is of trivially copyable type, we are able to copy the entire array of records using just a single invocation of std::memcpy.

Let's now suppose we want to copy a sequence of FixedCapacityString objects from one array (e.g., original) to another (e.g., duplicate):

```
const FixedCapacityString<30> original[] = { "one", "two", "three", "four" };
const std::size_t numStrings = sizeof original/sizeof *original;  // array size

FixedCapacityString<30> duplicate[numStrings];  // array same size as original
```

Notice above that we have used the C idiom to calculate, at compile time, the number of elements in our original array and store that value in a const integral variable, numStrings, suitable for declaring the `duplicate` array; see also Section 2.1."**constexpr** Variables" on page 302.

Let's now create a function, `f2`, that uses our custom `copyArrayOfRecords` function template to first propagate the record values stored in `original` to `duplicate` and then verify them at run time:

```
void f2()
{
    copyArrayOfRecords(duplicate, original, numStrings);  // fast array copy

    for (std::size_t i = 0; i < numStrings; ++i)  // for each copied string
    {
        assert(original[i] == duplicate[i]);  // Verify strings have same value.
    }
}
```

Rather than being specialized for `FixedCapacityString` arrays, as was `copyArrayOfRecords` above, a high-performance library might instead provide a **generic** array-copy function template, `copyArray`, that employs the `std::is_trivially_copyable` metafunction to *automatically* choose — at compile time — whether to apply the `std::memcpy` optimization or fall back on element-by-element assignment.

The two overloads of `copyArray` below have the same signature and thus would be ambiguous, except that they each employ the C++11 Standard Library **metafunction** `std::enable_if` (defined in `<type_traits>`) to eliminate one of the overloads based on the deduced type of `T`. As used here, `std::enable_if` yields a type, **void** by default, only if the predicate is **true**. This use of `enable_if` makes the function declaration ill formed if the predicate is **false**, taking that declaration out of consideration during overload resolution thanks to the **SFINAE** rule. In all cases, exactly one of the two overloads of `copyArray` will be well-formed, and that is the overload that will be selected for a particular template argument:

```
#include <cstring>       // std::memcpy
#include <type_traits>   // std::is_trivially_copyable, std::enable_if

template <typename T>
typename std::enable_if<!std::is_trivially_copyable<T>::value>::type
copyArray(T* dst, const T* src, std::size_t n)
    // Copy src array of size n to dst array element by element.
{
    for ( ; n > 0; --n)
    {
        *dst++ = *src++;  // Invoke T's copy-assignment operator.
    }
}
```

```
template <typename T>
typename std::enable_if<std::is_trivially_copyable<T>::value>::type
copyArray(T* dst, const T* src, std::size_t n)
    // Copy src array of size n to dst array by dint of trivial copyability.
{
    std::memcpy(dst, src, n * sizeof *dst);  // Copy all Ts at once quickly.
}
```

The first overload is selected for types that are *not* trivially copyable; each dst array element is individually assigned a value from src. The second overload is selected *only* for trivially copyable types, providing an optimized assignment from src to dst via a single call to std::memcpy.

We can now use our generic copyArray to replace copyArrayOfRecords for assigning the value of an array of FixedCapacityString objects:

```
void f3()
{
    copyArray(duplicate, original, numStrings);   // generic fast array copy

    for (std::size_t i = 0; i < numStrings; ++i)  // same as in f2 (above)
    {
        assert(original[i] == duplicate[i]);
    }
}
```

The call to copyArray in f3() (above) invokes the optimized (memcpy-based) overload because FixedCapacityString<30> is a trivially copyable type. Similar code using std::string, being of *non*-trivially copyable type, would choose the unoptimized (element-by-element assignment) overload instead and, hence, would not be an appropriate record type for this use case.

Another potential benefit of trivially copyable types is that they can be safely copied into an array of **unsigned char** and inspected — e.g., for debugging purposes — as a "bag of bits," provided we don't access any bytes having indeterminate value. When copying an object of trivially copyable type to an **unsigned char** array, indeterminate values can come from two sources: (1) **padding bytes** and (2) any bytes in the object representation that correspond to uninitialized non**static** data members; see *Potential Pitfalls — Conflating arbitrary values with indeterminate values* on page 493. Our FixedCapacityString template was deliberately engineered to obviate padding bytes, but any unused bytes in d_buffer will have indeterminate value. If we want to make the entire footprint of FixedCapacityString inspectable as raw bytes, we will need to initialize the entire d_buffer in every user-provided constructor, e.g., using std::memset(d_buffer, 0, N). Because only the *default* and *value* constructors are affected, the object remains trivially copyable albeit somewhat less runtime efficient to construct.

Elements of fixed-capacity string (trivial)

A string class need not necessarily contain elements of type **char**. For example, an std::basic_string containing elements of type **char32_t**, defined in <uchar.h>, can hold UTF-32 **code units**. For added flexibility, let's modify the FixedCapacityString template from the previous use case so that, in addition to the maximum number of characters, N, it is parameterized on the desired character type, T, which defaults to **char**:

```
#include <iostream>   // std::basic_ostream, std::wcout
#include <algorithm>  // std::equal

template <std::size_t N, typename T = char>
class FixedCapacityString
{
    static_assert(N <= 255, "Capacity N is too large.");  // requirement check

    unsigned char d_size;
    T             d_buffer[N + 1];

public:
    FixedCapacityString() : d_size(0) { d_buffer[0] = T(); }
    FixedCapacityString(const T* str)  // The length of str must be less than N.
    {
        const T nullChar = T();
        for (d_size = 0; str[d_size] != nullChar; ++d_size)
        {
            d_buffer[d_size] = str[d_size];
        }
        d_buffer[d_size] = nullChar;  // null terminator
    }

    std::size_t size() const { return d_size; }
    const T* c_str() const { return d_buffer; }

    // free functions (employing the hidden-friend idiom)
    friend bool operator==(const FixedCapacityString& lhs,
                           const FixedCapacityString& rhs)
    {
        if (lhs.d_size != rhs.d_size) return false;
        return std::equal(lhs.d_buffer, lhs.d_buffer+lhs.d_size, rhs.d_buffer);
    }

    friend bool operator!=(const FixedCapacityString& lhs,
                           const FixedCapacityString& rhs)
    {
        return !(lhs == rhs);
    }
```

```
    friend std::basic_ostream<T>&
            operator<<(std::basic_ostream<T>& os, const FixedCapacityString& s)
    {
        return os << s.c_str();  // might require additional support for some Ts
    }
};
```

We can now define a function, f1, that creates an object s, of an instantiation of FixedCapacityString holding a maximum of 15 characters, each of type **wchar_t**:

```
#include <cassert>  // standard C assert macro

void f1()
{
    FixedCapacityString<15, wchar_t> s(L"hello");  // L: wide-character literal
    assert(5 == s.size());
    std::wcout << s << L'\n';  // Print "hello\n" using only wide characters.
}
```

Next, let's consider the requirements for the "character" element type, T, in our FixedCapacityString class template above. Recall that we designed FixedCapacityString in the previous use case to be trivially copyable (and, hence, trivially destructible) so that containers could bitwise-copy objects of this type more efficiently (e.g., using std::memcpy). For FixedCapacityString to remain trivially copyable, T must also be trivially copyable. But consider that, in a robust high-performance implementation, we will want to avoid necessarily initializing every element in d_buffer on construction of an object of FixedCapacityString<N, T>. Unless T is trivially default constructible, the compiler will automatically invoke T's constructor for each element of FixedCapacityString<N, T>'s d_buffer before even entering the body of *any* user-provided constructor of FixedCapacityString<N, T>. It therefore behooves us to require that T be trivially default constructible. All of these constraints taken together imply that T must be a trivial type.

Interestingly, the constraint on T of being trivial is satisfied not only by narrow- and wide-character types, but by trivial UDTs as well. For example, consider a trivial class (e.g., Word) consisting of a single pointer member (e.g., d_word) having equality-comparison operators (== and !=) implemented as hidden friends:

```
#include <cstring>      // std::strcmp, std::memcpy
#include <type_traits>  // std::is_trivial

struct Word  // trivial type
{
    const char* d_word;  // does not own pointed-to string

    friend bool operator==(const Word& lhs, const Word& rhs)  // hidden friend
    {
        if (lhs.d_word == rhs.d_word) return true;        // same address value
```

```
        if (!lhs.d_word || !rhs.d_word) return false;    // (only) one nullptr
        return 0 == std::strcmp(lhs.d_word, rhs.d_word); // distinct addresses
    }

    friend bool operator!=(const Word& lhs, const Word& rhs)  // hidden friend
    {
        return !(lhs == rhs);
    }
};

static_assert(std::is_trivial<Word>::value, "");  // Verify our assumptions.
static_assert(std::is_trivially_copyable<FixedCapacityString<10, Word>
                                                    >::value, "");
```

Next we'll create two FixedCapacityString<10, Word> objects (e.g., source and destination). The source object is initialized with an array (e.g., rawData) of four Word objects, three being aggregate initialized from string literals and the fourth being value initialized to act as a null terminator. The destination object is **default constructed** and is thus empty:

```
Word wordArray[] = { {"alpha"}, {"beta"}, {"gamma"}, {} };  // raw data
FixedCapacityString<10, Word> source(wordArray);  // Construct from array.
FixedCapacityString<10, Word> destination;        // empty destination
```

Now we can demonstrate, in the body of a function (e.g., f2), that all of the desired functionality works as before, including the use of std::memcpy to transfer the value from source to destination:

```
void f2()
{
    assert(3 == source.size());             // Check source length.
    assert(source.c_str()[1] == Word{"beta"});     // Check middle word.

    assert(0 == destination.size());        // Check destination length.

    std::memcpy(&destination, &source, sizeof source);  // trivially copyable

    assert(3 == destination.size());        // Check destination length.
    assert(destination.c_str()[1] == Word{"beta"}); // Check middle word.
    assert(destination == source);          // Check equality.
}
```

The Word class does not need a **user-provided** constructor or destructor because it does not allocate or deallocate resources; the d_word member is initialized to point to a null-terminated string in externally managed memory (e.g., a string literal, which has **static storage duration**). The Word type is, thus, trivial — in fact, it's a POD **class** — so it meets the constraints for the character-type parameter, T, of our updated FixedCapacityString template. The `std::basic_string` template requires a **char-like object** as its character type, defined as a nonarray POD type.[29]

Though using a UDT as a string element is an unlikely scenario, there appears to be little reason to forbid it. We could broaden the set of allowed types by relaxing the **trivially constructible** requirement from `T` and suffer no ill consequences for types that are **trivial**. Moreover, we will achieve nearly the same runtime performance for those newly admitted types that are **trivially copyable** but *not* **trivially default constructible**. Such relaxation of requirements typically needs to be balanced against the simplicity of specification and the implementation latitude (including the flexibility for future enhancements) afforded by constraining `T` to being fully **trivial**. Whatever the eventual requirement on `T` might be, the implementer can enforce it with a compile-time check — e.g., `static_assert(std::is_trivial<T>::value, "");` — within the body of the `FixedCapacityString<N, T>` class template.

Note that the `std::basic_ostream<T>` argument to the streaming operator (**operator<<**) for a `FixedCapacityString` of `Word` elements will fail to instantiate unless we provide, at least, a custom template specialization for `std::basic_streambuf<Word>`. Even without such a specialized streaming implementation, `FixedCapacityString<Word>` is fully usable provided the streaming operator is not invoked.

Potential Pitfalls

Exporting bitwise copies of PODs

Historically, PODs were the category of types one might have thought to try to externalize directly because (1) the data bits represent the value directly (**trivial**) and (2) we know where the piece parts reside within the POD (**standard layout**). However, the set of things that programmers might like to do with such data and the things that they are *actually* permitted to do with that data are different — the legality is difficult to discern from reading the Standard and tends to be policed differently on different compiler versions and systems; see *Annoyances — The C++ Standard has not yet stabilized in this area* on page 521.

The C++ language is specified in terms of an abstract machine. Any data arriving from outside that machine, such as by network or file I/O, does not benefit from the permissions granted to data originating within that machine, even if it was originally produced by that same process. There is simply *no* guaranteed safe way to copy the **object representation** of a POD out of process and read it back in — even to the same process, let alone to a different program written in another language — using persistent storage, shared memory, or a network byte stream. Any such use of PODs has **undefined behavior** in C++, carrying the possibility of unanticipated results.

Nonetheless, PODs — more specifically, **trivially copyable types** — that do not refer to the address of other in-process objects are a useful concept from an engineering perspective as they most closely identify the kinds of types that can be sent outside of a running process

---

[29]In C++20, **char-like object** was redefined equivalently as a nonarray trivial standard-layout type.

via, say, a socket, shared memory, or file I/O, and then quickly reconstituted in, say, another process on an identical machine running an identical build of the same program.

Once we consider different builds of the same program, even when operating on the same machine, we lose many of the guarantees (such as consistent size and alignment of data members) that are implicit when operating within a single process. Interoperating between C and C++ translation units within a single process has defined behavior for a well-specified subset of PODs, but as soon as the communication crosses process boundaries, we are again necessarily dealing with distinct builds. When C++ programs interact with C programs in this manner, having a single back-end toolchain for assembling and linking the programs can help to minimize surprises.

Communicating across a network of heterogeneous architectures provides even more opportunities for the underlying **object representation** to differ in subtle ways. In addition to the native sizes of scalar types potentially being different on different platforms, the byte ordering (a.k.a. endianness), alignment and padding requirements, floating-point representations, and representations of non-numeric types such as **bool** might differ as well. Even being aware of these differences, attempting to compensate for them is error-prone and can lead to surprisingly subtle errors.

Finally, saving data in persistent storage as the raw **object representation** of a POD leaves such data at risk should any of the specific details of the in-process data representation change, say, as a result of a new version of a compiler, and is rarely advisable. Reading or writing binary data (e.g., of JPEG files) is best done as a byte stream, where each scalar value is decoded/encoded separately from/to an array of raw bytes with a well-defined arrangement.

In short, externalizing the **object representation** of PODs is not a substitute for proper network programming; see *Appendix — A cautionary tale: PODs are not just "bags of bits"* on page 530.

Requiring PODs or even just trivial types

This pitfall comes in two forms: (1) requiring a larger subset of type properties than is necessary and (2) creating a UDT that is overly general for the contracts it is expected to satisfy.

1. **Needlessly enforcing type contracts[30] that are overly restrictive** — First, imagine that we are writing a function template, `byteCopy1`, to copy the underlying representation from a supplied object of type `T`, and return the raw bytes by value as an `std::vector<char>`, such that byte copies of different types may reside within a single homogeneous data structure (such as an `std::map<KeyType, std::vector<char> >`):

---

[30] C++20 introduces the notion of **concepts** — a syntactic feature that can be used to concisely characterize the subset of allowed types suitable for a given template type parameter.

```
#include <cstring>      // std::memcpy
#include <type_traits>  // std::is_pod, std::is_trivially_copyable
#include <vector>       // std::vector

template <typename T>
std::vector<char> byteCopy1(const T& obj)  // object buffer
{
    static_assert(std::is_pod<T>(), "T must be POD type");  // Too restrictive!

    std::vector<char> result('\0', sizeof(obj));
    std::memcpy(result.data(), &obj, sizeof(obj));
    return result;  // newly allocated buffer containing object representation
}
```

In the example above, we have required that template type argument, T, be a POD
type. The only constraint on T that would affect the validity of this function template,
however, is that T must be **trivially copyable**. Hence, there is a substantial variety of
types that one might expect to work with this `byteCopy1` function but which, for no
legitimate reason, do not compile:

```
struct B { int x; };       // The base class is a POD.
struct D : B { int y; };   // derived class is trivial but not standard layout

void test1()
{
    B b = {};
    D d = {};

    std::vector<char> vb = byteCopy1(b);  // OK
    std::vector<char> vd = byteCopy1(d);  // Error, D is not a POD.
}
```

In the example above, even though d is not of POD type, there's nothing in the
implementation of function template `byteCopy1` — other than the **static_assert** —
that would prevent it from working on d too.

A more general solution (e.g., `byteCopy2`) would be for the contract to provide,
again via a **static_assert**, just the minimal set of type constraints required, thereby
enabling the function template to work with a much wider variety of argument types:

```
template <typename T>
std::vector<char> byteCopy2(const T& obj)
{
    static_assert(std::is_trivially_copyable<T>(),  // appropriately
                  "T must be trivially copyable");   // restrictive

    // ...                   (same as in byteCopy1 above)
}
```

The `byteCopy2` function template, above, properly fails *only* if copying the bytes of objects of the type supplied for `T` would result in undefined behavior.

2. **Overly restricting a type that is intended for use in generic programming** — The converse of over-constraining the arguments of a generic function is over-constraining the design of a type intended for use in that function. We might have wanted to add a constructor to `B`, above, but omitted such a constructor to keep `B` trivial. Given the less restrictive requirements of `byteCopy2` (above), we needn't hesitate to define a type (e.g., `B2`) that is trivially copyable but does not necessarily have a trivial default constructor:

```
struct B2 { int x; B2() : x(0) { } };  // trivially copyable but not POD

void test2()
{
    B2 b;  // invokes default constructor
    std::vector<char> vb = byteCopy2(b);  // OK, b is trivially copyable.
}
```

Using the wrong type trait

The C++ Standard Library provides three type traits, `std::is_trivial`, `std::is_trivially_copyable`, and `std::is_standard_layout`, that correspond *directly* to terms used in the **core-language specification**, namely, trivial type, trivially copyable type, and standard-layout type, respectively. These three atypical traits indicated whether a (typically library) developer may exploit a particular type's intrinsic properties — most often as a manual optimization in the body of a generic function — without the possibility of a compiler subverting the developer's intentions via aggressive optimization. Additional standard traits, such as `std::is_trivially_copy_constructible` and `std::is_trivially_copy_assignable`, afford more fine-grained classification — most often as a constraint in the interface of a generic function — and are also somewhat different in their characteristics. In particular, these interface-oriented traits impose additional constraints beyond checking that the corresponding operation is trivial. Hence, the similar-sounding names across these distinct trait categories can lead to subtle defects when a fine-grained **interface trait** is naively used in contexts where one of the **core traits** is needed, and vice versa.

The three **core traits** above are distinct from all the other, similarly sounding **interface traits** in that the **core traits** do not require any publicly accessible operations. That is, if a **struct**, `AllPublic`, having all of its user-declared members publicly accessible satisfies one or more of these traits, then a **class** `AllPrivate` declaring precisely the same members as **private** will satisfy that trait too. Such is not the case for the more fine-grained **interface traits**, which typically require the particular functionality in question to (1) be publicly accessible and (2) be **invocable** (i.e., *non*deleted and unambiguous). Note that all traits are context insensitive in that there is no relative notion of privileged (e.g., **private**) access, say, by dint of being a **friend**.

For example, consider a class, C, that declares a private copy constructor and a public deleted copy-assignment operator:

```
#include <type_traits>  // std::is_trivially_copyable
                        // std::is_trivially_copy_constructible (etc.)

class C  // trivially copyable but not trivially copy constructible
{
    C(const C&)             = default;  // nonpublic trivial copy constructor
public:
    C& operator=(const C&) = delete;    // public deleted copy assignment op
};

static_assert( std::is_trivially_copyable<C>::value, "");           // OK
static_assert(!std::is_trivially_copy_assignable<C>::value, "");    // OK
static_assert(!std::is_trivially_copy_constructible<C>::value, ""); // OK
```

In the example above, class C satisfies all the core language requirements for being trivially copyable as it has an implicitly declared *non*deleted trivial destructor, no *non*-trivial copy operations, and at least one *non*deleted trivial copy operation irrespective of that operation being private. The more specific interface trait std::is_trivially_copy_constructible evaluates to **false** when applied to C, because the constructor in question is not publicly accessible. The std::is_trivially_copy_assignable trait similarly evaluates to **false** because, though publicly accessible, the assignment is not invocable due to it being **deleted**. Note that all three compile-time assertions above would have succeeded without the negation (!) in the latter two had C's copy constructor been publicly accessible and its assignment operator been **defaulted** instead of deleted.

The traits that check for the core language properties (i.e., std::is_trivial, std::is_trivially_copyable, and std::is_standard_layout) are mandated to match exactly what the standard definitions require and pertain only to what liberties the implementation of a generic function may take for an object of a given type (e.g., use of std::memcpy) as well as what liberties the compiler itself might take when optimizing uses of a type. The other traits, which do not have a standard term associated with them (e.g., std::is_trivially_constructible, std::is_trivially_copy_constructible, std::is_trivially_copy_assignable, and std::is_trivially_destructible), also require — among other things — public accessibility, are more articulate and fine-grained, and are immune to subtle details of the core language; hence, these interface traits are typically better suited to checking relevant type properties as constraints in a generic function's *interface* rather than its implementation.

As an illustration of usage for these two distinct categories of type traits, consider a class, S, that is of **trivially copyable type** and yet cannot be assigned:

```
#include <type_traits>  // std::is_trivially_copyable

struct S  // trivially copyable but not assignable
{
    S() {}                                  // non-trivial default constructor
    S(const S&)            = delete;   // deleted copy constructor
    S(S&&)                 = default;  // trivial move constructor
    S& operator=(const S&) = delete;   // deleted assignment operator
};

static_assert(std::is_trivially_copyable<S>::value, "");  // OK
```

The author of class S — by explicitly deleting both the copy constructor and the copy assignment operator — clearly intended not to support having multiple active copies of objects of type S. Note, however, that the addition of a *non*deleted trivial move constructor makes type S trivially copyable nonetheless. Although using std::memcpy to assign values to objects of type S is well defined in the language, it goes against the design intent if the original object is used after the assignment, possibly leading to bugs due to the type's design choices not being respected:

```
#include <utility>  // std::move
#include <cstring>  // std::memcpy

void f1()
{
    S s1, s2;            // Construct two objects of type S.
    S s3(s1);            // Error, copy constructor is deleted.
    s2 = s1;             // Error, assignment operator is deleted.
    S s4(std::move(s1)); // OK, move construction

    std::memcpy(&s2, &s1, sizeof s1);  // Bug, backdoor copying is suspect.
}
```

Using std::memcpy (in the final line of f1, above) to copy from one S object, s1, to another, s2, is well defined because S just so happens to be trivially copyable; such valid use of std::memcpy, however, would subvert the programmer's intent that the value of an S object may be moved, but not copied. Consider also that, should the move constructor or destructor someday become *non*-trivial (since there was no express or implied promise that couldn't happen), any hard-coded std::memcpy, such as shown above, would silently manifest undefined behavior.

We can, however, employ the appropriate core trait, std::is_trivially_copyable, in a generic function's body to ensure that std::memcpy is applied *only* where it would not result in undefined behavior and then separately use the appropriate interface trait, `std::is_copy_assignable`, in the function's interface to indicate when using `std::memcpy` would violate the intended **contract** with the caller. For example, let's create a function template (e.g., `optimizedCopy`) that copies one array of `T` to another, using assignment semantics:

```
#include <cstring>      // std::memcpy
#include <type_traits>  // std::is_copy_assignable, std::is_trivially_copyable

template <typename T>
void optimizedCopy(T* dest, const T* first, const T* last)
    // Copy elements from range [first, last) to the range starting at dest.
    // requires that std::is_copy_assignable<T>::value is true
{
    static_assert(std::is_copy_assignable<T>::value, "T must be assignable");

    if (std::is_trivially_copyable<T>::value)  // Check for optimizability.
    {
        std::memcpy(dest, first, (last - first) * sizeof(T));  // FAST
    }
    else  // Type T is not trivially copyable, so no std::memcpy for it.
    {
        while (first != last)
        {
            *dest++ = *first++;  // (presumably) slower than std::memcpy
        }
    }
}
```

An instantiation of `optimizedCopy` will result in a compile-time assertion failure indicating a **contract violation** if the caller attempts to provide a type, `T`, that is not **copy assignable**. Presuming that the object in question does support conventional **copy assignment**, the algorithm for `optimizedCopy` will then check to see if an object of type `T` is trivially copyable and, if so, employ `std::memcpy` to copy the entire range at once. Otherwise, since `std::memcpy` would result in **undefined** behavior, `optimizedCopy` will instead perform element-by-element assignment, using `T`'s assignment operator. Thus, in our function template, we make complementary use of both the **interface trait**, `std::is_copy_assignable`, in the interface and the **core trait**, `std::is_trivially_copyable`, in the implementation. This sort of optimization is particularly useful for arrays of **trivially copyable types**; see *Use Cases — Fixed-capacity string (trivially copyable)* on page 470.

An alternative to employing just a **static_assert** for enforcing a compile-time contract is to — in addition — use the Standard Library metafunction `std::enable_if` (e.g., in `optimizedCopy2`) to disallow a call to `optimizedCopy2` if `T` is deduced not to be **copy assignable**:

```
template <typename T>
typename std::enable_if<std::is_copy_assignable<T>::value>::type
optimizedCopy2(T* dest, const T* first, const T* last)
    // Copy elements from range [first, last) to the range starting at dest.
    // This function does not participate in overload resolution unless
    // std::is_copy_assignable<T>::value is true.
{
    // ... (body including static_assert unchanged from optimizedCopy above)
}
```

In the example above, the return type of `optimizedCopy2` will be **void** if `std::is_copy_assignable<T>::value` is **true** and ill formed otherwise. Unlike our previous use of a **static_assert** in the body of the original `optimizedCopy`, an ill formed specialization of a function template does not necessarily result in a compile-time error but, instead, eliminates that specialization from the overload set, thereby allowing another, viable overload, if any, to be selected instead. In particular, note that this way, the **static_assert** in the body of an ill formed specialization never fires and is therefore an entirely redundant defensive check. An additional advantage of using `std::enable_if` in this example is that the copy assignable constraint is expressed, in addition to any English documentation, directly in the programmatic interface. On the other hand, for a function template such as `optimizedCopy2`, having just a **static_assert** might produce a more comprehensible error message than, e.g., "Error - no matching function for `optimizedCopy2`."[31]

There are vanishingly few cases in practice where `std::is_trivially_copy_constructible` or `std::is_trivially_copy_assignable` would be appropriate in the implementation of a function template as there's nothing special in the core language that comports with them. (Satisfying the requirements of one or both of these interface traits is neither necessary nor sufficient for the argument type to be trivially copyable.) What's more, a type that is trivially copyable might not satisfy either of these interface traits, e.g., due to the trait's additional requirements, such as public accessibility, invocability, etc. Conversely, `std::is_trivially_copyable` identifies precisely the superset of trivial types that, for example, may be safely copied via `std::memcpy` because this core trait takes into account all *five* (including the destructor) of the relevant special member functions associated with being trivially copyable, and yet it would be rare to see `std::is_trivially_copyable` used properly in the *interface* of a well-specified function template unless that template provides a low-level service. Hence, core traits properly belong to the implementation of generic functions, whereas interface traits almost always reside in the interface (but see *Potential Pitfalls — Ineligible use of `std::memcpy`* on page 497).

When it comes to class templates, there are other kinds of appropriate uses of `std::is_trivially_copy_assignable` and its ilk. Suppose, for example, that we want to guarantee that a class template that wraps some other type (e.g., `Wrap<T>`) is *non*assignable, copy assignable, or **trivially copy assignable** corresponding to the existence and triviality of the copy assignment operation defined for its template type argument, `T`. The

---

[31] In C++20, a **requires** clause (part of the *concepts* feature) provides an easier-to read alternative to `std::enable_if` and also produces a more comprehensible error message when the requirement is not met.

std::is_trivially_copy_assignable trait may be used to constrain a template partial specialization or, as in the example below, used to define a **user-provided** copy assignment operator *only* for *non*-trivially copy assignable types, T, used to instantiate Wrap:

```
#include <iostream>     // std::cout
#include <type_traits>  // std::is_trivially_copy_assignable,
                        // std::is_copy_assignable, std::is_reference

template <typename T>
class Wrap  // trivially copy assignable when possible
{
    T d_data;  // member object of type being wrapped

    struct Dummy { };  // local type (not usable outside of this class)

    typedef typename std::conditional<
            (    std::is_trivially_copy_assignable<T>::value
              && !std::is_reference<T>::value)
            || !std::is_copy_assignable<T>::value,
            const Dummy&,  // parameter for useless assignment operator
            const Wrap&    // parameter for copy assignment operator
        >::type MaybeCopyAssignType;  // parameter type for assignment operator

public:
    Wrap() = default;
    explicit Wrap(const T& d) : d_data(d) { }
    Wrap(const Wrap&) = default;

    Wrap& operator=(MaybeCopyAssignType rhs)  // maybe copy assignment operator
    {
        d_data = rhs.d_data;
        std::cout << "non-trivial copy assignment\n";
        return *this;
    }
};
```

In the Wrap class template above, the std::conditional metafunction is used to choose between one of two types for the MaybeCopyAssignType type alias: If T is trivially copy assignable but not a reference or if T is not copy assignable at all, then the aliased type, MaybeCopyAssignType, will be **const** Dummy&; otherwise, it will be **const** Wrap&. If MaybeCopyAssignType is aliased to **const** Dummy&, the declared **operator**= will be useless and will *not* have a signature appropriate for a copy-assignment operator, resulting in the implicit generation of a **defaulted** trivial copy-assignment operator, which will be **deleted** if T is not copy assignable; otherwise, the declared **operator**= *will* have a proper signature for a copy-assignment operator and, because it is **user-provided**, will not be trivial. Thus, the std::is_copy_assignable and std::is_trivially_copy_assignable traits for Wrap<T> mostly mirror those for T:

```
struct X { X& operator=(const X&); }; // not trivially copy assignable
struct Y { int& a; };                 // not copy assignable

static_assert( std::is_copy_assignable           <    int >::value, "");
static_assert( std::is_copy_assignable           <Wrap<int>>::value, "");
static_assert( std::is_trivially_copy_assignable<    int >::value, "");
static_assert( std::is_trivially_copy_assignable<Wrap<int>>::value, "");

static_assert( std::is_copy_assignable           <    X >::value, "");
static_assert( std::is_copy_assignable           <Wrap<X>>::value, "");
static_assert(! std::is_trivially_copy_assignable<    X >::value, "");
static_assert(! std::is_trivially_copy_assignable<Wrap<X>>::value, "");

static_assert(! std::is_copy_assignable           <    Y >::value, "");
static_assert(! std::is_copy_assignable           <Wrap<Y>>::value, "");
static_assert(! std::is_trivially_copy_assignable<    Y >::value, "");
static_assert(! std::is_trivially_copy_assignable<Wrap<Y>>::value, "");

static_assert( std::is_copy_assignable           <    int& >::value, "");
static_assert( std::is_copy_assignable           <Wrap<int&>>::value, "");
static_assert( std::is_trivially_copy_assignable<    int& >::value, "");
static_assert(! std::is_trivially_copy_assignable<Wrap<int&>>::value, "");
```

As the example code above shows, both **int** and **Wrap<int>** have *trivial* copy assignment operators. Given that X has a user-provided and, hence, *non*-trivial copy-assignment operator, so too does class **Wrap<X>**. But notice the apparent counterexample illustrated in the final two lines above. The std::is_trivially_copy_assignable trait applied to an **int&** evaluates to **true** but, when applied to the wrapped version (**Wrap<int&>**), is **false**. Had we allowed the assignment operator to be defaulted (i.e., by not checking std::is_reference), **Wrap<int&>** would have been **deleted**, which is not what we want. We therefore chose to design **Wrap** to have a *non*-trivial copy-assignment operator when T is a reference type.

Using sloppy terminology

Another misstep would be conflating terms, such as trivial or trivially copyable, that have well-defined meaning in the language standard, with similar-sounding but purely descriptive terms, like trivially destructible or **trivially copy constructible**, that have no corresponding core language meaning. For example, saying that a type, T, is trivially destructible could be interpreted to mean either (1) that T satisfies the subset of properties required of a trivial or trivially copyable type pertaining to the destructor or (2) that the interface trait std::is_trivially_destructible, when applied to T, evaluates to **true**. In particular, consider that std::is_trivially_copyable<T> doesn't necessarily imply std::is_trivially_destructible<T>:

```
#include <type_traits> // std::is_trivially_copyable,
                        // std::is_trivially_destructible,
                        // std::is_trivially_copy_assignable

class X  // X is trivially copyable but is X trivially destructible?
{
    ~X() = default;  // inaccessible trivial destructor
};

static_assert( std::is_trivially_copyable<X>::value, "");       // OK
static_assert(!std::is_trivially_destructible<X>::value, "");   // OK
static_assert( std::is_trivially_copy_assignable<X>::value, ""); // OK
```

In the example code above, class X is trivially copyable even though its trivial destructor is not **publicly accessible**. The std::is_trivially_copyable trait corresponds exactly to the language definition of trivially copyable, which is independent of the access levels of the destructor and any copy operations, whereas the std::is_trivially_destructible trait is **true** only if the destructor is both trivial and publicly accessible. Hence, the set of requirements that must be satisfied for std::is_trivially_copyable to be **true** is *not* a superset of those for std::is_trivially_destructible. Depending on one's terminology, X could be considered trivially destructible (because it has a nondeleted trivial destructor) or not (because std::is_trivially_destructible evaluates to **false**).

In this book, we consistently apply *non*standard descriptive terms, such as "trivially destructible," to mean exactly the set of types for which the corresponding standard interface trait, in this case is_trivially_destructible, would evaluate to **true** — just as we *must* with the standard ones. Thus, X is not considered trivially destructible because std::is_trivially_destructible<X>::value is **false**, whereas X *is* trivially copy assignable because std::is_trivially_copy_assignable<X>::value is **true**.

Be mindful that the difference between precise and sloppy is incontrovertibly subtle. When talking at a sufficiently high level, it is easy enough to misspeak and assert that the set of trivially copyable types is a proper subset of trivially destructible ones. To be correct, however, we must instead say that the set of trivially copyable types is a proper subset of types having a *non*deleted trivial destructor.

Using memcpy on objects having const or reference subobjects

From a user perspective, a bitwise copy from object a to object b can be seen as an assignment operation, b = a, or as destroying a and reconstructing it from b using copy construction — an operation similar to using placement ::**operator new**. For the most part, the distinction is irrelevant provided that all of those operations are trivial and any needed operation is available to be used (i.e., nondeleted, publicly accessible, and unambiguous). Note that a trivially copyable type guarantees a subset of that requirement — e.g., the *copy* and *move* assignment, the *copy* and *move* constructor, and the destructor are all guaranteed to be trivial but not necessarily usable, and only the destructor and one of the copy operations is declared and not deleted:

```cpp
#include <cassert>  // standard C assert macro
#include <new>      // placement new
#include <cstring>  // std::memcpy

void copy1a()
{
    int a = 1, b = 2;
    a = b;                          // assignment
    assert(2 == a);
}

void copy1b()
{
    int a = 1, b = 2;
    new(&a) int(b);                 // copy construction using placement new
    assert(2 == a);
}

void copy1c()
{
    int a = 1, b = 2;
    std::memcpy(&a, &b, sizeof b);  // bitwise copy
    assert(2 == a);
}
```

All three of the functions above produce well-defined results that are indistinguishable from one another.

Let's now consider a **struct** (e.g., S) that is of trivial type and yet contains a *non*static **const** data member (e.g., **const int** i) and another **struct** (e.g., B) that is of trivial type and yet contains a *non*static data member of reference type (e.g., **int&** r). In both cases, the implicitly declared default constructor, copy-assignment operator, and move-assignment operator are deleted:

```cpp
#include <type_traits>  // std::is_trivially_copyable
                        // std::is_trivially_copy_constructible (etc.)

struct S  // S is trivial yet neither default constructible nor assignable.
{
    const int i;  // const member i must be initialized at construction.
};

static_assert( std::is_trivial<S>::value, "");                          // OK
static_assert(!std::is_trivially_default_constructible<S>::value, "");  // OK
static_assert(!std::is_default_constructible<S>::value, "");            // OK
```

```
static_assert( std::is_trivially_copyable<S>::value, "");              // OK
static_assert( std::is_trivially_destructible<S>::value, "");          // OK
static_assert( std::is_trivially_copy_constructible<S>::value, "");    // OK
static_assert(!std::is_trivially_copy_assignable<S>::value, "");       // OK
static_assert(!std::is_copy_assignable<S>::value, "");                 // OK

struct B  // B is trivial yet neither default constructible nor assignable.
{
    int& r;      // Reference member r must be initialized at construction.
};

static_assert( std::is_trivial<B>::value, "");                         // OK
static_assert(!std::is_trivially_default_constructible<B>::value, "");  // OK
static_assert(!std::is_default_constructible<B>::value, "");           // OK

static_assert( std::is_trivially_copyable<B>::value, "");              // OK
static_assert( std::is_trivially_destructible<B>::value, "");          // OK
static_assert( std::is_trivially_copy_constructible<B>::value, "");    // OK
static_assert(!std::is_trivially_copy_assignable<B>::value, "");       // OK
static_assert(!std::is_copy_assignable<B>::value, "");                 // OK
```

Notice that, although **struct** S is of trivial type, and therefore of trivially copyable type, it has neither a *usable* default constructor nor a *usable* assignment operator; hence, employing std::memcpy to assign the value of such a type — even though it purports to be trivially copyable — would be a way of modifying a **const** subobject after it has been created. Similarly, **struct** B is of trivial type, but using std::memcpy to assign the value of a B object would be a way of rebinding a reference, perhaps to a different object. For these sorts of types, the semantics of copy construction and assignment are vastly different. Since assignment doesn't make sense, trivial destruction followed by copy construction is the only viable interpretation of std::memcpy. Unfortunately, in C++11 and C++14, destroying an object having a **const** or reference subobject and re-creating an object of the type at the same location invalidates all previous references to that object:

```
void copy2a()  // attempting to use the assignment operator
{
    S a = { 1 }, b = { 2 };
    a = b;                   // Error, assignment is not allowed.

    int i1 = 1, i2 = 2;
    B c = { i1 }, d = { i2 };
    c = d;                   // Error, assignment is not allowed.
}

void copy2b()  // using in-place copy construction with placement new
{
    S a = { 1 }, b = { 2 };
    S* pa = new (&a) S(b);   // OK, copy construction
```

```
    int x1 = a.i;            // Bug (UB), cannot refer to new object through a
    int x2 = pa->i;          // OK, can access through value returned from new
    assert(x2 == 2);         // OK, const member S::i was overwritten.

    int i1 = 1, i2 = 2;
    B c = { i1 }, d = { i2 };
    B* pc = new (&c) B(d);   // OK, copy construction
    int& y1 = c.r;           // Bug (UB), cannot refer to new object through c
    int& y2 = pc->r;         // OK, can access through return value of new
    assert(&y2 == &i2);      // OK, reference member B::r was rebound.
}

void copy2c()  // using std::memcpy
{
    S a = { 1 }, b = { 2 };
    std::memcpy(&a, &b, sizeof b);  // OK, bitwise copy
    int x = a.i;             // Bug (UB), cannot refer to new object through a

    int i1 = 1, i2 = 2;
    B c = { i1 }, d = { i2 };
    std::memcpy(&c, &d, sizeof d);  // OK, bitwise copy
    int& y = c.r;            // Bug (UB), cannot refer to new object through c
}
```

In copy2a, the assignment operation fails at compile time. In copy2b, using copy construction and placement **new** works. Moreover, it is valid to access the newly created object via the value returned from placement ::**operator new**, but not directly through the original name — even though they refer to the same address. In copy2c, it is also valid to std::memcpy from one object to another of the same trivially copyable type. Attempting to access the data members via the original names, however, leads similarly to UB, but, unlike with placement **new**, there is no valid new pointer available to use to access the newly created object. Hence, although it is not **undefined behavior** to use std::memcpy, it can serve no well-defined useful purpose.

Note, however, that as of C++20, reusing the name, reference, or pointer to an object that was destroyed and re-created (e.g., via std::memcpy or placement std::**operator new**) is now considered valid, even if the object contains a *non***static** member of **const**-qualified or reference-qualified type, thus eliminating the **undefined behavior** in both copy2b and copy2a, yet std::memcpy remains effectively unusable on such types in C++11 and C++14 (and C++17) as originally specified; see *Annoyances — The C++ Standard has not yet stabilized in this area* on page 521.

As a workaround on older compilers, one might try to mitigate such dangerous optimization in the implementation by combining std::is_trivially_copyable with std::is_assignable to prevent applying std::memcpy to types like S having **const** subobjects:

```
static_assert(   std::is_trivially_copyable<T>::value
              && std::is_assignable<T,T>::value, "");
```

Note that some legitimate cases might be rejected by the above **static_assert** — e.g., types that have no **const** or reference members but that declare **private** trivial assignment operators.

Conflating arbitrary values with indeterminate values

The C++ language makes an important distinction between an arbitrary POD value that has been written to (via initialization or assignment) versus one that is uninitialized. As a concrete example, consider two local scalar POD variables, x and y:

```
#include <cstdint>  // std::uintptr_t

void func()
{
    unsigned short x;                                         // indeterminate
    unsigned short y = reinterpret_cast<std::uintptr_t>(&x);  // arbitrary

    ++x;  // Bug, undefined behavior
    ++y;  // OK, defined behavior
}
```

In the example above, x is implicitly **default initialized**, which — having a trivial default constructor — means it will not be given a value. By contrast, y is assigned a value that might well change every time func is called. One might naively conclude that such distinctions are pedantic — they aren't. The value of y after being incremented is *guaranteed* to be one greater (modulo **unsigned short** wrap-around) than it was before. No such claim can be made for x.

During development, however, there might be times when we find it helpful to deliberately invoke an operation having **undefined behavior**. For example, inadvertently reading from an uninitialized memory location on the program stack — which itself has **undefined behavior** — can lead to a common form of security hole. Ironically, we might be able to exploit this same **undefined behavior** — in development — to detect and thereby prevent it elsewhere (e.g., in the hands of our customers).

Let's suppose we are writing a function, productionFunc, that begins by creating a moderately large fixed-size array of zero-initialized integers on the program stack. Instead of using a loop, it is suggested that we employ a new feature of C++11, **braced initialization** (see Section 2.1."Braced Init" on page 215), to achieve this zero initialization. As engineers, we will want to make sure that we have used the feature properly, so we write a small test function, cleanStack, that exercises this novel syntax to ostensibly **value-initialize** the array and then print each of its elements for visual inspection:

```
#include <iostream>  // std::cout

void cleanStack()  // function that creates and initializes an array of 4 ints
{
    int a[4]{};  // Does this syntax reliably create an array of zeros?
    std::cout << "cleanStack: " << a[0] << a[1] << a[2] << a[3] << " (OK)\n";
}  // expected output: cleanStack: 0000 (OK)
```

When running this function, we observe that, after initialization, each of the elements has a zero value. But, what if we haven't correctly initialized the array and the indeterminate values of the elements coincidentally evaluate to 0 (e.g., because the corresponding garbage data on the stack just happens to be all zeros — a common case if our process has never written to that location in memory)? As it turns out, we can exploit behavior that is not guaranteed by the Standard and yet often occurs in practice — especially at low levels of optimization.[32]

Let's now create a valid helper function, dirtyStack, that we have no doubt will initialize a similar **int** array to nonzero values and then print them just to be sure:

```
void dirtyStack()  // Dirty the stack (well-defined behavior).
{
    int ds[4];  // default initialized (uninitialized)
    ds[0] = ds[1] = ds[2] = ds[3] = -999;
    std::cout << "dirtyStack: " << ds[0]<<ds[1] << ds[2] << ds[3] << " (OK)\n";
}      // expected output: dirtyStack: -999-999-999-999 (OK)
```

Invoking dirtyStack, above, consistently produces the expected result. Suppose now we create a function, exercise, to invoke dirtyStack immediately before invoking cleanStack:

```
void exercise()  // well-defined behavior
{
    dirtyStack();  // OK, called first to try to dirty the stack
    cleanStack();  // OK, invoked on what we hope is a dirty stack
}   // expected output: dirtyStack: -999-999-999-999 (OK)
    //                  cleanStack: 0000 (OK)
```

Although observing the expected output of exercise might seem to give us some certainty that our newfangled C++11 initialization syntax is working as intended, we still don't know whether we are running in an environment that accidentally assigns old stack values to new uninitialized stack variables. To confirm that quintessential assumption, we will need to write a dubious function, readStack, to observe what happens when we read from a stack variable that is deliberately left uninitialized (**undefined behavior**):

```
void readStack()  // Observe stack (exploits manifest undefined behavior).
{
```

---

[32] An early pedagogical demonstration of this specific form of "useful" undefined behavior on typical computers of the day was suggested via an exercise in **dewhurst89**, section 1.8, "Exercises," pp. 25–28, specifically Exercise 1-6, p. 28.

```
    int r[4];  // default initialized
    std::cout << " readStack: " << r[0] << r[1] << r[2] << r[3] << " (UB)\n";
}
```

In the example above, we leave the `r` array deliberately uninitialized so that we can observe whether its values will correspond to the values left behind on the stack.

We can now put together a test program to establish the validity of our conjecture and therefore the correctness of our initialization by using `readStack` to observe uninitialized data at three critical points — before, *between*, and after the other two functions:

```
int main()
{
    readStack();   // UB, observe original stack (undefined behavior).
    dirtyStack();  // OK, dirty stack (and observe that it is dirty).
    readStack();   // UB, observe dirty stack (undefined behavior).
    cleanStack();  // OK, initialize stack (and observe zeroed values).
    readStack();   // UB, observe clean stack (undefined behavior).
    return 0;
}
```

By running `readStack` before and after running `dirtyStack` we can observe whether our current environment and optimization levels are such that uninitialized variables *will* be given the values left behind from previous similar function calls and thereby know that we have indeed "dirtied" the stack[33]:

```
 readStack: -133760-421480003 (UB)
dirtyStack: -999-999-999-999 (OK)
 readStack: -999-999-999-999 (UB)
cleanStack: 0000 (OK)
 readStack: 0000 (UB)
```

Now, when we run `cleanStack`, followed by `readStack` for good measure, we can be fairly certain that our `a` array in `cleanStack` was indeed correctly initialized. Running our example at a higher level of optimization, however, illustrates the importance of using `readStack`'s undefined behavior to validate our tenuous assumptions[34]:

```
 readStack: 0000 (UB)
dirtyStack: -999-999-999-999 (OK)
 readStack: 0000 (UB)
cleanStack: 0000 (OK)
 readStack: 0000 (UB)
```

Clearly the optimization level can affect the explicitly **undefined behavior** of attempting to access **indeterminate values**; moreover, the unpredictable behavior that may occur can be even more subtle and surprising.

---

[33]Output from GCC 7.4.0 (c. 2018) at optimization level 0: -O0
[34]Output from GCC 7.4.0 (c. 2018) at optimization level 1: -O1

A common misconception is that an uninitialized value is necessarily some random arbitrary value that just happens to be sitting in allocated memory at the time an object's lifetime begins and can otherwise be relied upon not to change spontaneously. Yet — even within a single code block of a running program — there is simply no guarantee that an indeterminate value will be the same the next time we try to access or observe it. For example, consider a program that calls a function, f, that has two **int** parameters, x and y, which are used to set the value of two non**static** local **int** variables, i and j — each initially of indeterminate value:

```
#include <cstdio>  // std::printf

void f(int x, int y)  // deliberately elicits undefined behavior
{
    int i, j;  std::printf("A: i: %3d, j: %3d\n", i, j);  // undefined behavior
    i = x;     std::printf("B: i: %3d, j: %3d\n", i, j);  //     "          "
    j = y;     std::printf("C: i: %3d, j: %3d\n", i, j);  // OK
}

int main()  // Behavior might change based on optimization levels.
{
    f(11, 22);  // Invoke function having undefined behavior.
    return 0;
}
```

At low levels of optimization,[35] it might appear as if an indeterminate value is guaranteed to be some unspecified arbitrary value, e.g., 32629 for i and -1410211896 for j:

```
A: i: 32629, j: -1410211896  // j is of indeterminate value.
B: i:  11, j: -1410211896    // <-- same value for j
C: i:  11, j:  22
```

Notice that, after assigning the value 11 to i on line B, the value of j (1184069128) appears to have remained the same. On the other hand, rebuilding and rerunning the program using a slightly higher optimization level[36] might produce qualitatively different results:

```
A: i:  22, j: 1184069128    // j is of indeterminate value.
B: i:  11, j:  0            // <-- changed
C: i:  11, j:  22
```

This time, immediately after assigning i the value 11 on line B, the uninitialized value of j, originally -1410211896, appears to change to 0 spontaneously. One possible explanation for this surprising behavior is that, at the code-generation level, the value of j is not established using a load instruction because the compiler has figured out that there is no useful value to

---

[35]E.g., Clang 9.0.1 (c. 2019) with optimization flag -O0
[36]E.g., Clang 9.0.1 (c. 2019) with optimization flag -O1

be loaded. Instead, the corresponding argument to `std::printf` is left uninitialized, having a different quasi-random value for each of the first two calls.

In short, **indeterminate values** are not *knowable*, and any attempt to access them or reason about their behavior is doomed to fail. Such values can, however, be copied, but only in special cases (e.g., **trivially copyable types**) and only in restrictive ways (e.g., via `std::memcpy`). Because the compiler is allowed to assume that no **indeterminate value** will ever be observed explicitly, copying of such a value (e.g., using `std::memcpy`) might result in no object code being executed; see *Ineligible use of std::memcpy* below and *Naive copying via other than std::memcpy* on page 501.

Ineligible use of `std::memcpy`

The C Standard Library functions `std::memcpy` and `std::memmove` are called out explicitly by the C++03 Standard as being special; using either of these functions to copy byte values does not in and of itself constitute reading or otherwise accessing the values of those bytes. Though not specifically called out in C++11 except in footnotes and examples, they retain their special behavior as a consequence of their specification in the C Standard on which the C++ Standard is based. Hence, the C++ language permits the use of `std::memcpy` (or `std::memmove`) to copy the underlying **object representation** of objects — even if of indeterminate value — under certain well-defined circumstances.

Well-defined use of `std::memcpy` to set the value of an object is limited to objects that are of trivially copyable type:

```cpp
#include <cassert>     // standard C assert macro
#include <cstring>     // std::memcpy, std::memmove, std::memset
#include <type_traits> // std::is_trivially_copyable

void ex1()
{
    int i = 5, j, k;
    std::memcpy(&j, &i, sizeof(int));  // OK, j has the same value as i.
    assert(i == j);
    std::memcpy(&j, &k, sizeof(int));  // OK, j has an indeterminate value.

    struct S0 { int i, j;   S0() { } } s0x, s0y; //    trivially copyable
    struct S1 { int i, j;  ~S1() { } } s1x, s1y; // not trivially copyable

    static_assert(true  == std::is_trivially_copyable<S0>::value, "");
    static_assert(false == std::is_trivially_copyable<S1>::value, "");

    std::memcpy(&s0x, &s0y, sizeof(S0)); // OK,  S0 is    trivially copyable.
    std::memcpy(&s1x, &s1y, sizeof(S1)); // Bug, S1 is not trivially copyable.
}
```

To use `std::memcpy` to populate an object of appropriate type, an initialized object of that type must exist:

```
void ex2()
{
    unsigned char a[sizeof(int)];     // array of characters
    std::memset(a, 0, sizeof(int));   // Set each char to numerical value 0.
    int i;                            // default-initialized indeterminate value
    std::memcpy(&i, a, sizeof(int));  // Bug (UB), copy indeterminate value
    assert(i == 0);                   // Maybe?!
}
```

C++ does not give permission, apart from cv-qualifiers, for the copied bytes to originate in a way other than being copied from an initialized object of that same object type; structural equivalence isn't good enough:

```
void ex3()
{
    const int i = 5;                  // const-qualified POD type
    int j;                            // nonqualified POD of same type
    std::memcpy(&j, &i, sizeof j);    // OK, source is const qualified.
    std::memcpy(&i, &j, sizeof j);    // Error, dest. is address of const object.

    float f;
    static_assert(sizeof i == sizeof f, "");  // true on most typical platforms
    std::memcpy(&f, &i, sizeof f);    // Bug (UB), arguments have different types.

    struct S1 { int i; } s1 = { 1 };  // POD struct having a single int
    struct S2 { int i; } s2 = { 2 };  // POD struct having same member types
    static_assert(sizeof s1 == sizeof s2, "");
    std::memcpy(&s1, &s2, sizeof s1); // Bug (UB), arguments of different types
    assert(s1.i == 2);                // Maybe?!
}
```

Note that there is simply no way to use `memcpy` to change the type or lifetime of an object:

```
#include <new>        // placement new

void ex4()
{
    unsigned char* bufPtr = new unsigned char[sizeof(float)];
    new (bufPtr) float(4.0);          // bufPtr now holds a float.
    int i = 5;
    std::memcpy(bufPtr, &i, sizeof(i)); // Bug (UB), float not int in bufPtr
    assert(*(int*)bufPtr == 5);        // Maybe?!
}
```

A common misinterpretation is that — because a POD type can be copied around as bytes — it is permissible to interpret any suitably aligned sequence of bytes as an object of that type:

```cpp
void ex5()
{
    struct S { short x, y; } s = { 1, 2 };  // POD type initialized to { 1, 2 }
    int i;
    static_assert(sizeof s == sizeof i, "");  // true on most platforms
    std::memcpy(&i, &s, sizeof s);            // Bug (UB), S is not int.
    assert(((S&)i).y == 2);                   // Maybe?!
}
```

Modifying a **const** object in any way has undefined behavior; hence, even a trivially copyable type that contains a nonstatic **const** data member is ineligible to be copied via std::memcpy:

```cpp
void ex6()
{
    struct S { const int x; int y; } s1 = {3, 4}, s2 = {};  // S is trivial.
    static_assert(std::is_trivially_copyable<S>::value, "");
    std::memcpy(&s2, &s1, sizeof(S));  // Bug (UB), changes the value of const x
    assert(s2.y == 4);                 // Maybe?!
}
```

A base-class object of even POD type is ineligible to be the source or destination of an std::memcpy:

```cpp
void ex7()
{
    struct Bx { char c; } bx1 = { 11 }, bx2 = { 22 };  // nonempty POD struct
    struct Dx : Bx { }    dx1 = {      }, dx2 = {     };  // nonempty POD struct

    // Bug (UB), copy from base-class subobject.
    std::memcpy(&bx1, static_cast<Bx*>(&dx2), sizeof(Bx));
    assert(bx1.c == 0);                                        // Maybe?!

    // Bug (UB), copy to base-class subobject.
    std::memcpy(static_cast<Bx*>(&dx1), &bx2, sizeof(Bx));  // Bug, UB
    assert(static_cast<Bx&>(dx1).c == 22);                     // Maybe?!
}
```

Note that if in, say, generic code we were to use std::memcpy to copy an empty POD object (e.g., by2 below) of nonzero size to a base class object of that same type, we might inadvertently clobber the first data member (e.g., c) in a derived-class object (e.g., dy1) that employs the **empty base optimization**:

```
void ex8()
{
    struct By { } by1 = {}, by2 = {};          // empty POD struct
    struct Dy : By { char c; } dy1, dy2;       // nonempty POD struct
    static_assert(sizeof(By) == sizeof(Dy), ""); // Both classes are of size 1.
    dy1.c = 33; dy2.c = 44;

    // Bug (UB), copy from base-class subobject.
    std::memcpy(&by1, static_cast<By*>(&dy2), sizeof(By));
    assert(dy2.c == 44); // probably true (source object unchanged)

    // Bug (UB), copy to base-class subobject.
    std::memcpy(static_cast<By*>(&dy1), &by2, sizeof(By));
    assert(dy1.c == 33); // probably false (first member clobbered)
}
```

The C++ Standard grants exclusive permission to use memcpy or memmove to copy the object representation of any eligible object (e.g., s below) to a byte buffer (e.g., cBuf) of the same size consisting of either **unsigned char** or **char** but nothing else.[37] Reversing the process leaves the value representation of the original object unchanged. What's more, copying from cBuf to a second object of the same type (e.g., s2) effectively copies the value representation of s to s2. The effect of memcpy-ing s to cBuf and then memcpy-ing cBuf to s2 is equivalent to memcpy-ing s to s2 directly:

```
void ex9()
{
    class S { int i; public: int j; S(int v):i(v) { } } s(0);
    static_assert(std::is_trivially_copyable<S>::value, "");

    unsigned char ucBuf[sizeof s]; // eligible as byte array
              char  cBuf[sizeof s]; //     "     "   "    "
      signed char scBuf[sizeof s]; // not eligible as byte array

    std::memcpy(ucBuf, &s, sizeof s);   // OK, unsigned char array
    std::memcpy( cBuf, &s, sizeof s);   // OK, char array
    std::memcpy(scBuf, &s, sizeof s);   // Bug, signed char not eligible

    S s1(1), s2(2), s3(3);              // distinct objects each of same type as s

    std::memcpy(&s ,  cBuf, sizeof s);  // OK, value rep. of s unchanged
    std::memcpy(&s1, ucBuf, sizeof s);  // OK,   "    "    "  s1 equals s
    std::memcpy(&s2,  cBuf, sizeof s);  // OK,   "    "    "  s2 equals s
    std::memcpy(&s3, scBuf, sizeof s);  // Bug, signed char not eligible
}
```

---

[37] As of C++17, std::byte is also included, along with **char** and **unsigned char**, in the set of types suitable as elements of an array for holding the object representation of objects of trivially copyable type.

Although rarely necessary and tightly regulated, it is possible to copy the object representation of an object of trivially copyable type to an array of unsigned ordinary characters
explicitly — i.e., other than via std::memcpy or std::memmove — and even to access the
*non*indeterminate values of the copied bytes within that array; see *Naive copying via other
than* std::memcpy below.

Naive copying via other than std::memcpy

Historically, the standard C library functions std::memcpy and std::memmove had been the
only explicitly sanctioned mechanisms for copying the underlying bytes from one object of
a trivially copyable type to another of the same type or to an intermediate byte buffer.
The Standard wording was changed for C++11 so as to clarify that these functions are
not the only sanctioned way to byte-copy trivially copyable types, so long as certain subtle
requirements are met.

There are three kinds of **ordinary character types**: **char**, **signed char**, and **unsigned char**.
The **implementation-defined underlying type** of the distinct C++ type **char** is either
unsigned char or **signed char**. Every bit pattern within an **unsigned char**, unlike a
signed char,[38] is required by the Standard to be representable and not, for example, trigger
a hardware trap or else otherwise misbehave when accessed, e.g., during **lvalue-to-rvalue
conversion**.

One might conclude that, because the Standard says that a **char** array can be used to hold
the underlying representation (copied via std::memcpy) of an object of trivially copyable
type, which can consist of any bit pattern, either (1) **signed char** on a given platform cannot
trap or (2) the underlying type for the distinct **char** type on the platform is **unsigned char**.
Such is not necessarily the case, however: Given a theoretical platform on which not all bit
patterns of **signed char** represent distinct values, it is likely safe for an array of such a
signed char type to hold arbitrary object representations so long as no attempt is made to
interpret the value of such an arbitrary bit pattern as a **signed char** object; see *Conflating
arbitrary values with indeterminate values* on page 493. Consequently, any operation that
does not interpret the value of a byte having arbitrary bit values (e.g., std::memcpy) can
have well-defined behavior even if **char** is signed and has a possible trap representation.

There are certain special allowances made for unsigned ordinary character types, which
always include **unsigned char** and may also include **char**, i.e., on platforms where type
char is unsigned. In particular, an object of an unsigned ordinary character type is permitted to represent and transfer — e.g., via initialization and copy assignment — object
representations of indeterminate value (see *Conflating arbitrary values with indeterminate
values* on page 493); such privileges are, however, distinctly limited and do not extend to
any other operations:

---

[38] As of C++20, a **signed char** too must be able to represent all 256 distinct bit patterns; see **bastien18**.

```
void test1()
{
    unsigned char u1;          // OK, u1 has indeterminate value.
    unsigned char u2(u1);      // OK, u2 has indeterminate value.
    u2 = 0;                    // OK, u2 has value 0 (0b00000000).
    u2 = u1;                   // OK, u2 has indeterminate value.
    bool bu = (u1 == u2);      // Bug, comparing indeterminate values
    int ui = u1;               // Bug, converting indeterminate value to int

    char c1;                   // OK, c1 has indeterminate value.
    char c2(c1);               // Bug, if char is signed
    c2 = 0;                    // OK, c2 has value 0 (0b00000000).
    c2 = c1;                   // Bug,  if char is signed
    bool bc = (c1 == c2);      // Bug, comparing indeterminate values
    int ci = c1;               // Bug, converting indeterminate value to int
}
```

When an uninitialized object of trivially copyable type is copied (e.g., using std::memcpy)
into an array of ordinary character type, all of the elements of the array will have indeterminate values. Regardless of whether the elements are signed or unsigned, the bytes can be
copied into an object of the original type. The bytes can be transferred via initialization or
assignment only if the array elements are unsigned:

```
#include <cstring>  // std::memcpy

struct S1 { short s; };  // (trivially copyable) POD struct of size 2

void test2()
{
    unsigned char ucBuf[sizeof(S1)];  // array of unsigned ordinary characters
    signed   char scBuf[sizeof(S1)];  //  "      "  signed        "         "

    S1 s0;                                 // uninitialized POD
    std::memcpy(ucBuf, &s0, sizeof s0);    // OK, copy indeterminate bytes.
    std::memcpy(scBuf, &s0, sizeof s0);    // OK, copy indeterminate bytes.

    S1 s1 = { 0 };  S1 s2 = { 0 };         // initialized PODs
    std::memcpy(&s1, ucBuf, sizeof s1);    // OK, s1 has indeterminate value.
    std::memcpy(&s2, scBuf, sizeof s2);    // OK, s2 has indeterminate value.

    unsigned char uc0 = ucBuf[0];          // OK, copy indeterminate value.
    unsigned char uc1 = ucBuf[1];          // OK, copy indeterminate value.

    signed char sc0 = scBuf[0];            // Bug, copy indeterminate value.
    signed char sc1 = scBuf[1];            // Bug, copy indeterminate value.
}
```

The value representation of an initialized, trivially copyable object comprises those bytes within the object's footprint that represent its value, i.e., all bytes except padding bytes. When such an object's object representation is copied into an array of ordinary character type, the bytes in the target array corresponding to the object's value representation (a.k.a. the *value-representing* bytes) will encode the object's value while the bytes corresponding to the object's padding bytes will have indeterminate value. Although both signed and unsigned ordinary character types are suitable targets for such a copy, only unsigned char values are guaranteed to be readable for value-representing bytes. Regardless of the character type, however, attempting to read a non-value-representing byte explicitly has undefined behavior.

As a concrete example, let's consider a trivially copyable POD struct, S2, consisting of just two data members: char c and short s:

```
struct S2  // (trivially copyable) POD struct - size = 4
{
    char  c;  // 1 byte  (offset 0)
              // 1 byte  (offset 1)  padding
    short s;  // 2 bytes (offset 2)
};
```

For the purposes of this example, we will need to define two character buffers, ucBuf and cBuf, having distinct character types as elements:

```
unsigned char ucBuf[sizeof(S2)];  // array of unsigned ordinary characters
         char  cBuf[sizeof(S2)];  //     "      "     ????     "        "
```

Note that both of the arrays above are guaranteed to be able to *hold* the object representation of S2 on any conforming platform. Elements of the ucBuf array, however, are further guaranteed always to support access to value-representing byte values, whereas those of the cBuf array can do so *only* on platforms where the underlying type of char is unsigned char. Let's now consider what happens when we properly copy (e.g., via std::memcpy) an initialized object of type S2 to both of the above buffers and then try to read and manipulate various individual bytes within those respective arrays:

```
#include <cassert>  // standard C assert macro

void test3()
{
    S2 s = { 'A', 5 };              // fully initialized
    std::memcpy(ucBuf, &s, sizeof s);  // OK
    std::memcpy( cBuf, &s, sizeof s);  // OK

    unsigned char uc0 = ucBuf[0];  // OK, copy value-representing byte.
    unsigned char uc1 = ucBuf[1];  // OK, copy padding byte (indeterminate).
    unsigned char uc2 = ucBuf[2];  // OK, copy value-representing byte.
    unsigned char uc3 = ucBuf[3];  // OK,   "       "          "
```

```
        char  c0 =  cBuf[0];  // OK, special case, char member of S2
        char  c1 =  cBuf[1];  // Bug? -- platform dependent (might be UB)
        char  c2 =  cBuf[2];  // "        "        "       "    "    "
        char  c3 =  cBuf[3];  // "        "        "       "    "    "

    assert('A' == ucBuf[0]);  // OK, corresponds to s.c
        int i1 = ucBuf[1];  // Bug (UB), convert from indeterminate value.
        int i3 = ucBuf[2];  // OK, convert from value-representing byte.
             ++ucBuf[3];  // OK, increment value-representing byte.

    assert('A' ==  cBuf[0]);  // OK, special case: corresponds to s.c
        int i2 =  cBuf[1];  // Bug (UB), convert from indeterminate value.
        int i4 =  cBuf[2];  // Bug? -- platform dependent (might be UB)
              ++cBuf[3];  // Bug? -- platform dependent (might be UB)
}
```

While it is always permissible to read *any* value-representing byte from an array of **unsigned char**, in the special case (e.g., cBuf[0] above) where the byte being read corresponds to an initialized **char** or **signed char** from the original object s, the initialized byte can be read reliably from an array of **char**, even if **char** is signed on the platform.

Note that we were able to reliably access the copy of s.c in both ucBuf and cBuf because the original initialized object (1) was of **standard-layout** type and (2) had a **char** as its first non**static** data member, which always has offset 0. Had that member not been first, we could have instead employed the offsetof macro to learn, in a portable way, its precise location within the array — one of the few unambiguously well-defined uses of offsetof; see *Aggressive use of offsetof* on page 520. In no event, however, are we permitted to "read" or operate on a byte corresponding to padding bytes as those are always of indeterminate value. What's more, if the original object was not of **standard-layout** type, none of the fields could be portably accessed through the byte array, although offsetof would work for many types and platforms.

Finally, now that we understand the special privileges afforded only to unsigned ordinary character types, let's explore the pitfalls that await the programmer who abuses this information in a misguided attempt to optimize copying of objects. For example, the myMemCpy function (below) provides a valid, albeit suboptimal, alternative implementation satisfying the functional requirements of std::memcpy (but not std::memmove):

```
#include <cstddef>  // std::size_t

void* myMemCpy(void* dstPtr, const void* srcPtr, std::size_t numBytes)
{
    unsigned char*       dp = reinterpret_cast<unsigned char*>(dstPtr);
    const unsigned char* sp = reinterpret_cast<const unsigned char*>(srcPtr);
```

```
    for (; numBytes; --numBytes)
    {
        *dp++ = *sp++;
    }
}
```

We have deliberately chosen to use **unsigned char** as it is the only ordinary character type that is guaranteed to represent a unique valid value for every possible bit pattern on every conforming platform.

Misuse of unions

It is a common misconception that it is *ever* well-defined behavior to write to a scalar member of a **union** and then read from another member of that union, sometimes referred to as a *union cast* or *type punning*, even when the two members are of identical type:

```
union U0  // Writing to a and then reading from b has undefined behavior.
{
    int a;  // scalar element of type int
    int b;  //    "        "      "    "    "
};
```

A motivation for this form of misuse would be to write a function that determines endianness:

```
union U1
{
    int           a;
    unsigned char b[sizeof a];
} const u1 = { 1 };

bool isBigEndian1() { return 0 == u1.b[0]; }  // Bug, type punning has UB.
```

A proper portable implementation can be achieved using, e.g., the Posix `htonl` function[39]:

```
#include <arpa/inet.h>  // htonl

bool isBigEndian2()
{
    return htonl(1) == 1;  // OK
}
```

No *reinterpretation* of the bit representation of a scalar value via access to parallel members of a **union** is *ever* well-defined behavior in C++. There are, however, other ways to accomplish this specific task natively; see *Abuse of **reinterpret_cast*** on page 506.

---

[39] As of C++20, we can query the `big` member of the standard **enum** std::endian, defined in the standard header <bit>, to resolve this question portably at compile time.

The only valid way to access the active member of a **union** through another member is via the common initial member sequence of standard-layout class types. Attempting to access a scalar as if it were a common first member — although ingrained in industry practice — nonetheless expressly has undefined behavior:

```
struct A { char type; /*...*/ };  // CIMS starts with char.
struct B { char type; /*...*/ };  //    "      "    "     "

union U2
{
    char type;  // scalar type
    A    a;     // standard-layout class type
    B    b;     //      "         "      "     "
};

void func()
{
    U2 u;
    u.a = A();          // OK, initialize union member with type A.
    char x = u.b.type;  // OK, b.type is part of CIMS.
    char y = u.type;    // Bug (UB), type is not part of CIMS.
}
```

In the example above, after **copy-initializing** the **union** u with a value-initialized object of type A, we properly access the common initial member type via the union member b. However, attempting to access that same value via the scalar type member of u has undefined behavior.

Finally, consider that adding even a trailing member that is not of standard-layout type to either A or B above would make the U2 **union** itself not standard layout and thus invalidate the property of having a common initial member sequence that A and B currently enjoy.

Abuse of `reinterpret_cast`

The **reinterpret_cast** keyword, used properly, has several important applications in correct code: (1) converting between typically unrelated valid pointer or reference types of *colocated* objects with the possibility of operating on the object through either pointer or reference; (2) converting between pointers to possibly invalid objects without ever accessing the object through the pointer; (3) converting between potentially unrelated pointer-to-member types, when both types are either data-member pointers or function-member pointers (but not one of each); (4) converting trivially copyable types to their underlying object representation (e.g., as an **unsigned char** array); and (5) converting between a pointer type and an integral or enumeration type of sufficient size (i.e., at least as large as the pointer).

Let's look at each of these valid uses in more detail.

1. **Between addresses to colocated valid objects** — There are a variety of circumstances in which the C++ language guarantees that two objects having **unrelated types** are colocated and can therefore be read and/or modified via a pointer and/or reference of the converted type. Specifically, (a) the first data member of any class of **standard**-layout type resides at the same address as the **class** object itself, and (b) every member of a **union** — regardless of its particular type characteristics — is guaranteed to reside at the same address as the **union** object itself[40]:

```
#include <cassert>  // standard C assert macro

struct C { int i; };          // standard-layout class type
union U { int i; double d; };  // union with two members

void func0()
{
    C c{ 3 };                               // C object; c.i initialized to 3
    int* ip = reinterpret_cast<int*>(&c);   // i resides at same address as c.
    *ip = 5;                                // OK, c.i is now 5.
    assert(5 == c.i);                       // OK,   "  "  "  "

    U u{ 5 };                               // u.i is the active member.
    int x = reinterpret_cast<int&>(u);      // OK, u.i has same address as u.
    assert(5 == x);                         // OK, x is a copy of u.i.

    reinterpret_cast<double&>(u) = 1.2;     // Bug (UB), no double there
    u.d = 3.5;                              // Make u.d the active member.
    reinterpret_cast<double&>(u) = 1.2;     // OK, u.d has same address as u.
    U& ru = reinterpret_cast<U&>(u.d);      // OK, ru has same address as u.d.
    assert(1.2 == ru.d);                    // OK
}
```

In this example, `c.i` has the same address as `c`; hence, a pointer (or reference) to one can be **reinterpret_cast** to a pointer (or reference) to the other, in both directions. Similarly, `u.i` and `u.d` have the same address as `u`, so **reinterpret_cast** can be used to convert pointers or references between them. Note that, even though `u` and `u.d` have the same address, it is not valid to modify `u.d` through a **reinterpret_cast** unless `u.d` is the active member of the **union**, i.e., after the assignment to `u.d`.

---

[40]C++17 wording clarifies that a **union** object always shares the same address as each of its members, even if the **union** is a non-standard-layout type; see CWG issue 2287 (**smith16c**).

2. **Between pointers to unrelated types** — Employing **reinterpret_cast** to convert between distinct pointer or reference types is always permitted provided no attempt is made to access the underlying object via the converted type:

```
void func1()
{
    int     i;                                    // uninitialized int
    float*  fp = reinterpret_cast<float*> (&i );  // OK, but cannot access *fp
    double& dr = reinterpret_cast<double&>( i );  // OK, but cannot access dr
    int&    ir = reinterpret_cast<int&>    (*fp); // OK, ir refers to i above.
    int*    ip = reinterpret_cast<int*>    (&dr); // OK, ip points to i above.

    ir = 4;                                       // OK, ir refers to an int.
    *fp = 2.1;                                    // Bug (UB), no float at *fp
}
```

It is valid to access the object through the pointer or reference resulting from a **reinterpret_cast** provided an object of the specified type exists at the specified address, as in the case of ir, above, which is the result of casting an **int*** to a **float***, dereferencing it, and then casting the **float&** to an **int&**. The **float*** does not point to a **float** object, so accessing the object pointed-to by fp has undefined behavior. Note that a C++ **reinterpret_cast** differs from a C-style cast in that it cannot be used to cast away cv-qualifiers:

```
const int ci  = 5;                                    // initialized const int
float&    fr = reinterpret_cast<float&>(  ci);  // Error, casts away const
const double* cdp = reinterpret_cast<const double*>(& ci);  // OK
const int&   cir = reinterpret_cast<const int&>   (*cdp);  // OK, &cir == &ci

void check1()
{
    assert((void*)&ci == (void*)&cir);  // C-style (void*) casts away const.
}
```

A common use of **reinterpret_cast** on pointer types is to restore the proper C++ type from a **void*** pointer as is typical in C-style callback programming. For example, consider a framework that provides a function, installHandlerFunction, taking as arguments a HandlerFunction and a **void*** pointer. When a particular event occurs, the supplied callback-handler function is invoked with the **void*** argument that was supplied when the handler was installed:

```
typedef void (*HandlerFunction)(void*);  // pointer to a handler function
void installHandlerFunction(HandlerFunction userFunction, void* userData);
int startEventLoop();  // Loop reads events and invokes callbacks.
```

The client supplying the function is forced to conform to the generic function API defined by the HandlerFunction **typedef** above, but, because the client is the one that supplied the data structure in the first place, the client is encouraged to use

reinterpret_cast to restore the proper type of the pointer from within the installed callback function, `MyCallbackFunc`:

```cpp
struct MyUserData  { /*...*/ };  // There's no restriction on this class type.

void MyCallbackFunc(void* dataptr)
{
    MyUserData* p = reinterpret_cast<MyUserData*>(dataptr);
    // ...     (use data at p)
}

int eventMain()
{
    MyUserData d{/*...*/};                       // Create local data.
    installHandlerFunction(&MyCallbackFunc, &d); // Register callback.
    return startEventLoop();                     // Cede control to event loop.
}
```

When calling `installHandlerFunction` above, we deliberately allowed the address of d to convert implicitly from `MyUserData*` to **void***, as implicit **standard conversion** to **void*** *never* causes the address value to change. Note that using a **static_cast** to restore the `MyUserData` type in the definition of `MyCallbackFunc` above would also have worked in the specific case of a **void***, as we are reversing a **standard conversion** between *related types* that is implicit in only one direction (see other uses of **static_cast** below); nonetheless, it is precisely when the value of the pointer is expected *not* to change that **reinterpret_cast** is indicated.

3. **Between pointer-to-member types** — It is always valid to cast a pointer to member to another pointer to member, provided that (1) both types are pointers to data members or both types are pointers to function members and (2) the resulting member-pointer is not applied to an object without being converted back to its original type:

```cpp
struct A { int   x; int   f();       };
struct B { float y; float g() const; };

A a{}; B b{};
float B::*ptfd = reinterpret_cast<float B::*>(&A::x);  // OK
int   A::*ptid = reinterpret_cast<int   A::*>(ptfd);   // OK
int&  i = a.*ptid; int i1 = i;  // OK, use x member of A.
float& f = b.*ptfd; int f1 = f;  // Bug (UB), does not point to a member of B

float (B::*ptff)() const = reinterpret_cast<float (B::*)() const>(&A::f); // OK
int   (A::*ptif)()       = reinterpret_cast<int   (A::*)()       >(ptff); // OK
int   i3 = (a.*ptif)();  // OK, f member function of A
float f3 = (b.*ptff)();  // Bug (UB), does not point to a member function of B

int A::*dp      = reinterpret_cast<int A::*>(ptif); // Error, function -> data
int (A::*fp)() = reinterpret_cast<int A::*>(ptid);  // Error, data -> function
```

509

4. **To the underlying** object representation — Just as we are always permitted to `std::memcpy` the underlying object representation of an object of trivially copyable type to an array of **unsigned char** of equal size (see *Ineligible use of std::memcpy* on page 497), so too are we permitted to **reinterpret_cast** the address of an object of such a type to a pointer of type **unsigned char***:

```
#include <cstring>  // std::memcpy

bool isLittleEndian1()
{
    const unsigned int x = 1;
    return reinterpret_cast<const unsigned char*>(&x)[0] == 1;
}
```

The example above suggests a portable way to detect at run time whether a given platform is little-endian. The pointer returned by the **reinterpret_cast** represents an array of bytes — typically four elements — holding the object representation of the integer x. If the first byte is 1, then the integer is assumed to be in little-endian format. An equivalent, albeit less efficient, implementation could have been written using `std::memcpy`:

```
bool isLittleEndian2()
{
    const unsigned int x = 1;
    unsigned char a[sizeof x];
    std::memcpy(a, &x, sizeof x);
    return a[0] == 1;
}
```

Note, however, that neither `std::memcpy` nor **reinterpret_cast** is well defined when getting the object representation of an object unless the original object is of trivially copyable type.

5. **Between pointer and integral types** — The Standard allows using **reinterpret_cast** to convert back and forth between integral types having at least as many bits as a **void*** and basic (nonmember) pointers. The only portable guarantee is that converting from a pointer to a sufficiently large integer and back to a pointer of the same kind as the original (e.g., function, object) will yield the same pointer value:

```
#include <cassert>  // standard C assert macro
#include <cstdint>  // std::uintptr_t, std::intptr_t, if supported

void test4()
{
```

```
    int x, *xp = &x;   // integer and pointer-to-integer variables

    // Convert pointer to various integral types.
    short int  si = reinterpret_cast<short int>(&x);  // Error, too small
    int         i = reinterpret_cast<int>      (&x);  // OK, if 32-bit void*
    long       li = reinterpret_cast<long>     (&x);  // OK, typically
    long      qli =         static_cast<long>  (&x);  // Error, static_cast
    long long lli = reinterpret_cast<long long>(&x);  // OK, typically
    __int128 llli = reinterpret_cast<__int128> (&x);  // OK, e.g., on GCC

    // Convert to optionally supported standard integral types.
    std::uintptr_t uipt = reinterpret_cast<std::uintptr_t>(&x);
                                                      // OK, if supported
    std::intptr_t  ipt = reinterpret_cast<std::intptr_t> (&x);
                                                      // OK, if supported

    // Convert integral values back to pointers:
    int*   lp = reinterpret_cast<int*>(  li);         assert(&x == lp);
    int*  llp = reinterpret_cast<int*>( lli);         assert(&x == llp);
    int* lllp = reinterpret_cast<int*>(llli);         assert(&x == lllp);

    int* p1  = reinterpret_cast<int*>(uipt);          assert(&x == p1);
    int* p2  = reinterpret_cast<int*>( ipt);          assert(&x == p2);
}
```

As the example code above shows, we can safely **reinterpret_cast** a pointer (e.g., &x) to an integral type of sufficient size *by value* and then back to the original pointer type. Note that **static_cast** can be used only for types that are implicitly convertible in at least one direction; hence, **static_cast** cannot be used to convert between pointers and integral values. Although optionally supported, most modern standard libraries provide standard types std::intptr_t and std::uintptr_t (in header <cstdint>), which are aliases for the platform-dependent signed and unsigned integer types, respectively, that are large enough to hold a pointer value:

```
#include <cstdint>  // std::uintptr_t, std::intptr_t, if supported

static_assert(sizeof(std::intptr_t) >=sizeof(void*),"");  // OK, if supported
static_assert(sizeof(std::uintptr_t)>=sizeof(void*),"");  // OK, if supported
```

Although modifying virtual memory addresses is not portable, we can often take advantage of "spare bits" in a pointer holding the address of a type T for which **alignof**(T) is 2 or or more — typically any scalar type larger than **char** and any class type having a nonstatic member of such a scalar type. In most implementations, casting a valid T* to an integral quantity always yields an even value:

```
#include <cassert>  // standard C assert macro
#include <cstdint>  // std::uintptr_t required

static_assert((alignof(double) & 1) == 0, "");  // assert even alignment

void alignmentCheck()
{
    struct { char c; double d; } x;

    assert((reinterpret_cast<std::uintptr_t>(&x.d) & 1) == 0); // OK, typically
}
```

Casting the address of a **double** to an `std::uintptr_t` typically yields a value whose low bit is 0 (i.e., the value is a multiple of 2). We can take advantage of this invariant — on platforms for which it is true — to hold a pointer and a Boolean value in the memory space of a single pointer (e.g., in a `PointerAndBool` class):

```
class PointerAndBool  // class to store a pointer and a bool in minimal space
{
    std::uintptr_t d_ptrAsInt;  // integral value of pointer ORed with bool

public:
    PointerAndBool(double* p, bool b)  // Store pointer and bool.
                  : d_ptrAsInt(reinterpret_cast<std::uintptr_t>(p) | b) { }

    bool getBool() const { return d_ptrAsInt & 1; }  // Retrieve bool.

    double* getPtr() const                           // Retrieve pointer.
    {
        return reinterpret_cast<double*>(d_ptrAsInt & ~std::uintptr_t(1));
    }
};

static_assert(sizeof(PointerAndBool) == sizeof(double*), "");  // Verify size.
```

The `PointerAndBool` constructor relies on the pointer (after conversion to `std::uintptr_t`) having a low-order bit value of zero and repurposes that bit to store the value of the Boolean parameter, `b`. The `getBool` accessor simply returns the value of this bit. Critically, `getPtr` restores the low-order bit to 0 before converting it back to a pointer via **reinterpret_cast**, thus ensuring that **reinterpret_cast** is being used symmetrically to convert back from the same integer obtained from the original pointer.

Now that we have an overview of the *valid* uses of **reinterpret_cast**, let's look at the ways that one can get in trouble by misapplying these subtle rules. Note that any

reinterpret_cast from one pointer type to another or from one reference type to another is valid, so long as the cast does not drop a cv-qualifier (which would be ill formed). It is only an *access* through the pointer or reference that might be invalid, leading to **undefined** behavior. The general rule is that an access to an object through the result of a **reinterpret_cast<T*>** is valid if and only if an object of type T exists at that address at the time it is accessed. Most of the pitfalls described below are violations of this concise, general, and widely applicable rule.

1. **Using reinterpret_cast for object conversions** — A **reinterpret_cast** operates between pointer types, between reference types, between pointer-to-member types, and between pointer types and integral types, but not between other object types. It is ill formed to use **reinterpret_cast**s to perform type conversions, even among types for which conversions exist. We cannot, for example, **reinterpret_cast** an **int** to a **float** or vice versa, nor can we **reinterpret_cast** a prvalue such as 3.14 to a reference of any kind:

   ```
   struct Class1 { explicit Class1(int); };   // explicitly convertible from int

   float         rc1 = reinterpret_cast<float>(3);              // Error
   int           rc2 = reinterpret_cast<int>(3.0);              // Error
   const double& rc3 = reinterpret_cast<const double&>(3.14);   // Error
   int&&         rc4 = reinterpret_cast<int&&>(3.14);           // Error, prvalue
   int           rc5 = reinterpret_cast<int>(3);                // OK, no-op
   unsigned      rc6 = reinterpret_cast<unsigned>(3);           // Error
   Class1        rc7 = reinterpret_cast<Class1>(5);             // Error

   float         sc1 = static_cast<float>(3);                   // OK, but unnecessary
   int           sc2 = static_cast<int>(3.0);                   // OK,   "        "
   const double& sc3 = static_cast<const double&>(3.14);        // OK,   "        "
   int&&         sc4 = static_cast<int&&>(3.14);                // OK, temporary obj
   int           sc5 = static_cast<int>(3);                     // OK, no-op
   unsigned      sc6 = static_cast<unsigned>(3);                // OK, but unnecessary
   Class1        sc7 = static_cast<Class1>(5);                  // OK
   ```

   Note that all of the ill formed uses of **reinterpret_cast** above are valid uses of **static_cast**.

2. **Accessing objects of unrelated types via reinterpret_cast** — Although **reinterpret_cast** between incompatible pointer and reference types is always valid, **undefined** behavior can arise when attempting to dereference such a converted pointer or reference: Unless there is somehow a valid object of the appropriate type at that address, accessing a value stored there has **undefined** behavior.

   To illustrate the austerity of this rule, consider that even though two different trivial **standard-layout** types, e.g., A and B below, might have precisely the same layout in memory, accessing the result of a **reinterpret_cast** of A* to B* explicitly has undefined behavior[41]:

```
struct A { int d_value; };  // POD struct of one int
struct B { int d_value; };  //  "     "    "   "  "

A a = { 5 };
void test1()
{
    reinterpret_cast<B&>(a).d_value = 6;  // Bug, A & B are unrelated types.
}
```

Now consider that the IEEE-754 floating-point format is specifically designed such that treating the contents of a **float** or **double** as a comparably sized integer type and incrementing it as an integer yields the next representable floating-point value:

```
#include <cassert>  // standard C assert macro
#include <limits>   // std::numeric_limits<float>::epsilon()

void test2()
{
    float f = 1.0f;                        // unity
    ++reinterpret_cast<int&>(f);  // Bug (UB), no int exists there.
    assert(f == 1.0f + std::numeric_limits<float>::epsilon());  // Maybe?!
}
```

As tempting as the shortcut above might be, at sufficiently high levels of optimization, compilers may determine that since such usage has **undefined behavior**, the program can be optimized by eliding it entirely. If we need this specific behavior reliably, we would call the Standard Library function std::nextafter defined in the standard header <cmath>:

```
#include <cassert>  // standard C assert macro
#include <cmath>    // std::nextafter
#include <limits>   // std::numeric_limits<float>::epsilon()

void test3()
{
    float f1 = 1.0f;
    float f2 = std::nextafter(f1, 2.0f);
    assert(f2 == 1.0f + std::numeric_limits<float>::epsilon());  // OK
}
```

3. **Accessing a nonactive member of a union via reinterpret_cast** — Because the address of a **union** is the same as the address of each of its members, we can reason that

---

[41]As of C++20, the std::bit_cast function template can be used to interpret objects of one type as another type of the same size when the target type has at least one eligible trivial default constructor and both the source and target types are trivially copyable.

all of the members of a union have the same address and we can **reinterpret_cast** between them. Having the address of a **union** member is not sufficient for accessing it, however; only the **active member** of the **union** can be validly accessed through the **union**'s address. For example, consider a **union** (e.g., U) of two identical POD **structs** (e.g., A and B):

```
struct A { int i; };  // POD struct having an int as its first data member
struct B { int j; };  // "     "      "      "  "  "  "      "      "

union U { A a; B b; } u;  // union of two structurally identical POD structs
```

Attempting to access the valid **int** via a **reinterpret_cast** through a *nonactive* member of the **union** has undefined behavior:

```
void func0()
{
    u.a = A();          // u.a is active; u.a.i has value 0.
    B& ub = reinterpret_cast<B&>(u);  // OK, but no object of type B there
    ub.j = 3;           // Bug (UB), accessing a non-existent B-type object
    int& ui = u.b.j;    // OK, in common initial member sequence
    ui = 5;             // OK, u.a.i now holds 5; u.a remains the active member.
}
```

As func0 above illustrates, accessing any part of u.b via the result of a **reinterpret_cast** of u to a reference to B (e.g., ub) has undefined behavior because there is no live object of type B at the same address as u; the permissions pertaining to a common initial member sequence apply *only* when access is through the **union** object, i.e., u.b.j. In particular, there is simply no way to change the active member of a **union** by assignment to a member whose address is obtained via a **reinterpret_cast**.

4. **Accessing an object's underlying** object representation **via reinterpret_cast** — A special exception is made for **unsigned ordinary character types** in that the underlying object representation of a valid trivially copyable object is assumed to coexist at the same address as the object itself:

```
bool f() { unsigned i=1; return reinterpret_cast<unsigned char&>(i); }  // OK
bool g() { unsigned i=1; return reinterpret_cast< signed char&>(i); }  // Bug
```

Note, however, that accessing the underlying object representation of an object is valid only if an object of trivially copyable type exists at that address and the byte being accessed isn't of indeterminate value:

```
struct Ntc { int k; Ntc(); ~Ntc(); };  // non-trivially copyable type
bool h1() { Ntc x;      return reinterpret_cast<unsigned char&>(x); } // Bug
bool h2() { int i;      return reinterpret_cast<unsigned char&>(i); } // Bug
bool h3() { int j = 1; return reinterpret_cast<unsigned char&>(j); } // OK
```

Function h1 above attempts to access the underlying object representation of object x, which is not of trivially copyable type, whereas h2 attempts to access the first byte of a trivially copyable object having indeterminate value. In h3, however, the returned reference is to the underlying object representation of a trivially copyable object having *non*indeterminate value.

5. **Casting a byte array to an object type** — Finally, irrespective of whether a type is considered trivial or standard layout, to **reinterpret_cast** an array of **unsigned char** to a T& (e.g., i) and then attempt to use that result as if it referred to a valid object has **undefined** behavior, unless an object of that type was constructed within the array and contains bytes appropriate to that type's object representation:

```
#include <new>  // placement new

void testIntBuffer()  // test int inside a suitably aligned character buffer
{
    alignas(int) unsigned char buffer[sizeof(int)];  // aligned to hold an int

    int& i = reinterpret_cast<int&>(buffer[0]);  // OK, but not OK to use
    i = 123;  // Bug (UB), no int is currently live in buffer.

    int& j = *new (buffer) int(123);  // int is created inside buffer.
    j = 456;  // OK, access to the int object via j is well defined.

    int& k = *reinterpret_cast<int*>(buffer);  // OK, now there's an int there.
    k = 789;  // OK, access via reinterpret_cast is now to a live int.
    i = 123;  // OK, i, j, and k refer to the same object at this point.
}
```

Note, however, that once we have started the lifetime of an **int** within that buffer — e.g., via placement `::operator new`[42] — we are free to use a reference to that object (e.g., j above) to access the integer. Moreover, once the lifetime of the integer has begun at the address of buffer, it is permissible to use **reinterpret_cast** (e.g., k) to access the **int** at that address. What's more, it is now valid to use the result returned from the previous **reinterpret_cast** (e.g., i) that occurred before the **int** existed!

We can use **reinterpret_cast** to treat an object of standard-layout type as though it were an array of **unsigned char**. Although one might assume that we could go in the other direction — i.e., converting from an array that contains the underlying object representation of an object of trivially copyable type to a pointer or reference to said object — such is not the case, even when the array has been initialized from the object representation of a trivially copyable object:

---

[42]"An *object* is created by a definition, by a *new-expression*, when implicitly changing the active member of a union, or when a temporary object is created"; see **iso17**, section 4.5, "The C++ object model," paragraph 1, p. 9. As of C++20, std::bit_cast implicitly creates objects nested within the return value. With the introduction of P0593 into the upcoming C++ Standard, certain other operations are deemed to implicitly create objects, including operations that begin the lifetime of an array of **unsigned char**, which would make all accesses via i in the testIntBuffer function above valid; see **smith20**.

```
#include <cstring>  // std::memcpy

int returnOne()  // invalid attempt to return (int) 1
{
    unsigned int x = 1;  // object of trivially copyable type
    alignas(int) unsigned char a[sizeof x];  // aligned array of bytes
    std::memcpy(a, &x, sizeof x);            // copy object representation
    int* x2 = reinterpret_cast<int*>(a);     // OK, but not OK to use
    return *x2;                              // Bug (UB), no int at x2
}
```

As previously mentioned, the **reinterpret_cast** itself is valid, but the resulting pointer (x2, above) does not refer to a valid object of type **int**; hence, dereferencing x2 has undefined behavior.[43]

6. **Accessing base or member subobjects via reinterpret_cast** — The C++ Standard guarantees that objects of **standard-layout class type** share the same address as certain subobjects when they exist, namely, the first *nonstatic* data member (including within any base class) and all base-class subobjects. This guarantee does *not*, however, hold for any *other* subobjects, nor for *any* subobjects of a *non*-standard-layout type. Note that the requirement that all base class subobjects of a standard-layout class type have the same address as the most-derived class object was not in the C++11 or C++14 Standards as published and was not codified until June 2018 with the resolution of CWG 2254 as a **defect report**[44]; not all compilers have yet implemented the resolution described in CWG 2254, however, resulting in unreliable placement of the second and subsequent base-class subobjects.

For example, suppose we have a **standard-layout** class type, D, that has two base classes, B1 and B2:

```
struct B1 { int i; int j; };  // first  base class (standard layout)
struct B2 { int f(); };       // second base class      "       "
struct D : B1, B2 { };        // multiple inheritance    "       "
```

A subobject of the first base class, B1, and the first nonstatic data member, i, will reside at the same address (e.g., b1p and i1p, respectively) as that of the derived class object (e.g., &d). Moreover, in compilers that conform to the changes in the resolution of CWG issue 2254, a subobject of the second base class, B2, will also reside at that address (e.g., b2p):

---

[43]As of C++20, we use `std::bit_cast<T>(x)` to implicitly create an object of the destination type, T, from the value representation of the source object, x, where **sizeof**(T) == **sizeof**(x) and both are trivially copyable. Future versions of C++ might someday render returning *x2 from the returnOne function valid, thereby obviating our writing `std::bit_cast<unsigned int>(*x2)`; see **smith20**.

[44]The resolution of CWG 2254 (**smith16a**) requires that all of the base class subobjects of an object of standard-layout type must have the same address as the object. Although not all compilers conform to this change and notably MSVC 19.29 (c. 2021) does not, all implementations at least ensure that the *first* base class subobject shares the address of the most-derived class object.

```
void test1()
{
    D d;                // object of standard-layout class type
    d.i = d.j = 0;    // Initialize d's members.

    B1*  b1p = reinterpret_cast<B1* >(&d);  // OK, we can dereference b1p.
    B2*  b2p = reinterpret_cast<B2* >(&d);  // OK, maybe can dereference b2p.
    int* i1p = reinterpret_cast<int*>(&d);  // OK, we can dereference i1p.

    b1p->i = 1;  // OK, set d.i to 1.
    b2p->f();    // OK, call d.f (unreliable before CWG2254).
    *i1p = 2;    // OK, set d.i to 2.

    B1& b1r = d;                            // OK, normal reference upcast
    D&   dr = reinterpret_cast<D&>(b1r);    // OK
    dr.i    = 3;                            // OK, set d.i to 3.
}
```

Using **reinterpret_cast** to cast a pointer from a D* to a B1*, or even to an **int***, works and produces dereferenceable pointers because objects of these types are guaranteed to reside at the *same* address. Similarly, casting to a B2* always works, but would produce a dereferenceable pointer only in compilers that have implemented the CWG 2254 resolution; otherwise, dereferencing the resulting pointer would yield **undefined** behavior. Finally, we can use address equivalence in reverse to **reinterpret_cast** from a base-class subobject reference to the derived-class reference (**b1r** and **dr**, respectively, above).

If the derived class is *not* of **standard-layout type**, then using a pointer to a base class object or first data member retrieved using **reinterpret_cast** has undefined behavior even though they might often share the same address:

```
struct B3 { int i; };   //   primary base class (standard layout)
struct B4 { int j; };   // secondary base class        "      "
struct E : B3, B4 { };  // multiple inheritance (non-standard-layout)

void test2()
{
    E e;                // object of nonstandard-layout class type
    e.i = e.j = 0;  // Initialize e's members.
    B3*  b3p = reinterpret_cast<B3* >(&e);  // OK, but can't dereference b3p
    B4*  b4p = reinterpret_cast<B4* >(&e);  // OK, "    "          "    b4p
    int* i3p = reinterpret_cast<int*>(&e);  // OK, "    "          "    i3p

    b3p->i = 3;  // Bug (UB), but might work as expected
    b4p->j = 4;  // Bug (UB), will not   "    "    "
    *i3p = 2;    // Bug (UB), but might   "    "    "
}
```

```
    B4& b4r = e;                              // OK, normal reference upcast
    E&  er = reinterpret_cast<E&>(b4r);       // OK, but can't use er
    er.i   = 3;                               // Bug (UB), won't work as expected
}
```

When we convert a derived-class pointer (or reference) to a base-class pointer (or reference) implicitly or using **static_cast**, the resulting pointer (or address of the reference) reflects a different address than the original. Hence, as the test3 function below illustrates, using **static_cast** to convert between pointers to a derived-class (e.g., e) object and a pointer to either base-class (e.g., B3 or B4) subobject, in either direction, produces well-defined results in those cases where **reinterpret_cast** would give us a pointer that cannot be dereferenced without leading to **undefined behavior**:

```
void test3()
{
    E e;             // object of nonstandard-layout class type
    e.i = e.j = 0;   // Initialize e's members.
    B3& b3r = e;     // implicit upcast
    B4& b4r = e;     //      "       "

    B3* b3p = static_cast<B3*>(&e);   // OK, explicit upcast
    B4* b4p = static_cast<B4*>(&e);   // OK,        "        "
    assert(b3p == &b3r);              // OK, static_cast respects hierarchy.
    assert(b4p == &b4r);              // OK,        "           "        "
    b3p->i = 3;                       // OK, e.i is now 3.
    b4p->j = 4;                       // OK, e.j is now 4.

    E& er1 = static_cast<E&>(b3r);    // OK, downcast requires static_cast.
    E& er2 = static_cast<E&>(b4r);    // OK,       "         "        "
    B4& ra = static_cast<B4&>(b3r);   // Error, B3 and B4 are unrelated types.
    B4& rb = reinterpret_cast<B4&>(b3r); // OK, but rb cannot be used.
    assert(&er1 == &e);               // OK, static_cast respects hierarchy.
    assert(&er2 == &e);               // OK,        "           "        "
    er1.i = 5;                        // OK, e.i is now 5.
    er1.j = 6;                        // OK, e.j is now 6.
    rb.j  = 7;                        // Bug (UB), rb does not refer to a B4.
}
```

Notice, in the test3 function above, that attempting to **static_cast** between reference types to unrelated base-class subobjects (e.g., b3r to ra) results in a welcome compile-time error, whereas the **reinterpret_cast** (e.g., b3r to rb) compiles without warning. Any subsequent attempt to dereference rb (e.g., rb.j) would, however, result in undefined behavior. When it comes to *non*-standard-layout types, only **static_cast** can be used to safely and portably cast between base-class and derived-class objects.

Aggressive use of `offsetof`

The `offsetof` macro is a C language facility, implemented as a macro, inherited by C++, and having a variety of subtle pitfalls that might lead to **undefined behavior**. In particular, the `offsetof` macro has defined behavior only when used with **standard-layout class types**. Using `offsetof` on classes that are not of **standard-layout** type has **undefined behavior**[45] — the compiler might produce a warning, `offsetof` might produce the expected results, or the program might exhibit random data corruption. The superset of **standard-layout class types** supported for `offsetof` by various compilers might differ; hence, even if the compiler produces reliable results when `offsetof` is used with a class that is not of **standard-layout** type, a program that depends on such use is not guaranteed to be portable.[46]

Because `offsetof` is specified as a macro, it fails to compile when invoked on class template instantiations having multiple template arguments (e.g., `Host<int, int>`) because the commas separating the template arguments are instead interpreted as separating macro arguments. As the constraints on `offsetof` are that the first macro parameter names a type, the usual workaround of enclosing the parameter in parentheses does not work — the argument is *not* an expression, and outer-level parentheses have no part in a type name. As a workaround, a type alias for the template instantiation can be used, or a **grouping macro** can be used to pass the type name as a macro argument:

```cpp
#include <cstddef>  // standard C offsetof macro

template <typename T, typename U>
struct MyPair  // standard-layout class template
{
    T first;
    U second;
};

const int badOffset1 = offsetof(MyPair<int, char>, first);
    // Error, three macro arguments: MyPair<int, char>, and first
const int badOffset2 = offsetof((MyPair<int, char>), second);
    // Error, (MyPair<int, char>) does not name a type

typedef MyPair<int, char> MyPairIC;                 // type alias
const int firstOffset = offsetof(MyPairIC, first);  // OK, two macro arguments
```

---

[45] As of C++17, use of `offsetof` on *non*-standard-layout class types is conditionally supported, meaning that a compiler must issue at least one diagnostic when `offsetof` is applied to a type that it cannot support; typically, C++11/14 compilers will at least warn in such cases.

[46] There have been some proposals to extend the set of types that a conforming compiler must support with `offsetof`, including P0897, which proposed support for all types; see **semashev18**. Discussion of this paper revealed that acceptance could prevent future ABI changes. Moreover, some of the features of the upcoming **reflection** feature would allow for a more complete `offsetof`-like function to be authored by the programmer. The proposal was abandoned.

```
#define GROUP_TYPE(...) __VA_ARGS__   // grouping macro
const int secondOffset = offsetof(GROUP_TYPE(MyPair<int, char>), second); // OK
```

Note that pointer arithmetic is well defined only within an array, making most uses of `offsetof` to calculate the position of a subobject relative to some address have undefined behavior. Although it is permitted to access the underlying byte representation of an object as a sequence of bytes, that representation is currently not considered an array by the Standard; hence, any pointer arithmetic within that underlying storage is dubious. Despite having undefined behavior, all relevant compilers currently allow for such pointer arithmetic to have the expected behavior[47]:

```
MyPair<int, char> thePair = { 4, 'F' };
unsigned char* pairRep = reinterpret_cast<unsigned char*>(&thePair);  // OK
unsigned char* secondRep = pairRep + secondOffset; // UB, but probably works
```

The `pairRep` pointer points to the object representation of `thePair`. The `secondRep` pointer will, in all relevant implementations, point to the object representation of `thePair.second`, but the Standard technically considers the pointer arithmetic to have undefined behavior.

The sanctioned way to access members of a class indirectly, where applicable, is via the pointer-to-member syntax, which also allows for pointers to member functions (but not to members that are references) and correctly handles complex class layouts including those having multiple inheritance, and especially virtual inheritance. Pointer-to-member objects are not restricted to standard-layout classes, thereby sidestepping undefined behavior associated with the C `offsetof` macro, but they do not support pointer-like arithmetic:

```
char MyPair<int, char>::*secondMemPtr = &MyPair<int, char>::second;
char* pc = &(thePair.*secondMemPtr);   // OK, access via a pointer to member
char c = thePair.*(secondMemPtr + 1);   // Error, arithmetic on member pointer
```

Annoyances

The C++ Standard has not yet stabilized in this area

The formal definitions for a **trivial class** and, in particular, a **trivially copyable class** were added in C++11 and have continued to evolve in succeeding Standards. Recall that a special member function is *non*-trivial if it is user-provided or if it invokes a *non*-trivial special member function for any base class or member variable; otherwise, it is trivial — even if it is deleted. C++11 had the definition of a trivially copyable class as one having a trivial destructor and not having any copy constructors, move constructors, or assignment

---

[47]There is an effort underway to make such address arithmetic well defined within the object representation of a class type that is (1) trivially copyable or (2) standard layout. If adopted, this proposal would make pointer arithmetic in conjunction with already valid use of `offsetof` within an object of standard-layout class type have well-defined behavior; see **stasiowski19**.

operators that are *non*-trivial — irrespective of whether any or all of them happened to be deleted (see Section 1.1."Deleted Functions" on page 53):

```cpp
struct S11  // was a trivially copyable struct in C++11 (as originally adopted)
{
    int i;                                // trivial data member
    ~S11()                    = delete;   // trivial destructor
    S11(const S11&)           = delete;   // trivial copy constructor
    S11& operator=(const S11&) = delete;  // trivial copy assignment operator
    S11(S11&&)                = delete;   // trivial move constructor
    S11& operator=(S11&&)     = delete;   // trivial move assignment operator
};
```

Note that **struct** S11 above was originally considered **trivially copyable** despite having *all* of its **copy operations** deleted. Moreover, since declaring and then immediately deleting any function makes it **trivial**, the **user-declared** explicitly **deleted destructor** is trivial.

Prior to C++11, the only way for an operation to be **trivial** was for it to be **implicitly declared** and therefore necessarily publicly accessible. The addition of **defaulted** member functions (see Section 1.1."Defaulted Functions" on page 33) means that we can now have *non***public** trivial operations:

```cpp
#include <type_traits>  // std::is_trivial, etc.

void f11();  // forward declaration of friend of C11 below

class C11  // is a trivially copyable class in C++11
{
    int i;
    C11(const C11&)           = default; // private trivial copy ctor
    C11& operator=(const C11&) = default; // private trivial copy assignment op

    friend void f11();  // has access to private copy operations

public:
    C11()                     = default;
    ~C11()                    = default;
};

static_assert(std::is_trivially_copyable<C11>::value, "");       // OK
static_assert(std::is_trivially_destructible<C11>::value, "");   // OK
static_assert(std::is_trivial<C11>::value, "");                  // OK
```

Hence, it was easy in C++11 and even C++14, as originally published, to create a **trivially copyable** user-defined type (UDT) that could be copied when treated as raw memory (e.g., using std::memcpy) yet had no valid **copy operations** defined within its public API.

During the development of C++17, there was an attempt to address these concerns.[48] The revised definition is that a trivially copyable class has a *non*deleted trivial destructor, that each of its declared copy and move operations is trivial, and that at least one copy or move operation is both trivial and *non*deleted (note that a **deleted function** is still trivial). Hence, there's now at least one *potentially* (e.g., it could be private or ambiguous) callable copy/move operation to better justify the validity of bitwise copying indicated by the `std::is_trivially_copyable` trait; see *Potential Pitfalls — Using the wrong type trait* on page 482. A similar contemporaneous change also required the destructor of both a trivially copyable class and, hence, a trivial class also be *non*deleted.[49] Applying these changes to the classes above, `S11` is no longer trivially copyable but `C11` remains so. Note, however, that an object of trivially copyable class type having **private** copy operations can be copied only by member and **friend** functions, unless exploiting the special permission to perform bitwise copies (e.g., using `std::memcpy`) granted for trivially copyable types:

```
C11 c1;        // OK, invokes public default constructor
C11 c2(c1);    // Error, invokes inaccessible private copy constructor

void f11()  // friend of C11
{
    C11 c3(c1);  // OK, invokes private copy constructor as a friend
    // ...
}

void g11()  // nonfriend of C11
{
    C11 c4;
    std::memcpy(&c4, &c1, sizeof c1);  // OK, C11 is still trivially copyable.
}
```

Another issue that evolved over multiple C++ versions was a concern that **volatile** data members may not have trivial semantics and therefore might require special copying semantics on certain platforms. This concern was addressed in C++14 by modifying the definitions of trivial copy/move constructors and assignment operators, in turn adding a further restriction to trivially copyable types that they do not have a **volatile**-qualified *non*static data member.[50] This change, however, was found to break compatibility with important platform ABIs, so the change was reverted via a **defect report** against C++14.[51]

```
class V  // trivially copyable in C++11, but might not be in C++14
{
    volatile int i;  // volatile-qualified nonstatic data member
};
```

---

[48] See **izvekov14**.
[49] See CWG issue 1734; **widman13**.
[50] See CWG issue 496; **maddock04**.
[51] See CWG issue 2094; **vandevoorde15**.

Class V above is trivially copyable in every version of C++, but the `std::is_trivially_copyable` trait might not reflect that on some older versions of C++14 compilers, depending on which interpretation of that Standard is in effect; see *Relevant standard type traits are unreliable* on page 527.

One might question what happens with trivially copyable types that have **const**-qualified or reference data members and whether bitwise copying (e.g., using `std::memcpy`) such objects has **undefined behavior** as these bitwise-copy operations inevitably overwrite a reference or **const** object. Performing a bitwise copy of such objects and then subsequently using that data in any way was modified in C++20, when a twofold change was made: (1) If a *non***const** object — referred to by a reference, pointer, or name (call it a *ref*) — is destroyed and a new object of the same type is subsequently constructed at the same location, the usability of the original *ref*, as of C++20, is not impacted by whether the object contains a **const** or reference subobject, whereas the existence of such a subobject, prior to C++20, would have rendered the *ref* unusable; and (2) `std::memcpy` and `std::memmove` implicitly create a new object in the destination location, making the previously introduced rule applicable to cases of bitwise copy using either `std::memcpy` or `std::memmove`.[52] Note that user-defined bitwise copy (e.g., using **unsigned char**s directly) still has UB as it does not begin the lifetime of the target object. Also note that a valid bitwise copy using `std::memcpy` or `std::memmove` implicitly creates a new object — i.e., has copy-construction semantics — even if the only *non*deleted trivial function conferring trivially copyable status is one of the assignment operators.

As an example of the kind of UB that might occur via optimization in C++11/14, consider that a compiler may cache the result of reading a **const** data member in a register, as the value may not change within the lifetime of the object in a well-defined program. Any attempt to replace that object via `std::memcpy` might be respected, but the stale value in the register will not necessarily be invalidated, so subsequent reads of that data member might produce the old value. A C++20 compiler, conversely, must now also allow for the possibly that such an object might be overwritten by `std::memcpy` or placement `::`**operator new** and inhibit this particular optimization in such cases.[53] For compilers implementing Standards prior to C++20, we can reduce risks in generic code by checking that a type is both trivially copyable *and* either copy assignable or **move assignable** (e.g., using `std::is_assignable`) before attempting to use `std::memcpy`, so as to avoid UB associated with **const**- and reference-qualified *non***static** data members. Note that the additional check for assignability will reject trivially copyable types having no publicly invocable assignment operators, even absent any **const** or reference *non***static** data members. Such rejection might better reflect the semantic intent of the class author anyway; see *Potential Pitfalls — Using memcpy on objects having **const** or reference subobjects* on page 489.

---

[52]See **smith20**.

[53]See CWG issue 1776; **finland13**.

A trivial type, in addition to being trivially copyable, is required to have at least one trivial default constructor and no *non*-trivial default constructors.[54] However, because every deleted function is trivial, a trivially copyable class in which all default constructors are deleted qualified as a trivial type in C++11 (as originally published), yet an object of such a type could never be default constructed. After the release of C++14, the definition of trivial class was amended to require that there be at least one *non*deleted trivial default constructor, and this change too was a defect report against C++14, with implementers typically propagating the fix back to C++11 as well.

This augmented restriction on what constitutes a trivial type doesn't solve the perceived problem in all cases because a class (e.g., B) that has more than one default constructor can still be trivial yet not be default constructible due to ambiguity:

```cpp
#include <type_traits>  // std::is_trivial, etc.

struct B  // B is considered trivial but cannot be default constructed.
{
    B()        = default;  // trivial default constructor #1
    B(int = 0) = delete;   //    "        "           "       #2
};

static_assert(std::is_trivial<B>::value, "");                      // OK
static_assert(std::is_trivially_default_constructible<B>::value, "");  // Error

B b;  // Error, ambiguous
```

Note that class B (above) qualifies as being trivial because, along with being trivially copyable, it has no *non*-trivial default constructors, and at least one *non*deleted default constructor, yet it can never be default constructed.[55] The ability to invoke the *default* constructor without invoking any *non*-trivial functions is reflected in the `std::is_trivially_default_constructible` trait (having the same additional invocability requirement as the `std::is_default_constructible` trait). Be aware, however, that the subset of default-constructor-related requirements on trivial types and the checks performed by the `std::is_trivially_default_constructible` trait are not the same; see *Potential Pitfalls — Using the wrong type trait* on page 482.

Interestingly, inheriting from a class, such as B, that has an ambiguous default constructor causes the default constructor of a derived class (e.g., D) to be implicitly deleted:

---

[54] A trivial class may have multiple default constructors and can even be default constructed successfully provided that it is unambiguous which one would be called after overload resolution. Such unorthodox designs might occur, say, by having multiple constructor templates using SFINAE constraints to ensure that exactly one of the overloads is viable.

[55] Note that for multiple popular compilers, other than GCC, the traits falsely report that class B (above) is *not* trivial.

```
struct D : B { };  // D is non-trivial even though B is.

static_assert(std::is_trivial<D>::value, "");                          // Error
static_assert(std::is_trivially_default_constructible<D>::value, "");  // Error
static_assert(std::is_trivially_copyable<D>::value, "");               // OK

D d;  // Error, default constructor of D is implicitly deleted.
```

Because D has a **deleted default constructor**, an up-to-date conforming C++11/14 (or later) implementation will report D (above) as being **trivially copyable**, but *not* of **trivial type**, yet older compilers might wrongly allow D to pass for a **trivial type**. Several workarounds exist. A library implementer could, for example, employ the `std::is_trivially_default_constructible` trait to ensure that the default constructor is in fact **invocable** (as well as being unambiguous and **accessible**) with respect to the type expression on which the trait is applied. Note that `std::is_trivially_default_constructible` does not distinguish between a type that cannot be default constructed at all (i.e., `std::is_default_constructible` evaluates to **false**) and a type whose default construction involves *non*-trivial functions.

Similarly, the definition of **standard-layout type** has matured since it was made distinct from **POD type** in C++11. After C++14 was released, the Standard clarified the requirement that there be at most one class in the derivation tree of a **standard-layout type** that "has" one or more *non***static** data members and extended the definition of a **standard-layout type** to include *unnamed* **bit fields** as well.[56]

The type of any base class of a standard-layout type cannot be the same as any nonstatic data member that would be at offset zero within objects of that type; otherwise, uniqueness of object address would be violated. C++17 provides a more rigorous, recursive definition of the set of types of all *non*-base-class subobjects that must be at offset zero, and requires that there be no overlap between this set and any direct or indirect base classes of a type to be considered a **standard-layout class**.[57] Subsequent Standards also make explicit that a **standard-layout class** has at most one base class subobject of any given type.[58] These later definitions also clarified what the first nonstatic data member means. Despite all of these clarifications being **defect reports** against C++14 and, in practice, against C++11, the `std::is_standard_layout` trait might not accurately represent the up-to-date definition of **standard-layout type**; again, see *Relevant standard type traits are unreliable* on page 527.

Finally, in C++03, allowing the flow of control to bypass (e.g., via a **goto**) the declaration of an automatic variable required that it be of POD type needing no initialization. As of C++11, the constraints on the type of such a variable were relaxed to no longer require that it be of either **standard-layout type** or **trivial type**, so long as the class had both a **trivial**

---

[56]See CWG issue 1881; **ranns14**.
[57]See CWG issue 1672 (**smith13**) and CWG issue 2120 (**tong15**).
[58]See CWG issue 1813; **vandevoorde13**.

default constructor and a trivial destructor (it needn't be trivially copyable). In 2019, the requirement on the trivial destructor was removed as a defect report[59]:

```
struct W  // has trivial constructor, but non-trivial destructor
{
    ~W() { } // user-provided (non-trivial) destructor
};


void func()  // Function that, in its body, jumps over a default-initialized
{            // automatic variable having a trivial default constructor.
    goto label;  // OK after DR fix
    W s;         // automatic variable having trivial constructor
label: ;
}
```

Note the body of func in the example code above is ostensibly valid C++, yet few C++11/14 compilers accept it due to the *non*-trivial destructor of class W. It is precisely these kinds of open-ended retroactive changes to previous Standards that lead to divergence among their implementations; see *Relevant standard type traits are unreliable* below.

Relevant standard type traits are unreliable

Depending on the vintage of our compiler, the Standard it is targeting, and the defect reports that it might or might not have addressed for that target, we might get different results when querying fundamental properties of types using the standard metafunctions found in the <type_traits> header. Specific evolutionary changes that might give inconsistent reports across compilers are described and documented in the preceding annoyance. What's more, not all implementations necessarily agree as to what the C++ Standard requires of various properties such as whether a given class (e.g., X) is considered trivial:

```
#include <type_traits>  // std::is_trivial


class X  // POD type having all special member functions defaulted private
{
    X()                   = default;
    X(const X&)           = default;
    X(X&&)                = default;
    ~X()                  = default;
    X& operator=(const X&) = default;
    X& operator=(X&&)     = default;
};


static_assert(std::is_trivial<X>::value, "private not trivial?");  // OK, maybe
```

---

[59]See CWG issue 2256; **smith16b**.

According to all C++ Standards, access control is not involved in determining whether a given class is a trivial type; hence, when compile-time asserting that trait using `std::is_trivial`, one might expect that we can rely on it across platforms. Although the example code above compiles for most platform and library combinations we've tested, it is not always so — even among popular compilers.[60]

An `std::pair` or `std::tuple` of PODs is not a POD

The C++ Standard Library provides two class templates, `std::pair` and `std::tuple`, that are designed to act like a generic **struct** of values that can be assembled and used in generic code. Given this design, it is tempting to imagine these **struct**-like templates would retain the POD-like properties of their template arguments. The Standard, however, requires only some of these properties to hold; moreover, many implementation strategies and some features of these types preclude the possibility of providing all of the properties, even when a handwritten **struct** with the same contents would have them.

For an operation provided by a Standard Library template to be trivial, it must be possible for an implicit or a user-declared but not user-provided implementation of that operation to meet the requirements that the Standard has for that operation.[61]

1. **Always defaulted operations** — When an operation is required by the Standard to use `=`**default**, it will naturally be trivial when it can be; see Section 1.1."Defaulted Functions" on page 33. This natural triviality is the case for the copy constructors and move constructors of `std::pair` and `std::tuple`. While the potential for non-trivial private data members of `std::pair` and `std::tuple` exists, it is commonly accepted that the intent of the defaulting of these members is that they should be trivial when the corresponding operations of the element types are trivial.[62]

2. **Required to be trivial operations** — The destructors of both `std::pair` and `std::tuple` are not required to use `=`**default** in all cases, but they are, however, explicitly required to be trivial when all elements have trivial destructors, thereby enabling these classes to meet one of the major requirements to be literal types (see Section 2.1."**constexpr** Functions" on page 257).[63]

3. **Never trivial or defaultable operations** — Operations with additional behavioral requirements that go beyond what a trivial implementation would do can never be

---

[60]The Microsoft compiler and library consistently fails the **static_assert** statement applied to `std::is_trivial<X>` above with every version of the tool chain we've tested.

[61]Much of the rationale for why `std::pair` and `std::tuple` are the way they are in modern C++ can be found in **krugler10b**.

[62]Despite the intent of the Standard, implementations vary with respect to the triviality of the copy and move constructors. GCC's standard library, libstdc++ 6.0.28 (c. 2020), offers a trivial copy constructor but not a **trivial move constructor** for an `std::tuple` of types with corresponding trivial operations, while the Microsoft implementation that ships with the MSVC 19.29 (c. 2021) compiler fails to provide triviality for either constructor. The standard library that ships with Clang, libc++ 13.0.0 (c. 2021), correctly provides both a trivial copy constructor and a trivial move constructor when possible.

[63]The requirement that destructors be trivial was clarified in LWG issue 2796 (**wakely16**).

made trivial by an implementation. The default constructors of both std::pair and std::tuple require that they value-initialize their elements, resulting in operations that can *never* be trivial.

4. **Conditionally defaultable operations** — The remaining operations are defined in such a way that they might be eligible to use =**default** for some potential template arguments. A noteworthy example is the assignment operators of std::pair and std::tuple, which are required to do a memberwise assignment, even when the member type is a reference. The defaulted assignment operation would be deleted in this case, so for at least some template arguments these operations will not be trivial. It would be possible to conditionally default these operations for nonreference types, but that involves **partial specialization** and complicated inheritance schemes or the need for an explosion of mildly varying implementations. This significant cost leads most library vendors to not attempt to make these operations trivial, and their being trivial is something that must be left as **QoI** and not a trait that can be portably depended upon.[64]

The Standard does not describe the layout of its classes, nor does it list the private members that may be used to implement them. In principle, the implementation of std::pair could have additional private members or declare first and second in different public base classes,[65] resulting in a conforming implementation that is never a **standard-layout type**. Similarly, std::tuple is often implemented through inheritance (recursively or through pack expansion) of a distinct type for each member element, resulting in a type that cannot be a **standard-layout type** for anything with more than one element. An implementation *could* provide distinct specializations for **standard-layout** fixed numbers of elements, but having multiple such specializations would be a labor-intensive solution to achieve **standard layout** for a subset of potential template arguments and is a QoI choice that standard library vendors do not seem to have made.

See Also

- "Aggregate Init '14" (§1.2, p. 138) introduces the notion of default member initialization to aggregates.

- "Braced Init" (§2.1, p. 215) provides additional insight into aggregates as well as other forms of braced initialization.

- "**constexpr** Functions" (§2.1, p. 257) shows how trivial types can be made usable at compile time.

---

[64]Modern versions of GCC, Clang, and MSVC always implement std::pair's copy and move-assignment operators as user-provided functions.

[65]An example of such an implementation can be found in the BDE open-source library implementation of pair maintained by the authors of this book. This implementation partially specializes pair for template arguments of reference type such that instantiations are trivially copyable if and only if both template arguments are of trivially copyable nonreference type; see **bde14**, /groups/bsl/bslstl/bslstl_pair.h.

- **"union** '11" (§3.1, p. 1174) expands on what classical C++ unions can encompass and comprise.

Further Reading

- For a vintage (c. 2010) but thorough introductory tutorial on this material, see **tsirunyan18**.

- To see the original standards paper that introduced the C++11 generalization, see **dawes07**.

- For the paper introducing a requirement (adopted for C++20) that mandates two's complement encoding for signed character types, see **maurer18**: "For narrow character types, each possible bit pattern of the object representation represents a distinct value."

Appendix

A cautionary tale: PODs are not just "bags of bits"

Adapted by Hyman Rosen[66]

The **float** data type is considered a POD by C++. That does not mean that it can hold arbitrary bit patterns.

When a big-endian representation of a floating-point number is stored in a **float** variable on a little-endian machine, that is, with the four bytes of the **float** in reverse order, many ordinary values will be mapped to NaN representations. Those values will be unstable because the Intel x86 (32-bit, not x86-64) instructions that compilers generate to load floating-point registers may flip bits inside the NaN representations.[67]

IEEE 754 and NaN representations

An IEEE 754 single-precision binary floating-point value is represented by a 23-bit fraction, an 8-bit exponent, and a sign bit in the following logical format (shown left to right from the most significant bit to the least):

```
| s|eeeeeeee|fffffffffffffffffffffff|
-------------------------------------
|+-|exponent| fraction (significand)|
|1b| 8 bits |        23 bits        |
```

---

[66]This appendix was adapted from internal documentation first written by Alexander Beels. The original document detailed the issue described herein, which was discovered during a technical analysis conducted by Beels at Bloomberg in 2018.

[67]Whether this change in the bit pattern amounts to a bug in x86 implementations is a matter of some debate. The compilers are somewhat limited by the legacy x87 floating-point instruction set; see **wilcox13**.

When all of the exponent bits are set to 1 and any of the significand bits are set to 1, the pattern is a NaN ("not-a-number"). It is easy to see that there are $2^{23} - 1$ significand patterns that yield a NaN, and when we add in the sign bit, we have $2^{24} - 2$ total **float** patterns that represent a NaN.

Implementations have a fair amount of freedom in how they deal with a NaN. In particular, implementations distinguish between **signaling NaN** patterns and **quiet NaN** patterns. A **signaling NaN** pattern tells the implementation that it should raise a signal, such as a floating-point exception, when the NaN is encountered in arithmetic. A quiet NaN calls for no special handling. Most processors follow the recommendations of the 2008 revision of IEEE 754 and use the most significant bit of the significand field for this purpose; if the most significant bit is 1, the NaN is *quiet*; otherwise, the NaN is *signaling*.

In the case of a 32-bit GCC toolchain using the Intel x87-compatible floating-point instructions, the compiler implementation will sometimes generate a **signaling NaN** in response to an illegal operation — such as taking the square root of a negative number — but then decide to "swallow" the exception by simply converting the **signaling NaN** to a **quiet NaN**:

```
float f = sqrt(-3.2);
```

In the code example above, the expression `sqrt(-3.2)` may yield a **signaling NaN** pattern in some temporary location, but that pattern could be converted to a **quiet NaN** by the time the assignment to `f` is complete. A C++ implementation has a lot of discretion here, and depending on various factors, including optimization, the **signaling NaN** could be stored in main memory, stored in an extended-precision floating-point register, passed to the x87-compatible floating-point unit, or never even be generated at all. In a typical program, we would probably never observe the change from *signaling* to *quiet*.

Comparison of big-endian and little-endian physical **float** layouts

Let's name each bit of a 32-bit **float**, using S for the sign bit, the uppercase letters A through H for the 8 exponent bits, and the lowercase letters a through w for the 23 bits of the significand:

```
|S|ABCDEFGH|abcdefghijklmnopqrstuvw|
|s|eeeeeeee|fffffffffffffffffffffff|        IEEE 754 format logical fields
|s|exponent|    significand        |
```

On a big-endian (BE) machine, the logical and physical layouts of an IEEE 754 floating-point number are the same:

```
|0       |8       |16      |24      |32
|SABCDEFG|Habcdefg|hijklmno|pqrstuvw|        physical bits in big-endian order
|seeeeeee|efffffff|ffffffff|ffffffff|        big-endian physical layout key
```

But on a little-endian (LE) machine (e.g., the Intel x86), the byte order is reversed:

```
|0       |8       |16      |24      |32
|pqrstuvw|hijklmno|Habcdefg|SABCDEFG|        physical bits in little-endian order
|ffffffff|ffffffff|efffffff|seeeeeee|        little-endian physical layout key
```

If bytes within a **float** are stored in big-endian order on a little-endian machine, the bits have different meanings than in the original **float**:

```
|0       |8       |16      |24      |32
|SABCDEFG|Habcdefg|hijklmno|pqrstuvw|       physical bits in BE order
|ffffffff|ffffffff|efffffff|seeeeeee|       interpretation of bits in LE order

|p|qrstuvwh|ijklmnoHabcdefgSABCDEFG|        Logical order of bits in a float
|s|eeeeeeee|fffffffffffffffffffffff|        IEEE 754 format logical fields
|s|exponent|       significand      |
```

Note that the seven least-significant bits (q–w) of the big-endian significand correspond to all but one bit of the little-endian exponent. Remember that setting all of the exponent bits to 1 indicates that a **float** is a NaN; this detail is where we are going to get ourselves into trouble.

Detailed example

Now let's consider code to take the value of a **float** from a big-endian machine and — taking the difference in byte order into account — move it into a **float** on a little-endian machine by serializing the **float** on the big-endian machine and reconstituting it on the little-endian machine. The sending machine writes out the bytes of a **float** to the network in big-endian order (a.k.a. *network* byte order), and the receiving machine first reads those bytes into a **float** *in the same order in which they were written* and then *reorders* the bytes within that **float** to put them into little-endian order, using a small set of library functions on the receiving end:

```
#include <algorithm>   // std::swap
#include <cstring>     // std::memcpy
#include <network.h>   // a library that includes the Network class

float read_float_from_network(Network* n)
{
    float f;
    n->read(&f);
    return f;
}

float fixup_float(float value)
{
    unsigned char buf[4];
    std::memcpy(buf, &value, 4);
    std::swap(buf[0], buf[3]);
    std::swap(buf[1], buf[2]);
```

```
    std::memcpy(&value, buf, 4);
    return value;
}

float deserialize(Network* n)
{
    return fixup_float(read_float_from_network(n));
}
```

Note that in this example, simplified for illustrative purposes, the `read_float_from_network` routine is returning a **float** value that still has its bytes in network byte order; it is `fixup_float` that will reverse those bytes.

Now, consider the number 98.8164, and the layout of the 32-bit IEEE 754 approximation of this value:

```
|0|10000101|10001011010000111111111|       logical layout
|s|eeeeeeee|fffffffffffffffffffffff|       IEEE 754 format logical fields

|01000010|11000101|10100001|11111111|      big-endian order layout
|seeeeeee|efffffff|ffffffff|ffffffff|      big-endian physical layout key
```

The sign bit is 0, the exponent is 133, and the significand is 4563455. The value of an ordinary **float** is given by the following equation:

$$value = (-1)^{sign} * (8388608 + significand) * 2^{(exponent-150)}$$

When we apply this formula to the value represented in our example, we get 98.81639862060546875, which is the closest value to 98.8164 representable in a 32-bit **float**:

$$value = (-1)^0 * (8388608 + 4563455) * 2^{(133-150)} = \frac{12952063}{131072} = 98.81639862060546875$$

If we write the four-byte big-endian **float** directly to the network and then read the representation in network byte order directly into a **float** on the little-endian machine (i.e., using `read_float_from_network`), the bytes will have reversed meanings:

```
|01000010|11000101|10100001|11111111|      bytes in network order
|seeeeeee|efffffff|ffffffff|ffffffff|      meaning of bits in big-endian format
|ffffffff|ffffffff|efffffff|seeeeeee|      meaning of bits in little-endian format

|1|11111111|01000011000010101000010|       network bits interpreted as LE float
|s|eeeeeeee|fffffffffffffffffffffff|       IEEE 754 format logical fields
```

The least-significant bits of the original significand have been read into the exponent field, and we have constructed a *signaling* NaN! When the GCC implementation notices the signaling NaN, it chooses not to emit a floating-point exception but rather to convert the signaling NaN into a **quiet** NaN by turning on the most-significant bit of the significand:

```
                v                     changed bit
|1|11111111|01000011100010101000010|   signaling NaN
|1|11111111|11000011100010101000010|   quiet NaN
|s|eeeeeeee|fffffffffffffffffffffff|   IEEE 754 format logical fields
```

The bytes of this value are then reversed by `fixup_float` into the order proper for the receiving machine, and the result is stored, now altered from its original value:

```
                v                     changed bit
|01000010|11000101|11100001|11111111|   physical layout before fixup_float
|ffffffff|ffffffff|efffffff|seeeeeee|   meaning of bits in little-endian format


                v                     changed bit
|11111111|11100001|11000101|01000010|   physical LE layout after fixup_float
|ffffffff|ffffffff|efffffff|seeeeeee|   meaning of bits in little-endian format


                v                     changed bit
|0|10000101|10001011110000111111111|   logical layout after fixup_float
|s|eeeeeeee|fffffffffffffffffffffff|   IEEE 754 format logical fields
```

The value of the sign and exponent have not changed, but the significand now has the value 4579839. We can now apply our formula to compute the actual value represented by this new **float**:

$$value = (-1)^0 * (8388608 + 4579839) * 2^{(133-150)} = \frac{12968447}{131072} = 98.94139862060546875$$

The value has mysteriously increased by 0.125 during transmission!

Conclusion

POD types do not grant a license to store arbitrary bits within them. Floating-point values may have NaN representations that change in the process of being moved. Pointers might have marker bits that do not represent parts of an address but other properties of the pointed-to memory. Signed integers on obscure architectures might have unused bits or strange representations. While C++ grants permission to copy PODs as streams of bytes out of and into objects of those types, those streams must represent proper values of those types.

Inheriting Base-Class Constructors

The term *inheriting constructors* refers to the use of a **using declaration** to expose nearly all of the constructors of a base class in the scope of a derived class.

Description

In a class definition, a **using** declaration naming a base class's constructor results in the derived class "inheriting" all of the nominated base class's constructors, except for *copy* and *move* constructors. Just like **using** declarations of member functions, the nominated base class's constructors will be considered when no matching constructor is found in the derived class. When a base class constructor is selected in this way, that constructor will be used to construct the base class, and the remaining bases and data members of the subclass will be initialized as if by the default constructor (e.g., applying default initializers; see Section 2.1."Default Member Init" on page 318).

```
struct B0
{
    B0() = default;    // public, default constructor
    B0(int)        { }  // public, one argument (implicit) value constructor
    B0(int, int)   { }  // public, two argument value constructor

private:
    B0(const char*) { }  // private, one argument (implicit) value constructor
};

struct D0 : B0
{
    using B0::B0;  // using declaration
    D0(double d);  // suppress implicit default constructor
};

D0 t(1);     // OK, inherited from B0::B0(int)
D0 u(2, 3);  // OK, inherited from B0::B0(int, int)
D0 v("hi");  // Error, Base constructor is declared private.
```

The only constructors that are explicitly *not* inheritable by the derived class are the potentially compiler-generated *copy* and *move* constructors:

```
#include <utility>  // std::move

B0 b1(1);              // OK, base-class object can be created.
B0 b2(2, 3);           // OK, base-class object can be created.
B0 b3(b1);             // OK, base-class object can be copied (from lvalue).
B0 b4(std::move(b1));  // OK, base-class object can be moved (from rvalue).
```

```
D0 w(b1);    // Error, base-class copy constructor is not inherited.
D0 v;        // OK, base-class default constructor is inherited.
D0 x(B0{});  // Error, base-class move constructor is not inherited.

D0 y(B0(4)); // Error, base-class move constructor is not inherited.
D0 z(t);     // OK, uses compiler-generated D0::D0(const D0&)
D0 j(D0(5)); // OK, uses compiler-generated D0::D0(D&&)
```

Note that we use braced initialization (see Section 2.1."Braced Init" on page 215) in
`D0 x(B0{});` to ensure that a variable x of type D0 is declared. `D0 x(B0());` would instead
be interpreted as a declaration of a function x returning D0 and accepting a pointer to a
nullary function returning B0, which is referred to as the **most vexing parse**.

The constructors inherited by the derived class have the same effect on whether the compiler implicitly generates special member functions as explicitly implemented ones would.
For example, D0's default constructor would be implicitly *deleted* (see Section 1.1."Deleted
Functions" on page 53) if B0 doesn't have a default constructor. Note that since the copy
and move constructors are *not* inherited, their presence in the base class wouldn't suppress implicit generation of copy and move assignment in the derived class. For instance,
D0's implicitly generated assignment operators **hide** their counterparts in B0:

```
void f()
{
    B0 b(0), bb(0);  // Create destination and source B0 objects.
    D0 d(0), dd(0);  //    "          "         "      "   D0    "

    b = bb;          // OK, assign base from lvalue base.
    b = B0(0);       // OK,    "     "     "  rvalue   "

    d = bb;          // Error, B0::operator= is hidden by D0::operator=.
    d = B0(0);       // Error,     "         "      "       "      "

    d.B0::operator=(bb);     // OK, explicit slicing is still possible.
    d.B0::operator=(B0(0));  // OK,     "         "     "    "      "

    d = dd;          // OK, assign derived from lvalue derived.
    d = D0(0);       // OK,    "      "       "  rvalue    "
}
```

Note that, when inheriting constructors, private constructors in the base class are accessed
as private constructors of that base class and are subject to the same access controls; see
Annoyances — Access levels of inherited constructors are the same as in base class on
page 549.

Inheriting constructors having the same **signature** from multiple base classes leads to ambiguity errors:

```
struct B1A { B1A(int); }; // Here we have two bases classes, each of which
struct B1B { B1B(int); }; // provides a converting constructor from an int.

struct D1 : B1A, B1B
{
    using B1A::B1A;
    using B1B::B1B;
};
```

```
D1 d1(0);  // Error, Call of overloaded D1(int) is ambiguous.
```

Each inherited constructor shares the same characteristics as the corresponding one in the nominated base class's constructor and then delegates to it. The characteristics preserved by constructor inheritance include the **access specifiers**, the **explicit** specifier, the **constexpr** specifier, the default arguments, and the exception specification; see Section 3.1. "**noexcept** Specifier" on page 1085 and Section 2.1. "**constexpr** Functions" on page 257. For constructor templates, the template parameter list and the default template arguments are preserved as well:

```
struct B2
{
    template <typename T = int>
    explicit B2(T) { }
};
```

```
struct D2 : B2 { using B2::B2; };
```

The declaration **using** B2::B2 above behaves as if a constructor template that delegates to its nominated base class's template was provided in D2:

```
// pseudocode
struct D2 : B2
{
    template <typename T = int>
    explicit D2(T i) : B2(i) { }
};
```

When deriving from a base class in which inheriting most (but not all) of its constructors is desirable, suppressing inheritance of one or more of them is possible by providing constructors in the derived class having the same signature as the ones that would be inherited:

```
struct B3
{
    B3()         { std::cout << "B3()\n"; }
    B3(int)      { std::cout << "B3(int)\n"; }
    B3(int, int) { std::cout << "B3(int, int)\n"; }
};
```

```
struct D3 : B3
{
    using B3::B3;
    D3(int) { std::cout << "D3(int)\n"; }
};

D3 d;        // prints "B3()"
D3 e(0);     // prints "D3(int)" --- The derived constructor is invoked.
D3 f(0, 0);  // prints "B3(int, int)"
```

In other words, we can suppress what would otherwise be an inherited constructor from
a nominated base class by simply declaring a replacement with the same signature in the
derived class. We can then choose to either implement it ourselves, **default** it (see Section 1.1."Defaulted Functions" on page 33), or **delete** it (see Section 1.1."Deleted Functions"
on page 53).

If we have chosen to inherit the constructors from multiple base classes, we can disambiguate
conflicts by declaring the offending constructor(s) explicitly in the derived class and then
delegating to the base classes if and as appropriate:

```
struct B1A { B1A(int); };  // Here we have two base classes, each of which
struct B1B { B1B(int); };  // provides a converting constructor from an int.

struct D3 : B1A, B1B
{
    using B1A::B1A;  // Inherit the int constructor from base class B1A.
    using B1B::B1B;  // Inherit the int constructor from base class B1B.

    D3(int i) : B1A(i), B1B(i) { }  // User-declare int converting constructor
};                                  // that delegates to bases.

D3 d3(0);  // OK, calls D3(int)
```

Lastly, inheriting constructors from a **dependent type** affords a capability over C++03
that is more than just convenience and avoidance of boilerplate code. In all of the example
code in *Description* on page 535 thus far, we know how to "spell" the base-class constructor; we are simply automating some drudge work. In the case of a *dependent* base class,
however, we do *not* know how to spell the constructors, so we *must* rely on **inheriting
constructors** if that is the forwarding semantic we seek:

```
template <typename T>
struct S : T  // The base type, T, is a *dependent type*.
{
    using T::T;  // inheriting constructors generically from a dependent type
};
```

```
#include <string>     // std::string
#include <vector>     // std::vector

S<std::string>        ss("hello");      // OK, uses constructor from base
S<std::vector<char>> svc("goodbye");    // Error, no suitable constructor in base
```

In this example, we created a class template, S, that derives publicly from its template argument, T. Then, when creating an object of type S parameterized by std::string, we were able to pass it a string literal via the inherited std::string constructor overloaded on a **const char***. Notice, however, that no such constructor is available in std::vector; hence, attempting to create the derived class from a literal string results in a compile-time error. See *Use Cases — Incorporating reusable functionality via a mix-in* on page 545.

A decidedly more complex alternative affording a different set of trade-offs would involve variadic constructor templates (see Section 2.1."Variadic Templates" on page 873) having forwarding references (see Section 2.1."Forwarding References" on page 377) as parameters. In this alternative approach, all of the constructors from the **public**, **protected**, and **private** regions of the bases class would now appear under the same access specifier — i.e., the one in which the perfectly forwarding constructor is declared. What's more, this approach would not retain other constructor characteristics, such as **explicit**, **noexcept**, **constexpr**, and so on. The forwarding can, however, be restricted to inheriting just the **public** constructors (without characteristics) by constraining on std::is_constructible using **SFINAE**; see *Annoyances — Access levels of inherited constructors are the same as in base class* on page 549.

Use Cases

Employing this form of **using** declaration to inherit a nominated base class's constructors — essentially verbatim — suggests that one or more of those constructors is sufficient to initialize the *entire* derived-class object to a valid useful state. Typically, such will pertain only when the derived class adds no member data of its own. While additional derived-class member data could possibly be initialized if by a *defaulted* default constructor, this state must be *orthogonal* to any modifiable state initialized in the base class, as such state is subject to independent change via **slicing**, which might in turn invalidate **object invariants**. Derived-class data will be either default-initialized or have its value set using member initializers (see Section 2.1."Default Member Init" on page 318). Hence, most typical use cases will involve wrapping an existing class by deriving from it (either publicly or privately), adding only defaulted data members having orthogonal values, and then adjusting the derived class's behavior via **overriding** its virtual or **hiding** its nonvirtual member functions.

Avoiding boilerplate code when employing structural inheritance

A key indication for using inheriting constructors is that the derived class addresses only auxiliary or optional, rather than required or necessary, functionality to its self-sufficient base class. As an interesting, albeit mostly pedagogical, example, suppose we want to provide a proxy for an `std::vector` that performs explicit checking of indices supplied to its index operator:

```cpp
#include <cassert>  // standard C assert macro
#include <vector>   // std::vector

template <typename T>
struct CheckedVector : std::vector<T>
{
    using std::vector<T>::vector;      // Inherit std::vector's constructors.

    T& operator[](std::size_t index)    // Hide std::vector's index operator.
    {
        assert(index < std::vector<T>::size());
        return std::vector<T>::operator[](index);
    }

    const T& operator[](std::size_t index) const   // Hide const index operator.
    {
        assert(index < std::vector<T>::size());
        return std::vector<T>::operator[](index);
    }
};
```

In the example above, inheriting constructors allowed us to use public structural inheritance to readily create a distinct new type having all of the functionality of its base type except for a couple of functions where we chose to augment the original behavior.

Although this example might be compelling, it suffers from inherent deficiencies making it insufficient for general use in practice: Passing the derived class to a function — whether by value or reference — will strip it of its auxiliary functionality. When we have access to the source, an alternative solution would be to use conditional compilation to add explicit checks in certain build configurations (e.g., using C-style `assert` macros).[1]

Avoiding boilerplate code when employing implementation inheritance

Sometimes it can be cost effective to adapt a **concrete class** having virtual functions to a specialized purpose by using inheritance. Useful design patterns exist where a **partial implementation** class, derived from a **pure abstract interface** (a.k.a. a **protocol**), con-

---

[1] A more robust solution along these same lines is anticipated for a future release of the C++ Language Standard and will be addressed in **lakos23**.

tains data, constructors, and pure virtual functions.[2] Such inheritance, known as **implementation inheritance**, is decidedly distinct from pure **interface inheritance**, which is often the preferred design pattern in practice.[3] As an example, consider a base class, `NetworkDataStream`, that allows overriding its virtual functions for processing a stream of data from an expanding variety of arbitrary sources over the network:

```
class NetworkDataStream
{
private:
    // ...                      (member data)

public:
    explicit NetworkDataStream(TCPConnection* tcpConnection);
    explicit NetworkDataStream(UDPConnection* udpConnection);
    explicit NetworkDataStream(RawDataStreamHandle* rawDataStreamHandle);

    virtual ~NetworkDataStream();

    virtual void onPacketReceived(DataPacket& dataPacket) = 0;
        // Derived classes must override this method.
};
```

The `NetworkDataStream` class above provides three constructors, with more under development, that can be used assuming no per-packet processing is required. Now, imagine the need for logging information about received packets (e.g., for auditing purposes). Inheriting constructors make deriving from `NetworkDataStream` and overriding (see Section 1.1. "**override**" on page 104) `onPacketReceived(DataPacket&)` more convenient because we don't need to reimplement each of the constructors, which are anticipated to increase in number over time:

```
class LoggedNetworkDataStream : public NetworkDataStream
{
public:
    using NetworkDataStream::NetworkDataStream;

    void onPacketReceived(DataPacket& dataPacket) override
    {
        LOG_TRACE << "Received packet " << dataPacket;      // local log facility
        NetworkDataStream::onPacketReceived(dataPacket);    // Delegate to base.
    }
};
```

Implementing a strong typedef

Classic **typedef** declarations — just like C++11 **using** declarations (see Section 1.1. "**using** Aliases" on page 133) — are just synonyms; they offer absolutely no additional type safety

---

[2]A discussion of this topic is planned for **lakos2a**, section 4.7.
[3]A discussion of this topic is planned for **lakos2b**, section 4.6.

over using the original type name. A commonly desired capability is to provide an alias to an existing type T that is uniquely interoperable with itself, explicitly convertible from T, but not implicitly convertible from T. This somewhat *more* type-safe form of alias is sometimes referred to as a **strong typedef**. A typical implementation of a **strong typedef** suppresses implicit conversions both from the new type to the type it wraps and vice versa via **explicit** converting constructors and **explicit** conversion operators. In this respect, the relationship of **strong typedef** with the type it wraps is analogous to that of a scoped enumeration (**enum class**) to its **underlying type**; see Section 2.1."Underlying Type '11" on page 829.

As a practical example, suppose we are exposing, to a fairly wide and varied audience, a class, PatientInfo, that associates two Date objects to a given hospital patient:

```cpp
class Date
{
    // ...

public:
    Date(int year, int month, int day);

    // ...
};

class PatientInfo
{
private:
    Date d_birthday;
    Date d_appointment;

public:
    PatientInfo(Date birthday, Date appointment);
        // Please pass the birthday as the first date and the appointment as
        // the second one!
};
```

For the sake of argument, imagine that our users are not as diligent as they should be in reading documentation to know which constructor argument is which:

```cpp
PatientInfo client1(Date birthday, Date appointment)
{
    return PatientInfo(birthday, appointment);  // OK
}

int client2(PatientInfo* result, Date birthday, Date appointment)
{
    *result = PatientInfo(appointment, birthday);  // Oops! wrong order
    return 0;
}
```

Now suppose that we continue to get complaints, from folks like `client2` in the example above, that our code doesn't work. What can we do?

Although this example is presented lightheartedly, misuse by clients is a perennial problem in large-scale software organizations. Choosing the same type for both arguments might well be the right choice in some environments but not in others. We are not advocating use of this technique; we are merely acknowledging that it exists.

One way is to force clients to make a conscious and explicit decision in their own source code as to which `Date` is the birthday and which is the appointment. Employing a **strong typedef** can help us to achieve this goal. Inheriting constructors provide a concise way to define a **strong typedef**; for the example above, they can be used to define two new types to uniquely represent a birthday and an appointment date:

```cpp
struct Birthday : Date  // somewhat type-safe alias for a Date
{
    using Date::Date;  // Inherit Date's three integer ctor.
    explicit Birthday(Date d) : Date(d) { }  // explicit conversion from Date
};

struct Appointment : Date  // somewhat type-safe alias for a Date
{
    using Date::Date;  // Inherit Date's three integer ctor.
    explicit Appointment(Date d) : Date(d) { }  // explicit conv. from Date
};
```

The `Birthday` and `Appointment` types expose the same interface of `Date`, yet, given our inheritance-based design, `Date` is not implicitly convertible to either. Most importantly, however, these two new types are not implicitly convertible to each other:

```cpp
Birthday b0(1994, 10, 4);  // OK, thanks to inheriting constructors
Date d0 = b0;              // OK, thanks to public inheritance
Birthday b1 = d0;          // Error, no implicit conversion from Date
Appointment a0;            // Error, Appointment has no default ctor.
Appointment a1 = b0;       // Error, no implicit conversion from Birthday
Birthday n2(d0);           // OK, thanks to an explicit constructor in Birthday
Appointment a2(1999, 9, 17); // OK, thanks to inheriting constructors
Birthday    b3(a2);        // OK, an Appointment (unfortunately) is a Date.
```

We can now reimagine a `PatientInfo` class that exploits this newfound (albeit artificially manufactured) type-safety:

```cpp
class PatientInfo
{
private:
    Birthday d_birthday;
    Appointment d_appointment;
```

```
public:
    PatientInfo(Birthday birthday, Appointment appointment);
        // Please pass the birthday as the first argument and the appointment as
        // the second one!
};
```

Now our clients have no choice but to make their intentions clear at the call site. The previous implementation of the client functions no longer compile:

```
PatientInfo client1(Date birthday, Date appointment)
{
    return PatientInfo(birthday, appointment);      // Error, doesn't compile
}

int client2(PatientInfo* result, Date birthday, Date appointment)
{
    *result = PatientInfo(appointment, birthday);  // Error, doesn't compile
    return 0;
}
```

Because the clients now need to explicitly convert their `Date` objects to the appropriate strong **typedef**s, it is easy to spot and fix the defect in `client2`:

```
PatientInfo client1(Date birthday, Date appointment)
{
    return PatientInfo(Birthday(birthday), Appointment(appointment));  // OK
}

int client2(PatientInfo* result, Date birthday, Date appointment)
{
    Birthday b(birthday);
    Appointment a(appointment);
    *result = PatientInfo(b, a);  // OK
}
```

In this example, the client functions failed to compile after the introduction of the strong **typedef**s, which is the intended effect. However, if `Date` objects were *implicitly* constructed when client functions created `PatientInfo`, the defective code would continue to compile because both strong **typedef**s can be implicitly constructed from the same arguments; see *Potential Pitfalls — Inheriting* implicit *constructors* on page 546.

Replicating types that have identical behavior in the name of type safety can run afoul of interoperability. Distinct types that are otherwise physically similar are often most appropriate when their respective behaviors are inherently distinct and unlikely to interact in practice (e.g., a `CartesianPoint` and a `RationalNumber`, each implemented as having two integral data members).[4]

---

[4]A discussion of this topic is planned for **lakos2a**, section 4.4.

Incorporating reusable functionality via a mix-in

Some classes are designed to generically enhance the behavior of a class just by inheriting from it; such classes are sometimes referred to as *mix-ins*. If we want to adapt a class to support the additional behavior of the mix-in, with no other change to its behavior, we can use simple **structural inheritance** (e.g., to preserve reference compatibility through function calls). To preserve the public interface, however, we will need it to inherit the constructors as well.

Consider, for example, a simple class to track the total number of objects created:

```
template <typename T>
struct CounterImpl  // mix-in used to augment implementation of arbitrary type
{
    static int s_constructed;  // count of the number of T objects constructed

    CounterImpl()                     { ++s_constructed; }
    CounterImpl(const CounterImpl&) { ++s_constructed; }
};

template <typename T>
int CounterImpl<T>::s_constructed;  // required member definition
```

The class template `CounterImpl`, in the example above, counts the number of times an object of type `T` was constructed during a run of the program. We can then write a generic adapter, `Counted`, to facilitate use of `CounterImpl` as a *mix-in*:

```
template <typename T>
struct Counted : T, CounterImpl<T>
{
    using T::T;
};
```

Note that the `Counted` adapter class inherits all of the constructors of the *dependent* class, `T`, that it wraps, without its having to know what those constructors are:

```
#include <string>   // std::string
#include <vector>   // std::vector
#include <myfoo.h>  // MyFoo

Counted<std::string>        cs ("ABC");   // Construct a counted string.
Counted<std::vector<char>> cvc(3, 'a'); // Construct a counted vector of char.
Counted<MyFoo>              cmf;          // Construct a counted MyFoo object.
```

While inheriting constructors are a convenience in nongeneric programming, they can be an essential tool for generic idioms.

Potential Pitfalls

Newly introduced constructors in the base class can silently alter program behavior

The introduction of a new constructor in a base class might silently change a program's run-time behavior if that constructor happens to be a better match during overload resolution of an existing instantiation of a derived class. Consider a `Session` class that initially provides only two constructors:

```
struct Session
{
    Session();
    explicit Session(RawSessionHandle* rawSessionHandle);
};
```

Now, imagine that a class, `AuthenticatedSession`, derived from `Session`, inherits the two constructors of its base class and provides its own constructor that accepts an integral authentication token:

```
struct AuthenticatedSession : Session
{
    using Session::Session;
    explicit AuthenticatedSession(long long authToken);
};
```

Finally, consider an instantiation of `AuthenticatedSession` in user-facing code:

```
AuthenticatedSession authSession(45100);
```

In the example above, `authSession` will be initialized by invoking the constructor accepting a **long long** (see Section 1.1."**long long**" on page 89) authentication token. If, however, a new constructor having the signature `Session(int fd)` is added to the base class, it will be invoked instead because it is a better match to the literal `45100` (of type `int`) than the constructor taking a **long long** supplied explicitly in the derived class; hence, adding a constructor to a base class might lead to a potential latent defect that would go unreported at compile time.

Note that this problem with implicit conversions for function parameters is not unique to inheriting constructors; any form of **using** declaration or invocation of an overloaded function carries a similar risk. Imposing stronger typing — e.g., by using strong **typedef**s (see *Use Cases — Implementing a strong typedef* on page 541) — might sometimes, however, help to prevent such unfortunate missteps.

Inheriting *implicit* constructors

Inheriting from a class that has implicit constructors can cause surprises. Consider again using inheriting constructors to implement a strong **typedef** from *Use Cases — Implement-*

*ing a strong **typedef*** on page 541. This time, however, let's suppose we are exposing a class, `PointOfInterest`, that associates the name and address of a given popular tourist attraction:

```
#include <string>  // std::string

class PointOfInterest
{
private:
    std::string d_name;
    std::string d_address;

public:
    PointOfInterest(const std::string& name, const std::string& address);
        // Please pass the name as the *first* and the address *second*!
};
```

Again imagine that our users are not always careful about inspecting the function prototype:

```
PointOfInterest client1(const std::string& name, const std::string& address)
{
    return PointOfInterest(name, address);  // OK
}

int client2(PointOfInterest*   result,
            const std::string& name,
            const std::string& address)
{
    *result = PointOfInterest(address, name);  // Oops! wrong order
    return 0;
}
```

We might think to again use strong **typedefs** here as we did for `PatientInfo` in *Use Cases — Implementing a strong **typedef*** on page 541:

```
struct Name : std::string  // somewhat type-safe alias for an std::string
{
    using std::string::string;  // Inherit, as is, all of std::string's ctors.
    explicit Name(const std::string& s) : std::string(s) { }  // conversion
};

struct Address : std::string  // somewhat type-safe alias for an std::string
{
    using std::string::string;  // Inherit, as is, all of std::string's ctors.
    explicit Address(const std::string& s) : std::string(s) { }  // conversion
};
```

The `Name` and `Address` types are not interconvertible; they expose the same interfaces as `std::string` but are not implicitly convertible from it:

```
Name n0 = "Big Tower";   // OK, thanks to inheriting constructors
std::string s0 = n0;     // OK, thanks to public inheritance
Name n1 = s0;            // Error, no implicit conversion from std::string
Address a0;              // OK, unfortunately an std::string has a default ctor.
Address a1 = n0;         // Error, no implicit conversion from Name
Name n2(s0);             // OK, thanks to an explicit constructor in Name
Name b3(a0);             // OK, an Address (unfortunately) is an std::string.
```

We can rework the `PointOfInterest` class to use the **strong typedef** idiom:

```
class PointOfInterest
{
private:
    Name    d_name;
    Address d_address;

public:
    PointOfInterest(const Name& name, const Address& address);
};
```

Now if our clients use the base class itself as a parameter, they will again need to make their intentions known:

```
PointOfInterest client1(const std::string& name, const std::string& address)
{
    return PointOfInterest(Name(name), Address(address));
}


int client2(PointOfInterest*   result,
            const std::string& name,
            const std::string& address)
{
   *result = PointOfInterest(Name(name), Address(address)); // Fix forced.
    return 0;
}
```

But suppose that some clients pass the arguments by **const char*** instead of **const** std::string&:

```
PointOfInterest client3(const char* name, const char* address)
{
    return PointOfInterest(address, name);  // Bug, compiles but runtime error
}
```

In the case of `client3` in the code snippet above, passing the arguments through *does* compile because the **const char*** constructors are inherited; hence, there is no attempt to convert to an `std::string` before matching the *implicit* conversion constructor. Had the `std::string` conversion constructor been declared to be **explicit**, the code would not have compiled. In short, inheriting constructors from types that perform implicit conversions can seriously undermine the effectiveness of the strong **typedef** idiom.

Annoyances

Inherited constructors cannot be selected individually

The inheriting-constructors feature does not allow the programmer to select a subset of constructors to inherit; all of the base class's eligible constructors are always inherited unless a constructor with the same signature is provided in the derived class. If the programmer desires to inherit all constructors of a base class except for perhaps one or two, the straightforward workaround would be to declare the undesired constructors in the derived class and then use deleted functions (see Section 1.1."Deleted Functions" on page 53) to explicitly exclude them.

For example, suppose we have a general class, Datum, that can be constructed from a variety of types:

```
struct Datum
{
    Datum(bool);
    Datum(char);
    Datum(short);
    Datum(int);
    Datum(long);
    Datum(long long);
};
```

If we wanted to create a version of Datum, call it NumericalDatum, that inherits all but the one constructor taking a **bool**, our derived class would (1) inherit publicly, (2) declare the unwanted constructor, and then (3) mark it with =**delete**:

```
struct NumericalDatum : Datum
{
    using Datum::Datum;              // Inherit all the constructors
    NumericalDatum(bool) = delete;  // except the one taking a bool.
};
```

Note that the subsequent addition of any non-numerical constructor to Datum (e.g., a constructor taking std::string) would defeat the purpose of NumericalDatum unless that inherited constructor were explicitly excluded from NumericalDataum by use of =**delete**.

Access levels of inherited constructors are the same as in base class

Unlike base-class member functions that can be introduced with a **using** directive with an arbitrary access level into the derived class (as long as they are accessible by the derived class), the access level of the **using** declaration for inherited constructors is ignored. The inherited constructor overload is instead accessible *if* the corresponding base-class constructor would be accessible:

```
struct Base
{
private:
    Base(int) { }  // This constructor is declared private in the base class.
    void pvt0() { }
    void pvt1() { }

public:
    Base() { }     // This constructor is declared public in the base class.
    void pub0() { }
    void pub1() { }
};
```

Note that, when employing **using** to (1) inherit constructors or (2) elevate base-class definitions in the presence of private inheritance, public clients of the class might find it necessary to look at what are ostensibly private implementation details of the derived class to make proper use of that type through its public interface:

```
struct Derived5 : private Base
{
    using Base::Base;  // OK, inherited Base() as public constructor
                       // and Base(int) as private constructor

private:
    using Base::pub0;  // OK, pub0 is declared private in derived class.
    using Base::pvt0;  // Error, pvt0 was declared private in base class.

public:
    using Base::pub1;  // OK, pub1 is declared public in derived class.
    using Base::pvt1;  // Error, pvt1 was declared private in base class.
};

void client()
{
    Derived x(0);  // Error, Constructor was declared private in base class.
    Derived d;     // OK, constructor was declared public in base class.
    d.pub0();      // Error, pub0 was declared private in derived class.
    d.pub1();      // OK, pub1 was declared public in derived class.
    d.pvt0();      // Error, pvt0 was declared private in base class.
    d.pvt1();      // Error, pvt1 was declared private in base class.
}
```

---

[5] Alisdair Meredith, one of the authors of the Standards paper that proposed this feature (**meredith08**), suggests that placing the **using** declaration for inheriting constructors as the first member declaration and preceding any access specifiers might be the least confusing location. Programmers might still be confused by the disparate default access levels of **class** versus **struct**.

This C++11 feature was itself created because the previously proposed solution — which also involved a couple of features new in C++11, namely, forwarding the arguments to base-class constructors with forwarding references (see Section 2.1."Forwarding References" on page 377) and variadic templates (see Section 2.1."Variadic Templates" on page 873) — made somewhat different trade-offs and was considered too onerous and fragile to be practically useful:

```cpp
#include <utility>  // std::forward

struct Base
{
    Base(int) { }
};

struct Derived : private Base
{
protected:
    template <typename... Args>
    Derived(Args&&... args) : Base(std::forward<Args>(args)...)
    {
    }
};
```

In the example above, we have used forwarding references (see Section 2.1."Forwarding References" on page 377) to properly delegate the implementation of a constructor that is declared **protected** in the derived class to a **public** constructor of a privately inherited base class. Although this approach fails to preserve many of the characteristics of the inheriting constructors (e.g., **explicit**, **constexpr**, **noexcept**, and so on), the functionality described in the code snippet above is simply not possible using the C++11 inheriting-constructors feature.

Flawed initial specification led to diverging early implementations

The original specification of inheriting constructors in C++11 had a significant number of problems with general use.[6] As originally specified, inherited constructors were treated as if they were redeclared in the derived class. For C++17, a significant rewording of this feature[7] happened to instead find the base class constructors and then define how they are used to construct an instance of the derived class, as we have presented here. With a final fix in C++20 with the resolution of CWG issue 2356,[8] a complete working feature was specified. All of these fixes for C++17 were accepted as **defect reports** and thus apply retroactively

---

[6]For the detailed analysis of the issues that were the consequence of the flawed initial C++11 specification of inheriting constructors, see emcpps.com.

[7]**smith15b**

[8]CWG issue 2356; **smith18**

to C++11 and C++14. For the major compilers, applying this **defect report** was either standardizing already existing practice or quickly adopting the changes.[9]

See Also

- "Defaulted Functions" (§1.1, p. 33) explains how defaulted functions are used to implement functions that might otherwise have been suppressed by inherited constructors.

- "Delegating Ctors" (§1.1, p. 46) discusses how delegating constructors are used to call one constructor from another from within the same user-defined type.

- "Deleted Functions" (§1.1, p. 53) describes how deleted functions can be used to exclude inherited constructors that are unwanted entirely.

- "**override**" (§1.1, p. 104) explains how **override** can be used to ensure that a member function intended to override a virtual function actually does so.

- "Default Member Init" (§2.1, p. 318) discusses how defaulted member initializers can be used to provide nondefault values for data members in derived classes that make use of inheriting constructors.

- "Forwarding References" (§2.1, p. 377) describes how forwarding references are used as an alternative (workaround) when access levels differ from those for base-class constructors.

- "Variadic Templates" (§2.1, p. 873) explains how variadic templates are used as an alternative (workaround) when access levels differ from those for base-class constructors.

---

[9] For example, GCC 7.0 (c. 2017) and later and Clang 4.0 (c. 2017) and later all have the modern behavior fully implemented regardless of which standard version is chosen when compiling.

List Initialization: `std::initializer_list<T>`

The C++ Standard Library's `std::initializer_list` class template supports lightweight, compiler-generated arrays of nonmodifiable values that are initialized in source code similarly to built-in, C-style arrays using the generalized braced initialization syntax.

Description

C++, and C before it, allows built-in arrays to be initialized via brace-enclosed lists of values:

```cpp
int data[] = { 0, 1, 1, 2, 3, 5, 8, 13 }; // initializer list of 8 int values
```

C++11 extends this concept to allow such lists of values to be provided to **user-defined types (UDTs)** in a variety of circumstances. The compiler arranges for the values to be stored in an unnamed C-style array of **const** elements and provides access to that array via an object of type `std::initializer_list` instantiated on the element type. This object is a *lightweight* proxy to the elements of the array that provides a familiar API to both iterate over the elements of the array and query its size. Note that copying the `std::initializer_list` object does not copy the array elements. The C++ Standard provides a reference definition that comprises **typedef**s, accessors, and an explicitly declared default constructor, along with implicit definitions of the other five **special member functions**; see Section 1.1."Defaulted Functions" on page 33:

```cpp
namespace std
{

template <typename E>
class initializer_list  // illustration of programmer-accessible interface
{

public:
    typedef E value_type;              // C++ type of each array element
    typedef const E& reference;        // There is no nonconst reference.
    typedef const E& const_reference;  // const lvalue reference type
    typedef size_t size_type;          // type returned by size()

    typedef const E* iterator;         // There is no nonconst iterator.
    typedef const E* const_iterator;   // const element-iterator type

    constexpr initializer_list() noexcept;  // default constructor

    constexpr size_t size() const noexcept;       // number of elements
    constexpr const E* begin() const noexcept;    // beginning iterator
    constexpr const E* end() const noexcept;      // one-past-the-last iterator
};
```

```
// initializer list range access
template <typename E> constexpr const E* begin(initializer_list<E> il) noexcept;
template <typename E> constexpr const E* end(initializer_list<E> il) noexcept;

} // close std namespace
```

The code example above illustrates the public functionality available for direct use by the compiler and programmers alike and elides the private machinery used by the compiler to initialize objects other than an empty initializer list. Objects of this template, instantiated for element type E, act as lightweight proxies for compiler-supplied arrays. When these proxy objects are copied or assigned, they do not copy the elements of their underlying array. Note that std::initializer_list satisfies the Standard Library requirements of a range with random access iterators.

The public interface of the std::initializer_list class template, in the code example above, also employs two other C++11 language features: **constexpr** and **noexcept**. The **constexpr** keyword allows the compiler to consider using a function so decorated as part of a **constant expression**; see Section 2.1.“**constexpr** Functions” on page 257. The **noexcept** specifier indicates that the function is not allowed to throw an exception; see Section 3.1. “**noexcept** Specifier” on page 1085.

As an introductory example, consider a function, printNumbers, that prints the elements of a given sequence of integers that is represented by its std::initializer_list<**int**> parameter, il:

```
#include <initializer_list>  // std::initializer_list
#include <iostream>          // std::cout

void printNumbers(std::initializer_list<int> il)  // prints given list of ints
{
    std::cout << "{";
    for (const int* ip = il.begin(); ip != il.end(); ++ip)  // classic for loop
    {
        std::cout << ' ' << *ip;  // output each element in given list of ints
    }
    std::cout << " } [size = " << il.size() << ']';
}
```

Using member functions begin and end, the printNumbers function in the code snippet above employs, for exposition purposes, the classic **for** loop to iterate through the supplied initializer list, printing each of the elements in turn to stdout, eventually followed by the size of the list. Note that il is passed by value rather than by **const** reference; this style of passing arguments is used purely as a matter of convention, because std::initializer_list is designed to be a small *trivial* type that many C++ implementations can optimize by efficiently passing such function arguments using CPU registers.

We can now write a test function to invoke this printNumbers function on a **braced-initializer** list; see Section 2.1.“Braced Init” on page 215:

```
void test()
{
    printNumbers({ 1, 2, 3, 4 });  // prints "{ 1 2 3 4 } [size = 4]"
}
```

In the test function above, the compiler transforms the braced-initializer list { 1, 2, 3, 4 } into a **temporary** unnamed C-style array of value of type **const int**, which is then passed via an std::initializer_list<int> to printNumbers for processing. While the std::initializer_list temporary does not own the temporary array, their lifetimes are the same, so there is no risk of a dangling reference.

Using the initializer_list class template

When an std::initializer_list is used, either by mentioning it explicitly or having it implicitly created by the compiler, the <initializer_list> header must be included — directly or indirectly — lest the program be ill formed:

```
std::initializer_list<int> x = { };   // Error, <initializer_list> not included
void f(std::initializer_list<int>);   // Error,        "         "   "       "
auto il1a = {1, 2, 3};                // Error,        "         "   "       "
auto il2a = { };                      // Error,        "         "   "       "
auto il3a = {1};                      // Error,        "         "   "       "
auto il4a{1, 2, 3};                   // Error, direct-list-init deduction fails.
auto il5a{ };                         // Error, direct-list-init deduction fails.
auto il6a{1};                         // OK, but direct-list-init deduces int.

#include <initializer_list>           // Provide std::initializer_list.

std::initializer_list<int> y = { };   // OK
void g(std::initializer_list<int>);   // OK
auto il1b = {1, 2, 3};                // OK, std::initializer_list<int>
auto il2b = { };                      // Error, cannot deduce element type
auto il3b = {1};                      // OK, std::initializer_list<int>
auto il4b{1, 2, 3};                   // Error, direct-list-init deduction fails.
auto il5b{ };                         // Error, direct-list-init deduction fails.
auto il6b{1};                         // OK, but direct-list-init deduces int.
```

In the example code above, any explicit or implicit use of the std::initializer_list requires the compiler to have first seen its definition — even when the type is deduced using **auto**; see Section 2.1."**auto** Variables" on page 195. Note, in particular, that std::initializer_list is not deduced when **direct-list initialization** rather than **copy-list initialization** is used. Instead, **auto** deduces the element's type if the list contains a single element (il6a and il6b above) and fails to compile otherwise (il4a, il4b, il5a, and il5b above); see Section 2.1."Braced Init" on page 215.

For a given element type, E, the std::initializer_list<E> class defines several type aliases, similar to how they are defined for standard-library containers:

```
#include <initializer_list>  // std::initializer_list

struct E { };
std::initializer_list<E>::size_type       ts;        // ts  of type std::size_t
std::initializer_list<E>::value_type      tv;        // tv  of type E
std::initializer_list<E>::reference       tr  = tv;  // tr  of type const E&
std::initializer_list<E>::const_reference tcr = tv;  // tcr of type const E&
std::initializer_list<E>::iterator        ti;        // ti  of type const E*
std::initializer_list<E>::const_iterator  tci;       // tci of type const E*
```

Note that both `reference` and `iterator` are declared **const**, just as are `const_reference` and `const_iterator`.

Compiler vendors are permitted to — and often do — provide alternative types for such aliases in general-purpose containers — e.g., a debugging iterator to assist in detecting errors such as dereferencing a past-the-end iterator. In the case of `std::initializer_list`, however, these type aliases are fixed in the C++ Standard, so they cannot vary.

A public default constructor is provided, which enables clients to create empty initializer lists:

```
std::initializer_list<E> x;  // x is an empty list of elements of type E.
```

Each of the other special member functions, such as the copy constructor and copy assignment operator, is implicitly generated and available to clients:

```
std::initializer_list<E> y(x);    // copy construction
void assignEmpty() { y = x; }     // copy assignment
```

Note that there is no public constructor for creating an `std::initializer_list` in any other way; the intention is that `std::initializer_list` objects are created behind the scenes — *by the compiler* — from braced-initializer lists:

```
E e0, e1, e2, e3;
std::initializer_list<E> z = {e0, e1, e2, e3};
```

The `size()` **const** member function returns the number of elements referenced by an initializer list:

```
int nX = x.size();  // OK, nX == 0
int nY = y.size();  // OK, nY == 0
int nZ = z.size();  // OK, nZ == 4
```

Note that accessing the elements or even just the size of an `std::initializer_list` after the associated temporary array has expired has **undefined behavior**; see *Potential Pitfalls — Dangling references to temporary underlying arrays* on page 566.

All member functions of `std::initializer_list` are declared **constexpr**, and `std::initializer_list` is a **literal type** (see Section 2.1."**constexpr** Functions" on page 257). Hence, `std::initializer_list` can be used during evaluation of **constant** expressions — e.g., compile-time assertions (see Section 1.1.“**`static_assert`**” on page 115) and array bounds:

```
static_assert(std::initializer_list<int>({0, 1, 2, 3}).size() == 4, "");   // OK

int a[(std::initializer_list<int>({2, 1, 0}).size())];   // a is an array of 3 int.
```

Accessing the members of the underlying array of an `std::initializer_list<E>` is accomplished via iterators of type **`const E*`**: two **`constexpr const`** member functions, `begin()` and `end()`, return pointers to the first and the one-past-the-end array-element positions, respectively:

```
#include <cassert>    // standard C assert macro
#include <iostream>   // std::cout

void test1()
{
    std::initializer_list<char> list = {'A', 'B', 'C'};
    assert(*list.begin()   == 'A');                      // front element
    assert(list.begin()[0] == 'A');                      // element 0
    assert(list.begin()[1] == 'B');                      // element 1
    assert(list.begin()[2] == 'C');                      // element 2
    assert(list.begin() + 3          == list.end());     // true in this case
    assert(list.begin() + list.size() == list.end());    // always true
}
```

In the `test1` function in the code example above, `list.begin()` evaluates to the address of the first element of the underlying contiguous array, which is suitable for use with the built-in subscript operator, `[]`. For a nonempty `std::initializer_list`, `begin()` returns the address of the first element of the range, `end()` returns the address of the one-past-last element, and `size() == end() - begin()`. If `size() == 0`, however, addresses returned by `begin()` and `end()` have unspecified but equal values.

The presence of the `begin()` and `end()` member functions enable an `std::initializer_list` to be used as the source of a range-based **`for`** loop; see Section 2.1.“Range **`for`**” on page 679:

```
void test2()  // Print "10 20 30 " to stdout.
{
    std::initializer_list<int> il = { 10, 20, 30 };

    for (int i : il)
    {
        std::cout << i << ' ';
    }
}
```

Moreover, these member functions enable us to specify a braced-initializer list as the source range of a range-based **`for`** loop:

```
void test3()  // Print "100 200 300 " to stdout.
{
    for (int i : {100, 200, 300})
    {
        std::cout << i << ' ';
    }
}
```

Note that the use of a `temporary std::initializer_list`, as in the example above, is supported in a range-based **for** loop only because lifetime extension (i.e., via binding to a reference as opposed to copying) of this library object is magically tied by the language to a corresponding lifetime extension of the underlying array. Without lifetime extension, this **for** loop too would have been considered to have **undefined** behavior; again, see *Pointer semantics and lifetimes of temporaries* below.

Finally, corresponding global `std::begin` and `std::end` **free function** templates are overloaded for `std::initializer_list` objects directly in the `<initializer_list>` header, but see *Annoyances — Overloaded free-function templates begin and end are largely vestigial* on page 570.

Pointer semantics and lifetimes of temporaries

An instance of the `std::initializer_list` class template is a lightweight proxy for a homogeneous array of values. This type does not itself contain any data but instead refers to the data via the address of that data. For example, `std::initializer_list` might be implemented as a pair of pointers or a pointer and a length.

When a nonempty braced list is used to initialize an `std::initializer_list`, the compiler generates a temporary array having the same lifetime as other **temporary** objects created in the same expression. The `std::initializer_list` object itself has a special form of *pointer semantics* understood by the compiler, such that the lifetime of the temporary array will be extended to the lifetime of the `std::initializer_list` object for which the underlying array was created. Importantly, the lifetime of this underlying array is *never* extended by copying its proxy initializer-list object.

Consider an `std::initializer<int>` initialized with three values, 1, 2, and 3:

```
std::initializer_list<int> iL = {1, 2, 3};  // initializes il with 3 values
```

The compiler first creates a **temporary** array holding the three values. That array would normally be destroyed at the end of the outermost expression in which it appears, but initializing `il` to refer to this array extends its lifetime to be coterminous with `il`.

No such lifetime extension occurs under any other circumstances:

```
void assign3InitializerList()  // BAD IDEA
{
    iL = { 4, 5, 6, 7 };  // iL has dangling reference to a temporary array.
}
```

The temporary array created in the assignment expression above is not used to initialize iL, so that temporary array's lifetime is not extended; it will be destroyed at the end of the assignment expression, leaving iL having a dangling reference to an array that no longer exists; see *Potential Pitfalls — Dangling references to temporary underlying arrays* on page 566.

Initialization of `std::initializer_list<E>` objects

The underlying array of an `std::initializer_list<E>` is a **const** array of elements of type E, with length determined by the number of items in the braced list. Each element is copy initialized by the corresponding expression in the braced list, and if user-defined conversions are required, they *must* be accessible at the point of construction. Following the rules of copy list initialization, narrowing conversions and explicit conversions are ill formed; see Section 2.1."Braced Init" on page 215:

```
struct X { operator int() const; };
void f(std::initializer_list<int>);

void testCallF()
{
    f({ 1, '2', X() });  // OK, 1 is int.
                         //     '2' has a language-defined conversion to int.
                         //      X has a user-defined conversion to int.

    f({ 1, 2.0 });       // Error, 2.0 has a narrowing conversion to int.
}
```

Note that, since the initializer is a constant expression, narrowing conversions from integer literal constant expressions of a wider type are permitted, provided that they are lossless:

```
#include <initializer_list>  // std::initializer_list

constexpr long long lli = 13LL;
const     long long llj = 17LL;

void g(const long long arg)
{
    std::initializer_list<int> x = { 0LL };  // OK, integral constant
    std::initializer_list<int> y = { lli };  // OK, integral constant
    std::initializer_list<int> z = { llj };  // OK, integral constant
    std::initializer_list<int> w = { arg };  // Error, narrowing conversion
}
```

Type deduction of `initializer_list`

An `std::initializer_list` will not be deduced for a braced-initializer argument to a function template having an *unconstrained* template parameter, but a braced-initializer argument can be a match for a template parameter specifically declared as an std::initializer_list<E>. In such a case, the supplied list must not be empty, and the type deduced must be the same for each item of the list; otherwise, the program is ill formed.

```
#include <initializer_list> // std::initializer_list

void f(std::initializer_list<int>);
template <typename E> void g(std::initializer_list<E>);
template <typename E> void h(E);

void test()
{
    f({ });                 // OK, empty list of int requires no deduction.
    f({ 1, '2' });          // OK, all list initializers convert to int.

    g({ 1, 2, 3 });         // OK, std::initializer_list<int> deduced.
    g({ });                 // Error, cannot deduce an E from an empty list
    g({ 1, '2' });          // Error, different deduced types

    h({ 1, 2, 3 });         // Error, cannot deduce an std::initializer_list
}
```

Note that the problem with an empty std::initializer_list when calling g is entirely due to the inability to deduce the type of the parameter; there is no problem passing an empty std::initializer_list to f since no type deduction is required. Similarly, heterogeneous lists can be passed to a known instantiation of std::initializer_list as long as all supplied list elements are implicitly convertible to its element type.

Unlike an unconstrained template argument, an **auto** variable (see Section 2.1. "**auto** Variables" on page 195) will deduce an std::initializer_list in copy list initialization. However, to resolve potential ambiguity in favor of a copy constructor, direct list initialization of an **auto** variable requires a list of exactly one element and is deduced to be a copy of the same type:

```
#include <initializer_list> // std::initializer_list

auto a = {1, 2, 3}; // OK, a is std::initializer_list<int>.
auto b{1, 2, 3};    // Error, too many elements in list
auto c = {1};       // OK, c is std::initializer_list<int>.
auto d{1};          // OK, d is int.
auto e = {};        // Error, cannot deduce element type from empty list
auto f{};           // Error, cannot deduce variable type from empty list
```

Note that the declarations of b and d were interpreted differently in the original C++11 Standard to both be valid and deduce as std::initializer_list<int>. However, this behavior was changed in C++17 with N3922 and applied retroactively to previous standards as a **defect report**. Early C++11 compilers might still display the original behavior, although most compilers adopted the **defect report** before completing their C++14 implementation.

Overload resolution and `std::initializer_list`

When name lookup finds an overload set containing `std::initializer_list` parameters, the ranking rules now prefer to match braced lists to the `std::initializer_list` overloads rather than interpret them as other forms of list initialization, unless a default constructor would be selected; see Section 2.1."Braced Init" on page 215.

Use Cases

Convenient population of standard containers

The original design intent of `std::initializer_list` was to make initializing a container with a sequence of values as simple as initializing a built-in array:

```
#include <vector>  // std::vector

std::vector<int> v{1, 2, 3, 4, 5};
```

Note that because `std::vector` deliberately makes available this form of initialization, the `<vector>` header is required to transitively **#include** `<initializer_list>` so that the user does not need to. This transitive inclusion is the case for the header of any standard library container, which means we do not generally see explicit inclusion of the `<initializer_list>` header in application code, since most uses are through standard containers.

Similarly, the standard containers provide operators to assign from `std::initializer_list`, thereby obviating temporaries that would be passed to the move-assignment operator:

```
void test1()
{
    v = {2, 3, 5, 7, 11, 13, 17};
}
```

Finally, because `std::initializer_list` satisfies the requirements of a random access range, all container member function templates that take a pair of iterators to denote a range were overloaded to also accept an `std::initializer_list` of the corresponding type:

```
void test2()
{
    v.insert(v.end(), {23, 29, 31});
}
```

Note that since the rules for braced initialization are recursive, more complex containers can also use this syntax, which might be especially convenient for providing initial data to **const** objects:

```cpp
#include <map>     // std::map
#include <string>  // std::string

const std::map<std::string, int> m{{"a", 1}, {"b", 2}, {"c", 3}};
```

Providing support for braced lists in user code

Certain user-defined types support an intuitive notion of initialization via a homogeneous list of values of a specific type. For example, the C++ Standard Library supports initializing container types, such as **vector** or **map**, using braced initialization — an unambiguous API from which many clients will benefit. Consider how we might support such initialization for a class holding a dynamic array of **int**s, which, for exposition purposes, we will implement using an **std::vector**:

```cpp
class DynIntArray
{
    // DATA
    std::vector<int> d_data;

  public:
    DynIntArray(const DynIntArray&) = delete;
    DynIntArray& operator=(const DynIntArray&) = delete;

    // CREATORS
    DynIntArray() : d_data() {}
    DynIntArray(std::initializer_list<int> il) : d_data(il) {}

    // MANIPULATORS
    DynIntArray& operator=(std::initializer_list<int> il)
    {
        d_data = il;

        return *this;
    }

    DynIntArray& operator+=(std::initializer_list<int> il)
    {
        d_data.insert(d_data.end(), il);

        return *this;
    }

    void shrink(std::size_t newSize)
```

```
    {
        assert(newSize <= d_data.size());

        d_data.resize(newSize);
    }

    // ACCESSORS
    bool isEqual(std::initializer_list<int> rhs) const
    {
        // std::equal will produce highly optimized comparison code.
        return d_data.size() == rhs.size() &&
               std::equal(d_data.begin(), d_data.end(), rhs.begin());
    }
};

inline
bool operator==(const DynIntArray& lhs, std::initializer_list<int> rhs)
{
    return lhs.isEqual(rhs);
}

inline
bool operator!=(const DynIntArray& lhs, std::initializer_list<int> rhs)
{
    return !lhs.isEqual(rhs);
}
```

There are many opportunities to provide rich support for braced lists beyond just constructors and assignment operators. Let's exercise this class in **main**, highlighting its support for braced lists:

```
int main()
{
    DynIntArray x = { 1, 2, 3, 4, 5 };

    std::initializer_list<int> il = { 1, 2, 3, 4, 5 };

    assert(x == il);

    assert((x == { 1, 2, 3, 4, 5 }));    // Error, not an std::initializer_list
    assert((x != { 1, 2, 3 }));          // Error, not an std::initializer_list

    assert( x.isEqual({ 1, 2, 3, 4, 5 }));
    assert(!x.isEqual({ 1, 2, 3, 4, 6 }));
    assert(!x.isEqual({ 1, 2, 3, 4 }));
    assert(!x.isEqual({ }));

    x += { 6 };
```

```
        assert(x != il);
        assert( x.isEqual({ 1, 2, 3, 4, 5, 6 }));

        x.shrink(2);

        std::initializer_list<int> ilB = { 1, 2 };

        assert(!x.isEqual({ 1, 2, 3, 4, 5, 6 }));
        assert( x.isEqual({ 1, 2 }));
        assert( x.isEqual(ilB));
        assert(x == ilB);

        assert((x == { 1, 2 }));  // Error, not an std::initializer_list

        x += { 8, 9, 10 };

        assert(!x.isEqual({ 1, 2 }));
        assert( x.isEqual({ 1, 2, 8, 9, 10 }));
    }
```

Note that due to a quirk of the C++ grammar for certain operators, using *braced-init-list* as the right-hand side of the argument of an **operator**== does not implicitly deduce an *initializer-list*, even if the **operator**== takes an *initializer-list* as the parameter; see Section 2.1."Braced Init" on page 215.

Functions consuming a variable number of arguments of the same type

Suppose we want a function that takes an arbitrary number of arguments all of the same type. In our example, we write a function that concatenates a number of input strings together separated by commas:

```
#include <initializer_list> // std::initializer_list
#include <string>           // std::string

std::string concatenate(std::initializer_list<std::string> ils)
{
    std::string separator;
    std::string result;
    for (const std::string* p = ils.begin(); p != ils.end(); ++p)
    {
        result.append(separator);
        result.append(*p);
        separator = ",";
    }
    return result;
}

std::string hex_digits = concatenate({"A", "B", "C", "D", "E"});
```

An example from the C++ Standard Library would be the additional overload for `std::min` provided by C++11 to take a list of arguments:

```
#include <algorithm>          // std::min
#include <initializer_list>   // std::initializer_list

constexpr int n = std::min({3,2,7,5,-1,3,9});   // min is constexpr in C++14.
static_assert(n == -1, "Error: wrong value?!");
```

Iterating over a fixed number of objects

`std::initializer_list` was designed from the start to model a standard library range, which is the same set of requirements for a type to support the C++11 range-based **for** loop (see Section 2.1."Range **for**" on page 679). Range-based **for** loops acquire their meaning through a translation equivalence; it is instructive to examine that as an example of the synergy of several new language features. Suppose that the compiler encounters a range-based **for** loop having the following form:

```
for (declaration : { list }) statement
```

Such a loop would be translated as follows:

```
{
    auto &&__r = { list };
    for (auto __b = __r.begin(), __e = __r.end(); __b != __e; ++__b)
    {
        declaration = *__b;
        statement
    }
}
```

Note the use of **auto&&** to perfectly deduce the type and value category of the range, avoiding the creation of unnecessary temporary objects.

Thus, __r is deduced to be an `std::initializer_list<E>`. By the special rule for creating `std::initializer_list` objects directly from a braced list and the corresponding lifetime extension rules for the reference __r to the deduced `std::initializer_list`, the lifetime of the array is extended to the lifetime of __r, which also encompasses the lifetime of the loop. Ultimately, that lifetime extension makes things work as expected; the array exists while the loop is executing and is destroyed immediately after.

Now suppose we want to iterate over a fixed set of objects. Using initializer lists lets us avoid the tedious boilerplate of creating our own array of data for the iteration. In our example, we analyze a character string to see if it begins with one of the numeric base prefix indicators[1]:

---

[1]To avoid unnecessary string copies, the standard C++17 `std::string_view` facility could be used in place of `std::string` in the `hasBasePrefix` example.

```
bool hasBasePrefix(const std::string& number)
{
    if (number.size() < 2) { return false; }

    for (const char* prefix : {"0x", "0X", "0b", "0B"})
    {
        if (std::equal(prefix, prefix + 2, number.begin()))
        {
            return true;
        }
    }

    return false;
}
```

Note that this pattern might often be seen feeding values to a test driver.

Potential Pitfalls

Dangling references to temporary underlying arrays

Because `std::initializer_list` has pointer semantics, it has all the pitfalls associated
with regular pointers with respect to dangling references, i.e., referring to an object after its
lifetime has ended. These problems arise when the lifetime of an `std::initializer_list`
object is greater than the lifetime of its underlying array. As a simple example, the following
risks undefined behavior and does not work as the developer might expect:

```
void test()
{
    std::initializer_list<int> il;
    il = { 1, 2, 3 };  // BAD IDEA, bound to a temporary that is about to expire
}
```

In this example, the temporary array created for the brace-enclosed list does not have its
lifetime extended, because `il` is being assigned, not initialized. At best, the compiler will
warn us:

```
warning: assignment from temporary 'initializer_list' does not extend the lifetime
of the underlying array
```

Furthermore, caution is required when initializing variables of type `std::initializer_list`.
There are several ways one might try to initialize such a variable:

```
typedef std::initializer_list<int> Ili;
Ili iL0 = {1, 2, 3};   // OK, copy initialization (implicit ctors only)
Ili iL0ne {1, 2, 3};   // OK, direct    "       (even explicit ctors)
Ili iL1 = (1, 2, 3);   // Error, conversion from int to nonscalar requested
Ili iL1ne (1, 2, 3);   // Error, no matching function call for (int, int, int)
```

```
Ili jL2 = ({1, 2, 3});  // Error, illegal context for statement expression
Ili jL2ne ({1, 2, 3});  // Bug, direct initialization from a copy
Ili jL3 = ((1, 2, 3));  // Error, conversion from int to nonscalar requested
Ili jL3ne ((1, 2, 3));  // Error, no matching function call for (int)

Ili kL4 = {{1, 2, 3}};  // Error, conversion from brace-enclosed list requested
Ili kL4ne {{1, 2, 3}};  // Error,      "      "    "       "       "      "
Ili kL5 = {(1, 2, 3)};  // Bug, copy initialization to single-int  init list
Ili kL5ne {(1, 2, 3)};  // Bug, direct      "       "     "      "     "
```

As can be inferred from the code example above, the language treats direct and copy initialization of an `std::initializer_list` the same — i.e., as if the inaccessible constructor used by the compiler to populate an `std::initializer_list` is declared without the explicit keyword; see Section 2.1."Braced Init" on page 215. If the list of values is enclosed in parentheses instead of braces, the list will be interpreted as either the use of the comma operator (`iL1`, `jL3`, `jL3ne`, `kL5`, and `kL5ne` above) or a function call (`iL1ne` above). Furthermore, it is important to avoid creating unnecessary copies, such as for `jL2ne` above: If the copy is not elided by the compiler, `jL2ne` refers to an array whose lifetime has ended.[2]

Annoyances

Initializer lists must sometimes be homogeneous

Though an `std::initializer_list<E>` is clearly always homogeneous, the initializer list used to create it in many cases can be a heterogeneous list of initializers convertible to the common type `E`. When the value type `E` needs to be deduced, however, the braced list must strictly be homogeneous:

```
#include <initializer_list>  // std::initializer_list

void f(std::initializer_list<int>) {}

template <typename E>
void g(std::initializer_list<E>) {}

int main()
{
    f({1, '2', 3});  // OK, heterogeneous list converts
    g({1, '2', 3});  // Error, cannot deduce heterogeneous list
    g({1,  2 , 3});  // OK, homogeneous list

    auto x = {1, '2', 3};  // Error, cannot deduce heterogeneous list
    auto y = {1,  2 , 3};  // OK, homogeneous list
    std::initializer_list<int> z = {1, '2', 3};  // OK, converts
}
```

---

[2]In C++17, direct initialization of `std::initializer_list` from an implicitly created temporary `std::initializer_list` will always work due to guaranteed copy elision.

`std::initializer_list` constructor suppresses the implicitly declared default

The declaration of a constructor with an *initializer-list* argument will suppress the implicit declaration of a default constructor, as one would expect. Without a default constructor, the `std::initializer_list` constructor will be called when the object is initialized from an empty list but not in other circumstances where a default constructor might be called. If such a type is then used as the type of a subobject, it would result in an implicitly declared default constructor of the outer object being deleted. These rules can make initialization from a pair of empty braces a bit counterintuitive:

```cpp
#include <cassert>  // standard C assert macro
#include <vector>   // std::vector

struct X
{
    std::vector<int> d_v;

    X(std::initializer_list<int> il) : d_v(il) {}
};

struct Y
{
    long long d_data;

    Y() : d_data(-1) {}
    Y(std::initializer_list<int> il) : d_data(il.size()) {}
};

struct Z1 : X { };

struct Z2 : X
{
    Z2() = default;        // BAD IDEA, implicitly deleted
};

struct Z3 : X
{
    using X::X;
};

struct Z4
{
    X data;

    Z4() = default;
};
```

```
void demo()
{
    X a;                        // Error, no default constructor

    X b{};                      // OK
    assert(b.d_v.empty());

    X c = {};                   // OK
    assert(c.d_v.empty());

    X d = { 1, 2, 7 };    // OK
    assert(3 == d.d_v.size() && 7 == d.d_v.back());

    X ax[5];                    // Error, no default constructor
    X bx[5]{};                  // OK, initializes each element with {}
    X cx[5] = {};               // OK, initializes each element with {}

    Y e;                        // OK
    assert(-1 == e.d_data);

    Y f{};                      // OK, default constructor!
    assert(-1 == f.d_data);

    Y g = {};                   // OK, default constructor!
    assert(-1 == g.d_data);

    Y h({});                    // OK, using std::initializer_list
    assert(0  == h.d_data);

    Y i = { 7, 8, 9 };    // OK, using std::initializer_list
    assert(3  == i.d_data);

    Z1 j1{};        // Error, calls implicitly deleted default constructor
    Z2 j2{};        // Error, calls deleted default constructor
    Z3 j3{};        // Error, calls implicitly deleted default constructor
    Z4 j4{};        // OK, aggregate initialization, empty list for X

    Z1 k1 = {};     // Error, calls implicitly deleted default constructor
    Z2 k2 = {};     // Error, calls deleted default constructor
    Z3 k3 = {};     // Error, calls implicitly deleted default constructor
    Z4 k4 = {};     // OK, aggregate initialization, empty list for X

    Z1 m1 = {{}};   // Error, not an aggregate, no initializer_list constructor
    Z2 m2 = {{}};   // Error, not an aggregate, no initializer_list constructor
    Z3 m3 = {{}};   // OK, initializer_list constructor with one int
    Z4 m4 = {{}};   // OK, aggregate initialization, empty list for X
}
```

Note that most of the Z1, Z2, and Z3 examples are "OK" in C++17 as the definition of aggregate evolves. Some of those examples are errors again in C++20 as will all of the Z4 examples above because Z4 ceases to be an aggregate in C++20 due to the user-declared default constructor.

On the other hand, with regard to nondefault constructors, if a nonempty pair of braces is supplied, the *initializer-list* constructor is favored over all others; see Section 2.1."Braced Init" on page 215:

```
void test()
{
    std::vector<int> v{ 12, 3 };
    assert(2 == v.size() && v.front() == 12);
    std::vector<int> w( 12, 3 );
    assert(12 == w.size() && w.front() == 3);
}
```

Initializer lists represent const objects

The underlying array of an initializer list is **const**, so the objects in that list cannot be modified. In particular, it is not possible to *move* elements out of the lists that are typically consumed just once, despite their being temporaries.

```
#include <vector>   // std::vector

std::vector<std::vector<int>> v = {{1, 2, 3},
                                   {4, 5, 6},
                                   {7, 8},
                                   {9}};
```

In this example, the vector, v, is initialized by an *rvalue* that is an std::initializer_list comprising four temporary vectors, each allocating memory for their internal array. However, the constructor for v must again copy each vector, allocating a fresh copy of each array, rather than take advantage of move-related optimizations, since each temporary is effectively **const**-qualified.

Another consequence of the **const** nature of std::initializer_list renders them useless when instantiated on **move-only** types, such as std::unique_ptr.

Overloaded free-function templates begin and end are largely vestigial

The range-based **for** feature initially required the free functions begin and end; see *Appendix* on page 571 for why they are no longer needed. The begin and end free functions were already provided by the <iterator> header, but because the <initializer_list> header is **freestanding** unlike the <iterator> header, it was necessary to also add specific overloads to the <initializer_list> header. Historically, due to the perceived range-based **for** dependency, the aforementioned free functions in the `<iterator>` header were also added to many other headers, including those for all of the standard containers.

As subsequent editions of the Standard have added to the set of related, free function overloads (for example, `empty`, added in C++17), those additional overloads have been added to multiple headers so that idiomatic generic code does not need to include additional headers. However, due to the **freestanding** requirement, none of those additional overloads are available through the `<initializer_list>` header.

See Also

- "Braced Init" (§2.1, p. 215) provides further details regarding object initialization and construction using braced lists and `std::initializer_list`s.

Further Reading

- An overview of the myriad problems associated with initialization is presented in **stroustrup05a**.

- The original proposal to achieve a uniform initialization syntax based on initializer lists can be found in **stroustrup05b**.

- Andrzej Krzemieński details why and how `std::initializer_list` can incur insidious runtime overhead due to excessive copying in **krzemienski16**.

Appendix

A brief history of user customization to support range-based `for`

The original incarnation of the range-based **for** loop was built around the proposed **concepts** language feature. The range argument to the **for** loop would satisfy the range `concept`, which the user could customize with a `concept_map` to adapt third-party libraries that did not have `begin` and `end` member functions.

When concepts were pulled after the first ISO ballot, the committee did not want to lose range-based **for**, so a new scheme was invented: The compiler would look for `begin` and `end` free functions. The Standard Library would provide the primary template for these functions, and `#include <iterator>` would be required for the range-based **for** loop to work, much like `#include <typeinfo>` is required to enable the **typeid** operator. Suggestions were made — and rejected — that the core feature should look for the member functions (just like the template) before looking for the free functions as the last resort. To make the standard library easy to use, the primary template for the `begin` and `end` functions was added to every standard container header, to `<regex>`, to `<string>`, and would be added on an ongoing basis to any new headers for types representing a range.

The Core Working Group then met the original request, so that range-based **for** never uses the `<iterator>` templates but directly looks for member functions and, failing that, performs an **ADL** lookup to find **begin** and **end**. The need to scatter these templates in every header is gone, but that core language change was not communicated to the Library Working Group in time. The only reason these functions remain in so many headers today is backward compatibility from when they were redundantly specified in C++11.

While the **begin** and **end** free functions are never required to support the range-based **for** loop, subsequent evolution of the Standard Library has embraced these functions as a means of expressing generic code. When called in a context that supports ADL, arbitrary third-party types can be adapted to satisfy the requirements of a Standard Library range. Further overloads for constant and reverse iterators were added for C++14 and for a broader range of queries, such as **empty** and **size**, in C++17. Unfortunately, due to the way the Standard Library specification is drafted, all of these additional overloads are scattered across the same set of additional headers, despite being totally unrelated to the vanished motivation of supporting range-based **for**.

Anonymous Function Objects (Closures)

Lambda expressions provide a means of defining function objects at the point where they are needed, enabling a powerful and convenient way to specify callbacks or local functions.

Description

Generic, object-oriented, and functional programming paradigms all place great importance on the ability of a programmer to specify a *callback* that is passed as an argument to a function. For example, the Standard Library algorithm, `std::sort`, accepts a callback argument specifying the sort order:

```
#include <algorithm>    // std::sort
#include <functional>   // std::greater
#include <vector>       // std::vector

template <typename T>
void sortDescending(std::vector<T>& v)
{
    std::sort(v.begin(), v.end(), std::greater<T>());
}
```

The function object, `std::greater<T>()`, is callable with two arguments of type `T` and returns **true** if the first is greater than the second and **false** otherwise. The Standard Library provides a small number of similar **functor types**, but, for more complicated cases, programmers must write a **functor** themselves. If a container holds a sequence of `Employee` records, for example, we might want to sort the container by either name or salary:

```
#include <string>  // std::string
#include <vector>  // std::vector

struct Employee
{
    std::string name;
    long        salary;  // in whole dollars
};

void sortByName(std::vector<Employee>& employees);
void sortBySalary(std::vector<Employee>& employees);
```

The implementation of `sortByName` can delegate the sorting task to the standard algorithm, `std::sort`. However, to achieve sorting by the desired criterion, we will need to supply `std::sort` with a callback that compares the names of two `Employee` objects. We can implement this callback as a pointer to a simple function that we pass to `std::sort`:

```
#include <algorithm>  // std::sort

bool nameLt(const Employee& e1, const Employee& e2)
    // returns true if e1.name is less than e2.name
{
    return e1.name < e2.name;
}

void sortByName(std::vector<Employee>& employees)
{
    std::sort(employees.begin(), employees.end(), &nameLt);
}
```

The `sortBySalary` function can similarly delegate to `std::sort`. For illustrative purposes, we will use a **function object** (i.e., `functor`) rather than a function pointer as the callback to compare the salaries of two `Employee` objects. Every **functor class** must provide a **call operator** (i.e., **operator()**), which, in this case, compares the salary fields of its arguments:

```
struct SalaryLt
{
    // functor whose call operator compares two Employee objects and returns
    // true if the first has a lower salary than the second, false otherwise

    bool operator()(const Employee& e1, const Employee& e2) const
    {
        return e1.salary < e2.salary;
    }
};

void sortBySalary(std::vector<Employee>& employees)
{
    std::sort(employees.begin(), employees.end(), SalaryLt());
}
```

Although it is a bit more verbose, a call through the function object is easier for the compiler to analyze and automatically inline within `std::sort` than is a call through the function pointer. Function objects are also more flexible because they can carry state, as we'll see shortly. Furthermore, if a function object is stateless, it is cheaper to pass around than a function pointer because nothing needs to be copied. The sorting example illustrates how small bits of a function's logic must be factored out into special-purpose auxiliary functions or functor classes that are often not reusable. It is possible, for example, that the `nameLt` function and `SalaryLt` class are not used anywhere else in the program.

When callbacks are tuned to the specific context in which they are used, they become both more complicated and less reusable. Let's say, for example, that we want to count the number of employees whose salary is above the average for the collection. Using Standard

Library algorithms, this task seems trivial: (1) sum all of the salaries using `std::accumulate`, (2) calculate the average salary by dividing this sum by the total number of employees, and (3) count the number of employees with above-average salaries using `std::count_if`. Unfortunately, both `std::accumulate` and `std::count_if` require callbacks to return the salary for an `Employee` and to supply the criterion for counting, respectively. The callback for `std::accumulate` must take two parameters — the current running sum and an element from the sequence being summed — and must return the new running sum:

```
struct SalaryAccumulator
{
    long operator()(long currSum, const Employee& e) const
        // returns the sum of currSum and the salary field of e
    {
        return currSum + e.salary;
    }
};
```

The callback for `std::count_if` is a **predicate** (i.e., an expression that yields a Boolean result in response to a yes-or-no question) that takes a single argument and returns **true** if an element having that value should be counted and **false** otherwise. In this case, we are concerned with `Employee` objects having salaries above the average. Our **predicate functor** must, therefore, carry around that average so it can compare the average to the salary of the employee that is supplied as an argument:

```
class SalaryIsGreater  // function object constructed with a threshold salary
{
    const long d_thresholdSalary;

public:
    explicit SalaryIsGreater(long ts) : d_thresholdSalary(ts) { }
        // construct with a threshold salary, ts

    bool operator()(const Employee& e) const
        // return true if the salary for Employee e is greater than the
        // threshold salary supplied on construction, false otherwise
    {
        return e.salary > d_thresholdSalary;
    }
};
```

Note that, unlike our previous functor classes, `SalaryIsGreater` has a member variable; i.e., it has *state*. This member variable must be initialized, necessitating a constructor. The call operator compares its input argument against this member variable to compute the predicate value.

With these two functor classes defined, we can finally implement the simple three-step algorithm for determining the number of employees with salaries greater than the average:

```
#include <algorithm>  // std::count_if
#include <numeric>    // std::accumulate

std::size_t numAboveAverageSalaries(const std::vector<Employee>& employees)
{
    const long sum = std::accumulate(employees.begin(), employees.end(), 0L,
                                     SalaryAccumulator());

    const long average = sum / employees.size();
    return std::count_if(employees.begin(), employees.end(),
                         SalaryIsGreater(average));
}
```

We now turn our attention to a syntax that allows us to rewrite these examples much more simply and compactly. Returning to the sorting example, the rewritten code has the name-comparison and salary-comparison operations expressed in place, within the call to std::sort:

```
void sortByName2(std::vector<Employee>& employees)
{
    std::sort(employees.begin(), employees.end(),
              [](const Employee& e1, const Employee& e2)
              {
                  return e1.name < e2.name;
              });
}

void sortBySalary2(std::vector<Employee>& employees)
{
    std::sort(employees.begin(), employees.end(),
              [](const Employee& e1, const Employee& e2)
              {
                  return e1.salary < e2.salary;
              });
}
```

In each case, the third argument to std::sort — beginning with [] and ending with the nearest closing } — is called a **lambda expression**. Intuitively, for this case, one can think of a lambda expression as an *operation* that can be invoked as a callback by the algorithm. The example shows a function-style parameter list — matching that expected by the std::sort algorithm — and a function-like body that computes the needed predicate. Using lambda expressions, a developer can express a desired operation directly at the point of use rather than defining it elsewhere in the program.

The compactness and simplicity afforded by using **lambda expressions** is even more evident when we rewrite the average-salaries example:

```
std::size_t numAboveAverageSalaries2(const std::vector<Employee>& employees)
```

```
{
    if (employees.empty()) { return 0; }
    const long sum = std::accumulate(employees.begin(), employees.end(), 0L,
                            [](long currSum, const Employee& e)
                            {
                                return currSum + e.salary;
                            });

    const long average = sum / employees.size();
    return std::count_if(employees.begin(), employees.end(),
                    [average](const Employee& e)
                    {
                        return e.salary > average;
                    });
}
```

The first lambda expression, above, specifies the operation for adding another salary to a running sum. The second lambda expression returns true if the Employee argument, e, has a salary that is larger than **average**, which is a local variable *captured* by the lambda expression. A lambda capture is a set of local variables that are usable within the body of the lambda expression, effectively making the lambda expression an extension of the immediate environment. We will look at the syntax and semantics of lambda captures in more detail in the next section, *Parts of a lambda expression*, below.

Note that the lambda expressions replaced a significant portion of code that was previously expressed as separate functions or functor classes. Some of that code reduction is in the form of documentation (comments), which increases the appeal of lambda expressions to a surprising degree. Creating a named entity such as a function or class imposes on the developer the responsibility to give that entity a meaningful name and sufficient documentation for a future human reader to understand its *abstract* purpose, outside the context of its use, even for one-off, nonreusable entities. Conversely, when an entity is defined right at the point of use, it might not need a name at all, and it is often self-documenting, as in both the sorting and average-salaries examples above. Both the original creation and maintenance of the code are simplified.

Parts of a lambda expression

A lambda expression has a number of parts and subparts, many of which are optional. For exposition purposes, let's look at a sample lambda expression that contains all of the parts:

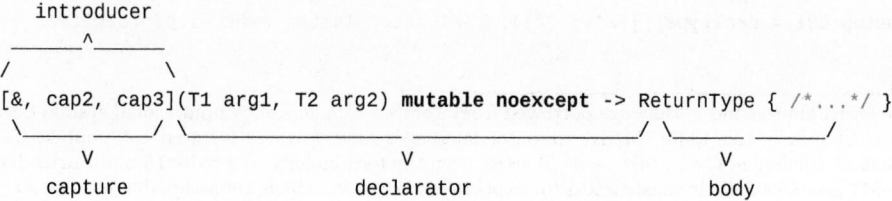

Evaluating a lambda expression creates a temporary **closure** object of an unnamed type called the **closure type**. Each part of a lambda expression is described in detail in the subsections below.

Closures

A lambda expression looks a lot like an unnamed function definition, and it is often convenient to think of it that way, but a lambda expression is actually more complex than that. First, a lambda expression, as the name implies, is an *expression* rather than a *definition*. The result of evaluating a lambda expression is a special function object called a closure[1]; it is not until the closure is *invoked* — which can happen immediately but often occurs later (e.g., as a callback) — that the *body* of the lambda expression is executed.

Evaluating a lambda expression creates a temporary **closure object** of an unnamed type called the **closure type**. The closure type encapsulates captured variables (see Section 2.2. "Lambda Captures" on page 986) and has a **call operator** that executes the body of the lambda expression. Each lambda expression has a unique closure type, even if it is identical to another lambda expression in the program. If the lambda expression appears within a template, the closure type for each instantiation of that template is unique. Note, however, that, although the closure object is an unnamed temporary object, it can be saved in a named variable whose type can be queried. Closure types are copy constructible and move constructible, but they have no other constructors and have deleted assignment operators.[2] Interestingly, it is possible to *inherit* from a closure type, provided the derived class constructs its closure type base class using only the copy or move constructors. This ability to derive from a closure type allows taking advantage of the empty-base optimization (EBO):

```
#include <utility>  // std::move

template <typename Func>
int callFunc(const Func& f) { return f(); }

void f1()
{
    int   i   = 5;
    auto  c1  = [i]{ return 2 * i; };    // OK, deduced type for c1
    using C1t = decltype(c1);            // OK, named alias for unnamed type
    C1t   c1b = c1;                      // OK, copy of c1
    auto  c2  = [i]{ return 2 * i; };    // OK, identical lambda expression
    using C2t = decltype(c2);
    C1t   c2b = c2;                      // Error, different types, C1t & C2t
    using C3t = decltype([]{/*...*/});   // Error, lambda expr within decltype
```

---

[1] The terms *lambda* and *closure* are borrowed from *Lambda Calculus*, a computational system developed by Alonzo Church in the 1930s. Many computer languages have features inspired by Lambda Calculus, although most (including C++) take some liberties with the terminology. See **rojas15** and **barendregt84**.

[2] C++17 provides default constructors for captureless lambdas, which are assignable in C++20.

```
    auto  c4 = []{ return 2; };        // OK, captureless lambda expression
    using C4t = decltype(c4);

    class C4Derived : public C4t       // OK, inherit from closure type.
    {
        int d_auxValue;
    public:
        C4Derived(C4t c4, int aux) : C4t(std::move(c4)), d_auxValue(aux) { }
        int aux() const { return d_auxValue; }
    };

    static_assert(sizeof(C4Derived) == sizeof(int), "");  // OK, EBO applied

    int ret = callFunc([i]{ return 2 * i; });  // OK, deduced arg type, Func

    c1b = c1;  // Error, assignment of closures is not allowed.
}
```

The types of c1 and c2, above, are different, even though they are token-for-token identical. As there is no way to explicitly name a closure type, we use **auto** in the case of c1 and c2 in f1 (see Section 2.1."**auto** Variables" on page 195) or template-argument deduction in the case of f in callFunc to create variables directly from the lambda expression, and we use **decltype** (see Section 1.1."**decltype**" on page 25) to create aliases to the types of existing closure variables (C1t and C2t). Note that using **decltype** directly on a lambda expression is ill formed, as shown with C3t, because there would be no way to construct an object of the resulting unique type.[3] The derived class, C1Derived, uses the type alias C1t to refer to its base class. Note that its constructor forwards its first argument to the base-class move constructor.

There is no way to specify a closure type prior to creating an actual closure object of that type. Consequently, there is no way to declare callFunc with a parameter of the actual closure type that will be passed; hence, it is declared as a template parameter. As a special case, however, if the lambda capture is *empty* (i.e., the lambda expression begins with []; see Section 2.2."Lambda Captures" on page 986), then the closure is implicitly convertible to an ordinary function pointer having the same signature as its call operator:

```
char callFuncPtr(char (*f)(const char*)) { return f("x"); }  // not a template

char c = callFuncPtr([](const char* s) { return s ? s[0] : '\0'; });
    // OK, closure argument is converted to function-pointer parameter.

char d = callFuncPtr([c](const char* s) { /*...*/ });
    // Error, lambda capture is not empty; no conversion to function pointer.
```

---

[3]Since C++20, lambda expression are allowed to appear in unevaluated contexts, including operands of **decltype** and **sizeof**.

The `callFuncPtr` function takes a callback in the form of a pointer to function. Even though it is not a template, it can be called with a lambda argument having the same parameter types, the same return type, and an empty lambda capture; the closure object is converted to an ordinary pointer to function. This conversion is *not* available in the second call to `callFuncPtr` because the lambda capture is not empty.

Conversion to function pointer is considered a user-defined conversion operator and thus cannot be implicitly combined with other conversions on the same expression. It can, however, be invoked *explicitly*, as needed:

```
using Fp2 = int(*)(int);  // function-pointer type

struct FuncWrapper
{
    FuncWrapper(Fp2) { /*...*/ }  // implicit conversion from function-pointer
    // ...
};

int f2(FuncWrapper);
int i2 = f2([](int x) { return x; });  // Error, two user-defined conversions
int i3 = f2(static_cast<Fp2>([](int x) { return x; }));  // OK, explicit cast
int i4 = f2(+[](int x) { return x; });  // OK, forced conversion
```

The first call to `f2` fails because it would require two implicit user-defined conversions: one from the closure type to the `Fp2` function-pointer type and one from `Fp2` to `FuncWrapper`. The second call succeeds because the first conversion is made explicit with the **static_cast**. The third call is an interesting shortcut that takes advantage of the unary **operator**+ being defined as the identity transformation for pointer types. Thus, the closure-to-pointer conversion is invoked for the operand of **operator**+, which returns the unchanged pointer, which, in turn, is converted to `FuncWrapper`; the first and third steps of this sequence use only one user-defined conversion each. The Standard Library `std::function` class template provides another way to pass a function object of unnamed type, one that does not require the lambda capture to be empty; see *Use Cases — Use with* `std::function` on page 601.

The compile-time and runtime phases of defining a closure type and constructing a closure object from a single lambda expression resembles the phases of calling a function template; what looks like an ordinary function call is actually broken down into a compile-time instantiation and a runtime call. The closure type is deduced when a lambda expression is encountered during compilation. When the control flow passes through the lambda expression at run time, the closure object is *constructed* from the list of captured local variables. In the `numAboveAverageSalaries` example on page 576, the `SalaryIsGreater` class can be thought of as a closure type — created by hand instead of by the compiler — whereas the call to `SalaryIsGreater(average)` is analogous to constructing the closure object at run time.

Finally, the purpose of a closure is to be invoked. It can be invoked immediately by supplying arguments for each of its parameters:

```
#include <iostream>  // std::cout
void f3()
{
    [](const char* s) { std::cout << s; }("hello world\n");
        // equivalent to std::cout << "hello world\n";
}
```

The closure object, in this example, is invoked immediately and then destroyed, making the above just a complicated way to say std::cout << "hello world\n";. More commonly, the lambda expression is used as a local function for convenience and to avoid clutter:

```
#include <cmath>  // std::sqrt

double hypotenuse(double a, double b)
{
    auto sqr = [](double x) { return x * x; };
    return std::sqrt(sqr(a) + sqr(b));
}
```

Note that the closure's call operator cannot be overloaded:

```
auto sqr = [](int x) { return x * x; };     // OK, store closure in sqr.
auto sqr = [](double x) { return x * x; };  // Error, redefinition of sqr
```

The most common use of a lambda expression, however, is as a callback to a function template, e.g., as a functor argument to an algorithm from the Standard Library:

```
#include <algorithm>  // std::partition

template <typename FwdIt>
FwdIt oddEvenPartition(FwdIt first, FwdIt last)
{
    using value_type = decltype(*first);
    return std::partition(first, last, [](value_type v) { return v % 2 != 0; });
}
```

The oddEvenPartition function template moves odd values to the start of the sequence and even values to the back. The closure object is invoked repeatedly within the std::partition algorithm.

Lambda capture and lambda introducer

The purpose of the lambda capture is to make certain local variables from the environment available to be used (or, more precisely, **ODR-used**, which means that they are used in a potentially evaluated context) within the **lambda body**. Each local variable can be **captured by copy** or **captured by reference**. Orthogonally, each variable can be **explicitly captured** or **implicitly captured**. We'll examine each of these aspects of lambda capture in turn.

Syntactically, the lambda capture consists of an optional **capture default** followed by a comma-separated list of zero or more identifiers (or the keyword **this**), which are **explicitly captured**. The capture default can be one of = or & for **capture by copy** or **capture by reference**, respectively. If there is a **capture default**, then **this** and any local variables in scope that are ODR-used within the lambda body and not explicitly captured will be implicitly captured.

```
void f1()
{
    int a = 0, b = 1, c = 2;
    auto c1 = [a, b]{ return a + b; };
        // a and b are explicitly captured.
    auto c2 = [&]{ return a + b; };
        // a and b are implicitly captured.
    auto c3 = [&, b]{ return a + b; };
        // a is implicitly captured, and b is explicitly captured.
    auto c4 = [a]{ return a + b; }
        // Error, b is ODR-used but not captured.
}
```

The Standard defines the **lambda introducer** as the lambda capture together with its surrounding [and]. If the **lambda introducer** is an empty pair of brackets, no variables will be captured, and the lambda is stateless:

```
auto c1 = []{ /*...*/ };  // empty lambda capture
```

The **lambda capture** enables access to portions of the local stack frame. As such, only variables with *automatic storage duration* — i.e., nonstatic local variables — can be captured, as we'll see in detail later in this section and the lambda body section. An explicitly captured variable whose name is immediately preceded by an & symbol in the **lambda capture** is **captured by reference**; without the &, it is **captured by copy**. If the capture default is &, then all implicitly captured variables are **captured by reference**. Otherwise, if the capture default is =, all implicitly captured variables are **captured by copy**:

```
void f2()
{
    int a = 0, b = 1;
    auto c1 = [&a]{ /*...*/ return a; };  // a captured by reference
    auto c2 = [a] { /*...*/ return a; };  // a captured by copy
    auto c3 = [a, &b] { return a + b; };
        // a is explicitly captured by copy, and b is explicitly
        // captured by reference.
    auto c4 = [=]{ return a + b; };
        // a and b are implicitly captured by copy.
    auto c5 = [&]{ return &a; };
        // a is implicitly captured by reference.
```

```
    auto c6 = [&, b]{ return a * b; };
        // a is implicitly captured by reference, and b is explicitly
        // captured by copy.
    auto c7 = [=, &b]{ return a * b; };
        // a is implicitly captured by copy, and b is explicitly
        // captured by reference.
    auto c8 = [a]{ return a * b; };
        // Error, a is explicitly captured by copy, but b is not captured.
}
```

When a lambda expression appears within a nonstatic member function, the **this** pointer can be captured as a special case:

```
class Class1
{
public:
    void mf()
    {
        auto c12 = [this]{ return this; };   // Explicitly capture this.
        auto c13 = [=]    { return this; };   // Implicitly capture this.
    }
};
```

Both implicit and explicit capture of **this** capture the pointer value of **this** and do not make a copy of the object pointed to by **this**. Redundant captures are not allowed; the same name (or **this**) cannot appear twice in the lambda capture. Moreover, if the capture default is &, then none of the explicitly captured variables may be captured by reference, and if the capture default is =, then any explicitly captured entities can be neither captured by copy nor **this**[4]:

```
class Class2
{
public:
    void mf()
    {
        int a = 0;
        auto c1 = [a, &a]{ /*...*/ }; // Error, a is captured twice.
        auto c2 = [=, a]{ /*...*/ };
            // Error, explicit capture of a by copy is redundant.
        auto c3 = [&,&a]{ /*...*/ };
            // Error, explicit capture of a by reference is redundant.
        auto c4 = [=, this]{ return this; };
            // Error, explicit capture of this with = capture default
    }
};
```

---

[4]C++20 removed the prohibition on explicit capture of **this** with an = capture default. In fact, C++20 deprecated implicit capture of **this** when the capture default is = and instead requires [=, **this**] to capture **this** in such situations.

We'll use the term *primary variable* to refer to the block-scope local variable outside of the lambda expression and *captured variable* to refer to the variable of the same name as viewed from within the lambda body. For every object that is captured by copy, the **lambda closure** will contain a member variable having the same type, after stripping any reference qualifier (except reference-to-function); this member variable is initialized from the primary variable by direct initialization and is destroyed when the **closure object** is destroyed. Any ODR-use of the captured name within the **lambda body** will refer to the closure's corresponding member variable. Thus, for an entity that is captured by copy, the primary and captured variables refer to distinct objects with distinct lifetimes. By default, the **call** operator is **const**, providing read-only access to members of the **closure object** (i.e., captured variables that are captured by copy); mutable (non**const**) call operators are discussed in *Lambda declarator* on page 591:

```
void f3()
{
    int a = 5;
    auto c1 = [a]       // a is captured by copy.
    {
        return a;       // return value of copy of a
    };
    a = 10;             // Modify a after it was captured by c1.
    assert(5 == c1());  // OK, a within c1 had value from before the change.

    int& b = a;
    auto c2 = [b]       // b is int (not int&), captured by copy.
    {
        return b;       // return value of copy of b
    };
    b = 15;             // Modify a through reference b.
    assert(10 == c2()); // OK, b within c2 is a copy, not a reference.

    auto c3 = [a]       // a is captured by copy.
    {
        ++a;            // Error, a is const within the lambda body.
    };
}
```

In the example above, the first **lambda expression** is evaluated to produce a **closure object**, c1, that captures a *copy* of a. Even when the primary a is subsequently modified, the captured a in c1 remains unchanged. When c1 is invoked, the **lambda body** returns the *copy*, which still has the value 5. The same applies to c2, but note that the copy of b is *not a reference* even though b is a reference. Thus, the copy of b in c2 is the value of a that b referred to at the time that c2 was created.

When a variable is captured by reference, the captured variable is simply an alias to the primary variable; no copies are made. Therefore, it is possible to modify the primary variable and/or take its address within the lambda body:

```cpp
void f4()
{
    int a = 5;
    auto c1 = [&a]        // a is captured by reference.
    {
        a = 10;           // Modify a through the captured variable.
        return &a;        // return address of captured a
    };
    assert(c1() == &a); // OK, primary and captured a have the same address.
    assert(10 == a);    // OK, primary a is now 10.

    int& b = a;
    auto c2 = [&b]        // b is captured by reference.
    {
        return &b;        // return address of captured b
    };
    assert(c2() == &b); // OK, primary and captured b have the same address.
    assert(c2() == &a); // OK, captured b is an alias for a.
}
```

In contrast to the f3 example, the c1 closure object above does *not* hold a copy of the captured variable, a, though the compiler might choose to define a member of type int& that refers to a. Within the lambda body, modifying a modifies the primary variable, and taking its address returns the address of the primary variable; i.e., the captured variable is an alias for the primary variable. With respect to variables that are captured by reference, the lambda body behaves much as though it were part of the surrounding block. The lifetime of a variable that is captured by reference is the same as that of the primary variable (since they are the same). In particular, if a copy of a closure object outlives a primary variable that is captured by reference, then the captured variable becomes a *dangling reference*; see *Potential Pitfalls — Dangling references* on page 607.

If **this** appears in the lambda capture, then (1) the current **this** pointer is captured by copy, and (2) within the lambda body, member variables accessible through **this** can be used without prefixing them with **this->**, as though the lambda body were an extension of the surrounding member function. The lambda body cannot refer to the closure directly; the captured **this** does not point to the closure but to the *this object of the function within which it is defined:

```cpp
class Class1
{
    int d_value;
```

```
public:
    // ...
    void mf() const
    {
        auto c1 = []{ return *this; };        // Error, this is not captured.
        auto c2 = []{ return d_value; };      // Error, this is not captured.
        auto c3 = [d_value]{ /*...*/; };      // Error, cannot capture member
        auto c4 = [this]{ return this; };     // OK, returns this
        auto c5 = [this]{ return d_value; };  // OK, returns this->d_value
        assert(this == c4());                 // OK, this is captured correctly.
    }
};
```

Note that c4 returns **this**, which is the address of the Class3 object for which mf was called. That **this** is the address of the Class3 object and not of the closure itself is one way in which the closure type is different from a named functor type — there is no way for an object of closure type to refer to itself directly. Because the closure type is unnamed and because it does not supply its own **this** pointer, it is difficult (but not impossible) to create a *recursive* lambda expression; see *Use Cases — Recursion* on page 604.

If **this** is captured (implicitly or explicitly), the lambda body will behave much like an extension of the member function in which the lambda expression appears, with direct access to the class's members:

```
#include <algorithm> // std::count_if
#include <vector>    // std::vector
#include <cstddef>   // std::size_t

class Class4
{
    int d_value;

public:
    std::size_t mf(const std::vector<int>& v) const
    {
        auto f = []{ return d_value; };
            // Error, this not captured; can't see d_value.
        return std::count_if(v.begin(), v.end(),
                        [this](int element){ return element < d_value; });
            // OK, uses this->d_value
    }
};
```

Note that capturing **this** does not copy the class object that it points to, but only the **this** pointer itself; the original **this** and the captured **this** will point to the same object:

```
class Class3
{
    int d_value;
```

```cpp
public:
    void mf()
    {
        auto c1 = [this]{ ++d_value; };   // Increment this->d_value.
        d_value = 1;
        c1();
        assert(2 == d_value);             // Change to d_value is visible.
    }
};
```

Here, we captured **this** in c1 but then proceeded to modify the object pointed to by **this** within the lambda body.[5]

A lambda expression can occur wherever other expressions can occur, including within other lambda expressions. The set of entities that can be captured in a valid lambda expression depends on the surrounding scope. A lambda expression that does not occur immediately within **block scope** cannot have a lambda capture:

```cpp
namespace ns1
{
    int v = 10;
    int w = [v]{ /*...*/ }();
                // Error, capture in global/namespace scope.

    void f5(int a = [v]{ return v; }());  // Error, capture in default argument.
}
```

When a lambda expression occurs in block scope, it can capture any local variables with *automatic* (i.e., nonstatic) storage duration in its **reaching scope**. The Standard defines the reaching scope of the lambda expression as the set of enclosing scopes up to and including the innermost enclosing function and its parameters. Static variables can be used without capturing them; see *Lambda body* on page 595:

```cpp
void f6(const int& a)
{
    int b = 2 * a;
    if (a)
    {
        int c;
        // ...
    }
    else
    {
        int d = 4 * a;
        static int e = 10;
```

---

[5]In C++17, it is possible to capture ***this**, which results in the entire class object being copied, not just the **this** pointer; for an example of why capturing ***this** might be useful, see *Annoyances — Can't capture *this by copy* on page 611.

```
    auto c1 = [a]{ /*...*/ };        // OK, capture argument a from f5.
    auto c2 = [=]{ return b; };      // OK, implicitly capture local b.
    auto c3 = [&c]{ /*...*/ };       // Error, c is not in reaching scope.
    auto c4 = [&]{ d += 2; };        // OK, implicitly capture local d.
    auto c5 = [e]{ /*...*/ };        // Error, e has static duration.
}

struct LocalClass
{
    void mf()
    {
        auto c6 = [b]{ /*...*/ };  // Error, b is not in reaching scope.
    }
};
}
```

The reaching scope of the lambda expressions for c1 through c5, above, includes the local variable d in the **else** block, b in the surrounding function block, and a from f6's arguments. The local variable, c, is not in their reaching scope and cannot be captured. Although e *is* in their reaching scope, it cannot be captured because it does not have automatic storage duration. Finally, the lambda expression for c6 is within a member function of a local class. Its reaching scope ends with the innermost function, LocalClass::mf, and does not encompass the surrounding block that includes a and b.

Only when the innermost enclosing function is a nonstatic class member function can **this** be captured:

```
void f7()
{
    auto c1 = [this]{ /*...*/ };  // Error, f5 is not a member function.
}

class Class6
{
    static void sfa()
    {
        auto c2 = [this]{ /*...*/ };  // Error, sf1 is static.
    }

    void mf()
    {
        auto c3 = [this]{ /*...*/ };  // OK, mf is nonstatic member function.

        struct LocalClass
        {
            static void sf2()
            {
```

```
            auto c4 = [this]{ /*...*/ };
                // Error, innermost function, sf2, is static.
        }
    };
    }
};
```

When a lambda expression is enclosed within another lambda expression, then the reaching scope includes all of the intervening lambda bodies. Any variable captured (implicitly or explicitly) by the inner lambda expression must be either defined or captured by the enclosing lambda expression:

```
void f8()
{
    int a = 0, b = 0;
    const char* d = "";
    auto c1 = [&a]                    // Capture a from function block.
    {
        int  d = 0;                   // Local definition of d hides outer def.
        auto c2 = [&a]{ /*...*/ };    // OK, a is captured by lambda c1.
        auto c3 = [d]{  /*...*/ };    // OK, capture local int d.
        auto c4 = [&]{ return d; };   // OK,    "       "      "  "
        auto c5 = [b]{  /*...*/ };    // Error, b not captured by lambda c1.
    };
    auto c6 = [=]
    {
        auto c7 = [&]{ return b; };
            // OK, ODR-use of b causes implicit capture in c7 and c6.
        auto c8 = [&d]{ return &d; };
            // d is captured by copy in c6; c8 returns address of copy.
    };
}
```

Note that there are two variables named d: one at function scope and one within the body of the first lambda expression. Following normal rules for unqualified name lookup, the inner lambda expressions used to initialize c3 and c4 capture the *inner* d (of type **int**), not the *outer* d (of type **const char***). Because it is not captured, primary variable b is *visible* but not *usable* — an important distinction that we'll discuss in *Lambda body* on page 595 — within the body of c1 and cannot, therefore, be captured by c5.

The lambda body for c7 ODR-uses b, thus causing it to be implicitly captured. This capture by c7 constitutes an ODR-use of b within the enclosing lambda expression, c6, in turn causing b to be implicitly captured by c6. In this way, a single ODR-use can trigger a *chain* of implicit captures from an enclosed lambda expression through its enclosing lambda expressions. Critically, when a variable is captured by copy in one lambda expression, any enclosed lambda expressions that capture the same name will capture the *copy*, not the primary variable, as we see in the lambda expression for c8.

Note that a variable named in a lambda capture isn't automatically *captured*. A variable is captured only if it is ODR-used within the lambda expression:

```cpp
#include <algorithm>  // std::min

void f9()
{
        int a = 0;  // a is not a compile-time constant.
    const int b = 2;  // b is     a compile-time constant.

    auto c1 = [&]{ return 2 * a; };      // a is ODR-used; implicitly captured.
    auto c2 = [&]{ return sizeof(a); };  // a is not ODR-used; not captured.
    auto c3 = [&]{ return 2 * b; };      // b is not ODR-used; not captured.
    auto c4 = [&]{ return &b; };         // b is ODR-used; implicitly captured.
    auto c5 = [&]{ std::min(b, 5); };    // b is ODR-used; implicitly captured.
}
```

In the above example, the lambda body for c1 ODR-uses a by reading its value and thus captures a. Conversely, c2 does *not* capture a despite its name being used in the lambda body because it is only used in the unevaluated operand of the **sizeof** operator, which does not constitute the variable's ODR-use. Similarly, c3 does *not* capture b because (1) b is a compile-time constant and (2) c3 only uses b's value, which also does not constitute ODR-use of b (see Section 2.1."**constexpr** Variables" on page 302). Finally, taking the address of or binding a reference to a variable *always* constitutes the variable's ODR-use; hence, both c4, which directly takes the address of b, and c5, which passes b by **const&** to std::min, capture b.

Finally, a lambda capture within a **variadic function template** (see Section 2.1."Variadic Templates" on page 873) may contain a **pack expansion**:

```cpp
#include <utility>  // std::forward

template <typename... ArgTypes>
int f10(const char* s, ArgTypes&&... args);

template <typename... ArgTypes>
int f11(ArgTypes&&... args)
{
    const char* s = "Introduction";
    auto c1 = [=]{ return f8(s, args...); };  // OK, args... captured by copy
    auto c2 = [s,&args...]{ return f8(s, std::forward<ArgTypes>(args)...); };
        // OK, explicit capture of args... by reference
}
```

In the example above, the variadic arguments to f11 are implicitly captured using capture by copy in the first lambda expression. Capturing by copy means that, regardless of the **value category** (*rvalue*, *lvalue*, and so on) of the original arguments, the captured variables are all *lvalue* members of the resulting *closure*. Conversely, the second lambda expression captures the set of arguments using **capture by reference**, again resulting in captured variables that are *lvalues*. The `ArgTypes` **pack expansion** designates a list of *types*, not *variables*, and does not, therefore, need to be captured to be used within the lambda expression, nor would it be valid to attempt to capture it. Because `ArgTypes` is specified using a forwarding reference (`&&`, see Section 2.1."Forwarding References" on page 377), the Standard Library `std::forward` function can be used to cast the captured variables to the **value category** of their corresponding arguments.

Lambda declarator

The **lambda declarator** looks a lot like a function declaration and is effectively the declaration of the **closure type's call operator**. The lambda declarator comprises the **call operator's** parameter list, mutability, exception specification, and return type:

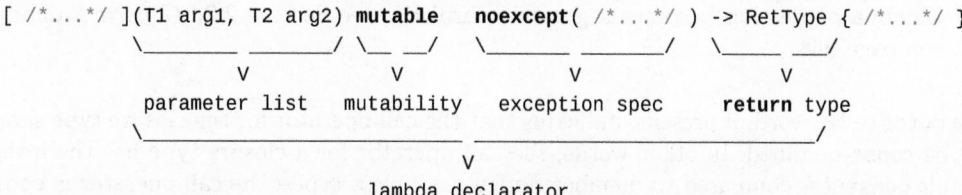

Although the **lambda declarator** looks similar to a function declaration, we cannot forward declare any part of a **lambda expression**; we can only define it.

The entire **lambda declarator** is optional. However, if *any* part is present, the parameter list must be present (even if it declares no parameters):

```cpp
void f0()
{
    [](int x) noexcept {/*...*/};   // OK, exception spec with parameter list
    []() -> int { return 5; };      // OK, return type with empty parameter list
    [] -> double {/*...*/};         // Error, return type with no parameter list
}
```

The parameter list for a **lambda expression** is the same as a parameter list for a function declaration, with minor modifications.

1. A parameter is not permitted to have the same name as an explicitly captured variable:

   ```cpp
   void f1()
   {
       int a;
       auto c1 = [a](short* a){ /*...*/ }; // Error, parameter shadows captured a.
       auto c2 = [ ](short* a){ /*...*/ }; // OK, local a is not captured.
       auto c3 = [=](short* a){ /*...*/ }; // OK, parameter hides local a.
   }
   ```

In the definition of c1, the lambda expression explicitly captures a and then improperly tries to declare a parameter by the same name. When a is not captured, as in the lambda expression for c2, having a parameter named a does not pose a problem; within the lambda body, the declaration of a in the parameter list will prevent name lookup from finding the declaration in the enclosing scope. The situation with c3 is essentially the same as for c2; because name lookup finds a in the parameter list rather than the enclosing scope, it does not attempt to capture it.

2. In C++11, none of the parameters may have default arguments. This restriction does not apply to C++14 and after:

```
auto c4 = [](int x, int y = 0){ /*...*/ };  // Error in C++11.  OK in C++14.
```

3. If the type of any of the parameters contains the keyword **auto**, then the lambda expression becomes a **generic lambda**; see Section 2.2."*Generic* Lambdas" on page 968.

The **mutable** keyword, if present, indicates that the call operator for the closure type should *not* be **const**-qualified. In other words, the call operator for a closure type has the inverse default **const**ness compared to member functions of class types: the call operator is **const**-qualified *unless* the lambda declarator is decorated with **mutable**. In practice, this rule means that member variables of the closure object, i.e., variables that were captured by copy, are **const** by default and cannot be modified within the lambda body unless the **mutable** keyword is present:

```
void f2()
{
    int a = 5;
    auto c1 = [a]()          { return ++a; };  // Error, copy of a is const.
    auto c2 = [a]() mutable { return ++a; };  // OK, increment copy of a
    assert(6 == c2());                         // OK, captured a incremented
    assert(5 == a);                            // OK, primary a not changed
    assert(7 == c2());                         // OK, captured a incremented
}
```

The two lambda expressions above are identical except for the **mutable** keyword. Both use capture by copy to capture local variable a, and both try to increment a, but only the one decorated with **mutable** can perform that modification. When the call operator on closure object c2 is invoked, it increments the *captured copy* of a, leaving the primary a untouched. If c2() is invoked again, it increments its copy of a a second time. A variable *not* captured by copy can be modified within the lambda body regardless of the presence of the **mutable** keyword on the lambda expression provided that the variable is modifiable in the enclosing scope. Such variables include non**const** automatic variables and function parameters captured by reference, as well as class data members that can be modified by the member function wherein the lambda capturing the **this** pointer is created:

```
class Class2
{
    int d_value;
public:
    // ...
    void mf()
    {
        d_value = 1;
        int a = 0;
        auto c1 = [&a,this]{
            a = d_value;    // OK, a is a reference to a nonconst object.
            d_value *= 2;   // OK, this points to a nonconst object.
        };
        c1();
        assert(1 == a && 2 == d_value);   // values updated by c1
        c1();
        assert(2 == a && 4 == d_value);   // values updated by c1 again
    }

    void cmf() const
    {
        int a = 0;
        auto c2 = [=]() mutable {
            ++a;         // OK, increment mutable captured variable
            ++d_value;   // Error, *this is const within cmf.
        };
    }
};
```

The lambda expression for c1 is not decorated with **mutable** yet both a and d_value can be modified, the first because it was captured by reference and the second because it was accessed through **this** within a non**const** member function, mf. Conversely, the lambda expression for c2 cannot modify d_value even though it is declared **mutable** because the captured **this** pointer points to a **const** object within the surrounding member function, cmf.

The lambda declarator may include an **exception specification**, consisting of a **noexcept** clause, after the **mutable** specifier, if any. The syntax and meaning of the exception specification are identical to that of a normal function; see Section 3.1."**noexcept** Specifier" on page 1085.

The return type of the call operator can be determined either by a **trailing return type** or by a **deduced return type**. Every example we have seen up to this point has used a deduced return type whereby the return type of the closure's call operator is deduced by the type of object returned by the **return** statement(s). If there are no **return** statements in the lambda body or if the **return** statements have no operands, then the return type is **void**. If there are multiple **return** statements, they must agree with respect to the return type. The rules for a deduced return type are the same for a lambda expression as they are for an ordinary function in C++14; see Section 3.2."**auto** Return" on page 1182:

```
void f3()
{
    auto c1 = [](int& i){ i = 0; };     // The deduced return type is void.
    auto c2 = []{ return "hello"; };    // The deduced return type is const char*.
    auto c3 = [](bool c)                // The deduced return type is int.
    {
        if (c) { return 5; }
        else   { return 6; }
    };
    auto c4 = [](bool c)
    {
        if (c) { return 5; }            // The deduced return type is int.
        else   { return 6.0; }          // Error, double does not match int.
    };
}
```

All four of the lambda expressions above have a deduced return type. The first one deduces a return type of **void** because the lambda body has no **return** statements. The next one deduces a return type of **const char*** because the string literal, **"hello"**, decays to a **const char*** in that context. The third one deduces a return type of **int** because all of the **return** statements return values of type **int**. The last one fails to compile because the two branches return values of different types. Note that the original C++11 Standard did not allow a deduced return type for a lambda body containing anything other than a single **return** statement. This restriction was lifted by a **defect report** and is no longer part of C++11. Compiler versions that predate ratification of this **defect report** might reject lambda expressions having multiple statements and a deduced return type.

If return type deduction fails or results in an undesired type (see Section 3.2."**auto** Return" on page 1182 for a description of why this feature needs to be used with care), a trailing return type can be specified (see Section 1.1."Trailing Return" on page 124):

```
#include <utility>  // std::pair

void f4()
{
    auto c1 = [](bool c) -> double {
        if (c) { return 5; }            // OK, int value converted to double
        else   { return 6.0; }          // OK, double return value
    };
    auto c2 = []() -> std::pair<int, int> {
        return { 5, 6 };                // OK, brace-initialize returned pair
    };
}
```

In the first lambda expression above, we specify a trailing return type of **double**. The two branches of the **if** statement would return different types (**int** and **double**), but because the return type has been specified explicitly, the compiler converts the return values to the known return type (**double**). The second lambda expression returns a value by brace initialization, which is insufficient for deducing a return value. Again, the issue is resolved by specifying the return type explicitly. Note that, unlike ordinary functions, a lambda expression cannot have a return type specified before the lambda introducer or lambda declarator:

```
auto c5 = int []      ()           { return 0; };  // Error, return type misplaced
auto c6 =       [] int ()           { return 0; };  // Error, return type misplaced
auto c7 =       []     () -> int { return 0; };  // OK, trailing return type
```

Attributes (see Section 1.1."Attribute Syntax" on page 12) that appertain to the *type* of call operator can be inserted in the lambda declarator just before the trailing return type. If there is no trailing return type, the attributes can be inserted before the open brace of the lambda body. Unfortunately, these attributes do not appertain to the call operator itself, but to its type, ruling out some common attributes:

```
#include <cstdlib>  // std::abort
auto c1 = []() noexcept [[noreturn]] {  // Error, [[noreturn]] on a type
    std::abort();
};
```

Lambda body

Combined, the lambda declarator and the lambda body make up the declaration and definition of an **inline** member function that is the call operator for the closure type. For the purposes of name lookup and the interpretation of **this**, the lambda body is considered to be in the context where the lambda expression is evaluated (independent of the context where the closure's call operator is invoked).

Critically, the set of entity names that can be used from within the lambda body is not limited to captured local variables. Types, functions, templates, constants, and so on — just like for any other member function — do not need to be captured and, in fact, *cannot* be captured in most cases. To illustrate, let's create a number of entities in multiple scopes:

```
#include <iostream>  // std::cout

namespace ns1
{
    void f1() { std::cout << "ns1::f1" << '\n'; }
    struct Class1 { Class1() { std::cout << "ns1::Class1()" << '\n'; } };
    int g0 = 0;
}

namespace ns2
{
    void f1() { std::cout << "ns2::f1" << '\n'; }

    template <typename T>
    struct Class1 { Class1() { std::cout << "ns2::Class1()" << '\n'; } };
```

```
    int const g1 = 1;
    int        g2 = 2;

    class Class2
    {
        int        d_value;   // nonstatic member variable
        static int s_mem;     // static member variable

        void mf1() { std::cout << "Class2::mf1" << '\n'; }

        struct Nested { Nested() { std::cout << "Nested()" << '\n'; } };

        template <typename T>
        static void print(const T& v) { std::cout << v << '\n'; }

    public:
        explicit Class2(int v) : d_value(v) { }

        void mf2();
        void mf3();
        void mf4();
        void mf5();
    };

    int Class2::s_mem = 0;
}
```

With these declarations, we first demonstrate the use of entities that are not variables and are accessible within the scope of a lambda body:

```
void ns2::Class2::mf2()
{
    using LocalType = const char*;

    auto c1 = []  // captureless lambda accessing nonvariables in scope
    {
        f1();             // Find ns2::f1 by unqualified name lookup.
        Class1<int> x1;   // Construct ns2::Class1<int> object.
        Nested      x2;   // Construct ns2::Class2::Nested object.
        print("print");   // Call static member function ns2::Class2::print.
        LocalType x3;     // Declare object of local type.
        ns1::f1();        // Find ns1::f1 func by qualified name lookup.
        ns1::Class1 x4;   // Find ns1::Class1 type by qualified lookup.
    };
}
```

We can see that, within the lambda body, nonvariables can be accessed normally, using either unqualified name lookup or, if needed, qualified name lookup.

Variables with static storage duration can also be accessed directly, without being captured:

```
void ns2::Class2::mf3()
{
    static int s1 = 3;

    auto c1 = []  // captureless lambda accessing static storage duration vars
    {
        print(g1);        // Print global constant ns2::g1.
        print(g2);        // Print global variable ns2::g2.
        print(ns1::g0);   // Print global variable ns1::g0.
        print(s_mem);     // Print static member variable s_mem.
        print(s1);        // Print static local variable s1.
    };
}
```

Here we see global constants, global variables, static member variables, and local static variables being used from the local scope.

Use Cases

Interface adaptation, partial application, and currying

Lambda expressions can be used to adapt the set of arguments provided by an algorithm to the parameters expected by another facility:

```
#include <algorithm>   // std::count_if
#include <string>      // std::string
#include <vector>      // std::vector

extern "C" int f1(const char* s, std::size_t n);

void f2(const std::vector<std::string>& vec)
{
    std::size_t n = std::count_if(vec.begin(), vec.end(),
        [](const std::string& s){ return 0 != f1(s.data(), s.size()); });
    // ...
}
```

Here we have a function, f1, that takes a C string and length and computes some predicate, returning zero for false and nonzero for true. We want to use this predicate with std::count_if to count how many strings in a specified vector match this predicate. The lambda expression in f2 adapts f1 to the needs of std::count_if by converting an std::string argument into **const char*** and std::size_t arguments and converting the **int** return value to **bool**.

A particularly common kind of interface adaptation is **partial application**, whereby we reduce the *parameter count* of a function by holding one or more of its arguments constant for the duration of the algorithm:

```
#include <algorithm>  // std::all_of

template <typename InputIter, typename T>
bool all_greater_than(InputIter first, InputIter last, const T& v)
    // returns true if all the values in the specified range [first, last)
    // are greater than the specified v, and false otherwise
{
    return std::all_of(first, last, [&v](const T& i) { return i > v; });
}
```

In the example above, the greater-than operator (>) takes two operands, but the `std::all_of` algorithm expects a functor taking a single argument. The lambda expression passes its single argument as the first operand to **operator>** and *binds* the other operand to the captured v value, thus resolving the interface mismatch.

Finally, let's touch on **currying**, a transformation borrowed from lambda calculus and functional programming languages. Currying is a flexible way to get results similar to partial application by transforming, for example, a binary function having parameters a and b into a unary function having just the first parameter, a, that returns a new function having just the second parameter, b. To apply this technique, we define a lambda expression whose call operator returns another lambda expression, i.e., a closure that returns another closure:

```
template <typename InputIter, typename T>
bool all_greater_than2(InputIter first, InputIter last, const T& v)
    // Return true if all the values in the specified range [first, last)
    // are greater than the specified v, and false otherwise.
{
    auto isGreaterThan = [](const T& v){
        return [&v](const T& i){ return i > v; };
    };
    return std::all_of(first, last, isGreaterThan(v));
}
```

The example above is another way to express the previous example. The call operator for isGreaterThan takes a single argument, v, and returns another single-argument closure object that can be used to compare i to v. Thus, `isGreaterThan(v)(i)` is equivalent to i > v.

Emulating local functions

Some programming languages allow functions to be defined within other functions. Such local functions are useful when the outer function needs to repeat a set of steps two or more times but where the repeated steps are meaningless outside of the immediate context and/or require access to the outer function's local variables. Using a lambda expression to produce a reusable closure provides this functionality in C++:

```
class Token { /*...*/ };

bool parseToken(const char*& cursor, Token& result)
    // Parse the token at cursor up to the next space or end-of-string,
    // setting result to the resulting token value.  Advance cursor to the
    // space or to the null terminator and return true on success.  Reset
    // cursor to its original value, set result to an empty token, and
    // return false on failure.
{
    const char* const initCursor = cursor;
    auto error = [&]
    {
        cursor = initCursor;
        result = Token{};
        return false;
    };
    // ...
    if (*cursor++ != '.')
    {
        return error();
    }
    // ...
}
```

The `error` closure object acts as a local function that performs all of the necessary error processing and returns **false**. Using this object, every error branch can be reduced to a single statement, `return error()`. Without lambda expressions, the programmer would likely resort to defining a custom class to store the parameters, using a **goto**, or, worse, cutting and pasting the three statements shown within the lambda body.

Emulate user-defined control constructs

Using a lambda expression, an algorithm can look almost like a new control construct in the language:

```
#include <mutex>    // std::mutex
#include <vector>   // std::vector

template <typename RandomIter, typename F>
void parallel_foreach(RandomIter first, RandomIter last, const F& op)
    // For each element, e, in [first, last), create a copy opx of op,
    // and invoke opx(e).  Any number of invocations of opx(e) might occur
    // concurrently, each using a separate copy of op.
{ /*...*/ }
```

```
void processData(std::vector<double>& data)
{
    double       beta    = 0.0;
    double const coef = 7.45e-4;
    std::mutex m;

    parallel_foreach(data.begin(), data.end(), [&](double e) mutable
    {
        if (e < 1.0)
        {
            // ...
        }
        else
        {
            // ...
        }
    });
}
```

The `parallel_foreach` algorithm is intended to act like a **for** loop except that all of the elements in the input range might potentially be processed in parallel. By inserting the "body" of this "parallel for loop" directly into the call to `parallel_foreach`, the resulting loop looks and feels a lot like a built-in control construct. Note that the capture default is **capture by reference** and will result in all of the iterations sharing the outer function's call frame, including, e.g., the mutex variable, m, used to prevent data races. Note that **capture by copy** is often preferred to **capture by reference** in parallel computations to deliberately *avoid* sharing. If an asynchronous computation might outlive its caller, then using **capture by copy** is a must for avoiding dangling references; see *Potential Pitfalls — Dangling references* on page 607.

Variables and control constructs in expressions

In situations where a single expression is required — e.g., member-initializers, initializers for **const** variables, and so on — an *immediately evaluated* lambda expression allows that expression to include local variables and control constructs such as loops:

```
#include <climits>  // SHRT_MAX

bool isPrime(long i);
    // Return true if i is a prime number.

const short largestShortPrime = []{
    for (short v = SHRT_MAX; ; v -= 2) {
        if (isPrime(v)) return v;
    }
}();
```

The value of `largestShortPrime` must be set at initialization time because it is a **const** variable with static storage duration. The loop inside the lambda expression computes the desired value, using a local variable, v, and a **for** loop. Note that the call operator for the resulting closure object is immediately invoked via the `()` argument list at the end of the lambda expression; the closure object is never stored in a named variable and goes out of scope as soon as the full expression is completely evaluated. This computation would formerly have been possible only by creating a single-use *named* function.

Use with `std::function`

As convenient as lambda expressions are for passing functors to algorithm *templates*, each closure having an unnamed and distinct typemakes it difficult to use them outside of a generic context. The C++11 Standard Library class template, `std::function`, bridges this gap (at a cost of runtime overhead) by providing a polymorphic invocable type that can be constructed from any type with a compatible invocation prototype, including but not limited to closure types.

As an example, consider a simple interpreter for a postfix input language that stores a sequence of instructions in an `std::vector`. Each instruction can be of a different type, but they all accept the current stack pointer as an argument and return the new stack pointer as a result. Each instruction is typically a small operation, ideally suited for being expressed as a lambda expression:

```cpp
#include <cstdlib>    // std::strtol
#include <functional> // std::function
#include <string>     // std::string
#include <vector>     // std::vector

using Instruction = std::function<long*(long* sp)>;

std::vector<Instruction> instructionStream;

std::string nextToken();                    // Read the next token.
char tokenOp(const std::string& token);  // operator for token

void readInstructions()
{
    std::string token;
    Instruction nextInstr;
    while (!(token = nextToken()).empty())
    {
        switch (tokenOp(token))
        {
            case 'i':
            {
```

```
                 // push integer literal
             long v = std::strtol(token.c_str(), nullptr, 10);
             nextInstr = [v](long* sp){ *sp++ = v; return sp; };
             break;
         }
         case '+':
         {
             // + operation: pop 2 longs and push their sum
             nextInstr = [](long* sp){
                 long v1 = *--sp;
                 long v2 = *--sp;
                 *sp++ = v1 + v2;
                 return sp;
             };
             break;
         }
         // ... more cases
     }

     instructionStream.push_back(nextInstr);
     }
 }
```

The `Instruction` type alias is an `std::function` that can hold, through a process called **type erasure**, any invocable object that takes a **long*** argument and returns a **long*** result. The `readInstructions` function reads successive string tokens and switches on the operation represented by the token. If the operation is `i`, then the token is an integer literal. The string token is converted into a **long** value, `v`, which is captured in a `lambda` expression. The resulting `closure` object is stored in the `nextInstr` variable; when called, it will push `v` onto the stack. Note that the `nextInstr` variable outlives the primary `v` variable, but, because `v` was captured by copy, the **captured variable**'s lifetime is the same as the `closure` object's. If the next operation is `+`, `nextInstr` is set to the `closure` object of an entirely different `lambda` expression, one that captures nothing and whose call operator pops two values from the stack and pushes their sum back onto the stack.

After the **switch** statement, the current value of `nextInstr` is appended to the instruction stream. Note that, although each `closure type` is different, they all can be stored in an `Instruction` object because the prototype for their call operator matches the prototype specified in the instantiation of `std::function`. The `nextInstr` variable can be created empty, assigned from the value of a `lambda` expression, and then later reassigned from the value of a different `lambda` expression. This flexibility makes `std::function` and `lambda` expressions a potent combination.

One specific use of `std::function` worth noting is to return a `lambda` expression from a nontemplate function:

```
std::function <int(int)> add_n(int n)
{
    return [n](int i) { return n + i; };
}

int result = add_n(3)(5);  // Result is 8.
```

The return value of add_n is a closure object wrapped in an std::function object. Note that add_n is not a template and that it is not called in a template or **auto** context. This example illustrates a runtime-polymorphic way to achieve currying; see the earlier example in *Interface adaptation, partial application, and currying* on page 597.

Event-driven callbacks

Event-driven systems tend to have interfaces that have an abundance of callbacks:

```
#include <memory>  // std::unique_ptr

class DialogBox { /*...*/ };

template <typename Button1Func, typename Button2Func>
std::unique_ptr<DialogBox> twoButtonDialog(const char* prompt,
                                           const char* button1Text,
                                           Button1Func button1Callback,
                                           const char* button2Text,
                                           Button2Func button2Callback)
{
    // ...
}
```

The twoButtonDialog factory function takes three strings and two callbacks and returns a pointer to a dialog box having two buttons. The dialog-box logic invokes one of the two callbacks, depending on which of the two buttons is pressed. These callbacks are often quite small pieces of code that can best be expressed directly in the program logic using lambda expressions:

```
void runModalDialogBox(DialogBox& db);

void launchShuttle(/*...*/)
{
    bool doLaunch = false;

    std::unique_ptr<DialogBox> confirm =
        twoButtonDialog("Are you sure you want to launch the shuttle?",
                        "Yes", [&]{ doLaunch = true; },
                        "No",  []{});
```

```
        runModalDialogBox(*confirm);

    if (doLaunch)
    {
        // ... Launch the shuttle!
    }
}
```

Here, the user is being prompted as to whether or not to launch a shuttle. Since the dialog box is processed entirely within the `launchShuttle` function, it is convenient to express two callbacks in place, within the function, using lambda expressions. The first lambda expression — passed as the callback for when the user clicks "Yes" — captures the `doLaunch` flag by reference and simply sets it to **true**. The second lambda expression — passed as the callback for when the user clicks "No" — does nothing, leaving the `doLaunch` flag having its original **false** value. The simplicity of these callbacks comes from their being effectively extensions of the surrounding block and, hence, have access (via the lambda capture) to block-scoped variables such as `doLaunch`.

Recursion

A lambda expression cannot refer to itself, so creating one that is recursive involves using one of a number of different possible workarounds. If the lambda capture is empty, recursion can be accomplished fairly simply by converting the lambda expression into a plain function pointer stored in a **static** variable:

```
void f1()
{
    static int (*const fact)(int) = [](int i)
    {
        return i < 2 ? 1 : i * fact(i - 1);
    };

    int result = fact(4);  // computes 24
}
```

In the above example, `fact(n)` returns the factorial of n, computed using a recursive algorithm. The variable, `fact`, becomes visible before its initializer is compiled, allowing it to be called from within the lambda expression. To enable the conversion to function pointer, the lambda capture must be empty; hence, `fact` must be static so that it can be accessed without capturing it.

If a recursive lambda expression is desired with a nonempty lambda capture, then the entire recursion can be enclosed in an outer lambda expression:

```
void f2(int n)
{
    auto permsN = [n](int m) -> int
    {
```

```
        static int (*const imp)(int, int) = [](int x, int m) {
            return m <= x ? m : m * imp(x, m - 1);
        };
        return imp(m - n + 1, m);
    };

    int a = permsN(5);  // permutations of 5 items, n at a time
    int b = permsN(4);  // permutations of 4 items, n at a time
}
```

In this example, permsN(m) returns the number of permutations of m items taken n at a time, where n is captured by the closure object. The implementation of permsN defines a nested imp function pointer that uses the same technique as fact, above, to achieve recursion. Since imp must have an empty lambda capture, everything it needs is passed in as arguments by the permsN enclosing lambda expression. Note that the imp pointer and the lambda expression from which it is initialized do not need to be scoped inside of the permsN lambda expression; whether such nesting is desirable is a matter of taste.

In C++14, additional approaches to recursion (e.g., the "Y Combinator" borrowed from lambda calculus[6]) are possible due to the availability of generic lambdas; see Section 2.2. "*Generic* Lambdas" on page 968.

Stateless lambdas

NB: This section was written in collaboration with Stephen Dewhurst. Any errors made in revising the draft are solely the authors'.

Stateless lambdas offer a convenient way of wrapping the invocation of functions and function-like macros, leading to their improved safety, efficiency, and usability in template contexts. Supplying a lambda that wraps a function invocation, rather than a function pointer, as an argument to a function template facilitates inlining and, consequently, the generation of more efficient code:

```
#include <algorithm>  // std::sort
#include <vector>     // std::vector

inline
bool greater(int lhs, int rhs)
{
    return lhs > rhs;
}

void test1(std::vector<int>& data)
{
    std::sort(data.begin(), data.end(), &greater);  // BAD IDEA!
}
```

---

[6]derevenets16

The specialization of `std::sort` invoked in the example above employs a function pointer as the comparison functor type, making it unlikely for calls to `greater` to be inlined unless the entire call to `std::sort` is inlined as well. Wrapping the invocation of the function with a stateless lambda, however, changes the specialization such that the comparison functor type is the compiler-generated type of the closure, enabling the compiler to inline calls to the comparator:

```
void test2(std::vector<int>& data)
{
    std::sort(data.begin(), data.end(), [](int lhs, int rhs) {
        return greater(lhs, rhs);                        // OK
    });
}
```

A similar use of stateless lambda is wrapping function-like macros, notorious for being visually indistinguishable from a function call yet lacking function-call semantics:

```
#define twice(E) ((E) + (E))  // BAD IDEA!

int test3(int value)  // Invoke functionality problematically as macro directly.
{
    return twice(++value);  // Bug, undefined behavior
}

int test4(int value)  // Invoke functionality properly via a stateless lambda.
{
    auto twoTimes = [](int arg) { return twice(arg); };

    return twoTimes(++value);  // OK, function-call semantics
}
```

Direct use of function-like macros, such as `twice` in the example above, can be made safer via wrapping the invocation in a stateless lambda, e.g., the `twoTimes` lambda above. Moreover, such wrapping enables the use of function-like macros as function objects in generic algorithms:

```
void test5(std::vector<int>& data)
{
    std::transform(data.begin(), data.end(), data.begin(),
                   [](int v) { return twice(v); });
}
```

If a function-like macro, such as `twice`, were used directly in function `test5` in the example above, the resulting program would fail to compile. Furthermore, when a particular name might refer to a regular function on one platform and to a function-like macro on another (which sometimes is the case for C Standard Library functions), wrapping the invocation with a stateless lambda might be useful to improve both inlining and *portability*:

```
#include <cassert>   // standard C assert macro
#include <numeric>   // std::accumulate
```

```cpp
#include <vector>    // std::vector
#include <utility>   // std::min

#ifdef _MSC_VER
#include <Windows.h> // defines the min macro when NOMINMAX is defined
#endif

int test6(const std::vector<int>& data)
{
    assert(!data.empty());
    return std::accumulate(
        data.begin() + 1, data.end(), data[0], [](int acc, int val) {
            using namespace std;   // Enable min to be called as a nonmacro.
            return min(acc, val);  // Note that min may or may not be a macro.
        });
}
```

Wrapping the invocation of min in a stateless lambda in the code example above will work irrespective of whether the min macro is defined by Windows.h. What's more, such wrapping enables proper overload resolution and template argument deduction for an std::min function should the min macro not be defined.

Being stateless, the closure type of this special form of lambda is eligible for **empty-base optimization (EBO)**. For types that need to store a function object, EBO can reduce object size compared to storing a function pointer. For example, the deleter stored by instances of the std::unique_ptr class template is eligible for such optimization:

```cpp
#include <memory>  // std::unique_ptr

void del(int* ptr) { /* Do some extra work, then delete. */ }
auto delWrap = [](int* ptr) { del(ptr); };

static_assert(
    sizeof(std::unique_ptr<int>)                   ==     sizeof(void*) &&
    sizeof(std::unique_ptr<int, decltype(&del)>)   == 2 * sizeof(void*) &&
    sizeof(std::unique_ptr<int, decltype(delWrap)>) ==    sizeof(void*), "");
```

Using the del function's type as the deleter for std::unique_ptr doubles the object size in contrast to using the default deleter. When the function is wrapped into a stateless lambda, however, the compiler is able to use EBO to avoid increasing the object size. Note that the compiler is, again, likely to inline calls to delWrap but not del.

Potential Pitfalls

Dangling references

Closure objects can capture references to local variables and copies of the **this** pointer. If a copy of the closure object outlives the stack frame in which it was created, these references can refer to objects that have been destroyed. The two ways in which a closure object can outlive its creation context are if (1) it is returned from the function or (2) it is stored in a data structure for later invocation:

```cpp
#include <functional>  // std::function
#include <vector>      // std::vector

class Class1
{
    int d_mem;

    static std::vector<std::function<double(void*)> > s_workQueue;

    std::function<void(int)> mf1()
    {
        int local;
        return [&](int i) -> void { d_mem = local = i; };  // Bug, dangling refs
    }

    void mf2()
    {
        double local = 1.0;
        s_workQueue.push_back([&,this](void* p) -> double {
                return p ? local : double(d_mem);
            });  // Bug, dangling refs
    }
};
```

The example above uses std::function to hold closure objects, as described in *Use Cases — Use with std::function* on page 601. In member function mf1, the lambda body modifies both the local variable and the member variable currently in scope. However, as soon as the function returns, the local variable goes out of scope, and the closure contains a dangling reference. Moreover, the object on which it is invoked can also go out of scope while the closure object continues to exist. Modifying either **this**->d_mem or local through the capture is likely to corrupt the stack, leading to a crash, potentially much later in the program.

The member function mf2, rather than *return* a closure with dangling references, stores it in a data structure, i.e., the s_workqueue static vector. Once again, local becomes a dangling reference when mf2 finishes and d_mem might become one when the object on which mf2 was called is destroyed, which can result in data corruption when the call operator for the stored closure object is invoked. It is safest to capture **this** and use capture by reference only when the lifetime of the closure object is clearly limited to the current function. Implicitly captured **this** is particularly insidious because, even if the capture default is capture by copy, member variables are not copied and are often referenced without the **this**-> prefix, making them hard to spot in the source code.

Overuse

The ability to write functions, especially functions with state, at the point where they are needed and without much of the syntactic overhead that accompanies normal functions and class methods, can potentially lead to a style of code that uses "lambdas everywhere," losing the abstraction and well-documented interfaces of separate functions. Lambda expressions are not intended for large-scale reuse. Sprinkling lambda expressions throughout the code can result in less well-factored, less maintainable code.

Mixing captured and noncaptured variables

A lambda body can access both automatic-duration local variables that were captured from the enclosing block and static-duration variables that need not and cannot be captured. Variables captured by copy are "frozen" at the point of capture and cannot be changed except by the lambda body (if **mutable**), whereas **static** variables can be changed independent of the lambda expression. This difference is often useful but can cause confusion when reasoning about a lambda expression:

```
void f1()
{
    static int a;
    int        b;

    a = 5;
    b = 6;

    auto c1 = [b]{ return a + b; };   // OK, b is captured by copy.
    assert(11 == c1());               // OK, a == 5 and b == 6.
    ++b;                              // Increment *primary* b.
    assert(11 == c1());               // OK, captured b did not change.
    ++a;                             // Increment static-duration a.
    assert(11 == c1());               // Fires, a == 6 and captured b == 6
}
```

When the closure object for c1 is created, the captured b value is frozen within the lambda body. Changing the primary b has no effect. However, a is not captured, nor is it allowed to be. As a result, there is only *one* a variable, and modifying that variable outside of the lambda body changes the result of invoking the call operator. In C++14, such lambda-capture expressions can be used to effectively capture a copy of such nonlocal variables if it is desired; see Section 2.2."Lambda Captures" on page 986.

Local variables in unevaluated contexts can yield surprises

To use a local variable, x, from the surrounding block as part of an unevaluated operand (e.g., **sizeof**(x) or **alignof**(x)), capturing x is generally unnecessary since it is not ODR-used within the lambda body. Whether or not x is captured, most expressions in unevaluated contexts behave as though x were *not* captured and the expression were evaluated directly in the enclosing block scope. This behavior is surprising because, for example, a captured variable in a non**mutable** lambda expression is **const**, whereas the primary variable might not be:

```cpp
#include <iostream>  // std::cout

short s1(int&)       { return 0; }
int   s1(const int&) { return 0; }

void f0()
{
    int x = 0;  // x is a nonconst lvalue.
    [x]{
        // captured x in nonmutable lambda is lvalue of type const int
        std::cout << sizeof(s1(x)) << '\n';  // prints sizeof(short)
        auto s1x = s1(x);                     // yields an int
        std::cout << sizeof(s1x) << '\n';     // prints sizeof(int)
    }();
}
```

The first print statement calls s1(x) in an unevaluated context, which ignores the captured x and returns the size of the result of s1(**int**&). The next statement actually *evaluates* s1(x), passing the *captured* x and calling s1(**const int**&) because the call operator is not decorated with **mutable**.

When using **decltype**(x), the result is the declared type of the *primary* variable, regardless of whether x was captured. However, if x had been captured by copy, **decltype**((x)), which returns the type of *expression* (x) (see Section 1.1."**decltype**" on page 25), would have yielded the *lvalue* type of the *captured* variable. There is some dispute as to what the correct results should be if x is *not* captured, with some compilers yielding the type of the primary variable and others complaining that it was not captured:

```cpp
void f1()
{
    int x = 0;  // x is a nonconst lvalue.
    auto c1 = [x]{ decltype((x)) y = x; };  // y has type const int&.
}
```

Finally, there is an unsettled question as to whether **typeid**(x) is an ODR-use of x and, therefore, requires that x be captured. Some compilers — e.g., GCC 11.2 (c. 2021) — will complain about the following code:

```cpp
#include <typeinfo>  // typeid
void f2()
```

```
{
    int x = 0;
    auto c1 = []() -> const std::type_info& { return typeid(x); };
        // Error on some platforms; "x was not captured."
}
```

One can avoid this pitfall simply by calling **typeid** outside of the lambda, capturing the result if necessary:

```
#include <typeinfo>  // typeid
void f3()
{
    int x = 0;
    const std::type_info& xid = typeid(x);
        // OK, typeid called outside of lambda.
    auto c1 = [&]() -> const std::type_info& { return xid; };
        // OK, return captured typeinfo.
}
```

Annoyances

Debugging

By definition, lambdas do not have names. Tools such as debuggers and stack-trace examiners typically display the compiler-generated names of the closure types even when the programmer stored the lambda in a variable with a descriptive name, making it difficult to discern where a problem occurred.

Can't capture *this by copy

A lambda expression can freeze the value of a surrounding local variable by using capture by copy, but no such ability is available directly to copy the object pointed to by **this**. To capture a copy of *this, it is necessary to create a variable external to the lambda expression (e.g., self in the example below) and capture *that* variable[7]:

---

[7]As of C++17, *this can be captured directly with **this** within the lambda body pointing to the *copy* rather than the original:

```
class Class2
{
    int d_value;

    void mf1()
    {
        auto c1 = [*this]{ return d_value; };
            // C++17: return d_value from copy of *this.
    }
};
```

```
class Class1
{
    int d_value;

    void mf1()
    {
        Class1& self = *this;
        auto c1 = [self]{ return self.d_value; };
    }
};
```

In C++14, it is possible to achieve the same effect in a terser manner using a lambda capture expression [self = *this] (see Section 2.2. "Lambda Captures" on page 986).

Confusing mix of immediate and deferred-execution code

The main selling point of lambda expressions — i.e., the ability to define a function object at the point of use — can sometimes be a liability. The code within a lambda body is typically not executed immediately but is deferred until some other piece of code, e.g., an algorithm, invokes it as a callback. The code that is immediately executed and the code whose invocation is deferred are visually intermixed in a way that could confuse a future maintainer. For example, let's look at a simplified excerpt from an earlier use case, *Use Cases — Use with* std::function on page 601.

```
#include <cstdlib>     // std::strtol
#include <functional>  // std::function
#include <string>      // std::string
#include <vector>      // std::vector

using Instruction = std::function<long*(long* sp)>;

std::vector<Instruction> instructionStream;

std::string nextToken();                      // Read the next token.
char tokenOp(const std::string& token);  // operator for token

void readInstructions()
{
    std::string token;
    Instruction nextInstr;
    while (!(token = nextToken()).empty())
    {
        switch (tokenOp(token))
        {
            // ... more cases
            case '+':
            {
                // + operation
```

```
                    nextInstr = [](long* sp){
                        long v1 = *--sp;
                        long v2 = *--sp;
                        *sp++ = v1 + v2;
                        return sp;
                    };
                    break;
                }
            // ... more cases
            }
        // ...
        }
}
```

A casual reading might lead to the assumption that operations such as `*--sp` are taking place within **case** `'+'`, when the truth is that these operations are encapsulated in a lambda expression and are not executed until the closure object is called (via `nextInstr`) in a relatively distant part of the code.

Trailing punctuation

The body of a lambda expression is a *compound statement*. When compound statements appear elsewhere in the C++ grammar, e.g., as the body of a function or loop, they are not followed by punctuation. A lambda expression, conversely, is invariably followed by some sort of punctuation, usually a semicolon or parenthesis but sometimes a comma or binary operator:

```
auto c1 = []{ /*...*/ };  // <-- The semicolon at the end is required.
```

When emulating a control construct using lambda expressions, the extra punctuation appears as a noticeable difference from a built-in language construct. Such is the case, for example, for `parallel_foreach` from *Use Cases — Emulate user-defined control constructs* on page 599:

```
void f(const std::vector<int>& data)
{
    // ...
    for (int e : data)
    {
        // ...              for loop body
    }  // <-- no punctuation after the closing brace

    parallel_foreach(data.begin(), data.end(), [&](int e)
    {
        // ...              parallel loop body
    });  // <-- The closing parenthesis and semicolon are required.
    // ...
}
```

In the above code snippet, the programmer would like the `parallel_foreach` algorithm to look as much like the built-in **for** loop as possible. However, the built-in **for** loop doesn't end with a closing parenthesis and a semicolon, whereas the `parallel_foreach` does.

See Also

- "`decltype`" (§1.1, p. 25) illustrates a form of type inference often used in conjunction with (or in place of) trailing return types.

- "`auto` Return" (§3.2, p. 1182) shows a form of type inference that shares syntactical similarities with trailing return types, leading to potential pitfalls when migrating from C++11 to C++14.

Further Reading

- Scott Meyers provides germane advice when implementing and using lambdas in his introductory book, *Effective Modern C++*; see **meyers15b**, Chapter 6, "Item 31: Avoid default capture modes," pp. 216–223; "Item 32: Use init captures to move objects into closures," pp. 224–229; "Item 33: Use `decltype` on `auto&&` parameters to `std::forward` them," pp. 229–232; and "Item 34: Prefer lambdas to `std::bind`," pp. 232–240.

Asking if an Expression Cannot `throw`

Using the **noexcept** keyword in its *operator* form affords a standard programmatic means of querying, at compile time, whether a given expression — typically involving a function call — can be relied upon never to emit a C++ exception.

Description

Some operations can choose significantly more efficient algorithms, e.g., having better asymptotic complexity, if they can identify that the expressions they will use will never emit exceptions.[1] The ability to query an expression for this property facilitates **generic programming**, especially with respect to *move* operations.

C++11 introduces a compile-time operator, **noexcept**, that, when applied to an arbitrary expression, evaluates to **true** if and only if *no* **potentially evaluated** subexpression within that expression *is allowed to* emit a C++ exception:

```
static_assert(noexcept(0), "");  // OK, 0 doesn't throw.
```

The **noexcept** operator is intentionally conservative in that the compiler must consider any potentially evaluated subexpression of its operand. Consider a **ternary operator** with a compile-time constant as its **conditional expression**:

```
static_assert(noexcept(1 ? throw : 0), "");  // Error, throw throws.
```

Clearly, this expression will always throw, so it is unsurprising that **noexcept** informs us of that. Perhaps counterintuitively, however, the similar expression that would never evaluate the **throw** at run time is also identified by the **noexcept** operator as potentially throwing:

```
static_assert(noexcept(0 ? throw : 0), "");  // Error, throw throws.
```

This inspection of subexpressions does not, thankfully, extend to **unevaluated operands** within the expression, such as those that are arguments of the **sizeof** operator[2]:

```
static_assert(noexcept(sizeof(throw, 1)), "");  // OK
```

In other words, if *any* individual potentially evaluated subexpression is capable of throwing, then the entire expression *must* be reported as potentially throwing.

Operator-produced exceptions

In addition to functions (see *Introducing **noexcept** exception specifications for functions* on page 619), certain operators in classical C++ have edge cases that might throw. Consider

---

[1] Note that the **noexcept** operator does not appertain to operating-system-level signals such as a floating-point exception, segmentation fault, and so on.

[2] The unevaluated operand of **sizeof** affects the result of the **noexcept** operator on the latest version of GCC 11.1 available at the time of this writing (c. 2021). A **defect report** has been filed; see **khlebnikov21**.

the familiar **new** operator used to allocate dynamic memory. Note that when we say "the **new** operator," we are talking about the C++ language construct that first calls the underlying function known as global `::operator new` and then invokes the appropriate constructor. The **contract** for **new** states that it will either allocate and return a pointer to the requested integral number of bytes or throw an `std::bad_alloc` exception defined in `<new>`. There is an overload of the underlying global **operator new** — and also the corresponding **operator new[]** — that takes an argument of type `std::nothrow_t` defined in `<new>`. This overload of **new** ignores the value of its `std::nothrow_t` argument but, instead of throwing on allocation failure, returns a *null* address value:

```
#include <new>  // std::nothrow

static_assert(!noexcept(new                int[1000]), ""); // OK, noexcept
                                                            // Result is false.

static_assert( noexcept(new(std::nothrow) int[1000]), ""); // OK, noexcept
                                                            // Result is true.
```

Performing a **dynamic_cast** on a reference (but not a pointer) to a **polymorphic type** will result in a runtime exception of type `std::bad_cast` if the referent is not of a class type that is publicly and unambiguously derived from the target type of the cast operation:

```
struct B         { virtual ~B();  };
struct BB        { virtual ~BB(); };
struct D1 : B    { };                      // one base class
struct D2 : B, BB { };                     // two base classes

D1 d1;
D2 d2;

B& b1r = d1;  // reference to B base class
B& b2r = d2;  // another reference to B base class

D1& d1r1 = dynamic_cast<D1&>(b1r);  // OK
D1& d1r2 = dynamic_cast<D1&>(b2r);  // throws std::bad_cast
D2& d2r1 = dynamic_cast<D2&>(b1r);  // throws std::bad_cast
D2& d2r2 = dynamic_cast<D2&>(b2r);  // OK

BB& bb1r = dynamic_cast<BB&>(b1r);  // throws std::bad_cast
BB& bb2r = dynamic_cast<BB&>(b2r);  // OK

// dynamic_cast to a pointer never throws.
B  *bp   = 0;
D1 *d1p  = dynamic_cast<D1*>(bp);    // dp == nullptr
D1 *d1p1 = dynamic_cast<D1*>(&b1r);  // OK
D1 *d1p2 = dynamic_cast<D1*>(&b2r);  // d1p2 == nullptr
D2 *d2p1 = dynamic_cast<D2*>(&b1r);  // d2p1 == nullptr
D2 *d2p2 = dynamic_cast<D2*>(&b2r);  // OK
```

```
BB *bb1p = dynamic_cast<BB*>(&b1r);  // bb1p == nullptr
BB *bb2p = dynamic_cast<BB*>(&b2r);  // OK
```

Observe that for bb2r in the example code above, the **dynamic_cast** of a reference to an object of type B, b2r, to a reference of type BB succeeds despite there being no direct inheritance relationship between these two types. In this particular case, it is possible to **dynamic_cast** between references to the specific objects of B and BB above because they are *both* polymorphic subobjects of the same parent object, d2, of derived-type D2. Indirect inheritance relationships, such as one between b2r and bb2r above, can be determined only at run time because not every reference to a B necessarily refers to a subobject of a D2. When no such cross-inheritance relationship exists for a particular reference to B, a **dynamic_cast** to a reference will throw std::bad_cast.

Because it is possible for a **dynamic_cast** to throw std::bad_cast, which is defined in <typeinfo>, on a reference but not a pointer, the **noexcept** operator discriminates between these two kinds of expressions:

```
static_assert( noexcept(dynamic_cast<D1*>(bp )), "");  // OK, never throws
static_assert(!noexcept(dynamic_cast<D1&>(b1r)), "");  // OK, can throw

static_assert( noexcept(dynamic_cast<D2*>(bp )), "");  // OK, never throws
static_assert(!noexcept(dynamic_cast<D2&>(b1r)), "");  // OK, can throw
```

In the example above, when the dynamic cast fails on a pointer, a *null* pointer value is returned. When the dynamic cast fails on a reference, however, the only other option would be to return a *null* reference, which is not allowed by the language, so throwing an exception is the only reasonable way of indicating a failure to the caller.

Runtime type identification (**RTTI**) exhibits similar behavior with respect to reference types. The **typeid** operator returns a **const** *lvalue* reference to an std::type_info object. If **typeid** queries a reference, it returns a reference to the **type_info** of the referenced object, and if the reference is to a polymorphic class, it returns a reference to the **type_info** of the complete object that is queried. A special rule allows for dereferencing a null pointer, which otherwise has undefined behavior, as the target of a **typeid** query. Since a dereference would involve a runtime query of the **vtable** if the declared type of the pointer refers to a polymorphic class, invoking **typeid** on a null pointer throws an std::bad_typeid exception. Note that this behavior would *not* occur if the pointer referred to a *non*polymorphic class. Hence, invoking **noexcept** on the **typeid** operator will return **true** unless the target is the result of dereferencing a pointer to a polymorphic class:

```
#include <typeinfo>  // typeid, std::typeinfo, std::bad_typeid

class B { virtual ~B() { } };
class C { };

B* bp = nullptr;
C* cp = nullptr;
```

```
static_assert( noexcept(typeid( cp)), ""); // OK, returns type_info for C*
static_assert( noexcept(typeid( bp)), ""); // OK, returns type_info for B*
static_assert( noexcept(typeid(*cp)), ""); // OK, returns type_info for C
static_assert(!noexcept(typeid(*bp)), ""); // OK, would throw std::bad_typeid
```

Deprecated, dynamic exception specifications for functions

Classic C++ provided what has now been renamed **dynamic exception specifications**, which can be used to decorate a function with the types of exception objects that a function was permitted to throw:

```
int f();            // Function f may throw anything.
int g() throw(int); // Function g may throw an integer.
int h() throw();    // Function h is not allowed to throw anything.
```

The **noexcept** operator looks *only* at the function declaration:

```
static_assert(!noexcept(f()), "");  // OK, may throw anything
static_assert(!noexcept(g()), "");  // OK, may throw an int
static_assert( noexcept(h()), "");  // OK, may not throw anything
```

Providing a *dynamic* exception specification does not prevent a function from *attempting* to throw or to rethrow a caught exception object. When an exception is thrown from within a function, the runtime system automatically checks to see if that function has an associated **dynamic exception specification** and, if so, looks up the type of the thrown exception. If the type of the thrown exception is listed, the exception is allowed to propagate outside of the function body; otherwise, **[[noreturn]] void** std::unexpected() is invoked, which calls std::terminate unless a user-supplied handler exits the program first. **[[noreturn]]** is an attribute that indicates the function will not return but may throw; see Section 1.1. "Attribute Syntax" on page 12 and Section 1.1. "noreturn" on page 95:

```
void f0()                 { throw 5;   } // throws int
void f1()                 { throw 5.0; } // throws double

void f2() throw(int)      { throw 5;   } // throws int
void f3() throw(int)      { throw 5.0; } // calls std::unexpected()

void f4() throw(double)   { throw 5;   } // calls std::unexpected()
void f5() throw(double)   { throw 5.0; } // throws double

void f6() throw(int, double) { throw 5;   } // throws int
void f7() throw(int, double) { throw 5.0; } // throws double

void f8() throw()         { throw 5;   } // calls std::unexpected()
void f9() throw()         { throw 5.0; } // calls std::unexpected()
```

The **noexcept** operator is unconcerned with the type of exceptions that might be thrown, reporting back only as to whether an exception of *any* type may escape the body of the function:

```
static_assert(!noexcept(f0()), "");  // doesn't say it doesn't throw
static_assert(!noexcept(f1()), "");  //    "       "   "    "      "

static_assert(!noexcept(f2()), "");  // f2 may throw an int.
static_assert(!noexcept(f3()), "");  // f3 "    "   "    "

static_assert(!noexcept(f4()), "");  // f4 may throw a double.
static_assert(!noexcept(f5()), "");  // f5 "    "   "    "

static_assert(!noexcept(f6()), "");  // f6 may throw int or double.
static_assert(!noexcept(f7()), "");  // f7 "    "   "    "     "

static_assert( noexcept(f8()), "");  // f8 may not throw.
static_assert( noexcept(f9()), "");  // f9 "   "    "
```

There are, however, practical drawbacks to dynamic exception specifications.

1. **Brittle** — These classic, fine-grained exception specifications attempt to provide excessively detailed information that is not programmatically useful and is subject to frequent changes due to otherwise inconsequential updates to the implementation.

2. **Expensive** — When an exception is thrown, a *dynamic*-exception list must be searched at run time to determine if that specific exception type is allowed.

3. **Disruptive** — When an exception reaches a *dynamic*-exception specification, the stack must be unwound, whether or not the exception is permitted by that specification, losing useful stack-trace information if the program is about to terminate.

These deficiencies proved, over time, to be insurmountable, and dynamic-exception specifications other than **throw()** were largely unused in practice.

As of C++11, dynamic-exception specifications are officially deprecated[3] in favor of the more streamlined **noexcept** specifier (see Section 3.1."**noexcept** Specifier" on page 1085), which we introduce briefly in the next section.

Introducing noexcept exception specifications for functions

C++11 introduces an alternative exception-specification mechanism for arbitrary free functions, member functions, and lambda expressions (see Section 2.1."Lambdas" on page 573):

```
void f() noexcept(expr);  // expr is a Boolean constant expression.
void f() noexcept;        // same as void f() noexcept(true)
```

Instead of specifying a *list* of exceptions that may be thrown, whether *any* exception may be thrown is specified. As with C++03, the lack of any annotation is the equivalent of saying anything might be thrown (except for destructors, which are **noexcept** by default):

---

[3]C++17 removes std::unexpected and all dynamic exception specifications other than **throw()**, which becomes a synonym for **noexcept** before **throw()** too is removed by C++20.

```
#include <exception>  // std::bad_exception
// C++03                              // C++11 equivalent

void f0();                          void g0();
void f1() throw();                  void g1() noexcept;
void f2() throw(std::bad_exception); void g2() noexcept(false);
void f3() throw(int, double);       void g3() noexcept(false);

static_assert(noexcept(f0()) == noexcept(g0()), "");  // OK, both are false.
static_assert(noexcept(f1()) == noexcept(g1()), "");  // OK, both are true.
static_assert(noexcept(f2()) == noexcept(g2()), "");  // OK, both are false.
static_assert(noexcept(f3()) == noexcept(g3()), "");  // OK, both are false.
```

The inability of the **noexcept** operator to distinguish among specific exceptions that can be thrown does not hamper its general applicability. By analogy, consider how we might address the Unix return-status convention of consistently returning 0 on success and a nonzero value otherwise:

```
void func(/*...*/)
{
    if (0 != doSomething(/*...*/))  // Quickly check if it failed.
    {
        // failure branch: handle, return, abort, etc.
    }

    // All good; continue on the good path.

    // ...
}
```

This long-standing convention exploits the realization that there can be many ways to fail but typically only one way to succeed. By comparing to 0 the return value of a called function, a calling function can quickly discriminate programmatically between two primary code paths — success and failure — irrespective of what specific nonzero error codes might be returned.

Much like a return status, generic libraries might need to choose from between just two algorithms having substantially different performance characteristics based solely on whether a given operation can be depended upon never to throw. By distilling the details of **dynamic-exception specifications** down to a simple binary **noexcept** specification, we sidestep most of the brittleness while preserving the ability to query programmatically for the essential information:

```
template <typename T>
void runAlgorithm(T t)
{
    if (noexcept(t.someFunction()))
    {
```

```
    // Use a faster algorithm that assumes no exception will be thrown.
}
else
{
    // Use a slower algorithm that can handle a thrown exception.
}
}
```

Notice that the primary, compile-time branch in the example above depends on *only* whether it can be reliably assumed that calling someFunction on an object of type T will never throw anything.

Although syntactically trivial, safe and effective use of the **noexcept** specifier fairly deserves substantial elaboration; see Section 3.1."**noexcept** Specifier" on page 1085.

Compatibility of dynamic and noexcept exception specifications

Dynamic exception specifications are required to unwind the program stack — a.k.a. **stack unwinding** — when an unexpected exception is encountered, whereas that behavior is left unspecified for violations of **noexcept** specifications:

```
#include <iostream>  // std::cout

struct S { ~S() { std::cout << "Unwound!" << std::endl; } };

int f() throw()  { S s; throw 0; }  // ~S is invoked.
int g() noexcept { S s; throw 0; }  // ~S might be invoked.
```

As of C++11, the *syntactic* meaning of **throw()** was made identical to **noexcept** and, hence, can coexist on declarations within the same translation unit:

```
int f() throw();    // OK
int f() noexcept;   // OK, redeclaration of same syntactic entity
```

If we now *define* the function, f, the nature of the **stack unwinding** behavior is left unspecified by the Standard.[4]

Compiler-generated special member functions

In C++11, exception specification on implicitly declared **special member functions** is still defined in terms of dynamic exception specification; this purely theoretical distinction

---

[4]On GCC, for example, the first declaration and, in fact, all pure declarations must be consistent (i.e., either all **noexcept** or all **throw()**), but they make no difference with respect to behavior. It is *only* the declaration on the function *definition* that governs. If the specification is dynamic and --std=c++17 is not specified, then **stack unwinding** will occur; otherwise, it will not. On Clang, **stack unwinding** always occurs. MSVC has never implemented specifying handlers with std::set_unexpected and doesn't perform stack unwinding. Intel (EDG) always calls the handler specified by std::set_unexpected and unwinds the stack.

is, however, unobservable via the **noexcept** operator. We will therefore speak only in terms of the observable binary property: **noexcept(true)** or **noexcept(false)**. For example, consider a class, A, containing only **fundamental types**, such as **int**, **double**, and **char***:

```
#include <utility>  // std::move

struct A { int i; double d; char* cp; } a, a2;  // built-ins only

static_assert(noexcept( A()              ), "");  // OK, default constructor
static_assert(noexcept( A(a)             ), "");  // OK, copy constructor
static_assert(noexcept( a = a2           ), "");  // OK, copy assignment
static_assert(noexcept( A(std::move(a))  ), "");  // OK, move constructor
static_assert(noexcept( a = std::move(a2) ), "");  // OK, move assignment
static_assert(noexcept( a.A::~A()        ), "");  // OK, destructor
```

Since this type neither contains nor inherits from other **user-defined types (UDTs)**, the compiler treats each of these implicit declarations as if they had been specified **noexcept**.

If a special member function is declared explicitly, then that declaration defines whether the function is to be considered **noexcept** irrespective of its definition (except when using =**default** on first declaration; see Section 1.1."Defaulted Functions" on page 33). Consider, for example, an empty class, B, that declares each of the six standard special member functions:

```
struct B  // empty class with all special members declared w/o exception spec.
{
    B();                      // default constructor: noexcept(false)
    B(const B&);              // copy constructor:    noexcept(false)
    B& operator=(const B&);   // copy assignment:     noexcept(false)
    B(B&&);                   // move constructor:    noexcept(false)
    B& operator=(B&&);        // move assignment:     noexcept(false)
    ~B();                     // destructor:          noexcept(true)
};
```

Without regard for their corresponding definitions, the **noexcept** operator will report each of these explicitly declared special member functions as being **noexcept(false)** with the lone exception of the **destructor**, which defaults to **noexcept(true)**; see *Annoyances — Destructors, but not move constructors, are **noexcept** by default* on page 653. More generally, all explicitly declared destructors default to **noexcept(true)** unless they have a base class or member with a **noexcept(false)** destructor. To indicate that the destructor of a class (e.g., BadIdea in the example below) may throw, it must be declared explicitly using the syntax **noexcept(false)** or a nonempty *dynamic* exception specification; see Section 3.1."**noexcept** Specifier" on page 1085:

```
struct BadIdea
{
    ~BadIdea() noexcept(false);  // destructor may throw
};
```

C++11 allows the user to declare a special member function and then request the compiler to provide its default implementation using the =**default** syntax; see Section 1.1."Defaulted Functions" on page 33. The resulting implementation will be *identical* to what it would have been had the special member function declaration been omitted rather than implicitly suppressed through the declaration of other special member functions:

```
struct C  // empty class declaring all of its special members to be =default
{
    C()                   = default;  // default constructor: noexcept(true)
    C(const C&)           = default;  // copy constructor:    noexcept(true)
    C& operator=(const C&) = default;  // copy assignment:     noexcept(true)
    C(C&&)                = default;  // move constructor:    noexcept(true)
    C& operator=(C&&)     = default;  // move assignment:     noexcept(true)
    ~C()                  = default;  // destructor:          noexcept(true)
};
```

When a user-defined type (e.g., D in the example below) contains or derives from types whose corresponding special member functions are all **noexcept(true)**, then so too will any implicitly defined special member functions of that type:

```
struct D : A { A v; } d, d2;  // All special members of A are noexcept(true).

static_assert(noexcept( D()              ), "");  // OK, default constructor
static_assert(noexcept( D(d)             ), "");  // OK, copy constructor
static_assert(noexcept( d = d2           ), "");  // OK, copy assignment
static_assert(noexcept( D(std::move(d))  ), "");  // OK, move constructor
static_assert(noexcept( d = std::move(d2)), "");  // OK, move assignment
static_assert(noexcept( d.D::~D()        ), "");  // OK, destructor
```

If, however, a special member function in any base or member type of a class (e.g., E in the example code below) is **noexcept(false)**, then the corresponding special member function of that class will be as well:

```
struct E { B b; } e, e2;  // All special members of B are noexcept(false) apart
                          // from the destructor.

static_assert(!noexcept( E()             ), "");  // OK, default constructor
static_assert(!noexcept( E(e)            ), "");  // OK, copy constructor
static_assert(!noexcept( e = e2          ), "");  // OK, copy assignment
static_assert(!noexcept( E(std::move(e)) ), "");  // OK, move constructor
static_assert(!noexcept( e = std::move(e2)), "");  // OK, move assignment
static_assert( noexcept( e.E::~E()       ), "");  // OK, destructor
```

It is permitted for an explicit **noexcept** specification to be placed on a special member of a class and then to use the =**default** syntax on first declaration to implement it. The explicit **noexcept** specification must then match that of the implicitly generated definition, else that special member function will be implicitly deleted:

```
struct F : B  // All special members of B are noexcept(false) apart
              // from the destructor.
{
    F()                     noexcept(false) = default;  // default constructor
    F(const F&)             noexcept       = default;  // copy constructor
    F& operator=(const F&)                 = default;  // copy assignment
    F(F&&)                  noexcept(true)  = default;  // move constructor
    F& operator=(F&&)                       = default;  // move assignment
    ~F()                    noexcept(true)  = default;  // destructor
};
```

Notice that, in class F in the code snippet above, both the *copy* and *move* constructors are mislabeled as being **noexcept(true)** when the defaulted declaration would have made them **noexcept(false)**. Such inconsistency is not in and of itself an error until an attempt is made to use that function; see Section 1.1.“Deleted Functions” on page 53:

```
void test()
{
    F f0, f1;            // OK,    default constructor
    F f2(f0);            // Error, copy constructor is deleted.
    f0 = f1;             // OK,    copy assignment
    F f3(std::move(f0)); // Error, move constructor is deleted.
    f0 = std::move(f1);  // OK,    move assignment
}                        // OK,    destructor
```

Note that the need for an *exact* match between explicitly declared and defaulted **noexcept** specifications is unforgiving in *either* direction. That is, had we, say, attempted to restrict the contract of the class F above by decorating its destructor with **noexcept(false)** when the defaulted implementation would have happened to have been **noexcept(true)**, that destructor would have nonetheless been implicitly deleted, severely crippling use of the class.

In C++20, mismatched explicit **noexcept** specification for a defaulted special member function no longer results in that member function being deleted. Instead, the explicit **noexcept** specification is accepted by the compiler.[5] This behavior change was accepted as a **defect report**, applying to C++11 and later, and is implemented, e.g., starting from Clang 9 (c. 2019), GCC 10.1 (c. 2020), and MSVC 16.8 (c. 2020).

Finally, the C++11 specification does not address directly the implicit exception specification for inheriting constructors (see Section 2.1.“Inheriting Ctors” on page 535), yet most popular compilers handle them correctly in that they take into account the exceptions thrown by the inherited constructor and all the member initialization involved in invocation of the inherited constructor.

In C++14, all implicitly declared special member functions, including inheriting constructors, are **noexcept(false)** if any function they invoke directly has an exception specification that allows all exceptions; otherwise, if any of these directly invoked functions has a dynamic exception specification, then the implicit member will have a dynamic exception specifica-

---

[5]See **smith19**.

tion that comprises all of the types that may be thrown by functions it invokes directly. In particular, when a constructor is inherited, its exception specification is nonthrowing if the base class constructor is nonthrowing, and the expressions initializing each of the derived class's additional bases and members are also nonthrowing. Otherwise, an inheriting constructor has a potentially throwing exception specification. Although the original text in the C++11 Standard was worded subtly differently, the wording was repaired via a **defect report** and incorporated directly into C++14. Note that all known implementations of the feature, even early prototypes, follow these corrected rules of C++14.

As a concrete example, let's suppose that we have a base class, BB, that has two *value* constructors, one throwing and the other *non*throwing:

```
struct BB  // base class having two overloaded value constructors
{
    BB(int)  noexcept(false);  //    throwing int  value constructor
    BB(char) noexcept(true);   // nonthrowing char value constructor
};
```

Applying the **noexcept** operator to these constructors produces the expected results:

```
int i;
char c;

static_assert(!noexcept( BB(i) ), "");  // noexcept(false)
static_assert( noexcept( BB(c) ), "");  // noexcept(true)
    // uses just base constructors' exception specifications
```

Next suppose we derive an empty class, D1, from BB that inherits BB's constructors:

```
struct D1 : BB  // empty derived class inheriting base class BB's ctors
{
    using BB::BB;  // inherits BB's ctors along with exception specs
};
```

Because the inherited constructors of the derived class are not required to invoke any other constructors, the exception specifications propagate unchanged:

```
static_assert(!noexcept( D1(i) ), "");  // noexcept(false)
static_assert( noexcept( D1(c) ), "");  // noexcept(true)
    // uses just the inherited constructors' exception specifications
```

Now imagine that we have some legacy class, SS, whose default constructor is implemented with a deprecated, dynamic exception specification that explicitly allows it to throw only an SSException (assumed defined elsewhere):

```
class SSException { /*...*/ };
struct SS  // old-fashioned type having deprecated, dynamic exception specs
{
    SS() throw(SSException);  // This ctor is allowed to throw only an SSException.
};
```

The **noexcept** operator, not caring about the type of a potential exception, reports **noexcept(false)**:

```
static_assert(!noexcept( SS() ),  "");  // throw(SSException)
    // uses the dynamic exception specification of the default constructor
```

Now suppose we derive a second type, D2, from base class BB but this time having, as a data member, ss, an object of type SS whose default constructor may throw an SSException:

```
struct D2 : BB  // nonempty derived class inheriting base class BB's ctors
{
    SS ss;        // data member having default ctor that may throw an SSException
    using BB::BB; // inherits BB's ctors along with exception specs
};
```

Both inherited constructors are now implicitly obliged to invoke the default constructor of ss, which may throw; hence, both inherited constructors are now potentially throwing:

```
static_assert(!noexcept( D2(i) ), "");  // BB(int) is noexcept(false).
static_assert(!noexcept( D2(c) ), "");  // SS() is throw(SSException).
    // uses both the inherited constructors' exception specifications and
    // the exception specification of the data member's default constructor
```

In the example above, the implicit exception specifications of the D2(**int**) and D2(**char**) constructors are, respectively, **noexcept(false)** and **throw**(SSException). Implicit dynamic exception specifications, despite being deprecated, are plausible since the invocation of an implicitly declared special member function, say, D2(**char**), will necessarily invoke all the other special member functions — i.e., BB(**char**) and SS() — that contribute to its implicit exception specification. If any of these implicitly invoked functions throws, the exception specification that will be checked first is that of the more restrictive invoked subfunction — i.e., that of SS() — and not the potentially more permissive caller.

Widening the exception specification of the implicitly declared special member functions, say, from **throw**(SSException) to **noexcept(false)**, would have no effect on which exceptions can propagate from the corresponding special member functions of bases and members. Even if we changed BB(**char**) to **noexcept(false)**, which would give D2(**char**) an implicit exception specification of **noexcept(false)** and allow exceptions of all types to pass, no other exception type thrown by SS() would ever propagate to a D2(**char**) constructor's potential exception specification check. Instead, the rogue exception would be stopped by the nonmatching exception specification of the subfunction SS() **throw**(SSException) invoked by the implicitly defined constructor.

Applying the noexcept operator to compound expressions

Recall from earlier in this feature section that the **noexcept** operator is applied to an expression, which might itself comprise other subexpressions. For example, consider a **noexcept** function f and non-**noexcept** function g, both operating on integers:

```
int f(int) noexcept;    // Function f is noexcept(false).
int g(int);             // Function g is noexcept(true).

static_assert( noexcept( f(17) ), "");   // OK, f is noexcept(true).
static_assert(!noexcept( g(17) ), "");   // OK, g is noexcept(false).
```

Now suppose that we have two function calls within a single expression:

```
static_assert( noexcept( f(1) + f(2) ), "");   // OK, f is noexcept(true).
static_assert(!noexcept( g(1) + g(2) ), "");   // OK, g is noexcept(false).
static_assert(!noexcept( g(1) + f(2) ), "");   // OK, "  "     "      "
static_assert(!noexcept( f(1) + g(2) ), "");   // OK, "  "     "  .   "
```

When we consider composing two functions, the overall expression is **noexcept** if and only if both functions are **noexcept**:

```
static_assert( noexcept( f(f(17)) ), "");   // OK, f is noexcept(true).
static_assert(!noexcept( g(g(17)) ), "");   // OK, g is noexcept(false).
static_assert(!noexcept( g(f(17)) ), "");   // OK, "  "     "     "
static_assert(!noexcept( f(g(17)) ), "");   // OK, "  "     "     "
```

The same applies to other forms of composition; recall from earlier that the specific operators applied in the expression do not matter, only whether any **potentially evaluated** subexpression might throw:

```
static_assert( noexcept( f(1) || f(2) ), "");   // OK, f is noexcept(true).
static_assert(!noexcept( g(1) || g(2) ), "");   // OK, g is noexcept(false).
static_assert(!noexcept( g(1) || f(2) ), "");   // OK, "  "     "      "
static_assert(!noexcept( f(1) || g(2) ), "");   // OK, "  "     "      "
static_assert(!noexcept( true || g(2) ), "");   // OK, note g is never called!
```

Importantly, note that the final expression in the example above is *not* **noexcept** even though the only subexpression that might throw is never evaluated. This deliberate language design decision eliminates variations in implementation that would trade off compile-time speed for determining whether the detailed logic of a given expression might throw, but see *Annoyances — Older compilers invade the bodies of **constexpr** functions* on page 654.

Applying the noexcept operator to move expressions

Finally, we come to the quintessential application of the **noexcept** operator. C++11 introduces the notion of a **move operation** — typically an adjunct to a **copy operation** — as a fundamentally new way to propagate the value of one object to another; see Section 2.1. "*Rvalue* References" on page 710. For objects that have well-defined **copy semantics** (e.g., **value semantics**), a valid copy operation typically satisfies *all* of the contractual requirements of the corresponding **move operation**, the only difference being that a requested *move* operation doesn't require that the value of the source object be preserved:

```
struct S  // Class S supports both copy and move operations.
{
    // ...
    S();                // default constructor
    S(const S&);        // copy constructor; noexcept(false)
    S(S&&) noexcept;    // move constructor; noexcept(true)
    // ...
};
```

When a value-preserving **copy operation** is not specifically needed, requesting that the value of an object be just *moved* could lead to a more runtime-efficient program. For example, a function that takes an argument by *rvalue* reference or by value is capable of exploiting a potentially more efficient move operation if one is available:

```
void f(const S&);  // passing object of type S by const lvalue reference
void f(S&&);       // passing object of type S by rvalue reference
```

However, note that *move* operations can lead to **memory diffusion** (i.e., memory blocks in the working set being spread throughout physical memory, causing cache misses and page faults), which in turn can severely impact the runtime performance of large, long-running programs.[6]

There are times when the compiler will automatically prefer a *move* operation over a *copy*, i.e., when it knows that the source object cannot be accessed after the end of the enclosing full expression:

```
S h();  // function returning an S by value
S s1;

void test()
{
    f(S());  // The compiler requests a move automatically.
    f(h());  // "      "        "      "  "     "       "

    S s2;
    f(s1);   // The compiler will not try to move automatically.
    f(s2);   // "      "      "   "  "   "    "      "
}
```

When an object such as s1 or s2 in the example code above has a name that can be used to access it, however, the programmer — knowing the value will no longer be needed — can request of the compiler that the object be moved:

---

[6]See **lakos16**, **bleaney16**, **lakos17a**, and **lakos17b**.

```
#include <utility> // std::move

void test2()
{
    S s2;
    f(std::move(s1));   // The compiler will now try to move from s1.
    f(std::move(s2));   // "      "      "   "   "   "   "     " s2.
}
```

When the programmer uses `std::move` to tell the compiler that the value of an object —
such as `s1` or `s2` in the code snippet above — is no longer needed, the compiler will invoke
the constructor variant taking `S` as an *rvalue* reference if one is available. If a class does not
provide a distinct move operation, requesting that an object be moved might have no effect
on the generated code:

```
struct C  // Class C supports copy but not move operations.
{
    C();                    // default constructor
    C(const C&);            // copy constructor
    C& operator=(const C&); // copy assignment
    ~C();                   // destructor
};

void f(C);

void test3()
{
    C c;

    C c1(c);                // invokes C's copy constructor
    C c2(std::move(c));     // invokes C's copy constructor

    f(c1);                  // invokes C's copy constructor
    f(std::move(c1));       // invokes C's copy constructor
}
```

Because class `C` in the example above has no distinct **move** operations, normal overload
resolution selects `C`'s *copy* constructor as the best match even when a *move* is requested
explicitly.

When using **noexcept** in conjunction with `std::move`, however, all that matters is whether
the *move* operation — whatever it might turn out to be — will be **noexcept(true)**; if so,

we can perhaps exploit that information to safely employ a more efficient algorithm that requires a nonthrowing move:

```
template <typename T>
void doSomething(T t)
{
    if (noexcept(T(std::move(t))))
    {
        // may assume no exception will be thrown during a move operation
    }
    else
    {
        // must use an algorithm that can handle a thrown exception
    }
}
```

Alternatively, we can simply *require* that any supplied type have a nonthrowing *move* operation:

```
template <typename T>
void doOrDie(T t)
{
    // may assume no exception will be thrown during a move operation

    static_assert(noexcept(T(std::move(t))), "");  // ill formed otherwise
}
```

Both class S and class C in the code snippets above have copy constructors that are declared **noexcept(false)**; however, class S also has a move constructor defined that is **noexcept(true)**, whereas C declared no move constructor at all:

```
S s1;  // declares a noexcept(true) move constructor
static_assert( noexcept(S(std::move(s1))), "");  // OK

C c1;  // declares only a noexcept(false) copy constructor
static_assert(!noexcept(C(std::move(c1))), "");  // OK
```

Although not recommended, we could define a class, S2, that is the same as S except that the *move* constructor is declared to be **noexcept(false)**:

```
S2 s2;  // declares noexcept(false) copy and move constructors
static_assert(!noexcept(S2(std::move(s2))), "");  // OK
```

Similarly, we could imagine a class, C2, that is the same as C except that the *copy* constructor is declared explicitly with **throw()**, making it **noexcept(true)**:

```
C2 c2;  // declares only a copy constructor decorated with throw()
static_assert(noexcept(C2(std::move(c2))), "");  // OK
```

There are many ways in which an object might or might not provide a nonthrowing *move* operation. As C2 in the example above suggests, even a C++03 class that happened to decorate its explicitly declared copy constructor with **throw()** would automatically satisfy the requirements of a nonthrowing *move*. A more likely scenario for a class designed prior to C++11 to wind up with a nonthrowing *move* operation is that it followed the **rule of zero**, thereby allowing each of the special member functions to be generated. In this case, all that might be needed to generate a nonthrowing *move* constructor is simply to recompile it under C++11! The takeaway here is that, irrespective of how a type is implemented, we can use the **noexcept** operator in combination with std::move to reliably determine, at compile time, whether an object of a given type *may* throw when we ask it to move. Note that while it is typical for C++03-targeted code to either have both copy and move operations nonthrowing, or both potentially throwing, a C++03 template instantiated with a C++11 type might have the **noexcept** specification of the copy and move operations be distinct, following those of the template argument type:

```
template <typename T>
struct NamedValue
{
    const char* d_name;
    T           d_value;
};
```

While NamedValue might be a class template shipping from a C++03-targeted library, the copy constructor for this class will clearly be **noexcept(false)**, but the move constructor might be throwing or not based solely on the properties of the template argument, T.

Applying the noexcept operator to functions in the C Standard Library

According to the C++03 Standard[7]:

> None of the functions from the Standard C library shall report an error by throwing an exception, unless it calls a program-supplied function that throws an exception.

This paragraph is accompanied by a footnote[8]:

> That is, the C library functions all have a **throw()** *exception-specification*. This allows implementations to make performance optimizations based on the absence of exceptions at runtime.

Note that this footnote applies only to functions in the C Standard Library, not to arbitrary functions having **extern "C"** linkage. It is not clear what the normative implications of the footnote might be, as it seems to be a non-normative note clarifying something not

---

[7]**iso03**, section 17.4.4.8, "Restrictions on exception handling," paragraph 2, p. 332
[8]Ibid., footnote 176, p. 332

obviously implied by the normative text. Given the extra costs associated with C++03 exception specifications, there are no known implementations that took advantage of this freedom.

For C++11, the footnote was revised to refer only to permitting the use of the new **noexcept** exception specification, without further clarification of the normative text. There is, however, also general permission to add a nonthrowing exception specification to any nonvirtual C++ Standard Library function, and it might be inferred that this provision gives implementations freedom to add such specifications to their C library wrappers too. Also note that functions taking callbacks, such as **bsearch** and **qsort**, will propagate exceptions thrown by the callback.

Again, there are no known implementations taking advantage of this freedom to add a nonthrowing exception specification to C library functions, although all of the functions in the <atomic> header intended for C interoperability are declared as **noexcept**, exploiting an arguable interpretation of the intent of this footnote.

Constraints on the **noexcept** specification imposed for **virtual functions**

When using C++03-style dynamic-exception specifications, the exception specification of any function override cannot be wider than that of the function being overridden:

```
struct BB03
{
    void n() throw();
    virtual void f();
    virtual void g1() throw();
    virtual void g2() throw();
    virtual void g3() throw();
    virtual void h()  throw(int, double);
};

struct DD03 : public BB03
{
    void n() throw(int);            // OK, hiding nonvirtual function
    void n(char) throw(int);        // OK, additional overload
    virtual void f();               // OK, base lacks exception spec.
    virtual void g1() throw();      // OK, same exception spec
    virtual void g2() throw(int);   // Error, wider exception spec (int)
    virtual void g3();              // Error, wider exception spec (all)
    virtual void h() throw(int);    // OK, tighter exception spec
};
```

Interestingly, the rules relating to **virtual** functions and **noexcept** are still defined by the C++11 and C++14 Standards in terms of dynamic exception specifications, despite that dynamic-exception specifications are deprecated. The C++14 Standard states[9]:

---

[9]**iso11a**, section 15.4, "Exception specifications," paragraph 5, p. 406

If a virtual function has an *exception-specification*, all declarations, including the definition, of any function that overrides that virtual function in any derived class shall only allow exceptions that are allowed by the *exception-specification* of the base class virtual function.

This specification means that the rules are straightforward from the perspective of **noexcept**. If the base function forbids exceptions by specifying **noexcept** or **noexcept(true)**, then the override must forbid exceptions by specifying one of **noexcept**, **noexcept(true)**, or **throw()**. In other words, if a base class virtual functions is **noexcept(true)**, then no derived class override of that function can have a throwing exception specification:

```
struct BB11
{
    void n() noexcept;
    virtual void f();
    virtual void g1() noexcept(true);
    virtual void g2() noexcept;
    virtual void g3() noexcept(true);
    virtual void g4() noexcept(true);
};

struct DD11 : public BB11
{
    void n();                            // OK, hiding nonvirtual function
    void n(char);                        // OK, additional overload
    void f() override;                   // OK, base lacks exception spec.
    void g1() noexcept override;         // OK, override is noexcept.
    void g2() throw() override;          // OK, override is noexcept.
    void g3() override;                  // Error, override allows exceptions.
    void g4() noexcept(false) override;  // Error, override allows exceptions.
};
```

These rules also apply to defaulted virtual functions, most notably destructors:

```
struct BB11a
{
    virtual ~BB11a() = default;  // noexcept(true)
};

struct DD11a : public BB11a
{
    virtual ~DD11a() noexcept(false);  // Error, BB11a::~BB11a() is noexcept(true).
};
```

Essentially, the envelope of what can be thrown from a virtual function in a derived class is constrained to be a subset of what can be thrown in each base class. This constraint can be quite restrictive since, in real-world systems, there are times when a base-class contract can serve a syntactic role and have a semantic approximation that can be relaxed if both the consumer and the supplier are in agreement regarding said relaxation; see *Annoyances — Exception-specification constraints in class hierarchies* on page 655.

Use Cases

Appending an element to an `std::vector`

There are certain cases where it is useful to know whether an expression, specifically one involving move operations, *may* throw so that an optimal algorithmic decision can be made. In fact, the reason *move* operations were thoughtfully added to C++11 was to support more efficient insertion of **allocating objects** into an `std::vector`. However, move operations alone turned out to be insufficient to achieve that goal without breaking existing code. Hence, the **noexcept** operator had to be hastily added just prior to shipping C++11; see *Appendix — Genesis of the **noexcept** operator: move operations* on page 658.

First, the original C++ Standard provided the **strong exception-safety guarantee** for any element inserted at the *end* of an `std::vector`, whether it be via the `insert` member function or the more popular `push_back`. Second, backward compatibility with C++03 meant that any type having explicitly defined copy operations would *not* be given implicit move operations, throwing or otherwise. Hence, when asked to move, any legacy C++ type would instead fall back on its copy operation, which, when it doesn't throw, satisfies all the requirements of an optimizing move operation.

Next, consider that some legacy code, having previously been promised the **strong guarantee**, fairly depends *at run time* on `std::vector::push_back` either succeeding or else throwing with no effect whatsoever on the state of the vector. To illustrate what is meant by the **strong exception-safety guarantee**, let's suppose we have a class, `S`, that has an explicitly declared copy constructor that *may* throw, thereby precluding an implicitly generated move constructor. For our purely pedagogical example, we will force the copy constructor to throw the third time the program attempts to copy an `S` object in the current process:

```
struct S
{
    static int s_nCopy;  // number of objects that have been copied
    int        d_uid;    // unique identifier for each copied object

    S()         : d_uid(-1) { }       // default constructor
    S(const S&) : d_uid(++s_nCopy)    // copy constructor
    {
        if (s_nCopy == 3) throw s_nCopy;  // throws on third attempt to copy
    }
};

int S::s_nCopy = 0; // initialization of static data member of class S
```

When inserting copies of `S` into an `std::vector<S>`, the **strong guarantee** ensures that the *entire* state of the vector — i.e., not just its **salient values** — remains unchanged despite the **throw**s occurring within the `push_back` operation. Pointers and references to the existing elements remain valid since the vector has not yet expanded, and the entire internal state of those elements too is unaltered:

```
#include <cassert>  // standard C assert macro
#include <vector>   // std::vector

int main()
{
    const S s;                    // default-constructed object (d_uid: -1)
    std::vector<S> v;             // container to fill

    v.reserve(2);                 // Do not reallocate until third push_back!
    assert(v.capacity() == 2);    // assert that capacity wasn't rounded higher

    v.push_back(s);
    v.push_back(s);

    // before:
    assert(v[0].d_uid == 1);
    assert(v[1].d_uid == 2);
    assert(v.capacity() == 2);    // assert that capacity is still the same

    // insert third (throwing) element:
    try
    {
        v.push_back(s);           // expected to throw constructing new element
        assert(!"Should have thrown an exception");
    }
    catch(int n)
    {
        assert(n == 3);           // Verify the expected exception value.
    }

    // after:
    assert(v[0].d_uid == 1);
    assert(v[1].d_uid == 2);
    assert(v.capacity() == 2);    // Even the vector's capacity is unchanged.
}
```

Importantly, when the exception is finally thrown, the entire state of the vector prior to attempting to add the third element remains unchanged, thus delivering on the **strong exception-safety guarantee** as has been required for `std::vector::push_back` by the C++ Standard since its inception. Had the third `push_back` not thrown, the *resize* would have occurred successfully, and each of the elements would have been *copied* into the newly allocated storage, which satisfies the letter of the original C++03 contract, but see *Annoyances — Change in unspecified behavior when an `std::vector` grows* on page 652.

The question now becomes how we should implement `std::vector::push_back` efficiently in modern C++.

Ignoring, for simplicity, C++11 memory allocators, recall that a standard vector maintains (1) the `data()` address of its dynamically allocated element storage, (2) the maximum `capacity()` of elements it can hold before having to resize, and (3) the `size()`, i.e., number of elements it currently holds. When the `size()` is either 0 or less than the current `capacity()`, there is no issue: An attempt is made to append the element after first allocating dynamic storage if the `capacity()` too was 0, and if an exception is thrown either during memory allocation or directly by the element's constructor, there is no effect on the state of the vector object. So far, so good.

Let's now consider what happens when the `size()` is not 0 and there is no more `capacity()` left, that is, `size() > 0 && size() == capacity()`. The first step, as ever, is to allocate a larger block of dynamic memory. If that allocation throws, there's nothing to do, and the **strong guarantee** is automatically satisfied. But what happens if that allocation succeeds? If we try to move an existing element to the newly allocated slab of memory and the move operation throws, we have no guarantee that the state of the element is unchanged in its original location. If the first move succeeds, then when we go to move a second element, we're past the point of no return: if the second move operation fails by throwing an exception, we have no way to go forward and similarly no guaranteed way to revert since attempting to move the first one back might throw as well. If this scenario were to occur, then the **strong exception-safety guarantee** would be violated and in the worst possible way: not at compile time, link time, or startup and not just under a heavy load, but nondeterministically at run time when the vector needs to grow and moving an existing element throws during that operation.

Alternatively, we could take the same conservative approach as in C++03 before move operations were standardized. That is, instead of even trying to efficiently move existing elements from the old dynamically allocated block to the new one, each element would instead be *copied*, e.g., using the **copy/swap idiom**, but now we are making a full copy of every existing element of the vector every time its capacity grows. The complexity of the operation could technically still be considered **amortized constant time**; depending on the complexity of the elements (e.g., whether or not they might allocate), however, the latency cost of a single `push_back` when additional capacity is needed could still be prohibitive. Unwilling to give up either the **strong guarantee** or the optimal performance in the increasingly typical case (support for nonthrowing move operations), the Standards Committee chose a third alternative: the **noexcept** operator.

Let's now consider how we might use the **noexcept** operator to implement an `std::vector`-like `push_back` member function that safely exploits the new *move* operations on potential elements, again, for simplicity of exposition, ignoring C++11 memory allocators. Let's start by considering a heavily elided definition of our class, `vector`:

```
#include <cstddef>  // std::size_t

namespace my {
```

```
template <typename T>
class vector
{
    T*          d_array_p;    // dynamic memory for elements of type T
    std::size_t d_capacity;   // maximum number of elements before resize
    std::size_t d_size;       // current number of elements in this array
public:
    vector() : d_array_p(0), d_capacity(0), d_size(0) { }  // created empty
    // ...
    void push_back(const T& value);   // safe, efficient implementation
    // ...
    void reserve(std::size_t capacity);   // make more space (might throw)
    void swap(vector& other) noexcept;    // swap state with other vector<T>
};
}
```

Assuming the existence of just the member functions in the example code above, let's look at implementing an efficient, exception-safe push_back method that preserves the **strong exception-safety guarantee** even for a type that, when asked just to move, *may* nonetheless throw:

```
#include <new>       // placement new
#include <utility>   // std::move

template <typename T>
void my::vector<T>::push_back(const T& value)   // safe, efficient implementation
{
    if (d_size < d_capacity)  // sufficient capacity in allocated memory
    {
        void* address = d_array_p + d_size;   // implicit conversion to void*
        ::new(address) T(value);              // may throw on copy
        ++d_size;                             // no throw
        return;                               // early return
    }

    // If we know that attempting to move an object may not throw, we can
    // improve performance compared to relying on a classically throwing copy.

    const std::size_t nextCapacity = d_capacity ? d_capacity * 2
                                                : 1;           // no throw

    if (noexcept(::new((void*)0) T(std::move(*d_array_p))))   // is no throw?
    {
        my::vector<T> tmp;                          // may throw
        tmp.reserve(nextCapacity);                  // may throw

        void* address = tmp.d_array_p + d_size;     // no throw
        ::new(address) T(value);                    // last potential throw
```

```
        for (std::size_t i = 0; i != d_size; ++i)  // for each existing element
        {
            void* addr = tmp.d_array_p + i;          // no throw
            ::new(addr) T(std::move(d_array_p[i]));  // no throw (move)
        }

        tmp.d_size = d_size + 1;  // no throw
        tmp.swap(*this);          // no throw, committed
    }
    else                                // otherwise employ the copy/swap idiom
    {
        my::vector<T> copy;             // may throw
        copy.reserve(nextCapacity);     // may throw
        copy = *this;                   // may throw
        copy.push_back(value);          // may throw on copy; capacity's good
        copy.swap(*this);               // no throw, committed
    }
}
```

As the code snippet above illustrates, as long as there is sufficient capacity in the current block of dynamic memory, there is no need for the **noexcept** operator to preserve the strong guarantee. Only when it becomes necessary to reallocate to a larger capacity does the need for the **noexcept** operator arise. At that point, we will need to know if, when we ask the object of type T to move-construct, it *may* throw, but see *Potential Pitfalls — Using the noexcept operator directly* on page 647:

```
    if (noexcept(::new((void*)0) T(std::move(*d_array_p))))  // no throw (move)
```

In the **else** clause, copying *may* throw, so we revert to the C++03 algorithm, which uses the familiar copy/swap idiom; notice that we call reserve to pre-allocate memory in a copy, rather than the current vector, to avoid problems with **aliasing** and redundant allocations.

But if we can know that moving (or copying if there's no move constructor) an object *may not* throw, then we might be able to avoid having to *copy* all the objects over to the newly allocated memory. First, we create a temporary vector and then reserve whatever the next larger capacity is intended to be. If either of these operations were to throw, then there would be no state change in the original vector, and, thus, the strong exception-safety guarantee would be preserved. Then we call **placement new** to construct the new element at the intended address. Note the specific syntax we use when calling **placement new**: Employing :: ensures that overloads of **new** in only the global namespace are considered, thus avoiding **ADL** finding any ill-advised, class-specific overloads. Moreover, we deliberately convert the address pointer to a plain **void*** to match exactly the specific, Standard-mandated overload of placement new we desire, thus preventing our accidentally calling any other, more specific overload in the global namespace. Note that we allow the pointer to implicitly convert to initialize a local **void*** variable rather than employing an explicit cast. If, when invoking the constructor for the new element, an exception is thrown, no new element will be created, the partially constructed temporary object will be destroyed as the exception leaves block scope, the temporary vector destructor will reclaim allocated memory, and again the **strong guarantee** is preserved. Note that the order of operations allows this member function to work properly even if the argument to **value** turns out to be a reference into this vector (a.k.a. aliasing).

We are now past the point at which it is possible for an exception to be thrown, so we proceed to move-construct each element in the new slab of memory. Once we're done moving all the elements over, we manually set the **d_size** data member of the temporary **vector**, **tmp**, and efficiently (no-throw) **swap** all of its members with those of the current vector. When **tmp** goes out of scope, it first destroys the moved-from, original elements before deleting the old, dynamically allocated block.

The use of the **noexcept** operator above, although correct, is subtle and not particularly easy to maintain. Almost all uses outside of **conditional noexcept specifications** (see Section 3.1."**noexcept** Specifier" on page 1085) involve move operations, the most common of which require even more arcane metaprogramming to make work properly; see *Implementing* `std::move_if_noexcept` on page 640 and *Implementing* `std::vector::push_back(T&&)` on page 644.

Enforcing a noexcept **contract using** static_assert

When writing a function template, the possibility of throwing an exception might be determined entirely by operations dependent on the template parameters. In such cases, we might want to have a contract that never throws an exception, so we use the **noexcept** specification. However, this behavior would lead to runtime enforcement of the contract, calling `std::terminate` if an exception is thrown from any of those operations involving the template parameters. If we want to enforce the contract at compile time, we would additionally use a **static_assert** testing the relevant expressions with the **noexcept** operator:

```
#include <cmath>  // std::sqrt
template <typename T>
T sine(T const& a, T const& b) noexcept
{
    static_assert(noexcept( T(b / std::sqrt(a * a + b * b)) ), "throwing expr");
    return b / std::sqrt(a * a + b * b);
}
```

Note that this approach will reject otherwise valid code that does not throw exceptions but is not yet marked up with an exception specification.

Preserving the **strong exception-safety guarantee** in `std::vector` by mandating that all elements inserted into a vector have a nonthrowing move constructor was rejected for concerns of breaking existing code. For a custom container, however, having such a restriction might be a reasonable design choice that could be similarly enforced with a **static_assert**:

```
#include <new>      // placement new
#include <utility> // std::move

template <typename T>
void my::vector<T>::push_back(const T& value)  // efficient implementation
{
    static_assert(noexcept(::new((void*)0) T(std::move(*d_array_p))),
                  "The element type must have a noexcept move constructor");

    if (d_size < d_capacity)  // sufficient capacity in allocated memory
    {
        void* address = d_array_p + d_size;  // implicit conversion to void*
        ::new(address) T(value);             // may throw on copy
        ++d_size;                            // no throw
        return;                              // early return
    }

    // We know that attempting to move an object may not throw, so we can
    // safely move rather than copy elements into the new storage.

    const std::size_t nextCapacity = d_capacity ? d_capacity * 2
                                                : 1;          // no throw

    my::vector<T> tmp;                         // may throw
    tmp.reserve(nextCapacity);                 // may throw

    void* address = tmp.d_array_p + d_size;    // no throw
    ::new(address) T(value);                   // last potential throw

    for (std::size_t i = 0; i != d_size; ++i)  // for each existing element
    {
        void* addr = tmp.d_array_p + i;          // no throw
        ::new(addr) T(std::move(d_array_p[i]));  // no throw (move)
    }

    tmp.d_size = d_size + 1;  // no throw
    tmp.swap(*this);          // no throw, committed
}
```

Implementing std::move_if_noexcept

The need for the **noexcept** operator is all but exclusively tied to *move* operations and yet — even for that purpose — the direct use of **noexcept** is almost always problematic. C++11 provides an extensive library of type traits that can precisely determine important, relevant properties of a type, such as whether it has an accessible constructor; see *Potential Pitfalls — Using the **noexcept** operator directly* on page 647.

Consider a broken implementation of a function intended to construct a new object at a given address, where the *move* constructor will be called if it is **noexcept**; otherwise, if the object type has an **accessible** copy constructor, call that, or, as a last resort, call the *move* constructor regardless since the type is simply not copyable (a.k.a. **move-only** type):

```
#include <new>           // placement new
#include <type_traits>   // std::is_copy_constructible
#include <utility>       // std::move


template <typename T>
void construct(void* address, T& object)
    // object passed by modifiable lvalue to enable both copy and move
{
    if (noexcept(::new(address) T(std::move(object))))  // noexcept move
    {
        ::new(address) T(std::move(object));   // OK, no-throw movable
    }
    else if (std::is_copy_constructible<T>::value)
    {
        ::new(address) T(object);  // Oops, compile-time error if not copyable
    }
    else // T is not declared copyable, is movable, and may throw.
    {
        ::new(address) T(std::move(object));  // move move-only type anyway
    }
}
```

The naive, straightforward implementation above fails to compile for move-only types because the copy branch of the **if** statement needs to compile even when the **else** branch is taken, as *all* branches are compiled for each template instantiation.[10] We need to force only one of each of the potential branches to be evaluated at compile time, which requires

---

[10]In C++17, the **if constexpr** language feature is a direct solution to such problems:

```
template <typename T>
void construct(void* address, T& object)
{
    if constexpr (noexcept(::new(address) T(std::move(object))))
    {
        ::new(address) T(std::move(object));
    }
    else if constexpr (std::is_copy_constructible<T>::value)
    {
        ::new(address) T(object);  // discarded if this branch is not taken
    }
    else // T is not declared copyable, is movable, and may throw.
    {
        ::new(address) T(std::move(object));
    }
}
```

selecting the chosen function through partial template specialization, rather than runtime branching in the function body itself. If it were allowed, we would opt to "partially specialize" the two-parameter `moveParameter` and `copyParameter` functions with respect to the value of its second, Boolean argument. As partial template specialization of functions is *not* permitted, we must *hoist* (factor out) the parameter to the would-be partially specialized function in a class template sporting the **static** function template to be called:

```
#include <new>            // placement new
#include <type_traits>    // std::is_copy_constructible
                          // std::is_nothrow_move_constructible
#include <utility>        // std::move

template <bool ShouldMove>
struct ImplementMoveOrCopy   // general declaration/definition of class template
{
    template <typename T>
    static void construct(void* address, T& object)
    {
        ::new(address) T(object); // copy
    }
};

template <>
struct ImplementMoveOrCopy<true>   // explicit specialization of class template
{
    template <typename T>
    static void construct(void* address, T& object)
    {
        ::new(address) T(std::move(object));    // move
    }
};

template <typename T>
void construct(void* address, T& object)
    // object passed by modifiable lvalue to enable both copy and move
{
    ImplementMoveOrCopy<std::is_nothrow_move_constructible<T>::value ||
        !std::is_copy_constructible<T>::value>::construct(address, object);
}
```

The example code above splits the once cohesive `construct` function template into three parts, two of which are intended as only private implementation details and hosted in a class template.

The C++ Standard Library provides the `std::move_if_noexcept` function to encapsulate such baroque metaprogramming code, which turns out to be surprisingly useful; see *Implementing std::vector::push_back(T&&)* on page 644:

```
#include <type_traits>  // std::conditional

template <typename T>
constexpr
typename std::conditional<!std::is_nothrow_move_constructible<T>::value
                          && std::is_copy_constructible<T>::value,
                          const T&,
                          T&&>::type
move_if_noexcept(T& x) noexcept
{
    return std::move(x);
}
```

There's a lot to unpack from the definition in the code snippet above, but the principle is simple: all of the work is done computing the return type of the function. The `std::conditional` return type is a standard library **metafunction** that evaluates a predicate and produces the second template parameter for its result type if the predicate is **true** and the final template parameter for its result type if the predicate is **false**. In this case, the predicate is using type traits to examine properties of the deduced type T to determine which result should be preferred. If a type is not copy constructible, indicated by the `std::is_copy_constructible` type trait, the `std::conditional` function should always return an *rvalue* reference. If a type is copy constructible, it should not return an *rvalue* reference unless the move constructor is **noexcept**. We use the type trait `is_nothrow_move_constructible` to determine whether a type has a **noexcept** *move* constructor, rather than attempting ourselves to implement the metaprogramming trickery inside a **noexcept** operator to avoid consideration of ancillary subexpressions.

A naive attempt to implement the `std::is_nothrow_move_constructible` trait using the **noexcept** operator might be:

```
#include <type_traits>  // std::integeral_constant
#include <utility>       // std::declval

template <typename T>
struct is_nothrow_move_constructible
    : std::integral_constant<bool,
                             noexcept(::new((void*)0) T(std::declval<T>()))>
{
};
```

Here, `std::declval` is a declared but not defined function that always returns an *rvalue* reference to the type of the template argument, avoiding the need to know of a valid constructor for an arbitrary type. However, this approach is still an approximation as we must use more complex template metaprogramming to return **false** when the move constructor is not public or is deleted. Due to the complexity of its implementation, the `move_if_noexcept` function is available as a part of the Standard Library.

Once we have the `move_if_noexcept` function, the `construct` example can be written even more simply and, this time, will compile without error:

```
template <typename T>
void construct(void* address, T& object)
    // object passed by modifiable lvalue to enable both copy and move
{
    ::new(address) T(std::move_if_noexcept(object));  // factored implementation
}
```

Note that the implementation of `construct` might also benefit from a conditional **noexcept** specification to indicate when the operation is **noexcept**; see Section 3.1. "**noexcept** Specifier" on page 1085.

Implementing `std::vector::push_back(T&&)`

In *Appending an element to an* `std::vector` on page 634, we discussed the primary motivation for having a **noexcept** operator, and in *Implementing* `std::move_if_noexcept` on page 640, we demonstrated how we could implement fully factored functionality that is eminently useful in a variety of *move*-related operations.

In addition to inserting a *copy* of a value into a vector, C++11 adds an overload to permit *moving* an element when inserting into the back of a vector, using the overload **void** `vector<T>::push_back(T&& value)` (see Section 2.1. "*Rvalue* References" on page 710). This function offers the same **strong exception-safety guarantee** as the "push-a-copy" overload but has to consider the additional case of a **move-only type** — i.e., a type having a **public** *move* constructor but no **accessible** *copy* constructor — where the *move* constructor *may* throw. In such cases, `push_back` offers only the **basic exception-safety guarantee**; that is, no resources will be leaked, and no invariants will be broken, but the state of the vector after the exception is thrown is otherwise unknown.

In addition to weakening the **strong exception-safety guarantee** in specific circumstances, the `push_back` of an *xvalue* — made possible by an *rvalue* reference (see Section 2.1. "*Rvalue* References" on page 710) — adds the complication of implementing a function template that in some circumstances wants to make a copy but in attempting to do so in other circumstances will fail to compile. This conundrum is precisely the problem the `std::move_if_noexcept` library function was designed to address.

Before digging into the implementation of the *rvalue*-reference overload of a vector-like container's `push_back`, we need to introduce the notion of being **exception agnostic**. C++ code is **exception safe** if it provides the **basic guarantee** that, if an exception is thrown out of a function, no resources are leaked and no invariants are broken; the code is **exception agnostic** if it is considered **exception safe** without having to resort to the use of exception-specific constructs, such as **try**, **catch**, or **throw**, that, in an exception-disabled build, might fail to compile. Striving for **exception agnosticism** in a library means relying on **RAII** as the means of avoiding resource leaks when an exception is injected into the code via, for example, a user-supplied callback function, a virtual function in a user-derived class, or an object of user-defined type supplied as a template parameter.

The term **scoped guard** is widely recognized as a category of object whose only purpose is to manage the lifetime of some other object, typically supplied at construction. When the guard object is destroyed, typically by dint of being an automatic variable leaving lexical scope, it destroys the object in its charge:

```cpp
template <typename T>
struct ScopedGuard
{
    T* d_obj_p;

    ScopedGuard(T* obj) : d_obj_p(obj) { }
    ~ScopedGuard() { delete d_obj_p; }
};
```

Even this `ScopedGuard`, a simplified version of C++11's `std::unique_ptr`, can be used beneficially to make sure that an object allocated using global **new** early in a function invocation will always be cleaned up, even when control flow leaves the function through an exception or an early return:

```cpp
#include <vector>  // std::vector

void test()
{
    ScopedGuard<std::vector<int>> sg(new std::vector<int>);  // guarded object
    sg.d_obj_p->push_back(123);
    // ...
    // ...                     (Something might throw.)

}  // Guarded object will be released automatically as guard leaves scope.
```

A special-case use for a scoped guard is one where it acts as an insurance policy up until some commit point, after which the guard is disabled. Consider a function, `evilFactory`, that dynamically allocates an `std::vector<int>`, populates it, and eventually returns a raw pointer to it, which is not recommended, unless an exception is thrown:

```cpp
std::vector<int>* evilFactory()  // Return raw address of dynamic memory (BAD).
{
    ScopedGuard<std::vector<int>> sg(new std::vector<int>);  // guarded object

    // ...                 (something might throw)

    std::vector<int>* tmp = sg.d_obj_p;  // Extract address of managed object.
    sg.d_obj_p = 0;                      // Release ownership to client.
    return tmp;                          // Return ownership of allocated object.
}
```

In this second example, the client makes use of the guard while the object is being configured. During that period, if an exception is thrown, the guard will automatically destroy and deallocate the dynamically allocated object entrusted to it as the exception exits scope. If, as would be the typical case, no exception is thrown, the object's address is extracted from the guard, the guard's pointer is zeroed out (releasing it from its guard responsibilities), and the raw address of the fully configured dynamic object is returned. (Note that this pedagogical example is not recommended.) We refer to a scoped guard that provides a way to release ownership of the managed object, typically via a **release** member function, as a **proctor**.

Let's now return to the principle task of implementing an *rvalue*-reference overload of a **push_back** member function for an **std::vector**-like container but, again for simplicity, ignoring memory allocators. First, we will need a simple **proctor class** that can own a dynamic object and ensure it is destroyed at the end of scope — such as when an exception is thrown — unless ownership is adopted by another object:

```
template <typename T>
class DestructorProctor  // generic "scoped guard" class with release method
{
    T* d_obj_p;  // address of object whose destructor might need to be called

    DestructorProctor(const DestructorProctor&) = delete;
    DestructorProctor& operator=(const DestructorProctor&) = delete;
public:
    explicit DestructorProctor(T* p) : d_obj_p(p) { }          // initialize
    ~DestructorProctor() { if (d_obj_p) { d_obj_p->~T(); } } // clean up
    void release() { d_obj_p = 0; }                            // disengage
};
```

With this **DestructorProctor** in hand, we can proceed to implement our **push_back** designed specifically for temporary values. Note that there is no longer a branch on the **noexcept** operator as all the necessary logic is handled by **move_if_noexcept** returning the right kind of reference:

```
template <typename T>
void my::vector<T>::push_back(T&& value)  // safe, efficient implementation
{
    if (d_size < d_capacity)  // if sufficient capacity in allocated memory...
    {
        void* address = d_array_p + d_size;  // implicit conversion to void*
        ::new(address) T(std::move(value));  // may throw on construction
        ++d_size;                            // no throw
        return;                              // early return
    }                                        // else...

    vector<T> tmp;                               // may throw
    tmp.reserve(d_capacity ? d_capacity * 2 : 1);  // may throw
```

```
    void* address = tmp.d_array_p + d_size;              // no throw
    T* newElement = ::new(address) T(std::move(value));  // ctor may throw
    DestructorProctor<T> guard(newElement);         // defend against exception

    for ( ; tmp.d_size != d_size; ++tmp.d_size)     // for each current element
    {
        void* addr = tmp.d_array_p + tmp.d_size;    // no throw
        ::new(addr) T(std::move_if_noexcept(d_array_p[tmp.d_size]));
            // may throw only if move is not noexcept
            // move if either move is noexcept or T is not copyable;
            // otherwise, copy to preserve strong exception-safety guarantee
    }

    guard.release();  // no throw
    ++tmp.d_size;     // no throw
    swap(tmp);        // no throw, committed
}
```

Note that if the above function copies, rather than moves, T and an exception is thrown, tmp will go out of scope, and the vector's destructor will take care of destroying all of the already-copied objects and deallocating the memory at tmp.d_array_p. As a result, the DestructorProctor is required to call only the destructor for the new element.

This same implementation strategy exploiting move_if_noexcept, used here for std::vector::push_back(T&&), could have also been used for the *lvalue*-reference version (see *Appending an element to an std::vector* on page 634), the only differences being that we would construct the new element without calling std::move — as ::new(address) T(value); — in two places. The use of std::move_if_noexcept would not be changed, as its purpose is to move construct the existing elements rather than necessarily copy construct the newly inserted element. Note that the loop variable to track the elements that are moved or copied is the d_size member of the tmp vector to ensure that any *copied* or *moved* objects are destroyed by the destructor of tmp if a subsequent move or copy operation throws. While the set of operations looks different because the two branches of the **if (noexcept(...))** statement in the original formulation of push_back appear incompatible, in fact the sequence of operations in this new version is almost identical since we have effectively inlined the reserve and copy-assignment operations of the original. The only difference is that, in the case of the nonthrowing move, the loop count is incrementing a member variable of the temporary vector rather than a local variable, and this difference should not be observable in practice.

Potential Pitfalls

Using the noexcept operator directly

One of the early discoveries in specifying the Standard Library was that, as the **noexcept** operator considers the whole expression, the result can be **false** due to side effects in subexpressions that were not intended as a direct part of the query. Consider the following constructor declaration:

```
template <typename T>
struct MyType
{
    // ...
    MyType(MyType&& rhs) noexcept(noexcept(T(T())));  // T is type of a member.
};
```

This declaration seems to illustrate a reasonable way to write an exception specification that is conditional on whether a member of type T has a nonthrowing move constructor. The expression under test creates a temporary object of type T from another default-constructed, temporary object of type T. How could this use of the **noexcept** operator not return the expected result?

First, this code assumes that T has an accessible default constructor in a best-effort attempt to create an *rvalue* of type T without knowing anything about it and specifically not knowing the syntax for an accessible constructor to initialize a temporary object. The Standard solves this problem by introducing the `declval` function into the `<utility>` header[11]:

```
#include <type_traits> // std::add_rvalue_reference
#include <utility>     // std::declval

template <typename T>
typename std::add_rvalue_reference<T>::type std::declval() noexcept;
```

While this function is declared by the Standard Library, using it in a context where it might be evaluated — i.e., outside a **decltype**, **noexcept**, **sizeof**, or similar — is an error. Note that the function is declared unconditionally **noexcept** to support its intended use in the **noexcept** operator without impacting the final result. This function generally returns an *rvalue* reference, but the use of the `add_rvalue_reference` type trait handles several corner cases. If instantiated with an *lvalue* reference, the reference-collapsing rules will be applied, and the result will be an *lvalue* reference. If instantiated with a type that does not support references, such as **void**, the type trait will simply return that same type. Note that as the function signature simply returns a reference but the function itself never defined, the question of how to create the returned *xvalue* at run time is avoided.

With the `declval` function in hand, we can rewrite our exception specification:

```
template <typename T>
struct MyType
{
    // ...
    MyType(MyType&&) noexcept(noexcept(T(std::declval<T>())));
};
```

---

[11] In C++17, **noexcept**(T(T())) does not check the **noexcept** specification of the move constructor *at all* due to **guaranteed copy elision**.

The use of std::declval solved the problem of type T not being default constructible, but this approach still has a subtle hidden problem. In addition to testing whether the move constructor for the temporary object of type T will not throw, we are testing the destructor of that temporary, since, by their nature, temporaries are destroyed at the end of the expression that creates them. This insight led to destructors having special rules, different from every other function, when declared without an exception specification (see *Annoyances — Destructors, but not move constructors, are **noexcept** by default* on page 653), which was important when recompiling code originally developed, tested, and validated against C++03. However, changing the rules for exception specifications on destructors still does not solve the problem when the destructor is explicitly declared as potentially throwing in new code. The workaround is to defer destruction of the temporary by using the **new** operator:

```
template <typename T>
struct MyType
{
    // ...
    MyType(MyType&&) noexcept(noexcept(::new((T*)0) T(std::declval<T>())));
};
```

Using the null pointer as the target address does not have undefined behavior here, as the expression is an unevaluated operand passed as an argument to the **noexcept** operator, so only the types involved in the expression, not the values, matter; see *Use Cases — Appending an element to an std::vector* on page 634.

The simple attempt to write the strongly motivating use case of a nonthrowing move constructor has turned into a complicated experts-only metaprogram. This pattern is generally observed by direct use of the **noexcept** operator, and typically such metaprograms are packaged up as clearly named **type traits** where they can be developed, tested, and deployed just once.

The noexcept **operator doesn't consider function bodies**

One source of confusion when first learning about the **noexcept** specification is assuming that the specification is determined by the expressions in the function body. This misconception is enhanced by the rules for implicitly declared, or **defaulted**, functions (see Section 1.1. "Defaulted Functions" on page 33) producing an exception specification based upon the corresponding exception specification of the bases and members of the class.

Similarly, that the compiler does not enforce **noexcept** by parsing the function definition and rejecting expressions that may throw was a deliberate language choice. If throwing out of a **noexcept** function were a compile-time error, exception specifications for function templates would have become particularly difficult for library authors, and it would be challenging to adopt any use of **noexcept** for projects compiling against C code or with legacy C++03 code. However, some compilers will issue warnings in cases where an exception is known to be thrown through a **noexcept** specification, i.e., in the case where all code paths lead to an exception and there is no regular return path:

```
void does_not_throw() noexcept
{
    throw "Oops!";  // OK, calls std::terminate, but a good compiler will warn
}

void should_not_throw(bool lie) noexcept
{
    if (lie)
    {
        throw "Fooled you!";  // OK, but conditional so compilers will not warn
    }
}
```

Annoyances

The noexcept operator is too sensitive for direct use

Given that the **noexcept** operator takes account of whole expressions, it can be surprisingly difficult to test just the operations about which the code is concerned. The C++ Standard Library provides a number of type traits that effectively package up the metafunctions necessary to determine such results in reusable components:

```
#include <type_traits>  // all of the std::* traits below

struct S { };  // Trivial object, all implicit operations are noexcept.

static_assert(std::is_nothrow_assignable<S,S>::value, "");          // OK
static_assert(std::is_nothrow_constructible<S>::value, "");         // OK
static_assert(std::is_nothrow_copy_assignable<S>::value, "");       // OK
static_assert(std::is_nothrow_copy_constructible<S>::value, "");    // OK
static_assert(std::is_nothrow_default_constructible<S>::value, ""); // OK
static_assert(std::is_nothrow_destructible<S>::value, "");          // OK
static_assert(std::is_nothrow_move_assignable<S>::value, "");       // OK
static_assert(std::is_nothrow_move_constructible<S>::value, "");    // OK
```

A sample implementation might look something like:

```
#include <new>          // placement new
#include <type_traits>  // std::integral_constant
#include <utility>      // std::declval

template <typename T, bool = std::is_move_constructible<T>::value>
struct is_nothrow_move_constructible__impl
    : std::integral_constant<bool, false> { };
```

```
template <typename T>
struct is_nothrow_move_constructible__impl<T,true>
    : std::integral_constant<bool,
          noexcept(::new((void*)0) T(std::declval<T>()))> { };


template <typename T>
struct is_nothrow_move_constructible
    : is_nothrow_move_constructible__impl<T> { };
```

See *Potential Pitfalls — Using the* **noexcept** *operator directly* on page 647. Notice that even this simple trait requires a level of indirection through a support class to avoid evaluating a **noexcept** expression that would not compile for a type that is not move constructible at all.

In addition to the traits supplied with C++11, a particular concern arose about determining whether a `swap` operation has a nonthrowing exception specification. The popular copy/swap idiom relies on a nonthrowing `swap` operation that is called via argument-dependent lookup (ADL) with the primary `std::swap` template also found by ordinary name lookup. This idiom is generally achieved with a **using** declaration within the scope of the code calling `swap`, but it is not possible to inject **using** `std::swap` within the single expression being tested by employing a **noexcept** operator. This issue was missed when specifying the Standard Library as the C++ library types themselves are all in namespace `std`, so they find the `std::swap` overload without requiring an additional **using**.[12]

However, unlike the C++11 traits, it is not possible for users to provide the equivalent functionality themselves without invading namespace `std`, something explicitly prohibited by the C++ Standard. These traits can be implemented *only* by the Standard Library itself.

In practice, use of the **noexcept** operator is often delegated to type traits, provided by either the Standard Library or user code, that can implement, test, debug, and package up the precise metaprogram clearly named for its intended usage.

The strong exception-safety guarantee itself

Much effort has gone into maintaining support for the strong exception-safety guarantee, and whether this guarantee buys significant benefit over the basic exception-safety guarantee to justify the cost is unclear. If an operation has failed such that an exception is thrown, the error recovery path typically catches at a granularity that will reattempt the whole transaction, including re-creating the objects that were providing the strong exception-safety guarantee for their use.

---

[12]This oversight was addressed in C++17 with the addition of two more type traits:

```
static_assert(std::is_nothrow_swappable<S>::value);        // OK, in C++17
static_assert(std::is_nothrow_swappable_with<S&, S&>::value);  // OK, in C++17
```

The intended benefit of the **strong exception-safety guarantee** is to enable transactional reasoning about code, where an operation must succeed, or leave the system in a good state. The **strong guarantee** requires that the "good state" be the state prior to starting the transaction, which raises the question of what is likely to change such that re-attempting the transaction would succeed on the second attempt. Generally, the fine-grained transactional guarantees give way to abandoning the whole transaction and starting over, in which case the state preserved by the **strong guarantee** is also lost. Note that fine-grained transactional reasoning does turn out to be important to atomic operations on concurrent code, but that is entirely distinct from the exception-safety guarantees.

In practice, the **strong guarantee** can prove useful when trying to diagnose problems in software, as it helps the debugging process to know that we can rely on inspecting an object to return the same state as before an operation was attempted. Of course, that relies on the assumption that the bug being diagnosed is not also impacting the **strong exception-safety guarantee** of the constituent code.

Change in unspecified behavior when an `std::vector` grows

One of the lesser known corner cases of C++03 is that when a vector grows, as it copies all of its elements into a new, larger array, state that is not copied by default is lost. For example, the capacity of a vector is generally not preserved when a vector is copied, even if the user has explicitly called **reserve** to ensure that the original vector object can grow without reallocating. Failing to preserve capacity can become an issue when trying to prepopulate a vector so that subsequent use in the program should not force a reallocation:

```cpp
#include <cassert>  // standard C assert macro
#include <vector>   // std::vector

void safe_append(std::vector<std::vector<int>>* target)
{
    assert(target);
    target->push_back(std::vector<int>());
    target->back().reserve(100);
}
```

This function ensures that every new **vector<int>** inserted into the **target** vector has a capacity of at least 100. However, if **target** itself is forced to grow, then all of the existing vectors in **target** will be copied and have a new capacity computed to reasonably hold the elements they already hold, which could well be a lower capacity, forcing new allocations to happen on later use, which this code was explicitly attempting to avoid.

C++11 addresses the common case where the move constructor for the element type of a vector is **noexcept**, as the vector will *move* rather than *copy* each element into the new array, and move operations frequently preserve more information about the state of the original object, including, in our example, the capacity of a vector.

Note that some programmers might think `std::vector<std::string>` would be a more common example to encounter this problem, but a confluence of fortunate design choices means that the issue presented above does not happen in practice. The design of `std::string` for C++03 enabled the copy-on-write optimization, which we believe all Standard Libraries implemented. This design means that when we copy a string, we share a reference-counted implementation and make a real copy only when either string calls a modifying operation (such as appending more characters) when the string being modified finally implements the deferred copy. However, manipulating a hidden shared state turns out to be a real performance problem for concurrent code, which was a major design goal for C++11, so the design of `std::string` changed to support the short-string optimization instead. A vector of this redesigned string would indeed display the original issue, if we had not simultaneously fixed `std::vector` to sidestep the problem using moves.

Destructors, but not move constructors, are noexcept by default

Once implementations of the **noexcept** operator were available with early compilers, it quickly became apparent that there were issues with common expressions involving temporary objects. These issues occurred because the **noexcept** operator included the whole lifetime of temporary objects, expressions involving temporaries would call their destructors, and the vast majority of existing C++03 code was written without exception specifications on their destructors.

In fact, the C++03 language did implicitly provide an exception specification for implicitly declared destructors, based upon the exception specification of their bases and members. Clearly the language was already trying to help us out, but as soon as the user wrote their own destructor, which is a common thing to do, that user would have to explicitly mark up that destructor as **noexcept**, or many potential uses of the **noexcept** operator would become irrelevant as it would always return **false**. The solution for this problem was to make destructors — and *only* destructors — special so that if there is no explicitly declared exception specification on a user-supplied destructor, it will be given the same exception specification as though it were implicitly declared. Note that many programmers misstate this rule as "destructors are implicitly **noexcept**." While it is the overwhelmingly common case that implicit destructors are **noexcept**, the rule allows for a class to explicitly mark its destructor as potentially throwing:

```
struct BadIdea
{
    ~BadIdea() noexcept(false) { }
};
```

Hence, any class that had a `BadIdea` base or member would also have an implicitly throwing destructor. However, unless someone explicitly writes a class like `BadIdea` in the first place, the commonly misstated rule that destructors generally have nonthrowing exception specifications holds.

The next question to arise is why move constructors do not get the same treatment as destructors and use the exception specification on an implicitly declared move constructor if there is no explicitly supplied specification. The simplest answer might be that nobody suggested it at the time.

noexcept arrived extremely late in the C++11 standardization process, and the need to address destructors was discovered only with early implementations of the new language feature interacting with the vast majority of existing code. Destructors are extremely common and a part of almost every object's lifetime. Move constructors were a new feature that required new code to be written so there was no large legacy of incompatible code to address. Move constructors are but one constructor of many, whereas a class could have only one destructor, so the rule that "destructors are special" was relatively easy to learn, whereas a new rule that "move constructors are an extra special constructor in the language" was less obvious. Also, there were more common cases where an implicit exception specification based upon the exception specification of the bases and members would give the wrong result for user-defined types. For example, the move constructor is responsible for restoring the invariants of any object whose state it consumes, and if one invariant is that an empty object always has an allocated object (e.g., a sentinel node in an implementation of `std::list`), then the user would be responsible for explicitly marking up that move constructor as **noexcept(false)**, or else the program would have a hidden termination condition, which did not seem as useful a default as one that merely misses a library optimization opportunity. Finally, without the large body of pre-existing code, it is not clear that even destructors would have been deemed special enough to have a different default to every other function in the language.

Older compilers invade the bodies of constexpr functions

It has always been clear that the **noexcept** operator was not permitted to infer from the body of an ordinary function, even an empty one, whether it would throw. However, for C++11 and C++14, the behavior for a function declared **constexpr** (see Section 2.1."**constexpr** Functions" on page 257) was underspecified, which meant that some compilers would inspect the body of a **constexpr** function when evaluating **noexcept**.

A clarification was made in C++17, and the specification is retroactive to C++11 and C++14, so we would expect all of the assertions in the following example to succeed on conforming compilers. Such is the case for all versions of Clang, but, for GCC versions before 9.1 (c. 2019) and MSVC up to 16.9 supplied with /std:c++latest (c. 2021), some of these cases have nonconforming results:

```
#include <stdexcept>  // std::runtime_error
          int f0()        { return 0; }
constexpr int f1()        { return 0; }
constexpr int f2(bool e)  { if (e) throw std::runtime_error(""); return 0; }
          int f3() noexcept { return 0; }
constexpr int f4() noexcept { return 0; }
```

```
static_assert(!noexcept(f0()),      ""); // OK
static_assert(!noexcept(f1()),      ""); // OK, but fails on old GCC and MSVC
static_assert(!noexcept(f2(false)), ""); // OK, but fails on old GCC and MSVC
static_assert(!noexcept(f2(true)),  ""); // OK
static_assert( noexcept(f3()),      ""); // OK
static_assert( noexcept(f4()),      ""); // OK
```

Exception-specification constraints in class hierarchies

There are occasions when we might want to legitimately override a function that never throws with a function that *can* throw. Such occasions are, perhaps, best illustrated by means of an example.

As background, a number of mathematical models using correlation matrices require that those matrices are **positive semidefinite**, a description of which is outside the scope of this book but can be found in most texts on statistics and matrix algebra.[13] Testing whether a matrix meets this requirement is a computationally expensive process for matrices of rank greater than 2, and this property automatically holds true for all rank 1, i.e., trivial, and rank 2 correlation matrices.

Suppose, as a hypothetical example, we have some form of mathematical model that depends on a matrix of correlation values requiring that the correlation matrix is **positive semidefinite**. For 2x2 matrices, the calculations are straightforward, and there is no need to check the validity of the input matrix.

When a more enhanced model is created that can handle arbitrarily large matrices, we have to check those matrices for validity:

```
class MySimpleCalculator
{

    // a mathematical model that can handle the simple case of only 1 or 2
    // assets


    virtual void setCorrelations(const SquareMatrix& correlations) noexcept
        // This function takes a correlation matrix that must be a valid 1x1
        // or 2x2 matrix.  If the matrix is larger than 2x2, then the behavior
        // is undefined.
    {
        // This simple calculator can handle only 2x2 correlations.
        assert(correlations.rank() <= 2);
        d_correlations = correlations;
    }
};
```

---

[13]See, for example, **vandenbos17**.

```
class MyEnhancedCalculator : public MySimpleCalculator
{
    // an enhancement that can handle arbitrarily large numbers of assets

    void setCorrelations(const SquareMatrix& correlations) override
        // This function takes an arbitrarily large correlation matrix,
        // satisfying a positive semidefiniteness constraint.  If the matrix
        // is not positive semidefinite, then an exception will be thrown.
    {
        // Check positive semidefiniteness only if rank > 2 because it is an
        // expensive calculation and is, by definition, true for correlations
        // when rank <= 2.
        if (correlations.rank() > 2 && !correlations.isPositiveSemiDefinite())
        {
            throw MyCorrelationExceptionClass();
        }

        d_correlations = correlations;
    }
};
```

We might think it would be a good idea to put **noexcept** on the base-class function, knowing that it can never throw. However, those plans would be foiled by the rules, which would force us to remove exception throwing from any overrides of this function.

So, given the above scenario, what are our options? There are, unfortunately, only three, none of which is ideal.

1. Remove the **noexcept** specifier from the base class. This option is arguably the easiest one, but we might have to sacrifice some compiler optimizations as a result of doing so or surprise clients who have come to depend on that function being **noexcept** in some way. Unfortunately, for base classes contained in third-party libraries, this option might not be viable.

2. Make the override function **noexcept** and change the **throw** into an **assert**. This option would be effectively kicking the problem of data validation upstream of the function call, saying to every caller, "If you don't want the program to die, don't pass bad data." It also means that unit testing could be done only by using "death tests," which has performance implications for the compilation/testing cycle.

3. Make the override function **noexcept** and simply fail to produce a useful result when given an invalid matrix, possibly with some other derived-class specific state to indicate being in an invalid state. This third alternative is, likewise, effectively kicking the problem upstream through indirect error reporting and handling and has added complications when it comes to unit testing.

Generally, if we are writing a class and there is any possibility that we or a client might consider inheriting from that class now or in the future and we are considering making any of the **virtual** member functions **noexcept**, we must consider carefully whether the benefits of **noexcept** outweigh the disadvantages.

Note that when we choose to remove a **noexcept** specifier from a base-class function, there might be cascading consequences:

```
class DataTable
{
    // This class has some data and appropriate virtual accessors.

    virtual Data getValue(/*...*/) const noexcept;
        // Return some of the held data based on arguments passed in.
};


class Calculator
{
    virtual double getUsefulStatistic(const DataTable& dt) noexcept;
        // given a DataTable dt, makes one or more calls to dt.getValue and
        // performs some calculation to generate a result
};
```

Suppose we want to do the same calculation on data in a database:

```
class LazyLoadingDataTable : public DataTable
{
    // holds a database connection and a mutable data cache

    Data getValue(/*...*/) const override;
        // queries the database for values not in cache and throws
        // DatabaseException in the event of any issues
};
```

Given the rules around **noexcept**, this code will cause a compilation error, which can be resolved by removing the **noexcept** specifier on the DataTable::getValue function. The revised code will now compile, so presumably all is well.

Let's examine what could happen if we have, for example, network congestion.

1. The program constructs a LazyLoadingDataTable with appropriate database connection information.

2. The program passes that into Calculator::getUsefulStatistic.

3. Calculator::getUsefulStatistic calls into LazyLoadingDataTable::getValue.

4. There is a database timeout, and an exception of type DatabaseException is thrown.

5. Because getUsefulStatistic is **noexcept**, the exception cannot propagate.

6. The program terminates.

The behavior outlined above can be problematic, not just in production systems, but also in unit testing. For example, suppose we want to test the above class with a mock database connection, which throws an exception; we would have to again resort to death testing.

See Also

- "**noreturn**" (§1.1, p. 95) describes a related annotation that implies a function will never return normally.

- "*Rvalue* References" (§2.1, p. 710) provides an in-depth discussion of the fundamental support for move operations.

- "**noexcept** Specifier" (§3.1, p. 1085) examines the issues surrounding the widespread, systemic use of **noexcept** beyond just move construction.

Further Reading

- For another perspective on both the genesis and effective use of the **noexcept** operator, see **krzemienski11**.

Appendix

Genesis of the noexcept operator: move operations

Late in the C++11 standardization process, a problem was discovered with the library optimizations that motivated the addition of *move* operations into C++. The problem was deemed serious enough to adopt a proposal[14] for a new language feature at the Pittsburgh meeting, March 2010, over a year after the cutoff for new features for C++11. That problem was breaking the strong exception-safety guarantee when inserting an element into a vector; see *Use Cases — Appending an element to an std::vector* on page 634. Much code has been written and tested expecting this guarantee to hold.

A simple fix would be to require that types provide a nonthrowing *move* constructor to establish the strong exception-safety guarantee. It is relatively simple to provide this guarantee when implementing a *move* constructor for our type, but that involves writing new code. What happens for code from the C++03 era when we recompile under the new rules? This code does not have any *move* constructors defined, as the C++03 language did not support them. Instead, when the vector tries to move each element, overload resolution will find the *copy* constructor and make copies. While we can expect a specially written *move* constructor to provide a no-throw guarantee, we cannot expect the same of *copy* constructors, which often need to allocate memory, such as when a type has an std::vector or std::string data member.

---

[14]gregor09

There are two parts to solving this problem for C++11, and both were adopted at the March 2010 meeting. The first part is an attempt to implicitly upgrade the existing C++03 code. Stroustrup suggested[15] providing implicitly declared *move* constructors and *move*-assignment operators for classes that follow the rule of zero, i.e., for classes that rely on the implicit declaration of the *copy* constructor, *copy*-assignment operator, and destructor. Implicit declaration was *not* desired in cases where users have themselves defined any of these functions, though, as that suggests that there is some internal state management that must be performed, such as releasing owned resources. The implicit definitions for the move operations are simple member-wise *move*-construct or *move*-assign operations, just as the implicitly defined copy operations call copy constructors/assignment operators. Note that C++03 code for the implicitly defined move operations will generally just *copy*, as the pre-existing C++03 code could not itself provide *move* overloads. However, C++03 class templates instantiated with C++11 move-optimized types will *move* correctly for their implicitly declared *move* operations. The important point is that move-optimized types rarely throw on move construction or move assignment, providing the guarantee that std::vector requires but for only that subset of user-supplied class types with optimized move operations.

The second part is Abrahams' introduction of the **noexcept** operator.[16] This operator acts upon expressions, much like the **sizeof** operator, to query whether *any* of the subexpressions that comprise the full expression *are allowed to* emit an exception. If it is known that calling a *move* constructor for the template parameter type, T, cannot throw, then there is no need to maintain a duplicate copy of each element when populating the new array after a vector grows to satisfy a new capacity. This guarantee allows the vector to attempt all the potentially throwing operations first (allocating the new array and constructing any new elements) and only then safely moving all the existing elements, preserving the strong exception-safety guarantee, even for old code recompiled with the new library optimization. Otherwise, as we know that a *move can* throw, the library falls back on the old nonoptimized behavior that makes a copy of each element into the array before updating the internal pointers to take ownership. Note that Abrahams' solution even guarantees that library optimization is available for some subset of C++03 types, but most such types will need updating to support nonthrowing *moves* to gain the benefit.

Abrahams also offered the final part of the puzzle: The **noexcept** exception specification fuels the **noexcept** operator[17]; see Section 3.1."**noexcept** Specifier" on page 1085.

---

[15]stroustrup10a
[16]abrahams10
[17]abrahams10

Opaque Enumeration Declarations

Any enumeration with a *fixed* **underlying type** can be declared without being defined, i.e., declared without its enumerators.

Description

Prior to C++11, enumerations could not be declared without the compiler having access to all of its enumerators, meaning that the definition of a specific **enum** had to be present in the **translation unit (TU)** prior to any declarations:

```
enum E0;                 // Error, incomplete enum type
enum E1 { e_A1, e_B1 };  // OK, definition
enum E1;                 // OK, redeclaration of existing enum in the same TU
```

Since C++11, enumerations can have a *fixed* **underlying type** (see Section 2.1."Underlying Type '11" on page 829), meaning that their integral representation does not depend on the values of their enumerators. Such enumerations can be declared without enumerators via an **opaque declaration**:

```
enum E2 : short;  // OK, opaque declaration with fixed char underlying type
enum E3;          // Error, opaque declaration without fixed underlying type
```

The declaration of the E2 enumeration above gives the compiler enough information to know that the size and alignment of the type is **sizeof(short)** and **alignof(short)**, respectively, even though the enumerators have not yet been seen. Conversely, the size, alignment, and signedness of a classic enumeration such as E3 is **implementation defined** and dependent on the specific enumerator values. The compiler cannot determine these properties until the enumerators are seen; hence, classic enumerations are not eligible for **opaque declaration**.

C++11 also introduced **scoped enumerations** (see Section 2.1."**enum class**" on page 332), declared with the keyword sequence **enum class** or **enum struct**. A scoped enumeration implicitly has an **underlying type** of **int** unless the user explicitly specifies a different **underlying type**. Because the underlying type of a **scoped enumeration** is always known at the point of declaration, it, too, can be declared with an **opaque declaration**:

```
enum class E4;          // OK, scoped enum, default int underlying type
enum class E5 : short;  // OK, scoped enum, fixed short underlying type
```

Within a single **translation unit**, the enumerators for an **enum** declared with an opaque declaration can be defined before the declaration, defined after it, or not provided at all:

```
enum E6 : unsigned { e_A6A, e_A6B };  // OK, enum definition
enum E6 : unsigned;                   // OK, redeclaration of existing enum
```

```
enum E7 : int;                      // OK, opaque enum declaration
enum E7 : int { e_A7 };             // OK, enum definition

enum E8 : short;                    // OK, opaque enum declaration
```

All the declarations of an enumeration within a single TU must agree on its **underlying type**; otherwise, the program is ill formed:

```
enum class E9;             // OK, fixed default underlying type of int
enum class E9 : int;       // OK, underlying type matches previous declaration.

enum E10 : short;          // OK, fixed explicit underlying type short
enum E10 : char { e_A10 }; // Error, redeclaration with different underlying type

enum class E11 : char;     // OK, fixed explicit underlying type char
enum class E11 : short;    // Error, redeclaration with different underlying type
```

Note that, as in C++03, multiple definitions of an enumeration are not allowed within a single TU:

```
enum E12 : char;           // OK, opaque enum declaration
enum E12 : char { e_A12 }; // OK, enum definition
enum E12 : char;           // OK, opaque enum redeclaration
enum E12 : char { e_A12 }; // Error, enum redefinition

enum class E13;            // OK, opaque enum declaration
enum class E13 { e_A13 };  // OK, enum definition
enum class E13;            // OK, opaque enum redeclaration
enum class E13 { e_A13 };  // Error, enum redefinition
```

An enumeration declared with an opaque declaration is a **complete type**. The type being complete means that, for example, we can request its size using **sizeof**, have a local, global, or member variable of the enumeration's type, and so on — all without having access to the enumeration's definition:

```
enum E14 : char;
static_assert(sizeof(E14) == 1, "");                // OK, sizeof of a complete type

enum class E15;
static_assert(sizeof(E15) == sizeof(int), "");  // OK, sizeof of a complete type

E14 a;  // OK, variable of a complete type
E15 b;  // OK,     "      "  "     "        "

struct S {
    E14 d_e14;  // OK, data member of a complete type
    E15 d_e15;  // OK,     "      "    "  "      "      "
};
```

```
  S(E14 e14, E15 e15)  // OK, by-value function arguments of complete types
  : d_e14(e14)
  , d_e15(e15)
  {
  }
};
```

Typical usage of opaque enumeration declarations often involves placing the **forward declar-ation** within a header and sequestering the complete definition within a corresponding .cpp (or a second header). A **forward declaration** can insulate clients from changes to the enumerator list (see *Use Cases — Using opaque enumerations within a header file* on page 663):

```
// myclass.h:
// ...

class MyClass {
    // ...
private:
    enum class State;  // forward declaration of State enumeration
    State d_state;
};

// ...

// myclass.cpp:

#include <myclass.h>
// ...
enum class MyClass::State { e_STATE1, e_STATE2, e_STATE3 };
    // complete definition compatible with forward declaration of MyClass::State
```

Note that such a **forward declaration** is distinct from a **local declaration**. A forward declaration is characterized by having a translation unit that deliberately comprises both the definition and the **opaque declaration** of the enumeration. This translation unit can result either from their direct colocation in the same file or via the inclusion of a header in the corresponding implementation file (as in the example above). For a local declaration, no such translation unit exists:

```
// library.h:
// ...

enum class E18 : short { e_A18, /*...*/ e_Z18 };

// client.cpp:

// Note that 'library.h' is not included

enum class E18;  // BAD IDEA: a local opaque enumeration declaration
```

A local declaration, such as E18 above, can be problematic; see *Potential Pitfalls — Redeclaring an externally defined enumeration locally* on page 675.

Use Cases

Using opaque enumerations within a header file

Physical design involves two related but distinct notions of information *hiding*: **encapsulation**[1,2] and **insulation**.[3,4] An implementation detail is *encapsulated* if changing it (in a semantically compatible way) does not require clients to rework their code but might require them to recompile it.

An *insulated* implementation detail, on the other hand, can be altered compatibly *without* forcing clients even to recompile, merely to relink their code against updated libraries. The advantages of avoiding such **compile-time coupling** transcend simply reducing compile time. For larger codebases in which various layers are managed under different release cycles, making a change to an *insulated* detail can be done with a .o patch and a relink the same day, whereas an *uninsulated* change might precipitate a waterfall of releases spanning days, weeks, or even longer.

As a first example of **opaque enumeration** usage, consider a non-**value-semantic mechanism** class, Proctor, implemented as a finite-state machine:

```
// proctor.h:

class Proctor
{
    int d_state;  // "opaque" but unconstrained int type (BAD IDEA)
    // ...

public:
    Proctor();
    // ...
};
```

Among other private members, Proctor has a data member, d_state, representing the current enumerated state of the object. We anticipate that the implementation of the underlying state machine will change regularly over time but that the **public** interface is relatively stable. We will, therefore, want to ensure that all parts of the implementation that are likely to change reside outside of the header. Hence, the complete definition of the enumeration of the states (including the enumerator list itself) is sequestered within the corresponding .cpp file:

---

[1] **liskov87**
[2] **liskov16, liskov09**
[3] **lakos96**, Chapter 6, pp. 327–471
[4] **lakos20**, sections 3.10–3.11, pp. 733–835

```
// proctor.cpp:
#include <proctor.h>

enum State { e_STARTING, e_READY, e_RUNNING, e_DONE };

Proctor::Proctor() : d_state(e_STARTING) { /*...*/ }
// ...
```

Prior to C++11, enumerations could not be **forward declared**. To avoid the unnecessary exposition of the enumerators in the header file, a completely unconstrained **int** would be used as a data member, and the enumeration would be defined in the .cpp file. With the advent of modern C++, we now have better options. First, we might consider adding an explicit underlying type to the enumeration in the .cpp file:

```
// proctor.cpp:
#include <proctor.h>

enum State : int { e_STARTING, e_READY, e_RUNNING, e_DONE };

Proctor::Proctor() : d_state(e_STARTING) { /*...*/ }
// ...
```

Now that the **component-local enum** has an explicit underlying type, we can **forward declare** it in the header file. The existence of proctor.cpp, which includes proctor.h, makes this declaration a **forward declaration** and not just a **local declaration**. Compilation of proctor.cpp guarantees that the declaration and definition are compatible. Having this **forward declaration** improves (somewhat) our type safety:

```
// proctor.h:
// ...
enum State : int;  // opaque declaration of enumeration (new in C++11)

class Proctor
{
    State d_state;  // opaque classical enumerated type (BETTER IDEA)
    // ...

public:
    Proctor();
    // ...
};
```

But we can do even better. First, we will want to nest the enumerated **State** type within the private section of the proctor to avoid needless namespace pollution. Then, because the numerical values of the enumerators are not relevant, we can more closely model our intent by nesting a more strongly typed **enum class** instead:

```
// proctor.h:
// ...
class Proctor
{
    enum class State;    // forward (nested) declaration of type-safe enumeration
    State d_current;     // opaque (modern) enumerated data type (BEST IDEA)
    // ...

public:
    Proctor();
    // ...
};
```

Next, we would then define the nested **enum class** accordingly in the .cpp file:

```
// proctor.cpp:
#include <proctor.h>

enum class Proctor::State { e_STARTING, e_READY, e_RUNNING, e_DONE };

Proctor::Proctor() : d_current(State::e_STARTING) { /*...*/ }
// ...
```

Finally, notice that in the header file of this example we first forward declared the nested **enum class** type within class scope and then separately defined a data member of the opaque enumerated type. We needed to do this separation because simultaneously *opaquely declaring* an enumeration and also defining an object of that type in a single statement is not possible:

```
enum E1 : int e1;  // Error, syntax not supported
enum class E2 e2;  // Error,    "       "        "
```

Fully defining an enumeration and simultaneously defining an object of the type in one stroke is, however, possible:

```
enum E3 : int { e_A, e_B } e3;  // OK, full type definition + object definition
enum class E4 { e_A, e_B } e4;  // OK,    "       "        "       "        "
```

Providing such a full definition, however, would have run counter to our intention to **insulate** the enumerator list of `Proctor::State` from clients including the header file defining `Proctor`.

Dual-Access: Insulating some external clients from the enumerator list

In previous use cases, the goal has been to insulate *all* external clients from the enumerators of an enumeration that is visible (but not necessarily programmatically reachable) in the defining component's header. Consider the situation in which a **component** (.h/.cpp pair) itself defines an enumeration that will be used by various clients within a single program, some of which will need access to the enumerators.

When an **enum class** or a classic **enum** having an explicitly specified underlying type (see Section 2.1."Underlying Type '11" on page 829) is specified in a header for direct programmatic use, external clients are at liberty to unilaterally redeclare it *opaquely*, i.e., without its enumerator list. A compelling motivation for doing so would be for a client who doesn't make direct use of the enumerators to insulate itself and/or its clients from having to recompile whenever the enumerator list changes.

Embedding any such local declaration in client code, however, would be highly problematic: If the underlying type of the declaration (in one translation unit) were somehow to become inconsistent with that of the definition (in some other translation unit), any program incorporating both translation units would immediately become silently **ill formed, no diagnostic required (IFNDR)**; see *Potential Pitfalls — Redeclaring an externally defined enumeration locally* on page 675. Unless a separate forwarding header file is provided along with (and ideally included by) the header defining the full enumeration, any client opting to exploit this opacity feature of an enumerated type will have no alternative but to redeclare the enumeration locally; see *Potential Pitfalls — Inciting local enumeration declarations: An attractive nuisance* on page 677.

For example, consider an **enum class**, Event, intended for public use by external clients:

```
// event.h:
// ...
enum class Event : char { /*... changes frequently ...*/ };
// ...              ^^^^
```

Now imagine some client header file, **badclient.h**, that makes use of the Event enumeration and chooses to avoid compile-time coupling itself to the enumerator list by embedding, for whatever reason, a local declaration of Event instead:

```
// badclient.h:
// ...
enum class Event : char;  // BAD IDEA: local external declaration
// ...
struct BadObject
{
    Event d_currentEvent; // object of locally declare enumeration
    // ...
};
// ...
```

Imagine now that the number of events that can fit in a **char** is exceeded and we decide to change the definition to have an underlying type of **short**:

```
// event.h:
// ...
enum class Event : short { /*... changes frequently ...*/ };
// ...              ^^^^^
```

Client code, such as in **badclient.h**, that fails to include the **event.h** header will have no automatic way of knowing that it needs to change, and recompiling the code for all cases where **event.h** isn't also included in the translation unit will not fix the problem. Unless every such client is somehow updated manually, a newly linked program comprising them will be IFNDR with the likely consequence of either a crash or, worse, the program continues to run and misbehaves. When providing a programmatically accessible definition of an enumerated type in a header where the **underlying type** is specified either explicitly or implicitly, we can give external clients a *safe* alternative to local declaration by also providing an auxiliary header containing *just* the corresponding opaque declaration:

```
// event.fwd.h:
// ...
enum class Event : char;
// ...
```

Here we have chosen to treat the forwarding header file as part of the same event component as the principal header but with an injected descriptive suffix field, .fwd.[5]

In general, having a forwarding header always included in its corresponding full header facilitates situations such as default template arguments where the declaration can appear at most once in any given translation unit; the only drawback is that the comparatively small forwarding header file must now also be opened and parsed if the full header file is included in a given translation unit. To ensure consistency, we thus **#include** this forwarding header in the original header defining the full enumeration:

```
// event.h:
// ...                         // Ensure opaque declaration (included here) is
#include <event.fwd.h>  // consistent with complete definition (below).
// ...
enum class Event : char { /*... changes frequently ...*/ };
// ...
```

---

[5]Using the compound *suffix* fwd.h (e.g., comp.fwd.h) for a forwarding header — instead of, say, comp_fwd.h or comp.fh — is advantageous in two ways. First, it preserves both the component's **base name** and the conventional **file extension** for headers on the host platform. Second, it informs the human reader that this is a *forwarding* header that might co-exist alongside a nonforwarding one. See **lakos20**, section 2.4, pp. 297–333.

In this way, every translation unit that includes the definition will serve to ensure that the forward declaration and definition match; hence, clients can incorporate safely only the presumably more stable forwarding header:

```
// goodclient.h:
// ...
#include <event.fwd.h>  // GOOD IDEA: consistent opaque declaration
// ...
class Client
{
    Event d_currentEvent;
    // ...
};
```

To illustrate real-world practical use of the opaque-enumerations feature, consider the various **components** that might depend on[6] an Event enumeration such as that above.

- Message — The component provides a *value-semantic* Message class consisting of just raw data,[7] including an Event field representing the type of event. This component never makes direct use of any enumeration values and thus needs to include only event.fwd.h and the corresponding opaque *forward* declaration of the Event enumeration.

- Sender and Receiver — These are a pair of components that, respectively, create and consume Message objects. To populate a Message object, a Sender will need to provide a valid value for the Event member. Similarly, to process a Message, a Receiver will need to understand the potential individual enumerated values for the Event field. Both of these components will include the primary event.h header and thus have the complete definition of Event available to them.

- Messenger — The final component, a general engine capable of being handed Message objects by a Sender and then delivering those objects in an appropriate fashion to a Receiver, needs a complete and usable definition of Message objects — possibly copying them or storing them in containers before delivery — but has no need for understanding the possible values of the Event member within those Message objects. This component can participate fully and correctly in the larger system while being completely *insulated* from the enumeration values of the Event enumeration.

By factoring out the Event enumeration into its own separate component and providing two distinct but compatible headers, one containing the opaque declaration and the other (which includes the first) providing the complete definition, we enable having different components choose not to compile-time couple themselves with the enumerator list without forcing them to *unsafely* redeclare the enumeration locally.

---

[6]**lakos20**, section 1.8, "The Depends-On Relation," pp. 237–243

[7]We sometimes refer to data that is meaningful only in the context of a higher-level entity as **dumb data**; see **lakos20**, section 3.5.5, pp. 629–633.

Cookie: Insulating all external clients from the enumerator list

A commonly recurring **design pattern**, commonly known as the "Memento pattern,"[8] manifests when a facility providing a service, often in a multi-client environment, hands off a packet of opaque information — a.k.a. a **cookie** — to a client to hold and then present back to the facility to enable resuming operations where processing left off. Since the information within the cookie will not be used substantively by the client, any unnecessary compile-time coupling of clients with the implementation of that cookie serves only to impede fluid maintainability of the facility issuing the cookie. With respect to not just *encapsulating* but *insulating* pure implementation details that are held but not used substantively by clients, we offer this Memento pattern as a possible use case for **opaque enumerations**.

Event-driven programming,[9] historically implemented using **callback functions**, introduces a style of programming that is decidedly different from that to which we might have become accustomed. In this programming paradigm, a higher-level agent (e.g., `main`) would begin by instantiating an `Engine` that will be responsible for monitoring for events and invoking provided callbacks when appropriate. Classically, clients might have registered a function pointer and a corresponding pointer to a client-defined piece of identifying data, but here we will make use of a C++11 Standard Library type, `std::function`, which can encapsulate arbitrary callable function objects and their associated state. This callback will be provided one object to represent the event that just happened and another object that can be used opaquely to reregister interest in the same event again, if appropriate for the application.

This opaque cookie and passing around of the client state might seem like an unnecessary step, but often the event management involved in software of this sort is wrapping the most often executed code in busy systems, and performance of each basic operation is therefore important. To maximize performance, every potential branch or lookup in an internal data structure must be minimized, and allowing clients to pass back the internal state of the engine when reregistering can greatly reduce the engine's work to continue a client's processing of events without tearing down and rebuilding all client state each time an event happens. More importantly, event managers such as this often become highly concurrent to take advantage of modern hardware, so performant manipulation of their own data structures and well-defined lifetime of the objects they interact with become paramount. This API makes the simple guarantee of, "If you don't reregister, then the engine will clean everything up; if you do, then the callback function will continue its lifetime," a tractable paradigm to follow.

```
// callbackengine.h:
#include <deque>          // std::deque
#include <functional>     // std::function

class EventData;          // information that clients will need to process an event
```

---

[8]**gamma95**, Chapter 5, section "Memento," pp. 283–291
[9]See also **gamma95**, Chapter 5, section "Observer," pp. 293–303.

```
class CallbackEngine;  // the driver for processing and delivering events

class CallbackData
{
    // This class represents a handle to the shared state associating a
    // callback function object with a CallbackEngine.

public:
    typedef std::function<void(const EventData&, CallbackEngine*,
        CallbackData)> Callback;
            // alias for a function object returning void and taking, as arguments,
            // the event data to be consumed by the client, the address of the
            // CallbackEngine object that supplied the event data, and the
            // callback data that can be used to reregister the client, should the
            // client choose to show continued interest in future instances of the
            // same event

    enum class State;  // GOOD IDEA
            // nested forward declaration of insulated enumeration, enabling
            // changes to the enumerator list without forcing clients to recompile

private:
    // ... (a smart pointer to an opaque object containing the state and the
    //      callback to invoke)

public:
    CallbackData(const Callback &cb, State init);

    // ... (constructors, other manipulators and accessors, etc.)

    State getState() const;
            // Return the current state of this callback.

    void setState(State state) const;
            // Set the current state to the specified state.

    Callback& getCallback() const;
            // Return the callback function object specified at construction.
};

class CallbackEngine
{
private:
    // ... (other, stable private data members implementing this object)

    bool d_isRunning;  // active state
```

```
        std::deque<CallbackData> d_pendingCallbacks;
            // The collection of clients currently registered for interest, or having
            // callbacks delivered, with this CallbackEngine.
            //
            // Reregistering or skipping reregistering when
            // called back will lead to updating internal data structures based on
            // the current value of this State.

    public:
        // ...    (other public member functions, e.g., creators, manipulators)

        void registerInterest(CallbackData::Callback cb);
            // Register (e.g., from main) a new client with this manager object.

        void reregisterInterest(const CallbackData& callback);
            // Reregister (e.g., from a client) the specified callback with this
            // manager object, providing the state contained in the CallbackData
            // to enable resumption from the same state as processing left off.

        void run();
            // Start this object's event loop.

        // ...  (other public member functions, e.g., manipulators, accessors)
    };
```

A client would, in **main**, create an instance of this **CallbackEngine**, define the appropriate functions to be invoked when events happen, register interest, and then let the engine **run**:

```
// myapplication.cpp:
// ...
#include <callbackengine.h>

static void myCallback(const EventData&    event,
                       CallbackEngine*     engine,
                       const CallbackData& cookie);
    // Process the specified event, and then potentially reregister the
    // specified cookie for interest in the same data.

int main()
{
    CallbackEngine engine;  // Create a configurable callback engine object.

    //...     (Configure the callback engine, e, as appropriate.)

    engine.registerInterest(&myCallback);  // Even a stateless function pointer can
                                            // be used with std::function.
```

```
    // ...create and register other clients for interest...

    engine.run();    // Cede control to e's event loop until complete.

    return 0;
}
```

The implementation of `myCallback`, in the example below, is then free to reregister interest in the same event, save the cookie elsewhere to reregister at a later time, or complete its task and let the `CallbackEngine` take care of properly cleaning up all now unnecessary resources:

```
void myCallback(const EventData&      event,
                CallbackEngine*       engine,
                const CallbackData&   cookie)
{
    int status = EventProcessor::processEvent(event);

    if (status > 0)  // Status is nonzero; continue interest in event now.
    {
        engine->reregisterInterest(cookie);
    }
    else if (status < 0)  // Negative status indicates EventProcessor wants
                          // to reregister later.
    {
        EventProcessor::storeCallback(engine, cookie);
                        // Call reregisterInterest later.
    }

    // Return flow of control to the CallbackEngine that invoked this
    // callback.  If status was zero, then this callback should be cleaned
    // up properly with minimal fuss and no leaks.
}
```

What makes use of the **opaque enumeration** here especially apt is that the internal data structures maintained by the `CallbackEngine` might be subtly interrelated, and any knowledge of a client's relationship to those data structures that can be maintained through callbacks is going to reduce the amount of lookups and synchronization that would be needed to correctly reregister a client without that information. The otherwise wide contract on `reregisterInterest` means that clients have no need themselves to directly know anything about the actual values of the `State` they might be in. More notably, a component like this is likely to be heavily reused across a large codebase, and being able to maintain it while minimizing the need for clients to recompile can be a huge boon to deployment times.

To see what is involved, we can consider the business end of the `CallbackEngine` implementation and an outline of what a single-threaded implementation might involve:

```
// callbackengine.cpp:
#include <callbackengine.h>

enum class CallbackData::State
{
    // Full (local) definition of the enumerated states for the callback engine.
    e_INITIAL,
    e_LISTENING,
    e_READY,
    e_PROCESSING,
    e_REREGISTERED,
    e_FREED
};

void CallbackEngine::registerInterest(CallbackData::Callback cb)
{
    // Create a CallbackData instance with a state of e_INITIAL and
    // insert it into the set of active clients.
    d_pendingCallbacks.push_back(CallbackData(cb, CallbackData::State::e_INITIAL));
}

void CallbackEngine::run()
{
    // Update all client states to e_LISTENING based on the events in which
    // they have interest.

    d_isRunning = true;
    while (d_isRunning)
    {
        // Poll the operating system API waiting for an event to be ready.
        EventData event = getNextEvent();

        // Go through the elements of d_pendingCallbacks to deliver this
        // event to each of them.
        std::deque<CallbackData> callbacks;
        callbacks.swap(d_pendingCallbacks);

        // Loop once over the callbacks we are about to notify to update their
        // state so that we know they are now in a different container.
        for (CallbackData& callback : callbacks)
        {
            callback.setState(CallbackData::State::e_READY);
        }

        while (!callbacks.empty())
```

```
            {
                CallbackData callback = callbacks.front();
                callbacks.pop_front();

                // Mark the callback as processing and invoke it.
                callback.setState(CallbackData::State::e_PROCESSING);

                callback.getCallback()(event, this, callback);

                // Clean up based on the new State.
                if (callback.getState() == CallbackData::State::e_REREGISTERED)
                {
                    // Put the callback on the queue to get events again.
                    d_pendingCallbacks.push_back(callback);
                }
                else
                {
                    // The callback can be released, freeing resources.
                    callback.setState(CallbackData::State::e_FREED);
                }
            }
        }
    }
}

void CallbackEngine::reregisterInterest(const CallbackData& callback)
{
    if (callback.getState() == CallbackData::State::e_PROCESSING)
    {
        // This is being called reentrantly from run(); simply update state.
        callback.setState(CallbackData::State::e_REREGISTERED);
    }
    else if (callback.getState() == CallbackData::State::e_READY)
    {
        // This callback is in the deque of callbacks currently having events
        // delivered to it; do nothing and leave it there.
    }
    else
    {
        // This callback was saved; set it to the proper state and put it in
        // the queue of callbacks.
        if (d_isRunning)
        {
            callback.setState(CallbackData::State::e_LISTENING);
        }
        else
```

```
        {
            callback.setState(CallbackData::State::e_INITIAL);
        }

        d_pendingCallbacks.push_back(callback);
    }
}
```

Note how the definition of `CallbackData::State` is visible and needed only in this implementation file. Also, consider that the set of states might grow or shrink as this `CallbackEngine` is optimized and extended, and clients can still pass around the object containing that state in a type-safe manner while remaining insulated from this definition.

Prior to C++11, we could not have *forward declared* this enumeration and so would have had to represent it in a *type-unsafe* way — e.g., as an **int**. Thanks to the modern **enum class** (see Section 2.1."**enum class**" on page 332), however, we can conveniently forward declare it as a nested type and then, separately, fully define it inside the `.cpp` implementing other noninline member functions of the `CallbackEngine` class. In this way, we are able to *insulate* changes to the enumerator list along with any other aspects of the implementation defined outside of the `.h` file without forcing any client applications to recompile. Finally, the basic design of the hypothetical `CallbackEngine` in the previous code example could have been used for any number of useful components: a parser or tokenizer, a workflow engine, or even a more generalized event loop.

Potential Pitfalls

Redeclaring an externally defined enumeration locally

An opaque enumeration declaration enables the use of that enumeration without granting visibility to its enumerators, reducing physical coupling between components. Unlike a **forward class declaration**, an opaque enumeration declaration produces a complete type, sufficient for substantive use (e.g., via the linker):

```
// client.cpp:
#include <cstdint>  // std::uint8_t
enum Event : std::uint8_t;
Event e;  // OK, Event is a complete type.
```

The *underlying type* specified in an opaque **enum** declaration must exactly match the full definition; otherwise, a program incorporating both is IFNDR. Updating an **enum**'s underlying type to accommodate additional values can lead to latent defects when these changes are not propagated to all local declarations:

```
// library.h:
enum Event : std::uint16_t { /* now more than 256 events */ };
```

Consistency of a local opaque **enum** declaration's underlying type with that of its complete definition in a separate translation unit cannot be enforced by the compiler, potentially leading to a program that is IFNDR. In the `client.cpp` example shown above, if the opaque declaration in `client.cpp` is not somehow updated to reflect the changes in `event.h`, the program will compile, link, and run, but its behavior has silently become undefined. The only robust solution to this problem is for `library.h` to provide two separate header files; see *Inciting local enumeration declarations: An attractive nuisance* on page 677.

The problem with local declarations is by no means limited to opaque enumerations. Embedding a local declaration for any object whose use might be associated with its definition in a separate translation unit via just the linker invites instability:

```
// main.cpp:                              // library.cpp:
extern int x;  // BAD IDEA!               int x;
// ...                                    // ...
```

The definition of object x (in the code snippets above) resides in the `.cpp` file of the library component while a supposed declaration of x is embedded in the file defining `main`. Should the type of just the definition of x change, both translation units will continue to compile, but, when linked, the resulting program will be IFNDR:

```
// main.cpp:                              // library.cpp:
extern int x;  // ILL-FORMED PROGRAM      double x;
// ...                                    // ...
```

To ensure consistency across translation units, the time-honored tradition is to place, in a header file managed by the supplier, a declaration of each external-linkage entity intended for use outside of the translation unit in which it is defined; that header is then included by both the supplier and each consumer:

```
// main.cpp:             // library.h:          // library.cpp:
#include <library.h>     // ...                 #include <library.h>
// ...                   extern int x;          int x;
                         // ...                  // ...
```

In this way, any change to the definition of x in `library.cpp` — the supplier — will trigger a compilation error when `library.cpp` is recompiled, thereby forcing a corresponding change to the declaration in `library.h`. When that happens, typical build tools will take note of the change in the header file's timestamp relative to that of the `.o` file corresponding to `main.cpp` — the consumer — and indicate that it too needs to be recompiled. Problem solved.

The maintainability pitfall associated with opaque enumerations, however, is qualitatively more severe than for other external-linkage types, such as a global **int**: (1) the full definition for the enumeration type itself needs to reside in a header for *any* external client to make use of its individual enumerators, and (2) typical components consist of just a .h/.cpp pair, i.e., exactly one .h file and usually just one .cpp file.[10]

Inciting local enumeration declarations: An attractive nuisance

Whenever we, as library component authors, provide the complete definition of an enumeration with a fixed underlying type and fail to provide a corresponding forwarding header having just the opaque declaration, we confront our clients with the difficult decision of whether to needlessly compile-time couple[11] themselves and/or their clients with the details of the enumerator list or to make the dubious choice to unilaterally redeclare that enumeration locally.

The problems associated with local declarations of data whose types are maintained in separate translation units is not limited to enumerations; see *Redeclaring an externally defined enumeration locally* on page 675. The maintainability pitfall associated with opaque enumerations, however, is qualitatively more severe than for other external-linkage types, such as a global **int**, in that the ability to elide the enumerators amounts to an *attractive nuisance* wherein a client — wanting to do so and having access to only a single header containing the complete definition — might be persuaded into declaring the enumeration locally!

Ensuring that library components that define enumerations whose enumerators can be elided also consistently provide a second forwarding header file containing the opaque declaration of each such enumeration would be one generally applicable way to sidestep this maintenance burden; see *Use Cases — Dual-Access: Insulating some external clients from the enumerator list* on page 665. Note that the attractive nuisance potentially exists even when the primary intent of the component is not to make the enumeration generally available.[12]

Annoyances

Opaque enumerations are not completely type safe

Making an enumeration opaque does not stop it from being used to create an object that is initialized opaquely to a zero value and then subsequently used (e.g., in a function call):

```
enum Bozo : int;   // forward declaration of enumeration Bozo
void f(Bozo);      // forward declaration of function f

void g()
{
```

---

[10]**lakos20**, sections 2.2.11–2.2.13, pp. 280–281

[11]For a complete real-world example of how compile-time coupling can delay a "hot fix" by weeks, not just hours, see **lakos20**, section 3.10.5, pp. 783–789.

[12]**wight**

```
    Bozo clown{};
    f(clown);      // OK, who knows if zero is a valid value?!
}
```

Though creating a zero-valued enumeration variable by default is not new, allowing one to be created without even knowing what enumerated values are valid is arguably dubious.

See Also

- "Underlying Type '11" (§2.1, p. 829) discusses the underlying integral representation for enumeration variables and their values.

- "**enum class**" (§2.1, p. 332) introduces an implicitly scoped, more strongly typed enumeration.

Further Reading

- For more on declaration versus definition, header files, .h and .cpp pairs, extracting actual dependencies, the depends-on relation, logical and physical name cohesion, avoiding unnecessary compile-time dependencies, and architectural insulation techniques, see **lakos20**.

- A complementary view of production software design can be found in **martin17**.

Range-Based **for** Loops

A more abstract form of **for** loops based on ranges provides a simplified and compact syntax for iterating through every member in a given sequence of objects.

Description

Iterating over the elements of a collection is a fundamental operation usually performed with a **for** loop:

```
#include <vector>  // std::vector
#include <string>  // std::string

void f1(const std::vector<std::string>& vec)
{
    for (std::vector<std::string>::const_iterator i = vec.begin();
         i != vec.end(); ++i)
    {
        // ...
    }
}
```

The code above iterates over the strings in an `std::vector`. Use of this classic iterator idiom is significantly more verbose than similar code in other languages because it uses a general-purpose construct, the **for** loop, to perform the specialized but common task of traversing a collection. In C++11, the definition of `i` can be simplified somewhat by using **auto**:

```
void f2(const std::vector<std::string>& vec)
{
    for (auto i = vec.begin(); i != vec.end(); ++i)
    {
        const std::string& s = *i;
        // ...
    }
}
```

Although **auto** does have a number of potential pitfalls, this use of **auto** to deduce the return type of `vec.begin()` is one of its safer idiomatic uses; see Section 2.1."**auto** Variables" on page 195. While this version of the loop is simpler to write, it still uses the fully general, three-part **for** construct. Moreover, `vec.end()` is evaluated each time through the loop.

The C++11 **range-based for loop** (sometimes colloquially referred to as the "foreach" loop) is a more concise loop notation tuned for traversing the elements of a container or other sequential range. A range-based **for** loop works with *ranges* and *elements* rather than *iterators* or *indexes*:

```
void f3(const std::vector<std::string>& vec)
{
    for (const std::string& s : vec)
    {
        // ...
    }
}
```

The loop in the example function above can be read as "for each element s in vec ...." There is no need to specify the name or type of the iterator, the loop-termination condition, or the increment clause; the syntax is focused purely on yielding each element of the collection for processing within the body of the loop.

Specification

The syntax for a range-based **for** loop declares a loop variable and specifies a range of elements to be traversed:

```
for ( for-range-declaration : range-expression ) statement
```

The compiler treats this high-level construct as though it were transformed into a lower-level **for** loop with the following pseudocode:

```
{
    auto&& __range = range-expression;
    for (auto __begin = begin-expr, __end = end-expr;
         __begin != __end;
         ++__begin)
    {
        for-range-declaration = *__begin;
        statement
    }
}
```

The variables __range, __begin, and __end, above, are for *exposition only*; i.e., the compiler does not necessarily generate variables with those names and user code is not permitted to access those variables directly.

The __range variable is defined as a **forwarding reference** (see Section 2.1."Forwarding References" on page 377); it will bind to any type of **range expression**, regardless of its **value category** (*lvalue* or *rvalue*). If the **range expression** yields a temporary object, its lifetime is extended, if necessary, until __range goes out of scope. Though this **lifetime extension** of temporary objects works in most cases, it is insufficient when __range doesn't bind directly to the temporary created by the **range expression**, potentially resulting in subtle defects; see *Potential Pitfalls — Lifetime of temporary objects in the range expression* on page 691.

The *begin-expr* and *end-expr* expressions used to initialize the __begin and __end variables, respectively, define a half-open range of elements starting with __begin and including any elements in __range up to but not including __end. The precise meaning of *begin-expr* and *end-expr* were clarified in C++14 but were essentially the same in C++11.[1]

- If __range refers to an array, then *begin-expr* is the address of the first element of the array and *end-expr* is the address of one past the last element of the array.

- If __range refers to a class object and begin and/or end are members of that class, then *begin-expr* is __range.begin() and *end-expr* is __range.end(). Note that if begin or end are found in the class, then both of these expressions must be valid or else the program is ill formed.

- Otherwise, *begin-expr* is begin(__range) and *end-expr* is end(__range), where begin and end are found using **argument-dependent lookup (ADL)**. Note that begin and end are looked up only in the namespaces associated with the expressions; names that are local to the context of the range-based **for** loop are not considered; see *Annoyances — Only ADL lookup* on page 707.

Thus, a container such as vector, with conventional begin and end member functions, provides everything necessary for a range-based **for** loop, as we saw in the f3 example on page 680. Note that *end-expr* — __range.end() in the case of the vector — is evaluated only once, unlike the idiomatic low-level **for** loop, where it is evaluated prior to every iteration.

Although the __begin and __end variables look and act like iterators, they need not conform to all of the iterator requirements in the Standard. Specifically, the type of __begin and __end must support prefix **operator++** but not necessarily postfix **operator++**, and it must support **operator!=** but not necessarily **operator==**. Note that in C++11 and C++14, __begin and __end are required to have the same type; see *Annoyances — No support for sentinel iterator types* on page 706.[2]

The *for-range-declaration* declares the loop variable. Any declaration that can be initialized with *__begin will work. For instance, if *__begin returns a reference to a modifiable object of, e.g., **int** type, then **int** j, **int&** j, **const int&** j, and **long** j would all be valid *for-range-declarations* declaring a loop variable j, but see *Potential Pitfalls — Inadvertent copying of elements* on page 696. Alternatively, the type of the loop variable can be deduced using **auto** — e.g., **auto** j, **auto&** j, **const auto&** j, or **auto&&** j (see Section 2.1."**auto** Variables" on page 195).

The sequence being traversed can be modified through the loop variable only if dereferencing __begin would return a reference to a modifiable type and the loop variable is similarly declared as a reference to a modifiable type (e.g., **int&**, **auto&**, or **auto&&**):

---

[1] The rules for interpreting *begin-expr* and *end-expr* were slightly unclear in C++11. A **defect report**, CWG issue 1442 (**miller12a**), clarified the wording retroactively. C++14 clarified the wording further.

[2] The C++17 Standard changes the defining code transformation of the range-based **for** loop so as to allow __begin and __end to have different types as long as they are comparable using __begin != __end; see *Annoyances — No support for sentinel iterator types* on page 706.

```
#include <vector>  // std::vector

void f1(std::vector<int>& vec)
{
    const std::vector<int>& cvec = vec;

    for (auto& i : cvec)
    {
        i = 0;  // Error, i is a reference to const int.
    }

    for (int j : vec)
    {
        j = 0;  // Bug, j is a loop-local variable; vec is not modified.
    }

    for (int& k : vec)
    {
        k = 0;  // OK, set element of vec to 0.
    }
}
```

Since cvec is **const**, the element type returned by *begin(cvec) is **const int**&. Thus, i is deduced as **const int**&, making invalid any attempt to modify an element through i. The second loop is valid C++11 code but has a subtle defect: j is not a reference — it contains a *copy* of the current element in the **vector** — so modifying j has no effect on the vector. The third loop correctly sets all of the elements of **vec** to zero; the loop variable k is a reference to the current element, so setting it to zero modifies the original vector.

Note that the *for-range declaration* must define a *new* variable; unlike a traditional **for** loop, it cannot name an existing variable already in scope:

```
void f2(std::vector<int>& vec)
{
    int m;
    for (    m : vec) { /*...*/ }  // Error, m does not define a variable.
    for (int& m : vec) { /*...*/ }  // OK, loop m hides function-scope m.
}
```

The *statement* that makes up the loop body can contain anything that is valid within a traditional **for** loop body. In particular, a **break** statement will exit the loop immediately, and a **continue** statement will skip to the next iteration.

Applying this transformation to a range-based **for** loop traversing a **vector** of **string** elements, we can see how the iterator idiom is hooked into for the traversal:

```
#include <string>  // std::string

void f3(const std::vector<std::string>& vec)
{
    // for (const std::string& s : vec) { /*...*/ }
    {
        auto&& __range = vec;  // reference to the std::vector
        for (auto __begin = __range.begin(), __end = __range.end();
            __begin != __end;
            ++__begin)
        {
            const std::string& s = *__begin;  // Get current string element.
            {
                // ...
            }
        }
    }
}
```

In this expansion, __range has type **const** std::vector<std::string>&, while __begin and __end have type std::vector<std::string>::const_iterator.

Traversing arrays and initializer lists

The <iterator> standard header defines array overloads for std::begin and std::end such that, when applied to a C-style array having a known number of elements, std::begin returns the address of the first element and std::end returns the address of one past that of the last element of the array. This functionality is built into the initialization of __begin and __end as a special case, in the expansion of a range-based **for** loop, so that it is possible to traverse the elements of an array without needing to #include <iterator>:

```
void f1()
{
    double data[] = {1.9, 2.8, 4.7, 7.6, 11.5, 16.4, 22.3, 29.2, 37.1, 46.0};
    for (double& d : data)
    {
        d *= 3.0;  // triple every element in the array
    }
}
```

In the above example, the reference d is bound, in turn, to each element of the array. The size of the array is not encoded anywhere in the loop syntax, either as a literal or as a symbolic value, simplifying the specification of the loop and preventing errors. Note that only arrays whose size is known at the point where the loop occurs can be traversed this way:

```
extern double data[];  // array of unknown size

void f2()
{
    for (double& d : data)  // Error, data is an incomplete type.
    {
        // ...
    }
}

double data[10] = { /*...*/ };  // too late to make the above compile
```

The above example would compile if **data** were declared having a size, e.g.,
extern double data[10], as that would be a complete type and provide sufficient information to traverse the array. The definition of **data** in the example *is* complete but is not
visible at the point that the loop is compiled.

An std::initializer_list is typically used to initialize an array or container using **braced
initialization**; see Section 2.1."Braced Init" on page 215. The std::initializer_list
template does, however, provide its own **begin** and **end** member functions and is, therefore,
directly usable as the *range-expression* in a range-based **for** loop:

```
#include <initializer_list>  // std::initializer_list

void f3()
{
    for (double v : {1.9, 2.8, 4.7, 7.6, 11.5, 16.4, 22.3, 29.2, 37.1, 46.0})
    {
        // ...
    }
}
```

The example above shows how a series of **double** values can be embedded right within the
loop header.

Use Cases

Iterating over all elements of a container

The motivating use case for this feature is looping over the elements in a container:

```
#include <list>  // std::list

void process(int* p);

void f1()
{
    std::list<int> aList{ 1, 2, 4, 7, 11, 16, 22, 29, 37, 46 };
```

```
    for (int& i : aList)
    {
        process(&i);
    }
}
```

This idiom takes advantage of all STL-compliant container types providing `begin` and `end` operations, which may be used to delimit a range encompassing the entire container. Thus, the loop above iterates from `aList.begin()` to `aList.end()`, calling `process` on each element encountered.

When iterating over an `std::map<Key, Value>` or `std::unordered_map<Key, Value>`, each element has type `std::pair<const Key, Value>`. To save typing and to avoid errors related to the first member of the pair being **const**, we declare **typedef** for the map type and use the `value_type` alias to refer to each element's type; see *Potential Pitfalls — Inadvertent copying of elements* on page 696:

```
#include <iostream>   // std::cout
#include <map>        // std::map
#include <string>     // std::string

typedef std::map<std::string, int> MapType;

MapType studentScores
{
    {"Emily", 89},
    {"Joel",  85},
    {"Bud",   86},
};

void printScores()
{
    for (MapType::value_type& studentScore : studentScores)
    {
        const std::string& student = studentScore.first;
        int&               score   = studentScore.second;
        std::cout << student << "\t scored " << score << '\n';
    }
}
```

This example prints each key/value pair in the `map`. We create two aliases, `student` for `studentScore.first` and `score` for `studentScore.second`, to better express the intent of the code.[3]

---

[3]In C++17, **structured bindings** allow two variables to be initialized from a single pair, each variable being initialized by the respective `first` and `second` members of the pair. A range-based **for** loop using a structured binding for the loop variables yields a clean and expressive way to traverse containers like map and unordered_map, e.g., using **for** (**auto**& [student, score] : studentScores).

Subranges

Using a classic **for** loop to traverse a container, c, allows a subrange of c to be specified beginning at some point after c.begin() — e.g., ++c.begin() — and/or ending at some point before c.end() — e.g., std::prev(c.end(), 3). To specify a subrange for a **range-based for** loop, we create a simple adapter to hold two iterators (or iterator-like objects) that define the desired subrange:

```
template <typename Iter>
class Subrange
{
    Iter d_begin, d_end;

public:
    using iterator = Iter;

    Subrange(Iter b, Iter e) : d_begin(b), d_end(e) { }

    iterator begin() const { return d_begin; }
    iterator end()   const { return d_end;   }
};

template <typename Iter>
Subrange<Iter> makeSubrange(Iter beg, Iter end) { return {beg, end}; }
```

The Subrange class above is a primitive start to a potentially rich library of range-based utilities.[4] It holds two externally supplied iterators that it can supply to a **range-based for** loop via its begin and end accessor members. The makeSubrange factory uses function template argument deduction to return a Subrange of the correct type.

Let's use Subrange to traverse a vector in reverse, omitting its first element:

```
#include <vector>    // std::vector
#include <iostream>  // std::cout, std::endl

template <typename Range>
void printRange(const Range& r)
{
    for (const auto& elem : r)
    {
        std::cout << elem << ' ';
    }
}
```

---

[4]The C++20 Standard introduces a new Ranges Library that provides powerful features for defining, combining, filtering, and manipulating ranges.

```
        std::cout << std::endl;
}

std::vector<int> vec{16, 3, 1, 8, 99};

void f1()
{
    printRange(makeSubrange(vec.rbegin(), vec.rend() - 1));
        // print "99 8 1 3"
}
```

The `printRange` function template will print out the elements of any range, provided the element type supports printing to an `std::ostream`. In `f1`, we use reverse iterators to create a `Subrange` starting from the last element of `vec` and iterating backward. By subtracting `1` from `vec.rend()`, we exclude the last element of the sequence, which is the first element of `vec`.

In fact, the iterators need not refer to a container at all. For example, we can use `std::istream_iterator` to iterate over "elements" in an input stream:

```
#include <iterator>   // std::istream_iterator
#include <sstream>    // std::istringstream

void f2()
{
    std::istringstream inStream("1 2 4 7 11 16 22 29 37 bad 46");
    printRange(makeSubrange(std::istream_iterator<int>(inStream),
                            std::istream_iterator<int>()));
}
```

In `f2`, the range being printed uses the `istream_iterator<T>` adapter template. Each time through the loop, the adapter reads another `T` item from its input stream. At end-of-file or if a read error occurs, the iterator becomes equal to the sentinel iterator, `istream_iterator<T>()`. Note that the range-based **for** loop feature and the `Subrange` class template do not require that the size of the subrange be known in advance.

Range generators

Iterating over a range does not necessarily entail traversing existing data elements. A range expression could yield a type that *generates* elements as it goes. A useful example is the `ValueGenerator`, an iterator-like class that produces a sequence of sequential values[5]:

---

[5]The `iota_view` and `iota` entities from the Ranges Library in the C++20 Standard provide a more sophisticated version of the `ValueGenerator` and `valueRange` facilities described here.

```
template <typename T>
class ValueGenerator
{
    T d_value;

  public:
    explicit ValueGenerator(const T& v) : d_value(v) { }

    T operator*() const { return d_value; }
    ValueGenerator& operator++() { ++d_value; return *this; }

    friend bool operator!=(const ValueGenerator& a, const ValueGenerator& b)
    {
        return a.d_value != b.d_value;
    }
};

template <typename T>
Subrange<ValueGenerator<T>> valueRange(const T& b, const T& e)
{
    return { ValueGenerator<T>(b), ValueGenerator<T>(e) };
}
```

Instead of referring to an element within a container, `ValueGenerator` is an iterator-like type that *generates* the value returned by **operator***. `ValueGenerator` can be instantiated for any type that can be incremented, e.g., integral types, pointers, or iterators. The `valueRange` function template is a simple factory to create a range comprising two `ValueGenerator` objects, using the `Subrange` class template defined in *Subranges* on page 686. Thus, to print the numbers from 1 to 10, simply use a **range-based for** loop, employing a call to `valueRange` as the **range expression**:

```
void f1()
{
    // prints "1 2 3 4 5 6 7 8 9 10 "
    for (int i : valueRange(1, 11))
    {
        std::cout << i << ' ';
    }
    std::cout << std::endl;
}
```

Note that the second argument to `valueRange` is one *past* the last item we want to iterate on, i.e., 11 instead of 10. With something like `ValueGenerator` as part of a reusable utility library, this formulation expresses the intent of the loop more cleanly and concisely than the classic **for** loop.

The ability to generate numbers means that a range need not be finite. For example, we might want to generate a sequence of random numbers of indefinite length:

```
#include <random>  // std::default_random_engine, std::uniform_int_distribution

template <typename T = int>
class RandomIntSequence {
    std::default_random_engine         d_generator;
    std::uniform_int_distribution<T> d_uniformDist;

public:
    class iterator {
        RandomIntSequence *d_sequence;
        T                  d_value;

        iterator() : d_sequence(nullptr), d_value() { }
        explicit iterator(RandomIntSequence *s)
            : d_sequence(s)
            , d_value(d_sequence->next()) { }

        friend class RandomIntSequence;

    public:
        iterator& operator++() { d_value = d_sequence->next(); return *this; }
        T operator*() const { return d_value; }

        friend bool operator!=(iterator, iterator) { return true; }
    };

    RandomIntSequence(T min, T max, unsigned seed = 0)
        : d_generator(seed ? seed : std::random_device()())
        , d_uniformDist(min, max) { }

    T next() { return d_uniformDist(d_generator); }

    iterator begin() { return iterator(this); }
    iterator end()   { return iterator(); }
};

template <typename T>
RandomIntSequence<T> randomIntSequence(T min, T max, unsigned seed = 0)
{
    return {min, max, seed};
}
```

The `RandomIntSequence` class template uses the C++11 random-number library to generate high-quality pseudorandom numbers.[6] Each call to its **next** member function produces a new random number of integral type, T, within the inclusive range specified

---

[6] An introduction to the C++11 random-number library can be found in Stephan T. Lavavej's excellent talk, **lavavej13**.

to the RandomIntSequence constructor. The nested `iterator` type holds a pointer to a RandomIntSequence and simply calls next each time it is incremented (i.e., via a call to **operator++**).

Of particular interest is **operator!=**, which returns **true** when comparing any two RandomIntSequence<T>::iterator objects. Thus, any range-based **for** loop that iterates over a RandomIntSequence is an infinite loop unless it terminates by some other means:

```
void f2()
{
    for (int rand : randomIntSequence(1, 10))
    {
        std::cout << rand << ' ';
        if (rand == 10) { break; }
    }

    std::cout << '\n';
}
```

This example prints a list of random numbers in the range 1 through 10, inclusive. The loop terminates after printing 10 for the first (and only) time.

Iterating over simple values

The ability to iterate over an `std::initializer_list` can be useful for processing a list of simple values or simple objects without first storing them in a container. Such a use case arises frequently when testing:

```
#include <limits>            // std::numeric_limits
#include <initializer_list>  // std::initializer_list

#define TEST_ASSERT(expr)  // ... assert that expr is true.

bool isEven(int i)
{
    return i % 2 == 0;
}

void testIsEven()
{
    // ...

    const int minInt = std::numeric_limits<int>::min();
    const int maxInt = std::numeric_limits<int>::max();

    for (int testValue : {minInt, -256, -2, 0, 2, 4, maxInt - 1})
    {
        TEST_ASSERT(isEven(testValue));
```

```
                    TEST_ASSERT(!isEven(testValue + 1));
        }
    }
```

The `testIsEven` function iterates over a sample of numbers within the domain of `isEven`, including boundary conditions, testing that each number is correctly reported as being even and that adding 1 to the number produces a result that is correctly reported as not being even.

Initializer lists are not limited to primitive types, so the test data set can contain more complex values:

```cpp
#include <initializer_list>  // std::initializer_list

#define TEST_ASSERT_EQ(expr1, expr2)  // ... assert that expr1 == expr2.

int half(int i)
{
    return i / 2;
}

struct TestCase
{
    int value;
    int expected;
};

void testHalf()
{
    for (const TestCase& test : std::initializer_list<TestCase>{
        {-2, -1}, {-1, 0}, {0, 0}, {1, 0}, {2, 1}
    })
    {
        TEST_ASSERT_EQ(test.expected, half(test.value));
    }
}
```

In this case, the range-based **for** loop iterates over an `std::initializer_list` holding `TestCase` structures. This paring of input(s) with expected output(s) of a component under test is common in unit tests.

Potential Pitfalls

Lifetime of temporary objects in the range expression

As shown in *Description* on page 679, if the range expression evaluates to a temporary object, that object remains valid, as a result of lifetime extension, for the duration of the range-based **for** loop. Unfortunately, there are some subtle ways in which lifetime extension is not always sufficient.

The basic notion of lifetime extension is that, when bound to a reference, the lifetime of a *prvalue* — i.e., an object created by a literal, constructed in place, or returned (by value) from a function — is *extended* to match the lifetime of the reference to which it is bound:

```cpp
#include <string>  // std::string

std::string strFromInt(int);

void f1()
{
    const std::string& s1 = std::string('a', 2);
    std::string&&      s2 = strFromInt(9);
    auto&&             i  = 5;

    // s1, s2, and i are "live" here.

    // ...

}  // s1, s2, and i are destroyed at end of enclosing block.
```

The first string is constructed in place. The resulting temporary string would normally be destroyed as soon as the expression was complete, but because it is bound to a reference, its lifetime is extended; its destructor is not called, and its memory footprint is not reused until s1 goes out of scope, i.e., at the end of the enclosing block. The strFromInt function returns by value; the result of calling it in the second statement produces a temporary variable whose lifetime is similarly extended until s2 goes out of scope. Finally, the forwarding reference, i, ensures that space in the current frame is allocated to hold the temporary copy of the (deduced) **int** value, 5; such space cannot be reused until i goes out of scope at the end of the enclosing block; see Section 2.1."Forwarding References" on page 377.

When the range expression for a range-based **for** loop is a *prvalue*, lifetime extension is vital to keeping the range object live for the duration of the loop:

```cpp
void f2(int i)
{
    for (char c : strFromInt(i))
    {
        // ...
    }
}
```

The return value from strFromInt is stored in a temporary variable of type std::string. The temporary string is destroyed when the loop completes, not when the expression evaluation completes. If the string were to go out of scope immediately, it would not be possible to iterate over its characters. This code would have **undefined behavior** were it not for the lifetime extension harnessed by the range-based **for** loop.

The limitation of lifetime extension is that it applies only if the reference is bound *directly* to the temporary variable itself or to a subobject (e.g., a member variable) of the temporary variable, in which case the lifetime of the entire temporary variable is extended. Note that initializing a reference from a reference or a pointer to either the temporary or one of its subobjects does not count as binding *directly* to the temporary variable and does not trigger lifetime extension. The danger of an object getting destroyed prematurely is generally seen when the **full expression** returns a reference, pointer, or iterator into a temporary object:

```cpp
#include <vector>    // std::vector
#include <string>    // std::string
#include <utility>   // std::pair
#include <tuple>     // std::tuple

struct Point
{
    double x, y;
    Point(double ax, double ay) : x(ax), y(ay) { }
};

struct SRef
{
    const std::string& str;
    SRef(const std::string& s) : str(s) { }
};


std::vector<int> getValues();   // Return a vector by value.

void f3()
{
    const Point& p1 = Point(1.2, 3.4);      // OK, extend Point lifetime.
    double&&     d1 = Point(1.2, 3.4).x;    // OK, extend Point lifetime.
    double&      d2 = Point(1.2, 3.4).y;    // Error, nonconst lvalue ref, d2

    using ICTuple = std::tuple<int, char>;
    const int&   i1 = getValues()[0];               // Bug, dangling reference
    const int&   i2 = std::get<0>(ICTuple{0,'a'});  // Bug, dangling reference
    auto&&       i3 = getValues().begin();          // Bug, dangling iterator
    const auto&  s1 = std::string("abc").c_str();   // Bug, dangling pointer
    const auto&  i4 = std::string("abc").length();  // OK, std::size_t extended

    SRef&&       sr = SRef("hello");    // Bug, string lifetime is not extended.
    std::string s2 = sr.str;            // Bug, string has been destroyed.
}
```

The first invocation of the **Point** constructor creates a temporary object that is bound to reference **p1**. The lifetime of this temporary object is extended to match the lifetime of the reference. Similarly, the lifetime of the second **Point** object is extended because a subobject, x, is bound to reference d1. Note that it is not permitted to bind a temporary to a non**const** *lvalue* reference, as is being attempted with d2, above.

The next four definitions do not result in useful lifetime extension at all.

1. In the case of i1, getValues() returns a *prvalue* of type std::vector<**int**>, resulting in the creation of a temporary variable. That temporary variable, however, is *not* the value being bound to the i1 reference; rather, the reference is bound to the result of the array-access operator (**operator**[]), which returns a reference into the temporary vector returned by getValues(). While we might consider an element of a vector logically to be a subobject of the vector, i1 is not bound directly to that subobject but rather to the reference returned by **operator**[]. The vector goes out of scope immediately at the end of the statement, leaving i1 to refer to an element of a destroyed object.

2. The identical situation occurs with i2 when accessing the member of a temporary std::tuple, this time via the nonmember function std::get<0>.

3. Rather than a reference, i3 is deduced to be an *iterator* as the result of the expression. The iterator's lifetime is extended, but the lifetime of the object to which it refers is not.

4. Similarly, for s1, the expression std::string("abc").c_str() yields a pointer into a temporary C-style string. Once again, the temporary std::string variable is not the object that is bound to the reference s1, so it gets destroyed at the end of the statement, invalidating the pointer.

Conversely, i4 binds directly to the temporary object returned by length, extending its life even though the string itself gets destroyed as before. Unlike i3 and s1, however, i4 is not an iterator or pointer and so does not retain an implicit reference to the defunct string object.

The last two definitions, for sr and s2, show how subtle the rules for lifetime extension can be. The "hello" literal is converted into a temporary variable of type std::string and passed to the constructor of SRef, which *also* creates a temporary object. It is only the SRef object that is bound to the sr reference, so it is only the SRef object whose lifetime is extended. The std::string("hello") temporary variable gets destroyed when the constructor finishes executing, leaving the object referenced by sr with a member, str, that refers to a destroyed object.

There are good reasons why lifetime extension applies only to the temporary object being bound to a reference. A lot of code depends on temporary objects going out of scope immediately, e.g., to release a lock, memory, or some other resource. For range-based **for** loops, however, a compelling argument has been made that the correct behavior would be to extend the lifetime of *all* of the temporaries constructed while evaluating the range expression.[7] Unless and until this behavior is changed in a future Standard, beware of using a range expression that returns a reference to a temporary variable:

---

[7]At the time of writing, Josuttis et al. seek to solve the issue when a range expression is a reference into a temporary; see **josuttis20a**, which references our original paper, **khlebnikov18**, motivating this book.

```
#include <iostream>   // std::istream, std::cout
#include <string>     // std::string
#include <vector>     // std::vector

class RecordList
{
    std::vector<std::string> d_names;
    // ...

public:
    explicit RecordList(std::istream& is);
        // Create a RecordList with data read from is.

    // ...

    const std::vector<std::string>& names() const { return d_names; }
};

void printNames(std::istream& is)
{
    // Bug, RecordList's lifetime is not extended.
    for (const std::string& name : RecordList(is).names())
    {
        std::cout << name << '\n';
    }
}
```

The `RecordList` constructed in the **range expression** is not bound to the implied __range reference within the **range-based for** loop, so its lifetime will end before the loop actually begins. Thus, the **const** std::vector<std::string>& returned by its `names` method becomes a dangling reference, the accessing of which has **undefined** behavior.

We can avoid this pitfall by creating a named object for each temporary whose lifetime would not be extended, i.e., any temporary not produced by the full **range expression**:

```
void printNames2(std::istream& is)
{
    {
        RecordList records(is);  // named variable
        for (const std::string& name : records.names())
        {
            std::cout << name << '\n';
        }

        // safe for records to go out of scope now
    }

    // ...
}
```

This minor rewrite of `printNames` creates an extra block scope in which we declare `records` as a named variable. The inner scope ensures that `records` gets destroyed immediately after the loop terminates.

Inadvertent copying of elements

When iterating through a container with a classic **for** loop, elements are typically referred to through an iterator:

```
void process(std::string&);

void f1(std::vector<std::string>& vec)
{
    for (std::vector<std::string>::iterator i = vec.begin();
         i != vec.end(); ++i)
    {
        process(*i);  // refer to element via iterator
    }
}
```

The range-based **for** loop gives the element a name and a type. If the type is not a reference, then each iteration of the loop will *copy* the current element. In many cases, this copy is inadvertent:

```
void f2(std::vector<std::string>& vec)
{
    for (std::string s : vec)
    {
        process(s);  // call process on copy of string element, potential
                     // bug
    }
}
```

The example above illustrates two issues: (1) there is an unnecessary expense in copying each string, and (2) the `process` function might modify or take the address of its argument, in which case this function will modify or take the address of the copy, rather than the original element; the strings in `vec` will remain unchanged.

This error appears to be especially common when using **auto** to deduce the loop variable's type:

```
void f3(std::vector<std::string>& vec)
{
    for (auto s : vec)
    {
        process(s);  // call process on *copy* of deduced string element,
                     // potential bug
    }
}
```

Copying an element is not always erroneous, but it might be wise to habitually declare the loop variable as a reference, making deliberate exceptions when needed:

```
void f4(std::vector<std::string>& vec)
{
    for (std::string& s : vec)
    {
        process(s);  // OK, call process on reference to string element
    }
}
```

If we want to avoid copying elements but also want to avoid modifying them, then a **const** reference will provide a good balance. Note, however, that if the type being iterated over is not the same as the type of the reference, a conversion might quietly produce the (undesired) copy anyway:

```
void f5(std::vector<char*>& vec)
{
    for (const std::string& s : vec)
    {
        // s is a reference to a copy of an element of vec.
    }
}
```

In this example, the elements of vec have type **char***. The use of **const** std::string& to declare the loop variable s correctly prevents modification of any elements of vec, but there is still a copy being made because each member access is converted to an object of type std::string.

Although the copying conversion in the examples above are discoverable with relative ease, iterating over an elaborate container coupled with implicit converting constructors can make subtle inadvertent copies difficult to detect. A classic example is that of iterating over the elements of an std::map or std::unordered_map. Suppose, for example, we define an IP table that maps 32-bit IPv4 addresses to domain name aliases; note that our use of digit separators (') in the IP addresses is valid only as of C++14, but can be omitted in C++11 without changing the meaning of the program (see Section 1.2."Digit Separators" on page 152):

```
#include <cstdint>       // std::int32_t, std::uint32_t
#include <string>        // std::string
#include <vector>        // std::vector
#include <unordered_map> // std::unordered_map

using IPTable = std::unordered_map<std::int32_t, std::vector<std::string>>;

IPTable iptable =
{
    { 0x12'dd'c3'31, { "domain.com", "www.domain.com" } },
```

```
    { 0x41'fe'f4'b4, { "domain.org", "www.domain.org" } },
    // ...
    // ...                    (additional entries)
    // ...
};
```

Subsequently, we set out to iterate over the map:

```
void process0()
{
    using int32_t = std::int32_t;
    for (const std::pair<int32_t, std::vector<std::string>>& entry : iptable)
    {
        // ...
    }
}
```

It might seem that this code takes all the necessary precautions to avoid unwittingly copying elements of the table by carefully duplicating the spelling of the key and value types and by using an *lvalue* reference for the loop variable. Moreover, the code uses **const** to ensure only read access to elements of the table. Alas, **process0** will nonetheless quietly copy the current **map** element on each iteration.

The culprit in this insidious and potentially significant performance defect is notoriously subtle. The element type of **iptable** is **std::pair<const int32_t, std::vector<std::string>>** — note the **const** in front of the key type. This **const** applies to only the key part of the **std::pair** instantiation, not to the entire **pair**. Hence, **const std::pair<int32_t, std::vector<std::string>>** is *not* a cv-qualified version of **std::pair<const int32_t, std::vector<std::string>>** and therefore cannot be used to form an *lvalue* reference to refer to the value type directly. These two **pair** types — the one used to declare **entry** and the one matching the value type of the **itable** map — are distinct and enjoy no special relationship other than that one is implicitly *convertible* to the other.

The type returned by *__begin in the loop expansion is an *lvalue* reference to **iptable**'s value type. To initialize **entry** to the mismatched element, the compiler must create a temporary variable holding the result of converting from **std::pair<const int32_t, std::vector<std::string>>&** to **std::pair<int32_t, std::vector<std::string>>**. This conversion is accomplished via an implicit converting constructor in **std::pair**:

```
template <typename U, typename V> pair(const pair<U, V>& p);
```

In this case, **U** is **const int32_t**, and **V** is **std::vector<std::string>**; hence, this constructor simply initializes **first** from **p.first** and **second** from **p.second**, effectively copying both parts. At the end of each iteration, the temporary object produced from this conversion is destroyed. Had both of the argument types for **std::pair** been scalars, there would be no significant performance issue for copying the **pair** value on each iteration of the loop. But, given that **std::vector** and **std::string** both have potentially expensive copy constructors and destructors that might allocate and deallocate memory, the performance loss due to copying as a result of the missing **const** in front of the integer key in the declaration of entry could be sizable.

Even when the element type is spelled correctly, the code lacks robustness. Suppose, during maintenance, the key type in iptable is changed from std::int32_t to std::uint32_t. Again, due to std::pair's implicit converting constructor, the loop will copy each element in turn, use it, and then destroy the copy.

Note that this pitfall is neither specific to range-based **for** loops nor new to C++11. Outside the context of this feature, however, client code seldom needs to name the element type of an std::map or std::unordered_map. Conversely, the programmer *must* supply a type for the loop variable in a range-based **for** loop, resulting in significantly more opportunities to misspell the pair type.[8]

There are several ways to avoid such problems. One is to avoid spelling the element type name and use the member type definition value_type instead:

```
void process1()
{
    for (const IPTable::value_type& entry : iptable)
    {
        // ...
    }
}
```

Another possibility is to use **decltype** to deduce the value type from an iterator expression (see Section 1.1."**decltype**" on page 25):

```
void process2()
{
    for (decltype(*iptable.begin()) entry : iptable)
    {
        // ...
    }
}
```

Using **auto**, along with the **const** and & modifiers, is perhaps the simplest, shortest, and most efficient way to express the loop (see Section 2.1."**auto** Variables" on page 195):

```
void process3()
{
    for (const auto& entry : iptable)
    {
        // ...
    }
}
```

---

[8]This error is common enough that Clang 12.0 (c. 2021) provides a warning when a misuse of pair results in an unwanted copy in a range-based **for** loop but does not provide such a warning for the classic **for** loop or for other cases of this pair mismatch.

For generic code that modifies a container, **auto&&** is the most general way to declare the loop variable. For generic code that does not modify the container, **const auto&** is safer[9],[10]:

```
template <typename Rng>
void f6(Rng& r)
{
    for (auto&& e : r)
    {
        // ...
    }

    for (const auto& cr : r)
    {
        // ...
    }
}
```

Because e is a forwarding reference and cr is a **const** reference, they will both correctly bind to the return type of *begin(Rng), even if that type is a *prvalue*.

Simple and reference-proxy behaviors can be different

Some containers have iterators that return proxies rather than references to their elements. Depending on how the loop variable is declared, the unwary programmer might get surprising results when the container's iterator type returns reference proxies.

An example of such a container is std::vector<**bool**>, whose reference type is a proxy class that emulates a reference to a single bit within the vector. The proxy class provides an **operator bool**() that returns the bit when the proxy is converted to **bool** and an **operator=**(**bool**) that modifies the bit when assigned a Boolean value.

Let's consider a set of loops, each of which iterates over a vector and attempts to set each element of the vector to **true**. We'll embed the loops in a function template so that we can compare the behavior of instantiating with a normal container (std::vector<**int**>) and with one whose iterator uses a reference proxy (std::vector<**bool**>):

```
#include <vector>  // std::vector

template <typename T>
void f1(std::vector<T>& vec)
{
    for (T     v : vec) { v = true; }  // (1)
    for (T&    v : vec) { v = true; }  // (2)
    for (T&&   v : vec) { v = true; }  // (3)
    for (auto  v : vec) { v = true; }  // (4)
```

---

[9] **meyers15b**, Chapter 2, "auto," pp. 37–48, and "Item 5: Prefer auto to explicit type declarations," pp. 37–42, in particular, p. 40

[10] **lavavej12**, starting at time 49:30

```
    for (auto&  v : vec) { v = true; }  // (5)
    for (auto&& v : vec) { v = true; }  // (6)
}

void f2()
{
    using IntVec  = std::vector<int>;   // has normal iterator
    using BoolVec = std::vector<bool>;  // has iterator with reference proxy

    IntVec  iv{ /*...*/ };
    BoolVec bv{ /*...*/ };

    f1(iv);
    f1(bv);
}
```

For each of the loops in `f1`, the difference in behavior between the `IntVec` and `BoolVec` instantiations hinges on what happens when `v` is initialized from `*__begin` within the loop transformation. For the `IntVec` iterator, `*__begin` returns a *reference* to the element within the container, whereas for the `BoolVec` iterator, it returns an *object* of the reference-proxy type.

1. Loop with `T` produces identical behavior from both instantiations. The loop makes a local copy of each element and then modifies the copy. The only difference is that the `BoolVec` version performs a conversion to **bool** to initialize v, whereas the `IntVec` version initializes v directly from the element reference. For both the `IntVec` or `BoolVec` version, the original vector remaining unchanged is a potential bug (see *Inadvertent copying of elements* on page 696).

2. Loop with `T&` modifies the container elements in the `IntVec` instantiation but fails to compile for the `BoolVec` instantiation. The compilation error comes from trying to initialize the non**const lvalue reference**, v, from an *rvalue* of the proxy type. The **bool** conversion operator does not help since the result would still be an *rvalue*.

3. Loop with `T&&` fails to compile for the `IntVec` iterator because the **rvalue reference**, v, cannot be initialized from `*__begin`, which is an lvalue reference. Surprisingly, the `BoolVec` instantiation *does* compile, but the loop does not modify the container. Here, **operator bool** is invoked on the proxy object returned by `*__begin`. The resulting temporary object is bound to v, and its lifetime is extended for the duration of the iteration. Because v is bound to a temporary variable, modifying v modifies only the temporary, not the original, element, resulting in a likely bug as in the case of loop with `T` (item 1).

4. Loop with **auto** compiles for both the `BoolVec` and `IntVec` cases but produces different results for each. For `IntVec` iterators, **auto** deduces the type of v as **int**, so assigning to v modifies a local copy of the element, as in loop with `T` (item 1). For `BoolVec`

iterators, the deduced type of v is the proxy type rather than **bool**. Assigning to the proxy *does* change the element of the container.

5. Loop with **auto&**, like loop with T& (item 2), works as expected for IntVec instantiation but fails to compile for the BoolVec instantiation. As before, the problem is that the BoolVec iterator yields an *rvalue* that cannot be used to initialize an lvalue reference.

6. Loop with **auto&&** produced identical behavior from both instantiations, modifying each of the **vector** elements. The type of v is deduced to be **int&** for IntVec instantiation and the proxy type for the BoolVec instantiation. Assigning through either the real reference or the reference proxy modifies the element in the container.

Let's now look at the situation with **const**-qualified loop variables:

```
template <typename T>
void f3(std::vector<T>& vec)
{
    for (const T     v : vec) { /*...*/ } // (7)
    for (const T&    v : vec) { /*...*/ } // (8)
    for (const T&&   v : vec) { /*...*/ } // (9)
    for (const auto  v : vec) { /*...*/ } // (10)
    for (const auto& v : vec) { /*...*/ } // (11)
    for (const auto&& v : vec) { /*...*/ } // (12)
}

void f4()
{
    using IntVec  = std::vector<int>;   // has normal iterator
    using BoolVec = std::vector<bool>;  // has iterator with reference proxy

    IntVec  iv{ /*...*/ };
    BoolVec bv{ /*...*/ };

    f3(iv);
    f3(bv);
}
```

7. Loop with **const** T works identically for both instantiations, converting the proxy reference to **bool** in the BoolVec case.

8. Loop with **const** T& works identically for both instantiations. For the IntVec case, the result of *__begin is bound directly to v. For the BoolVec case, *__begin produces proxy reference that is converted to a **bool** temporary that is then bound to v. Lifetime extension keeps the bool value alive.

9. Loop with **const** T&& fails to compile for IntVec but succeeds for BoolVec exactly as for loop with T&& (item 3) except that the temporary **bool** bound to v is **const** and

thus does not risk giving programmers the false belief that they are modifying the container.

10. Loop with **const auto** has the same behavior for both the IntVec and BoolVec instantiations. That mechanism is the same behavior as for loop with **auto** (item 4) except that, because v is **const**, *neither* instantiation can modify the container.

11. Loop with **const auto&** also works for both instantiations. For the IntVec case, the result of *__begin is bound directly to v. For the BoolVec case, v is deduced to be a **const** reference to the proxy type; *__begin produces a temporary variable of the proxy type, which is then bound to v. Lifetime extension keeps the proxy alive. In most contexts, a **const** proxy reference is an effective stand-in for a **const bool&**.

12. Loop with **const auto&&** fails to compile for IntVec but succeeds for BoolVec. The error with IntVec occurs because **const auto&&** is always a **const** rvalue reference (not a forwarding reference) and cannot be bound to the lvalue reference, *__begin. For BoolVec, the mechanism is identical to loop with **const auto&** (item 11) except that loop with **const auto&** (item 11) binds the temporary object to an lvalue reference, whereas loop with **const auto&&** (item 12) uses an rvalue reference. When the references are **const**, however, there is little practical differences between them.

Note that loop with **auto**, loop with **auto&&**, loop with **const auto**, loop with **const auto&**, and loop with **const auto&&** (items 4, 6, 10, 11, and 12) in the BoolVec instantiations bind a reference to a temporary proxy reference object, so taking the address of v in these situations is likely not to produce useful results. Additionally, loop with **T&&**, loop with **const T&**, and loop with **const T&&** (items 3, 8, and 9) bind v to a temporary **bool**. Users must be mindful of the lifetime of these temporary objects (a single iteration of the loop) and not allow the address of v to escape the loop.

Proxy objects emulating references to nonclass elements within a container are surprisingly effective, but their limitations are exposed when they are bound to references. In generic code, as a rule of thumb, **const auto&** is the safest way to declare a read-only loop variable if a reference proxy might be in use, while **auto&&** will give the most consistent results for a loop that modifies its container. Similar issues, unrelated to range-based **for** loops, occur when passing a proxy reference to a function taking a reference argument.

Annoyances

No access to the state of the iteration

When traversing a range with a classic **for** loop, the loop variable is typically an iterator or array index. Within the loop, we can modify that variable to repeat or skip iterations. Similarly, the loop-termination condition is usually accessible so that it is possible to, for example, insert or remove elements and then recompute the condition:

```
#include <unordered_set>   // std::unordered_set

void removeEvenNumbers(std::unordered_set<int>& data)
{
    for (auto it = data.begin(); it != data.end();) {
        if (*it % 2 == 0) {
            it = data.erase(it);
        } else {
            ++it;
        }
    }
}
```

The code above depends on (1) having access to the iterator, (2) being able to change the iterator, and (3) not having the iterator always incremented after each iteration. No similar function could be written using a range-based **for** loop since the __range, __begin, and __end variables are for exposition only and are not accessible from within the code.

A classic **for** loop can traverse more than one container at a time (e.g., to add corresponding elements from two containers and store them into a third). This feat is accomplished by either incrementing multiple iterators on each iteration or keeping a single index that is used to access multiple, random-access iterators concurrently. Trying to accomplish something similar with a range-based **for** loop usually involves using a hybrid approach:

```
#include <vector>   // std::vector
#include <cassert>  // standard C assert macro

void addVectors(std::vector<int>&       result,
                const std::vector<int>& a,
                const std::vector<int>& b)
    // For each element ea of a and corresponding element eb of b, set
    // the corresponding element of result to ea + eb.  The behavior is
    // undefined unless a and b have the same length.
{
    assert(a.size() == b.size());
    result.resize(a.size());

    std::vector<int>::const_iterator ia = a.begin();
    std::vector<int>::const_iterator ib = b.begin();
    for (int& sum : result)
    {
        sum = *ia++ + *ib++;
    }
}
```

Although result is traversed using the range-based **for** loop, a and b are effectively traversed manually using iterators. Whether this code is clearer to read or simpler to write than it would be with a classic **for** loop is debatable.

This situation can be improved through the use of a zip iterator — a type that holds multiple iterators and increments them in lock-step:

```cpp
#include <cassert>  // standard C assert macro
#include <tuple>    // std::tuple
#include <utility>  // std::declval
#include <vector>   // std::vector

template <typename... Iter>
class ZipIterator
{
    std::tuple<Iter...> d_iters;

    // ...

public:
    using reference = std::tuple<decltype(*std::declval<Iter>())...>;

    ZipIterator(const Iter&... i);

    reference operator*() const;
    ZipIterator& operator++();
    friend bool operator!=(const ZipIterator& a, const ZipIterator& b);
};

template <typename... Range>
class ZipRange
{
    using ZipIter =
        ZipIterator<decltype(begin(std::declval<Range>()))...>;

    // ...

public:
    ZipRange(const Range&... ranges);

    ZipIter begin() const;
    ZipIter end() const;
};

template <typename... Range>
ZipRange<Range...> makeZipRange(Range&&... r);
```

Using the `ZipIterator`, all three containers can be traversed using a single range-based **for** loop:

```
void addVectors2(std::vector<int>&       result,
                 const std::vector<int>& a,
                 const std::vector<int>& b)
{
    assert(a.size() == b.size());
    result.resize(a.size());

    for (std::tuple<int, int, int&> elems : makeZipRange(a, b, result))
    {
        std::get<2>(elems) = std::get<0>(elems) + std::get<1>(elems);
    }
}
```

Each iteration, instead of yielding a single element, yields an `std::tuple` of elements resulting from the traversal of multiple ranges simultaneously. To be used, the elements must be unpacked from the `std::tuple` using `std::get`. Zip iterators become much more attractive in C++17 with the advent of **structured bindings**, which allow multiple loop variables to be declared at once, without the need to directly unpack the `std::tuples`. The implementation and usage of `ZipRange` above is just a rough sketch: The full design and implementation of zip iterators and zip ranges are beyond the scope of this section.

Adapters are required for many tasks

In the usage examples above, we have seen a number of adapters, e.g., to traverse subranges, to traverse a container in reverse, to generate sequential values, and to iterate over multiple ranges at once. None of these adapters would be required for a classic **for** loop, which for a one-off situation might express the solution more simply. On the other hand, the adapters that we would create to make range-based **for** loops usable in more situations can lead to the development of a reusable *library* of adapters. Using the `ValueGenerator` class from Range generators, for example, produces simpler and more expressive code than using a classic **for** loop would.[11]

No support for sentinel iterator types

For a given range expression, __range, begin(__range) and end(__range) must return the same type to be usable with a range-based **for** loop. This limitation is problematic for ranges of indeterminate length, where the condition for ending a loop is not determined by comparing two iterators. For example, in the `RandomIntSequence` example (see *Use Cases — Range generators* on page 687), the end iterator for the infinite random sequence holds a null pointer and is never used, not even within **operator**!=. It would be more efficient and

---

[11]The Standard's Ranges Library, introduced in C++20, provides a sophisticated algebra for working with and adapting ranges.

convenient if the end iterator were a special, empty *sentinel* type. Comparing any iterator to the sentinel would determine whether the loop should terminate:

```
template <typename T = int>
class RandomIntSequence2
{
    // ...

public:
    class SentinelIterator { };

    class iterator {
        // ...
        friend bool operator!=(iterator, SentinelIterator) { return true; }
    };

    iterator        begin() { /*...*/ }
    SentinelIterator end() const { return {}; }
};
```

The above code shows an example of begin and end returning different types, where end returns an empty sentinel type. Unfortunately, using this formulation of RandomIntSequence2 with a C++11 range-based **for** loop will result in a compilation error complaining that begin and end return inconsistent types. [12]

Another type that could benefit from a sentinel iterator is std::istream_iterator, since the state of the end iterator is never used. It is unlikely that this interface will change, however, as std::istream_iterator has been with us since the first C++ Standard.

Only ADL lookup

The free functions begin and end are found using **argument-dependent lookup (ADL)** only. File-scope functions are not considered. If we wish to add begin and end functions for a range-like type that we do not own, we need to put those functions into the same namespace as the range-like type, inviting a potential name collision with other compilation units attempting to do the same thing:

---

[12]The limitation on the use of sentinel iterators was lifted in C++17. Sentinel iterators are supported directly by the C++20 Ranges Library. In C++17, the specification was modified to:

```
{
    auto&& __range = range-expression;
    auto __begin   = begin-expr;
    auto __end     = end-expr;
    for (; __begin != __end; ++__begin)
    {
        for-range-declaration = *__begin;
        statement
    }
}
```

```
// third_party_library.h:

namespace third_party
{

    class IteratorLike { /*...*/ };

    class RangeLike
    {
        // ... does not provide begin and end members
    };

    // ... does not provide begin and end free functions
}


// myclient.cpp:

#include <third_party_library.h>

static third_party::IteratorLike begin(third_party::RangeLike&);
static third_party::IteratorLike end(third_party::RangeLike&);

void f()
{
    third_party::RangeLike rl;
    for (auto&& e : rl)  // Error, begin not found by ADL
    {
        // ...
    }
}
```

The code above attempts to work around the absence of `begin(RangeLike&)` and
`end(RangeLike&)` in the third-party library by defining them locally within `myclient.cpp`.
This attempt fails because static functions are not found via ADL. A better workaround
that does work is to create a range adapter for the range-like class:

```
class RangeLikeAdapter
{
    // ...

public:
    RangeLikeAdapter(third_party::RangeLike&);
    third_party::IteratorLike begin() { /*...*/ }
    third_party::IteratorLike end()   { /*...*/ }
};
```

The adapter wraps the range-like type and provides the missing features. Beware, however, that if the wrapper stores a pointer or reference to a temporary `RangeLike` object, we don't run into the pitfall where the lifetime of temporary objects is not always extended; see *Potential Pitfalls — Lifetime of temporary objects in the range expression* on page 691.

See Also

- "**auto** Variables" (§2.1, p. 195) explains **auto**, often used in a range-based **for** loop to determine the type of the loop variable, and many of the pitfalls of **auto** apply when using it for that purpose.

- "Ref-Qualifiers" (§3.1, p. 1153) shows how to overload member functions to work differently on *rvalues* and *lvalues*.

Further Reading

- Scott Meyers identifies the benefits of using **auto** in range-based **for** loops, among other places, in **meyers15b**, "Item 5: Prefer **auto** to explicit type declarations," pp. 37–42.

Move Semantics and *Rvalue* References (&&)

A new form of reference, *rvalue* reference (&&), that complements C++03 *lvalue* references (&), is used via overloading to enable *move semantics*, a potential optimization in which the operation may safely assume that the internal representation of an object may be *repurposed* instead of copied.

Description

Rvalue references are perhaps the defining language feature of modern C++. To enable the introduction of move semantics, the C++ language evolved the notion of *lvalues* and non*lvalues* to three *disjoint* **value categories** (and two more, *overlapping* ones), allowing for a mostly smooth ability to capture the moment when an object's value is no longer needed, and consequently the object can have its internal (e.g., dynamically allocated) state *taken* rather than copied.

We will start by providing a high-level, conceptual overview of **rvalue references** and then introduce the new **value category**, *xvalues*, and describe the implications of **rvalue references** for **overload resolution** in C++11. Given this background, we will present **move operations** and explore the motivations behind their creation.

Having covered these higher-level concepts, we will then revisit, in greater detail, what changed in C++11 with respect to **value categories** and the subtleties of overload resolution involving the new *rvalue* form of reference. Next, we'll discuss the two new **special member functions**, namely the **move constructor** and the **move-assignment operator**.

Finally, we'll discuss both the theory and some practical heuristics for when explicitly casting — e.g., using `std::move` — the return value to an **rvalue reference** might be beneficial and, more importantly, when such a cast would likely pessimize runtime performance.

Readers unfamiliar with the role of **value categories**, the motivation for **move semantics**, or the practical use of **rvalue references** might benefit from a gentler, more approachable introduction, explicitly tailored to those familiar with C++03; see *Appendix — The evolution of value categories* on page 813.

Introduction to *rvalue* references

Prior to C++11, the only kind of reference type in C++ was the **lvalue reference**. For any type `T`, the type `T&` is an **lvalue reference** to `T`, and entities having this reference type act as alternate names for the objects to which they refer:

```
int  i;
int& ri  = i;    // lvalue reference to i
int* pi  = &i;
int& ri2 = *pi;  // also lvalue reference to i
```

Both a literal value — e.g., **5** — and the result of calling a function that returns by value — e.g., **f()** — are examples of a special kind of *rvalue* (a.k.a. non*lvalue*) known as a *prvalue*. A *prvalue* is not yet necessarily represented by an object in memory (i.e., it might not yet have a physical address); see *Prvalues in C++11/14* on page 720. Binding a **const** lvalue reference to a *prvalue* typically forces creation of a **temporary object** (**having identity**) whose lifetime will coincide with that of the reference itself; see *Appendix — Lifetime extension of a temporary bound to a reference* on page 819:

```
const int& rci = 5;      // lvalue reference to temporary having value 5

int f();                 // returns an int by value
const int& rci2 = f();   // lvalue reference to temporary returned by f
```

A non**const** lvalue reference cannot, however, bind to temporaries:

```
int& ri1 = 7;    // Error, cannot bind nonconst lvalue reference to temporary
int& ri2 = f();  // Error,    "      "      "      "       "      "       "
```

Being unable to bind non**const** lvalue references to temporaries protects programmers from inadvertently storing information in an object that is clearly at the end of its lifetime. On the other hand, this restriction also prevents programmers from taking advantage of the imminent destruction of the referent by assuming ownership of any resources that it might control.

To support creating references to objects that are at the end of their lifetimes and to enable modification of such objects, rvalue references were added in C++11. For any type **T**, the type **T&&** is an rvalue reference to **T**. The primary distinction between an lvalue reference and an rvalue reference is that non**const** rvalue references can bind to temporary objects:

```
int&& rri1 = 7;     // OK, rvalue reference to temporary having value 7
int&& rri2 = f();   // OK, rvalue reference to temporary returned by f
```

An rvalue reference will not, however, bind to *lvalues*:

```
int   j;
int&& rrj1 = j;    // Error, cannot bind rvalue reference to lvalue
int*  pj   = &j;
int&& rrj2 = *pj;  // Error, cannot bind rvalue reference to lvalue
```

Importantly, *lvalues* can be explicitly cast to rvalue references using a **static_cast**:

```
int&& rrj3 = static_cast<int&&>(j);     // OK
int&& rrj4 = static_cast<int&&>(*pj);   // OK
```

These rules help to prevent creating **rvalue references** to objects where there has been no implicit or explicit indication that the object's value is no longer going to be needed.

Introduction to *xvalues*

The purpose and effective use of **rvalue references** derive from both their syntactically distinct form and their conventional use of referring exclusively to objects whose values will not subsequently be needed. There are two distinct ways the compiler can be aware of such an expiring value: that value is held (1) in a compiler-generated (unreachable) temporary object, which is promptly destroyed after the value of an expression is used and (2) in a preexisting (potentially **reachable**) object that has been explicitly marked as being no longer needed.

When an expression produces a value that does not necessarily represent an object in physical memory, such as a function that returns by value or an arithmetic literal, that expression belongs to the *prvalue* **value category**. When an expression creates a **temporary object** and produces the location of that object or one of its subobjects, which the compiler knows it is going to promptly destroy, that expression belongs to the *xvalue* **value category**. When an expression evaluates to an **rvalue reference**, e.g., when an already existing object is explicitly cast to an **rvalue reference** or a function invocation returns one, that expression also belongs to the *xvalue* **value category**. Finally, any expression that references an existing object that is not known to be expiring belongs to the *lvalue* **value category**.

The categorization of values described above refines and adds to the C++03 **value categories** of just *lvalue* and non*lvalue* (*rvalue*). Any C++03 expression that produces an *rvalue* that does not necessarily create a **temporary object** is categorized in C++11 as a *prvalue*. If, however, the Standard requires that the *rvalue* be represented by a physical object (i.e., one having an address), then that value is classified as an *xvalue*. Any C++03 *lvalue* invariably remains an *lvalue* in C++11 (with just a few, highly esoteric shifts to *xvalues*).

As we saw in *Introduction to rvalue references* on page 710, an **rvalue reference** can be initialized with an expression that is a *prvalue*, in which case a **temporary object** will be created whose lifetime will be that of the reference:

```
struct S { /*...*/ };
S f();          // OK, function that returns by value
S&& rs1 = f();  // OK, rvalue reference binds to temporary S object.
```

Note, however, that once that temporary is bound to a named reference, that reference is not itself expiring and so, when used in an expression, does not belong to the *xvalue* value category:

```
S&& rs2 = rs1;  // Error, rs1 is not an xvalue or prvalue.
```

Alternatively, we can create an expression in the *xvalue* **value category** by invoking a function that returns an **rvalue reference** or via an explicit cast from lvalue to **rvalue reference**:

```
S&& g();
S&& rs3 = g();                  // OK
```

```
S s;
S&& rs4 = static_cast<S&&>(s);   // OK
```

Of particular note is the Standard Library utility `std::move`, which is a function returning an rvalue reference, like g in the example above, but with an implementation like the initializer for `rs4` above. In other words, `std::move` is effectively just a **static_cast** to an rvalue reference; see *The std::move utility* on page 731:

```
#include <utility>   // std::move

S&& rs5 = std::move(s);   // OK, same initialization as rs4
```

Casting an *lvalue* into an *xvalue* indicates explicitly that a **move operation** is allowed on the object being referenced and that its value is no longer going to be needed.

Requiring the address of a named subobject of a *prvalue* — just like a *prvalue* itself — will result in an *xvalue*:

```
S&& rs6 = f();   // OK, f returns S as a prvalue; initializing with an xvalue

struct D { S d_s; };
D h();
S&& rs7 = h().d_s;   // OK, h returns D as prvalue; initializing with xvalue
```

Importantly, what makes an *xvalue* useful in the context of **move semantics** is that (1) there's a constructed object underlining the value and (2) the compiler knows that value is **expiring**.

Introduction to modern overload resolution

During overload resolution, when choosing between a function having a matching rvalue reference parameter and one having a matching **const** lvalue reference parameter, the rvalue reference parameter has higher priority. This prioritization comes into play when the argument is a non*lvalue* — i.e., either an *xvalue* or a *prvalue*:

```
void f(const int&);   // (1) const lvalue reference
void f(int&&);        // (2) rvalue reference

void test()
{
    int i;
    f(i);             // lvalue, invokes (1)
    f(5);             // prvalue, invokes (2)
    f(std::move(i));  // xvalue, invokes (2)
}
```

Move operations

To take advantage of the new kind of reference type, C++11 also added two new **special member functions** to user-defined class types: the move constructor and the move-assignment operator. The move constructor of a class parallels the **copy constructor** but, instead of having an (typically **const**) lvalue reference parameter, has an (typically *non***const**) rvalue one:

```
struct S1
{
    S1(const S1&);  // copy constructor
    S1(S1&&);       // move constructor
};
```

Similarly, the move-assignment operator parallels the **copy-assignment operator** but takes an rvalue reference parameter instead:

```
struct S2
{
    S2& operator=(const S2&);  // copy-assignment operator
    S2& operator=(S2&&);       // move-assignment operator
};
```

Both of these new **special member functions** participate in overload resolution alongside the corresponding copy operations and are eligible and preferred for arguments that are either *xvalues* or *prvalues*. These move operations can then do what their name suggests and move the value of the source object, along with any resources that it owns, into the target object without regard for leaving the source object in a useful state, but see *Potential Pitfalls — Inconsistent expectations on moved-from objects* on page 794.

When programming with objects that support move operations, there is a conventional expectation of what these operations do to the target (moved-to) object relative to their C++03 copy counterparts: Either operation will result in the value previously held in the source (moved-from) object now being present in the target. While a copied-from object will generally remain unchanged, no such expectation exists for a moved-from object. What can be relied upon after an object is moved from is *governed* by that move operation's **contract**. Different types might derive maximal benefit from having any number of different guarantees on the state of such moved-from objects.

The most general assumption we could make about the state of a source object after a **move operation** would be to have absolutely *no* expectations, i.e., that it might not be valid to use with any of its operations, even destruction. Such generality, however, is not practically useful: Leaking such an object would then become the only safe course of action. A well-behaved type, therefore, must be *at least* safely destructible. A somewhat stronger presumption would be that a proper moved-from object will support assignment if the type supports assignment at all. However, not all types would necessarily benefit from providing such an enhanced guarantee.

At the other end of the spectrum, we could, for a particular type, guarantee that the source object retains its value, even after it is moved from — i.e., the same contract assumed for conventional copies. That is, a **copy operation** always implicitly satisfies the general requirements of a move operation. Simpler types that do not allocate additional resources, such as `int` or `std::complex<double>`, might see no benefit in doing anything other than letting their copy operations be used when a move operation is requested. In fact, any work to alter the source object would be unneeded and perhaps wasteful. Committing to such a strong contract for a move operation would, however, render it useless as an optimized copy; when no performance advantage can be gained from supplying move operations, they are typically omitted.

The more common expectation on the state of moved-from objects is somewhere in the middle, where they are left in a **valid but unspecified** state. For example, such is the fairly high degree of expectation that C++ Standard Library containers have for the element types they support. That is, every operation the containers might use on the element type, such as assignment, copying, or swapping, is valid to use on a moved-from object. Such strict requirements can, however, have undesirable runtime-performance consequences; see *Annoyances — Standard Library requirements on a moved-from object are overly strict* on page 807.

Although the source object of Standard-compliant move operations is always left in a valid state, that object's value is typically unspecified; hence, any operation — such as getting the first element of a container, e.g., `std::vector::front()` — having a **narrow contract** (i.e., one having preconditions) that is invoked obliviously on a moved-from object might well have **undefined behavior**.

Motivation

Move semantics, by dint of rvalue references, was introduced to address potentially expensive copying of data in situations where such copies were unnecessary. Consider, for example, the task of swapping the values of two vectors. A simple C++03 implementation would involve at least one allocation and deallocation as well as multiple element-wise copies:

```
#include <vector>  // std::vector

void swapVectors(std::vector<int>& v1, std::vector<int>& v2)
{
    std::vector<int> temp = v1;
    v1 = v2;
    v2 = temp;
}
```

Such allocations and copies are often unnecessary: After execution of `swapVectors`, the program continues to refer to two heap-allocated buffers containing the values, and simply exchanging the pointers within the vectors being swapped would have sufficed. Such gratuitous inefficiency would be further exacerbated if the elements of the vectors were expensive to copy, say, because they too allocated dynamic memory like `std::vector` or `std::string`. Similarly, when growing the buffer within an `std::vector<std::string>` (e.g., to accommodate an additional element), making a copy of each string despite a clear understanding that the old ones will be destroyed immediately after copying them is gallingly inefficient.[1] Finally, copying a temporary object that is about to be destroyed too is wasteful. **Move semantics** addresses these issues by allowing a potentially more efficient transfer (move) of resource ownership from one object to another in circumstances where a copy would be followed by discarding the original.

C++11 added rvalue references, move operations, and *xvalues* as a new **value category**, which conspire to enable the use of **move semantics** as an optimization of copy semantics in many common scenarios. By providing *only* move operations and *no* copy operations, we can develop **move-only types** whose unique form of semantics transcend mere optimization. The prototypical **move-only type**, `std::unique_ptr`, was introduced to supplant the highly problematic C++03 library component, `std::auto_ptr`. This new type allowed `std::auto_ptr` to be deprecated in C++11.[2]

Extended value categories in C++11/14

There are three disjoint **value categories** in modern C++: *lvalues*, *prvalues*, and *xvalues*.

1. An *lvalue* expression identifies a constructed object that already resides in physical memory, is potentially independently reachable from other parts of the program, and has *not* been designated as holding a value that is no longer needed. A distinguishing characteristic of this **value category** is that the unary address operator (&) may be applied to an *lvalue* to produce its address, e.g., for future reference. This **value category** includes named variables — such as the `i` and `a` in **double** `i, a[5];` as well as (non-bit-field) subobjects of an *lvalue* such as data members and array elements. It also includes string literals, such as `"Hello, World!"`.

2. A *prvalue* ("pure *rvalue*") is a value that typically has not yet been used to populate an object but could be used to do so. This **value category** includes arithmetic and character (but not string) literals such as `12`, `7.3e5`, **true**, and `'C'`. It also includes invocations of functions that return by value. Importantly, there is no way that such a value can be referred to from elsewhere in the program.

---

[1] Note that, for clarity, we're not involving the strong exception-safety guarantee provided by `std::vector` in this discussion. For more on moves, vectors, and the exception-safety guarantee, see Section 2.1. "**noexcept** Operator" on page 615.

[2] Unlike most other deprecations, `std::auto_ptr` has not lingered in the Standard and was completely removed in C++17.

3. An *xvalue*, like an *lvalue*, identifies an object in memory but is either not independently reachable or else has been explicitly tagged as **expiring**. This **value category** includes any expressions that produce **temporary objects** along with any expression that produces an unnamed **rvalue reference**, such as an explicit cast — e.g., **static_cast**<T&&>(v) (see *The std::move utility* on page 731) — or even the invocation of a function f() — declared as T&& f(); — that returns an **rvalue reference** explicitly.

To capture common properties among the three aforementioned disjoint (leaf) categories, C++11 defines two additional, overlapping **value categories**, *rvalues* and *glvalues*.

4. An *rvalue* (non*lvalue*) is either a *prvalue* or an *xvalue*. Importantly, **rvalue reference** can be bound to expressions in this category only.[3] An **rvalue reference** can bind to an *xvalue* directly, while a *prvalue* typically requires **materialization** first. From a programmer's perspective, however, the distinction between a *prvalue* and an *xvalue* is seldom important in C++11/14 because they interact with most other features in the same way.[4]

5. A *glvalue* ("generalized *lvalue*") is either an *lvalue* or an *xvalue* — i.e., not a *prvalue*. Importantly, all values in this category **have identity** and are, at least in principle,[5] represented by objects in physical memory. Most built-in operations require only a *prvalue* as an argument. When an operation, such as binding a reference, does require a *glvalue* and a *prvalue* is supplied, a process called **temporary materialization** initializes a temporary, effectively converting the *prvalue* into an *xvalue* and thus a *glvalue*.

Lvalues in C++11/14   An *lvalue* expression is one for which the built-in *address-of* operator, &, can be applied to obtain an address, typically resulting in the address of that *lvalue* in physical memory[6]:

---

[3]One exception is that **rvalue reference** will also bind to a function *lvalue*:

```
void f();  // Declaration of function: f is itself an lvalue.

void  (&lrf)() = f;  // can bind an lvalue reference to function lvalue
void  (&&rrf)() = f;  // "     "    " rvalue        "     "     "     "
```

[4]Guaranteed copy elision, introduced to C++17 through P0135R0 (**smith15c**), leverages the distinction between the two subcategories of *rvalues* to cause a *prvalue* returned from a function to be used to initialize the object representing the returned value directly, thereby sidestepping any intermediate temporary that might otherwise be copied, moved, or inconsistently elided.

[5]An object whose address is never observed might — especially after optimization — never reside in the address space of the final program, e.g., through application of the **as if** rule.

[6]The pointer-to-member formation expression — e.g., &Class::member — doesn't obtain a physical memory address; nonetheless, Class::member is an *lvalue* expression to which the unary address operator — & — may be applied.

```
// named lvalue          taking the address of an lvalue using &
// ------------          ----------------------------------------

double d;                double* dp          = &d;
                         double* dp2         = &(d += 0.5);

double& dr = d;          double*  dp3        = &dr;
                         double** dpp        = &dp3;

const int& cir = 1;      const int*  cip     = &cir;
                         const int** cipp    = &cip;

int f();                 int (*fp)()         = &f;

char a[10];              char (*ap)[10]      = &a;
                         char* cp            = &a[5];

struct S { int x; } s;   S* sp               = &s;
                         S* sp2              = &(s = s);
                         int* ip             = &s.x;

unsigned& g();           unsigned* up        = &g();

                         const char (*lp)[14] = &"Hello, World!";
                         const char* lp2      = &"Hello, World!"[5];
```

An *lvalue* expression identifies, by name or address, a potentially **reachable** object that, in a well-written program, outlives the end of the largest enclosing expression in which it resides. There exist well-defined ways, some dangerous, to form a *non***const** *lvalue* expression that refers to a temporary that would not otherwise outlive the enclosing expression:

```
// By cast: lifetime extension works.
int &r1 = (int&)(int&&)0;  // lvalue expression that refers to an int temporary

// By member function having no ref-qualifier: lifetime extension doesn't work.
#include <vector>  // std::vector
int &r2 = *std::vector<int>{1, 2, 3}.begin();
```

Note that use of `r2` above might lead to **undefined behavior**; see Section 2.1."Braced Init" on page 215 and Section 3.1."Ref-Qualifiers" on page 1153. Applying the built-in dereference operator `*` to any non**void**, non-null pointer variable produces an unnamed *lvalue*. In the example above, `*dp` and `*fp` are unnamed *lvalues*. Invoking a function that returns a reference, such as `g()` in the example above, also yields an *lvalue*.

Our ability to assign to or otherwise modify an *lvalue* of a built-in type is governed entirely by whether it is **const** qualified; for a user-defined type, assignment is additionally governed by whether the *copy* and/or *move* assignment is supported for that type; see *Special member function generation* on page 732. Finally, note that character-string literals (e.g., "Hello, World!"), unlike other literals, are considered *lvalues*, as illustrated by initializing lp and lp2 with extracted addresses, also shown in the example above.

The invocation of assignment or compound assignment operators on built-in types produces an *lvalue* as does the invocation of any user-defined function or operator that returns an lvalue reference:

```
struct S
{
    S& operator+=(const S&);  // operator returning lvalue reference
};

int& h();   // h() is an lvalue of type int.
S& j();     // j() is an lvalue of type S.

void testAssignment()
{
    int x = 7;
    x = 5;      // x = 5 is an lvalue of type int.
    x *= 13;    // x *= 13 is an lvalue of type int.
    h() = x;    // h() = x is an lvalue of type int.

    S s;
    j() = s;    // j() = s is an lvalue of type S.
    s += s;     // s += s is an lvalue of type S.
}
```

As with lvalue references, we cannot take the address of an rvalue reference. Pointers, on the other hand, can be of any value category, and an lvalue reference or rvalue reference can be bound, as appropriate, to a pointer expression. Dereferencing any non**void** pointer, regardless of the value category of the pointer, yields an *lvalue*:

```
int* pf();  // pf() is a prvalue of type int*.
void testDereference()
{
    *pf();  // *pf() is an lvalue of type int.

    int* p = pf();  // p is an lvalue of type int*.
    *p;             // *p is an lvalue of type int.
}
```

Finally, the name of a variable is an *lvalue*, independent of whether that variable is a reference, even if it is itself an **rvalue** reference:

```
void testNames()
{
    int x   = 17;
    int& xr = x;
    int&& xrv = std::move(x);

    x;   // x   is an lvalue of type int.
    xr;  // xr  "  "    "    "    "   "
    xrv; // xrv "  "    "    "    "   "
}
```

Prvalues in C++11/14   A *prvalue*, or *pure rvalue*, expression represents a value that is not necessarily associated with an object in memory and cannot have its address taken without forcing a conversion that creates an object in memory. Such a conversion creates a **temporary object** that is destroyed at either (1) the end of the outermost enclosing expression or (2) the end of the lifetime of a reference that is bound directly to that temporary object or one of its subobjects per the rules of **lifetime extension**; see *Appendix — Lifetime extension of a temporary bound to a reference* on page 819. There is no requirement for the compiler to **materialize** a *temporary* underlying object representation unless and until one is needed (e.g., to be mutated, to be moved from, or to be bound to a named reference), and that need is fulfilled by converting the *prvalue* to an *xvalue*, possibly creating a temporary object in the process. One other property particular to a non**void** *prvalue* expression is that it must be of **complete type**, i.e., sufficient to determine any underlying object's *size* using the built-in **sizeof** operator.

All arithmetic literals are *prvalue* expressions:

```
void testLiterals()
{
    5;    // 5   is a literal prvalue of type int.
    1.5;  // 1.5 is a literal prvalue of type double.
    '5';  // '5' is a literal prvalue of type char.
    true; // true is a literal prvalue of type bool.
}
```

Enumerators are also *prvalues*:

```
enum E { B };        // B is a named prvalue of type E.
```

The results of all numeric operators on built-in types are also *prvalues*:

```
void testNumericExpressions()
{
    const int x = 3;   // x is a named, nonmodifiable lvalue of type int.
    int y = 4;         // y is a named, modifiable lvalue of type int.
```

```
    3 + 2;          // 3 + 2 is a compile-time prvalue of type int.
    x * 2;          // x * 2 is a compile-time prvalue of type int.
    y - 2;          // y - 2 is a prvalue of type int.
    x / y;          // x / y is a prvalue of type int.

    x && y;         // x && y is a prvalue of type bool.
    x == y;         // x == y is a prvalue of type bool.
}
```

A non-numeric operation can also produce a *prvalue*:

```
void testOtherOperations()
{
    const int x = 3;

    &x;  // &x is a prvalue of type const int*.
    static_cast<int>(x); // static_cast<int>(x) is a prvalue of type int.
}
```

Functions that return by value and explicit temporaries of user-defined types are *prvalues* too:

```
struct S { } s;  // s is a named, modifiable lvalue of type S.
int f();         // f is a named, nonmodifiable lvalue of type int().
S g();           // g is a named, nonmodifiable lvalue of type S().

void testCalls()
{
    S();  // S() is a prvalue of type S.
    f();  // f() is a prvalue of type int.
    g();  // g() is a prvalue of type S.
}
```

Xvalues in C++11/14   An *xvalue* expression, also known as an expiring value, is entirely new in C++11. The important, *representational* difference between an *xvalue* and a *prvalue* is that an *xvalue* expression is guaranteed to be represented — at least in principle — by the location of an underlying object; no such guarantee exists for a *prvalue* expression, leaving its internal representation an implementation detail of the compiler.

There are several ways in which an *xvalue* might arise. First, an *xvalue* expression results when an *lvalue* is explicitly cast to an **rvalue** reference:

```
void testXvalues()
{
    int x = 9;
    static_cast<int&&>(x);  // static_cast<int&&>(x) is an xvalue of type int.
    const_cast<int&&>(x);   // const_cast<int&&>(x) is an xvalue of type int.
    (int&&) x;              // (int&&) x is an xvalue of type int.
}
```

Second, a function or operator that returns an **rvalue reference** produces an *xvalue* when invoked:

```
int&& rf();  // rf() is an xvalue of type int.
S&& rg();    // rg() is an xvalue of type S.

S&& operator*(const S&, const S&);  // oddly defined operator

void testOperator()
{
    int i, j;
    i * j;  // i * j is a prvalue of type int.
    S a, b;
    a * b;  // a * b is an xvalue of type S.
}
```

Third, the Standard Library utility function `std::move` also produces *xvalues*, as it is nothing more than a function defined to return an **rvalue reference** to the type passed to it; see *The `std::move` utility* on page 731.

Finally, expressions that access subobjects of any non*lvalue* are *xvalues*, including nonstatic data member access, array subscripting, and dereferencing pointers to data members. Note that when any of these operations is applied to a *prvalue*, a temporary needs to be created from that *prvalue* to contain the subobject, so the subobject is an *xvalue*[7]:

```
struct C  // C() is a prvalue of type C.
{
    int d_i;
    int d_arr[5];
};

C&& h();                   // h() is an xvalue of type C.
int C::* pd = &C::d_i;     // pointer to data member C::d_i

void testSubobjects()
{
    h().d_i;       // h().d_i is an xvalue of type int.
    C().d_i;       // C().d_i  "  "    "      "    "    "
    h().d_arr;     // h().d_arr is an xvalue of type int[5].
    C().d_arr;     // C().d_arr  "  "    "      "    "      "
    h().d_arr[0];  // h().d_arr[0] is an xvalue of type int.
    C().d_arr[0];  // C().d_arr[0]  "  "    "     "     "    "
```

---

[7] The identification of subobjects as *xvalues* rather than *prvalues* or, in some cases, *lvalues*, has been the subject of several core issues, all of which were accepted as **defect reports** between C++14 and C++20. Specifically, CWG issue 616 (**stroustrup07**) and CWG issue 1213 (**merrill10a**) deal with changes to the value categories of subobject expressions. Also note that compiler implementations of these clarifications took some time, with GCC not fully supporting them until GCC 9 (c. 2019).

```
    h().*pd;        // h().*pd is an xvalue of type int.
    C().*pd;        // C().*pd  "  "      "     "   "   "
}
```

Rvalue references

C++11 introduced **rvalue references**, a new reference type that uses a double ampersand, &&, as part of its syntax (e.g., **int**&&):

```
int&& r = 5;  // r is an rvalue reference initialized with a literal int 5.
```

The goal of expanding the type system to include **rvalue references** is to allow function overloading on values that are safe to be moved from, i.e., non*lvalues*. What distinguishes an **rvalue reference** from the familiar **lvalue reference** is that an **rvalue reference** will bind to non*lvalues* (and functions) only. When initialized with an *xvalue*, an **rvalue reference** is bound to the object identified by that *xvalue*. When an **rvalue reference** is initialized with a *prvalue*, a temporary is implicitly created to represent that value and typically has the same lifetime as the reference itself; see *Appendix — Lifetime extension of a temporary bound to a reference* on page 819.

We can now exploit **value categories** to show exactly what binds to what in the presence of a **const** qualifier[8]:

```
struct S { /*...*/ };

      S         fs();        // returns prvalue of type       S
const S         fcs();       // returns prvalue of type const S
      S&        flvrs();     // returns lvalue of type        S
const S&        fclvrs();    // returns lvalue of type const S
      S&&       frvrs();     // returns xvalue of type        S
const S&&       fcrvrs();    // returns xvalue of type const S

    S&& r0 = fs();           // OK
    S&& r1 = fcs();          // Error, cannot bind to const prvalue
    S&& r2 = flvrs();        // Error, cannot bind to        lvalue
    S&& r3 = fclvrs();       // Error, cannot bind to const lvalue
    S&& r4 = frvrs();        // OK
    S&& r5 = fcrvrs();       // Error, cannot bind to const xvalue

    const S&& cr0 = fs();    // OK
    const S&& cr1 = fcs();   // OK
    const S&& cr2 = flvrs(); // Error, cannot bind to        lvalue
```

---

[8]If we were to include **volatile**, we would double the number of possible qualifier combinations that could, in theory, be applied to each of the three *value categories*; since any practical applications of **volatile** are rare, we leave combinations involving it as an exercise for the reader.

```
const S&& cr3 = fclvrs(); // Error, cannot bind to const lvalue
const S&& cr4 = frvrs();  // OK
const S&& cr5 = fcrvrs(); // OK
```

Note that, if we were to replace S with a scalar type such as **int** in the example above, the **const** in the **return** value of fcs() would have been ignored (because **cv-qualifiers** on scalar return types are ignored); hence, the corresponding initialization of r1, where S is instead a scalar, would have succeeded.

An *rvalue* returned from a function can be modified provided (1) it is of user-defined type and (2) there exists a mutating member function; see *Appendix — Modifiable rvalues!* on page 820. Assignment to fundamental types is not permitted for *rvalues*:

```
struct V
{
    int d_i;                                        // public int member
    V(int i) : d_i(i) { }                           // int value constructor
    V& operator=(int rhs) { d_i = rhs; return *this; } // assignment from int
};
      V  fv(int i) { return V(i); }  // returns nonconst prvalue of type V
const V fcv(int i) { return V(i); }  // returns    const prvalue of type V

void test1()
{
    fv(2).d_i = 5;        // Error, cannot assign to rvalue int
    fv(2).operator=(5);   // OK, member assignment can be invoked on an rvalue.
    fv(2) = 5;            // OK,   "         "          "    "   "    "  "     "

    fcv(2).d_i = 5;       // Error, cannot assign to const rvalue int
    fcv(2).operator=(5);  // Error, assignment is a nonconst member function.
    fcv(2) = 5;          // Error,   "         "  "        "         "
}
```

What's more, that modified value will be preserved until the end of the outermost expression containing the *rvalue* subexpression:

```
#include <cassert>  // standard C assert macro

void test2()
{
    int x = 1 + (V(0) = 2).d_i + 3 + (fv(0) = 4).d_i + 5;
    assert(15 == x);  // 15 == 1 + 2 + 3 + 4 + 5
}
```

The ability to modify an unnamed, **temporary** *rvalue* directly, however, is distinct from that of modifying a named, nontemporary rvalue reference, which is itself an *lvalue*. Binding any *rvalue* expression — such as a default-constructed object, e.g., S(), or a literal, e.g., 1 — to a **const** lvalue reference was always possible in C++, but subsequently modifying it through that reference was not:

```
void test3()
{
        S&  lvrs = S();      // Error, initializes nonconst lvalue ref w/rvalue
  const S& clvrs = S();      // OK, initializes const lvalue ref w/prvalue
           clvrs = S();      // Error, assigning via a const lvalue ref
  const S* pcs = &clvrs;     // OK, any const lvalue reference is an lvalue.

        int&  lvri = 5;      // Error, initializes nonconst lvalue ref w/rvalue
  const int& clvri = 5;      // OK, initializes const lvalue ref w/prvalue
             clvri = 5;      // Error, assigning via a const lvalue ref
  const int* pci = &clvri;   // OK, any const lvalue reference is an lvalue.
}
```

Notice, however, that each of the named references in the example above, when used in an expression, is itself an *lvalue*, and hence a programmer may use the built-in unary address-of operator, &, to take the address of the possibly temporary underlying object that initialized it.

Rvalue references behave similarly in that, when a *prvalue* initializes a named **rvalue** reference, that *prvalue* materializes a **temporary object** whose lifetime is the same as that of the reference. Unlike a non**const** lvalue reference, however, a non**const** rvalue reference can be bound to a non**const** *rvalue* of the same type, in which case that same underlying object can be subsequently modified via the reference:

```
void test4()
{
        S&&  rvrs = S();      // OK, initializes an rvalue ref with a prvalue
  const S&& crvrs = S();      // OK, initializes a const. rvalue ref with an prvalue
           rvrs = S();        // OK, can modify via a named nonconst. rvalue ref
          crvrs = S();        // Error, cannot modify via a const. rvalue ref
        S*  ps = & rvrs;      // OK, a named nonconst. rvalue ref is an lvalue.
  const S* pcs = &crvrs;      // OK, a named const. rvalue ref is a const. lvalue.

        int&&  rvri = 5;      // OK, initializes an rvalue ref with a prvalue
  const int&& crvri = 5;      // OK, initializes const. rvalue ref with a prvalue
             rvri = 5;        // OK, can modify via a named nonconst. rvalue ref
            crvri = 5;        // Error, cannot modify via any const. rvalue ref
        int*  pi = & rvri;    // OK, a named nonconst. rvalue ref is an lvalue.
  const int* pci = &crvri;    // OK, a named const. rvalue ref is an lvalue.
}
```

Recall that **rvalue references** were invented to allow library developers to discriminate — using overloaded functions — between *movable* arguments, i.e., those that can be moved from safely, and nonmovable arguments. For this reason, it was necessary to ensure that an **rvalue reference** of a given type never implicitly binds to an *lvalue* of corresponding type, as allowing such liberal binding would result in **move operations** cannibalizing the state of objects that had not been identified as ready for such activity. So although a **const** lvalue reference binds to *all* values, a **const** rvalue reference is deliberately designed *not* to bind to an *lvalue* of the *same* type but to happily bind to an *rvalue* that is the result of an implicit conversion, including an **integral promotion**, from any other sufficiently distinct type:

```
    double   d;          //   d is a named lvalue of type          double.
const double   cd = 0;   //  cd is a named lvalue of type    const double.
const double fcd();      // fcd returns a prvalue of type nonconst double.

const double& clr1 = d;        // Initialize with lvalue of type double.
const double& clr2 = cd;       // Initialize with lvalue of type const double.
const double& clr3 = double(); // Initialize with prvalue of type double.
const double& clr4 = fcd();    //     "       "      "     "     "    "
      double&  lr4 = fcd(); // Error, initializes nonconst lvalue ref w/rvalue

const double&& crr1 = d;          // Error, cannot init w/value of same type
const double&& crr2 = cd;         // Error,     "    "  "  "    "     "   "
const double&& crr3 = double();   // Initialize with prvalue of type double.
const double&& crr4 = fcd();      //     "       "      "     "     "    "
      double&&  rr4 = fcd();      //     "       "      "     "     "    "


      float   f;          //   f is a named lvalue of type          float.
const float   cf = 0.0;   //  cf is a named lvalue of type    const float.
const float fcf();        // fcf returns a prvalue of type nonconst float.

const double&& cfr1 = f;        // OK, f is converted to rvalue of type double.
const double&& cfr2 = cf;       // OK, cf is converted to rvalue of type double.
const double&& cfr3 = float();  // Initialize with prvalue of type double.
const double&& cfr4 = fcf();    //     "       "      "     "     "    "
      double&&  fr4 = fcf();    //     "       "      "     "     "    "

short z;             // z is a named lvalue of type short int.
const int&& czr = z; // OK, z is promoted to an rvalue of type int.
```

If the type T of the *lvalue* initializing the **rvalue reference** of type U is close enough that a match might reasonably have been intended, the initialization is still rejected. By "close enough" here, we mean that T is **reference related** to U — i.e., U and V differ in **cv-qualification** (at any level) only or U (without top-level cv-qualification) is a direct or indirect base class of T (without top-level cv-qualification):

```
long j;
const volatile int&  lrj = j;  // Error, j is not of type int.
const volatile int&& rrj = j;  // OK, j converted to temporary of type int

struct B { }                 b;   // base class B
struct C { operator B() const; } c;   // convertible to B
struct D : B { }             d;   // derived from B
const D                      e;   // const derived from B
```

```
B&  lrb = b;  // OK
B&& rrb = b;  // Error, initializing rvalue with lvalue of same type

B&  lrc = c;  // Error, convertible type B as an rvalue only
B&& rrc = c;  // OK

B&  lrd = d;  // OK              •
B&& rrd = d;  // Error, initializing rvalue ref with reference-related lvalue

      B&  lre = e;  // Error, init of nonconst lvalue ref w/const lvalue
const B&  clre = e;  // OK
      B&& rre = e;  // Error, init rvalue ref with reference-related lvalue
const B&& crre = e;  // Error,  "    "    "    "    "    "    "
```

If the type of the *lvalue* initializing an **rvalue reference** is of a sufficiently distinct type from that of the reference, a new underlying object will be **materialized**; any subsequent modification via the reference will have no effect on the original value:

```
#include <utility>  // std::move
#include <cassert>  // standard C assert macro

void test5()
{
         char c  = 1;
    unsigned char u  = 2;

    char&& rc = static_cast<         char&&>(c);  // rc refers to c.
    char&& ru = static_cast<unsigned char&&>(u);  // temporary char created

    assert(&rc == &c);                     // rc refers to c.
    assert(&ru != static_cast<void*>(&u));  // ru refers to a different char.

    rc = 7;  assert(7 == c);  // c modified through rc
    ru = 8;  assert(2 == u);  // u unchanged
}  // Temporary lifetime ends with all other variables here.
```

Note that, in the example above, we used the **static_cast** construct to convert both the c and u *lvalues* to their respective *xvalues*; in practice, however, std::move is more commonly used for this purpose; see *The std::move utility* on page 731.

Overloading on reference types A compelling motivation for having a new kind of reference that binds exclusively to *rvalues* is to allow existing overload sets employing a **const** lvalue reference to be augmented so that when the same named function is invoked with a non*lvalue*, the new overload will be given preference, which can then move from its argument. For example, consider a function, g, that takes an object of user-defined type c, which it *might* need to copy and manipulate internally before returning a value, e.g., an **int**:

```
class C { /*...*/ };  // some UDT that might benefit from being "moved"

int g(const C& c);  // (1) [original] takes argument by const lvalue reference.
int g(C&& c);       // (2) [additional] takes argument by nonconst rvalue ref.
```

Note that even if we were sometimes inclined to pass user-defined types by value, we would *not* want to do so here for fear we might end up making an expensive copy for no reason; see *Use Cases — Passing movable objects by value* on page 771.

Let's now consider calling this function g on expressions having various kinds of values, e.g., *lvalues* versus *rvalues* and **const** versus non**const**:

```
      C c;        // c is a named lvalue of type C.
const C cc;       // cc is a named lvalue of type const C.
const C fc();     // fc() is an unnamed rvalue of type const C.

int i1 = g(c);     // OK, invokes overload g(const C&) because c is an lvalue
int i2 = g(C());   // OK, invokes overload g(C&&) because C() is a prvalue
int i3 = g(cc);    // OK, invokes overload g(const C&) because cc is const
int i4 = g(fc());  // OK, invokes overload g(const C&) because fc() is const
```

In this scenario, if an argument to g in the code snippet above is a non**const** *rvalue* (and therefore known to be movable and potentially a *temporary*), it will bind more strongly to g(C&&). Non*rvalue* and **const** arguments to g will not be considered for g(C&&) at all but are viable to pass to g(**const** C&), so that overload will be chosen. Note that passing a *prvalue* to a function taking its argument by either **rvalue reference** or **const** lvalue reference will cause a temporary object to be created, which will be destroyed at the end of the outermost expression invoking that function.

Adding an **rvalue reference** overload of g does not add to the set of usable arguments for g. That is, anything that can bind to a C&& can also bind to a **const** C&. A corollary to this observation is that, given any function having an overload set that contains a **const** T& parameter, one can *safely* introduce a parallel overload having a T&& parameter in the corresponding position with the desired effect that, when that function is called with an argument that is **movable** (i.e., not an *lvalue*) in that position, the newly added rvalue-reference overload will be called instead.

In the most general case, there are five — nine if we consider **volatile** — combinations of ways to pass an argument to a function (see Table 1).

Table 1: Parameter types

	nonconst	const
value	T / **const** T	
lvalue reference	T&	**const** T&
rvalue reference	T&&	**const** T&&

Despite appearances, the two pass-by-value options, namely T and **const** T, in the table above aren't different ways to pass an argument to a function. The top-level **const** on a parameter is not part of the function's interface, doesn't affect its **signature**, and is not reflected at the object-code level. For a **defining declaration** for a function, a **top-level const** acts only as a constraint on what the implementation can do with the parameter; for a **nondefining declaration**, however, a top-level **const** has no meaning whatsoever:

```
void fx(const int);  // nondefining declaration
void fx(int i)       //    defining declaration
{
    i = 5;  // OK
}

void fy(int);        // nondefining declaration
void fy(const int i) //    defining declaration
{
    i = 5;  // Error, i is not modifiable.
}

void fz(     int) { }  // OK
void fz(const int) { }  // Error, fz(int) is multiply defined.
```

One could, in principle, overload a function, such as g, with all five, distinct, mutually overloadable variants shown in Table 1, but doing so would lead to ambiguity as passing by value — T — and passing by lvalue reference — T& or **const** T& — are equivalently good matches. Hence, in practice, one passes an object either by value or some subset of the four possible reference variants. Such broad flexibility, however, is seldom useful.

Consider, for example, a function h that is overloaded on a non**const** *lvalue* and a non**const** *rvalue*:

```
void h(C& inOut);   // (3) OK, accepts only nonconst lvalues
void h(C&& inOnly);  // (4) OK, accepts only nonconst rvalues
```

As was the explicit intent of the inventors of **rvalue references**, an overload set like h provides the ability to distinguish programmatically between non**const** objects that are (1) *lvalues*, and therefore are *not* known to be safe to be *moved from*, and (2) non*lvalues*, and therefore *are* presumed to be safe to be *moved from* yet exclude any object whose type is qualified with **const**:

```
void test6(C& lv, const C& clv, const C&& crv)
{
    h(lv);             // (5) OK, invokes (3) because lv is an lvalue
    h(C());            // (6) OK, invokes (4) because C() is an rvalue
    h(clv);            // (7) Error, clv is const. No overload of h matches.
    h(std::move(crv)); // (8) Error, crv is const. No overload of h matches.
}
```

But consider that having such an overload set is typically contraindicated. Without the rvalue reference overload, invoking **h** on a *temporary* would simply fail to compile, thereby avoiding a runtime defect. With the **rvalue-reference** overload present, the code will in fact compile, but now any output written to that *temporary* will silently disappear along with that temporary.

Although seldom needed, Table 2[9] provides the relative priority in which all four potential pass-by-reference members of an overload set would be selected.

Table 2: Overload resolution priorities

Value Category		g(C&)	g(const C&)	g(C&&)	g(const C&&)
non**const** *lvalue*	c	1	2	N/A	N/A
const *lvalue*	cc	N/A	1	N/A	N/A
non**const** *rvalue*	C()	N/A	3	1	2
const *rvalue*	fc()	N/A	2	N/A	1

Note that the equivalent function to **fc** for a built-in type, **const int fi()**, would return a non**const** *rvalue*, as fundamental types returned by **const** value are treated as if they had been returned by non**const** value. The only way to have a function that returns a **const** *rvalue* of primitive type **T** is to have it return **const T&&**, such as **const int&& fi2()**.

***Rvalue* references in expressions**   Recall from *Lvalues in C++11/14* on page 717 that any named variable, including an **rvalue reference**, is an *lvalue*:

```
#include <utility> // std::move

struct S { /*...*/ };

void test1()
{
    S   s1;                 // local variable of type S
    S&& s2 = s1;            // Error, s1 is an lvalue.
    S&& s3 = std::move(s1); // OK, std::move(s1) is an xvalue.
    S&& s4 = s3;            // Error, s3 is an lvalue.
    S&& s5 = std::move(s3); // OK, std::move(s3) is an xvalue.
}
```

That a named **rvalue reference** itself was deliberately categorized as an *lvalue* helps to ensure that such a reference is not accidentally consumed as an *xvalue* until its current value is no longer needed elsewhere:

---

[9]Though Table 2 was derived and verified independently, a strikingly similar table can be found in **josuttis20b**, section 8.3.1, "Overload Resolution with Rvalue References," pp. 133–134, Table 8.1, p. 134.

```
void f(const S& s);   // only reads the value of s
void f(S&& s);        // consumes the value of s

void test2(S&& s)
{
    f(s);                // invokes int f(const S&)
    f(std::move(s));     // invokes int f(S&&)
}
```

Although perhaps unintuitive at first glance, it is important to consider how the function test2 above would have behaved had an **rvalue reference** itself been treated as an *rvalue*: The invocation f(s) would invoke **void f(S&&)**, which would result in consuming the value of s and leaving it in an unspecified state. The subsequent invocation of f(std::move(s)) would then be attempting to process a moved-from object, which almost certainly would not be the intent of the writer of test2.

The final use of an rvalue reference in a given context could conceivably be treated as an *xvalue*, but up to this point in the evolution of C++, that opportunity has been exploited only in the relatively narrow case where variables having **automatic storage duration** are used in **return** statements or **throw** expressions; see *Implicit moves from lvalues in* **return** *statements* on page 735. Additional implicit moves might be added to the language in the future but only if the proposals brought to the Standards Committee make a convincing case that such additions carry little or no risk of silently doing harm.

The std::move utility   A large part of the original motivation for having a new value category, dubbed *xvalues*, was to intersect the notions of *reachability* and *movability*; see *Appendix — Why do we need a new value category?* on page 824. The way we typically unite these heretofore disjoint properties — e.g., in the case of moving an element in a vector from one position to another — is to cast a pre-existing *lvalue* to an rvalue reference. Until now we've used a **static_cast**, but a **const_cast** would work too:

```
struct S { /*...*/ } s;   // some UDT that might benefit from being moved

int f(const S&  s);   // (1) takes any kind of S but with lower priority
int f(      S&& s);   // (2) takes only movable kinds of S with high priority

int i1 = f(s);                    // calls (1); can copy-construct local S from s
int i2 = f(const_cast<S&&>(s));   // calls (2); can move-construct local S from s
```

Note that our use of a **const_cast** above would allow even a **const** S to be converted to a non**const** rvalue reference, while a **static_cast** would enable a conversion from a type convertible to S to be bound to an rvalue reference, either of which might have unintended consequences. Given that an essential part of the design of rvalue references involves a specialized *cast* that must preserve the C++ type and **const**ness, while changing the value category, it was decided that the best approach to performing the conversion would be to create a library utility (implemented as a function template) that deduces the C++ type, ignoring reference qualifiers, and then used a **static_cast**, as opposed to a **const_cast**, in its implementation. One plausible implementation — using **forwarding references**, **constexpr**, and the **noexcept** decorator — is provided here for concreteness (see Section 2.1. "Forwarding References" on page 377, Section 2.1."**constexpr** Functions" on page 257, and Section 3.1."**noexcept** Specifier" on page 1085):

```
// example implementation of the Standard Library's std::move utility:
namespace std
{
    template <typename T> struct __RemoveReference       { typedef T type; };
    template <typename T> struct __RemoveReference<T&>   { typedef T type; };
    template <typename T> struct __RemoveReference<T&&>  { typedef T type; };

    template <typename T>
    constexpr typename __RemoveReference<T>::type&& move(T&& expression) noexcept
    {
        return static_cast<typename __RemoveReference<T>::type&&>(expression);
    }
}
```

As the example implementation above indicates, the name of this standard function template is move, it resides in the std namespace, and it can be found in the Standard <utility> header file. This function template is used just as one would use a **static_cast** to convert an lvalue-reference expression to an unnamed, rvalue-reference expression, except that the C++ type is deduced automatically rather than giving the user the opportunity to accidentally misspecify it:

```
#include <utility>  // std::move

S t1, t2;  // two similar objects that are each movable

int i3 = f(static_cast<S&&>(t1));  // can move-construct a local S from t1
int i4 = f(std::move(t2));         // can move-construct a local S from t2
```

The choice of *move* for the name of this specialized cast to rvalue reference can, however, be confusing; see *Annoyances — std::move does not move* on page 805.

Special member function generation Given the new capability of having additional function overloads for rvalue reference parameters, two new special member functions were also added in C++11.

1. A move constructor for a type X is a nontemplate constructor that can be invoked with a single rvalue reference to X. There are two requirements: (1) The first parameter of the constructor must be a cv-qualified rvalue reference to X, i.e., either X&&, **const** X&&, **volatile** X&&, or **const volatile** X&&, and (2) the constructor must have exactly one parameter or all parameters after the first must have default arguments:

```
struct S1 { S1(S1&&); };                 // move constructor
struct S2 { S2(const S2&&); };           //    "        "
struct S3 { S3(S3&&, int i = 0); };      //    "        "
struct S4 { S4(S4&&, int i); };          // not a move constructor
struct S5 { S5(int&&); };                //   "  "   "      "
struct S6 { S6(S6&); };                  //   "  "   "      "
```

2. A move-assignment operator for a type X is a nonstatic, nontemplate member function named **operator**= with exactly one parameter that is a cv-qualified rvalue reference to X, i.e., either X&&, **const** X&&, **volatile** X&&, or **const volatile** X&&. Any return type and value is valid for a move-assignment operator, but the common convention is to have a return type of X& and to return ***this**.

Just as with other special member functions, when not declared explicitly, it is possible for the move constructor and move-assignment operator to be declared implicitly[10] for a **class**, or **struct**, X.

- Supplying any of a user-declared copy or move constructor, copy or move assignment operator, or destructor will suppress the implicit generation of both move operations.

- The default move constructor will have the **function prototype** X::X(X&&). The default move-assignment operator will have the signature X& **operator**=(X&&).

- The **exception specification** and triviality of both move operations are determined by the **exception specification** and **triviality** of the corresponding operation on all base classes and non**static** data members of X.

- The default implementation will apply the corresponding operation to each base class and non**static** data member.

The rules governing special-member-function generation for a **union** are similar to those for a **class** or **struct** with the added proviso that *any* of the **union**'s six special member functions that are not declared explicitly will be deleted (see Section 1.1."Deleted Functions" on page 53) if they correspond to a *nontrivial* special member function of one or more of the **union**'s *non*static data members:

```
struct S { S(S&&); };   // S has a user-provided (nontrivial) move ctor.
union U { S s; };       // U's implicitly declared move ctor is deleted.
```

Note that a **trivial move operation** and a **trivial copy operation** on a union have the same behavior: a bitwise copy. For a much more detailed discussion of both **union**s and triviality, see Section 3.1."**union** '11" on page 1174 and Section 2.1."Generalized PODs '11" on page 401.

---

[10]For more on the implicit generation of special member functions, see Section 1.1."Defaulted Functions" on page 33.

Moves from *rvalues* in `return` statements   When the expression returned from a function is a *prvalue*, the return value will be initialized via move construction:

```
struct S { };

S f1() { return S(); }  // returns a prvalue

void test1()
{
    S s = f1();
}
```

The local variable `s` in `test1` above might be initialized in one of two ways. At a minimum, a temporary will be created within the body of `f1` and used as an *rvalue* to copy construct `s` within `test1`. The example is a perfect example for what has come to be known as **return-value optimization (RVO)**. Instead of constructing the object within the function and then copying — or even moving — it to the caller, space for the **footprint** of the object is reserved in the caller's scope, and then the object is constructed just once, **in place**, and is initialized by the returned *prvalue*. This optimization reduces to zero the number of additional constructor calls beyond the initial call, the best number of operations to invoke from the perspective of the performance-minded.[11]

Return values can be move-constructed when the returned expression is an *xvalue* as well:

```
S f2()
{
    S s;
    return std::move(s);  // returns an xvalue
}
```

In this case, the object initialized by the return value of `f2` will be constructed using an rvalue reference to `s`. It's important to note, however, that explicitly making such *lvalues* into *xvalues* on return might not be needed and, in some cases, might even prevent the above **named return-value optimization (NRVO)**; see *Implicit moves from lvalues in* **return** *statements* on page 735.

Finally, if a *prvalue* expression is to be returned, it is strongly contraindicated to use `std::move` to force a move from that *prvalue*:

```
S f3()
{
    return std::move(S());  // BAD IDEA
}
```

---

[11]C++17 mandates that there be no additional object created when a function returns a *prvalue*, effectively guaranteeing **copy elision**.

Applying `std::move` as in `f3` in the example above does more than just cast an expression to a particular type; it requires that there be an object to pass to the utility function. In this case, a temporary will have to be **materialized** to be the argument to `std::move`, and thus there will no longer be the possibility of eliding all moves and applying RVO.

Implicit moves from *lvalues* in `return` statements   Any time the use of an object coincides with the last time that object can be referenced, it might be beneficial to treat that object as an *xvalue* instead of an *lvalue* so that the resources owned by that object can be reused before they are released by the object's destructor. **Temporaries** are the primary means by which *xvalues* are generated spontaneously.

In a **return** statement, however, the lifetime of all variables having **automatic storage duration** — namely, non**volatile** local variables and function parameters — ends implicitly after the statement. This defined behavior enables any **return** statement that names such a variable to treat the returned expression as an *xvalue* instead of an *lvalue*, resulting in move construction of the return value instead of copy construction[12]:

```
struct S { };
void g(const S&);
void g(S&&);

S f1()
{
    S s;
    g(s);     // s is not an xvalue and selects g(const S&).
    return s; // s is an xvalue.
}

S f2(S s)
{
    g(s);     // s is not an xvalue and selects g(const S&).
    return s; // s is an xvalue.
}
```

If all **return** statements in a function are of the form, say, **return** x; where x is an automatic variable of the same type as the return type of the function, then the copy implied by the

---

[12]C++20 introduced the concept of an **implicitly movable entity** for those automatic-storage-duration objects that will be moved, rather than copied, when returned in this way. This concept was also extended to include rvalue references (to non**volatile** objects):

```
S returnRefParam(S&& input)
{
    return input; // input is an lvalue in C++11-17 and an xvalue in C++20.
}
```

return statements can often be elided. Where applicable, x can be constructed directly in the footprint of the target of the return value:

```
S nrvo(S* p)  // function taking the address of an (uninitialized) S object
{
    S s1;                  // s1 is a local automatic variable of type S.
    assert(&s1 == p);  // The assert will succeed only if NRVO is in effect.
    return s1;             // Return s1 (maybe via NRVO).
}

void callNrvo()  // test function to provide address of final S object, s2
{
    S s2 = nrvo(&s2);  // Pass in address of the variable being initialized.
}
```

In the example above, notice that **callNrvo** explicitly passes the address of the yet-to-be-initialized automatic variable, s2, to the nrvo function, enabling it to determine, via an assert, if NRVO is taking place. If NRVO is not being applied, the address passed in, via p, will differ from that of the local automatic variable s1, and if asserts are enabled, the program will terminate with an error message. Otherwise, we can be assured that s1 is being constructed in the footprint of s2 in the calling function, **callNrvo**.

This conversion to *xvalue* from a **return** statement broadly overlaps the cases where returning an automatic variable is eligible for **copy elision**, otherwise known as the **named return-value optimization**. NRVO has many subtle restrictions, is not guaranteed, depends on the specific expressions in any other **return** statements within the same function, and might even be dependent on specific properties of the type in question. Even where applicable, any use of NRVO is left entirely up to the implementation.

Functions that are eligible for **NRVO** also meet the requirements for move-constructing their return values, even if NRVO does not take effect. Hence, functions like f1 and nrvo in the code snippets above will, at worst, invoke a single **move constructor** to initialize their return values and, at best, invoke nothing at all.

Let's now consider a function (e.g., f3) that invokes std::move to cast a named local variable (e.g., s) to an rvalue reference explicitly:

```
S f3()
{
    S s;
    return std::move(s);  // explicit cast to an rvalue reference
}
```

Here, by explicitly using std::move to move from the local variable to the return value, we have also made this function no longer eligible for NRVO, as the return expression is a function call and not just the name of a local variable. This use of std::move results in *always* invoking a **move constructor** to initialize the return value and never eliding the additional object at all.

In general, when an object's lifetime is about to end and it will potentially be treated implicitly as an *xvalue*, it is a reasonable, relatively future-proof, rule of thumb to *not* explicitly use `std::move`. Even in cases where NRVO does not apply today, the move will happen either way, and in future Standards the extra object might be elided completely as the language evolves.[13]

When the type of a local variable used in a **return** statement does *not* exactly match the nonreference C++ type being returned, then the explicit use of `std::move` *is* indicated[14]: A conversion to the return type will always occur in that case. The explicit cast to an rvalue reference guarantees that the result of the conversion will be created by *moving from* the object named in the **return** statement. Note that some types of *move conversions*, e.g., those resulting from *move construction*, would happen even without the explicit use of `std::move`, but there is, however, no situation where having an explicit `std::move` pessimizes the creation of the result object, but see *Potential Pitfalls — Returning* **const** *rvalues pessimizes performance* on page 786.

When something more complicated than the name of an automatic variable is used as the expression of a **return** statement, the explicit use of `std::move` is also indicated, as none of the rules that might enable copy elision are potentially applicable:

```
S f4(bool flag)
{
    S a, b;
    return flag ? std::move(a) : std::move(b);  // std::move needed
}

S f5()
{
    S a;
    return 1, std::move(a);  // std::move needed
}
```

When to move return values   What can a poor programmer do to ensure that (1) a copy is always avoided where possible and (2) copy elision is never pessimized by an explicit cast?

Following six simple rules of thumb will achieve both of these goals now, and the resulting code should remain future-proof in perpetuity.

   1. First, do no harm. If there is a possibility that a value might subsequently be referenced from some other part of the program, then an explicit cast is *not* indicated:

---

[13]Proposals such as **zhilin21**, which makes NRVO apply more broadly and be guaranteed in a fashion similar to RVO in C++17; **odwyer19**, which adds implicitly movable entities to C++20; and **odwyer21**, which improves the handling of implicitly movable entities, all lead to improvements to functions that do not explicitly move, while offering no changes or improvements to functions that do.

[14]Note that, in future versions of C++, such use of explicit moves in **return** statements, i.e., those having expressions whose types do not match the declared return type of the function, will become increasingly less *indicated* but are unlikely to become *contraindicated*.

```
S f1(S* s)
{
    return *s;  // explicit cast not indicated
}

S s1;  // externally reachable variable

S g1()
{
    return s1;  // explicit cast not indicated
}
```

Moving from such an object might result in unintended and possibly incorrect behavior.

2. If the expression being returned is a *prvalue* (e.g., the anonymous construction of an object or a call to a function returning an object by value), then an explicit cast is *not* indicated:

```
S f2()
{
    return S(/*...*/);  // explicit cast not indicated
}

S g2()
{
    return f2(/*...*/);  // explicit cast not indicated
}
```

It is precisely these cases in which the **return-value optimization (RVO)** is likely to kick in, thereby eliding even move construction; providing an explicit cast would effectively disable RVO, forcing two objects to be created instead of just one.

3. If the expression in a **return** statement consists of just the name of a locally declared nonreference variable, including a by-value parameter or one in a local **catch** clause, and exactly matches the return type of the function, an explicit cast is *not* indicated:

```
S f3()
{
    S s;
    return s;  // explicit cast not indicated
}

S g3(S s)
{
    return s;  // explicit cast not indicated
}

S h3()
{
```

```
    try
    {
        // ...
    }
    catch (S s)
    {
        return s;  // explicit cast not indicated
    }
}
```

In some cases, NRVO will cause local objects to be constructed directly in the result; otherwise, an implicit cast is guaranteed so the object will move if the type supports move construction. Although the argument of a **catch**-clause parameter will never be optimized away, it too will be moved implicitly, and attempting to explicitly cast it unnecessarily might even trigger compiler warnings.

4. If the expression in a **return** statement consists of the name of a locally declared nonreference variable that does not exactly match the return type of the function, an explicit cast *is* indicated:

```
struct T {
    T(S&&);  // S is convertible to T.
};

T f4()
{
    S s;
    return std::move(s);  // Explicit cast is indicated.
}
```

Not all move conversions are guaranteed to occur implicitly; since copy elision doesn't apply when the types do not match exactly, having an explicit cast cannot pessimize object creation but might enable a *move* instead of a *copy* operation.

5. If the expression being returned is any kind of reference and it is clear that it is appropriate to move the object being referenced, then an explicit cast *is* indicated:

```
S f5()
{
    S s;
    S& r = s;
    return std::move(r);  // Explicit cast is indicated.
}

S g5(S&& s)  // Being passed as an rvalue reference indicates s should be moved.
{
    return std::move(s);  // Explicit cast is indicated.
}
```

There are no implicit conversions from references; since copy elision doesn't apply either, having an explicit cast cannot pessimize object creation but might enable a move instead of a copy.[15]

6. Additionally, when an expression resides in a **throw** statement, an explicit cast *is* indicated but only when it is *safe* to do so:

```
void f6(S s)
{
    throw std::move(s);  // Explicit cast is indicated.
}

void g6()
{
    S s;
    S& r = s;
    throw std::move(r);  // Explicit cast is indicated.
}

void h6()
{
    S s;  // used below by f6

    try
    {
        throw s;  // Explicit cast is not indicated.
    }
    catch (...) { }

    f6(s);  // uses s after being thrown
}
```

An exception object will always be created, and, without an explicit cast, it is not guaranteed that a viable move constructor will be invoked, especially when the thrown expression is of reference type. There is practically no situation where using `std::move` pessimizes the creation of the exception object,[16] whereas *not* using `std::move` might result in its being *copied* instead of *moved*.

If, however, the thrown object were to be caught within the same function and later used, then an explicit cast would *not* be indicated.

---

[15] In C++20, with the adoption as defect reports of P0527 (**stone17**) and P1825 (**stone19**) non**volatile**, rvalue references with automatic storage duration are implicitly treated as *xvalues* in **return** statements. In a compiler that has implemented this change, the use of `std::move` simply makes explicit what would otherwise have been implicit, but since the object to which the reference is bound will have already been created elsewhere, there is no difference in the number of move operations that must occur.

[16] In theory, when the operand is the name of a non**volatile** automatic variable whose scope does not extend beyond the end of the innermost enclosing **try** block (if one exists), the Standard allows for such an operand to be constructed directly into the exception object. Using `std::move` in that specific case would disable this optimization; however, no such optimization has been observed in any of the popular compilers we tested.

Summary

The introduction of extended value categories in C++11 was fundamental to enabling move semantics in modern C++. There are now three disjoint value categories, *lvalue*, *xvalue*, and *prvalue*, that can be used to characterize any C++ expression.

Two of these categories, *lvalue* and *xvalue*, together make up the *glvalue* category of expressions; each of these expressions is represented as if by an object having identity, i.e., one that could produce an address in memory if asked properly.

Two of these categories, *xvalue* and *prvalue*, together make up the *rvalue* category of expressions, which is characterized by values that are not needed outside the current expression; if an *rvalue* happens to already be represented by an object, that object is movable.

Individually, *lvalue* expressions have identity. We can obtain the address of an *lvalue* using the & operator; an *lvalue* cannot be moved from. *Prvalue* expressions do not have identity and thus are guaranteed to be safe to be moved from; if a *prvalue* happens to be represented by an object, that object is movable. *Xvalue* expressions have identity; each *xvalue* is guaranteed to already be represented by an object that is movable.

Using rvalue-reference parameters, in overload sets, to complement those employing **const** lvalue references enables constructors, assignment operators, and other operations to distinguish between arguments potentially having resources available to be harvested for reuse (i.e., repurposed) and those that are *read only*. The ability to detect, cannibalize, and repurpose the allocated resources of only expiring objects avoids needless copies of temporaries and other objects whose values have been identified (implicitly or explicitly) as being expendable.

Use Cases

Move operations as optimizations of copying

With the introduction of rvalue references, we are now able to discriminate between a reference bound to an object that is eligible to be moved from, i.e., an rvalue reference, and one that is bound to an object that must be copied, i.e., an lvalue reference. That is, we are now able to **overload** our constructors and assignment operators for both *rvalues* and *lvalues*.

Constructing an object from an *lvalue* expression of the same type is called *copy construction*. Constructing an object from an *rvalue* expression of the same type is called *move construction*. The term *move* colloquially expresses the idea of transferring **owned resources**, typically dynamically allocated memory blocks, from one object to another as opposed to that of somehow duplicating, e.g., allocating and copying, them.

In most practical applications, *moving* can be reasonably interpreted and properly implemented as an *optimization* of *copying* in that the requirements on the target object are the same, whereas the requirements on the source object are relaxed such that it need not retain the same state — or **value**, where applicable — after the operation completes.

Importantly, knowing that the semantics of *move* operations can be fully defined in terms of their corresponding *copy* operations makes them easy to understand. What's more, these newly added **move-semantic** operations can be tested using unit tests that are modified only slightly from their existing **copy-semantic** counterparts; see *Potential Pitfalls — Making a noncopyable type movable without just cause* on page 788.

Repurposing internal resources from an object that no longer needs them can lead to faster *copy*-like operations, especially when dynamic allocation and deallocation of memory is involved. Countervailing considerations, such as **locality of reference**, can, however, suggest that preferring *move* operations to *copy* operations might, in some circumstances, be contraindicated for overall optimal runtime performance, especially at scale.[17]

Properly implementing *move* operations that, for **expiring** objects, act like optimized **copy operations** will depend on the specifics of how we chose to implement a type, e.g., an object that (1) is written to manage its own resources explicitly (see *Creating a low-level value-semantic type (VST)* below) or (2) delegates resource management to its subobjects (see *Description — Special member function generation* on page 732).

Creating a low-level value-semantic type (VST)   Often, we want to create a **user-defined type (UDT)** that represents what we'll call a **platonic value**, i.e., one whose meaning is independent of its representation within the current process. When implemented properly, we refer to such a type as a **value-semantic type (VST)**. Although there are some cases where a VST might be implemented as a simple **aggregate type** (see *Description — Special member function generation* on page 732), there are other cases where a VST might, instead, manage its internal resources directly. The latter explicit implementation of a VST is the subject of this subsection.

For illustration purposes, consider a simple VST, **class** String, that maintains, as an **object invariant**, a null-*terminated* string value; i.e., this string class explicitly does *not* support having a *null* pointer value. In addition to a *value* constructor and a single **const** member function to access the value of the object, each of the four C++03 special member functions — default constructor, copy constructor, assignment operator, and destructor — are **user provided**, i.e., defined explicitly by the programmer. To keep this example focused, however, we will *not* store separately the length of the string, and we'll omit the notion of *excess* capacity altogether, leaving just a single non**static const char*** data member, d_str_p, to hold the address of the dynamically allocated memory:

```
class String { const char* d_str_p; /*...*/ };  // null-terminated-string manager
```

One practical aspect that we preserve is that default-constructed container types — going back to C++03 — are well advised, on purely performance grounds, never to pre-allocate resources, lest creating a large array of such empty containers be impracticably runtime-intensive to construct:

---

[17] **halpern21c**

```
String s;  // No memory is allocated.
```

To avoid having to check, internally, on each access whether a given string representation is a **null pointer value**, we instead create a common **static** *empty* string, s_empty, nested within our **String** class, and install its address during default construction or when we would otherwise want to represent an empty string. This address serves as a **sentinel** whose requisite runtime checking is properly relegated to more costly and/or presumably less frequent operations, such as copy construction, assignment, and destruction. Thus, an added **object invariant** is that a string value whose representation is dynamically allocated is never empty.

Finally, to provide better factoring, the definition of our **value-semantic** String class declares a private **static** member function, dupStr, that dynamically allocates and populates a new block of memory exactly sized to hold a supplied, nonempty **null-terminated-string** value:

```
// my_string.h:
// ...

class String  // greatly simplified null-terminated-string manager
{
    const char* d_str_p;  // immutable value, often allocated dynamically

    static const char s_empty[1];  // empty, used as sentinel indicating null

    static const char* dupStr(const char* str);  // allocate/return copy of str

public:
    // C++03
    String();                           // default constructor
    String(const char* value);          // value constructor
    String(const String& original);     // copy constructor
    ~String();                          // destructor
    String& operator=(const String& rhs); // copy-assignment operator
    const char* str() const;

    /* C++11 (to be added later)
    String(String&& expiring) noexcept;   // move constructor
    String& operator=(String&& expiring); // move-assignment operator
    */
};
```

Perhaps the best way to unpack the C++03 class definition of String in the code snippet above is to define its members in order of declaration in a corresponding .cpp file, realizing, of course, that all but the definition of the **static** data member, s_empty, would most likely be moved to the .h file as **inline** functions:

```
// my_string.cpp:
#include <my_string.h>   // Component header is routinely included first.
#include <cstddef>       // std::size_t
#include <cstring>       // std::memcpy, std::strlen
#include <cassert>       // standard C assert macro

const char String::s_empty[1] = {'\0'};  // const needs explicit initialization.
```

The static helper, dupStr, provides a factored implementation to create a copy of a *nonempty* null-terminated string. Note that, although this function would work on an empty string, our object invariant is that all empty strings are represented by the sentinel, s_empty, thus avoiding any gratuitous memory allocation:

```
const char* String::dupStr(const char* str)
{
    assert(str && *str);                     // strs are expected to be nonempty.
    std::size_t capacity = strlen(str) + 1;  // Calculate capacity.
    char* tmp = new char[capacity];          // Allocate memory.
    memcpy(tmp, str, capacity);              // Copy all chars through final '\0'.
    return tmp;                              // Return duplicate of str.
}
```

Our deliberate choice to avoid coupling the clean implementation of dupStr with the s_empty sentinel above — and thereby further reduce the amount of repetitive source code — allows us to express explicitly and more precisely detailed design and coding decisions that are generally applicable. For example, calling dupStr on either a null pointer value, e.g., 0, or an empty string, e.g., "", is **out of contract** and, in a debug build, would be flagged as an error. Given a defect-free implementation of String, however, this assertion can never be triggered as it is a *manifestly* **defensive check**.

With these *independent* primitive utilities in hand, we are now ready to implement the client-facing interface. The simplest and most straightforward member function is the default constructor, which simply installs the sentinel, s_empty, as its string value:

```
String::String() : d_str_p(s_empty) { }  // Set d_str_p to null value.
```

We say that the object is effectively set to a "null" value internally because s_empty, although not literally a null pointer value, consumes no dynamic-memory resources; externally, however, it represents efficiently an empty string value ("").

Next let's consider the value constructor, which allocates memory only when the supplied string buffer is neither a null pointer value (0) nor empty (""):

```
String::String(const char* value)
    // Value constructor allocates only if nonempty and then exactly as needed.
{
    if (!value || !*value)        // if value is null or empty
    {
```

```
        d_str_p = s_empty;          // no dynamic memory allocation
    }
    else                            // not empty
    {
        d_str_p = dupStr(value);    // allocated copy
    }
}
```

If the supplied `value` is either a null pointer value or an empty string, the `sentinel` is stored; otherwise, our trusty `dupStr` function will dynamically allocate and populate an appropriately sized **char** array to be managed by the `String` object going forward.

Next, let's consider what it means to copy construct a `String` object from another. In this case, we know that the internal representation of the other string cannot be a null address or even a dynamically allocated empty string; `d_str_p` holds either the `sentinel`, `s_empty`, or else a nonempty dynamically allocated string:

```
String::String(const String& original)
    // Copy constructor allocates exactly what's needed.
{
    if (s_empty == original.d_str_p)        // if original is null
    {
        d_str_p = s_empty;                  // no dynamic allocation
    }
    else                                    // not empty
    {
        d_str_p = dupStr(original.d_str_p); // allocated copy
    }
}
```

If the original object is *null*, then so too will be a copy; otherwise, a new resource will be allocated via `dupStr` to be managed by this object.

The destructor needs to deallocate when the object being managed isn't *null*:

```
String::~String()
    // Destructor deallocates only if needed.
{
    if (s_empty != d_str_p) // if not null
    {
        delete[] d_str_p;       // deallocate dynamic memory
    }
}
```

Thus, an empty `String` object, or an array thereof, requires no allocation on construction and no corresponding deallocation on destruction.

By far the most complex of the special member functions to implement explicitly is the copy-assignment operator. First, we must guard against classic aliasing in which the source and the destination of the assignment refer to the same object, or, if it is a possibility with the type in question, overlapping parts of the same object; in such cases, no state change is indicated. Second, we must secure any needed resources; that way, if an exception is thrown (e.g., due to being out of available memory), the destination will be unaffected. Third, we can now proceed to deallocate any resource currently managed by the object. Fourth, we install the new resource into the destination object. Fifth, we must remember to return a reference to the destination object:

```
String& String::operator=(const String& rhs)
    // Copy-assignment operator deallocates and allocates if and as needed.
{
    if (&rhs != this)                   // (1) Avoid assignment to self.
    {
        const char* tmp;                // (2) Hold preallocated resource.

        if (s_empty == rhs.d_str_p)     // If the rhs string is null,
        {
            tmp = s_empty;              // make this string null too.
        }
        else                            // rhs string is not empty.
        {
            tmp = dupStr(rhs.d_str_p);  // allocated copy
        }

        if (s_empty != d_str_p)         // (3) If this object isn't null,
        {
            delete[] d_str_p;           // deallocate storage.
        }

        d_str_p = tmp;                  // (4) Assign the resource.
    }

    return *this;                       // (5) lvalue reference
}
```

The comparatively greater complexity of copy assignment derives, in part, from there being two objects involved, either of which might be managing dynamically allocated memory resources. Implementing assignment operations becomes even more challenging in the presence of locally supplied memory allocators.[18] Again, to ensure exception safety (in this case, the **strong guarantee**), we must *always* remember to allocate any new resource before modifying the state of the destination object.

One last function needed to complete the example is the **str** accessor, which affords direct, efficient access to a *null*-terminated string representing the value managed by a **String** object:

---

[18]lakos17a, lakos17b, lakos19, halpern20

```
const char* String::str() const { return d_str_p; }
    // Value accessor returns null-terminated string with maximal efficiency.
```

Note that much of the prep work that was done already was in anticipation of making the implementation of this accessor function as streamlined and runtime efficient as possible, e.g., no conditional branching on each access.

The C++03 example above was written in a style that is consistent with sound C++03 design. We can, for example, create a large array of empty strings without having to separately allocate dynamic memory for each element:

```
String a[10000] = {};  // allocates no dynamic memory
```

```
static_assert(sizeof a == sizeof(char*) * 10000,"");
```

For a fixed-size array, we're in good shape; we'll allocate memory if and when we want to install a nonempty string. For a dynamically growing container, however, substantial runtime inefficiencies can manifest. For example, suppose we create an empty `std::vector<String>` object, `vs`, and then append, using `push_back`, five nonempty `String` objects having, say, values `"a"`, `"bb"`, `"ccc"`, `"dddd"`, and `"eeeee"`. In the end, the `vector` will hold five string elements in contiguous memory. Assuming geometric growth, the process of growing the initially empty `vector` to its final state requires allocating successively larger chunks of memory (e.g., 1, 2, 4, 8, ...) as measured in the size of the footprint of the contained element.

Each time we append a nonempty `String` element, a separate block of memory will necessarily be allocated dynamically to represent its value. Hence, a minimum of five memory allocations will be required irrespective of the `std::vector`'s growth strategy. When we combine these two separate allocation needs, one might reason that only nine separate blocks need be allocated: the five allocations to represent the individual string values and four more allocations to hold successively larger blocks until a block size sufficient to hold five elements is reached — e.g., $0 \rightarrow 1$, $1 \rightarrow 2$, $2 \rightarrow 4$, and $4 \rightarrow 8$. Without **move semantics**, however, the number of allocations required (e.g., in C++03) is 21.

To illustrate the copious allocations that ensue when a non-move-enabled, allocating type is stored in an `std::vector`, we have annotated in `test1` the bytes allocated (positive) and deallocated (negative) with each successive operation. For concreteness, we are assuming 8-byte char pointers, which dictate the footprint size of our `String` object. What's more, objects are *always* destroyed in reverse order of their construction. With respect to elements in an `std::vector`, the order of element destruction is **implementation defined**.[19] Here, we show their destruction from lowest to highest index:

---

[19]Note that libstdc++ 6.0.29 (c. 2021) destroys objects from lowest to highest index while libc++ 14 (c. 2021) does so from highest to lowest. For a built-in array or an `std::array`, however, the elements are proper subobjects that are required to be constructed from lowest to highest index; hence, destruction of these elements would always be from highest to lowest index.

```
#include <my_string.h>
#include <vector>          // std::vector

void test1() // using C++03's vector::push_back with C++03 String
{
    std::vector<String> vs;  // no dynamic allocation or deallocation
    vs.push_back("a");       // 2 8 2 -2
    vs.push_back("bb");      // 3 16 3 2 -2 -8 -3
    vs.push_back("ccc");     // 4 32 4 2 3 -2 -3 -16 -4
    vs.push_back("dddd");    // 5 5 -5
    vs.push_back("eeeee");   // 6 64 6 2 3 4 5 -2 -3 -4 -5 -32 -6
} // -2 -3 -4 -5 -6 -64
```

In the `test1` function above, an empty `std::vector`, `vs`, is created without any memory being allocated dynamically. The first time we "push back" a value, `"a"`, a temporary `String` object is constructed, requiring an allocation of 2 bytes. The vector `vs` is then resized from a capacity of zero to one, allocating 8 bytes on a 64-bit platform, and then the temporary `String` is copy constructed into this dynamic array of one element, requiring another 2 bytes to be allocated. When the original temporary is destroyed, those two bytes are reclaimed (-2 bytes).

Adding a second string, `"bb"`, to `vs` requires a reallocation by `std::vector` to a capacity of two `String` objects (16 bytes). So, altogether, appending `"a"` will require allocating four separate blocks of dynamic memory: 3 bytes for a temporary to hold `"bb"`, 16 bytes for the new capacity, 3 bytes to copy construct the temporary into the array, and 2 bytes to copy over the `String` representing `"a"`. After that, the original string holding `"a"` in the array of smaller capacity is destroyed (-2 bytes), the old capacity is deallocated (-8 bytes), and the original temporary used to "push back" the `"bb"` value is destroyed (-3 bytes).

Adding `"ccc"` is again similar. However, adding `"dddd"` is different in that, for the first time, there is sufficient capacity in the array *not* to have to resize. The temporary `String` needed to hold `"dddd"` is created (5 bytes), it is copied into the vector (5 bytes), and the temporary is then destroyed (-5 bytes). Adding `"eeeee"` is analogous to adding `"ccc"`.

Finally, when `vs` goes out of scope, there are five calls to the `String` destructor, each requiring a deallocation, plus a call to the destructor of `std::vector`, deallocating the 64-byte-capacity buffer stored within.

The excessive cost due to copying results from two distinct causes: (1) having to construct a temporary string object before copying it into the vector and (2) having to copy each string from the old-capacity buffer to the new one each time the vector is resized.

As of C++11, the Standard Library version of `std::vector` provides a more efficient member function, `emplace_back`, that makes use of forwarding references (see Section 2.1. "Forwarding References" on page 377) to construct the string only once *in place*, thus reducing the number of allocations resulting from constructing just the `String` objects from 17 to 12 (21 to 16 overall):

```
void test2() // using C++11's vector::emplace_back with C++03 String
{
    std::vector<String> vs;     // no dynamic allocation or deallocation
    vs.emplace_back("a");       // 8 2
    vs.emplace_back("bb");      // 16 3 2 -2 -8
    vs.emplace_back("ccc");     // 32 4 2 3 -2 -3 -16
    vs.emplace_back("dddd");    // 5
    vs.emplace_back("eeeee");   // 64 6 2 3 4 5 -2 -3 -4 -5 -32
} // -2 -3 -4 -5 -6 -64
```

But the real win comes from adding the two missing move operations to the C++03 version of class `String` without changing a single character in the existing class members. Note the *essential* use of **noexcept** following the parameter list in the move constructor, which enables `std::vector` to choose to *move* rather than *copy*; see Section 3.1."**noexcept** Specifier" on page 1085:

```
String::String(String&& expiring) noexcept
    // Move constructor never allocates or deallocates.
  : d_str_p(expiring.d_str_p)      // Assign address of expiring's resource.
{
    expiring.d_str_p = s_empty;  // expiring is now null but valid/empty.
}
```

The *move* constructor above never allocates or deallocates memory; instead, it simply propagates whatever resource was employed by the *expiring* source to the destination. Then, to establish unique ownership by the destination, the address of the **sentinel** value, s_empty, is used to overwrite the previous address in the expiring source.

The move-assignment operator, not necessary for this demonstration, is again somewhat more involved in that it must (1) guard against move assignment to self, (2) ensure that the resource is deallocated if the destination is managing a nonempty string, (3) assign the `expiring` object's resource to the destination object, (4) unconditionally overwrite the previous resource with the empty-string **sentinel**, and (5) always return an lvalue, not an rvalue, reference to the destination object:

```
String& String::operator=(String&& expiring) noexcept
    // Move-assignment operator never allocates; deallocates if necessary.
{
    if (&expiring != this)           // (1) Avoid assignment to self.
    {
        if (s_empty != d_str_p)      // (2) If this object isn't null,
        {
            delete[] d_str_p;        // deallocate dynamic storage.
        }

        d_str_p = expiring.d_str_p;  // (3) Assign address of expiring's resource.
```

```
    expiring.d_str_p = s_empty;  // (4) expiring is now null but valid/empty.
}

    return *this;                // (5) lvalue reference
}
```

Note that, although not strictly necessary, we have chosen to provide the **noexcept** specifier here because this operation (1) does not and never will throw, (2) has a **wide contract**, and (3) being **noexcept** provides some collateral value. Affording the **strong exception safety guarantee** is often predicated on using a **noexcept** operator (see Section 2.1."**noexcept** Operator" on page 615) to query the exception specification of both the **move constructor** and **move assignment operator**. Moreover, the **move assignment operator** is among the few functions whose **noexcept** status might affect compile-time algorithmic selection in generic code (**move construction** and swap being the other two).

As a brief aside, if our **move assignment operator** for `String` might (now or someday) throw and hence were not declared **noexcept**, the **move assignment operation** of, say, an **aggregate** involving our type won't provide the **strong exception safety guarantee** even though our `String` type does. Consider an aggregate type, e.g., A, containing two `String` objects, d_x and d_y:

```
#include <utility>  // std::move

struct A { String d_x, d_y; };  // aggregate class containing two String objects

void f(A& a, A& b)  // function performing move assignment
{
    a = std::move(b);  // Move assign value of b to object a.
}
```

If `b.d_x` is successfully moved but moving `b.d_y` throws, then we will end up with `b` in a half-moved-from state and `a` in a half-overwritten state as the exception leaves `f`.

Note, however, that the **noexcept** specifier is not always appropriate for **move assignment**. A potentially allocating **move assignment operator**, such as any that might copy on a change of allocator, would provide the alternate runtime-checkable guarantee: "If my allocator is changing, I will copy and potentially throw; otherwise, I will move and not throw." Such a guarantee would allow a compound object endeavoring to provide the **strong guarantee** to determine beforehand (at run time) whether *all* subobjects are capable of moving without throwing and, if so, choose to *move* them or else fall back on *copy* operations; see Section 3.1. "**noexcept** Specifier" on page 1085.

Now that the `String` class has been properly augmented with the two missing C++11 move operations (**move construction**, in particular), the number of allocations resulting from constructing just `String` objects under the same **test2** goes from 12 to 5 (16 to 9 overall), where the 5 allocations result from constructing each unique object from its literal string value exactly once. Importantly, allocation and deallocation resulting from copying elements from the old to the new storage in the `std::vector<String>` are eliminated entirely:

```
void test2() // using C++11's vector::emplace_back with C++11 String
{
    std::vector<String> vs;      // no dynamic allocation or deallocation
    vs.emplace_back("a");        // 8 2
    vs.emplace_back("bb");       // 16 3 -8
    vs.emplace_back("ccc");      // 32 4 -16
    vs.emplace_back("dddd");     // 5
    vs.emplace_back("eeeee");    // 64 6 -32
}  // -2 -3 -4 -5 -6 -64
```

The use of the **noexcept** specifier in the implementation of the move constructor is essential because of the **strong exception-safety guarantee** promised by the Standard when inserting or emplacing an element at the end of an `std::vector`; see Section 2.1."**noexcept** Operator" on page 615. It will turn out that, once our `String` class is outfitted with a *move* constructor, the rvalue reference of `vector::push_back` will avoid the dynamic allocation and deallocation of a copy, substituting just a single additional *move* operation; `vector::emplace_back` avoids even that tiny overhead.

Finally, the design of a class that supports *move* operations follows from the general idea that construction of an empty container should be inexpensive (i.e., not require memory allocation), as was done here. One could imagine making other trade-offs that would simplify the implementation at the expense of necessitating that every *valid* object maintains allocated resources, which would undermine a primary advantage of *move* operations, i.e., faster copy operations. For move operations to be both efficient and generally applicable, it is essential that the object has at least one valid state that does not require it to be managing external resources; see *Potential Pitfalls — Requiring owned resources to be valid* on page 803.

Creating a high-level VST   Implementing move operations for higher-level types, such as aggregates, that merely comprise other move-enabled types is fairly straightforward when compared with lower-level types that manage resources explicitly. Because the resources are managed independently by the move-operation-enabled base class and/or member subobjects themselves, all that's required is to ensure that those move operations are employed.

In the numbered list that follows, we will examine eight variants of a UDT that comprises two independent strings, `firstName` and `lastName`, describing a person. We start with the implicit definitions of all **special member functions** (i.e., `Person`, in item 1 below), followed by adding a value constructor (`Person2`), and then adding each of six **special member functions** (`Person3` through `Person8`).

1. No special member functions are **user provided**. For this application, there is no special constraint between the two string data members, and we will want to provide *write* as well as *read* access to each member unless the object of that class is itself **const** or accessed via a **const** pointer or reference. We will therefore elect to implement our class as a **struct** having two public data members of a **regular**, value-semantic type, such as `std::string`, that manages its own resources. For concreteness of exposition,

however, we will use the `String` class developed in *Creating a low-level value-semantic type (VST)* on page 742:

```
struct Person  // C++03 and C++11 aggregate type
{
    String firstName;
    String lastName;
};
```

The `Person` class above does not declare any explicit constructors of its own, yet it can be **default constructed** and **braced initialized** (see Section 2.1."Braced Init" on page 215):

```
Person w1;                                  // w1 holds { "", "" }.
Person x1 = {};                             // x1 holds { "", "" }.
Person y1 = { "Slava" };                    // y1 holds { "Slava", "" }.
Person z1 = { "Alisdair", "Meredith" };     // z1 holds { "Alisdair", "Meredith" }.
```

Note that, in the code sample above, `w1` is **default initialized** by an implicitly generated default constructor, whereas `x1`, `y1`, and `z1` follow the rules of **aggregate initialization**; see Section 2.1."Braced Init" on page 215.

Once constructed, the individual members of a `Person` object can be manipulated directly:

```
void test1()
{
    w1.firstName = "Vittorio";   // OK, w1 holds { "Vittorio", "" }.
    w1.lastName = "Romeo";       // OK, w1 holds { "Vittorio", "Romeo" }.
}
```

Moreover, a `Person` object, as a whole, can be both **copy constructed** and **copy assigned** via its corresponding, implicitly generated **special member functions**:

```
void test2()
{
    Person x(z1);  // x holds { "Alisdair", "Meredith" }; z1 is unchanged.
    x = w1;        // x now holds { "Vittorio", "Romeo" }; w1 is unchanged.
}                  // x destroys both of its member objects as it leaves scope.
```

What's more, when a `Person` object, e.g., `x` in `test2` above, leaves scope, its respective members are destroyed by its implicitly generated **destructor**. That is, a C++03 aggregate that comprises objects that individually support all of the needed special member functions will tacitly make the corresponding operations available to the overall aggregate type.

To update the `Person` object to support **move operations**, there is literally nothing to do. Provided that each member (and base) subobject supports the desired move operations for itself (as we know to be the case for `String` objects), the compiler generates them implicitly for the `Person` **struct** as well:

```
#include <utility> // std::move

void test3()
{
    Person p(z1);               // p holds { "Alisdair", "Meredith" }.
                                // z1 still holds { "Alisdair", "Meredith" }.

    Person q(std::move(p));     // q holds { "Alisdair", "Meredith" }.
                                // p might now hold { "", "" }.

    p = std::move(q);           // p now holds { "Alisdair", "Meredith" }.
                                // q might now hold { "", "" }.
}
```

The example above demonstrates that moving from an object that has been explicitly designated as **expiring** enables the `Person` class to, in turn, *allow* its members to steal resources from the corresponding individual members of the other object during both move construction and move assignment. The result is just a more efficient copy provided that we no longer rely on knowing the value of the moved-from object.

With respect to the specific state of moved-from `String` data members of a `Person`, the example code above — though illustrative of what we know to be the currently implemented behavior of our own `String` — would not necessarily be true of another string type, e.g., the vendor-supplied implementation of `std::string`, or even a future version of `String`; see *Potential Pitfalls — Inconsistent expectations on moved-from objects* on page 794.

Although pure **aggregate types** often suffice, we might sometimes find that we need to augment such an **aggregate type** with one or more **user-provided special member functions** or other constructors; doing so, however, might affect the implicit generation of other such functions and/or strip the type of its **aggregate type** status.

In what follows, we will proceed to add a **value constructor** (see item 2) followed by each of the six **special member functions** in turn (see items 3–8). After adding each function, we will observe the consequences of having added it and then default back whatever was removed. We will repeat this process until all of the missing functionality is restored. The process provides insight into the deeper meaning embedded in Hinnant's **special-member-function** table (see page 44) in Section 1.1. "Defaulted Functions" on page 33.

2. **User-provided value constructor.** As it stands now, there is no **value constructor** that takes the two member values and constructs a `Person` object:

```
Person nonGrata("John", "Lakos");  // Error, no matching constructor
```

Suppose we want to make it possible for a person class, e.g., `Person2`, to be constructed in this way. We will, at a minimum, need to provide a **value constructor** for that purpose:

```
struct Person2  // We want to add a value constructor.
{
    String firstName;
    String lastName;

    Person2(const char* first, const char* last)  // value constructor
    : firstName(first), lastName(last) { }
};
```

By adding this **value constructor** in the example above, we necessarily suppress the implicit declaration of the **default constructor**. Moreover, a class having a **user-provided** constructor of any kind is automatically no longer considered an **aggregate**; see Section 2.1."Braced Init" on page 215:

```
Person2 w2("John", "Lakos");            // OK, invokes value constructor
Person2 x2;                             // Error, no default constructor
Person2 y2 = { "Vittorio" };            // Error, no longer an aggregate
Person2 z2 = { "Vittorio", "Romeo" };   // OK, calls value ctor as of C++11
```

As the example above illustrates, we can now **direct-initialize** w2 via the new, user-provided value constructor, but there is now no implicitly declared default constructor for x2. Since Person2 is no longer considered an aggregate, we cannot use **aggregate initialization** to initialize (in this case, just some of) the members of y2. C++11, however, extends what can be done via braced initialization and thus allows this value constructor to be invoked; see Section 2.1."Braced Init" on page 215 and also Section 2.1."initializer_list" on page 553.

Still, we would like a way to somehow support the functionality provided by the implicit implementation of all *six* of the C++11 **special member functions**. Fortunately, C++11 offers a companion feature that allows us to declare and default the compiler-generated implementation of each special member function explicitly (see Section 1.1. "Defaulted Functions" on page 33):

```
struct Person2a  // We want to add a value constructor (Revision a).
{
    String firstName;
    String lastName;

    Person2a(const char* first, const char* last)  // value constructor
    : firstName(first), lastName(last) { }

    // New here in Person2a.
    Person2a() = default;                           // default constructor
};
```

Notice that Person2a differs from Person2 in the earlier example only in the addition of a *defaulted* default constructor on the final line of its class definition, thus restoring default construction but not aggregate initialization:

```
Person2a w2a("John", "Lakos");            // OK, invokes value constructor
Person2a x2a;                             // OK, invokes default constructor
Person2a y2a = { "Vittorio" };            // Error, still not an aggregate
Person2a z2a = { "Vittorio", "Romeo" };   // OK, calls value ctor as of C++11
```

Adding *any* nonspecial constructor would have the same effect on the implicit generation of the six special member functions, which in this case was to suppress implicit generation of only the **default constructor**. This sort of suppressive behavior invites the question, what effect does explicitly declaring the **default constructor** have on other special functions, e.g., **move construction**? The answer in this specific case is none, but that's the exception; the ultimate answer for each of the other five special member functions is elucidated in items 3–8.

3. User-provided default constructor. We might, at times, need to augment an **aggregate** with one or more **user-provided special member functions**, e.g., for debugging or logging purposes, that would *not* alter how we would have the compiler generate the remaining ones.

   Suppose that, for whatever reason, we'd like to add some metrics-gathering code to the **default constructor** of our original, **aggregate Person** class; we'll call this modified class **Person3**:

```
struct Person3  // We want to employ a user-provided default constructor.
{
    String firstName;
    String lastName;

    Person3() { /* user-provided */ }  // default constructor
};
```

   No other **special member function** is affected, but because we have provided a non-default implementation of a constructor (namely, the **default constructor**), the class is no longer an aggregate:

```
Person3 w3("abc", "def");     // Error, no value constructor is provided.
Person3 x3;                   // OK, invokes user-provided default ctor
Person3 y3 = { "abc" };       // Error, not an aggregate and no 1-arg ctor
Person3 z3 = { "abc", "def" };  // Error, not an aggregate and no value ctor
```

4. User-provided destructor. More typically, augmenting an **aggregate** with a **user-provided special member function** will suppress the implicit generation of others. In such cases, we can apply the same = **default** approach used in item 2 to automatically generate the default implementations of those special member functions that were suppressed.

   A **user-provided destructor**, unlike a **default constructor**, has far-reaching implications on the implicit generation of both **move operations** that, absent thorough unit testing, might go unnoticed and remain latent defects even after being released to production.

Suppose we'd like to add some benign code to the **destructor** of the **aggregate** class
Person and call the new class Person4:

```
struct Person4  // We want to employ a user-provided destructor.
{
    String firstName;
    String lastName;

    ~Person4() { /* user-provided */ }  // destructor
};
```

Declaring the destructor suppresses the declaration and implicit generation of both
the **move constructor** and **move-assignment operator** but leaves the object of **aggregate**
type. Absent proper unit testing, the object might appear to work as before, though
it silently *copies* rather than *moves* its subobjects:

```
Person4 x4 = { "abc", "def" };  // OK, still an aggregate
Person4 y4;                     // OK, default constructor is still available.
Person4 z4(std::move(x4));      // Bug, invokes implicit copy constructor
void test4()
{
    y4 = std::move(z4);         // Bug, invokes implicit copy assignment
}
```

Although we can still **aggregate-initialize** (x4) and **default construct** (y4) a Person4
object, no *move* operations are declared, so when we try to **move construct** (z4) or
move assign (y4) a Person4, the corresponding implicitly generated *copy* operations
are invoked automatically instead. The result is that each of the three objects —
x4, y4, and z4 — now manages its own dynamically allocated memory to represent
needlessly the same overall person value, namely, { "abc", "def" }:

```
#include <cstring>  // std::strcmp
#include <cassert>  // standard C assert macro

void test5()
{
    assert(strcmp(x4.firstName.str(), ""));      // Bug, still holds "abc"
    assert(strcmp(y4.firstName.str(), "abc"));   // OK, holds "abc"
    assert(strcmp(z4.firstName.str(), ""));      // Bug, still holds "abc"
}
```

Suppose we now decide to default both of these suppressed **move operations** explicitly
in Person4a:

```
struct Person4a  // adding user-provided destructor (Revision a)
{
    String firstName;
    String lastName;

    ~Person4a() { /* user-provided */ }         // destructor
```

```
    Person4a(Person4a&&) = default;              // move constructor
    Person4a& operator=(Person4a&&) = default;   // move assignment
};
```

By explicitly declaring the **move-assignment operator** to be **defaulted**, we restore that capability but implicitly **delete** (see Section 1.1."Deleted Functions" on page 53) both the copy constructor and copy-assignment operator. By explicitly defaulting the move constructor, however, not only do we implicitly suppress both copy operations, but we also suppress default construction. However, because no constructor has been user-provided (merely defaulting and/or **deleting** them would not be considered user-provided), the overall object remains of **aggregate** type:

```
Person4a x4a = { "abc", "def" }; // OK, still an aggregate
Person4a y4a;                     // Error, default constructor is not declared.
Person4a z4a(x4a);                // Error, copy constructor is deleted.
void test6()
{
    x4a = z4a;                    // Error, copy assignment is deleted.
}
```

Defaulting both copy operations and the **default constructor**, e.g., `Person4b`, restores the type to its previous functionality as a proper aggregate[20]:

```
struct Person4b  // adding a user-provided destructor (Revision b)
{
    String firstName;
    String lastName;

    ~Person4b() { /* user-provided */ }          // destructor

    // already added to Person4a
    Person4b(Person4b&&) = default;              // move constructor
    Person4b& operator=(Person4b&&) = default;   // move assignment

    // new here in Person4b
    Person4b() = default;                        // default constructor
    Person4b(const Person4b&) = default;         // copy constructor
    Person4b& operator=(const Person4b&) = default;  // copy assignment
};
```

To recap, adding the **user-provided destructor** in `Person4` suppressed both **move operations**. Defaulting these **move operations** in `Person4a`, in turn, suppressed both **copy operations** and, because of the **move constructor** specifically, the **default constructor** as well. Defaulting those three operations in `Person4b` restores everything we had in the original `Person` aggregate yet allows us to add benign metrics to a **user-provided destructor** as we see fit.

---

[20]To remain an aggregate in C++20, any defaulted constructors should simply be left undeclared.

5. User-provided copy constructor. Once we understand the consequences of defining our own destructor (e.g., `Person4` in the most recent example), the story behind adding a copy constructor to our original aggregate `Person` class will seem remarkably similar. Rather than repeat that laborious discovery process in all its detail, starting with `Person5` (the original aggregate + the copy constructor, not shown), we'll instead provide only the end result, namely, `Person5c` with all special member functionality restored:

```
struct Person5c  // adding a user-provided copy constructor
{
    String firstName;
    String lastName;

    Person5c(const Person5c& original)              // copy constructor
    : firstName(original.firstName)
    , lastName(original.lastName) { /* user-provided */ }

    // already added to Person5a (not shown)
    Person5c() = default;                           // default constructor

    // already added to Person5b (not shown)
    Person5c(Person5c&&) = default;                 // move constructor
    Person5c& operator=(Person5c&&) = default;      // move assignment

    // new here in Person5c
    Person5c& operator=(const Person5c&) = default; // copy assignment
};
```

Though we don't show the revisions to `Person5`, `Person5a`, and `Person5b` in the example above, we'll walk through those changes. The class necessarily forfeits its aggregate status in the first revision to `Person`, namely, `Person5a`, by user-providing a copy constructor or a constructor of any kind. What's more, explicitly declaring a copy constructor (in any way) suppresses implicit generation of the default constructor. Hence, any unit test expecting to construct the newly augmented person object using either a default constructor or aggregate initialization will not compile.

By defaulting the default constructor in `Person5a`, we regain the ability to compile our unit test driver and can now observe that, by having declared the copy constructor explicitly, we had suppressed both move construction and move assignment, thus introducing a potentially latent performance defect. Defaulting the two move operations in `Person5b` restores their respective move capabilities. Defaulting move assignment in particular, however, now causes copy assignment to be implicitly deleted; see Section 1.1."Deleted Functions" on page 53.

Finally, by defaulting the copy-assignment operator in Person5c (shown in the example above), we regain all of the regular functionality of the original aggregate class, but because of the user-provided copy constructor, Person5c is no longer amenable to aggregate initialization. Note that the destructor is *never* suppressed by the explicit declaration of any other function.

6. User-provided copy-assignment operator. Once we understand the consequences of user-providing a copy constructor (e.g., Person5c in the example in item 4), there are no surprises here. Again, we'll provide, for reference, only the final, transitive result, Person6b:

```
struct Person6b  // adding a user-provided copy-assignment operator
{
    String firstName;
    String lastName;

    Person6b& operator=(const Person6b& rhs)  // copy assignment
    {
        firstName = rhs.firstName;
        lastName  = rhs.lastName;
        return *this;
    }

    // already added to Person6a (not shown)
    Person6b(Person6b&&) = default;            // move constructor
    Person6b& operator=(Person6b&&) = default;  // move assignment

    // new here in Person6b
    Person6b() = default;                      // default constructor
    Person6b(const Person6b&) = default;       // copy constructor
};
```

Again, we've omitted Person6 and Person6a from the example above, but we'll walk through those revisions. Providing a user-defined copy-assignment operator in Person6, unlike providing a copy constructor, leaves the class of aggregate type but similarly suppresses the declaration of both the move constructor and move-assignment operator. Restoring move assignment in Person6a has no further suppressive effects, but restoring move construction in turn suppresses both default construction and copy construction. Class Person6b above provides the same functionality as the original aggregate Person class, i.e., including aggregate initialization, along with the ability to add a benign implementation, affecting no other special-member implementations, to the user-provided copy-assignment operator.

7. User-provided move constructor. Instrumenting a move constructor during development, if just to ensure that it is being called when expected, isn't a bad idea. Again, we will provide the final result and an appropriate analysis of how we got here:

```cpp
struct Person7b  // adding a user-provided move constructor
{
    String firstName;
    String lastName;

    Person7b(Person7b&& expiring)                       // move constructor
    : firstName(std::move(expiring.firstName))
    , lastName (std::move(expiring.lastName)) { /* user-provided */ }

    // already added to Person7a (not shown)
    Person7b() = default;                               // default constructor
    Person7b(const Person7b&) = default;                // copy constructor
    Person7b& operator=(const Person7b&) = default;     // copy assignment

    // new here in Person7b
    Person7b& operator=(Person7b&&) = default;          // move assignment
};
```

First note the use of `std::move` in the user-provided implementation of the **move constructor** in the example above. Recall that a parameter of type rvalue reference (`&&`) is itself an *lvalue*, so `std::move` is *required* to enable a move from such a parameter. Not employing `std::move` would mean that these data members would be individually copied rather than moved. Absent a thorough unit test, such inadvertent, pessimizing omissions might well find their way into widespread use.

In the original enhanced version (`Person7a`, which is not shown in the example), the user-provided move constructor immediately renders the class to be of nonaggregate type. Moreover, both the copy constructor and the copy-assignment operator are deleted, and the default constructor and the move-assignment operator are not implicitly generated. Since there is no way to create an object and then learn that the move-assignment operator is missing (short of knowing, as we do here), the first step is to get the unit test driver to compile, which is accomplished by defaulting the default constructor, copy constructor, and copy-assignment operator in `Person7a`.

After that, our thorough unit tests can observe that what should be move assignment is falling back on copy assignment, which needlessly allocates new resources rather than transferring them when the source is expiring. By now also defaulting the move-assignment operator, we arrive at a class that again has all the regular functionality of the original `Person` class, namely, `Person7b` (shown in the code snippet above), but absent the ability to be aggregate initialized.

8. User-provided move-assignment operator. Instrumenting a move-assignment operator during development, just like a move constructor, can be useful:

```
struct Person8b  // adding a user-provided move-assignment operator
{
    String firstName;
    String lastName;

    Person8b& operator=(Person8b&& expiring)          // move assignment
    {
        firstName = std::move(expiring.firstName);
        lastName  = std::move(expiring.lastName);
        return *this;
    }

    // previously added to Person8a (not shown)
    Person8b(const Person8b&) = default;              // copy constructor
    Person8b& operator=(const Person8b&) = default;   // copy assignment
    Person8b(Person8b&&) = default;                   // move constructor

    // new here in Person8b
    Person8b() = default;                             // default constructor
};
```

Again, we've omitted `Person8` and `Person8a`, but we'll discuss those revisions nonetheless, below. Importantly, let's again note the use of `std::move` in the implementation of the **user-provided move-assignment operator**; without it, the members would instead be *copied* undesirably rather than *moved*. In the original version (`Person8`), the user-provided move-assignment operator results in the deletion of both copy operations as well as the suppression of the implicit declaration of the move constructor. However, unlike the user-provided move constructor, the user-provided move-assignment operator doesn't affect the **aggregate** nature of the overall type nor does it immediately suppress the default constructor.

Since there is neither a copy constructor nor a move constructor available, both omissions would likely show up as compile-time errors in a thorough unit-test suite. By subsequently defaulting all three missing **special member functions** (`Person8a`), we would discover that the defaulting of the copy and move constructors has, in turn, suppressed the implicit declaration of the default constructor.

Finally, by defaulting the default constructor (`Person8b`), we regain all of the original functionality of the aggregate `Person` class including the ability to **aggregate-initialize** it.[21]

In summary: We can create a higher-level, **value-semantic type** (VST) quickly and reliably by combining lower-level ones. These higher-level VSTs can be aggregate initialized, default initialized, copied, and moved as a unit, provided the types of the respective, lower-level base and member subobjects support the needed operations.

---

[21] As with `Person4b`, to remain an **aggregate** in C++20, any defaulted constructors should simply be left undeclared.

Sometimes a user will need to provide a custom implementation of one or more of these special member functions, which might affect implicit generation of other member functions and/or the ability to **aggregate-initialize** the object; see Section 2.1."Braced Init" on page 215.

One might reasonably decide to just explicitly **default** *all* of the remaining **special member functions**, and that works well in most practical cases. Note, however, that, unlike suppression of the **copy operations**, when the **default constructor** or either **move operation** is suppressed by an explicit declaration of some other function, it is left undeclared rather than being *declared* but **deleted**, which in turn can have subtle implications.

Explicitly or implicitly **defaulting** (see Section 1.1."Defaulted Functions" on page 33) or **deleting** (see Section 1.1."Deleted Functions" on page 53) a function ensures that it *is* **declared** and, hence, participates in overload resolution and might affect the outcome of certain compile-time type traits, such as `std::is_literal_type`,[22] which can be found in the standard header `<type_traits>` (see Section 2.1."**constexpr** Functions" on page 257).

Explicitly **defining** a special member function to have the same implementation as would have been generated had that function been declared implicitly will produce the same behavior locally but might affect the outcome of certain type-wide traits such as `std::is_aggregate`, which also can be found in `<type_traits>`.[23]

Creating a generic value-semantic container type   A primary motivation for the introduction of rvalue references into C++11 was the desire to provide ubiquitous, uniform support for a pair of **special member functions**, parallel to the **copy constructor** and the **copy-assignment operator**, that distinguish when it is permissible to *steal* resources from the source object.

In particular, a standard container, such as `std::vector`, that is required to provide the **strong exception-safety guarantee** for public member functions, such as `push_back`, was deemed unacceptably inefficient in C++03. This poor performance occurred when resizing capacity because the **strong guarantee** necessitated copying over all of the original element subobjects only to then immediately (and wastefully) destroy the original ones. The gratuitous copying made necessary to preserve the **strong guarantee** could be sidestepped provided the element-type argument supplied to the **vector** template sports a nonthrowing **move constructor**.

Proper implementation of `std::vector` requires the ability to detect, at compile time, whether the **move constructor** of the specified element type is permitted to throw; a thorough discussion of how to implement robust `std::vector`-like operations, such as `push_back` and `emplace_back`, along with the **strong guarantee** is provided in Section 2.1."**noexcept** Operator" on page 615. Here, we will introduce a simplified, fixed-size-array type to illus-

---

[22]The `std::is_literal_type` type trait is deprecated in C++17 and removed in C++20.

[23]Rule C.20 of the *C++ Core Guidelines* advises, "If you can avoid defining default operations, do." See **stroustrup21**.

trate the straightforward benefits of **rvalue references** while sidestepping distractions arising from the **strong guarantee**, resizing capacity, and local memory allocators.[24]

Let's now consider the class definition for a simple generic container type, `FixedArray<T>`, that provides a minimal set of capabilities to manage a dynamically allocated, "fixed-size" array of elements of type `T`. The implementations of all six special member functions are user-provided, along with an "extra" (**explicit**) *size* constructor, used to set the fixed capacity of the array at construction. Note that only the *copy-* and *move*-assignment operators may change the size and capacity of an existing array object.

Finally, three more member functions are provided to access array elements by index of a non**const** and **const** array, along with a **const** member function to access the array's size. Note that the behavior is undefined unless the user-supplied element index is less than the array size:

```cpp
#include <cstddef>  // std::size_t

template <typename T>
class FixedArray
{
    T*          d_ary_p;  // dynamically allocated array of fixed size
    std::size_t d_size;   // number of elements in dynamically allocated array

public:
    FixedArray();                                     // default constructor
    explicit FixedArray(std::size_t size);            // size constructor
    ~FixedArray();                                    // destructor
    FixedArray(const FixedArray& original);           // copy constructor
    FixedArray& operator=(const FixedArray& rhs);     // copy-assignment
    FixedArray(FixedArray&& expiring) noexcept;       // move constructor
    FixedArray& operator=(FixedArray&& expiring) noexcept;  // move-assignment

    T& operator[](std::size_t index);                 // modifiable element access
    const T& operator[](std::size_t index) const;     // const element access
    std::size_t size() const;                         // number of array elements
};
```

The class definition in the example above — apart from the two C++11 **move operations** — would be the same in C++03. Moreover, we can instantiate and use a `FixedArray` on any VST that supports at least the four classic special member functions:

```cpp
FixedArray<double> ad;        // empty array of double objects
FixedArray<int>    ai(5);     // array of 5 zero-valued int objects

#include <string>             // std::string
FixedArray<std::string> as(10);  // array of 10 empty std::string objects
```

---

[24]A thorough description of the practical use of C++11 **memory allocators** and, especially, C++17 pmr **allocators** is anticipated in **lakos22**.

Note that if the element type supplied for the template parameter, T, does not support C++11 move operations, then neither will the FixedArray<T> container itself.

Let's now consider the implementation, which — apart from the two move operations — is the same as it would have been in C++03. Notably, creating a default-constructed container ideally allocates no resources (if just for performance reasons), and the **size constructor** is deliberately made explicit to avoid inadvertently creating a fixed array via an unexpected implicit conversion from an **int** (see Section 1.1."**explicit** Operators" on page 61):

```
template <typename T>  // default constructor
FixedArray<T>::FixedArray() : d_ary_p(0), d_size(0) { }

template <typename T>                       // size constructor
FixedArray<T>::FixedArray(std::size_t size) : d_size(size)
{
    d_ary_p = size ? new T[size]() : 0;  // value-initialize each element
}
```

When allocating a resource, we always consistently do so using array **new**. Notice that we have deliberately **value-initialized** — i.e., **new** T[size]() — the dynamically allocated array. For an object that has a default constructor, that constructor would be called regardless; for scalar or user-defined **aggregate** types, failing to value-initialize — i.e., **new** T[size] — could leave the elements, or parts thereof, in an uninitialized state.

Placing **defensive checks** for **object invariants** at the top of the body of a destructor is common because such placement guarantees their execution for every object before it is destroyed:

```
#include <cassert>  // standard C assert macro

template <typename T>  // destructor
FixedArray<T>::~FixedArray()
{
    assert(!d_ary_p == !d_size);  // assert object invariant
    delete[] d_ary_p;             // resource released as an array of T
}
```

Our object invariant for this FixedArray type requires that a memory resource is allocated if and only if the array size is nonzero. Notice also that every allocation is presumed to be allocated by array **new** and never directly, e.g., via **operator new**.

When it comes to **copy construction**, the implementation is mostly straightforward. For exception-safety purposes, we'll use the C++11 library component std::unique_ptr as a **scoped guard**. If the size of the original object is nonzero, we allocate enough memory to hold the requisite number of elements — nothing more — and then proceed to copy assign them one by one; if the original object was empty, then we make this object's resource handle *null* too:

```
#include <memory>  // std::unique_ptr

template <typename T>  // copy constructor
FixedArray<T>::FixedArray(const FixedArray& original) : d_size(original.d_size)
{
    if (d_size)  // if original array is not empty
    {
        std::unique_ptr<T> p(new T[d_size]); // Default-initialize each element.

        for (std::size_t i = 0; i < d_size; ++i)  // for each array element
        {
            p.get()[i] = original.d_ary_p[i];     // Copy-assign value.
        }

        d_ary_p = p.release();  // Release from exception-safety guard.
    }
    else  // else original array is empty
    {
        d_ary_p = 0;  // Make this array null too.
    }
}  // Note that we already set d_size in the initializer list up top.
```

Notice that here we have allocated the array using **default initialization** to minimize unnecessary initializations prior to copy assigning them. In a more efficient implementation, we might consider using **operator new** directly and then copy constructing each object in place, but we would then need to destroy each element in a loop as well where we currently use **operator delete[]**; see Section 2.1."**noexcept** Operator" on page 615. What's more, we could even check whether the element type is **trivially copyable** and, if so, use memcpy instead; see Section 2.1."Generalized PODs '11" on page 401.

As ever, copy assignment inherently has the most complex implementation of all the special member functions. First we must guard against assignment to self. If the two objects are not the same size, then we will need to make them so. If the target object holds a resource, we'll need to free it before allocating another. Once the two resources are the same size, we'll need to copy the elements over:

```
template <typename T>  // copy-assignment operator
FixedArray<T>& FixedArray<T>::operator=(const FixedArray& rhs)
{
    if (&rhs != this)  // guard against self-aliasing
    {
        if (d_size != rhs.d_size)  // If sizes differ, make this same as other.
        {
            if (d_ary_p)  // If this array was not null, clear it.
            {
```

```
                delete[] d_ary_p;  // Release resource as an array of T.
                d_ary_p = 0;       // Make null. (Note size isn't yet updated.)
                d_size  = 0;       // Make empty. (Reestablish obj. invariant.)
            }

            assert(!d_ary_p == !d_size);  // Assert object invariant.
            d_ary_p = new T[rhs.d_size];  // Default-initialize each element.
            d_size  = rhs.d_size;         // Make this size same as rhs size.
        }

        assert(d_size == rhs.d_size);  // The two sizes are now the same.

        for (std::size_t i = 0; i < d_size; ++i)  // for each element
        {
            d_ary_p[i] = rhs.d_ary_p[i];  // Copy-assign value.
        }
    }
    return *this;  // lvalue reference to self
}
```

Notice that we (1) released any current resources assuming that they were allocated using array **new** and (2) deliberately default-initialized each allocated element prior to copy assigning to it. Also notice that we have introduced two **defensive checks** in the middle of our implementation to serve as "active commentary" to state that, no matter how we got here, either what is asserted is **true** or else the program itself is defective.

Let's now turn to what is new in C++11. Unlike other containers that store their elements in their footprint, such as std::array, that require moving the individual elements from one region of memory to the other, this FixedVector will simply transfer ownership of the entire block from one object to the other. Hence, we will not need to **#include** the standard header that defines std::move, namely, <utility>. To implement the **move constructor**, we'll use the member-initializer list to copy the size and address of the resource to the object. After that, we'll just assign those values to render the source object *null*, i.e., managing no resources, as if it had just been **default constructed**:

```
template <typename T>      // move constructor
FixedArray<T>::FixedArray(FixedArray&& expiring) noexcept
 : d_size(expiring.d_size)
 , d_ary_p(expiring.d_ary_p)
{
    expiring.d_ary_p = 0;  // Relinquish ownership.
    expiring.d_size  = 0;  // Reestablish object invariant.
}
```

In this case, we always know that the value of a moved-from FixedArray object will be empty, but see *Potential Pitfalls — Inconsistent expectations on moved-from objects* on page 794.

Next, we consider **move assignment**. We must, as ever, first check for assignment to self. If not, we unconditionally delete our resource, knowing that it is a no-op if the resource handle is *null*. We then copy over the resource address and size from `expiring` and restore `expiring` to its default-constructed state:

```
template <typename T>          // move-assignment operator
FixedArray<T>& FixedArray<T>::operator=(FixedArray&& expiring) noexcept
{
    if (&expiring != this)  // Guard against self-aliasing.
    {
        delete[] d_ary_p;  // Release resource from this obj. as array of T.
        d_ary_p = expiring.d_ary_p;  // Copy address of resource.
        d_size  = expiring.d_size;   // Copy size of resource.
        expiring.d_ary_p = 0;        // Make expiring relinquish ownership.
        expiring.d_size  = 0;        // Re-establish object invariants in expiring.
    }

    return *this;  // Return lvalue (not rvalue) reference to self.
}
```

Note that the **move-assignment operator** takes an rvalue reference but, like its copy-assignment counterpart, returns an lvalue reference.

Finally, for completeness, we show the three methods to access the modifiable and **const** elements and the size of the array, respectively:

```
template <typename T>                           // modifiable element access
T& FixedArray<T>::operator[](std::size_t index)
{
    assert(index < d_size);  // Assert precondition.
    return d_ary_p[index];   // Return lvalue reference to modifiable element.
}

template <typename T>                           // const element access
const T& FixedArray<T>::operator[](std::size_t index) const
{
    assert(index < d_size);  // Assert precondition.
    return d_ary_p[index];   // Return lvalue reference to const element.
}

template <typename T>                           // number of array elements
std::size_t FixedArray<T>::size() const { return d_size; }
```

Note that the functionality provided by each of the three member functions above is entirely independent of the augmented functionality afforded by the two **move-semantic special member** functions, the **move constructor**, and the **move-assignment operator**.

For an industrial-strength implementation example involving a `push_back` operation overloaded on rvalue reference for an `std::vector`, see Section 2.1."**noexcept** Operator" on page 615.

Move-only types

It is sometimes useful for a class to represent **unique ownership** of a particular noncopyable resource. Without intrinsic copyability, the standard copy operations would not make sense. In such cases, implementing only the move operations provides a way to ensure that only one object retains ownership of the resource at any given time. Provided that typical use of such types does not involve being referenced (e.g., from external data structures), move operations can be useful for transporting the internal state of object that is inherently noncopyable, but see *Potential Pitfalls — Making a noncopyable type movable without just cause* on page 788.

For example, `std::thread`, introduced in C++11, represents an underlying operating system thread. There is no way to create a second copy of a running operating system thread, and it would be significantly unintuitive if `std::thread` objects could be easily copied when the underlying resource was not going to be duplicated. On the other hand, since an `std::thread` is primarily a handle to the underlying resource, its own identity does not need to be set in stone, so moving that handle to a different instance of `std::thread` is natural. This objective is accomplished by defining a **move constructor** and then deleting the **copy constructor**; see Section 1.1."Deleted Functions" on page 53 and Section 3.1."**noexcept** Specifier" on page 1085:

```
class thread
{
    // ...
    thread() noexcept;
    thread(thread&& other) noexcept;
    thread(const thread&) = delete;  // This line is optional.
    // ...
};
```

Note that supplying a **move operation** will implicitly delete both the **copy constructor** and copy-assignment operator; see Section 1.1."Defaulted Functions" on page 33.

To transfer the ownership of a thread, we must use `std::move`:

```
#include <thread>    // std::thread
#include <iostream>  // std::cout
#include <utility>   // std::move

void test1()
{
    std::thread t{[] { std::cout << "hello!"; }};
    std::thread tCopy  = t;             // Error, cannot copy
    std::thread tMoved = std::move(t);  // OK
}
```

If we want to transfer the ownership of the thread to another `std::thread` object, we are forced to explicitly convert t to an rvalue reference. By using `std::move` we communicate to the compiler and to those reading the code that a new object will now assume ownership of the underlying operating system resource and that the old object will be put into an empty state.

A related type, `std::unique_lock`, exemplifies the ability to move responsibility between objects, specifically the responsibility to release a lock when destroyed. Combining movability with standard **RAII** affords increased flexibility, enabling the passing and returning of a particular responsibility, such as freeing the resource, without the risk of failing to execute it when the unique owner is destroyed:

```
#include <mutex>    // std::mutex, std::unique_lock
#include <cassert>  // standard C assert macro

void test2()
{
    std::mutex m;
    std::unique_lock<std::mutex> ul{m};

    {
        std::unique_lock<std::mutex> ulMoved = std::move(ul);  // OK
    }  // ulMoved destroyed, lock released

    assert(ul.mutex() == nullptr);  // ul is moved-from.
}
```

Finally, the Standard provides `std::unique_ptr` to manage unique ownership of a resource, identified by a pointer, with a compile-time customizable deleter that will be used to free that resource when an `std::unique_ptr` is destroyed without having had its resource moved away. The default (and most common) use for this type is to manage heap-allocated memory, where the default deleter will simply invoke **delete** on the pointer. C++14 also adds a helper utility, `std::make_unique`, that encapsulates heap allocation with **new**:

```
#include <memory>  // std::unique_ptr, std::make_unique

void test3()
{
    std::unique_ptr<int> up1{new int(1)};       // OK, heap alloc #1
    up1 = std::make_unique<int>(2);             // OK, frees #1, new alloc #2

    std::unique_ptr<int> up2 = std::move(up1);  // OK, up2 now owns #2.
    assert( up1 == std::unique_ptr<int>());     // OK, up1 is moved-from.
    assert(*up2 == 2);                          // OK
}  // Destruction of up2 deletes alloc #2; destruction of up1 does nothing.
```

`std:unique_ptr` can be particularly useful when an object that cannot be copied needs to be referenced by an object whose ownership might need to move around. While one pre-C++11 solution to this need might be to dynamically allocate the object and track the object's lifetime with a reference-counted smart pointer (such as `std::tr1::shared_ptr` or boost::shared_ptr), the addition of that tracking incurs additional overhead that might not be warranted. Using std::unique_ptr instead will manage the lifetime of the heap-allocated object correctly, allowing it to remain in a stable location from construction to destruction and letting the client's handle to the object — an std::unique_ptr — move to where it needs to be.

Implementing a move-only type   For general purposes, the standard library templates already capture in a reusable fashion the proper implementation of a move-only type, e.g., std::unique_ptr, but see *Potential Pitfalls — Implementing a move-only type without employing std::unique_ptr* on page 791.

To understand what is involved in such implementations, let's explore how we might implement a subset of the functionality of std::unique_ptr. The declaration of our UniquePtr with no support for custom deleters simply needs to =**delete** the copy constructor and provide the appropriate move constructor and move-assignment operator. Along with the basic accessors to implement a typical **smart pointer**, a complete implementation of a move-only owning pointer is not especially involved:

```
#include <utility>  // std::swap

template <typename T>
class UniquePtr  // simple move-only owning pointer
{
    T* d_ptr_p;  // owned object

public:
    UniquePtr() : d_ptr_p{nullptr} { }          // construct an empty pointer
    UniquePtr(T* p) noexcept : d_ptr_p(p) { } // value ctor, take ownership

    UniquePtr(const UniquePtr&) = delete;       // not copyable

    UniquePtr(UniquePtr&& expiring) noexcept    // move constructor
    : d_ptr_p(expiring.release()) { }

    ~UniquePtr()                                // destructor
    {
        reset();
    }

    UniquePtr& operator=(const UniquePtr&) = delete;    // no copy assignment

    UniquePtr& operator=(UniquePtr&& expiring) noexcept // move assignment
    {
        reset();
        std::swap(d_ptr_p, expiring.d_ptr_p);
        return *this;
    }
```

```
    T& operator*() const          { return *d_ptr_p; }  // dereference
    T* operator->() const noexcept { return d_ptr_p; }   // pointer

    explicit operator bool() const noexcept
    { return d_ptr_p != nullptr; }                       // conversion to bool

    T* release()  // Release ownership of d_ptr_p without deleting it.
    {
        T* p     = d_ptr_p;
        d_ptr_p = nullptr;
        return p;
    }

    void reset()  // Clear the value of this object.
    {
        T* p     = d_ptr_p;
        d_ptr_p = nullptr;
        delete p;
    }
};
```

Note that we could choose to reimplement the **reset** function above by invoking another public member of `UniquePtr`:

```
template <typename T>
void UniquePtr<T>::reset() { delete release(); }  // Invoke public member.
```

We might also choose to reimplement the **release** function using the C++14 library function template `std::exchange`:

```
#include <utility>  // std::exchange

template <typename T>
T* UniquePtr<T>::release() {  return std::exchange(d_ptr_p, nullptr); }  // C++14
```

Even our straightforward implementation can then be used for a variety of purposes. With little overhead, RAII principles can be used for managing heap-allocated objects. `UniquePtr<T>` also meets the requirements for being placed in a standard container, letting it be used to build containers of types that are not themselves eligible to be placed in a container, such as creating an `std::vector` of nonmovable noncopyable objects. Marking the move operations **noexcept** will also allow standard containers to provide the strong exception guarantee even though our `UniquePtr` cannot be copied; see Section 3.1. "**noexcept** Specifier" on page 1085.

Passing around resource-owning objects by value

Passing movable objects by value   Prior to the introduction of move semantics, if we passed objects around by value, we would incur the cost of a lot of copies. With move semantics, this cost might be lower. There are several ways that resource-owning objects can be passed around.

Overload sets consisting of corresponding parameters that are passed by both reference and value, e.g., poor in the example below, are possible, but attempts to invoke such a function can result in overload resolution failures and, hence, are not typically useful in practice:

```cpp
void poor(int);        // (1) pass by nonconst  value
void poor(int&);       // (2) pass by nonconst lvalue reference
void poor(int&&);      // (3) pass by nonconst rvalue reference

void testPoor()
{
    int       i;       //   i is a    modifiable lvalue.
    const int ci = i;  //  ci is a nonmodifiable lvalue.
    int&      ri = i;  //  ri is a    modifiable lvalue reference.
    const int& cri = i; // cri is a nonmodifiable lvalue reference.

    poor(3);    // Error, ambiguous: (1) or (3)
    poor(i);    // Error, ambiguous: (1) or (2)
    poor(ci);   // OK, invokes (1)
    poor(ri);   // Error, ambiguous: (1) or (2)
    poor(cri);  // OK, invokes (1)
}
```

In the next example, we see the benefits of an overload set, e.g., **good** in the example below, that consists of corresponding parameters declared as both a nonmodifiable **lvalue reference** (**const** T&) and a modifiable **rvalue reference** (T&&):

```cpp
struct S // some UDT that might benefit from being "moved"
{
    S();           // default constructor
    S(const S&);   // copy constructor
    S(S&&);        // move constructor
};

int good(const S& s);  // (4) binds to any S object, but with lower priority
int good(S&& s);       // (5) binds to movable S objects with high priority

void testGood()
{
    S       s;         //   s is a    modifiable lvalue.
    const S cs = s;    //  cs is a nonmodifiable lvalue.
    S&      rs = s;    //  rs is a    modifiable lvalue reference.
    const S& crs = s;  // crs is a nonmodifiable lvalue reference.

    good(S());         // OK, invokes (5) - guts of S() available
    good(s);           // OK, invokes (4) - read only
    good(cs);          // OK, invokes (4) - read only
```

```
    good(rs);                    // OK, invokes (4) - read only
    good(crs);                   // OK, invokes (4) - read only
    good(static_cast<S&&>(s));   // OK, invokes (5) - guts of s available
    good(std::move(s));   // OK, invokes (5) as move returns S&&
    good(std::move(cs));  // OK, invokes (4) as move returns const S&&
}
```

In the example code above, we have called function good with six different expressions involving the user-defined type S. Notice that passing anything other than the modifiable *prvalue* S() or the modifiable *xvalue* static_cast<S&&>(s) invokes the overload (4) that accepts the object by **const** lvalue reference, not modifying it. If a copy is needed internally within the function good, it can be made in the usual way using S's *copy* constructor.

If the object being passed is either a *temporary* or an explicitly cast, unnamed *xvalue*, overload (5) is invoked, and the object is passed as a non**const** rvalue reference. If a "copy" is needed internally, it can now be made safely — and *perhaps*[25] more efficiently — using S's *move* constructor. See, however, *Potential Pitfalls — Failure to std::move a named rvalue reference* on page 784.

Let's now consider the alternative of having just one overload (e.g., func) in which a potentially *movable*, e.g., user-defined or generic, type is passed *by value*:

```
template <typename T>
int func(T t);  // (6) single "overload" that binds to any T object

void testFunc()
{
    S       s;       // s is a    modifiable lvalue.
    const S cs = s;  // cs is a nonmodifiable lvalue.
    S&      rs = s;  // rs is a    modifiable lvalue reference.
    const S& crs = s; // crs is a nonmodifiable lvalue reference.

    func(S());                  // OK, invokes (6) - constructed in func
    func(s);                    // OK, invokes (6) - copied into func
    func(cs);                   // OK, invokes (6) - copied into func
    func(rs);                   // OK, invokes (6) - copied into func
    func(crs);                  // OK, invokes (6) - copied into func
    func(static_cast<S&&>(s));  // OK, invokes (6) - moved into func
}
```

A function or function template, such as func in the example above, that accepts a movable object *by value* behaves, in some ways, similarly to the more traditional two-overload set, e.g., good in the previous example. If the object being passed in is a *prvalue* (i.e., a typically

---

[25]When data that is initially proximate in the virtual address space is allowed to *diffuse* due to either deallocation/reallocation or a *move* operation, *locality* of reference can suffer. Depending on the relative frequency with which the moved data is subsequently accessed, overall performance might be served by performing a *copy* instead, even when the *move* operation itself would be faster. We plan to discuss memory allocation and, specifically, *diffusion*, in **lakos22**.

not-yet-constructed **temporary**), it can be constructed *in place* as a local variable with no copy or move overhead at all. If the object is an *xvalue* (i.e., it already exists either as an unnamed *temporary* or as the result of an explicit cast to an unnamed **rvalue reference**), then S's **move constructor** will be invoked to "copy" it. In all other cases, S's **copy constructor** will be invoked. The net result is twofold: (1) From the perspective of the user of **func**, an efficient copy will always be made from the arguments supplied; (2) from the implementer's perspective, a mutable copy for internal use will always be available as an automatic variable.

Passing a potentially movable argument by value to a function, however, is not generally indicated. Even when the **contract** for the function states or implies that a potentially movable argument will necessarily be copied, passing that argument *by value* might incur gratuitous runtime overhead; see *Potential Pitfalls — Sink arguments require copying* on page 782. In cases where it is appropriate, passing specifically a *prvalue* — e.g., just the first call to **func**, in the example above, which passes S() — will cause the object to be constructed within the function itself, thereby avoiding even a *move* operation but has absolutely no runtime performance benefit for any of the other calls where a *glvalue*, i.e., *xvalue* or *lvalue*, is passed.

Passing movable objects *by value*, where applicable, means that only a single function overload need be written. This alternative becomes even more attractive when we consider a function taking multiple movable arguments:

```
int good2(const S&  s1, const S&  s2);  // both passed by const lvalue ref
int good2(const S&  s1,       S&& s2);  // passed by const lvalue, rvalue
int good2(      S&& s1, const S&  s2);  // passed by rvalue, const lvalue
int good2(      S&& s1,       S&& s2);  // both passed by rvalue reference

int func2(      S   s1,       S   s2);  // both passed by value
```

When passing potentially movable objects *by value* is either not applicable or otherwise undesirable, the general approach is to employ forwarding references (see Section 2.1."Forwarding References" on page 377) to preserve the **value category** of the argument through to the implementation:

```
template <typename T1, typename T2, typename T3>
int great3(T1&& t1, T2&& t2, T3&& t3);  // each passed by forwarding reference
```

See *Annoyances — Visual similarity to forwarding references* on page 806.

Return by value   Now that we have covered the ideas behind passing around resource-owning objects by value, we provide more realistic examples of these principles at work.

Our first example illustrates a simple output parameter for a function that creates a temporary filename. We consider two ways in which such a function might be designed. First, we pass in an output argument by address:

```
#include <string>  // std::string

void generateTemporaryFilename(std::string* outPath, const char* prefix)
```

```
{
    char suffix[8];
    // ... Create a unique suffix.

    *outPath = prefix;
    outPath->append(suffix);
}
```

Alternately, we can return an output `std::string` by value:

```
#include <string>    // std::string
#include <cstring>   // strlen

std::string generateTemporaryFilename(const char* prefix)
{
    char suffix[8];
    // ... Create a unique suffix.

    std::string rtnValue;
    rtnValue.reserve(strlen(prefix) + strlen(suffix));
    rtnValue.assign(prefix);
    rtnValue.append(suffix);
    return rtnValue;
}
```

In the first implementation, the caller must create an `std::string` on the stack and pass its address to the function. The second version presents an arguably clearer interface for the caller. In C++03, without move semantics, this second version would have had more allocations and copying, but with **rvalue references** and **move semantics**, there is only a single additional move. This example illustrates where **rvalue references** and move semantics come into effect and enable us to have interfaces that are easier and more natural for many to use but do not incur the often hidden penalties that these patterns can contain; however, see *Potential Pitfalls — Sink arguments require copying* on page 782 and *Potential Pitfalls — Disabling NRVO* on page 783.

In the second version, we always create an `std::string` object to return, which could become a performance issue if we are repeatedly invoking this function. In cases where a function might be called many times in a loop, a much more efficient alternative is to reuse the same capacity in the string.

Sink arguments

A **sink argument** is an argument to a function that will be retained or consumed. Before C++11, it was common to pass **sink arguments** as **const&** and copy them. For example, consider how a class, such as `HttpRequest`, might have been written in C++03:

```
#include <string>   // std::string

class HttpRequest
{
    std::string d_url;

public:
    HttpRequest(const std::string& url) : d_url(url) { }

    // url is a sink argument.
    void setUrl(const std::string& url)
    {
        d_url = url;
    }
};
```

With that interface, even in C++11, if an *rvalue*, e.g., a temporary, is passed, there is no way to avoid a copy. However, we can support move operations for sink arguments to prevent these unnecessary copies, e.g., writing `HttpRequest` another way:

```
#include <string>   // std::string
#include <utility>  // std::move

class HttpRequest
{
    std::string d_url;

public:
    HttpRequest(const std::string& url) : d_url(url) { }  // as before

    HttpRequest(std::string&& url) : d_url(std::move(url)) { }

    void setUrl(const std::string& url)  // as before
    {
        d_url = url;
    }

    void setUrl(std::string&& url)
    {
        d_url = std::move(url);
    }
};
```

In this case, we have provided overloads for rvalue references in the constructor and the `setUrl` function. Having the extra overloads is optimal for users of `HttpRequest`. Note, however, that implementations of both the copy constuctor and `setUrl` are essentially repeated. In addition, this approach can become cumbersome; to provide this behavior in our classes, we have to write 2^N overloads for functions taking N arguments, that is, an overload for each combination of **const** lvalue and **rvalue reference** types for each argument. Reducing code bulk is the motivation for the "pass-by-value and move" idiom:

```cpp
class HttpRequest
{
    std::string d_url;

public:
    HttpRequest(std::string url) : d_url(std::move(url)) { }

    void setUrl(std::string url)
    {
        d_url = std::move(url);
    }
};
```

We achieve close-to-optimal behavior by taking **sink arguments** by value and unconditionally moving them. This idiom adds only the cost of a limited number of move operations per argument over the fully general case with 2^N overloads and, importantly, does not add any extraneous copies.

With this version, if a user passes an *lvalue* to **setUrl**, the *lvalue* will be copied in the **url** argument, and then the argument will be moved into the data member: There will be one copy plus one move. If a user passes an *rvalue* to **setUrl**, the *rvalue* will be moved into the **url** argument, and then the argument will be moved into the data member: There will be two moves. In both cases, there is one more move than would be needed for the multioverload implementation.

The perfect-forwarding solution for **HttpRequest** will produce all possible overloads for qualified parameters at the cost of needing to be a template:

```cpp
#include <utility>  // std::forward

class HttpRequest
{
    std::string d_url;

public:
    template <typename S>
    HttpRequest(S&& url) : d_url(std::forward<S>(url)) { }

    template <typename S>
    void setUrl(S&& url)
    {
        d_url = std::forward<S>(url);
    }
};
```

Importantly, taking a **sink argument** by value will *always* make a copy. When that copy will be retained (such as the initialization of a member variable above), there is no additional cost. When there is a code path where the copy is not retained, this copy becomes unnecessary and, hence, unnecessarily inefficient; see *Potential Pitfalls — Sink arguments require copying* on page 782.

Finally, when we are dealing exclusively with move-only types, such as an std::unique_ptr, there are two ways to pass the argument in a manner that enables its resources to be consumed: (1) by value and (2) by rvalue reference. As previously discussed, passing the argument by value ensures that its resources will be consumed whereas passing it by rvalue reference enables the resources to be viewed and perhaps, but not necessarily, consumed.

Hence, one might imagine creating a suite of functions, e.g, f1, f2, f3, each taking a move-only type, e.g., M, having a known moved-from state, by rvalue reference and then applying each of them in turn to an object of type M:

```cpp
#include <utility>  // std::move

struct M;  // incomplete move-only type having known moved-from state

void f1(M&& m);       // function that can view and might consume m
void f2(M&& m);       //     "      "    "    "    "    "     "   "
void f3(M&& m);       //     "      "    "    "    "    "     "   "

void process(M&& m)   //     "      "    "    "    "    "     "   "
{
    f1(std::move(m));  // if m not yet consumed, and appropriate, consume it.
    f2(std::move(m));  // "  "  "   "     "      "    "      "      "    "
    f3(std::move(m));  // "  "  "   "     "      "    "      "      "    "
}
```

Observe, in the example above, that the potential for consumption is highlighted at each call site by the need to call std::move. By not building the consumption into the function signature, we leave more flexibility in each f*i*'s contract with its caller.

Factories having sink arguments Occasionally, a **factory function** is designed to take an object of a particular type and produce a modified version of the same object. Classically, the input to such a function would be taken by **const&**, and the output would be a named local variable that would be initialized and eventually returned:

```cpp
#include <cctype>  // std::toupper
#include <string>  // std::string

std::string toUppercase(const std::string& input)
{
    std::string result;
    result.resize(input.size());

    for (int i = 0; i < input.size(); ++i)  // Copy input.
    {
```

```
    result[i] = toupper(static_cast<unsigned char>(input[i]));
    }

    return result;
}
```

This implementation has the downside of making an extraneous copy when passed a temporary:

```
#include <cassert>  // Include standard C assert macro.

void testToUppercase()
{
    std::string upperHi = toUppercase("Hi");  // Copy twice.
    assert(upperHi == "HI");
}
```

Alternatively, the same pattern used for **sink arguments** can be used to initialize what will be our return value; take a **sink argument** by value:

```
// by-value version
std::string toUppercase(std::string input)
{
    for (int i = 0; i < input.size(); ++i)
    {
        input[i] = toupper(static_cast<unsigned char>(input[i]));
    }

    return input;
}

std::string output = toUppercase("hello");
```

This pass-by-value approach avoids extraneous copies, at the often acceptable cost of always requiring an extra move. As with the previous **sink argument** examples, higher maintenance options, which come with different associated compile-time costs, would be to (1) provide both **const** std::string& and std::string&& overloads, minimizing both moves and copies, or (2) reimplement the function as a template having a forwarding reference parameter; see Section 2.1."Forwarding References" on page 377.

Identifying value categories

Understanding the rules for which **value** category a particular expression belongs to can be challenging, and having a concrete tool to identify how a compiler will interpret an expression can be helpful. Building such a tool requires functionality that will behave in a distinct and observably different fashion for each of the three disjoint **value categories**: *lvalue*, *xvalue*, and *prvalue*. An operator that has such distinct behavior is the **decltype** operator; see Section 1.1."**decltype**" on page 25. When applied to a non-**id-expression**, e, having an underlying type of T, **decltype** will return one of exactly three types.

1. If e is a *prvalue*, then **decltype**(e) is T.

2. If e is an *lvalue*, then **decltype**(e) is T&.

3. If e is an *xvalue*, then **decltype**(e) is T&&.

We can apply **decltype** to various expressions, using std::is_same to verify that the type produced by the **decltype** operator is what we expect. When passed an id-expression naming an entity, we get the type of that entity, which is not helpful in identifying the value category of the id-expression, so we will always use an additional set of parentheses to obtain only the value-category-based determination of the type produced by **decltype**:

```
#include <type_traits>  // std::is_same
#include <utility>       // std::move

int x = 5;
int& y = x;
int&& z = static_cast<int&&>(x);
int f();
int& g();
int&& h();

// prvalues
static_assert( std::is_same< decltype(( 5 )),     int >::value, "" );
static_assert( std::is_same< decltype(( x + 5 )), int >::value, "" );
static_assert( std::is_same< decltype(( y + 5 )), int >::value, "" );
static_assert( std::is_same< decltype(( z + 5 )), int >::value, "" );
static_assert( std::is_same< decltype(( f() )),   int >::value, "" );

// lvalues
static_assert( std::is_same< decltype(( x )),   int& >::value, "" );
static_assert( std::is_same< decltype(( y )),   int& >::value, "" );
static_assert( std::is_same< decltype(( z )),   int& >::value, "" );
static_assert( std::is_same< decltype(( g() )), int& >::value, "" );

// xvalues
static_assert( std::is_same< decltype(( std::move(x) )), int&& >::value, "" );
static_assert( std::is_same< decltype(( std::move(y) )), int&& >::value, "" );
static_assert( std::is_same< decltype(( std::move(z) )), int&& >::value, "" );
static_assert( std::is_same< decltype(( h() )),          int&& >::value, "" );
```

Note the importance of adding the additional set of ( )s around the expression when it is an id-expression, i.e., just a single qualified or unqualified identifier. For all expressions that are not just id-expressions, an extra pair of ( )s will not alter the type produced by **decltype**.

Without the extra parenthesization, the reference qualifiers, or lack thereof, of the entity named by an **id-expression** become part of the type produced by **decltype**:

```
static_assert( std::is_same< decltype( x ),   int   >::value, "" );
static_assert( std::is_same< decltype( y ),   int&  >::value, "" );
static_assert( std::is_same< decltype( z ),   int&& >::value, "" );
```

Encapsulating this logic to build a utility will require working with expressions as operands. We do not have the ability to do high-level manipulation of expressions in the language, but we can use a lower-level and less-structured tool to do so in this case, building macros to identify value categories of expressions passed to them. To better handle any expression, including those with commas that are not nested within ( )s, we use a new feature that C++11 inherited from the C99 preprocessor, **variadic macros**:

```
#include <type_traits>  // std::is_reference, std::is_lvalue_reference,
                         // std::is_rvalue_reference
#include <utility>       // std::move

#define IS_PRVALUE( ... ) \
   (!std::is_reference< decltype(( __VA_ARGS__ )) >::value)

#define IS_LVALUE( ... ) \
    (std::is_lvalue_reference< decltype(( __VA_ARGS__ )) >::value)

#define IS_XVALUE( ... ) \
    (std::is_rvalue_reference< decltype(( __VA_ARGS__ )) >::value)

template <typename T, typename U>
struct S { };

S<int, long> s = {};

static_assert( IS_PRVALUE( S<int, int>() ), "");  // OK, needs __VA_ARGS__
static_assert( IS_LVALUE(  s ),             "");  // OK
static_assert( IS_XVALUE(  std::move(s) ),  "");  // OK
```

Finally, for completeness, we can see how macros can be written to identify the remaining value categories:

```
#define IS_RVALUE( ... ) (IS_XVALUE(__VA_ARGS__) || IS_PRVALUE(__VA_ARGS__))
#define IS_GLVALUE( ... ) (IS_LVALUE(__VA_ARGS__) || IS_XVALUE(__VA_ARGS__))

int x = 17;

static_assert( IS_RVALUE(x + 5),                                        "");  // OK
static_assert( IS_GLVALUE(x),                                           "");  // OK
static_assert( IS_GLVALUE(std::move(x)) && IS_RVALUE(std::move(x)), "");  // OK
```

Potential Pitfalls

Sink arguments require copying

As we saw in *Use Cases — Sink arguments* on page 775, passing by value and moving can offer certain advantages. If, however, we design a class, settle on an implementation, decide to use pass-by-value in the constructor, and then later decide to change the underlying representation, we might wind up with worse performance. If a copy is inevitable in the implementation and there is no chance that will change, passing by value might be beneficial. If we don't need to make the copy, then providing both **const&** and **&&** overloads or a template using **forwarding references** is needed to mitigate the risk.

For example, here we have written a class S that holds an std::string data member. We decide to take an std::string by value in the constructor and initialize our data member by applying std::move to the argument. Later, we decide to change our implementation to use our own String class. Our String has a converting constructor that takes an std::string and copies it (and does whatever else presumably motivated the change to our String). If we fail to update the constructor of class S (i.e., it still takes an std::string by-value and initializes the member with std::move of that string), we will wind up with less efficient code:

```
#include <string>  // std::string

class S
{
    std::string d_s;  // initial implementation

public:
    S(std::string s) : d_s(std::move(s)) { }  // sink argument constructor
};

std::string getStr();

int main()
{
    std::string lval;

    S s1(lval);      // copy and move
    S s2(getStr());  // move and move
}
```

In the code above, we incur a copy and a move if we pass an *lvalue* to the S constructor, and we experience two moves if we pass a temporary.

Suppose we then change S to use our own String class, but we neglect to change the constructor:

```
class String
{
public:
    String(const std::string&);  // Copy the contents of string.
};

class S
{
    String d_s;  // Implementation changed.

public:
    S(std::string s) : d_s(std::move(s)) { }  // Implementation did not change.
};

std::string getStr();

int main()
{
    std::string lval;

    S s1(lval);     // 2 copies
    S s2(getStr()); // 1 move and 1 copy
}
```

The problem is that now we are copying the argument twice: once into the `lval` parameter and then again into the `String` data member, `d_s`. Had we written the requisite overloads, we would not be in this situation:

```
class S
{
    String d_s;

public:
    S(const std::string& s) : d_s(s)             { }
    S(std::string&& s)      : d_s(std::move(s)) { }
};
```

So, unless we are absolutely certain that we will never change the implementation of our class, designing a constructor to take a sink argument by value can be suboptimal.

Disabling NRVO

Named return value optimization (NRVO) can occur only if the expression being returned from all paths through the function is the name of the same local variable. If we use `std::move` in a return statement, we are returning the return value of another function, i.e., `std::move`, and not a local variable by name, even though as developers we know that std::move is going to amount to no more than a cast applied to the argument we provide to it:

```cpp
#include <string>  // std::string

std::string expectingNRVO()
{
    std::string rtn;
    // ...
    return std::move(rtn);  // pessimization, no NRVO
}

std::string enablingNRVO()
{
    std::string rtn;
    // ...
    return rtn;             // optimization, NRVO possible
}
```

In the example above, the return value of the function is std::string, but after invoking std::move, the return expression is of type std::string&&. In general, when returning an object by value, we avoid std::move. While moving was once thought to be a faster way to return values from a function, testing validates that this is not the case.[26]

Failure to std::move a named *rvalue* reference

It is important to remember that we must use std::move on a named **rvalue reference** if we wish to move, as opposed to copy, the referenced object's contents somewhere. Even if the type of a function parameter is an **rvalue reference**, that parameter — by virtue of having a name — is, in fact, an *lvalue*. If an **rvalue reference** overload has the same implementation as the corresponding **const** lvalue reference overload, then it will likely be invoking the same *lvalue* overloads of any functions it calls. If the final use of the **rvalue reference** parameter does not employ std::move, then the function is failing to take advantage of whatever move operations the parameter type provides and is instead falling back to a higher-overhead copy operation.

Consider a large user-defined type, C, and an associated API that has a well-designed overload set that takes objects of type C by either **const** lvalue reference or rvalue reference:

```cpp
class C { /*...*/ };  // some UDT that might benefit from being "moved"

void processC(const C&);  // lvalue reference overload for processing C objects
void processC(C&&);       // rvalue reference overload for processing C objects

void applicationFunction(const C& c)
{
```

---

[26]See **orr18**.

```
    // ...
    processC(c);  // OK, invokes const C& overload of processC
}

void applicationFunction(C&& c)
{
    // ...
    processC(c);  // Bug, invokes const C& overload of processC
}
```

The intent of the second overload of `applicationFunction` was to move the contents of `c` into the appropriate *rvalue* overload of `processC`, but as the function parameter is itself an *lvalue*, the wrong overload is invoked. The proper solution is for the *rvalue* overload of `applicationFunction` to make an *xvalue* out of `c` before passing it to `processC`, since the state of `c` is no longer needed by the function:

```
#include <utility>  // std::move

void applicationFunction(C&& c)
{
    // ...
    processC(std::move(c));  // OK, invokes C&& overload of processC
}
```

Repeatedly calling `std::move` on a named *rvalue* reference

Utilizing `std::move` on rvalue reference parameters in a function is necessary but might result in defects if done ubiquitously. Recall (see *Description — Rvalue references in expressions* on page 730) that once an object has been moved from, the object's state should be considered unspecified, and, importantly, the object is certainly capable of no longer having the same value it originally had. When applying the same transformation from a **const** `C&` overload of a function to a `C&&` overload, as we did in *Failure to `std::move` a named rvalue reference* on page 784, it can be easy to falsely assume that all uses of the rvalue reference parameter should be wrapped in `std::move`:

```
void processTwice(const C& c)  // original lvalue reference overload
{
    processC(c);
    processC(c);
}

void processTwice(C&& c)  // naive transformation to rvalue overload
{
    processC(std::move(c));  // OK, invokes C&& overload of processC
    processC(std::move(c));  // Bug, c is already moved-from.
}
```

The proper approach here is to always be aware that `std::move` should be used only when an object's state is no longer needed. Though any call without `std::move` might result in a copy (depending on what `processC` does), using `std::move` solely on the last use of `c` in `processTwice` is the only approach that will keep this overload correct and consistent with the original overload:

```
void processTwice(C&& c)  // fixed rvalue overload
{
    processC(c);                // OK, invokes const C& overload of processC
    processC(std::move(c));  // OK, invokes C&& overload of processC
}
```

Returning const *rvalues* pessimizes performance

Prior to the introduction of move semantics, marking objects **const** when returning by value was sometimes recommended as good practice. For example, applying postfix **operator++** to a temporary is arguably not only useless but also almost certainly a bug.[27] In the specific case of postfix **operator++**, because the operator returns the previous value, an object must be returned, i.e., not a reference but a **temporary**. It was further recommended that the operator return a **const** object to prevent the application of postfix **operator++** twice.

The goal was to prevent postfix **operator++** as well as any other non**const** member function from being applied to a returned temporary object:

```
struct A
{
    // ...
    A& operator++();     // prefix operator++
    A operator++(int);   // postfix operator++

};
const A operator+(const A&, const A&);  // Return by const value.

void test1()
{
    A a, b;
    (a + b)++;  // Error, result of a + b is const A.
}
```

Perhaps a more common example of accidentally modifying an *expiring* **temporary** is applying **operator=** to a *prvalue* of a class type:

```
struct S { };  // arbitrary class type supporting copy assignment
S f();         // function returning prvalue of class type
```

---

[27] See **meyers96**, Item 6, "Distinguish between prefix and postfix forms of increment," pp. 31–34.

```
void test2()
{
    f() = S();       // valid but obviously wrong
}
```

The collateral damage of returning by **const** value, however, is that operations that seek to make use of the contents of the returned temporary will instead risk silently making additional copies, which can have unexpected and significant overhead:

```
void processA(const A& x);   // Copy x and send it off for processing.
void processA(A&& x);        // Move contents of x to be sent for processing.

void test3()
{
    A a, b;
    processA(a + b);  // Bug, invokes processA(const A&)
}
```

Overall, though the advice to return by **const** value produced some minor benefits in averting highly dubious modifications of temporaries prior to modern C++, it is now a form of antipattern. For cases where explicitly calling out operations that should not be invoked on temporaries is helpful, consider using reference qualifiers; see Section 3.1. "Ref-Qualifiers" on page 1153.

If presented with a library that still chooses to return by **const** value, one might be tempted to work around the problem by using a **const_cast** to move out of the **const** temporary return value:

```
void test4()  // This function uses a const_cast leading to undefined behavior.
{
    A a, b;
    processA(const_cast<A&&>(a + b));  // Bug (UB), modifies const object
}
```

Modifying a **const** object, however, is **undefined behavior**. The compiler's optimizer would be within its rights to elide **test3** entirely. What's more, external static analyzers (e.g., a code sanitizer) may (but might not) report such use as defective.

Move operations that throw

A move constructor that can throw is not useful in generic contexts where operations seek to provide the **strong exception-safety guarantee**; i.e., the operation will either succeed or throw an exception while leaving the object in its prior, valid state. Algorithms providing the **strong guarantee** would need to copy objects rather than move them, since they need to maintain the ability to unwind their work when an exception is thrown without risking further exceptions. This issue was, in fact, the very reason for the introduction of the **noexcept** keyword. Late in the development of C++11, this issue was discovered specifically with std::vector reallocations; see Section 2.1."**noexcept** Operator" on page 615.

Some moves are equivalent to copies

There is no need to provide move operations for a type for which copying and moving have the same effect, and doing so simply increases the maintenance cost of a type, the cost of compilation, and the risk of errors. In particular, built-in types do not have move operations, as there is no advantage to employing `std::move` over just copying them. For example, suppose we have a `Date` type comprising three **int** fields:

```cpp
class Date
{
    int day;
    int month;
    int year;

public:
    // ...
};
```

There is no added value in writing move operations for `Date` in the example above because copying cannot be optimized via move-like adoption of resources from the source object.

Given a move operation and a copy operation that have identical effects, eliminating the move operation will produce the same results in all situations with half the code. In general, it is best to avoid writing either operation and to let the compiler choose to generate both by following the **rule of zero**, and for a type such as `Date` in the example above, that is likely what we would do.

Making a noncopyable type movable without just cause

Copyable types will typically already have a valid default state, whereas noncopyable ones might not. Often, a **move operation** will reset a **moved-from object** to this default state. Adding such a state to an existing noncopyable type — e.g, just to support **move operations** — can break the assumptions of existing client code.

The addition of **move operations** to optimize the copying of *copyable* types has clearly defined semantics and wide applicability. Preexisting code is easy to retrofit and ideally will behave just as it did before, often with enhanced runtime performance. Note, however, that client code might sometimes require some modification if it is to take full advantage of the performance optimizations afforded by newly added **move operations**.

Existing documentation and unit tests will continue to be applicable for newly movable previously copyable types. What's more, the testing of move operations will be greatly facilitated by the tests for the copy operations as the only difference will be the relaxation of the strict post condition that the **moved-from object** retain its original value.

Although adding move operations to a previously copyable object would never degrade the performance associated with making the (destructive) copy itself, such degradation in subsequent accesses, due to **memory diffusion**, is a distinct possibility; hence, one might reasonably choose to copy values across nonlocal regions of memory even when **move operation** are available.[28]

On the other hand, making a *noncopyable* type movable introduces a distinct new semantic. If we know what it means to *copy* an object, then we have a complete specification for what it means to *move* it. Without that specification, we're charting new waters. Some of the reasons why a given type is noncopyable might well apply to moves too. Again, some noncopyable types might not have a natural uninitialized or "empty" state, so an appropriate **moved-from state** will need to be designed, documented, and tested — irrespective of whether the details of that state are made available to clients.

In practice, we find that most types of objects fall into two broad categories: (1) those that are used to represent a **platonic value** (VST) and (2) those that perform some sort of service (**mechanism**). Well-factored software components typically serve one or the other of these roles, but not both. For example, `std::complex<double>` is a VST, whereas `std::thread` is a **mechanism**. A standard container, such as `std::vector`, carries with it a fair amount of machinery, but most of that is in support of its **value**, which is typically a sequence of VSTs, whereas a **scoped guard** has no **value** whatsoever and serves only as a manager of the lifetime of some externally created resource.

Objects that have been made noncopyable are typically so because there's no **platonic value** to copy. If all that's needed is to share access to such **mechanisms**, then raw pointers might be sufficient. If, however, the need is to pass around unique ownership of such a noncopyable object, then that's another story; see *Use Cases — Passing around resource-owning objects by value* on page 771. In most cases, `std::unique_ptr` provides a standard and well-understood idiom for passing around unique ownership of noncopyable objects without the risks and development costs associated with crafting our own **move-only type**; see *Implementing a move-only type without employing `std::unique_ptr`* on page 791.

For example, suppose we have a preexisting (possibly C++03) **mechanism** that currently meets our needs. As this type doesn't try to represent a value, it doesn't implement any copy operations, equality comparison operations, etc. Suppose also that this type allocates dynamic memory. Although our **mechanism** cannot meaningfully be copied, it does have a reasonable default constructed state and, with the advent of **move semantics** in C++11, we could — in theory — implement arguably plausible **move operations**. Should we? What would be the return on our investment?

Adding move operations to such an inherently noncopyable type is unlikely to yield any meaningful utility that could not otherwise be achieved, far more safely and affordably, by an external application of `std::unique_ptr`. In addition, any attempt to retrofit an existing **mechanism** with move operations will invariably involve substantial development effort. Moreover, great care would be needed to ensure that (1) the documentation reflects the modified behavior, (2) appropriate new unit tests are added, and (3) the moved-from state of the object behaves sensibly. What's more, given that this **mechanism** might already be in wide use, such an invasive enhancement might break preexisting client code, designed

---

[28]See **halpern21c**.

based on assumptions that might no longer apply: Any client holding a pointer to such an object might be disheartened to learn that the object's implementation has been moved out from under it.

Let's now suppose we have some preexisting noncopyable type, `Nct`, and we find that we want to place objects of that type into a container such as an `std::vector`. We might think to add **move operations** to `Nct` as C++11 containers now support such move-only types, but that would be overkill as simply dynamically allocating the value (in a location whence it will then not move) and then managing its lifetime using an `std::unique_ptr` will get the job done:

```
#include <vector>   // std::vector
#include <memory>   // std::unique_ptr
#include <nct.h>    // Nct -- some noncopyable type, defined elsewhere

void f()  // function illustrating effective external use of std::unique_ptr
{
    std::vector<Nct> v1;
    v1.push_back(Nct(/*...*/));   // Error, no copy or move constructor
    v1.emplace_back(/*...*/);     // Error, move needed to grow buffer

    std::vector<std::unique_ptr<Nct>> v2;
    v2.push_back(std::make_unique<Nct>(/*...*/));      // OK
    v2.emplace_back(std::make_unique<Nct>(/*...*/));   // OK (same as above)

}
```

One might opine that such use of `std::unique_ptr` doesn't always play nicely with standard algorithms, such as `std::sort` or range-based **for** (see Section 2.1."Range **for**" on page 679). However, given that such algorithms are all but invariably used for VSTs and not for **mechanisms**, these concerns are not typically borne out in practice.

Separately, any **mechanism** such as an `std::pmr::memory_resource` — whose typical usage involves its client's storing the addresses of objects of that type — makes this ilk of inherently noncopyable types especially poor candidates to be **move-only**; moving from such a type would likely invalidate assumptions made by its clients. Similarly, making **mechanisms**, such as a concurrent lock or a shared cache, move-only would also be problematic as moving from a multiply referenced object of such a type would require coordination among all its active clients.

Factory functions offer up a special excuse for an arbitrary **mechanism** to be move-only: Such objects are constructed and configured within the factory function and then moved out of the function to what will typically become their final location as any subsequent move is likely to break active clients. Annoyingly, the compiler can often arrange to return such an object from a **factory function** without a move via either RVO or NRVO, but the C++11/14 standards require that a **move constructor** be **accessible** (even if it isn't implemented); see *Annoyances — RVO and NRVO require a declared copy or move constructor* on page 804. The good news is that this issue is at least partially addressed in C++17 with **guaranteed copy**

elision; until then, simply declaring but *not* defining a publicly accessible **move constructor** is sufficient to allow these long-standing optimizations to kick in or, if for some reason they do not, the program will fail to link — i.e., fail *safely*.

There are, however, pragmatic reasons for wanting to have **move-only types**, but the financial bar for creating them is fairly high; hence, the prerequisites are correspondingly formidable. Typically, a newly minted **move-only type** will need to be one where ease of use by unsophisticated clients (e.g., those unfamiliar with `std::unique_ptr`) is perceived to offset the substantial development and maintenance costs that come with creating a custom **move-only type**.

Implementing a move-only type without employing `std::unique_ptr`

Let's suppose that we aren't overly constrained by either budget or delivery date and we want to provide the optimal user experience for our resource wrapper types. What might be the safest and most cost-effective approach to implementing our own **move-only type**?

The go-to implementation for a **move-only type** — particularly one that allocates dynamic memory — is to use `std::unique_ptr` as a data member:

```cpp
#include <memory>    // std::unique_ptr
#include <cassert>   // standard C assert macro

class Mechanism;     // any nonmovable resource

class Wrapper
{
    std::unique_ptr<Mechanism> d_managed;
public:
    // ...     (public interface, no user-declared special member functions)

    void doWork()
    {
        assert(d_managed != nullptr);
        d_managed->doWork();
    }
};
```

Using this well-known Standard Library component is idiomatic and relatively easy for library developers to understand, test, and maintain. The public interface of `Wrapper` will still need to be enhanced beyond that of `Mechanism` to handle the **moved-from state** (where `d_managed == nullptr`), but the basic mechanics of moving will all be handled correctly via the default implementations of the **special member functions** of `Wrapper`. Importantly, using `std::unique_ptr` as the basis for our implementation of a **move-only type** automatically gives us a *canonical* "empty" representation to use as our **moved-from state**.

Again, any attempt to add move operations to a noncopyable type presumes that there is some demonstrated need to move the type. For a noncopyable type that either never needs to move or whose effective movement can be adequately synthesized via external application of `std::unique_ptr`, there is simply no engineering or business justification for adding **move operations** to the type itself — irrespective of how they might be implemented internally; see *Making a noncopyable type movable without just cause* on page 788. When a genuine need *does* exist, using `std::unique_ptr` under the covers is almost always the implementation of choice.

In rare cases, however, creating a move-only type, `M`, that does *not* involve `std::unique_ptr` might be justifiable; such a fully customized move-only class will, however, have a demonstrable need for maximal performance and satisfy *all* of several other criteria.

- The move operation for `M` can be made **noexcept(true)** (see Section 3.1.“**noexcept** Specifier” on page 1085); otherwise, to avoid such an undesirable move property, sticking with an `std::unique_ptr` implementation is likely indicated.

- The overhead of a single additional heap allocation is too high for the strict performance requirements of `M`; otherwise, using `std::unique_ptr` will not have a sufficiently negative impact on runtime performance.

- `M` itself is small and simple, such as a class holding a single **int** or pointer, where the move operations would be especially fast; otherwise, `std::unique_ptr`'s efficient move operations will be as fast or faster.

The archetypal **move-only type** that does *not* make use of `std::unique_ptr` in its implementation would be a nonallocating wrapper (e.g., `Socket`) for a lightweight handle (e.g., an integer descriptor) to some form of system resource (e.g, a socket), which needs to be owned and managed. Moreover, when ownership of the managed resource is transferred, there will typically be no computation (e.g., incrementing and decrementing of a counter) and absolutely no effect on the managed resource (or any other resource) — i.e., no allocation/deallocation, no open/close, no flush, etc.

For example, `std::thread` is a well-known standard move-only class that manages a lightweight handle to a system resource. Similarly, `std::unique_lock` is a standard class template that provides support for acquiring, transferring, and releasing ownership of a lock on a lockable type, such as `std::mutex`, as a lightweight move-only **handle type**. Such move-only *handles* “own” a resource and are responsible for ensuring said resource is appropriately flushed, closed, released, and/or deallocated when the last handle to which ownership was transferred is destroyed, while typically having no observable effect when ownership is transferred.

To better appreciate the costs and risks associated with developing a full-custom **move-only type** independently of `std::unique_ptr`, suppose we have evaluated an existing noncopyable type, `Mechanism`, and somehow determined that (1) it must be made **movable**, and (2) implementing that movability via an indirection through `std::unique_ptr` would not be sufficiently performant for our needs.

To make a **movable** version of `Mechanism`, we'll first have to design and implement **move operations**. This task is made challenging by having no precedent in the implementation of

Mechanism for migrating state from one object to another, along with the need to identify a distinct, new, **moved-from state**; see *Inconsistent expectations on moved-from objects* on page 794.

Next, all other **member functions** —including special member functions and especially the destructor — will need to handle objects in this new **moved-from state** and do so in a reliable and consistent way as **narrowing the contract** of a member function often has unacceptable downsides; see *Move operations that throw* on page 787.

Finally, all publicly accessible aspects of the **API** of Mechanism will somehow need to handle an object in a **moved-from state**, which can range from **narrowing contracts** to adding error return values or else alternative failure modes; see *Requiring owned resources to be valid* on page 803.

As our final concrete example, consider an implementation of a **move-only type**, MovableMechanism, that provides a movable version of some arbitrary preexisting, noncopyable nonmovable type, Mechanism:

```cpp
class MovableMechanism
{
    bool d_movedFrom;  // flag to indicate the moved-from state

    // ... (existing other private parts from Mechanism)

public:
    MovableMechanism()
    : d_movedFrom(false)
    {
        // existing constructor implementation
    }

    // ...      (Update all other existing constructors to
    // ...          properly manage the value of d_movedFrom.)

    MovableMechanism(MovableMechanism&& source) noexcept // Note use of noexcept.
    : d_movedFrom(false)
    {
        // Move/copy all state from source.
        source.d_movedFrom = true;
    }

    MovableMechanism& operator=(MovableMechanism&& rhs) noexcept // Note noexcept.
    {
        if (this != &rhs)
        {
            if (!d_movedFrom)
            {
                // Adapt original logic of Mechanism.
            }
```

```
            if (!rhs.d_movedFrom)
            {
                // Move/copy all state from rhs.
            }
            d_movedFrom = rhs.d_movedFrom;
            rhs.d_movedFrom = true;
        }
        return *this;
    }

    ~MovableMechanism()
    {
        if (!d_movedFrom)
        {
            // ... (existing implementation of Mechanism)
        }
    }

    void doWork()
    {
        assert(!d_movedFrom);  // needs to be added to ALL public functions
        // ... (existing implementation of doWork)
    }
};
```

As the sketch of the `MovableMechanism` class implementation above suggests, adding movability to a nonmovable noncopyable type, `Mechanism`, requires modifications to almost every aspect of of the type — at least all publicly accessible aspects of it. Should any of the original special member functions of `Mechanism` have been defaulted (see Section 1.1. "Defaulted Functions" on page 33), they might now need to become user provided to properly handle the new moved-from state. Moreover, changes to preconditions or essential behavior will necessarily invalidate any corresponding documentation. What's more, robust software implementing defensive checks (e.g., using standard C `assert` macros) will naturally want to implement new checks for all the newly established preconditions. Finally, all behavioral changes will require thorough updating of existing tests along with addressing all functionality that previously did not exist, including the **negative testing** of all newly added defensive checks.

Inconsistent expectations on moved-from objects

When creating a type that supports move operations, a key decision to be made is in what states moved-from objects of that type may be left and what operations will be valid on such objects. When writing code that uses a movable type, especially generic code, it is also important to understand and document the requirements on the template parameters. When a generic type has higher expectations for what can be done with moved-from objects than are actually supported, then possibly subtle runtime defects will likely arise. Importantly, this conundrum is entirely about objects in a certain state (moved-from) not being valid for certain operations (e.g., destruction, copying, assignment, comparison, user-defined utility functions, and so on), which is entirely a runtime property and, hence, a source of runtime defects that are potentially difficult to track down.

The choice of which of a type's operations should be valid on moved-from objects of that type has numerous ramifications on the user-friendliness of the type and what algorithms will safely work with the type. Let's explore, with example types that manage a simple heap-allocated **int** in different ways, five various choices that can be made regarding support for objects in a moved-from state. While these examples all fail in a common manner that is seemingly easily alleviated (dereferencing a **nullptr**), the structure of what works and what doesn't for these types will often occur in much larger contexts, and the considerations of what operations a type can and should support for moved-from objects apply equally to more involved scenarios.

1. The C++ language makes no explicit requirements that any operation in particular should be valid for moved-from objects. This freedom leads to the possibility of implementing a type that supports no operations on moved-from objects of that type, including destruction. Our first example type, S1 below, was originally written with the assumption that a heap-allocated **int** resource was always owned by every S1 object. At a later time, **move operations** were added to S1 that leave moved-from objects no longer managing a resource, and, furthermore, all operations were modified to have **undefined behavior** when invoked on moved-from objects. A misguided attempt to always set the value of a heap-allocated **int** to -1 prior to its being deleted then makes even the destructor invalid for moved-from objects:

```
#include <utility>  // std::move

class S1  // BAD IDEA: misguided attempt makes non-movable class movable
{
    int* d_r_p;  // owned heap-allocated resource

public:
    S1() : d_r_p(new int(1)) { }  // Allocate on construction.

    S1(const S1& original)
    : d_r_p(new int(*original.d_r_p)) { }  // no check for nullptr

    ~S1() { *d_r_p = -1; delete d_r_p; }   // no check for nullptr

    S1& operator=(const S1& rhs)
    {
        *d_r_p = *rhs.d_r_p;   // no check for either nullptr
        return *this;
    }
```

```
    void set(int i) { *d_r_p = i; }       // no check for nullptr
    int get() const { return *d_r_p; }  //   "    "    "    "    "

S1(S1&& expiring) : d_r_p(expiring.d_r_p)
{
    expiring.d_r_p = nullptr;  // expiring now invalid for most operations
}

S1& operator=(S1&& expiring)
{
    *d_r_p = -1;  // no check for nullptr
    delete d_r_p;
    d_r_p = expiring.d_r_p;
    expiring.d_r_p = nullptr;  // expiring now invalid for most operations
    return *this;
}
};

void test1()
{
    S1 s1;
    S1 s2 = std::move(s1);  // OK, s1.d_r_p == nullptr
    s1.set(17);             // Bug, dereferences nullptr s1.d_r_p
} // destruction of s1 dereferences nullptr
```

A type such as `S1` becomes difficult to use in many places where an implicit move might occur:

```
S1 createS1(int i, bool negative)
{
    S1 output1, output2;
    output1.set(i); output2.set(-i);
    return negative ? output2 : output1;  // no NRVO possible
}

void test2()
{
    S1 s;
    s = createS1(17, false);  // creates rvalue temporary and move-assigns to s
                              // destruction of temporary dereferences nullptr

}
```

In general, a type having an unforgiving state like that of a moved-from `S1` object is possible, but using it without the greatest of care is difficult. Most object creation, by design, leads to invocation of destructors, and many common programming constructs can lead to the creation of temporaries that are then moved from and destroyed. The only advantage of intentionally designing a type of this sort is that it pays no cost in checks for **nullptr** to support the moved-from state.

2. The primary downside of the fully unforgiving moved-from state can be alleviated by only making the destructor safe to invoke on a moved-from object:

```
class S2
{
    // ...            (similar to S1 above)

    ~S2() { delete d_r_p; }  // safe to use if d_r_p == nullptr
};
```

While silent use of S2 temporaries will not directly result in runtime defects, this minimal support for the moved-from state still leaves S2 unusable in a number of algorithms. Consider the following use of std::swap on S2 objects, an operation performed internally by many standard algorithms:

```
#include <utility>  // std::swap

void test3()
{
    S2 a, b;
    std::swap(a, b);  // Bug!
}
```

Internally, the invocation of std::swap would expand:

```
void test4()
{
    S2 a, b;
    S2 temp = std::move(a);  // OK, makes a.d_r_p == nullptr
    a = std::move(b);        // Bug, dereferences nullptr a.d_r_p and
                             //      makes b.d_r_p == nullptr
    b = std::move(temp);     // Bug, dereferences nullptr b.d_r_p
}
```

Note that, even though S2 is move-constructible and move-assignable, std::swap has **undefined behavior** when applied to S2 objects. Supporting only destruction and no other operations allows for basic use of a type but still fails to work correctly with even the simplest of standard algorithms.

3. To enable our type to be used with std::swap and, consequently, many common algorithms, the *copy-* and *move*-assignment operators can be made safe for objects in the moved-from state. This extra measure of safety allows std::swap and many other algorithms that either rely on std::swap or directly move objects around within a container to work safely with objects that have been previously moved from:

```
class S3
{
    // ...           (similar to S2 above)

    S3& operator=(const S3& rhs)
    {
        if (d_r_p == nullptr)
        {
            d_r_p = new int(*rhs.d_r_p);   // no check for rhs.d_r_p == nullptr
        }
        else
        {
            *d_r_p = *rhs.d_r_p;           // no check for rhs.d_r_p == nullptr
        }
        return *this;
    }

    S3& operator=(S3&& expiring)
    {
        delete d_r_p;
        d_r_p = expiring.d_r_p;
        expiring.d_r_p = nullptr;  // expiring now in moved-from state
        return *this;
    }
};
```

With the assignment operators now modified to support assignment *to* an object in the moved-from state (but not necessarily *from* an object in the moved-from state), we can now safely use `std::swap` and build algorithms on top of that:

```
void test5()
{
    S3 a, b;
    std::swap(a, b);
}

void sort3(S3& a, S3& b, S3& c)
{
    if (a.get() > b.get()) std::swap(a, b);
    if (b.get() > c.get()) std::swap(b, c);
    if (a.get() > b.get()) std::swap(a, b);
}
```

The moved-from state of S3 is not, however, valid for all operations expected of an element of a standard container, so S3 is not supported in any standard container;

see *Annoyances — Standard Library requirements on a moved-from object are overly strict* on page 807.

That an `S3` object in the moved-from state cannot itself be moved implies that all objects of unknown provenance must be treated with great care. Any object that client code might have moved from cannot be used for any purpose other than as the target of an assignment, and, in the case of `S3`, there is not even a way to safely identify if an object has been moved from:

```
void test6(const S3& inputS)
{
    S3 localS = inputS;   // UB if inputS is in moved-from state
}
```

The inability to detect the moved-from state could be addressed simply by giving a function, such as `test6`, a **narrow contract** requiring that its argument not be in the moved-from state. This stipulation, however, cannot typically be enforced at compile time and might be hard to diagnose at run time. The moved-from state can also make otherwise **wide-contract** operations on a container into a source of problems if an element is put into such an arguably poisonous state:

```
#include <vector>  // std::vector

void test7()
{
    std::vector<S3> vs1;  // OK
    vs1.push_back(S3());  // OK
    vs1.push_back(S3());  // OK

    S3 s = std::move(vs1[0]);  // OK

    std::vector<S3> vs2 = vs1;  // Bug, copying moved-from vs1[0]
}
```

Ensuring that types are well-behaved even in the moved-from state is one way to avoid such bugs, but see *Annoyances — Standard Library requirements on a moved-from object are overly strict* on page 807.

4. Fully supporting moving objects in the moved-from state removes a significant source of defects when dealing with objects of unknown provenance. In `test7` above, we attempted to *copy construct* an object, `vs2`, from another, `vs1`, that had already been moved from. If we want to fully defend against moved-from objects, we will have to expend considerably more development effort. Let's now take a look at what it might take to implement just the copy and move *assignment operators*:

```
class S4
{
    // ...            (similar to S3 above)

    S4& operator=(const S4& rhs)
    {
        if (rhs.d_r_p == nullptr)
        {
            delete d_r_p;
            d_r_p = nullptr;
        }
        else if (d_r_p == nullptr)
        {
            d_r_p = new int(*rhs.d_r_p);
        }
        else
        {
            *d_r_p = *rhs.d_r_p;
        }

        return *this;
    }

    S4& operator=(S4&& expiring)
    {
        if (this != &expiring)
        {
            delete d_r_p;
            d_r_p = expiring.d_r_p;
            expiring.d_r_p = nullptr; // expiring now in moved-from state
        }
        return *this;
    }
};
```

This additional support for use of the moved-from state allows basic algorithms to manipulate collections of objects with no concern for their value or whether they are in a moved-from state. In general, though, without a way to identify the moved-from state, it is still not viable to make use of objects of unknown provenance. Before considering altering a type's functionality to make more operations valid for objects in the moved-from state, see *Requiring owned resources to be valid* on page 803.

5. Making additional user-defined operations usable for objects in a moved-from state can be accomplished in several ways. The most common guidance — and what is expected by the Standard Library containers for the operations they require of their type arguments — is for the moved-from state to be **valid but unspecified**; i.e., all operations that have **wide contracts** can still be invoked on objects in the moved-from state, but there is no guarantee what results those operations will have. We can adjust the remaining operations of S4 accordingly:

```cpp
#include <cstdlib>  // std::rand

class S5a
{
    // ...            (similar to S4 above)

    void set(int i)
    {
        if (d_r_p == nullptr)
        {
            d_r_p = new int(i);
        }
        else
        {
            *d_r_p = i;
        }
    }

    int get() const
    {
        return (d_r_p == nullptr) ? std::rand() : *d_r_p;
    }
};
```

Class S5a in the example above is the first type that meets the full requirements for being an element in a standard container. Yet, calling `get()` on a moved-from object and subsequently using the value returned would almost certainly be a bug. What's more, S5a does nothing to facilitate identifying such a defect.

An alternate approach is to make the moved-from state fully specified, which we could do by replacing the call to `std::rand()` above with a fixed return value, such as 0. This attempt to have a reliable moved-from state can lead to confusion, as it cannot always be determined if a move, a copy, or nothing has happened when a move has been requested:

```
#include <cassert>  // standard C assert macro

class S5b
{
    // ...            (identical to S5a above)

    int get() const
    {
        return (d_r_p == nullptr) ? 0 : *d_r_p;
    }
};

void mightMove(S5b&&);   // function that might move from its argument

void test8()
{
    S5b s;
    s.set(17);
    mightMove(std::move(s));
    assert(s.get() == 0);   // Bug, if mightMove did not actually move
}
```

Consider the example of the standard containers themselves. An `std::vector` that has been moved from will be in unspecified state, e.g., unchanged or empty. All of the **wide-contract** operations of `std::vector`, e.g., `push_back` or `size()`, can be applied to an `std::vector` that has been moved from. These operations can, in turn, be used to identify the full state of the object and to check the preconditions of all of the other **narrow-contract** operations of `std::vector`, such as `front` or **operator[]**.

The various options available for what functionality a type might support for its moved-from objects must be matched to the requirements of any given algorithm involving that type. This need for sufficiently well-defined behavior in the case of moved-from objects applies broadly to both concrete algorithms using types supplied by other libraries and generic algorithms using types that have not yet been written.

The most general approach is to require the minimum functionality from a type and to require only that functionality of the values that will actually be passed to a particular algorithm. This choice can lead to narrow contracts requiring that a client not pass in objects in a moved-from state but maximizes the flexibility available to the client as to what they need to support.

The most restrictive approach and the one taken by the Standard Library is to require all moved-from objects be in a valid state. This choice can make it far less likely for **undefined behavior** to manifest when combining an algorithm having these requirements with an arbitrary type also meeting these requirements yet significantly inhibits the ability for code **sanitizers** and other debugging tools to detect defects when a moved-from object is in play.

When writing a type that will be used in a wide variety of scenarios, failing to meet the broadest possible set of requirements is often risky unless there is a compelling reason to do so. An algorithm is maximally applicable when it has the fewest possible requirements on the types it will work with.

Requiring owned resources to be valid

Objects that manage resources and support move operations will generally transfer ownership of their owned resource to the moved-to object when possible in lieu of somehow duplicating the owned resource. Fundamental to the design of such a resource-owning type that might move is deciding what the moved-from state should be and whether the moved-from state should also own a resource. Often, this moved-from state can match the default-constructed state and involves similar trade-offs. Maintaining as an invariant that a resource is always owned can bring with it significant costs, namely, the cost of acquiring a resource even if it will never be used. This price has to be weighed against the advantage of never needing to verify that the resource is there, simplifying some code and avoiding some branches.

Though it doesn't own resources outside of its own footprint, an important type worth considering is a common one, **int**, or, in general, any of the various **fundamental types**. Moving from an **int** leaves it unchanged, more because of the cheaper cost of leaving a source **int** unchanged than it being fundamental to the design. The default-initialized state of an **int**, however, is fraught with **undefined behavior** any time an attempt is made to use its value. This state is, in many ways, similar to a moved-from state that is not valid for any operations other than destruction and being assigned to. The value of an uninitialized **int** cannot be used in any meaningful way, and there is no way to query if a particular **int** object is properly initialized. This behavior comes with the advantage of keeping **int** trivial and the associated performance advantage of not having to do any writes when creating an **int** that will never be read:

```
void populate(int* i);
    // Populate the location pointed to by i with a value.

void test9()
{
    int i;          // OK, leave i uninitialized.
    populate(&i);   // OK, i is never read by populate.
}
```

The author of a heap-allocating movable type can learn an important lesson from **int** as to what the type's default-constructed state should be and, consequently, what its moved-from state should be. Consider the type **S4** discussed in *Inconsistent expectations on moved-from objects* on page 794, which supports assignment and destruction of moved-from objects and no other operations. Rather than have the default constructor allocate, we can instead make the default-constructed state be the same as the moved-from state:

```
class S4b
{
    // ...            (identical to S4 above)

    S4b() : d_r_p(nullptr) { }  // same state as the moved-from state
};
```

This implementation has a big advantage over the versions presented earlier that attempted to have a resource allocated for the default-constructed state in that it avoids that allocation completely. Any situation in which an object is default constructed and then immediately assigned a new value from a different object offers a potentially major performance improvement. The `String` example in *Use Cases — Creating a low-level value-semantic type (VST)* on page 742 achieved the same benefit by using a **sentinel** value with static storage duration for the moved-from and default-constructed states, with slightly different trade-offs and similar benefits.

Annoyances

RVO and NRVO require a declared copy or move constructor

To create a **factory function** for a type that returns objects of that type by value, the type is required to have an accessible *copy* or *move* constructor, either implicitly or explicitly declared. Frustratingly, even if the copy or move is always elided by RVO or NRVO, at least one of the constructors must still be either implicitly generated or have an accessible declaration:

```
class S1   // noncopyable nonmovable type
{
    S1() = default;  // private constructibility needed by factory

public:
    S1(const S1&);            // declared but never defined
    S1& operator=(const S1&);  // declared but never defined

    static S1 factory()
    {
        S1 output;
        return output;
    }
};

int test1()
{
    S1 s1 = S1::factory();  // OK, links without definition of S1(const&)
    S1 s2 = s1;             // Link-Time Error
    return 0;
}
```

The publicly accessible copy operation needed to facilitate the static `factory` function, however, will cause link-time errors in any code that *does* attempt to copy an object of the noncopyable `S1` type. This delay until link time of what ideally should be a compile-time error can make use of types like this burdensome.[29] Move operations slightly mitigate this annoyance as declaring, but not defining, move operations (e.g., `S2`, below) instead of copy operations (e.g., `S1`, above) will both suppress implicit copy operations and make attempting to copy (but not move) objects a compile-time error; attempting to move, however, will remain a link-time error:

```
class S2  // noncopyable nonmovable type
{
    S2() = default;  // private constructibility needed by factory

public:
    S2(const S2&&);              // never defined
    S2& operator=(const S2&&);   // never defined

    static S2 factory()
    {
        return S2();
    }
};

int test2()
{
    S2 s1 = S2::factory();  // OK, links without definition of S2(const&)
    S2 s2 = s1;             // Error, no copy constructor
    S2 s3 = std::move(s1);  // Link-Time Error
    return 0;
}
```

`std::move` does not move

Despite the name, `std::move` does not *move* anything and is simply an unconditional cast to an rvalue reference; see *Description — The `std::move` utility* on page 731:

```
template <typename T>
void swap(T& t1, T& t2)
{
    T temp = std::move(t1);
    t1 = std::move(t2);
    t2 = std::move(temp);
}
```

---

[29]C++17 introduced **guaranteed copy elision** not requiring declared copy and move constructors; copy and move constructors and assignment operators can be private or deleted, and factory functions can still be implemented to return such objects by value. C++23 seems likely to extend this guarantee to a limited number of NRVO eligible cases as well.

The invocations of `std::move` just unconditionally cast the arguments to rvalue references. The constructor and assignment operator for `T` found through overload resolution that take a single rvalue reference to `T`, which might well be the copy constructor and copy-assignment operator, are what do the work of `std::swap`, and though those might be move operations, nothing about that is guaranteed. This function can be written in a more verbose, less expressive yet identical way:

```
template <typename T>
void swap(T& t1, T& t2)
{
    T temp = static_cast<T&&>(t1);
    t1 = static_cast<T&&>(t2);
    t2 = static_cast<T&&>(temp);
}
```

Perhaps `std::move` might have been more aptly named `std::make_movable`, `std::as_xvalue`, or any similar name that conveyed that the qualities of the object are changed, but no explicit runtime action is being performed.

Visual similarity to forwarding references

The syntax for rvalue references has been overloaded with the similar but distinct concept of a forwarding reference; see Section 2.1."Forwarding References" on page 377. In hindsight, having a distinct syntax for forwarding references — even one as possibly distasteful as `&&&` — would have allowed for a clear distinction, preventing the case of *not* having a forwarding reference when one is intended.

To be a forwarding reference, a parameter's type must be an rvalue reference to a function template parameter that is *not* cv-qualified:

```
template <typename T>
void f1(T&& t);  // t is a forwarding reference.
```

Thus, using a class template parameter, adding a **const** or **volatile** qualifier, or using a concrete type will all make a function parameter an rvalue reference and not a forwarding reference:

```
template <typename T>
struct S
{
    void f2(T&& t);    // t is not a forwarding reference.
};

template <typename T>
void f4(const T&& t);  // t is not a forwarding reference.
void f5(int&& i);      // i is not a forwarding reference.
```

In practice, when implementing **perfect forwarding**, making a mistake in any one of these facets will result in not having a **forwarding reference** and compilation errors. Being unable to state clearly the intent to have a forwarding reference makes misuse by developers more likely and compilation errors more difficult to diagnose.

Value categories are a moving target

C++03 had just *lvalues* and *rvalues*. In the original design of C++11, the only *xvalues* were once *lvalues*. In C++14, members of *prvalue* user-defined types also became *xvalues*. In C++17 even more *prvalues* were identified as *xvalues*. Some of these changes have been adopted as **defect reports** against older standards, and some have introduced subtle changes in behavior between language standards.

In any case, the progression is in one direction: there were no *rvalues* in C++03 that were not *prvalues* in C++11, and then the demarcation between *prvalue* and *xvalue* continued to drift so that the categories of non*lvalues* that were deemed to be *xvalues* grew. The criterion now is *not* that an *xvalue* is a non*lvalue* that is reachable but that it is a non*lvalue* that refers to an object in memory; a *prvalue* now becomes everything else that isn't an *lvalue* and, unless **void**, must be a complete type. Once something becomes an *xvalue* in the Standard, it can never go back to being a *prvalue*. Understanding the evolution is helpful to understanding how the C++ language is evolving; see the *Appendix — The evolution of value categories* on page 813.

Overall, what the literature has lacked and the Standard's evolution has made difficult to understand is a clear designation of what the value categories are and what their purpose is. The realization that the *xvalue* category needed to encompass all objects whose data is no longer needed — whether due to being a temporary whose lifetime is ending or due to an explicit cast in code — took a great deal of time to clarify, with various edge cases continuing to surface.[30]

Standard Library requirements on a moved-from object are overly strict

By Sean Parent

Given an object, rv, of type T that has been moved from, the C++14[31] Standard specifies the required postconditions of a moved-from object[32]:

> rv's state is unspecified [*Note*: rv must still meet the requirements of the library component that is using it. The operations listed in those requirements must work as specified whether rv has been moved from or not. — *end note*]

---

[30]Though the distinction between a *prvalue* and an *xvalue* is largely academic prior to C++17, with the adoption of proposal P0135R0 (**smith15c**), knowing the difference becomes important in light of guaranteed copy elision and, in particular, **mandatory RVO** for *prvalues*.

[31]Similar wording having the same intent appears in every version of the C++ Standard since C++11.

[32]**iso14**, Table 20, p. 427

The requirement applies to both move construction and move assignment for types used with the Standard Library containers and algorithms. The note is not **normative** but does clarify that the requirements on a moved-from object are not relaxed.

To understand how this requirement causes an issue in practice, consider the following simple class definition. The intent of `my_type` is to create a class that always holds a valid value, is copyable and equality comparable, and happens to contain a remote part. The remote part in this example is held as an `std::unique_ptr` to an `implementation` object. A remote part might be employed to improve compile times by separating the implementation from the interface, to allow a polymorphic implementation using inheritance, or to trade off a slower copy for a faster move:

```
class implementation;

class my_type
{
    std::unique_ptr<implementation> d_remote;  // remote part

public:
    explicit my_type(int a)
    : d_remote{std::make_unique<implementation>(a)}
    { }

    my_type(const my_type& a)
    : d_remote{std::make_unique<implementation>(*a.d_remote)}
    { }

    my_type& operator=(const my_type& a)
    {
        *d_remote = *a.d_remote;
        return *this;
    }

    friend bool operator==(const my_type& a, const my_type& b)
    {
        return *a.d_remote == *b.d_remote;
    }
};
```

We can add the ability to move the object by using a default **move constructor** and **move-assignment operator**:

```
class my_type
{
    //...
public:
```

```
    //...
    my_type(my_type&&) noexcept = default;          // move constructor
    my_type& operator=(my_type&&) noexcept = default;  // move assignment
    // ...
};
```

If we ignore the library requirements and consider only the language requirements, this implementation is sufficient. The only language requirement is that a moved-from object be destructible because, without a cast, the only operation the compiler will perform on a moved-from object is to destroy it. By definition, an *rvalue* is a temporary object, and no other operations will be performed. The assignment x = f(), where x is of type my_type and f() returns a value of type my_type, will work correctly with the default member-wise implementations.

However, using my_type in a standard container or algorithm will likely fail. Consider inserting an element into a vector at a position, p:

```
#include <vector>  // std::vector
void test1(std::vector<my_type>* v,
           std::vector<my_type>::const_iterator p)
{
    my_type x{42};
    //...
    v->insert(p, x); // undefined behavior
}
```

If p is not at the end of v, the implementation of std::vector might move the range of elements [p, end(v)) and then copy x over a moved-from object. Implementations of the Standard Library may use a different approach to implementing insert that would not encounter this issue.[33] The copying of x results in a statement with the effect of *p = x where *p is a moved-from instance of my_type. The copy operation is likely to crash because of the implementation of copy assignment:

```
my_type& my_type::operator=(const my_type& rhs)
{
    *d_remote = *rhs.d_remote;
    return *this;
}
```

Following the move of the range of elements starting at p, d_remote of *p is equal to **nullptr**, and dereferencing d_remote has undefined behavior. There are multiple ways to fix the copy-assignment operator; for illustration purposes, we'll simply add a conditional to test d_remote and, if it is equal to **nullptr**, use an alternative implementation:

---

[33]The 11.0.1 version of the libc++ Standard Library does use the described approach and will result in a crash.

```
my_type& my_type::operator=(const my_type& rhs)
{
    if (d_remote == nullptr)
    {
        *this = my_type(rhs);   // copy-construct and move-assign
    }
    else
    {
        *d_remote = *rhs.d_remote;
    }

    return *this;
}
```

The additional check is sufficient to make *all* of the standard containers and algorithms work correctly. Unfortunately, this check is not sufficient to satisfy a strict reading of the Standard's requirements for element types.

- Copy construction from a moved-from object will fail.

- Copy assignment from a moved-from object will fail.

- Equality will fail if either operand has been moved from.

All of these operations would cause a **nullptr** to be dereferenced. The Standard Library states that these operations must be valid for *all* values of a given type.

The implementations of functions associated with the containers and algorithms in the Standard Library will never perform any operation on a moved-from object other than to destroy it or assign a new value to it *unless* called with an object that has already been moved from, i.e., by the caller directly. The operations in the list above will never be invoked.

The `std::swap` algorithm imposes one additional requirement. Consider swapping a value — e.g., `std::swap(x, x)` — with itself:

```
void test2()
{
    my_type x;
    // inlined std::swap(x, x):
    my_type tmp = std::move(x);
    x = std::move(x); // self-move-assignment of a moved-from object
    x = std::move(tmp);
}
```

The expression `x = std::move(x)` is a self-move-assignment of a moved-from object. The default move-assignment in the implementation of `my_type` above will work correctly for self-move-assignment of a moved-from object. The default implementation satisfies the post-conditions for both the right-hand and left-hand sides of the arguments and does not affect the value of x. The left-hand side of the argument of move assignment must be equal to the prior value of the right-hand side of the argument. The containers and algorithms in the Standard Library do not self-swap objects, but std::swap annoyingly provides the guarantee that self-swap will work if the arguments satisfy the requirements for the *move-constructible* and *move-assignable* concepts. The requirement for self-swap is both a legacy requirement from when std::swap was implemented in terms of copy and follows from a general requirement in the Standard that, unless otherwise specified, operations should work even if reference arguments alias each other in whole or in part. There is no known value in supporting self-swap, and a self-swap usually indicates a defect in the algorithm.

Adding the additional checks to satisfy the Standard's wording has an otherwise unnecessary performance impact and proves to be error-prone to implement. Beyond that, the additional code introduces a new *empty* state for my_type, which must be considered if we introduce an ordering with **operator**<() or any other operation the Standard Library might invoke. The gratuitously induced empty state defeats the purpose of **value semantics** because coding with an object that might or might not be empty is equivalent to coding with a pointer that might or might not be null.

The root cause of this issue is broader than just the postconditions of move operations. There is a Standard proposal to address these issues.[34] Until the proposal is adopted (and it might not be), a type must include these additional checks to adhere to the standard requirements.

Lack of destructive move

As far back as Hinnant's proposal,[35] the paper that first brought a complete approach to rvalue references to C++ in 2002, a gap was recognized: the lack of a single function that can both move the contents out of an object and also destroy it. The ability to combine moving from an object and destroying that same object into one operation would enable the design of types that do not have a resourceless moved-from state, avoiding the need for many of the considerations brought up in *Potential Pitfalls — Inconsistent expectations on moved-from objects* on page 794.

The complications in providing this form of destructive move or relocation functionality are numerous, and no refined proposal for a complete solution, that we are aware of, has come forward in the years since **rvalue references** were first officially proposed. A complete solution would need to address at least three items.

1. A syntactic and semantic mechanism to distinguish this new form for destroying an object from other ways in which an object can be passed and not destroyed would need to be designed.

2. The ability to apply operations of this sort to automatic variables would seem necessary to make the cost of another new language feature worth the benefits, but that would

---

[34]parent21
[35]hinnant02

require some mechanism to ensure that destructively moved objects can no longer be referenced once destroyed. This mechanism would involve potentially complex changes to name-lookup rules and object-lifetime rules.

3. The definition of destructive moves in a class hierarchy would be complicated by the requirement that the destruction of the members and bases of an expiring object and the construction of the corresponding members and bases of a new object must happen in the opposite order and thus cannot be done in parallel. Such remediation was, perhaps, one of the biggest unsolved sticking points when Hinnant[36] explored this design space.

Many of these problems are not applicable when relocation can be accomplished with a trivial copy operation combined with simply not invoking a destructor on the source object. A surprising number of types meet this criteria since any type that uniquely owns a resource by pointer is a potential candidate, including most common implementations of std::string, std::vector, and std::unique_ptr. Various production platforms have observed and leveraged this behavior, e.g., BDE[37] and Folly.[38] This partial approach to enabling types to support a limited form of destructive move is being considered for standardization.[39] The great benefit of having a trivial operation of this sort is that mass moves of objects between blocks of memory, such as that done by std::vector on insertions and resizes, can become single invocations of std::memcpy with no loss of correctness.

See Also

- "**decltype**" (§1.1, p. 25) describes an operator that depends heavily on the **value category** of its arguments.

- "Defaulted Functions" (§1.1, p. 33) expands on the details of defaulting the special member functions related to moving.

- "Deleted Functions" (§1.1, p. 53) expands on the details of deleting special member functions related to moving.

- "Forwarding References" (§2.1, p. 377) describes another use of the double-ampersand (&&) syntax, closely related but distinct from **rvalue references**.

- "**noexcept** Operator" (§2.1, p. 615) illustrates a feature that is commonly used to query the **noexcept** specification of move operations.

---

[36] **hinnant02**

[37] The BDE library from Bloomberg (**bde14**) identifies types that can support this form of relocation with a user-specializable type trait, bslmf::IsBitwiseMoveable, and takes advantage of that trait in many of the containers it provides.

[38] Facebook's Folly library (**facebook**) has a type trait, folly::isRelocatable, that identifies trivially relocatable objects, which is used to advantage in Folly containers such as fbvector.

[39] **odwyer20**

- "**noexcept** Specifier" (§3.1, p. 1085) describes the specifier commonly applied to move operations indicating that they do not throw exceptions.

- "Ref-Qualifiers" (§3.1, p. 1153) explains a feature that allows for overloading member functions on the **value category** of the object on which they are invoked.

Further Reading

- For the definitive retrospective on value category naming in C++11 by Stroustrup himself, see **stroustrup**.

- For the trail of papers that introduced move semantics, rvalue references, and the refined C++11 value categories, start with N1377 (**hinnant02**) and continue to N3055 (**miller10**). Produced in 2006 during the evolution of the feature, N2027 (**hinnant06**) gives an overview of the basics and cites many of the papers that contributed to how the feature took shape.

- For a solid treatment of the theory value semantics along with its practical applications, see **lakos15a** and **lakos15b**.

- *Effective Modern C++* (**meyers15b**) contains an excellent discussion of value categories, rvalue references, move semantics, and perfect forwarding.

- *C++ Move Semantics — The Complete Guide* is a recent attempt by a world-renowned author to capture all things related to move semantics, including value categories, rvalue references, and perfect forwarding; see **josuttis20b**.

Appendix

The evolution of value categories

What is a value category?   In C++, we use declaration statements to introduce named objects and functions into a scope:

```
const int i = 5;    // variable i of type const int having the value 5
double d = 3.14;    // variable d of type double having the value 3.14
double* p = &d;     // variable p of type double* holding the address of d
char f();           // function f returning a value of type char
enum E { A } e;     // variable e of type E enumerating A
```

We can then combine these functions and objects along with literals to form expressions. Some of these expressions might identify an object, and these expressions are all collectively known as *lvalues*:

```
void testExpressions1()
{
    i;      // a nonmodifiable int value whose address can be taken
    (i);    // "          "        "     "    "       "   "   "   "
    d;      // a modifiable double value whose address can be taken
    p;      // "         "    double*   "    "       "   "   "   "
    *p;     // "         "    double    "    "       "   "   "   "
    e;      // a modifiable E value whose address can be taken
}
```

The "l" in *lvalue* is often taken to mean "left" since these expressions can all conceivably appear on the left-hand side of an assignment operator. Even expressions with **const**-qualified type, which actually makes them ineligible to be the target of assignment, are considered *lvalues* since they identify an object in memory. Another common interpretation of the "l" is "live" since the objects, in general, reside in memory throughout the duration of their lifetime. However, being an *lvalue* is a compile-time property that is not dependent on the runtime value of the expression; for example, even if an expression dereferences a null pointer, it is still considered an *lvalue*.

All other expressions are then collectively known as non*lvalues*. Often, this category is identified as *rvalues*, with the "r" taken to mean "right" since these expressions are those that can appear on the right-hand side of an assignment operator:

```
void testExpressions2()
{
    5;          // int value whose address cannot be taken
    (i + 1);    // "    "    "       "       "      "   "
    (d + i);    // double value whose address cannot be taken
    f();        // char value whose address cannot be taken
    f() + 1;    // int     "    "       "       "     "   "
    A;          // E value whose address cannot be taken
}
```

Each of these non*lvalue* expressions identifies a value but not necessarily an object that resides in memory. All *lvalues* can also be implicitly converted to *rvalues*, referred to as **lvalue-to-rvalue conversion**, which is how the value in an *lvalue* is accessed. Another common interpretation for the "r" in *rvalue* is "read-only," as these values can be used to initialize other objects but cannot generally be modified.

Value categories prior to C++11   Early on — well before C++ — the classic, pre-Standard C programming language had already made the distinction between *lvalues* and non*lvalues*, a.k.a. *rvalues*.[40] In that characterization, the "l" in *lvalue* stood for "left" (as in what could appear on the left-hand side of an assignment operator); similarly, the "r" in *rvalue* stood for "right," as in what could appear on (only) the right-hand side. Along with the introduction of ANSI C,[41] the common characterization of an *lvalue* had evolved: "l" had

---

[40]**kernighan78**, Appendix A, section 5, "Objects and lvalues," p. 183

[41]**kernighan88**, Appendix A, section A.5, "Objects and Lvalues," p. 197

come to stand for where the object "lives," as in *object identity*. That is, an *lvalue* became one having an address, whereas a non*lvalue* has none. One can think of an *lvalue* as an expression — e.g., a named variable, an element of an array, or a (nonbit) field of a **struct** or **union** — whose address can be taken using the built-in (unary) address-of operator (&).

C also identified a third category, **function designator**, that — except when used as the operand of & (address-of operator), **sizeof**, and _Alignof — **decays**, i.e., is converted automatically, to the non*lvalue* address of the designated function, much like how a C-style array **decays** to the address of its first element. As all function-like behavior became part of the C++ type system, anything C identified as a **function designator** became a nonmodifiable *lvalue* in classical C++.

C++ restored the term "*rvalue*," replacing "non*lvalue*," to refer to any value not associated with physical storage, e.g., an arithmetic literal, enumerator, or nonreference value returned from a function.

Lvalue-reference declarations prior to C++11   C++ introduced the notion of an lvalue reference that can be declared **const** or non**const**.[42] Lvalue references allow for giving a name to the result of an *lvalue* expression, which can later be used wherever the *lvalue* expression could be used:

```
        int    i;        // modifiable lvalue
  const int    ci = 5;   // nonmodifiable lvalue initialized to value 5

        int&  ri1 = i;   // OK
        int&  ri2 = ci;  // Error, modifiable reference to const object
  const int&  rci1 = i;  // OK
  const int&  rci2 = ci; // OK
```

The original use case motivating references in C++ was to declare overloaded operators for user-defined types:

```
struct Point  // user-defined value type
{
    int d_x;
    int d_y;
    Point(int x, int y) : d_x(x), d_y(y) { }  // value constructor
};


Point operator+(const Point& lhs, const Point& rhs)
    // Return the vector sum of the specified lhs and rhs objects.
{
    return Point(lhs.d_x + rhs.d_x, lhs.d_y + rhs.d_y);
}
```

---

[42]Independently of whether the reference is declared **const**, it can also be declared **volatile**; similar to **const** qualifiers and *pointer* variables, a non**volatile** *reference* might not be initialized with the address of a **volatile** object. As the **volatile** qualifier is seldom used (productively) in practice, we will omit further consideration of it here.

The example above suggests a degree of convenience but not necessity. The `Point` arguments in the **operator+** above could have just as easily been passed by value, but pass-by-value would be problematic for its copy constructor. For an allocating object, such as an `std::string`, the arguments to its **operator+**, implementing string concatenation, could have been passed as efficiently via pointer.

The true value of references is illustrated by operators — such as the array-index operator, **operator[]**, and especially the common **assignment operator**, **operator=** — that return *access* to an independent object, not an *address* or *copy*:

```
void test()
{
    int         x, y, z;  x = y = z = 0;   // chaining in C and C++
    struct S { } a, b, c;  a = b = c = S();  // chaining in C++ only
}
```

That said, lvalue references in C++ also make it possible for the value returned by a function to be an *lvalue*:

```
Point& singletonPoint()  // Scott Meyers is known for this pattern of singleton.
{
    static Point meyersSingleton(0, 0);
    return meyersSingleton;  // Return reference to function-local static Point.
}


Point *address = &singletonPoint();  // address of function-local static Point
```

What's more, many expressions involving built-in operators that were considered non*lvalues* in C became *lvalues* in C++:

```
#include <cassert>  // standard C assert macro
void f0()
{
    int x = 1, y = 2;  // modifiable int variables
                       assert(1 == x);  assert(2 == y);
    (x = y) += 1;      assert(3 == x);  assert(2 == y);
    ++x += y;          assert(6 == x);  assert(2 == y);
    --x -= 2;          assert(3 == x);  assert(2 == y);
    x++ *= 3;          // Error, x++ is a nonlvalue (even in C++).
    (y, x) = 6;        assert(6 == x);  assert(2 == y);
    (x ? x : y) = 7;   assert(7 == x);  assert(2 == y);
}
```

As illustrated above, the affected operations include each of the built-in assignment operators (e.g., x *= 2), the built-in *prefix* but not *postfix* increment (++x) and decrement (--x) operators, potentially the comma operator (x, y), and potentially the ternary operator (x ? y : z):

```
void f1()
{
```

```
int x, y = 0;    // modifiable int variables
x = 1;           // lvalue in C++ (but not in C)
x *= 2;          //      "      "   "    "    "    "  "
++x;             //      "      "   "    "    "    "  "
--x;             //      "      "   "    "    "    "  "
x, y;            //      "      "   "    "    "    "  "
1, x;            //      "      "   "    "    "    "  "
x ? x : y;       //      "      "   "    "    "    "  "

x++;             // nonlvalue in C++ (and C too)
x--;             //      "      "   "    "    "    "
x, 1;            //      "      "   "    "    "    "
x ? 1 : y;       //      "      "   "    "    "    "
y ? x : 1;       //      "      "   "    "    "    "
}
```

With *lvalue* originally deriving from "left," intuition might lead one to think that being an *lvalue* is fundamentally tied to modifiability through assignment. C++ instead focuses on whether an expression represents an object in memory and whether taking the address of that object is a wise decision. Expressions that resolve to **const** built-in types or to user-defined types that fail to find a matching overload of **operator=** cannot be on the left-hand side of an assignment expression. However, class types that do support assignment can be on the left-hand side, which is the default for all class types:

```
struct S { /*...*/ };  // arbitrary class type supporting copy assignment

void f2()
{
    S() = S();  // OK, default behavior for all class types
}
```

Interestingly, for admittedly odd, user-defined types with a **const** overload of **operator=**, even a **const** non*lvalue* can be placed on the left-hand side of an assignment expression:

```
struct Odd
{
    const Odd& operator=(const Odd& rhs) const { return *this; }
};

void test()
{
    Odd() = Odd();  // rvalue assignment to rvalue

    const int x = 7;
    x = 8;          // Error, cannot assign to const int lvalue
}
```

Note, however, that if the assignment attempted to alter the state of any non**mutable** member of **Odd**, the program would surely fail to compile.

The address-of operator, &, is the primary language tool that is applicable only to *lvalues*. Any *lvalue* expression identifies an object in memory, generally one that has a lifetime beyond that expression, so the address-of operator is allowed to apply to such expressions:

```cpp
void f3(bool e)
{
    int a = 1, b = 2;    // modifiable integer variables

    &(a);        // OK
    &(++a);      // OK

    &(a + 5);    // Error, a + 5 is a nonlvalue.
    &(a++);      // Error, a++ is a nonlvalue.
    &(b, a);     // OK
    &(e ? a : b); // OK
}
```

Temporaries: nonreference values returned from a function   When a function returns an object via a nonreference type, an object might be created in memory whose lifetime will generally end after the statement invoking the function. Expressions that create and refer to such temporary objects are a form of non*lvalue*:

```cpp
double f() { return 3.14; }  // function returning a nonref. type by value
```

The lifetime of a temporary will typically, with some notable exceptions, last until the end of the largest expression in which it is contained, after which the temporary is destroyed:

```cpp
#include <iostream>  // std::cout
void g() { std::cout << "pi = " << f() << '\n'; }  // prints: pi = 3.14
```

When function g() above is invoked, the **temporary** used to represent the value returned by f() as an argument to the << operator's **const** lvalue reference parameter will persist until the end of the single statement in g's body.

In some cases, the lifetime of the **temporary** will be extended beyond the outermost expression in which it resides; see *Lifetime extension of a temporary bound to a reference* on page 819. On the other hand, when initializing elements of an array, if construction of an element requires creating a **temporary** for a default argument, said **temporary** will be destroyed *before* the next array element is created.

If more than one **temporary**'s lifetime ends at the same point, they are destroyed in the reverse order in which they were created:

```cpp
struct S  // This struct prints upon each construction and destruction.
{
    int d_i;  // holds constructor argument
    S(int i) : d_i(i) { std::cout << " C" << d_i; }  // print: Ci.
    S(const S&) { std::cout << "COPY";  exit(-1); }  // never called
```

```
    ~S()                { std::cout << " D" << d_i; }  // print: Di.
};

S f(int i) { return S(i); }  // factory function returning S(i) by value

void g()  // demonstrates relative order of ctor/dtor of temporary objects
{
    f(1);               // prints: C1 D1
    f(2), f(3);         // prints: C2 C3 D3 D2
    f(4), f(5), f(6);   // prints: C4 C5 C6 D6 D5 D4
}
```

In the example above, S prints a C_i on construction and a corresponding D_i when the object is destroyed. Notice that, despite the factory function constructing and returning an S by value, no copy operation occurs due to an optimization known as **return-value optimization (RVO)**. Although neither of the C++11 and C++14 Standards mandates it, this optimization has been implemented by virtually every popular C++ compiler since the early 2000s, provided an accessible *copy* or *move* constructor is declared, even if none is defined.

Lifetime extension of a temporary bound to a reference   Whenever a temporary object or a subobject of a **temporary object** is bound to a **const** lvalue reference (since C++98) or to an rvalue reference (since C++11), the lifetime of the **temporary object** is extended to be that of the reference to which it is bound:

```
struct S  // example struct containing data members and accessor functions
{
    int d_i;                    // integer data member
    int d_a[5];                 // integer array data member
    int i() { return d_i; }     // function returning data by value
    int& ir() { return d_i; }   // function returning data by reference
};

S f()  // example function constructing temporaries of varying lifetimes
{
    S();                        // temporary S destroyed after the semicolon
    const   S& r0 = S();        //     "     "     "     when r0 leaves scope
    const int& r1 = S().d_i;    //     "     "     "     when r1 leaves scope
    const int& r2 = S().d_a[3]; //     "     "     "     when r2 leaves scope
    const int& r3 = S().i();    //     "     "     "     after the semicolon
    const int& r4 = S().ir();   //     "     "     "     after the semicolon

    int i1 = r3;                // OK, copies from lifetime-extended temporary
    int i2 = r4;                // Bug, undefined behavior

    return S();                 // temporary S returned as rvalue to caller
}
```

Note that binding a reference to a member keeps the entire temporary object alive. Similarly, binding a reference to an element of an array keeps the array alive, and transitively keeps the complete object alive. There is no such connection between the return value of a function, such as the return values of i() and ir() above, and the object on which that function is invoked, so the S objects used to initialize r3 and r4 do not offer anything that extends their lifetimes beyond the statement in which they are created. In the case of r3, a temporary **int** *is* created, and the lifetime of that **int** extends to the end of the scope. In the case of r4, the referenced **int** is destroyed in the statement where r4 is initialized, making access through r4 have **undefined behavior** anywhere later in the function.

A temporary's lifetime is not necessarily tied to that of a reference to which it is bound. When binding to a reference member in a constructor initializer list, the temporary is destroyed at the end of the constructor. When binding to a reference parameter of a function, a **return** value, or in the initializer of a **new** expression, the **temporary**'s lifetime will end at the end of the **outermost expression** in which it resides:

```cpp
struct A { int&& d_r; };  // aggregate type having rvalue-reference member
int&& f() { return 3; }   // function returning rvalue-reference to temporary
void g(int&& r);          // function having rvalue-reference parameter

void h()
{
    A *p = new A{3};   // Temporary has shorter lifetime than reference.
    int &&r = f();     //     "        "   shorter   "        "        "
    delete new A{3};   //     "        "   longer    "        "        "
    g(3);              //     "        "   longer    "        "        "
}
```

Modifiable *rvalues*!   Given *rvalue*'s historical roots in C, some might find it incongruous that an "rvalue" (i.e., *rvalue* expression) could ever be modified because many used to think the "r" stood for "read-only." Before expounding on modern C++ value categories in the next section, let's observe that modifiability is, and always has been, a separable property of a C++ expression that is largely orthogonal to its value category. User-defined, non**const** operators can be invoked on temporary objects capable of modifying — or even relinquishing the address of — such temporaries:

```cpp
struct S
{
    int d_i;

    S() : d_i(0) { }

    S* addr() { return this; }           // accessor mostly equivalent to &
    S& incr() { ++d_i; return *this; }   // manipulator
};
```

```
void test()
{
    S* tempPtr = S().addr();   // address of temporary acquired
                               // tempPtr invalidated

    int i = S().incr().d_i;    // temporary created, modified, and accessed
    assert(i == 1);
}
```

Importantly, this sort of access to **temporaries** does not alter their fundamental nature; they are temporary. Even though the address of a temporary is acquired in **tempPtr** in the example above, the temporary itself will be destroyed after the statement is completed. Similarly, the member variable **d_i** of the temporary in the initializer for **i** is initialized itself, modified, accessed, and then destroyed, all within the same expression.

Rvalues of fundamental types in C++03, however, are not modifiable. The reason is twofold: (1) *rvalues* are not permitted to bind to non**const** lvalue references, and (2) fundamental types have no member functions. Hence, all operations that mutate fundamental types behave as if they were passed in as the first argument to a free operator with the first parameter passed as a non**const** lvalue reference:

```
// pseudocode illustrating how operators on fundamental types behave

int& operator=(int& lhs, const int& rhs);   // free operator function
    // Assign the value of rhs to the modifiable int object bound to lhs,
    // and return an lvalue reference to lhs.

int& operator+=(int& lhs, const int& rhs);  // free operator function
    // Assign the value that is the sum of rhs and lhs to the modifiable
    // int object bound to lhs, and return an lvalue reference to lhs.
```

In the same way that a member function can be restricted, using a **const** qualifier, to apply to **const** objects only, in C++11 a member function can be restricted, using an lvalue-reference qualifier, to apply to *lvalues* only; see Section 3.1. "Ref-Qualifiers" on page 1153. Applying such a reference qualifier to the assignment operator is the only way to get the same behavior for the assignment operator on a user-defined type that exists for fundamental types.

Occasionally, the ability to modify — and typically cannibalize — the state of a temporary is eminently useful. This ability will turn out to be the driving force behind the addition of rvalue references and the expansion of value categories to include *xvalues* in C++11.

Rationale: Why do we want move semantics?   As with many engineering solutions, necessity is the mother of invention. Make no mistake: The very notion of an **rvalue reference** was *invented* as part of a much larger feature engineered to solve a common, objectively verifiable performance problem involving (1) gratuitous memory allocations and deallocations and (2) excessive data copying. Consider the following program that does nothing more than build up an `std::vector` of `std::vector`s of `std::string`s, either by appending to the nested vectors or by inserting them at the front:

```
#include <vector>    // std::vector
#include <string>    // std::string
#include <cstdlib>   // std::atoi, std::abs

int main(int argc, char *argv[])
{
    int k = argc > 1 ? std::atoi(argv[1]) : 8;
    bool front = k < 0;
    int N = 1 << std::abs(k);

    std::string s = "The quick brown fox jumped over the lazy dog.";
        // string value that is too long for short-string optimization

    std::vector<std::string> vs;
    for (int i = 0; i < N; ++i) { vs.push_back(s); }
        // Create an (inner) vector-of-strings exemplar of size N.

    std::vector<std::vector<std::string> > vvs;
        // Create an empty vector of vectors of strings to be loaded in two ways.

    for (int i = 0; i < N; ++i)  // Make the outer vector of size N as well.
    {
        if (front)
        {
            vvs.insert(vvs.begin(), vs);  // Insert copy of vs at the beginning.
        }
        else
        {
            vvs.push_back(vs);             // Append copy of vs at the end.
        }
    }

    return 0;
}
```

This program, valid in both C++03 and C++11, behaves differently with the changes in C++11, and algorithms such as this were the intended target of the introduction of **move operations** to the language.

In C++03, the calls to **push_back** will, when needed, grow the internal capacity buffer of **vvs** a logarithmic number of times, e.g., capacity $= 1, 2, 4, \ldots, 2^N$, and copy all of the already-added elements to the new storage on each resize. Alternatively, when inserting at the front, each individual `insert` operation must copy all elements in vvs to the next element in the capacity buffer and then put the new element at index 0.

In C++11, both of these operations are vastly improved by the addition of **move semantics** to `std::vector`. Independently of the mechanics of the language feature, when an `std::vector` is moved from one location to another, it gives ownership of the allocated data buffer to the target object and leaves the source object empty (with 0 size and capacity and no data buffer). This constant-time operation, consisting of nothing more than the assignment of a small number of data members having fundamental types, replaces a linear-time operation involving many allocations but comes at the cost of altering the state of the source object. When possible, growing the data buffer in C++11 can take advantage of this moving behavior to move elements from the older, smaller data buffer to the newer, larger-capacity buffer. A constant-time move operation allows insertion at the front of the vector to become a linear-time operation, with no need to perform any extra operations regardless of the contents of the contained elements.

Running this program on a range of input values, all on the same host and compiler,[43] can show dramatic differences in performance for the same source code; see Table 3.

Table 3: Runtime impact of move semantics

		push_back		insert	
k	$N = 2^k$	C++03	C++11	C++03	C++11
8	256	0.029s	0.030s	0.028s	0.030s
9	512	0.037s	0.033s	0.235s	0.032s
10	1,024	0.065s	0.039s	1.560s	0.048s
11	2,048	0.179s	0.114s	13.704s	0.112s
12	4,096	0.628s	0.359s	99.057s	0.373s
13	8,192	2.409s	1.338s	764.613s	1.364s
14	16,384	9.728s	5.347s	5,958.029s	5.463s
15	32,768	66.789s	35.418s	40,056.858s	34.318s
16	65,576	core dump	97.943s	core dump	92.920s

This dramatic improvement comes from the **move semantics** of `std::vector`'s move operations enabling a constant-time move, instead of a linear-time copy, combined with the language facilitating `std::vector` being able to generically take advantage of that functionality when its `value_type` supports it. While nothing about these algorithms is impossible in C++03, having generic types able to reliably express and take advantage of this kind of improvement was deemed worth the cost of dramatically changing the language.

---

[43]The numbers shown were generated by timing the program on a T480 Thinkpad laptop with GCC 7.4.0 (c. 2018), setting optimization to -O2, and using `-std=c++03` or `-std=c++11` appropriately.

Why do we need *rvalue* references?   The ability to *move* the internal data structure of an allocating type from one object to another in C++11 — rather than always having to *copy* it, in the C++03 sense — can, under appropriate circumstances, lead to profoundly superior performance characteristics.

Classic C++, i.e., C++03, did not provide a systematic syntactic means for indicating that it was OK to extract the *guts* of an object and transplant them into another object of like type. The only time that doing such a thing would have been guaranteed to be safe in C++03 was when the object was a *temporary*, but there was no way to overload the copy constructor or assignment operator so that they would behave differently (and more optimally) when passed a *temporary*.

Classic C++ did, however, provide one Standard Library type, `std::auto_ptr`, that attempted to implement move semantics. This ill-fated, smart pointer type had a non**const** lvalue reference copy constructor that would take ownership from and reset its source object when "copied." While `std::auto_ptr` functioned as a pioneer for move semantics in C++03, it also helped to identify the dangers of attempting to implement move semantics without the more fundamental changes that came with rvalue references. Many attempts to work with containers of `std::auto_ptr` or to leverage standard algorithms with `std::auto_ptr` showed how easy it was for generic code to assume that copies were safe to make and promptly destroy the data on which they were attempting to operate. Move semantics enabled the introduction of `std::unique_ptr` as a true move-only type without the pitfalls of `std::auto_ptr`, and at the same time, `std::auto_ptr` was deprecated[44] and then finally removed in C++17.[45]

The introduction of rvalue references, using a syntax of && instead of the single & used for lvalue references, provided the key way in which implementations that take advantage of objects being in a movable state can be written in a safe and robust manner. `std::auto_ptr` showed that modifiable lvalue references were not sufficient for this task, and thus a new reference type was introduced to enable move operations. A new reference type facilitated new rules for what it could bind to and how it integrated with overload resolution and template argument deduction and provided a distinct format to identify implementations of move operations that would have minimal risk of changing the meaning of existing types.

Why do we need a new value category?   Simply put, the challenge for the designers of this C++11 feature was to enable move operations to occur when either (1) the compiler knows for certain that it is safe to do so or (2) the programmer takes responsibility for explicitly authorizing the compiler to enable a **move operation** that the compiler would not otherwise consider safe on its own. Their solution was twofold.

---

[44] **hinnant05**
[45] **baker14**

1. Invent the notion of an **rvalue reference** as a means for binding more aggressively than a **const** lvalue reference to expressions that are eligible to be moved from during overload resolution.

2. Invent a new **value category**, known as an *xvalue*, that could distinguish when an expression identifies an object that is eligible to be moved from, including temporary objects that are about to be implicitly destroyed and will no longer be reachable as well as objects manually identified, through an explicit cast to **rvalue reference**, as being eligible.

After a great deal of effort during the C++11 standardization process, the set of value categories that we have come to know today evolved and is represented in the Standard with the following chart[46],[47]:

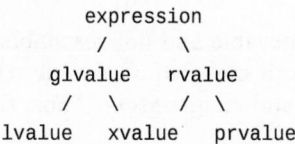

```
                    expression
                    /        \
               glvalue      rvalue
               /    \       /    \
          lvalue   xvalue  prvalue
```

This taxonomy helped greatly in formalizing the mechanics of **move operations** in the language, culminating in the final form of **value categories** in C++11.[48] A fundamental property that led to this categorization was identifying two primary, independent properties that could apply to a **value**.

1. A value can **have identity** or be **reachable** if it has an address and exists independently of the current expression.

2. A value can be **movable** if it is OK to cannibalize the internal representation of the object representing the value. Distinguishing values such as this was the primary goal of seeking to introduce **move semantics** into the language in the first place.

The two classical value categories, *lvalues* and non*lvalues*, both had opposite orientations for these two properties. An *lvalue* was **reachable** and not **movable**, whereas a non*lvalue* was not **reachable** and was **movable**. As the realization emerged that the goal was to treat these two properties orthogonally, it became apparent that the other pairings of these properties needed to be considered. A nonmovable, nonreachable value was deemed essentially not useful or worth considering, as nothing could fundamentally be done with such a value.

---

[46]**iso11a**, section 3.10, "Lvalues and rvalues," Figure 1, p. 78

[47]The motivation for what would become the terminology for the new value categories is explained by Bjarne Stroustrup himself (**stroustrup**).

[48]**miller10**

A **movable** and **reachable** object, however, was the missing piece of the puzzle needed to manually identify that an object was ready to be moved from.

Given this understanding, the task then became to identify reasonable names for values with these sets of properties.

- The category of *lvalue* was already formalized in the Standard and clearly embodied values that were **reachable** and not **movable**.

- At a fundamental level, historical work in computer science had trained people to intuitively conclude that *lvalues* and *rvalues* were a partitioning of the set of all values; i.e., every value was either an *lvalue* or an *rvalue*, and no value was both. This conclusion led to the *rvalue* category implicitly becoming all **movable** values, both **reachable** and not **reachable**.

- The set of values that are **movable** and not **reachable** matched well with many of the classical notions of *rvalue*, as it included *pure* values that had no object representation yet, such as integer literals and enumerators. Thus, this category was called *prvalues*, or *pure rvalues*.

- The set of all values that are **reachable** was also something that would need a name, as this category would come into play in the language in a number of places as a generalization of what was previously workable only with *lvalues*. Many fundamental operations that apply to an object in memory are worded in terms of the new *glvalue* category, or *generalized lvalues*.

- Finally, the category of **movable** objects that were **reachable** needed a name. As this category was a functionally new invention, a suitable name was not evident, and, perhaps serendipitously, the noncommittal letter "x" was chosen for the new *xvalue* category. Originally, this letter was chosen to represent "the unknown, the strange, the xpert only, or even the x-rated."[49] Over time, the "x" evolved to capture the **movability** of the values in this category, and it now stands for "expiring."

It is worth noting that the term *rvalue* changed meaning in C++11 by expanding to include *xvalues* that are reachable. This change coincides well with **rvalue references** being able to functionally bind to any *rvalue* but was a shift from classical C++ where *rvalues* were generally not **reachable**.[50] The change in terminology was deemed worth the potential confusion

---

[49]**stroustrup**

[50]Once an object of a class, even a temporary one, has its **this** pointer passed to a user-provided constructor, there are many side avenues by which that object might be referenced outside of the expression in which it was created:

```
struct A* p;                        // pointer to incomplete type
struct A  { A() { p = this; } };  // reachable whenever constructed
```

as it had far less impact than a similar change to *lvalue* would have had, and it kept *lvalue* and *rvalue* as a disjoint partition of the set of all values.

In C++11 as originally specified, the only way to arrive at an *xvalue* was via an explicit cast to an **rvalue reference** or by calling a function that returns an **rvalue reference**; hence, *xvalues* referencing unreachable temporaries were significantly harder to acquire. The original understanding many had was that an *xvalue* was essentially a *movable* nontemporary. Even as originally formulated, though, member functions invoked on temporaries were able to access and distribute *lvalue*, and thus *xvalue*, references to the temporaries through the **this** pointer. Two major core issues that impacted *xvalues*[51,52] were addressed in C++14 and applied retroactively as **defect reports** to C++11. These rule changes led to the treatment of subobjects of both *prvalues* and *xvalues* as *xvalues*, such as when doing data member access, pointer to data member dereferencing, and array subscripting.

As the understanding of where the differing value categories can have an impact has evolved, it has become clear that *xvalue* expressions identify **movable** objects that exist in memory, i.e., their lifetime has begun, but places no restrictions on whether the objects in question will continue their lifetimes beyond the end of the current statement.[53] In normal use, all *rvalues* — both *xvalues* and *prvalues* — bind equally well to **rvalue references** and are, for the most part, indistinguishable programmatically. One of the few places where they are treated differently is as a parenthesized expression used with the **decltype** operator (see Section 1.1. "**decltype**" on page 25), which can be leveraged to identify value categories (see *Use Cases — Identifying value categories* on page 779).

With this new set of value categories in hand, the only remaining pieces needed to integrate **move semantics** into the language were mechanisms to produce *xvalues* in code to which **rvalue references** may be bound. Given a *prvalue*, this mechanism could obviously be an implicit conversion, and thus many automatic benefits of **move semantics** could be enabled. Supporting only such implicit conversions and moving from only temporaries, however, was not going to solve strong motivational cases, like our std::vector<std::vector<std::string>> example described in *Rationale: Why do we want move semantics?* on page 821. To enable such cases, *xvalues* also needed to include *lvalues* that had been explicitly cast to **rvalue references**, enabling the moving of objects already stored in a data structure. To further enable the use of **rvalue references**, functions that return an **rvalue reference** also create *xvalues* when invoked, enabling Standard Library

---

[51]CWG issue 616; **stroustrup07**

[52]CWG issue 1213; **merrill10a**

[53]This same refinement of what is an *xvalue* and what is a *prvalue* inspired the formalization of guaranteed copy elision in C++17. The cases where no extra temporary needs to be created from the return value from a function are exactly the cases where a function call expression is a *prvalue* of the appropriate type, enabling the choice to simply materialize that *prvalue* in the location of the variable being initialized. This restructuring avoids the need to define intermediate temporaries and renders unnecessary the ability to optimize away those temporaries, making object lifetime more deterministic as well as enabling RVO for types that can be neither copied nor moved.

functions like `std::move` and other cases where encapsulating the ability to enable moving from a preexisting object is desired.

Explicit Enumeration Underlying Type

The underlying type of an enumeration is the fundamental **integral type** used to represent its enumerated values, which can be specified explicitly in C++11.

Description

Every enumeration employs an integral type, known as its **underlying type**, to represent its compile-time-enumerated values. By default, the **underlying type** of a C++03 **enum** is chosen by the implementation to be large enough to represent all of the values in the enumeration and is allowed to exceed the size of an **int** *only* if there are enumerators having values that cannot be represented as an **int** or **unsigned int**:

```
enum RGB { e_RED, e_GREEN, e_BLUE };                    // OK, fits any char

enum Port { e_LEFT = -81, e_RIGHT = -82 };              // OK, fits signed char

enum Mask { e_LOW = 32767, e_HIGH = 65535 };            // OK, fits unsigned short

enum Big { e_31 = 1U<<31 };                             // OK, fits unsigned int

enum Err { K = 1024, M = K*K, G = M*K, T = G*K };       // Error, G*K overflows int...

enum OK { K = 1<<10, M = 1<<20, G = 1<<30, T = 1LL<<40 }; // OK
```

The default underlying type chosen for an **enum** is always sufficiently large to represent *all* enumerator values defined for that **enum**. If the value doesn't fit in an **int**, it will be selected deterministically as the first type able to represent all values from the sequence: **unsigned int**, **long**, **unsigned long**, **long long**, **unsigned long long**; see Section 1.1. "**long long**" on page 89.

While specifying an enumeration's underlying type was impossible before C++11, the compiler could be forced to choose at least a 32-bit or 64-bit signed integral type by adding an enumerator having a sufficiently large negative value — e.g., **-1 << 31** for a 32-bit and **-1LL << 63** for a 64-bit signed integer (assuming such is available on the target platform).

The above applies only to C++03 **enum**s; the default underlying type of an **enum class** is ubiquitously **int**, and it is not implementation defined; see Section 2.1. "**enum class**" on page 332.

Note that **char** and **wchar_t**, like enumerations, are their own distinct types (as opposed to **typedef**-like aliases such as std::uint8_t) and have their own implementation-defined underlying integral types. With **char**, for example, the underlying type will always be either

signed char or **unsigned char** (both of which are also distinct C++ types). The same is true in C++11 for **char16_t** and **char32_t**.[1]

Specifying underlying type explicitly

As of C++11, we have the ability to specify the **integral type** that is used to represent an **enum** by providing the type explicitly in the **enum**'s declaration following the enumeration's (optional) name and preceded by a colon:

```
enum Port : unsigned char
{
    // Each enumerator of Port is represented as an unsigned char type.

    e_INPUT        =  37,  // OK, would have fit in a signed char too
    e_OUTPUT       = 142,  // OK, would not have fit in a signed char
    e_CONTROL      = 255,  // OK, barely fits in an 8-bit unsigned integer
    e_BACK_CHANNEL = 256,  // Error, doesn't fit in an 8-bit unsigned integer
};
```

If any of the values specified in the definition of the **enum** is outside the boundaries of what the provided **underlying type** is able to represent, the compiler will emit an error, but see *Potential Pitfalls — Subtleties of integral promotion* on page 832.

Use Cases

Ensuring a compact representation where enumerator values are salient

When an enumeration needs to have an efficient representation, e.g., when it is used as a data member of a widely replicated type, restricting the width of the underlying type to something smaller than would occur by default on the target platform might be justified.

As a concrete example, suppose that we want to enumerate the months of the year, in anticipation of placing that enumeration inside a date class having an internal representation that maintains the year as a two-byte signed integer, the month as an enumeration, and the day as an 8-bit signed integer:

```
#include <cstdint>  // std::int8_t, std::int16_t

class Date
{
    std::int16_t d_year;
    Month        d_month;
    std::int8_t  d_day;

public:
    Date();
```

---

[1]C++20 adds **char8_t**, which is a distinct type that has **unsigned char** as its underlying type.

```
    Date(int year, Month month, int day);

    // ...

    int year() const    { return d_year; }
    Month month() const { return d_month; }
    int day() const     { return d_day; }
};
```

Suppose that, within an application, a `Date` is typically constructed using values obtained through a GUI, where the month is always selected from a drop-down menu. The month is supplied to the constructor as an **enum** to avoid recurring defects where the individual fields of the date are supplied in month/day/year format. New functionality will be written to expect the month to be enumerated. Still, the date class will be used in contexts where the numerical value of the month is significant, such as in calls to legacy functions that accept the month as an integer. Moreover, iterating over a range of months is common and requires that the enumerators convert automatically to their integral underlying type, thus contraindicating use of the more strongly typed **enum class**:

```
enum Month // defaulted underlying type (BAD IDEA)
{
    e_JAN = 1, e_FEB, e_MAR, e_APR, e_MAY, e_JUN,
    e_JUL, e_AUG, e_SEP, e_OCT, e_NOV, e_DEC
};
static_assert(sizeof(Month) <= 4 && alignof(Month) <= 4, "");
```

As it turns out, date values are used widely throughout this codebase, and the proposed `Date` type is expected to be used in large aggregates. The underlying type of the **enum** in the code snippet above is implementation-defined and could be as small as a **char** or as large as an **int** despite all the values fitting in a **char**. Hence, if this enumeration were used as a data member in the `Date` class, `sizeof(Date)` would likely balloon to 12 bytes on some relevant platforms due to **natural alignment**! (See Section 2.1."**alignas**" on page 168.)

While reordering the data members of `Date` such that `d_year` and `d_day` were adjacent would ensure that `sizeof(Date)` would not exceed 8 bytes, a better approach is to explicitly specify the enumeration's underlying type to ensure `sizeof(Date)` is exactly the 4 bytes needed to accurately represent the value of a `Date` object. Given that the values in this enumeration fit in an 8-bit signed integer, we can specify its underlying type to be, e.g., std::int8_t or **signed char**, on every platform:

```
#include <cstdint>  // std::int8_t

enum Month : std::int8_t  // user-provided underlying type (GOOD IDEA)
{
    e_JAN = 1, e_FEB, e_MAR,
    e_APR    , e_MAY, e_JUN,
```

```
    e_JUL    , e_AUG, e_SEP,
    e_OCT    , e_NOV, e_DEC
};
```

```
static_assert(sizeof(Month) == 1 && alignof(Month) == 1, "");
```

With this revised definition of `Month`, the size of a `Date` class is 4 bytes, which is especially valuable for large aggregates:

```
Date timeSeries[1000 * 1000];  // sizeof(timeSeries) is now 4Mb (not 12Mb).
```

Potential Pitfalls

External use of opaque enumerators

Providing an explicit underlying type to an **enum** enables clients to declare it as a complete type without its enumerators. Unless the opaque form of its definition is exported in a header file separate from its full definition, external clients wishing to exploit the opaque version will be forced to locally declare it with its **underlying type** but without its enumerator list. If the underlying type of the full definition were to change, any program incorporating *its own* original and now inconsistent elided definition and the *new* full one would become silently **ill formed, no diagnostic required (IFNDR)**. (See Section 2.1."Opaque **enum**s" on page 660.)

Subtleties of integral promotion

When used in an arithmetic context, one might naturally assume that the type of a classic **enum** will first convert to its **underlying type**, which is not always the case. When used in a context that does not explicitly operate on the **enum** type itself, such as a parameter to a function that takes that enum type, **integral promotion** comes into play. For unscoped enumerations without an explicitly specified underlying type and for character types such as **wchar_t**, **char16_t**, and **char32_t**, integral promotion will directly convert the value to the first type in the list **int**, **unsigned int**, **long**, **unsigned long**, **long long**, and **unsigned long long** that is sufficiently large to represent all of the values of the underlying type. Enumerations having a fixed underlying type will, as a first step, behave as if they had decayed to their underlying type.

In most arithmetic expressions, this difference is irrelevant. Subtleties arise, however, when one relies on overload resolution for identifying the underlying type:

```
void f(signed char x);
void f(short x);
void f(int x);
void f(long x);
void f(long long x);
```

```
enum E1        { q, r, s, t, u };
enum E2 : short { v, w, x, y, z };

void test()
{
   f(E1::q);  // always calls f(int) on all platforms
   f(E2::v);  // always calls f(short) on all platforms
}
```

The overload resolution for f considers the type to which each *individual* enumerator can be directly integrally promoted. This conversion for E1 can be only to **int**. For E2, the conversion will consider **int** *and* **short**, and **short**, being an exact match, will be selected. Note that even though both enumerations are small enough to fit into a **signed char**, that overload of f will never be selected.

One might want to get to the implementation-defined underlying type, though, and the Standard does provide a trait to do that: std::underlying_type in C++11 and the corresponding std::underlying_type_t alias in C++14. This trait can safely be used in a cast without risking loss of value (see Section 2.1."**auto** Variables" on page 195):

```
#include <type_traits>  // std::underlying_type

template <typename E>
typename std::underlying_type<E>::type toUnderlying(E value)
{
    return static_cast<typename std::underlying_type<E>::type>(value);
}

void h()
{
    auto e1 = toUnderlying(E1::q); // might be anywhere from signed char to int
    auto e2 = toUnderlying(E2::v); // always deduced as short
}
```

Casting to the underlying type is not necessarily the same as direct integral promotion. If an enumerator is intended to be used in arithmetic operations,[2] a **constexpr** variable might be a better alternative (see Section 2.1."**constexpr** Variables" on page 302):

```
// enum { k_GRAMS_PER_OZ = 28 };   // not the best idea
constexpr int k_GRAMS_PER_OZ = 28;  // better idea

double gramsFromOunces(double ounces)
{
    return ounces * k_GRAMS_PER_OZ;
}
```

---

[2]As of C++20, using an expression of an unscoped enumerated type in a *binary* operation along with an expression of either some *other* enumerated type or any nonintegral type (e.g., **double**) is deprecated, with the possibility of being removed in C++23. Platforms might decide to warn against such uses retroactively.

See Also

- "**constexpr** Variables" (§2.1, p. 302) describes an alternative way of declaring compile-time constants.

- "**enum class**" (§2.1, p. 332) introduces a scoped, more strongly typed enumeration for which the default underlying type is **int** and can also be specified explicitly.

- "Opaque **enum**s" (§2.1, p. 660) offers a means to insulate individual enumerators from clients.

Further Reading

- Scott Meyers discusses the role of **underlying type** for modern, scoped enumerators as well as for classical, unscoped ones in **meyers15b**, "Item 10: Prefer scoped **enum**s to unscoped **enum**s," pp. 67-74.

User-Defined Literal Operators

C++11 allows developers to define a new suffix for a *numeric*, *character*, or *string* literal,
enabling a convenient lexical representation of the *value* of a **user-defined type** (UDT)
or even a novel notation for the value of a built-in type.

Description

A `literal` is a single token in a program that represents, in C and classic C++, a value of
an integer, floating-point, character, string, Boolean, or pointer type.

Examples of familiar literal tokens are integer literals `19` and `0x13`, each representing an
int having a value of 19; floating-point literals `0.19` and `1.9e-1`, each representing a **double**
having a value of 0.19; character literals `'a'` and `'\141'`, each representing a **char** having the
(ASCII) value for the letter "a"; string literal, `"hello"`, representing a null-terminated array
containing the six characters `'h'`, `'e'`, `'l'`, `'l'`, `'o'`, and `'\0'`; and Boolean keyword literals
true and **false**, representing the corresponding Boolean values. C++11 added the keyword
literal, **nullptr** (see Section 1.1."**nullptr**" on page 99), representing the null pointer value.

Both integer and floating-point literals have always had suffixes to identify other numeric
C++ types. For example, `123L` and `123ULL` are literals of type **signed long** and
unsigned long long, respectively, both having a decimal value 123, whereas `123.f` is a
literal of type **float** having the decimal value 123. We can easily distinguish programmatically between these different types of literals using, e.g., overload resolution:

```
void f(const int&);            // (1) overload for type int
void f(const long&);           // (2)    "     "    "  long
void f(const double&);         // (3)    "     "    "  double
void f(const float&);          // (4)    "     "    "  float
void f(const unsigned int&);   // (5)    "     "    "  unsigned int
void f(const unsigned long&);  // (6)    "     "    "  unsigned long

void test0()
{
    f(123);    // OK, calls (1)
    f(123L);   // OK, calls (2)
    f(123.);   // OK, calls (3)
    f(123.f);  // OK, calls (4)
    f(123U);   // OK, calls (5)
    f(123UL);  // OK, calls (6)
    f(123.L);  // Error, call to f(long double) is ambiguous
    f(123f);   // Error, invalid hex digit f in decimal constant
}
```

Notice that applying an `L` or `l` suffix to a floating-point literal (of default type **double**)
identifies it as being of type **long double**, which is a **standard conversion** away from

both **float** and **double**, making the call ambiguous. Applying F or f to an integer literal is, by default, not permitted unless a user-defined literal (UDL) of a compatible type can be found.

Classic C++ allowed values of only built-in types to be represented as compile-time literals. To express a hard-coded value of a UDT, a developer would need to use a **value constructor** or **factory function** and, unlike literals of built-in types, these *runtime* workarounds could never be used in a **constant expression**. For example, we might want to create a user-defined type, Name, that can construct itself from a null-terminated string:

```
class Name  // user-defined type constructible from a literal string
{
    // ...

public:
    Name(const char*);  // value constructor taking a null-terminated string
    //...
};
```

We can then initialize a variable of type Name from a string literal using the value constructor:

```
Name nameField("Maria");  // Name object having value "Maria"
```

Alternatively, we could create one or more **factory functions** that return a constructed object appropriately configured with the desired value. Multiple factory functions having different names can be created without necessarily adding new constructors to the definition of the returned type, although, in some cases, a factory function might be a **friend** of the type it configures:

```
#include <cassert>  // standard C assert macro

class Temperature { /*...*/ };

Temperature fahrenheit(double degrees);  // configured from degrees Fahrenheit
Temperature celsius(double degrees);     // configured from degrees Celsius

void test1()
{
    Temperature t1 = fahrenheit(32);  // Water freezes at this temperature.
    Temperature t2 = celsius(0.0);    //    "      "      "    "       "
    assert(t1 == t2);                 // Expect same type and same value.
}
```

Note that, as of C++11, the two functional constructs described above can be declared **constexpr** and thus be eligible to be evaluated as part of a **constant expression**; see Section 2.1."**constexpr** Functions" on page 257.

Although usable, the aforementioned C++03 workarounds for representing literal values of a UDT lack the compactness and expressiveness of those for built-in types. A fundamental design goal of C++ has always been to minimize such differences. To that end, C++11 extends the notion of **type suffix** to include user-definable identifiers with a leading underscore (e.g., _name, _time, _temp):

```
Temperature operator""_F(long double degrees) { /*...*/ }  // define suffix _F
Temperature operator""_C(long double degrees) { /*...*/ }  // define suffix _C

void test2()  // same as test1 above, but this time with user-defined literals
{
    Temperature t1 = 32.0_F; // Water freezes at 32 degrees Fahrenheit.
    Temperature t2 = 0.0_C;  //    "        "      "  0 degrees Celsius
    assert(t1 == t2);        // Expect same type and same value.
}
```

The example above demonstrates the basic idea of a **UDL** implemented as a new kind of operator: **operator**"" followed by a suffix name. A UDL is a literal token having a **UDL suffix** that names a **UDL operator**. A UDL *uses* a suffix, whereas a UDL operator *defines* a suffix. A UDL **suffix** must be a valid identifier that begins with an underscore (_). Note that suffixes without a leading underscore are reserved for the C++ Standard Library. A UDL is formed by appending a UDL **suffix** to a native literal of one of four **type categories**: integer literals (e.g., 2020_year), **floating-point literals** (e.g., 98.6_F), **character literals** (e.g., 'x'_ebcdic), and **string literals** (e.g., "1 Pennsylvania Ave"_validated). Regardless of the type category, a UDL can evaluate to any built-in or user-defined type. What's more, the same UDL **suffix** can apply to more than one of the four UDL type categories enumerated above, potentially yielding a different type for each category.

Each UDL operator is effectively a **factory function** that takes a highly constrained parameter list (see *UDL operators* on page 840) and returns an appropriately configured object. The defined UDL **suffix**, like postfix operators ++ and --, names a function to be called, but is parsed as part of the preceding literal (with no intervening whitespace) and cannot be applied to an arbitrary runtime expression. In fact, the compiler does not always produce an *a priori* interpretation of the literal before invoking the UDL **operator**.

Let's now see how we might create a UDL for our original user-defined type, Name. In this example, the UDL "function" operates on a string literal, rather than a floating-point literal:

```
Name operator""_Name(const char* n, std::size_t /* len */) { return Name(n); }
    // user-defined literal (UDL) operator for UDL suffix _Name

Name nameField = "Maria"_Name;  // Name object having value "Maria"
```

The UDL definition for string literals above, **operator**""_Name in this case, takes two arguments: a **const char*** representing a null-terminated character string and an std::size_t representing the length of that string excluding the null terminator. In our example, we ignore the second argument in the body of the UDL operator, but it must nonetheless be present in the parameter list.

UDL operators, like factory functions, can return a value of any type, including built-in types. Unit-conversion functions, for example, often return built-in types normalized to specific units:

```
#include <ctime>  // std::time_t

constexpr std::time_t minutes(int m) { return m * 60; }    // minutes to seconds
constexpr std::time_t hours(int h)   { return h * 3600; }  // hours to seconds
```

Each of the unit-conversion functions above returns an `std::time_t` (a standard type alias for a built-in integral type) representing a duration in seconds. We can combine such uniform quantities initialized from values in disparate units as needed:

```
std::time_t duration = hours(3) + minutes(15);    // 3.25 hours as seconds
```

Replacing the unit-conversion functions with UDLs allows us to express the desired value with a more natural-looking syntax. We now define two new UDL operators, creating suffixes _min for minutes and _hr for hours, respectively:

```
std::time_t operator""_min(unsigned long long m)
{
    return static_cast<std::time_t>(m * 60);  // minutes-to-seconds conversion
}

std::time_t operator""_hr(unsigned long long h)
{
    return static_cast<std::time_t>(h * 3600);  // hours-to-seconds conversion
}

std::time_t duration = 3_hr + 15_min;  // 3.25 hours as seconds
```

We are not done yet. Unlike built-in literals, UDLs that use the suffixes defined above cannot express arbitrary literal values that can be treated as compile-time constants usable in constant expressions such as sizing an array or within a `static_assert`:

```
int a1[5_hr];                    // Error, 5_hr is not a compile-time constant.
static_assert(1_min == 60, "");  // Error, 1_min " " " " " "
```

Typical definitions of UDLs will, therefore, also involve another C++11 feature, **constexpr** functions; see Section 2.1."**constexpr** Functions" on page 257. By simply adding **constexpr** to the declaration of our UDL operators, we enable them to be evaluated at compile-time and, hence, usable in constant expressions:

```
constexpr std::time_t operator""_Min(unsigned long long m)
{
    return static_cast<std::time_t>(m * 60);  // minutes-to-seconds conversion
}
```

```
constexpr std::time_t operator""_Hr(unsigned long long h)
{
    return static_cast<std::time_t>(h * 3600);  // hours-to-seconds conversion
}

int a2[5_Hr];                       // OK, 5_Hr is a compile-time constant.
static_assert(1_Min == 60, "");  // OK, 1_Min "  "     "       "       "
```

In short, a UDL operator is a new kind of **free operator** that (1) may be defined with certain specific signatures limited to a subset of the built-in types and (2) is invoked automatically when used as a suffix of a built-in literal. There are, however, multiple ways to define UDL operators — *precomputed-argument*, *raw*, and *template* — each more expressive and complex than the previous. The allowed variations on the definitions of UDL operators are elucidated below.

Restrictions on UDLs

A UDL suffix can be defined for only integer, floating-point, character, and string literals. Left deliberately unsupported are the two *Boolean* literals, **true** and **false**, and the *pointer* literal, **nullptr** (see Section 1.1."**nullptr**" on page 99). These omissions serve to sidestep lexical ambiguities — e.g., the Boolean literal, **true**, combined with the UDL suffix, _fact, would be indistinguishable from the identifier, true_fact.

We'll refer to the sequence of characters that make up a literal excluding any suffix as a **naked literal** — e.g., for literal "abc"_udl, the naked literal is "abc". UDL suffixes can be appended to otherwise valid lexical literal tokens only. That is, appending a UDL suffix to a token that wouldn't be considered a valid lexical literal without the suffix is not permitted. Though creating a suffix, _ipv4, to represent an IPv4 Internet address consisting of four octets separated by periods might be tempting, 192.168.0.1 would not be a valid lexical token in a program and, hence, neither would 192.168.0.1_ipv4. Interestingly, creating a UDL that would cause an overflow if interpreted without the suffix *is* permitted. Thus, for example, the UDL 0x123456789abcdef012345678_verylong, which comprises 24 hex digits and the UDL suffix, _verylong, would be valid even on an architecture whose native integers cannot exceed 64 bits (16 hex digits); see Section 1.1."**long long**" on page 89.

Note that there are no *negative* numeric literals in C++. The negative numeric value -123 is represented as two separate tokens: the negation operator and a positive literal, 123. Similarly, an expression like -3_t1 will attempt to apply the negation operator to the object of, say, Type1 produced by the 3_t1 UDL, which in turn comes from passing an **unsigned long long** having the positive value 3 to the UDL operator **operator**""_t1. Such an expression will be **ill formed** unless there is a negation operator that operates on *rvalues* of type Type1. None of the three forms of UDL operators (see *Cooked UDL operators* on page 843, *Raw UDL operators* on page 845, and *UDL operator templates* on page 849) needs, or is able, to handle a **naked** literal representing a negative number.

When two or more string literals appear without intervening tokens, they are concatenated and treated as a single string literal. If at least one of those strings has a UDL suffix, then the suffix is applied to the concatenation of the **naked literal** strings. If more than one of the strings has a suffix, then all such suffixes must be the same; concatenating string literals having different suffixes is not permitted, but strings having no suffix may be concatenated with strings having a UDL **suffix**:

```
#include <cstddef>  // std::size_t

struct XStr { /*...*/ };
XStr operator""_X(const char* n, std::size_t length);
XStr operator""_Y(const char* n, std::size_t length);

char a[] = "hello world";         // single native string literal
char b[] = "hello"      " world"; // native equivalent to "hello world"
XStr c   = "hello world"_X;       // user-defined string literal
XStr d   = "hello"_X    " world"; // UDL equivalent to "hello world"_X
XStr e   = "hello"      " world"_X; // "      "      "      "      "
XStr f   = "hello"_X    " world"_X; // "      "      "      "      "
XStr g   = "hel"_X "lo" " world"_X; // "      "      "      "      "
XStr h   = "hello"_X    " world"_Y; // Error, mixing UDL suffixes _X and _Y
```

Finally, combining a UDL **suffix** with a second built-in or user-defined suffix on a single token is not possible. Writing `45L_Min`, for example, in an attempt to combine the `L` suffix (for **long**) with the `_Min` suffix (for the user-defined minutes suffix described earlier) will simply yield the undefined and invalid suffix, `L_Min`.

UDL operators

A UDL **suffix** (e.g., `_udl`) is created by defining a UDL operator (e.g., **operator**""`_udl`) that follows a strict set of rules described in this section. In the declaration and definition of a UDL operator, the name of the UDL **suffix** *may* be separated from the quotes by whitespace; in fact, some older compilers might even *require* such whitespace due to a defect (since corrected and retroactively applied) in the original C++11 specification. Thus, for all but the oldest C++11 compilers, **operator**""`_udl`, **operator**"" `_udl`, and **operator** "" `_udl` are all valid spellings of the same UDL operator name. If a capital letter directly follows the underscore in the UDL **suffix**, however, having intervening whitespace after "" is **ill formed, no diagnostic required**. Such identifiers, e.g., `_F` or `_Min`, are reserved by the Standard for use by C++ implementations. Interestingly, even for the Standard Library implementations that are allowed to use **reserved identifiers**, omitting whitespace is still required for suffixes having the same spelling as a keyword, e.g., the `if` suffix for complex numbers. Note that whitespace is *not* permitted between a literal and its suffix in the *use* of a UDL. For example, `1.2 _udl` is ill formed; `1.2_udl` must appear as a single token with no whitespace.

A UDL generally consists of two parts: (1) a valid lexical literal token and (2) a user-defined suffix. The signature of each UDL operator must conform to one of three patterns, distinguished by the way the compiler supplies the **naked literal** to the UDL operator.

1. **Cooked UDL operator** — The naked literal is evaluated at compile time and passed into the operator as a value:

   ```
   Type1 operator""_t1(unsigned long long n);
   Type1 t1 = 780_t1;  // calls operator""_t1(780ULL)
   ```

2. **Raw UDL operator** — The characters that make up the naked literal are passed to the operator as a *raw*, unevaluated string (for numeric literals only):

   ```
   Type2 operator""_t2(const char* token);
   Type2 t2 = 780_t2;  // calls operator""_t2("780")
   ```

3. **UDL operator template** — The UDL operator is a template whose parameter list is a variadic sequence of **char** values (see Section 2.1."Variadic Templates" on page 873) that make up the **naked literal** (for numeric literals only):

   ```
   template <char...> Type3 operator""_t3();
   Type3 t3 = 780_t3;  // calls operator""_t3<'7', '8', '0'>()
   ```

Each of these three forms of UDL operators is expounded in more detail in its own separate section; see *Cooked UDL operators* on page 843, *Raw UDL operators* on page 845, and *UDL operator templates* on page 849.

When a UDL is encountered, the compiler prioritizes a cooked UDL operator over the other two. Given a UDL having suffix _udl, the compiler will look for any **operator""_udl** in the local scope (**unqualified name lookup**). If, among the operators found, there is a cooked UDL operator that exactly matches the type of the naked literal, then that UDL operator is called. Otherwise, for numeric literals only, the raw UDL operator or a UDL operator template is invoked; an ambiguity results if both operators are found. This set of lookup rules is deliberately short and rigid. Importantly, this lookup sequence differs from other operator invocations in that it does *not* involve **overload resolution** or argument conversions, nor does it employ **argument-dependent lookup (ADL)** to find operators in other namespaces.

Although ADL is never an issue for UDLs, common practice is to gather related UDL operators into a namespace (whose name often contains the word "literals"). This namespace is then typically nested within the namespace containing the definitions of the user-defined types that the UDL operators return. These literals-only nested namespaces enable a user to import just the literals into their scope via a single **using** directive, thereby substantially decreasing the likelihood of collisions with names in the enclosing **namespace**:

```
namespace ns1  // namespace containing types returned by UDL operators
{
    struct Type1 { };
    bool check(const Type1&);

    namespace literals  // nested namespace for UDL operators returning ns1 types
    {
        Type1 operator""_t1(const char*);
    }

    using namespace literals;  // Make literals available in namespace ns1.
}

void test1()  // file scope: finds UDL operator via using directive
{
    using namespace ns1::literals;  // OK, imports only the inner UDL operators
    check(123_t1);                  // OK, finds ns1::check via ADL
}
```

To use the _t1 UDL suffix above, test1 must somehow be able to find the declaration of
its corresponding UDL operator locally, which is accomplished by placing the operator in a
nested namespace and importing the entire namespace via a **using directive**. We could have
avoided the nested namespace and, instead, required each needed operator to be imported
individually:

```
namespace ns2  // namespace defining types returned by non-nested UDL operators
{
    struct Type2 { };
    bool check(const Type2&);

    Type2 operator""_t2(const char*);  // BAD IDEA: not nested
}

void test2()  // file scope: finds UDL operator via using declaration
{
    using ns2::operator""_t2;  // OK, imports just the needed UDL operator
    check(123_t2);             // OK, finds ns2::check via ADL
}
```

When multiple UDL operators are provided for a collection of types, however, the idiom of
placing just the UDL operators in a nested namespace (typically incorporating the name
"literals") obviates most of the commonly cited ill effects (e.g., accidental unwanted name collisions) attributed to more general use of **using** directives. In the interest of brevity, we will
freely omit the nested-literal namespaces in expository-only examples.

Finally, despite its use in the Standard for this specific purpose, there is never a need for
a namespace comprising only UDLs to be declared **inline** and doing so is contraindicated;
see Section 3.1."**inline namespace**" on page 1055.

Cooked UDL operators

Cooked UDL operators are supported for all four of the UDL type categories: integer, floating-point, character, and string. If this form of UDL operator is selected (see *UDL operators* on page 840), the compiler first determines which of the four UDL type categories applies to the naked literal, evaluates it without regard to the UDL suffix, and then passes the precomputed value to the UDL operator, which further processes its argument and returns the result of the UDL expression. Note that the UDL type category of the UDL operator refers to only the naked literal; its return value can be any arbitrary type, with or without an obvious relationship to its type category:

```
struct Smile { /*...*/ };  // arbitrary user-defined type

Smile operator""_fx(long double);  // floating-point literal returning Smile
float operator""_ix(unsigned long long);  // integer literal returning float
int operator""_sx(const char*, std::size_t);  // string literal returning int
```

The UDL type category for a cooked UDL operator is determined by the operator's signature; integer and floating-point UDL operators each take a single argument of, respectively, the largest unsigned integer and floating-point types defined by the language. Multiple cooked UDL operators may be declared in the same scope for the same UDL suffix (e.g., _aa) but different UDL type categories, and each may return a distinct arbitrary type (e.g., **short**, Smile):

```
short operator""_aa(unsigned long long n);  // integer literal operator
Smile operator""_aa(long double n);         // floating-point literal operator
bool  operator""_bb(long double n);         // floating-point literal operator
```

The naked literal is evaluated as an **unsigned long long** for integer literals (see Section 1.1. "**long long**" on page 89) or a **long double** for floating-point literals; the resulting value is then passed via the n parameter to the UDL operator. The compiler does the work of parsing and evaluating the sequence of digits, radix prefixes (e.g., 0 for octal and 0x for hexadecimal), decimal points, and exponents:

```
short v1 = 123_aa;  // OK, invokes operator""_aa(unsigned long long)
Smile v2 = 1.3_aa;  // OK, invokes operator""_aa(long double)
```

C++14 provides additional features related to built-in literals; see Section 1.2."Binary Literals" on page 142 and Section 1.2."Digit Separators" on page 152.

There is no overload resolution, **integer-to-floating-point conversion**, or **floating-point-to-integer conversion**, nor are UDL operators having numerically lower precision permitted:

```
Smile operator""_cc(double n);  // Error, invalid parameter list
```

If lookup does not find a UDL operator that matches the type category of the naked literal exactly, the match fails:

```
bool v3 = 123_bb;  // Error, unable to find integer literal _bb
bool v4 = 1.3_bb;  // OK, invokes operator""_bb(long double)
```

Because the **naked** literal is fully evaluated by the compiler, overflow and precision loss could become issues just as they are for native literals. These limitations vary by platform, but typical platforms are limited to 64-bit **unsigned long long** or 64-bit **long double** types in IEEE 754 format:

```
Smile v5 = 1.2e310_aa;                    // Bug, argument evaluates to infinity
Smile v6 = 2.5e-310_aa;                   // Bug, argument evaluates to denormalized
short v7 = 0x1234568790abcdef0_aa;        // Error, doesn't fit in any integer type
```

Note that the oversized integer initializer for **v7** in the code snippet above results in an error on some compilers but only a warning on others. Arbitrarily long literals are, however, supported by raw UDL operators and UDL operator templates; see *Raw UDL operators* on page 845 and *UDL operator templates* on page 849.

Each character and string literal in C++ has one of the available encodings identified with an **encoding prefix**. In addition to an empty prefix, C++03 supports the **L** encoding prefix for wide character and string literals. For example, the literals **'x'** and **"hello"** have (built-in) types **char** and **const char[6]**, respectively, whereas **L'x'** and **L"hello"** have the respective types **wchar_t** and **const wchar_t[6]**. C++11 added three more string encoding prefixes: **u** to indicate UTF-16 with a type of **const char16_t[N]**, **U** to indicate UTF-32 with a type **const char32_t[N]**, and **u8** to indicate UTF-8 with a type of **const char[N]**. The **u** and **U** prefixes can also be used on character literals; see Section 1.1."Unicode Literals" on page 129.[1]

The four C++11 encoding prefixes for character literals can each be supported by a distinct UDL operator signature (e.g., **_dd** below), each of which might return a distinct, arbitrary type:

```
int         operator""_dd(char     ch); // 'x'
double      operator""_dd(char16_t ch); // u'x'
const char* operator""_dd(char32_t ch); // U'x'
Smile       operator""_dd(wchar_t  ch); // L'x'
```

Any or all of the above forms can co-exist. A character **naked** literal (e.g., **'Q'**) is translated into the appropriate character type and value in the **execution character set** (i.e., the set of characters used at run time on the target operating system) and passed via the **ch** parameter to the body of the UDL operator. As ever, there are no narrowing or widening conversions, so the program is ill formed if the precise signature of the needed UDL operator is not found:

```
int    operator""_ee(char);        // 'x'
double operator""_ee(char32_t);    // U'x'

int    c1 = 'Q'_ee;  // OK, matches char parameter type
double c2 = U'Q'_ee; // OK, matches char32_t parameter type
```

---

[1]C++17 allows the **u8** prefix on character literals as well as on string literals, while C++20 changes the type for **u8**-prefixed string and character literals to use **char8_t** instead of **char**.

```
const char* c3 = u'Q'_ee;  // Error, no match for char16_t parameter type
Smile       c4 = L'Q'_ee;  // Error, no match for wchar_t parameter type
```

Similarly, there are four valid UDL operator signatures for string literals in C++11, each of which again might return a different type[2]:

```
bool  operator""_dd(const char*    str, std::size_t len);  //   "str"
int   operator""_dd(const char16_t* str, std::size_t len); //  u"str"
float operator""_dd(const char32_t* str, std::size_t len); //  U"str"
Smile operator""_dd(const wchar_t*  str, std::size_t len); //  L"str"
```

The string naked literal evaluates to a null-terminated character array. The address of the first element of that array is passed to the UDL operator via the str parameter, and its length — excluding the null terminator — is passed via len.

To recap, multiple cooked UDL operators can co-exist for a single UDL suffix, each having a distinct type category and each potentially returning a different C++ type. To show another example, the suffix _s on a floating-point literal could return an **double** to mean seconds, whereas the same suffix on a string literal might return an std::string. Moreover, string and character UDL operators that differ by character type (**char**, **char16_t**, and so on) often have different return types. Similar string UDL operators typically — but not necessarily — return similar types, such as std::string and std::u16string, that differ only in their underlying character type:

```
#include <string>    // std::string

double operator""_s(unsigned long long);  // integer UDL operator
double operator""_s(long double);          // floating-point UDL operator

std::string    operator""_s(const char*,    std::size_t); // string UDL
std::u16string operator""_s(const char16_t*, std::size_t); //    "    "

double         d = 12_s;        // yields double
std::u16string w = u"Hola"_s;   // yields std::u16string
std::string    s = "Hello"_s;   // yields std::string
```

Note again that these operators are often declared **constexpr** (see Section 2.1."**constexpr** Functions" on page 257) because they can *always* be evaluated at compile time because their arguments are frequently expressed *literally* in the source code.

Raw UDL operators

The *raw* pattern for UDL operators is supported for only the integer and floating-point UDL type categories. If this form of UDL operator is selected (see *UDL operators* on page 840),

---

[2]C++20 allows a fifth signature for string literals with the u8 prefix that takes a **const char8_t***.

the compiler packages up the **naked literal** as an unprocessed string — i.e., a sequence of raw characters transferred from the source — and passes it to the UDL operator as a null-terminated character string. All **raw UDL operators** (e.g., for suffix _rl below) have the same signature:

```
struct Type { /*...*/ };

Type operator""_rl(const char*);

Type t1 = 425_rl;   // invokes operator ""_rl("425")
```

This signature can be distinguished from a **cooked UDL operator** for string literals by the *absence* of an std::size_t parameter representing its length.

The raw string argument will be verified by the compiler to be a well-formed integer or floating-point literal token but is otherwise unmodified by the compiler. For any given UDL **suffix**, at most one matching **raw UDL operator** may be in scope at a time; hence, the return type cannot vary based on, e.g., whether the **naked literal** contains a decimal point. Such a capability *is*, however, available; see *UDL operator templates* on page 849.

A particular UDL **operator** might have a narrow contract and thus not accept some otherwise valid tokens. For example, we can define a UDL **suffix**, _3, to express base-3 integers using a raw UDL operator:

```
int operator""_3(const char* digits)
{
    // BAD IDEA: no error handling in the UDL operator

    int result = 0;

    while (*digits)
    {
        result *= 3;
        result += *digits - '0';
        ++digits;
    }

    return result;
}
```

We can now test this function at run time using the standard **assert** macro:

```
#include <cassert>   // standard C assert macro

void test()
{
    assert( 0 ==   0_3);
    assert( 1 ==   1_3);
```

```
    assert( 2 ==   2_3);
    assert( 3 ==  10_3);
    assert( 4 ==  11_3);
    // ...
    assert( 8 ==  22_3);
    assert( 9 == 100_3);
    assert(10 == 101_3);
}
```

Note that we could have declared our _3 raw UDL operator **constexpr** and replaced all of the (runtime) **assert** statements with (compile-time) **static_assert** declarations. Also observe that, as written, **constexpr operator""_3** requires C++14's relaxed **constexpr** function restrictions (see Section 2.1."**constexpr** Functions" on page 257), but it could be reimplemented to work in C++11.

Let's now consider valid lexical integer literals representing values outside of what would be considered valid of base-3 integers:

```
int i1 = 22_3;                     // (1) OK,  returns (int) 8
int i2 = 23_3;                     // (2) Bug, returns (int) 9
int i3 = 21.1_3;                   // (3) Bug, returns (int) 58
int i4 = 22211100022211100022_3;   // (4) Bug, too big for 32-bit int
```

In the example code above, (1) is a valid base-3 integer; (2) is a valid integer literal but contains the digit 3, which is *not* a valid base-3 digit; (3) is a valid floating-point literal, but the UDL operator returns values of only type **int**; and (4) is in principle a valid integer literal but represents a value that is too large to fit in a 32-bit **int**. Because cases (2), (3), and (4) are valid lexical literals, it is up to the implementation of the UDL operator to reject invalid values.

Let's now consider a more robust implementation of a base-3 integer UDL, _3b, that throws an exception when the literal fails to represent a valid base-3 integer:

```
#include <stdexcept>  // std::out_of_range, std::overflow_error
#include <limits>     // std::numeric_limits

int operator""_3b(const char* digits)
{
    int ret = 0;

    for (char c = *digits; c; c = *++digits)
    {
        if ('\'' == c)  // Ignore the C++14 digit separator.
        {
            continue;
        }
```

```
    if (c < '0' || '2' < c)  // Reject non-base-3 characters.
    {
        throw std::out_of_range("Invalid base-3 digit");
    }

    if (ret >= (std::numeric_limits<int>::max() - (c - '0')) / 3)
    {
        // Reject if 3 * ret + (c - '0') would overflow.
        throw std::overflow_error("Integer too large");
    }

    ret = 3 * ret + (c - '0');  // Consume c.
  }

    return ret;
}
```

In this implementation of a raw UDL operator for a suffix _3b, the first **if** statement looks for the C++14 digit separator and ignores it. The second **if** statement checks for characters outside the valid range for base-3 and, e.g., for cases (2) and (3), throws an out_of_range exception. The third **if** statement determines whether the computation is about to overflow and, e.g., for case (4), throws an overflow_error exception. The absence of compiler interpretation makes raw UDL operators potentially difficult to write but also powerful. Interpreting existing literal characters in a new way and accepting literals that would otherwise overflow or lose precision confers additional expressiveness on raw UDLs; e.g., the base-3 raw UDL operator shown above could not be expressed having the same domain using a cooked UDL operator. The downside of this additional expressiveness is the need to implement, debug, and maintain custom token parsing, including error checking.

If the intent is to consume integer literals, a raw UDL operator needs to either process or reject not only the decimal digits '0' to '9', but also the hex digits 'a'–'f' and 'A'–'F' as well as radix prefixes 0, 0x, and 0X. In C++14, the operator must also handle the 0b (binary) radix prefix and the digit separator '\''.

For floating-point literals, the raw UDL operator needs to handle the decimal digits, decimal point, exponent prefix ('e' or 'E'), and optional exponent sign ('+' or '-'). It is possible to handle both integer and floating-point literals in a single raw UDL operator, provided the return type is the same for both. In all cases, it is usually wise to reject *any* unexpected character, including characters that are not currently legal within numeric literals, in case the set of legal characters is enlarged in the future, e.g., by adding a new radix.

A raw UDL operator can be declared **constexpr**, but be aware that the rules for what is allowed in a **constexpr** function differ significantly between C++11 and C++14, as described in Section 2.1."**constexpr** Functions" on page 257. In particular, the loop-based implementation of **operator""**_3 (above) can be declared **constexpr** in C++14 but not in C++11, though it is possible to define a **constexpr** UDL operator in C++11 that has the same behavior by using a recursive implementation. If the literal is evaluated as part of a constant expression and if the literal contains errors that would result in exceptions being thrown (i.e., an invalid character or overflow), the compiler will reject the invalid literal at compile time. If, however, the literal is not part of a constant expression, an exception will still be thrown at run time:

```
constexpr int i4 = 25_3;  // Error, "throw" not allowed in constant expression
          int i5 = 25_3;  // Bug, exception thrown at run time
```

To ensure that every invalid literal is detected at compile time, use UDL operator templates, as described in the next section.

UDL operator templates

A UDL operator template, known as a *literal operator template* in the Standard, is a variadic template (see Section 2.1."Variadic Templates" on page 873) having a template parameter list consisting of a pack of an arbitrary number of **char** parameters and an empty runtime parameter list:

```
struct Type { /*...*/ };

template <char...> Type operator""_udl();
```

UDL operator templates support only the integer and floating-point type categories.[3] If this form of UDL operator is selected (see *UDL operators* on page 840), the compiler breaks up the naked literal into a sequence of raw characters and passes each one as a separate template argument to the instantiation of the UDL operator:

```
Type t1 = 42.5_udl;  // calls operator""_udl<'4', '2', '.', '5'>()
```

As in the case of raw UDL operators, the raw sequence of characters will be verified by the compiler to be a well-formed integer or floating-point literal token, but the UDL operator must deduce meaning from those characters. Unlike raw UDL operators, a UDL operator template can return different types based on the content of the naked literal. For example, the UDL operator _bignum (in the code snippet below) returns a **BigInteger** for integral literals and an **ArbitraryPrecisionFloat** for floating-point ones. The compile-time template logic needed to make this selection requires template metaprogramming, which in turn requires partial template specialization. Function templates, including UDL operator templates, cannot have partial specializations, so the selection logic is delegated to a helper class template, **MakeBigNumber**:

---

[3]C++20 added support for user-defined string literal operator templates, albeit with a different syntax.

```
class BigInteger { /*...*/ };
class ArbitraryPrecisionFloat { /*...*/ };

template<char... Cs> struct MakeBigNumber;

template<char... Cs>
constexpr typename MakeBigNumber<Cs...>::ReturnType
operator""_bignum() { return MakeBigNumber<Cs...>::factory(); }
```

`MakeBigNumber<Cs...>::ReturnType` is the template metafunction used to compute the
return type. In C++14, the return type can be deduced directly from the **return** statement;
see Section 3.2."**auto** Return" on page 1182. The implementation of `MakeBigNumber` relies
on helper metafunction that checks whether a numeric literal is integral:

```
template <char C>
struct IsIntegralLiteralChar
{
    static constexpr bool value = ('0' <= C && C <= '9') || C == '\'';

    static_assert(C != 'X' && C != 'x' && C != 'B' && C != 'b',
                  "Hex and binary literals are not supported.");
};

template <char C, char... Cs>
struct IsIntegralLiteral       // primary template
{
    static constexpr bool value = IsIntegralLiteralChar<C>::value &&
                                  IsIntegralLiteral<Cs...>::value;
};

template <char C>
struct IsIntegralLiteral<C>  // specialize for a single digit
{
    static constexpr bool value = IsIntegralLiteralChar<C>::value;
};
```

The primary `IsIntegralLiteral` template checks whether the first character in the `Cs...`
sequence can be a part of an integral literal (a digit or a digit separator `'`) and recursively
uses `IsIntegralLiteral` to check the rest of the sequence. A partial specialization for the
base case of the entire sequence comprising a single character is used to end the recursion.
Note that this simplified example does not recognize hexadecimal or binary literals. The
description of fixed-point literals in *Use Cases — User-defined numeric types* on page 858
provides a more complete exposition of this sort of return-type selection, including details of
the recursive template metaprogramming used to determine the return type and its value.

`MakeBigNumber` uses the `IsIntegralLiteral` metafunction to select between two specializations of the `MakeBigNumberImp` template — one intended for integral literals and one for
floating-point ones:

```
template <bool isIntegral, char... Cs>
struct MakeBigNumberImp;                   // primary template (unimplemented)

template <char... Cs>
struct MakeBigNumberImp<true, Cs...>   // specialize for integral literals
{
    using ReturnType = BigInteger;
    static constexpr ReturnType factory();
};

template <char... Cs>
struct MakeBigNumberImp<false, Cs...>  // specialize for float literals
{
    using ReturnType = ArbitraryPrecisionFloat;
    static constexpr ReturnType factory();
};

template <char... Cs>
struct MakeBigNumber : MakeBigNumberImp<IsIntegralLiteral<Cs...>::value, Cs...>
{
};
```

The `MakeBigNumber` template inherits from the implementation template `MakeBigNumberImp`, instantiating it with the result of `IsIntegralLiteral` and the character sequence `Cs...`. The primary `MakeBigNumImpl` template is not defined and is used only to dispatch between its two partial specializations via the first Boolean template parameter, `isIntegral`. The `factory` function defined in the first partial specialization (for `isIntegral == true`) returns a `BigInteger`, whereas one in the second specialization (for `isIntegral == false`) returns an `ArbitraryPrecisionFloat`:

```
BigInteger              i1 = 2100_bignum;ArbitraryPrecisionFloat f1 = 1.33_bignum;
ArbitraryPrecisionFloat f2 = 1e-5_bignum;
```

As template arguments, the characters that make up the **naked** literal are constant expressions and can be used with **static_assert** to force error detection at compile time. Unlike raw UDL operators, there is no risk of throwing an exception at run time, even when initializing a non**constexpr** value:

```
constexpr auto i2 = 0x12_bignum;  // Error, constexpr value
          auto i3 = 0x12_bignum;  // Error, nonconstexpr value
```

Being able to select a context-specific return type and to force compile-time error checking makes UDL operator **templates** the most expressive pattern for defining UDL operators. However, these capabilities come at the cost of having to develop them using less-than-readable template metaprogramming.

UDLs in the C++14 Standard Library

This book is primarily about modern C++ *language* features, but a short description of UDL suffixes in the Standard *Library* provides context for better understanding and appreciating the UDL language feature. These new suffixes (starting with C++14) make it easier to write software using standard strings, units of time, and complex numbers. Note that, because these are *standard* UDL suffixes, their names do not have a leading underscore.

A native string literal, without a suffix, describes a C-style array of characters, which decays to a pointer-to-character when passed as a function argument. The C++ Standard Library has had, from the start, string classes (the `std::basic_string` class template and its specializations, `std::string` and `std::wstring`) that improve on C-style character arrays by providing proper **copy semantics**, equality comparison, variable sizing, and so on. With the advent of UDLs, we can finally create literals of these library string types by utilizing the standard `s` suffix. The UDL operators for string literals are in header file `<string>` in namespace `std::literals::string_literals`[4]:

```cpp
#include <string>  // std::basic_string, related types, and UDL operators

using namespace std::literals::string_literals;  // std::basic_string UDLs
const char*     s1 =    "hello";    // Value decays to (const char*) "hello".
std::string     s2 =    "hello"s;   // value std::string("hello")
std::string     s3 = u8"hello"s;    // value std::string(u8"hello")
std::u16string  s4 =  u"hello"s;    // value std::u16string(u"hello")
std::u32string  s5 =  U"hello"s;    // value std::u32string(U"hello")
std::wstring    s6 =  L"hello"s;    // value std::wstring(L"hello")
```

Complex numbers can also be expressed using a more natural style, mimicking the notation used in mathematics. Within namespace `std::literals::complex_literals`, the suffixes `i`, `il`, and `if` are used to name **double**, **long double**, and **float** imaginary numbers, respectively. Note that all three suffixes work for both integer and floating-point literals:

```cpp
#include <complex>  // std::complex and UDL operators

using namespace std::literals::complex_literals; // std::complex UDLs
std::complex<double>       c1 = 2.4 + 3i;     // value 2.4, 3.0
std::complex<long double>  c2 = 1.2L + 5.1il; // value 1.2L, 5.1L
std::complex<float>        c3 = 0.1f + 2.if;  // value 0.1F, 2.0F
```

Unlike the built-in suffixes, however, UDL operators for complex numbers are provided only for lowercase suffixes:

```cpp
std::complex<double>       c4 = 2.4 + 3I;     // Error, invalid suffix I
std::complex<long double>  c5 = 1.2L + 5.1iL; // Error, invalid suffix iL
std::complex<float>        c6 = 0.1f + 2.If;  // Error, invalid suffix If
```

---

[4]C++20 adds **char8_t** and changes the type of s3 in the coding example from `std::string` to `std::u8string`.

The time utilities in the standard header, <chrono>, contain an elaborate and flexible system of units of duration. Each unit is a specialization of the class template std::chrono::duration, which is instantiated with a representation (either integral or floating-point) and a ratio relative to seconds. Thus, duration<**long**, ratio<3600, 1>> can represent an integral number of hours.

The <chrono> header also defines literal suffixes (in namespace std::literals::chrono_literals) having familiar names for time units such as s for seconds, min for minutes, and so on. Integer literals will yield a duration having an integral internal representation, and floating-point literals will yield one having a floating-point internal representation:

```
#include <chrono>  // std::literals::chrono_literals

using namespace std::literals::chrono_literals;  // std::chrono::duration UDLs
auto d1 = 2h;      // 2 hours   (integral internal representation)
auto d2 = 1.3h;    // 1.3 hours (floating-point internal representation)
auto d3 = 10min;   // 10 minutes (integral)
auto d4 = 30s;     // 30 seconds (integral)
auto d5 = 250ms;   // 250 milliseconds (integral)
auto d6 = 90us;    // 90 microseconds (integral)
auto d7 = 104.ns;  // 104.0 nanoseconds (floating-point)
```

In the example above, the **auto** keyword (see Section 2.1."**auto** Variables" on page 195) is used to allow the compiler to deduce the correct type from the literal expression. Although simple integer duration types have convenient aliases such as std::chrono::hours, some types do not have a standard name for the corresponding duration specialization; e.g., 1.2hr returns a value of type std::chrono::duration<T, std::ratio<3600>> where T is a signed integer of at least 23 bits and where the actual integer representation is implementation-defined. Naming a duration is even more complex when adding durations together; the resulting duration type is selected by the library to minimize loss of precision:

```
auto d8 = 2h + 35min + 20s;  // integral, 9320 seconds (2:35:20 in seconds)
auto d9 = 2.4s + 100ms;      // floating-point, 2500.0 milliseconds
```

We are certain to see more UDL suffixes defined in future Standards.

Use Cases

Wrapper classes

Wrappers can be used to add or remove capabilities for their (often built-in) underlying type. They assign *meaning* to a type and are thus useful in preventing programmer confusion or ambiguity in overload resolution. For example, an inventory-control system might track items by both part number and model number. Both numbers could be simple integers, but they have different meanings. To prevent programming errors, we create wrapper classes, PartNumber and ModelNumber, each holding an **int** value:

```
class PartNumber
{
    int d_value;

public:
    constexpr explicit PartNumber(int v) : d_value(v) { }
    // ...
};

class ModelNumber
{
    int d_value;

public:
    constexpr explicit ModelNumber(int v) : d_value(v) { }
    // ...
};
```

Neither `PartNumber` nor `ModelNumber` defines integer operations such as addition or multiplication, so any attempt to modify one (other than by assignment) or add two such values would result in a compile-time error. Moreover, having wrapper classes allows us to overload on the different types, preventing overload resolution ambiguities. Without UDLs, however, we must represent `PartNumber` or `ModelNumber` literals by explicitly casting **int** literals to the correct type:

```
// operations on model and part numbers:
int inventory(ModelNumber n) { int count = 0; /*...*/ return count; }
int inventory(PartNumber n)  { int count = 0; /*...*/ return count; }
void registerPart(const char* shortName, ModelNumber mn, PartNumber pn) { }

PartNumber pn1 = PartNumber(77) + 90;  // Error, no operator+(PartNumber, int)

int c1 = inventory(77);                 // Error, no matching function for call
int c2 = inventory(ModelNumber(77));    // OK, call inventory(ModelNumber)
int c3 = inventory(PartNumber(77));     // OK, call inventory(PartNumber)

void registerParts1()
{
    registerPart("Bolt", PartNumber(77), ModelNumber(77));  // Error, reversed
    registerPart("Bolt", ModelNumber(77), PartNumber(77));  // OK, correct args
}
```

The code above allows the compiler to detect errors that would be easy to make had part and model numbers been represented as raw **int** values. Attempting to add to a part number is rejected, as is the attempt to call `inventory` without specifying whether part-number inventory or model-number inventory is desired. Finally, the `registerPart` function cannot be called with its arguments accidentally reversed.

We can now create UDL suffixes, `_part` and `_model`, to simplify our use of hard-coded part and model numbers, making the code more readable:

```
#include <limits>    // std::numeric_limits
#include <stdexcept> // std::overflow_error

namespace inventory_literals
{
    constexpr ModelNumber operator"" _model(unsigned long long v)
    {
        if (v > std::numeric_limits<int>::max()) throw std::overflow_error("");
        return ModelNumber(static_cast<int>(v));
    }
    constexpr PartNumber operator"" _part(unsigned long long v)
    {
        if (v > std::numeric_limits<int>::max()) throw std::overflow_error("");
        return PartNumber(static_cast<int>(v));
    }
}

using namespace inventory_literals;  // Make literals available.
int c4 = inventory(77);              // Error, no matching function for call
int c5 = inventory(77_model);        // OK, call inventory(ModelNumber).
int c6 = inventory(77_part);         // OK, call inventory(PartNumber).

void registerParts2()
{
    registerPart("Bolt", 77_part, 77_model); // Error, reversed model & part
    registerPart("Bolt", 77_model, 77_part); // OK, arguments in correct order
}
```

A wrapper class can also be useful for tracking certain compile-time attributes of a general-purpose type such as `std::string`. For example, a system that reads input from a user must sanitize each input string before passing it to, e.g., a database. Raw input and sanitized input are both strings, but an unsanitized string must never be confused with a sanitized one. Thus, we create a wrapper class, `SanitizedString`, that can be constructed only by a member factory function, to which we give the easily-searchable name `fromRawString`:

```
#include <string> // std::string

class SanitizedString
{
    std::string d_value;

    explicit SanitizedString(const std::string& value) : d_value(value) { }

public:
    static SanitizedString fromRawString(const std::string& rawStr)
```

```
        return SanitizedString(rawStr);
    }

    // ...

    friend SanitizedString operator+(const SanitizedString& s1,
                                     const SanitizedString& s2)
    {
        return SanitizedString(s1.d_value + s2.d_value);
    }

    // ...
};
```

Calling `SanitizedString::fromRawString` is deliberately cumbersome in an attempt to make developers think carefully before using it. This call might, however, be *too* cumbersome in situations where the safety of a literal string is not in question:

```
std::string getInput();  // Read (unsanitized) string from input.
bool isSafeString(const std::string& s);  // Determine whether s is safe.

void process(const SanitizedString& instructions);
    // Run the specified instructions.

void processInstructions1()
    // Read instructions from input and process them.
{
    // Read instructions from input.
    std::string instructions = getInput();

    if (isSafeString(instructions))
    {
        // String is considered safe; sanitize it.
        SanitizedString sanInstr = SanitizedString::fromRawString(instructions);
        // ...

    // Prepend a "begin" instruction, then process the instructions.

    process("Instructions = begin\n" + sanInstr);
        // Error, no operator+(const char*, SanitizedString)

    process(SanitizedString::fromRawString("Instructions = begin\n") +
            sanInstr);
        // OK, but cumbersome
}
```

```
    else
    {
        // ...                        (error handling)
    }
}
```

The first call to **process** does not compile because, by design, we cannot concatenate a raw string and a sanitized string. The second call works but is unnecessarily cumbersome. Literal strings are *always* assumed to be safe (if there is proper code review) because they cannot originate from outside the program; there should be no need to call SanitizedString::fromRawString. Again, a UDL can make the code more compact and readable:

```
namespace sanitized_string_literals
{
    SanitizedString operator""_san(const char* str, std::size_t len)
        // Create a sanitized string.
    {
        return SanitizedString::fromRawString(std::string(str, len));
    }
}

void processInstructions2()
    // Read instructions from input and process them.
{
    using namespace sanitized_string_literals;

    // Read instructions from input.
    std::string instructions = getInput();

    if (isSafeString(instructions))
    {
        // The instructions string is considered safe; sanitize it.
        SanitizedString sanInstr = SanitizedString::fromRawString(instructions);
        // ...

        // Prepend a "begin" instruction, then process the instructions.

        process("Instructions = begin\n"_san + sanInstr);
            // OK, concatenate two sanitized strings.
    }
    // ...
}
```

This usage shows a case where the UDL is more than just convenient; because a UDL applies *only* to literals, it is largely immune to accidental misuse.

User-defined numeric types

Sometimes we need to represent arbitrarily large integers. A `BigInt` class, along with associated arithmetic operators, can represent such indefinite-magnitude integers:

```
namespace bigint
{
class BigInt
{
    // ...
};

BigInt operator+(const BigInt&);
BigInt operator-(const BigInt&);
BigInt operator+(const BigInt&, const BigInt&);
BigInt operator-(const BigInt&, const BigInt&);
BigInt operator*(const BigInt&, const BigInt&);
BigInt operator/(const BigInt&, const BigInt&);
BigInt abs(const BigInt&);
// ...
```

A `BigInt` literal must be able to represent a value larger than would fit in the largest built-in integral type, so we define the suffix using a raw UDL operator:

```
namespace literals
{
BigInt operator""_bigint(const char* digits)  // raw literal
{
    BigInt value;
    // ...        (Compute BigInt from digits.)
    return value;
}
} // Close namespace literals.

using namespace literals;
} // Close namespace bigint.

using namespace bigint::literals;  // Make _bigint literal available.
bigint::BigInt bnval  = 587135094024263344739630005208021231626182814_bigint;
bigint::BigInt bigone = 1_bigint;  // small value, but still has type BigInt
```

The `BigInt` class is appropriate for large integers, but numbers having fractional parts have a different problem: The IEEE standard **double** floating-point type cannot represent certain values exactly, e.g., 24692134.03. When **double**s are used to represent values, long summations may eventually produce an error in the hundredths place; i.e., the result will be off by .01 or more. In financial calculations, where values represent money, errors of just one or two pennies might be unacceptable. For this problem, we turn to decimal fixed-point (rather than binary floating-point) arithmetic.

A decimal fixed-point representation for a number is one where the number of decimal places of precision is chosen by the programmer and fixed at compile time. Within the specified size and precision, every decimal value can be represented exactly — e.g., a fixed-point number with two decimal digits of precision can represent the value 24692134.03 exactly but cannot represent the value 24692134.035. We'll define our FixedPoint class as a template, where the Precision parameter specifies the number of decimal places[5]:

```cpp
#include <limits>  // std::numeric_limits
#include <string>  // std::string, std::to_string

namespace fixedpoint
{

template <unsigned Precision>
class FixedPoint
{
    long long d_data;  // integral data = value * pow(10, Precision)

public:
    constexpr        FixedPoint() : d_data(0) { } // zero value
    constexpr explicit FixedPoint(long long);      // Convert from long long.
    constexpr explicit FixedPoint(double);         // Convert from double.

    constexpr FixedPoint(long long data, std::true_type /*isRaw*/)
        // Create a FixedPoint object with the specified data.  Note that
        // this is a "raw" constructor and no precision adjustment is made to
        // the data.
        : d_data(data) { }

    friend std::ostream& operator<<(std::ostream& stream, const FixedPoint& v)
        // Format the specified fixed-point number v, write it to the
        // specified stream, and return stream.
    {
        std::string str = std::to_string(v.d_data);
        // Insert leading '0's, if needed.
        if (str.length() < Precision)
            str.insert(0, (Precision - str.length()), '0');
        str.insert(str.length() - Precision, 1, '.');
        return stream << str;
    }
};
```

Our data representation is a **long long**, making the largest value that can be represented std::numeric_limits<**long long**>::max() / pow(10, Precision), assuming an integer pow function; see Section 1.1."**long long**" on page 89. The output function, **operator<<**, converts

---

[5]A more complete and powerful fixed-point class template was proposed for standardization in **mcfarlane19**.

d_data to a string and then inserts the decimal point into the correct location. The special "raw" constructor exists so that our UDL operator can easily construct a value without losing precision, as we'll see later; the unused second parameter is a dummy to distinguish it from other constructors.

We want to define a UDL operator template to return a FixedPoint type such that, for example, 12.34 would return a value of type FixedPoint<2> (for the two decimal places), whereas 12.340 would return a value of type FixedPoint<3>. We must first define a variadic helper template (see Section 2.1."Variadic Templates" on page 873) to compute both the type and the raw value of the fixed point number, given a sequence of digits:

```cpp
namespace literals  // fixed-point literals defined in this namespace
{

template <long long rawVal, int precision, char... c>
struct MakeFixedPoint;
```

This helper template will be recursively instantiated; at each level of recursion rawVal is the value computed so far, precision is the number of decimal places seen so far, and c... is the list of literal characters to be consumed. A special value of -1 for precision indicates that the decimal point has not yet been consumed.

The base case of our recursive template occurs when the parameter pack, c..., is empty — i.e., there are no more characters to consume. In this case, the computed type is simply FixedPoint<precision>, and the value of the UDL operator is computed from rawVal. We define the base case as a partial specialization of MakeFixedPoint where there is no character parameter pack:

```cpp
template <long long rawVal, int precision>
struct MakeFixedPoint<rawVal, precision>
{
    // base case when there are no more characters
    using type = FixedPoint<(precision < 0) ? 0 : precision>;
    static constexpr type makeValue() { return { rawVal, std::true_type{} }; }
        // Return the computed fixed-point number.
};
```

The other case occurs when there are one or more characters yet to be consumed. The helper must perform error checking for bad input characters and overflow before consuming the character and instantiating itself recursively:

```cpp
template <long long rawVal, int precision, char c0, char... c>
struct MakeFixedPoint<rawVal, precision, c0, c...>
{
private:
    static constexpr long long maxData = std::numeric_limits<long long>::max();
    static constexpr bool      c0isdig = ('0' <= c0 && c0 <= '9');

    // Check for out-of-range characters and overflow.
```

```
    static_assert(c0isdig || '\'' == c0 || '.' == c0,
                  "Invalid fixed-point digit");
    static_assert(!c0isdig || (maxData - (c0 - '0')) / 10 >= rawVal,
                  "Fixed-point overflow");

    // precision is
    // (1) < 0 if a decimal point was not seen,
    // (2) 0   if a decimal point was seen but no digits after the decimal point,
    // (3) > 0 otherwise, incremented once for each digit after the decimal point.
    static constexpr int nextPrecision = ('\'' == c0    ? precision :
                                          '.' == c0     ?         0 :
                                          precision < 0 ?        -1 :
                                          precision + 1);

    // Instantiate this template recursively to consume remaining characters.
    using RecurseType = MakeFixedPoint<(c0isdig ? 10 * rawVal + c0 - '0' :
                                        rawVal), nextPrecision, c...>;

  public:
    using type = typename RecurseType::type;
    static constexpr type makeValue() { return RecurseType::makeValue(); }
        // Return the computed fixed-point number.
};
```

This specialization consumes one character, `c0`, from the parameter pack. The first `static_assert` checks that `c0` is either a digit, digit separator (`'\''`), or decimal point (`'.'`). The second `static_assert` checks that the computation is not in danger of overflowing the maximum value of a **long long**. The constant, `nextPrecision`, which will be passed to the recursive instantiation of this template, keeps track of how many digits have been consumed after the decimal point (or `-1` if the decimal point has not yet been consumed). The `RecurseType` alias is the recursive instantiation of this template with the updated raw value (after consuming `c0`), the updated precision, and the input character sequence after having dropped `c0`. Thus, each recursion gets a potentially larger `rawVal`, a potentially larger `precision`, and a shorter list of unconsumed characters. The definitions of `type` and `makeValue` simply defer to the definitions in the recursive instantiation.

Finally, we define the `_fixed` UDL operator template, instantiating `MakeFixedPoint` with an initial `rawVal` of `0`, an initial `precision` of `-1`, and with a `c...` parameter pack consisting of all of the characters in the naked literal:

```
template <char... c>
constexpr typename MakeFixedPoint<0, -1, c...>::type operator""_fixed()
{
    return MakeFixedPoint<0, -1, c...>::makeValue();
}

}  // Close namespace literals.
}  // Close namespace fixedpoint.
```

Now the `_fixed` suffix can be used for decimal fixed-point UDLs where the precision of the returned type is automatically deduced based on the number of decimal places in the literal. Note that the literal can be used during **constant expression** evaluation:

```cpp
int fixedTest()
{
    using namespace fixedpoint::literals;

    constexpr auto fx1 = 123.45_fixed;    // return type FixedPoint<2>
    constexpr auto fx2 = 123.450_fixed;   // return type FixedPoint<3>
    std::cout << fx1 << '\n';             // prints "123.45"
    std::cout << fx2 << '\n';             // prints "123.450"
}
```

An effort is underway to define a standard **decimal floating-point** type, which, like our decimal fixed-point type, retains the benefit of precisely representing decimal fractions but where the precision is variable at run time. If implemented as a library type, a UDL **suffix** would allow such a type to have a natural representation in code.[6]

User-defined types having string representations

A universally unique identifier (UUID) is a 128-bit number that identifies specific pieces of data in computer systems. It can be readily expressed as an array of two 64-bit integers:

```cpp
#include <cstdint>  // std::uint64_t
class UUIDv4
{
    std::uint64_t d_value[2];
    // ...
};
```

A version-4 UUID has a canonical human-readable format consisting of five groups of hex digits separated by hyphens, e.g., `ed66b67a-f593-4def-9a9b-e69d1d6295ef`. Although storing this representation as a string would be easy, converting it using the packed, 128-bit integer format of the above `UUIDv4` class is more efficient and convenient. Moreover, UUIDs that are hard-coded into software are often generated by external tools — e.g., to identify the exact product build — and should therefore be compile-time constants. Using UDLs, we can readily express a UUID literal using the human-readable string format, converting it to a compile-time constant in the packed format:

```cpp
namespace uuid_literals
{
    constexpr UUIDv4 operator""_uuid(const char* s, std::size_t len)
    {
```

---

[6]kuhl12

```
        return { /* ... (decode UUID expressed in canonical format) */ };
    }
}

using namespace uuid_literals;
constexpr UUIDv4 buildId = "eeec1114-8078-49c5-93ca-fea6fbd6a280"_uuid;
```

Unit conversions and dimensional units

UDLs can be convenient for specifying a unit name on a numeric literal, providing a concise way both to convert the number to a normalized unit and to annotate a value's unit within the code. For example, the standard trigonometric functions all operate on **double** values where angles are expressed in radians. However, many people are more comfortable with degrees than radians, especially when expressing the value directly as a handwritten number:

```
#include <cmath>  // std::sin, std::cos

constexpr double pi = 3.1415926535897931159979634685;

double s1 = std::sin(30.0);     // Bug, intended sin(30 deg) but got sin(30 rad)
double s2 = std::sin(pi / 6);   // OK, returns sin(30 deg)
```

The normalized unit in this case is a radian, expressed as a **double**, but radians are generally fractions of π and are thus inconvenient to write. UDLs can provide convenient normalization from degrees or gradians to radians:

```
namespace trig_literals {

constexpr double operator""_rad(long double r)  { return r; }
constexpr double operator""_deg(long double d)  { return pi * d / 180.0; }
constexpr double operator""_grad(long double d) { return pi * d / 200.0; }

}

using namespace trig_literals;
double s3 = std::sin(30.0_deg);     // OK, returns sin(30 deg)
double s4 = std::sin(4.7124_rad);   // OK, returns approx -1.0
double s5 = std::cos(50.0_grad);    // OK, returns cos(50 grad) == cos(45 deg)
```

Unfortunately, the applicability of the above approach to unit normalization is limited. First, the conversion is one way — e.g., the expression `std::cout << 30.0_deg` will print out `0.524`, not `30.0`, necessitating a call to a radians-to-degrees conversion function when a human-readable value is desired. Second, a **double** does not encode any information about the units that it holds, so **double** `inputAngle` doesn't tell the reader (or program) whether the angle is expected to be input in degrees or radians.

A more robust way to use UDLs to express units is to define them as part of a comprehensive library of unit classes. Dimensional quantities (length, temperature, currency, and so on) often benefit from being represented by **dimensional unit types** that prevent confusion as to both the units and dimension of numeric values. For example, creating a function to compute kinetic energy from speed and mass seems simple:

```
double kineticE(double speed, double mass)
    // Return kinetic energy in joules given speed in m/s and mass in kg.
{
    return speed * speed * mass / 2.0;
}
```

Yet this simple function can be called incorrectly in numerous ways, with no compiler diagnostics to help prevent the errors:

```
double d1   = 15;              // distance in meters
double t1   = 4;               // time in seconds
double s1   = d1 / t1;         // speed in m/s (meters/second)
double m1   = 2045;            // mass in g
double m1Kg = m1 / 1000;       // mass in kg

double x1 = kineticE(d1, m1Kg);  // Bug, distance instead of speed
double x2 = kineticE(m1Kg, s1);  // Bug, arguments reversed
double x3 = kineticE(s1, m1);    // Bug, mass should be in kg, not g.
double x4 = kineticE(s1, m1Kg);  // OK, correct units --- m/s and kg
```

One way to detect some of these errors at compile time is to use a wrapper for each dimension:

```
struct Time     { constexpr Time(double sec);        /*...*/ };
struct Distance { constexpr Distance(double meters); /*...*/ };
struct Speed    { constexpr Speed(double mps);       /*...*/ };
struct Mass     { constexpr Mass(double kg);         /*...*/ };
struct Energy   { constexpr Energy(double joules);   /*...*/ };

// Compute speed from distance and time:
Speed operator/(Distance, Time);

Distance d2(15.0);         // distance in meters
Time     t2(4.0);          // time in seconds
Speed    s2(d2 / t2);      // speed in m/s (meters/second)
Mass     m2(2045.0);       // Bug, trying to get g, got kg instead
Mass     m2Kg(2045.0 / 1000);  // OK, mass in kg

Energy kineticE(Speed s, Mass m);
Energy x5 = kineticE(d2, m2Kg); // Error, 1st argument has an incompatible type.
Energy x6 = kineticE(m2Kg, s2); // Error, reversed arguments, incompatible types
Energy x7 = kineticE(s2, m2);   // Bug, mass should be in kg, not g.
Energy x8 = kineticE(s2, m2Kg); // OK, correct units --- m/s and kg
```

Note that the compiler correctly diagnoses an error in the initializations of x5 and x6 but still fails to diagnose the unit error in the initialization of x7. User-defined literals can amplify the benefits of dimensional unit classes by adding unit suffixes to numeric literals, eliminating implicit unit assumptions:

```
namespace si_literals
{
    constexpr Distance operator""_m  (long double meters);
    constexpr Distance operator""_cm (long double centimeters);
    constexpr Time     operator""_s  (long double seconds);
    constexpr Speed    operator""_mps(long double mps);
    constexpr Mass     operator""_g  (long double grams);
    constexpr Mass     operator""_kg (long double kg);
    constexpr Energy   operator""_j  (long double joules);
}

using namespace si_literals;
auto d3    = 15.0_m;    // distance in meters
auto t3    = 4.0_s;     // time in seconds
auto s3    = d3 / t3;   // speed in m/s (meters/second)
auto m3    = 2045.0_g;  // mass expressed as g but stored as kg
auto m3Kg = 2.045_kg;   // mass expressed as kg

Energy x9  = kineticE(s3, m3);    // OK, m3 has been normalized to kilograms.
Energy x10 = kineticE(s3, m3Kg);  // OK, correct units --- m/s and kg
```

Note that there are two UDLs that yield `Distance` and two UDLs that yield `Mass`. Typically, the internal representation of each of these dimensional types has a normalized representation; e.g., `Distance` might be represented in meters internally, so `25_cm` would be represented by a **double** data member with value `0.25`. It is also possible, however, for the unit to be stored alongside the value, thus avoiding rounding errors in certain cases. Better yet, the unit can be encoded as a template parameter at compile time:

```
#include <ratio>  // std::ratio
template <typename Ratio> class MassUnit;
using Grams     = MassUnit<std::ratio<1, 1000>>;
using Kilograms = MassUnit<std::ratio<1>>;

namespace unit_literals
{
    constexpr Grams     operator""_g  (long double grams);
    constexpr Kilograms operator""_kg (long double kg);
}
```

We now get *different* types for `100_g` and `0.1_kg`, but we can define `MassUnit` in such a way that they interoperate. The time-interval units that we saw previously in UDLs in the C++14 Standard Library provide a taste of what is possible with this approach.[7]

---

[7]Mateusz Pusz explores the topic of a comprehensive physical units library in **pusz20b**.

Test drivers

Because code is easier to maintain when "magic" values are expressed as named constants rather than literal values, a typical program does not contain many literals (see *Potential Pitfalls — Overuse* on page 868). The exception to this general rule is in unit tests where many different values are successively passed to a subsystem to test its behavior. For example, we define a `Date` class that supplies a subtraction operator returning the number of days between two `Dates`:

```
// date.h: (component header file)

class Date
{
    // ...
public:
    constexpr Date(int year, int month, int day);
    // ...
};


int operator-(const Date& lhs, const Date& rhs);
    // Return the number of days from rhs to lhs.
```

To test the subtraction operator, we need to feed it combinations of dates and compare the result with the expected result. We approach such testing by creating an array where each row holds a pair of dates and the expected result from subtracting them. Due to the large number of hard-coded values in the array, having a literal representation for the `Date` class would be convenient, even if the author of `Date` did not see fit to provide one:

```
// date.t.cpp: (component test driver)

#include <date.h>    // Date
#include <cstdlib>   // std::size_t
#include <cassert>   // standard C assert macro

namespace test_literals
{
    constexpr Date operator""_date(const char*, std::size_t);
        // UDL to convert date in "yyyy-mm-dd" format to a Date object
}

void testSubtraction()
{
    using namespace test_literals;  // Import _date UDL suffix.

    struct TestRow
    {
        Date lhs;  // left operand
```

```
        Date rhs;  // right operand
        int  exp;  // expected result
    };

    const TestRow testData[] =
    {
        { "2021-01-01"_date, "2021-01-01"_date,  0 },
        { "2021-01-01"_date, "2020-12-31"_date,  1 },
        { "2021-01-01"_date, "2021-01-02"_date, -1 },
        // ...
    };

    const std::size_t testDataSize = sizeof(testData) / sizeof(TestRow);

    for (std::size_t i = 0; i < testDataSize; ++i)
    {
        assert(testData[i].lhs - testData[i].rhs == testData[i].exp);
    }
}
```

Potential Pitfalls

Unexpected characters can yield bad values

Raw UDL operators and UDL operator templates must parse and handle every character from the *union* of the set of legal characters in integer and floating-point literals, even if the UDL operator is expecting only one of the two numeric type categories. Failure to generate an error for an invalid character is likely to produce an incorrect value, rather than a program crash or compilation error:

```
short operator""_short(const char* digits)
{
    short result = 0;
    for (; *digits; ++digits)
    {
        result = result * 10 + *digits - '0';
    }

    return result;
}

short s1 = 123_short;   // OK, value 123
short s2 = 123._short;  // Bug, '.' treated as digit value -2 ('.' - '0')
```

Testing only for the *expected* characters and rejecting any others is better than checking for *invalid* characters and accepting the rest:

```
#include <stdexcept>  // std::out_of_range

short operator""_shrt2(const char* digits)
{
    short result = 0;
    for (; *digits; ++digits)
    {
        if (*digits == '.')
        {
            throw std::out_of_range("Bad digit");  // BAD IDEA
        }

        if (!std::isdigit(*digits))
        {
            throw std::out_of_range("Bad digit");  // BETTER
        }

        result = result * 10 + *digits - '0';
    }

    return result;
}

short s3 = 123_shrt2;    // OK, value 123
short s4 = 123._shrt2;   // Error (detected), throws out_of_range("Bad digit")
short s5 = 0x123_shrt2;  // Error (detected), throws out_of_range("Bad digit")
```

The first **if** will catch an unexpected decimal point but not unexpected characters such as 'e', 'x', '\''. The second **if** will catch all unexpected characters. If a new radix or other currently illegal character is introduced in a future Standard, the second **if** will avoid processing it incorrectly. Note that, for example, after UDLs were added in C++11, both the 0b radix and the digit separator (') were introduced in C++14, potentially breaking any C++11-compliant UDL operator that didn't properly handle those characters.

Overuse

Although UDLs offer conciseness, they aren't necessarily the most effective way to create a literal value in a program. A regular constructor or function call might be almost as concise, simpler, and more flexible. For example, deg(90) is as readable as 90_deg and can be applied to runtime values as well as to literals.[8] If the constructor for a type naturally takes two or more arguments, a string UDL operator could theoretically parse a comma-separated list of

---

[8]**martin09**, Chapter 17, "Smells and Heuristics," section "G25: Replace Magic Numbers with Named Constants," pp. 300–301

arguments — e.g., `"(2.0, 6.0)"_point` to represent a 2-D coordinate — but is the literal really easier to read than `Point(2.0, 6.0)`?

Finally, even for simple cases, consider how *often* a literal is likely to be used. The use of "magic numbers" in code is widely discouraged. Numeric literals other than, say, `-1`, `0`, `1`, `2`, and `10` or string literals other than `""` are typically used only to initialize named constants. The speed of sound, for example, would probably be written as a constant, e.g., `speedOfSound`, rather than a literal, `343_mps`. Using literals to supply the special values used to initialize named constants provides little benefit by way of overall program readability:

```
constexpr Speed operator""_mps(unsigned long long speed);  // meters per second

constexpr Speed speedOfSound1 = 343_mps;   // OK, clear
constexpr Speed speedOfSound2(343);        // OK, almost as clear

constexpr Speed mach2 = 2 * speedOfSound1; // Literal is irrelevant.
constexpr Speed mach3 = 3 * speedOfSound2; // Literal is irrelevant.
constexpr Speed mach4 = 4 * 343_mps;       // Bad style: "magic" number
```

Often, the most common literal is the one that expresses the notion of an *empty* or *zero* value. A clearer, more descriptive alternative might be to create named constants, such as `constexpr Thing k_EMPTY_THING`, instead of defining a UDL `operator` just to be able to write `""_thing` or `0_thing`.

Preprocessor surprises

A string literal with a suffix, e.g., `"hello"_wrld`, is a single token in C++11 but was two tokens, `"hello"` and `_wrld`, in previous versions of the language. This change could manifest in a subtle difference in meaning, usually resulting in a compilation error, if `_wrld` is a macro:

```
#define _wrld " world"
const char* s = "hello"_wrld;  // "hello world" in C++03, UDL in C++11
```

Annoyances

No conversion from floating-point to integer UDL

Defining a cooked floating-point UDL `operator` does not make the corresponding suffix available to numeric literals that look like integers and vice versa:

```
double operator""_mpg(long double v);

double v1 = 12_mpg;   // Error, no integer UDL operator for _mpg
double v2 = 12._mpg;  // OK, floating-point UDL operator for _mpg found.
```

If the intention is to define a cooked UDL operator where numbers with and without a decimal point are accepted, then both forms of the UDL operator must be defined.

Potential suffix-name collisions

Using a UDL suffix requires bringing the corresponding UDL operator into the current scope, e.g., by means of a **using** directive. If the scope is large enough and if more than one imported namespace contains a UDL operator with the same name, a name collision can result:

```
using namespace trig_literals;         // _deg, _rad, and _grad suffixes
using namespace temperature_literals; // colliding _deg suffix

auto d = 12.0_deg;   // Error, ambiguous use of suffix, _deg
```

While it is possible to disambiguate the colliding suffixes via qualified name lookup, the ensuing verbosity might defeat the purpose of using a UDL in the first place:

```
auto a = trig_literals::operator""_deg(12.0);
auto b = temperature_literals::operator""_deg(12.0);
```

Confusing raw with string UDL operators

A UDL operator that takes a single **const char*** argument is a raw UDL operator for numeric literals but can be easily confused for a cooked UDL operator for string literals:

```
int operator""_udl(const char*);

int s = "hello"_udl;  // Error, no match for operator""(const char*, size_t)
```

Fortunately, such a problem will typically result in a compile-time error.

No UDL operator templates for string literals

UDL operator templates are called only for numeric literals; string literals are limited to the cooked UDL operators. It is thus not possible to choose, at compile time, different return types based on the contents of a string literal.[9]

No way to parse a leading - or +

As shown in *Description — Restrictions on UDLs* on page 839, a - or + before a numeric literal is a separate unary operation and not part of the literal. There are occasions, however,

---

[9] As of C++20, new syntax is added that removes the limitation of not being able to affect the return-type base on the contents of a literal string.

where it would be convenient to know whether the literal value is being negated. For example, if temperatures are being stored as **double** values in Kelvin and if the UDL suffix _C converts a floating-point literal from Celsius to Kelvin by calling a function, cToK(**double**), then the expression -10.0_C produces the nonsensical value -283.15 (-cToK(10.0)) rather than the intuitive value of +263.15 (cToK(-10.0)). Alas, parsing the - sign as part of the literal is simply not possible.

Parsing numbers is hard

Many of the benefits of raw UDL operators and UDL operator templates require parsing integer and/or floating-point values manually, in code, often using recursion. Getting this right is tedious at best. The Standard Library does not provide much support, especially for **constexpr** parsing.

See Also

- "**decltype**" (§1.1, p. 25) introduces a keyword often helpful for deducing the return type of a UDL operator template.

- "**nullptr**" (§1.1, p. 99) describes a keyword that unambiguously denotes the null pointer literal.

- "**auto** Variables" (§2.1, p. 195) shows how type inference can be used to declare a variable to hold the value of a UDL when the type of the UDL varies based on its contents.

- "**constexpr** Functions" (§2.1, p. 257) explains how most UDLs can be used as part of a constant expression.

- "Inheriting Ctors" (§2.1, p. 535) discusses a feature that allows wrapper types (or **strong typedefs**) to be constructible from the same arguments as the type they wrap.

- "Variadic Templates" (§2.1, p. 873) shows how templates can take an infinite number of parameters, which is required for implementing UDL operator templates.

- "**inline namespace**" (§3.1, p. 1055) describes a feature not recommended for UDL operators, yet the C++14 Standard Library puts UDL operators into **inline** namespaces.

Further Reading

- The motivation for having more flexible C++ literals, including improved compatibility with C99 and future C enhancements, can be found in **mcintosh08b**; the proposal with minimal wording changes to implement user-defined literals (with most non-wording-related discussion omitted) appears in **mcintosh08a**.

- For a discussion of user-defined literals with recommendations for idiomatic use, see **dewhurst19**.

Variable-Argument-Count Templates

By Andrei Alexandrescu

Language-level support for traditional templates is extended to enable both class and function templates to accept arbitrary numbers of template arguments and for function templates to access and process arbitrarily many argument objects of heterogeneous types via a new syntactic construct, the **parameter pack**.

Description

Experience with C++03 revealed a recurring need to specify a class template or function template that accepts an arbitrary number of arguments. The C++03 workarounds often require considerable boilerplate and hard-coded limitations that impede usability. Consider, for example, a function concat taking zero or more **const** std::string&, **const char***, or **char** arguments and returning an std::string that is the concatenation of that argument sequence:

```
#include <string>  // std::string

std::string s = "d";
std::string str0 = concat();          // str0 == "" (by definition)
std::string str1 = concat("apple");   // str1 == "apple"
std::string str2 = concat('b', "ccd"); // str2 == "bccd"
std::string str3 = concat(s, 'e', "fg"); // str3 == "defg"
```

One advantage of using a variadic function, such as concat, instead of repeatedly using the + operator is that the concat function can build the destination string exactly once, whereas each invocation of + creates and returns a new std::string object.

A simpler example is a variadic function, **add**, that calculates the sum of zero or more integer values supplied to it:

```
int v0 = add();       // v0 == 0 (by definition)
int v1 = add(3);      // v1 == 3
int v2 = add(-6, 2);  // v2 == -4
int v3 = add(7, 1, 4); // v3 == 12
// ...
```

Historically, variadic functions, such as concat and add (above), were implemented as a suite of related nonvariadic functions accepting progressively more arguments, up to some arbitrary limit (e.g., 20) chosen by the implementer:

```
int add();
int add(int);
int add(int, int);
int add(int, int, int);
// ...
// ...                    (declarations from 4 to 19 int parameters elided)
// ...
int add(int, int, int, /* 16 more int parameters elided, */ int);
```

Given the existence of an identity value (zero for addition), an alternative approach would be to have a single add function but with each of the parameters defaulted:

```
int add(int=0, int=0, /* 17 more defaulted parameters omitted */ int=0);
```

However, concat cannot use the same approach because each of its arguments might be a **char**, a **const char***, or an std::string (or types convertible thereto), and no single type accommodates all of these possibilities. To accept an arbitrary mix of arguments of the allowed types with maximal efficiency, the brute-force approach would require the definition of an exponential number of overloads taking any combination of **char**, **const char***, and **const** std::string&, again up to some implementation-chosen maximum number of parameters, N.

With such an approach, the number of required overloads is $O(3^N)$, which means that accommodating a maximum of just 5 arguments would require 364 overloads, and 10 arguments would require $88,573$ overloads![1] Defining a suite of N function *templates* instead is one approach to avoiding this combinatorial explosion of overloads:

```
#include <string>  // std::string

std::string concat();                                      // 0 parameters

template <typename T1>
std::string concat(const T1&);                             // 1 parameter

template <typename T1, typename T2>
std::string concat(const T1&, const T2&);                  // 2 parameters

template <typename T1, typename T2, typename T3>
std::string concat(const T1&, const T2&, const T3&);       // 3 parameters

// ...
// ...              (similar declarations taking up to, say, 20 parameters)
// ...
```

---

[1] The std::string_view Standard Library type introduced with C++17 would help here because it accepts conversion from both **const char*** and std::string and incurs no significant overhead. However, std::string_view cannot be initialized from a single **char**, so we'd be looking at $O(2^N)$ instead of $O(3^N)$ — not a dramatic improvement.

Using conventional function templates, we can drastically reduce the volume of source code required, albeit with some manageable increase in implementation complexity.

Each of the $N + 1$ templates can be written to accept any combination of its M arguments ($0 \leq M \leq N$) such that each parameter will independently bind to a **const char***, an std::string, or a **char** with no unnecessary conversions or extra copies at run time. Of the exponentially many possible concat template instantiations, the compiler generates — on demand — only those overloads that are actually invoked.

With the introduction of variadic templates in C++11, we are now able to represent variadic functions such as add or concat with just a single template that expands automatically to accept any number of arguments of any appropriate types — all by, say, **const** *lvalue* reference:

```
template <typename... Ts>
std::string concat(const Ts&...);
    // Return a string that is the concatenation of a sequence of zero or
    // more character or string arguments --- each of a potentially distinct
    // C++ type --- passed by const lvalue reference.
```

A variadic function template will typically be implemented with **recursion** to the same function with fewer parameters. Such function templates will typically be accompanied by an overload (templated or not) that implements the lower limit, in our case, the overload having exactly zero parameters:

```
std::string concat();
    // Return an empty string ("") of length 0.
```

The nontemplate overload above declares concat taking no parameters. Importantly, this overload will be preferred for calls to concat having no arguments because the nontemplate function is a better match than the variadic declaration, even though the variadic declaration would also accept zero arguments.

Having to write just two overloads to support any number of arguments has clear advantages over writing dozens of overloaded templates: (1) there is no hard-coded limit on argument count, and (2) the source is dramatically smaller, more regular, and easier to maintain and extend — e.g., it would be easy to add support for efficiently passing by forwarding reference (see Section 2.1."Forwarding References" on page 377). A second-order effect should be noted as well. The costs of defining variadic functions with C++03 technology are large enough to discourage such an approach in the first place, unless overwhelming efficiency motivation exists; with C++11, the low cost of defining variadics often makes them the simpler, better, and more efficient choice altogether. We return to the concat function template and provide a complete implementation later; see *Use Cases — Processing variadic arguments in order* on page 926.

Variadic *class* templates are another important motivating use case for this language feature.

A tuple is a generalization of std::pair that, instead of comprising just two objects, can store an arbitrary number of objects of heterogeneous types:

```
Tuple<int, double, std::string> tup1(1, 2.0, "three");
    // tup1 holds an int, a double, and an std::string.

Tuple<int, int> tup2(42, 69);
    // tup2 holds two ints.
```

Tuple provides a container for a specified set of types, in a manner similar to a **struct**, but without the inconvenience of needing to introduce a new **struct** definition with its own name. As shown in the example above, the tuples are also initialized correctly according to the specified types (e.g., **tup2** contains two integers initialized, respectively, with 42 and 69).

In C++03, an approximation to a tuple could be improvised by composing an **std::pair** with itself:

```
#include <utility>  // std::pair
std::pair<int, std::pair<double, long> > v;
    // Define a holder of an int, a double, and a long, accessed as
    // v.first, v.second.first, and v.second.second, respectively.
```

Composite use of **std:pair** types could, in theory, be scaled to arbitrary depth; defining, initializing, and using such types, however, is not always practical. Another approach commonly used in C++03 and similar to the one suggested for the **add** function template above is to define a template class, e.g., **Cpp03Tuple**, having many parameters (e.g, 9), each defaulted to a special marker type (e.g., **None**), indicating that the parameter is not used:

```
struct None { };  // empty "tag" used as a special "not used" marker in Cpp03Tuple

template <typename T1 = None, typename T2 = None, typename T3 = None,
          typename T4 = None, typename T5 = None, typename T6 = None,
          typename T7 = None, typename T8 = None, typename T9 = None>
class Cpp03Tuple;
    // struct-like class containing up to 9 data members of arbitrary types
```

Cpp03Tuple can be used to store, access, and modify up to nine values together; e.g., **Cpp03Tuple<int, int, std::string>** would consist of two **int**s and an **std::string**.

Cpp03Tuple's implementation uses a variety of **metaprogramming** tricks to detect which of the nine type slots are used. This approach is taken by **boost::tuple**,[2] an industrial-strength tuple implemented using C++03-era technology. In contrast, the variadic-template-based declaration (and definition) of a modern C++ tuple is much simpler:

```
template <typename... Ts>
class Cpp11Tuple;  // class template storing an arbitrary sequence of objects
```

C++11 introduced the Standard Library class template **std::tuple**, declared in a manner similar to **Cpp11Tuple**.

---

[2]https://github.com/boostorg/tuple/blob/develop/include/boost/tuple/tuple.hpp

An `std::tuple` can be used, for example, to return multiple values from a function. Suppose we want to define a function, `minAverageMax`, that — given a **range** of double values — returns, along with its cardinality, its minimum, average, and maximum values. The interface for such a function in C++03 might have involved multiple output parameters passed, e.g., by non**const** *lvalue* reference:

```
#include <cstddef> // std::size_t

template <typename Iterator>
void minAverageMax(std::size_t& numValues,  // (out only) number of inputs
                   double& minimum,         // (out only) minimum value
                   double& average,         // (out only) average value
                   double& maximum,         // (out only) maximum value
                   Iterator b, Iterator e); // input range
    // Load into the specified numValues, minimum, average, and maximum
    // the corresponding values extracted from the specified range [b, e).
```

Alternatively, one could have defined a separate **struct** (e.g., `MinAverageMaxRes`) and incorporated that into the interface of the `minAverageMax` function:

```
#include <cstddef>  // std::size_t

struct MinAverageMaxRes  // used in conjunction with minAverageMax (below)
{
    std::size_t count;   // number of input values
    double      min;     // minimum value
    double      average; // average value
    double      max;     // maximum value
};

template <typename Iterator>
MinAverageMaxRes minAverageMax(Iterator b, Iterator e);
```

Adding a helper **aggregate** such as `MinAverageMax` (above) works but demands a fair amount of boilerplate coding that might not be reusable or otherwise worth naming. The C++11 library abstraction `std::tuple` allows code to define such simple collections of objects on the fly:

```
#include <tuple>    // std::tuple
#include <cstddef>  // std::size_t

typedef std::tuple<std::size_t, double, double, double> MinAverageMaxRes;
    // type alias for a standard tuple of four specific scalar values

template <typename Iterator>
MinAverageMaxRes minAverageMax(Iterator b, Iterator e);
    // Return the cardinality, min, average, and max of the range [b, e).
```

We can now use our `minAverageMax` function to extract the relevant fields from a vector of **double** values:

```
#include <vector>  // std::vector

void test(const std::vector<double>& v)
{
    MinAverageMaxRes res = minAverageMax(v.begin(), v.end());  // Calculate.
    std::size_t num = std::get<0>(res);  // Fetch slot 0, the number of values.
    double       min = std::get<1>(res);  // Fetch slot 1, the minimum value.
    double       ave = std::get<2>(res);  // Fetch slot 2, the average value.
    double       max = std::get<3>(res);  // Fetch slot 3, the maximum value.
    // ...
    std::get<2>(res) = 0.0;               // Store 0 in slot 2 (just FYI).
    // ...
}
```

Note that elements in a tuple are accessed in a numerically indexed manner (beginning with slot 0) using the standard function template `std::get` for both reading and writing. Thus, an `std::tuple` works like an array of heterogenous elements indexed by a compile-time integer. The use of numeric indexes instead of member names can hinder readability, however, as member names can be self-documenting in a way that indexes cannot.

There are other motivating uses of variadic templates, such as allowing generic code to forward arguments to other functions, notably constructors, without the need to know in advance the number of arguments required. Related artifacts added to the C++ Standard Library include `std::make_shared`, `std::make_unique`, and the `emplace_back` member function of `std::vector` (see *Use Cases — Object factories* on page 929).

There is a lot to unpack here. We will begin our journey by understanding variadic *class* templates as **generic types** that provide a solid basis for understanding variadic *function* templates. In practice, however, variadic *function* templates are arguably more frequently applicable outside of advanced metaprogramming; see *Variadic function templates* on page 888.

Variadic class templates

Suppose we want to create a class template `C` that can take zero or more template type arguments:

```
template <typename... Ts> class C;
    // The class template C can be instantiated with a sequence of zero or
    // more template arguments of arbitrary types.
```

First we point out that the ellipsis (`...`), just like `++` or `==`, is parsed as a separate token; hence, any whitespace around the ellipsis is optional. The common style, and the one used in the C++ Standard documents, follows the typographic convention in written prose: `...` abuts to the left and is followed by a single space as in the declaration of `C` above.

Note that, as with nonvariadic template parameters, providing a name to represent the supplied template parameters (a.k.a. **template parameter pack**, see below) is optional and is often omitted in forward declarations:

```
template <typename... Ts> class C;  // with    name identifying parameter pack
template <typename...> class C;      // without  "        "         "         "
```

When an ellipsis token (...) appears *after* **typename** or **class** and before the optional type-parameter name (e.g., Ts), it introduces a **template parameter pack**:

```
template <typename... Ts>  // Ts names a template parameter pack.
class C;
```

We call entities such as Ts **template parameter packs** to distinguish them from **function parameter packs** (see *Variadic function templates* on page 888). The phrase **parameter pack** is a conflation of the two and also a casual reference to either of them whenever there is no ambiguity. A **template parameter pack** typically expresses a list of type template parameters (see *Type template parameter packs* on page 880) but might instead express a list of non-type template parameters (see *Non-type template parameter packs* on page 901) or a list of template template parameters (see *Template template parameter packs* on page 903).

This syntactic form of ... is used primarily in **declarations** (including those associated with **definitions**):

```
template <typename... Ts>
class C { /*...*/ };  // definition of class C
```

The same ... token, when it appears to the *right* of an existing **template parameter pack** (e.g., Ts), is used to *unpack* it:

```
#include <vector>  // std::vector

template <typename... Ts> class C  // definition of class C
{
    std::vector<Ts...> d_data;
        // using ... to unpack a template parameter pack
};
```

In the example above, the *unpacking* results in a comma-separated list of the types with which C was instantiated. The ... token is used after the **template parameter pack** name Ts to re-create the sequence of arguments originally passed to the instantiation of C. Referring to our example above, we might choose to create an object, x, of type C<**int**>:

```
C<int> x;  // has data member, d_data, of type std::vector<int>
```

We might, instead, consider creating an object, y, that also passes std::allocator<**char**> to C's instantiation:

```
C<char, std::allocator<char>> y;
    // y.d_data has type std::vector<char, std::allocator<char>>.
```

And so on. That is, **class** C can be instantiated with any sequence of types that is supported by the d_data member variable.

An instantiation such as C<**float, double**> would correspondingly attempt to instantiate std::vector<**float, double**>, which is in error and would cause the instantiation of C to fail. Several other cases and patterns of *unpacking* of **template parameter packs** exist and are described in detail in *Type template parameter packs* below.

Continuing our pedagogical discussion, let's **define** an empty variadic class template, D:

```
template <typename...> class D { };  // empty variadic-class-template definition
```

We can now create explicit instantiations of class template D by providing it with any number of *type* arguments:

```
D<>              d0;  // instantiation of D with no type arguments
D<int>           d1;  // instantiation of D with a single int argument
D<int, int>      d2;  // instantiation of D with two int arguments
D<int, const int> d3; // Note that d3 is a distinct type from d2.
D<double, char>  d4;  // instantiation of D with a double and char
D<char, double>  d5;  // Note that d5 is a distinct type from d4.
D<D<>, D<int>>   d6;  // instantiation of D with two UDT arguments
```

The number and order of arguments are part of the instantiated type, so each of the objects d0 through d6 above has a distinct C++ type:

```
void f(const D<double, char>&);  // (1) overload of function f
void f(const D<char, double>&);  // (2)    "    "    "    "

void test()
{
    f(d4);  // invokes overload (1)
    f(d5);  // invokes overload (2)
}
```

The sections that follow examine in full detail how to

- Declare variadic *class* and *function* templates using **parameter packs**
- Make use of variadic parameter lists in the implementation of class definitions and function bodies

Type template parameter packs

A **type template parameter pack** is the name representing a list of zero or more parameters following **class...** or **typename...** within a variadic template declaration.

Let's take a closer look at just the *declaration* of a variadic class template, C:

```
template <typename... Ts> class C { };
```

Here, the identifier `Ts` names a **template parameter pack**, which — as we saw previously — can bind to any sequence of explicitly supplied types including the empty sequence:

```
C<> c0;                  // OK, instantiation of C with no type arguments
C<int> c1;               // OK, instantiation of C with a single int argument
C<float, bool> c2;       // OK, instantiation of C with two type arguments
```

Passing an argument to `C` that is not a type, however, is not permitted:

```
C<128> cx0;              // Error, expecting type template argument, 128 provided
C<std::vector> cx1;      // Error, expecting type argument, template name provided
C<int, 42, int> cx2;     // Error, expecting type argument in second position
```

Template parameter packs can appear together with simple template parameters, with one restriction: **Primary class template declarations** allow at most one variadic parameter pack at the end of the template parameter list. (Recall that in standard C++ terminology, the **primary declaration** of a class template is the first declaration introducing the template's name; all specializations and partial specializations of a class template require the presence of a primary declaration.)

```
template <typename... Ts>
class C0  { };  // OK

template <typename T, typename... Ts>
class C1  { };  // OK

template <typename T, typename U, typename... Ts>
class C2  { };  // OK

template <typename... Ts, typename... Us>
class Cx0 { };  // Error, more than one parameter pack

template <typename... Ts, typename T>
class Cx1 { };  // Error, parameter pack must be the last template parameter.
```

There is no way to specify a default for a parameter pack; however, a parameter pack can follow a defaulted parameter:

```
template <typename... Ts = int>
class Cx2 { };  // Error, a parameter pack cannot have a default.

template <typename T = int, typename... Ts = char>
class Cx3 { };  // Error, a parameter pack cannot have a default.

template <typename T = int, typename... Ts>
class C3  { };  // OK

C3<> c31;                    // OK, T=int, Ts=<>
C3<char> c32;                // OK, T=char, Ts=<>
C3<char, double, int> c33;   // OK, T=char, Ts=<double, int>
```

What can we do with a **template parameter pack**? Template parameter packs are of a so-called *kind* distinct from other C++ entities. They are not types, values, or anything else found in C++03. As such, parameter packs are not subject to any of the usual operations one might expect:

```
template <typename... Ts>
class Cx4
{
    Cx4<Ts>* next;        // Error, cannot use unexpanded parameter pack Ts
    Ts memberVariable;    // Error,     "    "     "        "         "   "
    typedef Ts Ts1;       // Error,     "    "     "        "         "   "
    using Ts2 = Ts;       // Error,     "    "     "        "         "   "
};
```

There is no way to use a **parameter pack** in unexpanded form. Once introduced, the name of a parameter pack can occur only as part of a **pack expansion**. We've already encountered the simple **pack expansion** Ts..., which expands to the list of types to which Ts is bound. That expansion is allowed only in certain contexts where multiple types would be allowed:

```
template <typename... Ts>
class Cx5
{
    Cx5<Ts...>* d_next;     // OK, instantiate Cx5 in definition of member.
    Cx5<Ts...> f0();        // OK, instantiate Cx5 in member function signature.
    void f1(Cx5<Ts...>&);   // OK,      "        "   "   "      "        "
    Ts... d_memberVariable; // Error, expansion as a member type
    typedef Ts... Ts1;      // Error, expansion as a typedef type
    using Ts2 = Ts...;      // Error, expansion as a using declaration argument
};
```

Note that the code above remains invalid even if Ts contains a single type, e.g., in the instantiation Cx5<**int**>. Pack expansion is not textual and not allowed everywhere; it is allowed only in certain well-defined contexts. The first such context, as showcased with the member variable d_next in the code example above, is inside a **template argument list**. Note how the pattern can be surrounded by other parameters or expansions:

```
#include <map> // std::map

template <typename... Ts>
class C4
{
    void arbitraryMemberFunction()      // for illustration purposes
    {
        C4<Ts...>            v0; // OK, same type as *this
        C4<int, Ts...>       v1; // OK, expand after another argument.
        C4<Ts..., char>      v2; // OK, expand before another argument.
        C4<char, Ts..., int> v3; // OK, expand in between.
        C4<void, Ts..., Ts...> v4; // OK, two expansions
```

```
        C4<char, Ts..., int, Ts...> v5;  // OK, no need for them to be adjacent
        C4<void, C4<Ts...>, int>    v6;  // OK, expansion nested within
        C4<Ts..., C4<Ts...>, Ts...> v7;  // OK, mix of expansions
        std::map<Ts...>             v8;  // OK, works with nonvariadic template
    }
};
```

The examples above illustrate how **pack expansion** is not done textually, like a macro expanded by the C preprocessor. A simple textual expansion of C4<**char**, Ts..., **int**> would be C4<**char**, , **int**> if Ts were empty (i.e., inside the instantiation C4<>). Pack expansion is syntactic, not just textual, and "knows" to eliminate any spurious commas caused by the expansion of empty **parameter packs**.

Within the context of a template argument list, Ts... is not the only pattern that can be expanded; any template instantiation using Ts (e.g., D<Ts>...) can be expanded as a unit. The result is a list of template instantiations using each of the types in Ts in turn. Note that, in the example below, the expansions D<Ts...> and D<Ts>... are both valid but produce different results:

```
#include <vector>  // std::vector

template <typename... Ts> class D
{
    void memberFunction()
    {
        D<Ts...> v0;             // OK, same type as *this
        D<D<Ts...>> v1;          // OK, expand to D<D<T0, T1, ...>>.
        D<D<Ts>...> v2;          // OK, expand to D<D<T0>, D<T1>, ...>.
        D<std::vector<Ts>...> v3;  // OK, expand to C1<std::vector<T0>, ...>.
    }
};
```

The second important **pack expansion context** for type parameter packs is in a **base-specifier list**. All patterns that form a valid base specifier are allowed:

```
template <typename... Ts>   // zero or more arguments
class D1 : public Ts...     // Publicly inherit T0, T1, ...
{ /*...*/ };

template <typename... Ts>
class D2 : public D<Ts>...  // Publicly inherit D<T0>, D<T1>, ...
{ /*...*/ };

template <typename... Ts>
class D3 : public D<Ts...>  // Publicly inherit D<T0, T1, ...>
{ /*...*/ };
```

The access control specifiers — **public**, **protected**, and **private** — can be applied as usual.

However, within a single expansion pattern, the access specifier must be the same for all expanded elements:

```
template <typename... Ts>
class D4 : private Ts...   // Privately inherit T0, T1, ...
{ /*...*/ };


template <typename... Ts>
class D5 : public Ts..., private D<int, Ts>...
    // Publicly inherit T0, T1, ...
    // and privately inherit D<int, T0>, D<int, T1>, ...
{ /*...*/ };
```

Pack expansions can be freely mixed with simple base specifiers:

```
class AClass1 { /*...*/ };  // arbitrary class definition
class AClass2 { /*...*/ };  //      "          "          "


template <typename... Ts>
class D6 : protected AClass1, public Ts...                // OK
{ /*...*/ };


template <typename... Ts>
class D7 : protected AClass1, private Ts..., public AClass2  // OK
{ /*...*/ };
```

If the parameter pack being expanded (e.g., `Ts`, in the code snippet above) is empty, the expansion does not introduce any base class. Notice, again, how the expansion mechanism is syntactic, not textual; e.g., in the instantiation `D7<>`, the fragment **private** `Ts...`, disappears entirely, leaving `D7<>` with `AClass1` as a **protected** base and `AClass2` as a **public** base.

To recap, the two essential parameter expansion contexts for `type template parameter packs` are inside a `template argument list` and in a `base-specifier list`.

Specialization of variadic class templates

Recall from C++03 that after a class template is introduced by a **primary class template** declaration, it is possible to create **specializations** and **partial specializations** of that class template. We can declare **specializations** of a variadic class template by supplying zero or more arguments to its parameter pack:

```
template <typename... Ts> class C0;  // primary class template declaration


template <> class C0<>;              // Specialize C0 for Ts=<>.
template <> class C0<int>;           // Specialize C0 for Ts=<int>.
template <> class C0<int, void>;     // Specialize C0 for Ts=<int, void>.
```

Similar specializations can be applied to class templates that have other template parameters preceding the **template parameter pack**. The nonpack template parameters must be matched exactly by the arguments, followed by zero or more arguments for the parameter pack:

```
template <typename T, typename... Ts>
class C1;                             // primary class template declaration

template <> class C1<int>;            // Specialize C1 for T=int, Ts=<>.
template <> class C1<int, void>;      // Specialize for T=int, Ts=<void>.
template <> class C1<int, void, int>; // Specialize for T=int, Ts=<void, int>.
template <> class C1<>;               // Error, too few template arguments
```

Partial specializations of a class template can take multiple parameter packs because some of the types involved in the partial specialization might themselves use parameter packs. Consider, for example, a variadic class template, **Tuple**, defined as having exactly one parameter pack:

```
template <typename... Ts> class Tuple // variadic class template
{ /*...*/ };
```

Further assume a primary declaration of a variadic class template, **C2**, also having one type parameter pack. We also introduce definitions in addition to declarations so we can instantiate **C2** later:

```
template <typename... Ts> class C2
    // (0) primary declaration of variadic class template C2
{ /*...*/ };
```

This simple setup allows a variety of partial specializations. First, we can partially specialize **C2** for exactly two **Tuple**s instantiated with the same exact types:

```
template <typename... Ts>
class C2<Tuple<Ts...>, Tuple<Ts...>> // (1) two identical Tuples
{ /*...*/ };
```

We can also partially specialize **C2** for exactly two **Tuple**s but with potentially different type arguments:

```
template <typename... Ts, typename... Us>
class C2<Tuple<Ts...>, Tuple<Us...>> // (2) any two Tuples
{ /*...*/ };
```

Furthermore, we can partially specialize **C2** for any **Tuple** followed by zero or more types:

```
template <typename... Ts, typename... Us>
class C2<Tuple<Ts...>, Us...> // (3) any Tuple followed by 0 or more types
{ /*...*/ };
```

The possibilities are endless; shown below is one more partial specialization of **C2** with three template parameter packs that will match two arbitrary **Tuple**s followed by zero or more arguments:

```
template <typename... Ts, typename... Us, typename... Vs>
class C2<Tuple<Ts...>, Tuple<Us...>, Vs...>
    // (4) Specialize C2 for Tuple<Ts...> in the first position,
    // Tuple<Us...> in the second position, followed by zero or more
    // arguments.
{ /*...*/ };
```

Now that we have definitions for the primary template C2 and four partial specializations of it, let's take a look at a few variable definitions that instantiate C2. **Partial ordering of class template specializations**[3] will decide the best match for each instantiation and also deduce the appropriate template parameters:

```
C2<int>                              c2a;  // uses (0), Ts=<int>
C2<Tuple<int>, Tuple<int>>           c2b;  // uses (1), Ts=<int>
C2<Tuple<int, char>, Tuple<char>> c2c;  // uses (2), Ts=<int,char>, Us=<char>
C2<Tuple<int, int>, char>            c2d;  // uses (3), Ts=<int,int>, Us=<char>
C2<Tuple<int>, Tuple<char>, void> c2e;  // uses (4), Ts=<int>, Us=<char>, Vs=<void>
```

Notice how partial ordering chooses (2) instead of (4) for the definition of c2c, although both (2) and (4) are a match; a matching nonvariadic template is always a better match than one involving deduction of a parameter pack.

Even in a partial specialization, if a template argument of the specialization is a `pack expansion`, it must be in the last position:

```
template <typename... Ts>
class C2<Ts..., int>;
    // Error, template argument int can't follow pack expansion Ts....
```

```
template <typename... Ts>
class C2<Tuple<Ts>..., int>;
    // Error, template argument int can't follow pack expansion Tuple<Ts>....
```

```
template <typename... Ts>
class C2<Tuple<Ts...>, int>;
    // OK, pack expansion Ts... is inside another template.
```

Parameter packs are a terse and flexible placeholder for defining partial specialization — a "zero or more types fit here" wildcard. The primary class template does not even need to be variadic. Consider, for example, a nonvariadic class template, Map, fashioned after the std::map class template:

```
template <typename Key, typename Value> class Map;  // similar to std::map
```

We would then want to partially specialize another nonvariadic class template, C3, for all maps, regardless of keys and values:

---

[3] **iso14**, section 14.5.5.2, "Partial ordering of class template specializations," pp. 339–340

```
template <typename T> class C3;    // (1) primary declaration; C3 not variadic

template <typename K, typename V>  // (2a) Specialize C3 for all Maps, C++03 style.
class C3<Map<K, V>>;
```

Variadics offer a terser, more flexible alternative:

```
template <typename... Ts>  // (2b) Specialize C3 for all Maps, variadic style.
class C3<Map<Ts...>>;
    // Note: Map works with pack expansion even though it's not variadic,
    // but Ts... must comprise the number and types of arguments appropriate
    // for instantiating one.
```

The most important advantage of (2b) over (2a) is flexibility. In maintenance, Map might acquire additional template arguments, such as a comparison functor and an allocator. Changing Map's arguments requires surgery on C3's specialization (2a), whereas (2b) will continue to work unchanged because Map<Ts...> will accommodate any additional template parameters Map might accummulate.

An application must use either the nonvariadic (2a) or the variadic (2b) partial specialization but not both. If both are present, (2a) is always preferred because an exact match is always more specialized than one that deduces a parameter pack.

Variadic alias templates

Alias templates (since C++11) are a new way to associate a name with a family of types without needing to define forwarding glue code. For full details on the topic, see Section 1.1. "**using** Aliases" on page 133. Here, we focus on the applicability of **template parameter packs** to alias templates.

Consider, for example, the Tuple artifact that can store an arbitrary number of objects of heterogeneous types:

```
template <typename... Ts> class Tuple;  // Declare Tuple.
```

Suppose we want to build a simple abstraction on top of Tuple — a "named tuple" that has an std::string as its first element, followed by anything a Tuple can store:

```
#include <string>  // std::string

template <typename... Ts>
using NamedTuple = Tuple<std::string, Ts...>;
    // Introduce alias for Tuple of std::string and anything.
```

In general, **alias templates** take **template parameter packs** following the same rules as primary class template declarations: An alias template is allowed to take at most one template parameter pack in the last position. Alias templates do not support specialization or partial specialization.

Variadic function templates

Let's first consider a variadic function template that accepts a `template parameter pack` in its `template parameter list` but does not use any of its template parameters in its `function parameter list`:

```
template <typename... Ts>
int f0a();      // does not use Ts in parameter list

template <typename... Ts>
int f0b(int);   // uses int but not Ts in parameter list

template <typename T, class... Ts>
int f0c();      // does not use T or Ts in parameter list
```

The only way to call the functions shown in the code snippet above is by using explicit template argument lists:

```
int a1 = f0a<int, char, int>();    // Ts=<int, char, int>
int a2 = f0b<double, void>(42);    // Ts=<double, void>
int a3 = f0c<int, void, int>();    // T=int, Ts=<void, int>
int e1 = f0a();                    // Error, cannot deduce Ts
int e2 = f0b(42);                  // Error, cannot deduce Ts
int e3 = f0c();                    // Error, cannot deduce T and Ts
```

The notation `f0a<int, char, int>()` means to explicitly instantiate template function `f0a` with the specified type arguments and to call that instantiation.

Invoking any of the instantiations shown above will, of course, require that the corresponding definition of the function template exist somewhere within the program:

```
template <typename...> void f0a() { /*...*/ }  // variadic template definition
```

This definition will typically be part of or reside alongside its declaration in the same header or source file, but see Section 2.1."**extern template**" on page 353.

With the notable exception of factory functions such as `make_shared`, such functions are rarely encountered in practice; most of the time a template function would use its template parameters in the function parameter list. Let's now consider a different kind of variadic function template — one that accepts an arbitrary number of template arguments and an arbitrary number of *function* arguments working in tandem with the template arguments.

Function parameter packs

The syntax for declaring a variadic function template that accepts an arbitrary number of function arguments makes two distinct uses of the ellipsis (...) token. The first use is to introduce the template parameter pack `Ts`, as already shown. Then, to make the function parameter list of a function template variadic, we introduce a `function parameter pack` by placing the ... to the left of the function parameter name:

```
template <typename... Ts>  // template parameter pack Ts
int f1a(Ts... values);     // function parameter pack values
   // f1a is a variadic function template taking an arbitrary sequence of
   // function arguments by value (explanation follows), each independently of
   // arbitrary heterogeneous type.
```

A function parameter pack is a function parameter that accepts zero or more function arguments. Syntactically, a function parameter pack is similar to a regular function parameter declaration, with two distinctions.

1. The type in the declaration contains at least one **template parameter pack**.

2. The ellipsis ... is inserted right before the function parameter name, if present, or replaces the parameter name, if absent, i.e., for unused parameters.

Therefore, the declaration of **f1a** above has one **template parameter pack**, Ts, and one **function parameter pack**, values. The function parameter declaration Ts... values indicates that **values** will match zero or more arguments of various types, all by value. Replacing the parameter declaration with **const** Ts&... values would result in passing the arguments by reference to **const**. Just as with nonvariadic function templates, variadic template parameter lists are permitted to include any legal combination of **qualifiers** (**const** and **volatile**) and **declarator operators** (i.e., pointer *, reference &, forwarding reference &&, and array []):

```
template <typename... Ts> void f1b(Ts&...);
   // accepts any number and types of arguments by reference

template <typename... Ts> void f1c(const Ts&...);
   // accepts any number and types of arguments by reference to const

template <typename... Ts> void f1d(Ts* const*...);
   // accepts any number and types of arguments by pointer to const
   // pointer to nonconst object

template <typename... Ts> void f1e(Ts&&...);
   // accepts any number and types of arguments by forwarding reference

template <typename... Ts> void f1f(const volatile Ts*&...);
   // accepts any number and types of arguments by reference to pointer to
   // const volatile objects
```

To best understand the syntax of variadic function template declarations, it is important to distinguish the distinct — and indeed complementary — roles of the two occurrences of the ... token. First, as discussed in *Template template parameter packs* on page 903, **typename**... Ts introduces a **template parameter pack** called Ts that matches an arbitrary sequence of types. The second use of ... is, instead, a **pack expansion** that transforms the pattern — whether it's Ts..., **const** Ts&..., Ts* **const**..., etc. — into a comma-separated

889

parameter list for the function, where the C++ type of each successive parameter is determined by the corresponding type in `Ts`. The resulting construct is a **function parameter pack**.

Conceptually, a single variadic template function declaration can be thought of as a multitude of similar declarations with zero, one, etc., parameters fashioned after the variadic declaration:

```
template <typename... Ts> void f1c(const Ts&...);
    // variadic, any number of arguments, any types, all by const &


void f1c();
    // pseudo-equivalent for variadic f1c called with 0 arguments


template <typename T0> void f1c(const T0&);
    // pseudo-equivalent for variadic f1c called with 1 argument


template <typename T0, typename T1>
void f1c(const T0&, const T1&);
    // pseudo-equivalent for variadic f1c called with 2 arguments


template <typename T0, typename T1, typename T2>
void f1c(const T0&, const T1&, const T2&);
    // pseudo-equivalent for variadic f1c called with 3 arguments


// ...                        (and so on ad infinitum)
```

A good intuitive model would be that the **pack expansion** in the function parameter list is like an "elastic" list of parameter declarations that expands or shrinks appropriately. Note that the types in a **pack expansion** may all be different from one another, but the qualifiers (**const** and/or **volatile**) and **declarator operators** (i.e., pointer *, reference &, *rvalue* reference &&, and array []) specified in the **function parameter pack** are applied to each argument.

A variadic function template can take additional template parameters as well as additional function parameters:

```
template <typename... Ts> void f2a(int, Ts...);
    // one int followed by zero or more arbitrary arguments by value


template <typename T, typename... Ts> void f2b(T, const Ts&...);
    // first by value, zero or more by const &


template <typename T, typename U, typename... Ts> void f2c(T, const U&, Ts...);
    // first by value, second by const &, zero or more by value
```

There are restrictions on such declarations; see *The Rule of Greedy Matching* on page 896 and *The Rule of Fair Matching* on page 898.

Note that with a function's parameter list, ... can be used only in conjunction with a template parameter pack. Attempting to use ... where there's no parameter pack to expand could lead to inadvertent use of the old C-style variadics:

```
template <typename T, typename... Ts>
void good(T, Ts...);                    // variadic template

template <typename T, typename... Ts>
void oops(T, T...);                     // old C-style variadic
```

Such a mistake might be caused by a simple typo in the declaration of `oops`, leading to a variety of puzzling compile-time or link-time errors; see *Potential Pitfalls — Accidental use of C-style ellipsis* on page 952.

It is possible to use the parameter pack name (e.g., `Ts`) as a template parameter:

```
template <typename> struct S1;    // declaration only

template <typename... Ts>         // parameter pack named Ts
int fs1(S1<Ts>...);
    // Pack expansion for explicit instantiation of S1 accepts any number of
    // independent explicit instantiations of S1 by value.
```

The parameter pack name `Ts` acts as though it were a separate type parameter for each function argument, thereby allowing a different instantiation for `S1` at each parameter position. To invoke `fs1` on arguments of user-defined type `S1`, however, `S1` will need to be a **complete type** — i.e., its definition must precede the point of invocation of the function in the current translation unit:

```
int s1a = fs1(S1<int>());               // Error, S1 declared but not defined

template <typename T>
struct S1 { /*...*/ };                   // Introduce definition for S1.

int s1b = fs1();                         // Ts is the empty pack.
int s1c = fs1(S1<const char*>());        // Ts=<const char*>
int s1d = fs1(S1<int>(), S1<bool>());    // Ts=<int, bool>
```

More complex setups are possible as well. For example, we can write a variadic function template that operates on instantiations of user-defined-type templates that take two independent type parameters:

```
template <typename, typename>
struct S2;                        // two-parameter class template declaration

template <typename... Ts>    // parameter pack named Ts
int fs2(S2<Ts, Ts>...);
    // The function fs2 takes by value any number of explicit instantiations
    // of S2 as long as they use the same type in both positions.
```

Calls to `fs2` work only if we supply instantiations of `S2` having the same type for both template parameters:

```
template <typename, typename> struct S2 { /*...*/ };  // S2's definition

int s2a = fs2();                                 // OK
int s2b = fs2(S2<char, char>());                 // OK
int s2c = fs2(S2<int, int>(), S2<bool, bool>()); // OK
int s2d = fs2(S2<char, int>());                  // Error
int s2e = fs2(S2<char, const char>());           // Error
```

The problem with the last two calls above is that the instantiations `S2<char, int>` and `S2<char, const char>` violate the requirement that the two types in the instantiation of `S2` be identical, so there is no way to provide or deduce some `Ts` in a way that would make the call work.

Variadic member functions

Member functions can be variadic in two orthogonal ways: The class that comprises them might be variadic, and they might be variadic themselves. The simplest case features a variadic member function of a nontemplate class:

```
struct S3                                 // nonvariadic nontemplate class
{
    template <typename... Ts> int f(Ts...);  // OK
};

int s3 = S3().f(1, "abc");                 // Ts=<int, const char*>
```

Expectedly, a nonvariadic **class template** can declare variadic member functions as well:

```
template <typename T>
struct S4                                            // class template
{
    template <typename... Ts> int f1(Ts...);          // OK, variadic member
                                                      // function template

    template <typename... Ts> int f2(T, const Ts&...); // OK
};

int s3b = S4<int>().f1(1, false, true);              // Ts=<int, bool, bool>
int s3c = S4<int>().f2(1, false, true);              // Ts=<bool, bool>
```

A **variadic class template** might have regular **member functions**, member functions that take their own template parameters, and **variadic member function templates**:

```
template <typename... Ts>
struct S5
```

```
{
    int f1();        // nontemplate member function of variadic class template

    template <typename T>
    int f2(T);       // member function template of variadic class template

    template <typename... Us>
    int f3(Us...);   // variadic member function template of variadic class template
};

int s5a = S5<int, char>().f1();
    // Ts=<int, char>

int s5b = S5<char, int>().f2(2.2);
    // Ts=<int, char>, T=double

int s5c = S5<int, char>().f3(1, 2.2);
    // Ts=<int, char>, Us=<int, double>
```

Although in a sense all member functions of a variadic class template (e.g., S5, above) are
variadic, the class's template parameter pack (e.g., Ts, above) is fixed at the time the class
is instantiated. The only truly variadic function is f3 because it takes its own template
parameter pack, Us.

The parameter list for a member function within a variadic class will often use the template
parameter pack of the class in which it is defined:

```
template <typename... Ts>
struct S6                    // variadic class template
{
    int f1(const Ts&...);   // OK, not truly variadic; Ts is fixed

    template <typename T>
    int f2(T, Ts...);        // OK, also not truly variadic; Ts is fixed

    template <typename... Us>
    int f3(Ts..., Us...);    // OK, variadic template member function
};

int s6a = S6<int, char>().f1(1, 'a');
    // Ts=<int, char>

int s6b = S6<char, int>().f2(true, 'b', 2);
    // Ts=<char, int>, T=bool

int s6c = S6<int, char>().f3(1, 2, "asd", 123.456);  // 2 converted to char
    // Ts=<int, char>, Us=<const char*, double>
```

Notice how, in the initialization of s6c, the type arguments Ts of class template S6 must be chosen explicitly, whereas the variadic template f3 need not have Us specified because they are deduced from the argument types. This last example takes us to the important topic of **template argument deduction**.

Template argument deduction

A popular feature of C++ ever since templates were incorporated into the language pre-standardization has been the ability of function templates to determine their template arguments from the types of arguments provided. Consider, for example, designing and using a function, print, that outputs its argument to the console. In most cases, just letting print deduce its template argument from the function argument's type has brevity, correctness, and efficiency advantages:

```
#include <string>  // std::string

template <typename T> void print(const T& value);  // prints value to stdout

void testPrint0(const std::string& s)
{
    print<const char*>("Hi");
        // verbose:   specifies template argument and function argument
        // Redundant: Function argument's type is the template argument.

    print<int>(3.14);
        // Error-prone: narrowing conversion (prints 3)

    print<std::string>("Oops");
        // inefficient: might incur additional expensive implicit conversions

    print("Hi");
    print(3.14);
    print(s);
        // All good: Let print deduce template argument from function argument.
}
```

What makes the shorter form of the call work is the magic of C++ **template argument deduction**, which, unsurprisingly, works with variadic template parameters as well. A detailed description of all rules for **template argument deduction**, including those inherited from C++03, is outside the scope of this book.[4] Here, we focus on the additions to the rules brought about by variadic function templates.

With that in mind, imagine we set out to redesign the API of print (in the code example above) to output any number of arguments to the console:

---

[4]**meyers15b**, Chapter 1, "Deducing Types," pp. 9–35

```
#include <string>  // std::string

template <typename... Ts>            // template parameter pack Ts
void print(const Ts&... values);     // prints each of values to stdout

void testPrint1(const std::string& s)  // arbitrary function
{
    print<const char*, int, std::string>("Hi", 3.14, "Oops");
        // Verbose:    We specify template arguments and function arguments.
        // Redundant:  Function arguments' types are the template arguments.
        // Error-prone: narrowing conversion (prints 3)
        // Inefficient: Additional expensive implicit conversations might arise.

    print("Hi", 3.14, s);
        // All good: Deduce template arguments from function arguments.
}
```

The compiler will independently deduce each type in `Ts` from the respective types of the function's argument `values`:

```
void testPrint2()  // arbitrary function
{
    print();                 // OK, Ts=<>
    print(42, true);         // OK, Ts=<int, bool>
    print(42.2, "hi", 5);    // OK, Ts=<double, const char*, int>
}
```

As shown in the first line of `testPrint2` (above), a **template parameter pack** can be specified in its entirety when instantiating a function template:

```
void testPrint3()  // arbitrary function
{
    print<>();                     // OK, exact match
    print<int, bool>(42, true);    // OK, exact match
    print<int, bool>('a', 'b');    // OK, arguments convertible to parameters
}
```

Interestingly, we can specify only the first few types of the template parameter pack and let the others be deduced, mixing together **explicit template argument specification** and template argument deduction:

```
void testPrint4()  // arbitrary function
{
    print<>(5, 'a');                  // OK, Ts=<int, char>
    print<unsigned int>(42, true);    // OK, Ts=<unsigned int, bool>
    print<int, int>('a', "ab", 1);    // Error, cannot deduce Ts
}
```

Such a mix of explicit and implicit might be interesting but is not new; it has been the case for function templates since C++ was first standardized. The new element here is that we get to specify a fragment of a template parameter pack.

In the general case, a function may mix **template parameter packs** with other template parameters and **parameter packs** with other function parameters in a variety of ways.

The Rule of Greedy Matching

The Rule of Greedy Matching for **template parameter packs** (but not **function parameter packs**) states that once a template starts matching one explicitly specified template argument, it also matches all template arguments following it. There's no way to tell a **template parameter pack** it matched enough. Template parameter packs are *greedy*.

Consequently, there is no syntactic way to explicitly specify any template argument following one that matches a template parameter pack; the first pack gobbles up all remaining arguments. Put succinctly, **template parameters** following a **template parameter pack** can *never* be explicitly specified as template arguments.

Notice that the rule applies only once a pack starts matching, i.e., it has matched at least one item; indeed, there are a few legitimate cases in which an argument list makes no match at all, which we'll discuss soon.

Using the Rule of Greedy Matching allows us to navigate with relative ease a variety of combinations of pack and nonpack template parameters.

In the simplest and overwhelmingly most frequently encountered situation, the function takes one template parameter pack and one function parameter pack, both in the last position:

```
template <typename T1, typename T2, typename... Ts>   // ... in last position
int f1(T1, T2, const Ts&...);                          // ... in last position
```

In such cases, the Rule of Greedy Matching doesn't need to kick in because there are no parameters following a pack. Template argument deduction can be used for all of `T1`, `T2`, and `Ts` or for just a subset. In the simplest case, no template parameters are specified, and template argument deduction is used for all:

```
int x1a = f1(42, 2.2, 'a', true);
    // T1=int, T2=double, Ts=<char, bool> (all deduced)
```

Explicitly specified template arguments, if any, will match template parameters in the order in which they are declared. Therefore, if we specify one type, it binds to `T1`:

```
int x1b = f1<double>(42, 2.2, 'a', true);
    // T1=double (explicitly), T2=double (deduced), Ts=<char, bool> (deduced)
```

If we specify two types, they will bind to `T1` and `T2` in that order:

```
int x1c = f1<double, char>(42, 65, "abc", true);
```

```
// T1=double (explicitly), T2=char (explicitly),
// Ts=<const char*, bool> (deduced)
```

Note how, in the two examples above, we also have implicit conversions going on; i.e., 42 is converted to **double** and 65 is converted to **char**. Furthermore, a call can specify T1, T2, and the entirety of Ts:

```
int x1d = f1<const char*, char, bool, double>("abc", 'a', true, 42U);
// T1=const char* (explicitly), T2=char (explicitly),
// Ts=<bool, double> (explicitly)
```

Last but not least, as mentioned, a call might specify T1, T2, and only the first few types in Ts:

```
int x1e = f1<const char*, char, bool, double>("abc", 'a', true, 42, 'a', 0);
// T1=const char* (explicitly), T2=char (explicitly),
// Ts=<bool, double, char, int> (first two explicitly, others deduced)
```

Let us now look at a function having a **template parameter pack** not in the last position. However, in the parameter list, the **function parameter pack** is still in the last position:

```
template <typename T, typename... Ts, typename U>  // ... not last
int f2(T, U, const Ts&...);
```

In such cases, by the Rule of Greedy Matching, there is no way to specify U explicitly, so the only way to call **f1** is to let U be deduced:

```
int x2a = f2(1, 2);
// T=int (deduced), U=int (deduced), Ts=<> (by arity)

int x2b = f2<long>(1, 2, 3);
// T=long (explicitly), U=int (deduced), Ts=<int> (deduced)
```

The first template argument passed to **f2**, if any, is matched by T. Note that inferring the empty template parameter pack in the initialization of x2a does not involve deduction; the empty length is inferred by the arity of the call. In contrast, in the initialization of x2b, a pack of length 1 is deduced.

Any subsequent template arguments will be matched *en masse* by Ts in concordance with the Rule of Greedy Matching:

```
int x2c = f2<long, double, char>(1, 2, 3, 4);
// T=long (explicitly), U=int (deduced), Ts=<double, char> (explicitly)

int x2d = f2<int, double>(1, 2, 3.0, "four");
// T=int (explicitly), U=int (deduced), Ts=<double, const char*>
// (partially explicit, partially deduced)

int x2e = f2<int, char, double>(1, 'a', 3.0);
// Error, no viable function for T=int, U=char, and Ts=<char, double>
```

In all cases, U must be deduced for the call to f2 to match during overload resolution and template argument deduction.

Another way to make a template parameter work even if it's positioned after a parameter pack is by assigning it a default argument:

```
template <typename... Ts, typename T = int>
T f3(Ts... values);
```

Due to the way f3 is defined, there is no way to either deduce or specify T, so it will always be **int** and thus serves no obvious purpose as a template parameter:

```
int x3a = f3("one", 2);
    // Ts=<const char*, int> (deduced), T=int (default)

int x3b = f3<const char*>("one", 2);
    // Ts=<const char*, int> (partially deduced), T=int (default)

int x3c = f3<const char*, int>("one", 2);
    // Ts=<const char*, int> (explicitly), T=int (default)
```

The Rule of Fair Matching

To further explore the varied ways in which parameter packs interact with the rest of C++, let's take a look at a function that has a type following a **template parameter pack** and also an ordinary function parameter following a **function parameter pack**:

```
template <typename... Ts, typename T>
int f4(Ts... values, T value);
```

Here, a new rule applies, the Rule of Fair Matching, which is to a good extent the converse of the Rule of Greedy Matching. When a **function parameter pack** (e.g., **values** in the code snippet above) is *not* at the end of a function's parameter list, its corresponding type parameter pack (e.g., Ts above) *cannot be deduced* ever.

This rule makes the **function parameter pack values** fair because function parameters following a function parameter pack have a chance to match function arguments.

Let's take a look at how the rule applies to f4. In calls with one argument, Ts is not deduced, so it forcibly matches the empty list, and T matches the type of the argument:

```
int x4a = f4(123);     // Ts=<> (forced nondeduced), T=int
int x4b = f4('a');     // Ts=<> (forced nondeduced), T=char
int x4c = f4('a', 2);  // Error, cannot deduce Ts
```

Calls with more than one argument can be made if and only if we provide Ts to the compiler explicitly:

```
int x4d = f4<int, char>(1, '2', "three");
    // Ts=<int, char> (explicitly), T=const char*
```

Incidentally, for f4 there is no way to specify T explicitly because of the Rule of Greedy Matching:

```
int x4e = f4<int, char, const char*>(1, '2', "three");
    // Error, Ts=<int, char, const char*> (explicitly), no argument for T value
```

Note that the two rules work simultaneously on the same function call; they do not compete because they apply in different places; the Rule of Greedy Matching applies to **template parameter packs**, and the Rule of Fair Matching applies to **function parameter packs**.

Let's now consider declaring a function with two consecutive parameter packs and see how the rules work together in calls:

```
template <typename... Ts, typename... Us>  // two template parameter packs
int f5(Ts... ts, Us... us);                //  "   function   "       "
```

By the Rule of Greedy Matching, we cannot specify Us explicitly, so us will rely on deduction exclusively. By the Rule of Fair Matching, Ts cannot be deduced. First, let's analyze a call with no template arguments:

```
int x5a = f5(1);
    // Ts=<> (forcibly), Us=<int>

int x5b = f5(1, '2');
    // Ts=<> (forcibly), Us=<int, char>

int x5c = f5(1, '2', "three");
    // Ts=<> (forcibly), Us=<int, char, const char*>
```

Whenever a call specifies no **template arguments**, Ts cannot be deduced so it can at best match the empty list. That leaves all of the arguments to us, and deduction will work as expected for Us. This right-to-left matching might surprise at first and requires close reading of different parts of the C++ Standard but is easy to explain by using the two rules.

Let's now issue a call that does specify template arguments:

```
int x5d = f5<int, char>(1, '2');
    // Ts=<int, char> (explicitly), Us=<>

int x5e = f5<int, char>(1, '2', "three");
    // Ts=<int, char> (explicitly), Us=<const char*>

int x5f = f5<int, char>(1, '2', "three", 4.0);
    // Ts=<int, char> (explicitly), Us=<const char*, double>
```

By the Rule of Greedy Matching, all explicit template arguments go to Ts, and, by the Rule of Fair Matching, there's no deduction for Ts, so, even before looking at the function arguments, we know that Ts is exactly **<int, char>**. From here on, it's easy: The first two arguments go to ts, and all others, if any, will go to us.

Corner cases of function template argument matching

There are cases in which a template function could be written that can never be called, whether with explicit template parameters or by relying on template argument deduction:

```
template <typename... Ts, typename T>
void odd1(Ts... values);
```

By the Rule of Greedy Matching applied to `Ts`, `T` can never be specified explicitly. Moreover, `T` cannot be deduced either because it's not part of the function's parameter list. Hence, `odd1` is impossible to call. According to standard C++, such function declarations are **ill formed, no diagnostic required (IFNDR)**. Current compilers do allow such functions to be defined without a warning. However, any conforming compiler will disallow any attempt to *call* such an ill-fated function.

Another scenario is one whereby a variadic function can be instantiated, but one or more of its parameter packs must always have length zero:

```
template <typename... Ts, typename... Us, class T>
int odd2(Ts..., Us..., T);  // specious
```

Any attempt to call `odd2` by relying exclusively on template argument deduction without any explicit template arguments will force both `Ts` and `Us` to the empty list because, by the Rule of Fair Matching, neither `Ts` nor `Us` can benefit from template argument deduction. So calls with two, three, or more arguments fail:

```
int x2a = odd2(1, 2.5);          // Error, Ts=<>, Us=<>, too many arguments
int x2b = odd2(1, 2.5, "three"); // Error, Ts=<>, Us=<>,  "    "        "
```

However, there seem to be ways to invoke `odd2`, at least on contemporary compilers. First, calls using deduction with exactly one argument will merrily go:

```
int x2c = odd2(42);  // Ts=<>, Us=<>, T=42
```

Moreover, functions that pass an explicit argument list for `Ts` also seem to work:

```
int x2d = odd2<int, double>(1, 2.0, "three");
    // Ts=<int, double>, Us=<>, T=const char*
```

The call above passes `Ts` explicitly as `<int, double>`. Then, as always, `Us` is forced to the empty list, and `T` is deduced as **const char*** for the last argument. That way, the call goes through!

Or does it? Alas, the declaration of `odd2` is IFNDR. By the C++ Standard, if all valid instantiations of a variadic function template require a specific template parameter pack argument to be empty, the declaration is IFNDR. Although such a rule sounds arbitrary, it does have a good motivation: If all possible calls to `odd2` require `Us` to be the empty list, why is `Us` present in the first place? Such code is more indicative of a bug than of a meaningful intent. Also, diagnosing such cases might be quite difficult in the general case, so no diagnostic is required. As it turns out, today's compilers do not issue such a diagnostic, so the onus is on the template writer to make sure the code does what it's supposed to do.

A simple fix for odd2 is to just eliminate the Us template parameter, in which case odd2 has the same signature as f4 discussed in *The Rule of Fair Matching* on page 898. Another possibility to "legalize" odd2 is to drop the nonpack parameter, in which case it has the same signature as f5 in that same section.

A function that has three parameter packs in a row would also be IFNDR:

```
template <typename... Ts, typename... Us, typename... Vs>
void odd3(Ts..., Us..., Vs...);  // impossible to instantiate
```

The reason odd3 cannot work is purely bureaucratic: Neither Ts nor Us benefit from deduction, and there is no way to specify Us explicitly because Ts is greedy. Consequently, Us is forced to be always of length zero.

It might seem there is no way to define a function template taking more than two parameter packs. However, recall that deducing variadic function template parameters from the (object) arguments passed to the function uses the full power of C++'s **template argument deduction**. Defining functions with any number of template parameter packs is entirely possible provided the parameter packs are themselves part of other template instantiations:

```
template <typename...> class Vct { };  // variadic class template definition

template <typename T, typename... Ts, typename... Us, typename... Vs>
int fvct(const T&, Vct<Ts...>, Vct<Us...>, Vct<Vs...>);
    // The first parameter matches any type by const&, followed by three
    // not necessarily related instantiations of Vct.
```

The function template fvct takes a fixed number of parameters (four), the last three of which are independent instantiations of a variadic class template Vct. For each of them, fvct takes a template parameter pack that it passes along to Vct. For each call to fvct, template argument deduction figures out whether the call is viable and also binds Ts, Us, and Vs to the packs that make the call work:

```
int x = fvct(5, Vct<>(), Vct<char, int, long>(), Vct<bool>());
    // OK, T=int, Ts=<>, Us=<char, int, long>, Vs=<bool>
```

For each argument in the call above, the compiler matches the type of the argument with the pattern required by the template parameter; the matching process deduces the types that would make the match work. The general algorithm for matching a concrete type against a type pattern is called **unification**.[5]

Non-type template parameter packs

Defining a variadic template that takes arguments other than types is also possible. Just as C++03 template parameters can be *types*, *values*, or *templates*, so can template parameter

---

[5]bendersky18

packs. We used **type template parameter packs** up until now to simplify exposition, but non-type template parameter packs apply to class templates and function templates as well.

To clarify terminology, the C++ Standard refers to template parameters that accept values as **non-type template parameters** and to template parameters that accept names of templates as **template template parameters** (to be discussed in subsection *Template template parameter packs* on page 903).

Non-type template parameter packs are defined analogously with non-type template parameters:

```
template <int...>
class Ci { };           // variadic int-parameter class template

Ci<>           ci0;  // OK, zero ints given
Ci<1>          ci1;  // OK, one int argument
Ci<2, 3>       ci2;  // OK, two int arguments
Ci<true, 'a', 3u> ci3;  // OK, converts to three int arguments
Ci<4.0>        ci4;  // Error, floating-point literal 4.0 is ineligible.
```

The type specifier of the template **non-type template parameter pack** need not be only **int**; the same rules as for **non-type parameters** apply, restricting the types of non-type parameters to

- Integral

- Enumerated

- Pointer to function or object

- *Lvalue* reference to function or object

- Pointer to member

- std::nullptr_t

These types are the value types allowed for C++03 non-type template parameters. In short, value parameter packs obey the same restrictions as the C++03 non-type template parameters:

```
#include <cstddef>  // std::nullptr_t
#include <string>   // std::string

enum Enum { /*...*/ };              // arbitrary enumerated type
class AClass { /*...*/ };           // arbitrary class type

template <long... ls>     class Cl;  // OK, integral
template <bool... bs>     class Cb;  // OK, integral
template <char... cs>     class Cc;  // OK, integral
template <Enum... es>     class Ce;  // OK, enumerated
```

```
template <int&... is>           class Cri;  // OK, reference
template <std::string*... ss>   class Csp;  // OK, pointer
template <void (*... fs)(int)>  class Cf;   // OK, pointer to function
template <int AClass::*... >    class Cpm;  // OK, pointer to member
template <std::nullptr_t... >   class Cnl;  // OK, std::nullptr_t

template <Ci<>... cis>          class Cu;   // Error, cannot be user defined
template <double... ds>         class Cd;   // Error, cannot be floating point⁶
template <float... fs>          class Cf;   // Error, cannot be floating point
```

In the example above, the declaration of class template `Cu` is not permitted because `Ci<>` is a *user-defined* type, whereas the declarations of both `Cd` and `Cf` are disallowed because **double** and **float** are floating-point types.[7]

Template template parameter packs

Template template parameter packs are the variadic generalization of C++03's template template parameters. Classes and functions may be designed to take **template template parameter packs** as parameters in addition to **type parameter packs** and non-type template parameter packs.

A template *template* parameter is a template parameter that names an argument that is itself a *template*. Consider, for example, two arbitrary class templates, `A1` and `A2`:

```
template <typename> class A1 { /*...*/ };  // some arbitrary class template
template <typename> class A2 { /*...*/ };  // another arbitrary class template
```

Now suppose that we have a *class* template, (e.g., `C1`) that takes, as its template parameter, a *class template*:

```
template <template<typename> class X>  // X is a template template parameter.
struct C1 : X<int>, X<double>          // Inherit X<int> and X<double>.
{ };
```

We can now create instances of class `C1` where the bases are obtained by instantiating whatever argument we pass to `C1` with **int** and **double**, respectively:

```
C1<A1> c1a;  // inherits A1<int> and A1<double>
C1<A2> c1b;  // inherits A2<int> and A2<double>
```

In the code snippet above, `X` is a template *template* parameter that takes one *type* parameter. The template classes `A1` and `A2` match `X` because each of these templates, in turn, takes one *type* parameter as well.

---

[6]Support for user-defined types for non-type template parameters has been proposed for a future standard; see **snyder18**.

[7]C++20 does allow *floating-point* non-type template parameters, which enable the definition and use of non-type template parameter packs using **float**, **double**, or **long double** (making, e.g., the final entry — `Ci<4.0> ci4;` — in the previous example above valid as well).

If an instantiation is attempted with a class template that does not take the same number of template parameters, the instantiation fails, even when there is no doubt as to what the intent might be:

```
template <typename, typename = char>
class A3 { /*...*/ };  // OK, two-parameter template, with second one defaulted

C1<A3> c1c;  // Error, parameters of A3 are different from parameters of X.
```

Although A3 could be instantiated with a single template argument (due to its second template parameter having a default argument) and A3**<int>** is valid, C1<A3> will not compile. The compiler complains that A3 has two parameters, whereas X has a single parameter.

The same limitation is at work when the argument to C1 is a variadic template:

```
template <typename...>
class A4 { /*...*/ };     // OK, arbitrary variadic template

C1<A4> c1d;  // Error, parameters of A4 are different from parameters of X.
```

Let's define a class C2 that is a variadic generalization of C1 in such a way that it allows instantiation with A3 and A4:

```
template <template<typename...> class X>  // template template parameter
struct C2 : X<int>, X<double>             // inherit X<int>, X<double>
{ };
```

Note that, although one can use **typename** and **class** interchangeably inside the template parameters of X above, one must always use **class** for X itself.[8]

The difference between C2 and C1 is literally one token: C2 adds one **...** after **typename** *inside* the parameter list of X. That one token makes all the difference: by using it, C2 signals to the compiler that it accepts templates with any number of parameters, be they fixed in number, defaulted, or variadic. In particular, it works just fine with A1 and A2 as well as A3 and A4:

```
C2<A1> c2a;
   // inherits A1<int> and A1<double> in that order
C2<A2> c2b;
   // inherits A2<int> and A2<double> in that order
C2<A3> c2c;
   // inherits A3<int, char> and A3<double, char> in that order
   // char is the default argument for A3's second type parameter.
C2<A4> c2d;
   // inherits A4<int> and A4<double> in that order
```

---

[8]Since C++17, code may use either **typename** or **class** for template template parameters and for type template parameter packs.

When C3 instantiates A3<**int**> or A3<**double**>, A3's default argument for its second parameter kicks in. A4 will be instantiated with the type parameter pack <**int**> and separately with the type parameter pack <**double**>.

In contrast with template template parameters that require exact matching with their arguments, variadic template template parameters specifying **typename**... work in a more "do what I mean" manner by matching templates with default arguments and variadic templates. Applications might need either style of matching depending on context.

There is an orthogonal other direction in which we can generalize C2: We can define a template, C3, that accepts zero or more template template arguments:

```
template <template<typename> class... Xs>  // template template parameter pack Xs
struct C3
    : Xs<int>...      // inherits X0<int>, X1<int>, ...
    , Xs<double>...   // inherits X0<double>, X1<double>, ...
{ };
```

We get to instantiate C3 with zero or more template classes, each of which takes exactly one type parameter:

```
C3<>           c3a;
    // no base classes at all; Xs=<>, all base specifiers vanish

C3<A1>         c3b;
    // inherits A1<int> and A1<double> in that order

C3<A1, A2>     c3c;
    // inherits A1<int>, A2<int>, A1<double>, and A2<double> in that order

C3<A2, A1>     c3d;
    // inherits A2<int>, A1<int>, A2<double>, and A1<double> in that order

C3<A1, A2, A1> c3e;
    // Error, cannot inherit A1<int> and A1<double> twice
```

Note that C3, just like C1, cannot be instantiated with A3, again due to mismatched template parameters:

```
C3<A3> c3f;
    // Error, parameters of A3 are different from parameters of Xs.
C3<A4> c3g;
    // Error, parameters of A4 are different from parameters of Xs.
```

If we want to make instantiations with A3 and A4 possible, we can combine the two generalization directions by placing the ... inside the Xs parameter declaration *and* on Xs as well:

```
template <template<typename...> class... Xs>   // two sets of ...
struct C4                                      // most flexible
    : Xs<int>...                               // X0<int>, X1<int>, ...
    , Xs<double>...                            // X0<double>, X1<double>, ...
{ };
```

C4 combines the characteristics of C2 and C3. It accepts zero or more arguments, which in turn are accepted in a "do what I mean" manner:

```
C4<>         c4a;
    // no base classes at all; Xs=<>, all base specifiers vanish

C4<A1>       c4b;
    // inherits A1<int> and A1<double> in that order

C4<A1, A2>   c4c;
    // inherits A1<int>, A2<int>, A1<double>, and A2<double> in that order

C4<A3, A1>   c4d;
    // inherits A3<int, char>, A1<int>, A3<double, char>, and A1<double>
    // in that order

C4<A1, A4, A2> c4e;
    // inherits A1<int>, A4<int>, A2<int>, A1<double>, A4<double>,
    // A2<double>, in that order
```

C4 can be instantiated with template arguments comprising any combination of A1, A2, A3, and A4 in any order. Quite a few other templates match C4's template argument, even though they will fail to instantiate with a single parameter:

```
template <typename, typename> class A5 { /*...*/ };
template <typename, typename, typename...> class A6 { /*...*/ };

C4<A5> err1;  // Error, matches, but A5<int> and A5<double> are invalid.
C4<A6> err2;  // Error, matches, but A6<int> and A6<double> are invalid.
```

Templates that do not take type template parameters, however, will *not* match C4 or, for that matter, any of C1 through C4:

```
template <typename, int>
class A7 { /*...*/ };             // one type parameter and one non-type parameter
template <typename, int = 42>
class A8 { /*...*/ };             // same, but non-type parameter defaulted
template <template<typename> class>
class A9 { /*...*/ };             // template template parameter

C4<A7> err3;  // Error, second template argument of C4 has a different kind.
C4<A8> err4;  // Error, second     "       "     "  "  "  "      "        "
C4<A9> err5;  // Error, first      "       "     "  "  "  "      "        "
```

In short, class templates that do not take specifically *types* as their template parameters cannot be used in instantiations of C4.

In the general case, template template parameter packs may appear together with other template parameters and follow the rules and restrictions discussed so far in the context of type parameter packs. Any number of subtle but nevertheless perfectly meaningful matching cases can be defined involving combinations of fixed and variadic template parameters. Suppose, for example, we want to define a class template C5 that accepts a template that takes *at least* two parameters and possibly more:

```
template <template<typename, typename, typename...> class X>
class C5
    // class template definition having one template template parameter
    // for which the template template accepts two or more type
    // arguments
{ /*...*/ };

// a few templates that match C5

template <typename, typename> class B1;
template <typename, typename, typename = int> class B2;
template <typename, typename = int, typename = int> class B3;
template <typename, typename, typename...> class B4;

C5<B1> c5a;  // OK
C5<B2> c5b;  // OK
C5<B3> c5c;  // OK
C5<B4> c5d;  // OK
```

However, templates that don't have two fixed type parameters in the first two positions will not match C5:

```
template <typename> class B5;
template <int, typename, typename...> class B6;
template <typename, typename, int, typename...> class B7;
template <typename, typename...> class B8;

C5<B5> c5d;  // Error, argument mismatch
C5<B6> c5e;  // Error, argument mismatch
C5<B7> c5f;  // Error, argument mismatch
C5<B8> c5g;  // Error, argument mismatch
```

To match C5's template parameter, a template must take types for its first two parameters, followed by zero or more type parameters (with default values or not). B5 does not match because it takes only one parameter. B6 does not match because it takes an **int** in the first position, as opposed to a type, as required. B7 fails to match because it takes an **int** in the third position instead of a type. Finally, B8 is not a match because its second argument is not fixed.

To summarize our findings, **template template parameter packs** generalize **template template parameters** in two distinct, orthogonal ways.

- The **...** at the template template parameter level allows zero or more template arguments to match.

- The **...** inside the parameter list of the template template parameter allows loose matching of templates with default arguments or variadic; however, type versus value versus template parameters are still checked, as in the example involving A7, A8, and A9.

Pack expansion

Now that we have a solid command of using parameter packs in type and function declarations, it is time to explore how to use parameter packs in function implementations.

As briefly mentioned in *Variadic class templates* on page 878, parameter packs belong to a *kind* distinct from any other C++ entity; they are not types, values, template names, and so on. As far as learning parameter packs goes, they cannot be related to existing entities, so they might as well come from another language with its own syntax and semantics.

Literally the only way to use a parameter pack is to make it part of a so-called **pack expansion**. A **pack expansion** consists of a fragment of code (a "pattern") followed by **...**. The code fragment must contain at least one pack name; otherwise, it does not qualify as an expansion. Exactly what patterns are allowed depends on the place where the expansion occurs. Depending on context, the pattern is syntactically a simple identifier, a parameter declaration, an expression, or a type.

The dual use of **...** — to both introduce a pack and expand it — might seem confusing at first, but distinguishing between the two uses of **...** is easy: When the ellipsis occurs *before* a previously undefined identifier, it is meant to introduce it as the name of a parameter pack; in all other cases, the ellipsis is an expansion operator.

We've already seen **pack expansion** at work in *Variadic function templates* on page 888. In a variadic function template declaration, the function argument list (e.g., `Ts... values`) is an expansion resulting in zero or more by-value parameters.

To introduce a simple example of **pack expansion** in an actual computation, recall the **add** example in *Description* on page 873, in which a variadic function adds together an arbitrary number of integers. The full implementation shown below uses **double** instead of **int** for better usability. The important part is the expansion that keeps the computation going:

```
double add()                              // base case, no arguments
{
    return 0.0;                           // identity element for addition
}

template <typename T, typename... Ts>     // recursive case
double add(const T& lhs, const Ts&... rest) // accepts 1 or more arguments
```

```
    {
        return lhs + add(rest...);              // recurse expanding rest
    }
```

The key to understanding how `add` works is to model the expansion `rest...` as a comma-separated list of **double**s, always invoking `add` with fewer arguments than it currently received; when `rest` becomes the empty pack, the expansion expands to nothing and `add()` is called, which terminates the recursion by providing the neutral value 0.

Consider the call:

```
    int x1 = add(1.5, 2.5, 3.5);
```

Computation proceeds in a typical recursive manner.

1. The top-level call goes to the variadic function template `add`.

2. `add` binds `T` to **double** and `Ts` to **<double, double>**.

3. The expression `add(rest...)` expands into the recursive call `add(2.5, 3.5)`.

4. That call binds `T` to **double** and `Ts` to **<double>**.

5. The second expansion of `add(rest...)` leads to the recursive call `add(3.5)`.

6. Finally, the last expansion will recurse to `add()`, which returns 0.

The result is constructed as the recursion unwinds.[9]

From an efficiency perspective, it should be noted that `add` is not recursive in a traditional computer science sense. It does not call itself. Each seemingly recursive call is a call to an entirely new function with a different arity generated from the same template. After inlining and other common optimizations, the code is as efficient as writing the statements by hand.

A few rules apply to all pack expansions irrespective of their kind or the context in which they are used.

First, any pattern must contain at least one parameter pack. Therefore, expansions such as `C<int...>` or `f(5...)` are invalid. This requirement can be problematic in function declarations because a typo in a name might switch the meaning of `...` from **pack expansion** to an old-style C variadic function declaration; see *Potential Pitfalls — Accidental use of C-style ellipsis* on page 952.

A single **pack expansion** can contain two or more parameter packs. In that case, expansion of multiple parameter packs within the same expansion is always carried *in lockstep*; i.e., all packs are expanded concomitantly. For example, consider a function modeled after a slightly modified `add`, and note how, instead of expanding just `rest`, we expand a slightly more complex pattern in which `rest` appears twice:

---

[9]C++17 adds fold expressions — **return** lhs + ... + rest; — that allow a more succinct implementation of add.

```
template <typename... Ts>
double add2(const Ts&... xs)    // accepts 0 or more arguments
{
    return add((xs * xs)...);   // Expand xs * xs in call to add.
}
```

This time add2 calls add with the expansion (xs * xs)..., not just xs..., so we're looking at two parameter packs (the two instances of xs) expanded in lockstep. The call add2(1.5, 2.5, 3.5) will forward to add(1.5 * 1.5, 2.5 * 2.5, 3.5 * 3.5), revealing that add2 computes the sum of squares of its arguments.

The parentheses around the pattern in the expansion (xs * xs)... are not needed; the expansion comprehends the full expression to the left of ..., so the call could have been written as add(xs * xs...).

For expansion to work, all parameter packs in one expansion must be of the same length; otherwise, an error will be diagnosed at compile time. Suppose we define a function f1 that takes two parameter packs and passes an expansion involving both to add2:

```
template <typename... Ts, typename... Us>
double f1(const Ts&... ts, const Us&... us)
{
    return add2((ts - us)...);
}
```

Here, the only valid invocations are those with the same number of arguments for ts and us:

```
double x1a = f1<double, double>(1, 2, 3, 4);
    // OK, Ts=<double, double> (explicitly), Us=<int, int> (deduced)

double x1b = f1<double, double>(1, 2, 3, 4, 5);
    // Error, parameter packs ts and us have different lengths.
    // Ts=<double, double> (explicitly), Us=<int, int, int> (deduced)
```

Every form of pack expansion produces a comma-separated list consisting of copies of the pattern with the parameter packs suitably expanded. Expansion is syntactic, not textual — that is, the compiler is "smarter" than a typical text-oriented preprocessor. If the pack expansion is within a larger comma-separated list and the parameter packs being expanded have zero elements, the commas surrounding the expansion are adjusted appropriately to avoid syntax errors. For example, if ts is empty, the expansion add(1, ts..., 2) becomes add(1, 2), not add(1, , 2).

Expansion constructs can be nested. Each nesting level must operate on at least one parameter pack:

```
template <typename... Ts>
double f2(const Ts&... ts)
{
    return add2((add2(ts...) + ts)...);
}
```

Expansion always proceeds "inside out," with the innermost expansion carried out first. In the call `f2(2, 3)`, the expression returned after the first, innermost `ts` is expanded is `add2((add2(2, 3) + ts)...)`. The second expansion results in the considerably heftier expression `add2(add2(2, 3) + 2, add2(2, 3) + 3)`. Nested expansions grow in a combinatorial manner, so care is to be exercised.

What forms of `pattern...` are allowed, and where in the source code is the construct allowed? Not all potentially useful contexts are supported, however; see *Annoyances — Limitations on expansion contexts* on page 954. **Pack expansions** are defined for a variety of well-defined contexts, each of which is described separately in subsequent subsections.

- A function parameter pack

- A function call argument list

- A braced-initializer list

- A template argument list

- A base-specifier list

- A member initializer list

- A lambda-capture list

- An alignment specifier

- An attribute list

- A `sizeof...` expression

- A template parameter pack that is a **pack expansion**

Expansion in a function parameter pack

An ellipsis in a function declaration's parameter list expands to a list of parameter declarations. The pattern being expanded is a parameter declaration.

We discussed this expansion at length in the preceding subsections, so let's quickly recap by means of a few examples:

```
template <typename... Ts>
void f1(Ts...);                // expands to T0, T1, T2,...

template <typename... Ts>
void f2(const Ts&...);         // const T0&, const T1&,...

template <typename... Ts>
void f3(const C<Ts>&...);      // Complex use, e.g., in templates, is allowed.
```

```
template <typename... Ts, typename... Us>
void f4(const C<Ts, Us>&...);  // const C<T0, U0>&, const C<T1, U1>&,...
```

Expansion in a function call argument list or a braced-initializer list

Expansion may occur in the argument list of a function call or in an initializer list — either parenthesized or *brace-enclosed* (see Section 2.1."Braced Init" on page 215). In these cases, the pattern is the *largest expression or braced initialization list* to the left of the ellipsis.

This expansion is the only one that expands into expressions (all others are declarative), so in a way it is the most important because it relates directly to runtime work getting done.

Let's look at a few examples of expansion. Suppose we have a library that comprises three variadic function templates, f, g, and h, and an ordinary class, C, having a variadic *value* constructor:

```
template <typename... Ts> int f(Ts...);  // variadic function template
template <typename... Ts> int g(Ts...);  //      "         "        "
template <typename... Ts> int h(Ts...);  //      "         "        "

struct C                                 // ordinary class
{
    template <typename... Ts> C(Ts...);  // variadic value constructor
};
```

Let's now suppose that we define another variadic function template, client1, that intends to make use of this library by expanding its own parameter pack, xs, in various contexts:

```
template <typename... Ts>
void client1(Ts... xs)
{
    f(xs...);              // (1) f(x0, x1, ...);
    f(C(xs...));           // (2) f(C(x0, x1, ...));
    f(C(xs)...);           // (3) f(C(x0), C(x1), ...);
    f(3.14, xs + 1 ...);   // (4) f(3.14, x0 + 1, x1 + 1, ...);
    f(3.14, xs * 2. ...);  // (5) f(3.14, x0 * 2., x1 * 2., ...);
}
```

In comments, we informally denote with x0, x1, ..., the elements of the pack xs. The first call, f(xs...), illustrates the simplest expansion; the pattern being expanded, xs, is simply the name of a function parameter pack. The expansion results in a comma-separated list of the arguments received by client1.

The other examples illustrate a few subtleties. Examples (2) and (3) show how the positioning of ... determines how expansion unfolds. In (2), the expansion is carried out inside the call to C's constructor, so f is called with exactly one object of type C. In (3), the ellipsis occurs outside the constructor call, so f gets called with zero or more C objects, each constructed with exactly one argument.

Examples (4) and (5) show how whitespace might be important. If the space before ...
were missing, the C++ parser would encounter 1... and 2...., both of which are incorrect
floating-point literals.

Let's now look at a few more complex examples in another function, client2:

```cpp
template <typename... Ts>
void client2(Ts... xs)
{
    f("hi", xs + xs..., 3.14);   //  (6) f("hi", x0 + x0, x1 + x1, ..., 3.14);
    f(const_cast<Ts&>(xs)...);   //  (7) f(const_cast<T0&>(x0), ...);
    f(g(xs)..., h(xs...));       //  (8) f(g(x0), g(x1), ..., h(x0, x1, ...));
    C object1(*xs...);           //  (9) C object1(*x0, *x1, ...);
    C object2{*xs...};           // (10) C object2{*x0, *x1, ...};
    int a[] = { xs..., 0 };      // (11) int[] a = { x0, x1, ..., 0 };
}
```

Examples (6) and (7) feature simultaneous expansion of two packs. In (6), xs is expanded
twice. In (7), template parameter pack Ts and function parameter pack xs are both
expanded. In all cases of simultaneous expansion, the two or more packs are expanded
in lockstep; i.e., the first element in Ts together with the first element in xs form the first
element in the expansion, and so on. Attempting a single pack expansion with multiple
packs of unequal lengths results in a compile-time error. Example (6) also shows how an
expansion could be somewhere in the middle of a function's argument list.

Example (8) shows two sequential expansions that look similar but are quite different.
The two expansions are independent and can be analyzed separately. In g(xs)..., the
pattern being expanded is g(xs) and results in the list g(x0), g(x1), ... In contrast, in
the expansion h(xs...), the expansion is carried inside the call to h — h(x0, x1, ...).

Example (9) shows that expansion is allowed inside special functions as well. The expansion
C(*xs...) results in C's constructor called with *x0, *x1, and so on.

Last but not least, examples (10) and (11) illustrate expansion inside a braced-initialization
list. Example (10) calls the same constructor as (9), and example (11) initializes an array
of **int** with the content of xs followed by a 0.

For each of these examples to compile, the code resulting from **pack expansions** needs to
pass the usual semantic checks; for example, the **int** array initialization in (11) would fail
to compile if xs contained a value with a type not convertible to **int**. As is always the case
with templates, some instantiations work, whereas some don't.

In the examples above, the functions involved are all variadic. However, a function doesn't
need to be variadic — or a template for that matter — to be called with an expansion. The
expansion is carried out in the function call expression, and then the usual lookup rules
apply to decide whether the call is valid:

```cpp
int f1(int a, double b);   // simple function with two parameters

int f2();                  // no parameters
int f2(int a, double b);   // overload with two parameters
```

```
template <typename... Ts>
void client3(const Ts&... xs)
{
    f1(xs...);   // Works if and only if xs has exactly two elements
                 // convertible to int and double, respectively.

    f2(xs...);   // Works if and only if xs is empty or has exactly two elements
                 // convertible to int and double, respectively.
}
```

Expansion in a template argument list

We have already encountered **pack expansion** in the argument list of a template instantiation; if C is a class template and Ts is a template parameter pack, C<Ts...> instantiates C with the contents of Ts. There is no need for the template C to accept a variadic list of parameters. The resulting expansion must be appropriate for the template instantiated.

For example, suppose we define a variadic class Lexicon that uses its parameter pack in an instantiation of std::map:

```
#include <map>      // std::map
#include <string>   // std::string

template <typename... Ts>                     // template parameter pack
class Lexicon                                 // variadic class template
{
    std::map<Ts...> d_data;                   // Use Ts to instantiate std::map.
    // ...
};

Lexicon<std::string, int> c1;                 // (1) OK, std::map<std::string, int>
Lexicon<int> c2;                              // (2) Error, std::map<int> invalid
Lexicon<int, long, std::less<int>> c3;        // (3) OK
Lexicon<long, int, 42> c4;                    // (4) Error, 42 instead of comparator
```

Given that Lexicon forwards all of its template arguments to std::map, the only viable template arguments for Lexicon are those that would be viable for std::map as well. Therefore, (1) is valid because it instantiates std::map<std::string, int>. As usual, std::map's default arguments for its third and fourth parameters kick in; the **pack expansion** does not affect default template arguments. To wit, (3) passes three template arguments to std::map and leaves the last one (the allocator) to be filled with the default. Instantiations (2) and (4) of Lexicon are not valid because they would attempt to instantiate std::map with incompatible template arguments, i.e., the third argument should be a comparison functor, not an **int**.

Expansion in a base-specifier list

Suppose we set out to define a variadic template, `MB1`, that inherits all of its template arguments. This scheme is useful in applying design patterns such as Visitor[10] or Observer.[11] To enable such designs, expansion is allowed in a base-specifier list. The pattern under expansion is a base specifier, which includes an optional protection specifier (**public**, **protected**, or **private**) and an optional **virtual** base specifier. Let us define `MB1` to inherit all of its template arguments using **public** inheritance:

```
template <typename... Ts>   // template parameter pack
class MB1 : public Ts...     // multibase class, publicly inherit each of Ts
{
    // ...
};
```

The pattern **public** `Ts...` expands into **public** `T0`, **public** `T1`, and so on, for each type in `Ts`. All bases resulting from the expansion have the same protection level. If `Ts` is empty, the instantiation of `MB` has no base classes:

```
class S1 { /*...*/ };  // arbitrary class
class S2 { /*...*/ };  // arbitrary class


MB1<>            m1a;  // OK, no base class at all
MB1<S1>          m1b;  // OK, instantiate with S1 as only base.
MB1<S1, S2>      m1c;  // OK, instantiate with S1 and S2 as bases.
MB1<S1, S2, S1> m1d;   // Error, cannot directly inherit S1 twice
MB1<S1, int>    m1e;   // Error, cannot inherit from scalar type int
```

After expansion, the usual rules and restrictions apply; a class cannot inherit another one twice and cannot inherit types such as **int**.

Other bases can be specified before and/or after the pack. The other bases might specify other protection levels (and if they don't, the default protection level applies):

```
template <typename... Ts>   // parameter pack Ts
class MB2
    : virtual private S1    // S1 virtual private base
    , public Ts...          // Inherit each of Ts publicly.
{ /*...*/ };

template <typename... Ts>   // parameter pack Ts
class MB3
    : public S1             // S1 public base
    , virtual protected Ts... // each type in Ts a virtual protected base
```

---

[10]**alexandrescu01**, Chapter 10, "Visitor," pp. 235–262
[11]**gamma95**, Chapter 5, section "Observer," pp. 293–303

```
    , S2                        // S2 private base (uses default protection)
{ /*...*/ };

MB2<>   m2a;                     // (1) virtual private base S1
MB2<S2> m2b;                     // (2) virtual private base S1, public base S2
MB3<>   m3a;                     // public base S1, private base S2
MB3<S2> m3b;                     // Error, cannot inherit S2 twice
```

Expansions are not limited to simple pack names. The general pattern allowed in a base-specifier list is that of a full-fledged base specifier. For example, the parameter pack can be used to instantiate another template:

```
template <typename T>
class Act                        // arbitrary class template
{ /*...*/ };

template <typename... Ts>        // template parameter pack Ts
class MB4
    : public Act<Ts>...          // bases Act<T0>, Act<T1>, ...
{ /*...*/ };

MB4<>                     m4a;   // no base class
MB4<int, double>          m4b;   // bases Act<int>, Act<double>
MB4<MB4<int>, int>        m4c;   // bases Act<MB4<int>>, Act<int>
```

Arbitrarily complex instantiations can be specified in a base-specifier pack expansion, which opens up the opportunity for a variety of expansion patterns. Depending on where the ellipsis is placed, different expansion patterns can be created:

```
template <typename... Ts>
class Avct                       // arbitrary variadic class template
{ /*...*/ };

template <typename... Ts>        // template parameter pack Ts
class MB5                        // multibase class example
    : public Avct<Ts>...         // zero or more: Avct<T0>, Avct<T1>, ...
    , private Avct<Ts...>        // exactly one: Avct<T0, T1, ...>
{ /*...*/ };
```

Although the two expansions featured above are similar in syntax, they are semantically different. First, **public** Avct<Ts>... expands into multiple bases for MB5: **public** Avct<T0>, **public** Avct<T1>, and so on. The second expansion is completely different; in fact, it's not even an expansion in a base-specifier list. Its context is a template's argument list; see *Expansion in a template argument list* on page 914. The result of that expansion is a single class Avct<T0, T1, ...> that is an additional private base of MB5:

```
MB5<int, double> mb5a;
    // inherits publicly Avct<int>, Avct<double>
    // inherits privately Avct<int, double>

MB5<Avct<int, char>, double> mb5b;
    // inherits publicly Avct<Avct<int, char>>, Avct<double>,
    // inherits privately Avct<Avct<int, char>, double>

MB5<int> mb5c;
    // Error, cannot inherit Avct<int> twice
```

Expansion in a member initializer list

Allowing variadic bases on a class naturally creates the necessity of being able to initialize those bases accordingly. Consequently, **pack expansion** is allowed in a member initializer list. The pattern is a base initializer, i.e., the name of a base followed by a parenthesized list of arguments for its constructor:

```
template <typename... Ts>  // template parameter pack
struct S1 : Ts...          // Publicly inherit every type in the pack.
{
    S1() : Ts(0)...        // (1) Call constructor with 0 for each base.
    { /*...*/ }

    S1(int x) : Ts(x)...   // (2) Call constructor with x for each base.
    { /*...*/ }

    S1(const S1& original) : Ts(static_cast<const Ts&>(original))...
        // (3) Call the copy constructor for each base.
    { /*...*/ }
};
```

The default constructor (1) calls all bases' constructors, passing 0 to each. The second constructor (2) passes its one **int** argument to each base. The last constructor (3) of S implements the copy constructor and is rather interesting because it expands in turn to a call to the copy constructor for each member, passing it the result of a **static_cast** (which, in fact, is implicit) to the appropriate base type. Similar syntax can be used for defining the move constructor (see Section 2.1."*Rvalue* References" on page 710) and other constructors.

Let's embark on a more complex example. Suppose we want to define a class S2 with a constructor that accepts any number of arguments and forwards all of them to each of its base class constructors. To do so, that constructor itself needs to be variadic with a distinct parameter pack:

```
template <typename... Ts>      // template parameter pack
struct S2 : Ts...              // Publicly inherit every type in the pack.
{
    template <typename... Us>  // variadic constructor
    S2(const Us&... xs)        // accepts any number of arguments by const &
    : Ts(xs...)...             // (!) forwards them to each base constructor
    { }
};
```

The code above has at least one ellipsis on every significant line, and all are needed. Let's take a closer look.

First, class S2 inherits all of its template arguments. It has no exact knowledge about the types it would be instantiated with and, out of consideration for flexibility, defines a variadic constructor that forwards any number of arguments from the caller into each of its base classes. That constructor, therefore, is itself variadic with a separate template parameter pack, Us, and a corresponding argument pack, xs, that accepts arguments by reference to **const**. The key line, commented with (!) in the code, performs two expansions, which proceed inside out. First, xs... expands into the list of arguments passed to S2's constructor, leading to the pattern Ts(x0, x1, ...). In turn, that pattern itself gets expanded by the outer ... into a base initializer list: T0(x0, x1, ...), T1(x0, x1, ...), ...

What if passing by reference to **const** is too constraining and we want to define a more general constructor that can forward modifiable values as well? In that case, we need to use forwarding references (see Section 2.1."Forwarding References" on page 377) and the Standard Library function std::forward:

```
#include <utility>  // std::forward

template <typename... Ts>      // template parameter pack
struct S3 : Ts...              // Publicly inherit every type in the pack.
{
    template <typename... Us>  // variadic constructor
    S3(Us&&... xs)             // arguments by forwarding reference
    : Ts(std::forward<Us>(xs)...)...
                               // forwards them to each base constructor
    { }
};
```

S3's variadic constructor makes use of **forwarding references**, which automatically adapt to the type of the arguments passed. The library function std::forward ensures that each argument is forwarded with the appropriate type, qualifier, and *lvalue*ness to the constructors of each base class. The expansion process is similar to that in S2's constructor previously discussed, with the additional detail that std::forward<Us>(xs)... expands in lockstep Us and xs.

Expansion in a lambda-capture list

A C++ lambda expression, introduced with C++11 (see Section 2.1."Lambdas" on page 573), is an unnamed function object. A lambda can store internally some of the local variables present at the point of creation by a mechanism known as **lambda capture**. This important capability distinguishes lambdas from simple functions. Let's put it to use in defining a `tracer` lambda that is able to print a given variable to the console:

```
#include <iostream>  // std::cout, std::endl

template <typename T>  // single-parameter template
auto tracer(T& x)      // returns a lambda that, when invoked, prints x
{
    auto result = [&x]() { std::cout << x << std::endl; };
        // [&x] means the function object captures x by reference.
        // tracer must use auto to initialize the function object.
    return result;
}
```

Lambdas have a type chosen by the compiler, so we need **auto** to pass lambda objects around; see Section 2.1."**auto** Variables" on page 195. The code above might be a lot to absorb for someone new to lambdas, in which case reading Section 2.1."Lambdas" on page 573 along with Section 3.2."**auto** Return" on page 1182 before continuing would be in order.

The underlying idea is simple: A call such as `tracer(x)` saves a reference to x in a function object, which it then returns. Subsequent calls to that function object output the current value of x. It's important to save x by reference (hence the & in the capture), lest the lambda store x by value and uninterestingly print the same thing on each call.

Let's see `tracer` at work, tracing some variable in a function:

```
int process(int x)          // uses the trace facility
{
    auto trace = tracer(x);  // Initialize trace to follow x.
    trace();                 // prints current value of x
    ++x;                     // Change the value of x.
    trace();                 // prints current (changed) value of x
    return x;                // Return x back to the caller.
}

int x0 = process(42);        // prints 42, then 43, and initializes x0 to 43
```

What is the connection with variadics? Variadics are all about generalization, which applies here as well. Suppose we now set out to trace several variables at once. Instead of a one-argument function, `tracer` would then need to be variadic. Also, crucially, the lambda returned needs to store references to all arguments received in order to print them later. That means an expansion must be allowed inside a lambda-capture list.

First, let's assume a function, `print`, exists that prints any number of arguments to the console (*Use Cases — Generic variadic functions* on page 925 features an implementation of `print`):

```
template <typename... Ts>      // variadic function
void print(const Ts&... xs);   // prints each argument to std::cout in turn
```

The definition of `multitracer` uses `print` in a lambda with variadic capture:

```
template <typename... Ts>      // variadic template
auto multitracer(Ts&... xs)    // returns a lambda that, when invoked, prints xs
{
    auto result = [&xs...]() { print(xs...); };
        // [&xs...] means capture all of xs by reference.
        // result stores one reference for each argument.
    return result;
}
```

The entire API is enabled by the ability to expand `xs` inside the capture list. Expanding with `[&xs...]` captures by reference, whereas `[xs...]` captures the pack by value. Inside the lambda, `print` expands the pack as usual with `x...`.

Expansions in captures can be combined with all other captures:

```
template <typename... Ts> // variadic template
auto test(Ts&... xs)        // for illustration purposes
{
    int a = 0, b = 0;
    auto f1 = [&a, xs...]() { /*...*/ };
        // Capture a by reference and all of xs by value.

    auto f2 = [xs..., &a]() { /*...*/ };
        // same capture as f1

    auto f3 = [a, &xs..., &b]() { /*...*/ };
        // Capture a by value, all of xs by reference, and b by reference.

    auto f4 = [&, xs...]() { /*...*/ };
        // Capture all of xs by value and everything else by reference.

    auto f5 = [=, &xs..., &a]() { /*...*/ };
        // Capture a and all of xs by reference, and everything else by value.
}
```

The pattern must be that of a simple capture; init captures of parameter pack expansions is not allowed in C++11/14.[12]

Expansion in an alignment specifier

The **alignas** specifier is a feature new to C++11 that allows specifying the alignment requirement of a type or object; see Section 2.1."**alignas**" on page 168:

```
alignas(8)       float x1;   // Align x1 at an address multiple of 8.
alignas(double) float x2;    // Align x2 with the same alignment as a double.
```

Pack expansion inside the **alignas** specifier is allowed. The meaning in the presence of the pack is to specify the largest alignment of all types in the pack:

```
template <typename... Ts>  // variadic template
int test1(Ts... xs)        // for illustration purposes
{
    struct alignas(Ts...) S { };
        // Align S at the largest alignment of all types in Ts.
        // If Ts is empty, the alignas directive ignored.

    alignas(Ts...) float x1;
        // Align x1 at the largest alignment of all types in Ts.
        // If Ts is empty, the alignas directive ignored.

    alignas(Ts...) alignas(float) float x2;
        // Align x2 at the largest alignment of float and all types in Ts.

    alignas(float) alignas(Ts...) float x3;
        // same alignment as x2; order does not matter

    return 0;
}
```

As always with **alignas**, requesting an alignment smaller than the minimum alignment required by the declaration is an error:

```
int a1 = test1();        // OK, Ts empty, all alignas(Ts...) ignored
int a2 = test1('a', 1.0); // OK, align everything as a double.
int a3 = test1('a');     // Error (most systems), can't align float x1 to 1 byte
```

---

[12]C++20 introduces **pack expansion** in lambda initialization captures (see **revzin18**) that allows capturing variadics with a syntax such as [...us = vs] or [...us = std::move(vs)].

An idiom that avoids such errors is to use two **alignas** for a given declaration, one of which is the natural alignment of the declaration. That idiom is at work in the declarations of x2 and x3 in the definition of function template test1.

Using handwritten, comma-separated lists inside an **alignas** specifier is, however, not allowed. Expansion *outside* the specifier is also disallowed:

```
template <typename... Ts>  // variadic template
void test2(Ts... xs)        // for illustration purposes
{
    alignas(Ts)... float x4;
        // Error, cannot expand outside the alignas specifier

    alignas(double, Ts...) float x5;  // Error, syntax not allowed
    alignas(Ts..., double) float x6;  // Error,    "     "      "
    alignas(long, double)  float x7;  // Error,    "     "      "
}
```

To conclude, pack expansion in an **alignas** specifier allows choosing without contortions the largest alignment of a parameter pack. Combining two or more **alignas** specifiers facilitates a simple idiom for avoiding errors and corner cases.

Expansion in an attribute list

Attributes, introduced with C++11, are a mechanism for adding built-in or user-defined information about declarations; see Section 1.1."Attribute Syntax" on page 12.

Attributes are added to declarations using the syntax **[[attribute]]**. For example, **[[noreturn]]** is a standard attribute indicating that a function will not return:

```
[[noreturn]] void abort();  // Once called, it won't return.
```

Two or more attributes can be applied to a declaration either independently or as a comma-separated list inside the square brackets:

```
[[noreturn]] [[deprecated]] void finish();  // won't return, also deprecated
[[deprecated, noreturn]]     void finish();  //    "        "      "       "
```

For completeness and future extensibility, **pack expansion** is allowed inside an attribute specifier as in **[[attribute...]]**. However, this feature is not currently usable with any current attribute, standard or user-defined:

```
template <typename... Ts>
[[Ts()...]] void functionFromTheFuture();  // Error, nonworking code
```

The ability to expand packs inside attribute specifiers is reserved for future use and good to keep in mind for future additions to the language.

Expansion in a `sizeof...` expression

The **sizeof**... expression is an oddity in three ways. First, it has nothing to do with
classical **sizeof** in the sense that **sizeof**... does not yield the extent occupied in memory
by an object. Second, it is the only pack expansion that does *not* use the (by now familiar)
pack... syntax. Third, although it is considered an expansion, it does not expand a pack
into its constituents.

For any parameter pack P, **sizeof**...(P) yields to a compile-time constant of type size_t
equal to the number of elements of P:

```
template <typename... Ts>
std::size_t countArgs(Ts... xs)
{
    std::size_t x1 = sizeof...(Ts);         // x1 is the number of parameters.
    std::size_t x2 = sizeof...(xs);         // same value as x1
    static_assert(sizeof...(Ts) >= 0,"");   // sizeof...(Ts) is a constant.
    static_assert(sizeof...(xs) >= 0,"");   // sizeof...(xs) is a constant.
    return sizeof ... (Ts);                 // whitespace around ... allowed
}
```

Let's see countArgs in action:

```
std::size_t a0 = countArgs();           // initialized to 0
std::size_t a1 = countArgs(42);         // initialized to 1
std::size_t a2 = countArgs("ab", 'c');  // initialized to 2
```

Whitespace is allowed around the ..., but parentheses are not optional. Also, expansion is
disallowed inside **sizeof** and **sizeof**... alike:

```
template <typename... Ts>
void nogo(Ts... xs)
{
    std::size_t x1 = sizeof 42;         // OK, same as sizeof(int)
    std::size_t x2 = sizeof... Ts;      // Error, parens required around Ts
    std::size_t x3 = sizeof... xs;      // Error, parens required around xs
    std::size_t x4 = sizeof(Ts...);     // Error, cannot expand inside sizeof
    std::size_t x5 = sizeof...(Ts...);  // Error, cannot expand inside sizeof...
    std::size_t x6 = sizeof(xs...);     // Error, cannot expand inside sizeof
    std::size_t x7 = sizeof...(xs...);  // Error, cannot expand inside sizeof...
}
```

Expansion inside a template parameter list

Not to be confused with the case discussed in *Expansion in a template argument list* on
page 914, expansion in a template *parameter* list is a different case altogether. This *parameter* expansion is different from all other expansion cases because it involves two distinct
parameter packs: a type parameter pack and a non-type template parameter pack. To set

things up, suppose we define a class template, C1, that has a type parameter pack, Ts. Inside, we define a secondary class template, C2, that does *not* take any type parameters. Instead, it takes a non-type template parameter pack with types derived from Ts:

```
template <typename... Ts>    // type parameter pack
struct C1                     // class template
{
    template <Ts... vs>       // non-type parameters (attention: no typename!)
    struct C2 { };            // Ts expanded in C2's parameter list
};
```

Once C1 is instantiated with some types, the inner class C2 will accept *values* of the types used in the instantiation of C1. For example, if C1 is instantiated with **int** and **char**, its inner class template C2 will accept an **int** value and a **char** value:

```
C1<int, char>::C2<1, 'a'> x1;        // OK, C2 takes an int and a char.
C1<int, char>::C2<1> x2;             // Error, too few arguments for C2
C1<int, char>::C2<1, 'a', 'b'> x3;   // Error, too many arguments for C2
```

The only instantiations of C1 that are allowed are those that lead to valid declarations of C2. For example, user-defined types are not allowed as non-type template parameters, and, consequently, C1 cannot be instantiated with a user-defined type:

```
class AClass { };  // simple user-defined class

C1<int, AClass>::C2<1, AClass()> x1;
    // Error, a non-type template parameter cannot have type AClass.
```

No other expansion contexts

Note that what's missing is as important as what's present. **Pack expansion** is explicitly disallowed in any other context, even if it would make sense syntactically and semantically:

```
template <typename... Ts>
void bumpAll(Ts&... xs)
{
    ++xs...;  // Error, cannot expand xs in an expression-statement context
}
```

Annoyances — Limitations on expansion contexts on page 954 discusses this context further. Also recall that it is illegal to use pack names anywhere without expanding them, so they don't enjoy first-class status; see *Annoyances — Parameter packs cannot be used unexpanded* on page 956.

Summary of expansion contexts and patterns

To recap, expansion is allowed in only these few specific places:

Context	Pattern
function parameter pack	parameter declaration
function call argument list or a braced-initializer list	function argument
template argument list	template argument
base-specifier list	base specifier
member initializer list	base initializer
lambda-capture list	capture
alignment specifier	alignment specifier
attribute list	attribute
sizeof... expression	identifier
template parameter pack that is a **pack expansion**	parameter declaration

Use Cases

Generic variadic functions

A variety of functions of general utility are naturally variadic, either mathematically (min, max, sum) or as a programmer's convenience. Suppose, for example, we want to define a function, print, that writes its arguments to std::cout in turn followed by a newline[13]:

```cpp
#include <iostream>  // std::cout, std::endl

std::ostream& print()                  // parameterless overload
{
    return std::cout << std::endl;  // only advances to next line
}

template <typename T, typename... Ts>          // one or more types
std::ostream& print(const T& x, const Ts&... xs) // one or more args
{
    std::cout << x;                        // output first argument
    return print(xs...);                   // recurse to print rest
}

void test()
{
    print("Pi is about ", 3.14159265);         // "Pi is about 3.14159"
}
```

---

[13]C++20 introduces std::format, a facility for general text formatting.

The implementation follows a head-and-tail recursion that is typically used for C++ variadic function templates. The first overload of `print` has no parameters and simply outputs a newline to the console. The second overload does the bulk of the work. It takes one or more arguments, prints the first, and recursively calls `print` to print the rest. In the limit, `print` is called with no arguments, and the first definition kicks in, outputting the line terminator and also ending the recursion.

A variadic function's smallest number of allowed arguments does not have to be zero, and it is free to follow many other recursion patterns. For example, suppose we want to define a variadic function `isOneOf` that returns **true** if and only if its first argument is equal to one of the subsequent arguments. Calls to such a function are sensible for two or more arguments:

```
template <typename T1, typename T2>        // normal template function
bool isOneOf(const T1& a, const T2& b)  // two-parameter version
{
  return a == b;
}


template <typename T1, typename T2, typename... Ts>      // two or more arguments
bool isOneOf(const T1& a, const T2& b, const Ts&... xs)  // all by const&
{
  return a == b || isOneOf(a, xs...);                    // compare, recurse
}
```

Again, the implementation uses two definitions in a pseudorecursive setup but in a slightly different stance. The first definition handles two items and also stops recursion. The second version takes three or more arguments, handles the first two, and issues the recursive call only if the comparison yields **false**.

Let's take a look at a few uses of `isOneOf`:

```
#include <string>  // std::string

int a = 42;
bool b1 = isOneOf(a, 1, 42, 4);    // b1 is true.
bool b2 = isOneOf(a, 1, 2, 3);     // b2 is false.
bool b3 = isOneOf(a, 1, "two");    // Error, can't compare int with const char*
std::string s = "Hi";
bool b4 = isOneOf(s, "Hi", "a");   // b4 is true.
bool b5 = isOneOf(s);  // Error, no overload takes fewer than two parameters.
```

Processing variadic arguments in order

Let's now consider two possible implementations of the variadic string concatenation function `concat`, introduced in *Description* on page 873: one using a recursive approach, and the other taking advantage of **braced initialization** (see Section 2.1."Braced Init" on page 215) to avoid recursion.

Recall that `concat` takes a heterogeneous list of zero or more arguments — each of type `std::string`, **const char***, or **char** — and concatenates them into a single `std::string`:

```
#include <string>  // std::string

template <typename... Ts>
std::string concat(const Ts&... s);
```

To improve performance, we want to precompute the length of the resulting string by summing the lengths of all arguments to `concat`, allowing us to then reserve sufficient memory all at once. Since each argument to `concat` might have any of three types, we define a set of overloaded **extent** helper functions that compute the length of the **char** sequence appropriately for each possible argument type:

```
#include <string>   // std::string
#include <cstring>  // std::strlen

std::size_t extent(char)               { return 1; }
std::size_t extent(const char* s)      { return std::strlen(s); }
std::size_t extent(const std::string& s) { return s.length(); }
```

We still need the part of the computation that adds several extents together; a simple way to achieve that without adding another name is to allow **extent** to accept variadic arguments:

```
std::size_t extent() { return 0; }  // recursion base case

template <typename T, typename... Ts>
std::size_t extent(const T& arg, const Ts&... args)
{
    return extent(arg) + extent(args...);
}
```

The parameterless overload handles empty parameter packs. The variadic version peels off the first argument and adds its extent to the recursively computed sum of the remaining extents.

Once the final length is computed and an `std::string` object of appropriate capacity is constructed to hold the result, the return value of `concat` can be computed by a similar recursive function template, e.g., **stringAppend**, that appends each argument in turn to the result string:

```
void stringAppend(std::string&) { }  // recursion base case

template <typename S0, typename... S>
void stringAppend(std::string& result, const S0& s0, const S&... s)
{
    result += s0;
    stringAppend(result, s...);
}
```

The structure of stringAppend is familiar by now; it appends its second argument (s0) to result and then calls a recursive instantiation of itself to append the third and subsequent arguments. The final concat function template is not recursive but calls the two recursive templates we just defined:

```
template <typename... Ts>
std::string concat(const Ts&... args)
{
    // Create result string and reserve sufficient space to avoid reallocations.
    std::string result;
    result.reserve(extent(args...));

    // Append each string in parameter pack args to result.
    stringAppend(result, args...);

    return result;
}
```

In the implementation of concat above, sufficient capacity is reserved in the result string to hold the ultimate value before stringAppend is called, thus avoiding potential memory reallocations that can occur when appending repeatedly to a single string.

Alternatively, we can employ pack expansions in braced initializers to accumulate values as a side effect of those initializations, without helper functions having recursive instantiations:

```
template <typename... Ts>
std::string concat2(const Ts&... args)
{
    // Compute length of final concatenated string.
    std::size_t resultLen = 0;
    { bool unused[] = { ((resultLen += extent(args)), false)... }; }

    // Create result string and reserve sufficient space to avoid reallocations.
    std::string result;
    result.reserve(resultLen);

    // Append each string in parameter pack args to result.
    { bool unused[] = { ((result += args), false)... }; }

    return result;
}
```

The pack expansion ((resultLen += extent(args)), false)... in the concat2 function template above increments the value of resultLen by the extent of each argument in parameter pack args and then applies the comma operator to yield the value **false** for each expression; the expression is evaluated for only its side effect, not its resulting value. The unused array is thus initialized to all **false** values, with resultLen being set — as a side effect — to the sum of the lengths of the individual strings in parameter pack args. The unused array goes out of scope immediately after being initialized; an optimizing compiler need not even allocate space for **unused** on the stack, let alone initialize its elements.[14] Note that the pack expansion always calls **extent** with exactly one argument, so there is no need to define **extent**'s recursive variadic overload or parameterless base-case overload.

The technique used to compute **resultLen** is applied again to append each element of **args** — be it a **char**, a **const char***, or an **std::string** — to the end of **result**. Because the **pack expansion context** is an initializer list, the side effects of the expressions in the **pack expansion** are guaranteed to occur in order, unlike, say, a function argument list, which has no such ordering guarantee. Note that a **pack expansion** could be used to initialize a temporary object of type **std::initializer_list<bool>** to yield the same result by replacing { **bool** unused[] = { ... }; } with **(void)** initializer_list**<bool>**{ ... }; for the two uses of the idiom; see Section 2.1."**initializer_list**" on page 553.

Object factories

Suppose we want to define a generic **factory function** — a function able to create an instance of any given type by calling one of its constructors. Object factories[15,16] allow libraries and applications to centrally control object creation for a variety of reasons: using special memory allocation, tracing and logging, benchmarking, object pooling, late binding, deserialization, interning, and more.

The challenge in defining a generic object factory is that the type to be created (and therefore its constructors) is not known at the time of writing the factory. That's why C++03 object factories typically offer only default object construction, forcing clients to awkwardly use two-phase initialization, first to create an empty object and then to put it in a meaningful state.

Writing a generic function that can transparently forward calls to another function ("perfect forwarding") has been a long-standing challenge in C++03. An important part of the puzzle is making the forwarding function generic in the number of arguments, which is where variadic templates help in conjunction with forwarding references (see Section 2.1. "Forwarding References" on page 377):

```
#include <utility>   // std::forward

void log(const char* message);              // logging function

template <typename Product, typename... Ts>  // type to be created and params
Product factory(Ts&&... xs)                   // call by forwarding reference
{
    log("factory(): Creating a new object");  // Do some logging.
    return Product(std::forward<Ts>(xs)...);  // Forward arguments to ctor.
}
```

---

[14]Experiments with both Clang 12.0.0 (c. 2021) and GCC 11.1 (c. 2021) show that the unused array is entirely optimized away at optimization level -O2, even if the { and } braces surrounding the definition of unused are omitted.

[15]**gamma95**, Chapter 3, section "Factory Method," pp. 107–115

[16]**alexandrescu01**, Chapter 8, "Object Factories," pp. 197–218

`Ts&&... xs` introduces `xs`, a function parameter pack that represents zero or more forwarding references. As we know, the construct `std::forward<Ts>(xs)...` is a **pack expansion** that expands to a comma-separated list of `std::forward<T0>(x0)`, `std::forward<T1>(x1)`, and so on. The Standard Library function template `std::forward` passes accurate type information from the forwarding references `x0`, `x1`, ... to `Product`'s constructor.

To use the function, we must always provide the `Product` type explicitly; it is not a function parameter, so it cannot be deduced. The others are at best left to template argument deduction. In the simplest case, `factory` is usable with primitive types:

```
int i1 = factory<int>();    // Initialize i1 to 0.
int i2 = factory<int>(42);  // Initialize i2 to 42.
```

It also works correctly with overloaded constructors:

```
struct Widget
{
    Widget(double);         // constructor taking a double
    Widget(int&, double);   // constructor taking an int& and a double
};

int g = 0;
Widget w1 = factory<Widget>(g, 2.4);   // calls ctor with int& and double
Widget w2 = factory<Widget>(20);       // calls ctor with double
Widget w3 = factory<Widget>(20, 2.0);  // Error, cannot bind rvalue to int&
```

The last line introducing `w3` fails to compile because the *rvalue* `20` cannot convert to the non**const int**& required by `Widget`'s constructor — an illustration of perfect forwarding doing its job.

Many variations of object factories (e.g., using dynamic allocation, custom memory allocators, and special exceptions treatment) can be built on the skeleton of `factory` shown. In fact, Standard Library factory functions, such as `std::make_shared` and `std::make_unique`, use variadics and perfect forwarding in this same manner.

Hooking function calls

Forwarding is not limited to object construction. We can use it to intercept function calls in a generic manner and add processing such as tracing or logging. Suppose, for example, writing a function that calls another function and logs any exception it might throw:

```
#include <exception>  // std::exception
#include <utility>    // std::forward

void log(const char* msg);                    // Log a message.

template <typename Callable, typename... Ts>
auto logExceptions(Callable&& fun, Ts&&... xs)
    -> decltype(fun(std::forward<Ts>(xs)...))
```

```
{
    try
    {
        return fun(std::forward<Ts>(xs)...);    // perfect forwarding to fun
    }
    catch (const std::exception& e)
    {
        log(e.what());                          // log exception information
        throw;                                  // Rethrow the same exception.
    }
    catch (...)
    {
        log("Nonstandard exception thrown.");   // log exception information
        throw;                                  // Rethrow the same exception.
    }
}
```

Here, we enlist the help of `std::forward` and also that of the **auto -> decltype** idiom; see Section 1.1."Trailing Return" on page 124 and Section 1.1."**decltype**" on page 25. By using **auto** instead of the return type of `logExceptions` and following with -> and the trailing type **decltype**(fun(std::forward<Ts>(xs)...)), we state that the return type of `logExceptions` is the same as the type of the call fun(std::forward<Ts>(xs)...), which matches perfectly the expression that the function will actually return.

In case the call to `fun` throws an exception, `logExceptions` catches, logs, and rethrows that exception. So `logExceptions` is entirely transparent other than for logging the passing exceptions. Let's see it in action. First, we define a function, `assumeIntegral`, that is likely to throw an exception:

```
#include <stdexcept>  // std::runtime_error

long assumeIntegral(double d)            // throws if d has a fractional part
{
    long result = static_cast<long>(d);  // Compute the returned value.
    if (result != d)                     // Verify.
        throw std::runtime_error("Integral expected");
    return result;
}
```

To call `assumeIntegral` via `logExceptions`, we just pass it along with its argument:

```
void test()
{
    long a = logExceptions(assumeIntegral, 4.0);  // Initialize a to 4.
    long b = logExceptions(assumeIntegral, 4.4);  // throws and logs
}
```

Tuples

A *tuple* or a record is a type that groups together a fixed number of values of unrelated types. The C++03 Standard Library template `std::pair` is a tuple with two elements. The Standard Library template `std::tuple`, introduced in C++11, implements a tuple with the help of variadic templates. For example, `std::tuple<int, int, float>` holds two `int`s and a `float`.

There are many possible ways to implement a tuple in C++. C++03 implementations typically define a hard-coded limit on the number of values the tuple can hold and use considerable amounts of scaffolding, as described in *Description* on page 873:

```cpp
struct None { };  // empty "tag" used as a special "not used" marker

template <typename T1 = None, typename T2 = None, typename T3 = None,
          typename T4 = None, typename T5 = None, typename T6 = None,
          typename T7 = None, typename T8 = None, typename T9 = None>
class Cpp03Tuple;
    // tuple containing up to 9 data members of arbitrary types
```

Variadics are a key ingredient in a scalable, manageable tuple implementation. We discuss a few possibilities in approaching the core definition of a tuple, with an emphasis on data layout.

The definition of `Tuple1` (in the code snippet below) uses specialization and recursion to accommodate any number of types:

```cpp
template <typename... Ts>
class Tuple1;              // (0) incomplete declaration

template <>
class Tuple1<>            // (1) specialization for zero elements
{ /*...*/ };

template <typename T, typename... Ts>
class Tuple1<T, Ts...>   // (2) specialization for one or more elements
{
    T first;             // first element
    Tuple1<Ts...> rest;  // all other elements
    // ...
};
```

`Tuple1` uses composition and recursion to create its data layout. As discussed in *Description — Expansion in a base-specifier list* on page 915, the expansion `Tuple1<Ts...>` results in `Tuple1<T0, T1, ..., Tn>`. The specialization `Tuple1<>` ends the recursion.

The only awkward detail is that `Tuple1<int>` has member `rest` of type `Tuple1<>`, which is empty but is required to have nonzero size, so it ends up occupying space in the tuple.[17] Such

---

[17] On Clang 12.0.1 (c. 2021) and GCC 11.2 (c. 2021), `sizeof(Tuple1<int>)` is 8, twice the size of an `int`.

spatial inefficiencies can become problematic at scale — especially when cache-friendliness is at a premium.

A solution to avoid this issue is to partially specialize `Tuple1` for one element in addition to the two existing specializations:

```
template <typename T>
class Tuple1<T>              // (3) specialization for one element
{
    T first;
    // ...
};
```

With this addition, `Tuple1<>` uses the full specialization (1), `Tuple1<int>` uses the partial specialization (3), and all instantiations with two or more types use the partial specialization (2). For example, `Tuple1<int, long, double>` instantiates specialization (2), which uses `Tuple1<long, double>` as a member, which in turn uses the partial specialization (3) for member `rest` of type `Tuple1<double>`.

The disadvantage of the design above is that it requires similar code in the `Tuple1<T>` partial specialization and the general definition, leading to a subtle form of code duplication. Having to write some redundant code might not seem especially problematic, and yet a good tuple API typically has considerable scaffold: `std::tuple`, for example, has 25 member functions.

Let's address `Tuple1`'s problem by using inheritance instead of composition, thus benefitting from an old and well-implemented C++ layout optimization known as the **empty-base optimization**. When a base of a class has no state, that base is allowed, under certain circumstances, to occupy no room at all in the derived class. Let's design a `Tuple2` variadic class template that takes advantage of the **empty-base optimization**:

```
template <typename... Ts>
class Tuple2;                // incomplete declaration

template <>
class Tuple2<>              // specialization for zero elements
{ /*...*/ };

template <typename T, typename... Ts>
class Tuple2<T, Ts...>      // specialization for one or more elements
    : public Tuple2<Ts...>   // recurses in inheritance
{
    T first;
    //...
};
```

If we assess the size of `Tuple2<int>` with virtually any contemporary compiler, it is the same as **sizeof(int)**, so the base does not, in fact, add to the size of the complete object. One awkwardness with `Tuple2` is that with most compilers the types specified appear in the memory layout in reverse order; for example, in an object of type

`Tuple1<int, int, float, std::string>`, the string would be the first member in the layout, followed by the **float** and then by the two **int**s. (Compilers do have some freedom in defining layout, but most of today's compilers simply place bases first in their order, followed by members in the order of their declarations.)

To ensure a more intuitive layout, let's define `Tuple3` that uses an additional **struct** to hold individual elements, which `Tuple3` inherits before recursing:

```
template <typename T>
struct Element3  // element holder
{
    T value;      // no other data or member functions
};

template <typename... Ts>
class Tuple3;     // declaration to introduce the class template

template <>
class Tuple3<>    // specialization for zero elements
{ /*...*/ };

template <typename T, typename... Ts>  // one or more types
class Tuple3<T, Ts...>                  // one or more elements
    : public Element3<T>                // first in layout
    , public Tuple3<Ts...>              // Recurse to complete layout.
{ /*...*/ };
```

The `Tuple3` implementation (above) is close to what we need, but there is one additional problem to address: The instantiation `Tuple3<int, int>` will attempt to inherit `Element3<int>` twice, which is not allowed. One way to address this issue is by passing a so-called cookie to element template, an additional template parameter that uniquely tags each element differently. We choose `size_t` for the cookie type:

```
template <typename T, std::size_t cookie>
struct Element4      // Element holder also takes a cookie so the same element
                     // is not inherited twice; cookie is actually not used.
{
    T value;
};
```

The `Tuple4` class instantiates `Element4` with a decreasing value of **cookie** for each successive element:

```
template <typename... Ts>
class Tuple4;                        // (0) incomplete declaration
```

```
template <>
class Tuple4<>                          // (1) specialization for no elements
{ /*...*/ };

template <typename T, typename... Ts>
class Tuple4<T, Ts...>                  // (2) one or more elements
    : public Element4<T, sizeof...(Ts)> // first in layout, count is cookie
    , public Tuple4<Ts...>              // Recurse to complete layout.
{ /*...*/ };
```

To see how it all works, consider the instantiation `Tuple4<int, int, char>`, which matches specialization (2) with `T=int` and `Ts=<int, char>`. Consequently, `sizeof...(Ts)` — the number of elements in `Ts` — is 2. The specialization first inherits `Element4<int, 2>` and then `Tuple4<int, char>`. The latter, in turn, also uses specialization (2) with `T=int` and `Ts=<char>`, which inherits `Element4<int, 1>` and `Tuple4<char>`. Finally, `Tuple4<char>` inherits `Element4<char, 0>` and `Tuple4<>`, which kicks the first specialization into gear to terminate the recursion.

It follows that `Tuple4<int, int, char>` ultimately inherits (in order) `Element4<int, 2>`, `Element4<int, 1>`, and `Element4<char, 0>`. Most implementations of `std::tuple` are variations of the patterns illustrated by `Tuple1` through `Tuple4`.[18]

If `Element4` didn't take a distinct number for each member of the tuple type, `Tuple4<int, int>` would not work because it would inherit `Element4<int>` twice, which is illegal. With cookie, the instantiation works because it inherits the distinct types `Element4<int, 1>` and `Element4<int, 2>`.

The expanded templates for the above code example might look like this invalid but illustrative code:

```
class Tuple4<>
{ /*...*/ };
class Tuple4<char> : public Element4<char, 0>, public Tuple4<>
{ /*...*/ };
class Tuple4<int, char> : public Element4<int, 1>, public Tuple4<char>
{ /*...*/ };
class Tuple4<int, int, char> : public Element4<int, 2>, public Tuple4<int, char>
{ /*...*/ };
```

---

[18]libstdc++, the GNU C++ Standard Library, uses an inheritance-based scheme with increasing indexes (as opposed to `Tuple4` in which cookie values are decreasing). libc++, the LLVM Standard Library that ships with Clang, does not use inheritance for `std::tuple`, but its state implementation uses inheritance in conjunction with an increasing integral sequence. Microsoft's open-source STL (**microsoftb**) uses, at the time of this writing, the approach taken by `Tuple2`.

The complete implementation of a tuple type would contain the usual constructors and assignment operators as well as a *projection function* that takes an index i as a compile-time parameter and returns a reference to the ith element of the tuple. Let's see how to implement this rather subtle function. To get it done, we first need a helper template that returns the nth type in a template parameter pack:

```
template <std::size_t n, typename T, typename... Ts>
struct NthType              // yields nth type in the sequence <T, Ts...>
{
    typedef typename NthType<n - 1, Ts...>::type
        type;               // Recurse to smaller n.
};

template <typename T, typename... Ts>
struct NthType<0, T, Ts...>  // base case, 0th type in <T, Ts...> is T
{
    typedef T type;
};
```

NthType follows the now familiar pattern of recursive parameter pack handling. The first declaration introduces the recursive case. The specialization that follows handles the limit case n == 0 to stop the recursion. It is easy to follow that, for example, NthType<1, **short**, **int**, **long**>::type is **int**.

We are now ready to define the function get such that get<0>(x) returns a reference to the first element of a Tuple4 object called x:

```
template <std::size_t n, typename... Ts>  // n is the index. Ts is the tuple pack.
auto& get(Tuple4<Ts...>& x)               // top-level function
{
    typedef typename NthType<n, Ts...>::type
        ResultType;                       // Reference to this type is returned.
    typedef Element4<ResultType, sizeof...(Ts) - n - 1>
        ElementType;                      // element holding the value returned
    ElementType& r = x;                   // implicit conversion to get element
    return r.value;                       // Access the value from the Element4.
}
```

Calculating the cookie **sizeof**...(Ts) - n - 1 requires some finesse. Recall that the elements in a tuple come with cookies in the reverse order of their natural order, so the first element in a Tuple4<Ts...> has cookie **sizeof**...(Ts) - 1 and the last element has cookie 0. Therefore, when we compute the cookie of the nth element in the cookie, we use elementary algebra to get to the expression shown.

After all typing has been sorted out, the implementation itself is trivial; it fetches the appropriate Element4 base by means of an implicit cast and then returns its **value**. Let's put the code to test:

```
void test()
#include <cassert>  // standard C assert macro

{
    Tuple4<int, double, std::string> value;
    get<0>(value) = 3;
    get<1>(value) = 2.718;
    get<2>(value) = "hello";
    assert(get<2>(value) == "hello");
}
```

The example also illustrates why `get` is best defined as a nonmember function: A member function would have been forced to use the awkward syntax `value.template get<0>() = 3` to disambiguate the use of `<` as a template instantiation as opposed to the less-than operator.

Variant types

A *variant* type, sometimes called a *discriminated union*, is similar to a C++ **union** that keeps track of which of its elements is currently active and protects client code against unsafe uses. Variadic templates support a natural interface to express this design as a generic library feature.[19] For example, a variant type such as `Variant<int, float, std::string>` would be able to hold exactly one **int** or one **float** or one `std::string` value. Client code can change the current type by assigning to the variant object an **int**, a **float**, or an `std::string`, respectively.

To define a variant type, we need it to have enough storage to keep any of its possible values, plus a *discriminator* — typically a small integral that keeps the index of the currently stored type. For `Variant<int, float, std::string>`, the discriminator could be by convention 0 for **int**, 1 for **float**, and 2 for `std::string`.

We saw in the previous sections how to define data structures recursively for parameter packs, so let's try our hand at a variant layout in the `Variant1` design:

```
template <typename... Ts>              // parameter pack
class Variant1                         // can hold any in parameter pack
{
    template <typename...>             // union of all types in Ts
    union Store {};

    template <typename U, typename... Us>  // Specialize for >=1 types.
    union Store<U, Us...>
    {
        U head;              // Lay out a U object.
        Store<Us...> tail;   // all others at same address
```

---

[19]C++17's Standard Library type `std::variant` provides a robust and comprehensive implementation of a variant type.

```
        Store() {}            // User-provided constructor is required.
        ~Store() {}           // User-provided destructor is required.
    };

    Store<Ts...> d_data;      // Store for current datum.
    unsigned int d_active;    // index of active type in Ts

public:
    // ... (API goes here.)
};
```

C-style **union**s can be templates, too, and variadic ones at that. We take advantage of
this feature in `Variant1` to recursively define a variadic class template, `Store<Ts...>`,
that stores each of the types in the parameter pack `Ts` at the same address. One important C++11 feature that conveys flexibility to the design above is the relaxation on the
restrictions on types that can be stored in **union**s. In C++03, **union** members were not
allowed to have non-trivial constructors or destructors. Starting with C++11, any type
can be a member of a **union** provided the **union** has a user-provided constructor and/or
destructor, respectively; see Section 3.1."**union** '11" on page 1174. Therefore, types such as
`Variant1<std::string, std::map<int, int>>` work fine.

For the active index `d_active`, we use **unsigned int**, a reasonable compromise between
speed and size. (The `d_active` member should technically be an `std::size_t`, but we don't
need that large of an integral.) An even more layout-minded approach would choose among
`std::uint8_t`, `std::uint16_t`, `std::uint32_t`, and `std::uint64_t`, depending on the number of elements in the `Variant` instantiation and on space saving opportunities.

It is possible to define the `d_data` member of the `Variant1` class template, above, in a more
succinct manner as a fixed-size array of **char**. There are, however, two challenges to address.
First, the size of the array needs to be computed during compilation as the maximum of
the sizes of all types in `Ts`. Second, the array needs to have sufficient alignment to store any
of the types in `Ts`. Fortunately, both problems have simple solutions in idiomatic modern
C++:

```
#include <algorithm>  // std::max

template <typename... Ts> class Variant2;   // introducing declaration

template <> class Variant2<>                 // specialization for empty Ts
{ /*...*/ };

template <typename T, typename... Ts>
class Variant2<T, Ts...>                      // specialization for one or more types
{
    enum : std::size_t { size = std::max({sizeof(T), sizeof(Ts)...}) };
        // std::max takes std::initializer_list and is constexpr in C++14.
```

```
    alignas(T) alignas(Ts...) char  d_data[size];  // payload
    unsigned int                    d_active;      // index of active type in Ts

public:
    // ...                                  (API goes here.)
};
```

The code above showcases a new use of `std::max` — an overload introduced in C++14 that takes an initializer list as its parameter; see Section 2.1."`initializer_list`" on page 553. Another novelty is the use of `std::max` during compilation; see Section 2.1."**constexpr** Functions" on page 257. We apply `std::max` to **sizeof**(T) and to the **sizeof**(Ts)... expansion, which results in the comma-separated list **sizeof**(T), **sizeof**(T0), **sizeof**(T1), ... (Note that this expansion is not the same as **sizeof**...(Ts), which would just return the number of elements in Ts.)

In brief, d_data is an array of **char** as large as the maximum of the sizes of all of the types passed to Variant2. In addition, the **alignas** directives instructs the compiler to align d_data at the largest alignment of all types among T and all of Ts; see *Description — Expansion in an alignment specifier* on page 921 and Section 2.1."**alignas**" on page 168.

It is worth noting that both Variant1 and Variant2 are equally good from a layout perspective; in fact, even the implementation of their respective APIs are identical. The only use of d_data is to take its address and use it as a pointer to **void**, which the API casts appropriately.

The public interface ensures that when an element is stored in d_data, d_active will have the value of the index into the parameter pack Ts... that corresponds to that type. Hence, when a user attempts to retrieve a value from the variant, if the wrong type is requested, a runtime error will be reported.

Let's take a look at defining some relevant API functions — the default constructor, a value constructor, and the destructor:

```
#include <algorithm>  // std::max

template <typename... Ts>             // introducing declaration
class Variant;

template <> class Variant<>           // specialization for empty Ts
{ /*...*/ };

template <typename T, typename... Ts> // specialization for 1 or more
class Variant<T, Ts...>
{
    enum : std::size_t { size = std::max({sizeof(T), sizeof(Ts)...}) };
        // Compute payload size.
```

```
    alignas(T) alignas(Ts...) char d_data[size];  // approach in Variant1 fine too
    unsigned int                    d_active;      // index of active type in Ts

    template <typename U, typename... Us>
    friend U& get(Variant<Us...>& v);  // friend accessor

  public:
    Variant();                          // default constructor

    template <typename V>               // value constructor
    Variant(V&&);                       // V must be among T, Ts.

    ~Variant();                         // Destroy the current object.

    // ...
};
```

The implementation of the empty specialization, Variant<>, is trivial, so below we focus on the nonempty partial specialization with at least one type, Variant<T, Ts...>. The default constructor should put the object in a simple, meaningful state. A reasonable decision is to create (by default construction) the *first* object in Ts:

```
template <typename T, typename... Ts>
Variant<T, Ts...>::Variant()
{
    ::new(&d_data) T();  // default-constructed T at address of d_data
    d_active = 0;        // Set the active type to T, first in the list.
}
```

The default constructor in the example above uses **placement new** to create a default-constructed object at the address of **d_data**. The first element in the parameter pack is selected by means of partial specialization.

The value constructor is a bit more challenging because it needs to compute the appropriate value for **d_active** during compilation, for example, as an **enum** value. To that end, first we need a support metafunction that reports the index of a type in a template parameter pack. The first type is the sought type, followed by the types to be searched. If the first type is not among the others, a compile-time error is produced:

```
template <typename X, typename T, typename... Ts>  // Find X in T, Ts....
struct IndexOf                                      // primary definition
{
    enum : std::size_t { value = IndexOf<X, Ts...>::value + 1 };
};

template <typename X, typename... Ts>               // partial specialization 1
struct IndexOf<X, X, Ts...>                          // found X at front
{
```

```
    enum : std::size_t { value = 0 };               // found in position 0
};

template <typename X, typename... Ts>               // partial specialization 2
struct IndexOf<const X, X, Ts...>                   // found const X at front
{
    enum : std::size_t { value = 0 };               // also found in position 0
};
```

The : `size_t` syntax, new to C++11, specifies that the introduced anonymous **enum** has type `size_t` as its underlying type; see Section 2.1."Underlying Type '11" on page 829. The class template `IndexOf` follows a simple recursive pattern. In the general case, the first parameter type, X, which is the sought type, is different from the second parameter type, T, and `value` is computed recursively as a search through the remainder of the parameter list, `Ts`....

If the sought type is identical to the second template parameter, partial specialization 1 kicks in; if the sought type is a **const** variant of the second parameter, partial specialization 2 matches. (A complete implementation would also add a similar specialization for the **volatile** qualifier.) In either case, the recursion ends, and the value 0 is popped up the compile-time recursion stack:

```
std::size_t i1 = IndexOf<int, int, long>::value;          // i1 is 0.
std::size_t i2 = IndexOf<int, short, int, long>::value;   // i2 is 1.
std::size_t i3 = IndexOf<const int, short, int>::value;   // i3 is 1.
std::size_t i4 = IndexOf<int, float, double>::value;      // Error
```

If the type is not found in the pack at all, then the recursion will come to an end when `Ts` is empty and the recursion cannot find a specialization for just one type `T`, resulting in a compile-time error.

It is worth noting that `IndexOf` has an alternative implementation that uses `std::integral_constant`, a Standard Library facility introduced in C++11 that automates part of the `value` definition:

```
#include <type_traits> // std::integral_constant
template <typename X, typename T, typename... Ts>  // general definition
struct IndexOf2
    : std::integral_constant<std::size_t, IndexOf2<X, Ts...>::value + 1> {};

template <typename X, typename... Ts>
struct IndexOf2<X, X, Ts...>
    : std::integral_constant<std::size_t, 0u> {};   // partial specialization 1

template <typename X, typename... Ts>
struct IndexOf2<const X, X, Ts...>
    : std::integral_constant<std::size_t, 0u> {};   // partial specialization 2
```

The type `std::integral_constant<std::size_t, n>` defines a constant member named `value` of type `std::size_t` with value n, which simplifies to some extent the definition of `IndexOf` and clarifies its intent.

With this template at hand, we are ready to implement `Variant`'s value constructor, using **perfect forwarding** to create a `Variant` holding an object of the given type, with a compile-time error if the specified type is not found in the parameter pack `Ts`.

There is one more detail to handle. By design, we require `Ts` to contain only unqualified (no **const** or **volatile**), nonreference types, but the **value constructor** might deduce its type parameter as a reference type (such as **int&**). In such cases, we need to extract **int** from **int&**. The Standard Library template `std::remove_reference_t` was designed for exactly this task — both `std::remove_reference_t<int>` and `std::remove_reference_t<int&>` are aliases for **int**:

```
template <typename T, typename... Ts>  // definition for partial specialization
template <typename V>
Variant<T, Ts...>::Variant(V&& xs)      // value ctor using perfect forwarding
{
    typedef std::remove_reference_t<V> U;
         // Remove reference from V if any, e.g. transform int& into int.

    ::new(&d_data) U(std::forward<V>(xs));   // Construct object at address.
    d_active = IndexOf<U, T, Ts...>::value; // This code fails if U not in Ts.
}
```

Now we get to construct a `Variant` given any value of one of its possible types:

```
Variant<float, double> v1(1.0F);  // v1 has type float and value 1.
Variant<float, double> v2(2.0);   // v2 has type double and value 2.
Variant<float, double> v3(1);     // Error, int is not among allowed types.
```

A more advanced `Variant` implementation could support implicit conversions during construction as long as there is no ambiguity.[20]

Now that `Variant` knows the index of the active type in `Ts`, we can implement an accessor function that retrieves a reference to the active element, by a client that knows the type. For example, given a `Variant<short, int, long>` object named v, **int&** `get<int>(v)` should return a reference to the stored **int** if and only if the current value in v is indeed of type **int**; otherwise, `get` throws an exception:

```
template <typename T, typename... Ts>               // T is the assumed type.
T& get(Variant<Ts...>& v)                           // Variant<Ts...> by ref
{
    if (v.d_active != IndexOf<T, Ts...>::value) // Is the index correct?
        throw std::runtime_error("wrong type"); // If not, throw.
    void* p = &v.d_data;                        // If so, take store address
    return *static_cast<T*>(p);                 // and convert.
}
```

---

[20]Such functionality is supported by std::variant, introduced in C++17.

An overload of `get` that takes and returns **const** would be defined analogously.

Despite its simplicity, the `get` function (which needs to be a **friend** of `Variant` to access its **private** members) is safe and robust. If given a type not present in the `Variant`'s parameter pack, `IndexOf` fails to compile, and thus `get` does not compile either. If the type is present in the pack but is not the current type stored in the `Variant`, an exception is thrown. If everything works well, the address of `d_data` is converted to a reference to the target type with full confidence that the cast is safe to perform:

```
typedef Variant<long, double, std::string> Var;

Var x1(1L);                              // type long, value 1
Var x2(2.5);                             // type double, value 2.5
Var x3(std::string("hi"));               // type std::string, value "hi"

long y1(get<long>(x1));                  // OK, y1 is 1.
double y2(get<double>(x2));              // OK, y2 is 2.5.
std::string y3(get<std::string>(x3));    // OK, y3 contains "hi".
double y4(get<double>(x3));              // throws exception, wrong type
```

Writing `Variant`'s destructor is challenging because, in that case, we need to produce the compile-time type of the active element from the *runtime* index, `d_active`. The language offers no built-in support for such an operation, so we must produce a library-based solution instead.

One approach is to use a linear search: Starting with the active index `d_active` and the entire parameter pack, `Ts`, we reduce both successively until `d_active` becomes zero. At that point, we know that the dynamic type of the variant is the head of what's left of `Ts`, and we call the appropriate destructor. To implement such an algorithm, we define two overloaded functions, `destroyLinear`, that are each a friend of `Variant`:

```
template <unsigned int>
void destroyLinear(unsigned int, void*) { }  // terminates recursion

template <unsigned int i, typename T, typename... Ts>
void destroyLinear(unsigned int n, void* p)  // index and pointer to data
{
    if (n == i)
        static_cast<T*>(p)->~T();                    // found, call destructor manually
    else
        destroyLinear<i + 1, Ts...>(n, p);   // "recurse" with list tail
}
```

The second overload employs the idiom (used in several places in this feature section) of stripping the first element from the parameter pack on each successive call by using a named type parameter. If the runtime index is 0, then the destructor of `T`, the first type in the pack, is called against the pointer received. Otherwise, `destroyLinear` "recursively" calls a version of itself with the parameter pack reduced by 1 and the compile-time counter `i` correspondingly bumped. Note that "recursion" is not quite the correct term because the template instantiates a different function for each call.

The first overload simply terminates the recursion; it is never called in a correct program, but the compiler doesn't know that, so we need to provide a body for it.

Variant's destructor ensures that the variant object is not corrupt and then calls destroyLinear, passing the entire pack Ts... as the template argument (at compile time) and the current index and data address as function arguments (at run time):

```
template <typename T, typename... Ts>  // definition for partial specialization
Variant<T, Ts...>::~Variant()          // linear lookup destructor
{
    assert((d_active < 1 + sizeof...(Ts)));      // Check invariant.
    destroyLinear<0, T, Ts...>(d_active, &d_data); // Initiate destruction.
}
```

When presented with an algorithm with linear complexity, the natural reaction is to look for a similar solution with lower complexity, especially considering that the linear search will be performed at run time, not during compilation. In this case, we might try a *binary search* through the type parameter pack. In common usage, a variant does not have that many types, so a more scalable search algorithm might be considered overkill, but there are two reasons why this problem deserves our attention. First, there are variant types in common use that do have a large number of alternatives, such as the VARIANT type in the Windows operating system, having around 50 options in its union, and some data exchange formats that can have hundreds of types. Second, destructors are of particular importance because they tend to be called intensively, so destructors' size and speed can often affect performance of programs using them.

Let us now consider how we might create a function having logarithmic rather than linear complexity. We can implement such a function with relative ease provided that we carefully distinguish compile-time work from runtime work. The active index, d_active, in the binary search must, by necessity, be manipulated at run time; we can, however, manipulate the iteration limits during compilation. To that end, we define a function template, destroyLog, taking as template parameters the iteration limits, low and high, followed by the parameter pack containing the types being searched, Ts. Just like before, the runtime parameters are the search index, n, and the untyped pointer, p, to the object to be destroyed:

```
template <unsigned int low, unsigned int high, typename... Ts>
void destroyLog(unsigned int n, void* p)
{
    assert(n >= low && n < high);  // precondition

    static constexpr std::size_t mid = low + (high - low) / 2;
    if (n < mid)
    {
        destroyLog<low, (low >= mid ? high : mid), Ts...>(n, p);
    }
    else if (n > mid)
```

```
    {
        destroyLog<(mid + 1 >= high ? low : (mid + 1)), high, Ts...>(n, p);
    }
    else // (n == mid)
    {
        typedef typename NthType<mid, Ts...>::type Tn;
        static_cast<Tn*>(p)->~Tn();
    }
}
```

The implementation of destroyLog is reminiscent of a textbook recursive binary search algorithm, with the distinction that destroyLog takes extra care to separate compile-time work from runtime work. First, we compute the midpoint between low and high, which due to a **constexpr** variable (see Section 2.1."**constexpr** Variables" on page 302) can be accessed by compile-time constructs such as passing them as template arguments for further invocations of destroyLog.

The tests that follow decide whether the search continues for indices low (inclusive) through mid (exclusive), for indices mid+1 (inclusive) through high (exclusive), or not at all if the index has been found.

When recursing to the subranges below and above mid, care must be taken to ensure that destroyLog is invoked only for nonempty ranges. When the recursion would involve an instantiation of destroyLog that would have low >= high, we instead recurse to the same instantiation of destroyLog. We will never execute this infinite recursion at run time, and at compile time, the entire branch will likely be optimized away. Avoiding unneeded instantiations serves both to improve compilation time and to avoid instantiations that would not compile — e.g., the empty range at the end of the list of types, which would lead to attempting to use the invalid type NthType<**sizeof**...(Ts), Ts...>::type.

When the index has been found (i.e., n == mid), we finally have a compile-time constant matching the runtime index being searched. To fetch the type at index mid from parameter pack Ts, we use NthType, defined in *Tuples* on page 932. Once the type is extracted, the function is able to cast the **void*** pointer to the appropriate type and then invoke explicitly the correct destructor via that pointer.

The implementation of Variant's destructor that uses destroyLog is similar to the one using destroyLinear, with the difference being that it passes 0 and **sizeof**...(Ts) as additional arguments to prime the limits of the binary search:

```
#include <cassert>  // standard C assert macro

template <typename T, typename... Ts>
Variant<T, Ts...>::~Variant()  // logarithmic lookup destructor
{
    constexpr unsigned int variantCount = 1 + sizeof...(Ts);
    assert(d_active < variantCount);                        // invariant
    destroyLog<0, variantCount, T, Ts...>(d_active, &d_data);  // Initiate.
}
```

Although the time complexity of the runtime code is logarithmic, it is worth also looking at the number of *instantiations* created during the compilation of destroyLog. For a parameter pack Ts of length N, a distinct specialization of the destroyLog function itself is instantiated for every element of Ts. The instantiations of NthType<x, Ts...> for every x in the range between 0 and $N-1$ (inclusive), however, are the greater hidden cost. Each of these instantiations recursively refers to $x-1$ additional (distinct) instantiations of NthType, each with a smaller index and a shorter list. It follows that we have $O(N^2)$ instantiations of the NthType template, causing the compile time for destroyLog to increase quadratically with the number of types in the Variant; see also *Annoyances — Linear search for everything* on page 957.

Note that NthType, being just a template with a nested **typedef**, produces no code to be executed at run time; the size of the generated code is thus a function only of the number of distinct instantiations of destroyLog, which is $O(N)$. Despite the function template being instantiated recursively, the runtime code is not itself recursive — no instantiation will ever be re-invoked in a single call chain at run time, and thus the only theoretical recursion happens in dead branches. Aggressive inlining eliminates most of the individual instantiations, effectively resulting in a set of **if** statements having $O(\log N)$ nesting depth. As expected, contemporary compilers generate code virtually identical to a competently handwritten binary search.[21]

Of course, once we have a logarithmic implementation, we immediately wonder if we can do better, perhaps even a constant-time lookup. That brings us to an application of variadic templates in a braced initialization, as described in *Description — Expansion in a function call argument list or a braced-initializer list* on page 912. We use braced initialization to generate a table of function pointers, each pointing to a different instantiation of the same function template. For the table to work, each function must have the same signature. For the case of invoking a destructor, we will want to supply the object to be destroyed by using **void*** just like we did with destroyLinear and destroyLog. We can then write a function template taking a nondeduced type parameter to carry the necessary type information for the function implementation to cast the **void*** pointer to the necessary type:

```
template <typename T>
static void destroyElement(void* p)
{
    static_cast<T*>(p)->~T();
}
```

With this simple function template, we can populate a static array of function pointers by initializing an array of unknown bound (that will implicitly deduce the correct size) with a braced list produced by a **pack expansion**, taking the address of the destroyElement function

---

[21]The corresponding code has been tested with Clang 11.0.1 (c. 2021) and GCC 10.2 (c. 2020) at optimization level -O3.

template instantiated with the types in the pack. Once we have the array of destructor functions, matching the expected order of the runtime index d_active, we can simply invoke the function pointer at the current index to invoke the correct destructor for the currently active element:

```
template <typename... Ts>
void destroyCtTime(unsigned int n, void* p)   // same signature
{
    typedef void(*destructor)(void*);         // Simplify definition.
    static const destructor dt[] =            // array of function pointers
        { &destroyElement<Ts>... };           // Initialize with pack expansion.
    dt[n](p);                                 // Call appropriate destructor.
}
```

Note that this constant-time lookup is also the simplest of the three forms presented since it leans more heavily on integrating variadic **pack expansion** with other language features, in this case, braced array initialization.

It might appear that destroyCtTime is the best of the lot: It runs in constant time, it's small, it's simple, and it's easy to understand. However, upon a closer look, destroyCtTime has serious performance disadvantages. First, each destructor call entails an indirect call, which is notoriously difficult to inline and optimize except for the most trivial cases.[22]

Second, it is often the case that many types involved in a Variant have trivial destructors that do not perform any work at all. The functions destroyLinear and destroyLog have a white-box approach that naturally leads to the inlining and subsequent elimination of such destructors, leading to a massive simplification of the ultimately generated code. In contrast, destroyCtTime cannot take advantage of such opportunities; even if some destructors do no work, they will still be hidden beyond an indirect call, which is paid in all cases.

There is, however, a way to combine the advantages of destroyCtTime, destroyLinear, and destroyLog by using a meta-algorithmic strategy called **algorithm selection**[23]: Choose the appropriate algorithm depending on the Variant instantiation. The characteristics of instantiation can be inferred by using **compile-time introspection**. The criteria for selecting the best of three algorithms can be fairly complex. For instantiations with only a few types, most of which have trivial destructors, destroyLinear is likely to work best; for moderately large parameter pack sizes, destroyLog will be the algorithm of choice; finally, for large parameter pack sizes, destroyCtTime is best.

For a simple example, we can use the parameter pack size as a simple heuristic:

---

[22]GCC 11.2 (c. 2021) generates tables and indirect calls even for the most trivial uses. Clang 12.0.1 (c. 2021) is able to optimize away indirect calls for locally defined Variant objects only if the function has no control flow affecting Variant values. Both compilers were tested at optimization level -O3.

[23]**leyton-brown03**

```cpp
#include <cassert> // standard C assert macro

template <typename T, typename... Ts>  // definition for partial specialization
Variant<T, Ts...>::~Variant()          // improved destructor implementation
{
    constexpr unsigned int variantCount = 1 + sizeof...(Ts);

    assert(d_active < variantCount);  // Check invariant of variant.
    void* p = &d_data;                // d_data as void*

    if (variantCount <= 4)
        destroyLinear<0u, T, Ts...>(d_active, p);              // linear
    else if (variantCount <= 64)
        destroyLog<0u, variantCount, T, Ts...>(d_active, p);  // log
    else
        destroyCtTime<T, Ts...>(d_active, p);                 // O(1)
}
```

The constants 4 and 64 deciding the thresholds for choosing between algorithms are called **metaparameters** and are to be chosen experimentally. As mentioned, a more sophisticated implementation would eliminate from `Ts...` all types that have trivial destructors and focus on only the types that require destructor calls. Distinguishing between trivial and non-trivial destructors is possible with the help of the Standard Library introspection primitive `std::is_trivially_destructible` introduced in C++11.

Advanced traits

The use of **template template** parameters with variadic arguments allows us to create partial template specializations that match template instances with an arbitrary number of type parameters. This added flexibility allows the definition of traits that were not possible with prevariadics technology.

For example, consider the family of **smart pointer** templates. A smart pointer type is virtually always instantiated from a template having the pointed-to type as its first parameter:

```cpp
template <typename T>
struct SmartPtr1
{
    typedef T value_type;
    T& operator*() const;
    T* operator->() const;
    // ...
};
```

A more sophisticated smart pointer might take one or more additional template parameters, such as a deletion policy:

```
template <typename T, typename Deleter>
struct SmartPtr2
{
    T& operator*() const;
    T* operator->() const;
    // ...
};
```

SmartPtr2 still takes a value type as its first template parameter but also takes a Deleter functor for destroying the pointed-to object. (The Standard Library smart pointer std::unique_ptr added with C++11 also takes a deleter parameter.) Note that the author of SmartPtr2 did not add a nested value_type, yet the human reader can easily deduce that SmartPtr2's value type is T.

Now, we aim to define a traits class template that, given an arbitrary pointer-like type such as SmartPtr1<int> or SmartPtr2<double, MyDeleter>, can deduce the value type pointed to by the pointer (in our examples, uses int and double, respectively). Additionally, our traits class should allow us to "rebind" the pointer-like type, yielding a new pointer-like type with a different value type. Such an operation is useful, for example, when we want to use the same smart pointer facility as another library but rebound our own types.

Suppose, for example, a library defines a type Widget:

```
class Widget            // third-party class definition
{ /*...*/ };
```

Furthermore, the same library defines type WidgetPtr that behaves like a pointer to a Widget type but could be (depending on the library version, debug versus release builds, and so on) either SmartPtr1 or SmartPtr2:

```
class FastDeleter      // policy for performing minimal checking on SmartPtr2
{ /*...*/ };

class CheckedDeleter   // policy for performing maximal checking on SmartPtr2
{ /*...*/ };

#if !defined(DBG_LEVEL)
typedef SmartPtr1<Widget>                  WidgetPtr;  // release mode, fastest
#elif DBG_LEVEL >= 2
typedef SmartPtr2<Widget, CheckedDeleter> WidgetPtr;  // debug mode, safest
#else
typedef SmartPtr2<Widget, FastDeleter>    WidgetPtr;  // safety/speed compromise
#endif
```

In debug mode (DBG_LEVEL defined), the library uses a SmartPtr2 smart pointer that does additional checking around, for example, dereference and deallocation. There are two possible debugging levels, one with stringent checks and one that cuts a trade-off between safety and speed. In release mode, the library wants to run at full speed, so it uses SmartPtr1.

User code simply uses `WidgetPtr` transparently because the interfaces of the types are similar.

On the client side, we'd like to define a `GadgetPtr` type that behaves like a pointer to our own type `Gadget` but automatically adjusts to use the same smart pointer underpinnings, if any, that `WidgetPtr` is using. However, we don't have control over `DBG_LEVEL` or over the code introducing `WidgetPtr`. The strategies used by the definition of `WidgetPtr` might change across releases. How can we robustly figure out what kind of pointer — smart or not — `WidgetPtr` is representing?

Let's begin by declaring a primary class template with no body and then specializing it for native pointer types:

```
template <typename Ptr>
struct PointerTraits;      // incomplete declaration

template <typename T>
struct PointerTraits<T*>   // partial specialization for all raw pointers
{
    typedef T value_type; // normalized alias for T
    template <typename U>
    using rebind = U*;    // rebind<U> is an alias for U*.
};
```

The new **using** syntax has been introduced in C++11 as a generalized **typedef**; see Section 1.1."**using** Aliases" on page 133. `PointerTraits` provides a basic traits API. For any built-in pointer type, P, `PointerTraits<P>::value_type` resolves to whatever type P points to. Moreover, for some other type, X, `PointerTraits<P>::rebind<X>` is an alias for X*; i.e., it propagates the information that P is a built-in pointer to X:

```
#include <type_traits>  // std::is_same

static_assert(std::is_same<int, PointerTraits<int*>::value_type>::value, "");
static_assert(std::is_same<double*,
                      PointerTraits<int*>::rebind<double>>::value, "");
```

`PointerTraits` has a nested type, `value_type`, and a nested alias template, `rebind`. The first **static_assert** shows that, when Ptr is **int***, value_type is **int**. The second **static_assert** shows that, when Ptr is **int***, rebind<**double**> is **double***. In other words, `PointerTraits` can determine the pointed-to type for a raw pointer and provides a facility for generating a raw pointer type pointing to a *different* value type.

For now, however, `PointerTraits` is not defined for any type that is not a built-in pointer. For `PointerTraits` to work with an arbitrary smart pointer class (such as `SmartPtr1` and `SmartPtr2` above but also `std::shared_ptr`, `std::unique_ptr`, and `std::weak_ptr`), we must partially specialize it for a template instantiation, `PtrLike<T, X...>`, where T is assumed to be the value type and X... is a parameter pack of zero or more additional type parameters to PtrLike:

```cpp
template <
    template <typename, typename...> class PtrLike,
    typename T, typename... X>
struct PointerTraits<PtrLike<T, X...>>     // partial specialization for template
{
    using value_type = T;                  // Extract pointee type.
    template <typename U>
    using rebind = PtrLike<U, X...>;        // Rebind to some other type U.
};
```

This partial specialization will produce the correct result for any pointer-like class template that takes one or more type template parameters, where the first parameter is the value type of the pointer. First, it correctly deduces the value_type from the first argument to the template:

```cpp
typedef SmartPtr2<Widget, CheckedDeleter>  WP1;  // fully checked
typedef SmartPtr2<Widget, FastDeleter>     WP2;  // minimally checked

static_assert(std::is_same<
    PointerTraits<WP1>::value_type,   // Fetch the pointee type of WP1.
    Widget>::value, "");              // should be Widget

static_assert(std::is_same<
    PointerTraits<WP2>::value_type,   // Fetch the pointee type of WP2.
    Widget>::value, "");              // should also be Widget
```

Second, rebind is able to reinstantiate the original template, SmartPtr2, replacing T with a different type but retaining Deleter unchanged:

```cpp
class Gadget { /*...*/ };

static_assert(std::is_same<
    PointerTraits<WP1>::rebind<Gadget>,    // Rebind WP1 to Gadget.
    SmartPtr2<Gadget, CheckedDeleter>>     // fully checked, just like WP1
::value, "");

static_assert(std::is_same<
    PointerTraits<WP2>::rebind<Gadget>,    // Rebind WP2 to Gadget.
    SmartPtr2<Gadget, FastDeleter>>        // minimally checked, like WP2
::value, "");
```

The Standard Library facility std::pointer_traits, introduced with C++11, is a superset of our PointerTraits example.

Potential Pitfalls

Accidental use of C-style ellipsis

Inside the function parameters declaration, ... can be used only in conjunction with a template parameter pack. However, there is an ancient use of ... in conjunction with C-style variadic functions such as `printf`. That use can cause confusion. Say we set out to declare a simple variadic function, `process`, that takes any number of arguments by pointer:

```cpp
class Widget;                      // declaration of some user-defined type

template <typename... Widgets>  // parameter pack named Widgets
int process(Widget*...);        // meant as a pack expansion, but is it?
```

The author meant to declare `process` as a variadic function taking any number of pointers to objects. However, instead of `Widgets*...`, the author mistakenly typed `Widget*...` (note the missing "s"). This typo took the declaration into a completely different place: It is now a C-style variadic function in the same category as `printf`. Recall the `printf` declaration in the C Standard Library:

```cpp
int printf(const char* format, ...);
```

The comma and the parameter name are optional in C and C++, so omitting both leads to an equivalent declaration:

```cpp
int printf(const char*...);
```

Comparing `process` (with the typo in tow) with `printf` makes it clear that `process` is a C-style variadic function. Runtime errors of any consequence are quite rare because the expansion mechanisms are different across the two kinds of variadics. However, the compile- and link-time diagnostics can be puzzling. In addition, if the variadic function ignores the arguments passed to it, calling it might even compile, but the call will likely use a different calling convention than what was intended or assumed.

As an anecdote, a similar situation occurred during the review stage of this feature section. A simple misunderstanding caused a function to be declared inadvertently as a C-style variadic instead of C++ variadic template, leading to numerous indecipherable compile-time and link-time errors in testing that took many emails to figure out.

Undiagnosed errors

Description — Corner cases of function template argument matching on page 900 shows definitions of variadic template functions that are in error according to the C++ Standard yet pass compilation on contemporary compilers — that is, IFNDR. In certain cases, they can even be called. Such situations are most assuredly latent bugs:

```
template <typename... Ts, typename... Us, typename T>
int process(Ts..., Us..., T);
    // Ill-formed declaration: Us must be empty in every possible call.
int x = process<int, double>(1, 2.5, 3);
    // Ts=<int, double>, Us=<>, T=int
```

In virtually all cases, such code reflects a misplaced expectation; an always-empty parameter pack has no reason to exist in the first place.

Compiler limits on the number of arguments

The C++ Standard recommends that compilers support at least 1,024 arguments in a variadic template instantiation. Although this limit seems generous, real-world code might bump up against it, especially in conjunction with generated code or combinatorial uses.

This limit might lead to a lack of portability in production — for example, code that works with one compiler but fails with another. Suppose, for example, we define `Variant` that carries all possible types that can be serialized in a large application:

```
typedef Variant<
    char,
    signed char,
    unsigned char,
    short,
    unsigned short
    // ...                    (more built-in and user-defined types)
>
WireData;
```

We release this code to production and then, at some later date, clients find it fails to build on some platforms, leading to a need to reengineer the entire solution to provide full cross-platform support.

Annoyances

Unusable functions

Before variadics, any properly defined template function could be called by using explicit template argument specification, type deduction, or a combination thereof. Now it is possible to define variadic function templates that pass compilation but are impossible to call (either by using explicit instantiation, argument deduction, or both). Such unusable functions could cause confusion and frustration. Consider, for example, a few function templates, none of which take any function parameters:

```
template <typename T>              // template with one parameter
int f1();

template <typename T, typename U>  // template with two parameters
int f2();

template <typename... Ts>          // template with parameter pack
int f3();

template <typename T, typename... Ts>  // parameter pack at the end
int f4();

template <typename... Ts, typename T>  // pack followed by type parameter
int f5();
```

The first four functions can be called by explicitly specifying their template arguments:

```
int a1 = f1<int>();              // T=int
int a2 = f2<int, long>();        // T=int, U=long
int a3 = f3<char, int, long>();  // Ts=<char, int, long>
int a4 = f4<char, int, long>();  // T=char, Ts=<int, long>
```

However, there is no way to call f5 because there is no way to specify T:

```
int a5a = f5();            // Error, cannot infer type argument for T
int a5b = f5<int>();       // Error, cannot infer type argument for T
int a5c = f5<int, long>(); // Error, cannot infer type argument for T
```

Recall that by the Rule of Greedy Matching (see *Description — The Rule of Greedy Matching* on page 896), Ts will match all of the template arguments passed to f5, so T is starved. Such uncallable functions are IFNDR. There are several other variations that render variadic function templates uncallable and therefore IFNDR. Note that most contemporary compilers do allow compilation of f5.[24]

Limitations on expansion contexts

As discussed in *Description — Pack expansion* on page 908 and in the sections that follow it, expansion contexts are prescriptive. The standard enumerates all expansion contexts exhaustively: There is no other place in a C++ program where a parameter pack is allowed to occur, even if it seems syntactically and semantically correct.

For example, consider a variadic function template, bump1, that attempts to expand and increment each of the arguments in its parameter pack:

---

[24]The corresponding code has been tested with Clang 12.0.1 (c. 2021) and GCC 11.2 (c. 2021).

```
template <typename... Ts>
void bump1(Ts&... vs)   // some variadic function template
{
    ++vs...;            // Error, can't expand parameter pack at statement level
}
```

Attempting to expand a parameter pack at the statement level is simply not among the allowed expansion contexts; hence, the example function body above fails to compile.

Such limitations can be worked around by artificially creating an expansion context. For example, we can achieve our goal by replacing the erroneous line in bump1 (above) with one in bump2 (below) that, say, creates a local class with a constructor that takes Ts&... as parameters:

```
template <typename... Ts>
void bump2(Ts&... vs)
{
    struct Local            // local struct
    {
        Local(Ts&...) {}    // constructor takes each of Ts by reference
    }                       // no semicolon here, will create an object
    local(++vs...);         // OK, expansion allowed in constructor call
}
```

The code above creates a local **struct** called Local with a constructor and immediately constructs an object of that type called local. Expansion is allowed inside the argument list for the constructor call, which makes the code work.

A possibility to achieve the same effect with terser code is to create a lambda expression, [](Ts&...){}, and then immediately call it with the expansion ++vs... as its arguments:

```
template <typename... Ts>
void bump3(Ts&... vs)                // some variadic function template
{
    ([](Ts&...){})(++vs...);  // OK, pack expansion allowed in lambda call
}
```

The function above works, albeit awkwardly, by making use of another feature of C++11 that essentially allows us to define an anonymous function *in situ* and then invoke it; see Section 2.1."Lambdas" on page 573.[25] The other popular expansion context for evaluating and discarding a variadic expression expansion is using the expansion to initialize an std::initializer_list; see Section 2.1."initializer_list" on page 553.

---

[25]C++17 adds *fold expressions* that allow easy pack expansion at the expression and statement level. The semantics desired for the example shown would be achieved with a fold over the comma operator, using the syntax (... , ++vs);.

Parameter packs cannot be used unexpanded

As discussed in *Description — Pack expansion* on page 908, the name of a parameter pack cannot appear on its own in a correct C++ program; the only way to use a parameter pack is as part of an expansion by using `...` or **sizeof**. Such behavior is unlike types, template names, or values.

It is impossible to pass parameter packs around or to give them alternative names (as is possible with types by means of **typedef** and **using** and with values by means of references). Consequently, it is also impossible to define them as "return" values for metafunctions following conventions such as `::type` and `::value` that are commonly used in the `<type_traits>` standard header.

Consider, for example, sorting a type parameter pack by size. This simple task is not possible without a few helper types because there is no way to return the sorted pack. One necessary helper would be a typelist:

```
template <typename...> struct Typelist { };
```

With this helper type in hand, it is possible to encapsulate parameter packs, give them alternate names, and so on — in short, give parameter packs the same maneuverability that C++ types have:

```
typedef Typelist<short, int, long, float, double, long double> Numbers;
    // can be used to give a pack an alternate name

template <typename L>
struct SortBySize
{
    using type = Typelist< /*...*/ >;  // computed sorted-by-size version of
                                       // the Typelist L
};

typedef SortBySize<Numbers>::type SortedNumbers;
    // can be used to "return" a pack from a metafunction
```

Currently no `Typelist` facility has been standardized. An active proposal[26] introduces `parameter_pack` along the same lines as `Typelist` above. Meanwhile, compiler vendors have attempted to work around the problem in nonstandard ways.[27] A related proposal[28] defines `std::bases` and `std::direct_bases` but has, at the time of writing, been rejected.

---

[26]**spertus13**

[27]GNU defines the nonstandard primitives `std::tr2::__direct_bases` and `std::tr2::__bases`. The first yields a list of all direct bases of a given class, and the second yields the transitive closure of all bases of a class, including the indirect ones. To make these artifacts possible, GNU defines and uses a helper `__reflection_typelist` class template similar to `Typelist` above.

[28]**spertus09**

Expansion is rigid and requires verbose support code

There are only two syntactic constructs that apply to parameter packs: **sizeof...** and expansion via .... The latter underlies virtually all treatment of variadics and, as discussed, requires handwritten support classes or functions as scaffolding toward building a somewhat involved recursion-based pattern.

There is no expansion in an expression context, so it is not possible to write functions such as print in a concise, single-definition manner; see *Use Cases — Generic variadic functions* on page 925. In particular, expressions are not expansion contexts, so the following code will not work:

```cpp
#include <iostream>  // std::cout, std::ostream, std::endl

template <typename... Ts>
std::ostream& print(const Ts&... vs)
{
    std::cout << vs...;              // Error, invalid expansion
    return std::cout << std::endl;
}
```

Linear search for everything

One common issue with parameter packs is the difficulty of accessing elements in an indexed manner. Getting to the nth element of a pack is a linear search operation by necessity, which makes certain uses awkward and potentially time-consuming during compilation. Refer to the implementation of destroyLog in *Use Cases — Variant types* on page 937 as an example.

See Also

- "Braced Init" (§2.1, p. 215) illustrates one of the expansion contexts for function parameter packs.

- "Forwarding References" (§2.1, p. 377) describes a feature used in conjunction with **variadic function templates** to achieve **perfect forwarding**.

- "Lambdas" (§2.1, p. 573) introduces a feature that supports **pack expansion** in its capture list.

Further Reading

- "F.21: To return multiple 'out' values, prefer returning a struct or tuple," **stroustrup21**
- **vandevoorde18**

Relaxed Restrictions on constexpr Functions

C++14 lifts restrictions regarding the use of many language features in the body of a **constexpr** function (see Section 2.1."**constexpr** Functions" on page 257).

Description

The cautious introduction (in C++11) of **constexpr** functions — i.e., functions eligible for compile-time evaluation — was accompanied by a set of strict rules that made life easier for compiler implementers but severely narrowed the breadth of valid use cases for the feature. In C++11, **constexpr** function bodies were restricted to essentially a single **return** statement and were not permitted to have any modifiable local state (variables) or **imperative** language constructs (e.g., assignment), thereby reducing their usefulness:

```cpp
constexpr int fact11(int x)
{
    static_assert(x >= 0, "");  // Error, x is not a constant expression.
    static_assert(sizeof(x) >= 4, "");     // OK in C++11/14
    return x < 2 ? 1 : x * fact11(x - 1);  // OK in C++11/14
}
```

Notice that recursive calls were supported, often leading to convoluted implementations of algorithms compared to an **imperative** equivalent; see *Use Cases — Nonrecursive **constexpr** algorithms* on page 961.

The C++11 **static_assert** feature (see Section 1.1."**static_assert**" on page 115) was permitted in a C++11 **constexpr** function body. However, because the input variable x in fact11 above is inherently not a compile-time constant expression, it can never appear as part of a **static_assert** predicate. Note that a **constexpr** function returning **void** was also not permitted:

```cpp
constexpr void no_op() { }  // Error in C++11; OK in C++14
```

Experience gained from the release and subsequent real-world use of C++11 emboldened the Standards Committee to lift most of these restrictions for C++14, allowing the use of a large subset of C++ language constructs in the body of a **constexpr** function. In C++14, familiar control-flow statements, such as **if** and **while**, are also available, as are modifiable local variables and assignment operations:

```cpp
constexpr int fact14(int x)
{
    if (x <= 2)          // Error in C++11; OK in C++14
    {
        return 1;
    }
```

```
    int temp = x - 1;  // Error in C++11; OK in C++14
    return x * fact14(temp);
}
```

Some useful features remain disallowed in C++14 **constexpr** function bodies even if control flow does not reach them during compile-time evaluation.[1]

1. **asm** declarations

2. **goto** statements

3. Statements with labels other than **case** and **default**

4. **try** blocks

5. Definitions of variables

    (a) of other than a **literal type** (i.e., fully evaluable at compile time)
    (b) decorated with either **static** or **thread_local**
    (c) left uninitialized

The restrictions on what can appear in the body of a **constexpr** function that remain in C++14 are reiterated here in codified form. Note that the manner in which these remaining forbidden features are reported varies substantially from one compiler to the next:

```
#include <fstream>  // std::ifstream

template <typename T>
constexpr void f()
try {                    // Error, try outside body isn't allowed (until C++20).
    std::ifstream is;    // Error, objects of nonliteral types aren't allowed.
    int x;               // Error, uninitialized vars. disallowed (until C++20)
    static int y = 0;    // Error, static variables are disallowed.
    thread_local T t;    // Error, thread_local variables are disallowed.
    try{}catch(...){}    // Error, try/catch disallowed (until C++20)
    goto here;           // Error, goto statements are disallowed.
here: ;                  // Error, labels (except case/default) aren't allowed.
    asm("mov %r0");      // Error, asm directives are disallowed (until C++20).
} catch(...) { }         // Error, try outside body disallowed (until C++20)
```

---

[1]In C++20, even more restrictions were lifted — both on what is allowed to appear in the function body and on what can be a part of **constant expression** (i.e., what can be evaluated at compile time). For example, some limited forms of dynamic allocation are permitted as part of **constant expressions**, which, in combination with corresponding modifications to the Standard Library, allows compile-time use of container types, such as std::string and std::vector.

Use Cases

Nonrecursive constexpr algorithms

The C++11 restrictions on **constexpr** functions often forced programmers to implement naturally iterative algorithms in a recursive manner. Consider, as a familiar example, a naive C++11-compliant implementation of a **constexpr** function, `fib11`, returning the nth Fibonacci number:

```
constexpr long long fib11(long long x)
{
    return
        x == 0 ? 0
            : (x == 1 || x == 2) ? 1
                            : fib11(x - 1) + fib11(x - 2);
}
```

For a more efficient (yet less intuitive) C++11 algorithm, see *Recursive Fibonacci* in *Appendix — Optimized C++11 example algorithms* on page 965.

We used **long long** (instead of **long**) here to ensure a unique C++ type having at least 8 bytes on all conforming platforms for simplicity of exposition. We deliberately chose *not* to make the value returned **unsigned** because the extra bit does not justify changing the **algebra** (from **signed** to **unsigned**). For more discussion on these specific topics, see Section 1.1."**long long**" on page 89.

The implementation of the `fib11` function (above) has several undesirable properties.

1. **Reading difficulty** — Because it was implemented using a single **return** statement, branching requires a chain of *ternary operators*, leading to a single long expression that might impede human comprehension. This particular example can be written more concisely:

   ```
   constexpr long long fib11(long long x)
   {
       return x <= 1 ? x : fib11(x - 1) + fib11(x - 2);
   }
   ```

   However, not all such recurrence relations admit such simplification, and in any event, such cosmetic modifications have no effect on efficiency.

2. **Inefficiency and poor scaling** — The explosion of recursive calls is taxing on compilers: (1) the time to compile is markedly longer for the *recursive* C++11 algorithm than it would be for its *iterative* C++14 counterpart, even for modest inputs,[2] and (2)

---

[2]As an example, Clang 12.0.1 (c. 2021), running on an x86-64 machine, required more than 80 times longer to evaluate `fib(27)` implemented using the *recursive* (C++11) algorithm than to evaluate the same functionality implemented using the *iterative* (C++14) algorithm.

the compiler might simply refuse to complete the compile-time calculation if it exceeds some internal (platform-dependent) *threshold* for the allowed number of operations.[3]

3. **Redundancy** — Even if the recursive implementation were suitable for small input values during compile-time evaluation, it would be unlikely to be suitable for any run-time evaluation, thereby requiring programmers to provide and maintain *two* separate versions of the same algorithm: a compile-time *recursive* one and a runtime *iterative* one.

In contrast, an *imperative* implementation of a **constexpr** function returning the nth Fibonacci number in C++14, **fib14**, does not have any of the deficiencies discussed above:

```
constexpr long long fib14(long long x)
{
    if (x == 0) { return 0; }

    long long a = 0;
    long long b = 1;

    for (long long i = 2; i <= x; ++i)
    {
        long long temp = a + b;
        a = b;
        b = temp;
    }

    return b;
}
```

As one would expect, the compile time required to evaluate the iterative implementation above is manageable[4]; of course, far more computationally efficient — e.g., closed form[5] — solutions to this classic exercise are available.

---

[3] As an example, Clang 12.0.1 (c. 2021), running on an x86-64 machine, fails to compile **fib11(28)**:

```
error: static_assert expression is not an integral constant expression
    static_assert(fib11(28) == 317811, "");
                  ^~~~~~~~~~~~~~~~~~~~
```

note: constexpr evaluation hit maximum step limit; possible infinite loop?

GCC 11.2 (c. 2021) fails at **fib(36)**, with a similar diagnostic:

```
error: 'constexpr' evaluation operation count exceeds limit of 33554432
       (use '-fconstexpr-ops-limit=' to increase the limit)
```

Clang 12.0.1 (c. 2021) fails to compile any attempt at constant evaluation of **fib11(28)**, with the following diagnostic message:

note: constexpr evaluation hit maximum step limit; possible infinite loop?

[4] Both GCC 11.2 (c. 2021) and Clang 12.0.1 (c. 2021) evaluated **fib14(46)** correctly in less than 20ms on a machine running Windows 10 x64 and equipped with an Intel Core i7-9700k CPU.

[5] E.g., see http://mathonline.wikidot.com/a-closed-form-of-the-fibonacci-sequence.

Optimized metaprogramming algorithms

C++14's relaxed **constexpr** restrictions enable the use of modifiable local variables and imperative language constructs for metaprogramming tasks that were historically often implemented by using Byzantine recursive template instantiations, notorious for their voracious consumption of compilation time.

Consider, as a simple example, the task of counting the number of occurrences of a given type inside a **type list** represented here as a variadic template (see Section 2.1. "Variadic Templates" on page 873) that can be instantiated using a variable-length sequence of arbitrary C++ types:

```cpp
template <typename...> struct TypeList { };
    // empty variadic template instantiable with arbitrary C++ type sequence
```

Explicit instantiations of this variadic template could be used to create objects:

```cpp
TypeList<>                  emptyList;
TypeList<int>               listOfOneInt;
TypeList<int, long, double> listOfThreeIntLongDouble;
```

A naive C++11-compliant implementation of a **metafunction** Count, used to ascertain the number of times a given C++ type was used when creating an instance of the TypeList template (above), would usually make recursive use of involved **partial class template specialization** to satisfy the single-return-statement requirements:

```cpp
#include <type_traits> // std::integral_constant, std::is_same

template <typename X, typename List> struct Count;
    // general template used to characterize the interface for the Count
    // metafunction

    // Note that this general template is an incomplete type.

template <typename X>
struct Count<X, TypeList<>> : std::integral_constant<int, 0> { };
    // partial class template specialization of the general Count template
    // (derived from the integral-constant type representing a compile-time
    // 0), used to represent the base case for the recursion --- i.e., when
    // the supplied TypeList is empty

    // The payload (i.e., the enumerated value member of the base class)
    // representing the number of elements of type X in the list is 0.

template <typename X, typename Head, typename... Tail>
struct Count<X, TypeList<Head, Tail...>>
    : std::integral_constant<int,
        std::is_same<X, Head>::value + Count<X, TypeList<Tail...>>::value> { };
    // partial class template specialization of the general Count template
    // for when the supplied list is not empty
```

```
// In this case, the second argument will be partitioned as the first
// type in the sequence and the possibly empty remainder of the
// TypeList. The compile-time value of the base class will be either the
// same as or one greater than the value accumulated in the TypeList so
// far, depending on whether the first element is the same as the one
// supplied as the first type to Count.
```

```
static_assert(Count<int, TypeList<int, char, int, bool>>::value == 2, "");
```

Notice that we made use of a C++11 **parameter pack**, Tail... (see Section 2.1. "Variadic Templates" on page 873), in the implementation of the simple template specialization to package up and pass along any remaining types.

The C++11 restrictions encourage both somewhat rarefied metaprogramming-related knowledge and a *recursive* implementation that can be compile-time intensive in practice. For a more efficient C++11 version of Count, see ***constexpr*** *type list Count algorithm* in *Appendix — Optimized C++11 example algorithms* on page 966. By exploiting C++14's relaxed **constexpr** rules, a simpler and typically more compile-time friendly *imperative* solution can be realized:

```cpp
template <typename X, typename... Ts>
constexpr int count()
{
    bool matches[sizeof...(Ts)] = { std::is_same<X, Ts>::value... };
        // Create a corresponding array of bits where 1 indicates sameness.

    int result = 0;
    for (bool m : matches)  // (C++11) range-based for loop
    {
        result += m;        // Add up 1 bits in the array.
    }

    return result;  // Return the accumulated number of matches.
}
```

The implementation above — though more efficient and comprehensible — will require some initial learning for those unfamiliar with C++ variadic templates. The general idea here is to use **pack expansion** in a nonrecursive manner (see Section 2.1. "Variadic Templates" on page 873) to initialize the matches array with a sequence of zeros and ones (representing, respectively, mismatches and matches between X and a type in the Ts... pack) and then iterate over the array to accumulate the number of ones as the final result. This **constexpr**-based solution is both easier to understand and typically faster to compile.[6]

---

[6]For a type list containing 1,024 types, the imperative (C++14) solution compiles about twice as fast on GCC 11.2 (c. 2021) and roughly 2.6 times faster on Clang 12.0.1 (c. 2021).

See Also

- "**constexpr** Functions" (§2.1, p. 257) describes fundamentals of compile-time function evaluation.

- "**constexpr** Variables" (§2.1, p. 302) introduces variables usable as constant expressions.

- "Variadic Templates" (§2.1, p. 873) introduces a feature that allows templates to accept an arbitrary number of template arguments.

Further Reading

- Scott Meyers advocates for aggressive use of `constexpr` in **meyers15b**, "Item 15: Use constexpr whenever possible," pp. 97–103.

Appendix

Optimized C++11 example algorithms

Recursive Fibonacci Even with the restrictions imposed by C++11, we can write a more efficient recursive algorithm to calculate the nth Fibonacci number:

```cpp
#include <utility>  // std::pair

constexpr std::pair<long long, long long> fib11NextFibs(
    const std::pair<long long, long long> prev,  // last two calculations
    int count)                                   // remaining steps
{
    return (count == 0) ? prev : fib11NextFibs(
        std::pair<long long, long long>(prev.second,
                                        prev.first + prev.second),
        count - 1);
}
```

```
constexpr long long fib11Optimized(long long n)
{
    return fib11NextFibs(
        std::pair<long long, long long>(0, 1), // first two numbers
        n                                      // number of steps
    ).second;
}
```

constexpr type list Count algorithm   As with the `fib11Optimized` example, providing a more efficient version of the `Count` algorithm in C++11 is also possible, by accumulating the final result through recursive **constexpr** function invocations:

```
#include <type_traits>  // std::is_same

template <typename>
constexpr int count11Optimized() { return 0; }
    // Base case: always return 0.

template <typename X, typename Head, typename... Tail>
constexpr int count11Optimized()
    // Recursive case: compare the desired type (X) and the first type in
    // the list (Head) for equality, turn the result of the comparison
    // into either 1 (equal) or 0 (not equal), and recurse with the rest
    // of the type list (Tail...).
{
    return std::is_same<X, Head>::value + count11Optimized<X, Tail...>();
}
```

This algorithm can be optimized even further in C++11 by using a technique similar to the one shown for the iterative C++14 implementation. By leveraging an `std::array` as compile-time storage for bits where 1 indicates equality between types, we can compute the final result with a fixed number of template instantiations:

```
#include <array>        // std::array
#include <type_traits>  // std::is_same

template <int N>
constexpr int count11VeryOptimizedImpl(
    const std::array<bool, N>& bits,  // storage for "type sameness" bits
    int i)                            // current array index
{
    return i < N
        ? bits[i] + count11VeryOptimizedImpl<N>(bits, i + 1)
            // Recursively read every element from the bits array and
            // accumulate into a final result.
        : 0;
}
```

```
template <typename X, typename... Ts>
constexpr int count11VeryOptimized()
{
    return count11VeryOptimizedImpl<sizeof...(Ts)>(
        std::array<bool, sizeof...(Ts)>{ std::is_same<X, Ts>::value... },
            // Leverage pack expansion to avoid recursive instantiations.
        0);
}
```

Note that, despite being recursive, `count11VeryOptimizedImpl` will be instantiated only once with `N` equal to the number of elements in the `Ts...` pack. Recursion is used only to tally the results from that array.

Lambdas Having a Templated Call Operator

C++14 extends the **lambda expression** syntax of C++11 to allow a *templated* definition of the function call operator belonging to the **closure type**.

Description

Generic lambdas are a C++14 extension of C++11 lambda expressions (see Section 2.1. "Lambdas" on page 573) for which the function call operator is a member function template, which enables the deduction of template argument types at the point of invocation.

Consider two **lambda expressions**, each of which simply returns its argument:

```
auto identityInt = [](int  a) { return a; };  // nongeneric lambda
auto identity =    [](auto a) { return a; };  // generic lambda
```

Generic lambdas are characterized by the presence of one or more **auto** parameters, accepting arguments of any type. In the example above, the first version is a nongeneric lambda having a parameter of concrete type **int**. The second version is a **generic lambda** because its parameter uses the placeholder type **auto**. Unlike `identityInt`, which is callable only for arguments implicitly convertible to **int**, `identity` can be applied to any type that can be passed by value:

```
int        a1 = identityInt(42);    // OK, a1 == 42
double     a2 = identityInt(3.14);  // Bug, a2 == 3, truncation warning
const char* a3 = identityInt("hi"); // Error, cannot pass "hi" as int
int        a4 = identity(42);       // OK, a4 == 42
double     a5 = identity(3.14);     // OK, a5 == 3.14
const char* a6 = identity("hi");    // OK, strcmp(a6, "hi") == 0
```

Generic lambdas accomplish this compile-time polymorphism by defining their function call operator — **operator()** — as a *template*. Recall that the result of a **lambda expression** is a **closure object**, an object of unique type having a function call operator; i.e., the **closure type** is a unique **functor** class. The parameters defined in the **lambda expression** become the parameters to the function call operator. The following code transformation is roughly equivalent to the definitions of the `identityInt` and `identity` closure objects from the example above:

```
struct __lambda_1 // compiler-generated name; not visible to the user
{
    int operator()(int x) const { return x; }
    // ...
};
```

```
struct __lambda_2  // compiler-generated name; not visible to the user
{
    template <typename __T>
    __T operator()(__T x) const { return x; }
    // ...
};

__lambda_1 identityInt = __lambda_1();
__lambda_2 identity    = __lambda_2();
```

Note that the names __lambda_1, __lambda_2, and __T are for descriptive purpose and are not available to the user; the compiler might choose any name or no name for these entities.

A generic lambda is any lambda expression having one or more parameters declared using the placeholder type **auto**. The compiler generates a template parameter type for each **auto** parameter in the generic lambda, and that type is substituted for **auto** in the function-call operator's parameter list. In the identity example above, **auto** x is replaced with __T x, where __T is a new template parameter type. When user code subsequently calls, e.g., identity(42), normal template type deduction takes place, and **operator()<int>** is instantiated.

Lambda capture and mutable closures

The closure type produced by a generic lambda is not a class template. Rather, its function call operator and its conversion-to-function-pointer operator (as we'll see later in *Conversion to a pointer to function* on page 974) are function templates. In particular, the **lambda capture**, which creates member variables within the closure type, has the same syntax and semantics for all lambda expressions, generic or not. Similarly, the **mutable** qualifier has the same effect for generic lambdas as for nongeneric lambdas:

```
#include <algorithm>  // std::for_each
#include <iterator>   // std::next

template <typename FwdIter>
auto secondBiggest(FwdIter begin, FwdIter end)
    // Return the second-largest element in the range [begin, end),
    // assuming at least two elements and that all values in the range
    // are distinct.
{
    auto second = std::next(begin);  // Refer to second element.
    auto ret = *second;              // Set to second element.
    std::for_each(second, end,
        [biggest = *begin, &ret](const auto& element) mutable
        {
            if (biggest <= element) {
```

```
                    ret = biggest;
                    biggest = element;
                }
                else if (ret < element) {
                    ret = element;
                }
            });

        return ret;
    }
```

The declarations of second and ret use the placeholder **auto** (see Section 2.1."**auto** Variables" on page 195) to deduce the variables' types from their respective initializers. The return type of secondBiggest is also declared **auto** and is deduced from the type of ret (see Section 3.2. "**auto** Return" on page 1182). The generic lambda being passed to std::for_each uses the C++14 init-capture (see Section 2.2."Lambda Captures" on page 986) to initialize biggest to the largest value known so far. Because the lambda is declared **mutable**, it can update biggest each time a larger element is encountered. The ret variable is also captured — by reference — and is updated with the previous biggest value when a new biggest value is encountered. Note that, at the point where ret appears in the lambda capture, its type has already been deduced. When for_each invokes the function call operator, the type of the **auto** parameter, element, is conveniently deduced to be the element type for the input range and is thus the same reference type as ret except with an added **const** qualifier.

Constraints on deduced parameters

A generic lambda can accept any mix of **auto** and non**auto** parameters:

```
void g1()
{
    auto y1 = [](auto& a, int b, auto c) { a += b * c; };

    int    i = 5;
    double d = 1;

    y1(i, 2, 2);    // i is now 9.
    y1(d, 3, 0.5);  // d is now 2.5.
}
```

If the **auto** placeholder in a generic lambda parameter is part of a type declaration that forms a potentially cv-qualified reference, pointer, pointer-to-member, pointer-to-function, or reference-to-function type, then the allowable arguments will be restricted accordingly:

```
struct C1 { double d_i; };
double f1(int i);
```

```
auto y1 = [](const auto& r) { };    // Match anything (read only).
auto y2 = [](auto&& r)      { };    // Match anything (forwarding reference).
auto y3 = [](auto& r)       { };    // Match only lvalues.
auto y4 = [](auto* p)       { };    // Match only pointers.
auto y5 = [](auto(*p)(int)) { };    // Match only pointers to functions.
auto y6 = [](auto C1::* pm) { };    // Match only pointers to data members of C1.

void g2()
{
    int     i1 = 0;
    const int i2 = 1;

    y1(i1);        // OK, r has type const int&.
    y2(i1);        // OK, r has type int&.

    y3(5);         // Error, argument is not an lvalue.
    y3(i1);        // OK, r has type int&.
    y3(i2);        // OK, r has type const int&.

    y4(i2);        // Error, i2 is not a pointer.
    y4(&i2);       // OK, p has type const int*.

    y5(&f1);       // OK, p has type double (*)(int).

    y6(&C1::d_i);  // OK, pm has type double C1::*.
}
```

To understand how y1 and y2 match any argument type, recall that **auto** is a placeholder for a template type argument, say, __T. As usual, **const** __T& r can bind to a **const** or non**const** *lvalue* or a temporary value created from an *rvalue*. The argument __T&& r is a **forwarding reference** (see Section 2.1."Forwarding References" on page 377); __T will be deduced to an *rvalue* if the argument to y2 is an *rvalue* and to an *lvalue* reference otherwise. Because the parameter type for r is unnamed — we invented the name __T for descriptive purposes only — we must use **decltype**(r) to refer to the type of r:

```
#include <utility>  // std::move, std::forward
#include <cassert>  // standard C assert macro

struct C2
{
    int d_value;

    explicit C2(int i)     : d_value(i)                { }
    C2(const C2& original) : d_value(original.d_value) { }
    C2(C2&& other)         : d_value(other.d_value)    { other.d_value = 99; }
};
```

```
void g3()
{
    auto y1 = [](const auto& a) { C2 v(a); };
    auto y2 = [](auto&&       a) { C2 v(std::forward<decltype(a)>(a)); };

    C2 a(1);

    y1(a);            assert(1  == a.d_value); // copies from a
    y1(std::move(a)); assert(1  == a.d_value); //    "    "   a
    y2(a);            assert(1  == a.d_value); //    "    "   a
    y2(std::move(a)); assert(99 == a.d_value); // moves    "  a
}
```

In this example, y1 always invokes the copy constructor for C2 because a has type **const** C2&
regardless of whether we instantiate it with an *lvalue* or *rvalue* reference to C2. Conversely,
y2 forwards the **value category** of its argument to the C2 constructor using std::forward
according to the common idiom for forwarding references. If passed an *lvalue* reference, the
copy constructor is invoked; otherwise, the move constructor is invoked. We can tell the difference because C2 has a move constructor that puts the special value 99 into the moved-from
object.

The **auto** placeholder in a generic lambda parameter cannot be a type argument in a template specialization, a parameter type in the prototype of a function reference or function
pointer, or the class type in a pointer to member[1]:

```
#include <vector> // std::vector
auto y7 = [](const std::vector<auto>& x) { };  // Error, invalid use of auto
auto y8 = [](double (*f)(auto)) { };           // Error,    "     "   "   "
auto y9 = [](int auto::* m) { };                // Error,    "     "   "   "
```

Because of this restriction, there are no contexts where more than one **auto** is allowed to
appear in the declaration of a single lambda parameter. Template parameters *are* allowed
in these contexts for regular function templates, so **generic lambdas** are less expressive than
handwritten functor objects in this respect:

```
struct ManualY7
{
    template <typename T>
    void operator()(const std::vector<T>& x) const { } // OK, can deduce T
};

struct ManualY8
{
    template <typename T>
```

---

[1]GCC 10.2 (c. 2020) does allow **auto** in both template arguments and function prototype parameters
and deduces the template parameter type in the same way as for a regular function template. MSVC 19.29
(c. 2021) allows **auto** in the parameter list for a function reference or function pointer but not in the other
two contexts.

```
    void operator()(double (*f)(T)) const { }  // OK, can deduce T
};

struct ManualY9
{
    template <typename R, typename T>
    void operator()(R T::* m) const { }  // OK, can deduce R and T
};
```

ManualY7, ManualY8, and ManualY9 benefit of type deduction for their template arguments, whereas y7, y8, and y9 are unable to deduce **auto**. In addition, ManualY9 deduces two template arguments for a single function parameter. There is a trade-off between the benefits of lambda expressions, such as defining a function in place at the point of use, and the pattern-matching power of manually written function templates. See *Annoyances — Cannot use full power of template-argument deduction* on page 981.

A default value on an **auto** parameter, while allowed, is not useful because it defaults only the *value* and not the *type* of the parameter. Invocation of such a generic lambda requires the programmer to either supply a value for the argument, which defeats the point of a defaulted argument, or explicitly instantiate **operator()**, which is gratuitously awkward:

```
void g4()
{
    auto y = [](auto a = 3) { return a * 2; };
    y(5);                     // OK, returns an int with value 10
    y();                      // Error, cannot deduce type for parameter a
    y.operator()<int>();      // OK, returns an int with value 6
    y.operator()<double>();   // OK, returns a double with the value 6.0
}
```

Variadic generic lambdas

If a placeholder argument to a generic lambda is followed by an ellipsis (...), then the parameter becomes a variadic parameter pack, and the function call operator becomes a variadic function template; see Section 2.1.“Variadic Templates” on page 873:

```
#include <tuple>  // std::tuple, std::make_tuple
auto y11 = [](int i, auto&&... args)
{
    return std::make_tuple(i, std::forward<decltype(args)>(args)...);
};

std::tuple<int, const char*, double> tpl1 = y11(3, "hello", 1.2);
```

The y11 closure object forwards all of its arguments to std::make_tuple. The first argument must have type convertible to **int**, but the remaining arguments can have any type. Assuming the invented name __T for the template parameter pack, the generated function call operator for y11 would have a variadic template parameter list:

```
struct __lambda_3
{
    template <typename... __T> auto operator()(int i, __T&&... args) const
    {
        return std::make_tuple(i, std::forward<decltype(args)>(args)...);
    }
};
```

The standard limitations on variadic function templates apply. For example, only a variadic parameter pack at the end of the parameter list will match function call arguments at the point of invocation. In addition, because **auto** is not permitted in a template-specialization parameter, the usual methods of defining function templates with multiple variadic parameter packs do not work for generic lambdas:

```
// Attempt to define a lambda expression with two variadic parameter packs.
auto y12 = [](std::tuple<auto...>&, auto...args) { };
    // Error, auto is a template argument in tuple specialization.
```

Conversion to a pointer to function

A nongeneric lambda expression with an empty lambda capture can be converted implicitly to a function pointer with the same signature. A generic lambda with an empty lambda capture can similarly be converted to a regular function pointer, where the parameters in the prototype of the target pointer type drive deduction of the appropriate **auto** parameters in the generic lambda signature:

```
auto y1 = [](int a, char b) { return a; };   // nongeneric lambda
int (*f1)(int, char) = y1;                    // OK, conversion to pointer

auto y2 = [](auto a, auto b) { return a; };  // generic lambda
int    (*f2)(int, int)   = y2;  // OK, instantiates operator()<int, int>
double (*f3)(double, int) = y2; // OK, instantiates operator()<double, int>
char   (*f4)(int, char)  = y2;  // Error, incorrect return type
```

If the function target pointer is a variable template (see Section 1.2."Variable Templates" on page 157), then the deduction of the arguments is delayed until the variable template itself is instantiated:

```
template <typename T> int (*f5)(int, T) = y2;  // variable template
int (*f6)(int, short) = f5<short>;             // instantiate f5<short>
```

Each function pointer is produced by calling a conversion operator on the closure object. In the case of a generic lambda, the conversion operator is also a template. Template-argument deduction and return-type deduction are performed on the conversion operator; then the conversion operator instantiates the function call operator. Intuitively, it is as though the function call operator were a static member function template of the closure and the conversion operator returned a pointer to that member function.

Use Cases

Reusable lambda expressions

One of the benefits of lambda expressions is that they can be defined within a function, close to the point of use. Saving a lambda expression in a variable allows it to be reused within the function. This reusability is greater for generic lambdas than for nongeneric lambdas, just as function templates are more reusable than ordinary functions. Consider, for example, a function that partitions a vector of strings and a vector of vectors based on the length of each element:

```
#include <vector>     // std::vector
#include <string>     // std::string
#include <algorithm>  // std::partition

void partitionByLength(std::size_t                        pivotLen,
                       std::vector<std::vector<int>>& v1,
                       std::vector<std::string>&      v2)
{
    auto condition = [pivotLen](const auto& e) { return e.size() < pivotLen; };

    std::partition(v1.begin(), v1.end(), condition);
    std::partition(v2.begin(), v2.end(), condition);
}
```

The condition generic lambda can be used to partition both vectors because its function call operator can be instantiated on either element type. The capture of pivotLen is performed only once, when the lambda expression is evaluated to yield condition.

Applying a lambda to each element of a tuple

An std::tuple is a collection of objects having heterogeneous types. We can apply a functor to each element of a tuple by using some metaprogramming features of the C++14 Standard Library:

```
#include <utility> // std:::index_sequence, std::make_index_sequence
#include <tuple>   // std::tuple, std::tuple_size, std::get

template <typename Tpl, typename F, std::size_t... I>
void visitTupleImpl(Tpl& t, F& f, std::index_sequence<I...>)
{
```

```
        auto discard = { (f(std::get<I>(t)), 0)... };
}

template <typename Tpl, typename F>
void visitTuple(Tpl& t, F f)
{
    visitTupleImpl(t, f,
                   std::make_index_sequence<std::tuple_size<Tpl>::value>());
}
```

The `visitTuple` function uses `make_index_sequence` to generate a compile-time pack of sequential indexes, from 0 up to, but not including, the number of elements in the `tuple`-like argument `t`. The original arguments, along with this pack of indexes, are passed to `visitTupleImpl`, which applies each index to `t` and then calls the functor `f` on the resulting element, i.e., `f` "visits" that element of the tuple.[2] The implementation uses an idiom that discards the sequence of return values (if any) from the calls to `f`: Regardless of the type of value returned by `f(std::get<I>(t))`, even if it's **void**, the comma expression `(f(std::get<I>(t)), 0)` always yields the integer 0. The order of evaluation of elements in an `initializer_list` is guaranteed to be left to right. The result of this expansion is an `initializer_list` used to initialize `discard`, which, as its name suggests, is then discarded.

Once we have a `visitTuple` function, we can use it to apply a **generic lambda** to the elements of a `tuple`:

```
#include <ostream>  // std::ostream, std::endl
void test(std::ostream& os)
{
    std::tuple<int, float, const char*> t{3, 4.5, "six"};
    visitTuple(t, [&os](const auto& v){ os << v << ' '; });
    os << std::endl;
}
```

The first line of `test` constructs a `tuple`, `t`, with three different element types. The second line calls `visitTuple` to visit each element of `t` and apply a lambda function to it. The lambda **capture** stores a reference to the output stream, and the **lambda body** prints the current element to the output stream. This code would not work if the lambda were not generic because the type of `v` is different for each element in `t`.

Terse, robust lambdas

Often, function objects are more convenient to write as **generic lambdas**, rather than non-generic lambdas, even if they are used only once and their genericity is not fully exploited. Consider the case where a lambda's parameters have long, elaborate types:

---

[2]This pattern for using `make_index_sequence` with `tuple`-like objects is documented in a number of places (see **prowl13**); a basic knowledge of variadic templates (see Section 2.1."Variadic Templates" on page 873) is needed for understanding this idiom.

```
#include <iterator>   // std::iterator_traits
#include <algorithm>  // std::sort

template <typename Iterator>
void f1(Iterator begin, Iterator end)
    // Sort [begin, end) using a nongeneric lambda.
{
    std::sort(begin, end,
              [](typename std::iterator_traits<Iterator>::reference a,
                 typename std::iterator_traits<Iterator>::reference b)
              {
                  return a < b;
              });
}
```

The types for parameters a and b of the comparison lambda expression are not easy to type or read. Compare the code above with similar code using generic lambdas:

```
template <typename Iterator>
void f2(Iterator begin, Iterator end)
    // Sort [begin, end) using a generic lambda.
{
    std::sort(begin, end,
              [](const auto& a, const auto& b) { return a < b; });
}
```

The code is simpler to write and read because it takes advantage of the lambda expression being defined at the point of use; even though the argument types are not written out, their meaning is still clear. A generic lambda is also more robust when the types involved change, even in a small way, as it adapts to changes in argument types as long as they support the same interface.

Recursive lambdas

Since neither generic nor nongeneric lambda expressions have names, defining a lambda that calls itself recursively is tricky. One way to accomplish recursion is by passing the lambda as an argument to itself. This technique requires a generic lambda so that it can deduce its own type from its argument:

```
auto fib = [](auto self, int n) -> int  // Compute the nth Fibonacci number.
{
    if (n < 2) { return n; }
    return self(self, n - 1) + self(self, n - 2);
};

int fib7 = fib(fib, 7);  // returns 13
```

Notice that when we invoke the recursive lambda, we pass it as an argument to itself, both to the external call and to the internal recursive calls. To avoid this somewhat awkward interface, a special function object called a **Y Combinator** can be used.[3] The Y Combinator object holds the closure object to be invoked recursively and passes it to itself:

```
#include <utility>  // std::move, std::forward

template <typename Lambda>
class Y_Combinator {
    Lambda d_lambda;

public:
    Y_Combinator(Lambda&& lambda) : d_lambda(std::move(lambda)) { }

    template <typename... Args>
    decltype(auto) operator()(Args&&...args) const
    {
        return d_lambda(*this, std::forward<Args>(args)...);
    }
};

template <typename Lambda>
Y_Combinator<Lambda> Y(Lambda lambda) { return std::move(lambda); }
```

The function call operator for `Y_Combinator` is a **variadic function template** (see Section 2.1."Variadic Templates" on page 873) that passes itself to the stored closure object, `d_lambda`, along with zero or more additional arguments supplied by the caller. Thus, `d_lambda` and the `Y_Combinator` are mutually recursive functors. The `Y` function template constructs a `Y_Combinator` from a lambda expression.

To use a `Y_Combinator`, pass a recursive generic lambda to `Y`; the resulting object is the one that we would call from code:

```
auto fib2 = Y([](auto self, int n) -> int
{
    if (n < 2) { return n; }
    return self(n - 1) + self(n - 2);
});

int fib8 = fib2(8);  // returns 21
```

Note that the recursive lambda still needs to take `self` as an argument, but because `self` is a `Y_Combinator`, it does not need to pass `self` to itself. Unfortunately, we must now specify the return type of the lambda because the compiler cannot deduce the return type of the mutually recursive invocations of `self`. The usefulness of a Y Combinator in C++

---

[3]hindley86

is debatable given alternative and often simpler ways to achieve recursion, including using ordinary function templates instead of lambda expressions.[4]

Conditional instantiation

Because a generic lambda defines a function template that is not instantiated unless it is called, it is possible to put code into a generic lambda that would not compile for certain argument types. We can, thus, selectively instantiate calls to generic lambdas based on some compile-time conditional expression similar to the **if constexpr** feature introduced in C++17:

```cpp
#include <type_traits> // std::true_type, std::false_type
#include <utility>     // std::forward

// Identity functor: Each call to operator() returns its argument unchanged.
struct Identity
{
    template <typename T>
    decltype(auto) operator()(T&& x) { return std::forward<T>(x); }
};

template <typename F1, typename F2>
decltype(auto) ifConstexprImpl(std::true_type, F1&& f1, F2&&)
    // Call f1, which is the "then" branch of ifConstexpr.
{
    return std::forward<F1>(f1)(Identity{});
}

template <typename F1, typename F2>
decltype(auto) ifConstexprImpl(std::false_type, F1&&, F2&& f2)
    // Call f2, which is the "else" branch of ifConstexpr.
{
    return std::forward<F2>(f2)(Identity{});
}

template <bool Cond, typename F1, typename F2>
decltype(auto) ifConstexpr(F1&& f1, F2&& f2)
    // If the compile-time condition Cond is true, return the result of
    // invoking f1, else return the result of invoking f2.  The
    // invocations of f1 and f2 are each passed an instance of Identity
    // as their sole argument.
{
    using CondT = std::integral_constant<bool, Cond>;
    return ifConstexprImpl(CondT{}, std::forward<F1>(f1), std::forward<F2>(f2));
}
```

---

[4]Derevenets suggested that y_combinator should be part of the C++ Standard Library (see **derevenets16**), but the proposal was rejected for addressing a problem deemed not worth solving.

The `Identity` functor class, as its name suggests, returns its argument unchanged, preserving both its type and its value category (*lvalue* or *rvalue*). This functor exists solely to be passed to a generic lambda, which will then invoke it as described below.

The two overloads of `ifConstexprImpl` each take two functor arguments, only one of which is used. The first overload invokes only its first argument; the second overload invokes only its second argument. In both cases, an `Identity` object is passed as the only argument to the functor invocation.

The `ifConstexpr` function template, in addition to taking two functor arguments, must be instantiated with an explicit compile-time Boolean value. It calls one of the two `ifConstexprImpl` functions such that its first argument is instantiated and invoked if the condition is **true** — the "then" clause of the simulated **if constexpr**. The second argument is instantiated and invoked otherwise — the "else" clause of the simulated **if constexpr**.

To see how `ifConstexpr` achieves conditional instantiation, let's write a function that dereferences an object. The object being dereferenced can be a pointer, an `std::reference_wrapper`, or a class that behaves like `reference_wrapper`. We present both a C++17 version that uses **if constexpr** and a C++14 version that uses `ifConstexpr`, above:

```
#include <type_traits>  // std::is_pointer

template <typename T>
decltype(auto) objectAt(T ref)
    // Generalized dereference for pointers and reference_wrapper-like
    // objects: If T is a pointer type, return *ref; otherwise, return
    // ref.get().
{
#if __cplusplus >= 201703
    // C++17 version
    if constexpr (std::is_pointer<T>::value) { return *ref; }
    else                                     { return ref.get(); }
#else
    // C++14 version
    return ifConstexpr<std::is_pointer<T>::value>(
        [=](auto dependent) -> decltype(auto) { return *dependent(ref); },
        [=](auto dependent) -> decltype(auto) { return dependent(ref).get(); });
#endif
}
```

Looking at the C++17 version first, we see that if `ref` is a pointer, and then we return `*ref`; otherwise, we return `ref.get()`. In both cases, the code would not compile if the branch not taken were instantiated; i.e., `*ref` is ill formed for `std::reference_wrapper`, and `ref.get()` is ill formed for pointers. The code depends on the ill-formed branch being discarded at compile time.

The C++14 version needs to follow a specific idiom whereby each conditional branch is represented as a generic lambda with one **auto** parameter that is expected to be an `Identity` object. Because it is a template parameter, `dependent` is a **dependent type**. In C++ template parlance, a **dependent type** is one that cannot be known until template instantiation. Critically, the compiler will not check semantic correctness of an expression containing a value of **dependent type** unless and until the template is instantiated. Any such expression that uses a value of **dependent type** also has a **dependent type**. By wrapping `ref` in a call to `dependent`, therefore, we ensure that the compiler will not test if `*ref` or `ref.get()` is valid until the **generic lambda** is instantiated. Our implementation of `ifConstexpr` ensures that only the *correct* lambda is instantiated, thus preventing a compiler error.[5]

A simple test for `objectAt` instantiates it with both pointer and `reference_wrapper` arguments and verifies that the value returned has both the correct value and address:

```
#include <cassert>      // standard C assert macro
#include <functional>   // std::reference_wrapper
void f1()
{
    int i = 8;

    int&      i1 = objectAt(&i);
    int&      i2 = objectAt(std::reference_wrapper<int>(i));
    const int& i3 = objectAt(std::reference_wrapper<const int>(i));

    assert(8 == i1);
    assert(&i1 == &i);
    assert(&i2 == &i);
    assert(&i3 == &i);
}
```

Potential Pitfalls

Although the generic feature is generally safe, **generic lambdas** are an incremental advance over regular **lambda expressions**. All pitfalls of the nongeneric feature apply to this feature as well; see Section 2.1."Lambdas" on page 573.

Annoyances

Cannot use full power of template-argument deduction

Function templates allow constraining their argument types to having a specific structure, e.g., cv-qualified references, pointers to members, or instantiations of class templates:

```
#include <vector>  // std::vector
template <typename T> void f1(std::vector<T>& v) { }  // T is the element type.
```

---

[5]Paul Fultz suggested the idea for using an identity functor to mark expressions as having **dependent** type (**fultz14**).

Not only is the argument v constrained to being a **vector**, but the deduced element type **T** is available for use within the function. The same sort of pattern matching is not available portably for **generic lambdas**:

```
auto y1 = [](std::vector<auto>& v) { };  // Error, auto as template parameter
```

Constraining the deduced type of an **auto** parameter using metaprogramming, e.g., through the use of **std::enable_if**, is sometimes possible:

```
#include <type_traits>  // std::enable_if_t, std::is_same,
                        // std::remove_reference_t
auto y2 = [](auto& v) -> std::enable_if_t<
    std::is_same<
        std::vector<typename std::remove_reference_t<decltype(v)>::value_type>&,
        decltype(v)
    >::value> { };
```

The y2 **closure** can be called only with a vector. Any other type will fail substitution because **is_same** will return **false** if substitution even gets that far; substitution might fail earlier if the type for v does not have a nested **value_type**. Passing non**vector** arguments to this constrained lambda will now fail at the call site, rather than, presumably, failing during instantiation of y2(v):

```
void g1()
{
    int              i;
    std::vector<int>   v1;
    std::vector<float> v2;

    y2(i);   // Error, cannot call y2 on a nonvector
    y2(v1);  // OK, v1 is a vector
    y2(v2);  // OK, v2 is a vector
}
```

For all of the additional complication in y2, the element type for our **vector** is still not available within the lambda body, as it was for the function body for f1, above; we would need to repeat the type name **typename** std::remove_reference_t<**decltype**(v)>::value_type if the element type became necessary.

This annoyance is of no practical significance because **lambda expressions** cannot be overloaded. In the absence of overloading, there is little benefit to removing a call from the overload set compared to simply letting the instantiation fail, especially as most **lambda expressions** are defined at the point of use, making it comparatively easy to diagnose a compilation problem if one occurs. Moreover, this point-of-use definition is already tuned to ts expected use case, so constraints are often redundant, adding little additional safety to the code.

Difficulty in constraining multiple arguments

Often, we want to restrict function template arguments such that two or more arguments have related types. For example, an operation might require two iterators of the same type or one argument to be a pointer to the type of the other argument. Generic lambdas provide only limited support for interargument patterns. Each parameter to a generic lambda that contains **auto** is entirely independent of the other parameters, so the normal mechanism used for function templates — using the same named type parameter (e.g., T or U) in multiple places — is unavailable:

```
void g1()
{
    auto y = [](auto a, auto b) { };  // No interargument constraints
    y(1, 2);            // OK, arguments of type int and int
    y("one", "two");   // OK,      "       "   "  const char* and const char*
    y(1, "two");        // OK,      "       "   "  int and const char*
}
```

Limited constraints are possible — e.g., requiring that arguments have the same type — by using the **decltype** operator to declare subsequent parameters based on the types of earlier parameters; see Section 1.1."**decltype**" on page 25:

```
void g2()
{
    auto y = [](auto a, decltype(a) b) { };  // a and b have the same type.
    y(1, 2);            // OK, both arguments are of type int.
    y("one", "two");   // OK,    "       "        "    "    "  const char*.
    y(1, "two");        // Error, mixed argument types int and const char*
}
```

If the relationship between the parameter types is even slightly different than an exact match, expressing it can become complicated. For example, if parameter a is a pointer and we want parameter b to be a value of the type pointed to by a, our first approach might be to try **decltype(*a)**:

```
int i = 0;
```

```
void g3()
{
    auto y = [](auto* a, decltype(*a) b) { *a = b; };
    y(&i, 5);  // Error, can't bind rvalue 5 to int& b
    int j;
    y(&i, j);  // OK
}
```

Unfortunately, as we see, **decltype(*a)** yields a non**const** *lvalue* reference, which cannot bind to the *rvalue* 5. Our next attempt is to **const**-qualify b, since **const** references *can* bind to *rvalues*:

```
void g4()
{
    auto y = [](auto* a, const decltype(*a) b) { *a = b; };
    y(&i, 5);  // Error, const applied to reference is ignored.
}
```

This approach fails because **const** can be applied only to the *referred-to* type; applying **const** to the reference has no effect. If we use the standard metafunction std::remove_reference_t, we can finally get to the type to which a points, without any reference specifiers:

```
#include <type_traits>  // std::remove_reference_t

void g5()
{
    auto y = [](auto* a, std::remove_reference_t<decltype(*a)> b)
    {
        *a = b;
    };
    y(&i, 5); // OK, pass 5 by value for int b.
}
```

Note that y takes argument b by value, which can be inefficient for types having an expensive copy constructor. When the type of an argument is unknown, we usually pass it by **const** reference:

```
void g6()
{
    auto y = [](auto* a, const std::remove_reference_t<decltype(*a)>& b)
    {
        *a = b;
    };
    y(&i, 5); // OK, bind 5 to const int& b.
}
```

In the previous example, parameter b is always a **const** *lvalue* reference, never an *rvalue* reference. When constraining a type this way, we forfeit the possibility of perfect forwarding.

See Also

- "**decltype**" (§1.1, p. 25) describes the only way to name the type of an **auto** parameter in a generic lambda.

- "**auto** Variables" (§2.1, p. 195) introduces a **placeholder type** that allows a lambda expression, which has an unnamed type, to be saved in a variable and also details the rules for deducing an **auto** parameter from its argument expression.

- "Forwarding References" (§2.1, p. 377) provides the most general way to declare a generic lambda's parameters, preserving their types and value categories.

- "Lambdas" (§2.1, p. 573) introduces the facility for locally defined anonymous function objects that generic lambdas expand on.

- "Variadic Templates" (§2.1, p. 873) demonstrates how templated entities, such as generic lambdas, can accommodate a variable number of arguments.

- "Lambda Captures" (§2.2, p. 986) describes the init-capture syntax added to lambda captures in C++14.

- "**auto** Return" (§3.2, p. 1182) explains how a function, including the function call operator for a lambda expression, can deduce its return type from its **return** statements.

Further Reading

- A thorough introduction to the underlying theory of combinators and lambda calculus can be found in **hindley86**.

- Adding Y combinators to the generic lambda feature to facilitate recursion is proposed in **derevenets16**.

Lambda-Capture Expressions

An **init capture** expression enables a lambda to add a data member, initialized with an arbitrary expression, to its closure.

Description

In C++11, lambda expressions can capture variables in the surrounding scope either *by copy* or *by reference*:

```
void test0()
{
    int i = 0;
    auto f0 = [i]{ };   // Capture i by copy.
    auto f1 = [&i]{ };  // Capture i by reference.
}
```

Here, we use the familiar C++11 feature **auto** (see Section 2.1."**auto** Variables" on page 195) to deduce a closure's type since there is no way to name such a type explicitly.

Although one could specify *which* and *how* existing variables were captured, the programmer had no control over the creation of new variables within a **closure** (see Section 2.1. "Lambdas" on page 573). C++14 extends the **lambda-introducer** syntax to support implicit creation of data members inside a **closure** using an arbitrary initializer:

```
auto f2 = [i = 10]{ /* body of closure */ };
    // Synthesize an int data member, i, copy-initialized with 10.
```

```
auto f3 = [c{'a'}]{ /* body of closure */ };
    // Synthesize a char data member, c, direct-initialized with 'a'.
```

Note that the identifiers i and c above do not refer to any existing variables; they are specified by the programmer creating the closure. For example, the **closure** type bound to f2 above is similar in functionality to an **invocable struct** containing an **int** data member:

```
struct f2LikeInvocableStruct
{
    auto i = 10;  // The type int is deduced from the initialization expression.
    auto operator()() const { /* closure body */ }  // The struct is invocable.
};
```

The type of the data member is deduced from the initialization expression provided as part of the capture in the same vein as **auto** (see Section 2.1."**auto** Variables" on page 195) type deduction; hence, it's not possible to synthesize an uninitialized **closure** data member:

```
void test1()
{
    auto f4 = [u]{ };     // Error, u initializer is missing for lambda capture.
    auto f5 = [v{}]{ };   // Error, v's type cannot be deduced.
}
```

It is possible, however, to use variables outside the scope of the lambda as part of a lambda-capture expression and even to capture them *by reference* by prepending the & token to the name of the synthesized data member:

```
int i = 0;   // zero-initialized int variable defined in the enclosing scope
```

```
auto f6 = [j   = i]{ };   // OK, capture i by copy as j.
auto f7 = [&ir = i]{ };   // OK, capture i by reference as ir.
```

Though capturing *by reference* is possible, enforcing **const** on a lambda-capture expression is not:

```
auto f8 = [const i = 10]{ };                  // Error, invalid syntax
auto f9 = [const auto i = 10]{ };             // Error, invalid syntax
auto fA = [i = static_cast<const int>(10)]{ };  // OK, const is ignored.
```

The initialization expression is evaluated during the *creation* of the closure, not during its *invocation*:

```
#include <cassert>   // standard C assert macro

void test2()
{
    int i = 0;

    auto fB = [k = ++i]{ };   // ++i is evaluated at creation only.
    assert(i == 1);   // OK

    fB();   // Invoke fB (no change to i).
    assert(i == 1);   // OK
}
```

Finally, using the same identifier as an existing variable is possible for a synthesized capture, resulting in the original variable being shadowed (essentially **hidden**) in the lambda expression's body but not in its declared interface. The example below uses the C++11 compile-time operator **decltype** (see Section 1.1."**decltype**" on page 25) to infer the type of a variable in the enclosing scope to create a parameter of that same type as part of its declared interface[1]:

---

[1]Note that, in the shadowing example defining fC, GCC 11.2 (c. 2021) incorrectly evaluates **decltype**(i) inside the body of the lambda expression as **const char**, rather than **char**; see *Potential Pitfalls — Forwarding an existing variable into a closure always results in an object (never a reference)* on page 992.

```
#include <type_traits>  // std::is_same

int i = 0;

auto fC = [i = 'a'](decltype(i) arg)
{
    static_assert(std::is_same<decltype(arg), int>::value, "");
        // i in the interface refers to the int object in the outer scope.

    static_assert(std::is_same<decltype(i), char>::value, "");
        // i in the body refers to the char data member deduced at capture.
};
```

Notice that we have again used **decltype**, in conjunction with the standard is_same meta-function (which is **true** if and only if its two arguments are the same C++ type). This time, we're using **decltype** to demonstrate that the type (**int**), extracted from the variable i in the outer scope, is distinct from the type (**char**) extracted from the i within fC's body. In other words, the effect of initializing a variable in the capture portion of the lambda is to hide the name of an existing variable that would otherwise be accessible in the lambda's body.[2]

Use Cases

Moving (as opposed to copying) objects into a closure

Lambda-capture expressions can be used to *move* (see Section 2.1."*Rvalue* References" on page 710) an existing variable into a closure (as opposed to capturing it *by copy* or *by reference*).

Though possible, it is surprisingly difficult in C++11 to *move* from an existing variable into a closure. Programmers are forced either to pay the price of an unnecessary copy or to employ esoteric and fragile techniques, such as writing a wrapper that hijacks the behavior of its copy constructor to do a *move* instead:

```
#include <utility>  // std::move
#include <memory>   // std::unique_ptr

template <typename T>
struct MoveOnCopy  // wrapper template used to hijack copy ctor to do move
{
    T d_obj;
```

---

[2]Also note that since the deduced **char** member variable, i, is not materially used (**ODR-used**) in the body of the lambda expression assigned (bound) to fC, some compilers, e.g., Clang, might warn:

```
warning: lambda capture 'i' is not required to be captured for this use
```

```
      MoveOnCopy(T&& object) : d_obj(std::move(object)) { }
      MoveOnCopy(MoveOnCopy& rhs) : d_obj(std::move(rhs.d_obj)) { }
  };

  void f()
  {
      std::unique_ptr<int> handle(new int(100));  // move-only
          // Create an example of a handle type with a large body.

      MoveOnCopy<decltype(handle)> wrapper(std::move(handle));
          // Create an instance of a wrapper that moves on copy.

      const auto &c1 = [wrapper]{ /* use wrapper.d_obj */ };
          // Create a "copy" from a wrapper that is captured by copy.
  }
```

In the example above, we make use of the bespoke ("hacky") `MoveOnCopy` class template to wrap a movable object; when the lambda-capture expression tries to *copy* the wrapper, the wrapper in turn *moves* the wrapped `handle` into the body of the closure.

As an example of *needing* to move from an existing object into a closure, consider the problem of accessing the data managed by `std::unique_ptr` (movable but not copyable) from a separate thread — for example, by enqueuing a task in a thread pool:

```
ThreadPool::Handle processDatasetAsync(std::unique_ptr<Dataset> dataset)
{
    return getThreadPool().enqueueTask([data = std::move(dataset)]
    {
        return processDataset(data);
    });
}
```

As illustrated above, the `dataset` smart pointer is moved into the closure passed to `enqueueTask` by leveraging lambda-capture expressions — the `std::unique_ptr` is *moved* to a different thread because a copy would have not been possible.

Providing mutable state for a closure

Lambda-capture expressions can be useful in conjunction with **mutable** lambda expressions to provide an initial state that will change across invocations of the closure. Consider, for instance, the task of logging how many TCP packets have been received on a socket (e.g., for debugging or monitoring purposes). In this example, we are making use of the C++11 **mutable** feature of lambdas to enable the counter to be modified on each invocation:

```
void listen()
{
    TcpSocket tcpSocket(27015);  // some well-known port number
    tcpSocket.onPacketReceived([counter = 0]() mutable
    {
        std::cout << "Received " << ++counter << " packet(s)\n";
        // ...
    });
}
```

Use of counter = 0 as part of the lambda introducer tersely produces a **function object** that has an internal counter initialized with zero and incremented on every received packet. Compared to, say, capturing a counter variable *by reference* in the closure, the solution above limits the scope of counter to the body of the lambda expression and ties its lifetime to the closure itself, thereby preventing any risk of dangling references.

Capturing a modifiable copy of an existing const variable

Capturing a variable *by copy* in C++11 does not allow the programmer to control its **const** qualification; the generated closure data member will have the same **const** qualification as the captured variable, irrespective of whether the lambda is decorated with **mutable**:

```
#include <type_traits> // std::is_same

void f()
{
    int i = 0;
    const int ci = 0;

    auto lc = [i, ci]              // This lambda is not decorated with mutable.
    {
        static_assert(std::is_same<decltype(i), int>::value, "");
        static_assert(std::is_same<decltype(ci), const int>::value, "");
    };

    auto lm = [i, ci]() mutable    // Decorating with mutable has no effect.
    {
        static_assert(std::is_same<decltype(i), int>::value, "");
        static_assert(std::is_same<decltype(ci), const int>::value, "");
    };
}
```

In some cases, however, a lambda capturing a **const** variable *by copy* might need to modify that value when invoked. As an example, consider the task of comparing the output of two Sudoku-solving algorithms, executed in parallel:

```cpp
template <typename Algorithm> void solve(Puzzle&);
    // This function template mutates a Sudoku grid in place to the solution.

void performAlgorithmComparison()
{
    const Puzzle puzzle = generateRandomSudokuPuzzle();
        // const-correct: puzzle is not going to be mutated after being
        // randomly generated.

    auto task0 = getThreadPool().enqueueTask([puzzle]() mutable
    {
        solve<NaiveAlgorithm>(puzzle);  // Error, puzzle is const-qualified.
        return puzzle;
    });

    auto task1 = getThreadPool().enqueueTask([puzzle]() mutable
    {
        solve<FastAlgorithm>(puzzle);  // Error, puzzle is const-qualified.
        return puzzle;
    });

    waitForCompletion(task0, task1);
    // ...
}
```

The code above will fail to compile as capturing **puzzle** will result in a **const**-qualified closure data member, despite the presence of **mutable**. A convenient workaround is to use a lambda-capture expression in which a local modifiable copy is deduced:

```cpp
void performAlgorithmComparison2()
{
    // ...

    const Puzzle puzzle = generateRandomSudokuPuzzle();

    auto task0 = getThreadPool().enqueueTask([p = puzzle]() mutable
    {
        solve<NaiveAlgorithm>(p);  // OK, p is now modifiable.
        return p;
    });

    // ...
}
```

Note that the use of p = puzzle above is roughly equivalent to the creation of a new variable using **auto** (i.e., **auto** p = puzzle;), which guarantees that the type of p will be deduced as a non**const** Puzzle. Furthermore, if we wanted to avoid introducing a new name, we could use the same name in the lambda-capture expression as that of the copied variable — e.g., [puzzle = puzzle]. Capturing an existing **const** variable as a mutable copy is possible, but doing the opposite is not easy; see *Annoyances — There's no easy way to synthesize a* **const** *data member* on page 993.

Potential Pitfalls

Forwarding an existing variable into a closure always results in an object (never a reference)

Lambda-capture expressions allow existing variables to be **perfectly forwarded** (see Section 2.1."Forwarding References" on page 377) into a closure:

```
#include <utility>  // std::forward

template <typename T>
void f(T&& x)  // x is of type forwarding reference to T.
{
    auto c1 = [y = std::forward<T>(x)]
        // Perfectly forward x into the closure.
    {
        // ... (use y directly in this lambda body)
    };
}
```

Because std::forward<T> is typically used to preserve the **value category** of the argument, programmers might incorrectly assume that a capture such as y = std::forward<T>(x) (above) is somehow either a capture *by copy* or a capture *by reference*, depending on the original value category of x.

Remembering that lambda-capture expressions work similarly to **auto** type deduction for variables, however, reveals that such captures will *always* result in an object, *never* a reference:

```
// pseudocode (auto is not allowed in a lambda introducer.)
auto c1 = [auto y = std::forward<T>(x)] { };
    // The capture expression above is semantically similar to an auto
    // (deduced-type) variable.
```

If x was originally an *lvalue*, then y will be equivalent to a *by-copy* capture of x. Otherwise, y will be equivalent to a *by-move* capture of x. Note that both *by-copy* and *by-move* capture communicate **value** for **value-semantic types**.

If the desired semantics are to capture x *by move* if it originated from an **rvalue** and *by reference* otherwise, then the use of an extra layer of abstraction (using, e.g., std::tuple) is required:

```
#include <tuple>  // std::tuple

template <typename T>
void f(T&& x)
{
    auto c1 = [y = std::tuple<T>(std::forward<T>(x))]
    {
        // ... (Use std::get<0>(y) instead of y in this lambda body.)
    };
}
```

In the revised code example above, T will be an **lvalue reference** if x was originally an *lvalue*, resulting in the std::tuple containing an lvalue reference being the type of y, which — in turn — has semantics equivalent to x's being captured *by reference*. Otherwise, T will not be a reference type, and x will be *moved* into the closure.

Annoyances

There's no easy way to synthesize a const data member

Consider the hypothetical case where the programmer desires to capture a copy of a non-**const** integer k as a **const** closure data member:

```
void test1()
{
    int k = 0;
    [kcpy = static_cast<const int>(k)]() mutable  // const is ignored.
    {
        ++kcpy;  // "OK" -- i.e., compiles anyway even though we don't want it to
    };
}

void test2()
{
    int k = 0;
    [const kcpy = k]() mutable  // Error, invalid syntax
    {
        ++kcpy;  // no easy way to force this variable to be const
    };
}
```

The language simply does not provide a convenient mechanism for synthesizing, from a modifiable variable, a **const** data member. The simplest workaround is to create a **const** copy of the object in question and then capture it with traditional lambda-capture expressions:

```
int test3()
{
    int k;
    const int kcpy = k;

    [kcpy]() mutable
    {
        ++kcpy;  // Error, increment of read-only variable kcpy
    };
}
```

Alternatively, we can either use `tuple<const T>`, create a `ConstWrapper` **struct** that adds **const** to the captured object, or write a full-fledged function object in lieu of the leaner lambda expression.

std::function supports only copyable callable objects

Any lambda expression capturing a move-only object produces a closure type that is itself movable but *not* copyable:

```
void f()
{
    std::unique_ptr<int> moo(new int);        // some move-only object
    auto c1 = [moo = std::move(moo)]{ };  // lambda that does move capture

    static_assert(!std::is_copy_constructible<decltype(c1)>::value, "");
    static_assert( std::is_move_constructible<decltype(c1)>::value, "");
}
```

Lambdas are sometimes used to initialize instances of `std::function`, which requires the stored **callable object** to be copyable:

```
std::function<void()> f = c1;  // Error, la must be copyable.
```

Such a limitation — which is more likely to be encountered when using lambda-capture expressions — can make `std::function` unsuitable for use cases where move-only closures might conceivably be reasonable. Possible workarounds include (1) using a different type-erased, **callable object** wrapper type that supports move-only callable objects,[3] (2) taking a performance hit by wrapping the desired **callable object** into a copyable wrapper (such as `std::shared_ptr`), or (3) designing software such that noncopyable objects, once constructed, never need to move.[4]

---

[3]The `any_invocable` library type, proposed for C++23, is an example of a type-erased wrapper for move-only callable objects; see **calabrese20**.

[4]We plan to offer an in-depth discussion of how large systems can benefit from a design that embraces local arena memory allocators and, thus, minimizes the use of moves across natural memory boundaries identified throughout the system; see **lakos22**.

See Also

- "**auto** Variables" (§2.1, p. 195) offers a model with the same type deduction rules.

- "Braced Init" (§2.1, p. 215) illustrates one possible way of initializing the captures.

- "Forwarding References" (§2.1, p. 377) describes a feature that contributes to a source of misunderstanding of this feature.

- "Lambdas" (§2.1, p. 573) provides the needed background for understanding the feature in general.

- "*Rvalue* References" (§2.1, p. 710) gives a full description of an important feature used in conjunction with movable types.

Further Reading

- Scott Meyers discusses exploiting this modern feature of C++ to *move* an object (see Section 2.1."*Rvalue* References" on page 710) into a **lambda expression** in **meyers15b**, "Item 32: Use init capture to move objects into closure," pp. 224–229.

Chapter 3

Unsafe Features

Caveat emptor. A few modern C++ language features provide potential value in a few fairly specific, niche use cases, yet expose even experienced engineers to ample opportunities for misuse, often with nonobvious, far-reaching, and sometimes dire consequences. This chapter introduces C++11 and C++14 features that in specific cases can be used profitably but at disproportionately high risk. Moreover, the effort required to understand these features, the subtleties surrounding their effective use, and the risks of misusing them go beyond what many organizations would consider cost effective. Though no modern feature of C++ is inherently "unsafe," these few have an especially unattractive risk–reward ratio. An organization's leadership must be circumspect when supporting any use of this chapter's features. Even if they are used properly, code employing such *unsafe* features might be unmaintainable by engineers lacking the requisite mastery of the original authors. Furthermore, the presence of these features in a codebase might lead less experienced developers to employ them in new situations where such use would be strongly contraindicated.

"Unsafe" features are characterized by being of very high risk and little value. Recall from "An *Unsafe* Feature" in Chapter 0 that **final** (p. 1007) was our exemplar for an *unsafe* feature. When appropriate, this feature is exactly what's needed; ironically, unlike its *safe* cousin **override** (p. 104), both from the same Standards proposal, **final** is easily misused and seldom appropriate. Another *unsafe* feature is the **noexcept** specifier (p. 1085); unlike its related *conditionally safe* feature the **noexcept** operator (p. 615), misuse of this feature can render a codebase brittle and exception unfriendly. Yet another example of an *unsafe* yet useful feature is **friend** (p. 1031). Idiomatic use of this feature (e.g., in CRTP) can be of substantial value (e.g., in avoiding copy-paste errors), but most other uses (e.g., involving *long-distance friendship*) can lead to code that does not scale and is inordinately difficult to understand, test, and maintain. The benefit of fully teaching any of these features as part of even an advanced general training course is dubious. Although most of the features presented in this chapter have the potential to add value, all come with a profoundly high risk of being misused or a disproportionately high training cost — not only for implementors, but for maintainers too — and thus are considered *unsafe*.

In short, widespread adoption of *unsafe* features offers no sensible risk–reward ratio and thus is contraindicated. An organization considering incorporating *unsafe* features into a predominantly C++03 codebase would be well advised to adopt strict standards as to whether and under what circumstances such features shall be used. Even if you're an expert in modern C++, you'd be well advised to fully understand and appreciate the pitfalls in each *unsafe* feature you might want to employ.

The [[carries_dependency]] Attribute

Associating the [[carries_dependency]] attribute with individual parameters or the return value of a function provides a means to manually identify them as components of **data dependency chains** to enable, primarily across translation units, use of the lighter-weight **release-consume** synchronization paradigm as an optimization over the more conservative **release-acquire** paradigm.[1]

Description

C++11 ushered in support for multithreading by introducing a rigorously specified memory model. The Standard Library provides support for managing threads, including their execution, synchronization, and intercommunication. As a part of the new memory model, the Standard defines various synchronization operations that are classified as either *sequentially consistent*, *release*, *acquire*, *release-and-acquire*, or *consume* operations. These operations play a key role in making changes in data in one thread visible in another.

The modern C++ memory model describes two **synchronization paradigms** that are used to coordinate data flow among concurrent threads of execution. The current suite of supported **synchronization paradigms** comprises release-acquire and release-consume, although in practice **release-consume** is implemented in terms of **release-acquire** in all known implementations. In particular, the **release-consume** paradigm requires that the compiler be given fine-grained understanding of the **intra-thread dependencies** among the reads and writes within a program and relates those to atomic *release stores* and *consume loads* that happen concurrently across multiple threads of execution. Dependency chains in the **release-consume** synchronization paradigm specify which evaluations following the *consume load* are ordered after a corresponding *release store*.

The release-acquire paradigm

A *release* operation writes a value to a memory location, and an *acquire* operation reads a value from a memory location. Although many have referred to the release-acquire paradigm as *acquire-release*, the proper, standard, time-ordered nomenclature is *release-acquire*. In a **release-acquire** pair, the acquire operation reads the value written by the release operation, which means that all of the reads and writes to *any* memory location *before the release operation* happen before *all* of the reads and writes *after the acquire operation*. Note that this paradigm does *not* use dependency chains or the [[carries_dependency]] attribute. See *Use Cases — Producer-consumer programming pattern* on page 1000 for a complete example that implements this paradigm.

---

[1] The authors would like to thank Michael Wong, Paul McKenney, and Maged Michael for reviewing and contributing to this feature section.

Data dependency

In the current revisions of C++, **data dependency** is defined as existing whenever the output of one evaluation is used as the input of another. When one evaluation has a data dependency on another evaluation, the second evaluation is said to **carry dependency** to the other. The Standard Library function `std::kill_dependency` is also related and can be used to *break* a data dependency chain. Naturally the compiler must ensure that any evaluation that depends on another must not be started until the first evaluation is complete. A **data dependency chain** is formed when multiple evaluations carry dependency transitively; the output of one evaluation is used as the input of the next evaluation in the chain.

The release-consume paradigm

Some systems use the read-copy-update (RCU) synchronization mechanism. This approach preserves the order of *loads* and *stores* that form in a **data dependency chain**, which is a sequence of *loads* and *stores* in which the input to one operation is an output of another. A compiler can use guaranteed order of loads and stores provided by the RCU synchronization mechanism for performance purposes by omitting certain **memory-fence instructions** that would otherwise be required to enforce the correct ordering. In such cases, however, ordering is guaranteed only between those operations making up the relevant **data dependency chain**. The C++ definition of data dependency is intended to mimic the data dependency on RCU systems. Note, however, that C++ currently defines data dependency in terms of evaluations, while RCU data dependency is defined in terms of loads and stores.

This optimization was intended to be available in C++ through use of a *release-consume* pair, which, as its name suggests, consists of a *release-store* operation and a *consume-load* operation. A *consume* operation is much like an *acquire* operation, except that it guarantees only the ordering of those evaluations in a **data dependency chain**, starting with the consume-load operation.

Note, however, that currently no known implementation is able to take advantage of the current C++ *consume* semantics; hence, all current compilers promote *consume* loads to *acquire* loads, effectively making the `[[carries_dependency]]` attribute redundant. Revisions to render this feature implementable and therefore usable are currently under consideration by the C++ Standards Committee. Prototypes for various approaches have been produced. When a usable feature with real implementations is delivered, it quite possibly will not work exactly as described in the examples here; see *Use Cases* on page 1000.

Using the [[carries_dependency]] attribute

Data dependency chains can and do propagate into and out of called functions. If one of these interoperating functions is in a separate translation unit, the compiler will have no way of seeing the dependency chain. In such cases, the user can apply the `[[carries_dependency]]` attribute to imbue the necessary information for the compiler to track the propagation of dependency chains into and out of functions across translation units, thus possibly avoiding unnecessary memory-fence instructions; see *Use Cases* below. Note that the Standard Library function std::kill_dependency is also related and can be used to *break* a data dependency chain.

The [[carries_dependency]] attribute can be applied to a function declaration as a whole by placing it in front of the function declaration, in which case the attribute applies to the **return** value:

```
[[carries_dependency]] int* f();  // attribute applied to entire function f
```

In the example above, the [[carries_dependency]] attribute was applied to the declaration of function f to indicate that the **return** value carries a dependency out of the function. The compiler might now be able to avoid emitting a memory-fence instruction for the return value of f.

The [[carries_dependency]] attribute can also be applied to one or more of the function's parameter declarations by placing it immediately after the parameter name:

```
void g(int* input [[carries_dependency]]); // attribute applied to input
```

In the declaration of function g in the example above, the [[carries_dependency]] attribute is applied to the input parameter to indicate that a dependency is carried through that parameter into the function, which might obviate the compiler's having to emit an unnecessary memory-fence instruction for the input parameter; see Section 1.1."Attribute Syntax" on page 12.

In both cases, if a function or a parameter declaration specifies the [[carries_dependency]] attribute, the first declaration of that function shall specify that attribute. Similarly, if the first declaration of a function or one of its parameters specifies the [[carries_dependency]] attribute in one translation unit and the first declaration of the same function in another translation unit doesn't, the program is **ill formed, no diagnostic required (IFNDR)**.

It is important to note that while the [[carries_dependency]] attribute informs the compiler about the presence of a dependency chain, it does not itself create one. The dependency chain must be present in the implementation to have any effect on synchronization.

Use Cases

Producer-consumer programming pattern

The popular producer-consumer programming pattern uses *release-acquire* pairs to synchronize between threads:

```
// my_shareddata.h:
void initSharedData();
    // Initialize the shared data of my_shareddata.o to a well-known
    // aggregation of values.

void accessSharedData();
    // Confirm that the shared data of my_shareddata.o have been initialized
    // and have their expected values.


// my_shareddata.cpp:
#include <my_shareddata.h>

#include <atomic>  // std::atomic, std::memory_order_release, and
                   // std::memory_order_acquire
#include <cassert> // standard C assert macro

struct S
{
    int    i;
    char   c;
    double d;
};

static S                data;     // static for insulation
static std::atomic<int> guard(0); // static for insulation

void initSharedData()
{
    data.i = 42;
    data.c = 'c';
    data.d = 5.0;

    guard.store(1, std::memory_order_release);
}

void accessSharedData()
{
    while(0 == guard.load(std::memory_order_acquire))
        /* empty */ ;

    assert(42  == data.i);
    assert('c' == data.c);
    assert(5.0 == data.d);
}
```

```
// my_app.cpp:
#include <my_shareddata.h>
#include <thread>  // std::thread

int main()
{
    std::thread t2(accessSharedData);
    std::thread t1(  initSharedData);

    t1.join();
    t2.join();
}
```

When this *release-acquire synchronization paradigm* is used, the compiler must maintain the statements' ordering to avoid breaking the *release-acquire* guarantee; the compiler must also insert memory-fence instructions to prevent the hardware from breaking this guarantee.

If we wanted to modify the example above to use *release-consume* semantics, we would somehow need to make the `assert` statements a part of the dependency chain on the `load` from the `guard` object. We can accomplish this goal because reading data through a pointer establishes a dependency chain between the reading of that pointer value and the reading of the referenced data. Since *release-consume* allows the developer to specify that data of concern, using that policy instead of *release-acquire* policy (in the code example above) allows the compiler to be more selective in its use of memory fences:

```
// my_shareddata.cpp (use _*consume, not *_acquire):
#include <my_shareddata.h>

#include <atomic>  // std::atomic, std::memory_order_release, and
                   // std::memory_order_consume (not *_acquire)
#include <cassert> // standard C assert macro

struct S
{
    /* definition not changed */
};

static S                data;        // static for insulation (as before)
static std::atomic<S*> guard(nullptr); // guards just one struct S.

void initSharedData()
{
    data.i = 42;   // as before
    data.c = 'c';  // as before
    data.d = 5.0;  // as before

    guard.store(&data, std::memory_order_release);  // Set &data, not 1.
}
```

```
void accessSharedData()
{
    S* sharedDataPtr = nullptr;

    // Load using *_consume, not *_acquire.
    while (nullptr == (sharedDataPtr = guard.load(std::memory_order_consume)))
        /* empty */ ;

    assert(&data == sharedDataPtr);

    assert(42  == sharedDataPtr->i);
    assert('c' == sharedDataPtr->c);
    assert(5.0 == sharedDataPtr->d);
}
```

Finally, if we want to start to refactor the work of the `my_sharedata` component into multiple functions across different translation units, we would want to carefully apply the `[[carries_dependency]]` attribute to the newly refactored functions, so calling into these functions might conceivably be better optimized:

```
// my_shareddataimpl.h:

struct S
{
    int    i;
    char   c;
    double d;
};

[[carries_dependency]] S* getSharedDataPtr();
    // Return the address of the shared data in this translation unit.

void releaseSharedData(S* sharedDataPtr [[carries_dependency]]);
    // Release the shared data in this translation unit.  The behavior is
    // undefined unless getSharedDataPtr() == sharedDataPtr.

[[carries_dependency]] S* accessInitializedSharedData();
    // Return the address of the initialized shared data in this translation
    // unit.

void checkSharedDataValue(S* s [[carries_dependency]],
                          int    i,
                          char   c,
                          double d);
    // Confirm that data at the specified s has the specified i, c, and
    // d as constituent values.
```

```cpp
// my_shareddataimpl.cpp:

#include <my_shareddataimpl.h>

#include <cassert>  // standard C offsetof macro
#include <atomic>    // std::atomic, std::memory_order_*

static S              data;         // static for insulation
static std::atomic<S*> guard(nullptr); // guards one struct S.

[[carries_dependency]] S* getSharedDataPtr()
{
    return &data;
}

void releaseSharedData(S* sharedDataPtr [[carries_dependency]])
{
    assert(&data == sharedDataPtr);

    guard.store(sharedDataPtr, std::memory_order_release);
}

[[carries_dependency]] S* accessInitializedSharedData()
{
    S* sharedDataPtr = nullptr;

    while (nullptr == (sharedDataPtr = guard.load(std::memory_order_consume)))
        /* empty */ ;

    assert(&data == sharedDataPtr);

    return sharedDataPtr;
}

void checkSharedDataValue(S*      s [[carries_dependency]],
                          int     i,
                          char    c,
                          double d)
{
    assert(i == s->i);
    assert(c == s->c);
    assert(d == s->d);
}
```

```
// my_shareddata.cpp (re-factored to use *impl)
#include <my_shareddataimpl.h>

void initSharedData()
{
    S* sharedDataPtr = getSharedDataPtr();

    sharedDataPtr->i = 42;
    sharedDataPtr->c = 'c';
    sharedDataPtr->d = 5.0;

    releaseSharedData(sharedDataPtr);
}

void accessSharedData()
{
    S* sharedDataPtr = accessInitializedSharedData();
    checkSharedDataValue(sharedDataPtr, 42, 'c', 5.0);
}
```

Potential Pitfalls

No practical use on current platforms

All known compilers promote *consume* loads to *acquire* loads, thus failing to omit superfluous memory-fence instructions. Developers writing code with the expectation that it will be run under the more efficient **release-consume synchronization paradigm** will find that their code will continue to work — as expected — under the more conservative **release-acquire** guarantees until such time as a theoretical, not-yet-existent compiler that properly supports the **release-consume synchronization paradigm** becomes widely available. In the meantime, applications that require the potential performance benefits of *consume* semantics typically make careful use of platform-specific functionality instead.[2]

---

[2]Since C++17, the use of memory_order_consume has been explicitly discouraged after the acceptance of **boehm16**. The specific note in the standard now says, "Prefer memory_order_acquire, which provides stronger guarantees than memory_order_consume. Implementations have found it infeasible to provide performance better than that of memory_order_acquire. Specification revisions are under consideration" (**iso17**, section 32.4 "Order and Consistency," paragraph 1.3, Note 1, p. 1346).

See Also

- "Attribute Syntax" (§1.1, p. 12) provides an in-depth discussion of how attributes pertain to C++ language entities.

- "noreturn" (§1.1, p. 95) offers an example of another *attribute* that *is* implemented ubiquitously.

Further Reading

- A high-level implementation of the *read-copy-update* pattern for C++ is presented in **marton17**.

- Ideas for exploiting the *read-copy-update* pattern in C++ are presented in **marton18**.

Prohibiting Overriding and Derivation

The **final** specifier can be used to disallow either (1) overriding one or more virtual member functions from within derived types or (2) deriving from a type altogether.

Description

The ability to extend an arbitrary (**class** or **struct**) user-defined type (**UDT**) via inheritance and then to override any virtual functions declared therein is a hallmark of the C++ object-oriented model. There might, however, be cases where the author of such a UDT will find a legitimate need to intentionally restrict clients' abilities in this regard. The **final** specifier serves such a purpose.

When applied to a virtual-function declaration, **final** prevents derived-class authors from overriding that specific function. When used on a virtual function, **final** is syntactically similar to the **override** specifier (see Section 1.1."**override**" on page 104) but with different semantics. Separately, **final** can be applied to the declaration of a user-defined type as a whole, thereby preventing prospective clients from deriving from it. Finally, note that **final**, like **override**, is not a reserved keyword but rather a **contextual keyword** — i.e., an identifier with special meaning in certain contexts — and can still be used as a C++ identifier wherever the language grammar allows an identifier:

```
struct final final                          // struct named "final"
{
    final() = default;                      // default constructor
    virtual ~final() final;                 // final destructor
};
struct S1 { ::final* final; };              // data member named "final"
struct S2 { virtual ::final final() final; };  // function named "final"
final final;                                // object named "final"
```

The admittedly problematic example above is syntactically legal, defining several different entities named **final**, some of which also have the **final** specifier attached.

final virtual member functions

When applied to a virtual-function declaration, the **final** specifier prevents derived-class authors from *overriding* that function:

```
struct B0  // Each function in B0 is explicitly declared virtual.
{
    virtual void f();
    virtual void g() final;  // prevents overriding in derived classes
    virtual void g() const;
};
```

```
struct D0 : B0        // D0 inherits publicly from B0.
{
    void f();         // OK, overrides void B0::f()
    void g();         // Error, void B0::g() is final.
    void g() const;   // OK, void B0::g() const is not final.
};
```

As the simple example above illustrates, decorating a virtual member function — e.g., `B::g()` — with **final** precludes overriding only that specific function signature. Note that when redeclaring a **final** function outside the class definition (e.g., to define the function), the **final** specifier is not permitted:

```
void B0::g() final { }  // Error, final not permitted outside class definition
void B0::g() { }        // OK
```

final **on destructors**

The use of **final** on a virtual destructor precludes inheritance entirely, as any derived class must have either an implicit or explicit destructor that will attempt to override the **final** base class destructor:

```
struct B1
{
    virtual ~B1() final;
};

struct D1a : B1 { };    // Error, implicitly tries to override B1::~B1()

struct D1b : B1
{
    virtual ~D1b() { }  // Error, explicitly tries to override B1::~B1()
};
```

Any attempt to suppress the destructor in the derived class, e.g., using `=`**delete** (see Section 1.1."Deleted Functions" on page 53), will be in vain. If the intent is to suppress derivation entirely, a direct way would be to declare the type itself **final**; see *final user-defined types* on page 1011.

final **pure virtual functions**

Although declaring a **pure virtual function final** is allowed, doing so makes the type an **abstract class** and also prevents making any derived type a **concrete class**:

```
struct B2  // abstract class
{
    virtual void f() final = 0;  // OK, but probably not useful
};

B2 b;  // Error, B2 is an abstract type.

struct D2a : B2  // also an abstract class
{
};

D2a d;  // Error, D2a is an abstract type.

struct D2b : B2
{
    void f() {};  // Error, void B2::f() is final.
};
```

By declaring the pure virtual member function, `B2::f()` in the example above, to be final, we have effectively precluded ever extending the uninstantiable abstract class, B2, to *any* instantiable concrete class.

final and its interactions with virtual and override

When we apply **final** to nonvirtual functions, the **final** specifier will always force a compilation error:

```
struct B3a
{
    void f() final;  // Error, f is not virtual.
};

struct B3b
{
    void g();  // OK, g is not virtual.
};

struct D3 : B3b
{
    void g() final;  // Error, g is not virtual and hides B3b::g.
};
```

The **final** keyword combines with the **virtual** and **override** keywords to produce various effects. For example, a function declared **virtual** in a base class, e.g., each of the functions below in B4, automatically also makes virtual a function having the same name and signature in a derived class, e.g., the corresponding functions in D4, irrespective of whether the **virtual** keyword is repeated in D4:

```
struct B4  // Each of the functions in B4 is explicitly declared virtual.
{
    virtual void f();  // explicitly declared virtual
    virtual void g();  //       "         "        "
    virtual void h();  //       "         "        "
};

struct D4 : B4  // Each of the functions in D4 is explicitly declared final.
{
    void f() final;          // OK, because B4::f is declared virtual
    virtual void g() final;  // OK, explicitly declared virtual (no effect)
    void h() final override; // OK, because B4::h is declared virtual
    virtual void i() final;  // OK, explicitly declared virtual (necessary)
    void j() final;          // Error, nonvirtual function j declared final
};
```

Notice that D4::g() is annotated with the keyword **virtual**, but D4::f() is not. Redundantly adding **virtual** to the declaration of a function in a derived class when there is a matching function declared **virtual** in a base class is not necessary. In a manner similar to **override**, leaving off the explicit **virtual** will prevent removing the base-class function or even altering its signature.

Given the availability of the **override** specifier (see Section 1.1."**override**" on page 104), however, a common coding standard has emerged: Use **virtual** only to *introduce* a virtual function in a class hierarchy, and then *require* that any functions attempting to *override* a virtual function in a derived class be decorated with *either* **override** or **final** and explicitly *not* **virtual** because **virtual** is unambiguously implied:

```
struct B5  // base class consisting of virtual and nonvirtual functions
{
    virtual void f1();  // OK, virtual function
    virtual void f2();  // OK, virtual function
            void g1();  // OK, nonvirtual function
            void g2();  // OK, nonvirtual function
};

struct D5a  // "derived class" attempting to override virtual functions f1 and f2
{
    void f1() override;  // Error, f1 marked override but doesn't override
    void f2() final;     // Error, f2 marked final but isn't virtual
};
```

The astute reader will have noticed that in the example above we failed to make D5a inherit publicly from B5. Catching such a flaw early is the main benefit of following this convention.

If we try again, this time with D5b, we will observe a second benefit of always supplying either **override** or **final**:

```
struct D5b : B5  // This time we remembered to inherit from B5.
{
    void f1() override;  // OK
    void f2() final;     // OK
    void g1() override;  // Error, g1 marked override but doesn't override
    void g2() final;     // Error, g2 marked final but isn't virtual
};
```

Finally, one could imagine deliberately declaring a base-class function to be both **virtual** and **final** — e.g., just to prevent a derived class from hiding it:

```
struct B6
{
    virtual void f() final;  // OK
};

static_assert(sizeof(B6) == 1, "");  // Error, B6 holds a vtable pointer.

struct D6a : B6
{
    void f() const;  // OK, D6a::f doesn't override.
    void f();        // Error, B6::f is final.
};

struct D6b : B6
{
    void f(int i = 0);  // OK, even though it hides B6::f
};
```

Declaring, for the first time, the member function B6::f in the example above to be both **virtual** and **final** has limited practical effect. Attempts to hide f in a subclass will be blocked but only when the hiding function has *exactly* the same signature; a function that hides f can still be written with different member function qualifiers or even slightly different, possibly optional parameters. Adding **virtual** to f also makes B6 a **polymorphic type**, bringing with it the need for a **vtable pointer** in every object and making it non-**trivial**; see Section 2.1."Generalized PODs '11" on page 401. The compiler will likely be able to **devirtualize** calls to B6::f but might fail to do so, resulting in invocations of B6::f having the runtime overhead associated with **dynamic dispatch**; see *Potential Pitfalls — Attempting to defend against the hiding of a non***virtual** *function* on page 1026.

final user-defined types

The use of **final** is not limited to individual member functions; **final** can also be applied to an entire user-defined type to explicitly disallow *any* other type from inheriting from it. Preventing a type from being inheritable closes the gap between what is possible with built-in types, such as **int** and **double**, and what can additionally be done with typical user-defined ones — specifically, inherit from them. See *Use Cases — Suppressing derivation to ensure portability* on page 1014, i.e., **Hyrum's law**.

Although other use cases might be plausible, widespread, systemic use can run afoul of stable **reuse** in general and **hierarchical reuse** in particular; see *Potential Pitfalls — Systemic lost opportunities for reuse* on page 1023. Hence, the decision to use **final** on an entire class even rarely — let alone routinely — is not to be taken lightly.

Prior to C++11's introduction of the **final** specifier, there was no convenient way to ensure that a **user-defined type (UDT)** was *uninheritable*, although Byzantine idioms to approximate this restriction existed. For example, a virtual base class needs to be initialized in each constructor of all concrete derived types, and that can be leveraged to prevent useful inheritance. Consider a trio of classes, the first of which, **UninheritableGuard**, has a private constructor and befriends its only intended derived class; the second, **Uninheritable**, derives privately and virtually from **UninheritableGuard**; and the third, **Inheriting**, is a misguided class that tries in vain to inherit from **Uninheritable**:

```
struct UninheritableGuard  // private, virtual base class
{
private:
    UninheritableGuard();         // private constructor
    friend struct Uninheritable;  // constructible only by Uninheritable
};

struct Uninheritable : private virtual UninheritableGuard
{
    Uninheritable() : UninheritableGuard() { /*...*/ }
};

struct Inheriting : Uninheritable  // Uninheritable is effectively final.
{
    Inheriting()
    : Uninheritable()  // Error, Uninheritable() is inaccessible.
    { /*...*/ }
};
```

Any attempt to define — either implicitly or explicitly — a constructor for **Inheriting** will fail with the same error due to the inaccessibility of the constructor for **UninheritableGuard**. Using **virtual** inheritance typically requires each object of type **Uninheritable** to maintain a virtual table pointer; hence, this solution does not come without overhead. Note also that this workaround prior to **final** does not prevent the derivation itself, but merely the instantiation of any ill-fated derived classes.

In the special case where all of the data members of the type are trivial, i.e., have no user-provided **special member functions** (see Section 2.1."Generalized PODs '11" on page 401), we could have instead created a type, e.g., **Uninheritable2**, that is implemented as a **union** consisting of just a single **struct**:

```
union Uninheritable2  // C++ does not yet permit inheritance from union types.
{
    struct  // anonymous class type
    {
        int     i;
        double d;
    } s;

    Uninheritable2()
    {
        s.i = 0;
        s.d = 0;
    }
};

struct S : Uninheritable2 { };  // Error, unions cannot be base classes.
```

With the introduction of the **final** specifier, no such contortions are needed. When added to the *definition* of either a **class** or **struct**, the **final** specifier adeptly prevents prospective clients from deriving from that type:

```
struct S1 { };        // nonfinal user-defined type
struct S2 final { };  // final user-defined type

struct D1 : S1 { };   // OK, S1 is not declared final.
struct D2 : S2 { };   // Error, S2 is declared final.
```

The **final** specifier may be applied to a type's declaration only when it is part of that type's definition:

```
class C1;              // OK, C1 is (as of now) an incomplete type.
class C1 final;        // Error, attempt to declare variable of incomplete type
class C1 final { };    // OK, C1 is now a complete type.
class C1;              // OK, C1 is known to be a final type.
```

Once a type is complete, any attempt to redeclare that type using the **final** specifier will be a valid declaration of an object of that type named **final**; hence, a type that has been defined as *non***final** cannot subsequently be redeclared as **final**:

```
class C2 { };          // OK, C2 is a nonfinal complete type.
class C2 final;        // Bug? C2 object named final.
```

As the last line above illustrates, **final**, being a contextual keyword, is a valid name for an object of non**final** class C2; see *Potential Pitfalls — Contextual keywords are contextual* on page 1023.

The **final** specifier, in addition to decorating a **class** or **struct**, can also be applied to a **union**. Since derivation from a **union** isn't permitted anyway, declaring a union to be **final** has no effect.

final

The Standard C++14 Library header `<type_traits>` defines the trait `std::is_final`, which can be used to determine whether a given user-defined type is specified as **final**. This trait can be used to distinguish between a non**final** and **final union**. The argument to `std::is_final`, however, must be a complete type.

Use Cases

Suppressing derivation to ensure portability

A rare but compelling use of **final** for a user-defined type as a whole occurs when that type is used to simulate a feature that is or might some day be implemented as a **fundamental type**, subject to platform capabilities. By specifying the user-defined type to be **final**, we avoid locking it into forever being represented as a user-defined type.

As a real-world example, consider an early implementation of a family of floating-point decimal types: `Decimal32_t`, `Decimal64_t`, and `Decimal128_t`. Initially these types (as type aliases) are implemented in terms of user-defined types:

```
class DecimalFloatingPoint32  { /*...*/ };
class DecimalFloatingPoint64  { /*...*/ };
class DecimalFloatingPoint128 { /*...*/ };

typedef DecimalFloatingPoint32  Decimal32_t;
typedef DecimalFloatingPoint64  Decimal64_t;
typedef DecimalFloatingPoint128 Decimal128_t;
```

Once released in this form, there is nothing to stop users from inheriting from these **typedef**s to derive their own custom types, and, in fact, Hyrum's law predicts that such inheritance will happen:

```
class MyDecimal32    : public Decimal32_t      { /*...*/ };
class YourDecimal64  : private Decimal64_t     { /*...*/ };
class TheirDecimal128 : protected Decimal128_t { /*...*/ };
```

Hardware support will someday arrive — and on some platforms it already has — that will likely allow these **typedef**s to become aliases to fundamental types rather than aliases to user-defined types:

```
typedef __decimal32_t  Decimal32_t;
typedef __decimal64_t  Decimal64_t;
typedef __decimal128_t Decimal128_t;
```

When that day comes and we try to leverage the possibly large performance benefits of using a natively supported type, a small number of clients of this library will prevent the majority of users from enjoying the performance advantages of the new platform. The end result is that person-years of effort might be required to unravel the code that now depends on inheritance. That price could have been avoided had we just declared our *not necessarily* user-defined types **final** from the start:

```
class DecimalFloatingPoint32 final  { /*...*/ };
class DecimalFloatingPoint64 final  { /*...*/ };
class DecimalFloatingPoint128 final { /*...*/ };
```

Using **final** here would have avoided advertising more than we were prepared to support in perpetuity.

Improving performance of concrete classes

Object-oriented programming (OOP) encompasses two important aspects of software design: (1) inheritance and (2) **dynamic binding** (which is usually implemented by **virtual dispatch**). For a language to claim that it supports OOP, it must support both.[1,2] No overhead is associated with inheritance *per se*, but the same cannot be said in general for dynamic binding.

Irrespective of the various implications of an implementation consisting of a mixture of *interface*, *implementation*, and *structural* inheritance, consider the classic Shape, Circle, and Rectangle example illustrating **object orientation**:

```
class Shape   // abstract base class
{
    int d_x;  // x-coordinate of origin
    int d_y;  // y-coordinate of origin

public:
    Shape(int x, int y) : d_x(x), d_y(y) { }   // value constructor
    virtual ~Shape() { }                       // destructor

    void move(int dx, int dy) { d_x += dx; d_y += dy; }
                                               // concrete manipulator

    int xOrigin() const { return d_x; }        // concrete accessor
    int yOrigin() const { return d_y; }        // concrete accessor

    virtual double area() const = 0;           // abstract accessor
};

class Circle : public Shape  // concrete derived class
{
    int d_radius;  // radius of this circle

public:
    Circle(int x, int y, int radius) : Shape(x, y), d_radius(radius) { }
                                               // value constructor
```

---

[1]stroustrup91a, section 1.4.6, "Multiple Implementations," pp. 35–36
[2]stroustrup91b

```
    double area() const { return 3.14 * d_radius; }
                                        // concrete accessor (nonfinal)
};

class Rectangle: public Shape     // concrete derived class
{
    int d_length;  // length of this rectangle
    int d_width;   // width of this rectangle

public:
    Rectangle(int x, int y, int length, int width) :
                    Shape(x, y), d_length(length), d_width(width) { }
                                        // value constructor

    double area() const final { return d_length * d_width; }
                                        // concrete accessor (final)
};
```

Note that Shape acts both as an interface and as a base class offering a proper value constructor. Inheriting classes have to override Shape::area to provide a *concrete accessor* for their respective area values. The two classes inheriting from Shape, namely, Circle and Rectangle, differ substantially in just one aspect: Rectangle::area() is annotated with **final**, whereas Circle::area() is not.

Now imagine a client accessing the *concrete implementations* of Shape::area through a base-class reference:

```
void client1(const Shape& shape)
{
    int x = shape.xOrigin();     // inlines (e.g., Clang -O2, GCC -O1)
    double area = shape.area();  // Inline requires whole program optimization.
}
```

The call to Shape::xOrigin can be inlined at a fairly low level of optimization whereas the call to Shape::area cannot because it is subject to *virtual dispatch*. The same ability to inline the call to get the xOrigin applies for objects of either derived type — Circle as well as Rectangle — irrespective of whether the type's implementation of Shape::area has been annotated with **final**.

If the compiler can locally infer the runtime type of the derived object, the function calls can be inlined at a fairly low optimization level too, again irrespective of any annotation with **final**:

```
void client2()
{
    Circle c(3, 2, 1);
```

```
    Rectangle r(4, 3, 2, 1);
    const Shape& s1 = c;
    const Shape& s2 = r;

    double cArea = c.area();  // inlines (e.g., Clang -O2, GCC -O1)
    double rArea = r.area();  // inlines (e.g., Clang -O2, GCC -O1)

    double s1Area = s1.area();  // inlines (e.g., Clang -O2, GCC -O1)
    double s2Area = s2.area();  // inlines (e.g., Clang -O2, GCC -O1)
}
```

The difference facilitated by **final** comes to light when accepting references of these types
in a separate function. Because only `Rectangle` prohibits further overriding of the `area`
function, it is the only one of the three types that can know at compile time the runtime
type of its object and therefore bypass virtual dispatch:

```
void client3(const Shape& s, const Circle& c, const Rectangle& r)
{
    double sArea = s.area();  // must undergo virtual dispatch
    double cArea = c.area();  // must undergo virtual dispatch
    double rArea = r.area();  // inlines (Clang -O2, GCC -O1)
}
```

Note that a compilation system that is aware of the entirety of a program might be able
to turn that into knowledge that `Circle` is effectively final — e.g., by observing that no
other classes derive from it — and thus similarly bypass virtual dispatch in `client3`. Such
an optimization, however, is expensive, doesn't scale, and would be thwarted by common
practices, such as the possibility of loading shared objects at run time, which might contain
classes derived from `Circle` that are then passed to `client3`.

Restoring performance lost to mocking

In most cases, a component cannot be fully isolated from its dependencies in order to be
able to test it in complete isolation. An object-oriented approach widely used to artificially
circumvent such limitations is often colloquially referred to as **mocking**.

As an example, consider a custom file-handling class, `File`, that depends on a custom local
file system, `LocalFS`:

```
class FileHandle;

struct LocalFS  // lower-level file system
{
    FileHandle* open(const char* path, int* errorStatus = 0);
};
```

```
class File  // higher-level file representation
{
    LocalFS* d_lfs;  // pointer to concrete filesystem object

public:
    File(LocalFS* lfs) : d_lfs(lfs) { }

    int open(const char* path);
    // ...
};
```

In the design above, class `File`'s direct dependency on the local file system impedes testing `File`'s behavior in response to, say, a rarely occurring and difficult-to-induce system event.

To be able to test our `File` class thoroughly, we will need some way to control what the `File` class does when it receives input back from what it perceives to be the local file system. One approach would be to extract a pure abstract (a.k.a. **protocol**) class, e.g., `AbstractFileSystem`, from `LocalFS`. We can then make our `File` class depend on the protocol instead of `LocalFS` and make `LocalFS` implement it:

```
class AbstractFileSystem  // lower-level pure abstract interface
{
public:
    virtual FileHandle* open(const char* path, int* errorStatus = 0) = 0;
};


class File  // uses lower-level abstract file system
{
    AbstractFileSystem* d_afs;  // pointer to abstract filesystem object

public:
    File(AbstractFileSystem* afs) : d_afs(afs) { }

    int open(const char* path);
    // ...
};


class LocalFS : public AbstractFileSystem  // implements abstract interface
{
public:
    FileHandle* open(const char* path, int* errorStatus = 0);
};
```

With this more elaborate design, we are now able to create an independent concrete, "mock" implementation derived from `AbstractFileSystem`, which we can then use to orchestrate arbitrary behavior, thereby enabling us to test `File` both (1) in isolation and (2) under abnormal circumstances:

```
class MockedFS : public AbstractFileSystem  // test-engineer-controllable class
{
public:
    FileHandle* open(const char* path, int* errorStatus = 0) { /* mocked */ }
};

void test()  // test driver that orchestrates mock implementation to test File
{
    MockedFS mfs;  // mock AbstractFileSystem used to thoroughly test File
    File f(&mfs);  // f installed with mock instead of actual LocalFS

    int rc = f.open("dummyPath");  // mock used to supply handle
    // ...
}
```

Although this technique does enable independent testing, it comes with the performance cost of dynamic dispatch on all calls to the underlying `AbstractFileSystem` object. In certain situations where the concrete implementation doesn't have to be exchangeable for the mock, performance can be recovered by declaring some or all of the concrete, now-virtual functions of `localFS` **final**. This way, when we pass the concrete implementation — e.g., `LocalFS` — to a function explicitly, at least the functions that are declared **final** and were previously inline can again be inline:

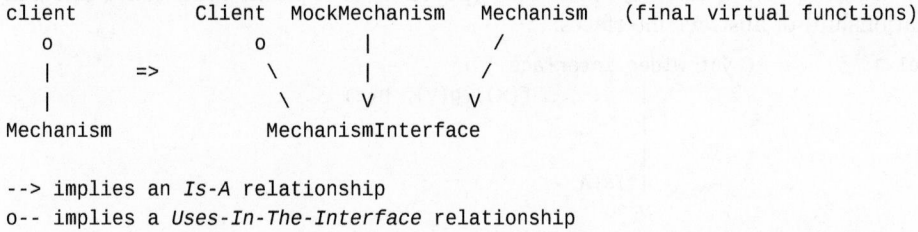

```
client          Client  MockMechanism   Mechanism   (final virtual functions)
  o               o          |           /
  |      =>         \        |          /
  |                  \       V         V
Mechanism             MechanismInterface


--> implies an Is-A relationship
o-- implies a Uses-In-The-Interface relationship
```

Alternatively, we might create a new component that adapts an existing library to a new interface suitable for mocking without having to alter it in any way:

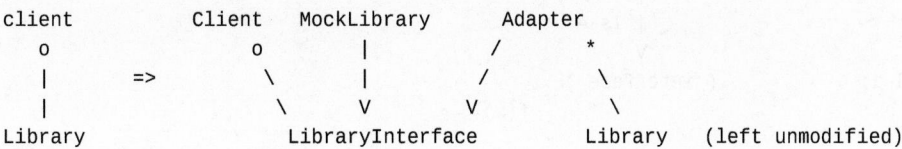

```
client          Client  MockLibrary     Adapter
  o               o          |          /        *
  |      =>         \        |         /          \
  |                  \       V        V            \
Library               LibraryInterface      Library   (left unmodified)


*-- implies a Uses-In-The-Implementation (only) relationship
```

However, it has become commonplace in the industry "to make a mockery of one's design through mocking"[3] by artificially declaring all nonconstructor member functions of a class

---

[3] Jonathan Wakely has expressed to John Lakos that indiscriminate and excessive use of mocking "is to make a mockery of one's design."

virtual (without extracting a protocol) just to be able to provide a "mock" implementation derived from the original concrete class:

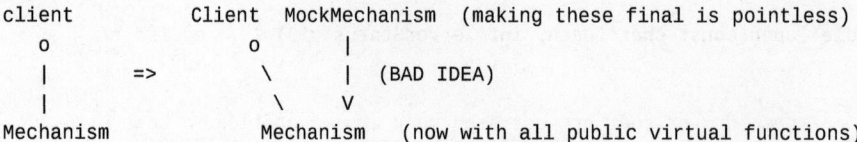

```
client              Client  MockMechanism  (making these final is pointless)
   o                   o       |
   |        =>          \      |   (BAD IDEA)
   |                     \     V
Mechanism               Mechanism  (now with all public virtual functions)
```

As the diagrams above suggest, much of the virtual function overhead associated with mocking can be reduced significantly by *not* deriving the mock from the original class. Instead, we can either (1) extract a **protocol** for all of the public nonconstructor member functions of that class and mark those specific functions **final** or (2) adapt the original concrete implementation unchanged to the new protocol for use by File and any other facilities that choose to opt in for the purposes of thoroughly testing their code. With either of these approaches, all clients that continue to use the concrete, possibly now-derived class by its original name do not need to pay for *any* virtual function overhead to support the ability to mock that class's interface where needed.

Improving performance in a protocol hierarchy

A **protocol hierarchy**[4,5] is a generalization of the **composite pattern**[6] in which a pure abstract interface (a.k.a. protocol) is the root (**level 1**) of a public inheritance hierarchy (*Is-A* relationship) of abstract interfaces:

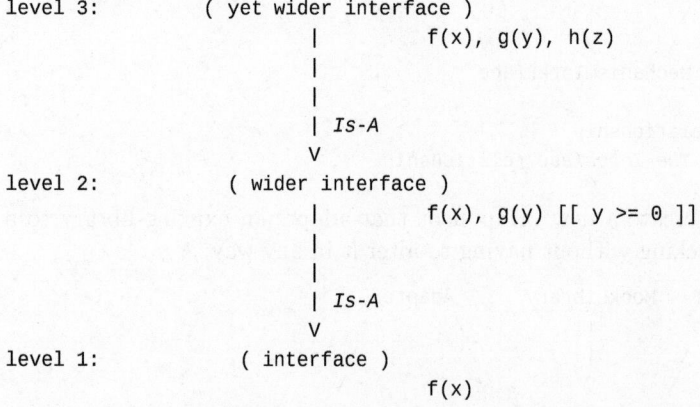

```
level 3:          ( yet wider interface )
                            |              f(x), g(y), h(z)
                            |
                            |
                            | Is-A
                            V
level 2:          ( wider interface )
                            |              f(x), g(y) [[ y >= 0 ]]
                            |
                            |
                            | Is-A
                            V
level 1:          ( interface )
                               f(x)
```

At each successive level, the *pure* interface is a proper superset of the one at the previous level from which it derives. None of the classes in the hierarchy contributes any implementation; each member function — except for the destructor — is implemented as **pure virtual**. In

---

[4]**lakos96**, Appendix A, pp. 737–768

[5]A discussion of this topic is planned for **lakos2a**, section 2.7.

[6]**gamma95**, Chapter 2, section "Composite," pp. 163–174

particular, notice that g(y) is not accessible at level 1, can be used only with non-negative values at level 2 (i.e., g(y) has a **narrow contract**), and is usable with all syntactically legal values at level 3 (i.e., g(y) has a **wide contract**). Note that this same sort of interface widening can apply in the absence of virtual functions through judicious use of hiding nonvirtual functions; see *Potential Pitfalls — Systemic lost opportunities for reuse* on page 1023.

Concrete leaf nodes can then be derived from the protocol hierarchy to implement the desired level of service as efficiently as practical. In cases where multiple concrete nodes need to share the same implementation of one or more functions, we can derive an intermediate node from the appropriate *protocol* that doesn't widen the interface at all but does implement one or more of the pure abstract functions; such an *impure* abstract node is known as a **partial implementation**. When the implementation of one of these functions is trivial, declaring that **virtual** function to also be **inline** might be sensible. Since, by design, there will be no need to further override that function, we can declare it to be **final** as well.

For performance-critical clients that would otherwise consume the concrete object via the pure abstract interface from which this partial implementation derives, we might decide to instead take the partial implementation itself as the reference type. Because one or more functions are both **inline** and **final**, the client can dispense with runtime dispatch and inline the virtual functions directly as discussed in *Restoring performance lost to mocking* on page 1017.

As a real-world example, consider a simplified **protocol hierarchy** for memory allocation:

```cpp
#include <cstddef>  // std::size_t

struct Allocator
{
    virtual void* allocate(std::size_t numBytes) = 0;
        // Allocate a block of memory of at least the specified numBytes.

    virtual void deallocate(void* address) = 0;
        // Deallocate the block at the specified address.
};

struct ManagedAllocator : Allocator
{
    virtual void release() = 0;
        // Reclaim all memory currently allocated from this allocator.
};
```

A **monotonic allocator** is a kind of **managed allocator** that allocates memory sequentially in a buffer subject to alignment requirements. In this class of allocators, the **deallocate** method is always a no-op; memory is reclaimed only when the managed allocator is destroyed or its **release** method is invoked:

```
struct MonotonicAllocatorPartialImp : ManagedAllocator
{
    inline void deallocate(void* address) final { /* empty */ }
        // Deallocate the block at the specified address.
};
```

Notice that we have specified the empty **inline** deallocate member function of
MonotonicAllocatorPartialImp to be **final**. A concrete monotonic allocator — e.g., a
BufferedSequentialAllocator — can then derive from this partial implementation:

```
struct BufferedSequentialAllocator : MonotonicAllocatorPartialImp
{
    BufferedSequentialAllocator();
        // Create a default version of a buffered-sequential allocator.

    void* allocate(std::size_t numBytes);
        // Allocate a block of memory of at least the specified numBytes.

    void release();
        // Reclaim all memory currently allocated from this allocator.
};
```

Now consider two allocator-aware types, TypeA and TypeB, each of which is always constructed with some flavor of managed allocator:

```
struct TypeA
{
    TypeA(ManagedAllocator* a);
    // ...
};

struct TypeB
{
    TypeB(MonotonicAllocatorPartialImp* a);
    // ...
};
```

We now construct each of the types using the same concrete allocator object:

```
void client()
{
    BufferedSequentialAllocator a;  // Concrete monotonic allocator object

    TypeA ta(&a);  // deallocate is a virtual call to an empty function.
    TypeB tb(&a);  // deallocate is an inline call to an empty function.
}
```

When TypeA invokes deallocate, it goes through the nonfinal, virtual function interface
of ManagedAllocator and is subject to the runtime overhead of dynamic dispatch. Note

that even if the virtual `deallocate` function were inline, unless it is declared **final** or the runtime type is somehow known at compile time, there is no sure way for the compiler to know that the function isn't overridden by a derived type.

In the case of `TypeB`, however, the function is both *declared* **final** and *defined* **inline**; hence, the virtual dispatch can be reliably sidestepped, the empty function can be inlined, and a true no-op is achieved with no runtime overhead.

Potential Pitfalls

Contextual keywords are contextual

Historically, the Standards Committee has taken different approaches to adding new keywords to the language. C++11 added ten new keywords to the language — **alignas**, **alignof**, **char16_t**, **char32_t**, **constexpr**, **decltype**, **noexcept**, **nullptr**, **static_assert**, and **thread_local**[7] — and thus made ten potential tokens no longer usable as identifiers. When considering new keywords, much effort is expended to determine the impact of that word's change in status on existing codebases. Two identifiers, **override** and **final**, were not made keywords and were instead given special meaning when used in contexts where previously identifiers were not syntactically allowed. This approach avoided possible code breakage for any existing codebases using these words as identifiers, at the cost of occasional confusion.

When used after a function declaration, **override** and **final** do not add any significant parsing ambiguity to the language; arbitrary identifiers were not syntactically valid in that position anyway, so confusion is minimal. When used on a **class** declaration, however, **final**'s meaning is not determined until tokens after it are parsed to distinguish between a variable declaration and a class definition:

```
struct S1 final;       // Error, variable named final of incomplete type
struct S2 final { };   // OK, final class definition
struct S2 final;       // OK, variable named final of complete type S2
```

Notice that the variable declarations in the example above both look like they might be an attempt to forward-declare a **struct** that is final but are instead a totally different language construct.

Systemic lost opportunities for reuse

Both **final** and **override** are similar in their complexity yet different in the potential adverse implications that widespread use can impose. Such ubiquitous use will depend heavily on the scale and nature of the development process employed. In some development

---

[7]C++14 and C++17 added no new keywords. C++20 added **char8_t**, **co_await**, **co_return**, **co_yield**, **concept**, **consteval**, **constinit**, and **requires**, notably mixing some words potentially already used as identifiers (**concept** and **requires**) with a collection of more obscure words that had little chance of conflicting with existing codebases.

environments, such as a small organization overseeing a closed-source codebase where clients are able to request timely code changes, encouraging liberal use of **final** might not be problematic. Instead of promising everything up front, even when much of what is offered is not immediately useful, the default development approach might reasonably be to provide only what is immediately necessary and then quickly expose more if and as needed.

For other organizations, however, request-based code changes might not be a viable option and can result in unacceptable delays in responding to client needs. Systemic use of **final** *inherently* prevents opportunistic reuse that involves inheritance. Consequently, clients wishing to adapt an immutable component are often forced to wrap it or else create a redundant copy. Gratuitously forbidding clients from doing what they deem appropriate — and what they would otherwise be able to do for free — might well be perceived as unnecessary nannyism.[8]

Consider, for example, the Standard Template Library (STL) and, in particular, std::vector. One might argue that std:vector was designed to facilitate generic programming, has no virtual functions, and therefore should be specified as **final** to ensure its "proper" use and no other. Suppose, on the other hand, that teachers wanting to teach their students the value of **defensive programming**[9] were to create an exercise to implement a CheckedVector<T>, derived publicly from std::vector<T>.[10] By inheriting constructors (see Section 2.1."Inheriting Ctors" on page 535), it is simple to implement this derived class with an alternate implementation for just **operator[]**:

```
#include <vector>    // std::vector
#include <cassert>   // standard C assert macro

template <typename T>
class CheckedVector : public std::vector<T>
{
public:
    using std::vector<T>::vector;   // Inherit all ctors of std::vector<T>.

    using reference       = typename std::vector<T>::reference;
    using const_reference = typename std::vector<T>::const_reference;
    using size_type       = typename std::vector<T>::size_type;
```

---

[8]"Unnecessary nannyism" is a phrase Bjarne Stroustrup used to characterize his initial decision to restrict operators [], (), and -> to be members; see **stroustrup94**, Chapter 3, section 3.6.2, "Members and Friends," pp. 81–83, particularly p. 83.

[9]See **lakos14a** and **lakos14b**.

[10]Bjarne Stroustrup stated (via email, April 11, 2021) that he himself has employed a class exercise in which the only two functions in the derived type (that he typically calls "Vector") hide the **operator[]** overloads of std::vector. These implementations perform additional checking so that if they are ever called out of their valid range, instead of resulting in **undefined behavior**, they do something sensible, e.g., throw an exception or, even better, print an error message and then call abort to terminate the program. By not employing assert, as we do in our example, Stroustrup avoids using conditional compilation, which is not essential to the didactic purpose of this exercise. When necessary, Stroustrup removes Vector from production use.

```
    reference operator[](size_type pos)              // Hide base-class function.
    {
        assert(pos < this->size());                  // Check bounds.
        return this->std::vector<T>::operator[](pos);
    }

    const_reference operator[](size_type pos) const  // Hide base-class function.
    {
        assert(pos < this->size());                  // Check bounds.
        return this->std::vector<T>::operator[](pos);
    }
};
```

In the implementation above, we have chosen to use the standard C assert macro instead of hard-coding the check and then, if needed, explicitly printing a message and calling abort. Note that this check will occur in only certain build modes, i.e., when NDEBUG is not defined for the current translation unit. Finally, the use of **this->** is purely stylistic to show that we are invoking a member function on this object and can be omitted with no change in behavior.

For local use with the goal of exploring and learning, allowing such **structural inheritance** — involving no virtual functions — can be an expeditious way of uncovering client misuse. This disciplined use of **structural inheritance** adds no data members; it merely widens some of the narrow interfaces in the base class, thereby benignly enhancing the defined behavior already provided yet leaving unchanged the behavior of all other functions of vector. We can now deploy our derived CheckedVector by replacing instances of std::vector with those of our derived CheckedVector, including those in interfaces where potential misuse might occur; simple interaction with the parts of the system not so modified will continue to operate as before. Functions that take an std::vector passed by value are not recommended but will continue to work as before via **slicing**, as will those passed by pointer or reference via implicit standard conversion to base type:

```
void myApi(const CheckedVector<int> &data);      // checked local API
void otherApi1(const std::vector<int> &data);    // by-reference standard API
void otherApi2(std::vector<int> data);           // by-value standard API
template <typename T>
void genericApi(const T& data);                  // generic API

void myFunction()
{
    CheckedVector<int> myData;
    // ...                 ( populate myData )

    myApi(myData);        // checked operations within implementation
    otherApi1(myData);    // normal usage, unchecked operation
    otherApi2(myData);    // normal usage, unchecked operation, slices on copy
```

```
    std::vector<int>& uncheckedData = myData;
    genericApi(myData);         // checked call to templated API
    genericApi(uncheckedData); // unchecked call to same API
}
```

Were std::vector declared **final**, this form of investigation would be entirely prevented, harming those who wished to learn or needed to diagnose defects in their systems using std::vector. Such compulsive use of **final**, even in local libraries, often leads to what is arguably the worst possible result: The client makes a local copy of the library class. Such gratuitously forced duplication of source code systemically exacerbates the already high cost of software maintenance and denies the use of any future enhancements or bug fixes made to that library class.

Finally, contrary to popular belief, the strict notion of substitutability afforded by **structural inheritance** is far more in keeping with that characterized by Barbara Liskov in her pioneering work on subtyping[11] than the *variation in behavior*[12] afforded by virtual functions. Thinking that a class must never be derived from just because it doesn't sport a virtual destructor is misguided. Many metaprogramming idioms rely on structural inheritance; for example, the class template std::integral_constant serves as the base class for most C++ type traits. Structurally inheriting a const_iterator from an iterator achieves implicit convertibility without consuming a user-defined conversion and thereby avoids needless asymmetry; see *Annoyances — Making empty types **final** precludes the empty-base-class optimization* on page 1028.

The decision to make use of **final** the default — absent any specific engineering reason — is dubious as it directly precludes reuse in general and hierarchical reuse in particular. In any event, such a policy, to achieve its intended purpose, fairly belongs with an organization as a whole rather than with each individual developer within that organization. If, however, some specific reason precludes overriding a virtual function or class inheritance, then the use of **final** is indicated to actively document our intent. Lacking such forceful documentation initially, Hyrum's law will ultimately subvert our ability to make the choice to prevent overriding and/or inheritance at a later date.

Attempting to defend against the hiding of a nonvirtual function

Deliberately hiding virtual functions is typically not recommended[13]; when it is done, it is often by accident. Declaring an otherwise nonvirtual function to be both virtual and final does in fact prevent a derived class author from overriding that specific function; a derived class's version of the function will never be invoked through dynamic dispatch. final does *not*, however, prevent a function of the same name having any distinct signature (or a member or type declaration) from inadvertently hiding it.

---

[11]liskov87

[12]Tom Cargill observed that data members are for variation in value, whereas virtual functions are for variation in behavior; see **cargill92**, section "Value versus Behavior," pp. 16–19, specifically p. 17 (see also p. 83 and p. 182).

[13]**meyers96**, Chapter 6, "Item 37, Avoid Hiding Inherited Names," pp. 131–132

As an illustrative example, suppose we were to have a simple output-device type, `Printer`, that contains a set of overloaded non`virtual` print functions to display various types of information on a common device:

```
struct Printer
{
    void print(int number);
    void print(bool boolean);
};
```

Now suppose an inexperienced programmer is about to extend `Printer` to support another parameter type and accidentally hides the base-class functions:

```
struct ExtendedPrinter : public Printer
{
    void print(long c);
};
```

Calling `ExtendedPrinter::print` with an argument having a type that is implicitly convertible to **long** — such as both of the existing supported types of **int** and **bool** — will still compile but fail to work as expected.

We might incorrectly try to defend against such misuse by declaring all functions of the base class both **virtual** and **final** as well:

```
struct Printer2
{
    virtual void print(int number) final;
    virtual void print(bool boolean) final;
};
```

Such machinations do, in fact, make it a compile-time error should we accidentally supply a function matching *exactly* that signature in a derived class, but it does not prevent a function of the same name having any other signature from doing so:

```
struct ExtendedPrinter2 : public Printer2
{
    void print(int number);    // Error, Printer2::print(int) is final.
    void print(char c);        // OK, still hides base-class functions
};
```

Making a function virtual in a class where previously there was none also forces the compiler to maintain a pointer to a **static** virtual-function table in each object. Consequently, *any* use of **virtual** and **final** to decorate the same function with a class has efficiency costs.

Annoyances

Making empty types `final` precludes the empty-base-class optimization

Whenever a user-defined type derives from another that has no data members, that base type does not typically consume any additional memory in the derived type. This optimization is called the **empty-base-class optimization (EBO)** and is often exploited when applying policy-based design. Consider this slightly modified version of a classic example[14] in which an `ObjectCreator` relies on a specific `CreationPolicy` type for implementing the acquisition of memory and construction of objects:

```cpp
#include <cstddef>  // std::size_t

template <typename T, template<typename> class CreationPolicy>
class ObjectCreator : CreationPolicy<T>
{
    std::size_t objectCount = 0;  // Keep track of allocated objects.

public:
    T* create()
    {
        ++objectCount;
        return CreationPolicy<T>().create();  // Delegate to CreationPolicy.
    }
};
```

Each of the associated policies is implemented as an empty class, i.e., a class having no data members:

```cpp
template <typename T>
class OpNewCreator  // sizeof(OpNewCreator) by itself is 1 byte.
{
public:
    T* create()
    {
        // Allocate memory using placement new and return address.
    }
};

template <typename T>
class MallocCreator  // sizeof(MallocCreator) by itself is 1 byte.
{
public:
    T* create()
```

---

[14]**alexandrescu01**, Chapter 1, section 1.5, "Policies and Policy Classes," pp. 8–11

```
    {
        // Allocate memory using malloc and return address.
    }
};


static_assert(sizeof(ObjectCreator<int,OpNewCreator>) == sizeof(std::size_t),"");
static_assert(sizeof(ObjectCreator<int,MallocCreator>)== sizeof(std::size_t),"");
```

Since `OpNewCreator` and `MallocCreator` do not have any data members, inheriting from either of them does not increase the size of `ObjectCreator` on any compiler that implements the empty base optimization. If someone later decides to declare them as **final**, inheriting becomes impossible, even if just privately as an optimization:

```
template <typename T>
class OpNewCreator final { /*...*/ };   // subsequently declared final

template <typename T>
class MallocCreator final { /*...*/ }; //       "          "        "

template <typename T, template<typename> class CreationPolicy>
class ObjectCreator : CreationPolicy<T>  // Error, derivation is disallowed.
{ /*...*/ };
```

By declaring the empty bases class **final**, a valid use case is needlessly prohibited. Using composition instead of **private inheritance** consumes at least one extra byte in the footprint of `ObjectCreator`,[15] which will inevitably also come at the cost of additional padding imposed by alignment requirements:

```
template <typename T, template<typename> class CreationPolicy>
class LargeObjectCreator
{
    CreationPolicy<T> policy;  // now consumes an extra byte &
    std::size_t objectCount = 0;  // with padding 8 extra bytes

public:
    T* create()
    {
        ++objectCount;
```

---

[15]C++20 adds a new attribute, `[[no_unique_address]]`, that allows the compiler to avoid consuming additional storage for data objects of empty classes:

```
struct A final { /* no data members */ };
struct S {
    [[no_unique_address]] A a;   static_assert(sizeof(a) >= 1, "");
    int x;                       static_assert(sizeof(x) == 4, "");
};                               static_assert(sizeof(S) == 4, "");
```

```
        return policy.allocate();
    }
};

static_assert(
    sizeof(LargeObjectCreator<int, OpNewCreator>) > sizeof(std::size_t), "");

static_assert(
    sizeof(LargeObjectCreator<int, MallocCreator>) > sizeof(std::size_t), "");
```

Alternatively, the author of `OpNewCreator` and `MallocCreator` might reconsider and remove **final**.

See Also

- "**override**" (§1.1, p. 104) describes a related contextual keyword that verifies the existence of matching virtual functions in base classes instead of preventing matching virtual functions in derived classes.

Further Reading

- Barbara Liskov discusses in her seminal 1987 keynote paper a remarkable number of issues relevant to the ongoing design and development of modern C++; see **liskov87**.

- Barbara Liskov and Jeanette Wing followed up with a precise notion of subtyping in which any property provable about objects of a supertype would necessarily hold for objects of proper subtypes; see **liskov94**. This notion of proper subtyping (which is manifestly distinct from C++-style inheritance) would later come to be known as the Liskov Substitution Principal (LSP)[16]:

  Let $\phi(x)$ be a property provable about objects x of type T. Then $\phi(y)$ should be true for objects y of type S where S is a subtype of T.

---

[16]**liskov94**, section 1, "Introduction," p. 1812

Extended friend Declarations

The target of a **friend** *declaration* has been extended to allow designation of (1) a **type alias**, (2) a named **template parameter**, or (3) any previously declared **class type** such that if the target is not found the **friend** declaration will simply fail to compile rather than introduce a new declaration into the enclosing scope.

Description

A **friend** declaration located within a given **user-defined type (UDT)** grants a designated type (or *free* function) access to private and protected members of that class. Because the extended **friend** syntax does not affect *function* friendships, this feature section addresses extended friendship only between *types*.

Prior to C++11, the Standard required an *elaborated type specifier* to be provided after the **friend** keyword to designate some other *class* as being a **friend** of a given type. An elaborated type specifier for a class is a syntactical element having the form **<class|struct|union> <identifier>**. Elaborated type specifiers can be used to refer to a previously declared entity or to declare a new one, with the restriction that such an entity is one of **class**, **struct**, or **union**:

```cpp
// C++03

struct S;
class C;
enum E { };

struct X0
{
    friend S;         // Error, not legal C++03
    friend struct S;  // OK, refers to S above
    friend class S;   // OK, refers to S above (might warn)
    friend class C;   // OK, refers to C above
    friend class C0;  // OK, declares C0 in X0's namespace
    friend union U0;  // OK, declares U0 in X0's namespace
    friend enum E;    // Error, enum cannot be a friend.
    friend enum E2;   // Error, enum cannot be forward-declared.
};
```

This restriction prevents other potentially useful entities, e.g., type aliases and template parameters, from being designated as friends:

```
// C++03
```

```
struct S;
typedef S SAlias;
```

```
struct X1
{
    friend struct SAlias;  // Error, using typedef-name after struct
};
```

```
template <typename T>
struct X2
{
    friend class T;        // Error, using template type parameter after class
};
```

Furthermore, even though an entity belonging to a namespace other than the class containing a **friend** declaration might be visible, explicit qualification is required to avoid unintentionally declaring a new type:

```
// C++03
```

```
struct S;  // This S resides in the global namespace.
```

```
namespace ns
{
    class X3
    {
        friend struct S;
            // OK, but declares a new ns::S instead of referring to ::S
    };
}
```

C++11 relaxes the aforementioned *elaborated type specifier* requirement and extends the classic **friend** syntax by instead allowing either a *simple type specifier*, which is any unqualified type or type alias, or a *typename specifier*, e.g., the name of a template *type* parameter or dependent type thereof:

```
struct S;
typedef S SAlias;
```

```
namespace ns
{
    template <typename T>
    struct X4
    {
        friend T;          // OK
```

```
        friend S;            // OK, refers to ::S
        friend SAlias;       // OK, refers to ::S
        friend decltype(0);  // OK, equivalent to friend int;
        friend C;            // Error, C does not name a type.
    };
}
```

Notice that now it is again possible to declare as a **friend** a type that is expected to have already been declared, e.g., S, without having to worry that a typo in the spelling of the type would silently introduce a new type declaration, e.g., C, in the enclosing scope.

Finally, consider the hypothetical case in which a class template, C, befriends a *dependent* (e.g., nested) type, N, of its type parameter, T:

```
template <typename T>
class C
{
    friend typename T::N;      // N is a dependent type of parameter T.
    enum { e_SECRET = 10022 }; // This information is private to class C.
};

struct S
{
    struct N
    {
        static constexpr int f()  // f is eligible for compile-time computation.
        {
            return C<S>::e_SECRET;  // Type S::N is a friend of C<S>.
        }
    };
};

static_assert(S::N::f() == 10022, "");  // N has private access to C<S>.
```

In the example above, the nested type S::N — but not S itself — has private access to C<S>::e_SECRET.[1]

Use Cases

Safely declaring a previously declared type to be a friend

In C++03, to befriend a type that was already declared required *redeclaring* it. If the type were misspelled in the friend declaration, a new type would be declared:

---

[1]Note that the need for **typename** in the **friend** declaration in the example above to introduce the dependent type N is relaxed in C++20. For information on other contexts in which **typename** will eventually no longer be required, see **meredith20**.

```
class Container { /*...*/ };

class ContainerIterator
{
    friend class Contianer;  // Compiles but wrong: ia should have been ai.
    // ...
};
```

The code above will compile and appear to be correct until `ContainerIterator` attempts to access a **private** or **protected** member of `Container`. At that point, the compiler will surprisingly produce an error. As of C++11, we have the option of preventing this mistake by using extended **friend** declarations:

```
class Container { /*...*/ };

class ContainerIterator
{
    friend Contianer;  // Error, Contianer not found
    // ...
};
```

Befriending a type alias used as a customization point

In C++03, the only option for friendship was to specify a particular **class** or **struct** when granting private access. Let's begin by considering a scenario in which we have an **in-process value-semantic type (VST)** that serves as a *handle* to a platform-specific object, such as a `Window` in a graphical application. (When used to qualify a VST, the term in-process, also called *in-core*, refers to a type that has typical value-type–like operations but does not refer to a value that is meaningful outside of the current process.[2]) Large parts of a codebase might seek to interact with `Window` objects without needing or obtaining access to the internal representation.

A small part of the codebase that handles platform-specific window management, however, needs privileged access to the internal representation of `Window`. One way to achieve this goal is to make the platform-specific `WindowManager` a **friend** of the `Window` class; however, see *Potential Pitfalls — Long-distance friendship* on page 1041:

```
class WindowManager;  // forward declaration enabling extended friend syntax

class Window
{
private:
```

---

[2] A discussion of this topic is planned for **lakos2a**, section 4.2.

```
    friend class WindowManager;   // could instead use friend WindowManager;
    int d_nativeHandle;           // in-process (only) value of this object

public:
    // ... all the typical (e.g., special) functions we expect of a value type
};
```

In the example above, class `Window` befriends class `WindowManager`, granting it private access. Provided that the implementation of `WindowManager` resides in the same physical **component** as that of class `Window`, no **long-distance friendship** results. The consequence of such a monolithic design would be that every client that makes use of the otherwise lightweight `Window` class would necessarily depend physically on the presumably heavier-weight `WindowManager` class.

Now consider that the `WindowManager` implementations on different platforms might begin to diverge significantly. To keep the respective implementations maintainable, one might choose to factor them into distinct C++ types, perhaps even defined in separate files, and to use a *type alias* determined using platform-detection preprocessor macros to configure that alias:

```
// windowmanager_win32.h:

#ifdef WIN32
class Win32WindowManager { /*...*/ };
#endif
```

```
// windowmanager_unix.h:

#ifdef UNIX
class UnixWindowManager { /*...*/ };
#endif
```

```
// windowmanager.h:

#ifdef WIN32
#include <windowmanager_win32.h>
typedef Win32WindowManager WindowManager;
#else
#include <windowmanager_unix.h>
typedef UnixWindowManager WindowManager;
#endif
```

```
// window.h:
#include <windowmanager.h>

class Window
{
private:
    friend WindowManager;  // C++11 extended friend declaration
    int d_nativeHandle;

public:
    // ...
};
```

In this example, class `Window` no longer befriends a specific class named `WindowManager`; instead, it befriends the `WindowManager` type alias, which in turn has been set to the correct platform-specific window manager implementation. Such extended use of **friend** syntax was not available in C++03.

Note that this use case involves long-distance friendship inducing an implicit cyclic dependency between the `component` implementing `Window` and those implementing `WindowManager`; see *Potential Pitfalls — Long-distance friendship* on page 1041. Such designs, though undesirable, can result from an emergent need to add new platforms while keeping tightly related code sequestered within smaller, more manageable physical units. An alternative design would be to obviate the long-distance friendship by widening the API for the `Window` class, the natural consequence of which would be to invite public client abuse vis-a-vis Hyrum's law.

Using the `PassKey` idiom to enforce initialization

Prior to C++11, efforts to grant private access to a class defined in a separate physical unit required declaring the higher-level type itself to be a **friend**, resulting in this highly undesirable form of friendship; see *Potential Pitfalls — Long-distance friendship* on page 1041. The ability in C++11 to declare a template *type* parameter or any other type specifier to be a friend affords new opportunities to enforce selective private access (e.g., to one or more individual functions) without explicitly declaring another type to be a **friend**; see also *Granting a specific type access to a single **private** function* on page 1038. In this use case, however, our use of extended **friend** syntax to befriend a template parameter is unlikely to run afoul of sound physical design.

Let's say we have a commercial library, and we want it to verify a software-license key in the form of a C-style string, prior to allowing use of other parts of the API:

```
// simplified pseudocode
LibPassKey initializeLibrary(const char* licenseKey);
int utilityFunction1(LibPassKey object /* ... (other parameters) */);
int utilityFunction2(LibPassKey object /* ... (other parameters) */);
```

Knowing full well that this approach is not *secure* and that innumerable deliberate, malicious ways exist to get around the C++ type system, we nonetheless want to create a plausible regime where no *well-formed* code can *accidentally* gain access to library functionality other than by legitimately initializing the system using a valid license key. We could easily cause a function to **throw**, **abort**, and so on, at run time when the function is called prior to the client's license key being authenticated. However, part of our goal, as a friendly library vendor, is to ensure that clients do not *inadvertently* call other library functions prior to initialization. To that end, we propose the following protocol.

1. Use an instantiation of the PassKey class template[3] that only our API *utility* **struct**[4] can create.

2. Return a constructed object of this type only upon successful validation of the license key.

3. Require that clients present this (constructed) passkey *object* every time they invoke any other function in the API.

Here's an example that encompasses all three aforementioned points:

```cpp
template <typename T>
class PassKey  // reusable standard utility type
{
    PassKey() { }  // private default constructor (no aggregate initialization)
    friend T;      // Only T is allowed to create this object.
};

struct BestExpensiveLibraryUtil
{
    class LicenseError { /*...*/ };  // thrown if license string is invalid

    using LibPassKey = PassKey<BestExpensiveLibraryUtil>;
        // This is the type of the PassKey that will be returned when this
        // utility is initialized successfully, but only this utility is able
        // to construct an object of this type. Without a valid license string,
        // the client will have no way to create such an object and thus no way
        // to call functions within this library.

    static LibPassKey initializeLibrary(const char* licenseKey)
        // This function must be called with a valid licenseKey string prior
        // to using this library; if the supplied license is valid, a
        // LibPassKey object will be returned for mandatory use in all
        // subsequent calls to useful functions of this library. This function
        // throws LicenseError if the supplied licenseKey string is invalid.
```

---

[3]**mayrand15**

[4]**lakos20**, section 2.4.9, "Only Classes, **struct**s, and Free Operators at Package-Namespace Scope," pp. 312–321, specifically Figure 2-23, p. 316

```
    {
        if (isValid(licenseKey))
        {
            // Initialize library properly.

            return LibPassKey();
                // Return a default-constructed LibPassKey. Note that only
                // this utility is able to construct such a key.
        }

        throw LicenseError();  // Supplied license string was invalid.
    }

    static int doUsefulStuff(LibPassKey key /*...*/);
        // The function requires a LibPassKey object, which can be constructed
        // only by invoking the static initializeLibrary function, to be
        // supplied as its first argument. ...

private:
    static bool isValid(const char* key);
        // externally defined function that returns true if key is valid
};
```

Other than going outside the language with invalid constructs or circumventing the type system with esoteric tricks, this approach, among other things, prevents invoking the doUsefulStuff function without a proper license. What's more, the C++ type system *at compile time* forces a prospective client to have initialized the library before any attempt is made to use any of its other functionality.

Granting a specific type access to a single `private` function

When designing in purely logical terms, wanting to grant some other logical entity special access to a type that no other entity enjoys is a common situation. Doing so does not necessarily become problematic until that friendship spans physical boundaries; see *Potential Pitfalls — Long-distance friendship* on page 1041.

As a simple approximation to a real-world use case,[5] suppose we have a lightweight object-database class, Odb, that is designed to operate collaboratively with objects, such as MyWidget, that are themselves designed to work collaboratively with Odb. Every compliant UDT suitable for management by Odb will need to maintain an integer object ID that is read/write accessible by an Odb object. Under no circumstances is any other object permitted to access, let alone modify, that ID independently of the Odb API.

---

[5] For an example of a real-world database implementation that requires managed objects to befriend that database manager, see **codesyn15**, section 2.1, "Declaring Persistent Classes."

Prior to C++11, the design of such a feature might require every participating class to define a data member named d_objectId and to declare the Odb class a **friend** (using old-style **friend** syntax):

```cpp
class MyWidget  // grants just Odb access to all of its private data
{
    int d_objectId;    // required by our collaborative-design strategy
    friend class Odb;  //     "      "  "          "            "       "
    // ...

public:
    // ...
};

class Odb
{
    // ...

public:
    template <typename T>
    void processObject(T& object)
        // This function template is generally callable by clients.
    {
        int& objId = object.d_objectId;
        // ... (process as needed)
    }

    // ...
};
```

In this example, the Odb class implements the public member function template, processObject, which then extracts the objectId field for access. The collateral damage is that we have exposed all of our private details to Odb, which is at best a gratuitous widening of our sphere of encapsulation.

Using the PassKey pattern allows us to be more selective with what we share:

```cpp
template <typename T>
class Passkey
    // Implement this eminently reusable Passkey class template again here.
{
    Passkey() { }  // prevent aggregate initialization
    friend T;      // Only the T in Passkey<T> can create a Passkey object.
    Passkey(const Passkey&) = delete;              // no copy/move construction
    Passkey& operator=(const Passkey&) = delete;   // no copy/move assignment
};
```

We are now able to adjust the design of our systems such that only the minimum private functionality is exposed to `Odb`:

```cpp
class Odb;        // Objects of this class have special access to other objects.

class MyWidget  // grants just Odb access to only its objectId member function
{
    int d_objectId;  // must have an int data member of any name we choose
    // ...

public:
    int& objectId(const Passkey<Odb>&) { return d_objectId; }
        // Return a non-const reference to the mandated int data member.
        // objectId is callable only within the scope of Odb.

    // ...
};

class Odb
{
    // ...

public:
    template <typename T>
    void processObject(T& object)
        // This function template is generally callable by clients.
    {
        int& objId = object.objectId(Passkey<Odb>());
        // ...
    }

    // ...
};
```

Instead of granting `Odb` private access to *all* encapsulated implementation details of `MyWidget`, this example uses the `PassKey` idiom to enable just `Odb` to call the (syntactically **public**) `objectId` member function of `MyWidget` with no private access whatsoever. As a further demonstration of the efficacy of this approach, consider that we are able to create and invoke the `processObject` method of an `Odb` object from a function, `f`, but we are blocked from calling the `objectId` method of a `MyWidget` object directly:

```cpp
void f()
{
    Odb mgr;          // object receiving fine-grained privileged access
    MyWidget widget;  // object granting selective private access to just Odb
    mgr.processObject(widget);
```

```
    int& objId = widget.objectId(PassKey<Odb>());  // cannot call out of Odb
      // Error, Passkey<T>::Passkey() [withT = Odb] is private within
      // this context.
}
```

Notice that use of the extended **friend** syntax to befriend a template parameter and thereby enable the PassKey idiom here improved the granularity with which we effectively grant privileged access to an individually named type but didn't fundamentally alter the testability issues that result when private access to specific C++ types is allowed to extend across physical boundaries; again, see *Potential Pitfalls — Long-distance friendship* below.

Curiously recurring template pattern

Befriending a template parameter via extended **friend** declarations can be helpful when implementing the **curiously recurring template pattern (CRTP)**. For use-case examples and more information on the pattern itself, see *Appendix — Curiously Recurring Template Pattern Use Cases* on page 1042.

Potential Pitfalls

Long-distance friendship

Since before C++ was standardized, granting private access via a **friend** declaration across physical boundaries, known as long-distance friendship, was observed[6],[7] to potentially lead to designs that are qualitatively more difficult to understand, test, and maintain. When a user-defined type, X, befriends some other specific type, Y, in a separate, higher-level translation unit, testing X thoroughly without also testing Y is no longer possible. The effect is a test-induced cyclic dependency between X and Y. Now imagine that Y depends on a sequence of other types, C1, C2, ..., CN-2, each defined in its own physical component, CI, where CN-2 depends on X. The result is a physical design cycle of size N. As N increases, the ability to manage complexity quickly becomes intractable. Accordingly, the two design imperatives that were most instrumental in shaping the C++20 **modules** feature were (1) to have no cyclic module dependencies and (2) to avoid intermodule friendships.

See Also

- **"using** Aliases" (§1.1, p. 133) describes a means to create type aliases and alias templates which can be befriended via the extended friend declarations.

---

[6]**lakos96**, section 3.6.1, ""Long-Distance Friendship and Implied Dependency," pp. 141–144
[7]**lakos20**, section 2.6, "Component Design Rules," pp. 342–370, specifically p. 367 and p. 362

Further Reading

- For yet more potential uses of the extended friend pattern in metaprogramming contexts, such as using CRTP, see **alexandrescu01**.

- **lakos96**, section 3.6, pp. 136–146, is dedicated to the classic use (and misuse) of friendship.

- A synopsis of the history and process by which the prestandardization form of a **friend** declaration in which the **class** specifier may be omitted is delineated in **miller05**.

- **lakos20** provides extensive advice on *sound* **physical design**, which generally precludes long-distance friendship.

Appendix

Curiously Recurring Template Pattern Use Cases

Refactoring using the curiously recurring template pattern Avoiding code duplication across disparate classes can sometimes be achieved using a strange template pattern first recognized in the mid-90s, which has since become known as the curiously recurring template pattern (CRTP). The pattern is *curious* because it involves the surprising step of declaring as a base class, such as B, a template that *expects* the derived class, such as C, as a template argument, such as T:

```
template <typename T>
class B
{
    // ...
};

class C : public B<C>
{
    // ...
};
```

As a trivial illustration of how the CRTP can be used as a refactoring tool, suppose that we have several classes for which we would like to track, say, just the number of active instances:

```
class A
{
    static int s_count;  // declaration
    // ...

public:
    static int count() { return s_count; }

    A()          { ++s_count; }
    A(const A&)  { ++s_count; }
```

```
    A(const A&&) { ++s_count; }
    ~A()         { --s_count; }

    A& operator=(A&)  = default;  // see special members
    A& operator=(A&&) = default;  //  "        "        "
    // ...
};

int A::s_count;  // definition (in .cpp file)

class B { /* similar to A (above) */ };
// ...

void test()
{              // A::s_count = 0, B::s_count = 0
    A a1;  // A::s_count = 1, B::s_count = 0
    B b1;  // A::s_count = 1, B::s_count = 1
    A a2;  // A::s_count = 2, B::s_count = 1
}              // A::s_count = 0, B::s_count = 0
```

In this example, we have multiple classes, each repeating the same common machinery. Let's now explore how we might refactor this example using the CRTP:

```
template <typename T>
class InstanceCounter
{
protected:
    static int s_count;  // declaration

public:
    static int count() { return s_count; }
};

template <typename T>
int InstanceCounter<T>::s_count;  // definition (in same file as declaration)

struct A : InstanceCounter<A>
{
    A()            { ++s_count; }
    A(const A&)    { ++s_count; }
    A(const A&&)   { ++s_count; }
    ~A()           { --s_count; }

    A& operator=(const A&)  = default;
    A& operator=(A&&)       = default;
    // ...
};
```

Notice that we have factored out a common counting mechanism into an `InstanceCounter` class template and then derived our representative class A from `InstanceCounter<A>`, and we would do similarly for classes B, C, and so on. This approach works because the compiler does not need to see the derived type until the point at which the template is instantiated, which will be *after* it has seen the derived type.

Prior to C++11, however, there was plenty of room for user error. Consider, for example, forgetting to change the base-type parameter when copying and pasting a new type:

```
struct B : InstanceCounter<A>  // Oops! We forgot to change A to B in
                               // InstanceCounter: The wrong count will be
                               // updated!
{
    B() { ++s_count; }
};
```

Another problem is that a client deriving from our class can mess with our protected `s_count`:

```
struct AA : A
{
    AA() { s_count = -1; }  // Oops! Hyrum's Law is at work again!
};
```

We could inherit from the `InstanceCounter` class privately, but then `InstanceCounter` would have no way to add to the derived class's public interface, for example, the public `count` static member function.

As it turns out, however, both of these missteps can be erased simply by making the internal mechanism of the `InstanceCounter` template private and then having `InstanceCounter` befriend its template parameter, T:

```
template <typename T>
class InstanceCounter
{
    static int s_count;  // Make this static data member private.
    friend T;            // Allow access only from the derived T.

public:
    static int count() { return s_count; }
};

template <typename T>
int InstanceCounter<T>::s_count;
```

Now if some other class does try to derive from this type, it cannot access this type's counting mechanism. If we want to suppress even that possibility, we can declare and default (see Section 1.1."Defaulted Functions" on page 33) the `InstanceCounter` class constructors to be private as well.

Synthesizing equality using the curiously recurring template pattern   As a second example of code factoring using the CRTP, suppose that we want to create a factored way of synthesizing **operator**== for types that implement just an **operator**<.[8] In this example, the CRTP base-class template, E, will synthesize the homogeneous **operator**== for its parameter type, D, by returning **false** if either argument is *less than* the other:

```
template <typename D>
class E { }; // CRTP base class used to synthesize operator== for D

template <typename D>
bool operator==(const E<D>& lhs, const E<D>& rhs)
{
    const D& d1 = static_cast<const D&>(lhs);  // derived type better be D
    const D& d2 = static_cast<const D&>(rhs);  //    "      "      "    " "
    return !(d1 < d2) && !(d2 < d1);           // assuming D has an operator<
}
```

A client that implements an **operator**< can now reuse this CRTP base case to synthesize an **operator**==:

```
struct S : E<S>
{
    int d_size;
};

bool operator<(const S& lhs, const S& rhs)
{
    return lhs.d_size < rhs.d_size;
}

void test1()
{
    S s1; s1.d_size = 10;
    S s2; s2.d_size = 10;

    assert(s1 == s2);  // compiles and passes
}
```

As this code snippet suggests, the base-class template, E, is able to use the template parameter, D (representing the derived class, S), to synthesize the homogeneous free **operator**== function for S.

Prior to C++11, no means existed to guard against accidents, such as inheriting from the wrong base and then perhaps even forgetting to define the **operator**<:

---

[8]This example is based on a similar one found on stackoverflow.com; see **tsirunyan10**.

```
struct P : E<S>  // Oops! should have been E(P) -- a serious latent defect
{
    int d_x;
    int d_y;
};

void test2()
{
    P p1; p1.d_x = 10; p1.d_y = 15;
    P p2; p2.d_x = 10; p2.d_y = 20;

    assert( !(p1 == p2) );  // Oops! This fails because of E(S) above.
}
```

Again, thanks to C++11's extended **friend** syntax, we can defend against these defects at compile time simply by making the CRTP base class's default constructor *private* and befriending its template parameter:

```
template <typename D>
class E
{
    E() = default;
    friend D;
};
```

Note that the goal here is not security but simply guarding against accidental typos, copy-paste errors, and other occasional human errors. By making this change, we will soon realize that there is no **operator<** defined for P.

Compile-time polymorphism using the curiously recurring template pattern   Object-oriented programming provides certain flexibility that at times might be supererogatory. Here we will exploit the familiar domain of abstract/concrete shapes to demonstrate a mapping between runtime polymorphism using virtual functions and compile-time polymorphism using the CRTP. We begin with a simple abstract **Shape** class that implements a single, pure, virtual **draw** function:

```
class Shape
{
public:
    virtual void draw() const = 0;  // abstract draw function (interface)
};
```

From this abstract **Shape** class, we now derive two concrete shape types, **Circle** and **Rectangle**, each implementing the *abstract* **draw** function:

```
#include <iostream>  // std::cout

class Circle : public Shape
{
    int d_radius;

public:
    Circle(int radius) : d_radius(radius) { }

    void draw() const  // concrete implementation of abstract draw function
    {
        std::cout << "Circle(radius = " << d_radius << ")\n";
    }
};

class Rectangle : public Shape
{
    int d_length;
    int d_width;

public:
    Rectangle(int length, int width) : d_length(length), d_width(width) { }

    void draw() const  // concrete implementation of abstract draw function
    {
        std::cout << "Rectangle(length = " << d_length << ", "
                             "width = " << d_width  << ")\n";
    }
};
```

Notice that a `Circle` is constructed with a single integer argument, i.e., `radius`, and a `Rectangle` is constructed with two integers, i.e., `length` and `width`.

We now implement a function that takes an arbitrary shape, via a **const** *lvalue* reference to its abstract base class, and prints it:

```
void print(const Shape& shape)
{
    shape.draw();
}

void testShape()
{
    print(Circle(1));        // OK, prints: Circle(radius = 1)
    print(Rectangle(2, 3));  // OK, prints: Rectangle(length = 2, width = 3)
    print(Shape());          // Error, Shape is an abstract class.
}
```

Now suppose that we didn't need all the runtime flexibility offered by this system and wanted to map just what we have in the previous code snippet onto templates that avoid the spatial and runtime overhead of virtual-function tables and dynamic dispatch. Such transformation again involves creating a CRTP base class, this time in lieu of our abstract interface:

```
template <typename T>
struct Shape
{
    void draw() const
    {
        static_cast<const T*>(this)->draw();  // assumes T derives from Shape
    }
};
```

Notice that we are using a **static_cast** to the address of an object of the **const** template parameter type, T, assuming that the template argument is of the same type as some derived class of this object's type. We now define our types as before, the only difference being the form of the base type:

```
class Circle : public Shape<Circle>
{
    // same as above
};
```

```
class Rectangle : public Shape<Rectangle>
{
    // same as above
};
```

We now define our **print** function, this time as a function template taking a **Shape** of arbitrary type T:

```
template <typename T>
void print(const Shape<T>& shape)
{
    shape.draw();
}
```

The result of compiling and running **testShape** above is the same, including that **Shape()** doesn't compile.

However, opportunities for undetected failure remain. Suppose we decide to add a third shape, **Triangle**, constructed with three sides:

```
class Triangle : public Shape<Rectangle>  // Oops!
{
    int d_side1;
```

```
    int d_side2;
    int d_side3;

public:
    Triangle(int side1, int side2, int side3)
        : d_side1(side1), d_side2(side2), d_side3(side3) { }

    void draw() const
    {
        std::cout << "Triangle(side1 = " << d_side1 << ", "
                             "side2 = " << d_side2 << ", "
                             "side3 = " << d_side3 << ")\n";
    }
};
```

Unfortunately, we forgot to change the base-class type parameter when we copy-pasted from `Rectangle`.

Let's now create a new test that exercises all three and see what happens on our platform:

```
void test2()
{
    print(Circle(1));        // prints: Circle(radius = 1)
    print(Rectangle(2, 3));  // prints: Rectangle(length = 2, width = 3)
    print(Triangle(4, 5, 6)); // prints: Rectangle(length = 4, width = 5) ?!
    Shape<int> bug;          // Compiles?!
}
```

As should by now be clear, a defect in our `Triangle` implementation results in *hard* **undefined behavior** that could have been prevented at compile time by using the extended **friend** syntax. Had we defined the CRTP base-class template's default constructor to be *private* and made its type parameter a **friend**, we could have prevented the copy-paste error with `Triangle` and suppressed the ability to create a `Shape` object without deriving from it (e.g., see `bug` in the previous code snippet):

```
template <typename T>
class Shape
{
    Shape() = default;  // Default the default constructor to be private.
    friend T;           // Ensure only a type derived from T has access.
};
```

Generally, whenever we are using the CRTP, making just the default constructor of the base-class template **private** and having it befriend its type parameter is typically a trivial local change, is helpful in avoiding various forms of accidental misuse and is unlikely to induce long-distance friendships where none previously existed: Applying extended **friend** syntax to an existing CRTP is typically *safe*.

Compile-time visitor using the curiously recurring template pattern   As more real-world applications of compile-time polymorphism using the CRTP, consider implementing traversal and visitation of complex data structures. In particular, we want to facilitate employing *default-action* functions, which allow for simpler code from the point of view of the programmer who needs the results of the traversal. We illustrate our compile-time visitation approach using binary trees as our data structure.

We begin with the traditional node structure of a binary tree, where each node has a left and right subtree plus a label:

```
struct Node
{
    Node* d_left;
    Node* d_right;
    char  d_label;  // label will be used in the pre-order example.

    Node() : d_left(0), d_right(0), d_label(0) { }
};
```

Now we wish to have code that traverses the tree in one of the three traditional ways: *pre-order*, *in-order*, *post-order*. Such traversal code is often intertwined with the actions to be taken. In our implementation, however, we will write a CRTP-like base-class template, `Traverser`, that implements empty stub functions for each of the three traversal types, relying on the CRTP-derived type to supply the desired functionality:

```
template <typename T>
class Traverser
{
private:
    Traverser() = default;  // Make the default constructor private.
    friend T;               // Grant access only to the derived class.

public:
    void visitPreOrder(Node*)  { }  // stub-functions & placeholders
    void visitInOrder(Node*)   { }  // (Each of these three functions
    void visitPostOrder(Node*) { }  // defaults to an inline "no-op.")

    void traverse(Node* n)  // factored subfunctionality
    {
        T* t = static_cast<T*>(this);  // Cast this to the derived type.

        if (n) { t->visitPreOrder(n);    }  // optionally defined in derived
        if (n) { t->traverse(n->d_left); }  //     "        "      "     "
```

```
            if (n) { t->visitInOrder(n);      }  // optionally defined in derived
            if (n) { t->traverse(n->d_right); }  //       "       "      "      "
            if (n) { t->visitPostOrder(n);    }  //       "       "      "      "
        }
    };
```

The factored traversal mechanism is implemented in the `Traverser` base-class template. A proper subset of the four customization points, that is, the four member functions invoked from the *public* `traverse` function of the `Traverser` base class, is implemented as appropriate in the derived class, identified by `T`. Each of these customization functions is invoked in order. Notice that the `traverse` function is safe to call on a **nullptr** as each individual customization-function invocation will be independently bypassed if its supplied `Node` pointer is null. If a customization function is defined in the derived class, that version of it is invoked; otherwise, the corresponding empty **inline** base-class version of that function is invoked instead. This approach allows for any of the three traversal orders to be implemented simply by supplying an appropriately configured derived type where clients are obliged to implement only the portions they need. Even the traversal itself can be modified, as we will soon see, where we create the very data structure we're traversing.

Let's now look at how derived-class authors might use this pattern. First, we'll write a traversal class that fully populates a tree to a specified depth:

```cpp
struct FillToDepth : Traverser<FillToDepth>
{
    using Base = Traverser<FillToDepth>;  // similar to a local typedef

    int d_depth;          //  final "height" of the tree
    int d_currentDepth;   //  current distance from the root

    FillToDepth(int depth) : d_depth(depth), d_currentDepth(0) { }

    void traverse(Node*& n)
    {
        if (d_currentDepth++ < d_depth && !n)  // descend; if not balanced...
        {
            n = new Node;     // Add node since it's not already there.
        }

        Base::traverse(n);    // Recurse by invoking the base version.

        --d_currentDepth;     // Ascend.
    }
};
```

The derived class's version of the `traverse` member function acts as if it overrides the `traverse` function in the base-class template and then, as part of its re-implementation, defers to the base-class version to perform the actual traversal.

Importantly, note that we have re-implemented **traverse** in the derived class with a function by the same name but having a *different* **signature** that has more capability (i.e., it's able to modify its immediate argument) than the one in the base-class template. In practice, this signature modification is something we would do rarely, but part of the flexibility of this design pattern, as with templates in general, is that we can take advantage of **duck typing** to achieve useful functionality in somewhat unusual ways. For this pattern, the designers of the base-class template and the designers of the derived classes are, at least initially, likely to be the same people, and they will arrange for these sorts of signature variants to work correctly if they need such functionality. Or they might decide that overridden methods should follow a proper contract and signature that they determine is appropriate, and they might declare improper overrides to be undefined behavior. In this example, we aim for illustrative flexibility over rigor:

```
void traverse(Node* n);    // as declared in the Traverser base-class template
void traverse(Node*& n);   // as declared in the FillToDepth derived class
```

Unlike virtual functions, the signatures of corresponding functions in the base and derived classes need not match exactly *provided* the derived-class function can be called in the same way as the corresponding one in the base class. In this case, the compiler has all the information it needs to make the call properly:

```
static_cast<FillToDepth *>(this)->traverse(n);  // what the compiler sees
```

Suppose that we now want to create a type that labels a *small* tree, balanced or not, according to its pre-order traversal:

```
struct PreOrderLabel : Traverser<PreOrderLabel>
{
    char d_label;

    PreOrderLabel() : d_label('a') { }

    void visitPreOrder(Node* n)  // This choice controls traversal order.
    {
        n->d_label = d_label++;
            // Each successive label is sequential alphabetically.
    }
};
```

The simple pre-order traversal class, **PreOrderLabel**, labels the nodes such that it visits each parent *before* it visits either of its two children.

Alternatively, we might want to create a read-only derived class, **InOrderPrint**, that simply prints out the sequence of labels resulting from an *in-order* traversal of the, e.g., previously pre-ordered, labels:

```
#include <cstdio>  // std::putchar

struct InOrderPrint : Traverser<InOrderPrint>
```

```
{
    ~InOrderPrint()
    {
        std::putchar('\n');  // Print single newline at the end of the string.
    }

    void visitInOrder(const Node* n) const
    {
        std::putchar(n->d_label);  // Print the label character exactly as is.
    }
};
```

The simple `InOrderPrint`-derived class, shown in the example above, prints out the labels of a tree *in order*: left subtree, then node, then right subtree. Notice that since we are only examining the tree here — not modifying it — we can declare the overriding method to take a **const** `Node*` rather than a `Node*` and make the method itself **const**. Once again, compatibility of signatures, not identity, is the key.

Finally, we might want to clean up the tree. We do so in *post-order* since we do not want to delete a node before we have cleaned up its children!

```
struct CleanUp : Traverser<CleanUp>
{
    void visitPostOrder(Node*& n)
    {
        delete n;    // always necessary
        n = 0;       // might be omitted in a "raw" version of the type
    }
};
```

Putting it all together, we can create a `main` program that creates a balanced tree to a depth of four and then labels it in *pre-order*, prints those labels in *in-order*, and destroys it in *post-order*:

```
int main()
{
    Node* n = 0;                  // tree handle

    FillToDepth(4).traverse(n);   // (1) Create balanced tree.
    PreOrderLabel().traverse(n);  // (2) Label tree in pre-order.
    InOrderPrint().traverse(n);   // (3) Print labels in order.
    CleanUp().traverse(n);        // (4) Destroy tree in post-order.
    return 0;
}
```

Running this program results in a binary tree of height 4, as illustrated in the code snippet below, and has reliably consistent output:

```
dcebgfhakjlinmo

Level 0:                                    a
                                   .       '       .
Level 1:                 b '                        ' i
                       .   '     .              .  '    '  .
Level 2:        c                f           j              m
             /   \            /   \        /   \          /   \
Level 3:    d     e          g     h      k     l        n     o
```

This use of the CRTP for traversal truly shines when the data structure to be traversed is especially complex, such as an abstract-syntax-tree (AST) representation of a computer program, where tree nodes have many different types, with each type having custom ways of representing the subtrees it contains. For example, a translation unit is a sequence of declarations; a declaration can be a type, a variable, or a function; functions have return types, parameters, and a compound statement; the statement has substatements, expressions, and so on. We would not want to rewrite the traversal code for each new application. Given a reusable CRTP-based traverser for our AST, we don't have to.

For example, consider writing a type that visits each integer literal node in a given AST:

```cpp
struct IntegerLiteralHandler : AstTraverser<IntegerLiteralHandler>
{
    void visit(IntegerLiteral* iLit)
    {
        // ... (do something with this integer literal)
    }
};
```

The AST traverser, which would implement a separate empty `visit` overload for each syntactic node type in the grammar, would invoke our derived `visit` member function with every integer literal in the program, regardless of where it appeared. This CRTP-based traverser would also call many other `visit` methods, but each of those would perform no action at all by default and would likely be elided at even modest compiler-optimization levels. Be aware, however, that although we ourselves are not rewriting the traversal code each time, the compiler is still doing it because every CRTP instantiation produces a new copy of the traversal code. If the traversal code is large and complex, the consequence might be increased program size, that is, **code bloat**.

Finally, the CRTP can be used in a variety of situations for many purposes,[9] which explains both its *curiously recurring* nature and nomenclature. Those uses invariably benefit from (1) declaring the base-class template's default constructor *private* and (2) having that template befriend its type parameter, which is possible only by means of the extended **friend** syntax. Thus, the CRTP base-class template can ensure, at compile time, that its type argument is actually derived from the base class as required by the pattern.

---

[9] fluentcpp17

Transparently Nested Namespaces

An **inline** namespace is a nested namespace whose member entities closely behave as if they were declared directly within the enclosing namespace.

Description

To a first approximation, an **inline namespace** (e.g., v2 in the code snippet below) acts a lot like a conventional nested namespace (e.g., v1) followed by a **using** directive for that namespace in its enclosing namespace[1]:

```
// example.cpp:
namespace n
{
    namespace v1  // conventional nested namespace followed by using directive
    {
        struct T { };     // nested type declaration (identified as ::n::v1::T)
        int d;            // ::n::v1::d at, e.g., 0x01a64e90
    }

    using namespace v1;   // Import names T and d into namespace n.
}

namespace n
{
    inline namespace v2   // similar to being followed by using namespace v2
    {
        struct T { };     // nested type declaration (identified as ::n::v2::T)
        int d;            // ::n::v2::d at, e.g., 0x01a64e94
    }

    // using namespace v2;  // redundant when used with an inline namespace
}
```

---

[1]C++17 allows developers to concisely declare nested namespaces with shorthand notation:

```
namespace a::b { /*...*/ }
// is the same as
namespace a { namespace b { /*...*/ } }
```

C++20 expands on the above syntax by allowing the insertion of the **inline** keyword in front of any of the namespaces, except the first one:

```
namespace a::inline b::inline c { /*...*/ }
// is the same as
namespace a { inline namespace b { inline namespace c { /*...*/ } } }

inline namespace a::b { }  // Error, cannot start with inline for compound namespace names
namespace inline a::b { }  // Error, inline at front of sequence explicitly disallowed
```

Four subtle details distinguish these approaches.

1. Name collisions with existing names behave differently due to differing name-lookup rules.

2. **Argument-dependent lookup (ADL)** gives special treatment to **inline** namespaces.

3. Template specializations can refer to the primary template in an **inline** namespace even if written in the enclosing namespace.

4. Reopening namespaces might reopen an **inline** namespace.

One important aspect that all forms of namespaces share, however, is that (1) nested symbolic names (e.g., n::v1::T) at the **API** level, (2) **mangled names** (e.g., _ZN1n2v11dE, _ZN1n2v21dE), and (3) assigned relocatable addresses (e.g., 0x01a64e90, 0x01a64e94) at the **ABI** level remain unaffected by the use of either **inline** or **using** or both. To be precise, source files containing, alternately, **namespace** n { **inline namespace** v { **int** d; } } and **namespace** n { **namespace** v { **int** d; } **using namespace** v; }, will produce identical assembly.[2] Note that a **using** directive immediately following an **inline** namespace is superfluous; name lookup will always consider names in **inline** namespaces before those imported by a **using** directive. Such a directive can, however, be used to import the contents of an **inline** namespace to some other namespace, albeit only in the conventional, **using direc-tive** sense; see *Annoyances — Only one namespace can contain any given **inline** namespace* on page 1082.

More generally, each namespace has what is called its ***inline** namespace set*, which is the transitive closure of all **inline** namespaces within the namespace. All names in the **inline** namespace set are roughly intended to behave as if they are defined in the enclosing namespace. Conversely, each **inline** namespace has an *enclosing namespace set* that comprises all enclosing namespaces up to and including the first non**inline** namespace.

Loss of access to duplicate names in enclosing namespace

When both a type and a variable are declared with the same name in the same scope, the variable name hides the type name — such behavior can be demonstrated by using the form of **sizeof** that accepts a nonparenthesized *expression* (recall that the form of **sizeof** that accepts a *type* as its argument requires parentheses):

```
struct A { double d; };  static_assert(sizeof( A) == 8, "");  // type
                      // static_assert(sizeof  A == 8, "");  // Error

int A;                   static_assert(sizeof( A) == 4, "");  // data
                         static_assert(sizeof  A == 4, "");  // OK
```

---

[2]These mangled names can be seen with GCC by running g++ -S <file>.cpp and viewing the contents of the generated <file>.s. Note that Compiler Explorer is another valuable tool for learning about what comes out the other end of a C++ compiler: see https://godbolt.org/.

Unless both type and variable entities are declared within the same scope, no preference is given to variable names; the name of an entity in an inner scope hides a like-named entity in an enclosing scope:

```
void f()
{
    double B;               static_assert(sizeof(B) == 8, "");  // variable
    {                       static_assert(sizeof(B) == 8, "");  // variable
        struct B { int d; }; static_assert(sizeof(B) == 4, "");  // type
    }                       static_assert(sizeof(B) == 8, "");  // variable
}
```

When an entity is declared in an enclosing **namespace** and another entity having the same name hides it in a *lexically* nested scope, then (apart from **inline** namespaces) access to a hidden element can generally be recovered by using scope resolution:

```
struct C { double d; };  static_assert(sizeof(  C) == 8, "");

void g()
{                       static_assert(sizeof(  C) == 8, "");  // type
    int C;              static_assert(sizeof(  C) == 4, "");  // variable
                        static_assert(sizeof(::C) == 8, "");  // type
}                       static_assert(sizeof(  C) == 8, "");  // type
```

A conventional nested namespace behaves as one might expect:

```
namespace outer
{
    struct D { double d; }; static_assert(sizeof(         D) == 8, ""); // type

    namespace inner
    {                       static_assert(sizeof(         D) == 8, ""); // type
        int D;              static_assert(sizeof(         D) == 4, ""); // var
    }                       static_assert(sizeof(         D) == 8, ""); // type
                            static_assert(sizeof(inner::D) == 4, ""); // var
                            static_assert(sizeof(outer::D) == 8, ""); // type
    using namespace inner;//static_assert(sizeof(         D) == 0, ""); // Error
                            static_assert(sizeof(inner::D) == 4, ""); // var
                            static_assert(sizeof(outer::D) == 8, ""); // type
}                           static_assert(sizeof(outer::D) == 8, ""); // type
```

In the example above, the inner variable name, D, hides the outer type with the same name, starting from the point of D's declaration in inner until inner is closed, after which the unqualified name D reverts to the type in the outer namespace. Then, right after the subsequent **using namespace** inner; directive, the meaning of the unqualified name D in outer becomes ambiguous, shown here with a **static_assert** that is commented out; any attempt to refer to an unqualified D from here to the end of the scope of outer will fail to compile. The type entity declared as D in the outer namespace can, however, still be accessed — from inside or outside of the `outer` namespace, as shown in the example — via its qualified name, `outer::D`.

If an **inline** namespace were used instead of a nested namespace followed by a **using** directive, however, the ability to recover by name the hidden entity in the enclosing namespace is lost. Unqualified name lookup considers the inline namespace set and the used namespace set simultaneously. Qualified name lookup first considers the **inline** namespace set and *then* goes on to look into used namespaces. These lookup rules mean we can still refer to `outer::D` in the example above, but doing so would still be ambiguous if `inner` were an inline namespace. This subtle difference in behavior is a byproduct of the highly specific use case that motivated this feature and for which it was explicitly designed; see *Use Cases — Link-safe ABI versioning* on page 1067.

Argument-dependent–lookup interoperability across inline namespace boundaries

Another important aspect of **inline** namespaces is that they allow ADL to work seamlessly across **inline** namespace boundaries. Whenever unqualified function names are being resolved, a list of *associated namespaces* is built for each argument of the function. This list of associated namespaces comprises the namespace of the argument, its enclosing namespace set, plus the **inline** namespace set.

Consider the case of a type, `U`, defined in an `outer` namespace, and a function, `f(U)`, declared in an `inner` namespace nested within `outer`. A second type, `V`, is defined in the `inner` namespace, and a function, `g`, is declared, after the close of `inner`, in the `outer` namespace:

```
namespace outer
{
    struct U { };

    // inline              // Uncommenting this line fixes the problem.
    namespace inner
    {
        void f(U) { }
        struct V { };
    }

    using namespace inner;  // If we inline inner, we don't need this line.

    void g(V) { }
}

void client()
{
    f(outer::U());          // Error, f is not declared in this scope.
    g(outer::inner::V());   // Error, g is not declared in this scope.
}
```

In the example above, a `client` invoking `f` with an object of type `outer::U` fails to compile because `f(outer::U)` is declared in the nested `inner` namespace, which is not the same as declaring it in `outer`. Because ADL does not look into namespaces added with the **using** directive, ADL does not find the needed `outer::inner::f` function. Similarly, the type `V`, defined in namespace `outer::inner`, is not declared in the same namespace as the function `g` that operates on it. Hence, when `g` is invoked from within `client` on an object of type `outer::inner::V`, ADL again does not find the needed function `outer::g(outer::V)`.

Simply making the `inner` namespace **inline** solves both of these ADL-related problems. All transitively nested **inline** namespaces — up to and including the most proximate non-**inline** enclosing namespace — are treated as one with respect to ADL.

The ability to specialize templates declared in a nested inline namespace

The third property that distinguishes **inline** namespaces from conventional ones, even when followed by a **using** directive, is the ability to specialize a class template defined within an **inline** namespace from within an enclosing one; this ability holds transitively up to and including the most proximate non**inline** namespace:

```
namespace out                        // proximate noninline outer namespace
{
    inline namespace in1             // first-level nested inline namespace
    {
        inline namespace in2         // second-level nested inline namespace
        {
            template <typename T>    // primary class template general definition
            struct S { };

            template <>              // class template full specialization
            struct S<char> { };
        }

        template <>                  // class template full specialization
        struct S<short> { };
    }

    template <>                      // class template full specialization
    struct S<int> { };
}

using namespace out;                 // conventional using directive

template <>
struct S<int> { };                   // Error, cannot specialize from this scope
```

Note that the conventional nested namespace `out` followed by a **using** directive in the enclosing namespace does not admit specialization from that outermost namespace, whereas all of the **inline** namespaces do. Function templates behave similarly except that — unlike class templates, whose definitions must reside entirely within the namespace in which they are declared — a function template can be *declared* within a nested namespace and then be *defined* from anywhere via a **qualified name**:

```
namespace out                          // proximate noninline outer namespace
{
    inline namespace in1               // first-level nested inline namespace
    {
        template <typename T>          // function template declaration
        void f();

        template <>                    // function template (full) specialization
        void f<short>() { }
    }

    template <>                        // function template (full) specialization
    void f<int>() { }
}

template <typename T>                  // function template general definition
void out::in1::f() { }
```

An important takeaway from the examples above is that every template entity — be it class or function — *must* be declared in *exactly* one place within the collection of namespaces that comprise the **inline** namespace set. In particular, declaring a class template in a nested **inline** namespace and then subsequently defining it in a containing namespace is not possible because, unlike a function definition, a type definition cannot be placed into a namespace via name qualification alone:

```
namespace outer
{
    inline namespace inner
    {
        template <typename T>          // class template declaration
        struct Z;                      // (if defined, must be within same namespace)

        template <>                    // class template full specialization
        struct Z<float> { };
    }

    template <typename T>              // inconsistent declaration (and definition)
    struct Z { };                      // Z is now ambiguous in namespace outer.

    const int i = sizeof(Z<int>);      // Error, reference to Z is ambiguous.

    template <>                        // attempted class template full specialization
```

```
    struct Z<double> { };           // Error, outer::Z or outer::inner::Z?
}
```

Reopening namespaces can reopen nested `inline` ones

Another subtlety specific to **inline** namespaces is related to reopening namespaces. Consider a namespace `outer` that declares a nested namespace `outer::m` and an **inline** namespace `inner` that, in turn, declares a nested namespace `outer:inner::m`. In this case, subsequent attempts to reopen namespace `m` cause an ambiguity error:

```
namespace outer
{
    namespace m { }         // opens and closes ::outer::m

    inline namespace inner
    {
        namespace n { }     // opens and closes ::outer::inner::n
        namespace m { }     // opens and closes ::outer::inner::m
    }

    namespace n             // OK, reopens ::outer::inner::n
    {
        struct S { };        // defines ::outer::inner::n::S
    }

    namespace m             // Error, namespace m is ambiguous.
    {
        struct T { };        // with clang defines ::outer::m::T
    }
}

static_assert(std::is_same<outer::n::S, outer::inner::n::S>::value, "");
```

In the code snippet above, no issue occurs with reopening `outer::inner::n` and no issue would have occurred with reopening `outer::m` but for the `inner` namespaces having been declared **inline**. When a new namespace declaration is encountered, a lookup determines if a matching namespace having that name appears anywhere in the ***inline** namespace set* of the current namespace. If the namespace is ambiguous, as is the case with `m` in the example above, one can get the surprising error shown.[3] If a matching namespace is found

---

[3]Note that reopening already declared namespaces, such as `m` and `n` in the `inner` and `outer` example, is handled incorrectly on several popular platforms. Clang, for example, performs a name lookup when encountering a new namespace declaration and give preference to the outermost namespace found, causing the last declaration of `m` to reopen `::outer::m` instead of being ambiguous. GCC, prior to 8.1 (c. 2018), does not perform name lookup and will place *any* nested namespace declarations directly within their enclosing namespace. This defect causes the last declaration of `m` to reopen `::outer::m` instead of `::outer::inner::m` and the last declaration of `n` to open a new namespace, `::outer::n`, instead of reopening `::outer::inner::n`.

unambiguously inside an **inline** namespace, n in this case, then it is that nested namespace that is reopened — here, ::outer::inner::n. The inner namespace is reopened even though the last declaration of n is not lexically scoped within inner. Notice that the definition of S is perhaps surprisingly defining ::outer::inner::n::S, not ::outer::n::S. For more on what is *not* supported by this feature, see *Annoyances — Inability to redeclare across namespaces impedes code factoring* on page 1079.

Use Cases

Facilitating API migration

Getting a large codebase to *promptly* upgrade to a new version of a library in any sort of timely fashion can be challenging. As a simplistic illustration, imagine that we have just developed a new library, parselib, comprising a class template, Parser, and a function template, analyze, that takes a Parser object as its only argument:

```cpp
namespace parselib
{
    template <typename T>
    class Parser
    {
        // ...

    public:
        Parser();
        int parse(T* result, const char* input);
            // Load result from null-terminated input; return 0 (on
            // success) or nonzero (with no effect on result).
    };

    template <typename T>
    double analyze(const Parser<T>& parser);
}
```

To use our library, clients will need to specialize our Parser class directly within the parselib namespace:

```cpp
struct MyClass { /*...*/ };  // end-user-defined type

namespace parselib  // necessary to specialize Parser
{
    template <>              // Create full specialization of class
    class Parser<MyClass> // Parser for user-type MyClass.
    {
        // ...
```

```
    public:
        Parser();
        int parse(MyClass* result, const char* input);
            // The contract for a specialization typically remains the same.
    };

    double analyze(const Parser<MyClass>& parser);
}
```

Typical `client` code will also look for the `Parser` class directly within the `parselib` namespace:

```
void client()
{
    MyClass result;
    parselib::Parser<MyClass> parser;

    int status = parser.parse(&result, "...( MyClass value )...");
    if (status != 0)
    {
        return;
    }

    double value = analyze(parser);
    // ...
}
```

Note that invoking `analyze` on objects of some instantiated type of the `Parser` class template will rely on ADL to find the corresponding overload.

We anticipate that our library's API will evolve over time, so we want to enhance the design of `parselib` accordingly. One of our goals is to somehow encourage clients to move essentially all at once, yet also to accommodate both the early adopters and the inevitable stragglers that make up a typical adoption curve. Our approach will be to create, within our outer `parselib` namespace, a nested **inline** namespace, `v1`, which will hold the current implementation of our library software:

```
namespace parselib
{
    inline namespace v1              // Note our use of inline namespace here.
    {
        template <typename T>
        class Parser
        {
            // ...
```

```
    public:
        Parser();
        int parse(T* result, const char* input);
            // Load result from null-terminated input; return 0 (on
            // success) or nonzero (with no effect on result).
    };

    template <typename T>
    double analyze(const Parser<T>& parser);
  }
}
```

As suggested by the name **v1**, this namespace serves primarily as a mechanism to support library evolution through API and ABI versioning (see *Link-safe ABI versioning* on page 1067 and *Build modes and ABI link safety* on page 1071). The need to specialize **class** Parser and, independently, the reliance on ADL to find the free function template analyze require the use of **inline** namespaces, as opposed to a conventional namespace followed by a **using** directive.

Note that, whenever a subsystem starts out directly in a first-level namespace and is subsequently moved to a second-level nested namespace for the purpose of versioning, declaring the inner namespace **inline** is the most reliable way to avoid inadvertently destabilizing existing clients; see also *Enabling selective **using** directives for short-named entities* on page 1074.

Now suppose we decide to enhance **parselib** in a non–backwards-compatible manner, such that the signature of **parse** takes a second argument **size** of type **std::size_t** to allow parsing of non–null-terminated strings and to reduce the risk of buffer overruns. Instead of unilaterally removing all support for the previous version in the new release, we can create a second namespace, **v2**, containing the new implementation and then, at some point, make **v2** the **inline** namespace instead of **v1**:

```
#include <cstddef>  // std::size_t

namespace parselib
{
    namespace v1  // Notice that v1 is now just a nested namespace.
    {
        template <typename T>
        class Parser
        {
            // ...

        public:
            Parser();
            int parse(T* result, const char* input);
```

```
                   // Load result from null-terminated input; return 0 (on
                   // success) or nonzero (with no effect on result).
        };

        template <typename T>
        double analyze(const Parser<T>& parser);
    }

    inline namespace v2     // Notice that use of inline keyword has moved here.
    {
        template <typename T>
        class Parser
        {
            // ...

        public:  // Note incompatible change to Parser's essential API.
            Parser();
            int parse(T* result, const char* input, std::size_t size);
                // Load result from input of specified size; return 0
                // on success) or nonzero (with no effect on result).
        };

        template <typename T>
        double analyze(const Parser<T>& parser);
    }
}
```

When we release this new version with v2 made **inline**, all existing clients that rely on the version supported directly in parselib will, by design, break when they recompile. At that point, each client will have two options. The first one is to upgrade the code immediately by passing in the size of the input string (e.g., 23) along with the address of its first character:

```
void client()
{
    // ...
    int status = parser.parse(&result, "...( MyClass value )...", 23);
    // ...                                            ^^^^ Look here!
}
```

The second option is to change all references to parselib to refer to the original version in v1 explicitly:

```
namespace parselib
{
    namespace v1  // specializations moved to nested namespace
    {
```

```
        template <>
        class Parser<MyClass>
        {
            // ...

        public:
            Parser();
            int parse(MyClass* result, const char* input);
        };

        double analyze(const Parser<MyClass>& parser);
    }
}

void client1()
{
    MyClass result;
    parselib::v1::Parser<MyClass> parser;  // reference nested namespace v1

    int status = parser.parse(&result, "...( MyClass value )...");
    if (status != 0)
    {
        return;
    }

    double value = analyze(parser);
    // ...
}
```

Providing the updated version in a new **inline** namespace v2 provides a more flexible migration path — especially for a large population of independent client programs — compared to manual targeted changes in client code.

Although new users would pick up the latest version automatically either way, existing users of `parselib` will have the option of converting immediately by making a few small syntactic changes or opting to remain with the original version for a while longer by making all references to the library namespace refer explicitly to the desired version. If the library is released before the **inline** keyword is moved, early adopters will have the option of opting in by referring to v2 explicitly until it becomes the default. Those who have no need for enhancements can achieve stability by referring to a particular version in perpetuity or until it is physically removed from the library source.

Although this same functionality can sometimes be realized without using **inline** namespaces (i.e., by adding a **using namespace** directive at the end of the `parselib` namespace), any benefit of ADL and the ability to specialize templates from within the enclosing `parselib` namespace itself would be lost. Note that, because specialization doesn't kick in until overload resolution is completed, specializing overloaded functions is dubious at best; see *Potential Pitfalls — Relying on **inline** namespaces to solve library evolution* on page 1077.

Providing separate namespaces for each successive version has an additional advantage in an entirely separate dimension: avoiding inadvertent, difficult-to-diagnose, latent linkage defects. Though not demonstrated by this specific example, cases do arise where simply changing which of the version namespaces is declared **inline** might lead to an **ill formed, no-diagnostic required (IFNDR)** program. This issue might ensue when one or more of its translation units that use the library are not recompiled before the program is relinked to the new static or dynamic library containing the updated version of the library software; see *Link-safe ABI versioning* below.

For distinct nested namespaces to guard effectively against accidental link-time errors, the symbols involved have to (1) reside in object code (e.g., a **header-only library** would fail this requirement) and (2) have the same **name mangling** (i.e., linker symbol) in both versions. In this particular instance, however, the signature of the **parse** member function of **parser** did change, and its mangled name will consequently change as well; hence the same **undefined symbol** link error would result either way.

Link-safe ABI versioning

inline namespaces are not intended as a mechanism for source-code versioning; instead, they prevent programs from being **ill formed** due to linking some version of a library with client code compiled using some other, typically older version of the same library. Below, we present two examples: a simple pedagogical example to illustrate the principle followed by a more real-world example. Suppose we have a library component my_thing that implements an example type, Thing, which wraps an **int** and initializes it with some value in its default constructor defined out-of-line in the cpp file:

```
struct Thing  // version 1 of class Thing
{
    int i;    // integer data member (size is 4)
    Thing();  // original noninline constructor (defined in .cpp file)
};
```

Compiling a source file with this version of the header included might produce an object file that can be incompatible yet linkable with an object file resulting from compiling a different source file with a different version of this header included:

```
struct Thing  // version 2 of class Thing
{
    double d;  // double-precision floating-point data member (size is 8)
    Thing();   // updated noninline constructor (defined in .cpp file)
};
```

To make the problem that we are illustrating concrete, let's represent the client as a main program that does nothing but create a Thing and print the value of its only data member, i.

```
// main.cpp:
#include <my_thing.h>  // my::Thing (version 1)
#include <iostream>    // std::cout

int main()
{
    my::Thing t;
    std::cout << t.i << '\n';
}
```

If we compile this program, a reference to a locally undefined linker symbol, such as _ZN2my7impl_v15ThingC1Ev,[4] which represents the my::Thing::Thing constructor, will be generated in the main.o file:

```
$ g++ -c main.cpp
```

Without explicit intervention, the spelling of this linker symbol would be unaffected by any subsequent changes made to the implementation of my::Thing, such as its data members or implementation of its default constructor, even after recompiling. The same, of course, applies to its definition in a separate translation unit.

We now turn to the translation unit implementing type my::Thing. The my_thing **component** consists of a .h/.cpp pair: my_thing.h and my_thing.cpp. The header file my_thing.h provides the physical interface, such as the definition of the principal type, Thing, its member and associated free function declarations, plus definitions for inline functions and function templates, if any:

```
// my_thing.h:
#ifndef INCLUDED_MY_THING
#define INCLUDED_MY_THING

namespace my                  // outer namespace (used directly by clients)
{
    inline namespace impl_v1  // inner namespace (for implementer use only)
    {
        struct Thing
        {
            int i;    // original data member, size = 4
            Thing();  // default constructor (defined in my_thing.cpp)
        };
    }
}
```

---

[4]On a Unix machine, typing nm main.o reveals the symbols used in the specified object file. A symbol prefaced with a capital U represents an undefined symbol that must be resolved by the linker. Note that the linker symbol shown here incorporates an intervening **inline** namespace, impl_v1, as will be explained shortly.

```
    }

#endif
```

The implementation file `my_thing.cpp` contains all of the non**inline** function bodies that will be translated separately into the `my_thing.o` file:

```
// my_thing.cpp:
#include <my_thing.h>

namespace my                    // outer namespace (used directly by clients)
{
    inline namespace impl_v1    // inner namespace (for implementer use only)
    {
        Thing::Thing() : i(0)   // Load a 4-byte value into Thing's data member.
        {
        }
    }
}
```

Observing common good practice, we include the header file of the component as the first substantive line of code to ensure that — irrespective of anything else — the header always compiles in isolation, thereby avoiding insidious include-order dependencies.[5] When we compile the source file `my_thing.cpp`, we produce an object file `my_thing.o` containing the definition of the same linker symbol, such as `_ZN2my7impl_v15ThingC1Ev`, for the default constructor of `my::Thing` needed by the client:

```
$ g++ -c my_thing.cpp
```

We can then link `main.o` and `my_thing.o` into an executable and run it:

```
$ g++ -o prog main.o my_thing.o
$ ./prog

0
```

Now, suppose we were to change the definition of `my::Thing` to hold a **double** instead of an **int**, recompile `my_thing.cpp`, and then relink with the original `main.o` without recompiling `main.cpp` first. None of the relevant linker symbols would change, and the code would recompile and link just fine, but the resulting binary **prog** would be IFNDR: the client would be trying to print a 4-byte, **int** data member, i, in `main.o` that was loaded by the library component as an 8-byte, **double** into d in `my_thing.o`. We can resolve this problem by changing — or, if we didn't think of it in advance, by adding — a new **inline** namespace and making that change there:

---

[5]See **lakos20**, section 1.6.1, "Component Property 1," pp. 210–212.

```
// my_thing.cpp:
#include <my_thing.h>

namespace my                   // outer namespace (used directly by clients)
{
    inline namespace impl_v2   // inner namespace (for implementer use only)
    {
        Thing::Thing() : d(0.0) // Load 8-byte value into Thing's data member.
        {
        }
    }
}
```

Now clients that attempt to link against the new library will not find the linker symbol, such as _Z...impl_v1...v, and the link stage will fail. Once clients recompile, however, the undefined linker symbol will match the one available in the new my_thing.o, such as _Z...impl_v2...v, the link stage will succeed, and the program will again work as expected. What's more, we have the option of keeping the original implementation. In that case, existing clients that have not as yet recompiled will continue to link against the old version until it is eventually removed after some suitable deprecation period.

As a more realistic second example of using **inline** namespaces to guard against linking incompatible versions, suppose we have two versions of a Key class in a security library in the enclosing namespace, auth — the original version in a regular nested namespace v1, and the new current version in an **inline** nested namespace v2:

```
#include <cstdint> // std::uint32_t, std::unit64_t

namespace auth        // outer namespace (used directly by clients)
{
    namespace v1      // inner namespace (optionally used by clients)
    {
        class Key
        {
        private:
            std::uint32_t d_key;
                // sizeof(Key) is 4 bytes.

        public:
            std::uint32_t key() const;  // stable interface function

            // ...
        };
    }

    inline namespace v2    // inner namespace (default current version)
    {
        class Key
```

```
    {
  private:
      std::uint64_t d_securityHash;
      std::uint32_t d_key;
          // sizeof(Key) is 16 bytes.

  public:
      std::uint32_t key() const;  // stable interface function

      // ...
    };
  }
}
```

Attempting to link together older binary artifacts built against version 1 with binary artifacts built against version 2 will result in a link-time error rather than allowing an ill formed program to be created. Note, however, that this approach works only if functionality essential to typical use is defined out of line in a `.cpp` file. For example, it would add absolutely no value for libraries that are shipped entirely as header files, since the versioning offered here occurs strictly at the binary level (i.e., between object files) during the link stage.

Build modes and ABI link safety

In certain scenarios, a class might have two different memory layouts depending on compilation flags. For instance, consider a low-level `ManualBuffer` class template in which an additional data member is added for debugging purposes:

```
template <typename T>
struct ManualBuffer
{
private:
    alignas(T) char d_data[sizeof(T)];  // aligned and big enough to hold a T

#ifndef NDEBUG
    bool d_engaged;  // tracks whether buffer is full (debug builds only)
#endif

public:
    void construct(const T& obj);
        // Emplace obj. (Engage the buffer.) The behavior is undefined unless
        // the buffer was not previously engaged.

    void destroy();
        // Destroy the current obj. (Disengage the buffer.) The behavior is
        // undefined unless the buffer was previously engaged.

    // ...
};
```

Note that we have employed the C++11 **alignas** attribute (see Section 2.1."**alignas**" on page 168) here because it is exactly what's needed for this usage example.

The d_engaged flag in the example above serves as a way to detect misuse of the ManualBuffer class but only in debug builds. The extra space and run time required to maintain this Boolean flag is undesirable in a release build because ManualBuffer is intended to be an efficient, lightweight abstraction over the direct use of **placement new** and explicit destruction.

The linker symbol names generated for the methods of ManualBuffer are the same irrespective of the chosen build mode. If the same program links together two object files where ManualBuffer is used — one built in debug mode and one built in release mode — the **one-definition rule (ODR)** will be violated, and the program will again be IFNDR.

Prior to **inline** namespaces, it was possible to control the ABI-level name of linked symbols by creating separate template instantiations on a per-build-mode basis:

```
#ifndef NDEBUG
enum { is_debug_build = 1 };
#else
enum { is_debug_build = 0 };
#endif


template <typename T, bool Debug = is_debug_build>
struct ManualBuffer { /*...*/ };
```

While the code above changes the interface of ManualBuffer to accept an additional template parameter, it also allows debug and release versions of the same class to coexist in the same program, which might prove useful, e.g., for testing.

Another way of avoiding incompatibilities at link time is to introduce two **inline** namespaces, the entire purpose of which is to change the ABI-level names of the linker symbols associated with ManualBuffer depending on the build mode:

```
#ifndef NDEBUG            // perhaps a BAD IDEA
inline namespace release
#else
inline namespace debug
#endif
{
    template <typename T>
    struct ManualBuffer
    {
        // ... (same as above)
    };
}
```

The approach demonstrated in this example tries to ensure that a linker error will occur if any attempt is made to link objects built with a build mode different from that of manualbuffer.o. Tying it to the NDEBUG flag, however, might have unintended consequences; we might introduce unwanted restrictions in what we call **mixed-mode builds**. Most modern platforms support the notion of linking a collection of object files irrespective of their optimization levels. The same is certainly true for whether or not C-style assert is enabled. In other words, we might want to have a mixed-mode build where we link object files that differ in their optimization and assertion options, as long as they are binary compatible — i.e., in this case, they all must be uniform with respect to the implementation of ManualBuffer. Hence, a more general, albeit more complicated and manual, approach would be to tie the noninteroperable behavior associated with this "safe" or "defensive" build mode to a different switch entirely. Another consideration would be to avoid ever inlining a namespace into the global namespace since no method is available to recover a symbol when there is a collision:

```
namespace buflib  // GOOD IDEA: enclosing namespace for nested inline namespace
{
#ifdef SAFE_MODE  // GOOD IDEA: separate control of non-interoperable versions
    inline namespace safe_build_mode
#else
    inline namespace normal_build_mode
#endif
    {
        template <typename T>
        struct ManualBuffer
        {
        private:
            alignas(T) char d_data[sizeof(T)];  // aligned/sized to hold a T

#ifdef SAFE_MODE
            bool d_engaged;  // tracks whether buffer is full (safe mode only)
#endif

        public:
            void construct(const T& obj);  // sets d_engaged (safe mode only)
            void destroy();                // sets d_engaged (safe mode only)
            // ...
        };
    }
}
```

And, of course, the appropriate conditional compilation within the function bodies would need to be in the corresponding .cpp file.

Finally, if we have two implementations of a particular entity that are sufficiently distinct, we might choose to represent them in their entirety, controlled by their own bespoke conditional-compilation switches, as illustrated here using the my::VersionedThing type (see *Link-safe ABI versioning* on page 1067):

```
// my_versionedthing.h:
#ifndef INCLUDED_MY_VERSIONEDTHING
#define INCLUDED_MY_VERSIONEDTHING

namespace my
{
#ifdef MY_THING_VERSION_1  // bespoke switch for this component version
    inline
#endif
    namespace v1
    {
        struct VersionedThing
        {
            int d_i;
            VersionedThing();
        };
    }

#ifdef MY_THING_VERSION_2  // bespoke switch for this component version
    inline
#endif
    namespace v2
    {
        struct VersionedThing
        {
            double d_i;
            VersionedThing();
        };
    }
}
#endif
```

However, see *Potential Pitfalls—**inline**-namespace-based versioning doesn't scale* on page 1076.

Enabling selective using directives for short-named entities

Introducing a large number of small names into client code that doesn't follow rigorous nomenclature can be problematic. Hoisting these names into one or more nested namespaces so that they are easier to identify as a unit and can be used more selectively by clients, such as through explicit qualification or using directives, can sometimes be an effective way of organizing shared codebases. For example, `std::literals` and its nested namespaces, such as `chrono_literals`, were introduced as **inline** namespaces in C++14. As it turns out, clients of these nested namespaces have no need to specialize any templates defined in these namespaces nor do they define types that must be found through ADL, but one can at least imagine special circumstances in which such tiny-named entities are either templates that require specialization or operator-like functions, such as swap, defined for local types within those nested namespaces. In those cases, **inline** namespaces would be required to preserve the desired "as if" properties.

Even without either of these two needs, another property of an **inline** namespace differentiates it from a non**inline** one followed by a **using** directive. Recall from *Description — Loss of access to duplicate names in enclosing namespace* on page 1056 that a name in an outer namespace will hide a duplicate name imported via a **using** directive, whereas any access to that duplicate name within the enclosing namespace would be ambiguous when that symbol is installed by way of an **inline** namespace. To see why this more forceful clobbering behavior might be preferred over hiding, suppose we have a communal namespace abc that is shared across multiple disparate headers. The first header, abc_header1.h, represents a collection of logically related small functions declared directly in abc:

```
// abc_header1.h:
namespace abc
{
    int i();
    int am();
    int smart();
}
```

A second header, abc_header2.h, creates a suite of many functions having tiny function names. In a perhaps misguided effort to avoid clobbering other symbols within the abc namespace having the same name, all of these tiny functions are sequestered within a nested namespace:

```
// abc_header2.h:
namespace abc
{
    namespace nested  // Should this namespace have been inline instead?
    {
        int a();  // lots of functions with tiny names
        int b();
        int c();
        // ...
        int h();
        int i();  // might collide with another name declared in abc
        // ...
        int z();
    }

    using namespace nested;  // becomes superfluous if nested is made inline
}
```

Now suppose that a client application includes both of these headers to accomplish some task:

```
// client.cpp:
#include <abc_header1.h>
#include <abc_header2.h>

int function()
{
    if (abc::smart() < 0) { return -1; }  // uses smart() from abc_header1.h
    return abc::z() + abc::i() + abc::a() + abc::h() + abc::c();  // Oops!
        // Bug, silently uses the abc::i() defined in abc_header1.h
}
```

In trying to cede control to the client as to whether the declared or imported abc::i() function is to be used, we have, in effect, invited the defect illustrated in the above example whereby the client was expecting the abc::i() from abc_header2.h and yet picked up the one from abc_header1.h by default. Had the nested namespace in abc_header2.h been declared **inline**, the qualified name abc::i() would have automatically been rendered *ambiguous* in namespace abc, the translation would have failed *safely*, and the defect would have been exposed at compile time. The downside, however, is that no method would be available to recover nominal access to the abc::i() defined in abc_header1.h once abc_header2.h is included, even though the two functions (e.g., including their mangled names at the ABI level) remain distinct.

Potential Pitfalls

inline-namespace–based versioning doesn't scale

The problem with using **inline** namespaces for ABI link safety is that the protection they offer is only partial; in a few major places, critical problems can linger until run time instead of being caught at compile time.

Controlling which namespace is **inline** using macros, such as was done in the my::VersionedThing example in *Use Cases — Link-safe ABI versioning* on page 1067, will result in code that directly uses the unversioned name, my::VersionedThing being bound directly to the versioned name my::v1::VersionedThing or my::v2::VersionedThing, along with the class layout of that particular entity. Sometimes details of using the **inline** namespace member are not resolved by the linker, such as the object layout when we use types from that namespace as member variables in other objects:

```
// my_thingaggregate.h:

// ...
#include <my_versionedthing.h>
// ...

namespace my
{
```

```
    struct ThingAggregate
    {
        // ...
        VersionedThing d_thing;
        // ...
    };
}
```

This new `ThingAggregate` type does not have the versioned **inline** namespace as part of its mangled name; it does, however, have a completely different layout if built with `MY_THING_VERSION_1` defined versus `MY_THING_VERSION_2` defined. Linking a program with mixed versions of these flags will result in runtime failures that are decidedly difficult to diagnose.

This same sort of problem will arise for functions taking arguments of such types; calling a function from code that is wrong about the layout of a particular type will result in stack corruption and other undefined and unpredictable behavior. This macro-induced problem will also arise in cases where an old object file is linked against new code that changes which namespace is **inline**d but still provides the definitions for the old version namespace. The old object file for the client can still link, but new object files using the headers for the old objects might attempt to manipulate those objects using the new namespace.

The only viable workaround for this approach is to propagate the **inline** namespace hierarchy through the entire software stack. Every object or function that uses `my::VersionedThing` needs to also be in a namespace that differs based on the same control macro. In the case of `ThingAggregate`, one could just use the same `my::v1` and `my::v2` namespaces, but higher-level libraries would need their own `my`-specific nested namespaces. Even worse, for higher-level libraries, every lower-level library having a versioning scheme of this nature would need to be considered, resulting in having to provide the full cross-product of nested namespaces to get link-time protection against mixed-mode builds.

This need for layers above a library to be aware of and to integrate into their own structure the same namespaces the library has removes all or most of the benefits of using **inline** namespaces for versioning. For an authentic real-world case study of heroic industrial use — and eventual disuse — of **inline**-namespaces for versioning, see *Appendix — Case study of using **inline** namespaces for versioning* on page 1083.

Relying on `inline` namespaces to solve library evolution

Inline namespaces might be misperceived as a complete solution for the owner of a library to evolve its API. As an especially relevant example, consider the C++ Standard Library, which itself does not use inline namespaces for versioning. Instead, to allow for its anticipated essential evolution, the Standard Library imposes certain special restrictions on what is permitted to occur within its own `std` namespace by dint of deeming certain problematic uses as either ill formed or otherwise engendering **undefined behavior**.

Since C++11, several restrictions related to the Standard Library were put in place.

- Users may not add any new declarations within namespace `std`, meaning that users cannot add new *functions*, *overloads*, *types*, or *templates* to `std`. This restriction gives the Standard Library freedom to add new *names* in future versions of the Standard.

- Users may not specialize member functions, member function templates, or member class templates. Specializing any of those entities might significantly inhibit a Standard Library vendor's ability to maintain its otherwise encapsulated implementation details.

- Users may add specializations of top-level Standard Library templates only if the declaration depends on the name of a nonstandard user-defined type and only if that user-defined type meets all requirements of the original template. Specialization of function templates is allowed but generally discouraged because this practice doesn't scale since function templates cannot be partially specialized. Specializing of standard class templates when the specialization names a nonstandard user-defined type, such as `std::vector<MyType*>`, is allowed but also problematic when not explicitly supported. While certain specific types, such as `std::hash`, are designed for user specialization, steering clear of the practice for any other type helps to avoid surprises.

Several other good practices facilitate smooth evolution for the Standard Library.[6]

- Avoid specializing variable templates, even if dependent on user-defined types, except for those variable templates where specialization is explicitly allowed.[7]

- Other than a few specific exceptions, avoiding the forming of pointers to Standard Library functions — either explicitly or implicitly — allows the library to add overloads, either as part of the Standard or as an implementation detail for a particular Standard Library, without breaking user code.[8]

- Overloads of Standard Library functions that depend on user-defined types are permitted, but, as with specializing Standard Library templates, users must still meet the requirements of the Standard Library function. Some functions, such as `std::swap`, are designed to be customization points via overloading, but leaving functions not specifically designed for this purpose to vendor implementations only helps to avoid surprises.

Finally, upon reading about this **inline** namespace feature, one might think that all names in namespace `std` could be made available at a global scope simply by inserting an

---

[6]These restrictions are normative in C++20, having finally formalized what were long identified as best practices. Though these restrictions might not be codified in the Standard for pre-C++20 software, they have been recognized best practices for as long as the Standard Library has existed and adherence to them will materially improve the ability of software to migrate to future language standards irrespective of what version of the language standard is being targeted.

[7]C++20 limits the specialization of variable templates to only those instances where specialization is explicitly allowed and does so only for the mathematical constants in `<numbers>`.

[8]C++20 identifies these functions as `addressable` and gives that property to only `iostream` manipulators since those are the only functions in the Standard Library for which taking their address is part of normal usage.

inline namespace std {} before including any standard headers. This practice is, however, explicitly called out as ill-formed within the C++11 Standard. Although not uniformly diagnosed as an error by all compilers, attempting this forbidden practice is apt to lead to surprising problems even if not diagnosed as an error immediately.

Inconsistent use of `inline` keyword is ill formed, no diagnostic required

It is an ODR violation, IFNDR, for a nested namespace to be **inline** in one translation unit and non**inline** in another. And yet, the motivating use case of this feature relies on the linker to actively complain whenever different, incompatible versions — nested within different, possibly **inline**-inconsistent, namespaces of an ABI — are used within a single executable. Because declaring a nested namespace **inline** does not, by design, affect linker-level symbols, developers must take appropriate care, such as effective use of header files, to defend against such preventable inconsistencies.

Annoyances

Inability to redeclare across namespaces impedes code factoring

An essential feature of an **inline** namespace is the ability to declare a template within a nested **inline** namespace and then specialize it within its enclosing namespace. For example, we can declare

- a type template, S0

- a couple of function templates, f0 and g0

- and a member function template h0, which is similar to f0

in an **inline** namespace, inner, and specialize each of them, such as for **int**, in the enclosing namespace, outer:

```
namespace outer                                          // enclosing namespace
{
    inline namespace inner                               // nested namespace
    {
        template<typename T> struct S0;                  // declarations of
        template<typename T> void f0();                  // various class
        template<typename T> void g0(T v);               // and function
        struct A0 { template <typename T> void h0(); };  // templates
    }

    template<> struct S0<int> { };                       // specializations
    template<> void f0<int>() { }                        // of the various
    void g0(int) { }  /* overload not specialization */  // class and function
    template<> void A0::h0<int>() { }                    // declarations above
}                                                        // in outer namespace
```

Note that, in the case of g0 in this example, the "specialization" **void g0(int)** is a non-template *overload* of the function template g0 rather than a specialization of it. We *cannot*, however, portably[9] declare these templates within the outer namespace and then specialize them within the inner one, even though the inner namespace is **inline**:

```
namespace outer                                     // enclosing namespace
{
    template<typename T> struct S1;                 // class template
    template<typename T> void f1();                 // function template
    template<typename T> void g1(T v);              // function template

    struct A1 { template <typename T> void h1(); }; // member function template

    inline namespace inner                          // nested namespace
    {                                               // BAD IDEA
        template<> struct S1<int> { };              // Error, S1 not a template
        template<> void f1<int>() { }               // Error, f1 not a template
        void g1(int) { }                            // OK, overloaded function
        template<> void A1::h1<int>() { }           // Error, h1 not a template
    }
}
```

Attempting to declare a template in the outer namespace and then define, effectively redeclaring, it in an **inline** inner one causes the name to be inaccessible within the outer namespace:

```
namespace outer                                         // enclosing namespace
{                                                       // BAD IDEA
    template<typename T> struct S2;                     // declarations of
    template<typename T> void f2();                     // various class and
    template<typename T> void g2(T v);                  // function templates

    inline namespace inner                              // nested namespace
    {
        template<typename T> struct S2 { };             // definitions of
        template<typename T> void f2() { }              // unrelated class and
        template<typename T> void g2(T v) { }           // function templates
    }

    template<> struct S2<int> { };      // Error, S2 is ambiguous in outer.
    template<> void f2<int>() { }       // Error, f2 is ambiguous in outer.
    void g2(int) { }                    // OK, g2 is an overload definition.
}
```

---

[9]GCC provides the -fpermissive flag, which allows the example containing specializations within the inner namespace to compile with warnings. Note again that g1(**int**), being an *overload* and not a *specialization*, wasn't an error and, therefore, isn't a warning either.

Finally, declaring a template in the nested **inline** namespace inner in the example above and then subsequently defining it in the enclosing outer namespace has the same effect of making declared symbols ambiguous in the outer namespace:

```
namespace outer                                        // enclosing namespace
{                                                      // BAD IDEA
    inline namespace inner                             // nested namespace
    {
        template<typename T> struct S3;                // declarations of
        template<typename T> void f3();                // various class
        template<typename T> void g3(T v);             // and function
        struct A3 { template <typename T> void h3(); };// templates
    }

    template<typename T> struct S3 { };                // definitions of
    template<typename T> void f3() { }                 // unrelated class
    template<typename T> void g3(T v) { }              // and function
    template<typename T> void A3::h3() { }             // templates

    template<> struct S3<int> { };       // Error, S3 is ambiguous in outer.
    template<> void f3<int>() { }        // Error, f3 is ambiguous in outer.
    void g3(int) { }                     // OK, g3 is an overload definition.
    template<> void A3::h3<int>() { }    // Error, h2 is ambiguous in outer.
}
```

Note that, although the definition for a member function template must be located directly within the namespace in which it is declared, a class or function template, once declared, may instead be defined in a different scope by using an appropriate name qualification:

```
template <typename T> struct outer::S3 { };          // OK, enclosing namespace
template <typename T> void outer::inner::f3() { }     // OK, nested namespace
template <typename T> void outer::g3(T v) { }         // OK, enclosing namespace
template <typename T> void outer::A3::h3<T>() { }     // Error, ill-formed

namespace outer
{
    inline namespace inner
    {
        template <typename T> void A3::h3() { }    // OK, within same namespace
    }
}
```

Also note that, as ever, the corresponding definition of the declared template must have been seen before it can be used in a context requiring a complete type. The importance of ensuring that all specializations of a template have been seen before it is used substantively (i.e., **ODR-used**) cannot be overstated, giving rise to the only limerick, which is actually part of the normative text, in the C++ Language Standard[10]:

---

[10]See **iso11a**, section 14.7.3, "Explicit specialization," paragraph 7, pp. 375–376, specifically p. 376.

> When writing a specialization,
> be careful about its location;
> or to make it compile
> will be such a trial
> as to kindle its self-immolation.

Only one namespace can contain any given inline namespace

Unlike conventional **using** directives, which can be used to generate arbitrary many-to-many relationships between different namespaces, **inline** namespaces can be used only to contribute names to the sequence of enclosing namespaces up to the first non**inline** one. In cases in which the names from a namespace are desired in multiple other namespaces, the classical **using** directive must be used, with the subtle differences between the two modes properly addressed.

As an example, the C++14 Standard Library provides a hierarchy of nested **inline** namespaces for literals of different sorts within namespace std.

- std::literals::complex_literals

- std::literals::chrono_literals

- std::literals::string_literals

- std::literals::string_view_literals

These namespaces can be imported to a local scope in one shot via a **using** std::literals or instead, more selectively, by **using** the nested namespaces directly. This separation of the types used with user-defined literals, which are all in namespace std, from the user-defined literals that can be used to create those types led to some frustration; those who had a **using namespace** std; could reasonably have expected to get the user-defined literals associated with their std types. However, the types in the nested namespace std::chrono did *not* meet this expectation.[11]

Eventually *both* solutions for incorporating literal namespaces, **inline** from std::literals and non**inline** from std::chrono, were pressed into service when, in C++17, a **using namespace** literals::chrono_literals; was added to the std::chrono namespace. The Standard does not, however, benefit in any objective way from any of these namespaces being **inline** since the artifacts in the literals namespace neither depend on ADL nor are templates in need of user-defined specializations; hence, having all non**inline** namespaces with appropriate **using** declarations would have been functionally indistinguishable from the bifurcated approach taken.

---

[11]CWG issue 2278; **hinnant17**

See Also

- "**alignas**" (§2.1, p. 168) provides properly aligned storage for an object of arbitrary type T in the example in *Use Cases — Build modes and ABI link safety* on page 1071.

Further Reading

- **sutter14a** uses inline namespaces as part of a proposal for a portable ABI across compilers.

- **lopez-gomez20** uses inline namespaces as part of a solution to avoid ODR violation in an interpreter.

Appendix

Case study of using `inline` namespaces for versioning

By Niall Douglas

Let me tell you what I (don't) use them for. It is not a conventional opinion.

At a previous well-regarded company, they were shipping no less than forty-three copies of Boost in their application. Boost was not on the approved libraries list, but the great thing about header-only libraries is that they don't obviously appear in final binaries, unless you look for them. So each individual team was including bits of Boost quietly and without telling their legal department. Why? Because it saved time. (This was C++98, and `boost::shared_ptr` and `boost::function` are both extremely attractive facilities.)

Here's the really interesting part: Most of these copies of Boost were not the same version. They were varying over a five-year release period. And, unfortunately, Boost makes no API or ABI guarantees. So, theoretically, you could get two different incompatible versions of Boost appearing in the same program binary, and BOOM! there goes memory corruption.

I advocated to Boost that a simple solution would be for Boost to wrap up their implementation into an internal inline namespace. That inline namespace ought to mean something.

- `lib::v1` is the *stable*, version-1 ABI, which is guaranteed to be compatible with all past and future `lib::v1` ABIs, forever, as determined by the ABI-compliance-check tool that runs on CI. The same goes for `v2`, `v3`, and so on.

- `lib::v2_a7fe42d` is the *unstable*, version-2 ABI, which may be incompatible with any other `lib::*` ABI; hence, the seven hex chars after the underscore are the git short **SHA**, permuted by every commit to the git repository but, in practice, per CMake configure, because nobody wants to rebuild everything per commit. This ensures that no symbols from any revision of `lib` will *ever* silently collide or otherwise interfere with any other revision of `lib`, when combined into a single binary by a dumb linker.

I have been steadily making progress on getting Boost to avoid putting anything in the global namespace, so a straightforward find-and-replace can let you "fix" on a particular version of Boost.

That's all the same as the pitch for **inline** namespaces. You'll see the same technique used in `libstdc++` and many other major modern C++ codebases.

But I'll tell you now, I don't use **inline** namespaces anymore. Now what I do is use a macro defined to a uniquely named namespace. My build system uses the git SHA to synthesize namespace macros for my namespace name, beginning the namespace and ending the namespace. Finally, in the documentation, I teach people to always use a namespace alias to a macro to denote the namespace:

```
namespace output = OUTCOME_V2_NAMESPACE;
```

That macro expands to something like `::outcome_v2_ee9abc2`; that is, I don't use **inline** namespaces anymore.

Why?

Well, for *existing* libraries that don't want to break backward source compatibility, I think **inline** namespaces serve a need. For *new* libraries, I think a macro-defined namespace is clearer.

- It causes users to publicly commit to "I know what you're doing here, what it means, and what its consequences are."

- It declares to *other* users that something unusual (i.e., go read the documentation) is happening here, instead of silent magic behind the scenes.

- It prevents accidents that interfere with ADL and other customization points, which induce surprise, such as accidentally injecting a customization point into `lib`, not into `lib::v2`.

- Using macros to denote namespace lets us reuse the preprocessor machinery to generate C++ modules using the exact same codebase; C++ modules are used if the compiler supports them, else we fall back to inclusion.

Finally, and here's the real rub, because we now have namespace aliases, if I were tempted to use an **inline** namespace, nowadays I probably would instead use a uniquely named namespace instead, and, in the `include` file, I'd alias a user-friendly name to that uniquely named namespace. I think that approach is less likely to induce surprise in the typical developer's likely use cases than **inline** namespaces, such as injecting customization points into the wrong namespace.

So now I hope you've got a good handle on **inline** namespaces: I was once keen on them, but after some years of experience, I've gone off them in favor of better-in-my-opinion alternatives. Unfortunately, if your type `x::S` has members of type `a::T` and macros decide if that is `a::v1::T` or `a::v2::T`, then no linker protects the higher-level types from ODR bugs, unless you also version `x`.

The noexcept **Function Specification**

A function having a **noexcept** exception specification denotes a programmatically observable, runtime-enforced guarantee that no thrown C++ exception will ever escape that function's body.

Description

C++, when first standardized in 1998, provided a mechanism to declare which specific exception types a function may throw including none at all (**throw( )**), and to detect any violations of that specification at runtime by terminating the program; see Section 2.1."**noexcept** Operator" on page 615. In practice, using this feature, known as **dynamic exception specifications**, led to more fragile and less efficient programs and, hence, was never used widely. This original foray into exception specifications was deprecated by C++11[1] in favor of a simpler scheme — employing a newly minted keyword, **noexcept** — that communicates only the critically important information of whether a thrown exception (of any kind) may ever escape from the body of a function so annotated.

Unconditional exception specifications

We may choose to decorate a function to indicate that it *cannot* exit via a thrown exception; any exception that would have escaped will instead be caught automatically at runtime, and std::terminate will be invoked (see *Potential Pitfalls — Overly strong contracts guarantees* on page 1112). We provide this **programmatically accessible** annotation by inserting the **noexcept** exception specification after the parameter list and (for a member function) any cv-ref qualifiers, but before any pure-virtual marker (= 0), any specifiers such as **override** (see Section 1.1."**override**" on page 104), or **final** (see Section 3.1."**final**" on page 1007), and, if present, any trailing return type (see Section 1.1."Trailing Return" on page 124):

```
struct B  // noexcept goes after any cv-ref qualifiers but before = 0.
{
    virtual int foo() const& noexcept = 0;  // The noexcept keyword goes thusly.
    virtual int bar() const& = 0;  // Derived classes may have an exception spec.
};

struct D1 : B  // noexcept goes before override or final.
{
    int foo() const& noexcept override;  // OK
    int bar() const& noexcept override;  // OK
};
```

---

[1] C++17 removed all support for dynamic exception specifications; only the **throw( )** spelling remained (until C++20 when that too was removed) and only as an alias for **noexcept**.

```
struct D2 : B  // The noexcept on an overriding function must be compatible.
{
    int foo() const& override;  // Error, incompatible exception specification
    int bar() const& override;  // OK
};

template <typename T>
auto sum(T a, T b) noexcept -> decltype(a + b);  // goes before trailing return
```

Note that exception specifications on overriding virtual functions must be compatible with (i.e., the same or stricter than) the corresponding virtual function declaration(s) in the corresponding base class(es) — e.g., see **struct**s D1 and D2 above. For additional details and a full example involving dynamic exception specifications, see Section 2.1."**noexcept** Operator" on page 615.

Decorating a function using just the keyword **noexcept** is equivalent to using the longer, conditional **noexcept** syntax, **noexcept(true)**. The absence of **noexcept**, other than for the special cases of *defaulted* **special member functions** (see Section 1.1."Defaulted Functions" on page 33), as well as *any* **destructors** and deallocation functions (see below), is equivalent to using the conditional **noexcept** syntax, **noexcept(false)**.

An implicitly declared **special member function** for a class type, T, will be **noexcept(true)** unless the implicitly generated function must invoke a function that is not **noexcept(true)**.

A **user-declared** special member function having no explicitly stated exception specification that is defaulted *in class scope* will have the same exception specification as if it had been declared implicitly. If a defaulted **user-declared** special member function *is* also decorated with an explicitly stated exception specification, the stated specification will be honored irrespective of what might have otherwise been generated implicitly.[2]

For example, consider a family of classes, S0 … S3, each having an explicitly stated exception specification for, say, its user-declared default constructor (but the same applies to the other five **special member functions** too)[3]:

---

[2]As originally designed for C++11, providing an exception specification on a defaulted **user-declared** **special member function** that did not match the implicit exception specification was ill formed. In 2014, a solution to CWG issue 1778 (**usa13**) was resolved — as a **defect report** — so that any such previously ill formed **special member functions** would become **deleted**. Implementing this change proved problematic because exception specifications — being a **complete-class context** — could not generally be determined implicitly before they were needed. Moreover, C++ developers might legitimately want to explicitly supersede the implicitly generated exception specification in either direction; see *Use Cases — Declaring nonthrowing move operations* on page 1094. In 2019, changes introduced by **smith19** — also as a **defect report** — enabled an explicit exception specification on a **defaulted** user-declared special member function to simply take precedence over the implicit specification.

[3]Note that on older compilers that predate the implementation of the aforementioned changes the constructor of S3 will be deleted, as will the corresponding implicit constructors of C3 and D3 below.

```
struct S0
{
    S0() noexcept(true);            // default constructor is noexcept
    virtual ~S0();                  // ensure nonaggregate (see below)
};

struct S1
{
    S1() noexcept(false);           // default constructor isn't noexcept
    virtual ~S1();                  // ensure nonaggregate (see below)
};

struct S2
{
    S2() noexcept(true)  = default; // default constructor is noexcept
    virtual ~S2();                  // ensure nonaggregate (see below)
};

struct S3
{
    S3() noexcept(false) = default; // default constructor isn't noexcept
    virtual ~S3();                  // ensure nonaggregate (see below)
};
```

In the pedagogical code above, S0 and S1 have **user-provided** default constructors, whereas the default constructors for S2 and S3 are **defaulted** and, hence, *not* user provided. Note that supplying an explicitly stated exception specification on a **defaulted** (see Section 1.1. "Defaulted Functions" on page 33) default constructor — just as with any other **defaulted** special member function — will supersede the implicitly generated exception specification.

Notice that, for the specific case of a default constructor (used above), we have chosen to incorporate a **user-provided** virtual destructor for each of the four classes, S0 ... S3 — to ensure that the **user declared** default constructor cannot be bypassed as a result of the type being an **aggregate** (see Section 2.1. "Braced Init" on page 215) or having **trivial** default initialization (see Section 2.1. "Generalized PODs '11" on page 401); deriving virtually from an empty base class would have worked too. By ensuring that value initialization uses the default constructor, we sidestep situations where the **noexcept** operator and the **noexcept** specifier subtly diverge; see Section 2.1. "**noexcept** Operator" on page 615:

```
static_assert( noexcept(S0()), "");  // employing the noexcept operator
static_assert(!noexcept(S1()), "");  //     "       "      "        "
static_assert( noexcept(S2()), "");  //     "       "      "        "
static_assert(!noexcept(S3()), "");  //     "       "      "        "
```

Let's now consider two more families of classes, C0 ... C3, which contain S0 ... S3, respectively, and D0 ... D3, which respectively derive from them:

```
struct C0 { S0 s; };   struct D0 : S0 { };   // default ctor is    noexcept
struct C1 { S1 s; };   struct D1 : S1 { };   // default ctor isn't noexcept
struct C2 { S2 s; };   struct D2 : S2 { };   // default ctor is    noexcept
struct C3 { S3 s; };   struct D3 : S3 { };   // default ctor isn't noexcept
```

Observe that, if a class Sn has a throwing default constructor, then so too will the implicitly generated default constructor for the corresponding class, Cn, containing Sn and similarly for the corresponding derived class, Dn, that publicly inherits from Sn.

User-provided functions that do *not* have an explicitly stated exception specification are presumed to be **noexcept(false)** apart from a couple of specific cases.

The default exception specification for a **user-provided** *destructor* is handled in a very special way: The absence of an exception specification implies that the destructor's exception specification is the same as if it had been generated implicitly — irrespective of the body of that destructor (e.g., Da, Dc):

```
struct Sx { ~Sx() noexcept(false); };              // destructor isn't noexcept
struct Sy { ~Sy() noexcept(true);  };              // destructor is    noexcept

struct Da : Sx { Sx s; ~Da(); };                   // destructor isn't noexcept
struct Db : Sx { Sx s; ~Db() noexcept; };          // destructor is    noexcept
struct Dc : Sy { Sy s; ~Dc(); };                   // destructor is    noexcept
struct Dd : Sy { Sy s; ~Dd() noexcept(false); };   // destructor isn't noexcept
```

Like most functions, all other **user-provided special member functions** having no explicitly stated exception specification are presumed to be **noexcept(false)**.

The other specific case where the absence of an explicitly stated exception specification does not imply **noexcept(false)** is on a deallocation function, such as a class-specific **delete**.[4] Here, the absence of an explicitly stated exception specification *always* implies **noexcept(true)**:

```
#include <cstddef>  // std::size_t

struct G  // implements class-specific new and delete
{
    void* operator new(std::size_t);  // class-specific new
    void  operator delete(void*);     // class-specific delete
};

static_assert(!noexcept(new G()), "");                          // OK
static_assert( noexcept(delete(static_cast<G*>(0))), "");  // OK
```

---

[4]Use of **class-specific memory management** is dubious; see **berger02**.

In C++11 and C++14, **noexcept** exception specifications, just like C++03 dynamic exception specifications before it, are not part of the type system.[5] Hence, we cannot use either form in type aliases, such as **typedef** (or **using**, see Section 1.1. "**using** Aliases" on page 133); see *Annoyances — Exception specifications are not part of a function's type* on page 1147:

```
typedef bool ft(int);              // OK
typedef bool ft(int);              // OK, typedef declaration repeated
typedef bool ft(int) noexcept;     // Error, exception spec. in type alias
typedef bool gt(int) noexcept(true);  // Error,     "      "   "   "    "
typedef bool ht(int) noexcept(false); // Error,     "      "   "   "    "
```

Similarly, functions cannot be overloaded on exception specifications:

```
bool f(int);                   // OK
bool f(int) noexcept(false);   // OK, proper redeclaration of throwing f
bool f(int) noexcept;          // Error, mismatched redeclaration
```

This inability to overload on **noexcept** is reminiscent of how the return type is not part of a function's **signature** and, hence, cannot be used for overloading purposes.[6] Unlike the return type, however, a function's exception specification is not consulted when determining a viable candidate during overload resolution, and, hence, function templates cannot exploit **SFINAE** (e.g., using `std::enable_if`) in an exception specification; see *Annoyances — Exception specifications do not trigger SFINAE* on page 1149.

Function pointers and references

Although not a part of the type system, **noexcept** exception specifications — just as with dynamic exception specifications — can be applied to a variable declaration of type function pointer, function reference, or pointer-to-member function:

```
bool ff(int) noexcept;                    // free (nonmember) function, ff
struct S { bool mf(int) noexcept; };      // member function, mf, of S

bool (*fPtr)(int) noexcept    = ff;       // pointer to free function ff
bool (&fref)(int) noexcept    = ff;       // reference to free function ff
bool (S::*gPTMF)(int) noexcept = &S::mf;  // pointer-to-member function mf
```

---

[5]As of C++17, exception specifications enter the type system. Among other benefits, such a change means exception specifications can be used in type aliases and overloading; see **maurer15**. Moreover, being part of the type system, in turn, affects name mangling and therefore the **ABI** (e.g., of function pointers and functions having function-pointers as parameters); see *Annoyances — ABI changes in future versions of C++* on page 1148.

[6]Even in C++17 and later, it will not be possible to overload arbitrary functions based solely on them being either **noexcept(true)** or **noexcept(false)**; it will, however, be possible to overload functions — irrespective of their own exception specifications — based on the exception specifications of any parameters that are of type function pointer, function reference, or pointer-to-member function.

A function having a **noexcept** exception specification, just as with **throw( )**, may be bound to a function pointer having no such specification but *not* vice versa (e.g., qf and qg below, respectively)[7]:

```
void f() noexcept;      // f may not throw.
void g();               // g may throw.

void (*pf)()       = f;  // OK, dissimilar yet compatible exception specs
void (*pg)()       = g;  // OK, pg is not declared noexcept.
void (*qf)() noexcept = f;  // OK, f is not permitted to throw.
void (*qg)() noexcept = g;  // Error, g may throw but qg is noexcept.
```

This behavior with respect to **noexcept** exception specifications parallels compatible-pointer assignments involving **dynamic exception specifications**, but see *Annoyances — Exception specifications are not part of a function's type* on page 1147.

Notice that, because exception specifications cannot be used in type aliases until C++17 (see *Unconditional exception specifications* on page 1085), we are forced, in the example code above, to spell the declarations for qf and qg (and, for consistency, did so for pf and pg as well).

Exception specifications — though not yet part of the type of a function, function pointer, etc. — are nonetheless required to be compatible when initializing or assigning to a function pointer, and most compilers make a best-effort attempt to verify compatibility at compile time:

```
void f1() { }          //    throwing function
void f2() noexcept { } // nonthrowing      "

void (*p1)()          = f1; // holds    throwing function
void (*p2)() noexcept = f2; //   "    nonthrowing function

void test()  // Function pointers of like type are interoperable.
{
    p1 = p1;  // OK,     throwing assigned from    throwing
    p2 = p2;  // OK,   nonthrowing      "      " nonthrowing
    p1 = p2;  // OK,     throwing       "      " nonthrowing
    p2 = p1;  // Error, nonthrowing     "      "    throwing
}
```

In particular, notice (above) that it is ill formed to assign the value of a function pointer that is *not* declared **noexcept** (e.g., p1) to one that *is* (e.g., p2).

Similarly, we can pass an arbitrary function pointer to a function via a function-pointer parameter of like type only if the exception specifications are compatible:

---

[7]Some compilers, most notably GCC, never implemented pointer-compatibility checks for C++03 dynamic **exception specifications** and therefore do not diagnose errors for the **noexcept** form either. Note that — even with GCC 11.1 (c. 2021) — when specifying Standards before C++17, this tool chain continues to allow incompatible pointer assignment without warning.

```
void g1 (void (*p)()          ) { }  //    throwing function-pointer parameter
void g2 (void (*p)() noexcept) { }  // nonthrowing    "         "         "

void test2()
{
    g1(f1);  // OK,    passing    throwing function via   throwing parameter
    g2(f2);  // OK,      "      nonthrowing    "       " nonthrowing    "
    g1(f2);  // OK,      "      nonthrowing    "       "   throwing     "
    g2(f1);  // Error,   "        throwing     "       " nonthrowing    "
}
```

Notice that, in the `test2()` function above, we are able to pass a potentially throwing function (e.g., `f1`) via a function-pointer parameter of corresponding type to a function (e.g., `g1`) accepting a throwing function but not to one (e.g., `g2`) requiring a nonthrowing function.

Interpreting and implementing the exception specification compatibility requirements on function pointers was unclear prior to C++17, but the rules were trivial enough to implement once exception specifications became part of the type system in C++17.

Conditional exception specifications

As introduced in the previous section, a function can clearly indicate whether it potentially throws exceptions by adding a compile-time predicate to the **noexcept** exception specification. For example, by using this predicate on a destructor, we can override the default and indicate that said destructor may throw:

```
void f() noexcept(true);  // equivalent to void f() noexcept

struct S
{
    ~S() noexcept(false);  // destructor may throw
};
```

In addition to **true** and **false**, the predicate can be any integral **constant expression** that can be implicitly converted to **bool**, which can include the use of compile-time operators such as the **sizeof** operator, the value of a type trait, or the evaluation of a **constexpr** function (see Section 2.1. "**constexpr** Functions" on page 257):

```
template <typename T>
void process(T& obj) noexcept(sizeof(T) < 1024);
```

Though any **constant expression** that can be converted to **bool** is allowed, many compilers will warn or error if a **narrowing conversion** is performed; hence, to ensure portability, it is necessary to employ expressions of type **bool** and add an explicit **static_cast<bool>** when using expressions of types other than **bool**.

Such predicates are especially useful in generic code, where it is known that the only opportunities to throw exceptions come from operations dependent on the template arguments. A common example might be using type traits to mark constructors as nonthrowing:

```
#include <utility>  // std::is_nothrow_copy_constructible
                    // std::is_nothrow_move_constructible


template <typename T>
class Wrap {
    T d_data;
public:
    Wrap(const Wrap&) noexcept(std::is_nothrow_copy_constructible<T>::value);
    Wrap(Wrap&&)      noexcept(std::is_nothrow_move_constructible<T>::value);
};
```

Exception specifications employing the noexcept operator

The primary motivation to add the **noexcept** exception specification was to support the **noexcept** operator (Section 2.1."**noexcept** Operator" on page 615), which queries expressions to ascertain, at compile time, whether any of their constituent subexpressions might throw. This operator has a natural synergy back to declaring exception specifications, where the **noexcept** operator is ideal for use in the predicate of a **noexcept** exception specification:

```
template <typename T, typename U>
void grow(T& lhs, const U& rhs) noexcept(noexcept(lhs += rhs))
{
    lhs += rhs;  // expression that might or might not throw
}
```

Notice the cumbersome, repetitive use of **noexcept(noexcept(...))** qualifying the grow function above. This use has nonetheless become idiomatic, and there has not yet been a proposal for a shorthand notation (e.g., noexcept2(...)) to combine the two.[8] As it turns out, it is rare, in practice, to query just a single expression to determine the **noexcept** status of a non-trivial expression — e.g., **noexcept(noexcept(T()) && noexcept(U()) && noexcept(lhs * rhs))**. Many of the more common single-expression queries are, however, wrapped up by standard type traits, such as std::is_nothrow_move_constructible. What's more, there is an important distinction to be made between the two forms, **noexcept(f())** and **noexcept(noexcept(f()))**; see *Potential Pitfalls — Forgetting to use the noexcept operator in the noexcept specifier* on page 1129.

1. **noexcept(f())** — the exception specification is determined at compile time by evaluating a **constexpr** function, f; see Section 2.1."**constexpr** Functions" on page 257.

---

[8]There have, however, been proposals to (re)consider the syntax **noexcept(auto)** to denote an exception specification that is a reflection of what's in the function body, rather than the "laborious and error-prone" alternative of having to repeat it in the exception specification itself; see **voutilainen15**.

2. **noexcept(noexcept(f()))** — the exception specification reflects whether the invocation of function **f** is permitted to emit an exception; see Section 2.1."**noexcept** Operator" on page 615.

Violating an exception specification

Although a **noexcept(true)** exception specification ensures that no thrown exception will escape from a call to that function, there are no syntactic or semantic rules for the compiler to diagnose when code might throw an exception that would attempt to violate that guarantee and thus result in a call to **std::terminate()**. Absolute enforcement of such guarantees is a runtime property of the program, and the compiler must ensure that all exceptions trying to pass out of a function having a nonthrowing exception specification result in the invocation of **std::terminate**.

When a (now deprecated) **dynamic exception specification** is violated, the compiler is required to complete stack unwinding of the function with the violated specification before invoking the installed **std::unexpected_handler**. This unwinding puts the program in a position where **std::unexpected** is called, which is then permitted to attempt to throw a new exception that does *not* violate the dynamic exception specification.

When a **noexcept(true)** exception specification is violated, it is **implementation defined** whether a compiler will perform stack unwinding, and **std::terminate** will always be invoked regardless. Importantly, note that — unlike with a **dynamic exception specification** — the program will *always* terminate execution of the program without any prospect of returning to the caller of the function whose exception specification was violated.

Potential efficiencies when expressions cannot throw

When designing a runtime-efficient program, it is often important to choose the best algorithm before digging down to the details of its implementation. Some algorithms are faster than others but fail to provide the same degree of exception safety guarantees. In some cases where it can be determined at compile time that an operation will not throw, we can replace a slower algorithm with a faster one. Using **noexcept** exception specifications to label the exception throwing nature of a particular operation, combined with the **noexcept** operator to query whether a particular operation is capable of throwing, enables a generic program to make the optimal choice when selecting the algorithm for a given type parameter. The advent of **move operations** (see Section 2.1."*Rvalue* References" on page 710) was the driving force behind the need to enable such considerations and was what emergently precipitated this feature; see *Use Cases — Declaring nonthrowing move operations* on page 1094. For a variety of detailed code examples, see Section 2.1."**noexcept** Operator" on page 615.

Additionally, the **noexcept** specifier serves as a hint to the compiler's optimizer; any guarantee that such a specifier affords is necessarily checked at runtime and can be considered reliable. If an exception is thrown and reaches the barrier at the call to a **noexcept** function, the compiler will exit the program by calling **std::terminate** and (although permitted) is not required to destroy any objects whose lifetime ends between the **throw** and the function entry. Skipping this unwinding allows the compiler to eliminate otherwise unused cleanup code, producing a smaller program. Moreover, when the compiler sees that a function has a nonthrowing exception specification, it can safely assume that no exceptions will be thrown when calling that function and so can eliminate other cleanup code associated with handling potentially thrown exceptions; see *Use Cases — Reducing object-code size* on page 1101.

Finally, explicit use of **noexcept** is not an entirely new code-elimination opportunity as the compiler could perform a similar analysis on, say, the body of an **inline** function (or, for smaller programs, on the compiled application during **link-time optimization**). However, because the **noexcept** specifier resides on the *declaration* of the function, that specifier is necessarily visible when the caller is compiled. As a result, explicit use of an exception specification simplifies the analysis a compiler would have to perform, making the potential optimization more viable when separately compiling each individual translation unit and, hence, more likely, but see *Potential Pitfalls — Overly strong contracts guarantees* on page 1112 and *Potential Pitfalls — Unrealizable runtime performance benefits* on page 1134.

Use Cases

Declaring nonthrowing move operations

The most common algorithmic benefits of the **noexcept** feature accrue to types having move and swap operations that are guaranteed not to throw. Operations such as resizing an **std::vector**, for example, can use move construction instead of copy construction to transfer elements from a smaller memory buffer to a larger one without concern that an exception will occur in the middle (e.g., due to potential dynamic memory allocation) and thus leave the vector in a half-moved state. It therefore behooves us to consider whether our classes can have such nonthrowing move and swap operations whenever runtime performance matters and annotate them with **noexcept** where applicable.

The first question we must ask ourselves when considering the move operations of a new class is whether the class can benefit from having a move constructor or move-assignment operator. A class that does not allocate resources seldom needs move operations that are distinct from its copy operations. If resources are managed by one or more member variables or base classes, the defaulted move operations are often sufficient. Note that any implicitly defaulted move operation will be suppressed by a user-declared copy operation; e.g., a user-declared copy constructor will suppress an implicit move constructor. See Section 1.1. "Defaulted Functions" on page 33.

A *user-provided* move operation will, by default, be **noexcept(false)**; it can and should be declared with the **noexcept** specifier whenever it does not invoke any throwing operation during the move. Let's, for example, define a smart pointer class, CloningPtr, that owns its pointed-to object and whose copy constructor and copy-assignment operator copy the owned object; two CloningPtr objects will never point to the same object:

```
template <typename T>
class CloningPtr
```

```
    {
        T* d_owned_p;   // pointer to dynamically allocated owned object, 0 if empty

    public:
        CloningPtr() : d_owned_p(nullptr) { }

        explicit CloningPtr(const T& val) : d_owned_p(new T(val)) { }

        CloningPtr(const CloningPtr& original)
        : d_owned_p(original.d_owned_p ? new T(*original.d_owned_p) : nullptr)
        {
        }

        CloningPtr(CloningPtr&& original) noexcept
        : d_owned_p(original.d_owned_p)
        {
            original.d_owned_p = nullptr;   // Remove ownership from original.
        }

        ~CloningPtr() { delete d_owned_p; }

        CloningPtr& operator=(const CloningPtr& rhs)
        {
            if (this != &rhs)
            {
                T* oldOwned_p = d_owned_p;
                d_owned_p = rhs.d_owned_p ? new T(*rhs.d_owned_p) : nullptr;
                delete oldOwned_p;
            }

            return *this;
        }

        CloningPtr& operator=(CloningPtr&& rhs) noexcept
        {
            if (&rhs == this) { return *this; }   // Check for self assignment.
            delete d_owned_p;

            d_owned_p     = rhs.d_owned_p;
            rhs.d_owned_p = nullptr;              // Remove ownership from rhs.

            return *this;
        }

        T& operator*() const { return *d_owned_p; }
        T* operator->() const { return d_owned_p; }
    };
```

CloningPtr has a default constructor that creates a null pointer and a value constructor that allocates a copy of its argument on the heap. When a CloningPtr object is copied using the copy constructor or copy-assignment operator, a new copy of the source's managed object is allocated for the target CloningPtr to manage. Copy construction and copy assignment are potentially throwing operations because they (1) allocate memory and (2) call T's copy constructor.

Now let's consider whether CloningPtr would benefit from defining move operations. A CloningPtr allocates a resource (the pointed-to object), and it can safely transfer that resource — via simple pointer moves — to the moved-to object without invoking any potentially throwing operations. We have, therefore, implemented a move constructor and move-assignment operator, both of which are decorated with the **noexcept** specifier. In both move operations, the d_owned_p pointer is copied from the moved-from object to the moved-to object, and then the moved-from object is set to null (to avoid having two CloningPtr objects attempting to own the same resource).

Note that std::swap<T> is declared such that when T's move constructor and move-assignment operator are both **noexcept**, std::swap<T> is **noexcept** automatically:

```
namespace std {

template <typename T>
void swap(T& left, T& right)  // Note use of conditional noexcept syntax.
    noexcept(is_nothrow_move_constructible<T>::value &&
             is_nothrow_move_assignable<T>::value);

} // close std namespace
```

Thus, we need not provide a custom swap function for CloningPtr because the global one, provided by the Standard Library as the default, will do the job:

```
#include <string>        // std::string
#include <utility>       // std::swap
#include <type_traits>   // std::is_nothrow_move_constructible,
                         // std::is_nothrow_move_assignable
#include <cassert>       // standard C assert macro

void f1()
{
    typedef CloningPtr<std::string> PtrType;

    PtrType p1("hello");
    PtrType p2(p1);             // Clones the string owned by p1
    assert(*p1 == "hello");
    assert(*p2 == "hello");

    static_assert(std::is_nothrow_move_constructible<PtrType>::value, "");
    static_assert(std::is_nothrow_move_assignable<PtrType>::value, "");
```

```
    static_assert(noexcept(std::swap(p1, p2)), "");   // noexcept for free
}
```

Defining a noexcept swap

Imagine an algorithm, strongSort(std::vector<T>& v), that sorts a vector of T while providing the **strong exception-safety guarantee**. If swap(T&, T&) is known *not* to throw, then the sort is performed in place; otherwise, v is copied, that copy is sorted, and then the sorted copy is swapped with v using the **copy/swap idiom**. That way, if swapping a pair of elements of the vector during the sort throws an exception, the original vector remains unchanged. Note that swapping std::vector objects never throws an exception, even if swapping individual elements might.

Let's define a variant of the CloningPtr class template from the previous use case. This variant, NonNullCloningPtr, is guaranteed never to have a null value. The default constructor for NonNullCloningPtr<T> will allocate a default-constructed T on the heap, and the move constructor will do the same for the new value of the moved-from object. Move assignment can avoid an allocation by just swapping the pointers, which are guaranteed to be non-null, in the moved-from and moved-to objects. The allocations in the constructors make decorating them with **noexcept** contraindicated (but see *A wrapper that provides* **noexcept** *move operations* on page 1099). However, even without a nonthrowing move operation we are not prevented from declaring a bespoke swap function that is **noexcept**:

```
#include <utility>   // std::swap

template <typename T>
class NonNullCloningPtr
{
    T* d_owned_p;   // pointer to dynamically allocated owned object, never null

public:
    NonNullCloningPtr() : d_owned_p(new T) { }   // might throw

    explicit NonNullCloningPtr(const T& val) : d_owned_p(new T(val)) { }

    NonNullCloningPtr(const NonNullCloningPtr& original)
    : d_owned_p(new T(*original.d_owned_p))
    {
    }

    NonNullCloningPtr(NonNullCloningPtr&& original)
    : d_owned_p(original.d_owned_p)
    {
        original.d_owned_p = new T;   // Remove ownership from original.
    }
```

```
    ~NonNullCloningPtr() { delete d_owned_p; }

    NonNullCloningPtr& operator=(const NonNullCloningPtr& rhs)
    {
        if (this != &rhs)
        {
            T* oldOwned_p = d_owned_p;
            d_owned_p = new T(*rhs.d_owned_p);
            delete oldOwned_p;
        }

        return *this;
    }

    NonNullCloningPtr& operator=(NonNullCloningPtr&& rhs) noexcept
    {
        std::swap(d_owned_p, rhs.d_owned_p);
        return *this;
    }

    T& operator*() const { return *d_owned_p; }
    T* operator->() const { return d_owned_p; }

    friend void swap(NonNullCloningPtr& a, NonNullCloningPtr& b) noexcept
    {
        std::swap(a.d_owned_p, b.d_owned_p);  // no allocation needed
    }
};
```

Just as with move assignment, the **swap** friend function simply swaps the **d_owned_p** pointers.
Thus, even though **NonNullCloningPtr**'s move constructor may throw, its **swap** operation
is guaranteed not to:

```
#include <string>          // std::string
#include <utility>         // std::swap
#include <type_traits>     // std::is_nothrow_move_constructible,
                           // std::is_nothrow_move_assignable
#include <cassert>         // standard C assert macro

void f2()
{
    typedef NonNullCloningPtr<std::string> PtrType;

    PtrType p1("hello");
    PtrType p2(std::move(p1));
    assert(*p1 == "");  // Moved-from object owns default-constructed string.
    assert(*p2 == "hello");

    static_assert(!std::is_nothrow_move_constructible<PtrType>::value, "");
```

```
    static_assert( std::is_nothrow_move_assignable<PtrType>::value, "");

    static_assert(!noexcept(std::swap(p1, p2)), "");   // std::swap explicitly
    static_assert( noexcept(swap(p1, p2)), "");        // friend swap via ADL
}
```

Calling `strongSort(std::vector<NonNullCloningPtr<U>>&)` will consequently use the faster algorithm. A number of techniques and algorithms depend on having a nonthrowing `swap`, so there is significant benefit to defining `swap` with an explicitly stated **noexcept** guarantee.

A wrapper that provides noexcept **move operations**

Looking at the implementation of `NonNullCloningPtr` in the previous use case, we can see that, when instantiated for `std::string`, the only reason its move constructor might throw would be due to an out-of-memory condition. If we assume that this condition can never occur or that, if it does occur, the only reasonable action is to terminate the program, then we can reasonably proceed as if the `NonNullCloningPtr<std::string>` cannot throw on move. To force algorithms to choose the faster **noexcept** path in situations like this one, we can create a *wrapper* class template that unconditionally decorates its move constructor and move-assignment operator with **noexcept**[9,10]:

```
#include <utility>  // std::move, std::forward

template <typename T>
class NoexceptMoveWrapper : public T
{
public:
    NoexceptMoveWrapper() = default;
    NoexceptMoveWrapper(const NoexceptMoveWrapper&) = default;
    NoexceptMoveWrapper& operator=(const NoexceptMoveWrapper&) = default;
```

---

[9]A similar wrapper class template, bslalg::NothrowMovableWrapper, is defined in Bloomberg's BDE library and is used to avoid some allocations in bsl::function, the BDE implementation of std::function. See **bde14**, /groups/bsl/bslalg_nothrowmovablewrapper.h.

[10]Prior to the implementation of **smith19** (in GCC 10, c. 2020, and Clang 9, c. 2019), the move operations for NoexceptMoveWrapper would be deleted or, with some compiler versions, **noexcept(false)**. One workaround would be to provide the implementations for these move operations explicitly:

```
template <typename T> NoexceptMoveWrapper<T>::
NoexceptMoveWrapper(NoexceptMoveWrapper<T>&& arg) noexcept
 : T(static_cast<T&&>(arg)) { }

template <typename T>
NoexceptMoveWrapper<T>& NoexceptMoveWrapper<T>::
operator=(NoexceptMoveWrapper<T>&& arg) noexcept
{
    static_cast<T&>(*this) = static_cast<T&&>(arg);
    return *this;
}
```

```
            // defaulted implementations

    NoexceptMoveWrapper(const T& val) : T(val) { }
        // implicit copy from a T

    template <typename... Us>
    explicit NoexceptMoveWrapper(Us&&... vals)
    : T(std::forward<Us>(vals)...) { }
        // perfect forwarding value constructor

    NoexceptMoveWrapper(T&& val) noexcept : T(std::move(val)) { }
    NoexceptMoveWrapper(NoexceptMoveWrapper&&) noexcept = default;
    NoexceptMoveWrapper& operator=(NoexceptMoveWrapper&&) noexcept = default;
        // moves terminate when the corresponding T operation throws
};
```

An instantiation of `NoexceptMoveWrapper<T>` inherits from `T` and defines constructors and assignment operators that forward to the corresponding operations within `T`. Note that the move constructor and move-assignment operator are explicitly defaulted but that the **noexcept** specifier is used to override the default exception specification; see *Description — Unconditional exception specifications* on page 1085. By wrapping a class type with `NoexceptMoveWrapper`, it is possible to coerce utilities to choose a faster algorithm that avoids the extra copying that would be needed to provide stronger exception guarantees:

```
#include <vector>        // std::vector
#include <string>        // std::string
#include <type_traits>   // std::is_nothrow_move_constructible
#include <cassert>       // standard C assert macro

void f3()
{
    typedef NonNullCloningPtr<std::string> PtrType;
    typedef NoexceptMoveWrapper<PtrType>    WrapperType;

    static_assert(!std::is_nothrow_move_constructible<PtrType>::value, "");
    static_assert( std::is_nothrow_move_constructible<WrapperType>::value, "");

    std::vector<PtrType> v1(3, PtrType("red"));        // "red", "red", "red"
    std::string* p1 = &*v1[0];
    v1.reserve(200);        // slow reallocation
    assert("red" == *v1[0]);
    assert(p1 != &*v1[0]);  // new string was allocated

    std::vector<WrapperType> v2(3, WrapperType("red"));  // "red", "red", "red"
    std::string* p2 = &*v2[0];
    v2.reserve(200);        // fast reallocation
    assert("red" == *v2[0]);
    assert(p2 == &*v2[0]);  // ownership transferred; no new string allocated
}
```

In the `f3` function, above, an `std::vector`, `v1`, is constructed holding three values of the unwrapped `NonNullCloningPtr<std::string>` type. When the `vector` is subsequently expanded using `reserve`, the elements are copied to a new location, and the original elements are then destroyed. Consequently, the string payloads are cloned to new locations, as evidenced by the `assert` statement showing that their addresses have changed. When the same set of operations is performed on an `std::vector` of wrapped objects (`v2`), the `reserve` method moves the elements rather than copying them because the move constructor is declared **noexcept**. Since move operations copy pointers rather than allocate new objects, no new string payloads need to be allocated, and the process of expanding the vector is made faster.

Finally, note that a wrapper in no way prevents exceptions from being thrown by the wrapped type's move operations. If we do not have sufficient global knowledge to know that exceptions will not be thrown during move operations, we must be content with program termination as the consequence when they do; see *Potential Pitfalls — Conflating **noexcept** with nofail* on page 1116.

Reducing object-code size

If we are used to programming for medium-to-large computers, such as desktop computers and servers, having terabytes of permanent storage and tens of gigabytes of program memory, we might not think to minimize overall executable program size. Yet consider that C++ is used widely throughout industry for many purposes beyond general-purpose computing. In particular, the inherently high degree of runtime performance afforded by C++ makes it an ideal language for use in small devices, such as cell phones, implanted medical devices, and wireless environmental monitors, where minimizing power consumption is of paramount importance. Often, the available memory on such devices is also limited, which makes reducing code size for **embedded systems** a valuable consideration in its own right; see *Annoyances — Algorithmic optimization is conflated with reducing object-code size* on page 1143.

Understanding the impact of **noexcept** on code size entails understanding the properties of typical contemporary exception handling implementations based on the **zero-overhead exception model**, which has become the de facto standard for essentially all modern 64-bit architectures.[11] The same general considerations affecting code size apply at least qualitatively to other, older exception handling models (e.g., some legacy 32-bit platforms).

Let's begin by observing the important difference between a C++11 **noexcept** specification and the C++03 dynamic exception specification, `throw()`.[12] When exception propagation encounters a **stack frame** within a function having a `throw()` exception specification, all local objects having non-**trivial destructors** (see Section 2.1.“Generalized PODs '11”

---

[11] For an introduction to how the zero-overhead exception model achieves essentially zero cost on the nonexceptional path, see **mortoray13**. The full details of the three levels of the Itanium exception API are delineated in **itanium16**.

[12] Note that this distinction disappeared in C++17 when `throw()` became an alias for `noexcept(true)` and was removed entirely in C++20.

on page 401) up to that frame must be destroyed, after which `std::unexpected` must be invoked. By contrast, when exception propagation encounters a frame within a function having a **noexcept** or **noexcept(true)** exception specification, the implementation is not required to do any unwinding. Although some implementations might choose to clean up the local stack frame, doing so is entirely optional, and in no event will control ever return to the caller after `std::terminate` is invoked:

```
struct Greeting
{
    Greeting() { std::cout << "Hello!\n"; }
    ~Greeting() { std::cout << "Goodbye!\n"; }
};

void greetAndTerminate() noexcept
{
    Greeting g;
    throw 0;
}
```

In the example above, compilers may generate code to output `"Goodbye!"` or not, subject to compiler version, optimization level, flags, and surrounding code.[13]

Hence, declaring a function with a **throw()** specification often *increases* the size of its compiled representation while the opposite is often true for **noexcept(true)**.[14]

In what follows, we will characterize when using a **noexcept** specifier might impact code size. To make the relative improvements more concrete, we will occasionally indicate the number of bytes in the object (`.o`) file created as the result of compiling (in both unoptimized and optimized modes), with a specific compiler-platform pair,[15] a separate translation unit containing only the small snippet of code shown. Of course, these numbers are the result of a particular compiler/optimizer, but because the Itanium ABI is ubiquitous, similar trends can be expected on other modern platforms.

Even in the absence of a **try**/**catch** block or **throw** statement, the compiler must nonetheless generate stack-unwinding code that calls destructors for any non-**trivially destructible** local variables in scope whenever a function that might throw is invoked. The simplest non-**trivially destructible** type is a class (e.g., **S**) having no members except for a user-provided destructor:

```
struct S  // empty non-trivially destructible class type
{
```

---

[13]Without any flags, GCC 11.2 (c. 2021) and MSVC 19.29 (c. 2021) output only `"Hello!"`, whereas Clang 12.0.1 (c. 2021) outputs both `"Hello!"` and `"Goodbye!"`.

[14]An insightful, high-level discussion of **noexcept** stack unwinding and how it differs from **throw()** can be found on StackOverflow; see **pradhan14**.

[15]To accommodate simultaneously both dynamic and **noexcept** exception specifications, we have chosen, as our demonstration compiler, GCC 7.4.0 (c. 2018) running on Cygwin on a T480s ThinkPad. The two compiler optimization modes are none (-O0) and highly optimized (-O3).

```
    ~S();   // user-provided, hence non-trivial destructor
};
```

For a function (e.g., `ff`) that constructs one or more objects of type `S` (e.g., `s1` and `s2`) and then invokes a potentially throwing operation (e.g., a call to function `gg`), the compiler must generate unwinding code to destroy those instances of `S` in the event that `gg` throws an exception:

```
void gg();   // declaration of potentially throwing function

void ff()    // definition of function having no exception specification
{
    S s1;
    gg();   // gg call #1
    S s2;
    gg();   // gg call #2
}
```

If, in the body of `ff` above, the first call to `gg` throws, then the unwinding logic must invoke the destructor for `s1`, but if the second call to `gg` throws, then the unwinding logic must invoke the destructors for both `s2` and `s1`, in that order. Nested blocks and conditional statements can complicate the unwinding logic, thereby producing a larger number of unwinding scenarios. Note that this unwinding logic appears on the **cold path** — i.e., it is invoked only if an exception is thrown at run time. Given the seemingly ubiquitous adoption of the **zero-overhead exception model**, this unwinding code bloats object size but does not compromise the performance of the **hot path**; see *Potential Pitfalls — Unrealizable runtime performance benefits* on page 1134.

Such unwinding logic is not always needed and is typically generated only when all three of the following conditions hold.

1. The function body contains one or more automatic variables of non-**trivially destructible** type (see Section 2.1.*"Rvalue* References" on page 710); otherwise, there are no destructors to invoke when unwinding.

2. There is at least one expression in the body of the function that might throw — e.g., the invocation of a function that is not **noexcept(true)**; otherwise, there is no need for unwinding logic.

3. The potentially throwing expression is invoked during the lifetime of one of the aforementioned variables, i.e., after it is constructed and before said variable leaves scope; otherwise, there is again no needed unwinding logic.

Note that there are other ways — unrelated to the exception specification — by which the compiler is able to reduce or eliminate stack-unwinding code. The other opportunities typically require the compiler to have visibility into the implementations of functions invoked from the function being compiled.

- If the body of a non-trivial destructor (e.g., `S::~S()`) is visible to the compiler and is found to be a no-op — whether or not it is declared **inline** — then the optimizer can treat it as trivial, eliminating condition (1), above.

- If the body of a potentially throwing operation is visible to the compiler and is determined not to throw, then the optimizer can treat that operation as not potentially throwing, possibly eliminating conditions (2) and (3), above.

For an exception specification to reduce the size of generated code, that specification must relieve the compiler of some obligation; specifically, the added specification must relieve the function of its obligation to generate some or all of the unwinding logic for a particular function. If function `ff`, above, were decorated with **noexcept**, then the compiler would have the option not to lay down code (1) to unwind the stack or (2) even to destroy `s1` and `s2` prior to calling `std::terminate` in the event that an invocation of `gg` throws. Hence — in theory — a compiler can presumably generate less unwinding code for a **noexcept** function simply by not destroying any local variables when an uncaught exception tries to escape. Adding a **noexcept** specification does, however, place one additional obligation on the function itself: The function must now take responsibility for ensuring that there is no possibility of an **exception** reaching the caller. If there are any potentially throwing expressions in the function, it is required to handle any attempt to unwind by ending with a call to `std::terminate()`, which will unconditionally end the program. Note that `std::terminate` invokes a `terminate_handler`, which can be set globally using `std::set_terminate`. It is **undefined behavior** if this function returns normally or does not terminate execution of the program. This additional call to `std::terminate` might result in a (typically small) increase in the size of the `.o` file, but not necessarily that of a final optimized program.[16]

Decorating a function with **noexcept** can also reduce the size of its *caller*, sometimes substantially, even if the called function sees little or no benefit, but see *Potential Pitfalls — Overly strong contracts guarantees* on page 1112 and *Accidental `terminate`* on page 1124. For example, consider what would happen if we were to decorate function `gg`, above, with **noexcept**: The two calls to function `gg` in the body of function `ff` would no longer be potentially throwing; thus, `ff` would no longer need any stack-unwinding code. This code-size reduction was observed in every compiler we tested with.[17] Note that no such size reduction would be expected if `S` were trivially destructible (condition #1) or if all invocations of `gg` took place prior to the construction of any non**static** local variables of non-trivially destructible type (condition #3), as no unwinding logic would be required in the first place.

A simple yet fairly general framework to investigate the effects of the **noexcept** specifier on generated-code size might consist of a non-trivially destructible class type, `S`; the *declaration*

---

[16]In our observations, GCC 8 (c. 2018) and higher and MSVC 14.x (c. 2019) typically generate less code, sometimes significantly less (but never more), on the cold path when a function meeting all three of the above conditions is declared **noexcept**. Conversely, Clang 12.0 (c. 2021), though generating smaller stack-unwinding code in general (compared to GCC), does generate slightly *more* object code with **noexcept** than without it to include a definition of the runtime-support function `__clang_call_terminate`.

[17]Experiments were performed with GCC 7.1.0 (c. 2017) GCC 11.1 (c. 2021), Clang 12.0 (c. 2021), and MSVC 19.29 (c. 2021).

of a lower-level function, g, that is typically *not* declared **noexcept**; and the definition of
the function f whose size we are endeavoring to minimize:

```
// minimal framework to measure code-size effects due to noexcept

struct S { ~S(); };  // non-trivially destructible class type

void g() G_EXCEPTION_SPEC;  // typically empty macro

void f() F_EXCEPTION_SPEC   // either empty or noexcept
{
    // ... (body of function under test)
}
```

In the example framework above, we have the simplest possible non-trivially destructible
but otherwise trivial class, S, which has, as its only user-declared member, the **declaration**
(though *not* the definition) of a user-provided destructor. Destructors, unlike any other user-
provided functions, default to **noexcept(true)**; see *Description — Unconditional exception
specifications* on page 1085. This observation is important as, by design, there is nothing
in S that might bias the experiment with an expression that may throw. Next we have the
declaration of a function g() followed by the macro G_EXCEPTION_SPEC, which allows us
to build this translation unit with g being **noexcept(true)** if we wish; typically, however,
we will choose it to be empty and hence default to **noexcept(false)**. Finally, we have
the **definition** of the function f() under test. This function is the only definition in the
translation unit and, hence, the only opportunity to contribute to runnable code size.

As a baseline, we note that the size of the .o that results from compiling just the definition
of S and the declaration of g on our reference platform is 32 bytes in either build mode
(unoptimized/optimized):

```
// base line translation unit is 32 bytes in either build mode
struct S { ~S(); };
void g() G_EXCEPTION_SPEC;
```

As our first substantive example, let's consider two functions, f1 and f2, each containing
one automatic variable of type S and one call to g. Let's start by calling g() first:

```
struct S { ~S(); };
void g() G_EXCEPTION_SPEC;
void f1() F_EXCEPTION_SPEC
{
    g();  // throwing expression comes before variable
    S s;  // non-trivially destructible automatic variable
}
```

In the example above, f1 has almost all the elements we need: (1) a local variable that has
a non-trivial destructor (e.g., s) and (2) an expression that may throw (e.g., g()). The only
missing ingredient is that the potentially throwing expression comes prior to the construction
of the first non-trivially destructible variable s.

Let's now consider what happens if we flip the order of `g()` and `s`:

```
struct S { ~S(); };
void g() G_EXCEPTION_SPEC;
void f2() F_EXCEPTION_SPEC
{
    S s;  // non-trivially destructible automatic variable
    g();  // throwing expression comes after variable
}
```

Lastly, we have a scenario in which declaring either **f2**, **g**, or both to be **noexcept** yields a potential net reduction in size for the resulting translation unit. Let's look at each of the four possible combinations of **noexcept** assignment in turn. If neither **f2** nor **g** is declared **noexcept**, then the compiler is obliged to generate unwind code to clean up **s** and propagate a potential exception thrown from **g** back to the caller of **f2**, which in turn can significantly increase the size of the body of **f2**. If **g** is declared **noexcept**, then, regardless of whether or not **f2** is declared **noexcept**, no additional code needs to be laid down to guard against the impossible case of an exception being thrown from **g**. Finally, if **f** is declared **noexcept** but **g** is not, most, if not all, of the size benefit is likely to be realized, but now there is the possibility of a small increase in the size of **f** resulting from the obligatory call to `std::terminate`.

A measurement of relative compiled-code sizes in both build modes (unoptimized/optimized) for each of the two function definitions, **f1** and **f2**, and for each of the four combinations of exception specifications on **g** and **f**, respectively, confirms our hypothesis, as shown in Table 1.[18]

Table 1: Comparing code sizes without/with noexcept on f and/or g

Candidate Function		G_S = noexcept F_S = noexcept		
void f1() F_S { g(); S s; }	88/84[a]	88/84	88/84	96/92
void f2() F_S { S s; g(); }	152/132	88/84	88/84	96/92

[a] Where, e.g., 88/84 means 88 bytes unoptimized / 84 bytes optimized

Looking at the data above, we observe that there was no opportunity to reduce the size of **f1** from a throwing **g** because the invocation of **g** preceded construction of any non-trivially destructible non**static** local variables. But, unless **g** is itself declared **noexcept** (or

---

[18] For information on how to approach benchmarking the impact of **noexcept**, see **dekker19b**.

is somehow inspectable by the **f1**'s compiler to confirm that it doesn't throw), the theoretical potential for a small increased size does exist (in our tests an 8-byte increase in the size of the resulting executable was observed for both build modes).

In the case of **f2**, however, the call to a throwing **g** *after* the construction of the non-trivially destructible s forces the compiler to lay down significant additional cold-path code (in our tests $152 - 88 == 64$ bytes unoptimized and $132 - 84 == 48$ bytes optimized) for a **noexcept(false)** f2 compared with a **noexcept(true)** one. Again observe that, with f2 as with f1, there is the possibility of a small code-size increase (in our tests $96 - 88 = 8/92 - 84 = 8$ bytes) when f2 is **noexcept(true)** and g is **noexcept(false)**, due to the call to std::terminate.

Our hypothesis is that the more complex the injection of potential exceptions, the more overhead in the form of additional generated cold-path code might be required. That is, two potentially throwing expressions that need to destroy different sets of local variables are more expensive than such expressions being called with the same set of variables in scope.

Finally, let's consider a family of functions, based on an initial function, **f00**, each having a sequence of definitions of six local variables of non-trivially destructible type, S, named s0–s5, interleaved with zero, one, or two calls to function g:

```
void f00() { S s0; S s1; S s2; S s3; S s4; S s5; }        // no exception source

void f01() { g(); S s0; S s1; S s2; S s3; S s4; S s5; }   // one exception source
void f02() { S s0; g(); S s1; S s2; S s3; S s4; S s5; }   //  "         "        "
//:    :    :                                      :  //  "         "        "
void f06() { S s0; S s1; S s2; S s3; S s4; g(); S s5; }   //  "         "        "
void f07() { S s0; S s1; S s2; S s3; S s4; S s5; g(); }   //  "         "        "

void f11() { g(); S s0; S s1; S s2; S s3; S s4; S s5; g(); } // two sources
//:    :    :                                       :  //  "         "
void f17() { S s0; S s1; S s2; S s3; S s4; S s5; g(); g(); } //  "         "
```

Assuming, for the moment, that g is an opaque declaration of a function that is *not* declared **noexcept** (and hence may throw), we wish to evaluate the effect on size for both unoptimized and optimized builds — this time using all three available exception specifications, **throw()**, none (i.e., **noexcept(false)**), and **noexcept** (i.e., **noexcept(true)**) — for each of the 15 family members, f00–f07 and f11–f17. For didactic purposes we have tabulated the size in bytes of the text and data segments of object files resulting from various compilations in Table 2.[19]

---

[19]All sizes are the size of the text+data segment of the object file in bytes, as reported by the size command. All data points were obtained using GCC 7.4.0 (c. 2018) with -O0 and -O3, respectively, on a Windows Cygwin platform hosted by a ThinkPad T480 laptop.

Table 2: Comparing text-segment sizes across various exception specifications

g is noexcept(false) configuration of f's body	Unoptimized			Optimized		
	throw()	none	noexcept	throw()	none	noexcept
f00 { s0 s1 s2 s3 s4 s5 }	152	152	152	132	132	132
f01 { g s0 s1 s2 s3 s4 s5 }	208	152	160	172	132	140
f02 { s0 g s1 s2 s3 s4 s5 }	232	200	160	212	180	140
f03 { s0 s1 g s2 s3 s4 s5 }	248	216	160	212	180	140
f04 { s0 s1 s2 g s3 s4 s5 }	264	236	160	228	196	140
f05 { s0 s1 s2 s3 g s4 s5 }	280	252	160	244	212	140
f06 { s0 s1 s2 s3 s4 g s5 }	280	252	160	244	216	140
f07 { s0 s1 s2 s3 s4 s5 g }	296	268	160	260	232	140
f11 { g s0 s1 s2 s3 s4 s5 g }	316	272	176	280	236	140
f12 { s0 g s1 s2 s3 s4 s5 g }	316	288	176	280	232	140
f13 { s0 s1 g s2 s3 s4 s5 g }	316	288	176	280	232	140
f14 { s0 s1 s2 g s3 s4 s5 g }	316	288	176	280	232	140
f15 { s0 s1 s2 s3 g s4 s5 g }	316	288	176	280	236	140
f16 { s0 s1 s2 s3 s4 g s5 g }	316	288	176	280	236	140
f17 { s0 s1 s2 s3 s4 s5 g g }	312	268	176	260	232	140
f07 but with g **noexcept**	152	152	152	132	132	132
f07 but with g visible/empty	188	188	188	164	164	164
f14 but with g **noexcept**	168	168	168	132	132	132
f14 but with g visible/empty	188	188	188	164	164	164

Here are a few things we can see in the data.

- f00 has no source of exceptions; hence, it defines a baseline for this experiment. Notice that the size of the object file is independent of the exception specifications, as no stack-unwinding code needs to be emitted.

- f01 calls g *before* any of the non-trivially **destructible** variables are created; hence, there is no opportunity for code reduction. Here we see that adding **throw()** substantially *increases* code size, whereas the only additional code size for a **noexcept** specification is due to the necessary exception table entry to call std::terminate.

- f02 calls g *after* s0 is constructed, and so substantial additional cleanup code is generated when no exception specification is provided. Declaring f02 **throw()** increases that overhead further. On the other hand, supplying f02 with a **noexcept** specifier reduces code size back to baseline plus the small overhead needed for the exception table entry to call std::terminate.

- f03–f07 demonstrate a monotonically nondecreasing space overhead as more and more variables must be unwound absent a **noexcept** specification. Interestingly, the place where the cost doesn't increase on our test platform is different between unoptimized (f06) and optimized (f03) builds.

- **f11** introduces a second source of exceptions before any local variables, adding a tiny increment to code size.

- **f12–17** demonstrate that the location where the second source of potential exceptions is inserted into the sequence makes no difference unless the two sources appear together (**f17**) in which case the **throw()** and implicit **noexcept(false)** specifications drop somewhat due to not needing extra exception table entries, whereas the **noexcept** specification version remains constant for both versions throughout this range.

- Finally we show the impact of **g** being itself **noexcept** or having a visible empty definition. Having **g** be **noexcept** produces the same code size as the smallest of the other variations explored here. Having it visible comes close, with the only difference being the space needed to include the definition of **g** itself within the translation unit.

Alternative compiler implementation strategies   When a function is declared **noexcept**, much of its responsibility to clean up local variables and unwind the stack is removed. Popular compilers appear to address this opportunity for optimization in one of two ways.

1. Leave all constructed variables on the current stack frame undestroyed and call std::terminate immediately. For this behavior, a shared exception handler that does no function-specific cleanup and instead immediately invokes std::terminate can be used, removing any need for the existence of the exception handler code in the built executable.[20]

2. Run the destructors of local variables and *then* call std::terminate. This technique requires exception handlers be emitted that match those that would handle unwinding in a **noexcept(false)** function, with the only difference being the final instruction to call std::terminate instead of continuing unwinding.[21]

Note that only approach (1) offers an opportunity for the body of the function decorated with **noexcept** to shrink in size; option (2) allows for no such saving. However, both options admit cold-path object-code shrinkage for a function (e.g., **f**) when a previously throwing function (e.g., **g**) called from **f** is declared **noexcept**.

Sample assembler listings   For concreteness, we provide here a simple example of a function for which adding **noexcept** offers an opportunity for the compiler to generate smaller code and then illustrate how contemporary versions of three popular compilers use that opportunity in their optimized generated assembler. Let's again look at the case where we have a non-trivially **destructible** non**static** variable, **s** of type **S**, followed by a call to a function, **g**, that is not known by the compiler to be **noexcept(true)**, in the body of a function, **f**, that we are considering declaring noexcept:

---

[20]This approach appears to be taken by both GCC and MSVC.
[21]This is the approach that appears to have been taken by Clang.

```
// isolated translation unit
struct S { ~S(); };         // has non-trivial destructor
void g();                   // is noexcept(false) by default
void f2() F_EXCEPTION_SPEC  // We will compile with and without noexcept.
{
    S s;  // non-trivially destructible automatic variable
    g();  // throwing expression comes after variable
}
```

As a final demonstration, we used Compiler Explorer[22] to compile the small translation unit above on contemporary versions of three popular platforms: GCC, Clang, and MSVC. On each of the three platforms we compiled the program above twice, first with F_EXCEPTION_SPEC=**noexcept**(**false**) and second with F_EXCEPTION_SPEC=**noexcept**(**true**). The side-by-side results for each platform — **noexcept**(**false**) and **noexcept**(**true**) — are presented below for reference.

GCC x86-064 11.1   With compiler flags -std=C++20 -O3. Note that the exception handling code is completely removed, and an entry in the exception handling table (not shown here) points directly to a built-in function that will call std::terminate:

```
F_EXCEPTION_SPEC=noexcept(false)              F_EXCEPTION_SPEC=noexcept(true)
--------------------------------              -------------------------------
f2():                                         f2():
  push rbp                                      sub rsp, 24
  sub rsp, 16                                   call g()
  call g()                                      lea rdi, [rsp+15]
  lea rdi, [rsp+15]                             call S::~S()
  call S::~S()                                  add rsp, 24
  add rsp, 16                                   ret
  pop rbp
  ret
  mov rbp, rax
  jmp .L2
f2() [clone .cold]:
.L2:
  lea rdi, [rsp+15]
  call S::~S()
  mov rdi, rbp
  call _Unwind_Resume
```

CLANG x86-064 12.0.1   With compiler flags -std=C++20 -O3. Note the only differences are the final instruction in the exception handler to call the included __clang_call_terminate function instead of the stack-unwinding intrinsic function _Unwind_Resume:

---

[22]https://godbolt.org

```
F_EXCEPTION_SPEC=noexcept(false)           F_EXCEPTION_SPEC=noexcept(true)
-------------------------------            -------------------------------
f2(): # @f2()                              f2(): # @f2()
  push rbx                                   push rbx
  sub rsp, 16                                sub rsp, 16
  call g()                                   call g()
  lea rdi, [rsp + 8]                         lea rdi, [rsp + 8]
  call S::~S()                               call S::~S()
  add rsp, 16                                add rsp, 16
  pop rbx                                    pop rbx
  ret                                        ret
  mov rbx, rax                               mov rbx, rax
  lea rdi, [rsp + 8]                         lea rdi, [rsp + 8]
  call S::~S()                               call S::~S()
  mov rdi, rbx                               mov rdi, rbx
  call _Unwind_Resume@PLT                    call __clang_call_terminate
                                           __clang_call_terminate:
                                             push rax
                                             call __cxa_begin_catch
                                             call std::terminate()
```

MSVC v19.29 VS16.11   With compiler flags /std:c++20 /O2. Again, we can see here that all of the exception handling code is removed when f is made **noexcept**:

```
MSVC 64 bit v19.29 VS16.11                 Compile options: /std:c++20 /O2
F_EXCEPTION_SPEC=noexcept(false)           F_EXCEPTION_SPEC=noexcept(true)
-------------------------------            -------------------------------
s$ = 48                                    s$ = 48
void f2(void) PROC                         void f2(void) PROC
$LN6:                                      $LN5:
    sub rsp, 40                                sub rsp, 40
    call void g(void)                          call void g(void)
    npad 1                                     lea rcx, QWORD PTR s$[rsp]
    lea rcx, QWORD PTR s$[rsp]                 call S::~S(void)
    call S::~S(void)                           npad 1
    add rsp, 40                                add rsp, 40
    ret 0                                      ret 0
void f2(void) ENDP                         void f2(void) ENDP
s$ = 48
int `void f2(void)'::`1'::dtor$0 PROC
    lea rcx, QWORD PTR s$[rdx]
    jmp S::~S(void) ; S::~S
int `void f2(void)'::`1'::dtor$0 ENDP
```

Potential Pitfalls

Overly strong contracts guarantees

A contract between human beings is a transactional agreement: "If you give me X, I will do Y." An important property of *software* contracts is that they don't change incompatibly for existing clients, which means the contract implicitly makes a somewhat stronger guarantee: "From now on, whenever you give me X, I will do Y." For example, consider a function, half, that simply uses the integer division operator (/) to divide a given value by 2:

```
int half(int value) { return value / 2; }
    // Return an integer that is numerically half of the specified value
    // rounded toward zero --- i.e., half(-3) is -1, not -2.
```

The half function defined above will reliably do what it promises to do for every possible (properly initialized) input value. When every expressible input to a function (including any relevant state) is valid, we say the function has a **wide contract**. Most nonmodifying member functions, such as length(), size(), and begin() (but not **operator[]**), on standard containers have wide contracts, assuming they are applied to a fully constructed object that has not yet been destroyed — even if the container has been moved from (see Section 2.1. "*Rvalue* References" on page 710).

Some functions *almost* have a wide contract, but not quite. For example, std::abs returns the absolute value of whatever integer is supplied to it unless that integer happens to be equal to INT_MIN (defined in <climits>) in which case for a platform that represents integers in two's complement (essentially all modern platforms), the behavior is undefined. Because not all expressible inputs are semantically valid for the std::abs function, we say that it has a **narrow contract**. A narrow contract provides guarantees on only the subset of expressible inputs that it deems valid: "From now on, whenever you give me X, I will do Y; but if you give me something other than X, I am not obliged to do Y or anything else for that matter; I'm allowed to do whatever I want, and you might not like it!"

As a simple illustration of a more typical narrow contract, consider a function sqrt that purports to return the square root of a given number, provided that it is non-negative:

```
double sqrt(double value);
    // Return the positive square root of the specified value.
    // The behavior is undefined unless value is nonnegative.
```

There are three benefits to *not* specifying what happens when sqrt is presented with a negative value.

1. The cost of designing, developing, documenting, testing, and maintaining **defined behavior** is typically reduced.

2. We leave open the option of mapping different behaviors onto the undefined behavior (e.g., in a debug, test, or "safe" build mode).

3. We keep open the option of extending the domain of **defined behavior** without compromising **backward compatibility**.

Suppose our aversion to **undefined behavior** were such that we felt compelled to define it so as to give sqrt a **wide** contract:

```
double sqrt(double value);
    // Return the square root of the specified value if nonnegative;
    // otherwise return -1.0.
```

For end-user APIs, always having a wide contract might well be the right decision; however, for internal, high-performance C++ libraries, it seldom is.

1. An artificially **wide contract** forces us to validate the input in every case — even when we know it's valid — thereby compromising runtime performance. If some client isn't sure, it's easy enough for that client to validate its own input before calling sqrt.

2. There is no opportunity to map out domain inputs to different behaviors, such as throwing a **bad_input** — e.g., in a "safe" build.

3. There is no opportunity for extension; e.g., we might find that returning 0 when given a negative works for every client and thereby avoids a useless status check.

For these reasons, we would not typically convert our **narrow contract** for sqrt to a wide one.

Next, let's consider a different interpretation of what it might mean for a contract to make an overly *strong guarantee*. Suppose we are trying to write a custom sort routine, businessSort, for a recurring data distribution particular to our business. The nature of the business places no real-time constraints on any one sort operation; the goal is to maximize throughput. For our first implementation, we have chosen to use insertion sort, which happens to have a complexity of $O(N \log N)$, so, without thinking ahead, we put that guarantee into the contract:

```
void businessSort(double* start, int n);
    // Modify the range of contiguous double values beginning at the specified
    // start address and extending n elements so that it is sorted in
    // ascending order in time that is O(n * log(n)).
```

Contracts that promise more than is necessary can gratuitously limit implementation alternatives, thereby impeding the evolution of a component to more efficient algorithms. The letter of the contract guarantee for businessSort (above) is overly strong because we are not concerned with a bound on any particular run, but on optimizing the overall throughput for a statistically large sample of many runs. Other algorithms, such as quicksort and randomized quicksort, do not absolutely guarantee an $O(N \log N)$ bound on every run but might well turn out to be a substantially better alternative on average. Once we publish the constraint in our contract, however, we cannot take it back without making a semantically incompatible change, something responsible library developers are loath to do.

Decorating a function with **noexcept** is another way to implicitly strengthen a contract: "From now on, whenever you give me something — irrespective of whatever else is in the explicit contract — I will not throw." If our motivation for using the **noexcept** specifier on a particular function f is to improve runtime performance algorithmically, we must presumably be anticipating that there is some prospective client that will apply the **noexcept** operator (see Section 2.1."**noexcept** Operator" on page 615) to an expression involving the invocation of f and, because that operator will evaluate to **true**, choose a different, more auspicious code path; see *Unrealizable runtime performance benefits* on page 1134. The overwhelmingly common idiomatic use case for employing **noexcept** to achieve more *algorithmically* runtime-efficient code is for a *move* or *swap* operation; see *Use Cases — Declaring nonthrowing move operations* on page 1094, *Defining a **noexcept** swap* on page 1097, and *A wrapper that provides **noexcept** move operations* on page 1099.

An eminently practical example of deliberately *not* specifying an overly strong contract guarantee by dint of **noexcept** — even for *move* operations[23] — can be found in the specification of std::list from the C++ Standard Library. Unlike std::vector and std::string, the move constructor for std::list is deliberately *not* specified as necessarily being declared **noexcept**, although several implementations take advantage of the freedom to add the more restrictive exception specification. Note that voluntarily adding **noexcept** at some future date does not usually result in ABI incompatibility[24]; adding **noexcept** after the fact can, however, alter code paths when recompiling preexisting client programs, which can lead to (typically benign) **ODR** violations if only some uses of a particular client template are recompiled.

The flexibility afforded by not specifying the **noexcept** for move (and default) constructors enables alternative implementation choices that would not otherwise be viable. One reason the implementation of std::list's move constructor might need to throw relates to how the empty node at the end of the list is represented.

One std::list implementation might dynamically allocate a **sentinel** node on default construction to represent the past-the-end position and treat the sentinel just like any other node in the list. This straightforward design choice implies that, if a list object is moved, a new **sentinel** node will need to be allocated and installed in the moved-from object, lest said object be left in a less-than-constructed state.

An alternative implementation would be to embed the past-the-end node directly into the **footprint** of the std::list object itself. This more complex design choice requires that we handle the tail node more carefully because (1) it has not been separately allocated like all other nodes and (2) pointers to this node will no longer be valid after moving the rest of the list into a new object.

The C++ Standard enables both implementation choices by specifically *not* making mandatory any **noexcept** guarantees on the move constructor (or default constructor) of std::list;

---

[23]As of C++17, move assignment for std::list becomes conditionally **noexcept** — i.e., it is **noexcept** whenever it is instantiated with a stateless allocator.

[24]Note that even when **noexcept** becomes part of the type system for functions, it is still not possible to overload on a **noexcept** qualifier. Hence, there's no need to incorporate that qualifier in the **mangled name** at the ABI level; see *Annoyances — ABI changes in future versions of C++* on page 1148.

vendors choosing the more involved implementation strategy have the freedom to add the **noexcept** guarantees to their own contracts if they so wish.[25]

Observe that the **noexcept** specifier doesn't always play nice with contracts, especially narrow contracts. Let's return to our `sqrt` function sporting a narrow contract but this time decorated with **noexcept**:

```
double sqrt(double value) noexcept;
    // Return the positive square root of the specified value.
    // The behavior is undefined unless value is nonnegative.
```

Recall that, in the previous contract for `sqrt`, the library implementer could choose to do anything well defined when a negative argument was passed to `sqrt`. This latitude in behavior could have included returning any **double** value, throwing an exception, invoking `std::abort()`, reformatting the user's hard drive, or executing code that itself had **language undefined behavior**. The **noexcept** on this version of `sqrt`, however, removes the option of throwing an exception.

Consider that, because we have made the **noexcept(true)** status of `sqrt` programmatically accessible to clients, we have — at least in principle — precluded writing a version of `sqrt` that, in a "safe" build mode, checks its argument and, if negative, throws an `std::invalid_argument` exception (defined in `<stdexcept>`). Some standard-library vendors provide a safe build mode that enables elaborate checking pertaining to misuse of standard containers, sometimes requiring additional dynamic memory allocation.[26] By changing the programmatically accessible interface to improve runtime checking, the code paths being checked in a safe build might be entirely different from those executed in a production one. Hence, for typical general-purpose computers, the use of **noexcept** for *any* purpose other than enabling the selection of an algorithmically superior code path is dubious; see *Unrealizable runtime performance benefits* on page 1134.

The term **undefined behavior** (UB) has a substantively different meaning in the context of a library contract than it does when applied to the language itself. By default, **undefined behavior** is typically considered **language undefined behavior** (a.k.a. **hard UB**), which gives the compiler license to elide code and assume conditions in branches, etc., on the assumption that *hard* UB cannot occur in a correct program. In the context of a function contract, however, **undefined behavior** means **library undefined behavior** (a.k.a. **soft UB**). Control over what happens when **library undefined behavior** (a.k.a. **soft UB**) occurs is in the hands of the library implementer and can range from any available well-defined behavior all the way up to executing code having **language undefined behavior** (a.k.a. **hard UB**). For a **noexcept** function, the library implementer loses the choice to throw an exception in such cases, in

---

[25]MSVC makes use of the flexibility afforded by the Standard's not requiring the move constructor of `std::list` to be **noexcept** and takes similar advantage of the flexibility afforded to other node-based containers, such as `std::map` and `std::unordered_map`. This simpler implementation choice also happens to ensure that the `end()` iterator of an `std::list` remains valid after a move.

[26]MSVC comes with a safe build mode that provides runtime checking for (mis)use of invalid iterators but requires additional memory allocation that would not be possible if **noexcept** specifications for functions that do not normally check such things were mandated; see **whitney16**.

the same way that the return value restricts the potential values that can be returned normally.[27]

Yet another consideration when marking as **noexcept** a function having a specifically **narrow contract** involves the relative ease of validating defensive precondition checks. Library authors will often want to respond to simple, easily detected violations of a contract by providing, in certain assertion-enabled build modes modes, a defensive check, e.g., using a C-style `assert`. A more sophisticated defensive-checking framework[28] might be configured to throw an exception (e.g., `contract_violation`) when an out-of-contract call is detected; such a configuration could be used within a unit-testing framework to test the defensive checks themselves without causing the test program to terminate. If, however, a function having a **narrow contract** is marked as **noexcept**, then such a framework would not work, as the attempt to throw `contract_violation` would always terminate the program.

Just prior to the release of C++11, the Standard Library adopted the cautious principle of deliberately *not* marking functions in the Standard Library having **narrow contracts** as **noexcept**, thereby granting implementers freedom to add such specifications where they believe their own implementation might benefit. This principle is known as the *Lakos Rule* after John Lakos, one of this book's authors, who originally put forward the guideline.[29]

Common best practice these days — especially given the increasingly wide adoption of the **zero-overhead exception model** — is to treat the use of exceptions in contracts as truly exceptional. Hence, we would not expect an exception to be thrown with any frequency in a modern, well-designed, defect-free program operating within the limits of its platform's available resources.

When acquiring relatively low-level system resources, such as opening a socket or a known-to-exist file, errors, though relatively rare, do occasionally occur. Despite their rarity, the inordinately large latency and inherent nonparallelizability associated with propagating an exception when it does occur can often prove prohibitive. Reproducible benchmarks using the zero-cost model show that a thrown exception is typically "orders of magnitude" slower than returning an error status.[30] Hence, it is not uncommon for such system-level features to opt for other means of communicating such infrequent but urgent information. Ironically, widespread use of **noexcept** is inconsistent with *any* use of exceptions to propagate exceptional failures up through enough stack frames to reach one where sufficient context exists to properly address the error; see *Accidental `terminate`* on page 1124.

Conflating noexcept with nofail

A function that is declared **noexcept** might not be **nofail**. Moreover, a function that happens to be **nofail** (today) might not be declared **noexcept**, and perhaps for good reason; see *Overly*

---

[27] See **lakos14b**, time 17:57.
[28] **bde14**, /bsl/bsls/bsls_assert
[29] **meredith11**
[30] See **nayar20**.

strong contracts guarantees on page 1112. Before we contrast the guarantees implied by **noexcept** with those of a function that is said to be nofail, it is essential that we understand precisely what it means for a function to (1) be nofail today and (2) provide a **nofail guarantee** — implicitly or otherwise — in its contract.

What do we even mean by nofail?   For most common purposes, a **nofail function** (such as sqrt, above) is one that has no failure mode: "Whenever you give me X, I will do Y." A contract that lacks any mention of what happens if the function fails suggests that it never fails. Now consider a contract having an **out clause**: "Whenever you give me X, I will do Y, *or tell you that I didn't*, and perhaps why I didn't." An example of such a status-reporting function is fopen from the C (and C++) Standard Library:

```
// in <cstdio>
FILE* fopen(const char* filename, const char* mode);
```

The contract for the fopen function would not be considered nofail as there is not one but two ways in which it reports that it might not have succeeded: (1) it returns a NULL file handle (pointer) and (2) it sets the global errno state (which gives an indication of why it failed). Note that errno is a preprocessor macro providing a separate value for each thread.

Given a function that doesn't provide a failure mode, we typically take that to mean that the function won't fail. To give us a concrete basis for discussion, let's start by considering three familiar, well-understood functions to see how they stack up:

```
int    half(int i);      // (#1) Return half of i (rounded toward 0).
int    abs(int i);       // (#2) Return the absolute value of i if not INT_MIN.
double sqrt(double v);   // (#3) Return the square root of v if nonnegative.
```

In each of the three example functions above, our intuition tells us that, unless given an *invalid* input, the function will always (a) adhere to its contract; (b) not throw, signal, terminate, or otherwise fail to return control to the caller; (c) return in a bounded amount of time; and (d) return the correct result within some agreed-upon tolerance (i.e., floating-point rounding). Assuming all of the preceding conditions hold *as implemented*, each of the three functions above can be said to be a **nofail function** (today) — irrespective of whether a **nofail guarantee** is stated explicitly in its contract.

One might argue that only the half function above is truly **nofail** because a client could erroneously call either of the other two functions **out of contract**, in which case the behavior would be undefined, and the function may terminate or worse. A natural conclusion might be that functions such as abs and sqrt — each having a **narrow contract** — cannot be considered **nofail** and that the only kinds of functions that can be truly **nofail** are those like half having a **wide contract**. Adopting such an overly restrictive approach is not useful because the only kinds of functions that can be entirely without preconditions are those that (1) inspect no external state, and (2) use no stack space or other resources — i.e., functions that do nothing.

For example, any function passed an **lvalue reference** or pointer to an object that had already been destroyed (especially if it has a **non-trivial destructor**) would necessarily be in violation of the implicit, language-imposed contract that no destroyed objects be passed and subsequently examined. Hence, any function taking an argument of any kind would mean that the function technically has preconditions and, therefore, a **narrow contract**. We conclude, therefore, that — to be useful — the definition of nofail does *not* apply to a function called with invalid input.

Next let's discuss what it means for a function's implementation to faithfully implement its contract. Whether it has an error-reporting contract or otherwise, the implementation of any function has a responsibility to honor that contract to the best of its ability. We will deliberately ignore defects in the implementation, be they accidental or deliberate. An academic measure of a *perfectly* **infallible implementation** for a function contract provides an extreme view.

1. The function must be known not to fail when run conceptually on C++'s **abstract machine**.[31]

2. No additional tangible resource (other than CPU) can be required in order for the function to complete.

Though objective and certainly sufficient, such an austere interpretation of the term **infallible implementation** would imply that virtually no function could be **infallible** in practice. Any function using exceptions as an error-reporting mechanism or allocating so much as a single local variable on the program stack would fail to meet such draconian criteria. Moreover, what might be tolerable in, say, a gaming application could well be entirely unacceptable in software controlling a nuclear reactor. For our purposes, any function (e.g., a recursive one) that must allocate more than a small, constant amount of computer resources to satisfy the contract — whether error-reporting or otherwise — would be considered **fallible**: "If you give me X, I promise I will try my best to do Y, but sometimes stuff happens, in which case I may not be able to return to keep my promise." Note that any function that is not capable of honoring its contract and yet returns anyway would be considered defective and/or dangerous.

To summarize what we've learned so far, both the contract and implementation separately contribute properties required by a **nofail function**: (1) the contract must not contain an **out clause** (i.e., one suggesting that the requested action may not be performed), and (2) the implementation must be (reasonably) infallible when dutifully implementing the contract on all relevant platforms; see Table 3.

---

[31]stroustrup04

Table 3: Interface and implementation properties pertaining to a *nofail* function

Reporting Contract	Fallible Implementation	Nickname	Example Function(s) Having These Properties
No	No	nofail	**int** half(**int**); or **double** sqrt(**double**);
Yes	No	reliable	FILE* fopen(**const char***, **const char***);
No	Yes	optimistic	**int** factorial(**int**); // recursive impl.
Yes	Yes	general	getGoodNewsPlease

As the table above summarizes, for a function overall to be nofail, it must be both **non-reporting** and have an infallible implementation, as was the case for half, std::abs, and sqrt. A function such as fopen that is infallible but reporting is, nonetheless, *reliable* in that we can call it from a nofail function and, if it fails, fall back on an infallible (albeit perhaps less efficient or otherwise less desirable) way to satisfy the contract. As an example, calculating the area of a polygon is always possible, but if we can quickly and reliably determine that it is a rectangle and access that representation, we can bypass the slower, more general algorithm.

Sometimes we might write a contract that is accidentally or, perhaps, even deliberately over constrained with no provision *in the contract* for reporting failure: "Whenever you call me, I promise to do Y (or die trying)." As an example, imagine a function, allocateMutex, that claims always to return a pointer to a newly allocated Muteax object:

```
class Mutex { /*...*/ };

Mutex* allocateMutex();
    // Allocate a distinct Mutex and return its address. Period. :)
```

If we were to place the allocateMutex function above in a loop that ran enough times, we could exhaust available memory on any physical machine. On the other hand, the intent of the function is for gainfully employed engineers to do their work without forcing them to test for running out of heap memory, a situation they might not intend to spend the time supporting in practice. For that reason, the part of the contract that says "...or, if I cannot, I will return **nullptr**" is deliberately omitted so as not to invite useless checks on the part of the caller. On the other hand, should this function ever fail to allocate a Mutex, returning normally would be an explicit violation of the contract. Ironically, failing to provide an escape clause in an English contract for human developers is analogous to what the compiler does at the object-code level when it sees a function marked **noexcept**; see *Use Cases — Reducing object-code size* on page 1101.

Finally, we will often encounter *general* functions, e.g., `getGoodNewsPlease`, which must rely on an *optimistic* function in their implementation but report other erroneous situations through reliably methods:

```
const char* getGoodNewsImp(Mutex* p);   // reliable function
    // Return good news; otherwise return nullptr.

const char* getGoodNewsPlease()          // general function
    // Return good news; otherwise return nullptr.
{
    Mutex* mtx = allocateMutex();  // fallible
    return getGoodNewsImp(mtx);    // reliable
}
```

In the admittedly contrived example above, a *reliable* function, `getGoodNewsImp`, having a **reporting contract** and an **infallible implementation**, is called from a function, `getGoodNewsPlease`, that calls an *optimistic* function having a fallible implementation. Consequently, the higher-level wrapper function has a **reporting contract** and a **fallible implementation**.

Determining whether a function overall is **nofail** can be challenging, especially with more involved reporting mechanisms than a simple return status. Recall that the `fopen` function returned status in two ways: (1) via the return and (2) via global state. To report success/ failure, only a single bit need be transmitted. Two other possible reporting channels would be to **signal** or to throw an exception.

As our next specimen, let's look at two seemingly similar member functions of `std::vector`:

```
#include <stdexcept>  // std::out_of_range

template <typename T>
class vector {
// ...
    T& operator[](std::size_t index);
        // Return a reference to the modifiable element at the specified index.
        // The behavior is undefined unless index < size().

    T& at(std::size_t index);
        // Return a reference to the modifiable element at the specified index
        // unless !(index < size()) in which case throw std::out_of_range.
// ...
};
```

Can we say that either of these contracts is **nofail**? The answer is yes, exactly one, but which one? Recall that answering this question involves answering two subquestions: (1) is the contract **nonreporting**, and (2) is the implementation **infallible**. When it is not immediately obvious, it can be helpful to translate a function that reports errors by some other mechanism to a canonical form that returns zero on success and a nonzero value otherwise, possibly storing additional information in global state (e.g., **errno**):

```
/* status */ int f(/* out parameter, */ /* input parameters */);  // pseudo code
```

The boilerplate pseudofunction above effectively reduces all functions to the same canonical form; by recasting interfaces to have (1) an out parameter and (2) an integer return type, we reframe the question of whether a function is nofail in a manner suitable for an easy, apples-to-apples comparison. Let's start by transforming `std::vector::operator[]`:

```
int fOperatorBrackets(T*& result, std::size_t index);  // was operator[]
    // Load, into the specified result, the address of the element at the
    // specified index. The behavior is undefined unless index < size().
```

Instead of returning a reference, a pointer argument is loaded (via *lvalue* reference). Notice that the function, as per our transformation, is declared to return an **int** by value, but the contract makes no mention of it. That's because, like **operator[]**, there's nothing in the contract that suggests that failure is an option.

Let's now look at converting `std::vector::at`:

```
int fAt(T*& result, std::size_t index);  // was std::vector::at
    // Load, into the specified result, the address of the element at the
    // specified index and return 0 unless !(index < size()), in which
    // case return a non-zero value with no effect on result.
```

When we look at these two functions in canonical form side-by-side, there can be absolutely no room for doubt: The classically narrow contract for fOperatorBrackets — corresponding to `std::vector::`**operator[]**`(std::size_t)` — has a contract that offers no way for the function to report failure even though there is a syntactic channel by which to do so. Hence, the contract is nonreporting — despite there being an open channel (the return value) by which an error *could* have been communicated. By contrast, the contract for fAt — corresponding to `std::vector::at(std::size_t)` — reports failure using the canonical error-reporting method of returning a nonzero value on failure. Therefore, `std::vector::`**operator[]** has a nonreporting contract, whereas `std::vector::at` does not. Since any plausible implementation of either function would be sufficiently infallible for any client, we conclude that `std::vector::`**operator[]** is nofail, whereas `std::vector::at` is merely *reliable*.

Irrespective of *how* a function's contract promises to report failure, that such a failure-reporting channel is mentioned disqualifies that function from being considered nofail. There is, however, a practical difference between returning an error status and throwing an exception on failure: In the case of returning a failure status, the client has one chance to check the status and react; otherwise, the program has a bug. In this second case, the client can either check the status via a **try**/**catch** block or else ignore it and *hope*[32] (1) that someone at a higher level will catch the exception and do something sensible, or (2) that terminating the program was a tolerable outcome for its end user. Of course, whether any particular client performs its due diligence or not is another matter; see *Accidental* `terminate` on page 1124.

---

[32]Hope is not a strategy; see **murphy16**, Chapter 1, "Introduction," pp. 3–12, specifically p. 3.

One additional issue that must be addressed is what happens when the primary action specified in a contract involves something that might appear to disqualify the function from being nofail:

```
int throwBadAlloc();  // nofail
    // Throw an std::bad_alloc exception.
```

```
void printByeAndQuit();  // optimistic
    // Output "Goodbye, World!\n" to std::cout and then call std::terminate().
```

In the case of `throwBadAlloc` above, there is no separate failure channel discussed in the contract; the principle request is to throw an exception. That there is, for whatever reason, an **int** return type changes nothing as the contract omits any discussion of what, if anything, might be returned. Any reasonable implementation will be infallible. Hence, `throwBadAlloc` is a nofail function. The second function, `printByeAndQuit`, also provides no discussion of what might happen if the function fails. In this case, however, the contract is incomplete because it does not address what will happen were `std::cout` to be closed. If we interpret not having the characters `"Goodbye, World!\n"` transmitted via standard output to be a failure, then an implementation could not be considered *infallible*; hence, this function cannot be considered *nofail*. Narrowing the contract to only promise an attempt to write to `std::cout` would allow us to consider this function nofail. Amending the contract to state that the function will invoke `std::terminate` (which cannot return) would essentially provide an out clause whenever the `printByeAndQuit` returned normally, making this function **reliable** but not nofail.

Summary so far   A contract can be said to be **nonreporting** *only* when it provides no means to report, via a mechanism accessible to the program, whether the operation was successful — irrespective of the current implementation or the specific syntax used to declare the function prototype. For a function to have an implementation that is considered **infallible**, the resources required by it to fulfill its contract must be sufficiently minimal for the application domain. For a function to be considered **nofail** overall, however, its contract must be **nonreporting** and its implementation **infallible**. Finally, absent an explicit nofail guarantee in the contract itself, a **nonreporting** function that happens to have an **infallible** implementation today might — due to maintenance over time — wind up having one that *isn't* necessarily **infallible** in the future.

noexcept versus nofail   When we have a function that doesn't throw, we can communicate that to human beings by either (1) not saying that it does throw or (2) explicitly stating that it doesn't throw. Hence, adding **noexcept** to a function having a wide contract that already promises not to throw does not materially affect either the pre- or post-conditions of that contract. For a function having a narrow contract, however, the verbal guarantee in the written contract would apply only when the function is called in contract — i.e., with all of its preconditions satisfied. Adding **noexcept** to a function with a narrow contract limits the implementation of the out-of-contract behavior of such a function, as it will have no well-defined way to throw an exception in such cases if it would choose to do so.

Given a nofail function, adding **noexcept** will not affect its in-contract behavior. For functions that use exceptions to report failure, adding **noexcept** can easily turn a *reliable* function having an infallible implementation into an optimistic one stripped of its ability to communicate any difficulties in satisfying the contract, should any arise. As an example, suppose we applied **noexcept** to the two functions of std::vector discussed above:

```
template <typename T>
class vector {
// ...
    T& operator[](std::size_t index) noexcept;
        // Return a reference to the modifiable element at the specified index.
        // The behavior is undefined unless index < size().

    T& at(std::size_t index) noexcept;
        // Return a reference to the modifiable element at the specified index
        // unless !(index < size()) in which case call std::terminate.
// ...
};
```

For std::vector::**operator[]**, adding **noexcept** has no effect on in-contract behavior but limits flexibility (e.g., to provide arbitrary behavior when called out of contract). In the case of std::vector::at, however, instead of detecting an out-of-range call and reporting it via an exception, the function will now be forced to call std::terminate. To be clear, adding **noexcept** to a function that might throw is not a means of suppressing (i.e., swallowing) exceptions.

In short, when we see a function declared **noexcept**, it does not necessarily — in and of itself — imply an *optimistic* let alone a nofail function. Decorating a function with **noexcept** implies merely that the function cannot, under no circumstances, throw an exception.

It is also important to note that nofail and **fault tolerant** are not the same thing. Achieving a fault-tolerant nofail guarantee in, say, an embedded system typically requires redundant, independently designed processes running on autonomous hardware. For example, to provide a fault-tolerant nofail guarantee in a vehicle-control system, there might be three or more redundant processes running on independent hardware that participate in a *voting system* to determine the best course of action or to decide whether to trust some surprising sensor data. The software is designed to fail hard if it detects that the subsystem in which it resides has becomes unreliable and to restart quickly and smoothly while the redundant processes continue voting and maintain control of the vehicle.

To be clear, nothing we have said above is about trying to defend against defects in our own software. Extensive code review followed by extensive unit, integration, system, and beta testing is how we do that. An effective technique for ensuring correctness that is complementary to unit testing and static analysis involves redundant (optional) runtime defensive checks. If one of these checks is enabled and determines that the software is no longer in a logically coherent state then, rather than attempting to work around the defect, the prevailing wisdom is to fail fast and loudly — but possibly after attempting to safely save any important in-process data.

Accidental **terminate**

As we know, if an exception is thrown from a function having a **noexcept** specification —
either within that function or from a function it calls — std::terminate will be invoked.

Suppose we want to make use of a third-party function within our **noexcept(true)** function.
The documented contract for that other library clearly states that all error conditions will
result in returning error codes rather than throwing exceptions, so we conclude that it's
safe to use this library within our function. It is, however, entirely plausible that the library
contains a bug and can, under certain circumstances that were not tested by the third
party, emit an exception. As the function has a **noexcept(true)** exception specification,
this scenario causes our program to terminate unexpectedly, eliminating any opportunity
for us to catch and process (or even suppress) that exception.

As an alternative scenario, suppose the **noexcept** function makes use of a function g from
a library maintained by another team. The contract for g doesn't mention throwing or not
throwing exceptions, but, upon reviewing the code for g, we deduce that it cannot throw
and so incorporate it into our **noexcept** function f. It is entirely plausible, however, that the
other team might discover an exceptional condition in g and, thus, add a **throw** — e.g., so
as not to affect preexisting documented status codes. Such undocumented exceptions would
cause our program to terminate.

To better illustrate this scenario, imagine we start with some arbitrary but ostensibly initially correct code:

```
// From <otherteam.h> header file:
double g(double a, double b);
    // Do a calculation and return -1 on error.

// Code under development:
double f(double a, double b) noexcept
    // Do a slightly different calculation and return -1 on error.
{
    double c = a + b;
    double d = a - b;
    return g(c, d);  // Note: pass-through status might prove brittle.
}
```

Our use of g in the example code above creates a dependency on the other team's library,
which contains g's implementation:

```
// In other team's implementation file:
#include <iostream>  // std::cerr

double g(double a, double b)
{
    // ... (some non-throwing calculation)

    if (error)
```

```
    {
        std::cerr << "Some problem occurred\n";
        return -1.0;
    }

    return result;
}
```

Next, let's suppose that, unbeknownst to us, the maintainers of that library take it upon themselves to add additional, file-based logging using a third-party logging library, FILE_LOGGER, that emits an exception when it fails to write to the log file (due to, e.g., issues with permissioning or disk space):

```
// Library code file
double g(double a, double b)
{
    // ... (some non-throwing calculation)

    if (error)
    {
        FILE_LOGGER << "Some problem occurred" << FILE_LOGGER_ENDL;
        return -1.0;
    }

    return result;
}
```

Now, if the logging ever fails to write to a file and emits an exception, the **noexcept** specification on our **f** will force the entire program to terminate.

One straightforward way to prevent these unexpected terminations is to assume that any function that is not guaranteed not to throw might throw and thus wrap every such function in a try block:

```
// Code under development:
double f(double a, double b) noexcept
    // Do a slightly different calculation and return -1 on error.
{
    double c = a + b;
    double d = a - b;

    try
    {
        return g(c, d);  // Note: pass-through status might prove brittle.
    }
    catch (...) { return -1.0; }
}
```

With some analysis, it might be possible to determine whether terminating on the rare exception is acceptable and, if not, either avoid poorly documented third-party functions, catch and handle the exception internally, or else choose to omit the **noexcept** specifier. An even simpler rule of thumb would be to, by default, omit the **noexcept** specifier unless we have reason to believe that adding **noexcept** will cause clients to adopt alternative (e.g., *algorithmically* faster) code paths; see *Unrealizable runtime performance benefits* on page 1134.

Pragmatically speaking, the more uses of the **noexcept** specifier there are in a codebase, the greater the chances of an unexpected call to std::terminate. Generic code, in particular, will fall victim to this pitfall whenever unsubstantiated no-throw assumptions are made regarding template arguments. If a generic library is designed not to use exceptions, that need not be a problem in and of itself. However, if a generic library uses **noexcept** specifiers pervasively, client code might effectively be forced into a programming style where it too must avoid exceptions in order to prevent the generic library from calling std::terminate undesirably.

The generic containers in the C++ Standard Library seldom throw exceptions themselves, but they do provide guarantees regarding the consequences of client code throwing exceptions. Should an operation cause an object of parameter type T to throw an exception, e.g., during copy construction, then the container will remain in a sound state — sometimes guaranteed to be unchanged from before the operation — and will allow the exception to propagate. The term **exception safe** applies only to the contract as it pertains in a fully conforming implementation of a library; we use the term **exception agnostic** to imply a purely **RAII**-based implementation of an **exception-safe** function that would compile and operate equally well in, say, an embedded system with exceptions explicitly disabled. Such an **exception-agnostic** style imposes no particular style on the client regarding the client's use (or nonuse) of exceptions.

Sudden and unexpected program termination introduces compelling disadvantages, one of which is the possible loss of unsaved in-process data. A naive approach to mitigate this problem would be to simply install a terminate handler that calls the application's standard **save** function, but doing so can cause more problems than it solves: (1) the program's initial state might have been corrupted as a result of the error, so we could be overwriting good saved data with corrupt program state, or (2) if the program's initial failure was due to resource exhaustion or connectivity issues (for example, the loss of network connectivity to a database server), then the **save** function might itself fail or, even worse, perform a partial save, deleting or otherwise rendering corrupt previously saved, older but still valuable data. A safer, and more commonly adopted, approach is for the termination to trigger a "best efforts" save to a recovery file, which would then permit post-mortem validation and analysis to be carried out as required:

```
#include <cstdlib>      // std::abort
#include <exception>   // std::terminate_handler, std::set_terminate

static void emergencySave()
    // Make a best effort to save all existing instances of client data to
    // special recovery files. This function is intended to be called by
    // std::terminate during an emergency program shutdown, e.g., if an
    // unexpected exception occurs. Importantly, the save algorithm is
    // designed to work with just 5MB of available memory.
{
    // ...            (Save as much client data as possible.)

    std::abort();   // Kill the program immediately.
}

int main()
{
    std::terminate_handler prevTermHandler = std::set_terminate(&emergencySave);

    // ...                     (application code)

    std::set_terminate(prevTermHandler);   // Restore previous terminate handler.
}
```

In the example code above, an unexpected call to `std::terminate` anywhere in the application code, e.g., as a result of an exception in a **noexcept** function, calls the installed `terminate_handler`, namely, `emergencySave`. The `emergencySave` function will typically rely on as few system and external resources (e.g., databases or network drives) as possible, as such are not guaranteed to be available and whose unavailability might, in fact, have been the cause of the failure in the first place.

One particularly noteworthy exception is `std::bad_alloc`, which is typically thrown when **new** fails to allocate memory. Relying on an out-of-memory exception to propagate up through arbitrary stack frames to some centralized **try-catch** block that uniformly processes such resource-related exceptions would be like playing Russian roulette with our clients' data, especially when there is pervasive (perhaps unnecessary) use of the **noexcept** specifier.

Moreover, if the program runs out of global memory, then many of the operations required by a typical `emergencySave` function (such as opening files for writing) can also be expected to fail. The classic, time-honored approach to saving ephemeral, in-process data in the event of an out-of-memory failure is to reserve, at the start of the program, sufficient memory to permit an emergency save operation (or any other graceful shutdown as might be appropriate) and, in addition to setting a `terminate_handler` as above, set a `new_handler` whose task is to make that reserved memory available when required:

```cpp
#include <exception>  // std::terminate_handler, std::set_terminate
#include <new>        // std::new_handler, std::set_new_handler

static void emergencySave() { /*...*/ }          // same as before

static void* reservedMemoryBlock = nullptr;  // memory reserved for emergencies

static void handleOutOfMemory()
    // Free reserved memory block and call std::terminate.
{
    ::operator delete(reservedMemoryBlock);  // Make memory available.
    reservedMemoryBlock = nullptr;
    std::terminate();                        // (hopefully) graceful termination
}

int main()
{
    std::terminate_handler prevTermHandler = std::set_terminate(&emergencySave);

    // Reserve 10MB memory to use during graceful termination.
    reservedMemoryBlock = ::operator new(10U * 1024U * 1024U);
    std::new_handler prevNewHandler = std::set_new_handler(&handleOutOfMemory);

    // ...         (application code --- might exhaust memory)

    std::set_new_handler(prevNewHandler);  // Restore previous new handler.
    ::operator delete(reservedMemoryBlock);// Free reserved memory.
    reservedMemoryBlock = nullptr;
    std::set_terminate(prevTermHandler);   // Restore previous terminate handler.
}
```

The skeletal solution sketched out above, in addition to setting the terminate handler, allocates 10MB at the start of `main` and registers `handleOutOfMemory` as the **new** handler. In the event that an allocation fails, `handleOutOfMemory` frees that 10MB to give the `emergencySave` function more than enough headroom to allocate the memory it requires.

Note that `emergencySave`, `handleOutOfMemory`, and `reservedMemoryBlock` are all declared file-scope **static** and are thus visible only within the compilation unit that defines `main`, which is the only place from which these entities should be referenced. A slightly more robust implementation might encapsulate the setting of the terminate handler and **new** handler in RAII classes that would automatically restore the previous handlers as well as freeing the reserved memory.

Forgetting to use the noexcept operator in the noexcept specifier

The **noexcept** specifier is commonly used in conjunction with the **noexcept** *operator* to compute the exception specification of a function (or function template) from the exception specification of a particular expression. The tested expression typically involves variables of a type dependent on the template arguments, as otherwise the answer is known a priori given specific types:

```
template <typename T, typename U>
void grow(T& lhs, const U& rhs) noexcept(noexcept(lhs += rhs))
{
    lhs += rhs;
}
```

Using a nested **noexcept** — i.e., **noexcept(noexcept(***expression***))** — looks odd but is necessary; forgetting the inner **noexcept** — i.e., writing just **noexcept(***expression***)** — can, in some cases, lead to code that still compiles but not with the expected semantics. Such flawed exception specifications are easy to write yet often hard to spot in code review as they look like the familiar **noexcept** specifier. The **noexcept** specifier expects a `constant expression` that is `contextually convertible to bool`. Fortunately, when the inner **noexcept** is accidentally omitted, the common case is that *expression* is not a compile-time `constant expression` and will thus trigger a compiler error. There are a few such mistakes that do constitute valid code, however, and those mistakes can easily result in the function declaration having the wrong exception specification.

Consider, for example, a pair of **inline** functions g1 and g2 that simply return **false**, both declared as **noexcept**, but with g2 defined as **constexpr** (see Section 2.1.*"***constexpr** Functions" on page 257) while g1 is not. We then define two functions, f1 and f2, that simply delegate to g1 and g2, respectively. Each tries to infer its corresponding exception specification from the exception specification of its called function but neglects to nest the **noexcept** operator within the **noexcept** specification:

```
          bool g1() noexcept { return false; }
constexpr bool g2() noexcept { return false; }

bool f1() noexcept(g1()) { return g1(); }  // Error, g1() not a constant expr.
bool f2() noexcept(g2()) { return g2(); }  // Bug, noexcept(false)

static_assert(noexcept(f2()) == noexcept(g2()), "");  // Error, f2 not noexcept
```

In the example above, the declaration of f1 is ill formed, producing a compilation error, because the argument, g1(), to its **noexcept** specifier is not a `constant expression`. Hence, the compiler prevents us from this pitfall in this common case. In the case of f2, however, the expression specifier is valid because g2() is a `constant expression` returning a type convertible to **bool**. The correct declaration for two similar functions (e.g., **f3** and **f4**) would nest the **noexcept** operator within the **noexcept** specifier:

```
bool f3() noexcept(noexcept(g1())) { return g1(); }  // OK, noexcept(true)
bool f4() noexcept(noexcept(g2())) { return g2(); }  // OK, noexcept(true)

static_assert(noexcept(f3()) == noexcept(g1()), "");  // OK
static_assert(noexcept(f4()) == noexcept(g2()), "");  // OK
```

A less frequently encountered variant of this pitfall occurs when the function used in the exception specification is not invoked at all, i.e., by accidentally omitting the empty argument list (**()**). Consider three versions (e.g., **j1**, **j2**, and **j3**) of a function returning the result of calling a non-**noexcept** function **h1** and computing, in three different ways, an exception specification from **h1**:

```
double h1() noexcept(false) { return 1.0; }

double j1() noexcept(h1)           { return h1(); }  // Bug, noexcept(true)
double j2() noexcept(noexcept(h1))   { return h1(); }  // Bug, noexcept(true)
double j3() noexcept(noexcept(h1())) { return h1(); }  // OK, noexcept(false)

static_assert(noexcept(j1()) == noexcept(h1()), "");  // Error, j1 is noexcept.
static_assert(noexcept(j2()) == noexcept(h1()), "");  // Error, j2 is noexcept.
static_assert(noexcept(j3()) == noexcept(h1()), "");  // OK, j3 is not noexcept.
```

The declaration of **j1** omits the inner **noexcept** operator *and* omits the parentheses for the function call, so the argument to the **noexcept** specifier decays to a pointer-to-function, which, being non-null, is evaluated as a Boolean **true**, thus making the exception specification for **j1** be **noexcept(true)**.[33] The declaration of **j2** does apply the nested **noexcept** operator, but similarly misses the function-call parentheses so also gets the result of function-to-pointer decay; an unevaluated function pointer never throws, so the exception specification for **j2** is also **noexcept(true)**. Finally, the declaration of **j3** applies the **noexcept** operator to a *call* to **h1**, producing the intended result that the exception specification for **j3** matches the exception specification for **h1**.

The expression within a **noexcept** specifier is generally either an expression involving traits or an expression within a **noexcept** operator; a correct **noexcept** specification seldom contains a single function call, though it does happen.

Imprecise expressions in a noexcept specification

The **noexcept** specifier indicates whether a single function may throw an exception. Conversely, the **noexcept** operator, when applied to a function-call expression, determines

---

[33] As noted in *Description — Conditional exception specifications* on page 1091, some compilers might issue a diagnostic when a function address is converted to **bool** during compilation, e.g., GCC 9.1 (c. 2019) and later.

whether any part of the expression — the function as well any expressions used in its arguments — might throw. Failing to grasp this subtlety can result in a function being marked **noexcept(false)** even when the expression required by the implementation does not throw. Consider a function template eval1 that takes an invocable object f of the template parameter type F and calls it with a string argument, stringArg, of type **const** std::string&. We want eval1 to have the same exception specification as f::**operator**():

```
#include <string>  // std::string

template <typename F>
void eval1(F f, const std::string& stringArg) noexcept(noexcept(f("")))  // Bug
{
    f(stringArg);
}
```

Here, we are making a concerted effort to pass the exception specification from f through to the exception specification of eval1. For conciseness, we pass an empty string as a placeholder for the string argument in the expression given to the **noexcept** operator, reasoning that the expression is *unevaluated* and hence can be safely abbreviated. Alas, if the argument to f has type **const** std::string&, then passing "" requires a call to the potentially throwing **converting constructor**, std::string(**const char***). Consequently, **noexcept**(f("")) would be **false** because **noexcept**(std::string("")) is **false** regardless of whether the call to f is guaranteed not to throw when called with an already constructed std::string, such as the object referred to by stringArg.

The obvious fix in this case is to use exactly the same expression in the **noexcept** specifier that is used in the return statement, i.e., f(**stringArg**). Before we explore this approach, let's consider a couple of alternatives that might be more appealing in the case of more complex expressions. The argument to f must be a nonthrowing expression that can bind to a **const** std::**string**& without invoking any possibly throwing conversions. A simple fix in this case, therefore, would be to simply switch our placeholder string to an invocation of the default constructor for std::string, which is declared **noexcept**:

```
#include <string>  // std::string

template <typename F>
void eval2(F f, const std::string& stringArg)
    noexcept(noexcept(f(std::string())))    // OK
{
    f(stringArg);
}
```

This fix, however, does not generalize to the case where F is passed an argument that is dependent on a template parameter type, perhaps using **perfect forwarding** (see Section 2.1."Forwarding References" on page 377). Because the type of the argument to f is not known until the template is instantiated, it is not known whether it has a default constructor nor whether any such default constructor is **noexcept**. Rather than place an unnecessary default-constructible constraint on that type, the solution is to use the C++11 library function std::declval, defined within the <utility> header:

```
template <typename T>
typename std::add_rvalue_reference<T>::type std::declval() noexcept;
```

The std::declval function is not defined, so it is an error to call it in a context where it would actually be evaluated. Its purpose is to create a reference to a type that can be used in an **unevaluated context** such as within the **noexcept** operator, **decltype**, **alignof**, or **sizeof**. We can use std::declval to create a more general definition of eval2 (e.g., eval3) with a correctly deduced exception specification:

```
#include <utility>  // std::declval, std::forward

template <typename F, typename T>
void eval3(F f, T&& arg) noexcept(noexcept(f(std::declval<T>())))
{
    f(std::forward<T>(arg));
}
```

Note that calling this function can still throw if the copy or move constructor or destructor for the functor type F can throw. Avoiding an unnecessary copy of F is why, in practice, F would typically be passed by reference:

```
template <typename F, typename T>
void eval4(F&& f, T&& arg)
    noexcept(noexcept(std::declval<F>()(std::declval<T>())))
{
    std::forward<F>(f)(std::forward<T>(arg));
}
```

The observant reader will have noticed that all this trouble arises from trying to avoid using function parameters in the exception specification. These parameters are in scope, as the exception specification follows the function parameter list, so the simplest and most reliably correct form of the exception specification would simply contain a copy of the expression used in the body of the function:

```
template <typename F, typename T>
void eval5(F&& f, T&& arg)
    noexcept(noexcept(std::forward<F>(f)(std::forward<T>(arg))))
{
    std::forward<F>(f)(std::forward<T>(arg));
}
```

Because the **noexcept** specification exactly mirrors the expression of concern, there is no chance of a discrepancy between the two. Unfortunately, this idiom requires significant code duplication; see *Annoyances — Code duplication* on page 1144.

The example of eval1 incorrectly produced a **noexcept(false)** specification, but it is also possible to produce an erroneous **noexcept(true)** specification if an important part of the evaluation is accidentally omitted. Consider this alternative generalized revision of `eval1` that accepts any argument type that can be converted to an `std::string` and passes it to the `f` function object:

```cpp
#include <string>  // std::string

template <typename F, typename S>
void eval6(F f, S&& str)
    noexcept(noexcept(f(std::forward<S>(str))))  // Bug, omits string ctor
{
    std::string s(std::forward<S>(str));  // might throw
    f(s);                                 // Invoke f on the "copy" of str.
}
```

In the example above, the argument to `f`, called from within the body of `eval6`, is *constructed* from the `str` parameter of `eval6`. Constructing the local variable might or might not throw, depending on the type of `S` and whether it is an **lvalue** or **rvalue**; when `str` is passed as an `std::string` rvalue, the `std::string` constructor is nonthrowing, but when it is passed as an *lvalue*, the selected constructor might throw. Let's see what happens when we instantiate this function template with a functor type (e.g., `Consume`) that has a **noexcept** call operator taking an argument of type **const** `std::string&`:

```cpp
struct Consume  // function-object type with nonthrowing call operator
{
    void operator()(const std::string& s) noexcept { }
};

std::string hello = "hello";
static_assert( noexcept(eval6(Consume{}, std::move(hello))), "");  // OK
static_assert( noexcept(eval6(Consume{}, hello)), ""); // passes, but shouldn't
```

When instantiated with `Consume` and an rvalue of type `std::string`, `eval6` is correctly declared **noexcept(true)**, as we see in the first **static_assert** above. However, when instantiated with an lvalue, it is *also* declared **noexcept(true)** even though there is a constructor call in the function body that might throw, potentially leading to an accidental terminate (see *Accidental terminate* on page 1124).

Again, the solution is to ensure that all the necessary expressions are considered by the **noexcept** operator in the exception specification (e.g., to `eval7`):

```cpp
template <typename F, typename S>
void eval7(F f, S&& str)
    noexcept(noexcept(f(std::string(std::forward<S>(str)))))
{
    std::string s(std::forward<S>(str));  // might throw
    f(s);                                 // Invoke f on the "copy" of str.
}

static_assert( noexcept(eval7(Consume{}, std::move(hello))), "");  // OK
static_assert(!noexcept(eval7(Consume{}, hello)), "");            // OK
```

In the above final version, eval7, the subexpression std::string(std::forward<S>(str)) will be **noexcept(true)** if and only if it would invoke a **noexcept** constructor were it actually evaluated, thus expressing the correct predicate for the pass-through function.

Unrealizable runtime performance benefits

As we know (see *Use Cases — Reducing object-code size* on page 1101), using **noexcept** under certain well-understood circumstances can measurably reduce object-code size.

Conventional wisdom suggests that "less code runs faster" and "more code runs slower." When there is less object code, it typically means that fewer machine instructions are executed. When there is more code, there might be more *proximate* instructions that — even if seldom executed — can nonetheless put pressure on a limited hardware resource, namely, the instruction cache.

Historically, support for exceptions resulted in executing additional instructions along the **exception free path** — even when no exceptions were thrown. With the increasingly ubiquitous use of the **zero-cost exception model**, no additional proximate machine instructions are introduced to support exceptions when an exception is not thrown — a.k.a the **hot path**. In adopting this zero-cost model, we aggressively trade off both latency and throughput when an exception is actually thrown — a.k.a., the **cold path**.

Despite contributing no overhead on the **exception free path**, a call to a function that could potentially throw might, however, preclude otherwise beneficial optimizations. Short of disabling all support for exceptions ubiquitously (e.g, on the compiler's command line), the best we can do currently to reinstate such runtime optimization opportunities is either to (1) make the body of a nonthrowing function visible when compiling a function that calls it, or (2) declare the nonthrowing function as **noexcept**, but see *Annoyances — Algorithmic optimization is conflated with reducing object-code size* on page 1143.

It will turn out that — unlike algorithmic improvements — opportunistic use of **noexcept** *solely* as a hint to enable the compiler to optimize *runtime* performance will seldom provide *any* gains, let alone consequential ones; hence, its widespread use throughout a codebase for such a purpose would be highly dubious[34]; see *Overly strong contracts guarantees* on page 1112.

Chandler Carruth said it best[35]:

> If you didn't write a benchmark for your code, you do not care about performance. That's not an opinion, Okay? That's fact.

The hot path and the cold path   We call the code that runs in the common, or typical, case the **hot path** to reflect that it is the path that is almost always taken. We call the exceptional case the **cold path** because it is by far the path less traveled, is unlikely to be in

---

[34]On MSVC 19.29 (c. 2021), adding **noexcept(true)** to an **inline** function — especially a member function of a DLL-exported class — might yield a significant drop in runtime performance; see **dekker19a**.

[35]**carruth17**, time 3:56–4:38

cache, and — for larger programs — might not even be paged into the computer's **physical memory** (RAM). Regardless of the exception-handling implementation used, throwing an exception is presumed to be *exceptional* (atypical) — i.e., all of its handling properly resides on the cold path.

In a **try/catch** construct, the **try** block is *always* on the hot path of that construct, whereas the **catch** block is invariably on the cold path. Even in the absence of an explicit **try** in the source code, the compiler must, in certain cases, generate an implicit **try/catch** with a hot path when no exception is thrown and a cold path for **stack unwinding** — i.e., destroying live, local, non-trivially **destructible** automatic variables, which might include a rethrow.

Note that a single function might require multiple implicit **try** blocks — one for each cluster of such local variables that is followed by a potentially throwing expression; see *Use Cases — Reducing object-code size* on page 1101.

Contemporary compilers make an effort to segregate, within the **executable image**, what they believe to be seldomly executed sequences of machine instructions and might sequester them into a distant region of the virtual address space. The path where an exception is thrown, however, is known with 100% accuracy to be on the cold path, and modern compilers will strive to avoid interleaving such cold-path code alongside frequently executed instructions.

Older exception-handling implementations   Prior to the ubiquitous adoption of the zero-cost exception model (described below), most compilers would perform stack-based bookkeeping to dynamically track the currently active nested **try** blocks at any point in the execution of the function.

For example, one implementation[36] would create a new exception-registration record for each **try** block, including those generated implicitly. Each registration record would hold two pointers: one to the exception-handler code and the other to the previous exception registration record. On entry to each **try** block (implicit or otherwise), the compiler would insert instructions to construct the exception registration record, add it to the linked list of active **try** blocks, and update a thread-local pointer to the new exception registration record. If an exception were to be thrown, the exception-handling logic would walk the linked list of registered blocks, calling each handler in turn as it unwound the stack. The compiler would also insert code at the end of the **try** block to handle the normal (i.e., exception free) case of restoring the thread-local pointer to the previous registration record, thereby removing the block from the linked list and restoring the previous dynamic exception handling state.

In these old models, registration and deregistration instructions were executed on the hot path on, respectively, entry to and exit from each **try** block — even when no exception was thrown. The runtime burden of exception support strongly favored the normal, nonexception case, but the runtime cost was nonzero. These instructions added overhead on the hot path that many considered onerous enough to choose to forgo using exceptions entirely, building their programs with exceptions disabled (e.g., using a compiler switch).

---

[36]Compilers for 32-bit Windows platforms continue to use this non-zero-cost exception-handling model; see **pietrek97**.

The advent of the zero-cost exception model, which adopted a different set of trade-offs, eliminated literally *all* runtime overhead on the hot path at the expense of larger programs and significantly increased the relative latency on the cold path — e.g, due to likely cache misses and perhaps even page faults. This newer "zero-cost" model made allowing support for exception handling practical for a wider range of applications.

The zero-cost exception model   In the increasingly ubiquitous **zero-cost** model, employed by most modern compilers, the runtime cost of supporting exceptions on the normal (i.e., exception free) path is *effectively* zero. That is to say, compared with not supporting exceptions at all, there are no additional machine instructions inserted into the hot path as result of the model itself: all of the additional object code is implemented in the form of tables and cold-path code.[37]

We say *effectively* here because there exist both theoretical and practical cases where — if the optimizer somehow knows that a particular function cannot throw — one or more machine instructions having nothing to do with the exception model itself might be able to be reordered if not entirely elided from the active instruction stream on the hot path. These forms of potential collateral optimization are characterized below.

Note that the term zero cost refers to the elimination of bookkeeping on the hot path. Support for exceptions is never truly *free*, as there must always be code generated to handle exceptions and unwind the stack, including calling destructors for local variables.

Theoretical opportunities for performance improvement

There are at least two distinct categories of runtime-performance optimization that a compiler could theoretically employ when a called function, g, is known by the compiler not to throw: (1) when instructions in the generated code are known to be independent, the compiler has maximum flexibility to choose and order machine instructions (**instruction selection** and **code motion**) so as to to minimize latency and take optimal advantage of the parallelism and pipelining available in modern CPUs; and (2) when a sequence of instructions is free from unpredictable branches, the optimizer can discover and elide "dead code" (**code elision**), i.e., remove instructions whose effects are never used.

As a hypothetical illustration of this first type of optimization, consider the familiar example where we have a function, f, having one or more local variables of type S, this time having a visible and substantial **default constructor** body along with a potentially opaque non-trivial destructor. Furthermore, we have a subroutine, g, whose implementation is opaque, currently **noexcept(false)** (by default), but happens to not throw. Note that, without visibility into the body of the constructor of S, the compiler cannot know that there is no interaction between S and g. Also note that, had the body of g been available, there would be no need to explicitly state that g does not throw (see *Annoyances — Algorithmic optimization is conflated with reducing object-code size* on page 1143):

---

[37]For a more detailed yet approachable introduction to the zero-cost exception model, see **mortoray13**.

```
struct S
{
    S() { /*runtime intensive*/ }  // inline, i.e., visible to caller's compiler
    ~S();  // possibly opaque (non-trivial) user-provided destructor
};

void g();  // may throw (but doesn't)

void f()
{
    S s0;
    S s1;
    S s2;
    g();  // call #1
    g();  // call #2
}
```

In theory, if there is visibility into the body of `S::S()`, the compiler can identify when the construction of `s0`, `s1`, and `s2` are provably independent and independent of invoking `g`. The generated code can — in principle — be executed concurrently (or at least overlap):

```
CALL f -----> S s0; ----> S s1; ----> S s2; ----> g(); ----> g(); ---> RETURN


               +--> S s0; ----->-------->--+
CALL f --+--> S s1; ----->-------->--+--> RETURN
               +--> S s2; ----->-------->--+
               +--> g();  -----> g(); ->--+
```

The schematic diagram above illustrates a theoretical best case of concurrency; more likely, the visible constructors of each `S` would be **vectorized** or **pipelined**, and the calls to the opaque function `g()` would be serialized after.

Any such **code-motion**–like optimization requires that at least one of `f` or `g` be declared **noexcept**; otherwise, the potentially throwing `g` function could throw prior to the construction of one or more of the *non*-trivially destructible local `S` variables. By declaring `g` as **noexcept**, code-motion–like compiler optimizations are made possible. Note that, if `g` is known to the human caller not to throw (see *Conflating **noexcept** with nofail* on page 1116), declaring `f` **noexcept** can have a similar effect provided the compiler takes advantage of the latitude it is granted by the standard *not* to attempt to clean up the current stack frame before invoking `std::terminate`; see *Description — Potential efficiencies when expressions cannot throw* on page 1093.

The potential for the above **code motion** and/or **vectorization** optimizations are rare and ephemeral — there must be a perfect storm of optimization opportunities for a compiler to beneficially take advantage of reordering operations around an opaque function call. However, running a microbenchmark on a function `f`, which exhibits a real reduction in object-code size when a subroutine g is declared as **noexcept**, illustrates that code size alone does not necessarily adversely affect runtime performance.

For example, consider a series of functions, fN, each having the same canonical form:

```
struct S { ~S() noexcept; };   // defined (empty) in a separate translation unit
void g() G_EXCEPTION_SPEC;      // declared with and without noexcept
void fN() { g(); S s0; g(); S s1; g(); /*...*/ S sN; g(); }
```

In other words, each function fN (f0, f1, f2, ...) has N local variables of type S interleaved with $N + 1$ invocations of g():

```
void f0() { g(); }
void f1() { g(); S s0; g(); }
void f2() { g(); S s0; g(); S s1; g(); }
   :    :    :    :    :     :    :      :    :...
```

We tried invoking functions f0 ... f8 on various platforms *with* and *without* declaring g as **noexcept**; the results are presented in Table 4 as the ratio of the former divided by the latter for both the object size and the runtime to call f.

Table 4: f() contains N calls to g()

	Object Size				Run Time[a]			
	GCC[b]	Clang[b]	MSVC[b]		GCC[b]	Clang[b]	MSVC[b]	
N[c]	-O3	-O3	/Ot	/Os	-O3	-O3	/Ot	/Os
0	1.0000	1.0000	1.0000	1.0000	1.0076	0.9985	0.9947	1.0207
1	0.5448	0.4929	0.5326	0.5326	0.9470	1.0660	0.9923	1.0568
2	0.5227	0.5412	0.4961	0.4961	1.0047	0.9465	1.0255	1.0083
3	0.5054	0.5048	0.4759	0.4759	0.9690	1.0717	0.9417	1.0063
4	0.4880	0.5126	0.4631	0.4631	1.0873	1.0446	1.0119	0.9853
5	0.4749	0.4821	0.4542	0.4542	1.0114	0.9863	0.9791	0.9705
6	0.4651	0.4606	0.4477	0.4477	0.9694	0.9988	0.9897	1.0106
7	0.4567	0.4484	0.4427	0.4427	0.9818	1.0158	0.9807	1.0012
8	0.4492	0.4527	0.4387	0.4387	1.0361	0.9969	0.9946	0.9704
9	0.4434	0.4432	0.4356	0.4356	1.0103	1.0186	0.9955	0.9942

[a] Average of middle 80% of 100 runs using Google benchmark
[b] GCC 11.1.0 (c. 2021), Clang 12.1.0 (c. 2021), and MSVC 19.29 (c. 2021)
[c] Each entry depicts g declared **noexcept(true)**/**noexcept(false)**.

The table above contains raw data obtained by running a loop from a **translation unit (TU)**, main.cpp, that invokes a function, f, in a second TU, f.cpp, that in turn calls a function, g, defined in a third TU, g.cpp, where an empty S::~S() { } is also defined. Notice that the code *size* of f reliably decreases when g is declared as **noexcept** (after a local variable having a non-trivial **destructor**) but — as there's no plausible theoretical opportunity for runtime optimization to occur — no similar reduction is reflected in the *runtime* ratios.

One could reasonably point out that the data above comes from a microbenchmark that might not be reflective of a large, real-world program. That is true, but, on the other hand, unlike issues of scale that impact L1, L2, and L3 cache, this microbenchmark has nothing to do with accessing data that might be affected by **working-set** size. A program having a large executable might well put more pressure on the instruction cache, but the zero-cost model will keep **cold-path** exception handling code from adding to that pressure; hence, executable size alone — in theory — plays no role in determining runtime performance. While a large executable might have an impact in other ways — larger transfer times to distributed systems, resource limits on highly constrained systems, etc. – the **cold-path** code alone does not appear to directly impact runtime performance.

When pondering the benefits of **noexcept** on an application that makes no direct use of exceptions, a reliable way to see whether there is any benefit would be to rebuild the entire application with exceptions disabled entirely — an option most modern compilers provide. While theory would indicate that there will almost certainly be a reduction in executable size, runtime performance might exhibit little or no significant difference.

Practically realizable performance improvements   The other form of optimization, resulting from code elision on the hot path, derives from knowing that some particular *user-provided* code that prepares for handling an exception thrown from a subsequent expression will never be needed — and thus can be removed — because the compiler knows that no such exception will be thrown. Such elision-based optimizations are known to have a measurable improvement in runtime performance.[38]

Let's now consider a mechanism for dealing with exceptions, based on RAII, that doesn't involve any explicit **try**, **catch**, or **throw**. In this example we'll start by using the C++11 standard library component std::unique_ptr as a **scoped guard** in the body of a function, fu to **proctor** ownership of a dynamically allocated **int**:

```
#include <memory>  // std::unique_ptr

void g();          // noexcept(false) by default

int* fu(int* p)  // runtime optimizable if compiler knows g won't throw
{
    std::unique_ptr<int> u(p);     // #1 Initialize guard u'.
    g();                           // #2 This call to g may throw.
    return u.release();            // #3 Return the locally managed resource.
}
```

---

[38]For a quantitative analysis of optimizations based on assumption, see **amini21**.

In the function fu (above), the address of a dynamically allocated **int** is supplied to fu to be managed temporarily by a guard, u. An externally defined function, g, that may throw is then invoked. Provided g doesn't throw, the address of that supplied **int** object is returned; otherwise, it is deleted, and the exception is rethrown.

Under the covers, the compiler will implicitly generate a **try/catch** block to prepare for the case where g throws. For didactic purposes, we have rewritten the fu above as fv, stating all implicitly generated functionality explicitly:

```
int* fv(int* p)  // runtime optimizable if compiler knows g won't throw
{
    int* d_u = p;                    // #1 Initialize guard u.
    try // implicitly generated try/catch block.
    {
        g();                         // #2 This call to g may throw.
    }
    catch (...)
    {
        delete d_u;  // Invoke guard u's destructor.
        throw;       // Rethrow currently in-flight exception.
    }
                                     // #3 Return the locally managed resource.
    int* retval = d_u;  // release(): Save value to be returned.
    d_u = 0;            // release(): Clear internal pointer value.
    delete d_u;         // Invoke guard u's destructor.
    return retval;      // Return allocated resource.
}
```

Let's now consider what sort of optimizations are possible along the hot path if the compiler knows that g() doesn't throw. For starters, the **try** and all code in the **catch** clause can be eliminated as there's no possibility of an exception propagating from the call to g(). Next, we can trace p through d_u and retval to see that it is always the value returned, so the return statement can be replaced with **return** p. The **delete** operator applied to d_u is always passed a null pointer value, which does nothing, and so that can be elided. Finally, while d_u is assigned to twice (first to p at the top of the function, then to 0 before the return), its value is never read, so both assignments and the local variable itself can be eliminated. That is, just by knowing that g doesn't throw the compiler can elide the catch block, both local variables, two assignments, and the invocation of the **delete** operator.

After the optimizer is done, a similarly didactic rendering of the equivalent code would be noticeably smaller:

```
void g() noexcept;
int* fw(int* p)
{
    g();        // #2 This call to g may not throw.
    return p;   // Return allocated resource.
}
```

To illustrate the difference between less code on only the **cold path** versus less code on *both paths*, we created a microbenchmark similar to the one above, this time replacing the local variables of type S with instances of std::unique_ptr<int>, and following each call to g with a call to release before finally releasing the resource back to the caller.

```
#include <memory>  // std::unique_ptr

#ifndef NOEXCEPT  // useful CPP technique to enable command-line control
#define NOEXCEPT
#endif

void g() NOEXCEPT;  // noexcept(false) by default, but what if noexcept(true)?

int* fN(int* p)
{
    std::unique_ptr<int> u0(p);  // #1 Initialize guard u0.
    g();                         // #2 May this call to g throw?
    u0.release();                // #3 Release the locally managed resource.

    std::unique_ptr<int> u1(p);  // #1 Initialize guard u1.
    g();                         // #2 May this call to g throw?
    u1.release();                // #3 Release the locally managed resource.

    // ... (total of N blocks)

    std::unique_ptr<int> uN(p);  // #1 Initialize guard uN.
    g();                         // #2 May this call to g throw?
    uN.release();                // #3 Release the locally managed resource.

    return p;                    // #3 Return the locally managed resource.
}
```

To bolster our intuition, we again present the results of various microbenchmark runs in Table 5.

Table 5: f() contains N unique_ptr guards around calls to g()

	Object Size				Run Time[a]			
	GCC[b]	**Clang[b]**	**MSVC[b]**		**GCC[b]**	**Clang[b]**	**MSVC[b]**	
N[c]	**-O3**	**-O3**	**/Ot**	**/Os**	**-O3**	**-O3**	**/Ot**	**/Os**
0	1.0000	1.0000	1.0000	1.0000	1.0034	0.9903	1.0086	0.9934
1	0.4154	0.5036	0.7289	0.7644	1.1030	0.9913	0.9352	1.1360
2	0.3681	0.5000	0.6146	0.6652	1.0014	0.9222	0.9590	1.0597
3	0.3333	0.4969	0.5369	0.5932	0.7884	1.0011	1.0740	1.1428
4	0.3067	0.4942	0.4806	0.5385	0.8323	0.9021	0.9985	1.4772
5	0.2857	0.4918	0.4490	0.4955	0.9937	0.9579	1.0526	0.9639
6	0.2681	0.4897	0.4183	0.4609	1.0112	0.7729	1.0875	1.1388
7	0.2537	0.4878	0.3932	0.4367	0.9697	0.8690	0.9711	0.9500
8	0.2416	0.4861	0.3723	0.4142	0.9640	0.8690	0.9605	0.9732
9	0.2309	0.4846	0.3440	0.3932	0.9293	0.8951	1.0426	0.9684

[a] Average of middle 80% of 100 runs using Google benchmark

[b] GCC 11.1.0 (c. 2021), Clang 12.1.0 (c. 2021), and MSVC 19.29 (c. 2021)

[c] Each entry depicts g declared **noexcept(true)**/**noexcept(false)**.

Unlike the previous experiment, because the compiler knows that g does not throw, it can eliminate all of the local variables — removing at least the instructions needed to initialize each local variable on the hot path (the destructor call for each std::unique_ptr is elidable on the hot path even if g is *not* **noexcept**).[39]

Keep in mind that tiny changes in generated code can have disproportionate and unpredictable effects on run time — both positive and negative — because of highly chaotic occurrences such as causing or preventing a single cache miss or even a page fault on the hot path. Something that theoretically ought to speed up the code might well end up slowing it down simply because it moved an instruction into a different **cache line**. Making changes to source code to trigger small optimizations in the compiler might have a small benefit, have no benefit, or perhaps even be a pessimization. Such micro optimizations on local object code can be counterproductive unless (1) said code is known to underperform and (2) such optimizations are done in conjunction with careful measurement.

Conclusion   The noexcept specifier, in conjunction with the **noexcept** operator (see Section 2.1."**noexcept** Operator" on page 615), was invented primarily to leverage *algorithmically* move operations that cannot throw while still allowing for the possibility of move operations that *do* throw.

Knowing that a given move operation does not throw often enables *algorithmic* speedup, with a natural spillover into swap operations. (See *Use Cases — Declaring nonthrowing move operations* on page 1094, *Use Cases — Defining a **noexcept** swap* on page 1097, and *Use Cases — A wrapper that provides **noexcept** move operations* on page 1099.) In special

---

[39]For a brief introduction to similar benchmarking of the non*algorithmic* runtime effects of **noexcept** as measured on several popular platforms, see **dekker19a**.

circumstances (e.g., embedded systems), we might want to use **noexcept** to reduce object code size; see *Use Cases — Reducing object-code size* on page 1101.

The zero-cost exception model *itself* (unlike previous models) introduces absolutely no overhead into the (exception free) hot path, leaving only minimal opportunities for **noexcept** to inform the compiler of local "peephole" runtime performance optimization opportunities — e.g., by eliding unused code explicitly supplied on the hot path by the user. Effective use of **noexcept** solely for the purpose of local (*non*algorithmic) runtime object-code optimization fairly demands benchmarking to justify the risks associated with premature specification (see *Overly strong contracts guarantees* on page 1112) and unexpected program termination (see *Accidental terminate* on page 1124).

One possible workaround to avoid such pitfalls would be to make the body of the called function, g, visible to the calling function, f. Doing so, however, strongly compile-time couples the entire body of g to f, thereby reducing the independent malleability of g. Currently, there is no general solution that gives us local code optimization without making a permanent contractual agreement; see *Annoyances — Algorithmic optimization is conflated with reducing object-code size* below.

Annoyances

Algorithmic optimization is conflated with reducing object-code size

If a move or swap operation throws an exception in generic code, any modification of the original object is considered irreversible because neither the moved-from nor the moved-to object is known to have a useful value. The **noexcept** operator (see Section 2.1."**noexcept** Operator" on page 615) and the accompanying **noexcept** specifier were invented to allow algorithms — especially those using move or swap operations, such as std::sort and std::rotate — to choose the fastest way to perform a task without risk of falling into such nonrecoverable situations. An algorithm can use the **noexcept** operator to determine (at compile time) if the move or swap operations it needs to use may throw and, if so, opt to use copy instead of move so that the original objects remain unchanged in the event of a thrown exception.

Decorating a function with **noexcept** might lead to some optimizations; see *Use Cases — Reducing object-code size* on page 1101. This side effect of **noexcept** could perhaps provide an incentive for developers to use the **noexcept** specifier even when there is no algorithmic benefit to be had, possibly committing to nonthrowing interfaces too early and thereby limiting the evolution of the interface design; see *Potential Pitfalls — Overly strong contracts guarantees* on page 1112 and *Unrealizable runtime performance benefits* on page 1134.

Ideally, the compiler could be given enough information to perform optimizations leveraging a nonthrowing function implementation without contractually obligating the function *never* to throw in the future. For any function g whose body is visible in the current translation unit (e.g., function templates and **inline** functions from an included header file) or when using link-time optimization, the compiler can already determine that a function's implementation will never throw — even if it is not declared **noexcept**. Without inspecting the function body, however, the only way currently to give the compiler sufficient information to optimize for a nonthrowing implementation is to declare the function **noexcept**.

A language extension could easily be added — e.g., an attribute `[[does_not_throw]]` (see Section 1.1."Attribute Syntax" on page 12) — to communicate precisely this implementation-only property as an optimization hint across translation units.

```
void g0();                    // noexcept(false), no optimization possible
void g1() noexcept;           // noexcept(true), all optimizations possible
[[does_not_throw]] void g2(); // noexcept(false), compiler optimization only
```

Within a decorated function's implementation, this attribute would have the same effect as **noexcept(true)** — any thrown exception would result in a call to `std::terminate`. The essential distinction between `[[does_not_throw]]` and **noexcept** would arise in the interaction with the **noexcept** operator and the type system, which would be blind to the new attribute and treat function calls decorated with it (and without **noexcept** or **noexcept(true)**) as it would treat any other **noexcept(false)** function call:

```
static_assert(!noexcept(g0()), "");  // OK, noexcept(false)
static_assert( noexcept(g1()), "");  // OK, can identify noexcept function
static_assert(!noexcept(g2()), "");  // OK, operator ignores attribute
```

Adding or removing a **noexcept** specification from a function might make client code follow different code paths or perhaps even fail to compile. This change can happen through client use of the **noexcept** operator, assignment to a **noexcept** function pointer, or (in C++17) use of the function to deduce a template argument. In other words, a function's exception specification is part of its **programmatically accessible** interface and hence part of its de facto contract.

Unlike **noexcept**, adding or removing `[[does_not_throw]]` would have no semantic effect — i.e, it would neither alter the function's type nor be capable of altering algorithmic decisions (e.g., via the **noexcept** operator). By using `[[does_not_throw]]` instead of **noexcept** when algorithmic optimization is not the intent, any potential optimization remains a pure implementation detail — subject to change (by the implementer) without notice. Such an attribute would be a cross-translation-unit people-code-optimization hint and would explicitly *not* imply anything contractual to the caller.

Alas, no such feature exists today — either in the Standard or in any implementation known to the authors. At least for now, **noexcept** must do double-duty as both an interface specifier and a cross-translation-unit optimization hint. Consequently, today's developers are forced to balance the trade-off of reduced object-code size against the potential pitfalls of otherwise imprudent use of the **noexcept** specifier; see *Potential Pitfalls — Unrealizable runtime performance benefits* on page 1134.

Code duplication

Many modern C++ language features aid in writing small generic functions that primarily delegate their implementation to other functions may vary in many aspects based on parameter type. Using a **trailing return type** (see Section 1.1."Trailing Return" on page 124), **decltype** (see Section 1.1."**decltype**" on page 25), and the conditional **noexcept** specifier (see *Description — Conditional exception specifications* on page 1091) can all aid in writing a generic function declaration whose properties are narrowly determined by (1) the operations it performs and (2) its parameter types.

For example, consider a function template, **add**, that takes two arguments, identified by parameters **lhs** and **rhs**, of arbitrary types, **U** and **V**, and returns a value of the same type and **value category** (see Section 2.1."*Rvalue* References" on page 710) that results from applying the infix operator + to the supplied arguments:

```
template <typename T, typename U>                           // declaration
auto add(const T& lhs, const U& rhs) noexcept(noexcept(lhs + rhs))
                                -> decltype(lhs + rhs);

template <typename T, typename U>                           // definition
auto add(const T& lhs, const U& rhs) noexcept(noexcept(lhs + rhs))
                                -> decltype(lhs + rhs)
{
    return lhs + rhs;  // Return type is same as type of this expression.
}
```

This declaration (having two repetitions of the returned expression) and definition (having three such repetitions) reliably capture the return type and exception specification of adding two objects of arbitrary types. Having to repeat the same expression many times introduces clutter and can result in a significant maintenance burden should that expression change. Any maintenance that causes these expressions not to match might result in a compilation error but could easily result in an incorrect exception specification instead, leading to an unintended call to **std::terminate** in code that was expected to properly propagate an exception; see *Potential Pitfalls — Accidental **terminate*** on page 1124.

Plausible workarounds employ the use of preprocessor macros in at least two distinct ways. The first approach is to implement each boilerplate portion of the function as a **variadic macro** (available since C++11):

```
#define DECLARE_FUNCTION_RETURN(...)                        \
        noexcept(noexcept(__VA_ARGS__)) -> decltype(__VA_ARGS__)

#define DEFINE_FUNCTION_RETURN(...)                         \
        noexcept(noexcept(__VA_ARGS__)) -> decltype(__VA_ARGS__) \
        { return __VA_ARGS__; }

template <typename T, typename U>
auto add(const T& lhs, const U& rhs) DECLARE_FUNCTION_RETURN(lhs + rhs);

template <typename T, typename U>
auto add(const T& lhs, const U& rhs) DEFINE_FUNCTION_RETURN(lhs + rhs)
```

A second macro-based approach implements what's known as an **expression alias**. In this rendering, the expression is factored out into a single macro definition, and then the macro alias replaces each of the five instances of that expression in the declaration and definition of add:

```
#define XYZZY_ADD_EXPRESSION  (lhs + rhs)  // fully factored expression alias

template <typename T, typename U>                          // declaration
auto add(const T& lhs, const U& rhs) noexcept(noexcept(XYZZY_ADD_EXPRESSION))
                                -> decltype(XYZZY_ADD_EXPRESSION);

template <typename T, typename U>                          // definition
auto add(const T& lhs, const U& rhs) noexcept(noexcept(XYZZY_ADD_EXPRESSION))
                                -> decltype(XYZZY_ADD_EXPRESSION)
{
    return XYZZY_ADD_EXPRESSION;
}

#undef XYZZY_ADD_EXPRESSION  // no longer needed
```

In this second approach, there is no duplication of the expression, and the amount of text involving macros is pleasantly minimized. Note that, because this code is likely to reside in a header file, it is important in either case that we ensure that macro names we choose are not going to conflict with an existing macro, as suggested by the prefix XYZZY_, and that we don't leave defined these macros that will have no further use beyond the definition of our function.

A C++14 feature, deduced return types (see Section 3.2.“**auto** Return” on page 1182), does obviate the repetition associated with deducing the return type, but requires that the definition be made visible to callers:

```
template <typename T, typename U>               // declaration and definition
auto add(const T& lhs, const U& rhs) noexcept(noexcept(lhs + rhs))
{
    return lhs + rhs;  // Return type is deduced by inspecting function body.
}
```

During the evolution of C++11, the creation of a similar facility was suggested for deducing the exception specification from the function's implementation, either implicitly for any visible function body or explicitly with a decorator such as **noexcept(auto)**, but neither of those options was adopted by the Standards Committee.[40] Consider that, with such a feature, a small change to the implementation may result in changing a **noexcept(true)** specification to a **noexcept(false)** one, thereby violating the implicit contract established in a previous release. What's more, changing the exception specification either way would

---

[40]See **stroustrup10b** and **ottosen10** and finally **merrill10b**, rejected by WG21 in November 2010. A more recent paper advocating the (re)consideration of the **noexcept(auto)** feature can be found in **voutilainen15**.

potentially cause different code paths to occur in existing client code; see *Potential Pitfalls — Overly strong contracts guarantees* on page 1112.

An alternative proposed language extension, akin to the second macro-based solution above, is commonly referred to as **expression aliases**:

```
template <typename A, typename B>
using add_expression(A a, B b) = a + b;
```

In this frequently discussed language extension, the aliased expression `lhs + rhs` would be substituted for the associated alias, `add_expression(lhs, rhs)`, directly — as if enforced inline. Being a proper alias expression, both **noexcept** and **decltype** would report directly on the expression itself. Unlike **noexcept(auto)**, however, C++ expression aliases would likely be limited to a single expression, thus discouraging overly complex implicit contracts and avoiding the textual-replacement and scope-irreverence problems endemic to macros.

Exception specifications are not part of a function's type

A common issue with using function-pointer types is that their type declarations can be considered awkward, especially for functions returning function pointers. One popular way to simplify such declarations is to use a type alias — i.e., **typedef** or **using** (see Section 1.1. "**using** Aliases" on page 133) — for the function type. Unfortunately, as exception specifications are not part of a function's type until C++17, it is not possible to declare an alias for a function type that includes an exception specification. In addition, exception specifications cannot be added to a type alias — even when using a type alias that happens to be a function type. Hence, to declare a function pointer having an explicitly stated exception specification, we are forced to spell out the function pointer declaration completely:

```
void f() noexcept;  // function having an explicitly stated exception specification

typedef void fn_type();           // OK
typedef void fn_noexcept() noexcept;  // Error, noexcept not part of type

fn_type* ft = f;          // OK
fn_type noexcept* fno = f;  // Error, cannot write noexcept there
void (*fn)() noexcept = f;  // OK, exception specification on function pointer

struct S  // class having a member function that is not permitted to throw
{
    void mem_fn() noexcept;  // This member function can never throw.
};

typedef void (S::*mem_type)();            // OK
typedef void (S::*mem_noexcept)() noexcept;  // Error, noexcept not part of type

mem_type mem_t = &S::mem_fn;         // OK
mem_type noexcept mem_no = &S::mem_fn;  // Error, cannot write noexcept there
void (S::*mem_n)() noexcept = &S::mem_fn;  // OK, noexcept on mem-ptr
```

Similarly, when deducing a function type as a template parameter, the exception specification is lost. Hence, a function template, e.g., `testAlgorithm`, deducing the specific type argument, e.g., `F`, is unable to query the exception specifications of any function, e.g., `f1` or `f2`, with which it is supplied:

```
void f1();          // f1 promising nothing about whether it will throw
void f2() noexcept; // f2 is contractually/actively prevented from throwing.

template <typename F>
void testAlgorithm(F f)  // function template that dispatches on noexcept(f())
{
    if (noexcept(f()))   // This branch is dead code until C++17.
    {
        // ...           (faster, exception unsafe algorithm)
    }
    else                 // When in doubt, take this safer branch.
    {
        // ...           (slower, exception-safe algorithm)
    }
}

void test()  // Call testAlgorithm on noexcept(false) and noexcept functions.
{
    testAlgorithm(f1);  // runs slower code in every version of C++
    testAlgorithm(f2);  // runs faster code only as of C++17 and later
}
```

As stated previously, this annoyance has been addressed in C++17, which makes the declarations of `fn_noexcept` and `mem_noexcept`, above, valid, as well as enabling `testAlgorithm` to deduce a **noexcept** function type for `F` in the call to `testAlgorithm(f2)` in function `test`.

ABI changes in future versions of C++

In C++11, functions can have parameters that are function pointers with **noexcept** exception specifications; see *Description — Function pointers and references* on page 1089. It is not permitted to bind a pointer to a function with an exception specification (implicit or otherwise) that would allow it to throw to a pointer that is declared **noexcept**. This check for compatible exception specifications is not part of the type system; instead, it is local to each parameter.

Newer C++ Standards — C++17 and onward — handle **noexcept** more consistently by making the exception specification part of the type of the function to which it applies. As functions cannot be overloaded on the exception specification alone, this change does not affect the **name mangling** for most functions. However, for functions that have function-pointer parameters, the **name mangling** for the function pointer type will be affected if a parameter has a nonthrowing exception specification, producing an ABI incompatibility between language versions:

```
void f1() noexcept;  // This function is declared to be noexcept(true).

void f2(void (*fn)() );        // takes pointer to noexcept(false) function
void f2(void (*fn)() noexcept);  // Warning, mangling will change in C++17.
                               // 1 function in C++14, 2 overloads in C++17
void test()
{
    f2(f1);  // might need to recompile and relink for modern C++ Standards
}
```

Such incompatibilities can be resolved by recompiling all code consistently with the same language-standard option before linking.

Exception specifications do not trigger SFINAE

An important feature when using C++ templates is the SFINAE principle, Substitution Failure Is Not An Error. SFINAE allows the compiler to drop a function from an overload set before overload resolution when, on substituting the types required to instantiate a function declaration, the compiler discovers that the declaration would be ill formed:

```
template <typename T>
void fun(T x, typename T::type y);  // (1) function template
void fun(int x, double y);          // (2) ordinary function

struct X { typedef int type; };

void test_fun()  // Demonstrate how SFINAE works on simple parameter types.
{
    fun(X(), 0);  // OK, calls (1), matching 0 to X::type
    fun(0, 0.0);  // OK, calls (2) by means of an exact match
    fun(0, 0);    // OK, SFINAE disqualifies (1), calls (2)
}
```

In the example above, the first call to fun binds to overload (1) as the first argument binds to x, deducing T to be X and T::type to be **int**. The second call to fun binds to overload (2), as each of its parameters is an exact match with the types of its respective arguments being passed in. The third call to fun is not an exact match to overload (2), so overload (1) is considered, but because the deduced type **int**::type is ill formed, SFINAE causes (1) to be removed from the overload set, leaving (2) as the only function remaining in the overload set still suitable for invocation.

Attempting to use SFINAE in a similar manner on an exception specification does not work because the exception specification itself is not involved in overload resolution and is not evaluated until the function has already been selected, at which point SFINAE no longer applies and the ill formed value causes a hard error:

```
template <typename T>
void func(T x) noexcept(T::value);  // (1) function template
void func(double x);                // (2) ordinary function

struct Y { static const bool value = true; };  // compile-time constant value

void test_func()  // Demonstrate how SFINAE fails to work with exception specs.
{
    func(Y());  // OK, calls (1), evaluating T::value as true
    func(0.0);  // OK, calls (2) by means of an exact match
    func(0);    // Error, value is not a member of int
}
```

The first two calls to func are similar to those for fun (above): The first call, not being an exact match for the ordinary function overload, makes the function template a better match, while the second call is an exact match to the ordinary function, so it is preferred. For the third call to func, the templated overload (1) is the best match during overload resolution; because the (conditional) **noexcept** specifier is not considered by SFINAE, the function template is not removed from consideration, resulting in an ill formed program that attempts to reference **int**::value.

See Also

- "**noexcept** Operator" (§2.1, p. 615) describes using the similarly named operator to determine whether a given expression may throw.

Further Reading

- Andrzej Krzemienski provides a solid overview of using the **noexcept** specifier effectively in **krzemienski11**.

- Scott Meyers offers a gentle introduction to using **noexcept** on function declarations in **meyers15b**, "Item 14: Declare functions noexcept if they won't emit exceptions," pp. 90–96; in particular, see the discussion on stack unwinding, p. 91.

- A useful discussion of the *non*algorithmic code-efficiency aspects of declaring a function **noexcept** can be found on StackOverflow; see **pradhan14**.

- Bryce Adelstein Lelbach offers a best-practices approach to macrobenchmarking in **adelstein-lelbach15**.

- Chandler Carruth, in his classic CppCon 2015 talk on microbenchmarking ("Tuning C++: Benchmarks, and CPUs, and Compilers! Oh My!"), gives a detailed, comprehensive treatment of how to isolate and identify root causes of low-level inefficiencies, while avoiding various pitfalls along the way; see **carruth15**.

- Niels Dekker has created an entire project on GitHub dedicated to researching, objectively measuring, and characterizing, on various popular platforms, the (primarily *non*algorithmic) effects on runtime performance — positive and negative — of declaring functions **noexcept**; see **dekker19a**.

- A general discussion of the **zero-cost-exception** model and how it influences effective use of exceptions in modern C++ is provided in **mortoray13**.

- The complete reference for the three levels of the itanium exception API is delineated in **itanium16**.

- A proposal for an alternative zero-cost exception mechanism that attempts to unite the various ways of returning failure status can be found in **sutter19**.

Reference-Qualified Member Functions

Qualifying a non**static** member function with either an **&** or **&&** refines its **signature** based on the **value category** — i.e., *lvalue* or *rvalue*, respectively — of the expression used to evoke it, thus enabling two distinct overloaded implementations of that member function.

Description

C++ has always supported decorating nonstatic member functions with cv-qualifiers and allowed overloading on those qualifiers:

```
struct Class1
{
    void mf1() const;      // (1) const-qualified member function
    void mf2();            // (2) member function with no qualifiers
    void mf2() volatile;   // (3) volatile-qualified overload of (2)
};
void f1()
{
             Class1 uobj;
       const Class1 cobj;
    volatile Class1 vobj;
    uobj.mf1();  // calls function (1)
    cobj.mf1();  // calls function (1)
    uobj.mf2();  // calls overloaded function (2)
    vobj.mf2();  // calls overloaded function (3)
    vobj.mf1();  // Error, no mf1 overload matches a volatile object.
    cobj.mf2();  // Error,  " mf2      "       " const       "
}
```

The **cv-qualifiers**, **const** and **volatile**, optionally appearing after the parameter list of a nonstatic member function prototype apply to the object on which the member is called and allow us to overload on the cv-qualification of that object. Overload resolution will select the closest match whose **cv-qualifiers** are the same as, or more restrictive than, the object's cv-qualification; hence, uobj.mf1() calls a **const**-qualified member even though vu is not **const**. A qualifier cannot be dropped during overload resolution, however, so vobj.mf1() and cobj.mf2() are ill formed.

C++11 introduced a similar feature, adding optional qualifiers that indicate the valid **value categories** for the expression a member function may be invoked on. Declaring a member function overload specifically for *rvalue* expressions, for example, allows library writers to make better use of move semantics. Note that readers of this feature are presumed to be familiar with **value categories** and, in particular, the distinction between *lvalue* and *rvalue* references (see Section 2.1."*Rvalue* References" on page 710):

```
struct Class2
{
    void mf() &;    // (1)
    void mf() &&;   // (2)
};
```

Each member function with a trailing & or && is said to be **ref-qualified**; the trailing & and && tokens are called **ref-qualifiers**. The & ref-qualifier on overload (1), above, restricts that overload to *lvalue* expressions. The && ref-qualifier on overload (2) restricts that overload to *rvalue* expressions:

```
void f2()
{
    Class2 uobj;
    uobj.mf();       // calls overloaded function (1)
    Class2().mf();   // calls overloaded function (2)
}
```

The expression, uobj, is an *lvalue*, so uobj.mf calls the *lvalue*-ref-qualified overload of member, whereas the expression, Class2(), is an *rvalue*, so calling mf on it chooses the *rvalue*-ref-qualified overload.

At the heart of understanding both cv-qualifiers and ref-qualifiers on member functions is recognizing the existence of an implicit parameter by which the class object is passed to the function:

```
class Class3
{
    // ...
public:
    void mf(int) &;          // two parameters: [Class3&      ], int
    void mf(int) &&;         //  "         "    : [Class3&&    ],  "
    void mf(int) const &;    //  "         "    : [const Class3& ],  "
    void mf(int) const &&;   //  "         "    : [const Class3&&],  "
};
```

In each of the four overloads of mf, there is a hidden reference parameter (shown in square brackets in the comments) in addition to the explicitly declared **int** parameter. The qualifiers at the end of the declarator, i.e., after the parameter list, specify the cv-qualifiers and ref-qualifier for this implicit reference. The **this** pointer holds the address of the object passed for this implicit parameter:

```
void Class3::mf(/* [Class3& __self,] */ int i) &
{
    // implicit Class3* const this = &__self
    // ...
}

void Class3::mf(/* [Class3&& __self,] */ int i) &&
```

```
{
    // implicit Class3* const this = &__self
    // ...
}

void Class3::mf(/* [const Class3& __self,] */ int i) const &
{
    // implicit const Class3* const this = &__self
    // ...
}

void Class3::mf(/* [const Class3&& __self,] */ int i) const &&
{
    // implicit const Class3* const this = &__self
    // ...
}
```

For descriptive purposes, we will refer to the implicit reference parameter as __self throughout this section, just as we did in the example above. In reality, this implicit parameter has no name and cannot be accessed from code. The **this** pointer within the function is, therefore, the address of __self. Note that the type of **this** does not reflect whether __self is an *lvalue* reference or an *rvalue* reference; dereferencing a pointer always yields an *lvalue*.

When a member function of an object is called, overload resolution finds the best match for the value category and cv-qualification of all of its arguments, including the implicit __self argument:

```
#include <utility>  // std::move

Class3 makeObj();

void f3()
{
             Class3   uobj;
       const Class3   cobj;
    volatile Class3   vobj;
       const Class3&  clvref = uobj;
             Class3&& rvref = std::move(uobj);  // Note: rvref is an lvalue.

    uobj.mf(0);     // calls mf(int) &
    cobj.mf(0);     // calls mf(int) const &
    vobj.mf(0);     // Error, no overload, mf(int) volatile &
    clvref.mf(0);   // calls mf(int) const &
    rvref.mf(0);    // calls mf(int) &

    makeObj().mf(0);         // calls mf(int) &&
    std::move(uobj).mf(0);   // calls mf(int) &&
    std::move(cobj).mf(0);   // calls mf(int) const &&
}
```

The three objects, uobj, cobj, and vobj, are *lvalues*, so calls to mf will match only the *lvalue* reference overloads, i.e., those with a & ref-qualifier. As always, overload resolution will pick the version of mf that best matches the cv-qualification of the object, without dropping any qualifiers. Thus, the call to cobj.mf(0) selects the **const** overload, whereas the call to vobj.mf(0) is ill formed because all candidate functions would require dropping the **volatile** qualifier. The **const** *lvalue* reference clvref matches the **const** *lvalue*-ref-qualified __self even though the object to which clvref is bound is not **const**. Though declared as an *rvalue* reference, a named reference such as rvref is always an *lvalue* when used in an expression (see Section 2.1."*Rvalue* References" on page 710); hence, rvref.mf(0) calls the non**const** *lvalue*-ref-qualified overload of mf.

The function makeObj returns an *rvalue* of type Class3. When mf is called on that *rvalue*, the non**const** *rvalue* reference overload is selected. The expression std::move(uobj) also binds to an *rvalue* reference and thus selects the same overload. An *rvalue* reference to **const** occurs rarely in production code, but when it does, it is usually the result of calling std::move on a **const** object (e.g., cobj), especially in generic code. Note, however, that a **const** *lvalue* reference can be bound to an *rvalue*; thus, if a matching *rvalue* reference overload is not found and a **const** *lvalue* reference overload exists, then the latter will match an *rvalue* reference to the class object:

```
class Class4
{
    // ...

public:
    void mf1() &;
    void mf1() const &;
    void mf1() &&;
    // no void mf1() const && overload

    void mf2() &;
    void mf2() const &;
    // no void mf2() && overload
    // no void mf2() const && overload
};

void f4()
{
        Class4 uobj;
    const Class4 cobj;

    std::move(cobj).mf1();  // calls mf1() const &
    std::move(uobj).mf2();  // calls mf2() const &
}
```

Syntax and restrictions

A ref-qualifier is an optional part of a nonstatic member function declaration. If present, it must come after any cv-qualifiers and before any exception specification. A constructor or destructor may not have a ref-qualifier:

```
void f1() &;  // Error, ref-qualifier on a nonmember function

class Class1
{
    // ...
public:
    Class1() &&;        // Error, ref-qualifier on constructor
    ~Class1() &;        // Error, ref-qualifier on destructor
    void mf() & const;  // Error, ref-qualifier before cv-qualification
    void mf() noexcept&; // Error, ref-qualifier after exception specification
    void mf() & &&;     // Error, two ref-qualifiers
    static void smf() &; // Error, ref-qualifier on static member function

    void mf(int) const && noexcept;  // OK, ref-qualifier correctly placed
};
```

A member function that does not have a ref-qualifier can be called for *either* an *lvalue* or an *rvalue*. Thus, C++03 code continues to compile and work as before:

```
class Class2 {
    // ...
public:
    void mf();
    void mf() const;
};


const Class2 makeConstClass2();

void f2()
{
        Class2 uobj;
    const Class2 cobj;

    uobj.mf();              // calls mf()
    cobj.mf();              // calls mf() const
    Class2().mf();          // calls mf()
    makeConstClass2().mf(); // calls mf() const
}
```

For a set of overloads having the same name and the same parameter types, ref-qualifiers must be provided for *all* members in that set or for *none* of them:

```cpp
class Class3
{
    // ...
public:
    void mf1(int*);             //
    int  mf1(int*) const &;     // Error, prior mf1(int*) is not ref-qualified.
    int  mf2(int) const;        //
    void mf2(int);              // OK, neither mf2(int) is ref-qualified.
    int&       mf3() &;         //
    const int& mf3() const &;   // OK, all mf3() overloads are ref-qualified.
    int&&      mf3() &&;        //
    void mf4(int);              //
    void mf4(char*) &&;         // OK, mf4(int) and mf4(char*) are different.
    int mf5(int) &;             // OK, not overloaded
    int&& mf6() &&;             // OK, not overloaded
};
```

Note that the overload of `mf1` is ill formed even though the unqualified and ref-qualified versions have different return types and different cv-qualifiers.

Member function templates may also have ref-qualifiers:

```cpp
class Class4
{
    // ...
public:
    template <typename T> Class4&  mf(const T&) &;
    template <typename T> Class4&& mf(const T&) &&;
};
```

Within a member function's body, regardless of whether the member has a `&` ref-qualifier, a `&&` ref-qualifier, or no ref-qualifier at all, uses of `*this` and of any nonstatic data members yield *lvalues*. Although arguably counterintuitive, this behavior is identical to the way that other reference parameters work:

```cpp
#include <cassert>  // standard C assert macro

template <typename T> bool isLvalue(T&)  { return true; }
template <typename T> bool isLvalue(T&&) { return false; }

class Class5
{
    int d_data;
public:
    void mf(int&& arg) &&
    {
```

```
        assert(isLvalue(arg));      // OK, named reference is an lvalue.
        assert(isLvalue(*this));    // OK, pointer dereference is an lvalue.
        assert(isLvalue(d_data));   // OK, member of an lvalue is an lvalue.
    }

    void mf(int& arg) &
    {
        assert(isLvalue(arg));      // OK, named reference is an lvalue.
        assert(isLvalue(*this));    // OK, pointer dereference is an lvalue.
        assert(isLvalue(d_data));   // OK, member of an lvalue is an lvalue.
    }
};
```

If a member function calls another member function on the same object, only the *lvalue*-ref-qualified overloads are considered:

```
#include <cassert>  // standard C assert macro

struct Class6
{
    bool mf1() &  { return false; }  // Return false if called on lvalue.
    bool mf1() && { return true; }   //    "   true  "    "    " rvalue.

    void mf2() && { assert(!mf1()); }  // calls lvalue overload
};
```

Function `mf2`, although *rvalue*-ref-qualified, nevertheless calls the *lvalue*-ref-qualified overload of `mf1` because *`this`* is an *lvalue*. If the desired behavior is to propagate the **value** category of the object on which it was called, `std::move` (or another reference cast) must be used:

```
class Class7
{
    int d_data;

public:
    bool mf1() &  { return false; }  // Return false if called on lvalue.
    bool mf1() && { return true; }   //    "   true  "    "    " rvalue.

    void mf2(int&& arg) &&
    {
        assert(!isLvalue(std::move(arg)));
        assert(!isLvalue(std::move(*this)));
        assert(!isLvalue(std::move(d_data)));

        assert(std::move(*this).mf1());
    }
};
```

Each call to std::move in the example above *reconstitutes* the value category of the original object. Note that we must mention ***this** explicitly in order to call the *rvalue*-ref-qualified overload of mf1.

The ref-qualifier, if any, is part of a member function's signature and is, therefore, part of its type and the type of a corresponding pointer to member function:

```
struct Class8
{
    void mf1(int) &;    // (1)
    void mf1(int) &&;   // (2)

    void mf2(int);      // (3)
};

using Plqf = void (Class8::*)(int)&;    // pointer to lvalue-ref-qualified function
using Prqf = void (Class8::*)(int)&&;   //    "     "  rvalue-ref-qualified     "
using Puqf = void (Class8::*)(int);     //    "     "  unqualified              "

void f8()
{
    Plqf lq = &Class8::mf1;  // OK, pointer to member function (1)
    Prqf rq = &Class8::mf1;  // OK,    "      "      "        "      (2)
    Puqf xq = &Class8::mf1;  // Error, mf1 is ref-qualified but Puqf is not.

    Puqf uq = &Class8::mf2;  // OK, pointer to member function (3)
    Plqf yq = &Class8::mf2;  // Error, mf2 is not ref-qualified but Plqf is.

    Class8 v;
    (v.*lq)(0);              // calls v.mf1(int), overload (1)
    (Class8().*rq)(1);       // calls Class8().mf1(int), overload (2)
    (v.*rq)(2);              // Error, rq expects an rvalue object.
}
```

Note that Plqf, Prqf, and Puqf are three different, mutually incompatible, types that reflect the ref-qualifier of the member function they each point to.

Use Cases

Returning a subobject of an *rvalue*

Many classes provide accessors that return a reference to a member of the class. We can gain performance benefits if those accessors returned *rvalue* references when called on an *rvalue* object:

```
#include <string> // std::string
#include <utility> // std::move
```

```
class RedString
{
    std::string d_value;

public:
    RedString(const char* s = "") : d_value("Red: ") { d_value += s; }

          std::string&  value() &        { return d_value; }
    const std::string&  value() const & { return d_value; }
          std::string&& value() &&       { return std::move(d_value); }
    // Note that this third overload returns std::string by rvalue reference.

    // ...
};

void f1()
{
        RedString urs("hello");
    const RedString crs("world");

    std::string h1 = urs.value();                    // "Red: hello"
    std::string h2 = crs.value();                    // "Red: world"
    std::string h3 = RedString("goodbye").value();  // "Red: goodbye"

    std::string h4 = std::move(urs).value();         // "Red: hello"
    std::string h5 = urs.value();                    // Bug, unspecified value

    std::string h6 = std::move(crs).value();         // "Red: world"
    std::string h7 = crs.value();                    // OK, "Red: world"
}
```

The `RedString` class provides three ref-qualified overloads of `value`. When `value` is called on `urs` and `crs`, the non**const** and **const** *lvalue*-ref-qualified overloads, respectively, are selected. Both overloads return an *lvalue* reference to `std::string`, so `h1` and `h2` are constructed using the copy constructor, as usual. In the case of the temporary variable created by `RedString("goodbye")`, however, the *rvalue*-ref-qualified overload of `value` is selected. This overload returns an *rvalue* reference, so `h3` is constructed using the move constructor, which might be more efficient.

As in the case of most such code, it is assumed that an *rvalue* reference refers to an object whose state no longer matters after evaluation of the expression. When that assumption doesn't hold, unexpected results may occur, as in the case of `h5`, which is initialized from a moved-from string, yielding a valid but unspecified string value.

The `value` member function is not overloaded for a **const** *rvalue*-ref-qualified object. Invoking it for such a (rarely encountered) type selects the **const** *lvalue*-ref-qualified overload, as *rvalues* can always be bound to **const** *lvalue* references. As a result, `h6` is initialized from a **const** `std::string&`, invoking the copy constructor and leaving `crs` unmodified.

One downside of this design is that the reference returned from the *rvalue*-ref-qualified overload could outlive the RedString object:

```cpp
void f2()
{
    std::string&& s1 = RedString("goodbye").value();
    char c1 = s1[0];  // Bug, s1 refers to a destroyed string.

    const std::string& s2 = RedString("goodbye").value();
    char c2 = s2[0]; // Bug, s2 refers to a destroyed string too.
}
```

The temporary variable created by the expression RedString("goodbye") is destroyed at the end of the statement; **lifetime extension** does not come into play because s is not bound to the temporary object itself, but to a reference returned by the value member function. Returning a dangling reference can be avoided by returning by *value* rather than by reference:

```cpp
class BlueString
{
    std::string d_value;

public:
    BlueString(const char* s = "") : d_value("Blue: ") { d_value += s; }

          std::string& value() &        { return d_value; }
    const std::string& value() const & { return d_value; }
          std::string  value() &&       { return std::move(d_value); }
    // Note that this third overload returns std::string by value.

    // ...
};

void f3()
{
    std::string s1 = BlueString("hello").value();

    std::string&& s2 = BlueString("goodbye").value();
    char c = s2[0];  // OK, lifetime of s has been extended.
}
```

The expression BlueString("hello").value() yields a temporary std::string initialized via move-construction from the member variable d_value. The variable s1 is, in turn, move-constructed from that temporary. Compared to the RedString version of value that returned an *rvalue* reference, this sequence logically has one extra move operation (two move-constructor calls instead of one). This extra move does not pose a problem in practice because (a) move construction of `std::string` objects is cheap and (b) most compilers will *elide* the extra move anyway, yielding equivalent code to the `RedString` case.[1]

Similarly, the expression `BlueString("goodbye").value()` yields a temporary `std::string`, but in this case the temporary variable is bound to the reference, `s2`, which extends its lifetime until `s` goes out of scope. Thus, `s2[0]` safely indexes a string that is still live.

Note one more, rather subtle, difference between the behavior of `value` for `RedString` versus `BlueString`:

```
void f4()
{
    RedString  rs("hello");
    BlueString bs("hello");

    std::move(rs).value();   // rs.d_value is unchanged.
    std::move(bs).value();   // bs.d_value is moved from.
}
```

Calling `value` on an *rvalue* of type `RedString` doesn't actually change the value of `d_value`; it is not until the returned *rvalue* reference is actually used (e.g., in a move constructor) that `d_value` is changed. Thus, if the return value is ignored, nothing happens. Conversely, for `BlueString`, the return of `value` is always a move-constructed temporary `std::string` object, causing `d_value` to end up in a moved-from state, even if the return value is ultimately ignored. This difference in behavior is seldom important in practice, as reasonable code will assume nothing about the value of a variable after it was used as the argument to `std::move`.

Forbidding modifying operations on *rvalues*

Modifying an *rvalue* means modifying a temporary object that is about to be destroyed. A common example of a defect resulting from this behavior is accidental assignment to a temporary object. Consider a simple `Employee` class with a `name` accessor and a function that attempts to set the name:

```
#include <string>   // std::string

class Employee
{
public:
    // ...
    std::string name() const;
    // ...
};
```

---

[1]Beginning with C++17, the description of the way return values are initialized changed so as to no longer **materialize** a temporary variable in this situation. This change is sometimes referred to as **guaranteed copy elision** because, in addition to defining a more consistent and portable semantic, it effectively legislates the optimization that was previously optional.

```
void f1(Employee& e)
{
    e.name() = "Fred";
}
```

The author of f1 in the example above might have incorrectly assumed that the assignment to e.name() would result in updating the name of the Employee object referenced by e. Instead, it modifies the temporary string returned by e.name(), which has no effect.

One way to prevent these sorts of accidents is to design a class interface with ref-qualified modifiers that are callable only for non**const** *lvalues*:

```
class Name
{
    std::string d_value;

public:
    Name() = default;
    Name(const char* s) : d_value(s) {}
    Name(const Name&) = default;
    Name(Name&&) = default;

    Name& operator=(const Name&) & = default;  // lvalue-ref-qualified
    Name& operator=(Name&&) &     = default;  // lvalue-ref-qualified
    // ...
};
```

Note that both the copy- and move-assignment operators for Name are ref-qualified for *lvalues* only. Overload resolution will not find an appropriate match for assignment to an *rvalue* of type Name:

```
class Employee2
{
    Name d_name;

public:
    // ...
    Name name() const { return d_name; }
    // ...
};

void f2(Employee2& e)
{
    e.name() = "Fred";  // Error, cannot assign to rvalue of type Name
}
```

Now, assignment to the temporary returned by e.name() fails to find a matching assignment operator, so the accidental assignment is supplanted by an error message. The same approach can be used to avoid many other accidental modifications on *rvalues*, including inserting elements, erasing elements, etc. Note, however, that modifying a temporary is not always a defect; see *Potential Pitfalls — Forbidding modifications to rvalues breaks legitimate use cases* on page 1170.

Forbidding operations on *lvalues*

If an instance of a class is intended to exist only for the duration of a single expression, then disabling most operations on *lvalues* of that type might be desirable. For example, an object of type `LockedStream`, below, works like an `std::ostream` except that it acquires a mutex for the duration of a single streaming expression:

```cpp
#include <cassert>   // standard C assert macro
#include <iostream>  // std::ostream, std::cout, std::endl
#include <mutex>     // std::mutex

class LockedStream {
    std::ostream&                 d_os;
    std::unique_lock<std::mutex> d_lock;

public:
    LockedStream(std::ostream& os, std::mutex& mutex)
    : d_os(os)
    , d_lock(mutex)
    {
    }

    LockedStream(LockedStream&& other) = default;
    ~LockedStream()                    = default;

    LockedStream(const LockedStream&)             = delete;
    LockedStream& operator=(const LockedStream&)  = delete;
    LockedStream& operator=(LockedStream&&)       = delete;

    template <typename T>
    LockedStream operator<<(const T& value) &&  // rvalue-ref-qualified
    {
        assert(d_lock.owns_lock());  // assert *this is not in moved-from state.
        d_os << value;
        return std::move(*this);
    }
};
```

A `LockedStream` is a **move-only** (noncopyable), nonassignable type that holds a reference to an output stream, `d_os`, and the `d_lock` member of type `std::unique_lock` provided by the Standard Library. The defaulted move constructor of `LockedStream` simply move constructs `d_lock`, which transfers the ownership of the locked mutex to the newly constructed object. Upon destruction, the `d_lock` member unlocks the mutex if it owns it and does nothing otherwise. Finally, the streaming operator, **operator**<<, that can be invoked only on an *rvalue* outputs to the stored `std::ostream` and then returns ***this** by move construction. Therefore, when streaming operators are chained, all of them will be protected by the locked mutex, with the last `LockedStream` in the chain automatically unlocking it:

```cpp
std::mutex coutMutex;  // mutex for std::cout

void f1()
{
    LockedStream(std::cout, coutMutex) << "Hello, " << 2021 << '\n';

    LockedStream ls(std::cout, coutMutex);
    ls << 2021;  // Error, can't stream to lvalue
}
```

Similar code in other threads can concurrently print to a `LockedStream` protected by `coutMutex`, and the locking protocol will prevent them from creating a data race. The first statement in `f1` acquires the lock, prints `"Hello, 2021"` followed by a newline, and then releases the lock automatically. An attempt to break this sequence into multiple statements fails because an *lvalue* of type `LockedStream` cannot be used for streaming.

Note that this idiom is intended to protect the user from casual errors only. Local variables of type `LockedStream` can be created, initialized, and — with creative use of `std::move` — even streamed to.

To use `LockedStream` directly, we need to construct a temporary object of `LockedStream`, which requires always supplying the stream with the correct corresponding mutex. Instead, for convenience and to avoid potential defects, we can create a class, `LockableStream`, which associates the two:

```cpp
class LockableStream {
    std::ostream& d_os;
    std::mutex    d_mutex;

public:
    LockableStream(std::ostream& os)
    : d_os(os)
    {
    }

    template <typename T>
    LockedStream operator<<(const T& value)
    {
        return LockedStream(d_os, d_mutex) << value;
    }
};
```

A `LockableStream` holds a reference to an `std::ostream` object and an `std::mutex`. The streaming operator, **operator**<<, constructs a `LockedStream` object and delegates the actual streaming operation to the `LockedStream`. The return value of **operator**<< is an *rvalue* of type `LockedStream`. We can then create a `LockableStream`, supplying it only with the wrapped `std::ostream`, and print to it:

```
LockableStream lockableCout(std::cout);

void f2()
{
    lockableCout << "Hello, " << 2021 << '\n';
}
```

Optimizing immutable types and builder classes

An **immutable type** is a type that has no modifying operations. Among other benefits, the representation of an **immutable type** can be shared by all objects that have the same value, including in concurrent threads. Every object that logically "modifies" an object of **immutable type** does so by returning a new object having the modified value; the original object remains unchanged. An `ImmutableString` class, for example, might have an `insert` member function that takes a second string argument and returns a copy of the original string with the second string inserted in the specified location:

```
#include <memory>    // std::shared_ptr
#include <string>    // std::string
#include <iostream>  // std::ostream, std::cout, std::endl

class ImmutableString
{
    std::shared_ptr<std::string> d_dataPtr;

    static const std::string s_emptyString;

public:
    using size_type = std::string::size_type;

    ImmutableString() {}

    ImmutableString(const char* s)
        : d_dataPtr(std::make_shared<std::string>(s)) { }

    ImmutableString(std::string s)
        : d_dataPtr(std::make_shared<std::string>(std::move(s))) { }

    ImmutableString& operator=(const ImmutableString&) = delete;
```

```
    ImmutableString insert(size_type pos, const ImmutableString& s) const
    {
        std::string dataCopy(asStdString());       // Copy string from this object.
        dataCopy.insert(pos, s.asStdString());     // Do insert.
        return std::move(dataCopy);                // Move into return value.
    }

    const std::string& asStdString() const
    {
        return d_dataPtr ? *d_dataPtr : s_emptyString;
    }

    friend std::ostream& operator<<(std::ostream& os, const ImmutableString& s)
    {
        return os << s.asStdString();
    }
    // ...
};

const std::string ImmutableString::s_emptyString;
```

The internal representation of an `ImmutableString` is an `std::string` object allocated on the heap and accessed via an instantiation of the C++ Standard reference-counted smart pointer, `std::shared_ptr`. The copy and move constructors and assignment operators are defaulted; when an `ImmutableString` is copied or moved, only the smart pointer member is affected. Thus, even large string values can be copied in constant time.

The `insert` member function begins by making a copy of the *internal representation* of the immutable string. The copy is modified and then returned; the representation in the original `ImmutableString` is not modified:

```
void f1()
{
    ImmutableString is("hello world");
    std::cout << is << std::endl;                // Print "hello world".
    std::cout << is.insert(5, ",") << std::endl; // Print "hello, world".
    std::cout << is << std::endl;                // Print "hello world".
}
```

Immutable types are often paired with *builder* classes — mutable types that are used to "build up" a value, which is then "frozen" into an object of the immutable type. Let's define a `StringBuilder` class with mutating `append` and `erase` member functions that modify its internal state, and a conversion operator that returns an `ImmutableString` containing the built-up value:

```
class StringBuilder
{
    std::string d_string;
```

```
public:
    using size_type = std::string::size_type;

    StringBuilder&  append(const char* s) &  { d_string += s; return *this; }
    StringBuilder&& append(const char* s) && { return std::move(append(s)); }

    StringBuilder&  erase(size_type pos, size_type n) &
    {
        d_string.erase(pos, n);
        return *this;
    }
    StringBuilder&& erase(size_type pos, size_type n) &&
    {
        return std::move(erase(pos, n));
    }

    operator ImmutableString() && { return std::move(d_string); }
};
```

The `append` and `erase` member functions are each ref-qualified and overloaded for both
lvalues and *rvalues*. The only difference between the overloads is that the *lvalue* overloads
each return an *lvalue* reference and the *rvalue* overloads each return an *rvalue* reference. In
fact, in each case, the *rvalue* overload simply calls the corresponding *lvalue* overload and then
calls `std::move` on the result. This technique works and does not cause infinite recursion
within the *rvalue* overload, because `*this` is always an *lvalue*, just as a parameter of *rvalue*
reference is always an *lvalue* within a function.

The operator to convert from `StringBuilder` to `ImmutableString` is *destructive* in that it
moves the built-up value out of the builder into the returned string. The conversion operator
is ref-qualified for *rvalue* references only — if the builder is not an *rvalue*, then the user
must invoke `std::move` on it explicitly. This protocol acts a signal to the future maintainer
that the builder object is in a moved-from state after the conversion and cannot be reused
after its value has been extracted:

```
void f2()
{
    StringBuilder builder;
    builder.append("apples, pears, bananas");
    builder.erase(8, 7);
    ImmutableString s1 = builder;                // Error, can't convert lvalue
    ImmutableString s2 = std::move(builder);     // OK, convert rvalue reference.
    std::cout << s2 << std::endl;                // Print "apples, bananas".

    ImmutableString s3 = StringBuilder()         // Modify builder rvalue.
        .append("apples, pears, bananas")
        .erase(8, 7);                            // OK, convert pure rvalue.
    std::cout << s3 << std::endl;                // Print "apples, bananas".
}
```

The `builder` object is an *lvalue* and is intended to be modified several times before yielding a built-up `ImmutableString` value. After it is modified using `append` and `erase` — selecting the *lvalue* overloads in both cases — attempting to convert it directly to `ImmutableString` fails because there is no such conversion from an *lvalue* `builder`. The initialization of `s2`, conversely, succeeds, *moving* the value from the `StringBuilder` into the result.

The expression `StringBuilder()` constructs an *rvalue*, which is then modified by a chain of calls to `append` and `erase`. The *rvalue* overload of `append` is selected, which returns an *rvalue* reference that, in turn, drives the selection of the *rvalue* overload of `erase`. Because the result of the chain of modifiers is an *rvalue* reference, **operator** `ImmutableString` can be invoked without calling `std::move`. This usage is safe because the temporary `StringBuilder` object is destroyed immediately afterward, so there is no opportunity for improperly reusing the builder object.

Potential Pitfalls

Forbidding modifications to *rvalues* breaks legitimate use cases

An earlier use case, *Use Cases — Forbidding modifying operations on rvalues* on page 1163, is also the subject of a potential pitfall. Consider a string class with a `toLower` modifier member function:

```
class String
{
public:
    // ...
    String& toLower();
        // Convert all uppercase letters to lowercase, then return modified
        // *this object.
};

String x;    // variable of type String
String f();  // function returning String

void test()
{
    String& a = x.toLower();   // OK, a refers to x.
    f().toLower();             // Defect (1), modifies temporary variable; no-op
    String& b = f().toLower(); // Defect (2), b is a dangling reference.
}
```

Defect (1) arises from the statement modifying a temp variable and hence having no effect. Defect (2) results from `toLower` unintentionally acting as an *rvalue-to-lvalue* reference cast because it returns an *lvalue* reference to a possibly *rvalue* object. The *lvalue* reference, `b`, is bound to the modified temporary `String` returned by `f()`, after it is modified by `toLower`. At the end of the statement, the temporary object is destroyed, causing **b** to become a **dangling reference**.

Given these issues, it is tempting to add a ref-qualifier to `toLower` so that it can be called only on *lvalues*:

```
class String
{
public:
    // ...
    String& toLower() &;
};
```

Although this ref-qualification prevents do-nothing modifications to a temporary `String`, it also prevents legitimate uses of `toLower` on an *rvalue*:

```
String c = f().toLower();  // Error, toLower cannot be called on an rvalue.
```

Here, the return value of `toLower` would be used to initialize **c** to a copy of the modified `String`. Unfortunately, we've prohibited calling `toLower` with an *rvalue*, so the call is ill formed. This pitfall might manifest any time we suppress modification of *rvalues* for a member function that returns a value or has a side effect.

We could, of course, create ref-qualified overloads for *both lvalue* and *rvalue* objects, returning by *lvalue* reference or *by value*, respectively, as we saw in the `BlueString` class in *Use Cases — Returning a subobject of an rvalue* on page 1160, but doing so ubiquitously can be costly; see *Annoyances — Providing ref-qualified overloads may be a maintenance burden* below.

Annoyances

Providing ref-qualified overloads may be a maintenance burden

Having two or more ref-qualified overloads of a member function can confer expressiveness and safety to a class. The trade-off is that these overloads expand the class interface and usually require code duplication, which can become a maintenance burden:

```
#include <string>  // std::string
#include <vector>  // std::vector

class Thing
{
    std::string     d_name;
    std::vector<int> d_data;
    // ...
```

```
public
:
    // ...

    const std::string& name() const & { return d_name; }
          std::string  name() &&       { return std::move(d_name); }

          std::vector<int>& data() &       { return d_data; }
    const std::vector<int>& data() const & { return d_data; }
          std::vector<int>&& data() &&      { return std::move(d_data); }

    Thing& rename(const std::string& n) & { d_name = n; return *this; }
    Thing& rename(std::string&& n) & { d_name = std::move(n); return *this; }
    Thing  rename(const std::string& n) &&
    {
        d_name = n;
        return *this;  // Bug, should be return std::move(*this)
    }
    Thing  rename(std::string&& n) &&
    {
        return std::move(rename(std::move(n)));  // Delegate to lvalue overload.
    }
};
```

The name member function is a classic accessor. Overloading it based on ref-qualification provides an optimization so that the d_name string can be moved instead of copied when the Thing object is expiring. Because it is an accessor, only the **const** *lvalue* and non**const** *rvalue* overloads are needed; other cv-qualifications do not make sense.

A modifiable Thing object can be mutated via the return type of its data member function, but a **const** Thing cannot. We are accustomed to overloading based on **const**, but adding ref-qualification doubles the number of overload combinations.

Finally, the rename member function illustrates a different kind of combinatorial overload set. This member function is overloaded on the value category of both the Thing argument and the n argument. In addition to the total number of overloads for a single function, this example illustrates a potential performance bug that occurs easily when copying and pasting numerous similar function bodies: by returning *this instead of std::move(*this) in the first *rvalue*-ref-qualified overload, the return value is copy constructed instead of move constructed.

One way to mitigate the maintenance burden of having many overloads is for the *rvalue*-ref-qualified overloads to delegate to the *lvalue*-ref-qualified ones, as seen in the last *rvalue*-ref-qualified overload of rename. Note that *this is *always* an *lvalue*, even within the *rvalue*-ref-qualified overloads, so the call to rename within the *rvalue*-ref-qualified version does not result in a recursive call to itself but instead results in a call to the *lvalue*-ref-qualified version.

See Also

- "*Rvalue* References" (§2.1, p. 710) details the inner workings of references that can bind to *rvalue* expressions only.

Further Reading

- For a discussion of the interaction between **override** and reference-qualified member functions, see **meyers15b**, "Item 12: Declare overriding functions `override`," pp. 79–85.

Unions Having Non-Trivial Members

Any nonreference type is permitted to be a member of a **union**.

Description

Prior to C++11, only **trivial types** — e.g., **fundamental types**, such as **int** and **double**, enumerated or pointer types, or a C-style array or **struct** (a.k.a. a POD) — were allowed to be members of a **union**. This limitation prevented any user-defined type having a **non-trivial special member function** from being a member of a **union**:

```
union U0
{
    int        d_i;  // OK
    std::string d_s;  // compile-time error in C++03 (OK as of C++11)
};
```

C++11 relaxes such restrictions on **union** members, such as d_s above, allowing any type other than a **reference type** to be a member of a **union**.

A **union** type is permitted to have user-defined special member functions but — by design — does not initialize any of its members automatically. Any member of a **union** having a **non-trivial constructor**, such as **struct** Nt below, must be constructed manually (e.g., via **placement new**) before it can be used:

```
struct Nt  // used as part of a union (below)
{
    Nt();   // non-trivial default constructor
    ~Nt();  // non-trivial destructor

    // Copy construction and assignment are implicitly defaulted.
    // Move construction and assignment are implicitly deleted.
};
```

As an added safety measure, any non-trivial **special member function** defined — either implicitly or explicitly — for any **member** of a **union** results in the compiler implicitly deleting (see "Deleted Functions" on page 53) the corresponding special member function of the **union** itself:

```
union U1
{
    int d_i;   // fundamental type having all trivial special member functions
    Nt  d_nt;  // user-defined type having non-trivial special member functions
```

```
    // Implicitly deleted special member functions of U1:
    /*
        U1()                         = delete; // due to explicit Nt::Nt()
        U1(const U1&)                = delete; // due to implicit Nt::Nt(const Nt&)
        ~U1()                        = delete; // due to explicit Nt::~Nt()
        U1& operator=(const U1&) = delete; // due to implicit
                                            //    Nt::operator=(const Nt&)
    */
};
```

A special member function of a **union** that is implicitly deleted can be restored via explicit declaration, thereby forcing a programmer to consider how non-trivial members should be managed. For example, we can start providing a *value constructor* and corresponding *destructor*:

```
#include <new>   // placement new

struct U2
{
    union
    {
        int   d_i;    // fundamental type (trivial)
        Nt    d_nt;   // non-trivial user-defined type
    };

    bool d_useInt;   // discriminator

    U2(bool useInt) : d_useInt(useInt)
    {
        if (d_useInt) { new (&d_i) int(); }   // value initialized (to 0)
        else          { new (&d_nt) Nt(); }   // default constructed in place
    }

    ~U2()   // destructor
    {
        if (!d_useInt) { d_nt.~Nt(); }
    }
};
```

Notice that we have employed **placement new** syntax to control the lifetime of both member objects. Although assignment would be permitted for the trivial **int** type, it would be **undefined behavior** for the non-trivial Nt type:

```
    U2(bool useInt) : d_useInt(useInt)
    {
        if (d_useInt) { d_i = int(); }  // value initialized (to 0)
        else          { d_nt = Nt(); }  // BAD IDEA: undefined behavior (no
                                        // lhs object)

    }
```

Now if we were to try to copy-construct or assign one object of type U2 to another, the
operation would fail because we have not yet specifically addressed those **special member**
functions:

```
void f()
{
    U2 a(false), b(true);  // OK (construct both instances of U2)
    U2 c(a);               // Error, no U2(const U2&)
    a = b;                 // Error, no U2& operator=(const U2&)
}
```

We can restore these implicitly deleted special member functions too, simply by adding
appropriate copy-constructor and assignment-operator definitions for U2 explicitly:

```
class U2
{
    // ... (everything in U2 above)

    U2(const U2& original) : d_useInt(original.d_useInt)
    {
        if (d_useInt) { new (&d_i) int(original.d_i);  }
        else          { new (&d_nt) Nt(original.d_nt); }
    }

    U2& operator=(const U2& rhs)
    {
        if (this == &rhs) // Prevent self-assignment.
        {
            return *this;
        }

        // Resolve all possible combinations of active types between the
        // left-hand side and right-hand side of the assignment:

        if (d_useInt)
        {
            if (rhs.d_useInt) { d_i = rhs.d_i; }
            else              { new (&d_nt) Nt(rhs.d_nt); }  // int DTOR trivial
        }
        else
```

```
    {
        if (rhs.d_useInt) { d_nt.~Nt(); new (&d_i) int(rhs.d_i); }
        else              { d_nt = rhs.d_nt; }
    } d_useInt = rhs.d_useInt;

    // Resolve all possible combinations of active types between the
    // left-hand side and right-hand side of the assignment. Use the
    // corresponding assignment operator when they match; otherwise,
    // if the old member is d_nt, run its non-trivial destructor, and
    // then copy-construct the new member in place:

        return *this;
    }
};
```

Note that in the code example above, we ignore exceptions for exposition simplicity. Note also that attempting to restore a **union**'s implicitly deleted special member functions by using the =**default** syntax (see Section 1.1."Defaulted Functions" on page 33) will still result in their being deleted because the compiler cannot know which member of the union is active.

Use Cases

Implementing a sum type as a discriminated union

A **sum type** is an algebraic data type that provides a choice among a fixed set of specific types. A C++11 unrestricted union can serve as a convenient and efficient way to define storage for a sum type (also called a *tagged* or *discriminated* union) because the alignment and size calculations are performed automatically by the compiler.

As an example, consider writing a parsing function parseInteger that, given an std::string input, will return, as a **sum type** ParseResult (see below), containing either an **int** result (on success) or an informative error message on failure:

```
ParseResult parseInteger(const std::string& input)  // Return a sum type.
{
    int result;     // Accumulate result as we go.
    std::size_t i;  // current character index

    // ...

    if (/* Failure case (1). */)
    {
        std::ostringstream oss;
        oss << "Found non-numerical character '" << input[i]
            << "' at index '" << i << "'.";
```

```
        return ParseResult(oss.str());
    }

    if (/* Failure case (2). */)
    {
        std::ostringstream oss;
        oss << "Accumulating '" << input[i]
            << "' at index '" << i
            << "' into the current running total '" << result
            << "' would result in integer overflow.";

        return ParseResult(oss.str());
    }

    // ...

    return ParseResult(result);  // Success!
}
```

The implementation above relies on `ParseResult` being able to hold a value of type either
`int` or `std::string`. By encapsulating a C++ **union** and a *discriminator* as part of the
`ParseResult` sum type, we can achieve the desired semantics:

```
class ParseResult
{
    union  // storage for either the result or the error
    {
        int         d_value; // result type (trivial)
        std::string d_error; // error  type (non-trivial)
    };

    bool d_isError;  // discriminator

public:
    explicit ParseResult(int value);              // value constructor (1)
    explicit ParseResult(const std::string& error);  // value constructor (2)

    ParseResult(const ParseResult& rhs);          // copy constructor
    ParseResult& operator=(const ParseResult& rhs);  // copy assignment

    ~ParseResult();                               // destructor
};
```

If a **sum type** comprised more than two types, the discriminator would be an appropriately
sized integral or enumerated type instead of a Boolean.

As discussed in *Description* on page 1174, having a non-trivial type within a **union** forces the programmer to provide each desired special member function and define it manually; note that the use of placement **new** is not required for either of the two *value constructors* (above) because the initializer syntax (below) is sufficient to begin the lifetime of even a non-trivial object:

```
ParseResult::ParseResult(int value) : d_value(value), d_isError(false)
{
}

ParseResult::ParseResult(const std::string& error)
    : d_error(error), d_isError(true)
    // Note that placement new was not necessary here because a new
    // std::string object will be created as part of the initialization of
    // d_error.
{
}
```

Placement **new** and explicit destructor calls are still, however, required for destruction and both copy operations[1]:

```
ParseResult::~ParseResult()
{
    if (d_isError)
    {
        d_error.std::string::~string();
            // An explicit destructor call is required for d_error because its
            // destructor is non-trivial.
    }
}

ParseResult::ParseResult(const ParseResult& rhs) : d_isError(rhs.d_isError)
{
    if (d_isError)
    {
        new (&d_error) std::string(rhs.d_error);
            // Placement new is necessary here to begin the lifetime of a
            // std::string object at the address of d_error.
    }
    else
    {
        d_value = rhs.d_value;
            // Placement new is not necessary here as int is a trivial type.
    }
}
```

---

[1]For more information on initiating the lifetime of an object, see **iso14**, section 3.8, "Object Lifetime," pp. 66–69.

```
ParseResult& ParseResult::operator=(const ParseResult& rhs)
{
    if (this == &rhs) // Prevent self-assignment.
    {
        return *this;
    }
    // Destroy lhs's error string if existent:
    if (d_isError) { d_error.std::string::~string(); }

    // Copy rhs's object:
    if (rhs.d_isError) { new (&d_error) std::string(rhs.d_error); }
    else               { d_value = rhs.d_value; }

    d_isError = rhs.d_isError;
    return *this;
}
```

In practice, ParseResult would typically use a more general sum type[2] abstraction to support arbitrary value types and provide proper exception safety.

Potential Pitfalls

Inadvertent misuse can lead to latent undefined behavior at runtime

When implementing a type that makes use of an unrestricted union, forgetting to initialize a non-trivial object (using either a *member initializer list* or placement **new**) or accessing a different object than the one that was actually initialized can result in tacit **undefined behavior**. Although forgetting to destroy an object does not necessarily result in **undefined behavior**, failing to do so for any object that manages a resource such as dynamic memory will result in a *resource leak* and/or lead to unintended behavior. Note that destroying an object having a trivial destructor is never necessary; there are, however, rare cases where we may choose not to destroy an object having a non-trivial one.

---

[2]std::variant, introduced in C++17, is the standard construct used to represent a sum type as a *discriminated union*. Prior to C++17, boost::variant was the most widely used *tagged* union implementation of a sum type.

See Also

- "Deleted Functions" (§1.1, p. 53) expounds on what it means for a special member function of a **union** that corresponds to a non**trivial** one in any of its base classes or non**static** data members to be implicitly deleted.

Further Reading

- The original proposal extending the semantics of a **union** — detailing its motivation and providing standard wording for C++11 — can be found in **goldthwaite07**.

- A demonstration of (1) how unrestricted unions in C++11 enable implementation of **sum types** for arbitrary user-defined types and (2) why C++17's std::variant Standard Library component is still sorely needed can be found in **ouellet16**.

Function (auto) Return-Type Deduction

The return type of a function can be deduced from the **return** statements in its definition
if a **placeholder** (e.g., **auto**) is used in place of the return type in the function's prototype.

Description

C++11 provides a limited capability for determining the return type of a function from the
function's arguments using the **decltype** operator (see Section 1.1."**decltype**" on page 25),
typically in a trailing return type (see Section 1.1."Trailing Return" on page 124):

```
template <typename Container, typename Key>
auto search11(const Container& c, const Key& k) -> decltype(c.find(k))
{
    return c.find(k);
}
```

Note that the trailing return type specification effectively repeats the entire implementation
of the function template. As of C++14, the return type of a function can instead be deduced
directly from the **return** statement(s) inside the function definition:

```
template <typename Container, typename Key>
auto search14(const Container& c, const Key& k)
{
    return c.find(k);  // Return type is deduced here.
}
```

The return type of the search14 function template defined above is determined by the type
of the expression c.find(k). This feature provides a useful shorthand for return types that
are difficult to name or would add unnecessary clutter. The deduced return types feature in
C++14 is an extension of a similar feature already available for **lambda expressions**
in C++11:

```
auto iadd1 = [](int i, int j) { return i + j; };  // valid since C++11
auto iadd2(int i, int j)      { return i + j; }  // valid since C++14
```

Note that this use of **auto** is distinct from using **auto** with a trailing return type:

```
auto a()            { return 1; }  // deduced return type int
auto b() -> double { return 1; }  // specified return type double
```

Specification

When a function's return type is specified using **auto** with no trailing return type or using
decltype(auto), the return type of the function is deduced from the **return** statement(s)

in the function body following the same rules as for deducing a variable declaration from its initializer expression (see Section 2.1."**auto** Variables" on page 195 and Section 3.2. "**decltype(auto)**" on page 1205):

```
class C1 { /*...*/ };

C1   c;
C1   f1();
C1&  f2();
C1&& f3();

auto           v1 = c;              // deduced type C1
auto           g1() { return c; }   //    "    return type C1

decltype(auto) v2 = c;              //    "    type C1
decltype(auto) g2() { return c; }   //    "    return type C1

auto           v3 = (c);            //    "    type C1
auto           g3() { return (c); } //    "    return type C1

decltype(auto) v4 = (c);            //    "    type C1&
decltype(auto) g4() { return (c); } //    "    return type C1&

auto           v5 = f1();           //    "    type C1
auto           g5() { return f1(); } //   "    return type C1

decltype(auto) v6 = f1();           //    "    type C1
decltype(auto) g6() { return f1(); } //   "    return type C1

auto           v7 = f2();           //    "    type C1
auto           g7() { return f2(); } //   "    return type C1

decltype(auto) v8 = f2();           //    "    type C1&
decltype(auto) g8() { return f2(); } //   "    return type C1&

auto           v9 = f3();           //    "    type C1
auto           g9() { return f3(); } //   "    return type C1

decltype(auto) v10 = f3();          //    "    type C1&&
decltype(auto) g10() { return f3(); } //  "    return type C1&&
```

As with variable declarations, **auto** (but not **decltype(auto)**) can be cv-qualified and decorated to form a reference, pointer, pointer-to-function, reference-to-function, or pointer-to-member function:

```
const auto  g11() { return c; }  // return type const C1
auto&       g12() { return c; }  //   "     "  C1&
const auto& g13() { return c; }  //   "     "  const C1&
```

```
auto&&     g14() { return c; }      //    "     "  C1&
auto&&     g15() { return f3(); }   //    "     "  C1&&
auto*      g16() { return &c; }     //    "     "  C1*
auto    (*g17())()  { return &g12; } //   "     "  C1& (*)()
auto&      g18() { return f3(); }   // Error, can't bind C1&& to lvalue ref
```

Note that **auto**&& is a **forwarding reference**, which means that the **value category** of the return expression will determine whether an *lvalue* reference (in the case of g14) or *rvalue* reference (in the case of g15) will be deduced. The function declaration is ill formed if the specifiers added to **auto** would cause the return-type deduction to fail, as in the case of g18.

The same restrictions apply to an **auto** and **decltype(auto)** return-type deduction as to a similar variable-type deduction[1]:

```
#include <vector>  // std::vector

std::vector<int> v;

std::vector<auto>&  g19() { return v; }  // Error, auto as template argument
decltype(auto)&     g20() { return v; }  // Error, & with decltype(auto)
const decltype(auto) g21() { return v; } // Error, const with  "
```

There is an additional restriction that an **auto** return type cannot be deduced from a braced-initializer list:

```
#include <initializer_list>  // std::initializer_list

auto v22 = { 1, 2, 3 };              // OK, deduced type initializer_list<int>
auto g22() { return { 1, 2, 3 }; }   // Error, braced-initializer list not allowed
```

If the declaration of g22 deduced an initializer list return type instead of being disallowed, it would always return a dangling reference, as the initializer list would go out of scope before the function could return.

Deducing a void return type

If the **return** statement for a function having a deduced return type is empty (i.e., **return;**) or if there are no **return** statements at all, then the return type is deduced as **void**. In such cases, the declared return type must be **auto**, **const auto**, or **decltype(auto)**, without additional reference, pointer, or other qualifiers:

```
auto           g1() { }             // OK, deduced return type void
auto           g2() { return; }     // OK,    "      "      "    "
decltype(auto) g3() { }             // OK,    "      "      "    "
decltype(auto) g4() { return; }     // OK,    "      "      "    "
const auto     g5() { }             // OK,    "      "      "    "
```

---

[1]Version 10.2 (c. 2020) and earlier versions of GCC that support C++14 permit **const decltype(auto)** for both variable and function declarations, even though the Standard forbids it.

```
auto*      g6() { return; }  // Error, no pointer returned
auto&      g7() { return; }  // Error, no reference returned
```

Multiple **return** statements

When there are multiple **return** statements in a function having a deduced return type, the return type is deduced from the textually first **return** statement in the function. The second and subsequent **return** statements must deduce the same return type as the first **return** statement, or the program is ill formed[2]:

```
auto g1(int i)
{
    if (i & 1) { return 3 * i + 1; }  // Deduce return type int.
    else       { return i / 2; }      // OK, deduce return type int again.
}

auto g2(bool b)
{
    if (b) { return "hello"; }  // Deduce return type const char*.
    else   { return 0.1; }      // Error, deduced double does not match.
}
```

Type deduction on multiple **return** statements does not take conversions into account; all the deduced types must be identical:

```
auto g3(long li)
{
    if (li > 0) { return li; }  // Deduce return type long.
    else        { return 0; }   // Error, deduced int does not match long.
}

auto g4(bool b)
{
    if (b) { return "text"; }    // Deduce return type const char*.
    else   { return nullptr; }   // Error, std::nullptr_t does not match.
}

struct S { S(int = 0); };  // convertible from int
```

---

[2]In C++17, discarded statements, such as in the body of an **if constexpr** statement whose condition is **false**, are not used for type deduction:

```
auto f()  // deduces return type of const char*
{
    if constexpr (false) return 1;  // discarded return statement
    else return "hello";            // OK, nondiscarded return statement
}
```

```
auto g5(bool b)
{
    if (b) { return S(); }  // Deduced return type S
    else   { return 2; }    // Error, conversion to S not considered
}


int& f();

auto g6(int i)
{
    if (i > 0) { return i + 1; }  // Deduce return type int.
    else       { return f(); }    // OK, deduce return type int again.
}


decltype(auto) g7(int i)
{
    if (i > 0) { return i + 1; }  // Deduce return type int.
    else       { return f(); }    // Error, deduced int& doesn't match int.
}
```

Note that the second **return** statements in g3, g4, and g5 do not consider possible conversions from the second **return** expression to the type deduced from the first **return** expression. The bodies of functions g6 and g7 are identical, but the latter produces an error because **decltype(auto)** preserves the value category of the expression f(), resulting in a different deduced return type in the second **return** statement than in the first.

Unlike **if** statements, the ternary conditional operator uses the **common type** of its second and third operands. Thus, return-type deduction that would be invalid using **if** statements might be valid when using the ternary conditional operator:

```
auto g8(long li)  // valid rewrite of g3
{
    return (li > 0) ? li : 0;  // OK, deduce common return type long.
}
```

Once the return type has been deduced, it can be used later in the same function, i.e., as the return type of a recursive call. If the return type would be needed before the first **return** statement is seen, the program is ill formed:

```
decltype(auto) g9(int i)
{
    if (i < 1) { return 0; }          // Deduce return type int.
    else       { return i + g9(i - 1); }  // OK, use previously deduced return
                                          // type to deduce int again.
}
```

```
decltype(auto) g10(int i)
{
    if (i > 1) { return i + g10(i - 1); }  // Error, return type not known yet
    else       { return 0; }
}
```

Perhaps surprisingly, g9 cannot be rewritten using the ternary conditional operator because return-type deduction cannot occur until both the **true** and **false** branches of the ternary expression have been processed by the compiler:

```
decltype(auto) g11(int i)  // erroneous rewrite of g9
{
    return i < 1 ? 0 : i + g11(i - 1);
        // Error, g11 used before return deduced
}
```

It is not necessary to provide a **return** statement at the end of the function if non**void** return type has already been deduced. However, the control flow falling off the end of the function has **undefined behavior**:

```
auto g12(bool b) { if (b) return 1;        }  // Bug, UB if b is false
auto g13(bool b) { if (b) return 1; return; }  // Error, deduction mismatch
```

Type of a function having a deduced return type

Deduced return types are allowed for almost every category of function, including free functions, static member functions, nonstatic member functions, function templates, member function templates, and conversion operators. Virtual functions, however, cannot have deduced return types:

```
auto free();                                // OK, free function
template <typename T> auto templ();         // OK, function template

struct S
{
    static auto staticMember();             // OK, static member function
    decltype(auto) member();                // OK, nonstatic member function
    template <typename T> auto memberTempl();  // OK, member function template
    operator auto() const;                  // OK, conversion operator
    virtual auto virtMember();              // Error, virtual function
};
```

When one of these functions is later defined or redeclared, it must use the *same* placeholder for the return type, even if the actual return type is known at the point of definition:

```
auto free() { return 8; }  // OK, redeclare and define with auto return type.

int S::staticMember() { return 4; }  // Error, must be declared auto
auto S::member() { return 5; }       // Error, previously decltype(auto)
```

The return type for `S::staticMember` is known to be **int** at the point of definition because the function body returns 4, but hard-coding the return type to be **int** instead of **auto** causes the definition not to match the declaration. In the case of `S::member`, both the declaration and the definition use placeholders, but the declaration uses **decltype(auto)** whereas the definition uses **auto**.

The type of a function that employs a deduced return type is incomplete until the function body has been seen; to be called or to have its address taken, the function's definition must appear earlier in the translation unit:

```
auto f1();

auto caller()
{
    f1();       // Error, return type of f1 is not known.
    return &f1; // Error, f1 has an incomplete type.
}

auto f1() { return 1.2; }  // return type deduced as double but too late
```

Consequently, a function declared in a header (`.h`) file must have a definition in the same header file to be usable through the normal **#include** mechanism. In practice, such a function will typically be either a template or inline, lest the definition be imported into multiple translation units, violating the **ODR**:

```
// file1.h:
auto func1();                     // OK, declaration only

auto func2() { return 4; }        // noninline definition (dangerous)

inline auto func3() { return 'a'; } // OK, inline definition

template <typename T>
decltype(auto) func4(T* t)         // OK, function template
{
    return *t;
}

// file2.cpp:
#include <file1.h>         // Error, IFNDR, redefinition of func2
double local2a = func1();  // Error, func1 return type is not known.
```

```
int     local2b = func2();      // Valid? Call one of the definitions of func2.
char    local2c = func3();      // OK, call to inline function func3
char    local2d = func4("a");   // OK, call to instantiation func4<const char>

// file3.cpp:
#include <file1.h>              // Error, IFNDR, redefinition of func2
auto func1() { return 1.2; }    // OK, defined to return double
double local3a = func1();       // OK
int     local3b = func2();      // Valid? Call one of the definitions of func2.
char    local3c = func3();      // OK, call to inline function func3
char    local3d = func4("b");   // OK, call to instantiation func4<const char>
```

Because `func1` is declared in `file1.h` but defined in `file3.cpp`, `file2.cpp` does not have enough information to deduce its return type. Conversely, `func2` has the reverse problem: there is an ODR violation because `func2` is redefined in every translation unit that has **#include** `<file1.h>`. The compiler is not required to diagnose most ODR violations, but linkers will typically complain about multiply-defined public symbols. Finally, `func3` is **inline** and `func4` is a template; like `func1`, their definitions are visible in each translation unit, making the deduced return type available, but unlike `func2`, they do not create an ODR violation.

Placeholders in trailing return types

If **auto** or **decltype(auto)** is used in a trailing return type, the meaning is the same as using the same placeholder as a leading return type:

```
auto f1() -> auto;
auto f2() -> decltype(auto);
auto f3() -> const auto&;

auto            f1();  // OK, compatible redeclaration of f1
decltype(auto)  f2();  // OK, compatible redeclaration of f2
const auto&     f3();  // OK, compatible redeclaration of f3
```

When any trailing return type is specified, the leading return-type placeholder must be plain **auto**:

```
decltype(auto) f4() -> auto;   // Error, decltype(auto) with trailing return
auto&          f5() -> int&;   // Error, auto& with trailing return
```

Deduced return types for lambda expressions

As described in Section 2.1."Lambdas" on page 573, the return type of a closure call operator can be deduced automatically from its **return** statement(s):

```
auto y1 = [](int& i)                    { return i += 1; };  // Deduce int.
```

The semantics of return-type deduction for lambda expressions having no trailing return type is the same as for a function with declared return type **auto**. The semantics of **decltype(auto)** are available by using **decltype(auto)** in a trailing return type:

```cpp
auto y2 = [](int& i) -> decltype(auto) { return i += 1; };   // Deduce int&.
```

Note that, even though return-type deduction is available for lambda expressions in C++11, it is only since C++14 that **decltype(auto)** is available. Prior to that, the preceding lambda expression would have required a more cumbersome and repetitious use of the **decltype** operator:

```cpp
auto y3 = [](int& i) -> decltype(i+=1) { return i += 1; };   // C++11 compatible
```

Template instantiation and specialization

Function templates are instantiated when they are selected by overload resolution. If the function has a deduced return type, then the template must be fully instantiated to deduce its return type even if the instantiation causes the program to be ill formed. This instantiation behavior differs from function templates with defined return types, where failure to compose a valid return type will result in a substitution failure that will benignly remove the template from the overload set (**SFINAE**):

```cpp
struct S { };

int f1(void* p) { return 0; }          // matches any pointer type

template <typename T>
auto f1(T* p) -> decltype(*p *= 2)     // better match if T *= int is valid
{
    return *p *= 2;
}

int f2(void* p) { return 0; }          // matches any pointer type

template <typename T>
auto f2(T* p)                          // better match for nonvoid pointer type
{
    return *p *= 2;                     // OK, only if T *= int is valid
}

void g1()
{
    unsigned i;
    S        s;
```

```
    auto v1 = f1(&i);   // OK, calls f1<unsigned>(unsigned*)
    auto v2 = f1(&s);   // OK, calls f1(void*)

    auto v3 = f2(&i);   // OK, calls f2<unsigned>(unsigned*)
    auto v4 = f2(&s);   // Error, hard failure instantiating f2<S>(S*)
}
```

The first overload for **f1** accepts any pointer argument and returns integer 0. The second overload for **f1** is a better match for a non**void** pointer only if the return type **decltype**(*p *= 2) is valid. If not, then the template specialization is removed from the overload set. Thus, **f1**(&s) will discard the **f1** template from consideration and instead call the less-specific **f1**(**void***) function. Note that **auto** in combination with a trailing return type is not a deduced return type; the return type for the **f1** template is determined during overload resolution and does not require instantiation of the function body. The example takes advantage of the name of a function parameter being in scope of the trailing return type, unlike that of a leading return type.

Conversely, the prototype for the **f2** function template will match *any* pointer type, regardless of whether it can eventually deduce a valid return type. Once it has been selected as the best overload, the **f2** template is fully instantiated, and its return type is deduced. If, during instantiation, *p *= 2 fails to compile — as it does for **f2<S>** — the program is ill formed; overload resolution is complete, so it is too late to remove the template specialization from the overload set.

The use of deduced return types for function templates does not preclude explicit instantiation (see Section 2.1."**extern template**" on page 353). When an explicit instantiation is declared, no instantiation or return type deduction occurs. If, however, the function template is used in such a way that its return type must be deduced, then the template is instantiated implicitly:

```
template <typename T> auto f(T t) { return t; }

extern template auto f(int);   // explicit instantiation declaration of f<int>
int (*p)(int) = f;             // f<int> is instantiated to deduce its return type.
```

The **extern** explicit instantiation declaration of **f**(**int**) does not instantiate **f<int>**, nor does it determine its return type. When used to initialize **p**, however, the return type must be deduced; **f<int>** is instantiated just for that purpose, but that instantiation does not eliminate the requirement that **f**(**int**) be explicitly instantiated elsewhere in the program, typically in a separate translation unit:

```
template auto f(int); // must appear somewhere in the program
```

Note that the explicit instantiation fails on some popular compilers if it is encountered after the implicit instantiation in the *same* translation unit.[3]

Any specialization or explicit instantiation of a function template with deduced return type must use the same placeholder, even if the return type could be expressed simply without the placeholder:

```
template <typename T> auto g(T t) { return t; }

template <>
auto g(double d) { return 7; }  // OK, explicit specialization, deduced as int

template auto g(int);            // OK, explicit instantiation, deduced as int

template <>
char g(char)    { return 'a'; } // Error, must return auto

template <typename T>
T    g(T t, int) { return t; }  // OK, different template
```

Even though **auto** g(**char**) and **char** g(**char**) have the same return type, the latter is not a valid specialization of the former. If one of the contributors to this return-type mismatch occurs within a template, the error might not be diagnosed until the template is instantiated:

```
template <typename T>
class A
{
    static T s_value;  // private static member variable
    friend T h(T);     // Declare friend function with known return type.
};

template <typename T> T A<T>::s_value;

auto h(int i)
{
    return A<int>::s_value;
        // Error, h is redeclared with a different return-type specification.
        // Error, this function is not a friend of A<int>.
}
```

When A<**int**> is instantiated, the declaration of T h(T) within class template A fails because, although **auto** h(**int**) has the same prototype as T h(T), where T is **int**, they are not considered the same function.

---

[3]Both Clang 12.0 (c. 2021) and GCC 10.2 (c. 2020) have bugs whereby they fail to explicitly instantiate a function template having a deduced return type if the implicit instantiation needed to deduce its return type is visible. See Clang bug 19551 (**halpern21b**) and GCC bug 99799 (**halpern21a**).

Placeholder conversion functions

The name of a conversion operator can be a placeholder. Multiple conversion operators can be defined in a single class, provided that no two have the same declared or deduced return type:

```cpp
#include <cassert>  // standard C assert macro

struct S
{
    static const int i;

    operator auto() { return 1; }
    operator long() { return 2L; }
    operator decltype(auto)() const { return (i); }
    operator const auto*() { return &i; }
};

const int S::i = 3;

void f1()
{
    S        s{};
    const S cs{};

    int        i1 = s;   // Convert to int.
    long       i2 = s;   // Convert to long.
    const int& i3 = s;   // Convert to const int&.
    int        i4 = cs;  // Convert to const int&.
    long       i5 = cs;  // Convert to const int&.
    const int& i6 = cs;  // Convert to const int&.
    long&      i7 = cs;  // Error, cannot convert to long&
    const int* p1 = s;   // Convert to int*.

    assert(1  == i1);
    assert(2L == i2);
    assert(3  == i3);
    assert(3  == i4);
    assert(3  == i5);
    assert(3  == i6);

    assert(p1 == &i3);
    assert(p1 == &i6);
}
```

The same rules apply to these conversion operators as to placeholder return types of ordinary member functions. The last conversion operator, for example, combines **auto** with **const** and the pointer operator. Note, however, that because these operators do not have unique names, either their implementation must be inline within the class (as above) or they must be distinguishable in some other way, e.g., by cv-qualification:

```cpp
struct R
{
    operator auto();        // OK, deduced type not known
    operator auto() const;  // OK, const-qualified, deduced type not known
};

R::operator auto() { return "hello"; }  // OK, deduce type const char*.
R::operator auto() const { return 4; }  // OK, deduce type int.

void f2()
{
    R r;

    const char* s = r;  // OK, choose nonconst conversion to const char*.
    int         i = r;  // OK, choose const conversion to int.
}
```

In **struct** R, the two conversion operators can coexist even before their return types are deduced because one is **const** and the other is not. The deduced types must be known before the conversion operators are invoked, as usual.

Use Cases

Complicated return types

In their book *Scientific and Engineering C++*,[4] authors Barton and Nackman pioneered template techniques that are now widely used. They described a system for implementing SI units in which the individual unit exponents were held as template value parameters; e.g., a distance exponent of 3 would denote cubic meters. The type system was used to constrain unit arithmetic so that only correct combinations would compile. Addition and subtraction require units of the same dimensionality (e.g., square meters), whereas multiplication and division allow for mixed dimensions (e.g., dividing distance by time to get speed in meters per second).

We give a simplified version here, supporting three base unit types for distance in meters, mass in kilograms, and time in seconds:

```cpp
// unit type holding a dimensional value in the MKS system
template <int DistanceExp, int MassExp, int TimeExp>
class Unit
```

---

[4]barton94

```
    {
        double d_value;

    public:
        Unit() : d_value(0.0) { }
        explicit Unit(double v) : d_value(v) { }

        double value() const { return d_value; }
        Unit operator-() const { return Unit(-d_value); }
    };

    // predefined units, for convenience
    using Scalar    = Unit<0, 0, 0>;   // dimensionless quantity
    using Meters    = Unit<1, 0, 0>;   // distance in meters
    using Kilograms = Unit<0, 1, 0>;   // mass in Kg
    using Seconds   = Unit<0, 0, 1>;   // time in seconds
    using Mps       = Unit<1, 0, -1>;  // speed in meters per second
```

Each different dimensional unit type is a different instantiation of `Unit`. The basic units for distance, mass, and time are each one-dimensional, whereas speed has an exponent of `1` for distance and `-1` for time, thus representing the unit, meters/second.

Summing two dimensional quantities requires that they have the same dimensionality, i.e., that they be represented by the same `Unit` specialization. The addition and subtraction operators are, therefore, straightforward to declare and implement:

```
    template <int DD, int MD, int TD>
    Unit<DD,MD,TD> operator+(Unit<DD,MD,TD> lhs, Unit<DD,MD,TD> rhs)
        // Add two quantities of the same dimensionality.
    {
        return Unit<DD,MD,TD>(lhs.value() + rhs.value());
    }

    template <int DD, int MD, int TD>
    Unit<DD,MD,TD> operator-(Unit<DD,MD,TD> lhs, Unit<DD,MD,TD> rhs)
        // Subtract two quantities of the same dimensionality.
    {
        return Unit<DD,MD,TD>(lhs.value() - rhs.value());
    }
```

Multiplication and division are more complicated because it is possible to, for example, divide distance by time to get speed. When we multiply two dimensional quantities, the exponents are added; when we divide them, the exponents are subtracted:

```
    template <int DDL, int MDL, int TDL, int DDR, int MDR, int TDR>
    auto operator*(Unit<DDL,MDL,TDL> lhs, Unit<DDR,MDR,TDR> rhs)
        // Multiply two dimensional quantities to produce a new.
    {
        return Unit<DDL+DDR, MDL+MDR, TDL+TDR>(lhs.value() * rhs.value());
    }
```

```
template <int DDL, int MDL, int TDL, int DDR, int MDR, int TDR>
auto operator/(Unit<DDL,MDL,TDL> lhs, Unit<DDR,MDR,TDR> rhs)
{
    return Unit<DDL-DDR, MDL-MDR, TDL-TDR>(lhs.value() / rhs.value());
}
```

The return types for the multiplicative operators are somewhat awkwardly long, and without deduced return types, those long names would need to appear twice, once in the function declaration and once in the **return** statement.

As a workaround, **operator*** and **operator/** could introduce a defaulted template parameter to avoid the repetition of the return type:

```
template <int DD1, int MD1, int TD1, int DD2, int MD2, int TD2,
          typename R = Unit<DD1+DD2, MD1+MD2, TD1+TD2>>
R operator*(Unit<DD1,MD1,TD1> lhs, Unit<DD2,MD2,TD2> rhs)
{
    return R(lhs.value() * rhs.value());
}
```

However, the workaround does not apply to nontemplated functions, such as kineticEnergy.

We can now use these operations to implement a function that returns the kinetic energy of a moving object:

```
auto kineticEnergy(Kilograms m, Mps v)
    // Return the kinetic energy of an object of mass m moving at velocity v.
{
    return m * (v * v) / Scalar(2);
}
```

The return type of this formula is determined automatically, without expressing the Unit template arguments directly. The returned unit is a joule, which can also be described as a kilogram $* \text{meter}^2/\text{second}^2$, as our test program illustrates:

```
#include <type_traits>  // std::is_same

void f1()
{
    using Joules = Unit<2, 1, -2>;  // energy in joules

    auto ke = kineticEnergy(Kilograms(4.0), Mps(12.5));
    static_assert(std::is_same<decltype(ke), Joules>::value, "");
}
```

Because of automatic return-type deduction, naming the Unit instantiation of each intermediate computation within kineticEnergy was unnecessary. The **static_assert** in the code above proves that our formula has returned the correct final unit.

Let the compiler apply the rules

The C++ rules for type promotion and conversion in expressions are complex and not easy to express in a return type. For example, consider the difficulty in verbalizing the rule for determining the return type when adding a value of type **int** to a value of type **unsigned int**. Determining the correct return type for a function that returns the result of such an expression is similarly difficult. This complication is compounded when the computation takes place in a function template. An explicit return type computed with **decltype** can be used to determine the type of an expression, but such determination requires duplicating the expression in the function declaration or fabricating a simpler expression that ideally has the same type. When multiple **return** statements exist with different contents, there is no straightforward way to guarantee that they yield the same type.

Using a deduced return type eliminates the need to duplicate code or reconcile return expressions:

```
template <typename T1, typename T2>
auto add_or_subtract(bool b, T1 v1, T2 v2)
{
    if (b) { return v1 + v2; }
    else   { return v1 - v2; }
}
```

The template above deduces the return type of adding a value of type T2 to a value of type T1 and verifies that the same type is produced when subtracting a value of type T2 from a value of type T1. If the two deduced types differ, an error diagnostic is produced rather than a silent promotion or conversion to the (possibly incorrect) manually determined type.

Returning a lambda expression

A lambda expression generates a unique **closure** type that cannot be named and cannot appear as the operand of the **decltype** operator. The only way that a function can generate and return a **closure object** is through the use of a deduced return type. This capability lets us define functions that capture parameters and generate useful function objects:

```
#include <algorithm>   // std::is_partitioned
#include <vector>      // std::vector

template <typename T>
auto lessThanValue(const T& t)
{
    return [t](const T& u) { return u < t; };
}

bool f1(const std::vector<int>& v, int pivot)
    // Return true if v is partitioned around the pivot value.
{
    return std::is_partitioned(v.begin(), v.end(), lessThanValue(pivot));
}
```

The lessThanValue function generates a functor — i.e., a closure object — that returns **true** if its argument is less than the captured t value. This functor is then used as an argument to is_partitioned.

Note that it is not possible to return different lambda expressions in different **return** statements because each lambda expression intrinsically has a different type than that of every other lambda expression, thus violating the requirements for return-type deduction:

```
auto comparator(bool reverse)
{
    if (reverse)
    {
        return [](int l, int r) { return l < r; };
    }
    else
    {
        return [](int l, int r) { return l > r; };  // Error, inconsistent type
    }
}
```

A solution could be to use std::function<**void**(**int**, **int**)> as the return type of our comparator function.

Perfect returning of wrapped functions

A generic wrapper that performs some task before and/or after calling another function needs to preserve the type and **value category** of the returned value of the called function. Using **decltype(auto)** is the simplest method to achieve this "perfect returning" of the wrapped call. For example, a wrapper template might acquire a mutex lock, call an arbitrary function provided by the user, and return the value produced by the function:

```
#include <utility>  // std::forward
#include <mutex>    // std::mutex and std::lock_guard

template <typename Func, typename... Args>
decltype(auto) lockedInvoke(std::mutex& m, Func&& f, Args&&... args)
{
    std::lock_guard<std::mutex> mutexLock(m);
    return std::forward<Func>(f)(std::forward<Args>(args)...);
}
```

The mutex is released automatically by the destructor for mutexLock. The return value and **value category** from f is faithfully returned by lockedInvoke. Note that lockedInvoke relies on two other C++11 features — forwarding references (see Section 2.1."Forwarding References" on page 377) and variadic function templates (see Section 2.1."Variadic Templates" on page 873) — to achieve **perfect forwarding** of its arguments to f.

Delaying return-type deduction

Sometimes, determining the return type of a function template requires instantiating the template recursively until the leaf case is found. In certain situations, these instantiations can cause unbounded compile-time recursion even when, logically, the recursion should terminate normally. Consider the recursive function template n1, which returns its template argument, N, through recursive instantiation, stopping when it calls the leaf case of N == 0:

```cpp
template <int i>  struct Int { };  // compile-time integer

int n1(Int<0>) { return 0; }       // leaf case for terminating recursion

template <int N>
auto n1(Int<N>) -> decltype(n1(Int<N-1>{}))
    // Return N through recursive instantiation.
{
    return n1(Int<N-1>{}) + 1;   // call to recursive instantiation
}

int result1 = n1(Int<10>{});       // Error, excessive compile-time recursion
```

On the surface, it looks like recursion should terminate after only 11 instantiations. The problem, however, is that the compiler must determine the return type of n1 before it knows whether it will recurse or not. To compute return type **decltype**(n1(Int<N-1>{})), the compiler must build an overload set for n1. The compiler finds two names that match, the leaf case n1(Int<0>) and the template n1(Int<N>). Even if N is 0, the compiler must instantiate the latter in order to complete building the overload set. If N is 0, therefore, it will instantiate n1<-1>, even though it will never call it. Hence, the recursion will not stop until n1 has been instantiated with every **int** value (though, in practice, the compiler will abort long before then).

When the return type is deduced using **auto** or **decltype(auto)**, the compiler adds the function to the overload set without having to determine its return type. Since the return type itself does not determine the result of overload resolution, we can avoid unneeded instantiations. Return-type deduction will occur only for the function that is actually chosen by overload resolution, so the return type when N < 0 will terminate recursion as expected:

```cpp
int n2(Int<0>) { return 0; }       // leaf case for terminating recursion

template <int N>
auto n2(Int<N>)
    // return N through recursive instantiation
{
    return n2(Int<N-1>{}) + 1;   // call to recursive instantiation
}

int result2 = n2(Int<10>{});       // OK, returns 10
```

In the example above, the call to n2 when N is 1 selects the leaf case (nontemplate) version and does not recursively instantiate the template version of n2.

Potential Pitfalls

Negative impacts on abstraction and insulation

If a library function provides an abstract interface, the user needs to read and understand only the function's declaration and its documentation. Except when maintaining the library itself, the function's implementation details are unimportant.

If a program insulates a library user from the library's implementation by placing the implementation code in a separate translation unit, compile-time coupling between library code and client code is reduced. A library that does not include function implementations in its header files can be rebuilt to provide updates without needing to recompile clients; only a relink is needed. Compilation times for client code are minimized by not needing to recompile library source code within header files.

Deduced function return types interfere with both abstraction and insulation and thus with the development of large-scale, comprehensible software. Because the return type cannot be determined without its implementation being visible to the compiler, publicly visible functions having deduced return types cannot be insulated; they must necessarily appear in a header file as **inline** functions or function templates, thereby being recompiled for every client translation unit. In this regard, a function with deduced return type is no different than any other **inline** function or function template. What is new, however, is its impact on abstraction: To fully understand a function's interface — including its return type — the user must read its implementation.

To mitigate the loss of abstraction from deduced return types, the function author can carefully document the expected properties of the returned object, even in the absence of a specific concrete type. Interestingly, understanding the return value's *properties*, not merely its *type*, might yield a resulting function that is *more* abstract than one for which a known type had been specified.

Reduced clarity

Not having the return type of a function visible in its declaration can reduce the clarity of a program. Deduced return types work best when they appear on tiny function definitions, so that the determinative **return** statement is easily visible. Functions having deduced return types are also well suited for situations where the particulars of a return type are not especially useful, as in the case of iterator types associated with containers.

Annoyances

Implementation-order sensitivity

If a deduced return type is used for a recursive function or a pseudorecursive function template, the textually first **return** statement must be the base case of the recursion:

```cpp
auto fib(int n)
    // Compute the nth Fibonacci number.
{
    if (n < 2) { return n; }              // base case, deduces int
    else { return fib(n-2) + fib(n-1); }  // OK, return type already known
}
```

The same code can be rearranged in a way that seems functionally identical but would fail to compile due to return-type deduction happening too late:

```cpp
auto fib2(int n)
    // Compute the nth Fibonacci number.
{

    if (n >= 2) { return fib2(n-2) + fib2(n-1); }  // Error, unknown return type
    else        { return n; }                       // OK, but too late
}
```

Importantly, multiple **return** statements all deducing the same return type ensures that rearranging the order of **return** statements does not lead to subtle changes in the deduced return type of the function. For example, if the first **return** deduces the type **short** and the second **return** deduces the type **long**, it is probably preferable for the compiler to complain than to silently truncate the **long** to a **short**. This protection, therefore, prevents an occasional annoyance from becoming a dangerous pitfall.

No SFINAE in function body

Substitution Failure Is Not An Error is often employed to conditionally remove a function template from an overload set.[5] Consider an overload set that aims to output an object to an std::ostream using its print member function if the object has one and by using streaming operator otherwise:

---

[5] C++20 introduces **concepts**, a much more expressive system to restrict the applicability of a function template that relies less on understanding the subtleties of SFINAE.

```
#include <iostream>  // std::ostream, std::cout

template <typename T>
decltype(auto) printImpl(std::ostream& os, const T& t, long)
    // low-priority overload that uses streaming operator
{
    return os << t;
}

template <typename T>
auto printImpl(std::ostream& os, const T& t, int) -> decltype(t.print(os))
    // high-priority overload for types having a print member function
{
    return t.print(os);
}

template <typename T>
decltype(auto) print(std::ostream& os, const T& t)
    // dispatcher function to select between overloads of printImpl
{
    return printImpl(os, t, 0);
}
```

When the client invokes the free function `print`, it uses the `printImpl` overload set to select the proper printing method. This overload set depends on **SFINAE** to work properly. When `printImpl` is invoked on an object for which the expression `t.print(os)` is valid, template substitution will proceed without error, and the resulting template specialization will be the best match during overload resolution because `0` is an exact match for the third argument. When invoked on an object of a type for which `t.print(os)` is invalid, the template substitution will fail, and the would-be resulting specialization will be dropped from the overload set, leaving the function that simply streams to the `std::ostream` as the best overload match despite it requiring a standard conversion for its third argument:

```
struct S {
    std::ostream& print(std::ostream& o) const        { return o << "PRINT"; }
};
std::ostream& operator<<(std::ostream& o, const S& s) { return o << "STREAM"; }

void testPrint()
{
    print(std::cout, S());  // prints "PRINT"
    print(std::cout, 17);   // prints "17"
}
```

Looking at the implementation of `printImpl`, one might think to remove the duplication of the `t.print(os)` expression by leveraging a deduced return type. This change, however, will

move the substitution error from the declaration to the function body, making the program
ill formed rather than removing the offending instantiation from the overload set:

```
template <typename T>
decltype(auto) printImpl2(std::ostream& os, const T& t, long)
{
    return os << t;
}

template <typename T>
decltype(auto) printImpl2(std::ostream& os, const T& t, int)  // deduced return
{
    return t.print(os);  // valid only if t.print(os) is valid
}

template <typename T>
decltype(auto) print2(std::ostream& os, const T& t)
{
    return printImpl2(os, t, 0);
}

void testPrint2()
{
    print2(std::cout, S());  // OK, template instantiation succeeds.
    print2(std::cout, 17);   // Error, tries to call print on an int
}
```

When `print2(17)` is seen, the compiler must look at *both* overloads of `print2`. Since the
version that calls the `print` member function is the better match, it tries to instantiate it
but fails upon seeing `t.print(os)`. The error does not occur during overload resolution, so
it is not considered a substitution failure. Rather than choosing the next best overload, the
compilation fails.

See Also

- "**decltype**" (§1.1, p. 25) describes a feature that yields the type of an expression at
  compile time and is used implicitly for type deduction.

- "Trailing Return" (§1.1, p. 124) discusses a less flexible but more deterministic alternative to deduced return types.

- "**auto** Variables" (§2.1, p. 195) introduces the rules for deducing the type of an **auto**
  variable, which are almost the same rules as for deducing a return type declared with
  the **auto** placeholder.

- "Forwarding References" (§2.1, p. 377) illustrates an idiom used ubiquitously in C++11 and C++14 templates, especially function templates that wrap other function templates, often using deduced return types.

- "Lambdas" (§2.1, p. 573) introduces **lambda expressions**, which had deduced return types in C++11 before they were extended for regular functions in C++14.

- "**decltype(auto)**" (§3.2, p. 1205) catalogs the rules for deducing the type of a **decltype(auto)** variable, which are the same rules as for deducing a return type declared with the **decltype(auto)** placeholder.

Deducing Types Using decltype Semantics

In a C++14 variable declaration, **decltype(auto)** can act as a **placeholder type** that is deduced to exactly match the type of the variable's initializer, preserving the initializer's **value category**, unlike the **auto** placeholder.

Description

The type specifier **auto** (see Section 2.1."**auto** Variables" on page 195) can be used in C++11 as a placeholder to declare a variable whose type is deduced from the variable's initializer:

```
struct C { /*...*/ };

C f1();

auto a1 = 0;     // deduced type int
auto a2{f1()};   // deduced type C
```

C++14 introduced a new placeholder, **decltype(auto)**, which can be used in most of the same contexts as **auto**. For the example above, **decltype(auto)** behaves identically to **auto**:

```
decltype(auto) a3 = 0;     // deduced type int
decltype(auto) a4{f1()};   // deduced type C
```

The literal 0 has type **int**; initializing a3 with 0 thus yields a variable of type **int**. Similarly, the expression f1() has type C, yielding a variable of type C when used to initialize a4.

Unlike plain **auto**, the deduced type of a variable declared with type **decltype(auto)** is determined not by using template-argument deduction rules, but by applying the **decltype** operator to the initialization expression. In practice, the cv-qualifiers and value category (see Section 2.1."*Rvalue* References" on page 710) of the initializer are preserved for **decltype(auto)**, whereas they would be discarded for plain **auto**:

```
int&    f2();
C&&     f3();
C       c1;
const C cc1;

auto           v1 = 4;      // deduced as int
decltype(auto) v2 = 4;      //    "      " int

auto           v3 = f2();   //    "      " int
decltype(auto) v4 = f2();   //    "      " int&

auto           v5 = f3();   //    "      " C
decltype(auto) v6 = f3();   //    "      " C&&
```

```
auto           v7  = cc1;   //     "      " C
decltype(auto) v8  = cc1;   //     "      " const C

auto           v9  = (cc1); //     "      " C
decltype(auto) v10 = (cc1); //     "      " const C&
```

As with the **decltype** operator, **decltype(auto)** is one of the few constructs that preserves the distinction between the two categories of *rvalue* — *prvalues* (e.g., literal 4) and *xvalues* (e.g., f3()).

Both **auto** and **decltype(auto)** can be used as placeholders for a function return type, indicating that the return type should be deduced from the function's **return** statement(s). The deduced return-type feature is covered in its own section (see Section 3.2."**auto** Return" on page 1182). Note that the deduction rules described for function return types in that section refer to the ones described for variables here. Readers are, therefore, advised to read this section first.

Specification

The **decltype(auto)** placeholder can appear in most places where **auto** can appear.

1. As the type in the declaration of an initialized variable, including variables defined in the init-statement of a loop or **switch** statement

2. As the type of object allocated and initialized by a **new** expression

3. As the type returned by a function or conversion operator

The last one is the most common use of **decltype(auto)** and is described in detail in Section 3.2."**auto** Return" on page 1182. Note that **decltype(auto)** cannot be used to declare a parameter of a generic **lambda expression**; see Section 2.2."*Generic* Lambdas" on page 968.

For a variable, v, declared with **decltype(auto)** and initialized with an expression, expr, the type of v is deduced to be the type denoted by **decltype(**expr**)**; see Section 1.1."**decltype**" on page 25. This semantic means that the deduced type might be cv-qualified and/or a reference:

```
struct C1 { /*...*/ };

int&    lvref();
C1&&    rvref();
C1      c1;
const C1 cc1;
```

```
decltype(lvref()) v1  = lvref();   // deduced as int&
decltype(auto)    v2  = lvref();   // equivalent to v1

decltype(rvref()) v3  = rvref();   // deduced as C1&&
decltype(auto)    v4  = rvref();   // equivalent to v3

decltype(c1)      v5  = c1;        // deduced as C1
decltype(auto)    v6  = c1;        // equivalent to v4

decltype((c1))    v7  = c1;        // deduced as C1&
decltype(auto)    v8  = (c1);      // equivalent to v7

decltype(cc1)     v9  = cc1;       // deduced as const C1
decltype(auto)    v10 = cc1;       // equivalent to v9
decltype((cc1))   v11 = cc1;       // deduced as const C1&
decltype(auto)    v12 = (cc1);     // equivalent to v11

decltype({ 3 })   v13 = { 3 };     // Error, not an expression
decltype(auto)    v14 = { 3 };     // Error, not an expression
```

The semantics of the **decltype** operator, when applied to an expression consisting of a single variable, cause **decltype**(c1) to yield type C1 and **decltype**((c1)) to yield reference type C1&, as in the definitions of v5 and v7, respectively; variables v6 and v8, therefore, also have the types C1 and C1&. A braced-initializer list such as { 3 } is not an expression; thus, v13 and v14 are both invalid.

Note that functions returning **scalar types** discard top-level cv-qualifiers on their return types, so a type deduced from a call to such a function will not reflect top-level cv-qualifiers even when defined with **decltype(auto)**:

```
template <typename T> T f();

decltype(auto) v15 = f<const C1>();          // deduced as const C1
decltype(auto) v16 = f<const int>();         //    "     " int
decltype(auto) v17 = f<const int&>();        //    "     " const int&
decltype(auto) v18 = f<const char* const>(); //    "     " const char*
```

The top-level **const** qualifier on the class type, **const** C1, and on the reference type, **const int**&, are preserved but not on the scalar type, **const int**. The **const**ness of the pointer itself, in **const char* const**, is similarly discarded, as it is the top-level cv-qualifier on a scalar type.

When a function name is used as the initializer expression, it automatically decays to a pointer type when initializing a variable declared with type **auto** but does not decay when

the variable is declared with type **decltype(auto)**; thus, the deduced type of gx2 below is
a function type, which is not an allowed type for a variable. Initializer expressions having
pointer-to-function type or reference-to-function type, as seen with gx3, gx4, gx5, and gx6,
do not pose a problem:

```
int g();
auto            gx1 = g;     // OK, deduced as (decayed type) int (*)()
decltype(auto) gx2 = g;     // Error, cannot define variable of type int()

auto            gx3 = &g;    // OK, deduced as int (*)()
decltype(auto) gx4 = &g;    // OK,    "     " int (*)()

auto&           gx5 = *gx3;  // OK,    "     " int (&)()
decltype(auto) gx6 = *gx3;  // OK,    "     " int (&)()
```

Note that gx5 uses & to force the variable type to be a reference. The ability to add reference
specifiers and cv-qualifiers to a placeholder is not available for **decltype(auto)**, as described
in the next section.

Syntactic restrictions

When used as a type placeholder, **decltype(auto)** must appear alone, unadorned by cv-
qualifiers, reference type specifiers, pointer type specifiers, or function parameter lists:

```
int&& f1();
int i1 = 5;

decltype(auto)       v1   = f1();  // OK, deduced as int&&
const decltype(auto) v2   = f1();  // Error, const qualifier not allowed
decltype(auto)&&     v3   = f1();  // Error, reference operator not allowed
decltype(auto)*      v4   = &i1;   // Error, pointer operator not allowed
decltype(auto)       (*v5)() = &f1;  // Error, function parameters not allowed
```

All of the above definitions would be valid if **decltype(auto)** were replaced with **auto**:

```
auto        v6       = f1();  // OK, v6 deduced as int
const auto  v7       = f1();  // OK, v7    "      " const int
auto&&      v8       = f1();  // OK, v8    "      " int&&
auto*       v9       = &i1;   // OK, v9    "      " int*
auto        (*v10)() = &f1;   // OK, v10   "      " int&& (*)()
```

The **decltype(auto)** placeholder cannot be used to define a variable without an initializer
because there would be no way to deduce its type. If multiple variables are defined in a
single **decltype(auto)** definition, they must all have initializers of exactly the same type:

```
#include <utility> // std::move

decltype(auto) v11;                                  // Error, no initializer
decltype(auto) v12 = f1(), v13 = std::move(i1);  // OK, deduced as int&&
decltype(auto) v14 = 5, v15 = f1();              // Error, ambiguous deduction
```

A non**static** member variable cannot be declared using **decltype(auto)**, even if provided with a default member initializer (see Section 2.1."Default Member Init" on page 318):

```
struct C1
{
    decltype(auto) d_data = f();  // Error, decltype(auto) for member variable
};
```

A **constexpr** static member variable (see Section 2.1."**constexpr** Variables" on page 302) that is initialized at the point of declaration can be declared using **decltype(auto)**, but a non**constexpr** static member variable cannot, simply because non**constexpr** static members must be initialized outside the class definition, independently of the **decltype(auto)** feature:

```
constexpr int f2() { return 5; }

struct C2
{
    static constexpr decltype(auto) s_mem1 = f2();  // OK
    static           decltype(auto) s_mem2 = f2();  // Error, in-class init
};
```

A variable with static storage duration (either in namespace or class scope) can be declared using an explicit type and then redeclared and initialized using **decltype(auto)**. Note, however, that some popular compilers reject these redeclarations[1]:

```
extern int gi; // forward declaration

struct C3
{
    static decltype(f2()) s_mem1;  // type int
};

decltype(auto) gi =        f2();  // OK, compatible redeclaration
decltype(auto) C3::s_mem1 = f2();  // OK, compatible redeclaration
```

---

[1]GCC 10.2 (c. 2020) and MSVC 19.29 (c. 2021), among many other compilers, reject **auto** redeclaration of previously declared variables; see GCC bug 60352 (**pluzhnikov14**). However, nothing in the C++14 Standard appears to disallow such redeclarations, and an example in the C++20 Standard suggests that they are valid.

new **expressions**

When used in a **new** expression, **decltype(auto)** offers little benefit over plain **auto** and will sometimes cause otherwise valid code to not compile:

```
int   i;
int&& f1();

auto* p1 = new auto(5);              // OK, equivalent to new int(5)
auto* p2 = new decltype(auto)(5);    // OK, equivalent to new int(5)

auto* p3 = new auto(i);              // OK, equivalent to new int(i)
auto* p4 = new decltype(auto)(i);    // OK, equivalent to new int(i)

auto* p5 = new auto(f1());           // OK, equivalent to new int(f1())
auto* p6 = new decltype(auto)(f1()); // Error, equivalent to new int&&(f1())

auto* p7 = new auto((i));            // OK, equivalent to new int(i)
auto* p8 = new decltype(auto)((i));  // Error, equivalent to new int&(i)
```

In all of the examples above, the variable type is declared as **auto*** so that it could be deduced from the return type of the **new** expression; plain **auto**, **decltype(auto)**, or **int*** would all have been equivalent. The initializers for **p6** and **p8** fail to compile because **decltype(auto)** deduces to a reference type in each of those cases, causing the **new** expression to generate a pointer-to-reference type. The **auto** specifiers used to initialize **p5** and **p7**, conversely, discard the reference qualifiers, yielding valid types.

Use Cases

Exact capture of an expression's type and value category

Both **auto&&** and **decltype(auto)** can be used to declare a variable initialized to the result of any expression, but only **decltype(auto)** will capture the exact value category of an initializing expression:

```
int   f1();
int&  f2();
int&& f3();
int   i;

auto&&          v1 = f1();  // type int&&
decltype(auto) v2 = f1();  // type int

auto&&          v3 = f2();  // type int&
decltype(auto) v4 = f2();  // type int&
```

```
auto&&          v5 = f3();  // type int&&
decltype(auto) v6 = f3();  // type int&&

auto&&          v7 = i;     // type int&
decltype(auto) v8 = i;     // type int
```

Variables v1 and v5 have the same value category even though f1() is a *prvalue* and f3() is an *xvalue*, illustrating the limitation of **auto**&&, whereas v2 and v6 correctly capture the distinction. In addition, **auto**&& deduces v7 as a reference, whereas **decltype(auto)** deduces v8 as an object.

Return type of a proxy iterator or moving iterator

When an iterator is dereferenced, it usually returns an *lvalue* reference to an element within a sequence. An iterator might, however, return an object of proxy type by value, as in the case of std::vector<bool>. Alternatively, the iterator dereference operator might return an *rvalue* reference to a sequence element, as in the case of a *moving iterator* — i.e., for a sequence that will not be used again after it has been traversed. **decltype(auto)** can be used in generic code to faithfully capture a dereferenced iterator when the value category of the iterator's reference type is unknown:

```
#include <vector>  // std::vector

template <typename C, typename V>
void fill(C& container, const V& val)
    // Replace the value of every element in container with a copy of val.
{
    for (typename C::iterator iter = container.begin();
        iter != container.end();
        ++iter)
    {
        // auto& element = *iter;  // won't work for proxy or moving iterators
        decltype(auto) element = *iter;
        element = val;
    }
}

void f1(std::vector<bool>& v)
{
    fill(v, false);
    // ...
}
```

Instead of **decltype(auto)**, we could have used **auto**&& and gotten the same effect, although the semantics of **decltype(auto)** are slightly simpler to understand in this case. Although more verbose, it would be more descriptive to declare element as having type **typename** std::iterator_traits<**decltype**(iter)>::reference.

Potential Pitfalls

Hidden dangling references

An operation on an *rvalue* will sometimes return an *rvalue* reference that is valid only for the lifetime of the original *rvalue*. When the returned reference is saved in a named variable, there is a danger of the variable binding to a temporary object that will go out of scope before it can be used:

```
#include <list>  // std::list

template <typename T>
T&& first(std::list<T>&& s) { return std::move(*s.begin()); }
    // Return an rvalue reference to the first element in s.

std::list<int> collection();
    // Return (by value) a list of int values.

void f()
{
    int&&          r1 = first(collection());
    auto&&         r2 = first(collection());
    decltype(auto) r3 = first(collection());

    // Bug, r1, r2, and r3 are all dangling references to destroyed
    // objects.

    // ...
}
```

The variables r1, r2, and r3 all have type **int&&**, and all are **dangling references** because they refer to an element of a list that goes out of scope immediately after the reference is initialized. When a reference variable is initialized from a reference expression, it is important to be wary of the lifetime of the object being referenced. In this regard, **decltype(auto)** adds no new hazard. Note, however, that r1 and r2 are both *declared* as reference types, whereas r3 is only *deduced* to be a reference type. The reference being *hidden* makes this pitfall harder to avoid for **decltype(auto)** than for the other two cases.

Poor signaling of intent

Since C++11, a common set of idioms has emerged for the use of **auto** in generic code:

```
auto        copyVar     = expr1;  // copy of expr1
const auto& readonlyVar = expr2;  // read-only reference to expr2
auto&&      mutableVar  = expr3;  // possibly mutable reference to expr3
```

The copyVar object will be initialized from expr1 using direct initialization; if expr1 yields an *rvalue* or *lvalue* reference, then the move or copy constructor, respectively, is invoked. The readonlyVar reference provides read-only access to the object produced by expr2; if expr2 returns an *rvalue*, then **lifetime extension** ensures that it remains valid until readonlyVar goes out of scope. Finally, mutableVar allows modifying or moving from expr3 (unless expr3 is **const**); as in the case of **const auto&**, lifetime extension might come into play. Faithful use of these idioms provides safety and signals the programmer's intent regarding the expected use of the variable.

There is no way to create a similar set of idioms for **decltype(auto)** because **decltype(auto)** cannot be combined with **const** or reference type specifiers; see *Annoyances — decltype(auto) stands alone* below. For variable declarations, therefore, using **auto** in this idiomatic way might be preferable.

The situation is somewhat different for *function return* types, where the expected use of the return value is not always known at the point of declaration; see Section 3.2."**auto** Return" on page 1182.

Annoyances

decltype(auto) stands alone

When defining a variable with **auto**, we can add cv-qualifiers and reference type specifiers to the deduced type, even if the initializer expression has simpler qualifiers:

```
int f();

const auto& v1 = f();  // v1 is const int&.
```

Unfortunately, **decltype(auto)** must stand alone; the type of the variable is always exactly that of the initializer expression, with no extra decorations:

```
const decltype(auto) v2 = f();  // Error, const with decltype(auto)
```

Thus, deducing a variable type that is always read-only, for example, is not possible with **decltype(auto)**.

See Also

- "**decltype**" (§1.1, p. 25) describes the **decltype** operator, which determines the semantics of **decltype(auto)**.

- "**auto** Variables" (§2.1, p. 195) describes the C++11 feature on which **decltype(auto)** is based.

- "*Rvalue* References" (§2.1, p. 710) describes the complex world of value categories that distinguish **decltype(auto)** from **auto**.

- "**auto** Return" (§3.2, p. 1182) shows how to apply the same deduction rules described in this section to function return types.

Afterword: Looking Back and Looking Forward

Wow, that wasn't what we expected! When we — John and Vittorio — first conceived of this project, we figured that we could do the topic — comprising some 50-odd feature sections — justice in 300 to 400 pages with the assistance of Rostislav and Alisdair as reviewers. It sounded straightforward: Create a thorough exegesis, derived from own experience, of what C++11 and C++14 added to C++03. Well, more than 1,200 pages later, and with the addition of Rostislav and Alisdair as coauthors, we now see just how difficult it is to make it look easy. The composition of this book was a humbling and exhilarating experience, not just for the authors but for the many others who were involved in one way or another. Now that this work is in your hands, dear reader, we hope you will find the effort to have been worth it.

Throughout the trials and tribulations of collecting data, consulting domain experts, writing everything up, and reviewing material, there has been one invariant: quality. We have never for any reason compromised on the quality of any aspect of the book — even at the cost of delaying the schedule by half a year, to the dismay of our editor, publisher, and loved ones. If any mistake did slip through, it's not out of sloppiness. We have poured everything we have into every sentence of the book, the index, the glossary, and even the back cover.

In hindsight, the enormity of the task we set for ourselves is clear. But it was only through the detailed working out of the material that this clarity was achieved. The vast effort to attain this clarity, in itself, is a compelling reason *EMC++S* had to be written: The breadth and depth of the additions to an already complex language meant that many subtle implications do not lie at the surface. To reach our goal, we had to cast our net wide and plumb the depths.

The good news is we got it done! *EMC++S* is here, and the fruits of our collective labors, personal sacrifices, all-nighters, etc., are ready and waiting to be consumed.

There are many successful C++ software developers out there who have been amply productive with classical C++ and might not have had the time, or seen the need to spend the copious hours required, to learn the ins and outs of the monolithic Leviathan of new and varied features modern C++ comprises. How is one to know which features add value and are safe to use, and which are fraught with pitfalls and/or provide little practical value?

Well-established, successful C++ developers, team leads, and technical managers fluent or expert in C++03 are precisely the audience that we had in mind as we wrote this

Afterword: Looking Back and Looking Forward

book. Keeping this book at the ready will help to level the playing field when encountering an unfamiliar modern feature, or help when deliberating over whether and under what circumstances a modern C++ feature might be appropriate or, more importantly, perhaps a really bad idea. Finally, if nothing else, you can — with a glance at the TOC — know with authority, without overthinking it, whether a modern feature is safe to use or might require significant research before it can be used *safely*.

What's Next?

Perhaps we are gluttons for punishment, but looking forward, our intention is to update this book every three years, following the schedule of publication of the C++ Standard. Once the world has had at least seven years to work with a stable Standard, we will again attempt to distill the best practices of the best engineers in a second edition of this book including coverage of C++17.

But we need the help of our readers. The next edition will incorporate the accumulated experience of proactive readers who submit suggestions, examples, corrections, bug fixes, etc., to our website (emcpps.com). We have learned myriad lessons in the process and expect — again, perhaps foolishly — that these updated editions will come more easily than this first one.

We hope to see you there!

Glossary

Note: In the blue text at the end of each definition, the number inside parentheses indicates the page on which the glossary term is first used in a given feature.

ABI – short for **application binary interface**. Generalized PODs '11 (402), inline namespace (1056), noexcept Specifier (1089)

abstract class – one from which objects cannot be instantiated. In C++, the term **abstract class** is typically used to imply one that has at least one **pure virtual function**. Note that an object that is not instantiable for some other reason, say, having no usable constructor (other than a copy constructor), might be said to be not *concrete*; see also **concrete class**. final (1008)

abstract interface – a protocol.

abstract machine – a hypothetical nondeterministic computer defined by the C++ Standard to abstractly model real hardware and provide a basis for describing the semantics of the C++ language absent resource (e.g., memory) constraints. noexcept Specifier (1118)

access level – a property, i.e., *public*, *protected*, or *private*, of member m of a class C as determined by the access level in effect in C where m was declared. Generalized PODs '11 (489)

access specifier – one of three keywords, **private**, **protected**, or **public**, used to specify the prevailing access level, governing the situations under which base classes and *declared* members are accessible: *private* base classes and members may be accessed only from within that class or by friends, *protected* base classes and members may also be accessed by derived classes, and *public* base classes and members may be accessed from anywhere. Defaulted Functions (35), Inheriting Ctors (537)

accessible (from a context) – implies, for a given member m, that its name is not precluded from use in a given client context c due solely to the access level of m. For example, if m is declared **protected** within a class S and c is the body of a member function of a class derived from S, then m is accessible when used in c. Note that accessible doesn't necessarily imply usable, as m might be, e.g., *ambiguous*, deleted, or an ill-formed template specialization. Note that this term is sometimes used informally (and imprecisely) to mean publicly accessible. Generalized PODs '11 (410), noexcept Operator (641), *Rvalue* References (790)

active member – a unique non**static** data member of a union whose lifetime has begun and has not ended. Generalized PODs '11 (406)

address space – all of the typically sequential, often virtual, almost always byte-addressable computer memory in which objects can be referenced via pointers. Note that, on embedded systems and older computers, the size of the addressable memory can be severely constrained (e.g., by the width of the address bus).

ADL – short for **argument-dependent lookup**.

Glossary

aggregate – an **aggregate type** or an object thereof. Aggregate Init '14 (138), Braced Init (230), Default Member Init (330), Generalized PODs '11 (402), *Rvalue* References (750), Variadic Templates (877), `noexcept` Specifier (1087)

aggregate class – one of **aggregate type**. Generalized PODs '11 (415)

aggregate initialization – the initialization of an **aggregate** from a **braced-initializer** list. Aggregate Init '14 (138), Braced Init (221), `constexpr` Functions (273), Default Member Init (330), Generalized PODs '11 (463), *Rvalue* References (752)

aggregate type – (1) a class type having no **user-provided** or explicit constructors, no base classes, no private or protected non**static** data members, and no virtual functions, or (2) any array type. As of C++14, aggregates can have default member initializers for non**static** data members. As of C++17, public non**virtual** base classes are allowed, but inherited constructors are not; as of C++20, all user-declared constructors become disallowed. `constexpr` Functions (279), Generalized PODs '11 (410), *Rvalue* References (742)

algebra – a set of operations, often involving just a single type, that can be applied to object values, along with any rules governing those operations and how they interrelate; see also **value semantics**. `constexpr` Functions '14 (961)

algorithm selection – the process by which an algorithm is chosen from among a portfolio of potentially applicable algorithms, based on readily observable, especially compile-time, features of the input data set (see **leyton-brown03**). Variadic Templates (947)

alias template – one that defines a family of **type aliases** parameterized by one or more **template parameters**. `using` Aliases (135), Variadic Templates (887)

aliasing – having pointers or **references** to distinct objects (possibly of distinct type) whose footprints overlap in the **address space**. `noexcept` Operator (638)

alignment (of an address) – the largest integral power of 2 that evenly divides the numerical value of a given address in the **address space**. `alignas` (168)

alignment requirement (of a type) – the smallest **alignment** at which an object of a given type can reside in the **address space**; see also **natural alignment**. `alignas` (168), `alignof` (184)

allocating object – one that might itself allocate and manage dynamically allocated memory outside of its own footprint using **new**, `malloc`, or some other allocation interface, such as `std::allocator` or, as of C++17, `std::pmr::polymorphic_allocator`. `noexcept` Operator (634)

allocator aware – implies, for a given **allocating object's** type, that its API supports the ability to supply an external resource to the class's constructor, used by the object to obtain memory; see also **scoped allocator model**.

amortized constant time (of a repeated operation) – a bound on the runtime complexity of a given operation such that when it is repeated N times (where N is a sufficiently large number), the total time spent is proportional to N, leading to a constant *average* time spent per operation. Note that any single iteration might not have a fixed limit on its run time and thus not execute in **constant time**. The classic example involves populating a default-constructed `std::vector` with **allocating objects** via repeated calls to `push_back` (assuming dynamic memory allocation itself is slow but still considered a **constant-time** operation); see also **constant time**. `noexcept` Operator (636)

API – short for **application programming interface**. Generalized PODs '11 (402), *Rvalue* References (793), `inline namespace` (1056)

Glossary

application binary interface (ABI) – the object-code-level aspects of a given library that might be needed to link it into a client program, such as the layout of scalar and class objects, how function names are mangled (to produce *type-safe* linkage), as well as **parameter**-calling and return-value conventions; if two libraries (e.g., two versions of the same library) have the same ABI, then they are interchangeable (mutually substitutable), requiring a client application only to relink but specifically *not* recompile.

application programming interface (API) – the source-code-level aspects of a library that are programmatically accessible to client software such as type aliases, enumerations, class definitions, and so on; two libraries having the same API but different ABIs are interchangeable (mutually substitutable) provided that every **translation unit** directly or indirectly incorporating source code from the API — e.g., via a processor `#include` directive or, as of C++20, a module import **statement** — is recompiled before the library is relinked.

architectural insulation – an architectural-level form of insulation.

argument – a value or object that is supplied to a parameterized **entity** and subsequently referred to by the name of its corresponding (formal) **parameter** — e.g., a *type* argument supplied to a template, or an *object* argument supplied to a function.

argument-dependent lookup (ADL) – the process by which, when a function is invoked using its unqualified name, candidate functions that will form the **overload** set are mustered from all namespaces associated with the function **arguments** along with those **accessible** from the caller's scope. Generalized PODs '11 (472), `initializer_list` (572), **noexcept** Operator (638), Range **for** (681), User-Defined Literals (841), `inline namespace` (1056)

arithmetic type – any integral type or floating-point type. `enum class` (334)

array-to-pointer decay – the implicit conversion from an array (having either known or unknown bounds) to a pointer to its first element. Braced Init (222)

as-if – a rule that grants latitude to a compiler to transform code in any way that maintains the same observable behavior for **well-formed** programs — i.e., the same latitude granted to the optimizer. Note that every C++ compiler is required to emulate only the behavior of the **abstract machine** (modulo physical limitations) and makes no other guarantees regarding the operation of the **physical** hardware on which the program is run. `constexpr` Variables (307), *Rvalue* References (717)

assignable (type) – implies, for a given type, that it has a homogeneous assignment operator, which is either built-in or a usable public assignment special member function that may be implicitly declared, defaulted, or user provided. Common usage is to treat the term assignable as short for copy assignable and to call out move assignable explicitly where relevant, such as when an object supports move assignment but not copy assignment. Generalized PODs '11 (486)

assignment operator – (1) a member function named **operator**= taking exactly one **argument** or (2) the built-in assignment operator (=). Generalized PODs '11 (522), *Rvalue* References (816)

atomic – implies, for a given operation, that it is executed either completely or not at all — e.g., concurrent atomic reads and writes cannot be observed to be partially completed. Function `static` '11 (80)

automatic storage duration – the C++ storage class of a non**static**, non**thread_local** function-scope object; an object of this storage class is created when the thread of execution passes through its **definition** and is destroyed immediately when execution leaves the lexical (a.k.a. block) scope in which it was **defined**. Note that all unnamed **temporaries** generated by the compiler are of this storage class. Function `static` '11 (68), *Rvalue* References (731)

Glossary

automatic variable – a variable having automatic storage duration, as in a non**static**, non-**thread_local** local (i.e., function-scope) variable. Note that C++11 redefines the C++03 meaning of the keyword **auto**; see Section 2.1."**auto** Variables" on page 195.

backward compatibility – the property of a newer version of released software (e.g., a component or library) with respect to some previous version such that any program that might have depended on that previous version of the software would have the same essential behavior when rebuilt (relinked and perhaps recompiled) against the newer version. noexcept Specifier (1113)

barrier – a memory barrier a.k.a. fence. Function static '11 (82)

base name (of a component) – the root name of a component's header file, excluding any package prefix or filename extensions (e.g., bdlt_date in bdl/bdlt/bdlt_date.h); see **lakos20**, section 2.4.7, "Proprietary Software Requires an Enterprise Namespace," pp. 309–310, specifically the definition on p. 310. Opaque enums (667)

base specifier list – a list that specifies, in the definition of a **struct** or **class**, the sequence of base classes, along with their respective access levels, whether each is **virtual**, and, potentially, any associated attributes; see Section 1.1."Attribute Syntax" on page 12. Variadic Templates (883)

basic exception-safety guarantee – a (typically implicit) promise that, in the event an exception is somehow thrown during the execution of a given function, (1) each object involved in the computation remains in a valid state (i.e., with its object invariants preserved) and (2) no resources are leaked. noexcept Operator (644)

basic guarantee – short for basic exception-safety guarantee. noexcept Operator (644)

basic source character set – the abstract character set that must be available for expressing C++ source code, which consists of space, horizontal and vertical tab, form feed, newline, the uppercase and lowercase Latin alphabet [A...Z] and [a...z], the 10 digits [0...9], and the 29 essential punctuation marks, _, {, }, [,], #, (,), <, >, %, :, ;, ., ?, *, +, -, /, ^, &, |, ~, !, =, ,, \, ", and '. Raw String Literals (110), Unicode Literals (130)

benchmark test – a measure of quantifiable and ideally repeatable results, e.g., runtime performance, object-code size, or memory consumption, that serves as a point of reference for comparing components, libraries, programs, and so on; most typically, benchmark testing is used to compare aspects of a proposed future version of software with its current one; see also **microbenchmark** and **regression test**. Raw String Literals (114)

binary search – one in which the data in a sorted random-access data structure (e.g., a built-in array or an std::vector) is repeatedly partitioned into a pair of subsets of approximately equal size (e.g., differing by at most a constant) until the value is found or determined to be absent in $O(logN)$ time, where N is number of elements in the data structure. constexpr Functions (292)

bit field – a contiguous sequence of bits of a specified length, declared within a class definition and having an underlying representation of integral or **enum** type; adjacent bit fields may share a memory location, and unnamed bit fields (which may be of zero length) may be declared to force what would otherwise be an adjacent bit field into the next addressable memory location. Generalized PODs '11 (526)

block scope – one created by a compound **statement** bounded by { and } that forms or resides within a function's body; variables that are declared within block scope are found by name only *after* their declaration within the block. Lambdas (587)

Glossary

boilerplate code – significant sections of source code that occur (typically copied) in multiple places with little or no variation. `using` Aliases (136), Variable Templates (161), Default Member Init (322), `enum class` (333)

brace elision – the act, by a programmer, of omitting braces around the initialization of nested members of **aggregate** type during **aggregate initialization** of a compound **aggregate**. Aggregate Init '14 (140)

brace initialization – the initialization of an object using a **braced-initializer list**. Generalized PODs '11 (493), Range `for` (684), *Rvalue* References (752), Variadic Templates (926)

braced-initializer list – a possibly empty, comma-separated sequence of values between braces ({ and }) used as an object initializer. `initializer_list` (554)

byte – the fundamental storage unit in the C++ memory model, necessarily at least 8 bits and, on modern hardware, universally exactly 8 bits. Digit Separators (153)

C linkage – a form of linkage that allows for **declarations** and **definitions** written in C++ to match with callers and callees written and compiled in the C language. Generalized PODs '11 (403)

C++03 POD type – (1) a scalar type, (2) an **aggregate** type or **union** having no non**static** data members that are not themselves C++03 POD types, or (3) an array of such objects. Generalized PODs '11 (414)

C++11 memory allocator – a potentially stateful (as of C++11) object that provides operations for allocating and deallocating memory dynamically. An allocator type appears as an optional **template parameter** in many standard containers and can be used to control how memory is allocated, how elements are constructed, and how they are referenced; see also C++17 pmr allocator. *Rvalue* References (763)

C++11 POD type – a type that is both a **trivial** type and a **standard-layout** type. C++20 removes the notion of a POD type as it is no longer deemed necessary. Generalized PODs '11 (415)

C++17 pmr allocator – a form of stateful memory allocator that supports allocating memory dynamically via the `std::pmr::memory_resource` *abstract base class*, thus providing a common vocabulary for enabling custom memory allocation, especially allocation from local arenas; see **lakos16**, **lakos17a**, **lakos17b**, **lakos19**. *Rvalue* References (763)

cache associativity – the characterization of the mapping from cache lines to locations in physical memory, ranging in implementation from one-to-many (**direct mapped**) to many-to-many with no restrictions (**fully associative**).

cache hit – successfully finding needed data resident in a given level of cache, obviating its retrieval from outside that cache. `alignas` (181)

cache line – the smallest unit of memory read from or written to main memory by a cache in a single operation. `alignas` (174), Generalized PODs '11 (459), `noexcept` Specifier (1142)

cache miss – failing to find needed data resident in a given level of cache, thus requiring its retrieval from outside that cache. `alignas` (182)

call operator – a non**static** member function having the name **operator()** and taking zero or more **arguments**; see also callable object. Lambdas (574)

callable entity – one for which the call operator may be applied — e.g., function, callable object, reference to either, and pointer to function; see also invocable entity.

Glossary

callable object – one whose type has one or more call operators; such an object can be invoked as if it were a function. Function `static` '11 (70), Lambda Captures (994)

callback function – one whose address is supplied for the purpose of being invoked when some anticipated event occurs. Opaque `enums` (669)

capture default – an optional specifier in a lambda-capture list that is either = or &, where = implies that variables captured implicitly are captured by copy, whereas & implies that they are captured by reference. Lambdas (582)

captured by copy – the form of lambda capture whereby a variable named in the enclosing scope of a lambda expression is copied to a data member of the returned lambda closure; all uses of that name within the body of the lambda expression refer to that data member instead of the variable from the enclosing scope. Lambdas (582)

captured by reference – the form of lambda capture whereby a variable named in the body of a lambda expression is treated as an alias to a variable of the same name in the enclosing scope. Lambdas (582)

captured by value – a colloquial term meaning captured by copy.

captured variable – one captured by copy or captured by reference within a lambda expression. Lambdas (602)

carry dependency – one in which some evaluation has a data dependency on the result of some other evaluation. `carries_dependency` (999)

cast – an expression that performs an explicit type conversion to a named type, T: the C-style cast, (T)*expr*, the equivalent functional notation, T(*expr*), and the four C++-specific notations, **const_cast**<T>(*expr*), **static_cast**<T>(*expr*), **reinterpret_cast**<T>(*expr*), and **dynamic_cast**<T>(*expr*) each perform casts, but with varying limitations on the types and expressions to which they can be applied. `enum class` (345)

char-like object – an object of *non*array POD (i.e., trivial standard-layout) type, suitable for use as the element type of an `std::string`. Generalized PODs '11 (479)

character literal – a token having exactly one character between single quotes, e.g., `'q'`, that is of type **char**. Such a token can also be preceded by u, U, or L, and it will be of type **char16_t**, **char32_t**, or **wchar_t**, respectively. Note that some platforms support multicharacter literals, e.g., `'jsl'`, in which case the type will be **int**, and have implementation-defined behavior. User-Defined Literals (837)

CI – short for continuous integration. `inline namespace` (1083)

CIMS – short for common initial member sequence.

class key – a keyword (one of **class**, **struct**, or **union**) used to declare (and perhaps define) a non**enum** user-defined type. Generalized PODs '11 (414)

class-specific memory management – a seldom used strategy in which user-provided (implicitly **static**) *member* overloads of **operator new** and **operator delete** will be used for dynamic allocation and deallocation, respectively. `noexcept` Specifier (1088)

class template – one that declares a parameterized **class**, **struct**, or **union**. Variadic Templates (892)

class template argument deduction – a C++17 feature that enables the deduction of template arguments for a variable using its initializer combined with deduction guides and constructors that are part of the primary class template named by the variable's definition.

Glossary

class type – a kind of user-defined type (UDT) whose definition is introduced using a class key (one of **class**, **struct**, or **union**). `alignas` (168), Generalized PODs '11 (405), `friend` '11 (1031)

closure – a (1) closure object or (2) closure type. Local Types '11 (87), Lambdas (578), *Generic* Lambdas (982), Lambda Captures (986), `auto` Return (1197)

closure object – a callable object created via a lambda expression. Lambdas (578), *Generic* Lambdas (968), `auto` Return (1197)

closure type – the (unnamed) type of a closure object produced by a lambda expression. Lambdas (578), *Generic* Lambdas (968)

code bloat – excessive object code as might result from (1) the inlining of a large function body invoked from numerous call sites or (2) many similar but not identical instantiations of a function template, say, when employing perfect forwarding of string literals (see Section 2.1. "Forwarding References" on page 377). `extern template` (353), `friend` '11 (1054)

code elision – a compiler optimization whereby code that provably can never execute is simply omitted from the generated object code. `noexcept` Specifier (1136)

code motion – a general term for compiler optimizations that reorder provably independent evaluations to potentially improve performance, based on the capabilities of hardware on which the code will execute. `noexcept` Specifier (1136)

code point – a single character (e.g., glyph, control character, or modifier) in a character set. Unicode comprises 1,114,112 code points. ASCII comprises 128 code points. Unicode Literals (129)

code unit – the smallest subdivision of a code point for a specific encoding. In Unicode, for example, the UTF-8 encoding uses 8-bit code units (one to four code units to represent each code point), and the UTF-32 encoding uses 32-bit code units (one per code point). Generalized PODs '11 (476)

cold path – a segment of generated object code that is executed only rarely or in exceptional cases (e.g., code within a **catch** block); such exceptional code is sometimes relegated to physically separate locations in memory so as to eliminate *any* added runtime cost associated with its existence (e.g., zero-cost-exception model). `noexcept` Specifier (1103)

Collatz conjecture – one that states that for all positive integers N, the Collatz sequence is finite. Note that the length, however, varies widely with successive values N.

Collatz function – one that, given an integer N, returns $N/2$ if N is even, and $3N + 1$ if N is odd; see also Collatz conjecture. `constexpr` Variables (313)

Collatz length – the cardinality of the shortest Collatz sequence starting with N that contains 1; note that the length varies widely with successive values of N. `constexpr` Variables (313)

Collatz sequence – one in which each successive element is obtained by starting with N and repeatedly applying the Collatz function to obtain the next element in the sequence. `constexpr` Variables (313)

comma operator – (1) the built-in sequencing operator that evaluates and discards the result of its left-hand side expression and then unconditionally evaluates its right-hand side expression, which becomes the result of evaluating the operator or (2) an *overloaded* operator, having the name **operator,**, that unconditionally evaluates both of its arguments and returns a result as determined by its user-provided definition. `constexpr` Functions (268)

common initial member sequence (CIMS) – the longest *initial* sequence (in declaration order) of non**static** data members and bit fields within a class type that is the same between two standard-layout types. Generalized PODs '11 (406)

Glossary

common type – the one that, for two given types, results from applying the **ternary operator (?:)** to two **expressions** of those respective types. Note that, for **arithmetic types**, the common type is the same type that would result for binary arithmetic **operators** applied to those types; for **class types**, however, the **common type**, if one exists, must be one of the two given types (modulo **cv-qualifications**); i.e., either they are the same type or there exists an unambiguous implicit conversion sequence from one to the other but not vice versa. auto Return (1186)

compile-time constant – (1) a (typically named) constant suitable for evaluation in a **constant expression**; (2) the value of any **constant expression** that is computed and available for use at compile time. enum class (346)

compile-time coupling – a tight form of **physical interdependency** across **components** that necessitates the recompilation of one **component** when some aspect of another's implementation changes. Opaque enums (663)

compile-time dispatch – the implementation technique determining which operation to invoke, depending on operand types, based on compile-time operations, often accomplished using function overloading, SFINAE, and, as of C++20, **concepts**. static_assert (121)

compile-time introspection – the implementation technique of altering program behavior and code generation based on compile-time observable properties of other **entities**, particularly using templates and **type deduction**, and also the primary motivation for ongoing research into reflection. Variadic Templates (947)

complete-class context – a semantic region within the lexical scope of a class definition in which the class (as a whole) itself is considered to be a **complete type** — e.g., function bodies, *default* arguments, default member initializers (see Section 2.1."Default Member Init" on page 318), and **noexcept** specifiers (see Section 3.1."**noexcept** Specifier" on page 1085). Default Member Init (319), noexcept Specifier (1086)

complete type – one whose complete **definition** has been seen, thereby allowing a compiler to know the layout and **footprint** of objects of that type. alignof (184), Default Member Init (319), enum class (350), Opaque enums (661), *Rvalue* References (720), Variadic Templates (891)

component – a physical unit of design consisting of two files: a header (or .h) file and a source (or .cpp) file, often accompanied by an associated **test driver** (or .t.cpp) file. extern template (359), Opaque enums (665), friend '11 (1035), inline namespace (1068)

component local – implies, for a given (logical) entity (**class**, function, template, **typedef**, macro, etc.), that — even though it is programmatically accessible — it is not intended (often indicated by naming convention) for consumption outside of the **component** in which it is **defined** or otherwise provided. Opaque enums (664)

composite pattern – a recursive design pattern that allows a single object or a group of objects to be treated uniformly for a common subset of operations via a common supertype; this pattern is useful for implementing *part-whole* hierarchies, such as a file system in which an object of the abstract Inode supertype is either a concrete *composite* Directory object, containing zero or more Inode objects, or else a concrete *leaf* File object. final (1020)

concepts – a C++20 feature that provides direct support for compile-time constraints on template parameters (limiting which potential **template arguments** match) to appropriately narrow the applicability of a template. Additionally, **concepts** can be used to add ordering between constrained templates — i.e., more constrained and less constrained templates can be implemented differently, and the most constrained one that is applicable for a particular invocation will be preferred for instantiation. Moreover, concepts afford advantages with respect to compile-time error detection and especially diagnostics. Prior to C++20, much of the same functionality was available using SFINAE and other advanced template metaprogramming techniques, but, among other things, concepts make expressing the requirements on template parameters simpler and clearer and allow constraining nontemplate constructors of class templates. static_assert (122), auto Variables (208), Generalized PODs '11 (480), initializer_list (571), auto Return (1201)

concrete class – one from which objects can be instantiated; see also abstract class. Inheriting Ctors (540), final (1008)

conditional compilation – the selective compilation of contiguous lines of source code, controllable from the command line (e.g., using the -D switch with gcc and clang), by employing standard C and C++ preprocessor directives such as **#if**, **#ifdef**, **#ifndef**, **#else**, **#elif**, and **#endif**. Generalized PODs '11 (469)

conditional expression – one that (1) consists of an application of the ternary operator (?:) or (2) is contextually convertible to **bool** and used to determine the code path taken in control-flow constructs such as **if**, **while**, and **for**, or as the first argument to a short-circuit *logical* or *ternary* operator (&&, ||, or ?:). noexcept Operator (615)

conditional noexcept **specification** – one having the form **noexcept** (*<expr>*) where *<expr>* is both a conditional expression and a constant expression, used to determine at compile time whether that function is to be declared **noexcept(true)**. noexcept Operator (639)

conditionally compile – the act of performing conditional compilation. Generalized PODs '11 (469)

conditionally supported – implies, for a particular feature, that a conforming implementation may choose to either support that feature as specified or not support it at all; if it is not supported, however, the implementation is required to issue at least one error diagnostic. Attribute Syntax (13), Generalized PODs '11 (425)

conforming implementation – one (e.g., a compiler) that satisfies all of the requirements of the version of the C++ Standard it attempts to implement.

constant expression – one that can be evaluated at compile time. Deleted Functions (59), static_assert (115), Braced Init (224), constexpr Functions (257), constexpr Variables (302), Generalized PODs '11 (431), initializer_list (554), User-Defined Literals (836), constexpr Functions '14 (960), noexcept Specifier (1091)

constant initialization – initialization of an object (e.g., one having *static* or *thread* storage duration) with values and operations that are evaluable at compile time. Function static '11 (75)

constant time – a bound on the runtime complexity of a given operation such that execution completes within a constant time interval, regardless of the size of the input; see also amortized constant time.

contextual convertibility to bool – implies, for a given expression E, that the definition of a local variable b, such as **bool** b(E), would be well-formed; see also conditional expression. See also contextually convertible to **bool**. explicit Operators (63)

contextual keyword – an identifier, such as **override** (see Section 1.1."**override**" on page 104) or **final** (see Section 3.1."**final**" on page 1007), that has special meaning in certain specific

Glossary

contexts but can otherwise be used like any other identifier, e.g., to name a variable or function. override (104), final (1007)

contextually convertible to bool – implies, for a given expression E, that E may be used to direct-initialize — e.g., bool b(E); — a **bool** variable, where even an explicit conversion operator (see Section 1.1."**explicit** Operators" on page 61) to **bool** may be used, in contrast to implicit conversion, for which converting constructors and conversion operators that are declared as **explicit** are always excluded. Contextual conversion occurs when the core language must test an expression as **bool**, such as is required by an **if** or **while** statement, the condition of a ternary operator (?:), or a conditional **noexcept** specifier (see Section 3.1."**noexcept** Specifier" on page 1085). See also contextual convertibility to **bool**. noexcept Specifier (1129)

continuous integration (CI) – the (typically automated) practice of continually recompiling all source code and running all tests as changes are made to a code base.

continuous refactoring – the practice of making broad incremental changes to a legacy code base, often involving the consolidation of duplicative components at a lower level in the physical hierarchy. deprecated (147)

contract – a bilateral agreement between the human user of a function and its implementer such that, provided all preconditions are met, all postconditions (along with any other promised essential behavior) are guaranteed; see also contracts. Generalized PODs '11 (485), noexcept Operator (616), *Rvalue* References (714)

contract violation – the failure on the part of the caller of a function to satisfy all of its preconditions or, having satisfied all preconditions, the failure of that function to satisfy all of its postconditions and/or live up to its promised essential behavior. Generalized PODs '11 (485)

contracts – a highly anticipated feature in a future version of C++ that will provide for optional runtime checking of preconditions and postconditions as well as invaluable input to static analysis tools and perhaps, some day, even optimizers; see **amini21**.

controlling constant expression – a compile-time constant expression used in a conditional-compilation preprocessor directive such as **#if** or **#elif**. constexpr Functions (285)

conventional string literal – a token consisting of a sequence of characters delimited on each end by double-quote (") characters, creating a null-terminated sequence of objects of type **const char**. The string literal is of type **const char**[N], where N is exactly one more than the integral (possibly zero) number of **char**s in the string. Note that prefixing a conventional string-literal token (e.g., "foo") with an L (e.g., L"foo") creates a null-terminated sequence of four **const wchar_t** objects instead. See also raw string literal. Also note that the type of a string literal in C++ has always been **const**; however, C++03 had a deprecated implicit conversion to (non**const**) **char*** for compatibility with C, rendering string literals themselves dubiously mutable. Raw String Literals (113)

conversion operator – for a given class S and type T, a possibly **explicit** *member* operator of the form **operator** T() used to convert expressions from type S to type T; see Section 1.1. "**explicit** Operators" on page 61. explicit Operators (61)

converting constructor – any non**explicit** constructor, other than a *copy* or *move* constructor, invocable with a single **argument**. explicit Operators (61), noexcept Specifier (1131)

cooked UDL operator – a user-defined literal *operator* that is passed the information obtained from an already-parsed string in the form of an **unsigned long long**, **long double**, or null-terminated **const char***. User-Defined Literals (841)

cookie – an opaque value produced by an object or subsystem intended to be held by the client and potentially passed as an argument in some subsequent call into that same object or subsystem. Opaque enums (669)

copy assignable – property of a type where assignment from an *lvalue* of the same type is valid. Generalized PODs '11 (485)

copy assignment – the process of invoking the assignment operator with two arguments of the same type (modulo cv-qualifiers) where the right-hand side of the argument is an *lvalue*. Generalized PODs '11 (485), *Rvalue* References (752)

copy-assignment operator – a special member function of a class X named **operator=** and taking a single argument whose type is X or, more commonly, lvalue reference to possibly cv-qualified X, where common practice is for it to have a return type of X& and to return ***this**. Deleted Functions (54), Generalized PODs '11 (451), *Rvalue* References (714)

copy constructible – property of a type where construction from an *lvalue* of the same type is valid.

copy construction – construction of an object from an *lvalue* of the same type (modulo cv-qualifiers). *Rvalue* References (764)

copy constructor – one that, for a given type X, takes, as its first argument, a possibly cv-qualified lvalue reference to X; any subsequent parameters must have *default* arguments. Deleted Functions (54), Generalized PODs '11 (437), *Rvalue* References (714)

copy elision – an optimization in which copies (and moves) are permitted to be elided under some circumstances, even if the elided operation would have had an observable side effect. The compiler may treat the source and the destination object of such a notional *copy* or *move* as referring to the same object, even across function call boundaries; see also **return-value optimization**. Forwarding References (390), *Rvalue* References (734)

copy initialization – the initialization that occurs when using the = form of initialization, as well as when passing arguments to a function, returning *by value* from a function, throwing and handling exceptions, and in aggregate *member* initialization. auto Variables (211), Braced Init (215), Default Member Init (318), Generalized PODs '11 (506)

copy initialized – implies, for a given object, that copy initialization has been employed. Braced Init (221)

copy list initialization – copy initialization from a braced-initializer list. Braced Init (226), Default Member Init (318), initializer_list (555)

copy operation – either copy construction or copy assignment. Deleted Functions (53), Generalized PODs '11 (522), noexcept Operator (627), *Rvalue* References (715)

copy semantics – implies, for an operation on two objects (a *destination* and a *source*), that once an operation completes, the *destination* and *source* objects have the same value and the value of the *source* object remains unchanged. Deleted Functions (54), noexcept Operator (627), *Rvalue* References (742), User-Defined Literals (852)

copy/swap idiom – one, commonly used (perhaps overused) to achieve the strong exception-safety guarantee when propagating the value of an object having potentially throwing copy operations, in which a local copy of the source value is made and, if that operation does not fail via an exception, a nonthrowing swap operation is then used to exchange the value of the destination object with that of the local copy. Note that using this idiom with a throwing swap still offers the basic guarantee. noexcept Operator (636), noexcept Specifier (1097)

Glossary

copyable – implies, for a given object, that one or more copy operations can be applied.

core language specification – the part of the C++ Standard that does not describe the Standard Library: clauses 1–16 in C++11 and C++14, clauses 1–19 in C++17, and clauses 1–15 in C++20. Generalized PODs '11 (482)

core trait – a standard trait (e.g., `std::is_trivially_copyable`) that corresponds to a term (e.g., trivially copyable) used in the core language specification and whose implementation typically requires a *compiler intrinsic*; see also **interface trait**. Generalized PODs '11 (482)

critical section – a region of code that must be guarded to prevent race conditions (a.k.a. **data races**) resulting from concurrent execution by multiple threads. Function `static` '11 (71)

CRTP – short for curiously recurring template pattern.

curiously recurring template pattern (CRTP) – one in which a class template, B, parameterized by a single type, D, is intended also to be a base class of D — e.g., **template <typename T> class** Crtp; **class** Derived : **public** Crtp<Derived> { /*...*/ } — so named because it was allegedly discovered independently and used repeatedly throughout the 1990s; see Section 3.1."**friend** '11" on page 1031. friend '11 (1041)

currying – transforming a function that accepts multiple arguments into a sequence of functions that each takes a single **argument**, such that invoking each returned function with the same respective **argument** as presented in the original function will return the same **value** as did the original one — i.e., if `f(a,b,c)` == `curry(f)(a)(b)(c)` — presumably named after the logician Haskell Curry. Lambdas (598)

cv-qualification – the (possibly empty) set of **cv-qualifiers** of a given type. *Rvalue* References (726)

cv-qualifier – one of two keywords, **const** or **volatile**, used to qualify variables, types, and **nonstatic** member functions. Forwarding References (379), *Rvalue* References (724), Ref-Qualifiers (1153)

cyclic physical dependency – a dependency among two or more physical entities that implies all involved entities are directly or indirectly physically dependent on each other. extern template (374)

cyclically dependent – implies, for a set of entities, that there exists a direct or indirect (often physical) dependency among them; see also **cyclic physical dependency**. Function `static` '11 (75)

dangling reference – one to an object whose lifetime has ended. Ref-Qualifiers (1171), decltype(auto) (1212)

data dependency – one in which the evaluation of an operation requires the result of another to have already been computed. carries_dependency (999)

data-dependency chain – a chain of evaluations that has a **data dependency** between each consecutive evaluation in the chain. carries_dependency (998)

data member – a *member* variable of a **class**, **struct**, or **union**; if declared **static**, the variable will be shared among all objects of the type. alignas (168)

data race – a defect in a multithreaded program or system in which the ordering of events among threads or processes, respectively, is insufficiently constrained to guarantee correct operation. Function `static` '11 (68)

death test – a form of **unit test** that verifies program termination occurs when expected (and thus involves termination of the **test driver** itself); implementing such tests typically requires a **test driver** that forks and then performs the **death test** in the child process, observing (from the parent process) that the expected output and exit status were produced.

Glossary

debug build – a mode in which code can be compiled that favors the ability to detect and diagnose bugs, often including the enabling of assertions via `<cassert>` or other assertion libraries. Generalized PODs '11 (468)

decay (of a type) – a colloquial term for implicit trivial conversions such as array to pointer, function to pointer, and *lvalue* to *rvalue*. Rvalue References (815)

decimal floating-point (DFP) – a representation of floating-point numbers that involves storing the mantissa as a power of 10, as opposed to the classical (binary) floating-point representation in C and C++, which stores the mantissa as a power of 2. User-Defined Literals (862)

declaration – a statement that declares an entity, such as a variable, function, or type; a declaration might be part of a definition; see also nondefining declaration and opaque declaration. `static_assert` (121), `constexpr` Variables (315), Variadic Templates (879), `noexcept` Specifier (1105)

declarator operator – either `*`, `&`, `&&`, `::*`, `[]`, or `()`, any of which can be applied to form a compound type, respectively a pointer, an lvalue reference, an rvalue reference, a pointer to member, an array, or a function. Variadic Templates (889)

declare – to introduce into a scope the existence (and perhaps properties) of a (typically) named entity such as a variable, function, type, template, or type alias (such as a **typedef**). Deleted Functions (54), Forwarding References (390), Rvalue References (762)

declared type (of an object) – the type with which a (typically) named entity was declared. `decltype` (25)

deduced return type – a type that, for a given function whose return type is represented using the **auto** keyword, is deduced from (possibly implicit) **return** statements within the function definition (see Section 1.1."Trailing Return" on page 124); note that **auto** at the start of a function declaration might instead be used to introduce a trailing, but nonetheless explicit, return type (see Section 1.1."Trailing Return" on page 124). Lambdas (593)

deduction guide – an implicit or user-defined rule that tells the compiler how to deduce template arguments for a class template from a provided initializer — available as of C++17.

default constructed – implies, for a given object, that it has been created without an initializing expression. Generalized PODs '11 (478), Rvalue References (752)

default constructor – one that can be invoked without arguments. Generalized PODs '11 (437), Rvalue References (754), `noexcept` Specifier (1136)

default initialization – initialization that (1) for a class type, invokes the constructor that would be invoked if the initializer were empty parentheses (i.e., `()`), (2) for an array type, default initializes each of its elements, and (3) in all other cases, performs no initialization. Note that default initialization can occur either because no initializer is supplied or as the result of value initialization. Braced Init (216), `constexpr` Functions (273), Rvalue References (765)

default initialized – implies, for a given object, that it was initialized via default initialization. Defaulted Functions (36), Braced Init (221), Default Member Init (322), Generalized PODs '11 (493), Rvalue References (752)

default member initializer – one that is associated with the declaration of a non**static** data member of a class type that may be used during construction when no other initializer is provided (e.g., from a constructor's member initializer list). `constexpr` Functions (270), Default Member Init (318), Generalized PODs '11 (426)

defaulted (function) – implies a defaulted special member function. Generalized PODs '11 (483), `noexcept` Operator (649), Rvalue References (757), `noexcept` Specifier (1086)

Glossary

defaulted special member function – a (user-declared) special member function specified (see Section 1.1."Defaulted Functions" on page 33) to be implemented using its default (i.e., compiler-generated) definition. Note that, in some situations (e.g., see Section 3.1."**union** '11" on page 1174), the compiler may choose to delete an implicitly or explicitly declared and defaulted function.

defect report (DR) – an acknowledgment by the C++ Standards Committee of a defect in the current C++ Standard that is considered by ISO to apply to the currently active C++ Standard and is generally taken by implementers to apply to all previous versions of the C++ Standard where the change would be both applicable and practicable. Braced Init (218), `constexpr` Functions (280), Generalized PODs '11 (432), Inheriting Ctors (551), `initializer_list` (561), Lambdas (594), `noexcept` Operator (615), Range **for** (681), *Rvalue* References (722), `noexcept` Specifier (1086)

defensive check – one typically performed at runtime (e.g., using a C-style `assert` macro) to verify some condition that is impossible to occur in a correct program. A common use case is to verify, for a given function, that there has not been a contract violation — i.e., a precondition or postcondition violation — yet is entirely superfluous in a correctly implemented program. Generalized PODs '11 (468), *Rvalue* References (744)

defensive programming – a term, sometimes (mis)used, to suggest generally good programming practice implies the use of defensive checks to, for example, detect client misuse of a given function, by violating its preconditions when invoking it. `final` (1024)

define – to provide, for a given entity, any additional details, e.g., size, layout, address, etc., beyond just its declaration, needed to use that entity in a running process. Deleted Functions (58), Forwarding References (390), *Rvalue* References (762), Variadic Templates (880)

defined dehavior – (1) behavior that is unambiguously codified in terms of C++'s abstract machine or (2) the full set of behaviors defined for a given component or library. Note that invoking a component or library out of contract is library undefined behavior (a.k.a. soft UB), which might lead to language undefined behavior (a.k.a. hard UB). `noexcept` Specifier (1112)

defining declaration – one — such as **class** Foo { }; — that provides a complete definition of the entity being declared. Note that a **typedef** or **using** declaration (see Section 1.1."**using** Aliases" on page 133) would not be considered *defining* because, according to the C++ Standard, neither is a definition. Also note that an opaque enumeration declaration does not provide the enumerators corresponding to the complete definition and, although sufficient to instantiate opaque objects of the enumerated type, does not allow for interpretation of their values; hence, it too would not be considered *defining*; see also nondefining declaration. *Rvalue* References (729)

definition – a statement that fully characterizes an entity (e.g., type, object, or function); note that all definitions are subject to the one-definition rule. Function `static` '11 (68), `constexpr` Variables (315), Variadic Templates (879), `noexcept` Specifier (1105)

delegating constructor – one that, rather than fully initializing data members and base-class objects itself, invokes another constructor after which it might perform additional work in its own body (see Section 1.1."Delegating Ctors" on page 46). Delegating Ctors (46)

deleted – implies (1) for a given function, that it has been rendered inaccessible from *any* access level — either explicitly, by being annotated using = **delete** (see Section 1.1."Deleted Functions" on page 53) or implicitly (e.g., see Section 3.1."**union** '11" on page 1174); or (2) for a given pointer to a dynamically allocated object, that the (typically global) **delete** operator has been applied to it (and no new object has subsequently been reallocated at that same address). Deleted Functions (59), Generalized PODs '11 (483), *Rvalue* References (757), `noexcept` Specifier (1086)

deleted function – one that is either declared explicitly to be deleted or else is implicitly deleted (e.g., an aggregate that comprises a subobject whose corresponding special member function is unavailable). Defaulted Functions (33), Generalized PODs '11 (523)

dependent type – one referenced in a template whose identity cannot be determined without knowing one or more of the arguments to the template itself. Inheriting Ctors (538), *Generic Lambdas* (981)

design pattern – an abstract unit of commonly recurring design (e.g., *Singleton, Adapter, Iterator, Visitor*) that comprises a fairly small number of entities having distinct roles and identified interrelationships, is more general than can be expressed directly (e.g., as a **template**) in reusable code, and is often language agnostic (e.g., C++, D, Java, Python, Smalltalk). Note that CRTP, despite having a P (for pattern), is so formulaic and nonportable that it might be considered a C++ *idiom* instead. See **gamma95**: Chapter 3, section "Singleton," pp. 127–138; Chapter 4, section "Adapter," pp. 139–150; and Chapter 5, section "Iterator," pp. 257–271, and section "Visitor," pp. 331–349. Opaque enums (669)

destructor – a special member function of a class (e.g., S) declared using the same name as the class but preceded by a tilde character (e.g., ~S) that is invoked implicitly when the lifetime of an object of that type ends on leaving the block in which the object was defined (automatic storage duration), when the main function returns (static storage duration), when the thread for which it is defined ends (thread storage duration), when the **delete** operator is applied (dynamic storage duration), or when the destructor is invoked explicitly within the program. Note that a class's destructor automatically invokes the destructors for each of its non**static** data members and base-classs objects. Generalized PODs '11 (450), *Rvalue* References (752), noexcept Specifier (1086)

detection idiom – a pattern used with templates to detect whether certain expressions are valid or ill formed for a particular sequence of template arguments, frequently used for compile-time dispatch; see **otsuka20**.

devirtualize – replace, as a pure optimization of a given virtual-function call, the *indirect* invocation of that function, through the object's virtual-function table, with a *direct* one, assuming that the tool chain can somehow determine the dynamic type of the object at either compile or link time; in such cases, the viable body of a virtual function can be inlined. final (1011)

DFP – short for decimal floating point.

diffusion – see memory diffusion. alignas (183)

dimensional unit type – a type used for representing distinct kinds and dimensions of physical units, often providing protection against mixing units where such mixing would be erroneous. User-Defined Literals (864)

direct braced initialized – implies, for a given object, that it has been initialized using a braced-initializer list in a direct initialization context. Generalized PODs '11 (455)

direct initialization – initialization of an object using a parenthesized initializer, a braced-initializer list that is not preceded by =, a **static_cast**, or a type conversion using functional notation. explicit Operators (62), auto Variables (211), Braced Init (215), Default Member Init (318)

Glossary

direct initialized – implies, for a given object, that it has been initialized via direct initialization. Braced Init (230), *Rvalue* References (754)

direct list initialization – the use of list initialization during direct initialization. Braced Init (229), Default Member Init (318), `initializer_list` (555)

direct mapped – a form of cache associativity in which every region in main memory maps to exactly one cache line, resulting in evictions when a second region that maps to the same cache line is accessed. `alignas` (182)

disambiguator – something that can be used to distinguish between two otherwise identical entities. For example, an unused additional function parameter of varying type is used as a disambiguator in an overload set, where the type to use for the disambiguating parameter is determined through metaprogramming by the invoker. Disambiguators can also be found in the syntax of the C++ language itself, e.g., when **template** or **typename** are needed to facilitate a proper parse. `decltype` (29)

distinguishing sequence – a sequence of salient operations that, when applied to two objects of the same type having initially distinct platonic values — whose observable salient attributes might not be distinguishable — will eventually produce objects whose respective observable salient attributes are not the same. In other words, two value semantic objects of a given type do not have the same value if there exists a distinguishing sequence for them. Note that this sequence might vary depending on the initial values of the respective objects, which differs from the classical definition in finite automata theory in which the distinguishing sequence must be the same for all pairs of FSM states.

divide and conquer – an approach to problem-solving where a task (e.g., sorting a collection of values) is divided into roughly equal-sized smaller tasks whose individual solutions can be used to solve the original, larger problem (e.g., merge sort). `constexpr` Functions (297)

DR – short for defect report.

duck typing – determining the properties of a type, often in a template when choosing what algorithms to use with objects of that type, based solely on the *syntactic* interface it supports. As this approach has no way to check for or enforce semantic requirements, it must rely on the aphorism, "If it looks like a duck and walks like a duck, it must be a duck." friend '11 (1052)

dumb data – values, typically integral, whose specific meaning is defined and usable only in a higher-level context; see **lakos20**, section 3.5.5, "Dumb Data," pp. 629–633. Opaque `enums` (668)

dynamic binding – determining, for a given object, the appropriate (virtual member) function to call based on the dynamic type of the object, often implemented via virtual dispatch. `final` (1015)

dynamic dispatch – invoking the appropriate (virtual member) function based on the dynamic type of the object used to invoke it; see also virtual dispatch. `final` (1011)

dynamic exception specification – the classic approach to exception specification using **throw** on a function declaration to list all of the exception types that might be thrown by a function. Supplanted by **noexcept** (see Section 3.1."**noexcept** Specifier" on page 1085), this feature was deprecated in C++11, removed except for **throw()** as an equivalent of **noexcept** in C++17, and removed completely in C++20. noexcept Operator (618), noexcept Specifier (1085)

dynamic type – the *runtime type* (e.g., `Derived`) of an object, which might differ from the static type (e.g., `Base`) of a pointer or reference to it — e.g., `Base* p = new Derived();` — where class `Derived` publicly inherits from class `Base`. Generalized PODs '11 (416)

EBO – see empty-base optimization.

embedded development – writing, documenting, testing, and deploying software for embedded systems. Binary Literals (145)

embedded system – one that runs either on resource-limited hardware or in restricted environments, ranging from pacemakers to set-top entertainment devices. `long long` (93), `noexcept` Specifier (1101)

emplacement – an often more efficient alternative to copy construction in which the arguments to some value constructor of an object, rather than a reference to a constructed object itself, are used to construct a new object directly in its final destination — e.g., `template<typename T> push_back(const T&);` versus `template<typename... Args> void emplace_back(Args&&... args);` for the `std::vector` container; see, e.g., **hu20**. Forwarding References (390)

empty-base optimization (EBO) – a compiler optimization in which a base-class subobject that introduces no non`static` data members is assigned the same address as another subobject of the derived-class object, provided they do not have the same type, to avoid any size overhead that would otherwise be required. Since C++11, compilers are required to perform this optimization if the derived class is a **standard-layout class**; otherwise, this optimization is allowed but not required. Had the same empty base type been used instead to create a data member, at least one additional byte would have been required within the footprint of the outer class; hence, the preference for making empty types base classes rather than data members. Note that C++20 introduces an attribute to address the inefficiency of empty data members. `alignof` (185), Generalized PODs '11 (499), Lambdas (607), Variadic Templates (933), `final` (1028)

encapsulation – the colocation of (typically private) data along with manipulator and accessory functions used to act upon and retrieve that data; ideally the representation of the data can change, perhaps necessitating client code be recompiled, but without forcing any clients to rework their code; see also **insulation**. Opaque `enums` (663)

encoding prefix – one placed before a string or character literal used to indicate a literal having a character type other than **char**. C++03 supported L for **wchar_t**; C++11 added u for **char16_t**, U for **char32_t**, and u8 for **char** (with UTF-8 encoding). User-Defined Literals (844)

entity – one of the primary logical building blocks of a C++ program: value, *object*, reference, *function*, *enumerator*, *type*, class member, bit-field, *template*, *template* specialization, *namespace*, parameter pack, or **this**. `decltype` (25), Local Types '11 (84), deprecated (147)

equality comparable – implies, for a given type, that the homogeneous equality-comparison operators, **operator==** and **operator!=**, are defined and publicly accessible for the purpose of determining whether two objects of that type have (represent) the same value; see value semantics. Note that equality comparable is independent of homogeneous relational operators (<, <=, >, >=).

escalation – a form of refactoring (a.k.a. *escalation technique*) whereby parts of a pair of components that are mutually dependent are moved to a separate, higher-level component, enabling the removal of a potential cyclic physical dependency; see **lakos20**, section 3.5.2, "Escalation," pp. 604–614. `extern template` (374)

essential behavior – a superset of **postconditions** that includes aspects of the computation beyond the final result, such as runtime complexity, thread safety, exception safety, etc.

Glossary

exception agnostic – a particular style of implementation in which no exception-related syntax (**try**, **catch**, or **throw**) is used and hence no exceptions are thrown directly; nonetheless the code remains entirely exception safe with respect to injected exceptions (e.g., from derived classes or template arguments) through judicious use of RAII. Importantly, a fully exception agnostic library will be buildable and behave correctly, irrespective of whether support for exceptions in the compiler is enabled; note that exception and nonexception builds might not necessarily be ABI compatible. noexcept Operator (644), noexcept Specifier (1126)

exception free path – one in which the flow of control (e.g., leading up to an invocation of a function) does not involve the throwing (and potentially catching) of any exceptions. noexcept Specifier (1134)

exception safe – implies, for a given function, that no defects will manifest nor resources leak when an exception escapes the function, even when that exception is thrown by a different function. More generally, a class, template, component, or library is exception safe if no defects or resource leaks occur as the result of an exception thrown during the evaluation of any function they define. noexcept Operator (644), noexcept Specifier (1126)

exception specification – one of two forms — dynamic exception specification (deprecated) or **noexcept** (as of C++11) — used for a given function to indicate which or just whether, respectively, exceptions may be thrown by that function. Lambdas (593), *Rvalue* References (733)

excess N notation – a representation of a (typically *signed*) value v stored instead as $v + N$ in an *unsigned* integer or bit field; the range for v is $-N$ through $M - N$, where M is the largest value representable in that storage. IEEE floating-point formats make use of a form of this notation in which N (a.k.a. the *bias*) is one less than half the range of the unsigned storage: excess 127 [-126 to +127] for **float** and excess 1023 [-511 to +512] for **double**. Note, however, that the smallest and largest values are reserved and have special meaning, thereby reducing the range of representable exponents by 2. Digit Separators (155)

executable image – the representation of the program in relocatable binary format, typically stored in a file, that is (at least partially) loaded by the operating system into memory prior to execution of that program. noexcept Specifier (1135)

execution character set – that comprising all characters that can be interpreted by a running program on a specific platform including, at minimum, all of the characters in the source character set; control characters representing alert, backspace, and carriage return; and a null character (or null wide character), whose value is 0. Each character in the execution character set has an implementation-defined non-negative integral value, typically specified by a standard such as ASCII or Unicode. User-Defined Literals (844)

expiring object – implies, for a given object, that it no longer needs to hold either its value or the resources used to represent that value beyond the expression in which it is used. An object can be explicitly marked as expiring (e.g., using std::move), and expressions that designate objects so marked are xvalues. An object may also be implicitly deemed by a compiler to be expiring (e.g., for a temporary). *Rvalue* References (713)

explicit instantiation declaration – a directive (see Section 2.1."**extern template**" on page 353) that suppresses implicit instantiation of a function template for the specified template arguments in the local translation unit, instead relying on an explicit instantiation definition, provided in exactly one translation unit within the program, potentially reducing compilation time and object-code size (but having no effect on the linked program's executable size or run time); see also explicit instantiation definition. extern template (353)

Glossary

explicit instantiation definition – a directive (see Section 2.1."**extern template**" on page 353), for a given template and specific **template arguments**, to instantiate and emit, in the current translation unit, any associated object code for **entities** that the template **defines**. Note that at most one such directive per template **specialization** may appear in a program, *no diagnostic required*; see also explicit instantiation declaration and Ill Formed, No Diagnostic Required. extern template (353)

explicit instantiation directive – either an explicit instantiation declaration or an explicit instantiation definition. extern template (353)

explicit specialization – a declaration or complete definition of a template specialization, used instead of instantiating the corresponding *primary template* (or any partial specialization) that might be selected when supplied with those same **arguments** at the point of use; see primary class template declaration and partial ordering of class template specialization.

explicit template-argument specification – the specification, when invoking a function template — e.g., **template <typename T, typename U> func()** — with a sequence of template arguments (e.g., **int**, **double**) surrounded by < and >, e.g., func<**int, double**>(0, 0); such explicitly specified template arguments will be used as is and will not require **template argument deduction.** Variadic Templates (895)

explicitly captured – implies, for a given variable, that it is named in the capture list of a lambda. Lambdas (582)

expression – a valid sequence of **operators** and **operands** that specifies a computation; the evaluation of an **expression** may produce a value or cause side effects. Unlike a **statement**, expressions may be nested; see also outermost expression.

expression alias – an often considered, potential future feature of C++ that would support a parameterized alias for an **expression**. Such a feature would substitute the expression inplace, much like a hygienic macro, behaving like a forced inline function having automatically deduced result type and exception specification (see Section 3.1."**noexcept** Specifier" on page 1085), but without the possibility of separating declaration and definition. noexcept Specifier (1146)

expression SFINAE – the use of SFINAE to exclude a function template **specialization** from consideration during overload resolution or a (class) template **partial specialization** during template instantiation, based on the validity of a particular **expression**. This form of SFINAE enables programming patterns such as the detection idiom. decltype (29), static_assert (122), Trailing Return (126)

expression template – a template **metaprogramming** pattern in which overloaded **operators** return compound types that capture, within their **template parameters**, an entire **expression**. When these complex types are converted to a desired result type, an optimized implementation of the entire **expression** will be evaluated, instead of a potentially much less efficient evaluation of each individual subexpression. This general technique has been used often in libraries such as Eigen (**eigen**) to optimize computations involving large matrices. auto Variables (202)

extended alignment – an alignment larger than the alignment of std::max_align_t. alignas (168)

external linkage – linkage that allows a name to refer to the same entity across translation units; see also internal linkage.

factory function – one whose purpose is to construct, initialize, and return an object, often by value. *Rvalue* References (778), User-Defined Literals (836), Variadic Templates (929)

Glossary

fallible – implies, for a given function, that it might fail to satisfy its postconditions even when its preconditions are met; see also fallible implementation. noexcept Specifier (1118)

fallible implementation – one that might fail to meet its contract, i.e., one that is fallible. noexcept Specifier (1120)

false sharing – a pessimizing storage phenomenon where unrelated objects that happen to wind up on the same cache line in memory result in potentially severe runtime performance degradation when multiple threads attempt to access those respective objects concurrently; note that cache line access on typical hardware is automatically synchronized to avoid concurrent access from execution threads. alignas (174)

fault tolerant – implies, for a given distributed system (but never a function, component, or program), that failures are reliably handled (e.g., through graceful degradation rather than catastrophic failure) and often approximated through significant redundancy of interconnected hardware, design, and implementation so as to avoid any single point of failure. noexcept Specifier (1123)

fence – a memory barrier; see also memory fence instruction. Function static '11 (82)

file extension – the part of a filename after a final ., commonly used in modern operating systems to identify distinct file types. For example, typical standard practice for C++ developers is to use .h or .hpp for *header* files and .cpp, .cxx, or .cc for *implementation* (a.k.a. *source*) files. Opaque enums (667)

floating-point literal – a literal denoting a floating-point value — e.g., 5.0 (**double**), 5.0f (**float**), or 5.0L (**long double**). User-Defined Literals (837)

floating-point-to-integer conversion – an implicit (truncating) conversion defined from floating-point types to integral types. User-Defined Literals (843)

floating-point type – either **float**, **double**, or **long double**.

flow of control – the execution path (i.e., sequence of operations executed) within a program; e.g., a file-scope static variable is initialized the first time the flow-of-control passes through its definition. Function static '11 (68)

footprint – the contiguous block of sufficiently aligned memory, as quantified by the **sizeof** and **alignof** operators (see Section 2.1."**alignof**" on page 184), in which any non**static** data members, base-class objects, vtable pointers, virtual-base pointers, and padding bytes needed to achieve proper subobject alignment reside; note that an object's footprint is independent of any dynamically allocated memory that it might hold or own. extern template (357), Generalized PODs '11 (452), *Rvalue* References (734), noexcept Specifier (1114)

forward class declaration – a forward declaration of a **class**, **struct**, or **union**, often used in the header file of a component to increase insulation. Opaque enums (675)

forward declaration – a nondefining declaration that resides ahead of its definition in the same translation unit (TU); typical use is (1) as an opaque declaration in a header file to facilitate consistent use across TUs and (2) to accommodate mutually dependent entities (e.g., within a single TU); see also local declaration. Opaque enums (662)

forward declared – implies, for a given entity in a particular translation unit (TU), that a nondefining declaration of it precedes its definition in that TU; see also local declaration. Opaque enums (664)

forwarding reference – a function template *parameter* whose type is an unqualified rvalue reference to a template parameter (T&&). The deduced **template argument** corresponding to the template parameter will have the same value category as the function **argument**; reference collapsing will cause the function **parameter** of the instantiated function to be an lvalue reference or rvalue reference as appropriate. Forwarding References (377), Range **for** (680), *Rvalue* References (732), Variadic Templates (918), *Generic* Lambdas (971), **auto** Return (1184)

fragmentation – the process by which initially densely packed blocks of allocated memory, due to repeated allocation and deallocation, spread out across the **address space** over time — e.g., even when the total memory utilization does not increase. As a consequence, an allocation request for a sizable block of (contiguous) memory, which might have succeeded if requested earlier in the process lifetime, cannot be honored, despite there being an ample quantity of (noncontiguous) free memory available; see also **memory diffusion**. alignas (183)

free function – one that is *not* a member function; see also **hidden friend idiom**. Deleted Functions (58), Generalized PODs '11 (442), initializer_list (558)

free operator – a built-in or user-defined **operator** that is not implemented as a **member** of a class; see also **member operator**. User-Defined Literals (839)

freestanding – implies a subset of the C++ Standard Library and core language (due to missing pieces of the library) intended to be run on platforms (such as **embedded systems**) that might not have a fully functioning underlying operating system. initializer_list (570)

full expression – one that is not a subexpression of another **expression**; see **outermost expression**. Range **for** (693)

full specialization – a (colloquial) synonym for **explicit specialization**.

fully associative – a form of cache associativity where any cache line can reference any region in main memory, obviating evictions until every cache line has been populated. alignas (182)

fully constructed – implies, for a given object, that its initialization, if any, has been completed. In particular, if initialization requires invoking a nondelegating constructor, fully constructed implies that the constructor has finished running, whereas if initialization requires invoking a delegating constructor, fully constructed implies that the target constructor has finished running. Delegating Ctors (47)

function designator – a term in the C Standard used to describe an **expression** having function type. *Rvalue* References (815)

function object – a callable object (a.k.a. functor); see also **invocable** object. constexpr Functions (292), Default Member Init (328), Lambdas (574), Lambda Captures (990)

function parameter list – the parameter declarations that specify the **arguments** with which a function may be invoked and, along with the function's name, contribute to its **signature**.

function parameter pack – a pack expansion within a function parameter list that defines a function parameter for each element of a named **template parameter pack**. Variadic Templates (879)

function prototype – (the specification of) a nondefining declaration of a function, which includes its **signature**, return type, and any other features, such as a **noexcept** specification (see Section 3.1."**noexcept** Specifier" on page 1085) that would distinguish it from other like-named functions. *Rvalue* References (733)

function scope – used (colloquially within this book) to mean **block scope**. Note that the C++ Standard as published (through C++20) has an entirely different **definition** of this term,

Glossary

applying only to labels; that definition was removed from the Standard via a DR (see **her-ring20**). Function static '11 (68)

function template – one that defines a compile-time parameterized function.

function-template-argument type deduction – a process effected by the compiler during overload resolution whereby each function template in the overload set is matched to the specified arguments and, if a valid set of template parameters can be deduced from the argument types, that specialization for the function template remains in the overload set (to be compared with other functions remaining in the set to determine if a unique best match can be found); see also SFINAE. auto Variables (195)

function try block – one, including its **catch** clause, that serves as a function body, primarily used to provide exception handling in a constructor — e.g., C::C(X x) : d_x(x) **try** { /*...*/ } **catch** (...) { /*...*/ } — as exceptions thrown from the member initializer list will also be caught and acted upon (but not swallowed) by the exception handler of the function try block. constexpr Functions (268)

functor – a callable object. Lambdas (573), *Generic* Lambdas (968)

functor class – a class type that supports callable objects. Lambdas (574)

functor type – the type of a callable object. Lambdas (573)

fundamental alignment – any alignment that is not greater than std::max_align_t; note that an alignment is always an integral power of 2 (1, 2, 4, 8, ...). alignas (168)

fundamental integral type – a synonym for integral type. long long (89)

fundamental type – either an arithmetic type, **void**, or std::nullptr_t. noexcept Operator (622), *Rvalue* References (803), final (1014), union '11 (1174)

general-purpose machine – a kind of computer that is designed for general applications, used widely in a variety of organizations. long long (93)

generalized PODs – a superset of C++03 POD types that are characterized in modern C++ as the intersection of trivial types and standard-layout types; see Section 2.1."Generalized PODs '11" on page 401.

generic – implies, for a given class, function, object, or code fragment, that properties intrinsic to its behavior will be specified (at compile time) at the point where it is used (e.g., the relevant template is instantiated); see also generic programming. Generalized PODs '11 (474)

generic lambda – one having function **parameters** specified using **auto** so as to create a **closure** having a templated function-call **operator**. Lambdas (592), *Generic* Lambdas (968)

generic programming – writing and using software in which the types of the objects being manipulated are themselves parameterized (e.g., using C++ templates). noexcept Operator (615)

generic type – one that is itself parameterized to accept, at compile time, type (or even non-type) arguments at the point at which it is instantiated; generic types are typically implemented as class templates in C++. Variadic Templates (878)

glvalue – a value category that characterizes an expression as one from which the identity of an object or function can be determined; a value that is not a *glvalue* is necessarily an *rvalue*. *Rvalue* References (717), decltype(auto) (1259)

golden file – a file containing the expected output of a (regression) test program. The test program is run, creating an output file that is then compared to the golden file, and if the files match, the test passes. Raw String Literals (114)

grouping macro – one that expands all of its arguments using __VA_ARGS__; a grouping macro is useful for circumventing syntactic annoyances that occur when a conventional macro is supplied a multiparameter template and thus with macro arguments containing commas that are not themselves nested within parentheses; e.g., SOME_MACRO(SomeTemplate<A, B, C>) results in a syntax error. Generalized PODs '11 (520)

guaranteed copy elision – a form of copy elision that became mandatory in C++17: when an object is initialized with a *prvalue* of the same type (e.g., when returning from a function *by value*), no temporary object is created, and the destination object is constructed directly from the initializing expression, thereby eliminating any need for (accessible) copy operations. Braced Init (216), **noexcept** Operator (648), *Rvalue* References (791), Ref-Qualifiers (1163)

handle type – one that defines a (typically lightweight) *proxy* for a physically separate object or resource, often wrapping a lower-level API that interacts directly with a raw resource. *Rvalue* References (792)

hard UB – short for language undefined behavior (a.k.a. language UB). **noexcept** Specifier (1115)

has identity – states, for a given entity, that there is a way (e.g., by name or address) of identifying it (e.g., a *glvalue*) other than just reiterating its value (e.g., a *prvalue*). For example, a variable or data member thereof has identity, whereas a (nonstring) literal does not. *Rvalue* References (711)

header-only library – a library whose full implementation is contained in header files and all defined functions are **template** or **inline**, removing the need to link library-specific object files. inline namespace (1067)

heap memory – a synonym for dynamically allocated memory.

hidden-friend idiom – the design technique of declaring and defining a free function or free operator as a **friend** of a type within the scope of a class definition. A function implemented in this way is not visible to ordinary name lookup or even qualified lookup and will be found only through argument-dependent lookup — i.e., only when the type declaring the *hidden friend* is participating in overload resolution. Generalized PODs '11 (472)

hide – preventing access, by one entity, to another entity of the same name due to name lookup rules. For example, function-name hiding occurs when a member function in a derived class has the same name as one in the base class, but it is not overriding it due to a difference in the function signature or because the member function in the base class is not **virtual**; the *hidden* member function is accessible only via a pointer or reference to the base class. Another example occurs when a type S is hidden by a variable — e.g., **struct** S { } S; S s; (Error, S is not a type.) — i.e., one having the same name in the same scope. Inheriting Ctors (536), Lambda Captures (987)

hierarchical reuse – a central paradigm of effective large-scale software development in which reuse is not limited to client-facing components but instead extends downward recursively to apply to all of the parts comprised by every component; see also Software Capital. final (1012)

higher-order function – one that operates on other functions — i.e., takes a function as an argument or returns a function as its return value. Trailing Return (125)

horizontal encoding – a convention whereby the meaning of certain bits that occur throughout an encoding (e.g., the microcode of a computer) are independent of the values of bits that occur elsewhere in that encoding.

Glossary

hot path – the part of a program (specifically, generated object code) that is executed under normal and frequently encountered conditions; see also **cold path**. noexcept Specifier (1103)

Hyrum's law – the observation attributed to Hyrum Wright of Google that, given a sufficient number of users of an API, all observable behavior — notably including those that are undocumented, unintentional, nonessential, or unstable — will be depended upon by the user base. final (1012), friend '11 (1036)

id expression – a qualified id or unqualified id that can be used to name an **entity** or a set of entities, such as variable names, function names, and (after a . or ->) class member names. decltype (25), *Rvalue* References (780)

identity – a property of an **expression** that can be identified uniquely, e.g., by name or address, independently of its **value**; see also **has identity**.

IFNDR – short for ill formed, no diagnostic required.

ill formed – implies, for a given program, that it is not valid C++. A compiler is required to fail to compile such a program and issue an appropriate diagnostic (error) message unless the ill formed nature is explicitly identified as one where no diagnostic is required (a.k.a. IFNDR); see ill formed, no diagnostic required. static_assert (120), Braced Init (227), constexpr Variables (303), User-Defined Literals (839), inline namespace (1067), auto Return (1203)

ill formed, no diagnostic required (IFNDR) – implies, for a given program, that it is ill formed in a way where the compiler is not required to issue a diagnostic. Typical examples of IFNDR, such as violations of the ODR, do not require a diagnostic because identifying the problem would either drastically impact compile times or be otherwise impracticable (if not impossible) in general. Delegating Ctors (50), static_assert (117), alignas (177), constexpr Functions (262), enum class (350), Opaque enums (666), Underlying Type '11 (832), User-Defined Literals (840), Variadic Templates (900), carries_dependency (1000), inline namespace (1067)

immutable type – a user-defined type for which objects instantiated from that type, once fully constructed, cannot be changed. Ref-Qualifiers (1167)

imperative programming – implies, for a given language or programming paradigm, the use of a sequence of **statements** describing the evaluations of **expressions** that progressively *mutate* existing state (e.g., variables, objects) within a program instead of always creating new objects of immutable types as is common in *declarative* or *functional* programming. constexpr Functions '14 (959)

implementation defined – implies, for a given behavior, that it is not fully specified by the Standard but that an implementation must specify in its documentation. Attribute Syntax (12), nullptr (100), alignas (168), constexpr Functions (295), enum class (335), Generalized PODs '11 (501), Opaque enums (660), *Rvalue* References (747), noexcept Specifier (1093)

implementation inheritance – a form of inheritance in which the implementation of a non**virtual** or nonpure **virtual** function defined in a base class is inherited along with its interface in a derived class; note that inheriting the definitions of non**virtual** functions is sometimes referred to more specifically as **structural inheritance**; see also **interface inheritance**. Inheriting Ctors (541)

implicitly captured – implies, for given a variable, that it is captured by a closure by dint of it being named in the body of the lambda. Lambdas (582)

implicitly declared – implies, for a special member function, that it is declared (and defined) by the compiler, obviating, in certain cases, an explicit declaration within the class definition. Generalized PODs '11 (522)

implicitly movable entity – one that, as of C++20, will be treated as an *xvalue*, e.g., a variable having automatic storage duration that is either a non**volatile** object or an rvalue reference to a non**volatile** object. *Rvalue* References (735)

in contract – implies, for a given function invocation, that none of the preconditions in the function's contract are violated. noexcept Specifier (1122)

in place – implies, for a given object, its construction directly into a particular memory location, e.g., by emplacement, rather than being passed a constructed object and then copying or moving it into place. *Rvalue* References (734)

in-process – implies, for a given value (such as an object's address), that it is meaningful only within the currently running process. friend '11 (1034)

incomplete type – one that has been declared but not defined. Note that a class type is considered to be incomplete within its own class definition unless it is within a complete-class context for that type.

indeterminate value – one that cannot be relied upon in *any* way (e.g., not even to *not* change spontaneously); for example, any non**static** object of scalar type, such as **int**, that is not explicitly initialized has an indeterminate value, as do any bits within the footprint of an object used to ensure alignment (a.k.a. *padding*) or to hold a virtual table (or base) pointer. Most uses of an indeterminate value have undefined behavior; see Section 2.1."Generalized PODs '11" on page 401. Generalized PODs '11 (435)

infallible – implies, for a given function, that it will never fail to satisfy its contract (e.g., due to resource limitations); see infallible implementation. noexcept Specifier (1118)

infallible implementation – a function definition that can reasonably be expected to satisfy its contract on any relevant platform regardless of the availability of system resources (e.g., heap memory, stack memory, file handles, mutexes). noexcept Specifier (1118)

inheriting constructors – the C++11 feature (see Section 2.1."Inheriting Ctors" on page 535) whereby constructors can be inherited from a base class via **using** directives; each inherited constructor has essentially the same signature in the derived class, invokes the relevant base class constructor, and initializes derived-class data members in the same way an implicit default constructor would initialize them. Inheriting Ctors (538)

init capture – a form of *capture* in a lambda expression, since C++14 (see Section 2.2."Lambda Captures" on page 986), that specifies an initializer expression, essentially adding a new data member of deduced type to the closure object; see captured by copy and captured by reference. Lambda Captures (986)

inline namespace – a variant of **namespace**, since C++11 (see Section 3.1."**inline namespace**" on page 1055), in which a namespace declared using the **inline** keyword enables name lookup in an enclosing namespace (e.g., via ADL) to find names declared within a nested **inline** namespace, similar to providing a **using** (namespace) directive after the close of a conventionally nested namespace. What's more, an **inline** namespace enables templates to be specialized from within the enclosing namespace. Note that name conflicts that might arise with an enclosing name are addressed quite differently for an **inline** namespace compared to a conventional one. inline namespace (1055)

instantiation time – short for template instantiation time. static_assert (120)

instruction selection – a form of compiler optimization in which optimal (otherwise equivalent) sets of instructions are selected based on the target platform and other aspects of the context

Glossary

in which those instructions will execute — e.g., **vectorized** operations or operations that will exhibit superior pipelining on the target CPU. noexcept Specifier (1136)

insulate – reduce or eliminate compile-time coupling (e.g., an implementation detail); see insulation. noreturn (96), constexpr Functions (299), extern template (369), Opaque enums (665)

insulating – implies, for a given interface, that implementation details are insulated and can change without forcing clients to recompile, only relink.

insulation – a strong form of encapsulation in which the representation of private implementation details can change without forcing clients to recompile their code, but simply to relink it; see **lakos20**, section 3.11.1, "Formal Definitions of *Encapsulation* vs. *Insulation*," pp. 790–791. Opaque enums (663)

integer literal – one specifying an integral value. This value can be expressed (1) in decimal, in which case the literal sequence of (decimal) digits is in the range [0-9] and does not begin with 0; (2) in octal, in which case the (octal) digit sequence is limited to the range [0-7] and begins with 0; (3) in hexadecimal, in which case the literal begins with a 0x or 0X and is followed by one or more (hexadecimal) digits in the case-insensitive range [0-9a-f]; or, as of C++14, (4) in binary, in which case the literal begins with a 0b or 0B and is followed by one or more (binary) digits, 0 or 1 (see Section 1.2."Binary Literals" on page 142). An integer literal may have an optional suffix, which may contain a (case-insensitive) L or LL and may also contain a (case-insensitive) U, e.g., 1L, 0377uL, or 0xABCuL. As of C++14, digit separators (') (see Section 1.2."Digit Separators" on page 152) may be used to visually group digits (e.g., 1'000'000) and are especially useful in C++14 with binary literals (see Section 1.2. "Binary Literals" on page 142), e.g., 0b1100'1011. Note that every integer literal has a non-negative value; expressions such as -1, -02, and -0x3 apply the unary-minus (-) operator to the non-negative **int** value of that integer literal. Note that if the value is too large to fit in **int**, then **unsigned int**, **long**, **unsigned long**, **long long**, and **unsigned long long** may be tried (in that order); however, the set of possible types for an integer literal may be constrained by its suffix. In particular, a decimal literal without a suffix always has a signed type and overflows if the value cannot be represented as a **signed long long**. More generally, if the value of the integer literal is not representable in any type that is compatible with the prefix and suffix, it is ill formed. User-Defined Literals (837)

integer-to-floating-point conversion – an implicit conversion from an integral type to a floating-point type. User-Defined Literals (843)

integer type – a synonym for integral type.

integral constant – a constant expression of integral type such as an integer literal or **constexpr** variable of integral type (see Section 2.1."**constexpr** Variables" on page 302). Note that a **const**-qualified variable of integral type that is initialized with a constant expression can be an integral constant too. Braced Init (223), constexpr Variables (303)

integral constant expression – an expression of integral or unscoped enumeration type that is a constant expression, i.e., one that can be evaluated at compile time. alignas (169), alignof (184)

integral promotion – the implicit conversion of the type of an integral expression to a larger integral type that preserves value. In expressions, an integral bit field of less than the number of bits in an **int** is, by default, promoted to an **int**. In *integral* expressions, if a (binary) operation is applied to two integral expressions of different sizes, the smaller one will be promoted to the larger size before the operation is performed; see also integral constant,

integral constant expression, and **integral type**. Deleted Functions (56), **enum class** (334), *Rvalue References* (726), Underlying Type '11 (832)

integral type – a category of fundamental types, codified by the std::is_integral trait, denoting one of **bool**, **char**, **signed char**, **unsigned char**, **char16_t**, **char32_t**, **wchar_t**, and the familiar **signed** and **unsigned** variations on **short**, **int**, **long**, **long long** (see Section 1.1."**long long**" on page 89), and any implementation-defined extended-integer type; C++20 adds **char8_t** to this list. **long long** (89), Underlying Type '11 (829)

interface inheritance – a form of inheritance in which the interface (only) of one or more pure **virtual** functions declared in a base class is inherited in a derived class; see also implementation inheritance. Inheriting Ctors (541)

interface trait – a (typically standard) trait, such as std::is_trivially_destructible, that describes an aspect of the usable interface of a type but does *not* correspond to a property named in the core language specification; see also **core trait**. Generalized PODs '11 (482)

internal linkage – linkage that prevents an entity from being referenced by name from another translation unit. Multiple distinct entities having internal linkage may have the same name, provided each resides in a separate translation unit; see also **external linkage**. Function **static** '11 (77), **constexpr** Variables (307)

intra-thread dependency – a data dependency that exists between evaluations within a single thread. carries_dependency (998)

invocable – implies, for a given entity f and zero or more arguments t1, t2, ..., tN, that one of (t1.*f)(t2, ..., tN), ((*t1).*f)(t2, ..., tN), t1.*f, (*t1).*f, or f(t1, t2, ..., tN) is well formed at the point of invocation — i.e., f must be usable and either a (1) callable entity, (2) pointer-to-member function, or (3) pointer-to-data member. Generalized PODs '11 (482), Lambda Captures (986)

invocable entity – one that is invocable; see also **callable entity**.

join (a thread) – the operation by which execution of the current thread is suspended until execution of one or more other threads completes.

lambda body – the statements in a lambda expression that will form the body of a lambda closure's call operator. Lambdas (581), *Generic* Lambdas (976)

lambda capture – a syntax by which variables from a reaching scope are made available for use within the body of a lambda expression. See also **captured by copy** and **captured by reference**. Lambdas (577), Variadic Templates (919), *Generic* Lambdas (969)

lambda closure – the object created by evaluating a lambda expression. Lambdas (584)

lambda declarator – the function parameter list, mutability, exception specification, and return type of a lambda expression, all of which are imbued on the call operator of the lambda closure. Lambdas (591)

lambda expression – an anonymous *callable* type having unnamed data members used to store values that are, by default, captured by copy (=) or else captured by reference (&); see Section 2.1."Lambdas" on page 573. Local Types '11 (83), Lambdas (576), *Generic* Lambdas (968), Lambda Captures (995), **auto** Return (1182), **decltype(auto)** (1206)

lambda introducer – a possibly empty lambda capture list, surrounded by [], used to begin a lambda expression; e.g., [](){} is a lambda expression that captures nothing, takes no arguments, does nothing, and returns **void**. Lambdas (582), Lambda Captures (986)

Glossary

language undefined behavior – that which is not defined by the C++ Standard's specification of the abstract machine; such behavior can, in theory, be mapped onto *any* behavior that the target hardware supports and that the host operating system will allow (a.k.a. hard UB). To quote Marshall Clow, "Your cat can get pregnant — even if you don't have a cat!" (**clow14**, time 02:00). noexcept Specifier (1115)

leak – the phenomenon (often considered a defect) in which a limited system resource, most usually memory, is acquired but never released.

levelization technique – one of nine classic refactoring techniques — escalation, *demotion*, *opaque pointers*, dumb data, *redundancy*, *callbacks*, *manager class*, *factoring*, and escalating *encapsulation* — used to remove (or ideally avoid) cyclic physical dependencies within a code base; see **lakos20**, section 3.5, "Levelization Techniques," pp. 602–704.

library undefined behavior – that which is not specified (explicitly or otherwise) in the contract of a function. When library undefined behavior occurs, for example, by calling a function in a way that fails to satisfy one or more of its preconditions (e.g., passing a negative value to a square-root function), the behavior of the program, from a language perspective, might still be well defined; however, library undefined behavior often leads to language undefined behavior (e.g., attempting to use substantively, in the implementation of a function, a null pointer that was passed in erroneously by a client). noexcept Specifier (1115)

lifetime extension – that which may happen to a **temporary object** when it is used to initialize a reference having **automatic storage duration**; in such cases, the temporary's lifetime will be extended beyond its largest enclosing **expression** and instead will end along with that of the reference bound to it. Range **for** (680), *Rvalue* References (720), Ref-Qualifiers (1162), decltype(auto) (1213)

link-time optimization – optimization that occurs during *linking*, as opposed to that which occurs during compilation of an individual **translation unit** (TU), and thus has available the definition of an entire program. Though capable of performing transformations beyond what can typically be achieved locally within a TU, such global optimizations come at the cost of scaling poorly (e.g., superlinearly) with the size of a program. noexcept Specifier (1094)

linkage – a characterization that denotes whether and to what extent distinct **declarations** of the same name will refer to the same entity: (1) a name having **external linkage**, such as a global function or variable, can refer to an entity that is defined in a different **translation unit** (TU); (2) a name having **internal linkage**, such as a function declared in an **unnamed namespace**, can refer to an entity that is defined in the same TU only; (3) a name having *no* linkage, such as a variable at block scope, always refers to a distinct entity that cannot be defined elsewhere. Note that the notion of linkage does not apply to a nonentity such as a type alias. Local Types '11 (83)

list initialization – initialization using a braced-initializer list. Braced Init (215), constexpr Functions (260), Default Member Init (331)

literal – a token that represents a value (typically a constant expression) — e.g., an integer literal, floating-point literal, string literal, or user-defined literal (see Section 2.1."User-Defined Literals" on page 835). User-Defined Literals (835)

literal type – one whose objects can be constructed (and potentially manipulated and accessed) at compile time; see Section 2.1."**constexpr** Functions" on page 257. Deleted Functions (59), constexpr Functions (260), constexpr Variables (302), Generalized PODs '11 (431), initializer_list (556), constexpr Functions '14 (960)

local class – one defined within the body of a function (as opposed to at namespace or class scope).

local declaration – a nondefining declaration, at file or namespace scope, of an external-linkage entity — other than one supplied by the header of some other **component** — for which there is no corresponding definition within the same translation unit (TU). Hence, unlike a forward declaration — e.g., in a header file — there is never an opportunity for a conventional compiler to verify that this specific declaration matches its definition (in some other TU). Note that local declarations are especially problematic for global functions and variables, which can be used substantively via their nondefining declarations alone; see Section 2.1. "Opaque **enum**s" on page 660. Also note that this book's use of the term local declaration is in relation to **physical design** and distinct from the more common logical notion of *local* (e.g., *local type* or *local* variable), which pertains to an entity that is declared in block scope. Opaque enums (662)

local scope – a synonym for block scope — i.e., the scope implied by a *compound* statement, such as the body of a function or lambda expression.

locality of reference – the phenomenon whereby data that resides in close proximity in the address space is typically more likely to be accessed together (i.e., within close temporal proximity). alignas (181), *Rvalue* References (742)

logical – implies, for a given aspect of software design, the classical notions exclusive to language constructs such as classes, functions, inheritance, using relationships, and control-flow, as opposed to physical ones, e.g., involving files and libraries, compile- and link-time dependencies, and executable size.

logical design – the identification of relationships between (logical) entities, such as types, functions, and variables, irrespective of the specific (physical) files, translation units, and libraries in which those entities will eventually reside. "Fortunately, there is a serendipitous synergy between good logical design and good physical design. Given time, these two design goals will come to reinforce one another." See **lakos96**, section 5.11, "Summary," pp. 324–325, specifically p. 325 (bottom).

long-distance friendship – that which is granted to an entity not defined within the current component. friend '11 (1035)

lossy conversion – one that loses information and thus is not reversible for the entire domain upon which it is defined — e.g., converting a **double** to an **int**. Braced Init (222)

lvalue – the value category of an expression whose evaluation determines the identity of an entity (i.e., an object, bit field, or function) that is not expiring. For example, an *lvalue* might be the name of a variable, the result of operator . or -> applied to a (non-expiring) object to access a member, the result of dereferencing a pointer, a call to a function whose return type is an lvalue reference, or any expression of function type. The built-in address-of operator (&) requires an *lvalue* as its operand; however, an expression designating a bit field may not have its address taken, even if it is an *lvalue*. decltype (26), auto Variables (196), Braced Init (216), constexpr Functions (267), Forwarding References (377), Generalized PODs '11 (501), Lambdas (590), noexcept Operator (617), Range for (680), *Rvalue* References (710), Variadic Templates (875), *Generic* Lambdas (971), Lambda Captures (992), friend '11 (1047), noexcept Specifier (1133), Ref-Qualifiers (1153), auto Return (1184), decltype(auto) (1211)

lvalue reference – one formed, for a type X, as X&. A non**const** reference of this kind can be bound to only an *lvalue*, while a **const** lvalue reference can be bound to any expression having a type that is implicitly convertible to X, possibly resulting in the creation of a **temporary** and the

Glossary

associated lifetime extension that would ensue. Range **for** (701), *Rvalue* References (710), Lambda Captures (993), **noexcept** Specifier (1118)

lvalue-to-rvalue conversion – the implicit conversion that occurs when a *prvalue* is needed from an expression whose value category is *glvalue* — effectively, the process of reading the value of an object. Generalized PODs '11 (501), *Rvalue* References (814)

managed allocator – one that keeps track of each active allocation made through it such that it is able to unilaterally release all outstanding memory at destruction or, perhaps, via a single (e.g., **release**) operation (a.k.a. *winking out*). As of C++17, the C++ Standard Library supports this sort of functionality via two concrete classes derived from **std::pmr::memory_resource**: (1) a (special-purpose) monotonic-allocator resource that treats each individual deallocation as a no-op and (2) a (general-purpose) multipool-allocator resource that is substitutable for the global allocator supplied by the C++ run time. **final** (1021)

mandatory RVO – a requirement, as of C++17, for functions returning objects by value (a form of guaranteed copy elision) that, when the value in a unique **return** statement is a *prvalue*, the object, instead of being copied or moved, is constructed in place in its final destination in the calling function's context. *Rvalue* References (807)

mangled name – one created by the compiler and potentially used by the linker to uniquely identify distinct entities having the same name but defined in different contexts, e.g., entities having the same name but declared in multiple scopes or an (overloaded) function having multiple signatures. This feature of the ABI also enables *type-safe* linkage, which helps to avoid mismatches across translation units — e.g., that a function defined to take an **int** cannot be bound to (the use of) a declaration of a function having the same name but taking a **long**. A function template, in addition to its parameters, necessarily incorporates the return type as part of the mangled name. The use of C linkage eliminates such mangling, thereby preventing the overloading of such functions and function templates. Note that a global variable, e.g., a **double**, declared at file or namespace scope might, but is not required to, use a mangled name to identify its type in the ABI; hence, *type-safe* linkage cannot be relied upon to detect such mismatches; see local declarations. **inline namespace** (1056), **noexcept** Specifier (1114)

manifestly constant evaluated – implies, for a given expression, that it is used in a context that requires it be evaluated at compile time, such as an array bound or as an argument for a non-type template parameter; see also constant expression. **constexpr** Functions (258)

mantissa – the part of a floating-point representation that contains the significant digits; note that, when represented in binary, the leading 1 can be omitted. Digit Separators (155)

materialize – the act of temporary materialization — i.e., that of the compiler creating a temporary object in the address space to represent a given *prvalue*. *Rvalue* References (717), Ref-Qualifiers (1163)

maximal fundamental alignment – that of **std::max_align_t**, which, for any given platform, is at least as strict as that of every scalar type. **alignof** (193)

mechanism – a term used to characterize a class type capable of instantiating objects and whose purpose it is to provide a service, such as scoped guard, *lock*, *socket*, etc. A mechanism does not attempt to represent a platonic value, such as does **std::complex<double>**, nor even an in-process one (e.g., one whose value incorporates a memory address as a salient attribute). Delegating Ctors (51), Opaque **enums** (663), *Rvalue* References (789)

Glossary

member – an entity other than a **friend** function — such as a data member, member function, user-defined type, or type alias — that is declared to reside within the scope of a class type; see also hidden-friend idiom. union '11 (1174)

member function – one that is a member of a **class**, **struct**, or **union**; see also free function. *Rvalue* References (793), Variadic Templates (892)

member initializer list – the syntax used in constructors to initialize direct base classes, **virtual** base classes, and non**static** data members. Note that the initialization order is fixed by the relative order in which base classes and data members are declared (some compilers may warn if the relative orderings differ). Delegating Ctors (46), Braced Init (230), Default Member Init (318)

member operator – a user-defined (overloaded) operator (e.g., copy assignment) that is implemented as a member of a class and, unless implicitly **static** (e.g., class-specific operators **new** and **delete**), has access to the object's **this** pointer as an implicit argument.

memory barrier – a form of *synchronization primitive* that is used to enforce an observable modification order for one or more memory locations (a.k.a. a fence), facilitating the coordination of access to data from concurrent execution contexts; see also multithreading contexts. Function static '11 (80)

memory diffusion – the process by which the size of the working set increases over time, despite constant memory utilization; see also memory fragmentation. noexcept Operator (628), *Rvalue* References (788)

memory-fence instruction – a machine-level instruction enforcing an observable modification order for one or more memory locations; see also memory barrier. carries_dependency (999)

memory fragmentation – the process by which the maximum available contiguous chunk of dynamically allocatable memory decreases over time, despite consistent memory utilization; see also memory diffusion.

memory leak – a type of resource leak involving specifically a memory resource. Note that use of class-specific memory allocators (e.g., implemented in terms of class-specific **new** and **delete**) can create a *pseudo* memory leak that can be as problematic as a genuine one; see **lakos96**, section 10.3.4, "Class-Specific Memory Management," pp. 698–711, in particular, Figure 10-30, p. 709. Function static '11 (74)

metafunction – a compile-time operation whose parameters and results are code subject to compilation, such as functions, types, and compile-time constants, rather than runtime values. C++ metafunctions, such as the standard type traits provided in <type_traits>, are implemented as class, variable, and alias templates that compute types and/or compile-time constants based on the values of their metaparameters, supplied as template arguments. Note that modern C++ introduced a related feature; see Section 2.1."**constexpr** Functions" on page 257. Forwarding References (381), Generalized PODs '11 (469), noexcept Operator (643), constexpr Functions '14 (963)

metaparameter – a parameter that controls (a priori) the generation or the workings of an entity that is itself parameterized; for example, in a neural network, the number of layers is a metaparameter. Specifically (in C++), a metaparameter is a template parameter used at compile time to configure a section of code (e.g., one that defines a type or implements an algorithm). The allocator parameter in a C++11/14 standard container is a metaparameter that controls how memory is to be allocated and deallocated by the container. Note that, as of C++17, PMR provides a more flexible, runtime-based alternative for memory allocation. Variadic Templates (948)

Glossary

metaprogramming – the act of writing code whose input and output is, itself, code; specifically (in C++), a programming paradigm in which class and function **templates** are defined in such a way as to generate on-demand highly configurable interfaces and implementations under the control of their **template parameters (metaparameters)**. In this paradigm, the template programmer writes code that, in turn, controls a sophisticated code generator (the **template-instantiation** engine), which will generate source code when the template is instantiated. C++ *template* **metaprogramming** was ushered into classical C++ during the 2000s in large part by Andrei Alexandrescu (**alexandrescu01**). `decltype` (30), `constexpr` Functions (257), Variadic Templates (876)

Meyers' singleton – one that is implemented as a `static` variable in function scope, popularized by Scott Meyers; see **meyers96**, "Techniques," item 26, "Allowing Zero or One Objects," pp. 130–138. Function `static` '11 (72)

microbenchmark – a benchmark that is characterized by itself being small and typically performing one or a few operations many times in a loop; such benchmarks are often used to model real-world programs but might not be reflective of behavior in larger, long-running ones — e.g., due to memory diffusion.

mix-in – a type intended to provide a (perhaps partial) implementation of the desired derived type, often via (perhaps private) structural inheritance, such as in the CRTP (to achieve the EBO, at least until C++20); see Section 3.1."`final`" on page 1007. A derived (e.g., *adapter*) type might multiply inherit publicly from both a **mix-in** and an **abstract-interface**, which can then be used to access and manipulate the **mix-in** polymorphically; see **lakos96**, Appendix A, "The Protocol Hierarchy Design Pattern," pp. 737–768, specifically item 6, pp. 754–755.

mixed-mode build – one that comprises multiple **translation units** built using distinct but compatible *build modes* (compiler settings) — e.g., different levels of optimization. `inline namespace` (1073)

mock – an artificial, often highly configurable, implementation of an **abstract interface**, controllable by a higher-level agent, used for the testing technique known as **mocking**. A well-designed **mock** implementation will often (1) record its inputs from the client for analysis by the testing agent and (2) provide specific outputs to be consumed (e.g., in response to inputs) by the client; see also **mocking**.

mocking – a testing technique that involves spoofing a client of an **abstract interface** using an artificial implementation that acts at the will of a higher-level agent orchestrating the test of said client. This approach enables the testing agent to assess and evaluate the behavior of the client even under unusual, exceptional, or error conditions; see also **mock**. `final` (1017)

modules – a C++20 feature that introduces a new way to organize C++ code, which provides better **encapsulation** than do conventional headers. Note, however, that **modules**, as currently defined, do absolutely nothing new with respect to **insulation**. `friend` '11 (1041)

monotonic allocator – a managed allocator that dispenses memory from one or more contiguous regions of memory in a *sequential* fashion, yielding both fast allocations and dense memory utilization. Memory is reclaimed only when the allocator object itself is destroyed or its `release` method is invoked; individual deallocations are no-ops. Note that imprudent use of such an allocator can result in a pseudo **memory leak**. The C++17 Standard Library provides **monotonic allocator** functionality via the `std::pmr::monotonic_buffer_resource` class. `alignof` (190), `final` (1021)

most vexing parse – a subtle syntactic ambiguity in the grammar of the C++ language between (1) a function declaration and (2) a variable definition that is direct-initialized with, e.g., a result of a function-style cast or a default-constructed temporary object of a user-defined type. In cases where such an ambiguity arises, the compiler resolves it in favor of a function declaration. For example, the statement — `S s(int(my_obj));` — declares a function named `s` having a single parameter, of type `int`, and not, as one might reasonably think, a local variable `s`, of type `S`, that is initialized with `my_obj` cast to an `int` via a function-style cast. Similarly, the statement — `S s2(MyType());` — declares a function having the decayed function-pointer parameter `MyType (*)()` and returning an `S`. Uniform initialization, using braces instead of parentheses, is often touted as solving the most vexing parse problem in that, e.g., `MyType{}` is always interpreted as a value-initialized `MyType` object, but constructor arguments within braces sometimes have a different meaning than those within parentheses, such as when a constructor has an `initializer_list` parameter. Inheriting Ctors (536)

movable – implies, for a given object, that one or more move operations can be applied. *Rvalue* References (728)

move assignable – implies, for a given type, that assignment from an *rvalue* of that type is well formed. Note that all copy assignable types are also implicitly move assignable unless the move-assignment operator is explicitly deleted. Generalized PODs '11 (524)

move assignment – assignment that potentially harvests resources from an expiring source object to populate the target object more expeditiously (e.g., by avoiding memory allocation). *Rvalue* References (750)

move-assignment operator – an overload of **operator=** for a particular type, X, that takes a single argument that is a (potentially cv-qualified) rvalue reference to X. Common practice is to have a return type of X& and to return ***this**. *Rvalue* References (710)

move construction – construction of an object from an *rvalue* of the same type (modulo cv-qualifiers); resources allocated to the expiring source object may be harvested to expedite the transfer of value. Note that a class might not have a move constructor distinct from its copy constructor, in which case move construction is copy construction (if available). *Rvalue* References (750)

move constructor – a constructor for a particular type, X, that has, as a first parameter, a (potentially cv-qualified) rvalue reference to X; any subsequent parameters have default arguments. Generalized PODs '11 (437), *Rvalue* References (710)

move only – implies, for a given type, that it is a move-only type; i.e., objects of that type cannot be copied, only moved. `initializer_list` (570), **noexcept** Operator (641), *Rvalue* References (790), Ref-Qualifiers (1165)

move-only type – one that provides one or more move operations but no copy operations, such as `std::unique_ptr`. **noexcept** Operator (644), *Rvalue* References (716)

move operation – either a move constructor or a move-assignment operator. Defaulted Functions (43), Deleted Functions (53), **alignas** (183), **noexcept** Operator (627), *Rvalue* References (710), **noexcept** Specifier (1093)

move semantics – the conventional meaning associated with an object that exploits the framework afforded by C++ rvalue references and the two additional special member functions, move constructor and move-assignment operator, whereby the value of an expiring source object can be transferred to a target object, perhaps more runtime efficiently, by repurposing resources allocated to the source, such that the source object might no longer represent

Glossary

its original value. Note that copy semantics satisfy the requirements of move semantics, but not vice versa; consequently, any type that supports copy semantics naturally supports move semantics unless the *move* special member functions have been explicitly deleted; see also **value semantics**. *Rvalue* References (710)

moved-from object – one that has been the source argument of a move operation. Note that the state of such an object will *by definition* satisfy all of its intended object invariants but might be otherwise unspecified; see also **moved-from state**. *Rvalue* References (788)

moved-from state – the state of an object after it has been the source for a move operation. Depending on the object's type, this state can be (1) its pre-move state, (2) a well-documented (possibly unique) *empty* state, (3) the default-constructed state, (4) some finite number of designated post-move states, or (5) an unspecified state. Note that — by definition — a moved-from object satisfies all of its object invariants and, hence, remains a *valid* object; see Section 2.1."*Rvalue* References" on page 710. *Rvalue* References (789)

multithreading context – one in which there might be multiple threads of execution running concurrently in the same address space (e.g., a single process). Function static '11 (68)

naked literal – the initial sequence of characters comprising a user-defined literal token excluding the UDL suffix. Note that a naked literal is always a syntactically valid literal in its own right. User-Defined Literals (839)

name mangling – the creation of a mangled name by the compiler or other tooling such as a symbolic debugger. Mangled names, in addition to the name, may contain scope and type information, as well as other decorations that are specific to the ABI. inline namespace (1067), noexcept Specifier (1149)

named return-value optimization (NRVO) – a form of copy elision that can occur when the (entire) operand of a **return** statement is the name of a non**volatile** variable having automatic storage duration of the same type (ignoring cv-qualifiers) as the *return type*. In such a case, a compiler can often avoid creating a distinct local variable before either copying or moving it into the object representing it in the caller's context. Note that there is active interest for future versions of C++ (post C++20) in increasing opportunities for this optimized behavior and also making it mandatory — e.g., to facilitate the implementation of factory functions returning objects *by value* that are neither copyable nor movable. *Rvalue* References (734)

NaN – short for *Not a Number*, characterizing one of a fixed set of bit patterns in the representation of a floating-point type that do *not* represent a numeric value. In particular, equality and relational comparisons involving floating-point variables in this state always return **false** — even when applied reflexively, e.g., x == x. Hence, floating-point values do not fully obey all notions implied by value semantics. Generalized PODs '11 (530)

narrow contract – a function contract that contains one or more preconditions on its arguments or ambient program state, including, for a member function, any preconditions on the state of its underlying object (e.g., std::vector::front() requires, as a precondition, that it *not* be empty); see also **wide contract** and **library undefined behavior**. *Rvalue* References (715), final (1021), noexcept Specifier (1112)

narrowing conversion – one between scalar types that is known to be lossy, such as from **double** to **float**, or any conversion from an integral type to a floating-point type (e.g., **bool** to **long double**) or vice versa (e.g., **float** to **long long**) — even if it is not lossy on the current platform. Braced Init (222), noexcept Specifier (1091)

narrowing the contract – evolving a function contract by strengthening or otherwise adding new (nonduplicative) preconditions, thereby reducing the domain of the function, which might impact backward compatibility for its users; see also widening the contract. *Rvalue References* (793)

natural alignment – the minimum alignment for a given size that is sufficiently strict to accommodate any object of that size provided that neither it nor any of its subobjects has had its alignment requirements artificially strengthened via explicit use of an alignment specifier (see Section 2.1."**alignas**" on page 168). Numerically, the *naturalalignment* for size N is $gcd(N, \textbf{sizeof}(\text{std::max\_align\_t}))$ — in other words, the largest power of 2, not larger than **alignof**(std::max_align_t), that evenly divides N, e.g., *naturalalignment*(4) = 4, *naturalalignment*(5) = 1, and *naturalalignment*(6) = 2. Note that natural alignment is typically used when the size of an object is known but not its type; for example, allocating 4 bytes with natural alignment will result in 4-byte aligned storage because the computation cannot distinguish between, e.g., a single **int** (having a required alignment of 4) and a **struct** containing two **short** data members (having a required alignment of only 2). alignas (179), alignof (184), Underlying Type '11 (831)

negative testing – the testing practice of deliberately violating a precondition when invoking a function having a narrow contract in a unit test. Such testing is important in practice to ensure that any defensive checks are implemented as intended (e.g., without all-too-common off-by-one errors) and requires that the test harness be compiled in a mode in which such defensive checks would be expected to detect those specific contract violations at runtime (see production build). These tests are often implemented by configuring a suitable defensive checking framework to throw a specific *test* exception on a contract violation or else via death tests, in which case a process must be started for each individual successful trial. *Rvalue References* (794)

new handler – a callback function registered using the standard library function std::set_new_handler that will be invoked by standard allocation functions whenever a memory allocation attempt fails. Note that this callback function may try to free additional memory to allow for a retry of the allocation attempt. alignof (193)

nibble – half a byte, i.e., 4 bits. Digit Separators (153)

nofail – implies, for a given function or guarantee, that it is a nofail function or nofail guarantee, respectively. noexcept Specifier (1116)

nofail function – one that provides no failure mode (i.e., has no out clause in the contract describing its interface) and has an infallible implementation, irrespective of whether it provides a nofail guarantee. noexcept Specifier (1117)

nofail guarantee – one that, for a given function, implies it is now and always will be a nofail function. noexcept Specifier (1117)

nondefining declaration – one — such as **class** Foo; — that does not provide all of the collateral information, such as function or class body, associated with a complete definition. Note that a **typedef** or **using** declaration (see Section 1.1."**using** Aliases" on page 133) is *non*defining as type aliases are declared, not defined. Also note that an opaque enumeration declaration provides only the underlying type for that enumeration, sufficient to instantiate opaque objects of the enumerated type yet *not* sufficient to interpret its values; hence, it too is not (fully) defining and therefore is *nondefining*. Note that a nondefining declaration may be repeated within a single translation unit (TU); see also defining declaration. *Rvalue References* (729)

Glossary

nonprimitive functionality – implementable in terms of the publicly accessible functionality of a type or a set of types and, hence, does not require access to any of their encapsulated (private) implementation details. `explicit` Operators (67)

nonreporting contract – a function contract that does *not* specify an out clause — i.e., the contract (e.g., for `std::vector::push_back`) makes no mention of what happens if the operation were to fail. `noexcept` Specifier (1120)

nonreporting function – a function whose contract offers no mechanism to report whether the principal action requested was performed. `noexcept` Specifier (1119)

nonstatic data member – one declared without the **static** keyword, an instance of which appears in every object of the class. `constexpr` Variables (305)

non-trivial constructor – not a trivial constructor, such as a user-provided constructor (which is never trivial, even if the resulting generated code matches exactly what a trivial constructor would do). `union` '11 (1174)

non-trivial destructor – not a trivial destructor — e.g., a user-provided destructor or one whose implementation invokes some non-trivial destructor of a base-class or data-member subobject. `noexcept` Specifier (1118)

non-trivial special member function – one that is not trivial; see also special member function. `union` '11 (1174)

non-type parameter – short for non-type template parameter. Variadic Templates (902)

non-type parameter pack – a template parameter pack made up of non-type template parameters. Variadic Templates (902)

non-type template parameter – one whose argument is a constant expression, rather than a type or template; the parameter must have integral type, enumeration type, pointer type, pointer-to-member type, or lvalue reference type. C++20 broadens slightly this category of types to structural types, which includes floating-point types and class types comprising other structural types. Variadic Templates (902)

normative wording – implies, for wording in the Standard, that it forms part of the definition of ISO C++, as opposed to (nonnormative) notes, which exist only to make the Standard easier to read. *Rvalue* References (808)

notionally trivially destructible – implies, for a given class type, that it could (and would) have a trivial destructor if not for a desire to have some entirely optional operations that do not change the semantics of a correct program — e.g., defensive checks to verify that object invariants have been maintained properly throughout the lifetime of the object. Note that such a type might be written using, e.g., conditional compilation to have a trivial destructor in some build modes but not in others. Generalized PODs '11 (468)

NRVO – short for named return-value optimization. *Rvalue* References (736)

null address – the value of a pointer variable that represents the absence of a memory address; the bit pattern representing such a value, however, is implementation defined. See also null pointer value. `nullptr` (99)

null pointer value – a *singular* value in the domain of each pointer type that never represents the address of an object nor the address past the end of an object. Note that the object representation of a null pointer value is implementation defined and need not be all zero bits nor even the same between different pointer types. *Rvalue* References (743)

Glossary

null statement – an empty statement consisting of just a single semicolon (;). constexpr Functions (268)

null-terminated string – a sequence of characters whose end is marked by a terminating character having the numeric value of 0. *Rvalue* References (743)

object invariant – a property of an object that holds from the point at which it becomes fully constructed until its destructor begins to execute, except when the flow of control is within the body of a mutating public member (or friend) function of that object's class; in other words, every object invariant is implicitly a postcondition of every public member and friend function of its class. Generalized PODs '11 (472), Inheriting Ctors (539), *Rvalue* References (742)

object orientation – an object-centric (as opposed to a function-centric) approach to programming in which data serves to aggregate functions rather than vice versa. In this mindset, programmers view objects as the fundamental building blocks of logical design, where raw data is encapsulated in objects along with the functions that access and manipulate it. In C++, objects are defined in terms of classes; see also object-oriented programming. Note that this now antiquated term was popularized in the late 1980s and has since fallen into disuse. final (1015)

object-oriented programming – a paradigm of programming that extends object orientation to provide dynamic binding along with subtyping as a means of factoring interfaces as well as implementations of related types; see also object orientation. In C++, these *object-oriented* features are implemented via **virtual** functions and inheritance. Generalized PODs '11 (440)

object representation – the bytes of data within an object's footprint used to represent the object's state. Generalized PODs '11 (405)

ODR – short for one-definition rule. constexpr Variables (307)

ODR-used – implies, for a given entity, that it is referenced in a potentially evaluated expression; such entities are subject to the ODR and thus must have a definition for a program to be considered well formed. Lambdas (581), Lambda Captures (988), inline namespace (1081)

one-definition rule (ODR) – the C++ language constraint on a well-formed program that there must be exactly one definition for each entity that is ODR-used; otherwise, the program is IFNDR. Entities whose source-level definitions must appear in multiple translation units, such as inline functions, template definitions, and default arguments, may have multiple definitions, but all of those definitions must be generated from the same sequence of tokens. Note that, as of C++17, a definition need not exist for an entity that is ODR-used only within a *discarded statement*, i.e., a statement in the unused part of an **if constexpr** construct. constexpr Functions (263), extern template (374), inline namespace (1072), noexcept Specifier (1114), auto Return (1188)

opaque declaration – a nondefining declaration for a class type or enumeration. Note that such declarations expose minimal collateral information beyond the name of the type being declared, e.g., type aliases — such as **typedef int** size_type; — are not *opaque*; see also insulation. Opaque enums (660)

opaque enumeration declaration – a nondefining declaration of an enumeration, which does not specify its enumerators but fixes its underlying type so that its size and alignment can be determined and thus allows objects of that type to be created, copied, etc., opaquely. Note that such opaque enumeration declarations present a unique challenge with respect to physical design in that a component that defines an enumeration having a fixed underlying type

Glossary

might need to provide two header files — one containing the opaque enumeration declaration and a second (which may include the first) that provides the full definition; see Section 2.1. "Opaque **enums**" on page 660. Opaque enums (663)

operator – a kind of function that has a non-function-like syntax known to the compiler and consisting of either a keyword or other token (typically comprising just punctuation characters) that can used as part of an **expression** alongside its operands — e.g., **sizeof**(a + b), where both + and **sizeof** are operators. Token-based **operators** include assignment (=), equality comparison (==), member access, subscripting ([]), sequencing (,), conditional (?:), function call (()), etc. Keyword-based operators include **sizeof**, **new**, **delete**, **typeid**, and, as of C++11, **alignof**, **decltype**, and **noexcept**. Many of the built-in token-based **operators**, along with **new** and **delete**, can be overloaded for **class** types; notable exceptions include dot (.) and conditional (?:). constexpr Functions (265)

ordinary character type – one that is **char**, **signed char**, or **unsigned char**. Note that **char8_t** (introduced in C++20) is *not* an ordinary character type. Generalized PODs '11 (501)

out clause – in law, a clause that permits signatories to a **contract** to opt out of particular provisions or to terminate the contract early. In software contracts, it is a **statement** in a contract that (1) allows a function not to achieve its stated goal and (2) typically specifies a channel by which it will inform the caller of its failure to do so and perhaps also an explanation of what precipitated that failure. noexcept Specifier (1117)

out of contract – implies, for a given invocation of a function, that one or more of its **preconditions** (explicitly stated or otherwise) was not satisfied. *Rvalue* References (744), noexcept Specifier (1117)

outermost expression – the expression E, for a given expression S, such that S is a subexpression of E and E is not a subexpression of any other expression; see also **full expression**. *Rvalue* References (820)

over-aligned – implies, for a given type, that its **alignment requirement** exceeds that of what would otherwise be its minimal required **alignment**; see also **natural alignment**. alignof (185)

overload – (1) a member of a set of functions or **operators** that have the same name but different signatures or (2) the act of creating such a similarly named function or **operator** (see also **overloading**). *Rvalue* References (741)

overload resolution – the process by which, after name lookup, the C++ compiler determines which, if any, function from the set of candidate functions is the *unique* best match for a given **argument** list. Deleted Functions (53), *Rvalue* References (710), User-Defined Literals (841)

overload set – the set of (viable) candidates (**overloads**), for a given invocation of a function (or **operator**), that the compiler refines during **overload resolution** until it finds the *best viable function*, if one exists, for the supplied **argument** list.

overloading – the act of creating an **overload**.

overriding – providing, for a **virtual** function declared in a base type, a suitable implementation specific to a derived type. Inheriting Ctors (539)

owned resource – one, such as dynamic memory, a socket, or a shared-memory handle, that is managed by an object (a.k.a. the *owner*), typically with the expectation that the owner will release the resource when it no longer needs it, e.g., in the owner's **destructor**. Move operations typically transfer an **owned resource** from one owner to another. On occasion, a resource can have more than one owner — such as in the case of std::shared_ptr — in which case the last owner to be destroyed is typically responsible for releasing the resource. *Rvalue* References (741)

Glossary

pack expansion – the process of expanding a syntactic pattern followed by an ellipsis (...) that contains the name of at least one **parameter pack** into a comma-separated list of instantiations of that pattern, appropriate for that **pack expansion context**. Lambdas (590), Variadic Templates (882), `constexpr` Functions '14 (964)

pack-expansion context – the syntactic position at which a **pack expansion** occurs, which impacts both the kinds of **parameter packs** that can be expanded and the semantics of that expansion. Variadic Templates (883)

package prefix – an organization-wide unique (ideally very short) identifier that denotes the smallest unit of **physical design** larger than a **component** (e.g., `std`, `bsls`, `bslma`, `ball`). This name is often used for the **namespace** containing a collection of related logical entities, such as classes and functions. This same name can be used as the initial part of the name of a physical entity, such as a directory, a **component**, or a library, to associate it with the **namespace** that comprises its logical content; see **lakos20**, section 2.4, "Logical and Physical Name Cohesion," pp. 297–333, specifically section 2.4.10, "Package Prefixes Are Not Just Style," pp. 322–326.

padding byte – one supplied by the compiler in the **footprint** of an object of class type, typically to satisfy **alignment** requirements of individual **data members** or for the object as a whole. Each padding byte is of indeterminate value and, like a vtable pointer or virtual base pointer, does not contribute to the **value representation** of the object. Generalized PODs '11 (475)

parameter – the (formal) name declared within the **defining declaration** of an entity, such as a function or template, used locally within its **definition** to refer to the corresponding (actual) **argument** supplied when called or instantiated, respectively.

parameter declaration – The declaration of a **parameter** to a function within a function's **parameter list**. Variadic Templates (888)

parameter list – a sequence of formal **parameter declarations**, such as a function parameter list or a template parameter list.

parameter pack – a function **parameter pack** or a template **parameter pack**. Variable Templates (159), Variadic Templates (873), `constexpr` Functions '14 (964)

partial application – transforming an N-ary function into another of smaller arity, specifically by binding one or more **parameters** of the original function to fixed **arguments**, as commonly occurs in C++ when trailing **parameters** of a given function are declared to have default arguments or, more generally, when a higher-order function, e.g., $h(F, v)$, is applied to some function, e.g., $f(x, y, z)$, to yield another function, e.g., $g(x, y) = h(f(x, y, z), k)$, such that, for all a and b, $g(a, b) = f(a, b, k)$. Lambdas (597)

partial class-template specialization – the partial specialization of a class template. `constexpr` Functions '14 (963)

partial implementation – an abstract class that provides implementations for some (but not all) **virtual** functions of a protocol. Inheriting Ctors (540), `final` (1021)

partial ordering of class-template specialization – the process by which the compiler selects the most specialized candidate when instantiating a class template that has partial specializations. Variadic Templates (886)

partial specialization – a template specialization that is itself a template. Generalized PODs '11 (529), Variadic Templates (884)

partially constructed – implies, for a given object, that its constructor has begun executing, but has not yet completed. Delegating Ctors (47)

Glossary

perfect forwarding – the use of a combination of a forwarding reference and `std::forward` to enable a function `f` (e.g., a factory function) to call a different function (e.g., the constructor of a class) with one of `f`'s **arguments**, retaining both its type and its **value category**. Braced Init (240), *Rvalue* References (807), Variadic Templates (942), **noexcept** Specifier (1131), **auto** Return (1198)

perfectly forwarded – implies, for a given function **argument**, that it was passed into the function using **perfect forwarding**. Lambda Captures (992)

physical – implies, for a given aspect of design, that it involves files, libraries, or dependencies, in contrast to a purely **logical** one, e.g., that which pertains to classes, functions, **variables**, algorithms, or their relationships. Note that this term is also used to denote *physical* aspects of the program, tool chain, and supporting hardware, such as executable size, compilers, linkers, available memory, and so on.

physical dependency – implies, for two distinct **physical** entities (e.g., files, **components**, libraries), that one requires the other in order to be compiled, linked, tested, or used. In well-designed **component**-based software, an envelope of **physical dependencies** among **components** can be gleaned quickly by examining their relative **#include** directives. Generalized PODs '11 (443)

physical design – (1) implies, during software development, the factoring and partitioning of **logical** content into source files and libraries and (2) the **physical** aspects that characterize the design and architecture of the resulting software. Opaque enums (663), **friend** '11 (1042)

physical memory – storage that provides the **address space** available to a running process. **noexcept** Specifier (1135)

pipelined – implies, for a given computation, that a step that comes earlier in the serial ordering of subcomputations is allowed to begin processing a new data item while later steps continue to work concurrently on previous data items, yielding better throughput and/or reduced latency. Optimizing compilers often reorder instructions to better exploit the ability of modern CPUs to *pipeline* their execution so as to improve performance. **noexcept** Specifier (1137)

placeholder – short for **placeholder type**. **auto** Return (1182)

placeholder type – one of **auto** or, in C++14, **decltype(auto)** that can be used in a **declaration** to represent a type that will be deduced from the relevant initialization. As of C++20, a **placeholder** can be constrained by a **concept**. **auto** Variables (195), *Generic* Lambdas (984), **decltype(auto)** (1205)

placement new – an overload of the **new** operator, defined by the C++ Standard, that can be used to construct an object at a particular location in memory. Forwarding References (391), Generalized PODs '11 (452), **noexcept** Operator (638), Variadic Templates (940), **inline namespace** (1072), **union** '11 (1174)

plain old data (POD) – a now-deprecated term in the C++ Standard (replaced by the union of standard-layout type and trivial) used to describe C++ types that were C compatible, having the same layout and behavior in both languages.

platonic value – one whose *unique* meaning is understood outside of the current running process. Multiple variables in separate programs, processes, or databases — having different representations (e.g., `5u`, `5.0`, `'V'`, or `"five"`) — might each identify such a value, but that value (i.e., *the* integer 5) is itself unique. *Rvalue* References (742)

PMR – short for polymorphic memory resource.

POD – short for Plain Old Data, such as a C++03 POD type or C++11 POD type. Generalized PODs '11 (401), **union** '11 (1174)

point of instantiation – the source-code location where template arguments are supplied (either directly or via template argument deduction) to template parameters to form a template instantiation.

pointer semantics – a *proxy* or handle type with *in-core* (a.k.a. in-process) value semantics that behaves similarly to a built-in pointer in that a value of the type provides access — typically via the dereference operators, * or -> — to some resource (e.g., a separately allocated object, as is the case for std::shared_ptr) or else has a *null* value. If an object of *pointer-semantic* type is copied, the original and the *copy* will refer to the *same* resource; any modifications made to the resource through one will be reflected in accesses through the other. Two *pointer-semantic* objects will not have the same value unless they refer to the same resource or both are *null*. Note that *pointer-semantic* objects are more independent of their referenced entity than are reference-semantic objects in that the former can be modified (e.g., assigned) independently, have a separate notion of equality, and be *null*, whereas the latter approximate fixed aliases to their referenced entity, analogous to the difference between built-in pointers and references; in particular, assigning from a *pointer-semantic* object, unlike a reference-semantic one, does not imply copying its referenced resource.

pointer to member – a type (or a value of that type) that is able to identify (by its value) a specific non**static** member of a specific **class** type, such as an **int** data member of **class** X, or a possibly **virtual**, non**static** member function having a specific signature and return value. A class member cannot be accessed using the value of a pointer-to-member type alone, but instead it must be combined with the address of a live object of the specified (or derived) type. **explicit** Operators (64), Generalized PODs '11 (456)

polymorphic class – one having a **virtual** function or a **virtual** base class. noexcept Operator (617)

polymorphic memory resource (PMR) – (1) a class derived from the standard abstract base class std::pmr::memory_resource, used to customize memory allocation and deallocation when using classes that obtain memory from an std::pmr::polymorphic_allocator object; (2) colloquially, the facilities in the C++ Standard Library within the std::pmr namespace, including memory_resource, polymorphic_allocator, monotonic_buffer_resource, and unsynchronized_pool_resource. **alignof** (190), Default Member Init (328)

polymorphic type – one that, in C++, is implemented as a polymorphic class. noexcept Operator (616), **final** (1011)

positive semidefinite – implies, for a given matrix, that it is both Hermitian and all of its eigenvalues are non-negative; see **vandenbos17**. noexcept Operator (655)

POSIX epoch – 00:00:00 UTC on January 1, 1970, the reference time point against which POSIX time representations are typically based. constexpr Functions (291)

postcondition – a promise made in the contract of a function stating what conditions will hold once the flow of control leaves a function, provided that all of that function's (explicit or implicit) preconditions are met.

potentially evaluated – implies, for a given expression, that it is *not* an unevaluated operand or part of one. noexcept Operator (615)

precondition – a predicate, specified within a function's contract, that must hold when the function is invoked; otherwise, the behavior is undefined. See also library undefined behavior. Attribute Syntax (18), Generalized PODs '11 (472)

Glossary

predicate – a Boolean-valued expression, typically indicating whether some particular property holds; see also **predicate function**. Lambdas (575)

predicate function – one that returns a Boolean value; see also **predicate functor**. Local Types '11 (86)

predicate functor – a callable object that returns a Boolean value; see also **predicate**. Lambdas (575)

primary-class-template declaration – a declaration that introduces a class template into the current scope (and, hence, is neither a specialization nor a partial specialization). Variadic Templates (881)

primary declaration – short for **primary-class-template declaration**. Variadic Templates (881)

private inheritance – derivation (e.g., using the **private** keyword) from a base class such that inheritance does not afford programmatic access to the base class to any further derived classes or pubic clients. final (1029)

procedural – implies, for a given imperative programming paradigm or language, that the basic building blocks are functions that operate on raw data rather than, say, objects that encapsulate raw data along with relevant functionality; see also **object orientation**. Generalized PODs '11 (448)

proctor – an object of a **proctor class**. noexcept Operator (646), noexcept Specifier (1139)

proctor class – one that, like a scoped guard, uses RAII to take temporary ownership of a resource and ensure that the held resource is released when the flow of control exits scope unexpectedly, e.g., via a thrown exception. Unlike a scoped guard, however, a proctor class necessarily has an explicit *release* operation that allows ownership of the resource to be adopted by another (longer-lived) entity before the proctor is destroyed. Proctor objects are used for writing exception-safe code in an exception-agnostic programming style. noexcept Operator (646)

production build – one that employs a compilation mode that prioritizes the performance required of a production system, perhaps sacrificing niceties such as defensive checks or debugging information. Generalized PODs '11 (469)

programmatically accessible – implies, for a given (logical) entity (e.g., within some other entity), that it can be manipulated, accessed, or detected *programmatically* (i.e., using the C++ language) by clients. noexcept Specifier (1085)

protocol – a class whose (user-declared) members — apart from an empty destructor, possibly defined out of line in a source (.cpp) file — consist of only pure virtual functions and that does not inherit (either directly or indirectly) from any other class that is not itself a protocol. Generalized PODs '11 (440), Inheriting Ctors (540), final (1018)

protocol hierarchy – an inheritance hierarchy consisting exclusively of protocols, whereby higher-level protocols serve only to widen and augment the functionality available to public clients; see **lakos96**, Appendix A, "The Protocol Hierarchy Design Pattern," pp. 737–768. final (1020)

prvalue – short for *pure rvalue*; an expression of this value category — such as a function that returns *by value* or a numeric literal — has a value but no inherent identity; see also *lvalue* and *xvalue*. decltype (25), nullptr (99), auto Variables (206), constexpr Functions (282), enum class (346), Generalized PODs '11 (513), Range for (692), *Rvalue* References (711), decltype(auto) (1206)

publicly accessible – implies, for a given member of a user-defined type, that its access level is *public*. Generalized PODs '11 (489)

Glossary

pun – the act of type punning, i.e., accessing an object from other than a compatible type.

pure abstract interface – one that is a protocol, i.e., providing no implementation of any kind. Inheriting Ctors (540)

pure function – one that (1) produces no side effects and (2) returns a consistent value for a given set of arguments. Such functions can, for example, have their results *memoized* (reused for specific input arguments without having to reevaluate the function) with no observable change in the behavior of the program. Attribute Syntax (16)

pure virtual function – one that is a **virtual** function declared with a *pure* specifier, =0. Such a function need be **defined** only if it is called with (or as if with) its qualified id; see also protocol. `final` (1008)

qNaN – short for quiet NaN.

QoI – short for quality of implementation.

qualified id – an unqualified id following a (possibly empty) sequence of namespace or class specifiers, each separated by :: — e.g., `B::x`, **decltype**(a)::d_b, or `std::vector<int>`.

qualified name – one that contains the scope-resolution operator (::) — e.g., `::foo` (global scope) or `bar::baz` (bar scope). `inline namespace` (1060)

qualifier – (classically) short for cv-qualifier, one of **const** or **volatile**; see Section 3.1."Ref-Qualifiers" on page 1153. Variadic Templates (889)

quality of implementation (QoI) – a characterization with respect to a range of (e.g., compiler or library) implementation behaviors that are allowed by the Standard along with the possibly subjective measure of how well those implementations meet the intent of the Standard and the needs of the users. `constexpr` Functions (277), Generalized PODs '11 (529)

quiet NaN (qNaN) – a NaN value that is generated by certain computations (e.g., 0.0/0.0) and that, when used as an operand, yields a NaN result; e.g., $1.0 + NaN$ yields NaN. Contrast with signaling NaN. Generalized PODs '11 (531)

RAII – short for resource acquisition is initialization. Deleted Functions (54), Forwarding References (388), **noexcept** Operator (644), *Rvalue* References (769), **noexcept** Specifier (1126)

range – any object (e.g., an `std::vector`) that exposes a sequence of elements suitable for iteration using a range-based **for** loop. Note that C++20 elaborates on this notion via the addition of the *ranges* library. `decltype` (29), Variadic Templates (877)

range-based for loop – a variety of **for** loop, introduced in C++11 (see Section 2.1."Range **for**" on page 679), that provides a simpler, more abstract syntax — **for** (*declaration* : *range-expression*) — used to iterate through the elements of a range. Range `for` (679)

range expression – one that produces a range — i.e., one suitable for use in a range-based **for** loop. Range `for` (680)

raw string literal – a C++11 feature (see Section 1.1."Raw String Literals" on page 108) that allows a string literal to be interpreted *literally* — i.e., without escape sequences (commonly called a "here doc" in scripting languages). Raw String Literals (113)

raw UDL operator – a user-defined-literal operator that is passed the unparsed literal string as a null-terminated **const char***. User-Defined Literals (841)

Glossary

reachable – implies, for a given expression, that its value has identity and that the address of its underlying object representation is accessible. To a good approximation, an object is reachable if it is a *glvalue*, that is, an *lvalue* or an *xvalue* but not a *prvalue*; there are, however, pathological prvalues that are nonetheless reachable. Consider, for example, a type S that holds an **int** and stores its **this** pointer as a global variable on construction — **struct** S; S* p; **struct** S { **int** v; S(**int** i) : v(i) { p = **this**; } }; **int** x = (S(3), 2 * p->v); — and sets the value of x to 6. See Section 2.1."*Rvalue* References" on page 710. *Rvalue* References (712)

reaching scope – the set of enclosing scopes containing a lambda, up to and including the innermost enclosing function and its **parameters**. This scope defines the set of automatic-storage-duration variables that a lambda can *capture* or to which it can refer; see captured by copy and captured by reference. Lambdas (587)

recursion – (1) invoking a function that is called (directly or indirectly) from that same function — e.g., **int** f(**int** n) { **return** n > 0 ? n * f(n-1) : 1; } — or (2) defining an entity in terms of itself, e.g., a type list (see Section 2.1."Variadic Templates" on page 873). Variadic Templates (875)

redundant check – one that is superfluous in a defect-free program (a.k.a. defensive check). static_assert (115)

ref-qualifier – one of & or && applied to a non**static** member function declaration, thereby enabling overloading based on the value category of the object from which that member function is invoked. Forwarding References (380), Ref-Qualifiers (1154)

reference collapsing – the C++ language rule for applying & or && to a type alias or **decltype** expression that is itself a reference (T& or T&&), i.e., when there are two *reference* operators being applied to the same underlying type. The resulting reference will be an lvalue reference (T&) unless both operators are &&, in which case the result will be an rvalue reference (T&&). Forwarding References (380)

reference related – implies, for a given type T, that some other type U differs in only cv-qualification (at any level) or T is a direct or indirect base class of U. *Rvalue* References (726)

reference type – one that denotes an alias to an object of the referenced type and can be either an lvalue reference or an rvalue reference. alignof (184), union '11 (1174)

reflection – a language feature allowing a program to inspect and modify its own structure and behavior. The C++ Standards Committee, and specifically its Study Group 7, is actively working toward incorporating static (compile-time) reflection capabilities into a future version of C++. Generalized PODs '11 (520)

regression test – one designed to detect the recurrence of some previously corrected undesired property (e.g., a bug) in the software.

regular type – one that emulates syntactically the operations (and corresponding behaviors) of built-in types such as an **int**, e.g., that they be copy constructible, copy assignable, destructible, and equality comparable; see **stepanov09**, section 1.5, "Regular Types," pp. 6–8. Note that, due to being copyable, all such types are implicitly also movable. Though required by the definition of regular type, default construction is not typically needed in generic contexts. A type that does not provide equality-comparison operators but would otherwise be considered a regular type is called *semiregular*; see **stepanov15**, section 10.3, "Concepts," pp. 181–184, specifically p. 184. alignof (187), *Rvalue* References (751)

release-acquire – a synchronization paradigm in which all reads and writes on memory locations that appear in the source code before a *release* operation will occur before all reads and writes that appear after a subsequent *acquire* operation. carries_dependency (998)

release-consume – a synchronization paradigm within the release/acquire/consume memory model that guarantees that any modification to a memory location made visible by a *release* operation can be read after a *consume* operation on a (possibly different) memory location provided that there is a **data dependency chain** from the modified location to the consumed location. carries_dependency (998)

reliable – implies, for a given function having a **reporting contract**, that it has an **infallible implementation** and any failure to deliver fully on the outcome intended by the caller will always be reliably reported back to the caller in some well-defined way, e.g., via an error status. noexcept Specifier (1122)

reporting contract – a function **contract** having an **out clause** that specifies a channel by which an error is reported back to the caller. noexcept Specifier (1120)

reserved identifier – one commandeered for exclusive use by the C++ Standard Library and whose use by other code is **ill formed, no diagnostic required** — e.g., any identifier that contains (anywhere) double underscores (__), or any identifier having a leading _ in the **global namespace**. User-Defined Literals (840)

resource acquisition is initialization (RAII) – a C++ programming idiom for managing the lifetime of any allocated resource — e.g., dynamic or shared memory, socket, file — by acquiring it in the constructor of an object and then relying on that object's **destructor** to be responsible for releasing it, thereby tying proper management of the underlying resource to that of the lifetime of the object itself. This idiom is effective at avoiding common defects, compared with having to pair allocation and deallocations explicitly, especially with respect to early **return** statements and unexpectedly thrown exceptions.

return-type deduction – a feature by which the return type of a lambda expression (since C++11) or a function having a **placeholder type** (e.g., **auto**) as its return type (since C++14) is deduced from the possibly implicit **return** statement in the (necessarily visible) function body; see Section 2.1."Lambdas" on page 573 and Section 3.2."**auto** Return" on page 1182, respectively. decltype (28)

return-value optimization (RVO) – copy elision (guaranteed as of C++17) that can occur by constructing the return value of a function directly into the variable in the calling context that is initialized from said return value, rather than constructing a temporary; see also **named return-value optimization (NRVO)**. Forwarding References (390), *Rvalue* References (734)

reuse – utilizing a piece of software designed for one application or context in a different one. final (1012)

RTTI – short for runtime type identification. noexcept Operator (617)

rule of zero – a design guideline recommending to class authors that, when possible, the compiler be allowed to implicitly generate all five **special member functions** that are typically defined together (or not at all): destructor, copy constructor, copy-assignment operator, and where advantageous (e.g., for runtime performance), move constructor and move-assignment operator. Choosing data members of types, such as std::vector, std::shared_ptr, and std::unique_ptr, that properly manage their respective owned resources, obviates having to provide these functions explicitly, thereby automatically achieving the appropriate owned-resource lifetime management through effective use of RAII. Note, however, that having a

Glossary

data member of move-only type, such as `std::unique_ptr`, will result in a **move-only class** when adhering to this rule. `noexcept` Operator (631), *Rvalue* References (788)

runtime type – a synonym for dynamic type.

runtime type identification (RTTI) – a C++ language feature whereby an object's type, and thereby information associated with that type, can be determined at run time; this mechanism underlies type-safe casting using **`dynamic_cast`** and runtime querying of type information using **`typeid`**.

rvalue – any expression that is not an *lvalue* (i.e., either an *xvalue* or a *prvalue*) and, hence, can be passed to a function via an **rvalue reference**. **`decltype`** (26), Defaulted Functions (42), **`nullptr`** (99), Variable Templates (167), **`auto`** Variables (196), Braced Init (216), Forwarding References (377), Generalized PODs '11 (501), `initializer_list` (570), Lambdas (590), **`noexcept`** Operator (628), Range **`for`** (680), *Rvalue* References (710), Variadic Templates (890), *Generic* Lambdas (971), Lambda Captures (992), **`noexcept`** Specifier (1133), Ref-Qualifiers (1153), **`auto`** Return (1184), **`decltype(auto)`** (1206)

rvalue reference – a reference, formed for a type X as X&&, that can be bound to an *rvalue*; see Section 2.1. "*Rvalue* References" on page 710. Forwarding References (400), Range **`for`** (701), *Rvalue* References (710)

RVO – short for return-value optimization.

safe-bool idiom – a technique in class design (e.g., using an *unspecified-bool* type) that suppresses unwanted comparisons made available by the presence of a non**`explicit`** conversion function to **`bool`**. **`explicit`** Operators (64)

salient attribute – a (typically independently observable) property of an object (e.g., the *year* of a *date* or the *real* part of a *complex number*) that contributes to its overall semantic value, i.e., one that would be relevant in the result of a homogeneous equality-comparison **operator** (`==`) for its type.

salient operation – one, for a given value-semantic type, that is relevant to the algebra governing the set of platonic values it aims to represent.

salient value – a particular value corresponding to the salient attribute of a type. `noexcept` Operator (634)

sanitizer – a family of tools (e.g., AddressSanitizer, ThreadSanitizer) provided along with the GCC and especially Clang tool chains that can be run with an instrumented build of an application to identify various sorts of defects, such as dangling pointers, memory leaks, race conditions, and various forms of undefined behavior. *Rvalue* References (802)

scalar type – one that is an arithmetic type, enumeration type, pointer type, pointer-to-member type, `std::nullptr_t`, or any cv-qualified version of these types. `alignas` (168), Braced Init (217), Generalized PODs '11 (417), **`decltype(auto)`** (1207)

scoped allocator model – one comprising stateful customizable memory allocators in which all of an object of allocator-aware type and all of its allocator-aware subobjects are constructed using the same allocator, i.e., the allocator used by (and optionally passed into) the outermost object's constructor. Default Member Init (328)

scoped enumeration – one, declared using **enum class** or **enum struct**, for which the enumerator names are not automatically injected into the enclosing namespace. Opaque `enums` (660)

scoped guard – an object that uses RAII to take ownership of a resource and ensures that it is released when the object goes out of scope, typically used as a local variable in block scope to prevent a resource (such as a mutex lock or file handle) from being leaked in the event of an early `return` statement or a thrown exception; see also **proctor**. `noexcept` Operator (645), *Rvalue* References (764), `noexcept` Specifier (1139)

section – a segmented portion of an object file containing object-level code that can be incorporated by the linker into the final executable program, independently of any other such sections. `extern template` (361)

secure hash algorithms (SHA) – a family of cryptographic hash functions defined by the U.S. National Institute for Standards and Technology.

sentinel – a marker, such as an out-of-band value, often used to represent the end of a sequence, e.g., a null terminator to represent the end of a string or a null pointer or empty node to represent the end of a list. *Rvalue* References (743), `noexcept` Specifier (1114)

sequencing operator – a synonym for the comma operator. `constexpr` Functions (265)

serial date – one that is represented as a single number, generally days since a well-known epoch, as opposed to one represented by year, month, and day individually. Generalized PODs '11 (453)

set associative – implies, for a given hardware memory cache, that every address is directly mapped to exactly one *set* of (e.g., 2, 4, or 8) lines in the cache. The cache lines within each set are fully associative, obviating evictions from the set until all cache lines within it are full. A set-associative cache is a hybrid between a direct mapped cache and a fully associative cache, with a power-performance trade-off between the two. `alignas` (182)

SFINAE – short for substitution failure is not an error. `decltype` (28), `static_assert` (121), Forwarding References (397), Generalized PODs '11 (474), Inheriting Ctors (539), `noexcept` Specifier (1089), `auto` Return (1190)

SHA – short for secure hash algorithms. `inline namespace` (1083)

side effect – any observable modification of program state that occurs as the result of evaluating an expression. Attribute Syntax (16)

signal – a type of message that is sent to a process by the operating system, possibly indicating an error condition. The process may — depending on the type of signal — ignore it, have one of its threads interrupted so that it can execute a signal handler, or terminate. Note that signals first originated in Bell Labs UNIX (version 4) in 1973, are part of C, and are entirely independent of C++ exceptions. `noexcept` Specifier (1120)

signaling NaN (sNaN) – one of a subset of NaN values that, in theory, produces a signal (e.g., a floating-point exception) originating from the processor hardware when used as part of a computation. An sNaN is never generated from a computation (e.g., by 0.0/0.0) but must instead be explicitly set by the programmer. Theoretically, an sNaN could be injected into a computation to catch bugs such as use of freed memory, but examples of such use are rare in practice; moreover, many compilers implicitly convert sNaNs into qNaNs. Generalized PODs '11 (531)

signature – the information needed at the ABI level to uniquely identify a function (including an instantiation of a function template) from any other one that might coexist (e.g., be overloaded) having the same name. A function's signature comprises its fully qualified name (including enclosing namespace and class if any), function parameter list, and (for member functions) cv-qualifiers and ref-qualifiers; see Section 3.1."Ref-Qualifiers" on page 1153. If

Glossary

the function is a **specialization** of a function template, its **signature** includes its **template arguments**, whether explicitly specified or deduced. Though this term is seldom used for templates except when referring to an instantiation or **specialization**, the **signature** of an (unspecialized) **function template** further includes its return type and **template parameter list**. Trailing Return (124), Inheriting Ctors (536), *Rvalue* References (729), `friend` '11 (1052), `noexcept` Specifier (1089), Ref-Qualifiers (1153)

signed integer overflow – an evaluation (e.g., the result of a built-in operation on one or two signed integers) in which an **expression** or subexpression has *signed* integer **type** but its **value** is outside the range of **values** representable in that type. All overflow on signed integers has **undefined** behavior. In contrast, the same operations on unsigned integers, which follow modular arithmetic, do not have any cases where the result cannot be expressed in the same type; hence, most operations (other than division by 0) on unsigned integers are well defined. `long long` (90)

sink argument – one that is supplied to a function — either *by value* or by rvalue reference — typically with the intent of transferring ownership of a managed resource. Note that passing by rvalue reference leaves open the option to read but not move, whereas passing by **value** does not. *Rvalue* References (775)

size constructor – one, available on certain standard containers (e.g., `std::vector`), that takes an integral size and initializes the container with that many **value-initialized** elements. *Rvalue* References (764)

slicing – the outcome of copying or moving from a derived-class object, via a base-class **reference** to the original object, to a distinct base-class object. Note that the resulting object will be unable to hold any supplementary state that might exist in only the derived class; in the special case of a **move operation**, **object invariants** could be violated for either or both objects involved. Inheriting Ctors (539), `final` (1025)

smart pointer – a user-defined type, typically with overloads of `operator->` and `operator*`, intended to behave like a built-in pointer but with additional semantics or functionality, often to manage the lifetime of the referenced objects using RAII. The most commonly available examples are `std::shared_ptr`, which uses **reference** counting to manage ownership of shared objects, and `std::unique_ptr`, which is a **move-only type** that allows only one object at a time to own a given dynamically allocated object. *Rvalue* References (770), Variadic Templates (948)

sNaN – short for signaling NaN.

soft UB – short for library undefined behavior. `noexcept` Specifier (1115)

Software Capital – a proprietary suite of relevant, interoperable, reusable **components** that is an asset of an entire organization and does not belong to any one application or product; see **lakos20**, section 0.9, "Software Capital," pp. 86–97.

source character set – short for basic source character set.

special member function – one of the six member functions that the compiler knows how to generate: default constructor, copy constructor, move constructor, copy-assignment operator, move-assignment operator, and destructor. Defaulted Functions (33), Deleted Functions (53), `constexpr` Functions (266), Generalized PODs '11 (413), `initializer_list` (553), *Rvalue* References (710), `noexcept` Specifier (1086), `union` '11 (1174)

specialization – the class, function, or class member that results when supplying a template argument for every (nonoptional) template parameter of a template. The use of a specialization will trigger template instantiation of the *primary template* (or one of its partial specializations) unless there exists an explicit specialization for that template. Variadic Templates (884)

stack frame – a contiguous segment of memory within a running program that is used to hold local variables — i.e., objects having automatic storage duration. noexcept Specifier (1101)

stack memory – a synonym for automatically allocated memory.

stack unwinding – the process by which the runtime library destroys automatic variables when traversing the call stack from the point an exception is thrown to the point it is caught. Note that, if a thrown exception encounters a function having a **noexcept** specification, it is implementation defined whether stack unwinding occurs before the runtime library calls std::terminate; see Section 3.1."**noexcept** Specifier" on page 1085. noexcept Operator (621), noexcept Specifier (1135)

standard conversion – an *implicit conversion*, having built-in meaning, from one type to another, such as array to pointer decay or **short** to **int** promotion. Unlike a user-defined conversion, a standard conversion does not involve a converting constructor or conversion operator. Zero or more *implicit conversions* might be used when an expression is converted to a destination type, such as when direct initializing a variable, or when a function parameter is being initialized from a function argument. The Standard defines a *partial ordering* of conversions that is used, during overload resolution, to choose certain conversions over others, with sequences consisting entirely of standard conversions always preferred over those containing a user-defined conversion. Deleted Functions (56), **enum class** (334), Generalized PODs '11 (509), User-Defined Literals (835)

standard-layout – implies, for a given class type, that its physical layout (a.k.a. footprint in memory) has properties that can be relied upon portably (e.g., that the address of the first data member coincides with the address of the object overall), as well as being suitable for integration with other languages, C in particular; see also standard-layout class and standard-layout type. Generalized PODs '11 (420)

standard-layout class – a **class**, **struct**, or **union** having all non**static** data members at the same access level, no non**static** data members of reference type or non-standard-layout type, no base classes that are not standard-layout classes, and no **virtual** functions or **virtual** base classes; furthermore, if such a class is not a **union**, no two subobjects — i.e., base classes, non**static** data members, and subobjects thereof — of the same type will both have offset 0 within an object of the outermost type. Generalized PODs '11 (422)

standard-layout class type – a synonym for standard-layout class. Generalized PODs '11 (420)

standard-layout type – one that is a (possibly cv-qualified) scalar or standard-layout class type, or an array of such a type. alignas (178), alignof (186), Generalized PODs '11 (401)

statement – a unit of programming larger than an expression that typically governs the scope of temporaries created therein; unlike expressions, statements cannot be nested. An expression followed by a semicolon forms a statement (as does a semicolon alone). A label (within a function) is required to precede a statement. See also block scope.

static assertion declaration – one using the **static_assert** keyword to evaluate a constant expression at compile time. If the expression is **false**, the program is ill formed and the compiler outputs a required (optional, as of C++17) user-supplied diagnostic string. Such

Glossary

declarations are invaluable for enforcing compile-time assumptions (e.g., maximum object size) and especially in conjunction with standard traits (e.g., `std::is_trivially_copyable`). static_assert (115)

static data space – that memory region of a running program holding objects having static storage duration. Variable Templates (165)

static storage duration – the lifetime of a variable defined in namespace scope or declared with the **static** storage-class specifier, beginning sometime before its first use in the program and ending after the main function has completed. At program startup, such a variable is always zero-initialized, and if its initialization is a constant expression, such initialization is performed. If the variable is defined at block scope, any further initialization that it requires will be performed when control flow reaches its definition for the first time; otherwise, the implementation may complete such initialization at any time prior to its first use. Non-trivial destructors are run on normal program termination in (roughly) the reverse order of the corresponding constructor invocations. Function static '11 (68), Generalized PODs '11 (478)

storage-class specifier – one of **static**, **thread_local**, **extern**, or **mutable**, all of which control details of where and how an entity can be located. C++03 also allowed the (redundant) use of **auto** as a storage-class specifier for variables with automatic storage duration, which was removed in C++11. Up to C++14, the specifier **register** was allowed as a hint to store an object in registers in lieu of memory, but this was removed in C++17. auto Variables (195)

strict aliasing – a rule in C++ stating that accessing the value of an object of one type through a pointer or reference to a different type has undefined behavior unless that difference is limited to cv-qualifiers (at any level) and, for integral types only, **signed** versus **unsigned**; compilers may optimize based on this rule by assuming that any two pointers or references to objects of such dissimilar types do not refer to overlapping memory regions and, thus, modifications through one will not affect the state of the other. Note that accessing the individual bytes of the object representation of any object type through a pointer to **char** or **unsigned char** (and, as of C++20, `std::byte`) never violates the strict-aliasing rule; see Section 2.1."Generalized PODs '11" on page 401. Generalized PODs '11 (401)

string literal – a literal comprising a sequence of characters between quotation marks (`""`) that together form a null-terminated string. static_assert (115), deprecated (148), User-Defined Literals (837)

strong exception-safety guarantee – one provided by certain Standard Library container operations, e.g., `push_back` on an `std::vector`, stipulating that if an exception is emitted by the operation, then no changes to the state of the operands will be observed. noexcept Operator (634), *Rvalue* References (750), **noexcept** Specifier (1097)

strong guarantee – short for strong exception-safety guarantee. noexcept Operator (634), *Rvalue* References (746)

strong `typedef` – a user-defined type (UDT) implementing the strong typedef idiom, e.g., using inheriting constructors. Inheriting Ctors (542), User-Defined Literals (871)

strong `typedef` **idiom** – one that involves creating a user-defined type (UDT) wrapper having the same API as the type it wraps but which is not implicitly convertible *from* that type, thereby providing a greater degree of static type safety. In particular, this idiom is used for avoiding programming errors whereby one kind of value is passed where a different kind is expected when they are each represented by the same vocabulary type. A typical implementation of a strong typedef is in terms of a **struct** derived from the original type and then employing inheriting constructors (see Section 2.1."Inheriting Ctors" on page 535) to avoid having to rewrite the derived-class constructors explicitly. For integer types, a classical **enum** having the original type as its underlying type (see Section 2.1."Underlying Type '11" on page 829) can serve the same purpose. Function static '11 (74)

structural inheritance – a form of inheritance in which non-**virtual** functions are inherited by a derived class; see also **implementation inheritance**. Deleted Functions (57), **alignas** (180), Inheriting Ctors (545), **final** (1025)

structural type – a category of type, introduced in C++20, used to characterize the extended set of allowable types for values supplied as non-type template parameters, which include integral type, enumeration type, pointer type, pointer-to-member type, lvalue reference type, as well as floating-point type and class types made up of other structural types.

structured binding – a C++17 feature that introduces new names bound to the subobjects of the object produced by the expression that initializes them, i.e., **auto** [a,b] = std::make_tuple(17,42); where a will be initialized to 17 and b will hold the value 42. Range for (685)

substitution failure is not an error (SFINAE) – a property of C++ template instantiation that enables the technique of supplying **template arguments** to a function template to determine if the resulting function will participate in overload resolution or supplying template arguments to a template partial specialization to determine whether it is eligible to be instantiated; errors that result from substituting certain (e.g., syntactically incompatible) arguments for the **template parameters** result merely in that particular template instantiation being dropped from the overload set, and is not (in and of itself) ill formed.

sum type – an *abstract data type* allowing the representation of one of multiple possible alternative types. Each alternative has its own type (and state), and only one alternative can be active at any given point in time. Sum types keep track of which choice is active and properly implement (value-semantic) special member functions (even for non-trivial types). They can be implemented efficiently as a C++ **class** using a **union** and a separate (integral) discriminator. This sort of implementation is commonly referred to as a discriminating (or tagged) union and is available in C++17 as std::variant. union '11 (1177)

synchronization paradigm – the general approach used to coordinate memory reads and writes among two or more concurrent threads of execution. As used in this book, one of two approaches within the *release-acquire/consume* memory consistency model — release-acquire or **release-consume**. carries_dependency (998)

syntactic sugar – language and library features that ease the use of the language by providing more ergonomic interfaces that obviate more verbose or difficult-to-use syntax but do not themselves provide new functionality.

template argument – the type, template, or value mapped to a template parameter in the instantiation of a template. Variadic Templates (899)

template argument deduction – the process by which template arguments are determined from the types of the *function* arguments when calling a function template. Variadic Templates (894)

template argument list – the sequence of arguments — types, templates, or values, depending on the corresponding parameters — that are used to specify explicit, nondeduced arguments to a template instantiation. Variadic Templates (882)

template head – the keyword **template** and associated template parameter list used to introduce the declaration or definition of a template. Variable Templates (157)

Glossary

template instantiation – (1) the process of substituting template arguments into the template parameters of a template declaration or definition to produce a concrete entity declaration or definition, respectively, and (2) the entity produced by this process. Forwarding References (382)

template-instantiation time – the point at which, for a given template, the compiler performs template instantiation, triggered when encountering a point of instantiation for that template in the source code. Note that when a template definition is first encountered, certain semantic analysis and error detection — particularly those involving the template parameters — must be deferred until template-instantiation time. static_assert (116)

template parameter – one, for a given template, that is associated with a template argument (i.e., a type, template, or value) when that template is instantiated; see also point of instantiation. Variadic Templates (896), friend '11 (1031)

template parameter list – the list of template parameters, surrounded by angle brackets (< and >), in the template head of a template declaration or definition. Variadic Templates (888)

template parameter pack – a template parameter that accepts one or more template arguments, identified by an ellipsis (...) preceding the parameter name (if any) in the template head; the size of a parameter pack is determined by the number of template arguments supplied or deduced for the pack parameter at the point of instantiation for the template. Generalized PODs '11 (437), Variadic Templates (879)

template template parameter – a template parameter that expects a template argument that is itself a template: **template <template <typename> class** X> **class** Y; (declares a template template parameter, X, for a template class, Y). Variable Templates (165), Variadic Templates (902)

template template parameter pack – a template parameter pack of template template parameters: **template <template <typename> class** X...> (X is a template template parameter pack). Variadic Templates (903)

temporary – short for temporary object; see also expiring object. initializer_list (555), *Rvalue References* (724)

temporary materialization – the act, by the compiler, of creating a temporary object when needed, e.g., when binding a reference to a *prvalue*. *Rvalue* References (717)

temporary object – an unnamed object, created by evaluating an expression, whose lifetime generally extends until the end of the outermost enclosing expression in which the temporary is created. *Rvalue* References (711)

ternary operator – an operator, formed with ? and :, taking three operands: (1) a conditional expression before the ?, (2) an expression between the ? and the : to be evaluated to produce the result if the first argument is **true**, and (3) an expression after the : to be evaluated to produce the result if the first argument is **false**. The type of the complete expression is the common type of the second and third operands. constexpr Functions (268), noexcept Operator (615)

test driver – a program that, when invoked, will run unit tests for a component. Raw String Literals (114)

thrashing – profound performance degradation, resulting from excessive cache misses or page faults due to poor memory-access patterns. alignas (183)

thread storage duration – the lifetime of an object declared using the **thread_local** keyword; storage for these entities will be created when first used in a thread and will last for the duration of the thread in which it was allocated. Any reference to a variable of this type will be to one associated with the current thread. Note that, when declaring an object to have thread storage duration in function scope, providing the **static** keyword in addition avoids spurious warnings — e.g., "implicitly auto variable is declared ___thread."

top-level const – a **const** cv-qualifier — such as for the variable p in **int *const** p; — that pertains to a type overall. By contrast, a non-top-level const — such as for the variable q in **const int*** q; — pertains to the type of object to which q points, rather than to q itself. Note that reference types and function types, including member-function types, can never have a top-level cv-qualifier, and the top-level cv-qualifier of an array — such as **const int** x[5]; — is the top-level cv-qualifier of the type of its elements. *Rvalue* References (729)

trailing return type – the return type for a function or a lambda expression specified after the parameter list, cv-qualifiers, and **noexcept** specification and preceded by the -> token; for a function, the **auto** placeholder resides where the return type would traditionally have been specified. An important benefit of a **trailing return type** is that it is permitted to refer to function parameters, e.g., by using **decltype** on an expression involving them; see Section 1.1. "Trailing Return" on page 124. Lambdas (593), **noexcept** Specifier (1145)

translation unit (TU) – the combined text resulting from a source file and all header files incorporated via **#include** directives that are translated (at once) into a single object file. Function **static** '11 (71), Opaque **enums** (660), **noexcept** Specifier (1138)

trivial – implies, for a given entity, that it is especially simple in some manner that allows it to be treated specially; see also trivial class, trivial type, and trivial operation. Defaulted Functions (38), Deleted Functions (59), **constexpr** Functions (273), Generalized PODs '11 (409), *Rvalue* References (733), **final** (1011), **noexcept** Specifier (1087), **union** '11 (1181)

trivial class – one that is trivially copyable, has at least one nondeleted trivial default constructor, and has no default constructors that are not trivial. Generalized PODs '11 (521)

trivial constructor – a trivial default constructor, trivial copy constructor, or trivial move constructor. Generalized PODs '11 (408)

trivial copy-assignment operator – a copy-assignment operator that is not user provided, is for a nonpolymorphic type, and does not invoke any non-trivial copy-assignment operators for base classes or data members; it essentially performs a *bitwise copy* of the object representation. Generalized PODs '11 (470)

trivial copy constructor – a copy constructor that is not user provided, is for a nonpolymorphic type, and does not invoke any non-trivial constructors for base classes or data members; it essentially performs a *bitwise copy* of the object representation. Generalized PODs '11 (470)

trivial copy operation – one that is performed by directly calling a trivial copy constructor or trivial copy-assignment operator (or perhaps even a trivial move operation, if one should be chosen as a better fit during overload resolution). *Rvalue* References (733)

trivial default constructor – a default constructor that is not user provided, is for a nonpolymorphic type having no default member initializers, and does not invoke any non-trivial constructors for base classes or data members; when an object of class type having a trivial default constructor is default initialized, any of its scalar data members begin their lifetimes having indeterminate values. Generalized PODs '11 (461)

trivial destructibility – the quality, for a given type, as to whether it's trivially destructible. Generalized PODs '11 (468)

Glossary

trivial destructor – a destructor that is neither user provided nor **virtual** and that does not invoke any non-trivial destructors for base classes or data members. Generalized PODs '11 (408), **noexcept** Specifier (1101)

trivial move-assignment operator – a move-assignment operator that is not user provided, is for a nonpolymorphic type, and does not invoke any non-trivial move-assignment operators for base classes or members; it essentially performs a *bitwise copy* of the object representation.

trivial move constructor – a move constructor that is not user provided, is for a nonpolymorphic type, and does not invoke any non-trivial constructors for base classes or data members; it essentially performs a *bitwise copy* of the object representation. Generalized PODs '11 (528)

trivial move operation – one that is generated by the compiler and — just like a trivial copy operation — is essentially a *bitwise copy* of the underlying object representation. *Rvalue* References (733)

trivial operation – a special member function that is trivial — i.e., one having a compiler-provided implementation that conceptually does the absolute minimum amount of work: nothing (for a trivial default constructor or trivial destructor) or just a simple *bitwise copy* of the object representation (for a trivial copy constructor, trivial move constructor, trivial copy-assignment operator, or trivial move-assignment operator). Defaulted Functions (33)

trivial type – a scalar type, trivial class type, array of such a type, or cv-qualified version of such a type. Generalized PODs '11 (401), **union** '11 (1174)

triviality – the quality of an entity or operation being trivial or not. *Rvalue* References (733)

trivially constructible – implies, for a given type `T` and a (potentially empty) template parameter pack `A`, that the standard library type trait `std::is_trivially_constructible<T, A...>::value` is **true** — i.e., `T` is of scalar type, or both the destructor and *constructor* of `T` that would be called for arguments of the types specified by `A...` are trivial, **public**, nondeleted, and unambiguously invocable, or `T` is an array of such types. In common usage, the argument type is not specified, in which case the meaning is the same as **trivially default constructible**. Function **static** '11 (80), Generalized PODs '11 (431)

trivially copy assignable – implies, for a given type `T`, that the standard library type trait `std::is_trivially_copy_assignable<T>::value` is **true** — i.e., an *lvalue* of type `T` can be unambiguously assigned-to from a **const** *lvalue* of type `T` via a trivial, **public**, and nondeleted assignment operator. Note that a trivial or trivially copyable type is not required to have a public, unambiguous copy-assignment operator and is thus not necessarily trivially copy assignable. Generalized PODs '11 (486)

trivially copy constructible – implies, for a given type `T`, that the standard library type trait `std::is_trivially_constructible<T, const T&>::value` is **true** — i.e., `T` is of scalar type, both the copy constructor and destructor of `T` are trivial, **public**, nondeleted, and unambiguously invocable, or `T` is an array of such types. Note that a type that is trivially copy constructible might not be trivially copyable and vice versa. Generalized PODs '11 (488)

trivially copyable – implies, for a given type, that it is a trivially copyable type. Defaulted Functions (39), Generalized PODs '11 (401), *Rvalue* References (765)

trivially copyable class – one having a nondeleted trivial destructor and at least one of the four possible *copy* or *move* operations — i.e., one of copy constructor, move constructor, copy-assignment operator, or move-assignment operator — that is not deleted and none of which is non-trivial. Note that a trivially copyable class might not be trivially copy constructible and vice versa. Generalized PODs '11 (521)

trivially copyable type – a scalar type, trivially copyable class, array of such a type, or cv-qualified version of such a type; such types are **assignable** by external bitwise copying, e.g., using `std::memcpy`. Generalized PODs '11 (468)

trivially default constructible – implies, for a given type `T`, that the standard library type trait `std::is_trivially_default_constructible<T>::value` is **true**. In other words, `T` is a scalar type, or both the **default constructor** and **destructor** of `T` are trivial and usable (i.e., **public**, nondeleted, and unambiguously invocable), or `T` is an array of such types. Note that a trivial type is not required to have a public or unambiguous **default constructor** or **destructor** and is thus not necessarily **trivially default constructible**. Generalized PODs '11 (401)

trivially destructible – implies, for a given type, that it is a trivially destructible type, and, hence, failing to execute that **destructor** before deallocating or reusing an object's memory is typically of no practical consequence; see also **notionally trivially destructible**. constexpr Variables (305), Generalized PODs '11 (402), **noexcept** Specifier (1102)

trivially destructible type – one for which the standard library type trait `std::is_trivially_destructible<T>::value` is **true** — i.e., it is a class type with a trivial, **public**, and nondeleted destructor, a scalar type, an array of such types with known bound, or a reference type. Note that a trivial type is not required to have a public **destructor** and is thus not necessarily a trivially destructible type; see also **usable**. Generalized PODs '11 (430)

trivially move assignable – implies, for a given type `T`, that the standard library type trait `std::is_trivially_move_assignable<T>::value` is **true** — i.e., an *lvalue* of type `T` can be unambiguously assigned-to from an *rvalue* of type `T` via a trivial, **public**, and nondeleted assignment operator. Note that a trivial or trivially copyable type is *not* required to have a public unambiguous **move-assignment operator** and is thus *not* necessarily trivially move assignable; see also **usable**.

trivially move constructible – implies, for a given type `T`, that the standard library type trait `std::is_trivially_move_constructible<T>::value` is **true** — i.e., `T` is trivially destructible and can be unambiguously constructed from an *rvalue* of type `T` via a trivial, **public**, and nondeleted constructor. Note that a trivial or trivially copyable type is not required to have a public, unambiguous **move constructor** or **destructor** and is thus not necessarily trivially move constructible.

TU – short for translation unit.

type alias – an alternate name for a type, declared using a **typedef** or, as of C++11, a using declaration; see Section 1.1. "**using** Aliases" on page 133. friend '11 (1031)

type deduction – short for function-template-argument type deduction. Forwarding References (380)

type erasure – an idiom enabling dynamic polymorphism without requiring inheritance from a base class or overriding **virtual** functions. Type erasure in C++ involves creating a class `C` that defines an API via its (nonvirtual) public interface and supplies a constructor (or other member [or even friend] function) template that adapts an object of its **parameter** type `T` to that API. This approach allows `C` to be used as a **vocabulary type**, supporting polymorphism across API boundaries without requiring `T` objects to have a common base class nor requiring clients to be templates. For example, in the C++ Standard Library, `std::function` uses type erasure to erase the type of an invocable object, and `std::shared_ptr` uses it to erase the type of its deleter. Lambdas (602)

Glossary

type inference – the feature whereby the compiler substitutes the type of an **expression** for an **auto** placeholder or **decltype** specifier. `alignof` (193)

type list – a library (i.e., reusable) class template that can capture a sequence of types and exposes basic list operations on those types for use in compile-time **metaprogramming**. `constexpr` Functions '14 (963)

type parameter pack – short for type template parameter pack. Variadic Templates (903)

type punning – circumventing the type system to enable access to an object of a given type as though it were an object of a different type. Generalized PODs '11 (401)

type suffix – characters at the end of a literal token that affect its interpretation; a type suffix can be either a built-in suffix (e.g., `f`, `u`, `L`) or a UDL suffix; see Section 2.1."User-Defined Literals" on page 835. User-Defined Literals (837)

type template parameter – a template parameter that expects a type as its argument: in the declaration — `template <typename T> class C;` — `T` is a *type* parameter for class template `C`.

type template parameter pack – a template parameter pack that represents a sequence of template argument types: in the declaration — `template <typename... T> class C;` — `T` is a type template parameter pack for class template `C`. Variadic Templates (880)

type trait – a metafunction for providing a Boolean predicate on the properties of a type (for compile-time introspection) or else a transformed version of a type (facilitating generic programming). A type trait is typically defined as (1) a class template taking one or more type template parameters and having a `static constexpr bool` data member named `value` that holds the evaluated predicate, (2) a class template having a type alias member named `type` that represents the transformed type, (3) a `constexpr bool` variable template that yields the value of the evaluated predicate, or (4) an alias template that yields the transformed type. `static_assert` (119), `using` Aliases (136), Variable Templates (161), Forwarding References (378), Generalized PODs '11 (436), `noexcept` Operator (649)

UB – short for undefined behavior.

UDL – short for user-defined literal.

UDL operator – one having a name of the form `operator""`*<identifier>*, designating *<identifier>* as a UDL suffix. The UDL operator is invoked to produce the value of a user-defined literal having the specified *<identifier>* suffix. Declaring a UDL operator with an *<identifier>* that does not begin with _ is reserved for exclusive use by the Standard Library. User-Defined Literals (837)

UDL operator template – a family of UDL operators that is declared as a variadic function template (see Section 2.1."Variadic Templates" on page 873) having a single non-type template parameter pack of type `char` and taking no function arguments. Note that a distinct instantiation results for each unique string to which such an operator is applied, possibly resulting in code bloat. User-Defined Literals (841)

UDL suffix – the identifier at the end of a user-defined literal, used to locate an appropriate UDL operator. User-Defined Literals (837)

UDL type category – one characterizing the kind of naked literal that precedes the suffix part of a user-defined literal — i.e., one of (1) integer literal, (2) floating-point literal, (3) character literal, or (4) string literal. User-Defined Literals (837)

UDT – short for user-defined type. `final` (1007)

Glossary

undefined behavior (UB) – that which results from executing a piece of C++ code for which no behavior is defined by the language or library and, in theory, could be anything. A well-formed construct in the language, e.g., dereferencing a pointer to access an object, can result in language undefined behavior (a.k.a. hard UB) under certain conditions (e.g., if the pointer is null). A function having a **narrow contract** makes no guarantees when invoked with one or more of its **preconditions** unsatisfied; doing so results in library undefined behavior (a.k.a. soft UB), which is not in and of itself language UB but might well lead to it; see also **ill formed**. Attribute Syntax (18), Delegating Ctors (50), Function `static` '11 (70), `long long` (90), `noreturn` (97), `alignof` (190), Braced Init (218), Generalized PODs '11 (401), `initializer_list` (556), Range `for` (692), *Rvalue* References (715), `final` (1024), `friend` '11 (1049), `inline namespace` (1077), `noexcept` Specifier (1104), `union` '11 (1175), `auto` Return (1187)

undefined symbol – the name (possibly mangled) of an **entity** that has been **odr-used** but not defined. `extern template` (363)

underlying type (UT) – the integral type used to represent values of an enumeration. Unicode Literals (131), `alignas` (171), `constexpr` Variables (308), `enum class` (333), Generalized PODs '11 (501), Inheriting Ctors (542), Opaque `enums` (660), Underlying Type '11 (829)

unevaluated context – an unevaluated operand or subexpression thereof. Note that the expression (`0 ? a : b`) does not provide an unevaluated context for a, even though a will never be evaluated. `decltype` (31), `noexcept` Specifier (1132)

unevaluated operand – an expression used as an argument to a compile-time operator — e.g., `sizeof`, `typeid` (except for expressions of polymorphic type), `alignof`, `decltype`, or `noexcept` — that does not evaluate the expression but merely introspects some aspect of that expression's static type. An unevaluated operand is not ODR-used. As of C++20, either a `requires` expression or an expression used in a `requires` clause is also an unevaluated operand. `noexcept` Operator (615)

Unicode – an international standard encoding used to represent most text characters found in the world's various languages and writing systems, as well as special symbols and control characters. Unicode has a maximum of $1,112,064$ code points, of which $144,697$ were assigned as of Unicode 14.0.0; see **unicode**.

unification – the algorithmic process in C++ of finding the appropriate **template arguments** that can make two parameterized symbolic types equivalent, e.g., when identifying a type for a template parameter during template argument deduction. Variadic Templates (901)

uniform initialization – a colloquial term for a set of C++11 features, braced initialization in particular, that allow the use of braces (`{` and `}`) as a consistent syntax for initializing an object, whether of scalar type, class type, or array type — e.g., `int x{0}; S s{}; char a[]{'p', 'q'};` see also **most vexing parse**. Braced Init (215)

unique object address – implies, for a given object of a given type, that no other object of that type resides at that same address at the same time. In general, two non-bit-field objects having overlapping lifetimes must have distinct addresses unless one is nested within the other (e.g., a base class subobject and the enclosing derived class object, or an object and its first non`static` data member) or they are of different types and at least one is an empty base class (e.g., a base class and a non`static` data member with a different type at offset 0). As of C++20, the requirement for an object to have a distinct address may be relaxed under certain circumstances (e.g., for an empty **member** object of **class type**) through use of the `[[no_unique_address]]` attribute. Generalized PODs '11 (418)

Glossary

unique ownership – a resource-management model in which at most one object can claim ownership of a resource at any given time. The move operations for a type implementing this model (a.k.a. a move-only type) will typically transfer ownership of any allocated resource to the moved-to object, leaving the moved-from object resourceless. Destroying the current owner releases the resource entirely — e.g., `std::unique_ptr`. *Rvalue* References (768)

unit test – a (sometimes standalone) test intended to verify the correctness of the implementation of a single software component along with any of its inherent physical dependencies.

universal reference – a synonym for forwarding reference proposed by Scott Meyers, favored by some, and discouraged by the C++ Standards Committee. Forwarding References (400)

unnamed namespace – one introduced without a name (a.k.a. an *anonymous namespace*). Any entity that is declared within an unnamed namespace is unique to the translation unit in which it is defined, has internal linkage (which, for an object, is comparable to declaring it `static` at file scope), and can be used as if it were declared in the enclosing namespace without additional qualification (see Section 3.1."**inline namespace**" on page 1055). Function `static` '11 (77)

unqualified id – an identifier (e.g., x), operator name (e.g., **operator**=), or template id (e.g., `T<A,C::B>`) that is not preceded by a scope-resolution operator (`::`) or class member access operator (`.` or `->`).

unqualified name lookup – the process by which an unqualified ID is matched to an entity by searching through enclosing class and namespace scopes, as well as associated namespaces nominated by **argument-dependent lookup (ADL)**. User-Defined Literals (841)

unrelated types – types that are either (1) entirely unrelated by inheritance or (2) do not share a common polymorphic class as a base class (note that pointers and references to unrelated types are not interconvertible using **dynamic_cast**). Generalized PODs '11 (507)

unsigned ordinary character type – either **unsigned char** or, on platforms where **char** is *unsigned*, **char**. Generalized PODs '11 (515)

usable – implies, for a given member function, that it is accessible, defined, and, in the context in which it is called, *unambiguous*, i.e., overload resolution will identify it as the *best viable function*.

usable literal type – one that provides a nonempty set of operations beyond merely those required of it to be a literal type, enabling meaningful use in a constant expression. constexpr Functions (282)

user declared – implies, for a given function, that its declaration appears in the source code irrespective of whether it is deleted or defaulted; see Section 1.1."Deleted Functions" on page 53 and Section 1.1."Defaulted Functions" on page 33, respectively. constexpr Functions (274), Generalized PODs '11 (413), noexcept Specifier (1086)

user defined – implies, for a given special member function, that it is user provided. Note that such use of the term user defined is obsolete as of C++11, replaced by the more precise terms user declared and user provided. (Note also that *user defined* retains other valid meanings that are not obsolete.)

user-defined conversion – the result of invoking either a converting constructor or a conversion operator, explicitly or implicitly.

user-defined literal (UDL) – a string or numeric literal whose meaning is defined by either the user or the standard library. A UDL suffix at the end of the literal token identifies which UDL operator is used to interpret it and produce a value. Generalized PODs '11 (462), User-Defined Literals (837)

user-defined type (UDT) – a (1) **class**, (2) **struct**, (3) **union**, or (4) enumeration type (**enum** or **enum class**; see Section 2.1."**enum class**" on page 332). Delegating Ctors (46), **alignas** (168), Default Member Init (322), Generalized PODs '11 (462), **initializer_list** (553), **noexcept** Operator (622), *Rvalue* References (742), User-Defined Literals (835), **final** (1012), **friend** '11 (1031)

user provided – implies, for a given function, that it is user declared and is not explicitly defaulted or deleted on its first declaration. Function **static** '11 (80), Braced Init (217), Generalized PODs '11 (413), *Rvalue* References (742), **noexcept** Specifier (1087)

user-provided special member function – a special member function that is user provided. Defaulted Functions (33)

using declaration – one that begins with **using** and introduces an existing declaration into the current scope and is sometimes used colloquially to refer to the declaration of a type alias or alias template; see Section 1.1."**using** Aliases" on page 133. **constexpr** Functions (268), Inheriting Ctors (535)

using directive – short for using-namespace directive. **constexpr** Functions (268), User-Defined Literals (842), **inline namespace** (1056)

using-namespace directive – one — of the form **using namespace** *ns* — that makes all names in a nominated namespace *ns* usable in the current scope without namespace qualifiers; see Section 3.1."**inline namespace**" on page 1055.

UT – short for underlying type.

UTF-8 – a variable-width encoding for Unicode characters that uses one to four 8-bit code units for each code point and is designed to encode the first 128 Unicode code points using a 1-byte representation that is identical to that used by the ASCII character encoding. User-Defined Literals (844)

UTF-16 – a variable-width encoding for Unicode characters that uses one or two 16-bit code units for each code point. User-Defined Literals (844)

UTF-32 – a fixed-width encoding for Unicode characters that uses one 32-bit code unit for each code point. User-Defined Literals (844)

valid but unspecified – implies, for a given object, that it meets the C++ Standard Library's minimum requirements for a moved-from object; such an object must, in principle, meet all of the requirements of the specific Standard Library template with which it is used, especially that it can be assigned-to (if the template requires assignability), swapped (if the template requires swappability), compared (if the template requires comparison), and destroyed (often required, even if not documented); see also **moved-from state**. *Rvalue* References (715)

value – (1) the platonic value (or else the in-process value) represented by an object such as might affect the result of its associated homogeneous equality-comparison operator or (2) the bit pattern associated with its value representation. Delegating Ctors (51), **noexcept** Operator (625), *Rvalue* References (741), Lambda Captures (992), Ref-Qualifiers (1162)

value category – a characterization of a compile-time property of a (typically runtime-evaluable) expression. Every expression has one of three disjoint leaf value categories: *lvalue, xvalue,*

Glossary

and *prvalue*. In addition, two compound **value** categories — *glvalue* (comprising *lvalue* and *xvalue*) and *rvalue* (comprising *xvalue* and *prvalue*) — serve to characterize **values** that (1) have identity and (2) are expiring, respectively; see Section 2.1."*Rvalue* References" on page 710. `decltype` (25), Forwarding References (377), Lambdas (590), Range `for` (680), *Rvalue* References (710), *Generic* Lambdas (972), Lambda Captures (992), `noexcept` Specifier (1145), Ref-Qualifiers (1153), `auto` Return (1184), `decltype(auto)` (1205)

value constructor – one designed to *assemble* (as opposed to *copy* or *move*) an overall **value** from one or more supplied **arguments** and that (absent defaulted **arguments**) is never also a **default constructor, copy constructor, or move constructor**. Defaulted Functions (37), Generalized PODs '11 (450), *Rvalue* References (753), User-Defined Literals (836), Variadic Templates (942)

value initialization – a form of initialization, typically invoked by supplying an empty (rather than absent) initializer list, such as () or {}, that (1) performs zero initialization for scalar types as well as class types having a trivial default constructor, (2) invokes the default constructor for class types having a user-provided default constructor, or (3) performs zero initialization and then invokes the default constructor for all other class types, i.e., those that have a compiler-generated non-trivial default constructor. For an array type, each individual element is value initialized. Value initialization for a type having a deleted or *ambiguous* default constructor is ill formed — even if said initialization would not involve invoking the **default constructor**. Braced Init (216), `constexpr` Functions (273), Generalized PODs '11 (493)

value initialized – implies, for a given object, that it has undergone **value initialization**. Braced Init (221), Generalized PODs '11 (412), *Rvalue* References (764)

value representation – the bits in an object's footprint that represent its value, excluding, e.g., those used for padding or to represent a virtual-function-table pointer or virtual-base pointer. Generalized PODs '11 (405)

value semantic (of a type) – implies, for a given type, that it has **value semantics**. Defaulted Functions (36), Delegating Ctors (48), `alignof` (187), Opaque `enums` (663), *Rvalue* References (743)

value-semantic type (VST) – one, specifically a **class type**, that has **value semantics**. Forwarding References (386), Generalized PODs '11 (452), *Rvalue* References (742), Lambda Captures (992), `friend` '11 (1034)

value semantics – the fundamental, language-independent, mathematical principles that must be satisfied by any type that properly represents a platonic value; see **lakos15a**. Importantly, two objects of a **value-semantic type** do *not* have the same value (as defined by their respective **salient** attributes) if there exists a sequence of **salient** operations (a.k.a. a distinguishing sequence) that, when applied to each object separately, mutates the respective objects such that they can be observed not to have (i.e., represent) the same **value**. Note that a well-written C++ **value-semantic type** will also be a **regular type** (see **stepanov09**, section 1.5, "Regular Types," pp. 6–8) unless its (homogeneous) equality-comparison **operator** (==) would be too computationally complex; if it's omitted, the type becomes *semiregular* (see **stepanov15**, section 10.3, "Concepts," pp. 181–184, specifically p. 184); see also **lakos15b**. Also note, as of C++20, the Standard Library supports the concepts `std::regular` and `std::semiregular`. `noexcept` Operator (627), *Rvalue* References (811)

variable – a named object having *automatic*, *static*, or *thread* storage duration.

variable template – one — e.g., `template <typename T> T var;` — that can be instantiated to yield a family of like-named variables, each of distinct type, e.g., `var<int>`, `var<double>`; see Section 1.2."Variable Templates" on page 157. `constexpr` Variables (302)

Glossary

variadic class template – one that can be instantiated with a variable number of template arguments by virtue of having a parameter pack in its template parameter list. Variadic Templates (892)

variadic function template – one that can be instantiated with a variable number of template arguments by virtue of having a parameter pack in its template parameter list, typically callable with a variable number of function arguments, achieved by having a function parameter list that contains a function parameter pack. Lambdas (590), Variadic Templates (957), *Generic* Lambdas (978)

variadic macro – one that can be expanded with a variable number of macro arguments. Originally a C99 feature and incorporated into C++ as of C++11, a variadic macro is declared with an ellipsis (...) in its parameter list; within the macro, the special identifier __VA_ARGS__ expands to the macro arguments matching the ellipsis. Braced Init (249), *Rvalue* References (781), noexcept Specifier (1145)

variadic member function template – a variadic function template declared as a member of a class. Variadic Templates (892)

vectorization – the use, by the compiler, of special platform-specific CPU instructions that can perform (typically arithmetic) operations on multiple values at once. noexcept Specifier (1137)

vertical encoding – a data layout whereby the values of certain bits indicate the intended interpretation of other bits within the same data structure. Generalized PODs '11 (440)

virtual base pointer – a common implementation of **virtual** base classes where a derived-class object contains internal pointers to its **virtual** base class subobjects, which may be at different locations relative to the object depending on its concrete type. An alternative to a virtual base pointer, used in the Itanium ABI, is to include offsets to **virtual** bases within the virtual-function table. Generalized PODs '11 (409)

virtual dispatch – a form of dynamic dispatch achieved in C++ via inheritance and virtual functions, which are invariably implemented using virtual-function tables. final (1015)

virtual-function table – a compiler-generated data structure specific to each polymorphic class used to dispatch a **virtual** function call to the appropriate concrete function implementation at run time. The compiler assigns each member function that is declared **virtual** in a base class a distinct index that is used to look up a function pointer and an offset (typically zero in the case of non-**virtual** single inheritance) to be applied to the **this** pointer prior to invoking the function. The layout of a virtual function table is implementation-specific and might also store RTTI information and **virtual**-base class offsets. Note that each object of polymorphic type stores, within its footprint, an extra hidden pointer to its class's virtual-function table. Generalized PODs '11 (441)

vocabulary type – one that is used widely in the interfaces of functions to represent a common (typically concrete) data type (e.g., **int**, **double**, std::string) or (typically abstract) service (e.g., std::pmr::memory_resource in C++17). long long (91), Unicode Literals (131), constexpr Functions (291)

VST – short for value-semantic type.

vtable – short for virtual-function table. noexcept Operator (617)

vtable pointer – a pointer, hidden in the footprint of each object of polymorphic type, used to access the virtual function table that will be employed during virtual dispatch and, for some implementations, to access a **virtual** base class. Generalized PODs '11 (409), final (1011)

Glossary

well formed – implies, for a given program or program fragment, that it meets the language requirements for proper translation, i.e., that no part of it is ill formed. Note that being well formed does not imply that a program is correct; a well-formed program might still compute results incorrectly or have undefined behavior at runtime; see also IFNDR. `alignas` (169)

wide contract – one without preconditions. Note that restrictions imposed by the C++ language itself — e.g., that an input not have indeterminate value — are not considered preconditions for the purpose of determining whether a contract is wide; see also narrow contract. *Rvalue* References (750), `final` (1021), `noexcept` Specifier (1112)

widening the contract – the act of evolving the interface of a function having a narrow contract by weakening or removing preconditions to increase its domain in a way that will not invalidate any existing in contract call to the function. Note that a contract that has been widened is not necessarily a wide contract (i.e., some preconditions might still exist).

witness argument – a specific value used as an argument in a test to prove that a function is callable or has some other hard-to-discover but easy-to-verify behavior. `constexpr` Functions (283)

working set – the set of memory pages (or cache lines) currently needed by the program over some fixed time interval. If the working-set size is too large, the program will be subject to thrashing. `alignas` (182), `noexcept` Specifier (1139)

xvalue – a *glvalue* that denotes an object whose resources can be reused. `decltype` (26), `auto` Variables (206), Forwarding References (380), *Rvalue* References (710), `decltype(auto)` (1206)

Y combinator – a function object that indirectly holds a reference to itself, providing one form of expressing recursive lambda expressions. *Generic* Lambdas (978)

zero cost – implies, for a given implementation choice (e.g., exception-handling model), that, if not used (e.g, no exception is thrown), it imposes exactly *zero* additional runtime cost. In particular, the *zero-cost exception model* was chosen in service of a fundamental design criteria of C++ that, for a language feature to be adopted, it impose no general (i.e., no program-wide) runtime overhead, "What you don't use, you don't pay for (zero-overhead rule)" (**stroustrup94**, section 4.5, "Low-Level Programming Support Rules," pp. 120–121, specifically p. 121). Moreover, whenever such a feature is used, it (typically) couldn't be hand coded any better. See also zero-cost exception model. `noexcept` Specifier (1136)

zero-cost exception model – a technique for implementing C++ exception handling whereby no instructions related to possible exceptions are inserted into the nonexceptional code path (a.k.a. the hot path). This technique maximizes the speed of execution along the hot path by avoiding a test, on each function call return, to check whether the called function exited via an exception. Instead, the compiler generates tables that are used to lookup and jump to appropriate exception-handling code (a.k.a. the cold path) when an exception is thrown. Some compilers go so far as to put the cold path in entirely separate memory pages so that it is not loaded into memory unless and until an exception is thrown, at the cost of much lower runtime performance on the presumably rare occasions when the cold path code is taken. `noexcept` Specifier (1134)

zero initialized – a form of initialization in which (1) scalar objects are initialized as if from an integer literal 0, (2) all subobjects of array and class types are zero initialized, (3) the first data members of objects of union type are zero initialized, with any padding bits set to zero, and (4) reference types are *not* initialized. For example, objects having static storage duration or thread storage duration are zero initialized prior to any other initialization that might be performed. Function static '11 (75), Braced Init (218)

zero-overhead exception model – a synonym for zero-cost exception model. noexcept Specifier (1101)

Bibliography

abrahams09 David Abrahams, Rani Sharoni, and Doug Gregor, "Allowing Move Constructors to Throw." Technical Report N2983, International Standards Organization, Geneva, Switzerland, November 9, 2009
http://www.open-std.org/jtc1/sc22/wg21/docs/papers/2009/n2983.html

abrahams10 David Abrahams, Rani Sharoni, and Doug Gregor, "Allowing Move Constructors to Throw (Rev. 1)." Technical Report N3050, International Standards Organization, Geneva, Switzerland, March 12, 2010
http://www.open-std.org/jtc1/sc22/wg21/docs/papers/2010/n3050.html

adamczyk05 J. Stephen Adamczyk, "Adding the long long type to C++ (Revision 3)." Technical Report N1811, International Standards Organization, Geneva, Switzerland, April 2005
http://open-std.org/JTC1/SC22/WG21//docs/papers/2005/n1811.pdf

adelstein-lelbach15 Bryce Adelstein-Lelbach, "Benchmarking C++ Code." *CppCon: The C++ Conference* (Aurora, CO, 2015)
https://www.youtube.com/watch?v=zWxSZcpeS8Q

alexandrescu01 Andrei Alexandrescu, *Modern C++ Design: Generic Programming and Design Patterns Applied* (Boston: Addison-Wesley, 2001)

amini21 Parsa Amini and Joshua Berne, "Quantifying the Impact of Assuming Preconditions." Technical Report P2421R0, International Standards Organization, Geneva, Switzerland, forthcoming

baker14 Billy Baker, "Removing auto_ptr." Technical Report N4168, International Standards Organization, Geneva, Switzerland, October 2, 2014
http://www.open-std.org/jtc1/sc22/wg21/docs/papers/2014/n4168.html

ballman Aaron Ballman, "Rule 03. Integers (INT)." *SEI CERT C++ Coding Standard* (Pittsburgh, PA: Carnegie Mellon University Software Engineering Institute)
https://wiki.sei.cmu.edu/confluence/pages/viewpage.action?pageId=88046333

balog20 Pal Balog, "Make Declaration Order Layout Mandated." Technical Report P1847R3, International Standards Organization, Geneva, Switzerland, March 1, 2020
http://www.open-std.org/jtc1/sc22/wg21/docs/papers/2020/p1847r3.pdf

Bibliography

barendregt84 Henk Barendregt and Erik Barendsen, "Introduction to Lambda Calculus." *Nieuw Archief Voor Wiskunde*, January 1984, volume 4:pp. 337–372

barton94 John J. Barton and Lee R. Nackman, *Scientific and Engineering C++: An Introduction With Advanced Techniques and Examples* (Reading, MA: Addison-Wesley, 1994)

bastien18 JF Bastien, "Signed Integers are Two's Complement." Technical Report P0907R4, International Standards Organization, Geneva, Switzerland, October 6, 2018 http://www.open-std.org/jtc1/sc22/wg21/docs/papers/2018/p0907r4.html

bde14 "Basic Development Environment." Bloomberg https://github.com/bloomberg/bde/

bendersky18 Eli Bendersky, "Unification." Eli Bendersky's blog, November 12, 2018 https://eli.thegreenplace.net/2018/unification/

berger02 Emery D. Berger, Benjamin G. Zorn, and Kathryn S. McKinley, "Reconsidering Custom Memory Allocation." *Proceedings of the 17th ACM SIGPLAN Conference on Object-Oriented Programming, Systems, Languages, and Applications* (2002), pp. 1–12 https://doi.org/10.1145/582419.582421

bleaney16 Graham Bleaney, "Validation of Memory-Allocation Benchmarks." Technical Report P0213R0, International Standards Organization, Geneva, Switzerland, January 24, 2016 http://www.open-std.org/jtc1/sc22/wg21/docs/papers/2016/p0213r0.pdf

boccara20 Jonathan Boccara, "Virtual, final and override in C++." Fluent C++, February 21, 2020 https://www.fluentcpp.com/2020/02/21/virtual-final-and-override-in-cpp/

boehm16 Hans-J. Boehm, "Temporarily Discourage `memory_order_consume`." Technical Report P0371R1, International Standards Organization, Geneva, Switzerland, 2016 http://www.open-std.org/jtc1/sc22/wg21/docs/papers/2016/p0371r1.html

brown19 Walter E. Brown and Daniel Sunderland, "Recommendations for Specifying 'Hidden Friends'." Technical Report P1601R0, International Standards Organization, Geneva, Switzerland, 2019 http://www.open-std.org/jtc1/sc22/wg21/docs/papers/2019/p1601r0.pdf

calabrese20 Matt Calabrese and Ryan McDougall, "`any_invocable`." Technical Report P0288R6, International Standards Organization, Geneva, Switzerland, 2020 http://www.open-std.org/jtc1/sc22/wg21/docs/papers/2020/p0288r6.html

cargill92 Tom Cargill, *C++ Programming Style* (Reading, MA: Addison-Wesley, 1992)

carruth15 Chandler Carruth, "Tuning C++: Benchmarks, and CPUs, and Compilers! Oh My!" *CppCon: The C++ Conference* (Aurora, CO, 2015) https://www.youtube.com/watch?v=nXaxk27zwlk

Bibliography

carruth17 Chandler Carruth, "Going Nowhere Faster." *CppCon: The C++ Conference* (Aurora, CO, 2017)
https://www.youtube.com/watch?v=2EWejmkKlxs

clow14 Marshall Clow, "Undefined Behavior in C++: What is it, and why do you care?" *C++Now* (2014)
https://www.youtube.com/watch?v=uHCLkb1vKaY

codesyn15 "C++ Object Persistence with ODB." Technical Report Revision 2.4, Code Synthesis, February 2015
https://www.codesynthesis.com/products/odb/doc/manual.xhtml

cpprefa "`std::all_of, std::any_of, std::none_of`." C++ Algorithm Library, cppreference.com
https://en.cppreference.com/w/cpp/algorithm/all_any_none_of

cpprefb "`std::unordered_map`." C++ Containers Library, cppreference.com
https://en.cppreference.com/w/cpp/container/unordered_map

cpprefc "`std::any`." C++ Utilities Library, cppreference.com
https://en.cppreference.com/w/cpp/utility/any

cpprefd "`std::declval`." C++ Utilities Library, cppreference.com
https://en.cppreference.com/w/cpp/utility/declval

cpprefe "Reference declaration." C++ Language Declarations, cppreference.com
https://en.cppreference.com/w/cpp/language/reference

dawes07 Beman Dawes, "POD's Revisited; Resolving Core Issue 568 (Revision 5)." Technical Report N2342, C++ Standards Committee Working Group, Geneva, Switzerland, July 18, 2007
http://www.open-std.org/jtc1/sc22/wg21/docs/papers/2007/n2342.htm

dekker19a Niels Dekker, "`noexcept_benchmark`." published via GitHub, January 18, 2019
https://github.com/N-Dekker/noexcept_benchmark/blob/main/LICENSE

dekker19b Niels Dekker, "Lightning Talk: `noexcept` considered harmful???" *C++ on Sea* (2015)
https://www.youtube.com/watch?v=dVRLp-Rwg0k

derevenets16 Yegor Derevenets, "A Proposal to Add Y Combinator to the Standard Library." Technical Report P0200R0, C++ Standards Committee Working Group, Geneva, Switzerland, January 22, 2016
http://www.open-std.org/jtc1/sc22/wg21/docs/papers/2016/p0200r0.html

dewhurst89 Stephen Dewhurst and Kathy T. Stark, *Programming in C++* (Englewood Cliffs, NJ: Prentice Hall, 1989)

Bibliography

dewhurst19 Stephen Dewhurst, "TMI on UDLs: Mechanics, Uses, and Abuses of User-Defined Literals." *CppCon: The C++ Conference* (2019)
https://www.youtube.com/watch?v=gxMiiI19VnQ

dijkstra82 Edsger W. Dijkstra, "On the Role of Scientific Thought." *Selected writings on Computing: A Personal Perspective*, pp. 60–66 (NY: Springer-Verlag, 1982)

dimov18 Peter Dimov and Vassil Vassilev, "Allowing Virtual Function Calls in Constant Expressions." Technical Report P1064R0, C++ Standards Committee Working Group, Geneva, Switzerland, 2018
http://www.open-std.org/jtc1/sc22/wg21/docs/papers/2018/p1064r0.html

dosreis09 Gabriel Dos Reis, "Issue 981: Constexpr constructor templates and literal types." *C++ Standard Core Language Defect Reports and Accepted Issues, Revision 104* (Geneva, Switzerland: International Standards Organization, 2009)
http://www.open-std.org/jtc1/sc22/wg21/docs/cwg_defects.html#981

dosreis18 G. Dos Reis, J. D. Garcia, J. Lakos, A. Meredith, N. Myers, and B. Stroustrup, "Support for Contract Based Programming in C++." Technical Report P0542R4, C++ Standards Committee Working Group, Geneva, Switzerland, 2018
http://www.open-std.org/jtc1/sc22/wg21/docs/papers/2018/p0542r4.html

dusikova19 Hana Dusíková, "Compile Time Regular Expressions." Technical Report P1433R0, C++ Standards Committee Working Group, Geneva, Switzerland, 2019
http://www.open-std.org/jtc1/sc22/wg21/docs/papers/2019/p1433r0.pdf

eigen "Eigen." tuxfamily.org
http://eigen.tuxfamily.org/

ellis90 Margaret A. Ellis and Bjarne Stroustrup, *The Annotated C++ Reference Manual* (Reading, MA: Addison-Wesley, 1990)

facebook "Facebook folly library."
https://github.com/facebook/folly

finland13 Finland, "Issue 1776: Replacement of class objects containing reference members." *C++ Standard Core Language Defect Reports and Accepted Issues, Revision 104* (Geneva, Switzerland: International Standards Organization, 2013)
http://www.open-std.org/JTC1/SC22/WG21/docs/cwg_defects.html#1776

fluentcpp17 "What the Curiously Recurring Template Pattern Can Bring to Your Code." Fluent C++, May 16, 2017
https://www.fluentcpp.com/2017/05/16/what-the-crtp-brings-to-code/

freesoftwarefdn20 *Using the GNU Compiler Collection (GCC)* (Boston, MA: Free Software Foundation, Inc., 2020)
https://gcc.gnu.org/onlinedocs/gcc/

fultz14 Paul Fultz, "Is there interest in a `static if` emulation library?" Boost C++ Libraries online forum archive, August 13, 2014
https://lists.boost.org/Archives/boost/2014/08/216607.php

gamma95 *Design Patterns: Elements of Reusable Object-Oriented Software* (Reading, MA: Addison-Wesley, 1995)

goldthwaite07 Lois Goldthwaite, "Toward a More Perfect Union." Technical Report N2248, International Standards Organization, Geneva, Switzerland, May 7, 2007
http://www.open-std.org/jtc1/sc22/wg21/docs/papers/2007/n2248.html

gregor09 Douglas Gregor and David Abrahams, "Rvalue References and Exception Safety." Technical Report N2855, International Standards Organization, Geneva, Switzerland, March 23, 2009
http://www.open-std.org/jtc1/sc22/wg21/docs/papers/2009/n2855.html

grimm17 Rainer Grimm, "C++ Core Guidelines: Rules for Enumerations." Modernes C++, November 27, 2017
https://www.modernescpp.com/index.php/c-core-guidelines-rules-for-enumerations

gustedt13 Jens Gustedt, "right angle brackets: shifting semantics." Jens Gustedt's blog, December 18, 2013
https://gustedt.wordpress.com/2013/12/18/right-angle-brackets-shifting-semantics/

halpern20 Pablo Halpern and John Lakos, "Unleashing the Power of Allocator-Aware Software Infrastructure." Technical Report P2126R0, International Standards Organization, Geneva, Switzerland, March 2, 2020
http://www.open-std.org/jtc1/sc22/wg21/docs/papers/2020/p2126r0.pdf

halpern21a Pablo Halpern, "Bug 99799: Explicit instantiation function template with auto deduced return type fails if soft instantiation occurred." Bugzilla, March 27, 2021
https://gcc.gnu.org/bugzilla/show_bug.cgi?id=99799

halpern21b Pablo Halpern, "Bug 49751: Explicit instantiation function template with auto deduced return type fails if soft instantiation occurred." Bugzilla, March 28, 2021
https://bugs.llvm.org/show_bug.cgi?id=49751

halpern21c Pablo Halpern, "Move, Copy, and Locality at Scale." Technical Report P2329, International Standards Organization, Geneva, Switzerland, 2021
http://wg21.link/P2329

herring20 S. Davis Herring, "Declarations and where to find them." Technical Report P1787R6, International Standards Organization, Geneva, Switzerland, October 23, 2020
http://www.open-std.org/jtc1/sc22/wg21/docs/papers/2020/p1787r6.html

hindley86 J. Roger Hindley and Jonathan P. Seldin, *Introduction to Combinators and (lambda) Calculus* (Cambridge, England: Cambridge University Press, 1986)

Bibliography

hinnant02 Howard Hinnant, Peter Dimov, and Dave Abrahams, "A Proposal to Add Move Semantics Support to the C++ Language." Technical Report N1377, International Standards Organization, Geneva, Switzerland, September 10, 2002
http://www.open-std.org/jtc1/sc22/wg21/docs/papers/2002/n1377.htm

hinnant05 Howard Hinnant, "Rvalue Reference Recommendations for Chapter 20." Technical Report N1856, International Standards Organization, Geneva, Switzerland, August 26, 2005
http://www.open-std.org/jtc1/sc22/wg21/docs/papers/2005/n1856.html

hinnant06 Howard Hinnant, Bjarne Stroustrup, and Bronek Kozicki, "A Brief Introduction to Rvalue References." Technical Report N2027, International Standards Organization, Geneva, Switzerland, June 12, 2006
http://www.open-std.org/jtc1/sc22/wg21/docs/papers/2006/n2027.html

hinnant14 Howard Hinnant, "Everything You Ever Wanted To Know About Move Semantics (and Then Some)." *Conference of the ACCU* (Bristol, England, 2014)
https://accu.org/content/conf2014/Howard_Hinnant_Accu_2014.pdf

hinnant16 Howard Hinnant, "Everything You Ever Wanted To Know About Move Semantics." Bloomberg Engineering Distinguished Speaker Series, 2016
https://www.youtube.com/watch?v=vLinb2fgkHk&t=28s

hinnant17 Howard Hinnant, "Issue 2278: User-Defined Literals for Standard Library Types." Technical Report CWG2278, International Standards Organization, Geneva, Switzerland, September 10, 2017
https://cplusplus.github.io/LWG/issue2278

hruska20 Joel Hruska, "How L1 and L2 CPU Caches Work, and Why They're an Essential Part of Modern Chips." *Extreme Tech*, April 14, 2020
https://www.extremetech.com/extreme/188776-how-l1-and-l2-cpu-caches-work-and-why-theyre-an-essential-part-of-modern-chips

hu20 Yasen Hu, "C++ Diary #1 | emplace_back vs. push_back." Published via GitHub, Aug 13, 2020
https://yasenh.github.io/post/cpp-diary-1-emplace_back

ieee19 *IEEE Standard for Floating-Point Arithmetic* (New York, NY: Institute of Electrical and Electronics Engineers, Inc., 2019)
https://ieeexplore.ieee.org/document/8766229

inteliig "The Intel Intrinsics Guide." Intel Corporation
https://software.intel.com/sites/landingpage/IntrinsicsGuide/#

intel16 *Intel 64 and IA-32 Architectures Optimization Reference Manual.* Number 248966-033 (Santa Clara, CA: Intel Corporation, 2016)
https://www.intel.com/content/dam/www/public/us/en/documents/manuals/64-ia-32-architectures-optimization-manual.pdf

Bibliography

iso99 *ISO/IEC 9899:1999 Programming Languages — C* (Geneva, Switzerland: International Standards Organization, 1999)
http://www.open-std.org/jtc1/sc22/WG14/www/docs/n1256.pdf

iso03 *ISO/IEC 14882:2003 Programming Language C++* (Geneva, Switzerland: International Standards Organization, 2003)

iso11a *ISO/IEC 14882:2011 — Programming Language — C++* (Geneva, Switzerland: International Standards Organization, 2011)
http://www.open-std.org/jtc1/sc22/wg21/docs/papers/2011/n3242.pdf

iso11b *ISO/IEC 9899:2011 Information Technology — Programming Languages — C* (Geneva, Switzerland: International Standards Organization, 2011)
https://www.iso.org/standard/57853.html

iso14 *ISO/IEC 14882:2014 Programming Language C++* (Geneva, Switzerland: International Standards Organization, 2014)
http://www.open-std.org/JTC1/SC22/WG21/docs/papers/2013/n3797.pdf

iso17 *ISO/IEC 14882:2017 Programming Language C++* (Geneva, Switzerland: International Standards Organization, 2017)
http://www.open-std.org/jtc1/sc22/wg21/docs/papers/2017/n4659.pdf

iso18a "C++ Standard Core Language Active Issues, Revision 100." Technical report, International Standards Organization, Geneva, Switzerland, 2018
http://www.open-std.org/jtc1/sc22/wg21/docs/cwg_active.html

iso18b *ISO/IEC 9899:2018 Information Technology — Programming Languages — C* (Geneva, Switzerland: International Standards Organization, 2018)
https://www.iso.org/standard/74528.html

iso20a "Allow Duplicate Attributes." Technical Report P2156R1, International Standards Organization, Geneva, Switzerland, 2020
http://www.open-std.org/jtc1/sc22/wg21/docs/papers/2020/p2156r1.pdf

iso20b *ISO/IEC 14882:2020 Programming Languages — C++* (Geneva, Switzerland: International Standards Organization, 2020)
https://www.iso.org/standard/79358.html

itanium16 "Itanium C++ ABI: Exception Handling (Revision: 1.22)." Itanium, June 2, 2016
https://itanium-cxx-abi.github.io/cxx-abi/abi-eh.html

izvekov14 Matheus Izvekov, "Disallowing Inaccessible Operators From Trivially Copyable." Technical Report N4148, International Standards Organization, Geneva, Switzerland, September 24, 2014
http://www.open-std.org/jtc1/sc22/wg21/docs/papers/2014/n4148.html

Bibliography

johnson19 CJ Johnson, "Permitting trivial default initialization in constexpr contexts." Technical Report P1331R2, International Standards Organization, Geneva, Switzerland, July 15, 2019
http://www.open-std.org/jtc1/sc22/wg21/docs/papers/2019/p1331r2.pdf

josuttis20a Nicolai Josuttis, Victor Zverovich, Filipe Mulonde, and Arthur O'Dwyer, "Fix the Range-Based `for` Loop, Rev. 0." Technical Report P2012R0, International Standards Organization, Geneva, Switzerland, November 15, 2020
http://www.open-std.org/jtc1/sc22/wg21/docs/papers/2020/p2012r0.pdf

josuttis20b Nicolai Josuttis, *C++ Move Semantics — The Complete Guide* (Braunschweig, Germany: self-published, 2020)

kahan97 W. Kahan, "Lecture Notes on the Status of IEEE Standard 754 for Binary Floating-Point Arithmetic." Electrical Engineering and Computer Science Department, University of California, Berkeley, CA, 1997
https://people.eecs.berkeley.edu/ wkahan/ieee754status/IEEE754.PDF

kalev14 Danny Kalev, "Safety in Numbers: Introducing C++14's Binary Literals, Digit Separators, and Variable Templates." informit.com, May 14, 2014
https://www.informit.com/articles/article.aspx?p=2209021

keane20 Erich Keane, "Allow Duplicate Attributes." Technical Report P2156R0, C++ Standards Committee Working Group, Geneva, Switzerland, 2020
https://wg21.link/p2156r0

kernighan78 Brian W. Kernighan and Dennis M. Ritchie, *The C Programming Language.* 1st edition (Englewood Cliffs, NJ: Prentice Hall, 1978)
https://archive.org/details/TheCProgrammingLanguageFirstEdition

kernighan88 Brian W. Kernighan and Dennis M. Ritchie, *The C Programming Language.* 2nd edition (Englewood Cliffs, NJ: Prentice Hall, 1988)
https://archive.org/details/cprogramminglang00bria/mode/2up

kernighan99 Brian W. Kernighan and Rob Pike, *The Practice of Programming* (Reading, MA: Addison-Wesley, 1999)

khlebnikov18 Rostislava Khlebnikov and John Lakos, "Embracing Modern C++ Safely." Technical report, Bloomberg, New York, NY, March 29, 2018
http://bloomberg.github.io/bde-resources/pdfs/Embracing_Modern_Cpp_Safely.pdf

khlebnikov21 Rostislava Khlebnikov, "Bug 101087: Unevaluated operand of sizeof affects noexcept operator." Bugzilla, June 15, 2021
https://gcc.gnu.org/bugzilla/show_bug.cgi?id=101087

klarer04 Robert Klarer, John Maddock, Beman Dawes, and Howard Hinnant, "Proposal to Add Static Assertions to the Core Language (Revision 3)." Technical Report N1720, International Standards Organization, Geneva, Switzerland, October 20, 2004
http://www.open-std.org/jtc1/sc22/wg21/docs/papers/2004/n1720.html

krugler10a Daniel Krügler, "Issue 1071: Literal class types and trivial default constructors." *C++ Standard Core Language Defect Reports and Accepted Issues, Revision 104* (Geneva, Switzerland, 2010)
http://www.open-std.org/jtc1/sc22/wg21/docs/cwg_defects.html#1071

krugler10b Daniel Krügler, "Cleanup of `pair` and `tuple`." Technical Report N3140, C++ Standards Committee Working Group, International Standards Organization, Geneva, Switzerland, October 2, 2010
http://www.open-std.org/jtc1/sc22/wg21/docs/papers/2010/n3140.html

krzemienski11 Andrzej Krzemieński, "Using `noexcept`." Andrzej's C++ blog, June 10, 2011
https://akrzemi1.wordpress.com/2011/06/10/using-noexcept/

krzemienski16 Andrzej Krzemieński, "The Cost of `std::initializer_list`." Andrzej's C++ blog, July 7, 2016
https://akrzemi1.wordpress.com/2016/07/07/the-cost-of-stdinitializer_list/

kuhl12 Dietmar Kühl, "Proposal to Add Decimal Floating Point Support to C++." Technical Report N3407, International Standards Organization, Geneva, Switzerland, September 14, 2012
http://www.open-std.org/jtc1/sc22/wg21/docs/papers/2012/n3407.html

lakos96 John Lakos, *Large-Scale C++ Software Design* (Reading, MA: Addison-Wesley, 1996)

lakos14a John Lakos, "Defensive Programming Done Right, Part I." *CppCon* (2014)
https://www.youtube.com/watch?v=1QhtXRMp3Hg

lakos14b John Lakos, "Defensive Programming Done Right, Part II." *CppCon* (2014)
https://www.youtube.com/watch?v=tz2khnjnUx8

lakos15a John Lakos, "Value Semantics: It Ain't About the Syntax! — Part I." *CppCon* (2015)
https://www.youtube.com/watch?v=W3xI1HJUy7Q

lakos15b John Lakos, "Value Semantics: It Ain't About the Syntax! — Part II." *CppCon* (2015)
https://www.youtube.com/watch?v=0EvSxHxFknM

lakos16 John Lakos, Jeffrey Mendelsohn, Alisdair Meredith, and Nathan Myers, "On Quantifying Memory-Allocation Strategies (Revision 2)." Technical Report P0089R1, February 12, 2016
http://www.open-std.org/jtc1/sc22/wg21/docs/papers/2016/p0089r1.pdf

lakos17a John Lakos, "Local ('Arena') Memory Allocators — Part I." *Meeting C++* (2017)
https://www.youtube.com/watch?v=ko6uyw0C8r0

Bibliography

lakos17b John Lakos, "Local ('Arena') Memory Allocators — Part II." *Meeting C++* (2017)
https://www.youtube.com/watch?v=fN7nVzbRiEk

lakos19 John Lakos, "Value Proposition: Allocator-Aware (AA) Software." *C++Now* (2019)
https://www.youtube.com/watch?v=dDR93TfacHc

lakos20 John Lakos, *Large-Scale C++ — Volume I: Process and Architecture* (Boston: Addison-Wesley, 2020)

lakos22 John Lakos and Joshua Berne, *C++ Allocators for the Working Programmer* (Boston: Addison-Wesley, forthcoming)

lakos23 John Lakos and Rostislava Khlebnikhov, *Design by Contract for Large-Scale Software* (Boston: Addison-Wesley, forthcoming)

lakos2a John Lakos, *Large-Scale C++ — Volume II: Design and Implementation* (Boston: Addison-Wesley, forthcoming)

lakos2b John Lakos, *Large-Scale C++ — Volume III: Verification and Testing* (Boston: Addison-Wesley, forthcoming)

lavavej12 Stephan T. Lavavej, "STL11: Magic && Secrets." Going Native 2012, January 10, 2012
https://channel9.msdn.com/Events/GoingNative/GoingNative-2012/STL11-Magic-Secrets

lavavej13 Stephan T. Lavavej, "rand() Considered Harmful." Going Native 2013, August 17, 2013
https://channel9.msdn.com/Events/GoingNative/2013/rand-Considered-Harmful

leyton-brown03 Kevin Leyton-Brown, Eugene Nudelman, Galen Andrew, Jim McFadden, and Yoav Shoham, "A Portfolio Approach to Algorithm Selection." *IJCAI* (2003), pp. 1542–1543

liskov87 Barbara Liskov, "Data Abstraction and Hierarchy." *Addendum to the Proceedings on Object-Oriented Programming Systems, Languages, and Applications* (New York: Association for Computing Machinery, 1987), pp. 17–34
https://dl.acm.org/doi/10.1145/62138.62141

liskov94 Barbara Liskov and Jeannette M. Wing, "A Behavioral Notion of Subtyping." *ACM Transactions Programming Language Systems*, 1994, volume 16(6):pp. 1811–1841

liskov09 Barbara Liskov, "The Power of Abstraction." ACM SIGPLAN International Conference on Object-Oriented Programming, Systems, Languages, and Applications, October 27, 2009

liskov16 Barbara Liskov, "The Power of Abstraction." Bloomberg's Engineering Distinguished Speaker Series, October 24, 2016

lopez-gomez20 Javier López-Gómez, Javier Fernández, David del Rio Astorga, Vassil Vassilev, Axel Naumann, and J. Daniel García, "Relaxing the One Definition Rule in Interpreted C++." *Proceedings of the 29th International Conference on Compiler Construction*, CC 2020 (New York, NY, USA: Association for Computing Machinery, 2020), pp. 212–222
https://doi.org/10.1145/3377555.3377901

maddock04 John Maddock, "Issue 496: Is a volatile-qualified type really a POD?" *C++ Standard Core Language Defect Reports and Accepted Issues, Revision 104* (Geneva, Switzerland: International Standards Organization, 2004)
http://www.open-std.org/JTC1/SC22/WG21/docs/cwg_defects.html#496

martin09 Robert Martin, *Clean Code: A Handbook of Agile Software Craftsmanship* (Boston: Addison-Wesley, 2009)

martin17 Robert Martin, *Clean Architecture: A Craftsman's Guide to Software Structure and Design* (Boston: Addison-Wesley, 2017)

marton17 G. Márton, I. Szekeres, and Z. Porkoláb, "High-Level C++ Implementation of the read-copy-update Pattern." *IEEE 14th International Scientific Conference on Informatics* (2017), pp. 243–248

marton18 Gábor Márton, Imre Szekeres, and Zoltán Porkoláb, "Towards a High-Level C++ Abstraction to Utilize the Read-Copy-Update Pattern." *Acta Electrotechnica et Informatica*, 2018, volume 18(3):pp. 18–26

maurer15 Jens Maurer, "P0012R0: Make exception specifications be part of the type system, version 4." Technical Report P0012R0, International Standards Organization, Geneva, Switzerland, September 8, 2015
http://open-std.org/JTC1/SC22/WG21/docs/papers/2015/p0012r0.html

maurer18 Jens Maurer, "P1236R1: Alternative Wording for P0907R4 Signed Integers are Two's Complement." Technical Report P1236R1, International Standards Organization, Geneva, Switzerland, November 9, 2018
http://www.open-std.org/jtc1/sc22/wg21/docs/papers/2018/p1236r1.html

mayrand15 François Mayrand, "Passkey Idiom and Better Friendship in C++." Desktop Application Development, Spiria Digital Inc., May 21, 2015
https://www.spiria.com/en/blog/desktop-software/passkey-idiom-and-better-friendship-c/

mccormack94 Joel McCormack, Paul Asente, and Ralph R. Swick, "X Toolkit Intrinsics — C Language Interface, Version 11, Release 7.7." Technical report, X Consortium, Inc., 1994
https://www.x.org/releases/X11R7.7/doc/libXt/intrinsics.html

Bibliography

mcfarlane19 John McFarlane, "Fixed-Point Real Numbers." Technical Report P0037R7, International Standards Organization, Geneva, Switzerland, June 17, 2019
http://www.open-std.org/jtc1/sc22/wg21/docs/papers/2019/p0037r7.html

mcintosh08a Ian McIntosh, Michael Wong, Raymond Mak, Robert Klarer, Jens Maurer, Alisdair Meredith, Bjarne Stroustrup, and David Vandevoorde, "User-defined Literals (aka. Extensible Literals (revision 4))." Technical Report N2750-08-0260, International Standards Organization, Geneva, Switzerland, August 22, 2008
http://www.open-std.org/jtc1/sc22/wg21/docs/papers/2008/n2750.pdf

mcintosh08b Ian McIntosh, Michael Wong, Raymond Mak, Robert Klarer, Jens Maurer, Alisdair Meredith, Bjarne Stroustrup, and David Vandevoorde, "User-Defined Literals (Revision 5)." Technical Report N2765, International Standards Organization, Geneva, Switzerland, September 18, 2008
http://www.open-std.org/Jtc1/sc22/wg21/docs/papers/2008/n2765.pdf

meredith07 Alisdair Meredith, "Issue 644: Should a trivial class type be a literal type?" *C++ Standard Core Language Defect Reports and Accepted Issues, Revision 104* (Geneva, Switzerland: International Standards Organization, 2007)
http://www.open-std.org/jtc1/sc22/wg21/docs/cwg_defects.html#644

meredith08 Alisdair Meredith, M. Wong, and J. Maurer, "Inheriting Constructors (Revision 4)." Technical Report N2512, International Standards Organization, Geneva, Switzerland, April 2, 2008
http://www.open-std.org/jtc1/sc22/wg21/docs/papers/2008/n2512.html

meredith11 Alisdair Meredith and John Lakos, "Conservative use of noexcept in the Library." Technical Report N3279, International Standards Organization, Geneva, Switzerland, March 25, 2011
http://www.open-std.org/jtc1/sc22/wg21/docs/papers/2011/n3279.pdf

meredith16 Alisdair Meredith, "Deprecating Vestigial Library Parts in C++17." Technical Report P0174R2, International Standards Organization, Geneva, Switzerland, June 23, 2016
http://www.open-std.org/jtc1/sc22/wg21/docs/papers/2016/p0174r2.html

meredith20 Alisdair Meredith, "Down with ~~typename~~ in the Library!" Technical Report P2150R0, International Standards Organization, Geneva, Switzerland, April 14, 2020
http://open-std.org/JTC1/SC22/WG21/docs/papers/2020/p2150r0.html

merrill10a Jason Merrill, "Issue 1213: Array subscripting and xvalues." *C++ Standard Core Language Defect Reports and Accepted Issues, Revision 104* (Geneva, Switzerland, 2010)
http://www.open-std.org/jtc1/sc22/wg21/docs/cwg_defects.html#1213

merrill10b Jason Merrill, "noexcept(auto)." Technical Report N3207, International Standards Organization, Geneva, Switzerland, November 11, 2010
http://www.open-std.org/jtc1/sc22/wg21/docs/papers/2010/n3207.htm

mertz18 Arne Mertz, "Trailing Return Types, East Const, and Code Style Consistency." *Simplify C++!* (2018)
https://arne-mertz.de/2018/05/trailing-return-types-east-const-and-code-style-consistency/

meyers92 Scott Meyers, *Effective C++* (Reading, MA: Addison-Wesley, 1992)

meyers96 Scott Meyers, *More Effective C++* (Reading, MA: Addison-Wesley, 1996)

meyers98 Scott Meyers, *Effective C++*. 2nd edition (Reading, MA: Addison-Wesley, 1998)

meyers04a Scott Meyers and Andrei Alexandrescu, "C++ and the Perils of Double-Checked Locking: Part I." *Dr Dobb's Journal*, 2004, pp. 46–49

meyers04b Scott Meyers and Andrei Alexandrescu, "C++ and the Perils of Double-Checked Locking: Part II." *Dr Dobb's Journal*, 2004, pp. 57–61

meyers05 Scott Meyers, *Effective C++*. 3rd edition (Boston: Addison-Wesley, 2005)

meyers15a Scott Meyers, "The View from Aristeia: Breaking All the Eggs in C++." scottmeyers.blogspot.com, November 2015
http://scottmeyers.blogspot.com/2015/11/breaking-all-eggs-in-c.html

meyers15b Scott Meyers, *Effective Modern C++: 42 Specific Ways to Improve Your Use of C++11 and C++14*. 1st edition (Sebastopol, CA: O'Reilly, 2015)

microsofta "Guidelines Support Library." Microsoft
https://github.com/Microsoft/GSL

microsoftb "STL." Microsoft
https://github.com/microsoft/STL

microsoftc "Built-in types (C++)." Guidelines Support Library, Microsoft
https://docs.microsoft.com/en-us/cpp/cpp/fundamental-types-cpp

microsoftd "C26481 NO_POINTER_ARITHMETIC." Guidelines Support Library, Microsoft, April 29, 2020
https://docs.microsoft.com/en-us/cpp/code-quality/c26481?view=vs-2019

miller00 Mike Miller, "Issue 253: Why must empty or fully-initialized const objects be initialized?" *C++ Standard Core Language Active Issues, Revision 104* (Geneva, Switzerland: International Standards Organization, 2000)
http://www.open-std.org/jtc1/sc22/wg21/docs/cwg_defects.html#253

miller05 William M. Miller, "Extended `friend` Declarations (Rev. 3)." Technical Report N1791, International Standards Organization, Geneva, Switzerland, May 2005
http://www.open-std.org/JTC1/sc22/wg21/docs/papers/2005/n1791.pdf

Bibliography

miller07 David E. Miller, Herb Sutter, and Bjarne Stroustrup, "Strongly Typed Enums (Revision 3)." Technical Report N2347, International Standards Organization, Geneva, Switzerland, July 19, 2007
http://www.open-std.org/jtc1/sc22/wg21/docs/papers/2007/n2347.pdf

miller10 William M. Miller, "A Taxonomy of Expression Value Categories." Technical Report N3055, International Standards Organization, Geneva, Switzerland, March 12, 2010
http://www.open-std.org/jtc1/sc22/wg21/docs/papers/2010/n3055.pdf

miller12a Mike Miller, "Issue 1442: Argument-dependent lookup in the range-based `for`." *C++ Standard Core Language Defect Reports and Accepted Issues, Revision 104* (Geneva, Switzerland: International Standards Organization, 2012)
http://www.open-std.org/jtc1/sc22/wg21/docs/cwg_defects.html#1442

miller12b Mike Miller, "Issue 1542: Compound Assignment of braced-init-list." *C++ Standard Core Language Active Issues, Revision 104* (Geneva, Switzerland: International Standards Organization, 2012)
http://www.open-std.org/jtc1/sc22/wg21/docs/cwg_active.html#1542

miller13 Mike Miller, "Issue 1655: Line Endings in Raw String Literals." *C++ Standard Core Language Active Issues, Revision 100* (Geneva, Switzerland: International Standards Organization, 2013)
http://www.open-std.org/jtc1/sc22/wg21/docs/cwg_active.html#1655

miller17 Mike Miller, "Issue 2354: Extended Alignment and Object Representation." *Core Language Working Group Tentatively Ready Issues for the February, 2019 (Kona) Meeting* (Geneva, Switzerland: International Standards Organization, 2017)
http://www.open-std.org/jtc1/sc22/wg21/docs/papers/2019/p1359r0.html#2354

miller21 William M. Miller, "C++ Standard Core Language Defect Reports and Accepted Issues, Revision 104." Technical report, International Standards Organization, Geneva, Switzerland, February 24, 2021
http://www.open-std.org/jtc1/sc22/wg21/docs/cwg_defects.html

mortoray13 Edaqa Mortoray, "The true cost of zero cost exceptions." Musing Mortoray Blog, September 12, 2013
https://mortoray.com/2013/09/12/the-true-cost-of-zero-cost-exceptions/

murphy16 Niall Richard Murphy, Betsy Beyer, Chris Jones, and Jennifer Petoff, *Site Reliability Engineering: How Google Runs Production Systems* (Sebastopol, CA: O'Reilly Media, 2016)
https://sre.google/books/

narkive "Why internal linkage variables can't be used to instantiate an template?" Narkive, accessed February 4, 2021
https://comp.lang.cpp.moderated.narkive.com/PsCvujrV/why-internal-linkage-variables-can-t-be-used-to-instantiate-an-template

nayar20 Amit Nayar, "Investigating the Performance Overhead of C++ Exceptions." pspdfkit.com blog, 2020
https://pspdfkit.com/blog/2020/performance-overhead-of-exceptions-in-cpp/

niebler13 Eric Niebler, "Universal References and the Copy Constructor." ericniebler.com, August 7, 2013
https://ericniebler.com/2013/08/07/universal-references-and-the-copy-constructo/

odwyer18 Arthur O'Dwyer and JF Bastien, "Copying volatile subobjects is not trivial." Technical Report P1153R0, International Standards Organization, Geneva, Switzerland, October 4, 2018
http://www.open-std.org/jtc1/sc22/wg21/docs/papers/2018/p1153r0.html

odwyer19 Arthur O'Dwyer and David Stone, "More implicit moves." Technical Report P1155R3, International Standards Organization, Geneva, Switzerland, June 17, 2019
http://www.open-std.org/jtc1/sc22/wg21/docs/papers/2019/p1155r3.html

odwyer20 Arthur O'Dwyer, "Object Relocation in Terms of Move Plus Destroy." Technical Report P1144R5, International Standards Organization, Geneva, Switzerland, March 1, 2020
http://www.open-std.org/jtc1/sc22/wg21/docs/papers/2020/p1144r5.html

odwyer21 Arthur O'Dwyer, "Simpler implicit move." Technical Report P2266R1, International Standards Organization, Geneva, Switzerland, March 13, 2021
http://www.open-std.org/jtc1/sc22/wg21/docs/papers/2021/p2266r1.html

orr18 Roger Orr, "Nothing is Better than Copy or Move." *ACCU 2018* (2018)
https://www.youtube.com/watch?v=-dc5vqt2tgA

otsuka20 Kohei Otsuka, "C++ Detection Idiom explained." Published via gitconnected.com, July 24, 2020
https://levelup.gitconnected.com/c-detection-idiom-explained-5cc7207a0067

ottosen10 Thorsten Ottosen, "Please reconsider noexcept." Technical Report N3227, International Standards Organization, Geneva, Switzerland, November 23, 2010
http://www.open-std.org/jtc1/sc22/wg21/docs/papers/2010/n3227.html

ouellet16 Félix-Antoine Ouellet, "The joys and pains of unrestricted unions." /* Insert Code Here */ blog, August 18, 2016
https://faouellet.github.io/unrestricted-unions/

pacifico12 Stefano Pacifico, Alisdair Meredith, and John Lakos, "Toward a Standard C++ 'Date' Class." Technical Report N3344, International Standards Organization, Geneva, Switzerland, January 15, 2012
http://www.open-std.org/jtc1/sc22/wg21/docs/papers/2012/n3344.pdf

Bibliography

parent21 Sean Parent, "Relaxing Requirements of Moved-From Objects." Technical Report P2345R0, International Standards Organization, Geneva, Switzerland, April 14, 2021
http://www.open-std.org/jtc1/sc22/wg21/docs/papers/2021/p2345r0.pdf

pietrek97 Matt Pietrek, "A Crash Course on the Depths of Win32™ Structured Exception Handling." *Microsoft Systems Journal*, January 1997
http://bytepointer.com/resources/pietrek_crash_course_depths_of_win32_seh.htm

pluzhnikov14 Paul Pluzhnikov, "Bug 60352: Bogus 'error: conflicting declaration auto i.'" Bugzilla, February 27, 2014
https://gcc.gnu.org/bugzilla/show_bug.cgi?id=60352

pradhan14 Pradhan, "noexcept, stack unwinding and performance." StackOverflow online forum, September 27, 2014
https://stackoverflow.com/questions/26079903/noexcept-stack-unwinding-and-performance

prowl13 Andy Prowl, "Template tuple — calling a function on each element." StackOverflow online forum, May 5, 2013
https://stackoverflow.com/questions/16387354/template-tuple-calling-a-function-on-each-element/16387374#16387374

pusz20a Mateusz Pusz, "Enable variable template template Parameters." Technical Report P2008R0, C++ Standards Committee Working Group, International Standards Organization, Geneva, Switzerland, January 10, 2020
http://www.open-std.org/jtc1/sc22/wg21/docs/papers/2020/p2008r0.html

pusz20b Mateusz Pusz, "A Physical Units Library For the Next C++." *CppCon: The C++ Conference* (Aurora, CO, 2020)
https://www.youtube.com/watch?v=7dExYGSOJzo

ranns14 Nina Ranns, "Issue 1881: Standard-layout classes and unnamed bit-fields." *C++ Standard Core Language Defect Reports and Accepted Issues, Revision 104* (Geneva, Switzerland: International Standards Organization, 2014)
http://www.open-std.org/jtc1/sc22/wg21/docs/cwg_defects.html#1881

revzin18 Barry Revzin, "Allow pack expansion in lambda init-capture." Technical Report P0780R2, C++ Standards Committee Working Group, International Standards Organization, Geneva, Switzerland, March 14, 2018
http://www.open-std.org/jtc1/sc22/wg21/docs/papers/2018/p0780r2.html

rojas15 Ràul Rojas, "A Tutorial Introduction to the Lambda Calculus." *arXiv*, 2015
https://arxiv.org/pdf/1503.09060.pdf

seacord13 Robert C. Seacord, *Secure Coding in C and C++*. 2nd edition (Boston: Addison-Wesley, 2013)

semashev18 Andrey Semashev, "Supporting `offsetof` for All Classes." Technical Report P0897R0, C++ Standards Committee Working Group, International Standards Organization, Geneva, Switzerland, 2018
http://www.open-std.org/jtc1/sc22/wg21/docs/papers/2018/p0897r0.html

sharpe13 Chris Sharpe, "Contextually converted to bool." Chris's C++ Thoughts, July 28, 2013
http://chris-sharpe.blogspot.com/2013/07/contextually-converted-to-bool.html

smith11a Richard Smith, "Issue 1358: Unintentionally ill-formed `constexpr` function template instances." *C++ Standard Core Language Defect Reports and Accepted Issues, Revision 104* (Geneva, Switzerland: International Standards Organization, 2011)
http://www.open-std.org/jtc1/sc22/wg21/docs/cwg_defects.html#1358

smith11b Richard Smith, "Issue 1452: Value-initialized objects may be constants." *C++ Standard Core Language Closed Issues, Revision 104* (Geneva, Switzerland: International Standards Organization, 2011)
http://www.open-std.org/jtc1/sc22/wg21/docs/cwg_closed.html#1452

smith13 Richard Smith, "Issue 1672: Layout compatibility with multiple empty bases." *C++ Standard Core Language Closed Issues, Revision 104* (Geneva, Switzerland: International Standards Organization, 2013)
http://www.open-std.org/jtc1/sc22/wg21/docs/cwg_defects.html#1672

smith14 Richard Smith, "Issue 1951:Cv-qualification and literal types." *C++ Standard Core Language Defect Reports and Accepted Issues, Revision 104* (Geneva, Switzerland: International Standards Organization, 2014)
http://www.open-std.org/jtc1/sc22/wg21/docs/cwg_defects.html#1951

smith15a Richard Smith, "Attributes for namespaces and enumerators." Technical Report N4196, C++ Standards Committee Working Group, International Standards Organization, Geneva, Switzerland, 2015
http://www.open-std.org/jtc1/sc22/wg21/docs/papers/2014/n4196.html

smith15b Richard Smith, "Rewording Inheriting Constructors (Core Issue 1941 et al.)." Technical Report P0136R1, C++ Standards Committee Working Group, International Standards Organization, Geneva, Switzerland, 2015
http://www.open-std.org/jtc1/sc22/wg21/docs/papers/2015/p0136r1.html

smith15c Richard Smith, "Guaranteed Copy Elision through Simplified Value Categories." Technical Report P0135R, C++ Standards Committee Working Group, International Standards Organization, Geneva, Switzerland, 2015
http://www.open-std.org/jtc1/sc22/wg21/docs/papers/2015/p0135r0.html

smith16a Richard Smith, "Issue 2254: Standard-layout classes and bit-fields." *C++ Standard Core Language Defect Reports and Accepted Issues, Revision 104* (Geneva, Switzerland: International Standards Organization, 2016)
http://www.open-std.org/jtc1/sc22/wg21/docs/cwg_defects.html#2254

Bibliography

smith16b Richard Smith, "Issue 2256: Lifetime of trivially-destructible objects." *Core Language Working Group "ready" Issues for the February, 2019 (Kona) meeting* (Geneva, Switzerland: International Standards Organization, 2016)
http://www.open-std.org/jtc1/sc22/wg21/docs/papers/2019/p1358r0.html#2256

smith16c Richard Smith, "Issue 2287: Pointer-interconvertibility in non-standard-layout unions." *C++ Standard Core Language Defect Reports and Accepted Issues, Revision 104* (Geneva, Switzerland: International Standards Organization, 2016)
http://www.open-std.org/jtc1/sc22/wg21/docs/cwg_defects.html#2287

smith16d Richard Smith, "Issue 2827: `is_trivially_constructible` and non-trivial destructors." *C++ Standard Library Active Issues List (Revision D122)* (Geneva, Switzerland: International Standards Organization, 2016)
https://cplusplus.github.io/LWG/lwg-active.html#2827

smith18 Richard Smith, "Issue 2356: Base Class Copy and Move Constructors Should Not Be Inherited." *C++ Standard Core Language Defect Reports and Accepted Issues, Revision 104* (Geneva, Switzerland, 2018)
http://www.open-std.org/jtc1/sc22/wg21/docs/cwg_defects.html#2356

smith19 Richard Smith, "Contra CWG DR1778." Technical Report P1286R2, C++ Standards Committee Working Group, International Standards Organization, Geneva, Switzerland, 2019
http://www.open-std.org/jtc1/sc22/wg21/docs/papers/2019/p1286r2.html

smith20 Richard Smith, "Implicit Creation of Objects for Low-Level Object Manipulation." Technical Report P0593R6, C++ Standards Committee Working Group, International Standards Organization, Geneva, Switzerland, 2020
http://www.open-std.org/jtc1/sc22/wg21/docs/papers/2020/p0593r6.html

snyder18 Jeff Snyder and Louis Dionne, "Class Types in Non-Type Template Parameters." Technical Report P0732R2, International Standards Organization, Geneva, Switzerland, June 6, 2018
http://www.open-std.org/jtc1/sc22/wg21/docs/papers/2018/p0732r2.pdf

solihin15 Yan Solihin, *Fundamentals of Parallel Multi-Core Architecture* (Boca Raton, FL: CRC Press, 2015)

spertus09 Mike Spertus, "Type Traits and Base Classes." Technical Report N2965, International Standards Organization, Geneva, Switzerland, September 25, 2009
http://www.open-std.org/jtc1/sc22/wg21/docs/papers/2009/n2965.html

spertus13 Mike Spertus, "Packaging Parameter Packs (Rev. 2)." Technical Report N3728, International Standards Organization, Geneva, Switzerland, September 3, 2013
http://www.open-std.org/jtc1/sc22/wg21/docs/papers/2013/n3728.html

stasiowski19 Krystian Stasiowski, "Accessing Object Representations." Technical Report P1839R2, International Standards Organization, Geneva, Switzerland, November 11, 2019
http://www.open-std.org/jtc1/sc22/wg21/docs/papers/2019/p1839r2.pdf

stepanov09 Alexander Stepanov and Paul McJones, *Elements of Programming* (Boston: Addison-Wesley, 2009)

stepanov15 Alexander A. Stepanov and Daniel E. Rose, *From Mathematics To Generic Programming* (Boston: Addison-Wesley, 2015)

stevens93 W. Richard Stevens, *Advanced Programming in the UNIX Environment* (Reading, MA: Addison-Wesley, 1993)

stone17 David Stone, "Implicitly move from rvalue references in return statements." Technical Report P0527R1, International Standards Organization, Geneva, Switzerland, November 8, 2017
http://www.open-std.org/jtc1/sc22/wg21/docs/papers/2018/p0527r1.html

stone19 David Stone, "Merged wording for P0527R1 and P1155R3." Technical Report P1825R0, International Standards Organization, Geneva, Switzerland, July 19, 2019
http://www.open-std.org/jtc1/sc22/wg21/docs/papers/2019/p1825r0.html

stroustrup Bjarne Stroustrup, "'New' Value Terminology."
https://www.stroustrup.com/terminology.pdf

stroustrup91a Bjarne Stroustrup, *The C++ Programming Language*. 2nd edition (Reading, MA: Addison-Wesley, 1991)

stroustrup91b Bjarne Stroustrup, "What is 'Object-Oriented Programming'?" (1991 revised version). stroustrup.com, 1991
https://stroustrup.com/whatis.pdf

stroustrup94 Bjarne Stroustrup, *The Design and Evolution of C++* (Reading, MA: Addison-Wesley, 1994)

stroustrup04 Bjarne Stroustrup, "Abstraction and the C++ Machine Model." *Proceedings of the First International Conference on Embedded Software and Systems (ICESS '04)* (Berlin Heidelberg: Springer-Verlag, 2004), pp. 1–13
https://www.springer.com/gp/book/9783540281283#

stroustrup05a Bjarne Stroustrup and Gabriel Dos Reis, "Initialization and Initializers." Technical Report N1890, Geneva, Switzerland, September 22, 2005
http://www.open-std.org/jtc1/sc22/wg21/docs/papers/2005/n1890.pdf

stroustrup05b Bjarne Stroustrup and Gabriel Dos Reis, "Initializer Lists." Technical Report N1919, Geneva, Switzerland, December 11, 2005
http://www.open-std.org/jtc1/sc22/wg21/docs/papers/2005/n1919.pdf

Bibliography

stroustrup07 Bjarne Stroustrup, "Issue 616: Definition of 'indeterminate value'." *C++ Standard Core Language Defect Reports and Accepted Issues, Revision 104* (Geneva, Switzerland, 2007)
http://www.open-std.org/jtc1/sc22/wg21/docs/cwg_defects.html#616

stroustrup10a Bjarne Stroustrup and Lawrence Crowl, "Defining Move Special Member Functions." Technical Report N3053, International Standards Organization, Geneva, Switzerland, March 12, 2010
http://www.open-std.org/jtc1/sc22/wg21/docs/papers/2010/n3053.html

stroustrup10b Bjarne Stroustrup, "To which extent can `noexcept` be deduced?" Technical Report N3202, International Standards Organization, Geneva, Switzerland, November 7, 2010
http://www.open-std.org/jtc1/sc22/wg21/docs/papers/2010/n3202.pdf

stroustrup13 Bjarne Stroustrup, *The C++ Programming Language.* 4th edition (Boston: Addison-Wesley, 2013)

stroustrup21 Bjarne Stroustrup and Eds. Herb Sutter, *C++ Core Guidelines* (Standard C++ Foundation, 2021)
https://isocpp.github.io/CppCoreGuidelines/CppCoreGuidelines

sutter12 Herb Sutter, "Reader Q&A: What does it mean for [[attributes]] to affect language semantics?" Sutter's Mill: Herb Sutter on Software Development, April 5, 2012
https://herbsutter.com/2012/04/05/reader-qa-what-does-it-mean-for-attributes-to-affect-language-semantics/

sutter14a Herb Sutter, "Defining a Portable ABI." Technical Report N4028, International Standards Organization, Geneva, Switzerland, May 23, 2014
http://www.open-std.org/jtc1/sc22/wg21/docs/papers/2014/n4028.pdf

sutter14b Herb Sutter, Bjarne Stroustrup, and Gabriel Dos Reis, "Forwarding References." Technical Report N4164, International Standards Organization, Geneva, Switzerland, October 6, 2014
https://isocpp.org/files/papers/N4164.pdf

sutter19 Herb Sutter, "Zero-Overhead Deterministic Exceptions: Throwing Values." Technical Report P0709R4, International Standards Organization, Geneva, Switzerland, April 8, 2019
http://www.open-std.org/jtc1/sc22/wg21/docs/papers/2019/p0709r4.pdf

svoboda10 David Svoboda, "Supporting the `noreturn` property in C1x." Technical Report N1453, International Standards Organization, Geneva, Switzerland, April 27, 2010
http://www.open-std.org/jtc1/sc22/wg14/www/docs/n1453.htm

tong15 Hurbert Tong, "Issue 2120: Array as first non-static data member in standard-layout class." *C++ Standard Core Language Closed Issues, Revision 104* (Geneva, Switzerland: International Standards Organization, 2015)
http://www.open-std.org/jtc1/sc22/wg21/docs/cwg_defects.html#2120

tsirunyan10 Armen Tsirunyan, "What is the curiously recurring template pattern (CRTP)?" StackOverflow online forum, November 13, 2010
https://stackoverflow.com/questions/4173254/what-is-the-curiously-recurring-template-pattern-crtp

tsirunyan18 Armen Tsirunyan, "What are Aggregates and PODs and How/Why Are They Special?" StackOverflow online forum, June 11, 2018
https://stackoverflow.com/questions/4178175/what-are-aggregates-and-pods-and-how-why-are-they-special

unicode "Unicode 14.0.0." Unicode Consortium, Sep 14, 2021
https://www.unicode.org/versions/Unicode14.0.0/

usa13 USA, "Issue 1778: exception-specification in explicitly-defaulted functions." *C++ Standard Core Language Defect Reports and Accepted Issues, Revision 104* (Geneva, Switzerland: International Standards Organization, 2013)
http://www.open-std.org/jtc1/sc22/wg21/docs/cwg_defects.html#1778

vandenbos17 Adriaan van den Bos, *Appendix C: Positive Semidefinite and Positive Definite Matrices* (Wiley & Sons, 2007), pp. 259–263
https://onlinelibrary.wiley.com/doi/abs/10.1002/9780470173862.app3

vandevoorde05 Daveed Vandevoorde, "Right Angle Brackets." Technical Report N1757, Revision 2, C++ Standards Committee Working Group, International Standards Organization, Geneva, Switzerland, 2005
http://www.open-std.org/jtc1/sc22/wg21/docs/papers/2005/n1757.html

vandevoorde13 Daveed Vandevoorde, "Issue 1813: Direct vs indirect bases in standard-layout classes." *C++ Standard Core Language Defect Reports and Accepted Issues, Revision 104* (Geneva, Switzerland: International Standards Organization, 2013)
http://www.open-std.org/jtc1/sc22/wg21/docs/cwg_defects.html#1813

vandevoorde15 Daveed Vandevoorde, "Issue 2094: Trivial copy/move constructor for class with volatile member." *C++ Standard Core Language Defect Reports and Accepted Issues, Revision 104* (Geneva, Switzerland: International Standards Organization, 2015)
http://www.open-std.org/JTC1/SC22/WG21/docs/cwg_defects.html#2094

vandevoorde18 David Vandevoorde, Nicolai Josuttis, and Douglas Gregor, *C++ Templates: The Complete Guide* (Boston: Addison-Wesley, 2018)

voutilainen15 Ville Voutilainen, "noexcept(auto), again." Technical Report N4473, C++ Standards Committee Working Group, International Standards Organization, Geneva,

Bibliography

Switzerland, April 10, 2015
http://www.open-std.org/jtc1/sc22/wg21/docs/papers/2015/n4473

wakely13 Jonathan Wakely, "Compile-Time Integer Sequences." Technical Report N3493, C++ Standards Committee Working Group, International Standards Organization, Geneva, Switzerland, January 11, 2013
http://www.open-std.org/jtc1/sc22/wg21/docs/papers/2013/n3493.html

wakely15 Jonathan Wakely, "Bug 65685: Reducing alignment with alignas should be rejected." Bugzilla, April 7, 2015
https://gcc.gnu.org/bugzilla/show_bug.cgi?id=65685

wakely16 Jonathan Wakely, "Issue 2796: `tuple` should be a literal type." Technical report, Geneva, Switzerland, July 30, 2016
https://cplusplus.github.io/LWG/issue2796

whitney16 Tyler Whitney, Kent Sharkey, John Parente, Colin Robertson, Mike Blome, Mike Jones, Gordon Hogenson, and Saisang Cai, "Checked Iterators." Technical report, Redmond, WA, November 4, 2016
https://docs.microsoft.com/en-us/cpp/standard-library/checked-iterators?view=msvc-160

widman13 James Widman, "Issue 1734: Nontrivial deleted copy functions." *C++ Standard Core Language Defect Reports and Accepted Issues, Revision 104* (Geneva, Switzerland: International Standards Organization, 2013)
http://www.open-std.org/jtc1/sc22/wg21/docs/cwg_defects.html#1734

wight Hyrum Wight, "Hyrum's Law."
https://www.hyrumslaw.com/

wilcox13 Charles L. Wilcox, "Bug 57484: 'std::numeric_limits< T >::signaling_NaN()' signaling-bit is incorrect for x86 32-bit." Bugzilla, May 31, 2013
https://gcc.gnu.org/bugzilla/show_bug.cgi?id=57484

williams19 Anthony Williams, "The Power of Hidden Friends in C++." Just Software Solutions blog, June 25, 2019
https://www.justsoftwaresolutions.co.uk/cplusplus/hidden-friends.html

yasskin12 Jeffrey Yasskin, "Issue 1579: Return by Converting Move Constructor." *C++ Standard Core Language Active Issues, Revision 104*, number N4750 (Geneva, Switzerland, 2012)
http://www.open-std.org/jtc1/sc22/wg21/docs/cwg_defects.html#1579

yuan20 Zhihao Yuan, "Converting from `T*` to `bool` should be considered narrowing (re: US 212)." Technical Report P1957R2, C++ Standards Committee Working Group, International Standards Organization, Geneva, Switzerland, February 10, 2020
http://www.open-std.org/jtc1/sc22/wg21/docs/papers/2020/p1957r2.html

Bibliography

zhilin21 Anton Zhilin, "Guaranteed copy elision for return variables." Technical Report P2025R2, International Standards Organization, Geneva, Switzerland, March 14, 2021 http://www.open-std.org/jtc1/sc22/wg21/docs/papers/2021/p2025r2.html

Index

Symbols

{ } (braced-initialization syntax)
  annoyances, 247–255
    allowing narrowing conversions, 247–248
    auto deduction, 253–254
    broken macro-invocation syntax, 248–249
    copy list initialization in member initializer lists, lack of, 249–250
    explicit constructors passed multiple arguments, 250–252
    narrowing aggregate initialization, 247
    obfuscation with opaque usage, 252–253
    operator acceptance, 254–255
  C++03 aggregate initialization, 219–222
  C++03 initialization syntax, 215–219
  C++11 aggregate initialization, 224–225
  copy initialization and scalars, 235–236
  copy list initialization, 226–228
  default member initialization and, 233
  description of, 215
  direct list initialization, 228–231
  further reading for, 256
  list initialization, 233–234
  potential pitfalls, 242–247
    aggregates with deleted constructors, 247
    inadvertently calling initializer-list constructors, 242–244
    NRVO and implicit moves disabled, 244–246
  restrictions on narrowing conversions, 222–224
  support for, 562–564
  type name omissions, 234
  use cases, 236–242
    avoiding the most vexing parse, 237–238
    defining value-initialized variables, 236–237
    uniform initialization in factory functions, 239–241
    uniform initialization in generic code, 238–239
    uniform member initialization in generic code, 241–242
  variables in conditional expressions, 235

, (comma) operator, 268, 928, 955n25
  constexpr functions, 265
  rvalue references, 816
>> (consecutive right-angle brackets)
  description of, 21
  further reading for, 24
  potential pitfalls with, 22–24
  use cases, 22
=**default** syntax. *See also* deleted functions; rvalue references; **static_assert**
  annoyances, 42–43
  description of, 33–36
  first declaration of special member function, 34–35
  further reading for, 44
  implementation of user-provided special member function, 35–36
  implicit generation of special member functions, 44–45
  potential pitfalls, 41–42
  use cases, 36–41
    making explicit class APIs with no runtime cost, 38–39
    physically decoupling interface from implementation, 40–41
    preserving type triviality, 39–40
    restoring generation of suppressed special member function, 36–37
=**delete** syntax. *See also* defaulted functions; rvalue references
  annoyances, 58–59
  description of, 53
  further reading for, 60
  use cases, 53–57
    hiding structural base class member functions, 56–57
    preventing implicit conversion, 55–56
    suppressing special member function generation, 53–55
' (digit separator). *See also* binary literals
  description of, 152–153
  further reading for, 154
  loss of precision in floating-point literals, 154–156
  use cases, 153
(( )) (double parentheses) notation, 25, 30
> (greater-than) operator, 21–22

Index

|| (logical or) operator, 265
( ) (parentheses), with **decltype** operands, 25, 30
&& (rvalue references)
    annoyances, 804–812
        destructive move, lack of, 811–812
        evolution of value categories, 807
        moved-from object requirements overly
           strict, 807–811
        RVO and NRVO require declared
           copy/move constructors, 804–805
        std::move does not move, 805–806
        visual similarity to forwarding references,
           806–807
    decltype results as, 26
    description of, 710–741
    in expressions, 730–731
    extended value categories in C++11/14,
        716–723
    further reading for, 813
    lvalue references, comparison, 710–711
    modifiable, 820–821
    motivation for, 715–716
    move operations, 714–715
    moves in **return** statements, 734–740
    necessity of, 824
    overload resolution, 713
    overloading on reference types, 727–730
    potential pitfalls, 782–804
        disabling NRVO, 783–784
        failure to std::move named rvalue refer-
           ences, 784–785
        implementing move-only types without
           std::unique_ptr, 791–794
        inconsistent expectations on moved-from
           objects, 794–803
        making noncopyable type movable with-
           out just cause, 788–791
        move operations that throw, 787
        repeatedly calling std::move on named
           rvalue references, 785–786
        requiring owned resources to be valid,
           803–804
        returning **const** *rvalues* pessimizes per-
           formance, 786–787
        sink arguments require copying, 782–783
        some moves equivalent to copies, 788
    special member functions, 732–733
    std::move, 731–732
    use cases, 741–781
        identifying value categories, 779–781
        move operations as optimizations of copy-
           ing, 741–767
        move-only types, 768–771

        passing around resource-owning objects
           by value, 771–775
        sink arguments, 775–779
    value category evolution, 813–828
    xvalues, 712–713
[[ ]] (square brackets), 12
0b prefix. *See also* digit separator (')
    description of, 142–143
    further reading for, 146
    use cases, 144–146
        bit masking and bitwise operations, 144–
           145
        replicating constant binary data, 145–146

A

ABI link safety, build modes and, 1071–1074
ABI versioning
    exception specification incompatibility,
        1148–1149
    link-safe, 1067–1071
abstract classes, 1008, 1009
    extracting, 1018
    final contextual keyword, 1008–1009
    VShape as, 440
abstract interfaces, 1048, 1200
    deduced return types and, 1200
    pure, 540, 1020, 1021
abstract machine, 1118
abstract-syntax-tree (AST), 1054
access levels, 421, 489, 549–551, 550n5
access specifiers, 34, 35, 439, 537, 550n5, 884
accessible (from a context), 410
accessible copy constructor, 641, 644
accidental terminate, 1124–1128
acquire/release memory barrier, 80n7
active members, 406
adapter requirements in range-based **for** loops,
    706
aggregate class, 415
aggregate initialization. *See also* default member
        initializers
    annoyances, 140–141
    in C++03, 219–222
    in C++11, 224–225, 241
    constexpr functions, 273–274
    default member initializers, 330
    with deleted constructors, 247
    description of, 138–139
    narrowing, 247
    potential pitfalls, 140
    rvalue references, 752
    of scalar members, 463
    use cases, 139
aggregate types, 138, 1087
    direct list initialization, 230

Index

generalized PODs, 410
  as literal types, 279–280
aggregates, 877
  default member initializers, 330
  POD types, 402
algebra, 961
algorithm selection, 947
algorithms. *See also* functions
  configuring via lambda expressions, 86–87
  conflating optimization with code-size reduction, 1143–1144
  constexpr functions in, 294n19
  divide and conquer, 297
  nonrecursive **constexpr** algorithms, 961–962
  optimized C++11 example algorithms, 965–967
optimized metaprogramming algorithms, 963–964
alias templates, 887
aliases. *See also* inheriting constructors; trailing return
  creating with **using** declarations, 133–137
  description of, 133–134
  use cases, 134–137
    binding arguments to template parameters, 135–136
    simplified **typedef** declarations, 134–135
    type trait notation, 136–137
aliasing, 638–639
alignas specifier
  description of, 168–172
  memory allocation, 181–183
  natural alignment, 179–181
  pack expansion, 921–922
  potential pitfalls, 176–179
    ill-formed, no-diagnostic required (IFNDR), 176–177
    misleading applications to user-defined types (UDTs), 177–178
    overlooking alternatives to avoiding false sharing, 178–179
    underspecifying alignment, 176
  strengthening alignment
    of data members, 170–171
    of particular objects, 169–170
    of user-defined types (UDTs), 171
  supported alignments, 168–169
  type identifier as argument, 172
  use cases, 172–176
    false sharing, avoiding, 174–176
    proper alignment for architecture-specific instructions, 173–174
    sufficiently aligned object buffers, 172–173

alignment. *See also* **alignas** specifier; **alignof** operator
  for architecture-specific instructions, 173–174
  incompatibly specified, 176–177
  maximal fundamental, 193
  natural, 179–181, 193
  strengthening, 168
    of data members, 170–171
    of particular objects, 169–170
    of user-defined types (UDTs), 171
  supported, 168–169
  underspecifying, 176
alignment requirements, 168, 184
alignof operator. *See also* **alignas** specifier; **decltype**
  annoyances, 193–194
  description of, 184
  fundamental types, 184
  use cases, 186–193
    monotonic memory allocation, 190–193
    probing alignment of type during development, 186–187
    sufficiently aligned buffers, 187–190
  user-defined types, 185–186
allocating objects, 634
almost trivially destructible, 464–470
amortized constant time (of a repeated operation), 636
annotations. *See* attribute support; attributes
anonymous function objects. *See* closure objects; lambda expressions
API migration, facilitating, 1062–1067
Application Binary Interface (ABI)
  build modes and link safety, 1071–1074
  changes in future C++ versions, 1089n5, 1114, 1114n24, 1148–1149
  inline namespaces, 1056, 1064, 1083
  link-safe ABI versioning, 1067–1071
  POD types, 402
Application Programming Interface (API), 402, 445
arbitrary values, conflating with indeterminate values, 493–497
architecture-specific instructions, alignment for, 173–174
argument-dependent lookup (ADL), 472, 1056, 1058
  inline namespaces, 1056, 1058–1059
  range-based **for** loops, 681, 707–709
  user-defined literals (UDLs), 841
arguments
  passing multiple to explicit constructors, 250–252
  of same type, 564–565
  template, local/unnamed types, 83–88

Index

value initialization, avoiding the most vexing parse, 237–238

arithmetic operators, braced lists and, 254–255

arithmetic types

    enum class, 334, 337–339

    implicit conversion, avoiding, 337–339

array types

    alignof operator, 184

    as literal types, 280

    as standard-layout types, 417

    as trivial types, 425

arrays

    built-in, deducing, 211–212

    initialization with `std::initializer_list`

        annoyances, 567–571

        description of, 553–561

        further reading for, 571

        potential pitfalls, 566–567

        range-based **for** loops, 571–572

        use cases, 561–566

    size deduction, lack of, 330

    traversing with range-based **for** loops, 683–684

array-to-pointer decay, 220, 222

ASCII

    basic source character set, 130

    Unicode string literals, 129

as if, 307

assert, 656

assert statements in dependency chain, 1002

assignable (type), 486

assignment operator, 521–522

    braced lists and, 254–255

    lvalue references, 816

atomic (operation), 80–82

attribute lists, 922

attribute support. *See also* attributes

    description of

        attribute placement, 13

        attribute syntax, 12–13

        standardized compiler-specific attributes, 13–14

    potential pitfalls

        undefined behavior, 19

        unrecognized attributes, 18–19

    use cases

        control of external static analysis, 17–18

        hints for additional optimization opportunities, 15–16

        prompting of compiler diagnostics, 14–15

        statement of explicit assumptions, 16–17

        statements of semantic properties, 18

attributes. *See also* attribute support

    `[[carries_dependency]]`

        description of, 998–1000

        further reading for, 1006

        potential pitfalls, 1005

        use cases, 1000–1005

    `[[clang::no_sanitize]]`, 14

    definition of, 12

    `[[deprecated]]`, 14

        description of, 147–148

        potential pitfalls, 150

        use cases, 148–150

    `[[gnu::cold]]`, 15

    `[[gnu::const]]`, 16–17, 19

    `[[gnu::pure]]`, 14, 16

    `[[gnu::warn_unused_result]]`, 14–15, 15n7

    `[[gsl::suppress]]`, 17–18

    `[[noreturn]]`, 13

        description of, 95

        further reading for, 98

        potential pitfalls, 97–98

        use cases, 95–97

auto variables

    annoyances, 212–213

        nonstatic data members, not allowed, 212

        template argument deductions, not all allowed, 212–213

    braced initialization and, 253–254

    decltype(auto) placeholder

        annoyances, 1213

        description of, 1205–1210

        potential pitfalls, 1212–1213

        use cases, 1210–1212

    description of, 195–199

    further reading for, 214

    idioms for, 1213

    potential pitfalls, 204–212

        compromised readability, 204

        deducing built-in arrays, 211–212

        deduction for list initialization, 210–211

        hidden properties of fundamental types, 209–210

        interface restrictions, lack of, 208–209

        unexpected conversions, 206–208

        unintentional copies, 204–206

    return-type deduction

        annoyances, 1201–1203

        description of, 1182–1194

        potential pitfalls, 1200

        use cases, 1194–1200

    use cases, 200–203

        deeply nested variable types, 202–203

        ensuring variable initialization, 200

        implementation-defined or compiler-synthesized variable types, 202

        preventing unexpected implicit conversions, 201

Index

redundant type name repetition, avoiding, 200–201

resilience to library code changes, 203

auto&&, 383–384

automatic objects, 69

automatic storage duration, 68, 195, 582, 731, 735, 740n16

automatic variables, 526–527, 735–737

auxiliary variables, creating with **decltype**, 28

B

backward compatibility, 1113

barriers, 80n7

base classes, hiding member functions, 56–57

base name (of a component), 667n5

base specifier list, 883, 884, 915–917, 925

base-class constructors. *See* constructors

basic exception-safety guarantee, 644, 651

basic source character set, 110, 130

behavior, undefined. *See* undefined behavior

benchmark tests, 114

big-endian **float** layouts, 531–534

binary literals. *See also* digit separator (')

description of, 142–143

further reading for, 146

use cases, 144–146

bit masking and bitwise operations, 144–145

replicating constant binary data, 145–146

binary searches, 292, 294, 944–946

binary trees, 1050–1054

bind function, 14

bit fields, 329n4, 526

bit flags, 347–348

bit masking, 144–145

bit representation of PODs, 530–534

bitwise copies of PODs, exporting, 479–480

bitwise operations, 21–24, 144–145

block scope, 587

boilerplate code

aliases, 136–137

default member initializers, 322

enum class, 333

implementation inheritance, avoiding with, 540–541

repetition, avoiding, 323–325

structural inheritance, avoiding with, 540

variable templates, 161

Boost, 1083–1084

boost::variant, 1180n2

brace elision, 140, 220

braced initialization

annoyances, 247–255

allowing narrowing conversions, 247–248

auto deduction, 253–254

broken macro-invocation syntax, 248–249

copy list initialization in member initializer lists, lack of, 249–250

explicit constructors passed multiple arguments, 250–252

narrowing aggregate initialization, 247

obfuscation with opaque usage, 252–253

operator acceptance, 254–255

C++03 aggregate initialization, 219–222

C++03 initialization syntax, 215–219

C++11 aggregate initialization, 224–225

copy initialization and scalars, 235–236

copy list initialization, 226–228

default member initialization and, 233

description of, 215

direct list initialization, 228–231

further reading for, 256

list initialization, 233–234

potential pitfalls, 242–247

aggregates with deleted constructors, 247

inadvertently calling initializer-list constructors, 242–244

NRVO and implicit moves disabled, 244–246

range-based **for** loops, 684

restrictions on narrowing conversions, 222–224

support for, 562–564

type name omissions, 234

use cases, 236–242

avoiding the most vexing parse, 237–238

defining value-initialized variables, 236–237

uniform initialization in factory functions, 239–241

uniform initialization in generic code, 238–239

uniform member initialization in generic code, 241–242

variables in conditional expressions, 235

variadic templates, 926

braced initialized, 752

braced initializer lists, 554–557, 912–914

brackets ([ ]), 12

buffers

creating with sufficient alignment, 172–173

sufficiently aligned, 187–190

build modes, ABI link safety and, 1071–1074

builder classes, optimizing, 1167–1170

built-in arrays, deducing, 211–212

bytes, 153, 286–287, 503–505, 533–534, 748, 1107

Index

C

C linkage, 403–404

C Standard Library, **noexcept** operator and, 631–632

C++ Language Standard, limerick in, 1081–1082

The C++ Programming Language (Stroustrup), 4

C++03
aggregate initialization, 219–222, 247
double-checked-lock pattern, 81–82
dynamic exception specifications, 1089
explicit-instantiation directives, 353n1
initialization syntax, 215–219
nested templated types, 22
passing multiple arguments to **explicit** constructors, 250–252
POD types, 412–415
right-shift operator (>>), 22–24
unscoped enumerators, workarounds for, 332–333
user-declared, 413n6
weakly typed enumerators, drawbacks to, 333–335

C++11
aggregate initialization, 224–225, 241
conditionally safe features
    alignas specifier, 168–183
    alignof operator, 184–194
    auto variables, 195–214
    constexpr functions, 257–301
    constexpr variables, 302–317
    default member initializers, 318–331
    enum class, 332–352
    extern template, 353–376
    forwarding references, 377–400
    generalized plain old data types (PODs), 401–534
    inheriting constructors, 535–552
    lambda expressions, 573–614
    noexcept operator, 615–659
    opaque enumerations, 660–678
    range-based **for** loops, 679–709
    rvalue references, 26, 710–828
    std::initializer_list, 553–572
    underlying types (UTs), 829–834
    user-defined literals (UDLs), 835–872
    variadic templates, 873–958
interface test, 275
lvalue references, 717–720
lvalue-reference declarations prior to, 815–818
memory allocation, 763n25
new keywords in, 1023
optimized example algorithms, 965–967
POD types. *See* POD types

prvalues, 720–721
safe features
    attribute support, 12–20
    consecutive right-angle brackets (>>), 21–24
    decltype, 25–32
    defaulted functions, 33–45
    delegating constructors, 46–52
    deleted functions, 53–60
    explicit conversion operators, 61–67
    local/unnamed types, 83–88
    long long integral type, 89–94
    [[noreturn]] attribute, 13
    [[noreturn]] attribute in, 95–98
    nullptr keyword, 99–103
    override member-function specifier, 5, 104–107
    raw string literals, 108–114
    static_assert, 115–123
    thread-safe function-scope static variables, 68–82
    trailing return, 28. *See also* **decltype**; deduced return type
    trailing return types, 124–128
    type/template aliases, 133–137
    Unicode string literals, 129–132
scoped enumerations, 335–336
std::unique_ptr<T>, 42n3
unsafe features
    [[carries_dependency]] attribute, 998–1006
    final contextual keyword, 1007–1030
    friend declarations, 1031–1054
    inline namespaces, 1055–1084
    noexcept exception specification, 1085–1152
    ref-qualifiers, 1153–1173
    union type, 1174–1181
user-provided, 413n6
value categories prior to, 814–815
xvalues, 721–723

C++14
capturing *this by copy, 612
conditionally safe features
    constexpr functions, 959–967
    generic lambdas, 968–985
    lambda-capture expressions, 986–995
lvalue references, 717–720
new keywords in, 1023n7
prvalues, 720–721
safe features
    aggregate initialization, 138–141
    binary literals, 142–146
    [[deprecated]] attribute, 14, 147–151

Index

digit separator ('), 152–156
templated variable declarations, 157–166
std::index_sequence, 293
\<type_traits\> header, 1014
unsafe features
  auto return-type deduction, 1182–1204
  decltype(auto) placeholder, 1205–1214
user-defined literals (UDLs) in, 852–853
xvalues, 721–723

C++17
  capturing ***this** by copy, 611n7
  conditionally supported, 425n7
  dynamic exception specifications, 1085n1
  exception specifications and type system, 1089n5
  false sharing, avoiding, 175n6
  fold expressions, 955n25
  guaranteed copy elision, 216n1, 648n11, 805n30, 827n54
  if **constexpr** language feature, 641n10
  nested namespaces, 1055n1
  new keywords in, 1023n7
  pmr allocators, 763n25
  polymorphic memory resources, 190n3
  range-based **for** loops, 681n2
  sentinels, 707n12
  std::any, 187n2
  std::pmr::monotonic_resource, 468n27
  std::pmr::unsynchronized_pool_resource, 468n27
  std::string_view, 874n1
  std::variant, 452n19, 1180n2
  structured binding, 201n2, 685n3
  trivial types, 425n7
  type traits, 651n12

C++20
  bit field initialization, 329n4
  char-like object, 479n29
  concepts, 122n5, 208n3, 480n30, 1201n5
  constexpr functions as destructors, 463n25
  constexpr functions in algorithms, 294n19
  constinit keyword, 75n5, 304n1, 316n8
  contracts, 467n26
  deleted constructors, 247n8
  designated initializers, 139n1
  destructors, 407n3
  encapsulation of helper types, 85n3
  enumeration comparisons, 335n1
  floating-point non-type template parameters, 903n7
  generic lambdas, explicit parameter types, 193–194
  implicit conversion, 223n3
  implicitly movable entities, 735n13
  manifestly constant evaluated, 258n1

  moves in **return** statements, 740n16
  nested namespaces, 1055n1
  new keywords in, 1023n7
  [[no_unique_address]] attribute, 1029n15
  Ranges Library, 686n4, 687n5
  ranges library, 391–393
  relaxed restrictions on **constexpr** functions, 960n1
  reordering data members, 178n10
  requires clause, 486n31
  sentinels, 707n12
  Standard Library–related restrictions, 1078n6
  std::bit_cast, 514n41, 516n42
  std::is_constant_evaluated(), 297n20
  std::is_pod, 438n14
  std::remove_cvref\<T\>, 399n6
  terse concept notation syntax, 398n5
  trivially destructible types, 430n9
  typename disambiguator, 382n1
  unscoped enumerated types, 833n2
  user-declared constructors, 274n7

C++23
  guaranteed copy elision, 805n30
  reordering data members, 178n10

C++-only types, translating to C, 452–456
C99, flexible array members, 404n1
cache associativity, 182n11
cache hit, 181
cache lines, 174–175, 181–183, 459, 1142
cache miss, 182
call operators in functor classes, 574–575
callable objects, 70, 994
callback functions, 669. *See also* lambda expressions
callbacks, event-driven, 603–604
capture default, 582–583, 600, 608
captured by copy, 582, 611–612, 990–992
captured by reference, 582
captured by value. *See* captured by copy
captured variables, 582–585, 590–591, 602, 609–610, 990
[[carries_dependency]] attribute
  description of, 998–1000
  further reading for, 1006
  potential pitfalls, 1005
  use cases, 1000–1005
Carruth, Chandler, 1134
carry dependency, 999
cast, 345
character literals, 837, 844n1
char-like object, 479, 479n29
checkBalance function, 15
checksumLength function, 27, 28n1

Index

Clang
    acquire/release memory barrier, 80n7
    attribute support
        `[[gnu::cold]]` attribute, 15
        `[[gnu::const]]` attribute, 16–17, 19
        `[[gnu::warn_unused_result]]` attribute, 14–15, 15n7
        standardized compiler-specific attributes, 14
    compiler warnings, 150
    delegating constructors, 50n2
    explicit expression of type-consistency, 28n1
    incompatibly specified alignment, 177
    indirect calls, 947n22
    `inline` namespaces, 1061n3
    namespace-qualified name support, 13n2
    nonrecursive `constexpr` algorithms, 961n2, 962n3
    pair mismatches, 699n8
    reducing code size, 1104n16, 1110–1111
    stack unwinding, 621n4
    template instantiation with deduced return type, 1192n3
    trivial copy/move constructors, 528n62
    underspecifying alignment, 176
`[[clang::no_sanitize]]` attribute, 14
class APIs, making explicit, 38–39
class keys, 414–415
class member functions. *See* functions
class template specialization, 1059–1061
class templates, 892. *See also* variadic class templates
    preventing misuse of, 118–119
    `std::initializer_list` usage, 555–558
class types, 405
classes. *See also* constructors; templates
    constraints in hierarchies, 655–658
    enum
        annoyances, 351
        description of, 332–337
        further reading for, 352
        potential pitfalls, 344–350
        use cases, 337–344
    Packet, 27–28
    variadic class templates, 878–880
        member functions, 892–894
        non-type template parameter packs, 901–903
        specialization of, 884–887
        type template parameter packs, 880–884
class-specific memory management, 1088n4
clients
    API migration, facilitating, 1063
    inline namespaces, 1059

closure objects, 974, 978, 986. *See also* lambda expressions; lambda-capture expressions
    deduced return types and, 1197–1198
    forwarding variables into, 992–993
    identity, 968
    moving objects into, 988–989
    mutable state, 989–990
closure types, 87, 578–581, 968–970, 1197
code bloat, 1054
    extern template, 353, 364–365, 371–372, 375
    reducing in object files, 365–369
code duplication, 48–50, 1144–1147
code elision, 1136, 1139
code factoring, impeding with inline namespaces, 1079–1082
code motion, 1136, 1137
code point, 129, 131
code size, reducing, 1101–1111, 1143–1144
code units, 131, 476
cold path, 1103, 1104n16, 1134–1135
Collatz conjecture, 313
Collatz function, 313
Collatz length, 313
Collatz sequence, 313
collisions, 109–111
comma (,) operator, 268, 928, 955n25
    `constexpr` functions, 265
    rvalue references, 816
common initial member sequence (CIMS), 406, 421–423, 447
common type, 1186
compilation errors, forcing with `=delete` syntax. *See* defaulted functions; rvalue references
compiler diagnostics, prompting, 14–15
Compiler Explorer, 1110
compiler warnings, 150
compiler-generated special member functions, 621–626
compiler-synthesized types, 202
compile-time accessible variables. *See* `constexpr` variables
compile-time assertions with `static_assert`
    annoyances, 123
    description of, 115–118
    evaluation in templates, 116–118
    further reading for, 123
    potential pitfalls, 120–122
        misuse to restrict overload sets, 121–122
        unintended compilation failures, 120–121
    syntax and semantics, 115–116

Index

use cases, 118–119
    preventing misuse of class and function templates, 118–119
    verifying assumptions about target platform, 118
compile-time constants
    as conditional expression, 615
    in constant expressions, 838
    constexpr functions, 260–262
    enum class, 346–347
    enumerators as, 164
    pi, 160
    POD types, 463
    user-defined literals (UDLs), 862
compile-time constructible, literal types, 462–464
compile-time coupling, 6, 40–41, 663, 677n11, 1200
compile-time dispatch, 121
compile-time evaluation
    of data tables, 291–295
    diagnosing undefined behavior, 312–314
    low compiler limits, 295
    overhead costs of **constexpr** functions, 298–299
    penalizing run time for, 299–300
    string traversal, 287–291
compile-time introspection, 947
compile-time invocable functions. *See* **constexpr** functions
compile-time polymorphism, 1046–1050
compile-time visitation, 1050–1054
complete types, 184, 316, 832, 891, 1014, 1081
    alignof operator, 184
    default member initializers, 319
    enum class, 350
    opaque enumerations, 661
    prvalues, 720
    rvalue references, 720, 807
complete-class context, 319, 1086n2
component local, 664
components
    extern template, 359–360
    friend declarations, 1035–1036, 1041
    link-safe ABI versioning, 1068
    opaque enumerations, 665, 667
composite patterns, 1020
compound assignment operators, braced lists and, 254–255
compound expressions, **noexcept** operator and, 626–627
concepts, 122n5, 208n3, 480n30, 571, 1201n5
concrete classes, 56, 540
    final contextual keyword, 1008–1009
    mocking, 1017–1020
    performance, 1015–1017
concrete monotonic allocators, 1022

concurrent initialization, 68–69
conditional compilation, 403, 469, 540, 1024n10, 1073
conditional exception specifications, 1091–1092
conditional expressions
    compile-time constants as, 615
    noexcept operator, 615
    variables in, initialization, 235
conditional instantiation, 979–981
conditional **noexcept** specifications, 639, 644
conditionally compile, 469–470
conditionally safe features
    alignas specifier
        description of, 168–172
        memory allocation, 181–183
        natural alignment, 179–181
        potential pitfalls, 176–179
        use cases, 172–176
    alignof operator
        annoyances, 193–194
        description of, 184
        fundamental types, 184
        use cases, 186–193
        user-defined types, 185–186
    auto variables
        annoyances, 212–213
        description of, 195–199
        further reading for, 214
        potential pitfalls, 204–212
        use cases, 200–203
    braced initialization
        annoyances, 247–255
        C++03 aggregate initialization, 219–222
        C++03 initialization syntax, 215–219
        C++11 aggregate initialization, 224–225
        copy initialization and scalars, 235–236
        copy list initialization, 226–228
        default member initialization and, 233
        description of, 215
        direct list initialization, 228–231
        further reading for, 256
        list initialization, 233–234
        potential pitfalls, 242–247
        restrictions on narrowing conversions, 222–224
        type name omissions, 234
        use cases, 236–242
        variables in conditional expressions, 235
    constexpr functions
        annoyances, 299–300
        compile-time evaluation, 284–286
        constructor constraints, 269–276
        description of, 257–261, 959–960
        further reading for, 301, 965
        inlining and definition visibility, 262–265

Index

conditionally safe features (cont.)
  constexpr functions (cont.)
    literal types, 278–284
    member functions, 266–268
    optimized C++11 example algorithms, 965–967
    parameter and return types, 277–278
    as part of contract, 261–262
    potential pitfalls, 295–299, 314
    relaxed restrictions in C++14, 959–967
    restrictions on, 268–269
    templates, 276–277
    type system and function pointers, 265–266
    use cases, 286–295, 961–964
  constexpr variables
    annoyances, 314–316
    description of, 302–307
    potential pitfalls, 314
    use cases, 307–314
  default member initializers, 6
    annoyances, 328–330
    description of, 318–321
    potential pitfalls, 326–328
    use cases, 322–325
  definition of, 5–6
  enum class
    annoyances, 351
    description of, 332–337
    further reading for, 352
    potential pitfalls, 344–350
    use cases, 337–344
  extern template
    annoyances, 373–375
    description of, 353–365
    further reading for, 376
    potential pitfalls, 371–373
    use cases, 365–370
  forwarding references
    annoyances, 397–400
    description of, 377–385
    further reading for, 400
    potential pitfalls, 394–397
    use cases, 386–393
  generalized plain old data types (PODs)
    annoyances, 521–529
    bit representation, 530–534
    C++03 POD types, 412–415
    C++11 POD types, 415–417
    description of, 401–402
    further reading for, 530
    future direction, 438–439
    potential pitfalls, 479–521
    privileges, 402–412

    standard-layout class special properties, 420–425
    standard-layout types, 417–420
    trivial subcategories, 429–436
    trivial types, 425–429
    type traits, 436–438
    use cases, 439–479
  generic lambdas
    annoyances, 981–984
    description of, 968–975
    further reading for, 985
    potential pitfalls, 981
    use cases, 975–981
  inheriting constructors
    annoyances, 549–552
    description of, 535–539
    potential pitfalls, 546–549
    use cases, 539–545
  lambda expressions
    annoyances, 611–614
    description of, 573–597
    further reading for, 614
    potential pitfalls, 607–611
    use cases, 597–607
  lambda-capture expressions
    annoyances, 993–994
    description of, 986–988
    further reading for, 995
    potential pitfalls, 992–993
    use cases, 988–992
  noexcept operator
    annoyances, 650–658
    description of, 615–634
    further reading for, 658
    move operations, 658–659
    potential pitfalls, 647–650
    use cases, 634–647
  opaque enumerations
    annoyances, 677–678
    description of, 660–663
    further reading for, 678
    potential pitfalls, 675–677
    use cases, 663–675
  range-based **for** loops
    annoyances, 703–709
    description of, 679–684
    further reading for, 709
    potential pitfalls, 691–703
    use cases, 684–691
  rvalue references
    annoyances, 804–812
    decltype results as, 26
    description of, 710–741
    further reading for, 813
    potential pitfalls, 782–804

Index

use cases, 741–781

value category evolution, 813–828

std::initializer_list

  annoyances, 567–571

  description of, 553–561

  further reading for, 571

  potential pitfalls, 566–567

  range-based **for** loops, 571–572

  use cases, 561–566

underlying types (UTs)

  description of, 829–830

  further reading for, 834

  potential pitfalls, 832–833

  use cases, 830–832

user-defined literals (UDLs)

  annoyances, 869–871

  description of, 835–853

  further reading for, 872

  potential pitfalls, 867–869

  use cases, 853–867

variadic templates

  annoyances, 953–957

  description of, 873–925

  further reading for, 958

  potential pitfalls, 952–953

  use cases, 925–951

conditionally supported, 425n7

conditionally supported behavior, 13n2

configuration structs, 139

conforming implementations, 14n4, 171n2

consecutive right-angle brackets (>>)

  description of, 21

  further reading for, 24

  potential pitfalls with, 22–24

  use cases, 22

const data members

  difficulty of synthesizing, 993–994

  memcpy usage on, 489–493

  returning as *rvalues* pessimizes performance, 786–787

const default constructible, 218

const objects, representation by initializer lists, 570

const variables, capturing modifiable copy of, 990–992

constant binary data, replicating, 145–146

constant expressions, 115, 224, 257. *See also* **constexpr** functions; **constexpr** variables

  compile-time constants in, 838

  conditional exception specifications, 1091

  noexcept exception specifications, 1129

  trivially destructible types, 431

  user-defined literals (UDLs), 836

constant initialization, 75

constant time, 636, 823

constants, named, 346–347

  const-default-constructible, 218

  constexpr data structures, storing, 311–312

constexpr functions

  in algorithms, 294n19

  annoyances, 299–300

    implicit **const**-qualification, 300

    penalizing run time to enable compile time, 299–300

  compile-time evaluation, 284–286

  constructor constraints, 269–276

  description of, 257–261

  destructors, 463n25

  further reading for, 301

  inlining and definition visibility, 262–265

  literal types, 278–284

  member functions, 266–268

  noexcept operator and, 654–655

  parameter and return types, 277–278

  as part of contract, 261–262

  potential pitfalls, 295–299, 314

    implementation difficulties, 296–297

    low compiler limits, 295

    overhead costs, 298–299

    overzealous usage, 298

    premature commitment, 297–298

  relaxed restrictions in C++14, 959–967

    description of, 959–960

    further reading for, 965

    optimized C++11 example algorithms, 965–967

    use cases, 961–964

  relaxed restrictions on. *See* **constexpr** variables; variadic templates

  restrictions on, 268–269

  templates, 276–277

  type system and function pointers, 265–266

  use cases, 286–295

    alternative to function-like macros, 286–287

    compile-time data table evaluation, 291–295

    compile-time string traversal, 287–291

    user-defined literals (UDLs), 838–839

constexpr specifier, 28n1

constexpr variables

  annoyances, 314–316

    static **constexpr** member variables not defined in own class, 316

    static member variables require external definitions, 314–315

  description of, 302–307

  initializer undefined behavior, 306–307

  internal linkage, 307

Index

constexpr variables (cont.)
    potential pitfalls, 314
    use cases, 307–314
        alternative to enumerated compile-time
            integral constants, 307–310
        diagnosing undefined behavior at compile
            time, 312–314
        nonintegral symbolic numeric constants,
            310–311
        storing **constexpr** data structures, 311–
            312
constinit keyword, 75n5, 304n1, 316n8
const-qualified member functions, 300
constraining
    deduced parameters, 970–973
    multiple arguments, 983–984
constructors. *See also* copy constructors; move
        constructors
    boilerplate code repetition, avoiding, 323–
        325
    code duplication, avoiding, 48–50
    delegating
        description of, 46–48
        potential pitfalls, 50–51
        use cases, 48–50
    deleted in aggregates, 247
    explicit, passing multiple arguments, 250–
        252
    inheriting
        annoyances, 549–552
        description of, 535–539
        potential pitfalls, 546–549
        use cases, 539–545
    restrictions on, 269–276
    for std::initializer_list, inadvertently
        calling, 242–244
    as trivial, 437
    user-declared, 274n7, 1087
    value initializing arguments, avoiding the
        most vexing parse, 237–238
containers
    initialization, 561–562
    iterating all elements, 684–685
    nested, 22
contextual keywords, 1007. *See also* keywords
    override
        description of, 104–105
        further reading for, 107
        potential pitfalls, 106
        use cases, 105–106
    potential pitfalls, 1023
contextually convertible to **bool**, 63–65, 1129
continuous refactoring, 147

contract guarantees
    nofail functions, 1117–1122
    overly strong, 1112–1116
contract violations, 485
contracts, 467n26, 485
    constexpr functions as part of, 261–262
    new operator, 616
    overly restrictive, 480–482
    rvalue references, 714
control constructs
    emulating, 599–600
    in lambda expressions, 600–601
controlling constant expressions, 285
conventional string literals, 113
conversion operators
    explicit
        description of, 61–63
        potential pitfalls, 66–67
        use cases, 63–65
    as placeholders, 1193–1194
converting constructors, 61
cooked UDL operators, 841, 843–845, 870
cookies, 669–675
copy assignable, 485–486
copy assignment, 485, 758
copy assignment operator
    deleted functions, 54
    rvalue references, 714
    user-provided, 759
    vertical encoding, 451
copy constructible, 455
copy construction, 489–492
copy constructors
    declaring special member functions, 34
    deleted functions, 54
    hijacking with perfect-forwarding construc-
        tor, 395–397
    literal types and, 281
    rvalue references, 714
    RVO and NRVO requirements, 804–805
    as trivial, 437
    user-provided, 758–759
    vertical encoding, 450
copy elision, 390
copy initialization, 215–216
    in aggregate initialization, 221
    in generic code, 239
    for nonstatic data members, 318
    scalar type, 235–236
    unions, 506
copy list initialization, 226–228
    direct list initialization, compared, 231–232
    in factory functions, 240
    in generic code, 239
    in member initializer lists, 249–250

for nonstatic data members, 318
std::initializer_list, 555
copy operations, 522, 627
deleted functions, 53
move operations as optimization of, 741–767
rvalue references, 715
sink arguments, 782–783
some equivalent to moves, 788
copy semantics, 54, 627, 742, 852
copy/direct, 215
copy/swap idiom, 636, 1097
core constant expression, 960n1
core language specification, 482
core traits, 482
.cpp files, 41n2
critical section, 71
C-style ellipsis, 952
C-style functions, 158
curiously recurring template pattern (CRTP), 1042–1054
compile-time polymorphism, 1046–1050
compile-time visitation, 1050–1054
refactoring, 1042–1044
synthesizing equality, 1045–1046
currying, 597–598
cv-qualifiers, 1153–1154, 1157–1158, 1207–1208
forwarding references, 379
as literal types, 280
rvalue references, 724
as standard-layout types, 417
as trivial types, 425
cyclic physical dependency, 374
cyclically dependent, 75

D
d_engaged flag, 1072
dangling references, 566–567, 607–608, 1171, 1212
data dependency, 999
data dependency chains, 998–999, 1002
data members
const
difficulty of synthesizing, 993–994
memcpy usage on, 489–493
returning as *rvalues* pessimizes performance, 786–787
reordering, 178n10
strengthening alignment, 168, 170–171
data races, 68–69
data structures, **constexpr**, 311–312
data tables, compile-time evaluation, 291–295
death tests, 656
debug build, 468
debugging lambda expressions, 611
decay (of a type), 815
decimal floating-point (DFP), 862

declarations, 121, 315, 879
friend
curiously recurring template pattern (CRTP) use cases, 1042–1054
description of, 1031–1033
further reading for, 1042
potential pitfalls, 1041
use cases, 1033–1041
prior to C++11, 815–818
user-provided destructors, 1105
declarator operators, 889
declared interface, 987
declared type (of an object), 25
declaring
deleted functions, 58–59
function pointers, 127–128
decltype. *See also* **auto** variables; **decltype(auto)**
placeholder; rvalue references
annoyances, 31
description of
use with entities, 25
use with expressions, 25–26
potential pitfalls, 30
use cases
avoidance of explicit typenames, 26–27
creation of auxiliary variable of generic type, 28
explicit expression of type-consistency, 27–28, 28n1
validation of generic expressions, 28–30
decltype(auto) placeholder
annoyances, 1213
description of, 1205–1210
in new expressions, 1210
potential pitfalls, 1212–1213
specification, 1206–1208
syntactic restrictions, 1208–1209
use cases, 1210–1212
declval function, 31
deduced parameters, constraints on, 970–973
deduced return types, 593–594, 1146
annoyances, 1201–1203
description of, 1182–1194
for lambda expressions, 1189–1190, 1197–1198
potential pitfalls, 1200
use cases, 1194–1200
compiler-applied rules, 1197
complicated return types, 1194–1196
delaying return-type deduction, 1199–1120
perfect returning wrapped functions, 1198
returning lambda expressions, 1197–1198

Index

deducing
    built-in arrays, 211–212
    list initialization, 210–211
    pointer types, 197–198
    reference types, 198
deeply nested variable types, 202–203
default constructed, 478, 752
default constructors, 754, 1136
    declaring special member functions, 33–34
    suppressed by std::initializer_list, 568–570
    as trivial, 437
    user-provided, 755
default initialization, 216–219, 765
    in aggregate initialization, 221
    constexpr functions, 273
    for nonstatic data members, 322–323
default initialized, 493, 752
default member initialization, 233
default member initializers
    aggregate initialization with, 138–141
    annoyances, 328–330
        applicability limitations, 329
        array size deduction, lack of, 330
        loss of aggregate status, 330
        loss of triviality, 329–330
        parenthesized direct-initialization syntax, lack of, 328–329
    constexpr functions, 270
    description of, 318–321
    potential pitfalls, 326–328
        inconsistent subobject intialization, 326–328
        loss of insulation, 326
    safety of, 6
    trivial types, 426
    union interactions, 320–321
    use cases, 322–325
        boilerplate repetition, avoiding, 323–325
        documentation of default values, 325
        nonstatic data member initialization, 322–323
        simple struct initialization, 322
default values, documentation of, 325
defaulted default constructors, exception specifications and, 1087
defaulted functions, 522, 649. *See also* deleted functions; rvalue references; **static_assert**
    annoyances, 42–43
    description of, 33–36
    exception specifications and, 1086
    first declaration of special member function, 34–35
    further reading for, 44

implementation of user-provided special member function, 35–36
    implicit generation of special member functions, 44–45
    potential pitfalls, 41–42
    use cases, 36–41
        making explicit class APIs with no runtime cost, 38–39
        physically decoupling interface from implementation, 40–41
        preserving type triviality, 39–40
        restoring generation of suppressed special member function, 36–37
defaulted special member functions. *See* defaulted functions
defaulted template parameters, 31
default/value, 215
defect reports (DR), 432n10, 615n2, 722n8, 1086n2
defensive checks, 468, 744
defensive programming, 1024
defined behavior, 1112–1113
defining declarations, 729
definition (of objects), 68
definitions, 315, 879
delaying return-type deduction, 1199–1200
delegating constructors
    description of, 46–48
    potential pitfalls, 50–51
        delegation cycles, 50–51
        suboptimal factoring, 51
    use cases, 48–50
delegation cycles, 50–51
deleted functions, 33–34, 757, 1086n2. *See also* defaulted functions; rvalue references
    annoyances, 58–59
    description of, 53
    further reading for, 60
    as trivial, 523
    use cases, 53–57
        hiding structural base class member functions, 56–57
        preventing implicit conversion, 55–56
        suppressing special member function generation, 53–55
dependency. *See* data dependency
dependent base classes. *See* inheriting constructors
dependent types
    generic lambdas, 981
    inheriting constructors, 538
[[deprecated]] attribute, 14
    description of, 147–148
    potential pitfalls, 150
    use cases, 148–150

derived classes
    compile-time visitation, 1050–1054
    preventing with **final** contextual keyword, 1007, 1014–1015
design patterns, 669
designated initializers, 139n1
destructive move, lack of, 811–812
destructors
    in C++20, 407n3
    as **constexpr** functions, 463n25
    declaring special member functions, 34
    exception specifications and, 1086
    final contextual keyword, 1008
    noexcept by default, 653–654
    rvalue references, 752
    skippable, 464–470
    user-provided, 755–757
    vertical encoding, 450
devirtualize, 1011
diagnostics, compiler, 14–15
diffusion, 183n14
digit separator ('). *See also* binary literals
    description of, 152–153
    further reading for, 154
    loss of precision in floating-point literals, 154–156
    use cases, 153
dimensional unit types, 863–865
direct aggregate initialization, 493
direct braced initialized, 455
direct initialization, 215, 754
    explicit conversion operators, 62
    in factory functions, 240
    in generic code, 239
    of members, 241–242
    for nonstatic data members, 318
    syntax, 328–329
direct initialized, 230
direct list initialization, 228–231
    copy list initialization, compared, 231–232
    in factory functions, 240
    in generic code, 239
    of members, 241–242
    for nonstatic data members, 318
    std::initializer_list, 555
direct mapped, 182n11
disabling
    implicit moves, 244–246
    named return-value optimization (NRVO), 783–784
    NRVO, 244–246
disambiguators, 28–30
discriminated unions, 937–948, 1177–1180
divide and conquer, 297
documentation of default values, 325

double-checked-lock pattern (C++03), 81–82
duck typing, 1052
dumb data, 668n7
duplicate names, loss of access in namespaces, 1056–1058
dynamic binding, 1015
dynamic dispatch, 1011
dynamic exception specifications, 618–619, 1085, 1089, 1090
    compatibility with **noexcept** specifications, 621
    noexcept exception specification, compared, 1101–1102
    violating, 1093
dynamic types, 416

E

EBCDIC, 129n1
Effective C++ (Meyers), 3
elaborated type specifiers, 1031–1032
embedded development, 145
embedded systems, 1101
embedding code in C++ programs, 111–112
emplacement, 390–391
empty-base optimization (EBO), 185, 499, 607, 933, 1028–1030
encapsulation
    of helper types, 85n3
    of implementation details, 343–344
    opaque enumerations, 663
    types within functions, 84–85
encoding prefixes, 844
entities
    decltype use with, 25–26
    [[deprecated]] attribute, 147–150
enum class
    annoyances, 351
    description of, 332–337
    further reading for, 352
    potential pitfalls, 344–350
        bit flags, 347–348
        collections of named constants, 346–347
        external use of opaque enumerators, 350
        iteration, 348–350
        strong typing can be counterproductive, 344–346
    scoped enumerations, 335–336
    underlying types (UTs) and, 337
    unscoped C++03 enumerations, work-arounds for, 332–333
    use cases, 337–344
        encapsulating implementation details, 343–344
        implicit conversion to arithmetic types, avoiding, 337–339

Index

enum class (cont.)
 use cases (cont.)
  namespace pollution, avoiding, 339–340
  overloading disambiguation, 340–343
  weakly typed C++03 enumerators, drawbacks to, 333–335
enumerations. *See also* opaque enumerations
 comparisons in C++20, 335n1
 underlying types (UTs)
  description of, 829–830
  further reading for, 834
  potential pitfalls, 832–833
  use cases, 830–832
enumerators, as compile-time constants, 164
errors
 compiler warnings as, 150
 compile-time, 22
escalation, 374
essential behavior, 102
event-driven callbacks, 603–604
exception agnostic, 644, 1126
exception free path, 1134, 1136, 1143
exception safe, 644, 1126
exception specifications, 593. *See also* **noexcept**
  exception specifications
 conditional, 1091–1092
 constraints in class hierarchies, 655–658
 dynamic, 618–619
 function types and, 1147–1148
 text-segment size comparison, 1108
 type system and, 1089n5
 unconditional, 1085–1089
 violating, 1093
exceptions, 615–618, 1104
excess N notation, 155
executable images, 1135
execution character sets, 844
expansion. *See* pack expansion
expiring objects, 741–742, 749
expiring value
 rvalue references, 712–713
 xvalues, 721–723
explicit class APIs, 38–39
explicit constructors, passing multiple arguments, 250–252
explicit conversion operators
 description of, 61–63
 potential pitfalls, 66–67
 use cases, 63–65
explicit instantiation declarations
 annoyances, 373–375
  member validity, 374–375
  unrelated class definitions, 373–374
 description of, 353–365
 further reading for, 376

illustrative example, 355–359
.o files, effect on, 359–365
potential pitfalls, 371–373
 corresponding explicit-instantiation declarations and definitions, 371–372
 pessimization over optimization, 373
use cases, 365–370
 insulation from client code, 369–370
 reducing code bloat in object files, 365–369
explicit instantiation definitions, 353–355, 358–359, 363, 370–375
explicit instantiation directives, 353n1, 354–355, 369, 375
explicit template argument specifications, 895
explicit typenames, 26–27
explicitly captured, 582–583
explicitly copied, 583
explicitly declaring special member functions, 33–34
exporting bitwise copies of PODs, 479–480
expression alias, 1146–1147
expression SFINAE, 29n3, 122, 126
expression templates, 202–203
expressions. *See also* lambda expressions
 compound, **noexcept** operator and, 626–627
 decltype use with, 25–26
 decomposing complex, 391–393
 rvalue references in, 730–731
 validation of, 28–30
extended alignment, 168–170
extended **friend** declarations. *See* **friend** declarations
extended **typedef**. *See* aliases
extern template
 annoyances, 373–375
  member validity, 374–375
  unrelated class definitions, 373–374
 description of, 353–365
 further reading for, 376
 illustrative example, 355–359
 .o files, effect on, 359–365
 potential pitfalls, 371–373
  corresponding explicit-instantiation declarations and definitions, 371–372
  pessimization over optimization, 373
 use cases, 365–370
  insulation from client code, 369–370
  reducing code bloat in object files, 365–369
external definitions for static member variables, 314–315
external linkages, 307
external static analysis, control of, 17–18

Index

F

factory functions, 239–241, 929–930
  perfect forwarding, 388–389
  rvalue references, 790, 804–805
  sink arguments, 778–779
  uniform initialization in, 239–241
  user-defined literals (UDLs), 836–838, 851
  wrapping initialization in, 389–390
factory operator, 837
fallible, 1118
fallible implementation, 1120
false sharing, 174–179, 182
fault tolerant, 1123
fault-tolerant nofail guarantee, 1123
fences, 82
Feynman, Richard, 1
file extensions, 667n5
final contextual keyword
  annoyances, 1028–1030
  description of, 1007–1014
  further reading for, 1030
  override member-function specifier, interactions with, 1007, 1009–1011
  potential pitfalls, 1023–1027
    as contextual keyword, 1023
    hiding nonvirtual functions, 1026–1027
    systemic lost reusability, 1023–1026
  with pure virtual functions, 1008–1009
  as unsafe, 6
  use cases, 1014–1023
    performance of concrete classes, 1015–1017
    protocol hierarchy performance improvements, 1020–1023
    restoration of performance lost to mocking, 1017–1020
    suppressed derivation for portability, 1014–1015
  with user-defined types (UDTs), 1011–1014
  with virtual destructors, 1008
  virtual keyword, interactions with, 1009–1011
  with virtual member functions, 1007–1008
fixed-capacity strings, 470–479
flexible array members, 404n1
floating-point literals, 154–156, 837, 869–870
floating-point non-type template parameters, 903n7
floating-point types, 223
  big-endian and little-endian layouts, 531–534
  IEEE 754, 530–534
  precision of, 155
  user-defined literals (UDLs), 862
floating-point-to-integer conversion, 843

flow of control, 68
fold expressions, 955n25
footprint, 1114
  extern template, 357
  POD types, 452, 475
  rvalue references, 734, 747
for loops, range-based, 571–572
  annoyances, 703–709
  description of, 679–684
  further reading for, 709
  potential pitfalls, 691–703
  use cases, 684–691
for range declaration, 681–682
forward class declarations, 675
forward declarations, 662
forward declared, 664–665
forwarding references
  annoyances, 397–400
    metafunction requirements in constraints, 398–400
    similarity to rvalue references, 397–398
  auto return-type deduction, 1184
  auto&&, 383–384
  description of, 377–385
  function template argument type deduction, 379–380
  further reading for, 400
  generic lambdas, 971
  identifying, 382–383
  lambda-capture expressions, 992
  not forwarding, 384–385
  potential pitfalls, 394–397
    hijacking copy constructor, 395–397
    std::forward<T>, enabling move operations, 395
    template instantiations with string literals, 394–395
  range-based **for** loops, 680
  reference collapsing, 380–382
  rvalue references, 732, 806–807
  std::forward<T>, 385
  use cases, 386–393
    decomposing complex expressions, 391–393
    emplacement, 390–391
    forwarding expressions to downstream consumers, 386
    multiple parameter handling, 386–388
    perfect forwarding for generic factory functions, 388–389
    wrapping initialization in generic factory functions, 389–390
-fpermissive flag, 1080n9
fragmentation, 183n14

Index

free functions, 442
  declaring, 58
  overloading, 570–571
  range-based **for** loops, 571–572, 707–709
  std::initializer_list, 558
free operators, 839
freestanding, 570
friend declarations
  description of, 1031–1033
  further reading for, 1042
  potential pitfalls, 1041
  use cases, 1033–1041
    curiously recurring template pattern (CRTP), 1041–1054
    declaring previously declared type as friend, 1033–1034
    enforcing initiatlization with PassKey idiom, 1036–1038
    special type access, 1038–1041
    type aliases as customization point, 1034–1036
full expressions, 693
full specialization, 355–357, 1059–1062
fully associative, 182n11
fully constructed, 47
function call argument list, 912–914
function calls, hooking, 930–931
function declarations. *See also* functions
  [[carries_dependency]] attribute, 1000
  [[noreturn]] attribute in
    description of, 95
    further reading for, 98
    potential pitfalls, 97–98
    use cases, 95–97
  override keyword in
    description of, 104–105
    further reading for, 107
    potential pitfalls, 106
    use cases, 105–106
  trailing return types
    description of, 124–126
    further reading for, 128
    use cases, 126–128
  virtual, **override**, **final** keywords, 1009–1011
function definitions, reducing code size, 1105
function designators, 815
function objects, 328, 574, 990
function parameter packs, 879, 888–892
  pack expansion, 911–912
  Rule of Fair Matching, 898–899
function pointers
  calls through, 574
  generic lambda conversion to, 974–975
  noexcept and, 1089–1091

[[noreturn]] attribute misuse, 98
  readability of declarations, 127–128
  type system and, 265–266
function prototypes, 733
function references, **noexcept** and, 1089–1091
function template argument matching, 900–901
function template argument type deduction, 195, 379–380
function templates
  instantiation and specialization, 1190–1192
  preventing misuse of, 118–119
  return type dependent on parameter type, 126
functions. *See also* **constexpr** functions; constructors; defaulted functions; deleted functions; destructors; factory functions; special member functions
  arguments of same type, 564–565
  auto return-type deduction
    annoyances, 1201–1203
    description of, 1182–1194
    potential pitfalls, 1200
    use cases, 1194–1200
  bind, 14
  checkBalance, 15
  checksumLength, 27, 28n1
  declval, 31
  dynamic exception specifications, 618–619
  encapsulating types within, 84–85
  generic variadic functions, 925–926
  hereticalFunction, 17–18
  linearInterpolation, 16–17
  loggedSum, 28, 31
  myRandom, 19
  noexcept exception specifications, 619–621
  overloading, 1089n6
  preconditions, 18
  pure, 16
  ref-qualifiers
    annoyances, 1171–1172
    description of, 1153–1160
    further reading for, 1173
    potential pitfalls, 1170–1171
    use cases, 1160–1170
  reportError, 15
  sortRange, 28–30
  sortRangeImpl, 28–30
  start, 14
  std::kill_dependency, 999–1000
  unusable in variadic templates, 953–954
  variadic function templates, 888
    function parameter packs, 888–892
    function template argument matching, 900–901
    template argument deductions, 894–896

variadic member functions, 892–894
vectorLerp, 16–17
function-scope static variables
  annoyances, 80
  C++03 double-checked-lock pattern, 81–82
  concurrent initialization, 68–69
  description of, 68–71
  destruction, 69
  further reading for, 81
  logger example, 69–70
  multithreaded contexts, 70–71
  potential pitfalls, 75–80
    dangerous recursive initialization, 77
    dependence on order-of-destruction of local objects, 78–80
    initialization not guaranteed, 75–77
    recursion subtleties, 77–78
  use cases, 71–75
function-try-block, 268
functor classes, 574–575
functor types, 573
functors, 573
fundamental alignment, 168
fundamental integral types
  historical perspective on, 93–94
  long long
    description of, 89
    further reading for, 92
    potential pitfalls, 91–92
    use cases, 89–91
fundamental types, 803, 1014
  alignof operator, 184
  hidden properties of, 209–210
  union membership and, 1174

G
GCC
  acquire/release memory barrier, 80n7
  ambiguity errors, 340n2
  attribute support
    [[gnu::cold]] attribute, 15
    [[gnu::**const**]] attribute, 16–17, 19
    [[gnu::warn_unused_result]] attribute, 14–15, 15n7
    [[gsl::suppress]] attribute, 17–18
    standardized compiler-specific attributes, 14
  auto redeclaration, 1209
  binary literals, 142n1
  compiler warnings, 150
  deduced parameters, 972n1
  default initialization, 218
  delegating constructors, 50n2
  explicit expression of type-consistency in, 28n1

-fpermissive flag, 1080n9
incompatibly specified alignment, 177
indirect calls, 947n22
inline namespaces, 1061n3
namespace-qualified name support, 13n2
nonrecursive **constexpr** algorithms, 962n3
pointer compatibility, 1090n7
reducing code size, 1104n16, 1110
stack unwinding, 621n4
template instantiation with deduced return type, 1192n3
trivial copy/move constructors, 528n62
underspecifying alignment, 176
generalized attribute support. *See* attribute support
generalized plain old data types (PODs)
  annoyances, 521–529
    C++ Standard not stabilized, 521–527
    standard type traits unreliable, 527–528
    std::pair and std:tuple of PODs are not PODs, 528–529
  bit representation, 530–534
  C++03 POD types, 412–415
  C++11 POD types, 415–417
  description of, 401–402
  further reading for, 530
  future direction, 438–439
  potential pitfalls, 479–521
    abuse of **reinterpret_cast**, 506–519
    aggressive use of offsetof, 520–521
    conflating arbitrary and indeterminate values, 493–497
    exporting bitwise copies of PODs, 479–480
    ineligible use of std::memcpy, 497–501
    memcpy usage on **const** or reference subobjects, 489–493
    misuse of unions, 505–506
    naive copying other than std::memcpy, 501–505
    requiring PODs or trivial types, 480–482
    sloppy terminology, 488–489
    wrong type traits, 482–488
  privileges, 402–412
    bitwise copyability, 409–410
    contiguous storage, 405
    object lifetime begins at allocation, 407–409
    offsetof macro usage, 410–412
    predictable layout, 405–407
  standard-layout class special properties, 420–425
  standard-layout types, 417–420
  trivial subcategories, 429–436
  trivial types, 425–429

Index

generalized plain old data types (PODs) (cont.)
    type traits, 436–438
    use cases, 439–479
        compile-time constructible, literal types, 462–464
        fixed-capacity string elements, 476–479
        fixed-capacity strings, 470–475
        navigating compound objects with `offsetof`, 456–460
        secure buffers, 460–462
        skippable destructors, 464–470
        translating C++-only types to C, 452–456
        vertical encoding for non-trivial types, 448–452
        vertical encoding within a union, 439–448
general-purpose machines, 93
generic code
    member initialization in, 241–242
    uniform initialization in, 238–239
generic expressions, validating with **decltype**, 28–30
generic factory functions. *See* factory functions
generic lambdas
    annoyances, 981–984
        cannot use full power of template-argument deduction, 981–982
        difficulty constraining multiple arguments, 983–984
    constraints on deduced parameters, 970–973
    conversion to function pointer, 974–975
    description of, 968–975
    explicit parameter types, 193–194
    further reading for, 985
    lambda captures, 969–970
    mutable closures, 969–970
    potential pitfalls, 981
    use cases, 975–981
        applying lambdas to tuple elements, 975–976
        conditional instantiation, 979–981
        recursive lambdas, 977–979
        reusable lambda expressions, 975
        terse, robust lambdas, 976–977
    variadic, 973–974
generic programming, 615
generic types, 28, 878
generic value-semantic types (VSTs), creating, 762–767
generic variadic functions, 925–926
glvalues, 717
GNU, nonstandard primitives, 956n27
[[gnu::cold]] attribute, 15
[[gnu::**const**]] attribute, 16–17, 19

[[gnu::pure]] attribute, 14, 16
[[gnu::warn_unused_result]] attribute, 14–15, 15n7
golden files, 114
greater-than operator (>), 21–22
grouping macros, 520
gsl::span type, 17
[[gsl::suppress]] attribute, 17–18
guaranteed copy elision, 216n1, 567n2, 648n11, 717n4, 790–791, 805n30, 807n31, 827n54, 1163n1
Guidelines Support Library, 17

H
handle types, 792
hard UB. *See* language undefined behavior
header files, 41n2, 663–665
header-only library, 1067
helper functions. *See* functions
helper types, encapsulation of, 85n3
hereticalFunction, 17–18
hidden friend idiom, 472
hidden properties of fundamental types, 209–210
hiding
    member functions, 56–57
    nonvirtual functions, 1026–1027
hierarchical reuse, 1012, 1023–1026
higher-order functions, 125
high-level value semantic types (VSTs), creating, 751–762
hooking function calls, 930–931
horizontal microcode, 445n17
hot paths, 1134–1136, 1139, 1142
Hyrum's law, 85, 1012, 1014, 1036

I
ICC
    incompatibly specified alignment, 177
    underspecifying alignment, 176
identity closure objects, 968
identityInt, 968
id-expression, 25, 780
IEEE 754 floating-point types, 530–534
if constexpr language feature, 641n10
ill formed, 120, 1067, 1071, 1077, 1203
ill formed, no diagnostic required (IFNDR), 1000
    constexpr functions, 262–263
    delegating constructors, 50
    enum class, 350
    incompatibly specified alignment, 176–177
    inline namespaces, 1067, 1072, 1079
    [[noreturn]] attribute, 97
    opaque enumerations, 666, 675–676, 832
    static assertions in templates, 116–118
    variadic templates, 900

immutable types, optimizing, 1167–1170
imperative programming, 959
implementation defined, 1093
    alignments, 168–169
    NULL macro, 100
    opaque enumerations, 660
implementation inheritance, avoiding boilerplate
    code with, 540–541
implementation-defined behavior
    enum class, 335
    limits on, 295
    unrecognized attributes, 12, 18–19
implementation-defined types, 202, 501
implicit **const**-qualification, 300
implicit constructors, inheriting, 546–549
implicit conversion, 66, 223n3
    to arithmetic types, avoiding, 337–339
    preventing, 55–56, 201
implicit generation of special member functions,
    44–45
implicit moves
    disabling, 244–246
    in **return** statements, 735–737
implicitly captured, 582–583
implicitly declared, 522
implicitly declared default constructors, 568–570
implicitly movable entities, 735n13
in contract, 1122–1123
in place, 734
indentation of string literals, 112–113
indeterminate values, 435, 493–497
infallible, 1118
infallible implementation, 1118–1123
inheritance
    improving concrete class performance,
        1015–1017
    preventing with **final** contextual keyword,
        1008, 1012
inheriting constructors. *See also* default member
        initializers; defaulted functions; delegat-
        ing constructors; deleted functions; for-
        warding references; **override** member-
        function specifier; variadic templates
    annoyances, 549–552
        access levels same as in base class, 549–
            551
        cannot select individually, 549
        flawed initial specification, 551–552
    description of, 535–539
    potential pitfalls, 546–549
        implicit constructors, 546–549
        new constructors in base class alters
            behavior, 546

use cases, 539–545
    implementation inheritance, avoiding
        boilerplate code, 540–541
    reusable functionality through mix-ins,
        545
    strong **typedef** implementation, 541–544
    structural inheritance, avoiding boiler-
        plate code, 540
init capture, 986
initialization. *See also* aggregate initialization;
        braced initialization; copy initializa-
        tion; copy list initialization; default
        initialization; default member ini-
        tializers; direct initialization; direct
        list initialization; list initialization;
        std::initializer_list; uniform ini-
        tialization; value initialization
    of bit fields, 329n4
    concurrent, 68–69
    constant, 75
    enforcing with PassKey idiom, 1036–1038
    recursive, 77–78, 163–165
    of simple structs, 322
    subobject, inconsistency in, 326–328
    of subobjects, inconsistency in, 326–328
    thread-safe function-scope static variables,
        68–69
    trivial default, 1087
    of variables, 200
    wrapping in factory functions, 389–390
initializer lists. *See* std::initializer_list
initializer_list. *See* std::initializer_list
initializers, undefined behavior with **constexpr**
        variables, 306–307
inline namespace sets, 1056
inline namespaces. *See also* **alignas** specifier
    annoyances, 1079–1082
        code factoring, impeding, 1079–1082
        one-to-one relationship with namespaces,
            1082
    argument-dependent lookup (ADL) interop-
        erability, 1058–1059
    class template specialization, 1059–1061
    description of, 1055–1062
    duplicate names, loss of access to, 1056–
        1058
    further reading for, 1083
    potential pitfalls, 1076–1079
        inconsistent use of inline keyword, 1079
        lack of scalability, 1076–1077
        library evolution, 1077–1079
    reopening, 1061–1062

Index

inline namespaces (cont.)
    use cases, 1062–1076
        ABI link safety and build modes, 1071–1074
        API migration, facilitating, 1062–1067
        link-safe ABI versioning, 1067–1071
        selective **using** directives for short-named entities, 1074–1076
        versioning case study, 1083–1084
inline specifier, 262–265
in-process value-semantic type (VST), 1034
instantiation, conditional, 979–981
instantiation time, 120
instruction selection, 1136
insulate, 96, 299, 369, 665
insulation, 299, 1200
    from client code, 369–370
    loss of, 326
    opaque enumerations, 663, 665
int type, relative size of, 91–92
integer literals, 837, 869–870. *See also* binary literals
integer types. *See* integral types
integer-to-floating-point conversion, 843
integral constant expressions. *See also* **alignof** operator
    alignas specifier, 169
    alignof operator, 184
    constexpr variables as alternative, 307–310
    requirements, 303
integral constants, 223
integral promotion, 334, 726, 832–833
integral types. *See also* fundamental integral types
    enumerations, 829
    reinterpret_cast keyword, 510–512
interface inheritance, 541
interface test (C++11), 275
interface traits, 482–489
interface widening, 1021
interfaces. *See also* inheriting constructors
    adaptation with lambda expressions, 597–598
    gsl::span in, 17n10
    physically decoupling from implementation, 40–41
internal linkage, 307
intra-thread dependencies, 998
invocable, 482, 526, 986
ISO C++ Standards Committee, 4
iteration
    enum class and, 348–350
    lack of access to state, 703–706
    over all container elements, 684–685
    over fixed number of objects, 565–566
    over simple values, 690–691
    sentinels, lack of support, 706–707
iterators, vectors of, 26–27

K

keywords. *See also* functions; **using** declarations
    adding new, 1023
    auto
        annoyances, 212–213
        description of, 195–199
        further reading for, 214
        potential pitfalls, 204–212
        use cases, 200–203
    constinit, 75n5, 304n1, 316n8
    decltype
        annoyances, 31
        description of, 25–26
        potential pitfalls, 30
        use cases, 26–30, 28n1
    final
        annoyances, 1028–1030
        description of, 1007–1014
        further reading for, 1030
        potential pitfalls, 1023–1027
        as unsafe, 6
        use cases, 1014–1023
    nullptr
        description of, 99–100
        further reading for, 103
        use cases, 100–103
    override
        description of, 104–105
        further reading for, 107
        potential pitfalls, 106
        safety of, 5
        use cases, 105–106
    register, 195n1
    reinterpret_cast, 506–519
    static_assert
        annoyances, 123
        description of, 115–118
        further reading for, 123
        potential pitfalls, 120–122
        use cases, 118–119

L

L1 cache, 181–183
L2 cache, 181–183
L3 cache, 181–183
Lakos Rule, 1116
lambda body, 581, 595–597
lambda captures, 577, 581–591, 919, 969–970
lambda closure, 584
lambda declarators, 591–595

Index

lambda expressions
  annoyances, 611–614
    capturing ***this** by copy, 611–612
    debugging, 611
    mixing immediate and deferred-execution code, 612–613
    trailing punctuation, 613–614
  configuring algorithms via, 86–87
  decltype(auto) placeholders and, 1206
  deduced return types for, 1189–1190, 1197–1198
  description of, 573–597
  further reading for, 614
  generic lambdas
    annoyances, 981–984
    description of, 968–975
    further reading for, 985
    potential pitfalls, 981
    use cases, 975–981
  local/unnamed types, 83–84
  parts of, 577–578
    closures, 578–581
    lambda body, 595–597
    lambda captures, 581–591
    lambda declarators, 591–595
    lambda introducers, 581–591
  potential pitfalls, 607–611
    dangling references, 607–608
    local variables in unevaluated contexts, 610–611
    mixing captured and noncaptured variables, 609
    overuse, 609
  use cases, 597–607
    emulating local functions, 598–599
    emulating user-defined control constructs, 599–600
    event-driven callbacks, 603–604
    interface adaptation, partial application, currying, 597–598
    recursion, 604–605
    stateless lambdas, 605–607
    with **std::function**, 601–603
    variables and control constructs in expressions, 600–601
lambda introducers, 581–591, 986
lambda-capture expressions. *See also* **auto** variables; braced initialization; forwarding references; lambda expressions; rvalue references
  annoyances, 993–994
    difficulty of synthesizing **const** data members, 993–994
    std::function supports only copyable callable objects, 994

description of, 986–988
further reading for, 995
potential pitfalls, 992–993
use cases, 988–992
  capturing modifiable copy of **const** variable, 990–992
  moving objects into closure, 988–989
  providing mutable state for closure, 989–990
lambda-capture list, 919–921
language undefined behavior, 1115
libraries
  Guidelines Support Library, 17
  Ranges Library, 391–393, 686n4, 687n5
  resilience to code changes, 203
library undefined behaviors, 1115
lifetime extensions, 1162, 1213
  prvalues, 720
  range-based **for** loops, 680, 691–696
  temporary objects, 819–820
limerick in C++ Language Standard, 1081–1082
linear search in variadic templates, 957
linearInterpolation function, 16–17
linkage, 83
link-safe ABI versioning, 1067–1071
link-time optimization, 1094, 1143
Liskov, Barbara, 1026, 1030
Liskov Substitution Principal (LSP), 1030
list initialization
  braced initialization and, 215, 233–234
  deducing, 210–211
list initialized literal types, 260
literal types, 278–284
  aggregate types as, 279–280
  array types as, 280
  compile-time constructible, 462–464
  in constant expressions, 260–261, 273, 277–278
  constexpr constructors and, 281
  cv-qualifiers as, 280
  identifying, 282–284
  pointers as, 281
  reference types as, 279
  scalar types as, 278
  std::initializer_list, 556
  std::is_literal_type, 283n14
  trivially destructible types as, 431
  user-defined, 280
  variable templates of, 302
  void return type as, 280
literals
  binary
    description of, 142–143
    further reading for, 146
    use cases, 144–146

Index

literals (cont.)

  digit separators (') in

    description of, 152–153

    further reading for, 154

    loss of precision in floating-point literals, 154–156

    use cases, 153

  floating-point, 154–156, 837, 869–870

  integer, 837, 869–870

  raw string

    description of, 108–111

    potential pitfalls, 112–114

    use cases, 111–112

  Unicode

    description of, 129–130

    potential pitfalls, 130–132

    use cases, 130

  user-defined

    annoyances, 869–871

    description of, 835–853

    further reading for, 872

    potential pitfalls, 867–869

    use cases, 853–867

little-endian **float** layouts, 531–534

local declarations, 662, 675–677

local functions, emulating, 598–599. *See also* lambda expressions

local scope. *See* block scope

local variables in unevaluated contexts, 610–611

locality of reference, 181, 742, 773n26

local/unnamed types. *See also* **decltype**; lambda expressions

  description of, 83–84

  use cases, 84–87

    configuring algorithms via lambda expressions, 86–87

    encapsulating types within functions, 84–85

    instantiating templates with local function objects as type arguments, 85–86

loggedSum function, 28, 31

logical optimization, 365

logical or (||) operator, 265

long long integral type

  description of, 89

  further reading for, 92

  potential pitfalls, 91–92

  use cases, 89–91

long type, relative size of, 91–92

long-distance friendship, 1035–1036, 1041

loops. *See* range-based **for** loops

lossy conversions, restrictions on, 222–224

low-level value-semantic types (VSTs), creating, 742–751

lvalue references, 26, 716, 1118, 1133

  in C++11/14, 717–720

  declarations prior to C++11, 815–818

  evolution of, 807, 813–828

  forbidding operations on, 1165–1167

  implicit moves in **return** statements, 735–737

  range-based **for** loops, 703

  rvalue references, introduction to, 710–711

lvalue-to-rvalue conversion, 501

M

macro-defined namespaces, 1083–1084

macro-invocation syntax, 248–249

macros. *See also* functions

  alternatives to, 286–287

  offsetof

    aggressive usage, 520–521

    navigating compound objects, 456–460

    POD type usage, 410–412

    support for, 423–425

magic constants, 308

managed allocators, 1021–1022

mandatory RVO, 807n31

mangled names, 1056, 1114n24

manifestly constant evaluated, 258n1

mantissa, 155

materialization, 717

materialize, 1163n1

maximal fundamental alignment, 193

mebibyte conversion, 286–287

mechanisms, 51

member functions

  constexpr as implicitly **const**-qualified, 300

  hiding, 56–57

  overriding, 105–106

  variadic member functions, 892–894

member initialization lists, 230

member initializer lists

  copy list initialization in, 249–250

  delegating constructors, 46

  nonstatic data member initialization, 318

  pack expansion, 917–918

member initializers, default

  annoyances, 328–330

    applicability limitations, 329

    array size deduction, lack of, 330

    loss of aggregate status, 330

    loss of triviality, 329–330

    parenthesized direct-initialization syntax, lack of, 328–329

  description of, 318–321

Index

potential pitfalls, 326–328
  inconsistent subobject intialization, 326–328
  loss of insulation, 326
safety of, 6
union interactions, 320–321
use cases, 322–325
  boilerplate repetition, avoiding, 323–325
  documentation of default values, 325
  nonstatic data member initialization, 322–323
  simple **struct** initialization, 322
memcpy. *See* std::memcpy
memory allocation, 75n4, 181–183
  in C++11, 763n25
  monotonic, 190–193, 1021–1022
  secure buffers, 460–462
memory barriers, 80n7
memory diffusion, 628, 788
memory leak, 74
memory models, synchronization paradigms for, 998
memory_order_acquire, 1005n2
memory_order_consume, 1005n2
memory-fence instructions, 999–1000
metafunctions, 469, 963
  forwarding references, 381
  requirements in constraints, 398–400
  std::remove_cvref<T>, 399n6
metaparameters, 948
metaprogramming, 876, 963–964
metaprograms, 257
Meyers, Scott, 3
Meyers singleton, 71–75
microbenchmarks, 1137–1141
mixed-mode builds, 1073
mix-ins, reusable functionality through, 545
mocking, 1017–1020
mocks, 1017–1020
modifiable *rvalue*s, 820–821
modules, 85n3, 1041
monotonic allocators, 1021–1022
monotonic memory allocation, 190–193
Moore's law, 93n5
most vexing parse, avoiding, 237–238
move assignable, 524
move assignment, 750, 756
move construction, 750
move constructors
  literal types and, 281
  noexcept operator and, 653–654
  rvalue references, 710, 714, 732–733
  RVO and NRVO requirements, 804–805
  std::list, 1114

as trivial, 437
user-provided, 760
move operations
  avoiding, 183n14
  deleted functions, 53
  destructive move, lack of, 811–812
  enabling with std::forward<T>, 395
  noexcept operator, 627–631, 658–659
  on noncopyable types, 788–791
  nonthrowing, 1094–1097
  objects into closure, 988–989
  as optimization of copying, 741–767
  rvalue references, 710, 714–715
  some equivalent to copies, 788
  throwing in, 787
  wrappers for **noexcept**, 1099–1101
move semantics
  necessity of, 821–823
  rvalue references, 710, 715–716
move-assignment operator
  rvalue references, 710, 714, 733
  user-provided, 760–761
moved-from objects
  inconsistent expectations, 794–803
  overly strict requirements, 807–811
  rvalue references, 714–715, 788, 807–812
moved-from state, 789, 791–803
move-only types, 570, 641, 644
  implementing without std::unique_ptr, 791–794
  rvalue references, 716, 768–771, 790
moving iterators, return types of, 1211–1212
MSVC
  auto redeclaration, 1209
  compiler warnings, 150
  deduced parameters, 972n1
  incompatibly specified alignment, 177
  reducing code size, 1104n16, 1111
  stack unwinding, 621n4
  standardized compiler-specific attributes, 14
  trivial copy/move constructors, 528n62
  underspecifying alignment, 176
multiple arguments
  constraining, 983–984
  passing to explicit constructors, 250–252
multiple parameters, handling, 386–388
multiple **return** statements, 1185–1187
multithreaded programs, avoiding false sharing, 174–175
multithreading context, 68, 70–71
mutable closures, 969–970
mutable state, providing for closure, 989–990
myRandom function, 19

Index

N

naked literals, 839–846, 849, 851, 861

name collisions, 870

name mangling, 1067, 1089n5, 1149

named constants, **enum** class for collections of, 346–347

named functions, 66–67

named return-value optimization (NRVO), 805n30
   disabling, 244–245, 783–784
   requires declared copy/move constructors, 804–805
   rvalue references, 734, 736–739, 790, 804

namespace-qualified names, 13n2

namespaces
   inline
      annoyances, 1079–1082
      description of, 1055–1062
      further reading for, 1083
      potential pitfalls, 1076–1079
      use cases, 1062–1076
      versioning case study, 1083–1084
   pollution, avoiding, 339–340

NaN (Not a Number) representations, 530–534

narrow contracts, 715, 1021, 1112–1118, 1122

narrowing aggregate initialization, 247

narrowing conversions, 1091
   allowing, 247–248
   restrictions on, 222–224

narrowing the contract, 793

natural alignment, 179–181, 193, 831

negative testing, 794

nested containers, 22

nested namespaces. *See* inline namespaces

new expressions, **decltype(auto)** in, 1210

new handler, 193

new line encoding, 113–114

nibbles, 153–154

[[no_unique_address]] attribute, 1029n15

noexcept exception specifications, 619–621
   annoyances, 1143–1150
      ABI changes in future C++ versions, 1148–1149
      code duplication, 1144–1147
      exception specifications not part of function's type, 1147–1148
      optimization conflated with reducing code size, 1143–1144
      SFINAE triggering, 1149–1150
   compatibility with dynamic specifications, 621
   conditional exception specifications, 1091–1092
   constraints for virtual functions, 632–634
   description of, 1085–1094
   efficiencies with, 1093–1094

function pointers and references, 1089–1091

further reading for, 1151–1152

potential pitfalls, 1112–1143
   accidental terminate, 1124–1128
   conflating with nofail, 1116–1123
   forgotten **noexcept** operator, 1129–1130
   imprecise expressions, 1130–1134
   overly strong contract guarantees, 1112–1116
   theoretical opportunities for performance improvement, 1136–1143
   unrealizable runtime performance benefits, 1134–1136

unconditional exception specifications, 1085–1089

use cases, 1094–1111
   noexcept swap definition, 1097–1099
   nonthrowing move operations, 1094–1097
   reduction of object-code size, 1101–1111
   wrappers for **noexcept** move operations, 1099–1101

violating, 1093

noexcept operator
   annoyances, 650–658
      change in unspecified behavior when std::vector grows, 652–653
      destructors, not move constructors, **noexcept** by default, 653–654
      exception specification constraints in class hierarchies, 655–658
      older compilers invade **constexpr** function bodies, 654–655
      sensitivity for direct usage, 650–651
      strong exception-safety guarantee, 651–652
   C Standard Library functions and, 631–632
   compatibility of dynamic and **noexcept** exception specifications, 621
   compiler-generated special member functions, 621–626
   compound expressions and, 626–627
   constraints for virtual functions, 632–634
   description of, 615–634
   dynamic exception specifications for functions, 618–619
   exception specifications with, 1092–1093
   forgetting in **noexcept** exception specifications, 1129–1130
   further reading for, 658
   move operations, 627–631, 658–659
   noexcept exception specifications for functions, 619–621
   operator-produced exceptions, 615–618

potential pitfalls, 647–650
 direct usage, 647–649
 function bodies, lack of consideration, 649–650
 use cases, 634–647
  appending elements to std::vector, 634–639
  enforcing **noexcept** contract using **static_assert**, 639–640
  std::move_if_noexcept, 640–644
  std::vector::push_back(T&&), 644–647
noexcept swap, defining, 1097–1099
nofail functions, 1116–1123
nofail guarantee, 1117, 1122–1123
noncaptured variables, mixing with captured, 609
noncopyable types, making movable, 788–791
nondefining declarations, 729
nonintegral symbolic numeric constants, 310–311
nonprimitive functionality, 67
nonrecursive **constexpr** algorithms, 961–962
nonreporting contracts, 1120–1122
nonreporting functions, 1119, 1122
nonstatic data members
 auto not allowed, 212
 constexpr variables, 305
 initialization, 318, 322–323
nonthrowing move operations, 1094–1097
non-trivial, 1011
non-trivial constructors, union membership and, 1174
non-trivial destructors, 1101–1104, 1118, 1136
non-trivial special member functions, union type and, 1174–1181
non-trivial types, vertical encoding for, 448–452
non-trivially destructible, 1102–1109, 1137
non-type parameters, 902
non-type template parameter packs, 901–903
non-type template parameters, 901–903, 903n7
nonvirtual functions, hiding, 1026–1027
[[noreturn]] attribute, 13. *See also* attribute support
 description of, 95
 further reading for, 98
 potential pitfalls, 97–98
  inadvertently break working programs, 97
  misuse on function pointers, 98
 use cases, 95–97
  compiler diagnostics, 95–96
  runtime performance, 96–97
normative wording, 808
NRVO. *See* named return-value optimization (NRVO)
null address, 99–102
NULL macro, 100

null pointer value, 743
null statements, 268
null terminated strings, 743
null-pointer-literal. *See* **nullptr** keyword
nullptr keyword
 description of, 99–100
 further reading for, 103
 use cases, 100–103
  overload resolution, 101–102
  overloading literal null pointer, 102–103
  type safety, 100–101
numeric literals
 digit separators (') in
  description of, 152–153
  further reading for, 154
  loss of precision in floating-point literals, 154–156
  use cases, 153
 user-defined, 858–862

O
.o files
 extern template, effect on, 359–365
 reducing code bloat, 365–369
object factories, 929–930
object files
 extern template, effect on, 359–365
 reducing code bloat, 365–369
object invariants, 539, 742
object orientation, 1015
object representation
 POD types, 405
 reinterpret_cast keyword, 510, 515–516
object-oriented design, vertical encoding comparison, 440–441
object-oriented programming, 1015
objects
 creating, 516n42
 iterating over fixed number, 565–566
 moving into closure, 988–989
 reducing code size, 1101–1111, 1143–1144
 resource-owning, passing around, 771–775
 std::initializer_list<E> initialization, 559
 strengthening alignment, 169–170
obsolete entities, [[deprecated]] attribute for
 description of, 147–148
 potential pitfalls, 150
 use cases, 148–150
ODR-used, 581–582, 590, 988n2, 1081
offsetof macro
 aggressive usage, 520–521
 navigating compound objects, 456–460
 POD type usage, 410–412
 support for, 423–425

Index

one-definition rule (ODR), 263, 1072, 1079
    constexpr functions, 263
    extern template, 374
    violating, 1189
opaque declarations, 660–662
opaque enumerations
    annoyances, 677–678
    description of, 660–663
    external usage, 350, 832
    further reading for, 678
    potential pitfalls, 675–677
        inciting local enumeration declarations, 677
        redeclaring externally defined enumeration locally, 675–677
    use cases, 663–675
        cookies, 669–675
        insulating some external clients from enumerator list, 665–668
        within header files, 663–665
operands, for **decltype**
    ( ) versus (( )) notation for, 30
    entities, 25
    expressions, 25–26
operators. *See also* keywords
    || (logical or), 265
    alignof
        annoyances, 193–194
        description of, 184
        fundamental types, 184
        use cases, 186–193
        user-defined types, 185–186
    bitwise right-shift, 21–24
    braced lists and, 254–255
    decltype
        annoyances, 31
        description of, 25–26
        potential pitfalls, 30
        use cases, 26–30, 28n1
    explicit
        description of, 61–63
        potential pitfalls, 66–67
        use cases, 63–65
    greater-than (>), 21–22
    noexcept
        annoyances, 650–658
        description of, 615–634
        further reading for, 658
        move operations, 658–659
        potential pitfalls, 647–650
        use cases, 634–647
    sequencing, 265
    UDL operators, 840–842
        cooked, 843–845
        raw, 845–849

        templates, 849–851
optimization
    attributes for
        hints for additional optimization opportunities, 15–16
        statement of explicit assumptions, 16–17
    builder classes, 1167–1170
    conflating with reducing code size, 1143–1144
    immutable types, 1167–1170
optimized metaprogramming algorithms, 963–964
ordered after, 998
ordinary character types, 501–505
out clause, 1118
out of contract, 744, 1117
outermost expressions, 820
over-aligned, 185
overhead costs, single-threaded applications, 80
overload resolution
    deleted functions, 53
    nullptr keyword, 101–102
    priorities, 730
    rvalue references, 713
    std::initializer_list, 561
    user-defined literals (UDLs), 841
overloading, 741
    free functions, 570–571
    functions, 1089n6
    improving disambiguation, 340–343
    null pointer, 102–103
    reference types, 727–730
overloads, ref-qualified, 1171–1172
overly strong contract guarantees, 1112–1116
override member-function specifier
    as contextual keyword, 1023
    description of, 104–105
    final contextual keyword, interactions with, 1007, 1009–1011
    further reading for, 107
    potential pitfalls, 106
    safety of, 5
    use cases, 105–106
overriding, 539
    member functions, 105–106
    preventing with **final** contextual keyword, 1007
owned resources, 741, 803–804

P
pack expansion, 882, 908–911, 925, 964
    alignas specifier, 921–922
    attribute lists, 922
    base specifier list, 915–917
    braced initializer lists, 912–914

Index

cannot use unexpanded, 956
disallowed, 924
expansion is rigid and requires verbose support code, 957
function call argument list, 912–914
function parameter packs, 911–912
lambda-capture list, 919–921
limitations on contexts, 954–955
member initializer list, 917–918
sizeof... expressions, 923
template argument list, 914
template parameter list, 923–924
pack expansion context, 883, 929
Packet class, 27–28
`Packet::checksumLength`, 27, 28n1
padding bytes, 475
pages, 181–183
pair mismatches, 699n8
parameter count, 597
parameter declarations, 888, 1000
parameter pack expansion, 590
parameter packs, 879, 964
function parameter packs, 888–892
non-type template parameter packs, 901–903
pack expansion, 908–911, 925
alignas specifier, 921–922
attribute lists, 922
base specifier list, 915–917
braced initializer lists, 912–914
cannot use unexpanded, 956
disallowed, 924
expansion is rigid and requires verbose support code, 957
function call argument list, 912–914
function parameter packs, 911–912
lambda-capture list, 919–921
limitations on contexts, 954–955
member initializer list, 917–918
sizeof... expressions, 923
template argument list, 914
template parameter list, 923–924
Rule of Fair Matching, 898–899
Rule of Greedy Matching, 896–898
template template parameter packs, 903–908
type template parameter packs, 880–884
variable templates, 159
parameter types, return types dependent on, 126
parameterized constants, 160–161
parameters
constexpr functions, 277–278
handling multiple, 386–388
parentheses with **decltype** operands, 25, 30
partial application, 597–598

partial class template specialization, 963
partial implementation, 1021
partial implementation classes, 540
partial ordering of class template specialization, 886
partial specialization, 529, 884–887
partially constructed, 47
passing resource-owning objects, 771–775
PassKey idiom
enforcing initialization with, 1036–1038
special type access with, 1039–1041
perfect forwarding, 807, 942, 1131, 1198
expressions to downstream consumers, 386
in factory functions, 240
hijacking copy constructors, 395–397
lambda-capture expressions, 992
perfectly forwarded, 992
performance
of concrete classes, 1015–1017
of protocol hierarchy, 1020–1023
theoretical opportunities for improvement, 1136–1143
unrealizable runtime benefits, 1134–1136
pessimization, returning **const** *rvalues*, 786–787
physical dependency, 374
physical design, 663
physical memory, 1135
physical optimization, 365
pi, 160
pipelined, 1137
placeholder types, 195
placeholders, 1182
conversion functions, 1193–1194
decltype(auto)
annoyances, 1213
description of, 1205–1210
potential pitfalls, 1212–1213
use cases, 1210–1212
in trailing return types, 1189
placement **new**, 452, 638, 940, 1175, 1180
placement of attributes, 13
plain old data (POD). *See* POD types
platonic values, 742
pmr allocators in C++17, 763n25
POD types
annoyances, 521–529
C++ Standard not stabilized, 521–527
standard type traits unreliable, 527–528
`std::pair` and `std::tuple` of PODs are not PODs, 528–529
bit representation, 530–534
C++03 POD types, 412–415
C++11 POD types, 415–417
description of, 401–402
further reading for, 530

Index

POD types (cont.)

future direction, 438–439

potential pitfalls, 479–521

abuse of `reinterpret_cast`, 506–519

aggressive use of `offsetof`, 520–521

conflating arbitrary and indeterminate values, 493–497

exporting bitwise copies of PODs, 479–480

ineligible use of `std::memcpy`, 497–501

`memcpy` usage on **const** or reference sub-objects, 489–493

misuse of unions, 505–506

naive copying other than `std::memcpy`, 501–505

requiring PODs or trivial types, 480–482

sloppy terminology, 488–489

wrong type traits, 482–488

privileges, 402–412

bitwise copyability, 409–410

contiguous storage, 405

object lifetime begins at allocation, 407–409

`offsetof` macro usage, 410–412

predictable layout, 405–407

standard-layout class special properties, 420–425

standard-layout types, 417–420

trivial subcategories, 429–436

trivial types, 425–429

type traits, 436–438

use cases, 439–479

compile-time constructible, literal types, 462–464

fixed-capacity string elements, 476–479

fixed-capacity strings, 470–475

navigating compound objects with `offsetof`, 456–460

secure buffers, 460–462

skippable destructors, 464–470

translating C++-only types to C, 452–456

vertical encoding for non-trivial types, 448–452

vertical encoding within a union, 439–448

POD-struct, 405–407, 412–415

POD-union, 412–415

pointer semantics, 558–559

pointer types, deducing, 197–198

pointers. *See also* function pointers

as literal types, 281

`noexcept` and, 1089–1091

`nullptr` keyword

description of, 99–100

further reading for, 103

use cases, 100–103

`reinterpret_cast` keyword, 506–519

semantics, 558–559

smart pointers, 948–951

pointers to members, 456, 459, 509

polymorphic classes, 617

polymorphic memory resources, 190n3

polymorphic types, 616, 1011

polymorphism, compile-time, 1046–1050

portability with **final** contextual keyword, 1014–1015

positive semidefinite, 655

POSIX epoch, 291

postconditions, 807–811

potentially evaluated, 615

preconditions, 18, 472

predicate functions, 86

predicate functors, 575

predicates, 575

preprocessor macros. *See* macros

primary declarations, 881

primary-class-template declarations, 881

private functions, 1038–1041

private inheritance, 1029

proctor classes, 646

proctors, 646, 1139

producer-consumer programming pattern, 1000–1005

production build, 469

programmatically accessible, 1085, 1144

protocol hierarchy, performance of, 1020–1023

protocols, 440, 540, 1018, 1020

proxy iterators, return types of, 1211–1212

prvalues, 513, 716

in C++11/14, 720–721

evolution of, 807

passing to `decltype`, 25

publicly accessible, 489

pure abstract classes, extracting, 1018

pure abstract interfaces, 540, 1020, 1021

pure functions, 16

pure interfaces, 1020

pure virtual functions

final contextual keyword, 1008–1009

in protocol hierarchy, 1020

Q

qualified ids. *See* id-expression

qualified names, 127, 1060

qualifiers, 889

quality of implementation (QoI), 277, 529

quiet NaN (qNaN), 531

Index

R

range expressions
  lifetime of temporary objects, 691–696
  range-based **for** loops, 680
range generators, 687–690
range-based **for** loops, 571–572
  annoyances, 703–709
    adapter requirements, 706
    argument-dependent lookup (ADL), 707–709
    sentinel iterator types, lack of support, 706–707
    state of iteration, lack of access, 703–706
  description of, 679–684
  further reading for, 709
  potential pitfalls, 691–703
    differences in simple and reference-proxy behaviors, 700–703
    inadvertent element copying, 696–700
    lifetime of temporary objects, 691–696
  specification, 680–683
  traversing arrays and initializer lists, 683–684
  use cases, 684–691
    iterating all container elements, 684–685
    iterating simple values, 690–691
    range generators, 687–690
    subranges, 686–687
Ranges Library, 391–393, 686n4, 687n5
raw string literals
  collisions, 109–111
  description of, 108–111
  potential pitfalls, 112–114
    encoding new lines and whitespace, 113–114
    unexpected indentation, 112–113
  use cases, 111–112
raw UDL operators, 841, 845–849, 870
reachable, 712
reaching scope, 587–588
read-copy-update (RCU) synchronization mechanism, 999
recursion, 604–605, 875
recursive initialization, 77–78, 163–165
recursive lambdas, 977–979
reducing code size, 1101–1111, 1143–1144
redundant check, 115
refactoring with curiously recurring template pattern (CRTP), 1042–1044
reference collapsing, 380–382
reference related, 726
reference types
  alignof operator, 184
  deducing, 198
  gsl::span, 17
  as literal types, 279
  memcpy usage on, 489–493
  overloading, 727–730
  union membership and, 1174
references, **noexcept** and, 1089–1091
reflection, 520n46
ref-qualified, 1154
ref-qualified overloads, 1171–1172
ref-qualifiers
  annoyances, 1171–1172
  description of, 1153–1160
  forwarding references, 380
  further reading for, 1173
  potential pitfalls, 1170–1171
  syntax and restrictions, 1157–1160
  use cases, 1160–1170
    forbidding *lvalue* operations, 1165–1167
    forbidding *rvalue*-modifying operations, 1163–1165
    optimizing immutable types and builder classes, 1167–1170
    returning *rvalue* subobjects, 1160–1163
register keyword, 195n1
regular types, 187n2, 751. *See also* types
reinterpret_cast keyword, 506–519
relaxed restrictions on **constexpr** functions, 959–967. *See also* **constexpr** variables; variadic templates
  description of, 959–960
  further reading for, 965
  optimized C++11 example algorithms, 965–967
  use cases, 961–964
    nonrecursive **constexpr** algorithms, 961–962
    optimized metaprogramming algorithms, 963–964
release-acquire synchronization paradigm, 998, 1000–1002, 1005
release-consume synchronization paradigm, 998–999, 1002–1003, 1005
reopening inline namespaces, 1061–1062
reordering data members, 178n10
reportError function, 15
reporting contracts, 1120
representation, 480, 570
requires clause in C++20, 486n31
reserved identifiers, 840
Resource Acquisition is Initialization (RAII), 388
resource-owning objects, passing around, 771–775
return statements
  disabling NRVO and implicit move, 244–246
  moves in, 734–740
  multiple, 1185–1187

Index

return types
    auto deduction
        annoyances, 1201–1203
        description of, 1182–1194
        potential pitfalls, 1200
        use cases, 1194–1200
    constexpr functions, 277–278
    dependent on parameter type, 126
    of moving iterators, 1211–1212
    of proxy iterators, 1211–1212
    qualified names in, 127
    return by value, 774–775
    trailing return
        description of, 124–126
        further reading for, 128
        inferring type of, 28
        use cases, 126–128
return value optimization (RVO), 390
    requires declared copy/move constructors,
        804–805
    rvalue references, 734
return values, [[carries_dependency]] attribute,
    1000
return-type deduction, delaying, 1199–1200
reusable lambda expressions, 975
reuse, lost with **final** contextual keyword, 1023–
    1026
right-angle brackets (>>)
    description of, 21
    further reading for, 24
    potential pitfalls with, 22–24
    use cases, 22
risk-to-reward ratio. *See* safety of adoption
Rule of Fair Matching, 898–899
Rule of Greedy Matching, 896–898
rule of zero, 631, 788
runtime performance
    overhead costs of **constexpr** functions, 298–
        299
    penalizing to enable compile time, 299–300
runtime type identification (RTTI), 617
rvalue references, 1133
    annoyances, 804–812
        destructive move, lack of, 811–812
        evolution of value categories, 807
        moved-from object requirements overly
            strict, 807–811
        RVO and NRVO require declared
            copy/move constructors, 804–805
        std::move does not move, 805–806
        visual similarity to forwarding references,
            806–807
    decltype results as, 26
    description of, 710–741
    in expressions, 730–731

extended value categories in C++11/14,
    716–723
forbidding modifying operations, 1163–
    1165, 1170–1171
further reading for, 813
lvalue references, comparison, 710–711
modifiable, 820–821
motivation for, 715–716
move operations, 714–715
moves in **return** statements, 734–740
necessity of, 824
overload resolution, 713
overloading on reference types, 727–730
potential pitfalls, 782–804
    disabling NRVO, 783–784
    failure to std::move named rvalue refer-
        ences, 784–785
    implementing move-only types without
        std::unique_ptr, 791–794
    inconsistent expectations on moved-from
        objects, 794–803
    making noncopyable type movable with-
        out just cause, 788–791
    move operations that throw, 787
    repeatedly calling std::move on named
        rvalue references, 785–786
    requiring owned resources to be valid,
        803–804
    returning **const** *rvalues* pessimizes per-
        formance, 786–787
    sink arguments require copying, 782–783
    some moves equivalent to copies, 788
range-based **for** loops, 703
    returning subobjects of, 1160–1163
    similarity to forwarding references, 397–398
    special member functions, 732–733
    std::move, 731–732
    use cases, 741–781
        identifying value categories, 779–781
        move operations as optimizations of copy-
            ing, 741–767
        move-only types, 768–771
        passing around resource-owning objects
            by value, 771–775
        sink arguments, 775–779
    value category evolution, 813–828
    xvalues, 712–713

S

safe features
    aggregate initialization
        annoyances, 140–141
        description of, 138–139
        potential pitfalls, 140
        use cases, 139

Index

attribute support
  description of, 12–14
  potential pitfalls with, 18–19
  use cases, 14–18
binary literals
  description of, 142–143
  further reading for, 146
  use cases, 144–146
consecutive right-angle brackets (>>)
  description of, 21
  further reading for, 24
  potential pitfalls with, 22–24
  use cases, 22
decltype
  description of, 25–26
  potential pitfalls, 30
  use cases, 26–30
defaulted functions
  annoyances, 42–43
  description of, 33–36
  further reading for, 44
  implicit generation of special member
    functions, 44–45
  potential pitfalls, 41–42
  use cases, 36–41
definition of, 5
delegating constructors
  description of, 46–48
  potential pitfalls, 50–51
  use cases, 48–50
deleted functions
  annoyances, 58–59
  description of, 53
  further reading for, 60
  use cases, 53–57
[[deprecated]] attribute, 14
  description of, 147–148
  potential pitfalls, 150
  use cases, 148–150
digit separator (')
  description of, 152–153
  further reading for, 154
  loss of precision in floating-point literals,
    154–156
  use cases, 153
explicit conversion operators
  description of, 61–63
  potential pitfalls, 66–67
  use cases, 63–65
local/unnamed types
  description of, 83–84
  use cases, 84–87
long long integral type
  description of, 89
  further reading for, 92

potential pitfalls, 91–92
  use cases, 89–91
[[noreturn]] attribute, 13
  description of, 95
  further reading for, 98
  potential pitfalls, 97–98
  use cases, 95–97
nullptr keyword
  description of, 99–100
  further reading for, 103
  use cases, 100–103
override member-function specifier, 5
  description of, 104–105
  further reading for, 107
  potential pitfalls, 106
  use cases, 105–106
raw string literals
  description of, 108–111
  potential pitfalls, 112–114
  use cases, 111–112
static_assert
  annoyances, 123
  description of, 115–118
  further reading for, 123
  potential pitfalls, 120–122
  use cases, 118–119
thread-safe function-scope static variables
  annoyances, 80
  C++03 double-checked-lock pattern, 81–
    82
  description of, 68–71
  further reading for, 81
  potential pitfalls, 75–80
  use cases, 71–75
trailing return, 28
  description of, 124–126
  further reading for, 128
  inferring type of, 28
  use cases, 126–128
type/template aliases, creating with **using**
  declarations, 133–137
variable templates
  annoyances, 165
  description of, 157–160
  potential pitfalls, 163–165
  use cases, 160–163
safe-bool idiom, 64
safety of adoption, 2, 4–5. *See also* conditionally
  safe features; safe features; unsafe features
salient values, 634, 830–832
sanitizers, 802
scalar types, 1207
  aggregate initialization, 222
  braced lists and, 254–255

Index

aggregate initialization (cont.)
    in C++03, 414
    copy initialization, 235–236
    initialization, 217
    as literal types, 278
    as standard-layout types, 417
    as trivial types, 425
scope
    duplicate names, loss of access to, 1056–1058
    function-scope static variables
        annoyances, 80
        C++03 double-checked-lock pattern, 81–82
        description of, 68–71
        further reading for, 81
        potential pitfalls, 75–80
        use cases, 71–75
scoped allocator model, 328n3
scoped enumerations, 335–336, 660
scoped guard, 645–646
sections, **extern template**, 361
secure buffers, 460–462
Secure Hash Algorithms (SHA), 1083–1084
selective **using** directives for short-named entities, 1074–1076
semantics, 12, 18, 558–559
sentinels, 1114
    iterator types, lack of support, 706–707
    rvalue references, 743
sequencing operator, 265. *See also* comma (,) operator
serial dates, 453
set associative, 182n11
SFINAE (substitution failure is not an error), 400, 1089
    deduced return types and, 1201–1203
    exception specifications and, 1149–1150
    perfect forwarding, 397
    template instantiation and specialization, 1190
SFINAE evaluation context
    decltype with, 28–30
    expression SFINAE, 29n3
shadowed, 987
short-named entities, **using** directives for, 1074–1076
side effects, 16
signaling NaN (sNaN), 531
signals/signaling, 1120, 1213
signatures, 1052
    inheriting constructors, 536
    overloading functions, 1089
    rvalue references, 729
signed integer overflow, 90

simple structs, initialization, 322
simple type specifiers, 1032
single-thread-aware objects, avoiding false sharing, 175–176
single-threaded applications, overhead costs, 80
sink arguments, 775–779, 782–783
size constructors, 764
sizeof... expressions, 923
skippable destructors, 464–470
slicing, 539, 1025
SmallObjectBuffer, 118n4
smart pointers, 948–951
soft UB. *See* library undefined behaviors
sortRange function, 28–30
sortRangeImpl function, 28–30
space. *See* whitespace
special member functions. *See also* defaulted functions; deleted functions; functions; user-provided special member functions
    compiler-generated, 621–626
    constexpr, 266–268
    creating high-level value-semantic types (VSTs), 751–762
    declaring explicitly, 33–34
    defaulting first declaration of, 34–35
    exception specifications and, 1086
    implicit generation of, 44–45
    initializer lists, 553
    non-trivial, union type and, 1174–1181
    restoring suppressed, 36–37
    rvalue references, 710, 714, 732–733
    standard-layout types, 421
    suppressing generation of, 53–55
    as trivial, 1012
    user-declared versus user-provided, 413n6
specialization of variadic class templates, 884–887
specifiers and arguments. *See also* exception specifications; keywords
    alignas
        description of, 168–172
        memory allocation, 181–183
        natural alignment, 179–181
        potential pitfalls, 176–179
        use cases, 172–176
    inline, 262–265
square brackets ([[ ]]), 12
stable reuse, 1012
stack frame, 1101
stack unwinding, 621n4, 1135
standard conversion, 509
    enum class, 334
    user-defined literals (UDLs), 835
Standard Library–related restrictions, 1078
standardized compiler-specific attributes, 13–14

Index

standard-layout class types, special properties, 420–425

standard-layout classes, 422

standard-layout types, 178

    accessing subobjects via **reinterpret_cast**, 517–519

    alignof operator, 186

    generalized PODs, 401, 416, 417–420

    translating C++-only types to C, 452–456

    vertical encoding for, 448–452

start function, 14

stateless lambdas, 605–607

static assertion declarations, 115

static data space, 165

static member variables

    external definitions, 314–315

    not defined in own class, 316

static storage duration, 68, 478

static variables, function-scope

    annoyances, 80

    C++03 double-checked-lock pattern, 81–82

    description of, 68–71

    further reading for, 81

    potential pitfalls, 75–80

    use cases, 71–75

static_assert. *See also* trailing return

    annoyances, 123

    description of, 115–118

    enforcing **noexcept** contract, 639–640

    evaluation in templates, 116–118

    further reading for, 123

    potential pitfalls, 120–122

        misuse to restrict overload sets, 121–122

        unintended compilation failures, 120–121

    syntax and semantics, 115–116

    use cases, 118–119

        preventing misuse of class and function templates, 118–119

        verifying assumptions about target platform, 118

static-analysis tools, control of external, 17–18

std::any, 187n2

std::bit_cast, 514n41, 516n42

std::declval, 31

std::enable_if, 486n31

std::forward. *See* forwarding references

std::forward<T>, 385, 395

std::function

    lambda expressions with, 601–603

    limitations, 994

std::index_sequence, 293

std::initializer_list, 233

    annoyances, 567–571

        constructor suppresses implicitly declared default, 568–570

        homogeneous initializer lists, 567

        overloaded free function templates, 570–571

        representation of **const** objects, 570

    class template usage, 555–558

    description of, 553–561

    further reading for, 571

    inadvertently calling constructors, 242–244

    overload resolution, 561

    pointer semantics and temporary lifetimes, 558–559

    potential pitfalls, 566–567

    range-based **for** loops, 571–572

    std::initializer_list<E> object initialization, 559

    traversing with range-based **for** loops, 683–684

    type deduction, 559–561

    use cases, 561–566

        function arguments of same type, 564–565

        iterating over fixed number of objects, 565–566

        population of standard containers, 561–562

        support for braced lists, 562–564

std::initializer_list<E> object initialization, 559

std::is_constant_evaluated(), 297n20

std::is_final, 1014

std::is_literal_type, 283n14

std::is_lvalue_reference, 378

std::is_pod, 438n14

std::kill_dependency function, 999–1000

std::list, move constructors, 1114

std::literals, 1082

std::memcpy, 484–485

    const and reference subobject usage, 489–493

    ineligible usage, 497–501

std::move, 731–732

    failure to use with named rvalue references, 784–785

    lack of movement with, 805–806

    repeatedly calling on named rvalue references, 785–786

std::move_if_noexcept, 640–644

std::pair, 528–529

std::pmr, 190n3

std::pmr::monotonic_resource, 468n27

std::pmr::unsynchronized_pool_resource, 468n27

std::remove_cvref<T>, 399n6

std::set_terminate, 1104

std::string_view, 874n1

Index

`std::terminate`, 1104, 1109, 1124–1128
`std::thread`, 70
`std::tr2::__bases`, 956n27
`std::tr2::__direct_bases`, 956n27
`std::tuple`, 528–529
`std::uint8_t` value, 27
`std::uint16_t`, 27, 28n1
`std::unique_ptr`, implementing move-only types
    without, 791–794
`std::unique_ptr<T>`, 42n3
`std::unordered_map`, 135n1
`std::upper_bound`, 294n19
`std::variant`, 452n19, 1180n2
`std::vector`, 1024–1026
    appending elements, 634–639
    change in unspecified behavior, 652–653
`std::vector::push_back(T&&)`, 644–647
storage class specifiers, 195
storing **constexpr** data structures, 311–312
Streaming SIMD Extensions (SSE), 173–174
strengthening alignment, 168
    of data members, 170–171
    of particular objects, 169–170
    of user-defined types (UDTs), 171
strict aliasing, 401
string literals, 837, 862–863, 870
    compile-time traversal, 287–291
    [[deprecated]] attribute, 148
    raw
        description of, 108–111
        potential pitfalls, 112–114
        use cases, 111–112
    static_assert, 123
    template instantiations with, 394–395
    Unicode
        description of, 129–130
        potential pitfalls, 130–132
        use cases, 130
strong exception-safety guarantee
    noexcept operator, 634–639, 651–652, 658–
        659, 1097
    rvalue references, 750, 751, 762, 787
strong guarantee, 634, 746
strong **typedef** idiom, 73–74
strong **typedef** implementation, 541–544
strongly typed enumerations. *See* **enum** class
Stroustrup, Bjarne, 4
    undefined behavior, avoiding, 1024n10
    "unnecessary nannyism," 1024n8
structs, initialization, 322
structural base classes, hiding member functions,
    56–57
structural inheritance, 57, 180, 1025–1026
    boilerplate code with, avoiding, 540

    with mix-ins, 545
    natural alignment, 180
structured binding, 201n2, 685n3
subobjects
    initialization, inconsistency in, 326–328
    of *rvalues*, returning, 1160–1163
    value categories of, 722n8
subranges, 686–687
substitution failure is not an error. *See* SFINAE
sum type, 1177–1180
suppressed   constructors   by
    `std::initializer_list`, 568–570
suppressed special member functions, restoring,
    36–37
symbol demangler, 361n2
symbolic numeric constants, nonintegral, 310–311
synchronization paradigms, 998–999
syntax of direct initialization, 328–329
synthesizing equality with curiously recurring
    template pattern (CRTP), 1045–1046

T

`T&&` (forwarding references)
    annoyances, 397–400
        metafunction requirements in con-
            straints, 398–400
        similarity to rvalue references, 397–398
    auto&&, 383–384
    description of, 377–385
    function template argument type deduction,
        379–380
    further reading for, 400
    identifying, 382–383
    not forwarding, 384–385
    potential pitfalls, 394–397
        hijacking copy constructor, 395–397
        `std::forward<T>`, enabling move opera-
            tions, 395
        template instantiations with string liter-
            als, 394–395
    reference collapsing, 380–382
    `std::forward<T>`, 385
    use cases, 386–393
        decomposing complex expressions, 391–
            393
        emplacement, 390–391
        forwarding expressions to downstream
            consumers, 386
        multiple parameter handling, 386–388
        perfect forwarding for generic factory
            functions, 388–389
        wrapping initialization in generic factory
            functions, 389–390

template aliases. *See also* inheriting constructors; trailing return
    creating with **using** declarations, 133–137
    description of, 133–134
    use cases, 134–137
        binding arguments to template parameters, 135–136
        simplified **typedef** declarations, 134–135
        type trait notation, 136–137
template argument deductions, 212–213, 894–896
template argument list, 882, 914
template arguments, 899
template head, 157
template instantiation
    forwarding references, 382
    with string literals, 394–395
template instantiation time, 116, 120
template parameter list, 888, 923–924
template parameter packs, 437, 879–884, 896–898
template parameters, 135–136, 896
template template class parameters, 165
template template parameter packs, 903–908
template template parameters, 165, 902
template-argument expressions, 21–22
templated call operator. *See* generic lambdas
templated variable declarations. *See also* **constexpr** variables
    annoyances, 165
    description of, 157–160
    potential pitfalls, 163–165
    use cases, 160–163
        parameterized constants, 160–161
        reducing verbosity of type traits, 161–163
templates
    constexpr functions, 276–277
    evaluation of static assertions in. *See* **static_assert**
    extern
        annoyances, 373–375
        description of, 353–365
        further reading for, 376
        potential pitfalls, 371–373
        use cases, 365–370
    instantiation and specialization, 1190–1192
    local/unnamed types as arguments to
        description of, 83–84
        use cases, 84–87
    preventing misuse of, 118–119
    static assertion evaluation in, 116–118
    std::initializer_list usage, 555–558
    UDL operator templates, 841, 849–851
    variable
        annoyances, 165
        description of, 157–160

potential pitfalls, 163–165
    use cases, 160–163
variadic
    annoyances, 953–957
    description of, 873–925
    further reading for, 958
    potential pitfalls, 952–953
    use cases, 925–951
temporary materialization, 717
temporary objects, 818–819
    arrays, 555
    lifetime extensions, 819–820
    lifetime in range expressions, 691–696
    modifiable *rvalues*, 820–821
temporary rvalue references, 724
ternary operator, 268, 615, 1186–1187
test drivers, 114, 866–867
*this, captured by copy, 611–612
thrashing, 183n14
thread pool, 989
thread-safe function-scope static variables
    annoyances, 80
    C++03 double-checked-lock pattern, 81–82
    concurrent initialization, 68–69
    description of, 68–71
    destruction, 69
    further reading for, 81
    logger example, 69–70
    multithreaded contexts, 70–71
    potential pitfalls, 75–80
        dangerous recursive initialization, 77
        dependence on order-of-destruction of local objects, 78–80
        initialization not guaranteed, 75–77
        recursion subtleties, 77–78
    use cases, 71–75
top level **const**, 729
trailing punctuation in lambda expressions, 613–614
trailing return. *See also* **decltype**; deduced return type
    description of, 124–126
    further reading for, 128
    inferring type of, 28
    use cases, 126–128
        function template whose return type depends on parameter type, 126
        qualifying names, avoiding redundantly in return types, 127
        readability of declarations with function pointers, 127–128
trailing return types, 593–594, 1189

Index

translation unit (TU)
>   opaque enumerations, 660
>   thread-safe function-scope static variables, 71
translation-lookaside buffer (TLB), 182n13
transparently nested namespaces. *See* inline namespaces
trivial, 38
trivial classes, 521
trivial constructors, 273–274, 408n4
trivial copy constructors, 470, 528n62
trivial copy operation, 483, 733, 812
trivial copy-assignment operator, 470
trivial default constructors, 461
trivial default initialization, 1087
trivial destructibility, 468–469
trivial destructors, 408n4
trivial move constructors, 484, 528n62
trivial move operation, 733
trivial operations, 33
trivial types
>   in C++17, 425n7
>   fixed-capacity string elements, 476–479
>   future direction of PODs, 438–439
>   generalized PODs, 401, 416–417, 425–429
>   preserving, 39–40
>   requiring, 480–482
>   special member functions and, 1012
>   subcategories, 429–436
>   union membership and, 1174
triviality, loss of, 329–330
trivially constructible, 80n7
>   POD types, 431–432
>   secure buffers, 460–462
trivially copy assignable, 486–487
trivially copy constructible, 488
trivially copyable, 39, 41–42
>   C++ Standard not stabilized, 521–527
>   fixed-capacity strings, 470–475
>   ineligible use of std::memcpy, 497–501
>   memcpy usage on **const** or reference subobjects, 489–493
>   naive copying other than std::memcpy, 501–505
>   POD types, 401, 434–436
>   sloppy terminology, 488–489
>   wrong usage of type traits, 482–488
trivially copyable class, 521
trivially copyable types, 468
trivially default constructible, 401, 430–436
trivially destructible
>   compile-time constructible, literal types, 462–464
>   **constexpr** variables, 305
>   POD types, 402, 430–434

reducing code size, 1104
sloppy terminology, 488–489
trivially destructible types in C++20, 430n9
true sharing, 183n15
tuples, 932–937, 975–976
type aliases. *See also* inheriting constructors; trailing return
>   befriending as customization point, 1034–1036
>   creating with **using** declarations, 133–137
>   description of, 133–134
>   exception specifications and, 1090, 1147
>   use cases, 134–137
>>   binding arguments to template parameters, 135–136
>>   simplified **typedef** declarations, 134–135
>>   type trait notation, 136–137
type categories, 837, 843
type deduction
>   forwarding references, 379–380
>   of std::initializer_list, 559–561
type erasure, 602
type identifiers as **alignas** specifier argument, 172
type inference, 193
type lists, 963
type parameter packs, 903
type punning, 401
type safety, 100–101
type suffix, 837
type template parameter packs, 880–884
type template parameters, 902
type traits, 436–438
>   in C++17, 651n12
>   notation, 136–137
>   reducing verbosity, 161–163
>   **static_assert**, 119
>   std::is_lvalue_reference, 378
>   as unreliable, 527–528
>   wrong usage, 482–488
<type_traits> header, 1014
type-consistency, explicit expression of, 27–28, 28n1
typedef. *See also* aliases
>   capturing results of **decltype** expressions in, 31
>   in <cstdint>, 92
>   strong implementation, 541–544
typename disambiguator, 382n1
typename specifiers, 1032
typenames
>   explicit, 26–27
>   in **friend** declarations, 1033n1

types. *See also* POD types; trivial types; type
aliases; type safety; type traits; user-
defined types (UDTs); value-semantic
types (VSTs)

as **alignof** argument, 193–194

function pointers and, 265–266

historical perspective on, 93–94

literal, 278–284

local/unnamed

description of, 83–84

use cases, 84–87

long long

description of, 89

further reading for, 92

potential pitfalls, 91–92

use cases, 89–91

redundant repetition, avoiding, 200–201

relative sizes of, 91–92

scalar

aggregate initialization, 222

copy initialization, 235–236

initialization, 217

trailing return. *See also* **decltype**; deduced
return type

description of, 124–126

further reading for, 128

inferring type of, 28

use cases, 126–128

underlying types (UTs)

description of, 829–830

further reading for, 834

potential pitfalls, 832–833

use cases, 830–832

union

description of, 1174–1177

further reading for, 1181

potential pitfalls, 1180

use cases, 1177–1180

variant, 937–948

U

UDL operator templates, 841, 849–851, 870

UDL operators, 840–842

cooked, 843–845

raw, 845–849

templates, 849–851

UDL suffix, 837

UDL type categories, 843

UDTs. *See* user-defined types (UDTs)

unconditional exception specifications, 1085–1089

undefined behavior (UB), 1024n10, 1077, 1104,
1175

attributes and, 18–19

auto return-type deduction, 1187

constexpr variable initializers, 306–307

contract guarantees, 1115

delegating constructors, 50n2

diagnosing at compile time, 312–314

friend declarations, 1049

generalized PODs, 401

long long integral type, 90

[[noreturn]] attribute, 97

range-based **for** loops, 692

rvalue references, 715

thread-safe function-scope static variables,
70

uninitialized values, 218

union type and, 1180

undefined symbol links, 1068n4

undefined symbols, 363

underlying types (UTs)

constexpr variables, 308–309

description of, 829–830

enum class, 337

enumerations, 333–334

further reading for, 834

opaque enumerations, 660

potential pitfalls, 832–833

Unicode string literals, 131

use cases, 830–832

underspecifying alignment, 176

unevaluated contexts, std::declval used in, 31,
1132

unevaluated operands, 615

Unicode string literals

description of, 129–130

potential pitfalls, 130–132

embedding Unicode graphemes, 130–131

library support, lack of, 131

UTF-8, problematic treatment of, 131–
132

use cases, 130

unification, 901

uniform initialization, 215

in factory functions, 239–241

in generic code, 238–239

member initialization in generic code, 241–
242

union type

description of, 1174–1177

discriminated unions, 937–948

further reading for, 1181

misuse of, 505–506

potential pitfalls, 1180

use cases, 1177–1180

vertical encoding within, 439–448

unions

default member initializers and, 320–321

final contextual keyword in, 1013

unique object address, 418

Index

unique ownership, 768
unique-object-address requirement, 418
unit conversions, 863–865
universally unique identifier (UUID), 862–863
unnamed namespaces, 77
unprocessed string contents, syntax for. *See* raw
    string literals
unqualified name lookup, 841
unreachable rvalue references, 712
unrecognized attributes, implementation-defined
    behavior of, 18–19
unrelated types, 507
unsafe features
    auto return-type deduction
        annoyances, 1201–1203
        description of, 1182–1194
        potential pitfalls, 1200
        use cases, 1194–1200
    [[carries_dependency]] attribute
        description of, 998–1000
        further reading for, 1006
        potential pitfalls, 1005
        use cases, 1000–1005
    decltype(auto) placeholder
        annoyances, 1213
        description of, 1205–1210
        potential pitfalls, 1212–1213
        use cases, 1210–1212
    definition of, 6
    final contextual keyword, 6
        annoyances, 1028–1030
        description of, 1007–1014
        further reading for, 1030
        potential pitfalls, 1023–1027
        use cases, 1014–1023
    friend declarations
        curiously recurring template pattern
            (CRTP) use cases, 1042–1054
        description of, 1031–1033
        further reading for, 1042
        potential pitfalls, 1041
        use cases, 1033–1041
    inline namespaces
        annoyances, 1079–1082
        description of, 1055–1062
        further reading for, 1083
        potential pitfalls, 1076–1079
        use cases, 1062–1076
        versioning case study, 1083–1084
    noexcept exception specification
        annoyances, 1143–1150
        description of, 1085–1094
        further reading for, 1151–1152
        potential pitfalls, 1112–1143
        use cases, 1094–1111

ref-qualifiers
    annoyances, 1171–1172
    description of, 1153–1160
ref-qualifiers (cont.)
    further reading for, 1173
    potential pitfalls, 1170–1171
    use cases, 1160–1170
union type
    description of, 1174–1177
    further reading for, 1181
    potential pitfalls, 1180
    use cases, 1177–1180
unscoped C++03 enumerations, workarounds for,
    332–333
unsigned long long type
    description of, 89
    further reading for, 92
    potential pitfalls, 91–92
    use cases, 89–91
unsigned ordinary character types, 515
unspecified rvalue references, 715
unwinding logic, 1103
usable literal types, 282–284
user declared, 413n6, 1105
user provided
    defaulted functions, 33–36
    generalized PODs, 466–472, 477–478
    replacement for user declared, 413n6
    rvalue references, 742, 794
user-declared constructors, 274n7
user-declared default constructors, 1087
user-declared special member functions, 1086
user-defined control constructs, 599–600
user-defined conversion, 61, 580
user-defined literals (UDLs), 462
    annoyances, 869–871
        confusing raw and string operators, 870
        floating-point to integer, lack of conver-
            sion, 869–870
        parsing problems, 870–871
        potential suffix-name collisions, 870
        UDL operator templates for string liter-
            als, lack of, 870
    in C++14 Standard Library, 852–853
    description of, 835–853
    further reading for, 872
    operators, 840–842
        cooked, 843–845
        raw, 845–849
        templates, 849–851
    potential pitfalls, 867–869
        overuse, 868–869
        preprocessor surprises, 869
        unexpected characters yield bad values,
            867–868

restrictions on, 839–840
use cases, 853–867
    test drivers, 866–867
    unit conversions and dimensional units, 863–865
    user-defined numeric types, 858–862
    user-defined types with string representations, 862–863
    wrappers, 853–857
user-defined types (UDTs), 835
    alignas specifier, misleading application of, 177–178
    alignof operator, 185–186
    compile-time constructible, literal types, 462
    creating high-level value-semantic types (VSTs), 751–762
    default initialization, 322
    delegating constructors, 46
    final contextual keyword in, 1007, 1011–1015
    friend declarations
        curiously recurring template pattern (CRTP) use cases, 1042–1054
        description of, 1031–1033
        further reading for, 1042
        potential pitfalls, 1041
        use cases, 1033–1041
    initializer lists, 553
    as literal types, 280
    noexcept operator, 622
    numeric literals, 858–862
    strengthening alignment, 168, 171
    with string representations, 862–863
user-provided copy assignment operator, 759
user-provided copy constructors, 758–759
user-provided default constructors, 80, 217–219, 755, 1087
    exception specifications and, 1087
    initialization, 217–218
user-provided destructors, 755–756
    declaration of, 1105
    exception specifications and, 1088
user-provided functions, exception specifications and, 1088
user-provided move constructors, 760
user-provided move-assignment operator, 760–761
user-provided special member functions, 33, 751–753, 1012, 1088
    defaulting implementation of, 35–36
    exception specifications and, 1088
    rvalue references, 753, 755
user-provided value constructors, 753–755

using declarations, 535
    alias creation with, 133–137
    constexpr functions, 268
    with inline namespaces, 1055–1056
using directives, 842
    constexpr functions, 268
    for short-named entities, 1074–1076
using-namespace directives, 1066
UTF-8, 129–131, 844
UTF-16, 129–131, 844
UTF-32, 129–131, 844

V

valid but unspecified, 715, 801
value categories, 25, 26, 30, 590, 710, 1145. *See also* lvalue references; prvalues; rvalue references; xvalues
    auto return-type deduction, 1184, 1186
    evolution of, 807, 813–828
    exact capture with **decltype(auto)**, 1210–1211
    extended categories in C++11/14, 716–723
    forwarding references, 377
    generic lambdas, 972
    identifying, 779–781
    lambda-capture expressions, 992
    prior to C++11, 814–815
    range-based **for** loops, 680
    ref-qualifiers, 1153, 1155, 1159–1160, 1172
    of subobjects, 722n8
value constructors, 37, 942
    user-defined literals (UDLs), 836
    user-provided, 753–755
    vertical encoding, 450
value initialization, 216–219, 764
    constexpr functions, 273–274
    of constructor arguments, avoiding the most vexing parse, 237–238
value initialize, 493
value representation, 405, 409, 452, 500, 503, 517n43
value semantics, 627, 811
value-initialized variables, defining, 236–237
values, 51, 741
value-semantic classes, 36, 48n1, 187–188, 743
value-semantic mechanisms, 663
value-semantic types (VSTs), 51, 1034
    forwarding references, 386
    generic, creating, 762–767
    high-level, creating, 751–762
    lambda-capture expressions, 992
    low-level, creating, 742–751
    POD types, 452
    in-process, 1034
    rvalue references, 742, 751–752, 761

Index

variable templates. *See also* **constexpr** variables
  annoyances, 165
  description of, 157–160
  of literal type, 302
  potential pitfalls, 163–165
  specialization of, 1078n7
  use cases, 160–163
    parameterized constants, 160–161
    reducing verbosity of type traits, 161–163
variables. *See also* **auto** variables; **constexpr** variables; function-scope static variables
  auxiliary, 28
  in conditional expressions, initialization, 235
  const, capturing modifiable copy of, 990–992
  forwarding into closure, 992–993
  initialization, 200
  in lambda expressions, 600–601
  local, in unevaluated contexts, 610–611
  mixing captured and noncaptured, 609
  strengthening alignment, 168
  value-initialized, defining, 236–237
variadic alias templates, 887
variadic class templates, 875, 878–880
  member functions, 892–894
  non-type template parameter packs, 901–903
  specialization of, 884–887
  type template parameter packs, 880–884
variadic function templates, 878, 912, 926
  function parameter packs, 888–892
  function template argument matching, 900–901
  generic lambdas, 978
  lambda expressions, 590
  template argument deductions, 894–896
variadic generic lambdas, 973–974
variadic macros, 249, 781
variadic member function templates, 892
variadic member functions, 892–894
variadic templates. *See also* variadic class templates; variadic function templates
  annoyances, 953–957
    expansion is rigid and requires verbose support code, 957
    limitations on expansion contexts, 954–955
    linear search, 957
    parameter packs cannot be used unexpanded, 956
    unusable functions, 953–954
  description of, 873–925
  further reading for, 958

pack expansion, 908–911, 925
  alignas specifier, 921–922
  attribute lists, 922
  base specifier list, 915–917
  braced initializer lists, 912–914
  disallowed, 924
  function call argument list, 912–914
  function parameter packs, 911–912
  lambda-capture list, 919–921
  member initializer list, 917–918
  sizeof... expressions, 923
  template argument list, 914
  template parameter list, 923–924
potential pitfalls, 952–953
  accidental use of C-style ellipsis, 952
  compiler limits on number of arguments, 953
  undiagnosed errors, 952–953
Rule of Fair Matching, 898–899
Rule of Greedy Matching, 896–898
template template parameter packs, 903–908
use cases, 925–951
  advanced traits, 948–951
  generic variadic functions, 925–926
  hooking function calls, 930–931
  object factories, 929–930
  processing variadic arguments in order, 926–929
  tuples, 932–937
  variant types, 937–948
variadic alias templates, 887
variadic member functions, 892–894
variant types, 937–948
vectorization, 1137
vectorLerp function, 16–17
vectors of iterators, 26–27. *See also* std::vector
verbosity of type traits, reducing, 161–163
versioning
  with inline namespaces, 1083–1084
  lack of scalability, 1076–1077
vertical encoding, 439–452
  for non-trivial types, 448–452
  within a union, 439–448
  Xlib library, 445–448
vertical microcode, 445n17
virtual base pointers, 409, 416–417, 426
virtual destructors, 1008
virtual dispatch, 202, 1015–1017, 1023
virtual functions, 632–634
virtual keyword, with **final** contextual keyword, 1009–1011
virtual member functions, 1007–1008
  overriding
    description of, 104–105

Index

further reading for, 107
potential pitfalls, 106
use cases, 105–106
virtual memory, 181–183
virtual-function tables (vtables), 441, 617
vocabulary types, 91, 94, 131
void return type
deducing, 1184–1185
as literal types, 280
vtable pointers, 409, 416–417, 426, 441–442, 1011

W

-Wall (GCC), 28n1
weakly typed C++03 enumerators, drawbacks to, 333–335
well-formed programs, 147n1, 169, 276n8, 355, 371
-Wextra (GCC), 28n1
whitespace, 22, 113–114
wide contracts
final contextual keyword, 1021
noexcept operator, 1112–1113
rvalue references, 750
widgetIterators, 26–27

Wing, Jeanette, 1030
witness arguments, 283–284
witnesses, 284
working sets, 182–183, 183n14, 628, 1139
-Wpedantic (GCC), 28n1
wrappers, 853–857
for **noexcept** move operations, 1099–1101
perfect returning, 1198

X

Xlib library, 445–448
xvalues, 712–713, 717
in C++11/14, 721–723
evolution of, 807, 825–828

Y

y combinators, 605, 978, 979n4

Z

zero cost, 1101n11, 1136
zero initialized, 75, 77n6, 218, 222, 493
zero-cost exception model, 1134–1136
zero-overhead exception model, 1101

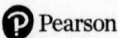